96
Sutre 3.
36145
Worn V 36
V. 40

AN ENGLISH INTERPRETATION OF THE HOLY QUR-AN
Arabic Text and Translation

AN ENGLISH INTERPRETATION

OF

THE

HOLY

QUR-AN

WITH FULL
ARABIC TEXT

BY

Abdullah Yusuf Ali

SH. MUHAMMAD ASHRAF
PUBLISHERS, BOOKSELLERS & EXPORTERS
LAHORE - PAKISTAN.

ISBN NO. 969-432-000-3

Published by
SH. MUHAMMAD ASHRAF
Publishers & Booksellers
7-Aibak Road (New Anarkali)
Lahore - Pakistan.
Printed at
ASHRAF PRINTING PRESS
Lahore - Pakistan.

SMA 11/95-23X36/16-55gm.4721/F

DEDICATION

To all who love and reverence the Book,
And earnestly strive to find in it,
Not a reflection of their own fancies,
But a clue to Unity, Discipline,
And the Call to higher matters of the spirit,
I dedicate this humble effort at Interpretation,
The fruit of my Life, Thought, and Study,

'Abdullah Yūsuf 'Ali
(Servant of Islam)

FROM THE PREFACE TO FIRST EDITION, 1934

...It may be asked: Is there any need for a fresh English translation? To those who ask this question I commend a careful consideration of the facts which I have set out in my Note on Translation. After they have read it, I would invite them to take any particular passage, say ii. 74 or ii. 102, or ii. 164 and compare it with any previous version they choose. If they find that I have helped them even the least bit further in understanding its meanings, or appreciating its beauty or catching something of the grandeur of the original, I would claim that my humble attempt is justified.

It is the duty of every Muslim, man, woman, or child to read the Qur-ān and understand it according to his own capacity. If any one of us attains to some knowledge or understanding of it by study, contemplation, and the test of life, both outward and inward, it is his duty, according to his capacity, to instruct others, and share with them the joy and peace which result from contact with the spiritual world. The Qur-ān—indeed every religious book—has to be read, not only with the tongue and voice and eyes, but with the best light that our intellect can supply, and even more, with the truest and purest light which our heart and conscience can give us. It is in this spirit that I would have my readers approach the Qur-ān.

It was between the age of four and five that I first learned to read its Arabic words, to revel in its rhythm and music and wonder at its meaning. I have a dim recollection of the _Khatm_ ceremony which closed that stage. It was called "completion": it really just _began_ a spiritual awakening that has gone on ever since. My revered father taught me Arabic, but I must have imbibed from him into my innermost being something more—something which told me that all the world's thoughts, all the world's most beautiful languages and literatures, are but vehicles for that ineffable message which comes to the heart in rare moments of ecstasy. The soul of mysticism and ecstasy is in the Qur-ān, as well as that plain guidance for the plain man which a world in a hurry affects to consider as sufficient. It is good to make this personal confession, to an age in which it is in the highest degree unfashionable to speak of religion or spiritual peace or consolation, an age in which words like these draw forth only dirision, pity, or contempt.

I have explored Western lands, Western manners, and the depths of Western thought and Western learning to an extent which has rarely fallen to the lot of an Eastern mortal. But I have never lost touch with my Eastern heritage. Through all my successes and failures I have learned to rely more and more upon the one true thing in all life—the voice that speaks in a tongue above that of mortal man. For me the embodiment of that voice has been in the noble words of the Arabic Qur-ān, which I have tried to translate for myself and apply to my experience again and again. The service of the Qur-ān has been the pride and the privilege of many Muslims. If felt that with such life-experience as has fallen to my lot, my service to the Qur-ān, should be to present it in a fitting garb in English. That ambition I have cherished in my mind for more than forty years. I have collected books and materials for it. I have visited places, undertaken journeys, taken notes, sought the society of men, and tried to explore their thoughts and hearts in order to equip myself for the task. Sometimes I have considered it too stupendous for me,—the double task of understanding the original, and reproducing its nobility, its beauty, its poetry, its grandeur, and its sweet, practical, reasonable application to everyday experience. Then I have blamed myself for lack of courage,—the spiritual courage of men who dared all in the Cause which was so dear to them.

Two sets of apparently accidental circumstances at last decided me. A man's life is subject to inner storms far more devastating than those in the physical world around him. In such a storm, in the better anguish of a personal sorrow which nearly unseated I my reason and made life seem meaningless, a new hope was born out of a systematic pursuit of my long-cherished project. Watered by tears, my manuscript began to grow in depth and earnestness if not in bulk. I guarded it like a secret treasure. Wanderer that I am, I carried it about, thousands of miles, to all sorts of countries and among all sorts of people. At length, in the city of Lahore, I happened to mention the matter to some young people who held me in respect and affection. They showed an enthusiasm and an eagerness which surprised me. They almost took the matter out of my hands. They asked for immediate publication. I had various bits ready, but not even one complete *Sīpāra*. They made me promise to complete at least one *Sīpāra* before I left Lahore. As if by magic, a publisher, a *kātib* (calligraphist, to write the Arabic Text), an engraver of blocks for such text, and a printer were found, all equally anxious to push forward the scheme. Blessed be youth, for its energy and determination! "Where others flinch, rash youth will dare!"

Gentle and discerning reader! what I wish to present to you is an English Interpretation, side by side with the Arabic Text. The English shall be, not a mere substitution of one word for another, but the best expression I can give to the fullest meaning which I can understand from the Arabic Text. The rhythm, music and exalted tone of the original should be reflected in the English Interpretation. It may be but a faint reflection, but such beauty and power as my pen commands shall be brought to its service. I want to make English itself an Islamic language, if such a person as I can do it. And I must give you all the necessary aid which I can....

The Text in English is printed... in parallel columns with the Arabic Text. Each *Sūra* and the verse of each *Sūra* is separately numbered, and the numbers are shown page by page. The system of numbering the verses have not been uniform in previous translations. European editors and translators have allowed their numbering to diverge considerably from that accepted in the East. This causes confusion in giving and verifying references. The different *Qīrāats* sometimes differ as to the punctuation stops and the numbering of the verses. This is not a vital matter, but it causes confusion in references. It is important that at least in Islamic countries one system of numbering should be adopted. I have adopted mainly that of the Egyptian edition published under the authority of the King of Egypt. This will probably be accepted in Egypt and in Arabic-speaking countries, as those countries generally look up to Egypt in matters of literature. I am glad to see that the text... published by the *Anjuman-i-Himayat-Islām* of Lahore is following the same system of numbering. I recommend to other publishers...the same good example. If once this is done, we shall have a uniform system of numbering. I have retained the numbering of Sections, as it is universally used in the Arabic copies, and marks a logical division of the *Sūras*. I have supplied a further aid to the reader in indicating sub-division of the Sections into paragraphs. They are not numbered, but are distinguished by the use of a flowery initial letter...

...Every earnest and reverent student of the Qur-ān, as he proceeds with his study, will find, with an inward joy difficult to describe, how this general meaning also enlarges as his own capacity for understanding increases. It is like a traveller climbing a mountain: the higher he goes, the farther he sees. From a literary point of view the poet Keats has described his feeling when he discovered Chapman's Homer:

> Then felt I like some watcher of the skies
> When a new planet swims into his ken,
> Or like stout Cortez when with eagle eyes
> He stared at the Pacific, and all his men
> Looked at each other with surmise,
> Silent, upon a peak in Darien.

How much greater is the joy and sense of wonder and miracle when the Qur-ān opens our spiritual eyes! The meaning which we thought we had grasped expands. New worlds are opened out. As we progress, still newer, and again newer worlds "swim into our ken".

The miracle deepens and deepens, and almost completely absorbs us. And yet we know that the "face of God"—our final goal—has not yet been reached. We are in the *mulk* of Sulaimān (Q.ii. 102), which the evil ones denied, belied, and even turned into blasphemy. But we can ignore blasphemy, ridicule and contempt, for we are on the threshold of Realities and a little perfume from the garden of the Holy One has already gladdened our nostrils....

The Arabic Text I have had printed from photographic blocks, made for me by Master Muhammad Sharif. The calligraphy is from the pen of Pir 'Abdul Hamīd, with whom I have been in touch and who has complied with my desire for a bold round hand, with the words clearly separated, the vowel points accurately placed over or under the letter to which they relate, and the verses duly numbered and placed in juxtaposition with their English equivalents. Calligraphy occupies an important place in Muslim Art, and it is my desire that my version should not in any way be deficient in this respect.

I have been fortunate in securing the co-operation of Professor Zafar Iqbāl in looking over the proofs of the Arabic Text. In connection with the Anjuman's edition of the Arabic Qur-ān he has devoted much time and thought to the correct punctuation of the Text, and he has also investigated its history and problems. I hope he will some day publish these valuable notes. I have been privileged to see the Anjuman's Text before its formal publication. I consider it the most carefully prepared Text of any produced in India and I have generally followed it in punctuation and the numbering of verses,—the only points on which my difficulties are likely to arise on the Quranic Text....

One final word to my readers. Read, study and digest the Holy Book. Read slowly and let it sink into your heart and soul. Such study will, like virtue, be its own reward. If you find anything in this volume to criticise please let it not spoil your enjoyment of the rest. If you write to me, quoting chapter and verse, I shall be glad to consider your citicism, but let it not vex you if I exercise my own judgment in deciding for myself. Any corrections accepted will be gratefully acknowledged. On the other hand, if there is something that specially pleases you or helps you, please do not hesitate to write to me. I have given up other interests to help you. It will be a pleasure to know that my labour has not been in vain. If you address me care of my Publisher at his Lahore address, he will always forward the letter to me.

LAHORE   A. YŪSUF 'ALĪ
4th April, 1934
=18th of the month of Pilgrimage 1352 H.

FROM THE PREFACE TO THIRD EDITION,
1938

... The zeal and energy which my publisher, Shaikh Muhammad Ashraf, has thrown into the work, require renewed acknowledgment. For four years he and I have co-operated in a great undertaking, and all processes connected with it have been carried out by loving Muslim hands.

Since I last greeted my readers collectively I have been able to perform the Pilgrimage to the holy city of Makkah and the sacred territory around it and seen with my own eyes the city and territory of Madina, with all the country around and between the holy Cities. I have realised for myself the scenes in which the revelations came which I have humbly sought to interpret. I hope that some glimpses of this experience will have been conveyed to my dear readers. Will they pray that God may give me strength to complete this work and to serve Islam in other ways!

A Yūsuf 'Ali

TRANSLATIONS OF THE QUR-ĀN

ALMOST all languages spoken by Muslims have translations of the Qur-ān in them. Usually the Text is printed with the Translation. If the language is undeveloped, many of the Arabic words of the Qur-ān are taken over bodily into it for want of corresponding words in that language. Even in cultivated languages like Persian or Turkish, the introduction of religious terms from Arabic gave a body of words which were common to the whole Islamic world, and thus cemented that unity of the Muslim Brotherhood which is typified by the Qibla. Where the notion itself is new to the speakers of polished languages, they are glad to borrow the Arabic word expressing that notion and all the associations connected with it. Such a word is *Qibla*. Where the language is undeveloped the translation is nothing more than a rough explanation of the Arabic Text. The translation has neither grammatical finish nor a form which can stand independently by itself. That is what happened with the earlier Urdu translations. They were really rough explanations. The ambition of every learned Muslim in to read the Qur'ān in Arabic. The ambition of every Muslim is to read the *sounds* of the Arabic Text. I wish that his or her ambition were also to *understand* the Qur-ān, either in Arabic or in the mother tongue or some well developed tongue which he or she understands. Hence the need for good and accurate translations.

The translations into non-European languages known to me are: Persian, Turkish, Urdu, Tamil (used by Moplas), Pashto (for Afghans), Bengali, Malay, some of the languages of the Eastern Archipelago and some of the African languages. I believe there is also a Chinese (dialectical) translation.

The earliest Urdu translation was by Shāh 'Abdul Qādir of Delhi (d. 1826). He has already been mentioned among the Indian Commentators. Since then numerous Urdu translations have followed, some of which have been left incomplete. Among the complete ones, much used at the present day, may be mentioned those of Shāh, Rafi'-ud-din of Delhi, Shāh Ashraf 'Ali Thānawī, and Maulvi Naẕir Ahmad (d. 1912) Personally I present the last...

Before the development of the modern European vernaculars the cultivated language of Europe was Latin. A Latin translation was made for the Monastery of Clugny about 1143 (in the sixth century of the Hijra) but not published till 1543. The place of publication was Basle and the publisher Bibliander. This was translated into Italian, German and Dutch. Schweigger's German translation was published at Nuremburg (Bavaria) in 1616. A French translation by Du Ryer was published at Paris in 1647, and a Russian one at St. Petersburg in 1776. Savary's French translation appeared in 1783, and Kasimirski's French translation (which has passed through several editions) first appeared in 1840, the French interest in Islam having been stimulated by French conquests in Algeria and North Africa. The Germans have followed up Schweigger, with Boysen's translation in 1773, Wahl's in 1828, and Ullmann's (first edition) in 1840....

Meanwhile Maracci had produced in 1689 a Latin version of the Qur-ān with the Arabic Text and quotations from various Arabic Commentaries, carefully selected and garbled, so as to give the worst possible impression of Islam to Europe. Maracci was a learned man, and there is no pretence about the object he had in view, viz. to discredit Islam by an elaborate show of quotations from Muslim authorities themselves. Maracci was himself a Confessor to Pope Innocent XI; his work is dedicated to the holy Roman Emperor Leopold I; and he introduces it by an introductory volume containing what he calls a "refutation of the Qur-ān."

The first English translation by A. Ross was but a translation of the first French translation of Du Ryer of 1647, and was published a few years after Du Ryer's. George Sale's translation (1734) was based on Maracci's Latin version, and even his notes and his Preliminary Discourse are based mainly on Maracci. Considering that Maracci's object was to discredit Islam in the eyes of Europe, it is remarkable that Sale's translation should be looked upon as a standard translation in the English-speaking world, and should pass through edition after edition, being even included in the series called the Chandos Classics and receiving the benediction of Sir E. Denison Ross. The Rev. J.M. Rodwell arranged the Suras in rough chronological order. His translation was first published in 1861. Though he tries to render the idiom fairly, his notes show the mind of a Christian clergyman, who was more concerned to "show up" the Book than to appreciate or expound its beauties. Prof. E.H. Palmer's translation (first published in 1876) suffers from the idea that the Qur-ān ought to be translated into colloquial language. He failed to realise the beauty and grandeur of style in the original Arabic. To him that style was "rude and rugged": we may more justifiably call his translation careless and slipshod.

The amount of mischief done by these versions of non-Muslim and anti-Muslim writers has led Muslim writers to venture into the field of English translation. The first Muslim to undertake an English translation was Dr. Muhammad 'Abdul Hakim Khan of Patiala, 1905; Mirzā Hairat of Delhi also published a translation (Delhi, 1919); the Commentary which he intended to publish in a separate volume of introduction was, as far as I know, never published. My dear friend the late Nawab 'Imād-ul-Mulk Sāiyid Hussain Bilgrāmī of Hyderabad Deccan, translated a portion, but he did not live to complete his work. The Aḥmadiya Sect has also been active in the field. Its Qadiyan Anjuman published a version of the first *Sīpāra* in 1915. Apparently no more was published. Its Lahore Anjuman has published Maulvi Muḥammad 'Ali's translation (first edition in 1917), which has passed through more than one edition...But the English of the Text is decidedly weak, and is not likely to appeal to those who know no Arabic. There are two other Muslim translations of great merit. But they have been published without the Arabic Text. Hafiẓ Ghulam Sarwar's translation (published in 1930 or 1929) deserved to be better known than it is. He has provided fairly fully summaries of the Sūras section by section....Mr. Marmaduke Pickthall's translation was published in 1930. He is an English Muslim, a literary man of standing, and an Arabic scholar....His rendering is "almost literal": it can hardly be expected that it can give an adequate idea of a Book which (in his own words) can be described as "that inimitable symphony the very sounds of which move men to tears and ecstasy". Perhaps the attempt to catch something of that symphony in another language is impossible. Greatly daring, I have made that attempt. We do not blame an artist who tries to catch in his picture something of the glorious light of a spring landscape.

The English language being widely spread over the world, many people interested in Islam will get their ideas of the Qur-ān from English translations. It is good that qualified Muslims should make the attempt to present the picture which their own mental and spiritual vision present to themselves.... Their non-Muslim fellow-countrymen judge—usually misjudge—their religion by the material which is available to them in English. We should improve and increase this material as much as we can and from as many points of view as we can. Some Muslim nations—like the Turks—have now determined to provide their religious literature (including the Holy Book) in their own national language. In order to keep them in touch with the thought and points of view of their brethren-in-faith, the English language would under present conditions be the most convenient medium. These are the considerations which have moved me to undertake the stupendous task of providing an English Interpretation of the Qur-ān. I pray for strength and light, so that I may be enabled to succeed in this service to Islam.

❋ ❋ ❋ ❋ ❋ ❋

TRANSLITERATION OF ARABIC WORDS AND NAMES

THE following table shows the system which I have followed in transliterating the letters of the Arabic alphabet:

١	= Alif	= a		ط	= Ṭā'	= ṭ		
		= ā (long vowel)		ظ	= Ẓā'	= ẓ		
ب	= Bā'	= b		ع	= 'Ayn	= '		(inverted apostrophe)
ت	= Tā'	= t		غ	= Ghayn	= gh		
ث	= Thā'	= th		ف	= Fā'	= f		
ج	= Jīm	= j		ق	= Qāf	= q		
ح	= Ḥā'	= ḥ		ك	= Kāf	= k		
خ	= Khā'	– kh		ل	– Lām	= l		
د	= Dāl	= d		م	= Mīm	= m		
ذ	= Dhāl	= dh		ن	= Nūn	= n		
ر	= Rā'	– r		ه	– Hā'	= h		
ز	= Zāy	= z		و	= Wāw	= w		(consonantal)
س	= Sīn	= s				= ū		(long vowel)
ش	= Shīn	= sh		ى	= Yā'	– y		(consonantal)
ص	– Ṣād	– ṣ				= i		(long vowel)
ض	= Ḍād	= ḍ		ء	= Hamzah	= '		(apostrophe)

Short vowels: ﹷ (fatḥah) = a

ﹻ (kasrah) = i

ﹹ (dammah) = u

1. In internationalised words and names I have used the spelling ordinarily current in English e.g., Mawlvi, Urdu, Islam, Israel, Abraham, Jacob. Here the boundary is thin and rather ill-defined, and possibly my practice and that of my proof readers, have not been absolutely uniform.

2. Some names, e.g., Ishmael, Hagar, etc., have acquired a contemptuous association in their European forms, while the persons they represent are sacred personages held in great honour in Islam. I have, therefore, avoided the European forms and used the Arabic forms, Ismā'īl, Hājar etc.

xiii

PUNCTUATION MARKS IN THE ARABIC TEXT

THE punctuation marks in the Arabic Text have been worked out by our 'Ulamā with care and minute attention to details. The earliest manuscripts had few or no punctuation marks. Their growth and development furnish an interesting history, on which I hope Professor Ẓafar Iqbāl, who has gone into the question, will publish his notes. In classical Europe, Greek had practically no punctuation marks. Later Latin had one or two rudimentary ones. In modern Europe they developed with printing. Aldus Manutius (16th century) was the first to work out a regular system. The Muslims were much earlier in the field for Quranic purposes, although in current Urdu, Persian, or Arabic punctuation is not a strong point.

Quranic punctuation is an elaborate system, in which three kinds of marks are used. First, there are marks to show the variations in the systems of Qiraat. The most important of these is what is known as the *Mu'ānaqa* معانقه. This literally means the action of two persons embracing each other shoulder to shoulder as in the ceremonious salute at the celebration of 'Īd. The technical meaning in connection with the Quranic Text is that a certain word or expressions so marked can be construed as going either with the words or expressions preceding it or with those following it. The word or expression in question is indicated by three dots ∴ placed before and after it, above other punctuation marks if any. An example will be found in ii.2, where the word *fī-hi* may be construed either as referring to the word *raib* in the preceding clause, or to the word *hudan* in the succeeding clause. Either or both constructions are admissible. Passages where such constructions occur are indicated in the margin of the Arabic Text by the abbreviation ع where this was worked out by the earlier Commentators (*Mutaqaddimīn*), or by the word معانقه in full, where it was worked out by the later commentators (*Mutaakhkhirin*). The numeral above it shows serial number of the *Mu'ānaqa* of each series.

Secondly, there are marginal marks showing divisions into sections or paragraphs. These are denoted by the letter *'ain* (ع) in the margin, and are explained under the heading "Divisions of the Qur-ān".

Thirdly, there are the ordinary punctuation marks in the Text. A knowledge of the most important of these is necessary for an intelligent reading of the Text. Most important of all is a big circle O to denote the end of one Āyat and the beginning of another. If the end of the Āyat is not also the end of a sentence, the mark of a smaller stop is put above it. Where one mark is put on the top of another, the former governs the letter. A warning not to stop is denoted by ﻻ .The letter ﻡ (*lāzim*) shows that a stop is absolutely necessary; otherwise the sense is spoilt. This is so important that it is also shown prominently in the margin as وقف لازم. ج. (*jaiz*) shows that a stop is optional, but if you do not stop, the sense is not spoiled. There are other marks to show the extent to which a stop is permissible, e.g. for taking breath, etc., or where option is allowed, whether it is better to stop or not to stop. The letter ط (*muṭlaq*) denotes a full stop, i.e. the end of a sentence, but not the end of an argument, as in the case of a paragraph or section (ع)

❧ ❧ ❧ ❧ ❧ ❧

DIVISIONS OF THE QUR-ĀN

THE reading of the Qur-ān is considered a pious duty by every Muslim and is actually performed in practice by every literate person, man, woman, and child. For the convenience of those who wish to complete the whole reading in a given time, the whole Text is divided in thirty equal parts or seven equal parts. The thirtieth part is called *Juz-un* in Arabic, and *Sīpāra* or simply *Pāra* in Persian and Urdu. If you read a *Sīpāra* every day, you complete the whole reading in a month of thirty days. The seventh part is called a *Manzil*. If one is read every day, the whole is complete in a week. Usually the arithmetical quarters of a *Sīpāra* (one-fourth, one-half, three-quarters) are also marked in the Arabic copies *Ar-rub'*, *An-nisf* and *Aththalātha*.

According to subject-matter the division is different. The whole of the Qur-ān is arranged in 114 Sūras of every unequal size. The Sūras are numbered and the consecutive number is shown just before the title of the Sūra, both in Arabic and English. In Arabic the figure just after the title shows the chronological order as usually accepted by Muslim writers. Each Sūra consists of a number of Āyats. Sūra I contains 7 Āyats and Sura II contains 286.... The most convenient form of quotation is to name the Sūra and the Āyat: thus ii. 120 means the 120th Āyat of the second Sūra. A Sūra is usually spoken of as a Chapter in English, but that translation is hardly satisfactory. If you examine the order you will find that each Sūra is a step in a gradation. I have left the word untranslated, as a technical term in our religious literature. The Āyat or verse division is usually determined by the rhythm and cadence in the Arabic Text. Sometimes an Āyat contains many sentences. Sometimes a sentence is divided by a break in an Āyat. But usually there is a pause in meaning at the end of an Āyat.

A division of the Sūra into Sections is shown in all Arabic Texts. There are logical divisions according to meaning. The word translated "Section" is in Arabic *Rukū'*, a "bowing of the head". The end of *Rukū'* is shown in Arabic by ع. Usually three figures are written with ع .The top figure shows the number of Ruku's completed in that Sura. The middle figure shows the number of Āyats in the *Rukū's* just completed. The Bottom figure shows the number of *Rukū's* completed in the *Sīpāra*, irrespective of Sūras. For example, the first ع in *Sīpāra* II which continues Sūra II from *Sīpāra* I is usually marked ع١ ·· It means that at that point 17 Rukū's of Sūra II have been completed, that the *Rukū'* of which it marks the close contains 6 Āyats, and that it is the first Rukū' that falls in *Sīpāra* II. I have further marked the subdivision of Rukū's into shorter paragraphs where necessary, by using in the English text a bold flowery initial; e.g. see the initial in p 2–2:6 or the initial in p 7–2:35.

❇ ❇ ❇ ❇ ❇ ❇

AN APPEAL TO OUR READERS

Every endeavour has been made and steps have been taken, as far as humanly possible, to avoid any error in this Holy Qur'an. In spite of this, there is the likelihood of errors, having inadvertently been overlooked, to err, is human.

The readers are earnestly requested that, in case they come across any errors, they will please point these out to us so that these may be corrected.

Publisher

CONTENTS

Al Fātiḥah (The Opening)

بِسْمِ اللهِ الرَّحْمٰنِ الرَّحِيْمِ ۚ ١

1. *In the name of Allah, Most
   Gracious, Most Merciful.*

٢- اَلْحَمْدُ لِلّٰهِ رَبِّ الْعٰلَمِيْنَ ۙ

2. Praise be to Allah
   The Cherisher and Sustainer   of
   　　　　　　　　the Worlds;

٣- الرَّحْمٰنِ الرَّحِيْمِ ۙ

3. Most Gracious, Most Merciful;

٤- مٰلِكِ يَوْمِ الدِّيْنِ ۗ

4. Master of the Day of Judgement.

٥- اِيَّاكَ نَعْبُدُ وَ اِيَّاكَ نَسْتَعِيْنُ ۗ

5. Thee do we worship,
   And Thine aid we seek.

٦- اِهْدِنَا الصِّرَاطَ الْمُسْتَقِيْمَ ۙ

6. Show   us the straight way,

٧- صِرَاطَ الَّذِيْنَ اَنْعَمْتَ عَلَيْهِمْ ۙ غَيْرِ
الْمَغْضُوْبِ عَلَيْهِمْ وَ لَا الضَّآلِّيْنَ ۧ

7. The way of those on whom
   Thou hast bestowed Thy Grace,
   Those whose (portion)
   Is not wrath,
   And who go not astray.

INTRODUCTION TO SŪRA II *(Baqara)* — 286 Verses

As the opening Sūra sums up in seven beautiful verses the essence of the Qur-ān, so this Sūra sums up in 286 verses the whole teaching of the Qur-ān. It is a closely reasoned argument.

Al Baqarah (The Heifer)

*In the name of Allah, Most Gracious,
Most Merciful.*

1. Alif Lām Mīm.

2. This is the Book;
   In it is guidance sure, without
               doubt,
   To those who fear Allah;

3. Who believe in the Unseen,
   Are steadfast in prayer,
   And spend out of what We
   Have provided for them;

4. And who believe in the
               Revelation
   Sent to thee,
   And sent before thy time,
   And (in their hearts)
   Have the assurance of the
               Hereafter

5. They are on (true guidance),
   From their Lord, and it is
   These who will prosper.

6. As to those who reject Faith,
   It is the same to them
   Whether thou warn them
   Or do not warn them;
   They will not believe.

7. Allah hath set a seal
   On their hearts and on their
               hearing,
   And on their eyes is a veil;
   Great is the penalty they
               (incur).

SECTION 2.

8. Of the people there are some

who say:
"We believe in Allah and the Last
day;"
But they do not (really) believe.

مَنْ يَّقُوْلُ اٰمَنَّا بِاللّٰهِ وَ
بِالْيَوْمِ الْاٰخِرِ وَمَا هُمْ بِمُؤْمِنِيْنَ ۟

9. Fain would they deceive
Allah and those who believe,
But they only deceive themselves,
And realize (it) not!

٩- يُخٰدِعُوْنَ اللّٰهَ وَ الَّذِيْنَ اٰمَنُوْا ۚ وَمَا
يَخْدَعُوْنَ اِلَّا اَنْفُسَهُمْ وَمَا يَشْعُرُوْنَ ۟

10. In their hearts is a disease;
And Allah has increased their
disease:
And grievous is the penalty they
(incur),
Because they are false
(to themselves).

١٠- فِيْ قُلُوْبِهِمْ مَّرَضٌ ۙ فَزَادَهُمُ اللّٰهُ مَرَضًا ۚ
وَ لَهُمْ عَذَابٌ اَلِيْمٌ ۙ بِمَا كَانُوْا
يَكْذِبُوْنَ ۟

11. When it is said to them:
"Make not mischief on the earth,"
They say: "Why, we only
Want to make peace!"

١١- وَ اِذَا قِيْلَ لَهُمْ لَا تُفْسِدُوْا فِي الْاَرْضِ ۙ
قَالُوْٓا اِنَّمَا نَحْنُ مُصْلِحُوْنَ ۟

12. Of a surety, they are the ones
Who make mischief,
But they realize (it) not.

١٢- اَلَآ اِنَّهُمْ هُمُ الْمُفْسِدُوْنَ وَ لٰكِنْ لَّا
يَشْعُرُوْنَ ۟

13. When it is said to them:
"Believe as the others believe:"
They say: "Shall we believe
As the fools believe?"—
Nay, of a surety they are the
fools,
But they do not know.

١٣- وَ اِذَا قِيْلَ لَهُمْ اٰمِنُوْا كَمَآ اٰمَنَ النَّاسُ
قَالُوْٓا اَنُؤْمِنُ كَمَآ اٰمَنَ السُّفَهَآءُ ۙ اَلَآ اِنَّهُمْ
هُمُ السُّفَهَآءُ وَ لٰكِنْ لَّا يَعْلَمُوْنَ ۟

14. When they meet those who
believe,
They say: "We believe;"
But when they are alone
With their evil ones,
They say: "We are really with you
We (were) only jesting."

١٤- وَ اِذَا لَقُوا الَّذِيْنَ اٰمَنُوْا قَالُوْٓا اٰمَنَّا ۖ وَ اِذَا
خَلَوْا اِلٰى شَيٰطِيْنِهِمْ ۙ قَالُوْٓا اِنَّا مَعَكُمْ ۙ اِنَّمَا
نَحْنُ مُسْتَهْزِءُوْنَ ۟

15. Allah will throw back
Their mockery on them,
And give them rope in
their trespasses;
So they will wander like blind
ones (to and fro).

١٥- اَللّٰهُ يَسْتَهْزِئُ بِهِمْ وَ يَمُدُّهُمْ فِيْ طُغْيَانِهِمْ
يَعْمَهُوْنَ ۟

16. These are they who have
bartered
Guidance for error:

١٦- اُولٰٓئِكَ الَّذِيْنَ اشْتَرَوُا الضَّلٰلَةَ بِالْهُدٰى ۖ

But their traffic is profitless,
And they have lost true direction.

فَمَا رَبِحَتْ تِّجَارَتُهُمْ وَمَا كَانُوْا مُهْتَدِيْنَ ٥

17. Their similitude is that of a
man
Who kindled a fire;
When it lighted all around him,
Allah took away their light
And left them in utter darkness.
So they could not see.

١٧- مَثَلُهُمْ كَمَثَلِ الَّذِى اسْتَوْقَدَ نَارًا ۚ فَلَمَّا أَضَاءَتْ مَا حَوْلَهُ ذَهَبَ اللّٰهُ بِنُوْرِهِمْ وَتَرَكَهُمْ فِىْ ظُلُمَاتٍ لَّا يُبْصِرُوْنَ ٥

18. Deaf, dumb, and blind,
They will not return (to the
path).

١٨- صُمٌّ بُكْمٌ عُمْىٌ فَهُمْ لَا يَرْجِعُوْنَ ٥

19. Or (another similitude)³⁹
Is that of a rain-laden cloud
From the sky: in it are zones
Of darkness, and thunder and
lightning:
They press their fingers in their
ears
To keep out the stunning
thunderclap,
The while they are in terror of
death.
But Allah is ever round
The rejecters of Faith!

١٩- أَوْ كَصَيِّبٍ مِّنَ السَّمَآءِ فِيْهِ ظُلُمَاتٌ وَّرَعْدٌ وَّبَرْقٌ ۚ يَجْعَلُوْنَ أَصَابِعَهُمْ فِىْ آذَانِهِمْ مِّنَ الصَّوَاعِقِ حَذَرَ الْمَوْتِ ۚ وَاللّٰهُ مُحِيْطٌ بِالْكٰفِرِيْنَ ٥

20. The lightning all but snatches
away
Their sight; every time the light
(Helps) them, they walk therein,
And when the darkness grows on
them,
They stand still,
And if Allah willed, He could
take away
Their faculty of hearing and
seeing;
For Allah hath power over all
things.

٢٠- يَكَادُ الْبَرْقُ يَخْطَفُ أَبْصَارَهُمْ ۚ كُلَّمَا أَضَاءَ لَهُمْ مَّشَوْا فِيْهِ ۙ وَإِذَا أَظْلَمَ عَلَيْهِمْ قَامُوْا ۚ وَلَوْ شَآءَ اللّٰهُ لَذَهَبَ بِسَمْعِهِمْ وَأَبْصَارِهِمْ ۚ إِنَّ اللّٰهَ عَلٰى كُلِّ شَىْءٍ قَدِيْرٌ ۙ ع

SECTION 3.

21. O ye people!
Adore your Guardian Lord,
Who created you
And those who came before you,
That ye may become righteous,

٢١- يٰٓأَيُّهَا النَّاسُ اعْبُدُوْا رَبَّكُمُ الَّذِىْ خَلَقَكُمْ وَالَّذِيْنَ مِنْ قَبْلِكُمْ لَعَلَّكُمْ تَتَّقُوْنَ ۙ

22. Who has made the earth your
couch

٢٢- الَّذِىْ جَعَلَ لَكُمُ الْأَرْضَ فِرَاشًا وَّالسَّمَآءَ

And the heavens your canopy;
And sent down rain from the
               heavens;
And brought forth therewith
Fruits for your sustenance;
Then set not up rivals unto
               Allah
When ye know (the truth).

23. And if ye are in doubt
As to what We have revealed
From time to time to Our servant,
Then produce a Sūrah
Like thereunto;
And call your witnesses or helpers
(If there are any) besides Allah,
If your (doubts) are true.

24. But if ye cannot—
And of a surety ye cannot—
Then fear the Fire
Whose fuel is Men and Stones—
Which is prepared for those
Who reject Faith.

25. But give glad tidings
To those who believe
And work righteousness,
That their portion is Gardens,
Beneath which rivers flow.
Every time they are fed
With fruits therefrom,
They say: "Why, this is
What we were fed with before,"
For they are given things in
               similitude;
And they have therein
Companions pure (and holy);
And they abide therein (forever).

26. Allah disdains not to use
The similitude of things,
Lowest   as well as highest.
Those who believe know
That it is truth from their Lord;
But those who reject faith say:
"What means Allah by this
               similitude?"

بِنَآءٌ ۚ وَّ اَنْزَلَ مِنَ السَّمَآءِ مَآءً فَاَخْرَجَ بِهٖ مِنَ الثَّمَرٰتِ رِزْقًا لَّكُمْ ۚ فَلَا تَجْعَلُوْا لِلّٰهِ اَنْدَادًا وَّ اَنْتُمْ تَعْلَمُوْنَ ۝

٢٣- وَاِنْ كُنْتُمْ فِیْ رَیْبٍ مِّمَّا نَزَّلْنَا عَلٰی عَبْدِنَا فَاْتُوْا بِسُوْرَةٍ مِّنْ مِّثْلِهٖ ۪ وَ ادْعُوْا شُهَدَآءَكُمْ مِّنْ دُوْنِ اللّٰهِ اِنْ كُنْتُمْ صٰدِقِیْنَ ۝

٢٤- فَاِنْ لَّمْ تَفْعَلُوْا وَ لَنْ تَفْعَلُوْا فَاتَّقُوا النَّارَ الَّتِیْ وَقُوْدُهَا النَّاسُ وَ الْحِجَارَةُ ۖ اُعِدَّتْ لِلْكٰفِرِیْنَ ۝

٢٥- وَ بَشِّرِ الَّذِیْنَ اٰمَنُوْا وَ عَمِلُوا الصّٰلِحٰتِ اَنَّ لَهُمْ جَنّٰتٍ تَجْرِیْ مِنْ تَحْتِهَا الْاَنْهٰرُ ۚ كُلَّمَا رُزِقُوْا مِنْهَا مِنْ ثَمَرَةٍ رِزْقًا ۙ قَالُوْا هٰذَا الَّذِیْ رُزِقْنَا مِنْ قَبْلُ ۙ وَ اُتُوْا بِهٖ مُتَشَابِهًا ۖ وَ لَهُمْ فِیْهَا اَزْوَاجٌ مُّطَهَّرَةٌ ۖ وَّ هُمْ فِیْهَا خٰلِدُوْنَ ۝

٢٦- اِنَّ اللّٰهَ لَا یَسْتَحْیٖ اَنْ یَّضْرِبَ مَثَلًا مَّا بَعُوْضَةً فَمَا فَوْقَهَا ۚ فَاَمَّا الَّذِیْنَ اٰمَنُوْا فَیَعْلَمُوْنَ اَنَّهُ الْحَقُّ مِنْ رَّبِّهِمْ ۚ وَ اَمَّا الَّذِیْنَ كَفَرُوْا فَیَقُوْلُوْنَ مَاذَا اَرَادَ اللّٰهُ

By it He causes many to stray,
And many He leads into the right
path;
But He causes not to stray,
Except those who forsake
(the path)—

بِهٰذَا مَثَلًا يُضِلُّ بِهِ كَثِيْرًا ۞
وَّيَهْدِىْ بِهِ كَثِيْرًا ۚ
وَمَا يُضِلُّ بِهٖ إِلَّا الْفٰسِقِيْنَ ۞

27. Those who break Allah's
Covenant
After it is ratified,
And who sunder what Allah
Has ordered to be joined,
And do mischief on earth:
These cause loss (only) to
themselves.

٢٧- اَلَّذِيْنَ يَنْقُضُوْنَ عَهْدَ اللّٰهِ مِنْۢ بَعْدِ
مِيْثَاقِهٖ وَيَقْطَعُوْنَ مَآ أَمَرَ اللّٰهُ بِهٖۤ أَنْ
يُّوْصَلَ وَيُفْسِدُوْنَ فِى الْاَرْضِ ۚ أُولٰٓئِكَ
هُمُ الْخٰسِرُوْنَ ۞

28. How can ye reject
The faith in Allah?—Seeing that
ye were without life,
And He gave you life;
Then will He cause you to die,
And will again bring you to life;
And again to Him will ye return.

٢٨- كَيْفَ تَكْفُرُوْنَ بِاللّٰهِ وَكُنْتُمْ اَمْوَاتًا
فَاَحْيَاكُمْ ۚ ثُمَّ يُمِيْتُكُمْ ثُمَّ يُحْيِيْكُمْ ثُمَّ
إِلَيْهِ تُرْجَعُوْنَ ۞

29. It is He Who hath created for
you
All things that are on earth;
Then He turned to the heaven
And made them into seven
firmaments.
And of all things
He hath perfect knowledge.

٢٩- هُوَ الَّذِىْ خَلَقَ لَكُمْ مَّا فِى الْاَرْضِ
جَمِيْعًا ثُمَّ اسْتَوٰۤى إِلَى السَّمَآءِ فَسَوّٰىهُنَّ
سَبْعَ سَمٰوٰتٍ ۚ
وَهُوَ بِكُلِّ شَىْءٍ عَلِيْمٌ ۞

SECTION 4.

30. Behold, thy Lord said to the
angels: "I will create
A vicegerent on earth." They
said:
"Wilt Thou place therein one
who will make
Mischief therein and shed
blood?—
Whilst we do celebrate Thy
praises
And glorify Thy holy (name)?"
He said: "I know what ye know
not."

٣٠- وَإِذْ قَالَ رَبُّكَ لِلْمَلٰٓئِكَةِ إِنِّىْ جَاعِلٌ
فِى الْاَرْضِ خَلِيْفَةً ۚ قَالُوْۤا أَتَجْعَلُ فِيْهَا
مَنْ يُّفْسِدُ فِيْهَا
وَيَسْفِكُ الدِّمَآءَ ۚ وَ
نَحْنُ نُسَبِّحُ بِحَمْدِكَ وَنُقَدِّسُ لَكَ ۚ قَالَ
إِنِّىْ اَعْلَمُ مَا لَا تَعْلَمُوْنَ ۞

31. And He taught Adam the
names

٣١- وَعَلَّمَ اٰدَمَ الْاَسْمَآءَ

Of all things; then He placed
them
Before the angels, and said: "Tell
Me
The names of these if ye are
right."

32. They said: "Glory to Thee: of
knowledge
We have none, save what Thou
Hast taught us: in truth it is
Thou
Who art perfect in knowledge
and wisdom."

33. He said: "O Adam! tell them
Their names." When he had told
them,
Allah said: "Did I not tell you
That I know the secrets of heaven
And earth, and I know what ye
reveal
And what ye conceal?"

34. And behold, We said to the
angels:
"Bow down to Adam:" and they
bowed down:
Not so Iblīs: he refused and was
haughty:
He was of those who reject Faith.

35. We said: "O Adam! dwell
thou
And thy wife in the Garden;
And eat of the bountiful things
therein
As (where and when) ye will; but
approach not this tree,
Or ye run into harm and
transgression."

36. Then did Satan make them slip
From the (Garden), and get them
out
Of the state (of felicity) in which
They had been. We said:
"Get ye down, all (ye people),
With enmity between yourselves.

On earth will be your dwelling
place
And your means of livelihood　—
For a time."

٣٧. Then learnt Adam from his Lord
Words of inspiration,　and his
Lord
Turned towards him; for He
Is Oft-Returning, Most Merciful.

مُسْتَقَرٌّ وَّمَتَاعٌ إِلٰى حِيْنٍ ۞

٣٧- فَتَلَقّٰى اٰدَمُ مِنْ رَّبِّهٖ كَلِمٰتٍ فَتَابَ
عَلَيْهِ ؕ اِنَّهٗ هُوَ التَّوَّابُ الرَّحِيْمُ ۞

٣٨. We said: "Get ye down all from
here:
And if, as is sure, there comes to
you
Guidance from Me, whosoever
Follows My guidance, on them
Shall be no fear, nor shall they
grieve.

٣٨- قُلْنَا اهْبِطُوْا مِنْهَا جَمِيْعًا ۚ
فَاِمَّا يَاْتِيَنَّكُمْ مِّنِّيْ هُدًى فَمَنْ تَبِعَ
هُدَايَ فَلَا خَوْفٌ عَلَيْهِمْ وَلَا هُمْ
يَحْزَنُوْنَ ۞

٣٩. "But those who reject Faith
And belie Our Signs,
They shall be Companions of the
Fire;
They shall abide therein."

٣٩- وَالَّذِيْنَ كَفَرُوْا وَكَذَّبُوْا بِاٰيٰتِنَآ اُولٰٓئِكَ
اَصْحٰبُ النَّارِ ۚ هُمْ فِيْهَا خٰلِدُوْنَ ۞

SECTION 5.

٤٠. ⑩ Children of Israel! call to mind
The (special) favour which I
bestowed
Upon you, and fulfil your
Covenant
With Me as I fulfil My Covenant
With you, and fear none but Me.

٤٠- يٰبَنِيْٓ اِسْرَآءِيْلَ اذْكُرُوْا نِعْمَتِيَ الَّتِيْٓ
اَنْعَمْتُ عَلَيْكُمْ وَاَوْفُوْا بِعَهْدِيْٓ اُوْفِ
بِعَهْدِكُمْ ۚ
وَاِيَّايَ فَارْهَبُوْنِ ۞

٤١. And believe in what I reveal,
Confirming the revelation
Which is with you,
And be not the first to reject
Faith therein, nor sell My Signs
For a small price; and fear Me,
And Me alone.

٤١- وَاٰمِنُوْا بِمَآ اَنْزَلْتُ مُصَدِّقًا لِّمَا مَعَكُمْ
وَلَا تَكُوْنُوْٓا اَوَّلَ كَافِرٍۭ بِهٖ ۫ وَلَا تَشْتَرُوْا
بِاٰيٰتِيْ ثَمَنًا قَلِيْلًا ۫
وَّاِيَّايَ فَاتَّقُوْنِ ۞

٤٢. And cover not Truth
With falsehood, nor conceal
The Truth when ye know
(what it is).

٤٢- وَلَا تَلْبِسُوا الْحَقَّ بِالْبَاطِلِ وَتَكْتُمُوا
الْحَقَّ وَاَنْتُمْ تَعْلَمُوْنَ ۞

٤٣. And be steadfast in prayer;

٤٣- وَاَقِيْمُوا الصَّلٰوةَ

Practise regular charity;
And bow down your heads
With those who bow down
(in worship).

وَأَقِيمُوا الزَّكَوٰةَ وَارْكَعُوا مَعَ الرَّاكِعِينَ ۞

44. Do ye enjoin right conduct
On the people, and forget
(To practise it) yourselves.
And yet ye study the Scripture?
Will ye not understand?

٤٤- أَتَأْمُرُونَ النَّاسَ بِالْبِرِّ وَتَنْسَوْنَ
أَنْفُسَكُمْ وَأَنْتُمْ تَتْلُونَ الْكِتَبَ
أَفَلَا تَعْقِلُونَ ۞

45. Nay, seek (Allah's) help
With patient perseverance
And prayer:
It is indeed hard, except
To those who bring a lowly
spirit—

٤٥- وَاسْتَعِينُوا بِالصَّبْرِ وَالصَّلٰوةِ وَإِنَّهَا
لَكَبِيرَةٌ إِلَّا عَلَى الْخَاشِعِينَ ۞

46. Who bear in mind the certainty
That they are to meet their Lord,
And that they are to return to
Him.

٤٦- الَّذِينَ يَظُنُّونَ أَنَّهُمْ مُّلَقُوا رَبِّهِمْ وَ
أَنَّهُمْ إِلَيْهِ رَاجِعُونَ ۞

SECTION 6.

47. ۞ Children of Israel! call to
mind
The (special) favour which I
bestowed
Upon you, and that I preferred
you
To all others (for My Message).

٤٧- يَبَنِى إِسْرَآءِيلَ اذْكُرُوا نِعْمَتِيَ الَّتِى
أَنْعَمْتُ عَلَيْكُمْ وَأَنِّى فَضَّلْتُكُمْ عَلَى
الْعَٰلَمِينَ ۞

48. Then guard yourselves against a
day
When one soul shall not avail
another
Nor shall intercession be accepted
for her,
Nor shall compensation be taken
from her,
Nor shall anyone be helped
(from outside).

٤٨- وَاتَّقُوا يَوْمًا لَّا تَجْزِى نَفْسٌ عَنْ
نَّفْسٍ شَيْئًا
وَلَا يُقْبَلُ مِنْهَا شَفَاعَةٌ
وَلَا يُؤْخَذُ مِنْهَا عَدْلٌ
وَلَا هُمْ يُنْصَرُونَ ۞

49. And remember, We delivered you
From the people of Pharaoh: they
set you
Hard tasks and punishments,
slaughtered

٤٩- وَإِذْ نَجَّيْنَكُمْ مِّنْ اٰلِ فِرْعَوْنَ يَسُومُونَكُمْ
سُوٓءَ الْعَذَابِ يُذَبِّحُونَ

Your sons and let your
womenfolk live;
Therein was a tremendous trial
from your Lord.

أَبْنَاءَكُمْ وَيَسْتَحْيُوْنَ نِسَاءَكُمْ وَفِيْ
ذٰلِكُمْ بَلَاءٌ مِنْ رَّبِّكُمْ عَظِيْمٌ ۝

50. And remember We divided
The Sea for you and saved you
And drowned Pharaoh's people
Within your very sight.

٥٠- وَإِذْ فَرَقْنَا بِكُمُ الْبَحْرَ فَأَنْجَيْنٰكُمْ وَ
أَغْرَقْنَا اٰلَ فِرْعَوْنَ وَأَنْتُمْ تَنْظُرُوْنَ ۝

51. And remember We appointed
Forty nights for Moses,
And in his absence ye took
The calf (for worship),
And ye did grievous wrong.

٥١- وَإِذْ وٰعَدْنَا مُوْسٰى أَرْبَعِيْنَ لَيْلَةً ثُمَّ
اتَّخَذْتُمُ الْعِجْلَ مِنْ بَعْدِهٖ
وَأَنْتُمْ ظٰلِمُوْنَ ۝

52. Even then We did forgive you,
There was a chance for you
To be grateful.

٥٢- ثُمَّ عَفَوْنَا عَنْكُمْ مِنْ بَعْدِ ذٰلِكَ لَعَلَّكُمْ
تَشْكُرُوْنَ ۝

53. And remember We gave
Moses the Scripture and the
Criterion
(Between right and wrong), there
was
A chance for you to be guided
aright.

٥٣- وَإِذْ اٰتَيْنَا مُوْسَى الْكِتٰبَ وَالْفُرْقَانَ
لَعَلَّكُمْ تَهْتَدُوْنَ ۝

54. And remember Moses said
To his people: "O my people!
Ye have indeed wronged
Yourselves by your worship of the
calf:
So turn (in repentance) to your
Maker,
And slay yourselves
(the wrongdoers);
That will be better for you
In the sight of your Maker."
Then He turned towards you
(in forgiveness):
For He is Oft-Returning, Most
Merciful.

٥٤- وَإِذْ قَالَ مُوْسٰى لِقَوْمِهٖ يٰقَوْمِ إِنَّكُمْ
ظَلَمْتُمْ أَنْفُسَكُمْ بِاتِّخَاذِكُمُ الْعِجْلَ فَتُوْبُوْا
إِلٰى بَارِئِكُمْ فَاقْتُلُوْا أَنْفُسَكُمْ
ذٰلِكُمْ خَيْرٌ لَّكُمْ عِنْدَ بَارِئِكُمْ
فَتَابَ عَلَيْكُمْ
إِنَّهٗ هُوَ التَّوَّابُ الرَّحِيْمُ ۝

55. And remember ye said:[70]
"O Moses!
We shall never believe in thee
Until we see Allah manifestly,"
But ye were dazed

٥٥- وَإِذْ قُلْتُمْ يٰمُوْسٰى لَنْ نُّؤْمِنَ لَكَ
حَتّٰى نَرَى اللّٰهَ جَهْرَةً فَأَخَذَتْكُمُ الصّٰعِقَةُ

By thunder and lightning
Even as ye looked on.

٥٦. Then We raised you up
After your death;
Ye had the chance
To be grateful.

٥٧. And We gave you the shade of
clouds
And sent down to you
Manna[71] and quails, saying:
"Eat of the good things
We have provided for you:"
(But they rebelled);
To Us they did no harm,
But they harmed their own souls.

٥٨. And remember We said:
"Enter this town, and eat
Of the plenty therein
As ye wish; but enter
The gate with humility,
In posture and in words,
And We shall forgive you your
faults
And increase (the portion of)
Those who do good."

٥٩. But the transgressors
Changed the word from that
Which had been given them;
So We sent on the transgressors
A plague from heaven,
For that they infringed
(Our command) repeatedly.

SECTION 7.

٦٠. And remember Moses prayed
For water for his people;
We said: "Strike the rock
With thy staff." Then gushed forth
Therefrom twelve springs.
Each group knew its own place
For water. So eat and drink
Of the sustenance provided by
Allah.
And do no evil nor mischief
On the (face of the) earth.

61. And remember ye said:
"O Moses! we cannot endure
One kind of food (always);
So beseech thy Lord for us
To produce for us of what the
earth
Groweth—its pot-herbs, and
cucumbers,
Its garlic, lentils, and onions."
He said: "Will ye exchange
The better for the worse?
Go ye down to any town,
And ye shall find what ye want!"
They were covered with
humiliation
And misery; they drew
On themselves the wrath of Allah.
This because they went on
Rejecting the Signs of Allah
And slaying His Messengers
Without just cause.
This because they rebelled
And went on transgressing.

SECTION 8.

62. Those who believe (in the
Qur'ān),
And those who follow the Jewish
(scriptures),
And the Christians and the
Sabians —
Any who believe in Allah
And the Last Day,
And work righteousness,
Shall have their reward
With their Lord; on them
Shall be no fear, nor shall they
grieve.

63. And remember We took
Your Covenant
And We raised above you
(The towering height
Of Mount (Sinai)
(Saying): "Hold firmly
To what We have given you
And bring (ever) to remembrance
What is therein:
Perchance ye may fear Allah."

١٦- وَإِذْ قُلْتُمْ يٰمُوْسٰى لَنْ نَّصْبِرَ عَلٰى
طَعَامٍ وَّاحِدٍ فَادْعُ لَنَا رَبَّكَ يُخْرِجْ لَنَا
مِمَّا تُنْبِتُ الْأَرْضُ مِنْ بَقْلِهَا وَقِثَّآئِهَا
وَفُوْمِهَا وَعَدَسِهَا وَبَصَلِهَا ۖ قَالَ أَتَسْتَبْدِلُوْنَ
الَّذِىْ هُوَ أَدْنٰى بِالَّذِىْ هُوَ خَيْرٌ ۚ
اهْبِطُوْا مِصْرًا فَإِنَّ لَكُمْ مَّا سَأَلْتُمْ ۗ
وَضُرِبَتْ عَلَيْهِمُ الذِّلَّةُ وَالْمَسْكَنَةُ ۖ
وَبَآءُوْ بِغَضَبٍ مِّنَ اللهِ ۗ
ذٰلِكَ بِأَنَّهُمْ كَانُوْا يَكْفُرُوْنَ بِآيٰتِ اللهِ
وَيَقْتُلُوْنَ النَّبِيِّنَ بِغَيْرِ الْحَقِّ ۗ
ذٰلِكَ بِمَا عَصَوْا وَّكَانُوْا يَعْتَدُوْنَ ۞

٦٢- إِنَّ الَّذِيْنَ اٰمَنُوْا وَالَّذِيْنَ هَادُوْا
وَالنَّصٰرٰى وَالصّٰبِئِيْنَ
مَنْ اٰمَنَ بِاللهِ وَالْيَوْمِ الْأٰخِرِ
وَعَمِلَ صَالِحًا
فَلَهُمْ أَجْرُهُمْ عِنْدَ رَبِّهِمْ ۖ
وَلَا خَوْفٌ عَلَيْهِمْ وَلَا هُمْ يَحْزَنُوْنَ ۞

٦٣- وَإِذْ أَخَذْنَا مِيْثَاقَكُمْ
وَرَفَعْنَا فَوْقَكُمُ الطُّوْرَ ۖ
خُذُوْا مَا اٰتَيْنٰكُمْ بِقُوَّةٍ
وَاذْكُرُوْا مَا فِيْهِ
لَعَلَّكُمْ تَتَّقُوْنَ ۞

64. But ye turned back thereafter;
Had it not been for the Grace
And Mercy of Allah to you,
Ye had surely been
Among the lost.

٦٤- ثُمَّ تَوَلَّيْتُمْ مِّنْ بَعْدِ ذٰلِكَ فَلَوْلَا فَضْلُ اللهِ عَلَيْكُمْ وَرَحْمَتُهُ لَكُنْتُمْ مِّنَ الْخٰسِرِيْنَ ۝

65. And well ye knew
Those amongst you
Who transgressed
In the matter of the Sabbath;
We said to them:
"Be ye apes,
Despised and rejected."

٦٥- وَلَقَدْ عَلِمْتُمُ الَّذِيْنَ اعْتَدَوْا مِنْكُمْ فِى السَّبْتِ فَقُلْنَا لَهُمْ كُوْنُوْا قِرَدَةً خٰسِئِيْنَ ۝

66. So We made it an example
To their own time
And to their posterity,
And a lesson
To those who fear Allah.

٦٦- فَجَعَلْنٰهَا نَكَالًا لِّمَا بَيْنَ يَدَيْهَا وَمَا خَلْفَهَا وَمَوْعِظَةً لِّلْمُتَّقِيْنَ ۝

67. And remember Moses said
To his people: "Allah commands
That ye sacrifice a heifer."
They said: "Makest thou
A laughing-stock of us?"
He said: "Allah save me
From being an ignorant (fool)!"

٦٧- وَاِذْ قَالَ مُوْسٰى لِقَوْمِهٖٓ اِنَّ اللهَ يَأْمُرُكُمْ اَنْ تَذْبَحُوْا بَقَرَةً قَالُوْٓا اَتَتَّخِذُنَا هُزُوًا قَالَ اَعُوْذُ بِاللهِ اَنْ اَكُوْنَ مِنَ الْجٰهِلِيْنَ ۝

68. They said: "Beseech on our
behalf
Thy Lord to make plain to us
What (heifer) it is!"
He said: "He says: the heifer
Should be neither too old
Nor too young, but of middling
Age: now do what ye are
commanded!"

٦٨- قَالُوا ادْعُ لَنَا رَبَّكَ يُبَيِّنْ لَّنَا مَا هِىَ قَالَ اِنَّهٗ يَقُوْلُ اِنَّهَا بَقَرَةٌ لَّا فَارِضٌ وَّلَا بِكْرٌ عَوَانٌ بَيْنَ ذٰلِكَ فَافْعَلُوْا مَا تُؤْمَرُوْنَ ۝

69. They said: "Beseech on our
behalf
Thy Lord to make plain to us
Her colour." He said: "He says:
A fawn-coloured heifer,
Pure and rich in tone,
The admiration of beholders!"

٦٩- قَالُوا ادْعُ لَنَا رَبَّكَ يُبَيِّنْ لَّنَا مَا لَوْنُهَا قَالَ اِنَّهٗ يَقُوْلُ اِنَّهَا بَقَرَةٌ صَفْرَآءُ فَاقِعٌ لَّوْنُهَا تَسُرُّ النّٰظِرِيْنَ ۝

70. They said: "Beseech on our
behalf
Thy Lord to make plain to us

٧٠- قَالُوا ادْعُ لَنَا رَبَّكَ يُبَيِّنْ لَّنَا مَا هِىَ

What she is: to us are all heifers
Alike: we wish indeed for
                guidance
If Allah wills."

اِنَّ الۡبَقَرَ تَشَٰبَهَ عَلَیۡنَا ؕ
وَ اِنَّاۤ اِنۡ شَآءَ اللّٰهُ لَمُهۡتَدُوۡنَ ۝

71. He said: "He says: a heifer
Not trained to till the soil
Or water the fields; sound
And without blemish." They
               said:
"Now hast thou brought
The truth." Then they offered
Her in sacrifice,
But not with goodwill.

۷۱ - قَالَ اِنَّهٗ یَقُوۡلُ اِنَّهَا بَقَرَةٌ لَّا ذَلُوۡلٌ تُثِیۡرُ
الۡاَرۡضَ وَ لَا تَسۡقِی الۡحَرۡثَ ۚ مُسَلَّمَةٌ لَّا
شِیَةَ فِیۡهَا ؕ قَالُوا الۡـٰٔنَ جِئۡتَ بِالۡحَقِّ ؕ فَذَبَحُوۡهَا
وَ مَا کَادُوۡا یَفۡعَلُوۡنَ ۝

SECTION 9.

72. Remember ye slew a man
And fell into a dispute
Among yourselves as to the
               crime:
But Allah was to bring forth
What ye did hide.

۷۲ - وَ اِذۡ قَتَلۡتُمۡ نَفۡسًا فَادّٰرَءۡتُمۡ فِیۡهَا ؕ
وَ اللّٰهُ مُخۡرِجٌ مَّا کُنۡتُمۡ تَکۡتُمُوۡنَ ۝

73. So We said: "Strike the (body)
With a piece of the (heifer)."
Thus Allah bringeth the dead
To life and showeth you His
               Signs:
Perchance ye may understand.

۷۳ - فَقُلۡنَا اضۡرِبُوۡهُ بِبَعۡضِهَا ؕ
کَذٰلِکَ یُحۡیِ اللّٰهُ الۡمَوۡتٰی ۙ
وَ یُرِیۡکُمۡ اٰیٰتِهٖ لَعَلَّکُمۡ تَعۡقِلُوۡنَ ۝

74. Thenceforth were your hearts
Hardened: they became
Like a rock and even worse
In hardness. For among rocks
There are some from which
Rivers gush forth; others
There are which when split
Asunder send forth water;
And others which sink
For fear of Allah. And Allah is
Not unmindful of what ye do.

۷۴ - ثُمَّ قَسَتۡ قُلُوۡبُکُمۡ مِّنۡ بَعۡدِ ذٰلِکَ
فَهِیَ کَالۡحِجَارَةِ اَوۡ اَشَدُّ قَسۡوَةً ؕ وَ اِنَّ مِنَ
الۡحِجَارَةِ لَمَا یَتَفَجَّرُ مِنۡهُ الۡاَنۡهٰرُ ؕ وَ اِنَّ
مِنۡهَا لَمَا یَشَّقَّقُ فَیَخۡرُجُ مِنۡهُ الۡمَآءُ ؕ وَ
اِنَّ مِنۡهَا لَمَا یَهۡبِطُ مِنۡ خَشۡیَةِ اللّٰهِ ؕ
وَ مَا اللّٰهُ بِغَافِلٍ عَمَّا تَعۡمَلُوۡنَ ۝

75. Can ye (O ye men of Faith)
Entertain the hope that they
Will believe in you?—
Seeing that a party of them
Heard the Word of Allah,
And perverted it knowingly
After they understood it.

۷۵ - اَفَتَطۡمَعُوۡنَ اَنۡ یُّؤۡمِنُوۡا لَکُمۡ وَ قَدۡ کَانَ
فَرِیۡقٌ مِّنۡهُمۡ یَسۡمَعُوۡنَ کَلٰمَ اللّٰهِ ثُمَّ
یُحَرِّفُوۡنَهٗ مِنۡ بَعۡدِ مَا عَقَلُوۡهُ وَ هُمۡ
یَعۡلَمُوۡنَ ۝

76. Behold! when they meet
The men of Faith, they say:
"We believe": but when
They meet each other in private,
They say: "Shall you tell them
What Allah hath revealed to you,
That they may engage you
In argument about it
Before your Lord?"—
Do ye not understand (their aim)?

٧٦ـ وَإِذَا لَقُوا الَّذِيْنَ اٰمَنُوْا قَالُوْا اٰمَنَّا ۖ وَ
إِذَا خَلَا بَعْضُهُمْ إِلَى بَعْضٍ قَالُوْا أَتُحَدِّثُوْنَهُمْ
بِمَا فَتَحَ اللّٰهُ عَلَيْكُمْ لِيُحَاجُّوْكُمْ بِهٖ عِنْدَ
رَبِّكُمْ ۚ
أَفَلَا تَعْقِلُوْنَ ۞

77. Know they not that Allah
Knoweth what they conceal
And what they reveal?

٧٧ـ أَوَلَا يَعْلَمُوْنَ أَنَّ اللّٰهَ يَعْلَمُ مَا يُسِرُّوْنَ
وَمَا يُعْلِنُوْنَ ۞

78. And there are among them
Illiterates, who know not the Book,
But (see therein their own) desires,
And they do nothing but
           conjecture.

٧٨ـ وَمِنْهُمْ أُمِّيُّوْنَ لَا يَعْلَمُوْنَ الْكِتٰبَ
إِلَّا أَمَانِيَّ وَإِنْ هُمْ إِلَّا يَظُنُّوْنَ ۞

79. Then woe to those who write
The Book with their own hands,
And then say: "This is from
             Allah,"
To traffic with it
For a miserable price!—
Woe to them for what their hands
Do write, and for the gain
They make thereby.

٧٩ـ فَوَيْلٌ لِّلَّذِيْنَ يَكْتُبُوْنَ الْكِتٰبَ بِأَيْدِيْهِمْ
ثُمَّ يَقُوْلُوْنَ هٰذَا مِنْ عِنْدِ اللّٰهِ لِيَشْتَرُوْا بِهٖ
ثَمَنًا قَلِيْلًا ۖ فَوَيْلٌ لَّهُمْ مِّمَّا كَتَبَتْ أَيْدِيْهِمْ
وَوَيْلٌ لَّهُمْ مِّمَّا يَكْسِبُوْنَ ۞

80. And they say: "The Fire
Shall not touch us
But for a few numbered days;"
Say: "Have ye taken a promise
From Allah, for He never
Breaks His promise?
Or is it that ye say of Allah
What ye do not know?"

٨٠ـ وَقَالُوْا لَنْ تَمَسَّنَا النَّارُ إِلَّا أَيَّامًا مَّعْدُوْدَةً ۚ
قُلْ أَتَّخَذْتُمْ عِنْدَ اللّٰهِ عَهْدًا فَلَنْ يُّخْلِفَ
اللّٰهُ عَهْدَهٗ أَمْ تَقُوْلُوْنَ عَلَى اللّٰهِ مَا لَا
تَعْلَمُوْنَ ۞

81. Nay, those who seek gain
In Evil, and are girt round
By their sins—
They are Companions of the Fire:
Therein shall they abide
(Forever).

٨١ـ بَلٰى مَنْ كَسَبَ سَيِّئَةً وَّ أَحَاطَتْ بِهٖ
خَطِيْئَتُهٗ فَأُولٰٓئِكَ أَصْحٰبُ النَّارِ ۚ
هُمْ فِيْهَا خٰلِدُوْنَ ۞

82. But those who have faith
And work righteousness.

٨٢ـ وَالَّذِيْنَ اٰمَنُوْا وَ عَمِلُوا الصّٰلِحٰتِ

They are Companions of the
                        Garden:
Therein shall they abide
(Forever).

SECTION 10.

83. And remember We took
A Covenant from the Children
Of Israel (to this effect):
Worship none but Allah;
Treat with kindness
Your parents and kindred,
And orphans and those in need;
Speak fair to the people;
Be steadfast in prayer;
And practise regular charity.
Then did ye turn back,
Except a few among you,
And ye backslide (even now).

84. And remember We took
Your Covenant (to this effect):
Shed no blood amongst you,
Nor turn out your own people
From your homes: and this
Ye solemnly ratified,
And to this ye can bear witness.

85. After this it is ye, the same people,
Who slay among yourselves,
And banish a party of you
From their homes; assist
(Their enemies) against them,
In guilt and transgression;
And if they come to you
As captives, ye ransom   them,
Though it was not lawful
For you to banish them.
Then is it only a part of the Book
That ye believe in,
And do ye reject the rest?
But what is the reward for those
Among you who behave like this
But disgrace in this life?—
And on the Day of Judgement
They shall be consigned
To the most grievous penalty.
For Allah is not unmindful
Of what ye do.

86. These are the people who buy
The life of this world at the price
Of the Hereafter: their penalty
Shall not be lightened
Nor shall they be helped.

SECTION 11.

87. We gave Moses the Book
And followed him up
With a succession of Messengers;
We gave Jesus, the son of Mary,
Clear (Signs) and strengthened him
With the Holy Spirit. Is it
That whenever there comes to you
A Messenger with what ye
Yourselves desire not, ye are
Puffed up with pride?—
Some ye called imposters,
And others ye slay!

88. They say, "Our hearts
Are the wrappings (which preserve
Allah's Word; we need no more)"
Nay, Allah's curse is on them
For their blasphemy:
Little is it they believe.

89. And when there comes to them
A Book from Allah, confirming
What is with them—although
From of old they had prayed
For victory against those
Without Faith—when there comes
To them that which they
(Should) have recognized.
They refuse to believe in it
But the curse of Allah
Is on those without Faith.

90. Miserable is the price
For which they have sold
Their souls, in that they
Deny (the revelation)
Which Allah has sent down,
In insolent envy that Allah
Of His Grace should send it

٨٦- أُولَٰٓئِكَ الَّذِينَ اشْتَرَوُا الْحَيَوٰةَ الدُّنْيَا بِالْأَخِرَةِ ۖ فَلَا يُخَفَّفُ عَنْهُمُ الْعَذَابُ وَلَا هُمْ يُنْصَرُونَ ۝

٨٧- وَلَقَدْ اٰتَيْنَا مُوسَى الْكِتٰبَ وَقَفَّيْنَا مِنْ بَعْدِهِ بِالرُّسُلِ ۖ وَاٰتَيْنَا عِيسَى ابْنَ مَرْيَمَ الْبَيِّنٰتِ وَاَيَّدْنٰهُ بِرُوحِ الْقُدُسِ ۗ اَفَكُلَّمَا جَاءَكُمْ رَسُولٌ بِمَا لَا تَهْوَىٰ اَنْفُسُكُمُ اسْتَكْبَرْتُمْ ۖ فَفَرِيقًا كَذَّبْتُمْ وَفَرِيقًا تَقْتُلُونَ ۝

٨٨- وَقَالُوا قُلُوبُنَا غُلْفٌ ۚ بَلْ لَعَنَهُمُ اللّٰهُ بِكُفْرِهِمْ فَقَلِيلًا مَا يُؤْمِنُونَ ۝

٨٩- وَلَمَّا جَاءَهُمْ كِتٰبٌ مِنْ عِنْدِ اللّٰهِ مُصَدِّقٌ لِمَا مَعَهُمْ ۙ وَكَانُوا مِنْ قَبْلُ يَسْتَفْتِحُونَ عَلَى الَّذِينَ كَفَرُوا ۖ فَلَمَّا جَاءَهُمْ مَا عَرَفُوا كَفَرُوا بِهِ ۚ فَلَعْنَةُ اللّٰهِ عَلَى الْكٰفِرِينَ ۝

٩٠- بِئْسَمَا اشْتَرَوْا بِهِ اَنْفُسَهُمْ اَنْ يَكْفُرُوا بِمَا اَنْزَلَ اللّٰهُ بَغْيًا اَنْ يُنَزِّلَ اللّٰهُ مِنْ فَضْلِهِ عَلَى مَنْ يَشَاءُ ۖ

To any of His servants He
pleases:
Thus have they drawn
On themselves Wrath upon
Wrath,
And humiliating is the
punishment
Of those who reject Faith.

91. When it is said to them,
"Believe in what Allah
Hath sent down," they say,
"We believe in what was sent
down
To us;" yet they reject
All besides, even if it be Truth
Confirming what is with them.
Say: "Why then have ye slain
The prophets of Allah in times
Gone by, if ye did indeed
Believe?"

92. There came to you Moses
With clear (Signs); yet
Ye worshipped the Calf
(Even) after that, and ye
Did behave wrongfully.

93. And remember We took
Your Covenant and We raised
Above you (the towering height)
Of Mount (Sinai):
(Saying): "Hold firmly
To what We have given you,
And hearken (to the Law)":
They said: "We hear,
And we disobey":
And they had to drink
Into their hearts
(Of the taint) of the Calf
Because of their Faithlessness.
Say: "Vile indeed
Are the behests of your Faith
If ye have any faith!"

94. Say: "If the last Home,
with Allah, be for you specially,
And not for anyone else,

Then seek ye for death,
If ye are sincere."

فَتَمَنَّوُا الْمَوْتَ اِنْ كُنْتُمْ صٰدِقِيْنَ ۟

95. But they will never seek
For death, on account of the
                              (sins)
Which their hands have sent
On before them.
And Allah is well-acquainted
With the wrongdoers.

٩٥- وَلَنْ يَّتَمَنَّوْهُ اَبَدًا بِمَا قَدَّمَتْ اَيْدِيْهِمْ ؕ وَاللّٰهُ عَلِيْمٌۢ بِالظّٰلِمِيْنَ ۟

96. Thou wilt indeed find them,
Of all people, most greedy
Of life—even more
Than the idolaters:
Each one of them wishes
He could be given a life
Of a thousand years:
But the grant of such life
Will not save him
From (due) punishment.
For Allah sees well
All that they do.

٩٦- وَلَتَجِدَنَّهُمْ اَحْرَصَ النَّاسِ عَلٰى حَيٰوةٍ ۛ وَمِنَ الَّذِيْنَ اَشْرَكُوْا ۛ يَوَدُّ اَحَدُهُمْ لَوْ يُعَمَّرُ اَلْفَ سَنَةٍ ۚ وَمَا هُوَ بِمُزَحْزِحِهٖ مِنَ الْعَذَابِ اَنْ يُّعَمَّرَ ؕ وَاللّٰهُ بَصِيْرٌۢ بِمَا يَعْمَلُوْنَ ۟

SECTION 12.

97. Say: Whoever is an enemy
To Gabriel—for he brings down
The (revelation) to thy heart
By Allah's will, a confirmation
Of what went before.
And guidance and glad tidings
For those who believe—

٩٧- قُلْ مَنْ كَانَ عَدُوًّا لِّجِبْرِيْلَ فَاِنَّهٗ نَزَّلَهٗ عَلٰى قَلْبِكَ بِاِذْنِ اللّٰهِ مُصَدِّقًا لِّمَا بَيْنَ يَدَيْهِ وَهُدًى وَّبُشْرٰى لِلْمُؤْمِنِيْنَ ۟

98. Whoever is an enemy to Allah
And His angels and prophets,
To Gabriel and Michael—
Lo! Allah is an enemy to those
Who reject Faith.

٩٨- مَنْ كَانَ عَدُوًّا لِّلّٰهِ وَمَلٰٓئِكَتِهٖ وَرُسُلِهٖ وَجِبْرِيْلَ وَمِيْكٰلَ فَاِنَّ اللّٰهَ عَدُوٌّ لِّلْكٰفِرِيْنَ ۟

99. We have sent down to thee
Manifest Signs (*āyāt*);
And none reject them
But those who are perverse.

٩٩- وَلَقَدْ اَنْزَلْنَآ اِلَيْكَ اٰيٰتٍۢ بَيِّنٰتٍ ۚ وَمَا يَكْفُرُ بِهَآ اِلَّا الْفٰسِقُوْنَ ۟

100. Is it not (the case) that
Every time they make a
                         Covenant,
Some party among them
Throw it aside?—Nay,
Most of them are faithless.

١٠٠- اَوَكُلَّمَا عٰهَدُوْا عَهْدًا نَّبَذَهٗ فَرِيْقٌ مِّنْهُمْ ؕ بَلْ اَكْثَرُهُمْ لَا يُؤْمِنُوْنَ ۟

101. And when there came to them
A Messenger from Allah,
Confirming what was with them,
A Party of the People of the
Book
Threw away the Book of Allah
Behind their backs.
As if (it had been something)
They did not know!

١٠١-وَلَمَّا جَآءَهُمْ رَسُوْلٌ مِّنْ عِنْدِ اللّٰهِ
مُصَدِّقٌ لِّمَا مَعَهُمْ
نَبَذَ فَرِيْقٌ مِّنَ الَّذِيْنَ اُوْتُوا الْكِتٰبَ ۚ كِتٰبَ
اللّٰهِ وَرَآءَ ظُهُوْرِهِمْ كَاَنَّهُمْ لَا يَعْلَمُوْنَ ۝

102. They followed what the evil
ones
Gave out (falsely)
Against the power
Of Solomon: the blasphemers
Were, not Solomon, but
The evil ones, teaching men
Magic, and such things
As came down at Babylon
To the angels Hārūt and
Mārūt.
But neither of these taught
anyone
(Such things) without saying:
"We are only for trial;
So do not blaspheme."
They learned from them[105]
The means to sow discord
Between man and wife.
But they could not thus
Harm anyone except
By Allah's permission.
And they learned what harmed
them,
Not what profited them.
And they knew that the
buyers
Of (magic) would have
No share in the happiness
Of the Hereafter. And vile
Was the price for which
They did sell their souls,
If they but knew!

١٠٢-وَاتَّبَعُوْا مَا تَتْلُوا الشَّيٰطِيْنُ عَلٰى
مُلْكِ سُلَيْمٰنَ ۚ وَمَا كَفَرَ سُلَيْمٰنُ وَلٰكِنَّ
الشَّيٰطِيْنَ كَفَرُوْا يُعَلِّمُوْنَ النَّاسَ
السِّحْرَ ۚ

وَمَآ اُنْزِلَ عَلَى الْمَلَكَيْنِ بِبَابِلَ هَارُوْتَ
وَمَارُوْتَ ۚ

وَمَا يُعَلِّمٰنِ مِنْ اَحَدٍ
حَتّٰى يَقُوْلَآ اِنَّمَا نَحْنُ فِتْنَةٌ فَلَا تَكْفُرْ ۚ
فَيَتَعَلَّمُوْنَ مِنْهُمَا مَا يُفَرِّقُوْنَ بِهٖ بَيْنَ
الْمَرْءِ وَزَوْجِهٖ ۚ

وَمَا هُمْ بِضَآرِّيْنَ بِهٖ مِنْ اَحَدٍ اِلَّا بِاِذْنِ اللّٰهِ ۚ
وَيَتَعَلَّمُوْنَ مَا يَضُرُّهُمْ وَلَا يَنْفَعُهُمْ ۚ
وَلَقَدْ عَلِمُوْا لَمَنِ اشْتَرٰىهُ مَا لَهٗ فِى
الْاٰخِرَةِ مِنْ خَلَاقٍ ۗ
وَلَبِئْسَ مَا شَرَوْا بِهٖٓ اَنْفُسَهُمْ ۚ
لَوْ كَانُوْا يَعْلَمُوْنَ ۝

103. If they had kept their Faith
And guarded themselves from
evil,
Far better had been
The reward from their Lord,

١٠٣-وَلَوْ اَنَّهُمْ اٰمَنُوْا وَاتَّقَوْا
لَمَثُوْبَةٌ مِّنْ عِنْدِ اللّٰهِ خَيْرٌ ۚ

If they but knew!

SECTION 13.

104. **O** ye of Faith!
Say not (to the Prophet)
Words of ambiguous import,
But words of respect;
And hearken (to him):
To those without Faith
Is a grievous punishment.

105. It is never the wish
Of those without Faith
Among the People of the Book,
Nor of the Pagans,
That anything good
Should come down to you
From your Lord.
But Allah will choose
For His special Mercy
Whom He will—for Allah is
Lord of grace abounding.

106. None of Our revelations
Do We abrogate
Or cause to be forgotten,
But We substitute
Something better or similar:
Knowest thou not that Allah
Hath power over all things?

107. Knowest thou not
That to Allah belongeth
The dominion of the heavens
And the earth?
And besides Him ye have
Neither patron nor helper.

108. **W**ould ye question
Your Messenger as Moses
Was questioned of old?
But whoever changeth
From Faith to Unbelief,
Hath strayed without doubt
From the even way.

109. Quite a number of the People
Of the Book wish they could
Turn you (people) back

لَوْ كَانُوا يَعْلَمُونَ ۞

١٠٤- يَا أَيُّهَا الَّذِينَ آمَنُوا
لَا تَقُولُوا رَاعِنَا
وَقُولُوا انْظُرْنَا وَاسْمَعُوا
وَلِلْكَافِرِينَ عَذَابٌ أَلِيمٌ ۞

١٠٥- مَا يَوَدُّ الَّذِينَ كَفَرُوا
مِنْ أَهْلِ الْكِتَابِ
وَلَا الْمُشْرِكِينَ
أَنْ يُنَزَّلَ عَلَيْكُمْ مِنْ خَيْرٍ مِنْ رَبِّكُمْ
وَاللّٰهُ يَخْتَصُّ بِرَحْمَتِهِ مَنْ يَشَاءُ
وَاللّٰهُ ذُو الْفَضْلِ الْعَظِيمِ ۞

١٠٦- مَا نَنْسَخْ مِنْ آيَةٍ
أَوْ نُنْسِهَا نَأْتِ بِخَيْرٍ مِنْهَا أَوْ مِثْلِهَا
أَلَمْ تَعْلَمْ أَنَّ اللّٰهَ عَلَى كُلِّ شَيْءٍ قَدِيرٌ ۞

١٠٧- أَلَمْ تَعْلَمْ أَنَّ اللّٰهَ لَهُ مُلْكُ السَّمٰوٰتِ
وَالْأَرْضِ ۗ وَمَا لَكُمْ مِنْ دُونِ اللّٰهِ مِنْ
وَلِيٍّ وَلَا نَصِيرٍ ۞

١٠٨- أَمْ تُرِيدُونَ أَنْ تَسْئَلُوا رَسُولَكُمْ
كَمَا سُئِلَ مُوسَى مِنْ قَبْلُ
وَمَنْ يَتَبَدَّلِ الْكُفْرَ بِالْإِيمَانِ
فَقَدْ ضَلَّ سَوَاءَ السَّبِيلِ ۞

١٠٩- وَدَّ كَثِيرٌ مِنْ أَهْلِ الْكِتَابِ

To infidelity after ye have
                    believed.

From selfish envy,
After the Truth hath become
Manifest unto them:
But forgive and overlook,
Till Allah accomplishes
His purpose: for Allah
Hath power over all things.

لَوۡ يَرُدُّوۡنَكُمۡ مِّنۡ بَعۡدِ اِيۡمَانِكُمۡ كُفَّارًا ۚ
حَسَدًا مِّنۡ عِنۡدِ اَنۡفُسِهِمۡ مِّنۡ بَعۡدِ مَا
تَبَيَّنَ لَهُمُ الۡحَقُّ ۚ
فَاعۡفُوۡا وَاصۡفَحُوۡا حَتّٰى يَاۡتِىَ اللّٰهُ بِاَمۡرِهٖ ؕ
اِنَّ اللّٰهَ عَلٰى كُلِّ شَىۡءٍ قَدِيۡرٌ ۝

110. And be steadfast in prayer
And regular in charity:
And whatever good
Ye send forth for your souls
Before you, ye shall find it
With Allah: for Allah sees
Well all that ye do.

١١٠- وَاَقِيۡمُوا الصَّلٰوةَ وَاٰتُوا الزَّكٰوةَ ؕ
وَمَا تُقَدِّمُوۡا لِاَنۡفُسِكُمۡ مِّنۡ خَيۡرٍ تَجِدُوۡهُ
عِنۡدَ اللّٰهِ ؕ
اِنَّ اللّٰهَ بِمَا تَعۡمَلُوۡنَ بَصِيۡرٌ ۝

111. And they say: "None
Shall enter Paradise unless
He be a Jew or a Christian."
Those are their (vain) desires.
Say: "Produce your proof
If ye are truthful."

١١١- وَقَالُوۡا لَنۡ يَّدۡخُلَ الۡجَنَّةَ اِلَّا مَنۡ
كَانَ هُوۡدًا اَوۡ نَصٰرٰى ؕ تِلۡكَ اَمَانِيُّهُمۡ ؕ قُلۡ
هَاتُوۡا بُرۡهَانَكُمۡ اِنۡ كُنۡتُمۡ صٰدِقِيۡنَ ۝

112. Nay—whoever submits
His whole self   to Allah
And is a doer of good—
He will get his reward
With his Lord;
On such shall be no fear,
Nor shall they grieve.

١١٢- بَلٰى ۚ مَنۡ اَسۡلَمَ وَجۡهَهٗ لِلّٰهِ
وَهُوَ مُحۡسِنٌ فَلَهٗۤ اَجۡرُهٗ عِنۡدَ رَبِّهٖ ۪
وَلَا خَوۡفٌ عَلَيۡهِمۡ وَلَا هُمۡ يَحۡزَنُوۡنَ ۝

SECTION 14.

113. The Jews say: "The Christians
Have naught (to stand) upon";
And the Christians say:
"The Jews have naught
(To stand) upon." Yet they
(Profess to) study the (same) Book.
Like unto their word
Is what those say who know
                      not;
But Allah will judge
Between them in their quarrel
On the Day of Judgement.

١١٣- وَقَالَتِ الۡيَهُوۡدُ لَيۡسَتِ النَّصٰرٰى عَلٰى
شَىۡءٍ ۖ وَّقَالَتِ النَّصٰرٰى لَيۡسَتِ الۡيَهُوۡدُ
عَلٰى شَىۡءٍ ۙ وَّهُمۡ يَتۡلُوۡنَ الۡكِتٰبَ ؕ
كَذٰلِكَ قَالَ الَّذِيۡنَ لَا يَعۡلَمُوۡنَ مِثۡلَ قَوۡلِهِمۡ ۚ
فَاللّٰهُ يَحۡكُمُ بَيۡنَهُمۡ يَوۡمَ الۡقِيٰمَةِ فِيۡمَا كَانُوۡا
فِيۡهِ يَخۡتَلِفُوۡنَ ۝

114. And who is more unjust

١١٤- وَمَنۡ اَظۡلَمُ مِمَّنۡ مَّنَعَ مَسٰجِدَ اللّٰهِ

Than he who forbids
That in places for the worship
Of Allah, His name should be
Celebrated?—whose zeal
Is (in fact) to ruin them?
It was not fitting that such
Should themselves enter them
Except in fear. For them
There is nothing but disgrace
In this world, and in the world
To come, an exceeding torment.

اَنْ يُّذْكَرَ فِيْهَا اسْمُهٗ وَسَعٰى فِيْ خَرَابِهَا
اُولٰٓئِكَ مَا كَانَ لَهُمْ اَنْ يَّدْخُلُوْهَآ اِلَّا
خَآئِفِيْنَ ۚ ۖ
لَهُمْ فِي الدُّنْيَا خِزْيٌ وَّلَهُمْ فِي الْاٰخِرَةِ
عَذَابٌ عَظِيْمٌ ۝

115. To Allah belong the East
And the West: whithersoever
Ye turn, there is Allah's
                    countenance.
For Allah is All-Embracing,
All-Knowing.

١١٥- وَلِلّٰهِ الْمَشْرِقُ وَالْمَغْرِبُ ۚ
فَاَيْنَمَا تُوَلُّوْا فَثَمَّ وَجْهُ اللّٰهِ ۚ
اِنَّ اللّٰهَ وَاسِعٌ عَلِيْمٌ ۝

116. They say: "Allah hath begotten
A son": Glory be to Him—Nay,
To Him belongs all
That is in the heavens
And on earth: everything
Renders worship to Him.

١١٦- وَقَالُوا اتَّخَذَ اللّٰهُ وَلَدًا ۙ
سُبْحٰنَهٗ ۚ بَلْ لَّهٗ مَا فِي السَّمٰوٰتِ وَالْاَرْضِ ۚ
كُلٌّ لَّهٗ قَانِتُوْنَ ۝

117. To Him is due
The primal origin
Of the heavens and the earth:
When He decreeth a matter,
He saith to it: "Be,"
And it is.

١١٧- بَدِيْعُ
السَّمٰوٰتِ وَالْاَرْضِ ۚ وَاِذَا قَضٰى اَمْرًا
فَاِنَّمَا يَقُوْلُ لَهٗ كُنْ فَيَكُوْنُ ۝

118. Say those without knowledge:
"Why speaketh not Allah
Unto us? Or why cometh not
Unto us a Sign?"
So said the people before them
Words of similar import.
Their hearts are alike.
We have indeed made clear
The Signs unto any people
Who hold firmly
To Faith (in their hearts).

١١٨- وَقَالَ الَّذِيْنَ لَا يَعْلَمُوْنَ لَوْلَا
يُكَلِّمُنَا اللّٰهُ اَوْ تَأْتِيْنَآ اٰيَةٌ ۘ
كَذٰلِكَ قَالَ الَّذِيْنَ مِنْ قَبْلِهِمْ مِّثْلَ
قَوْلِهِمْ ۚ
تَشَابَهَتْ قُلُوْبُهُمْ ۗ
قَدْ بَيَّنَّا الْاٰيٰتِ لِقَوْمٍ يُّوْقِنُوْنَ ۝

119. Verily, We have sent thee
In truth as a bearer

١١٩- اِنَّآ اَرْسَلْنٰكَ بِالْحَقِّ بَشِيْرًا وَّ

Of glad tidings and a warner:
But of thee no question
Shall be asked of the companions
Of the Blazing Fire.

نَذِيرًا
وَّلَا تُسْئَلُ عَنْ اَصْحٰبِ الْجَحِيْمِ ٥

120. Never will the Jews
Or the Christians be satisfied
With thee unless thou follow
Their form of religion. Say:
"The Guidance of Allah—that
Is the (only) Guidance,"
Wert thou to follow their desires
After the knowledge
Which hath reached thee,
Then wouldst thou find
Neither Protector nor Helper
Against Allah.

١٢٠- وَلَنْ تَرْضٰى عَنْكَ الْيَهُوْدُ وَلَا النَّصٰرٰى
حَتّٰى تَتَّبِعَ مِلَّتَهُمْ ۚ قُلْ
اِنَّ هُدَى اللّٰهِ هُوَ الْهُدٰى ۗ
وَلَئِنِ اتَّبَعْتَ اَهْوَآءَهُمْ بَعْدَ الَّذِىْ
جَآءَكَ مِنَ الْعِلْمِ ۙ
مَالَكَ مِنَ اللّٰهِ مِنْ وَّلِيٍّ وَّلَا نَصِيْرٍ ٥

121. Those to whom We have sent
The Book study it as it
Should be studied: they are
The ones that believe therein:
Those who reject faith therein—
The loss is their own.

١٢١- اَلَّذِيْنَ اٰتَيْنٰهُمُ الْكِتٰبَ يَتْلُوْنَهٗ حَقَّ
تِلَاوَتِهٖ ۗ اُولٰٓئِكَ يُؤْمِنُوْنَ بِهٖ ۗ وَمَنْ
يَّكْفُرْ بِهٖ فَاُولٰٓئِكَ هُمُ الْخٰسِرُوْنَ ٥

SECTION 15.

122. Children of Israel! call to mind
The special favour which I
bestowed
Upon you, and that I preferred
you
To all others (for My Message).

١٢٢- يٰبَنِىْ اِسْرَآءِيْلَ اذْكُرُوْا نِعْمَتِىَ الَّتِىْ
اَنْعَمْتُ عَلَيْكُمْ
وَاَنِّىْ فَضَّلْتُكُمْ عَلَى الْعٰلَمِيْنَ ٥

123. Then guard yourselves against
a Day
When one soul shall not avail
another.
Nor shall compensation be
accepted from her
Nor shall intercession profit her
Nor shall anyone be helped
(from outside).

١٢٣- وَاتَّقُوْا يَوْمًا
لَّا تَجْزِىْ نَفْسٌ عَنْ نَّفْسٍ شَيْئًا
وَّلَا يُقْبَلُ مِنْهَا عَدْلٌ
وَّلَا تَنْفَعُهَا شَفَاعَةٌ ۙ
وَّلَا هُمْ يُنْصَرُوْنَ ٥

124. And remember that Abraham
Was tried by his Lord
With certain Commands,
Which he fulfilled:
He said: "I will make thee
An Imam[124] to the Nations."

١٢٤- وَاِذِ ابْتَلٰٓى اِبْرٰهٖمَ رَبُّهٗ
بِكَلِمٰتٍ فَاَتَمَّهُنَّ ۗ
قَالَ اِنِّىْ جَاعِلُكَ

He pleaded: "And also
(Imāms) from my offspring!"
He answered: "But My Promise
Is not within the reach
Of evildoers."

125. Remember We made the House
A place of assembly for men
And a place of safety;
And take ye the Station
Of Abraham as a place
Of prayer; and We covenanted
With Abraham and Ismā'īl,
That they should sanctify
My House for those who
Compass it round, or use it
As a retreat, or bow, or
Prostrate themselves (therein
In Prayer).

126. And remember Abraham said:
"My Lord, make this a City
Of Peace,   and feed its People
With fruits   —such of them
As believe in Allah and the
                    Last Day."
He said: "(Yea), and such as
Reject Faith—for a while
Will I grant them their pleasure,
But will soon drive them
To the torment of Fire
An evil destination (indeed)!"

127. And remember Abraham
And Ismā'īl raised
The foundations of the House
(With this prayer): "Our Lord!
Accept (this service) from us:
For Thou art the All-Hearing,
The All-Knowing.

128. "Our Lord! make of us
Muslims, bowing to Thy (Will),
And of our progeny a people
Muslim, bowing to thy (Will);
And show us our places for
The celebration of (due) rites;
And turn unto us (in Mercy);
For Thou art the Oft-Returning,

لِلنَّاسِ اِمَامًا ۖ

قَالَ وَمِنْ ذُرِّيَّتِى ۖ

قَالَ لَا يَنَالُ عَهْدِى الظَّالِمِينَ ۝

١٢٥- وَاِذْ جَعَلْنَا الْبَيْتَ مَثَابَةً لِّلنَّاسِ وَاَمْنًا ۖ

وَاتَّخِذُوْا مِنْ مَّقَامِ اِبْرٰهٖمَ مُصَلًّى ۖ

وَعَهِدْنَا اِلٰۤى اِبْرٰهٖمَ وَاِسْمٰعِيْلَ

اَنْ طَهِّرَا بَيْتِىَ لِلطَّآئِفِيْنَ

وَالْعٰكِفِيْنَ وَالرُّكَّعِ السُّجُوْدِ ۝

١٢٦- وَاِذْ قَالَ اِبْرٰهٖمُ رَبِّ اجْعَلْ هٰذَا بَلَدًا اٰمِنًا وَّارْزُقْ اَهْلَهٗ مِنَ الثَّمَرٰتِ

مَنْ اٰمَنَ مِنْهُمْ بِاللّٰهِ وَالْيَوْمِ الْاٰخِرِ ۖ

قَالَ وَمَنْ كَفَرَ فَاُمَتِّعُهٗ قَلِيْلًا

ثُمَّ اَضْطَرُّهٗ اِلٰى عَذَابِ النَّارِ ۖ

وَبِئْسَ الْمَصِيْرُ ۝

١٢٧- وَاِذْ يَرْفَعُ اِبْرٰهٖمُ الْقَوَاعِدَ مِنَ الْبَيْتِ وَاِسْمٰعِيْلُ ۖ

رَبَّنَا تَقَبَّلْ مِنَّا ۖ

اِنَّكَ اَنْتَ السَّمِيْعُ الْعَلِيْمُ ۝

١٢٨- رَبَّنَا وَاجْعَلْنَا مُسْلِمَيْنِ لَكَ

وَمِنْ ذُرِّيَّتِنَا اُمَّةً مُّسْلِمَةً لَّكَ ۖ

وَاَرِنَا مَنَاسِكَنَا وَتُبْ عَلَيْنَا ۖ

اِنَّكَ اَنْتَ التَّوَّابُ

Most Merciful.

السَّحِيْمُ ۟

129. "Our Lord! send amongst
them
A Messenger of their own,
Who shall rehearse Thy Signs
To them and instruct them
In Scripture and Wisdom,
And sanctify them:
For Thou art the Exalted in Might
The Wise."

١٢٩- رَبَّنَا وَابْعَثْ فِيْهِمْ رَسُوْلًا مِّنْهُمْ يَتْلُوْا عَلَيْهِمْ اٰيٰتِكَ وَيُعَلِّمُهُمُ الْكِتٰبَ وَالْحِكْمَةَ وَيُزَكِّيْهِمْ ؕ اِنَّكَ اَنْتَ الْعَزِيْزُ الْحَكِيْمُ ۚ

SECTION 16.

130. And who turns away
From the religion of Abraham
But such as debase their souls
With folly? Him We chose
And rendered pure in this world:
And he will be in the Hereafter
In the ranks of the Righteous.

١٣٠- وَمَنْ يَّرْغَبُ عَنْ مِّلَّةِ اِبْرٰهٖمَ اِلَّا مَنْ سَفِهَ نَفْسَهٗ ؕ وَلَقَدِ اصْطَفَيْنٰهُ فِى الدُّنْيَا ۚ وَاِنَّهٗ فِى الْاٰخِرَةِ لَمِنَ الصّٰلِحِيْنَ ۟

131. Behold! his Lord said
To him: "Bow (thy will to Me):"
He said: "I bow (my will)
To the Lord and Cherisher
Of the Universe."

١٣١- اِذْ قَالَ لَهٗ رَبُّهٗۤ اَسْلِمْ ۙ قَالَ اَسْلَمْتُ لِرَبِّ الْعٰلَمِيْنَ ۟

132. And this was the legacy
That Abraham left to his sons,
And so did Jacob;
"Oh my sons! Allah hath chosen
The Faith for you; then die not
Except in the state of
submission (to Allah).

١٣٢- وَوَصّٰى بِهَآ اِبْرٰهٖمُ بَنِيْهِ وَيَعْقُوْبُ ؕ يٰبَنِيَّ اِنَّ اللّٰهَ اصْطَفٰى لَكُمُ الدِّيْنَ فَلَا تَمُوْتُنَّ اِلَّا وَاَنْتُمْ مُّسْلِمُوْنَ ؕ

133. Were ye witnesses
When Death appeared before
Jacob?
Behold, he said to his sons:
"What will ye worship after me?"
They said: "We shall worhip
Thy God and the God of thy
fathers, —
Of Abraham, Ismā'īl and Isaac—
The One (True) God:
To him we bow (in Islam)."

١٣٣- اَمْ كُنْتُمْ شُهَدَآءَ اِذْ حَضَرَ يَعْقُوْبَ الْمَوْتُ ۙ اِذْ قَالَ لِبَنِيْهِ مَا تَعْبُدُوْنَ مِنْۢ بَعْدِيْ ؕ قَالُوْا نَعْبُدُ اِلٰهَكَ وَ اِلٰهَ اٰبَآئِكَ اِبْرٰهٖمَ وَاِسْمٰعِيْلَ وَاِسْحٰقَ اِلٰهًا وَّاحِدًا ۚ وَّنَحْنُ لَهٗ مُسْلِمُوْنَ ۟

134. That was a People that hath
Passed away. They shall reap

١٣٤- تِلْكَ اُمَّةٌ قَدْ خَلَتْ ۚ لَهَا مَا

The fruit of what they did,
And ye of what ye do!
Of their merits
There is no question in your
             case!

كَسَبَتْ وَ لَكُمْ مَّا كَسَبْتُمْ ۚ وَلَا تُسْـَٔلُوْنَ عَمَّا كَانُوْا يَعْمَلُوْنَ ۞

135. They say: "Become Jews
Or Christians if ye would be guided
(To salvation)." Say thou:
"Nay! (I would rather) the
             Religion
Of Abraham, the True,
And he joined not gods with
             Allah."

١٣٥- وَ قَالُوْا كُوْنُوْا هُوْدًا اَوْ نَصٰرٰى تَهْتَدُوْا ۗ قُلْ بَلْ مِلَّةَ اِبْرٰهٖمَ حَنِيْفًا ۗ وَ مَا كَانَ مِنَ الْمُشْرِكِيْنَ ۞

136. Say ye: "We believe
In Allah, and the revelation
Given to us, and to Abraham,
Ismāʿīl, Isaac, Jacob,
And the Tribes, and that given
To Moses and Jesus, and that given
To (all) Prophets from their Lord:
We make no difference
Between one and another of them:
And we bow to Allah (in Islam)."

١٣٦- قُوْلُوْٓا اٰمَنَّا بِاللهِ وَمَآ اُنْزِلَ اِلَيْنَا وَمَآ اُنْزِلَ اِلٰٓى اِبْرٰهٖمَ وَاِسْمٰعِيْلَ وَاِسْحٰقَ وَ يَعْقُوْبَ وَالْاَسْبَاطِ وَمَآ اُوْتِيَ مُوْسٰى وَ عِيْسٰى وَمَآ اُوْتِيَ النَّبِيُّوْنَ مِنْ رَّبِّهِمْ ۚ لَا نُفَرِّقُ بَيْنَ اَحَدٍ مِّنْهُمْ ۖ وَنَحْنُ لَهٗ مُسْلِمُوْنَ ۞

137. So if they believe
As ye believe, they are indeed
On the right path; but if
They turn back, it is they
Who are in schism: but Allah will
Suffice thee as against them,
And He is the All-Hearing,
The All-Knowing.

١٣٧- فَاِنْ اٰمَنُوْا بِمِثْلِ مَآ اٰمَنْتُمْ بِهٖ فَقَدِ اهْتَدَوْا ۚ وَاِنْ تَوَلَّوْا فَاِنَّمَا هُمْ فِيْ شِقَاقٍ ۚ فَسَيَكْفِيْكَهُمُ اللهُ ۚ وَهُوَ السَّمِيْعُ الْعَلِيْمُ ۞

138. (Our religion is)
The Baptism of Allah:
And who can baptize better
Than Allah? And it is He
Whom we worship.

١٣٨- صِبْغَةَ اللهِ ۚ وَمَنْ اَحْسَنُ مِنَ اللهِ صِبْغَةً ۖ وَّنَحْنُ لَهٗ عٰبِدُوْنَ ۞

139. Say: Will ye dispute
With us about Allah, seeing
That He is our Lord
And your Lord; that we
Are responsible for our doings
And ye for yours; and that
We are sincere (in our faith)
In Him?

١٣٩- قُلْ اَتُحَاجُّوْنَنَا فِى اللهِ وَهُوَ رَبُّنَا وَرَبُّكُمْ ۚ وَلَنَآ اَعْمَالُنَا وَلَكُمْ اَعْمَالُكُمْ ۚ وَنَحْنُ لَهٗ مُخْلِصُوْنَ ۞

140. Or do ye say that
Abraham, Ismā'īl, Isaac,
Jacob and the Tribes were
Jews or Christians?
Say: Do ye know better
Than Allah? Ah! who
Is more unjust than those
Who conceal the testimony
They have from Allah?
But Allah is not unmindful
Of what ye do!

١٤٠- أَمْ تَقُولُونَ إِنَّ إِبْرَٰهِۦمَ وَإِسْمَٰعِيلَ
وَإِسْحَٰقَ وَيَعْقُوبَ وَالْأَسْبَاطَ كَانُوا
هُودًا أَوْ نَصَٰرَىٰ قُلْ ءَأَنتُمْ أَعْلَمُ أَمِ اللَّهُ
وَمَنْ أَظْلَمُ مِمَّن كَتَمَ شَهَٰدَةً عِندَهُۥ
مِنَ اللَّهِ
وَمَا اللَّهُ بِغَٰفِلٍ عَمَّا تَعْمَلُونَ ○

141. That was a people that hath
Passed away. They shall reap
The fruit of what they did
And ye of what ye do!
Of their merits
There is no question in your
case:

١٤١- تِلْكَ أُمَّةٌ قَدْ خَلَتْ
لَهَا مَا كَسَبَتْ وَلَكُم مَّا كَسَبْتُمْ
وَلَا تُسْأَلُونَ عَمَّا كَانُوا يَعْمَلُونَ ○ ﷼

SECTION 17

142. The Fools among the people
Will say: "What hath turned
Them from the Qiblah to which
They were used?" Say:
To Allah belong East and West:
He guideth whom He will
To a Way that is straight.

١٤٢- سَيَقُولُ السُّفَهَآءُ مِنَ النَّاسِ ﷽
مَا وَلَّىٰهُمْ عَن قِبْلَتِهِمُ الَّتِي
كَانُوا عَلَيْهَا قُل لِّلَّهِ الْمَشْرِقُ وَالْمَغْرِبُ
يَهْدِي مَن يَشَآءُ إِلَىٰ صِرَٰطٍ مُّسْتَقِيمٍ ○

143. Thus have We made of you
An *Ummah* justly balanced,
That ye might be witnesses
Over the nations,
And the Messenger a witness
Over yourselves;
And We appointed the Qiblah
To which thou wast used,
Only to test those who followed
The Messenger from those
Who would turn on their
heels
(From the Faith). Indeed it was
(A change) momentous, except
To those guided by Allah.
And never would Allah
Make your faith of no effect.
For Allah is to all people

١٤٣- وَكَذَٰلِكَ جَعَلْنَٰكُمْ أُمَّةً وَسَطًا
لِّتَكُونُوا شُهَدَآءَ عَلَى النَّاسِ
وَيَكُونَ الرَّسُولُ عَلَيْكُمْ شَهِيدًا
وَمَا جَعَلْنَا الْقِبْلَةَ الَّتِي كُنتَ عَلَيْهَا
إِلَّا لِنَعْلَمَ مَن يَتَّبِعُ الرَّسُولَ
مِمَّن يَنقَلِبُ عَلَىٰ عَقِبَيْهِ
وَإِن كَانَتْ لَكَبِيرَةً إِلَّا عَلَى الَّذِينَ هَدَى
اللَّهُ
وَمَا كَانَ اللَّهُ
لِيُضِيعَ إِيمَٰنَكُمْ

الجزء الثاني سورة البقرة ٢

Most surely full of kindness,
Most Merciful.

اِنَّ اللّٰهَ بِالنَّاسِ لَرَءُوْفٌ رَّحِيْمٌ ۞

144. We see the turning
Of thy face (for guidance)
To the heavens: now
Shall We turn thee
To a Qiblah that shall
Please thee. Turn then
Thy face in the direction
Of the Sacred Mosque:
Wherever ye are, turn
Your faces in that direction.
The people of the Book
Know well that that is
The truth from their Lord,
Nor is Allah unmindful
Of what they do.

١٤٤- قَدْ نَرٰى تَقَلُّبَ وَجْهِكَ فِى السَّمَآءِ ۚ
فَلَنُوَلِّيَنَّكَ قِبْلَةً تَرْضٰهَا ۚ
فَوَلِّ وَجْهَكَ شَطْرَ الْمَسْجِدِ الْحَرَامِ ۚ
وَحَيْثُ مَا كُنْتُمْ فَوَلُّوْا وُجُوْهَكُمْ شَطْرَهٗ ۗ
وَاِنَّ الَّذِيْنَ اُوْتُوا الْكِتٰبَ لَيَعْلَمُوْنَ اَنَّهُ
الْحَقُّ مِنْ رَّبِّهِمْ ۗ
وَمَا اللّٰهُ بِغَافِلٍ عَمَّا يَعْمَلُوْنَ ۞

145. Even if thou wert to bring
To the people of the Book
All the Signs (together),
They would not follow
Thy Qiblah; nor art thou
Going to follow their Qiblah;
Nor indeed will they follow
Each other's Qiblah. If thou
After the knowledge hath reached
              thee,
Wert to follow their (vain)
Desires—then wert thou
Indeed (clearly) in the wrong.

١٤٥- وَلَئِنْ اَتَيْتَ الَّذِيْنَ اُوْتُوا الْكِتٰبَ
بِكُلِّ اٰيَةٍ مَّا تَبِعُوْا قِبْلَتَكَ ۚ
وَمَآ اَنْتَ بِتَابِعٍ قِبْلَتَهُمْ ۚ
وَمَا بَعْضُهُمْ بِتَابِعٍ قِبْلَةَ بَعْضٍ ۚ
وَلَئِنِ اتَّبَعْتَ اَهْوَآءَهُمْ
مِّنْ بَعْدِ مَا جَآءَكَ مِنَ الْعِلْمِ ۙ
اِنَّكَ اِذًا لَّمِنَ الظّٰلِمِيْنَ ۘ

146. The people of the Book
Know this as they know
Their own sons; but some
Of them conceal the truth
Which they themselves know.

١٤٦- اَلَّذِيْنَ اٰتَيْنٰهُمُ الْكِتٰبَ يَعْرِفُوْنَهٗ كَمَا
يَعْرِفُوْنَ اَبْنَآءَهُمْ ۖ وَاِنَّ فَرِيْقًا مِّنْهُمْ
لَيَكْتُمُوْنَ الْحَقَّ وَهُمْ يَعْلَمُوْنَ ۞

147. The Truth is from thy Lord
So be not at all in doubt.

١٤٧- اَلْحَقُّ مِنْ رَّبِّكَ فَلَا تَكُوْنَنَّ
مِنَ الْمُمْتَرِيْنَ ۧ

SECTION 18

148. To each is a goal
To which Allah turns him;
Then strive together (as in a race)

١٤٨- وَلِكُلٍّ وِّجْهَةٌ هُوَ مُوَلِّيْهَا فَاسْتَبِقُوا

Towards all that is good.
Wheresoever ye are,
Allah will bring you
Together. For Allah
Hath power over all things.

الْخَيْرَاتِ ۚ أَيْنَ مَا تَكُونُوا
يَأْتِ بِكُمُ اللهُ جَمِيعًا ۚ
إِنَّ اللهَ عَلَى كُلِّ شَىْءٍ قَدِيرٌ ۝

149. From whencesoever
Thou startest forth   turn
Thy face in the direction
Of the Sacred Mosque;
That is indeed the truth
From thy Lord. And Allah
Is not unmindful
Of what ye do.

١٤٩- وَمِنْ حَيْثُ خَرَجْتَ فَوَلِّ
وَجْهَكَ شَطْرَ الْمَسْجِدِ الْحَرَامِ ۖ
وَإِنَّهُ لَلْحَقُّ مِنْ رَبِّكَ ۗ
وَمَا اللهُ بِغَافِلٍ عَمَّا تَعْمَلُونَ ۝

150. So from whencesoever
Thou startest forth, turn
Thy face in the direction
Of the Sacred Mosque;
And wheresoever ye are,
Turn your face thither:
That there be no ground
Of dispute against you
Among the people,
Except those of them that are
Bent on wickedness; so fear
Them not, but fear Me;
And that I may complete
My favours on you, and ye
May (consent to) be guided;

١٥٠- وَمِنْ حَيْثُ خَرَجْتَ فَوَلِّ
وَجْهَكَ شَطْرَ الْمَسْجِدِ الْحَرَامِ ۚ
وَحَيْثُ مَا كُنْتُمْ
فَوَلُّوا وُجُوهَكُمْ شَطْرَهُ ۙ
لِئَلَّا يَكُونَ لِلنَّاسِ عَلَيْكُمْ حُجَّةٌ ۗ
إِلَّا الَّذِينَ ظَلَمُوا مِنْهُمْ ۗ
فَلَا تَخْشَوْهُمْ وَاخْشَوْنِي ۗ
وَلِأُتِمَّ نِعْمَتِي عَلَيْكُمْ وَلَعَلَّكُمْ تَهْتَدُونَ ۝

151. A similar (favour
Have ye already received)
In that We have sent
Among you a Messenger
Of your own, rehearsing to you
Our Signs, and purifying
You, and instructing you
In Scripture and Wisdom,
And in new Knowledge.

١٥١- كَمَا أَرْسَلْنَا
فِيكُمْ رَسُولًا مِنْكُمْ يَتْلُوا عَلَيْكُمْ آيَاتِنَا
وَيُزَكِّيكُمْ وَيُعَلِّمُكُمُ الْكِتَابَ وَالْحِكْمَةَ
وَيُعَلِّمُكُمْ مَا لَمْ تَكُونُوا تَعْلَمُونَ ۝

152. Then do ye remember
Me; I will remember
You. Be grateful to Me,
And reject not Faith.
SECTION 19.

١٥٢- فَاذْكُرُونِي أَذْكُرْكُمْ
وَاشْكُرُوا لِي وَلَا تَكْفُرُونِ ۝

153. O ye who believe! seek help
With patient Perseverance

١٥٣- يَا أَيُّهَا الَّذِينَ آمَنُوا اسْتَعِينُوا بِالصَّبْرِ

And Prayer: for Allah is with those
Who patiently persevere.

وَالصَّلٰوةِ ۚ إِنَّ اللهَ مَعَ الصّٰبِرِيْنَ ٥

154. And say not of those
Who are slain in the way
Of Allah: "They are dead."
Nay, they are living,
Though ye perceive (it) not.

١٥٤- وَلَا تَقُوْلُوْا لِمَنْ يُّقْتَلُ فِىْ سَبِيْلِ اللهِ
أَمْوَاتٌ ۚ
بَلْ أَحْيَاءٌ وَّلٰكِنْ لَّا تَشْعُرُوْنَ ٥

155. Be sure we shall test you
With something of fear
And hunger, some loss
In goods or lives or the fruits
(Of your toil), but give
Glad tidings　to those
Who patiently persevere—

١٥٥- وَلَنَبْلُوَنَّكُمْ بِشَىْءٍ
مِّنَ الْخَوْفِ وَالْجُوْعِ وَنَقْصٍ مِّنَ الْأَمْوَالِ
وَالْأَنْفُسِ وَالثَّمَرٰتِ ۗ
وَبَشِّرِ الصّٰبِرِيْنَ ۙ

156. Who say, when afflicted
With calamity: "To Allah
We belong, and to Him
Is our return"

١٥٦- الَّذِيْنَ إِذَا أَصَابَتْهُمْ مُّصِيْبَةٌ ۙ
قَالُوْا إِنَّا لِلّٰهِ وَإِنَّا إِلَيْهِ رٰجِعُوْنَ ٥

157. They are those on whom
(Descend) blessings from their
Lord,
And Mercy,
And they are the ones
That receive guidance.

١٥٧- أُولٰٓئِكَ عَلَيْهِمْ صَلَوٰتٌ مِّنْ رَّبِّهِمْ
وَرَحْمَةٌ ۖ
وَأُولٰٓئِكَ هُمُ الْمُهْتَدُوْنَ ٥

158. Behold! Ṣafa and Marwah
Are among the Symbols
Of Allah. So if those who visit
The House　in the Season
Or at other times,
Should compass them round,
It is no sin in them.
And if any one obeyeth his own
Impulse to Good —
Be sure that Allah
Is He Who recogniseth
And knoweth.

١٥٨- إِنَّ الصَّفَا وَالْمَرْوَةَ مِنْ شَعَآئِرِ اللهِ ۚ
فَمَنْ حَجَّ الْبَيْتَ أَوِ اعْتَمَرَ
فَلَا جُنَاحَ عَلَيْهِ أَنْ يَّطَّوَّفَ بِهِمَا ۚ
وَمَنْ تَطَوَّعَ خَيْرًا ۙ
فَإِنَّ اللهَ شَاكِرٌ عَلِيْمٌ ٥

159. Those who conceal
The clear (Signs) We have
Sent down, and the Guidance,
After We have made it
Clear for the People
In the Book—on them
Shall be Allah's curse,

١٥٩- إِنَّ الَّذِيْنَ يَكْتُمُوْنَ
مَآ أَنْزَلْنَا مِنَ الْبَيِّنٰتِ وَالْهُدٰى
مِنْ بَعْدِ مَا بَيَّنّٰهُ لِلنَّاسِ فِى الْكِتٰبِ ۙ
أُولٰٓئِكَ يَلْعَنُهُمُ اللهُ

And the curse of those
Entitled to curse—

وَيَلْعَنُهُمُ اللّٰعِنُوْنَ ۞

160. Except those who repent
And make amends
And openly declare (the Truth):
To them I turn;
For I am Oft-Returning,
Most Merciful.

١٦٠- إِلَّا الَّذِيْنَ تَابُوْا وَأَصْلَحُوْا وَبَيَّنُوْا
فَأُولٰٓئِكَ أَتُوْبُ عَلَيْهِمْ ۚ
وَأَنَا التَّوَّابُ الرَّحِيْمُ ۝

161. Those who reject Faith,
And die rejecting—
On them is Allah's curse,
And the curse of angels,
And of all mankind;

١٦١- إِنَّ الَّذِيْنَ كَفَرُوْا وَمَاتُوْا وَهُمْ كُفَّارٌ
أُولٰٓئِكَ عَلَيْهِمْ لَعْنَةُ اللّٰهِ
وَالْمَلٰٓئِكَةِ وَالنَّاسِ أَجْمَعِيْنَ ۞

162. They will abide therein:
Their penalty will not
Be lightened, nor will
Respite be their (lot).

١٦٢- خٰلِدِيْنَ فِيْهَا ۚ لَا يُخَفَّفُ عَنْهُمُ الْعَذَابُ
وَلَا هُمْ يُنْظَرُوْنَ ۝

163. And your God
Is One God:
There is no god
But He,
Most Gracious,
Most Merciful.

١٦٣- وَإِلٰهُكُمْ إِلٰهٌ وَّاحِدٌ ۚ
لَّا إِلٰهَ إِلَّا هُوَ
الرَّحْمٰنُ الرَّحِيْمُ ۞

SECTION 20.

164. Behold! In the creation
Of the heavens and the earth;
In the alternation
Of the Night and the Day;
In the sailing of the ships
Through the Ocean
For the profit of mankind;
In the rain which Allah
Sends down from the skies,
And the life which He gives
therewith
To an earth that is dead;
In the beasts of all kinds
That He scatters
Through the earth;
In the change of the winds,
And the clouds which they
Trail like their slaves
Between the sky and the earth—
(Here) indeed are Signs

١٦٤- إِنَّ فِيْ خَلْقِ السَّمٰوٰتِ وَالْأَرْضِ
وَاخْتِلَافِ الَّيْلِ وَالنَّهَارِ
وَالْفُلْكِ الَّتِيْ تَجْرِيْ فِي الْبَحْرِ
بِمَا يَنْفَعُ النَّاسَ وَمَآ
أَنْزَلَ اللّٰهُ مِنَ السَّمَآءِ
مِنْ مَّآءٍ
فَأَحْيَا بِهِ الْأَرْضَ بَعْدَ مَوْتِهَا
وَبَثَّ فِيْهَا مِنْ كُلِّ دَآبَّةٍ ۠
وَّتَصْرِيْفِ الرِّيٰحِ وَالسَّحَابِ
الْمُسَخَّرِ بَيْنَ السَّمَآءِ وَالْأَرْضِ
لَأَيٰتٍ

For a people that are wise.

لِّقَوۡمٍ يَّعۡقِلُوۡنَ ۝

165. Yet 'there are men
Who take (for worship)
Others besides Allah,
As equal (with Allah):
They love them
As they should love Allah,
But those of Faith are
Overflowing in their love
For Allah. If only
The unrighteous could see,
Behold, they would see
The Punishment: that to Allah
Belongs all power, and Allah
Will strongly enforce
The Punishment.

١٦٥- وَمِنَ النَّاسِ مَنۡ يَّتَّخِذُ مِنۡ دُوۡنِ
اللّٰهِ اَنۡدَادًا
يُّحِبُّوۡنَهُمۡ كَحُبِّ اللّٰهِ ؕ
وَالَّذِيۡنَ اٰمَنُوۡۤا اَشَدُّ حُبًّا لِّلّٰهِ ؕ
وَلَوۡ يَرَى الَّذِيۡنَ ظَلَمُوۡۤا اِذۡ يَرَوۡنَ الۡعَذَابَ ۙ
اَنَّ الۡقُوَّةَ لِلّٰهِ جَمِيۡعًا ۙ
وَّاَنَّ اللّٰهَ شَدِيۡدُ الۡعَذَابِ ۝

166. Then would those
Who are followed
Clear themselves of those
Who follow (them):
They would see the Penalty,
And all relations
Between them would be cut off.

١٦٦- اِذۡ تَبَرَّاَ الَّذِيۡنَ اتُّبِعُوۡا مِنَ الَّذِيۡنَ
اتَّبَعُوۡا وَرَاَوُا الۡعَذَابَ
وَتَقَطَّعَتۡ بِهِمُ الۡاَسۡبَابُ ۝

167. And those who followed
Would say: "If only
We had one more chance,
We would clear ourselves
Of them, as they have
Cleared themselves of us."
Thus will Allah show them
(The fruits of) their deeds
As (nothing but) regrets.
Nor will there be a way
For them out of the Fire.

١٦٧- وَقَالَ الَّذِيۡنَ اتَّبَعُوۡا
لَوۡ اَنَّ لَنَا كَرَّةً فَنَتَبَرَّاَ مِنۡهُمۡ كَمَا تَبَرَّءُوۡا
مِنَّا ؕ
كَذٰلِكَ يُرِيۡهِمُ اللّٰهُ اَعۡمَالَهُمۡ حَسَرٰتٍ
عَلَيۡهِمۡ ؕ
وَمَا هُمۡ بِخٰرِجِيۡنَ مِنَ النَّارِ ۝

SECTION 21.

168. O ye people!
Eat of what is on earth,
Lawful and good;
And do not follow
The footsteps of the Evil One,
For he is to you
An avowed enemy.

١٦٨- يٰۤاَيُّهَا النَّاسُ كُلُوۡا مِمَّا فِى الۡاَرۡضِ
حَلٰلًا طَيِّبًا ۖ وَّلَا تَتَّبِعُوۡا خُطُوٰتِ الشَّيۡطٰنِ ؕ
اِنَّهٗ لَكُمۡ عَدُوٌّ مُّبِيۡنٌ ۝

169. For he commands you
What is evil

١٦٩- اِنَّمَا يَاۡمُرُكُمۡ

And shameful,
And that ye should say
Of Allah that of which
Ye have no knowledge.

170. When it is said to them:
"Follow what Allah hath
                    revealed:"
They say: "Nay! we shall follow
The ways of our fathers:"
What! even though their fathers
Were void of wisdom and
                        guidance?

171. The parable of those
Who reject Faith is
As if one were to shout
Like a goat-herd, to things
That listen to nothing
But calls and cries:[170]
Deaf, dumb, and blind,
They are void of wisdom.

172. O ye who believe!
Eat of the good things
That We have provided for you
And be grateful to Allah,
If it is Him ye worship.

173. He hath only forbidden you
Dead meat,   and blood,
And the flesh of swine,
And that on which
Any other name hath been invoked
Besides that of Allah.
But if one is forced by
                    necessity,
Without willful disobedience,
Nor transgressing due limits—
Then is he guiltless.
For Allah is Oft-Forgiving
Most Merciful.

174. Those who conceal
Allah's revelations in the Book,
And purchase for them
A miserable profit—
They swallow into themselves

Naught but Fire;
Allah will not address them
On the Day of Resurrection,
Nor purify them:
Grievous will be
Their Penalty.

175. They are the ones
Who buy Error
In place of Guidance
And Torment in place
Of Forgiveness.
Ah! what boldness
(They show) for the Fire!

176. (Their doom is) because
Allah sent down the Book
In truth but those who seek
Causes of dispute in the Book
Are in a schism
Far (from the purpose).

SECTION 22

177. It is not righteousness
That ye turn your faces
Towards East or West;
But it is righteousness—
To believe in Allah
And the Last Day,
And the Angels,
And the Book,
And the Messengers;
To spend of your substance,
Out of love for Him,
For your kin,
For orphans,
For the needy,
For the wayfarer,
For those who ask,
And for the ransom of slaves;
To be steadfast in prayer,
And practise regular charity,
To fulfil the contracts
Which ye have made;
And to be firm and patient,
In pain (or suffering)
And adversity,

أُولَـٰئِكَ مَا يَأْكُلُونَ فِى بُطُونِهِمْ إِلَّا النَّارَ
وَلَا يُكَلِّمُهُمُ اللّٰهُ يَوْمَ الْقِيَامَةِ
وَلَا يُزَكِّيهِمْ ۚ وَلَهُمْ عَذَابٌ أَلِيمٌ ٠

١٧٥- أُولَـٰئِكَ الَّذِينَ اشْتَرَوُا الضَّلَالَةَ
بِالْهُدَى
وَالْعَذَابَ بِالْمَغْفِرَةِ ۚ
فَمَا أَصْبَرَهُمْ عَلَى النَّارِ٠

١٧٦- ذَٰلِكَ بِأَنَّ اللّٰهَ نَزَّلَ الْكِتَابَ بِالْحَقِّ ۗ
وَإِنَّ الَّذِينَ اخْتَلَفُوا فِى الْكِتَابِ
لَفِى شِقَاقٍ بَعِيدٍ ٠

١٧٧- لَيْسَ الْبِرَّ أَنْ تُوَلُّوا وُجُوهَكُمْ
قِبَلَ الْمَشْرِقِ وَالْمَغْرِبِ
وَلَـٰكِنَّ الْبِرَّ مَنْ آمَنَ بِاللّٰهِ
وَالْيَوْمِ الْآخِرِ وَالْمَلَائِكَةِ وَالْكِتَابِ
وَالنَّبِيِّينَ ۚ
وَآتَى الْمَالَ عَلَى حُبِّهِ ذَوِى الْقُرْبَى
وَالْيَتَامَى وَالْمَسَاكِينَ
وَابْنَ السَّبِيلِ وَالسَّائِلِينَ وَفِى الرِّقَابِ ۚ
وَأَقَامَ الصَّلَاةَ وَآتَى الزَّكَاةَ ۚ
وَالْمُوفُونَ بِعَهْدِهِمْ إِذَا عَاهَدُوا ۖ
وَالصَّابِرِينَ فِى الْبَأْسَاءِ وَالضَّرَّاءِ

And throughout
All periods of panic.
Such are the people
Of truth, the God-fearing.

وَحِيْنَ الْبَأْسِ ۗ أُولٰۤئِكَ الَّذِيْنَ صَدَقُوْا ۗ وَأُولٰۤئِكَ هُمُ الْمُتَّقُوْنَ ۝

178. O ye who believe!
The law of equality
Is prescribed to you
In cases of murder:
The free for the free,
The slave for the slave,
The woman for the woman.
But if any remission
Is made by the brother
Of the slain, then grant
Any reasonable demand,
And compensate him
With handsome gratitude.
This is a concession
And a Mercy
From your Lord.
After this, whoever
Exceeds the limits
Shall be in grave penalty.

١٧٨۔ يٰۤاَيُّهَا الَّذِيْنَ اٰمَنُوْا كُتِبَ عَلَيْكُمُ الْقِصَاصُ فِى الْقَتْلٰى ۗ اَلْحُرُّ بِالْحُرِّ وَالْعَبْدُ بِالْعَبْدِ وَالْاُنْثٰى بِالْاُنْثٰى ۗ فَمَنْ عُفِىَ لَهٗ مِنْ اَخِيْهِ شَىْءٌ فَاتِّبَاعٌۢ بِالْمَعْرُوْفِ وَاَدَاۤءٌ اِلَيْهِ بِاِحْسَانٍ ۗ ذٰلِكَ تَخْفِيْفٌ مِّنْ رَّبِّكُمْ وَرَحْمَةٌ ۗ فَمَنِ اعْتَدٰى بَعْدَ ذٰلِكَ فَلَهٗ عَذَابٌ اَلِيْمٌ ۝

179. In the Law of Equality
There is (saving of) Life
To you, O ye men of
    understanding;
That ye may
Restrain yourselves.

١٧٩۔ وَلَكُمْ فِى الْقِصَاصِ حَيٰوةٌ يّٰاُولِى الْاَلْبَابِ لَعَلَّكُمْ تَتَّقُوْنَ ۝

180. It is perscribed,
When death approaches
Any of you, if he leave
Any goods, that he make a
    bequest
To parents and next of kin,
According to reasonable usage;
This is due
From the God-fearing.

١٨٠۔ كُتِبَ عَلَيْكُمْ اِذَا حَضَرَ اَحَدَكُمُ الْمَوْتُ اِنْ تَرَكَ خَيْرَا ۖ الْوَصِيَّةُ لِلْوَالِدَيْنِ وَالْاَقْرَبِيْنَ بِالْمَعْرُوْفِ ۚ حَقًّا عَلَى الْمُتَّقِيْنَ ۗ

181. If anyone changes the bequest
After hearing it,
The guilt shall be on those
Who make the change.
For Allah hears and knows
(All things).

١٨١۔ فَمَنْۢ بَدَّلَهٗ بَعْدَ مَا سَمِعَهٗ فَاِنَّمَاۤ اِثْمُهٗ عَلَى الَّذِيْنَ يُبَدِّلُوْنَهٗ ۚ اِنَّ اللّٰهَ سَمِيْعٌ عَلِيْمٌ ۝

182. But if anyone fears
Partiality or wrongdoing
On the part of the testator,
And makes peace between
(The parties concerned),
There is no wrong in him:
For Allah is Oft-Forgiving,
Most Merciful.

SECTION 23.

183. O ye who believe!
Fasting is prescribed to you
As it was prescribed
To those before you,
That ye may (learn)
Self-restraint—

184. (Fasting) for a fixed
Number of days;
But if any of you is ill,
Or on a journey,
The prescribed number
(Should be made up)
From days later.
For those who can do it
(With hardship), is a ransom,
The feeding of one
That is indigent
But he that will give
More, of his own free will—
It is better for him.
And it is better for you
That ye fast,
If ye only knew.

185. Ramaḍān is the (month)
In which was sent down
The Qur'ān, as a guide
To mankind, also clear (Signs)
For guidance and judgement
(Between right and wrong).
So every one of you
Who is present (at his home)
During that month
Should spend it in fasting,
But if any one is ill,
Or on a journey,
The prescribed period
(Should be made up)

١٨٢- فَمَنْ خَافَ مِنْ مُّوصٍ جَنَفًا أَوْ إِثْمًا
فَأَصْلَحَ بَيْنَهُمْ
فَلَا إِثْمَ عَلَيْهِ ۚ
إِنَّ اللّٰهَ غَفُورٌ رَّحِيمٌ ۚ ٥

١٨٣- يَـٰٓأَيُّهَا الَّذِيْنَ اٰمَنُوْا كُتِبَ عَلَيْكُمُ الصِّيَامُ
كَمَا كُتِبَ عَلَى الَّذِيْنَ مِنْ قَبْلِكُمْ
لَعَلَّكُمْ تَتَّقُوْنَ ۙ ٥

١٨٤- أَيَّامًا مَّعْدُوْدٰتٍ ۚ
فَمَنْ كَانَ مِنْكُمْ مَّرِيْضًا
أَوْ عَلٰى سَفَرٍ
فَعِدَّةٌ مِّنْ أَيَّامٍ أُخَرَ ۚ
وَعَلَى الَّذِيْنَ يُطِيْقُوْنَهُ فِدْيَةٌ طَعَامُ
مِسْكِيْنٍ ۖ فَمَنْ تَطَوَّعَ خَيْرًا فَهُوَ خَيْرٌ لَّهُ ۚ
وَأَنْ تَصُوْمُوْا خَيْرٌ لَّكُمْ
إِنْ كُنْتُمْ تَعْلَمُوْنَ ٥

١٨٥- شَهْرُ رَمَضَانَ الَّذِيْٓ أُنْزِلَ فِيْهِ الْقُرْاٰنُ
هُدًى لِّلنَّاسِ
وَبَيِّنٰتٍ مِّنَ الْهُدٰى وَالْفُرْقَانِ ۚ
فَمَنْ شَهِدَ مِنْكُمُ الشَّهْرَ فَلْيَصُمْهُ ۗ
وَمَنْ كَانَ مَرِيْضًا
أَوْ عَلٰى سَفَرٍ
فَعِدَّةٌ مِّنْ أَيَّامٍ أُخَرَ ۗ

By days later.
Allah intends every facility
For you; He does not want
To put you to difficulties.
(He wants you) to complete
The prescribed period,
And to glorify Him
In that He has guided you;
And perchance ye shall be
             grateful.

يُرِيْدُ اللهُ بِكُمُ الْيُسْرَ
وَلَا يُرِيْدُ بِكُمُ الْعُسْرَ
وَلِتُكْمِلُوا الْعِدَّةَ
وَلِتُكَبِّرُوا اللهَ عَلَى مَا هَدٰىكُمْ
وَلَعَلَّكُمْ تَشْكُرُوْنَ ٠

186. When My servants
Ask thee concerning Me,
I am indeed
Close (to them): I listen
To the prayer of every
Supplicant when he calleth on
             Me:
Let them also, with a will,
Listen to My call,
And believe in Me:
That they may walk
In the right way.

١٨٦- وَاِذَا سَاَلَكَ عِبَادِيْ
عَنِّيْ فَاِنِّيْ قَرِيْبٌ ؕ
اُجِيْبُ دَعْوَةَ الدَّاعِ
اِذَا دَعَانِ ۙ
فَلْيَسْتَجِيْبُوْا لِيْ
وَلْيُؤْمِنُوْا بِيْ لَعَلَّهُمْ يَرْشُدُوْنَ ٠

187. Permitted to you,
On the night of the fasts,
Is the approach to your wives.
They are your garments
And ye are their garments.
Allah knoweth what ye
Used to do secretly among
             yourselves;
But He turned to you
And forgave you;
So now associate with them,
And seek what Allah
Hath ordained for you,
And eat and drink,
Until the white thread
Of dawn appear to you
Distinct from its black thread;
Then complete your fast
Till the night appears;
But do not associate
With your wives
While ye are in retreat
In the mosques. Those are
Limits (set by) Allah:
Approach not nigh thereto.

١٨٧- اُحِلَّ لَكُمْ لَيْلَةَ الصِّيَامِ
الرَّفَثُ اِلٰى نِسَآئِكُمْ ؕ هُنَّ لِبَاسٌ لَّكُمْ
وَاَنْتُمْ لِبَاسٌ لَّهُنَّ ؕ عَلِمَ اللهُ اَنَّكُمْ كُنْتُمْ
تَخْتَانُوْنَ اَنْفُسَكُمْ فَتَابَ عَلَيْكُمْ
وَعَفَا عَنْكُمْ ۚ
فَالْـٰٔنَ بَاشِرُوْهُنَّ
وَابْتَغُوْا مَا كَتَبَ اللهُ لَكُمْ ۪ وَكُلُوْا وَاشْرَبُوْا
حَتّٰى يَتَبَيَّنَ لَكُمُ الْخَيْطُ الْاَبْيَضُ مِنَ الْخَيْطِ
الْاَسْوَدِ مِنَ الْفَجْرِ ۪
ثُمَّ اَتِمُّوا الصِّيَامَ اِلَى الَّيْلِ ۚ
وَلَا تُبَاشِرُوْهُنَّ وَاَنْتُمْ عٰكِفُوْنَ ۙ فِى الْمَسٰجِدِ ؕ
تِلْكَ حُدُوْدُ اللهِ فَلَا تَقْرَبُوْهَا ؕ
كَذٰلِكَ يُبَيِّنُ اللهُ اٰيٰتِهٖ

Thus doth Allah make clear
His Signs to men: that
They may learn self-restraint.

188. And do not eat up
Your property among yourselves
For vanities, nor use it
As bait for the judges,
With intent that ye may
Eat up wrongfully and knowingly
A little of (other) people's
property.

SECTION 24

189. They ask thee
Concerning the New Moons.
Say: They are but signs
To mark fixed periods of time
In (the affairs of) men,
And for Pilgrimage.
It is no virtue if ye enter
Your houses from the back:
It is virtue if ye fear Allah.
Enter houses
Through the proper doors:
And fear Allah:
That ye may prosper.

190. Fight in the cause of Allah
Those who fight you,
But do not transgress limits;
For Allah loveth not transgressors.

191. And slay them
Wherever ye catch them,
And turn them out
From where they have
Turned you out;
For tumult and oppression
Are worse than slaughter;
But fight them not
At the Sacred Mosque,
Unless they (first)
Fight you there;
But if they fight you,
Slay them.
Such is the reward
Of those who suppress faith.

192. But if they cease,
     Allah is Oft-Forgiving,
     Most Merciful.

١٩٢- فَاِنِ انْتَهَوْا
فَاِنَّ اللهَ غَفُوْرٌ رَّحِيْمٌ ۝

193. And fight them on
     Until there is no more
     Tumult or oppression,
     And there prevail
     Justice and faith in Allah;
     But if they cease,
     Let there be no hostility
     Except to those
     Who practise oppression.

١٩٣- وَقَاتِلُوْهُمْ حَتّٰى لَا تَكُوْنَ فِتْنَةٌ
وَّيَكُوْنَ الدِّيْنُ لِلّٰهِ ۚ
فَاِنِ انْتَهَوْا فَلَا عُدْوَانَ اِلَّا عَلَى
الظّٰلِمِيْنَ ۝

194. The prohibited month—
     For the prohibited month,
     And so for all things
                    prohibited—
     There is the law of equality.
     If then any one transgresses
     The prohibition against you,
     Transgress ye likewise
     Against him.
     But fear Allah, and know
     That Allah is with those
     Who restrain themselves.

١٩٤- اَلشَّهْرُ الْحَرَامُ بِالشَّهْرِ الْحَرَامِ
وَالْحُرُمٰتُ قِصَاصٌ ۚ
فَمَنِ اعْتَدٰى عَلَيْكُمْ
فَاعْتَدُوْا عَلَيْهِ بِمِثْلِ مَا اعْتَدٰى
عَلَيْكُمْ ۚ
وَاتَّقُوا اللهَ وَاعْلَمُوْا اَنَّ اللهَ مَعَ الْمُتَّقِيْنَ ۝

195. And spend of your substance
     In the cause of Allah,
     And make not your own hands
     Contribute to (your) destruction;
     But do good;
     For Allah loveth those
     Who do good.

١٩٥- وَاَنْفِقُوْا فِيْ سَبِيْلِ اللهِ وَلَا تُلْقُوْا
بِاَيْدِيْكُمْ اِلَى التَّهْلُكَةِ ۚ
وَاَحْسِنُوْا ۚ اِنَّ اللهَ يُحِبُّ الْمُحْسِنِيْنَ ۝

196. And complete
     The *Hajj* or *Umrah*
     In the service of Allah,
     But if ye are prevented
     (From completing it),
     Send an offering
     For sacrifice,
     Such as ye may find,
     And do not shave your heads
     Until the offering reaches
     The place of sacrifice.
     And if any of you is ill,

١٩٦- وَاَتِمُّوا الْحَجَّ وَالْعُمْرَةَ لِلّٰهِ ۚ
فَاِنْ اُحْصِرْتُمْ فَمَا اسْتَيْسَرَ مِنَ الْهَدْيِ ۚ
وَلَا تَحْلِقُوْا رُءُوْسَكُمْ
حَتّٰى يَبْلُغَ الْهَدْيُ مَحِلَّهٗ ۚ
فَمَنْ كَانَ مِنْكُمْ مَّرِيْضًا
اَوْ بِهٖٓ اَذًى مِّنْ رَّأْسِهٖ فَفِدْيَةٌ مِّنْ صِيَامٍ

Or has an ailment in his scalp,
(Necessitating shaving),
(He should) in compensation
Either fast, or feed the poor,
Or offer sacrifice;
And when ye are
In peaceful conditions (again),
If any one wishes
To continue the *Umrah*
On to the *Ḥajj*,
He must make an offering
Such as he can afford,
But if he cannot afford it,
He should fast
Three days during the *Ḥajj*
And seven days on his return,
Making ten days in all.
This is for those
Whose household
Is not in (the precincts
Of) the Sacred Mosque,
And fear Allah,
And know that Allah,
Is strict in punishment.

SECTION 25

197. For *Ḥajj*
Are the months well-known.
If any one undertakes
That duty therein,
Let there be no obscenity,
Nor wickedness,
Nor wrangling
In the *Ḥajj*
And whatever good
Ye do, (be sure)
Allah knoweth it.
And take a provision
(With you) for the journey,
But the best of provisions
Is right conduct.
So fear Me,
O ye that are wise.

198. It is no crime in you
If ye seek of the bounty
Of your Lord (during
pilgrimage).
Then when ye pour down

أَوْ صَدَقَةٍ أَوْ نُسُكٍ ۚ

فَإِذَآ أَمِنْتُمْ ۗ

فَمَنْ تَمَتَّعَ بِالْعُمْرَةِ إِلَى الْحَجِّ

فَمَا اسْتَيْسَرَ مِنَ الْهَدْيِ ۚ

فَمَنْ لَمْ يَجِدْ فَصِيَامُ ثَلٰثَةِ أَيَّامٍ فِي الْحَجِّ

وَسَبْعَةٍ إِذَا رَجَعْتُمْ ۗ

تِلْكَ عَشَرَةٌ كَامِلَةٌ ۗ

ذٰلِكَ لِمَنْ لَمْ يَكُنْ أَهْلُهُ حَاضِرِي الْمَسْجِدِ

الْحَرَامِ ۚ

وَاتَّقُوا اللّٰهَ

وَاعْلَمُوٓا أَنَّ اللّٰهَ شَدِيدُ الْعِقَابِ ۝

١٩٧- الْحَجُّ أَشْهُرٌ مَعْلُومٰتٌ ۚ

فَمَنْ فَرَضَ فِيهِنَّ الْحَجَّ فَلَا رَفَثَ

وَلَا فُسُوقَ ۙ

وَلَا جِدَالَ فِي الْحَجِّ ۗ

وَمَا تَفْعَلُوا مِنْ خَيْرٍ يَعْلَمْهُ اللّٰهُ ۗ

وَتَزَوَّدُوا فَإِنَّ خَيْرَ الزَّادِ التَّقْوٰى ۖ

وَاتَّقُونِ يَأُولِي الْأَلْبَابِ ۝

١٩٨- لَيْسَ عَلَيْكُمْ جُنَاحٌ أَنْ تَبْتَغُوا

فَضْلًا مِنْ رَبِّكُمْ ۚ فَإِذَآ أَفَضْتُمْ مِنْ

عَرَفٰتٍ

From (Mount) 'Arafāt,
Celebrate the praises of Allah
At the Sacred Monument,
And celebrate His praises
As He has directed you,
Even though, before this,
Ye went astray.

فَاذْكُرُوا اللّٰهَ عِنْدَ الْمَشْعَرِ الْحَرَامِ ۖ
وَاذْكُرُوهُ كَمَا هَدٰىكُمْ ۚ
وَاِنْ كُنْتُمْ مِّنْ قَبْلِهٖ لَمِنَ الضَّآلِّيْنَ ۟

199. Then pass on
At a quick pace from the place
Whence it is usual
For the multitude
So to do, and ask
For Allah's forgiveness.
For Allah is Oft-Forgiving,
Most Merciful.

١٩٩- ثُمَّ اَفِيْضُوْا مِنْ حَيْثُ اَفَاضَ
النَّاسُ
وَاسْتَغْفِرُوا اللّٰهَ ۚ
اِنَّ اللّٰهَ غَفُوْرٌ رَّحِيْمٌ ۟

200. So when ye have
Accomplished your holy rites,
Celebrate the praises of Allah,
As ye used to celebrate
The praises of your fathers —
Yea, with far more
Heart and soul.
There are men who say:
"Our Lord! Give us
(Thy bounties) in this world!"
But they will have
No portion in the Hereafter.

٢٠٠- فَاِذَا قَضَيْتُمْ مَّنَاسِكَكُمْ
فَاذْكُرُوا اللّٰهَ
كَذِكْرِكُمْ اٰبَآءَكُمْ اَوْ اَشَدَّ ذِكْرًا ۗ
فَمِنَ النَّاسِ مَنْ يَّقُوْلُ رَبَّنَآ اٰتِنَا فِى
الدُّنْيَا
وَمَالَهٗ فِى الْاٰخِرَةِ مِنْ خَلَاقٍ ۟

201. And there are men who say:
"Our Lord! Give us
Good in this world
And good in the Hereafter,
And defend us
From the torment
Of the Fire!"

٢٠١- وَمِنْهُمْ مَّنْ يَّقُوْلُ رَبَّنَآ اٰتِنَا
فِى الدُّنْيَا حَسَنَةً وَّفِى الْاٰخِرَةِ حَسَنَةً
وَّقِنَا عَذَابَ النَّارِ ۟

202. To these will be allotted
What they have earned;
And Allah is quick in account.

٢٠٢- اُولٰٓئِكَ لَهُمْ نَصِيْبٌ مِّمَّا كَسَبُوْا ۗ
وَاللّٰهُ سَرِيْعُ الْحِسَابِ ۟

203. Celebrate the praises of Allah
During the Appointed Days.
But if anyone hastens
To leave in two days,
There is no blame on him,
And if anyone stays on,

٢٠٣- وَاذْكُرُوا اللّٰهَ فِىْ اَيَّامٍ مَّعْدُوْدٰتٍ ۚ
فَمَنْ تَعَجَّلَ فِيْ يَوْمَيْنِ
فَلَاۤ اِثْمَ عَلَيْهِ ۚ

There is no blame on him,
If his aim is to do right.
Then fear Allah, and know
That ye will surely
Be gathered unto Him.

204. There is the type of man
Whose speech
About this world's life
May dazzle thee,
And he calls Allah to witness
About what is in his heart;
Yet is he the most contentious
Of enemies.

205. When he turns his back,
His aim everywhere
Is to spread mischief
Through the earth and destroy
Crops and cattle.
But Allah loveth not mischief.

206. When it is said to him,
"Fear Allah,"
He is led by arrogance
To (more) crime.
Enough for him is Hell—
An evil bed indeed
(To lie on)!

207. And there is the type of man
Who gives his life
To earn the pleasure of Allah;
And Allah is full of kindness
To (His) devotees.

208. O ye who believe!
Enter into Islam
Wholeheartedly;
And follow not
The footsteps
Of the Evil One;
For he is to you
An avowed enemy.

209. If ye backslide
After the clear (Signs)
Have come to you,

وَمَن تَأَخَّرَ فَلَا إِثْمَ عَلَيْهِ لِمَنِ اتَّقَى وَاتَّقُوا اللهَ وَاعْلَمُوا أَنَّكُمْ إِلَيْهِ تُحْشَرُونَ ٥

٢٠٤ - وَمِنَ النَّاسِ مَن يُعْجِبُكَ قَوْلُهُ فِي الْحَيَوةِ الدُّنْيَا وَيُشْهِدُ اللهَ عَلَى مَا فِي قَلْبِهِ وَهُوَ أَلَدُّ الْخِصَامِ ٥

٢٠٥ - وَإِذَا تَوَلَّى سَعَى فِي الْأَرْضِ لِيُفْسِدَ فِيهَا وَيُهْلِكَ الْحَرْثَ وَالنَّسْلَ وَاللهُ لَا يُحِبُّ الْفَسَادَ ٥

٢٠٦ - وَإِذَا قِيلَ لَهُ اتَّقِ اللهَ أَخَذَتْهُ الْعِزَّةُ بِالْإِثْمِ فَحَسْبُهُ جَهَنَّمُ وَلَبِئْسَ الْمِهَادُ ٥

٢٠٧ - وَمِنَ النَّاسِ مَن يَشْرِي نَفْسَهُ ابْتِغَاءَ مَرْضَاتِ اللهِ وَاللهُ رَؤُوفٌ بِالْعِبَادِ ٥

٢٠٨ - يَا أَيُّهَا الَّذِينَ آمَنُوا ادْخُلُوا فِي السِّلْمِ كَافَّةً وَلَا تَتَّبِعُوا خُطُوَاتِ الشَّيْطَنِ إِنَّهُ لَكُمْ عَدُوٌّ مُبِينٌ ٥

٢٠٩ - فَإِن زَلَلْتُمْ مِنْ بَعْدِ مَا جَاءَتْكُمُ

Then know that Allah
Is Exalted in Power, Wise.

البَيِّنٰتُ فَاعْلَمُوْا اَنَّ اللّٰهَ عَزِيْزٌ حَكِيْمٌ ○

210. Will they wait
Until Allah comes to them
In canopies of clouds,
With angels (in His train)
And the question
Is (thus) settled?
But to Allah
Do all questions
Go back (for decision).

٢١٠ - هَلْ يَنْظُرُوْنَ اِلَّا اَنْ يَّأْتِيَهُمُ اللّٰهُ
فِيْ ظُلَلٍ مِّنَ الْغَمَامِ
وَالْمَلٰٓئِكَةُ وَقُضِيَ الْاَمْرُ
وَاِلَى اللّٰهِ تُرْجَعُ الْاُمُوْرُ ○

SECTION 26

211. Ask the Children of Israel
How many Clear (Signs)
We have sent them.
But if anyone,
After Allah's favour
Has come to him,
Substitutes (something else),
Allah is strict in punishment.

٢١١ - سَلْ بَنِيْٓ اِسْرَآءِيْلَ كَمْ اٰتَيْنٰهُمْ مِّنْ
اٰيَةٍ بَيِّنَةٍ ۗ وَمَنْ يُّبَدِّلْ نِعْمَةَ اللّٰهِ
مِنْ بَعْدِ مَا جَآءَتْهُ
فَاِنَّ اللّٰهَ شَدِيْدُ الْعِقَابِ ○

212. The life of this world
Is alluring to those
Who reject faith,
And they scoff at those
Who believe.
But the righteous
Will be above them
On the Day of Resurrection;
For Allah bestows His
　　　　　　　　abundance
Without measure
On whom He will.

٢١٢ - زُيِّنَ لِلَّذِيْنَ كَفَرُوا الْحَيٰوةُ الدُّنْيَا
وَيَسْخَرُوْنَ مِنَ الَّذِيْنَ اٰمَنُوْا ۘ
وَالَّذِيْنَ اتَّقَوْا فَوْقَهُمْ يَوْمَ الْقِيٰمَةِ ۗ
وَاللّٰهُ يَرْزُقُ مَنْ يَّشَآءُ
بِغَيْرِ حِسَابٍ ○

213. Mankind was one single nation,
And Allah sent Messengers
With glad tidings and
　　　　　　　　warnings;
And with them He sent
The Book in truth,
To judge between people
In matters wherein
They differed;
But the People of the Book,
After the clear Signs
Came to them, did not differ
Among themselves,

٢١٣ - كَانَ النَّاسُ اُمَّةً وَّاحِدَةً ۗ
فَبَعَثَ اللّٰهُ النَّبِيّٖنَ مُبَشِّرِيْنَ وَمُنْذِرِيْنَ ۙ
وَاَنْزَلَ مَعَهُمُ الْكِتٰبَ بِالْحَقِّ
لِيَحْكُمَ بَيْنَ النَّاسِ
فِيْمَا اخْتَلَفُوْا فِيْهِ ۗ وَمَا اخْتَلَفَ فِيْهِ
اِلَّا الَّذِيْنَ اُوْتُوْهُ مِنْ بَعْدِ

Except through selfish
　　　　　　　　　contumacy.
Allah by His Grace
Guided the Believers
To the Truth,
Concerning that
Wherein they differed.
For Allah guides
Whom He will
To a path
That is straight.

مَا جَاۤءَتْهُمُ الْبَيِّنَاتُ بَغْيًۢا بَيْنَهُمْ

فَهَدَى اللّٰهُ الَّذِيْنَ اٰمَنُوْا

لِمَا اخْتَلَفُوْا فِيْهِ

مِنَ الْحَقِّ بِإِذْنِهِ ۚ وَاللّٰهُ يَهْدِيْ مَنْ

يَّشَاۤءُ اِلٰى صِرَاطٍ مُّسْتَقِيْمٍ ○

214. Or do ye think
That ye shall enter
The Garden (of Bliss)
Without such (trials)
As came to those
Who passed away
Before you?
They encountered
Suffering and adversity,
And were so shaken in spirit
That even the Messenger
And those of faith
Who were with him
Cried: "When (will come)
The help of Allah"
Ah! Verily, the help of Allah
Is (always) near!

٢١٤- اَمْ حَسِبْتُمْ اَنْ تَدْخُلُوا الْجَنَّةَ

وَلَمَّا يَأْتِكُمْ مَّثَلُ الَّذِيْنَ خَلَوْا مِنْ

قَبْلِكُمْ ۗ

مَسَّتْهُمُ الْبَأْسَاۤءُ وَالضَّرَّاۤءُ وَزُلْزِلُوْا

حَتّٰى يَقُوْلَ الرَّسُوْلُ وَالَّذِيْنَ اٰمَنُوْا

مَعَهٗ

مَتٰى نَصْرُ اللّٰهِ ۗ

اَلَاۤ اِنَّ نَصْرَ اللّٰهِ قَرِيْبٌ ○

215. They ask thee
What they should spend
(In charity). Say: Whatever
Ye spend that is good,
Is for parents and kindred
And orphans
And those in want
And for wayfarers.
And whatever ye do
That is good—Allah
Knoweth it well.

٢١٥- يَسْـَٔلُوْنَكَ مَاذَا يُنْفِقُوْنَ ۗ

قُلْ مَاۤ اَنْفَقْتُمْ مِّنْ خَيْرٍ

فَلِلْوَالِدَيْنِ وَالْاَقْرَبِيْنَ

وَالْيَتٰمٰى وَالْمَسٰكِيْنِ وَابْنِ السَّبِيْلِ ۗ

وَمَا تَفْعَلُوْا مِنْ خَيْرٍ

فَاِنَّ اللّٰهَ بِهٖ عَلِيْمٌ ○

216. Fighting is prescribed
Upon you, and ye dislike it.
But it is possible
That ye dislike a thing
Which is good for you,
And that ye love a thing

٢١٦- كُتِبَ عَلَيْكُمُ الْقِتَالُ وَهُوَ كُرْهٌ لَّكُمْ ۚ

وَعَسٰىٓ اَنْ تَكْرَهُوْا شَيْئًا وَّهُوَ خَيْرٌ لَّكُمْ ۚ

وَعَسٰىٓ اَنْ تُحِبُّوْا شَيْئًا وَّهُوَ شَرٌّ لَّكُمْ ۚ

Which is bad for you.
But Allah knoweth,
And ye know not.

SECTION 27.

217. They ask thee
Concerning fighting
In the Prohibited Month.
Say: "Fighting therein
Is a grave (offence);
But graver is it
In the sight of Allah
To prevent access
To the path of Allah,
To deny Him,
To prevent access
To the Sacred Mosque,
And drive out its members."
Tumult and oppression
Are worse than slaughter.
Nor will they cease
Fighting you until
They turn you back
From your faith
If they can.
And if any of you
Turn back from their faith
And die in unbelief,
Their works will bear no fruit
In this life
And in the Hereafter;
They will be
Companions of the Fire
And will abide therein.

218. Those who believed
And those who suffered exile
And fought (and strove and
struggled)
In the path of Allah—
They have the hope
Of the Mercy of Allah:
And Allah is Oft-Forgiving,
Most Merciful.

219. They ask thee

وَاللّٰهُ يَعْلَمُ وَاَنْتُمْ لَا تَعْلَمُوْنَ ۞

٢١٧- يَسْـَٔلُوْنَكَ عَنِ الشَّهْرِ الْحَرَامِ قِتَالٍ فِيْهِ ؕ
قُلْ قِتَالٌ فِيْهِ كَبِيْرٌ ؕ
وَصَدٌّ عَنْ سَبِيْلِ اللّٰهِ وَكُفْرٌ بِهٖ
وَالْمَسْجِدِ الْحَرَامِ ۙ
وَاِخْرَاجُ اَهْلِهٖ مِنْهُ اَكْبَرُ عِنْدَ اللّٰهِ ۚ
وَالْفِتْنَةُ اَكْبَرُ مِنَ الْقَتْلِ ؕ
وَلَا يَزَالُوْنَ يُقَاتِلُوْنَكُمْ حَتّٰى يَرُدُّوْكُمْ
عَنْ دِيْنِكُمْ اِنِ اسْتَطَاعُوْا ؕ
وَمَنْ يَّرْتَدِدْ مِنْكُمْ
عَنْ دِيْنِهٖ فَيَمُتْ
وَهُوَ كَافِرٌ
فَاُولٰٓئِكَ حَبِطَتْ اَعْمَالُهُمْ
فِى الدُّنْيَا وَالْاٰخِرَةِ ۚ
وَاُولٰٓئِكَ اَصْحٰبُ النَّارِ ۚ
هُمْ فِيْهَا خٰلِدُوْنَ ۞

٢١٨- اِنَّ الَّذِيْنَ اٰمَنُوْا وَالَّذِيْنَ هَاجَرُوْا
وَجٰهَدُوْا فِىْ سَبِيْلِ اللّٰهِ ۙ
اُولٰٓئِكَ يَرْجُوْنَ رَحْمَتَ اللّٰهِ ؕ
وَاللّٰهُ غَفُوْرٌ رَّحِيْمٌ ۞

٢١٩- يَسْـَٔلُوْنَكَ

Concerning wine and
                gambling.
Say: "In them is great sin,
And some profit, for men;
But the sin is greater
Than the profit."

They ask thee how much
They are to spend;
Say: "What is beyond
Your needs."

Thus doth Allah
Make clear to you
His Signs: in order that
Ye may consider—

220. (Their bearings) on
This life and the Hereafter

They ask thee
Concerning orphans.
Say: "The best thing to do
Is what is for their good;
If ye mix
Their affairs with yours,
They are your brethren;

But Allah knows
The man who means mischief
From the man who means good.
And if Allah had wished,
He could have put you
Into difficulties; he is indeed
Exalted in Power, Wise."

221. Do not marry
Unbelieving   women
Until they believe:
A slave woman who believes
Is better than an unbelieving
                    woman.
Even though she allure you.
Nor marry (your girls)
To unbelievers until
They believe:
A man slave who believes
Is better than an unbeliever
Even though he allure you.
Unbelievers do (but)
Beckon you to the Fire.
But Allah beckons by His Grace

To the Garden (of Bliss)
And forgiveness,
And makes His Signs
Clear to mankind:
That they may
Receive admonition.

SECTION 28

222. They ask thee
Concerning women's courses.
Say: They are
A hurt and a pollution:
So keep away from women
In their courses, and do not
Approach them until
They are clean.
But when they have
Purified themselves,
Ye may approach them
In any manner, time, or place
Ordained for you by Allah.
For Allah loves those
Who turn to Him constantly
And He loves those
Who keep themselves pure and
clean.

223. Your wives are
As a tilth   unto you
So approach your tilth
When or how you will;
But do some good act
For your souls beforehand;
And fear Allah,
And know that ye are
To meet Him (in the Hereafter),
And give (these) good tidings
To those who believe.

224. And make not
Allah's (name) an excuse
In your oaths against
Doing good, or acting rightly,
Or making peace
Between persons;
For Allah is One
Who hearest and knoweth
All things.

وَالْمَغْفِرَةِ بِإِذْنِهِ
وَيُبَيِّنُ آيٰتِهِ لِلنَّاسِ
لَعَلَّهُمْ يَتَذَكَّرُوْنَ ۞

٢٢٢ - وَيَسْـَٔلُوْنَكَ عَنِ الْمَحِيْضِ
قُلْ هُوَ أَذًى
فَاعْتَزِلُوا النِّسَاءَ فِى الْمَحِيْضِ
وَلَا تَقْرَبُوْهُنَّ حَتّٰى يَطْهُرْنَ
فَاِذَا تَطَهَّرْنَ
فَأْتُوْهُنَّ مِنْ حَيْثُ أَمَرَكُمُ اللّٰهُ
اِنَّ اللّٰهَ يُحِبُّ التَّوَّابِيْنَ
وَيُحِبُّ الْمُتَطَهِّرِيْنَ ۞

٢٢٣ - نِسَاؤُكُمْ حَرْثٌ لَّكُمْ
فَأْتُوْا حَرْثَكُمْ أَنّٰى شِئْتُمْ
وَقَدِّمُوْا لِأَنْفُسِكُمْ
وَاتَّقُوا اللّٰهَ
وَاعْلَمُوْٓا أَنَّكُمْ مُّلٰقُوْهُ
وَبَشِّرِ الْمُؤْمِنِيْنَ ۞

٢٢٤ - وَلَا تَجْعَلُوا اللّٰهَ عُرْضَةً
لِّأَيْمَانِكُمْ أَنْ تَبَرُّوْا
وَتَتَّقُوْا وَتُصْلِحُوْا بَيْنَ النَّاسِ
وَاللّٰهُ سَمِيْعٌ عَلِيْمٌ ۞

225. Allah will not
Call you to account
For thoughtlessness
In your oaths,
But for the intention
In your hearts,
And He is
Oft-Forgiving,
Most Forbearing.

٢٢٥- لَا يُؤَاخِذُكُمُ اللهُ
بِاللَّغْوِ فِىٓ أَيْمَانِكُمْ
وَلَٰكِنْ يُؤَاخِذُكُمْ بِمَا كَسَبَتْ قُلُوبُكُمْ
وَاللهُ غَفُورٌ حَلِيمٌ ٥

226. For those who take
An oath for abstention
From their wives,
A waiting for four months
Is ordained;
If then they return,
Allah is Oft-Forgiving,
Most Merciful.

٢٢٦- لِلَّذِينَ يُؤْلُونَ مِنْ نِسَآئِهِمْ
تَرَبُّصُ أَرْبَعَةِ أَشْهُرٍ
فَإِنْ فَآءُو
فَإِنَّ اللهَ غَفُورٌ رَّحِيمٌ ٥

227. But if their intention
Is firm for divorce,
Allah heareth
And knoweth all things.

٢٢٧- وَإِنْ عَزَمُوا الطَّلَاقَ
فَإِنَّ اللهَ سَمِيعٌ عَلِيمٌ ٥

228. Divorced women
Shall wait concerning themselves
For three monthly periods.
Nor is it lawful for them
To hide what Allah
Hath created in their wombs,
If they have faith
In Allah and the Last Day.
And their husbands
Have the better right
To take them back
In that period, if
They wish for reconciliation.
And women shall have rights
Similar to the rights
Against them, according
To what is equitable;
But men have a degree
(Of advantage) over them.
And Allah is Exalted in Power,
Wise.

٢٢٨- وَالْمُطَلَّقَاتُ يَتَرَبَّصْنَ
بِأَنْفُسِهِنَّ ثَلَٰثَةَ قُرُوٓءٍ
وَلَا يَحِلُّ لَهُنَّ
أَنْ يَكْتُمْنَ مَا خَلَقَ اللهُ فِىٓ أَرْحَامِهِنَّ
إِنْ كُنَّ يُؤْمِنَّ بِاللهِ وَالْيَوْمِ الْآخِرِ
وَبُعُولَتُهُنَّ أَحَقُّ بِرَدِّهِنَّ فِى ذَٰلِكَ إِنْ
أَرَادُوٓا إِصْلَاحًا
وَلَهُنَّ مِثْلُ الَّذِى عَلَيْهِنَّ بِالْمَعْرُوفِ
وَلِلرِّجَالِ عَلَيْهِنَّ دَرَجَةٌ
وَاللهُ عَزِيزٌ حَكِيمٌ ٥

SECTION 29

229. A divorce is only
Permissible twice: after that,

٢٢٩- الطَّلَاقُ مَرَّتَانِ فَإِمْسَاكٌ

The parties should either hold
Together on equitable terms,
Or separate with kindness.

It is not lawful for you,
(Men), to take back
Any of your gifts (from your wives),
Except when both parties
Fear that they would be
Unable to keep the limits
Ordained by Allah.
If ye (judges) do indeed
Fear that they would be
Unable to keep the limits
Ordained by Allah,
There is not blame on either
Of them if she give
Something for her freedom.
These are the limits
Ordained by Allah;
So do not transgress them
If any do transgress
The limits ordained by Allah,
Such persons wrong
(Themselves as well as others).

230. So if a husband
Divorces his wife
　　　　　　　(irrevocably),
He cannot, after that,
Remarry her until
After she has married
Another husband and
He has divorced her.
In that case there is
No blame on either of them
If they reunite, provided
They feel that they
Can keep the limits
Ordained by Allah.
Such are the limits
Ordained by Allah,
Which He makes plain
To those who understand.

231. When ye divorce[261]
Women, and they fulfil
The term of their ('*Iddah*),
Either take them back

On equitable terms
Or set them free
On equitable terms;
But do not take them back
To injure them, (or) to take
Undue advantage;
If any one does that,
He wrongs his own soul.
Do not treat Allah's Signs
As a jest,
But solemnly rehearse
Allah's favours on you,
And the fact that He
Sent down to you
The Book
And Wisdom,
For your instruction.
And fear Allah,
And know that Allah
Is well-acquainted
With all things.

SECTION 30.

232. When ye divorce
Women, and they fulfil
The term of their ('*Iddah*),
Do not prevent them
From marrying
Their (former) husbands,
If they mutually agree
On equitable terms.
This instruction
Is for all amongst you,
Who believe in Allah
And the Last Day.
That is (the course
Making for) most virtue
And purity amongst you.
And Allah knows,
And ye know not.

233. The mothers shall give suck
To their offspring
For two whole years,
If the father desires
To complete the term.
But he shall bear the cost
Of their food and clothing

On equitable terms.
No soul shall have
A burden laid on it
Greater than it can bear.
No mother shall be
Treated unfairly
On account of her child.
Nor father
On account of his child,
An heir shall be chargeable
In the same way,
If they both decide
On weaning,
By mutual consent,
And after due consultation,
There is no blame on them.
If ye decide
On a foster-mother
For your offspring
There is no blame on you,
Provided ye pay (the mother)
What ye offered,
On equitable terms.
But fear Allah and know
That Allah sees well
What ye do.

234. If any of you die
And leave widows behind,
They shall wait concerning
　　　　　　　　themselves
Four months and ten days:
When they have fulfilled
Their term, there is no blame
On you if they dispose
Of themselves in a just
And reasonable manner.
And Allah is well acquainted
With what ye do.

235. There is no blame
On you if you make
An offer of betrothal
Or hold it in your hearts.
Allah knows that ye
Cherish them in your hearts:
But do not make a secret
　　　　　　　　contract

With them except
That you speak to them
In terms honourable, nor resolve
        on the tie
Of marriage till the term
Prescribed is fulfilled.
And know that Allah
Knoweth what is in your hearts,
And take heed of Him;
And know that Allah is
Oft-Forgiving, Most Forbearing.

    SECTION 31.

أَنْ تَقُوْلُوْا
قَوْلًا مَّعْرُوْفًا وَلَا تَعْزِمُوْا عُقْدَةَ النِّكَاحِ
حَتّى يَبْلُغَ الْكِتَابُ أَجَلَهُ ؕ
وَاعْلَمُوْۤا أَنَّ اللّٰهَ يَعْلَمُ مَا فِىْۤ أَنْفُسِكُمْ
فَاحْذَرُوْهُ ؕ وَاعْلَمُوْۤا أَنَّ اللّٰهَ غَفُوْرٌ حَلِيْمٌۢ

236. There is no blame on you
If ye divorce women
Before consummation
Or the fixation of their dower;
But bestow on them
(A suitable gift),
The wealthy
According to his means,
And the poor
According to his means—
A gift of reasonable amount
Is due from those
Who wish to do the right thing.

٢٣٦ ۔ لَا جُنَاحَ عَلَيْكُمْ
اِنْ طَلَّقْتُمُ النِّسَآءَ
مَا لَمْ تَمَسُّوْهُنَّ
اَوْ تَفْرِضُوْا لَهُنَّ فَرِيْضَةً ۖ وَمَتِّعُوْهُنَّ ۚ
عَلَى الْمُوْسِعِ قَدَرُهُ وَعَلَى الْمُقْتِرِ قَدَرُهُ ۚ
مَتَاعًا بِالْمَعْرُوْفِ ۚ حَقًّا عَلَى الْمُحْسِنِيْنَ

237. And if ye divorce them
Before consummation,
But after the fixation
Of a dower for them,
Then the half of the dower
(Is due to them), unless
They remit it
Or (the man's half) is remitted
By him in whose hands
Is the marriage tie;
And the remission
(Of the man's half)
Is the nearest to righteousness
And do not forget
Liberality between yourselves.
For Allah sees well
All that ye do.

٢٣٧ ۔ وَاِنْ طَلَّقْتُمُوْهُنَّ
مِنْ قَبْلِ اَنْ تَمَسُّوْهُنَّ وَقَدْ فَرَضْتُمْ
لَهُنَّ فَرِيْضَةً فَنِصْفُ مَا فَرَضْتُمْ
اِلَّاۤ اَنْ يَّعْفُوْنَ
اَوْ يَعْفُوَا الَّذِىْ
بِيَدِهِ عُقْدَةُ النِّكَاحِ ؕ
وَاَنْ تَعْفُوْۤا اَقْرَبُ لِلتَّقْوٰى ؕ
وَلَا تَنْسَوُا الْفَضْلَ بَيْنَكُمْ ؕ
اِنَّ اللّٰهَ بِمَا تَعْمَلُوْنَ بَصِيْرٌ

238. Guard strictly
Your (habit) of prayers,

٢٣٨ ۔ حَافِظُوْا عَلَى الصَّلَوٰتِ

Especially the Middle Prayer;
And stand before Allah
In a devout (frame of mind).

239. If ye fear (an enemy),
Pray on foot, or riding,
(As may be most convenient),
But when you are
In security, celebrate
Allah's praises in the manner
He has taught you,
Which ye knew not (before).

240. Those of you
Who die and leave widows
Should bequeath
For their widows
A year's maintenance
And residence;
But if they leave
(The residence),
There is no blame on you
For what they do
With themselves,
Provided it is reasonable.
And Allah is Exalted in Power,
Wise.

241. For divorced women
Maintenance (should be provided)
On a reasonable (scale).
This is a duty
On the righteous.

242. Thus doth Allah
Make clear His Signs
To you: in order that
Ye may understand.

SECTION 32.

243. Didst thou not
Turn thy vision to those
Who abandoned their homes,
Though they were thousands
(In number), for fear of death?
Allah said to them: "Die":
Then He restored them to
life.
For Allah is full of bounty

وَالصَّلٰوةِ الْوُسْطٰى وَقُوْمُوْا لِلّٰهِ قٰنِتِيْنَ ۝

٢٣٩- فَاِنْ خِفْتُمْ فَرِجَالًا اَوْ رُكْبَانًا ۚ فَاِذَآ اَمِنْتُمْ فَاذْكُرُوا اللّٰهَ كَمَا عَلَّمَكُمْ مَّا لَمْ تَكُوْنُوْا تَعْلَمُوْنَ ۝

٢٤٠- وَالَّذِيْنَ يُتَوَفَّوْنَ مِنْكُمْ وَيَذَرُوْنَ اَزْوَاجًا ۖ وَّصِيَّةً لِّاَزْوَاجِهِمْ مَّتَاعًا اِلَى الْحَوْلِ غَيْرَ اِخْرَاجٍ ۚ فَاِنْ خَرَجْنَ فَلَا جُنَاحَ عَلَيْكُمْ فِيْ مَا فَعَلْنَ فِيْ اَنْفُسِهِنَّ مِنْ مَّعْرُوْفٍ ۗ وَاللّٰهُ عَزِيْزٌ حَكِيْمٌ ۝

٢٤١- وَلِلْمُطَلَّقٰتِ مَتَاعٌ ۢ بِالْمَعْرُوْفِ ۗ حَقًّا عَلَى الْمُتَّقِيْنَ ۝

٢٤٢- كَذٰلِكَ يُبَيِّنُ اللّٰهُ لَكُمْ اٰيٰتِهٖ لَعَلَّكُمْ تَعْقِلُوْنَ ۧ

٢٤٣- اَلَمْ تَرَ اِلَى الَّذِيْنَ خَرَجُوْا مِنْ دِيَارِهِمْ وَهُمْ اُلُوْفٌ حَذَرَ الْمَوْتِ ۖ فَقَالَ لَهُمُ اللّٰهُ مُوْتُوْا ثُمَّ اَحْيَاهُمْ ۗ اِنَّ اللّٰهَ لَذُوْ فَضْلٍ عَلَى النَّاسِ وَلٰكِنَّ اَكْثَرَ النَّاسِ

To mankind, but
Most of them are ungrateful.

لَا يَشْكُرُونَ ۝

244. Then fight in the cause
Of Allah, and know that Allah
Heareth and knoweth all things.

٢٤٤ ـ وَقَاتِلُوا فِي سَبِيلِ اللهِ وَاعْلَمُوا
أَنَّ اللهَ سَمِيعٌ عَلِيمٌ ۝

245. Who is he
That will loan to Allah
A beautiful loan,   which Allah
Will double unto his credit
And multiply many times?
It is Allah that giveth (you)
Want or Plenty,
And to Him shall be
Your return.

٢٤٥ ـ مَنْ ذَا الَّذِى
يُقْرِضُ اللهَ قَرْضًا حَسَنًا
فَيُضَاعِفَهُ لَهُ أَضْعَافًا كَثِيرَةً
وَاللهُ يَقْبِضُ وَيَبْسُطُ
وَإِلَيْهِ تُرْجَعُونَ ۝

246. Hast thou not
Turned thy vision to the Chiefs
Of the Children of Israel
After (the time of) Moses?
They said to a Prophet
(That was) among them:
"Appoint for us a King, that we
May fight in the cause of Allah."
He said: "Is it not possible,
If ye were commanded
To fight, that that ye
Will not fight?" They said:
"How could we refuse
To fight in the cause of Allah,
Seeing that we were turned out
Of our homes and our
                        families?"
But when they were commanded
To fight, they turned back,
Except a small band
Among them. But Allah
Has full knowledge of those
Who do wrong.

٢٤٦ ـ أَلَمْ تَرَ إِلَى الْمَلَإِ
مِنْ بَنِي إِسْرَائِيلَ مِنْ بَعْدِ مُوسَى
إِذْ قَالُوا لِنَبِيٍّ
لَهُمُ ابْعَثْ لَنَا مَلِكًا نُقَاتِلْ فِي سَبِيلِ
اللهِ قَالَ هَلْ عَسَيْتُمْ
إِنْ كُتِبَ عَلَيْكُمُ
الْقِتَالُ أَلَّا تُقَاتِلُوا
قَالُوا وَمَا لَنَا أَلَّا نُقَاتِلَ فِي سَبِيلِ اللهِ
وَقَدْ أُخْرِجْنَا مِنْ دِيَارِنَا وَأَبْنَائِنَا
فَلَمَّا كُتِبَ عَلَيْهِمُ الْقِتَالُ
تَوَلَّوْا إِلَّا قَلِيلًا مِنْهُمْ
وَاللهُ عَلِيمٌ بِالظَّالِمِينَ ۝

247. Their Prophet said to them:
"Allah hath appointed
Tālūt   as king over you."
They said: "How can he
Exercise authority over us
When we are better fitted
Than he to exercise authority,

٢٤٧ ـ وَقَالَ لَهُمْ نَبِيُّهُمْ
إِنَّ اللهَ قَدْ بَعَثَ لَكُمْ طَالُوتَ مَلِكًا
قَالُوا أَنَّى يَكُونُ لَهُ الْمُلْكُ عَلَيْنَا
وَنَحْنُ أَحَقُّ بِالْمُلْكِ مِنْهُ

And he is not even gifted,
With wealth in abundance?"
He said: Allah hath
Chosen him above you,
And hath gifted him
Abundantly with knowledge
And bodily prowess: Allah
Granteth His authority to whom
He pleaseth. Allah is
All-Embracing, and He knoweth
All things."

وَلَمۡ يُؤۡتَ سَعَةً مِّنَ الۡمَالِ ۚ

قَالَ إِنَّ اللّٰهَ اصۡطَفٰهُ عَلَيۡكُمۡ

وَزَادَهُ بَسۡطَةً فِى الۡعِلۡمِ وَالۡجِسۡمِ ؕ

وَاللّٰهُ يُؤۡتِىۡ مُلۡكَهُ مَنۡ يَّشَآءُ ؕ

وَاللّٰهُ وَاسِعٌ عَلِيۡمٌ ۟

248. And (further) their Prophet
Said to them: "A Sign
Of his authority
Is that there shall come
To you the Ark of the
                    Covenant,
With (an assurance) therein
Of security   from your Lord,
And the relics left
By the family of Moses
And the family of Aaron,
Carried by angels.
In this is a Symbol
For you if ye indeed
Have faith."

٢٤٨۔ وَقَالَ لَهُمۡ نَبِيُّهُمۡ

إِنَّ اٰيَةَ مُلۡكِهٖۤ

أَنۡ يَّأۡتِيَكُمُ التَّابُوۡتُ

فِيۡهِ سَكِيۡنَةٌ

مِّنۡ رَّبِّكُمۡ وَبَقِيَّةٌ مِّمَّا تَرَكَ اٰلُ مُوۡسٰى

وَاٰلُ هٰرُوۡنَ تَحۡمِلُهُ الۡمَلٰٓئِكَةُ ؕ

إِنَّ فِىۡ ذٰلِكَ لَاٰيَةً لَّكُمۡ

إِنۡ كُنۡتُمۡ مُّؤۡمِنِيۡنَ ۟

SECTION 33.

249. When Tālūt set forth
With the armies, he said:
"Allah will test you
At the stream; if any
Drinks of its water,
He goes not with my army;
Only those who taste not
Of it go with me;
A mere sip out of the hand
Is excused." But they all
Drank of it, except a few.
When they crossed the river—
He and the faithful ones with him,
They said: "This day
We cannot cope
With Goliath and his forces."
But those who were convinced
That they must meet Allah,
Said: "How oft, by Allah's will,

٢٤٩۔ فَلَمَّا فَصَلَ طَالُوۡتُ بِالۡجُنُوۡدِ ۙ

قَالَ إِنَّ اللّٰهَ مُبۡتَلِيۡكُمۡ بِنَهَرٍ ۚ

فَمَنۡ شَرِبَ مِنۡهُ فَلَيۡسَ مِنِّىۡ ۚ

وَمَنۡ لَّمۡ يَطۡعَمۡهُ فَإِنَّهُ مِنِّىۡۤ

إِلَّا مَنِ اغۡتَرَفَ غُرۡفَةً بِيَدِهٖ ۚ

فَشَرِبُوۡا مِنۡهُ إِلَّا قَلِيۡلًا مِّنۡهُمۡ ؕ فَلَمَّا جَاوَزَهُ

هُوَ وَالَّذِيۡنَ اٰمَنُوۡا مَعَهُ ۙ

قَالُوۡا لَا طَاقَةَ لَنَا الۡيَوۡمَ بِجَالُوۡتَ وَجُنُوۡدِهٖ ؕ

قَالَ الَّذِيۡنَ يَظُنُّوۡنَ أَنَّهُمۡ مُّلٰقُوا اللّٰهِ ۙ

كَمۡ مِّنۡ فِئَةٍ قَلِيۡلَةٍ

Hath a small force
Vanquished a big one?
Allah is with those
Who steadfastly persevere."

غَلَبَتْ فِئَةً كَثِيرَةً بِإِذْنِ اللهِ ۗ
وَاللهُ مَعَ الصَّبِرِينَ ۝

250. When they advanced
To meet Goliath and his forces,
They prayed: "Our Lord!
Pour out constancy on us
And make our steps firm:
Help us against those
They reject faith."

٢٥٠- وَلَمَّا بَرَزُوا لِجَالُوتَ وَجُنُودِهِ
قَالُوا رَبَّنَآ أَفْرِغْ عَلَيْنَا صَبْرًا
وَثَبِّتْ أَقْدَامَنَا
وَانْصُرْنَا عَلَى الْقَوْمِ الْكَفِرِينَ ۝

251. By Allah's will,
They routed them:
And David[286] slew Goliath:
And Allah gave him
Power and wisdom
And taught him
Whatever (else) He willed.
And did not Allah
Check one set of people
By means of another,
The earth would indeed
Be full of mischief:
But Allah is full of bounty
To all the worlds.

٢٥١- فَهَزَمُوهُمْ بِإِذْنِ اللهِ ۙ
وَقَتَلَ دَاوُدُ جَالُوتَ
وَآتَاهُ اللهُ الْمُلْكَ
وَالْحِكْمَةَ وَعَلَّمَهُ مِمَّا يَشَآءُ ۗ
وَلَوْلَا دَفْعُ اللهِ النَّاسَ بَعْضَهُمْ بِبَعْضٍ
لَفَسَدَتِ الْأَرْضُ
وَلَكِنَّ اللهَ ذُو فَضْلٍ عَلَى الْعَلَمِينَ ۝

252. These are the Signs
Of Allah: we rehearse them
To thee in truth; verily
Thou art one of the Messengers.

٢٥٢- تِلْكَ آيَتُ اللهِ نَتْلُوهَا عَلَيْكَ بِالْحَقِّ ۗ
وَإِنَّكَ لَمِنَ الْمُرْسَلِينَ ۝

253. Those Messengers
We endowed with gifts,
Some above others:
To one of them Allah spoke;
Others He raised
To degrees (of honour);
To Jesus, the son of Mary,
We gave Clear (Signs),
And strengthened him
With the holy spirit.
If Allah had so willed,
Succeeding generations
Would not have fought
Among each other, after
Clear (Signs) had come to them

٢٥٣- تِلْكَ الرُّسُلُ
فَضَّلْنَا بَعْضَهُمْ عَلَى بَعْضٍ ۘ مِنْهُمْ مَّنْ
كَلَّمَ اللهُ وَرَفَعَ بَعْضَهُمْ دَرَجَتٍ ۚ
وَآتَيْنَا عِيسَى ابْنَ مَرْيَمَ الْبَيِّنَتِ
وَأَيَّدْنَهُ بِرُوحِ الْقُدُسِ ۗ وَلَوْ شَآءَ اللهُ
مَا اقْتَتَلَ الَّذِينَ مِنْ بَعْدِهِمْ
مِّنْ بَعْدِ مَا جَآءَتْهُمُ الْبَيِّنَتُ وَلَكِنِ
اخْتَلَفُوا فَمِنْهُمْ مَّنْ آمَنَ وَمِنْهُمْ مَّنْ

But they (chose) to wrangle,
Some believing and others
Rejecting. If Allah had so willed,
They would not have fought
Each other; but Allah
Fulfilleth His plan.

SECTION 34.

254. **O** ye who believe!
Spend out of (the bounties)
We have provided for you,
Before the Day comes
When no bargaining
(Will avail), nor friendship
Nor intercession.
Those who reject Faith—they
Are the wrongdoers.

255. **Allah!** There is no god
But He—the Living,
The Self-subsisting, Eternal.
No slumber can seize Him
Nor sleep. His are all things
In the heavens and on earth.
Who is there can intercede
In His presence except
As He permitteth? He knoweth
What (appeareth to His
               creatures
As) Before or After
Or Behind them.
Nor shall they compass
Aught of His knowledge
Except as He willeth.
His Throne doth extend
Over the heavens
And the earth, and He feeleth
No fatigue in guarding
And preserving them
For He is the Most High,
The Supreme (in glory).

256. **Let** there be no compulsion
In religion: Truth stands out
Clear from Error: whoever
Rejects Evil and believes
In Allah hath grasped

The most trustworthy
Handhold, that never breaks.
And Allah heareth
And knoweth all things.

استمسك بالعروة الوثقى لا انفصام لها
والله سميع عليم ○

257. Allah is the Protector
Of those who have faith:
From the depths of darkness
He will lead them forth
Into light. Of those
Who reject faith the patrons
Are the Evil Ones: from light
They will lead them forth
Into the depths of darkness.
They will be Companions
Of the fire, to dwell therein
(Forever).

٢٥٧- الله ولي الذين امنوا
يخرجهم من الظلمت الى النور
والذين كفروا اوليٰٓئهم الطاغوت
يخرجونهم من النور الى الظلمت
اوليٰٓئك اصحب النار
هم فيها خلدون ○

SECTION 35.

258. Hast thou not
Turned thy vision to one
Who disputed with Abraham
About his Lord, because
Allah had granted him
Power? Abraham said:
"My Lord is He Who
Giveth life and death."
He said: "I give life and death."
Said Abraham: "But it is Allah
That causeth the sun
To rise from the East:
Do thou then cause him
To rise from the West?"
Thus was he confounded
Who (in arrogance) rejected
Faith. Nor doth Allah
Give guidance
To a people unjust.

٢٥٨- الم تر الى الذي حاجّ ابرهم في
ربه ان اتىٰه الله الملك ۘ
اذ قال ابرهم ربي الذي يحي و يميت ۙ
قال انا احي و اميت ۚ
قال ابرهم فان الله
ياتي بالشمس من المشرق
فات بها من المغرب
فبهت الذي كفر ۗ
والله لا يهدي
القوم الظلمين ○

259. Or (take) the similitude
Of one who passed
By a hamlet, all in ruins
To its roofs. He said:

٢٥٩- او كالذي مرّ على قرية
وهي خاوية على عروشها ۚ

"Oh! how shall Allah
Bring it (ever) to life,
After (this) its death?"
But Allah caused him
To die for a hundred years,
Then raised him up (again).
He said: "How long
Didst thou tarry (thus)?"
He said: "(Perhaps) a day
Or part of a day." He said:
"Nay, thou hast tarried
Thus a hundred years;
But look at thy food
And thy drink; they show
No signs of age; and look
At thy donkey; and that
We may make of thee
A Sign unto the people,
Look further at the bones,
How We bring them together
And clothe them with flesh."
When this was shown clearly
To him, he said: "I know
That Allah hath power
Over all things."

قَالَ أَنّٰى يُحْىِ هٰذِهِ اللّٰهُ بَعْدَ مَوْتِهَا ۚ
فَأَمَاتَهُ اللّٰهُ مِائَةَ عَامٍ
ثُمَّ بَعَثَهُ ۚ قَالَ كَمْ لَبِثْتَ ۚ
قَالَ لَبِثْتُ يَوْمًا أَوْ بَعْضَ يَوْمٍ ۚ
قَالَ بَلْ لَبِثْتَ مِائَةَ عَامٍ
فَانْظُرْ إِلٰى طَعَامِكَ
وَشَرَابِكَ لَمْ يَتَسَنَّهْ ۚ
وَانْظُرْ إِلٰى حِمَارِكَ
وَلِنَجْعَلَكَ آيَةً لِّلنَّاسِ
وَانْظُرْ إِلَى الْعِظَامِ كَيْفَ نُنْشِزُهَا
ثُمَّ نَكْسُوهَا لَحْمًا ۚ
فَلَمَّا تَبَيَّنَ لَهُ ۙ قَالَ أَعْلَمُ
أَنَّ اللّٰهَ عَلٰى كُلِّ شَيْءٍ قَدِيرٌ ۞

260. Behold! Abraham said:
"My Lord! Show me how
Thou givest life to the dead."
He said: "Dost thou not
Then believe?" He said:
"Yea! but to satisfy
My own understanding."
He said: "Take four birds;
Tame them to turn to thee;
Put a portion   of them
On every hill, and call to them;
They will come to thee,
(Flying) with speed.
Then know that Allah
Is Exalted in Power, Wise."

٢٦٠- وَإِذْ قَالَ إِبْرٰهِمُ رَبِّ أَرِنِي كَيْفَ
تُحْىِ الْمَوْتٰى ۚ قَالَ أَوَلَمْ تُؤْمِنْ ۚ
قَالَ بَلٰى وَلٰكِنْ لِّيَطْمَئِنَّ قَلْبِي ۚ
قَالَ فَخُذْ أَرْبَعَةً مِّنَ الطَّيْرِ
فَصُرْهُنَّ إِلَيْكَ
ثُمَّ اجْعَلْ عَلٰى كُلِّ جَبَلٍ مِّنْهُنَّ جُزْءًا
ثُمَّ ادْعُهُنَّ يَأْتِينَكَ سَعْيًا ۚ
وَاعْلَمْ أَنَّ اللّٰهَ عَزِيزٌ حَكِيمٌ ۞

SECTION 36.

261. The parable of those
Who spend their substance
In the way of Allah is that
Of a grain of corn: it groweth
Seven ears, and each ear

٢٦١- مَثَلُ الَّذِينَ يُنْفِقُونَ أَمْوَالَهُمْ
فِي سَبِيلِ اللّٰهِ كَمَثَلِ حَبَّةٍ أَنْبَتَتْ سَبْعَ
سَنَابِلَ فِي كُلِّ سُنْبُلَةٍ

Hath a hundred grains.
Allah giveth manifold increase
To whom He pleaseth:
And Allah careth for all
And He knoweth all things,

262. Those who spend
Their substance in the cause
Of Allah, and follow not up
Their gifts with reminders
Of their generosity
Or with injury—for them
Their reward is with their Lord;
On them shall be no fear,
Nor shall they grieve.

263. Kind words
And covering of faults
Are better than charity
Followed by injury.
Allah is Free of all wants,
And He is most Forbearing.

264. O ye who believe!
Cancel not your charity
By reminders of your generosity
Or by injury—like those
Who spend their substance
To be seen of men,
But believe neither
In Allah nor in the Last Day.
They are in Parable like a hard
Barren rock, on which
Is a little soil; on it
Falls heavy rain,
Which leaves it
(Just) a bare stone.
They will be able to do nothing
With aught they have earned.
And Allah guideth not
Those who reject faith.

265. And the likeness of those
Who spend their substance,
Seeking to please Allah
And to strengthen their souls,
Is as a garden, high

And fertile; heavy rain
Falls on it but makes it yield
A double increase
Of harvest, and if it receives not
Heavy rain, light moisture
Sufficeth it. Allah seeth well
Whatever ye do.

اَصَابَهَا وَابِلٌ فَاتَتْ اُكُلَهَا ضِعْفَيْنِ ۚ
فَاِنْ لَّمْ يُصِبْهَا وَابِلٌ فَطَلٌّ ؕ
وَاللّٰهُ بِمَا تَعْمَلُوْنَ بَصِيْرٌ ۟

266. Does any of you wish
That he should have a garden
With date palms and vines
And streams flowing
Underneath, and all kinds
Of fruit, while he is stricken
With old age, and his children
Are not strong (enough
To look after themselves)—
That it should be caught
In a whirlwind,
With fire therein,
And be burnt up?
Thus doth Allah make clear
To you (His) Signs:
That ye may consider.

٢٦٦- اَيَوَدُّ اَحَدُكُمْ اَنْ تَكُوْنَ لَهٗ جَنَّةٌ
مِّنْ نَّخِيْلٍ وَّاَعْنَابٍ
تَجْرِيْ مِنْ تَحْتِهَا الْاَنْهٰرُ ۙ
لَهٗ فِيْهَا مِنْ كُلِّ الثَّمَرٰتِ ۙ
وَاَصَابَهُ الْكِبَرُ وَلَهٗ ذُرِّيَّةٌ ضُعَفَآءُ ۖ
فَاَصَابَهَآ اِعْصَارٌ فِيْهِ نَارٌ فَاحْتَرَقَتْ ؕ
كَذٰلِكَ يُبَيِّنُ اللّٰهُ
لَكُمُ الْاٰيٰتِ لَعَلَّكُمْ تَتَفَكَّرُوْنَ ۟ ۣ

SECTION 37.

267. O ye who believe!
Give of the good things
Which ye have (honourably)
　　　　　　　earned,
And of the fruits of the earth
Which We have produced
For you, and do not even aim
At getting anything
Which is bad, in order that
Out of it ye may give away
Something, when ye yourselves
Would not receive it
Except with closed eyes.
And know that Allah
Is free of all wants,
And worthy of all praise.

٢٦٧- يٰٓاَيُّهَا الَّذِيْنَ اٰمَنُوْٓا
اَنْفِقُوْا مِنْ طَيِّبٰتِ مَا كَسَبْتُمْ
وَمِمَّآ اَخْرَجْنَا لَكُمْ مِّنَ الْاَرْضِ ۖ
وَلَا تَيَمَّمُوا الْخَبِيْثَ
مِنْهُ تُنْفِقُوْنَ
وَلَسْتُمْ بِاٰخِذِيْهِ
اِلَّآ اَنْ تُغْمِضُوْا فِيْهِ ؕ
وَاعْلَمُوْٓا اَنَّ اللّٰهَ غَنِيٌّ حَمِيْدٌ ۟

268. The Evil One threatens
You with poverty
And bids you to conduct
Unseemly. Allah promiseth

٢٦٨- اَلشَّيْطٰنُ يَعِدُكُمُ الْفَقْرَ
وَيَأْمُرُكُمْ بِالْفَحْشَآءِ ۚ

You His forgiveness
And bounties.
And Allah careth for all
And He knoweth all things.

وَاللهُ يَعِدُكُمْ مَغْفِرَةً مِنْهُ
وَفَضْلًا ۚ وَاللهُ وَاسِعٌ عَلِيمٌ ۞

269. He granteth wisdom
To whom He pleaseth;
And he to whom wisdom
Is granted receiveth
Indeed a benefit overflowing;
But none will grasp the Message
But men of understanding.

٢٦٩- يُؤْتِى الْحِكْمَةَ مَنْ يَّشَاءُ ۚ
وَمَنْ يُؤْتَ الْحِكْمَةَ
فَقَدْ أُوْتِىَ خَيْرًا كَثِيرًا ۚ
وَمَا يَذَّكَّرُ إِلَّا أُولُوا الْأَلْبَابِ ۞

270. And whatever ye spend
In charity or devotion,
Be sure Allah knows it all.
But the wrongdoers
Have no helpers.

٢٧٠- وَمَآ أَنْفَقْتُمْ مِنْ نَّفَقَةٍ
أَوْ نَذَرْتُمْ مِنْ نَّذْرٍ فَإِنَّ اللهَ يَعْلَمُهُ ۚ
وَمَا لِلظّٰلِمِينَ مِنْ أَنْصَارٍ ۞

271. If ye disclose (acts
Of) charity, even so
It is well,
But if ye conceal them,
And make them reach
Those (really) in need,
That is best for you:
It will remove from you
Some of your (stains
Of) evil. And Allah
Is well-acquainted
With what ye do.

٢٧١- إِنْ تُبْدُوا الصَّدَقَاتِ
فَنِعِمَّا هِىَ ۚ وَإِنْ تُخْفُوهَا
وَتُؤْتُوهَا الْفُقَرَآءَ
فَهُوَ خَيْرٌ لَّكُمْ ۚ
وَيُكَفِّرُ عَنْكُمْ مِنْ سَيِّاٰتِكُمْ ۚ
وَاللهُ بِمَا تَعْمَلُونَ خَبِيرٌ ۞

272. It is not required
Of thee (O Messenger),
To set them on the right path,
But Allah sets on the right path
Whom He pleaseth.
Whatever of good ye give
Benefits your own souls,
And ye shall only do so
Seeking the "Face"
Of Allah. Whatever good
Ye give, shall be
Rendered back to you,
And ye shall not

٢٧٢- لَيْسَ عَلَيْكَ
هُدَاهُمْ وَلٰكِنَّ اللهَ يَهْدِى مَنْ يَّشَاءُ ۚ
وَمَا تُنْفِقُوا مِنْ خَيْرٍ فَلِأَنْفُسِكُمْ ۚ
وَمَا تُنْفِقُونَ
إِلَّا ابْتِغَآءَ وَجْهِ اللهِ ۚ
وَمَا تُنْفِقُوا مِنْ خَيْرٍ
يُوَفَّ إِلَيْكُمْ وَأَنْتُمْ

Be dealt with unjustly.

لَا تُظْلَمُونَ ۟

273. (Charity is) for those
In need, who, in Allah's cause
Are restricted (from travel),
And cannot move about
In the land, seeking
(For trade or work):
The ignorant man thinks,
Because of their modesty,
That they are free from want.
Thou shalt know them
By their (unfailing) mark:
They beg not importunately
From all and sundry,
And whatever of good
Ye give, be assured
Allah knoweth it well.

٢٧٣- لِلْفُقَرَاءِ الَّذِينَ
أُحْصِرُوا فِى سَبِيلِ اللّٰهِ لَا يَسْتَطِيعُونَ
ضَرْبًا فِى الْأَرْضِ ۖ
يَحْسَبُهُمُ الْجَاهِلُ أَغْنِيَاءَ مِنَ التَّعَفُّفِ ۖ
تَعْرِفُهُمْ بِسِيمَاهُمْ ۚ
لَا يَسْئَلُونَ النَّاسَ إِلْحَافًا ۗ
وَمَا تُنْفِقُوا مِنْ خَيْرٍ
فَإِنَّ اللّٰهَ بِهِ عَلِيمٌ ۟

SECTION 38.

274. Those who (in charity)
Spend of their goods
By night and by day,
In secret and in public,
Have their reward
With their Lord:
On them shall be no fear,
Nor shall they grieve.

٢٧٤- الَّذِينَ يُنْفِقُونَ أَمْوَالَهُمْ بِاللَّيْلِ
وَالنَّهَارِ سِرًّا وَعَلَانِيَةً
فَلَهُمْ أَجْرُهُمْ عِنْدَ رَبِّهِمْ ۖ
وَلَا خَوْفٌ عَلَيْهِمْ وَلَا هُمْ يَحْزَنُونَ ۟

275. Those who devour usury
Will not stand except
As stands one whom
The Evil One by his touch
Hath driven to madness.
That is because they say:
"Trade is like usury,"
But Allah hath permitted trade
And forbidden usury.
Those who after receiving
Direction from their Lord,
Desist, shall be pardoned
For the past; their case
Is for Allah (to judge);
But those who repeat
(The offence) are Companions
Of the Fire; they will
Abide therein (forever).

٢٧٥- الَّذِينَ يَأْكُلُونَ الرِّبَوٰا لَا يَقُومُونَ
إِلَّا كَمَا يَقُومُ الَّذِى يَتَخَبَّطُهُ الشَّيْطَٰنُ
مِنَ الْمَسِّ ۚ ذٰلِكَ بِأَنَّهُمْ قَالُوا إِنَّمَا الْبَيْعُ
مِثْلُ الرِّبَوٰا ۘ وَأَحَلَّ اللّٰهُ الْبَيْعَ وَحَرَّمَ
الرِّبَوٰا ۚ فَمَنْ جَاءَهُ مَوْعِظَةٌ مِنْ رَبِّهِ
فَانْتَهَىٰ فَلَهُ مَا سَلَفَ ۚ
وَأَمْرُهُ إِلَى اللّٰهِ ۖ
وَمَنْ عَادَ فَأُولٰئِكَ أَصْحَٰبُ النَّارِ ۖ
هُمْ فِيهَا خَٰلِدُونَ ۟

276. Allah will deprive
Usury of all blessing,
But will give increase
For deeds of charity;
For He loveth not
Creatures ungrateful
And wicked.

٢٧٦ - يَمْحَقُ اللَّهُ الرِّبَوا
وَيُرْبِى الصَّدَقَٰتِ ۗ
وَاللَّهُ لَا يُحِبُّ
كُلَّ كَفَّارٍ أَثِيمٍ ۞

277. Those who believe,
And do deeds of righteousness,
And establish regular prayers
And regular charity,
Will have their reward
With their Lord:
On them shall be no fear,
Nor shall they grieve.

٢٧٧ - إِنَّ الَّذِينَ آمَنُوا وَعَمِلُوا الصَّٰلِحَٰتِ
وَأَقَامُوا الصَّلَوٰةَ وَآتَوُا الزَّكَوٰةَ
لَهُمْ أَجْرُهُمْ عِنْدَ رَبِّهِمْ ۖ
وَلَا خَوْفٌ عَلَيْهِمْ وَلَا هُمْ يَحْزَنُونَ ۞

278. O ye who believe!
Fear Allah, and give up
What remains of your demand
For usury, if ye are
Indeed believers.

٢٧٨ - يَٰٓأَيُّهَا الَّذِينَ آمَنُوا اتَّقُوا اللَّهَ
وَذَرُوا مَا بَقِيَ مِنَ الرِّبَوٰا
إِنْ كُنْتُمْ مُؤْمِنِينَ ۞

279. If ye do it not,
Take notice of war
From Allah and His Messenger:
But if ye turn back,
Ye shall have
Your capital sums;
Deal not unjustly,
And ye shall not
Be dealt with unjustly.

٢٧٩ - فَإِنْ لَمْ تَفْعَلُوا فَأْذَنُوا بِحَرْبٍ
مِنَ اللَّهِ وَرَسُولِهِ ۖ وَإِنْ تُبْتُمْ
فَلَكُمْ رُءُوسُ أَمْوَالِكُمْ
لَا تَظْلِمُونَ وَلَا تُظْلَمُونَ ۞

280. If the debtor is
In a difficulty,
Grant him time
Till it is easy
For him to repay.
But if ye remit it
By way of charity,
That is best for you
If ye only knew.

٢٨٠ - وَإِنْ كَانَ ذُو عُسْرَةٍ
فَنَظِرَةٌ إِلَىٰ مَيْسَرَةٍ ۚ
وَأَنْ تَصَدَّقُوا خَيْرٌ لَكُمْ ۖ
إِنْ كُنْتُمْ تَعْلَمُونَ ۞

281. And fear the Day
When ye shall be
Brought back to Allah.
Then shall every soul
Be paid what it earned,

٢٨١ - وَاتَّقُوا يَوْمًا تُرْجَعُونَ فِيهِ
إِلَى اللَّهِ ۖ
ثُمَّ تُوَفَّىٰ كُلُّ نَفْسٍ مَا كَسَبَتْ

And none shall be
Dealt with unjustly.

SECTION 39.

282. O ye who believe!
When ye deal with each other,
In transactions involving
Future obligations
In a fixed period of time,
Reduce them to writing
Let a scribe write down
Faithfully as between
The parties; let not the scribe
Refuse to write: as Allah
Has taught him,
So let him write.
Let him who incurs
The liability dictate,
But let him fear
His Lord Allah,
And not diminish
Aught of what he owes.
If the party liable
Is mentally deficient,
Or weak, or unable
Himself to dictate,
Let his guardian
Dictate faithfully.
And get two witnesses,
Out of your own men,
And if there are not two men,
Then a man and two women,
Such as ye choose,
For witnesses,
So that if one of them errs,
The other can remind her.
The witnesses
Should not refuse
When they are called on
(For evidence).
Disdain not to reduce
To writing (your contract)
For a future period,
Whether it be small
Or big: it is juster
In the sight of Allah,
More suitable as evidence,
And more convenient

وَهُمْ لَا يُظْلَمُونَ ۞

٢٨٢ - يَاۤأَيُّهَا الَّذِينَ اٰمَنُوۤا

اِذَا تَدَايَنْتُمْ بِدَيْنٍ

اِلٰٓى اَجَلٍ مُّسَمًّى فَاكْتُبُوهُ ۚ

وَلْيَكْتُبْ بَيْنَكُمْ كَاتِبٌ بِالْعَدْلِ ۚ

وَلَا يَاْبَ كَاتِبٌ

اَنْ يَّكْتُبَ كَمَا عَلَّمَهُ اللّٰهُ فَلْيَكْتُبْ ۚ

وَلْيُمْلِلِ الَّذِي عَلَيْهِ الْحَقُّ

وَلْيَتَّقِ اللّٰهَ رَبَّهُ

وَلَا يَبْخَسْ مِنْهُ شَيْئًا ۚ

فَاِنْ كَانَ الَّذِي عَلَيْهِ الْحَقُّ سَفِيهًا

اَوْ ضَعِيفًا اَوْ لَا يَسْتَطِيعُ

اَنْ يُّمِلَّ هُوَ فَلْيُمْلِلْ وَلِيُّهُ بِالْعَدْلِ ۚ

وَاسْتَشْهِدُوا شَهِيدَيْنِ

مِنْ رِّجَالِكُمْ ۚ

فَاِنْ لَّمْ يَكُونَا رَجُلَيْنِ

فَرَجُلٌ وَّامْرَاَتٰنِ

مِمَّنْ تَرْضَوْنَ مِنَ الشُّهَدَآءِ

اَنْ تَضِلَّ اِحْدٰىهُمَا

فَتُذَكِّرَ اِحْدٰىهُمَا الْاُخْرٰى ۚ

وَلَا يَاْبَ الشُّهَدَآءُ اِذَا مَا دُعُوا ۚ

وَلَا تَسْـَٔمُوۤا اَنْ تَكْتُبُوهُ

صَغِيرًا اَوْ كَبِيرًا اِلٰٓى اَجَلِهِ ۚ

ذٰلِكُمْ اَقْسَطُ عِنْدَ اللّٰهِ

وَاَقْوَمُ لِلشَّهَادَةِ وَاَدْنٰۤى اَلَّا تَرْتَابُوۤا

To prevent doubts
Among yourselves
But if it be a transaction
Which ye carry out
On the spot among yourselves
There is no blame on you
If ye reduce it not
To writing.
But take witnesses
Whenever ye make
A commercial contract;
And let neither scribe
Nor witness suffer harm.
If ye do (such harm),
It would be wickedness
In you. So fear Allah;
For it is Allah
That teaches you.
And Allah is well acquainted
With all things.

إِلَّا أَن تَكُونَ تِجَارَةً
حَاضِرَةً
تُدِيرُونَهَا بَيْنَكُمْ
فَلَيْسَ عَلَيْكُمْ جُنَاحٌ أَلَّا تَكْتُبُوهَا
وَأَشْهِدُوا إِذَا تَبَايَعْتُمْ
وَلَا يُضَارَّ كَاتِبٌ وَلَا شَهِيدٌ
وَإِن تَفْعَلُوا فَإِنَّهُ فُسُوقٌ بِكُمْ
وَاتَّقُوا اللَّهَ وَيُعَلِّمُكُمُ اللَّهُ
وَاللَّهُ بِكُلِّ شَيْءٍ عَلِيمٌ ٠

283. If ye are on a journey,
And cannot find
A scribe, a pledge
With possession (may serve
The purpose).
And if one of you
Deposits a thing
On trust with another,
Let the trustee
(Faithfully) discharge
His trust, and let him
Fear his Lord.
Conceal not evidence;
For whoever conceals it—
His heart is tainted
With sin. And Allah
Knoweth all that ye do.

٢٨٣- وَإِن كُنتُمْ عَلَىٰ سَفَرٍ
وَلَمْ تَجِدُوا كَاتِبًا
فَرِهَانٌ مَّقْبُوضَةٌ
فَإِنْ أَمِنَ بَعْضُكُم بَعْضًا
فَلْيُؤَدِّ الَّذِي اؤْتُمِنَ أَمَانَتَهُ
وَلْيَتَّقِ اللَّهَ رَبَّهُ
وَلَا تَكْتُمُوا الشَّهَادَةَ
وَمَن يَكْتُمْهَا فَإِنَّهُ آثِمٌ قَلْبُهُ
وَاللَّهُ بِمَا تَعْمَلُونَ عَلِيمٌ ٠

SECTION 40.

284. To Allah belongeth all
That is in the heavens
And on earth. Whether
Ye show what is in your minds
Or conceal it, Allah
Calleth you to account for it.
He forgiveth whom He pleaseth,
And punisheth whom He pleaseth.

٢٨٤- لِّلَّهِ مَا فِي السَّمَاوَاتِ وَمَا فِي الْأَرْضِ
وَإِن تُبْدُوا مَا فِي أَنفُسِكُمْ
أَوْ تُخْفُوهُ يُحَاسِبْكُم بِهِ اللَّهُ
فَيَغْفِرُ لِمَن يَشَاءُ وَيُعَذِّبُ مَن يَشَاءُ

For Allah hath power
Over all things.

والله عَلَى كُلِّ شَيْءٍ قَدِيْرٌ ۝

285. The Messenger believeth
In what hath been revealed
To him from his Lord,
As do the men of faith.
Each one (of them) believeth
In Allah, His angels,
His books, and His Messengers.
"We make no distinction (they say)
Between one and another
Of His Messengers." And they say:
"We hear, and we obey:
(We seek) Thy forgiveness,
Our Lord, and to Thee
Is the end of all journeys."

٢٨٥- اٰمَنَ الرَّسُوْلُ بِمَاۤ اُنْزِلَ اِلَيْهِ
مِنْ رَّبِّهٖ وَالْمُؤْمِنُوْنَ ؕ
كُلٌّ اٰمَنَ بِاللّٰهِ وَمَلٰٓئِكَتِهٖ
وَكُتُبِهٖ وَرُسُلِهٖ ۛ
لَا نُفَرِّقُ بَيْنَ اَحَدٍ مِّنْ رُّسُلِهٖ ۛ
وَقَالُوْا سَمِعْنَا وَاَطَعْنَا ۗ
غُفْرَانَكَ رَبَّنَا وَاِلَيْكَ الْمَصِيْرُ ۝

286. On no soul doth Allah
Place a burden greater
Than it can bear.
It gets every good that it earns,
And it suffers every ill that it earns.
(Pray:) "Our Lord!
Condemn us not
If we forget or fall
Into error; our Lord!
Lay not on us a burden
Like that which Thou
Didst lay on those before us,
Our Lord! lay not on us
A burden greater than we
Have strength to bear.
Blot out our sins,
And grant us forgiveness.
Have mercy on us.
Thou art our Protector;
Help us against those
Who stand against Faith."

٢٨٦- لَا يُكَلِّفُ اللّٰهُ نَفْسًا اِلَّا وُسْعَهَا ؕ
لَهَا مَا كَسَبَتْ وَعَلَيْهَا مَا اكْتَسَبَتْ ؕ
رَبَّنَا لَا تُؤَاخِذْنَاۤ اِنْ نَّسِيْنَاۤ
اَوْ اَخْطَأْنَا ۚ
رَبَّنَا وَلَا تَحْمِلْ عَلَيْنَاۤ
اِصْرًا كَمَا حَمَلْتَهٗ
عَلَى الَّذِيْنَ مِنْ قَبْلِنَا ۚ
رَبَّنَا وَلَا تُحَمِّلْنَا مَا لَا طَاقَةَ لَنَا بِهٖ ۚ
وَاعْفُ عَنَّا ۖ وَاغْفِرْ لَنَا ۖ
وَارْحَمْنَا ۗ اَنْتَ مَوْلٰىنَا
فَانْصُرْنَا عَلَى الْقَوْمِ الْكٰفِرِيْنَ ۝

INTRODUCTION TO SŪRA III (*Āl-i-'Imrān*) — 200 Verses

This Sūra is cognate to Sūra ii, but the matter is here treated from a different point of view. The references to Badr (Ramadlān, H. 2) and Uhud (Shawwāl, H. 3) give a clue to the dates of those passages.

Like Sūra ii, it takes a general view of the religious history of mankind, with special reference to the People of the Book, proceeds to explain the birth of the new People of Islam and their ordinances, insists on the need of struggle and fighting in the cause of Truth, and exhorts those who have been blessed with Islam to remain constant in Faith, pray for guidance, and maintain their spiritual hope for the Future.

The new points of view developed are: (1) The emphasis is here laid on the duty of the Christians to accept the new light; the Christians are here specially appealed to as the Jews were specially appealed to in the last Sūra; (2) the lessons of the battles of Badr and Uhud are set out for the Muslim community; and (3) the responsibilities of that community are insisted on both internally and in their relations to those outside.

Sūrah 3.

Āli 'Imrān (The Family of 'Imrān)

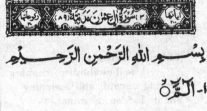

In the name of Allah, Most Gracious, Most Merciful.

بِسْمِ اللهِ الرَّحْمٰنِ الرَّحِيْمِ

1. Alif Lām Mīm.

١ـ الٓمّٓ ۚ

2. Allah! There is no god
But He—the Living,
The Self-Subsisting, Eternal.

٢ـ اَللهُ لَاۤ اِلٰهَ اِلَّا هُوَ الْحَيُّ الْقَيُّوْمُ ۙ

3. It is He Who sent down
To thee (step by step),
In truth, the Book,
Confirming what went before it,
And He sent down the Law
(Of Moses) and the Gospel
(Of Jesus)

٣ـ نَزَّلَ عَلَيْكَ الْكِتٰبَ بِالْحَقِّ مُصَدِّقًا لِّمَا بَيْنَ يَدَيْهِ وَاَنْزَلَ التَّوْرٰىةَ وَالْاِنْجِيْلَ ۙ

4. Before this, as a guide to
mankind,
And He sent down the Criterion
(Of judgement between right and
wrong).
Then those who reject
Faith in the Signs of Allah
Will suffer the severest
Penalty, and Allah
Is Exalted in Might,
Lord of Retribution.

٤ـ مِنْ قَبْلُ هُدًى لِّلنَّاسِ وَاَنْزَلَ الْفُرْقَانَ ۚ اِنَّ الَّذِيْنَ كَفَرُوْا بِاٰيٰتِ اللهِ لَهُمْ عَذَابٌ شَدِيْدٌ ؕ وَاللهُ عَزِيْزٌ ذُو انْتِقَامٍ ۗ

5. From Allah, verily
Nothing is hidden
On earth or in the heavens.

٥ـ اِنَّ اللهَ لَا يَخْفٰى عَلَيْهِ شَيْءٌ فِى الْاَرْضِ وَلَا فِى السَّمَاءِ ؕ

6. He it is Who shapes you
   In the wombs as He pleases.
   There is no god but He,
   The Exalted in Might,
   The Wise.

٦۔ هُوَ الَّذِىْ يُصَوِّرُكُمْ فِى الْاَرْحَامِ كَيْفَ يَشَآءُ ۚ لَآ اِلٰهَ اِلَّا هُوَ الْعَزِيْزُ الْحَكِيْمُ ۝

7. He it is Who has sent down
   To thee the Book;
   In it are verses
   Basic or fundamental
   (Of established meaning);
   They are the foundation
   Of the Book: others
   Are not of well-established
                meaning. But those
   In whose hearts is perversity
                          follow
   The part thereof that is not of
                well-established meaning.
   Seeking discord, and searching
   For its hidden meanings,
   But no one knows
   Its true meanings except Allah.
   And those who are firmly
                      grounded
   In knowledge say: "We believe
   In the Book; the whole of it
   Is from our Lord:" and none
   Will grasp the Message
   Except men of understanding.

٧۔ هُوَ الَّذِىْۤ اَنْزَلَ عَلَيْكَ الْكِتٰبَ مِنْهُ اٰيٰتٌ مُّحْكَمٰتٌ هُنَّ اُمُّ الْكِتٰبِ وَاُخَرُ مُتَشٰبِهٰتٌ ۚ فَاَمَّا الَّذِيْنَ فِىْ قُلُوْبِهِمْ زَيْغٌ فَيَتَّبِعُوْنَ مَا تَشَابَهَ مِنْهُ ابْتِغَآءَ الْفِتْنَةِ وَابْتِغَآءَ تَاْوِيْلِهٖ ۚ وَمَا يَعْلَمُ تَاْوِيْلَهٗۤ اِلَّا اللّٰهُ ۘ وَالرّٰسِخُوْنَ فِى الْعِلْمِ يَقُوْلُوْنَ اٰمَنَّا بِهٖ ۙ كُلٌّ مِّنْ عِنْدِ رَبِّنَا ۚ وَمَا يَذَّكَّرُ اِلَّاۤ اُولُوا الْاَلْبَابِ ۝

8. "Our Lord!" (they say),
   "Let not our hearts deviate
   Now after Thou hast guided us,
   But grant us mercy
   From Thine own Presence;
   For Thou art the Grantor
   Of bounties without measure.

٨۔ رَبَّنَا لَا تُزِغْ قُلُوْبَنَا بَعْدَ اِذْ هَدَيْتَنَا وَهَبْ لَنَا مِنْ لَّدُنْكَ رَحْمَةً ۚ اِنَّكَ اَنْتَ الْوَهَّابُ ۝

9. "Our Lord! Thou art He
   That will gather mankind
   Together against a Day about
                          which
   There is no doubt; for Allah
   Never fails in His promise."

٩۔ رَبَّنَاۤ اِنَّكَ جَامِعُ النَّاسِ لِيَوْمٍ لَّا رَيْبَ فِيْهِ ۚ اِنَّ اللّٰهَ لَا يُخْلِفُ الْمِيْعَادَ ۝

SECTION 2.

10. Those who reject Faith—
Neither their possessions
Nor their (numerous) progeny
Will avail them aught
Against Allah; they are
            themselves
But fuel for the Fire.

١٠- اِنَّ الَّذِيْنَ كَفَرُوْا لَنْ تُغْنِيَ عَنْهُمْ اَمْوَالُهُمْ وَلَا اَوْلَادُهُمْ مِّنَ اللهِ شَيْئًا ۚ وَاُولٰٓئِكَ هُمْ وَقُوْدُ النَّارِ ۙ

11. (Their plight will be)
No better than that
Of the people of Pharaoh,
And their predecessors:
They denied our Signs,
And Allah called them to
            account
For their sins.
For Allah is strict
In punishment.

١١- كَدَأْبِ اٰلِ فِرْعَوْنَ ۙ وَالَّذِيْنَ مِنْ قَبْلِهِمْ ۚ كَذَّبُوْا بِاٰيٰتِنَا ۚ فَاَخَذَهُمُ اللهُ بِذُنُوْبِهِمْ ۗ وَاللهُ شَدِيْدُ الْعِقَابِ ○

12. Say to those who reject Faith:
"Soon will ye be vanquished
And gathered together
To Hell—an evil bed
Indeed (to lie on)!

١٢- قُلْ لِّلَّذِيْنَ كَفَرُوْا سَتُغْلَبُوْنَ وَتُحْشَرُوْنَ اِلٰى جَهَنَّمَ ۚ وَبِئْسَ الْمِهَادُ ○

13. "There has already been
For you a Sign
In the two armies
That met (in combat):
One was fighting in the Cause
Of Allah, the other
Resisting Allah; these saw
With their own eyes
Twice their number.
But Allah doth support
With His aid whom He pleaseth.
In this is a warning
For such as have eyes to see."

١٣- قَدْ كَانَ لَكُمْ اٰيَةٌ فِيْ فِئَتَيْنِ الْتَقَتَا ۚ فِئَةٌ تُقَاتِلُ فِيْ سَبِيْلِ اللهِ وَاُخْرٰى كَافِرَةٌ ۚ يَّرَوْنَهُمْ مِّثْلَيْهِمْ رَأْىَ الْعَيْنِ ۚ وَاللهُ يُؤَيِّدُ بِنَصْرِهٖ مَنْ يَّشَاءُ ۗ اِنَّ فِيْ ذٰلِكَ لَعِبْرَةً لِّاُولِى الْاَبْصَارِ ○

14. Fair in the eyes of men
Is the love of things they covet:
Women and sons;
Heaped-up hoards
Of gold and silver; horses
Branded (for blood and
            excellence);
And (wealth of) cattle

١٤- زُيِّنَ لِلنَّاسِ حُبُّ الشَّهَوٰتِ مِنَ النِّسَاءِ وَالْبَنِيْنَ وَالْقَنَاطِيْرِ الْمُقَنْطَرَةِ مِنَ الذَّهَبِ وَالْفِضَّةِ وَالْخَيْلِ الْمُسَوَّمَةِ وَالْاَنْعَامِ وَالْحَرْثِ ۗ

And well-tilled land.
Such are the possessions
Of this world's life;
But in nearness to Allah
Is the best of the goals
(To return to).

15. Say: Shall I give you
Glad tidings of things
Far better than those?
For the righteous are Gardens
In nearness to their Lord,
With rivers flowing beneath;
Therein is their eternal home;
With Companions pure (and
                        holy)
And the good pleasure of Allah.
For in Allah's sight
Are (all) His servants—

16. (Namely), those who say;
"Our Lord! we have indeed
Believed: forgive us, then,
Our sins, and save us
From the agony of the Fire"—

17. Those who show patience,
Firmness and self-control;
Who are true (in word and deed);
Who worship devoutly;
Who spend (in the way of Allah);
And who pray for forgiveness
In the early hours of the
                        morning.

18. There is no god but He:
That is the witness of Allah,
His angels, and those endued
With knowledge, standing firm
On justice. There is no god but He
The Exalted in Power,
The Wise.

19. The Religion before Allah
Is Islam (submission to His Will):
Nor did the People of the Book
Dissent therefrom except
Through envy of each other,
After knowledge had come to
                        them.

ذٰلِكَ مَتَاعُ الْحَيٰوةِ الدُّنْيَا ۖ
وَاللهُ عِنْدَهٗ حُسْنُ الْمَاٰبِ ٥

١٥- قُلْ أَؤُنَبِّئُكُمْ بِخَيْرٍ مِّنْ ذٰلِكُمْ ۚ
لِلَّذِيْنَ اتَّقَوْا عِنْدَ رَبِّهِمْ جَنّٰتٌ
تَجْرِيْ مِنْ تَحْتِهَا الْأَنْهٰرُ
خٰلِدِيْنَ فِيْهَا وَأَزْوَاجٌ مُّطَهَّرَةٌ
وَّرِضْوَانٌ مِّنَ اللهِ ۗ
وَاللهُ بَصِيْرٌ بِالْعِبَادِ ۙ

١٦- أَلَّذِيْنَ يَقُوْلُوْنَ رَبَّنَاۤ
إِنَّنَاۤ اٰمَنَّا فَاغْفِرْ لَنَا ذُنُوْبَنَا
وَقِنَا عَذَابَ النَّارِ ۚ

١٧- أَلصّٰبِرِيْنَ وَالصّٰدِقِيْنَ
وَالْقٰنِتِيْنَ وَالْمُنْفِقِيْنَ
وَالْمُسْتَغْفِرِيْنَ بِالْأَسْحَارِ ٥

١٨- شَهِدَ اللهُ أَنَّهٗ لَاۤ إِلٰهَ إِلَّا هُوَ ۙ
وَالْمَلٰٓئِكَةُ وَأُولُوا الْعِلْمِ قَآئِمًا بِالْقِسْطِ ۚ
لَاۤ إِلٰهَ إِلَّا هُوَ الْعَزِيْزُ الْحَكِيْمُ ٥

١٩- إِنَّ الدِّيْنَ عِنْدَ اللهِ الْإِسْلَامُ ۗ
وَمَا اخْتَلَفَ الَّذِيْنَ أُوْتُوا الْكِتٰبَ
إِلَّا مِنْ بَعْدِ مَا جَآءَهُمُ الْعِلْمُ بَغْيًا بَيْنَهُمْ ۗ
وَمَنْ يَّكْفُرْ بِاٰيٰتِ اللهِ

But if any deny the Signs of Allah,
Allah is swift in calling to account.

فَإِنَّ اللّٰهَ سَرِيعُ الْحِسَابِ

20. So if they dispute with thee,
Say: "I have submitted
My whole self[360] to Allah
And so have those
Who follow me."
And say to the People of the Book
And to those who are unlearned:
"Do ye (also) submit yourselves?"
If they do, they are in right
guidance,
But if they turn back,
Thy duty is to convey the Message;
And in Allah's sight
Are (all) His servants.

٢٠- فَإِنْ حَآجُّوكَ فَقُلْ أَسْلَمْتُ وَجْهِىَ
لِلّٰهِ وَمَنِ اتَّبَعَنِ ۚ
وَقُلْ لِّلَّذِينَ أُوتُوا الْكِتَابَ
وَالْأُمِّيِّنَ ءَأَسْلَمْتُمْ ۚ
فَإِنْ أَسْلَمُوا فَقَدِ اهْتَدَوْا ۚ
وَإِنْ تَوَلَّوْا فَإِنَّمَا عَلَيْكَ الْبَلَاغُ ۚ
وَاللّٰهُ بَصِيرٌ بِالْعِبَادِ ۞

SECTION 3.

21. As to those who deny
The Signs of Allah, and in
defiance
Of right,   slay the prophets,
And slay those who teach
Just dealing with mankind,
Announce to them a grievous
penalty.

٢١- إِنَّ الَّذِينَ يَكْفُرُونَ بِآيَاتِ اللّٰهِ
وَيَقْتُلُونَ النَّبِيِّنَ بِغَيْرِ حَقٍّ ۙ
وَيَقْتُلُونَ الَّذِينَ يَأْمُرُونَ بِالْقِسْطِ
مِنَ النَّاسِ ۙ فَبَشِّرْهُمْ بِعَذَابٍ أَلِيمٍ ۝

22. They are those whose works
Will bear no fruit
In this world
And in the Hereafter,
Nor will they have
Anyone to help.

٢٢- أُولٰٓئِكَ الَّذِينَ حَبِطَتْ أَعْمَالُهُمْ
فِي الدُّنْيَا وَالْآخِرَةِ ۖ
وَمَا لَهُمْ مِّنْ نَاصِرِينَ ۝

23. Hast thou not turned
Thy vision to those
Who have been given a portion
Of the Book? They are
Invited to the Book of Allah,
To settle their dispute,
But a party of them
Turn back and decline
(The arbitration).

٢٣- أَلَمْ تَرَ إِلَى الَّذِينَ أُوتُوا نَصِيبًا مِّنَ
الْكِتَابِ يُدْعَوْنَ إِلَى كِتَابِ اللّٰهِ
لِيَحْكُمَ بَيْنَهُمْ ثُمَّ يَتَوَلَّى فَرِيقٌ مِّنْهُمْ
وَهُمْ مُّعْرِضُونَ ۝

24. This because they say:
"The Fire shall not touch us
But for a few numbered days";
For their forgeries deceive them

٢٤- ذٰلِكَ بِأَنَّهُمْ قَالُوا لَنْ تَمَسَّنَا النَّارُ
إِلَّا أَيَّامًا مَّعْدُودَاتٍ ۖ وَغَرَّهُمْ فِي دِينِهِمْ

As to their own religion.

مَا كَانُوْا يَفْتَرُوْنَ ۟

25. But how (will they fare)
When We gather them together
Against a Day about which
There is no doubt,
And each soul will be paid out
Just what it has earned,
Without (favour or) injustice?

٢٥- فَكَيْفَ إِذَا جَمَعْنٰهُمْ
لِيَوْمٍ لَّا رَيْبَ فِيْهِ ۙ
وَوُفِّيَتْ كُلُّ نَفْسٍ مَّا كَسَبَتْ
وَهُمْ لَا يُظْلَمُوْنَ ۟

26. Say: "O Allah!
Lord of Power (and Rule),
Thou givest Power
To whom Thou pleasest,
And Thou strippest off Power
From whom Thou pleasest:
Thou enduest with honour
Whom Thou pleasest,
And Thou bringest low
Whom Thou pleasest:
In Thy hand is all Good.
Verily, over all things
Thou hast power.

٢٦- قُلِ اللّٰهُمَّ مٰلِكَ الْمُلْكِ
تُؤْتِى الْمُلْكَ مَنْ تَشَآءُ
وَتَنْزِعُ الْمُلْكَ مِمَّنْ تَشَآءُ ۫
وَتُعِزُّ مَنْ تَشَآءُ
وَتُذِلُّ مَنْ تَشَآءُ ۗ
بِيَدِكَ الْخَيْرُ ۗ
إِنَّكَ عَلٰى كُلِّ شَىْءٍ قَدِيْرٌ ۟

27. "Thou causest the Night
To gain on the Day,
And Thou causest the Day
To gain on the Night;
Thou bringest the Living
Out of the Dead,
And Thou bringest the Dead
Out of the Living;
And Thou givest sustenance
To whom Thou pleasest,
Without measure."

٢٧- تُوْلِجُ الَّيْلَ فِى النَّهَارِ
وَتُوْلِجُ النَّهَارَ فِى الَّيْلِ ۫
وَتُخْرِجُ الْحَىَّ مِنَ الْمَيِّتِ
وَتُخْرِجُ الْمَيِّتَ مِنَ الْحَىِّ ۫
وَتَرْزُقُ مَنْ تَشَآءُ بِغَيْرِ حِسَابٍ ۟

28. Let not the Believers
Take for friends or helpers
Unbelievers rather than
Believers: if any do that,
In nothing will there be help
From Allah: except by way
Of precaution, that ye may
Guard yourselves from them.
But Allah cautions you
(To remember) Himself;
For the final goal
Is to Allah.

٢٨- لَا يَتَّخِذِ الْمُؤْمِنُوْنَ الْكٰفِرِيْنَ أَوْلِيَآءَ
مِنْ دُوْنِ الْمُؤْمِنِيْنَ ۚ
وَمَنْ يَّفْعَلْ ذٰلِكَ فَلَيْسَ مِنَ اللّٰهِ فِىْ
شَىْءٍ إِلَّا أَنْ تَتَّقُوْا مِنْهُمْ تُقٰةً ۗ
وَيُحَذِّرُكُمُ اللّٰهُ نَفْسَهٗ ۗ
وَإِلَى اللّٰهِ الْمَصِيْرُ ۟

29. Say: "Whether ye hide
What is in your hearts
Or reveal it,
Allah knows it all:
He knows what is
In the heavens,
And what is on earth.
And Allah has power
Over all things.

٢٩- قُلْ إِنْ تُخْفُوا مَا فِى صُدُورِكُمْ
أَوْ تُبْدُوهُ يَعْلَمْهُ اللهُ ۙ
وَيَعْلَمُ مَا فِى السَّمٰوٰتِ وَمَا فِى الْأَرْضِ ۙ
وَاللهُ عَلٰى كُلِّ شَىْءٍ قَدِيرٌ ۞

30. "On the Day when every soul
Will be confronted
With all the good it has done,
And all the evil it has done,
It will wish there were
A great distance
Between it and its evil.
But Allah cautions you
(To remember) Himself.
And Allah is full of kindness
To those that serve Him."

٣٠- يَوْمَ تَجِدُ كُلُّ نَفْسٍ
مَّا عَمِلَتْ مِنْ خَيْرٍ مُّحْضَرًا ۖۚ
وَمَا عَمِلَتْ مِنْ سُوءٍ ۚ
تَوَدُّ لَوْ أَنَّ بَيْنَهَا وَبَيْنَهُ أَمَدًا بَعِيدًا ۗ
وَيُحَذِّرُكُمُ اللهُ نَفْسَهُ ۗ
وَاللهُ رَءُوفٌ بِالْعِبَادِ ۞

SECTION 4.

31. Say: "If ye do love Allah,
Follow me: Allah will love you
And forgive you your sins;
For Allah is Oft-Forgiving,
Most Merciful."

٣١- قُلْ إِنْ كُنْتُمْ تُحِبُّونَ اللهَ
فَاتَّبِعُونِى يُحْبِبْكُمُ اللهُ
وَيَغْفِرْ لَكُمْ ذُنُوبَكُمْ ۗ وَاللهُ غَفُورٌ رَّحِيمٌ ۞

32. Say: "Obey Allah
And His Messenger":
But if they turn back,
Allah loveth not those
Who reject Faith.

٣٢- قُلْ أَطِيعُوا اللهَ وَالرَّسُولَ ۖ
فَإِنْ تَوَلَّوْا
فَإِنَّ اللهَ لَا يُحِبُّ الْكَافِرِينَ ۞

33. Allah did choose
Adam and Noah, the family
Of Abraham, and the family
Of 'Imrān above all people—

٣٣- إِنَّ اللهَ اصْطَفٰى آدَمَ وَنُوحًا وَآلَ
إِبْرَاهِيمَ وَآلَ عِمْرَانَ عَلَى الْعَالَمِينَ ۞

34. Offspring, one of the other;
And Allah heareth
And knoweth all things.

٣٤- ذُرِّيَّةً بَعْضُهَا مِنْ بَعْضٍ ۗ
وَاللهُ سَمِيعٌ عَلِيمٌ ۞

35. Behold! a woman of 'Imrān
Said: "O my Lord! I do
Dedicate unto Thee
What is in my womb

٣٥- إِذْ قَالَتِ امْرَأَتُ عِمْرَانَ رَبِّ إِنِّى
نَذَرْتُ لَكَ مَا فِى بَطْنِى مُحَرَّرًا

For Thy special service:
So accept this of me:
For Thou hearest
And knowest all things."

36. When she was delivered,
She said: "O my Lord!
Behold! I am delivered
Of a female child!"—
And Allah knew best
What she brought forth—
"And no wise is the male
Like the female.
I have named her Mary,
And I commend her
And her offspring
To Thy protection
From the Evil One,
The Rejected."

37. Right graciously
Did her Lord accept her:
He made her grow
In purity and beauty;
To the care of Zakarīya
Was she assigned.
Every time that he entered
(Her) chamber to see her,
He found her supplied
With sustenance. He said:
"O Mary! Whence (comes) this
To you?" She said:
"From Allah: for Allah
Provides sustenance
To whom He pleases,
Without measure."

38. There did Zakarīya
Pray to his Lord, saying:
"O my Lord! Grant unto me
From Thee a progeny
That is pure: for Thou
Art He that heareth prayer!"

39. While he was standing
In prayer in the chamber,
The angels called unto him:
"Allah doth give thee
Glad tidings of Yaḥya,
Witnessing the truth

فَتَقَبَّلْ مِنِّيْ ۚ
اِنَّكَ اَنْتَ السَّمِيْعُ الْعَلِيْمُ ۞

٣٦- فَلَمَّا وَضَعَتْهَا قَالَتْ رَبِّ اِنِّيْ وَضَعْتُهَآ
اُنْثٰى ۗ
وَاللّٰهُ اَعْلَمُ بِمَا وَضَعَتْ ۚ
وَلَيْسَ الذَّكَرُ كَالْاُنْثٰى ۚ
وَاِنِّيْ سَمَّيْتُهَا مَرْيَمَ
وَاِنِّيْٓ اُعِيْذُهَا بِكَ
وَذُرِّيَّتَهَا مِنَ الشَّيْطٰنِ الرَّجِيْمِ ۞

٣٧- فَتَقَبَّلَهَا رَبُّهَا بِقَبُوْلٍ حَسَنٍ
وَّاَنْۢبَتَهَا نَبَاتًا حَسَنًا ۙ وَّكَفَّلَهَا زَكَرِيَّا ۗ
كُلَّمَا دَخَلَ عَلَيْهَا زَكَرِيَّا الْمِحْرَابَ ۙ
وَجَدَ عِنْدَهَا رِزْقًا ۚ
قَالَ يٰمَرْيَمُ اَنّٰى لَكِ هٰذَا ۗ
قَالَتْ هُوَ مِنْ عِنْدِ اللّٰهِ ۗ
اِنَّ اللّٰهَ يَرْزُقُ مَنْ يَّشَآءُ
بِغَيْرِ حِسَابٍ ۞

٣٨- هُنَالِكَ دَعَا زَكَرِيَّا رَبَّهٗ ۚ قَالَ رَبِّ هَبْ
لِيْ مِنْ لَّدُنْكَ ذُرِّيَّةً طَيِّبَةً ۚ
اِنَّكَ سَمِيْعُ الدُّعَآءِ ۞

٣٩- فَنَادَتْهُ الْمَلٰۤئِكَةُ
وَهُوَ قَآئِمٌ يُّصَلِّيْ فِى الْمِحْرَابِ ۙ
اَنَّ اللّٰهَ يُبَشِّرُكَ بِيَحْيٰى

Of a Word from Allah,   and (be
Besides) noble, chaste,
And a Prophet—
Of the (goodly) company
Of the righteous."

مُصَدِّقًا بِكَلِمَةٍ مِنَ اللّٰهِ
وَسَيِّدًا وَّحَصُورًا
وَّنَبِيًّا مِنَ الصّٰلِحِيْنَ ۚ ۝

40. He said: "Oh my Lord!
How shall I have a son,
Seeing I am very old,
And my wife is barren?"
"Thus," was the answer,
"Doth Allah accomplish
What He willeth."

۴۰- قَالَ رَبِّ اَنّٰى يَكُوْنُ لِىْ غُلٰمٌ
وَّقَدْ بَلَغَنِىَ الْكِبَرُ
وَامْرَاَتِىْ عَاقِرٌ ۚ
قَالَ كَذٰلِكَ اللّٰهُ يَفْعَلُ مَا يَشَآءُ ۝

41. He said: "O my Lord!
Give me a Sign!"
"Thy Sign," was the answer,
"Shall be that thou
Shalt speak to no man
For three days
But with signals.
Then celebrate
The praises of thy Lord
Again and again,
And glorify Him
In the evening
And in the morning."

۴۱- قَالَ رَبِّ اجْعَلْ لِّىْ اٰيَةً ۚ
قَالَ اٰيَتُكَ اَلَّا تُكَلِّمَ النَّاسَ
ثَلٰثَةَ اَيَّامٍ
اِلَّا رَمْزًا ۚ
وَاذْكُرْ رَّبَّكَ كَثِيْرًا
وَّسَبِّحْ بِالْعَشِىِّ وَالْاِبْكَارِ ۞

SECTION 5.

42. Behold! the angels said.
"O Mary! Allah hath chosen
                          thee
And purified thee—chosen thee
Above the women of all
                     nations.

۴۲- وَاِذْ قَالَتِ الْمَلٰئِكَةُ يٰمَرْيَمُ اِنَّ اللّٰهَ
اصْطَفٰىكِ وَطَهَّرَكِ وَاصْطَفٰىكِ عَلٰى نِسَآءِ
الْعٰلَمِيْنَ ۝

43. "O Mary! worship
Thy Lord devoutly:
Prostrate thyself,
And bow down (in prayer)
With those who bow down."

۴۳- يٰمَرْيَمُ اقْنُتِىْ لِرَبِّكِ وَاسْجُدِىْ
وَارْكَعِىْ مَعَ الرّٰكِعِيْنَ ۝

44. This is part of the tidings
Of the things unseen,
Which We reveal unto thee
(O Prophet!) by inspiration:
Thou wast not with them
When they cast lots
With arrows,   as to which

۴۴- ذٰلِكَ مِنْ اَنْۢبَآءِ الْغَيْبِ
نُوْحِيْهِ اِلَيْكَ ۚ وَمَا كُنْتَ لَدَيْهِمْ
اِذْ يُلْقُوْنَ اَقْلَامَهُمْ
اَيُّهُمْ يَكْفُلُ مَرْيَمَ

Of them should be charged
With the care of Mary:
Nor wast thou with them
When they disputed (the point).

وَمَا كُنْتَ لَدَيْهِمْ
إِذْ يَخْتَصِمُونَ ٥

45. Behold! the angels said:
"O Mary! Allah giveth thee
Glad tidings of a Word
From Him: his name
Will be Christ Jesus.
The son of Mary, held in honour
In this world and the Hereafter
And of (the company of) those
Nearest to Allah;

٤٥- إِذْ قَالَتِ الْمَلَائِكَةُ يَامَرْيَمُ إِنَّ اللَّهَ
يُبَشِّرُكِ بِكَلِمَةٍ مِنْهُ ۖ
اسْمُهُ الْمَسِيحُ عِيسَى ابْنُ مَرْيَمَ
وَجِيهًا فِي الدُّنْيَا وَالْآخِرَةِ
وَمِنَ الْمُقَرَّبِينَ ۙ

46. "He shall speak to the people
In childhood and in maturity.
And he shall be (of the company)
Of the righteous."

٤٦- وَيُكَلِّمُ النَّاسَ فِي الْمَهْدِ وَكَهْلًا
وَمِنَ الصَّالِحِينَ ٥

47. She said: "O my Lord!¹³⁸⁹
How shall I have a son
When no man hath touched me?"
He said: "Even so:
Allah createth
What He willeth:
When He hath decreed
A Plan, He but saith
To it, 'Be,' and it is!

٤٧- قَالَتْ رَبِّ أَنَّى يَكُونُ لِي وَلَدٌ
وَلَمْ يَمْسَسْنِي بَشَرٌ ۖ
قَالَ كَذَلِكِ اللَّهُ يَخْلُقُ مَا يَشَاءُ ۚ
إِذَا قَضَى أَمْرًا
فَإِنَّمَا يَقُولُ لَهُ كُنْ فَيَكُونُ ٥

48. "And Allah will teach him
The Book and Wisdom,
The Law and the Gospel,

٤٨- وَيُعَلِّمُهُ الْكِتَابَ وَالْحِكْمَةَ
وَالتَّوْرَاةَ وَالْإِنْجِيلَ ۙ

49. "And (appoint him)
A messenger to the Children
Of Israel, (with this message):
"'I have come to you,
With a Sign from your Lord,
In that I make for you
Out of clay, as it were,
The figure of a bird,
And breathe into it,
And it becomes a bird
By Allah's leave:
And I heal those
Born blind, and the lepers,
And I quicken the dead,
By Allah's leave;

٤٩- وَرَسُولًا إِلَى بَنِي إِسْرَائِيلَ ۙ
أَنِّي قَدْ جِئْتُكُمْ بِآيَةٍ مِنْ رَبِّكُمْ ۖ
أَنِّي أَخْلُقُ لَكُمْ
مِنَ الطِّينِ كَهَيْئَةِ الطَّيْرِ
فَأَنْفُخُ فِيهِ فَيَكُونُ طَيْرًا
بِإِذْنِ اللَّهِ ۖ
وَأُبْرِئُ الْأَكْمَهَ وَالْأَبْرَصَ
وَأُحْيِ الْمَوْتَى بِإِذْنِ اللَّهِ ۖ

And I declare to you
What ye eat, and what ye
               store
In your houses. Surely
Therein is a Sign for you
If ye did believe;

وَاُنَبِّئُكُمْ بِمَا تَأْكُلُوْنَ وَمَا تَدَّخِرُوْنَ
فِىْ بُيُوْتِكُمْ اِنَّ فِىْ ذٰلِكَ لَاٰيَةً لَّكُمْ اِنْ
كُنْتُمْ مُّؤْمِنِيْنَ ۚ

50. "(I have come to you),
To attest the Law
Which was before me.
And to make lawful
To you part of what was
(Before) forbidden to you;
I have come to you
With a Sign from your Lord.
So fear Allah
And obey me.

٥٠۔ وَمُصَدِّقًا لِّمَا
بَيْنَ يَدَىَّ مِنَ التَّوْرٰىةِ
وَلِاُحِلَّ لَكُمْ بَعْضَ الَّذِىْ
حُرِّمَ عَلَيْكُمْ وَجِئْتُكُمْ بِاٰيَةٍ مِّنْ رَّبِّكُمْ
فَاتَّقُوا اللّٰهَ وَاَطِيْعُوْنِ

51. "It is Allah
Who is my Lord
And your Lord;
Then worship Him.
This is a Way
That is straight.'"

٥١۔ اِنَّ اللّٰهَ رَبِّىْ
وَرَبُّكُمْ فَاعْبُدُوْهُ
هٰذَا صِرَاطٌ مُّسْتَقِيْمٌ ۚ

52. When Jesus found
Unbelief on their part
He said: "Who will be
My helpers to (the work
Of) Allah?" Said the Disciples:
"We are Allah's helpers:
We believe in Allah,
And do thou bear witness
That we are Muslims.

٥٢۔ فَلَمَّآ اَحَسَّ عِيْسٰى مِنْهُمُ الْكُفْرَ
قَالَ مَنْ اَنْصَارِىْ اِلَى اللّٰهِ
قَالَ الْحَوَارِيُّوْنَ نَحْنُ اَنْصَارُ اللّٰهِ ۚ
اٰمَنَّا بِاللّٰهِ ۚ
وَاشْهَدْ بِاَنَّا مُسْلِمُوْنَ ۚ

53. "Our Lord! we believe
In what Thou hast revealed,
And we follow the Messenger;
Then write us down
Among those who bear witness."

٥٣۔ رَبَّنَآ اٰمَنَّا بِمَآ اَنْزَلْتَ
وَاتَّبَعْنَا الرَّسُوْلَ
فَاكْتُبْنَا مَعَ الشّٰهِدِيْنَ ۚ

54 And (the unbelievers)
Plotted and planned,
And Allah too planned,
And the best of planners
Is Allah.

٥٤۔ وَمَكَرُوْا وَمَكَرَ اللّٰهُ ۚ
وَاللّٰهُ خَيْرُ الْمَاكِرِيْنَ ۚ

SECTION 6.

55. Behold! Allah said:
"O Jesus! I will take thee
And raise thee to Myself
And clear thee (of the
           falsehoods)
Of those who blaspheme;
I will make those
Who follow thee superior
To those who reject faith,
To the Day of Resurrection:
Then shall ye all
Return unto me,
And I will judge
Between you of the matters
Wherein ye dispute.

٥٥- اِذْ قَالَ اللهُ يٰعِيْسٰى اِنِّىْ مُتَوَفِّيْكَ وَرَافِعُكَ اِلَىَّ وَمُطَهِّرُكَ مِنَ الَّذِيْنَ كَفَرُوْا وَجَاعِلُ الَّذِيْنَ اتَّبَعُوْكَ فَوْقَ الَّذِيْنَ كَفَرُوْٓا اِلٰى يَوْمِ الْقِيٰمَةِ ۚ ثُمَّ اِلَىَّ مَرْجِعُكُمْ فَاَحْكُمُ بَيْنَكُمْ فِيْمَا كُنْتُمْ فِيْهِ تَخْتَلِفُوْنَ ۝

56. "As to those who reject faith,
I will punish them
With terrible agony
In this world and in the
           Hereafter.
Nor will they have
Anyone to help.

٥٦- فَاَمَّا الَّذِيْنَ كَفَرُوْا فَاُعَذِّبُهُمْ عَذَابًا شَدِيْدًا فِى الدُّنْيَا وَالْاٰخِرَةِ ۖ وَمَا لَهُمْ مِّنْ نّٰصِرِيْنَ ۝

57. "As to those who believe
And work righteousness,
Allah will pay them (in full)
Their reward:
But Allah loveth not
Those who do wrong.

٥٧- وَاَمَّا الَّذِيْنَ اٰمَنُوْا وَعَمِلُوا الصّٰلِحٰتِ فَيُوَفِّيْهِمْ اُجُوْرَهُمْ ۗ وَاللهُ لَا يُحِبُّ الظّٰلِمِيْنَ ۝

58. "This is what we rehearse
Unto thee of the Signs
And the Message
Of Wisdom."

٥٨- ذٰلِكَ نَتْلُوْهُ عَلَيْكَ مِنَ الْاٰيٰتِ وَالذِّكْرِ الْحَكِيْمِ ۝

59. The similitude of Jesus
Before Allah is as that of
           Adam;
He created him from dust,
Then said to him: "Be":
And he was.

٥٩- اِنَّ مَثَلَ عِيْسٰى عِنْدَ اللهِ كَمَثَلِ اٰدَمَ ۗ خَلَقَهٗ مِنْ تُرَابٍ ثُمَّ قَالَ لَهٗ كُنْ فَيَكُوْنُ ۝

60. The Truth (comes)
From thy Lord alone;
So be not of those
Who doubt.

٦٠- اَلْحَقُّ مِنْ رَّبِّكَ فَلَا تَكُنْ مِّنَ الْمُمْتَرِيْنَ ۝

61. If anyone disputes

٦١- فَمَنْ حَآجَّكَ فِيْهِ

In this matter with thee,
Now after (full) knowledge
Hath come to thee,
Say: "Come! let us
Gather together—
Our sons and your sons,
Our women and your women,
Ourselves and yourselves:
Then let us earnestly pray,
And invoke the curse
Of Allah on those who lie!"

مِنۢ بَعْدِ مَا جَآءَكَ مِنَ الْعِلْمِ فَقُلْ تَعَالَوْا نَدْعُ اَبْنَآءَنَا وَاَبْنَآءَكُمْ وَنِسَآءَنَا وَنِسَآءَكُمْ وَاَنْفُسَنَا وَاَنْفُسَكُمْ ثُمَّ نَبْتَهِلْ فَنَجْعَلْ لَّعْنَتَ اللّٰهِ عَلَى الْكٰذِبِيْنَ ۝

62. This is the true account;
There is no god
Except Allah;
And Allah—He is indeed
The Exalted in Power,
The Wise.

٦٢- اِنَّ هٰذَا لَهُوَ الْقَصَصُ الْحَقُّ ۚ وَمَا مِنْ اِلٰهٍ اِلَّا اللّٰهُ ۚ وَاِنَّ اللّٰهَ لَهُوَ الْعَزِيْزُ الْحَكِيْمُ ۝

63. But if they turn back,
Allah hath full knowledge
Of those who do mischief.

٦٣- فَاِنْ تَوَلَّوْا فَاِنَّ اللّٰهَ عَلِيْمٌۢ بِالْمُفْسِدِيْنَ ۝

SECTION 7.

64. Say: "O People
Of the Book! come
To common terms
As between us and you:
That we worship
None but Allah;
That we associate
No partners with Him;
That we erect not,
From among ourselves,
Lords and patrons
Other than Allah."
If then they turn back,
Say ye: "Bear witness
That we (at least)
Are Muslims (bowing
To Allah's Will)."

٦٤- قُلْ يٰٓاَهْلَ الْكِتٰبِ تَعَالَوْا اِلٰى كَلِمَةٍ سَوَآءٍۢ بَيْنَنَا وَبَيْنَكُمْ اَلَّا نَعْبُدَ اِلَّا اللّٰهَ وَلَا نُشْرِكَ بِهٖ شَيْئًا وَّلَا يَتَّخِذَ بَعْضُنَا بَعْضًا اَرْبَابًا مِّنْ دُوْنِ اللّٰهِ ۚ فَاِنْ تَوَلَّوْا فَقُوْلُوا اشْهَدُوْا بِاَنَّا مُسْلِمُوْنَ ۝

65. Ye People of the Book!
Why dispute ye
About Abraham,
When the Law and the Gospel
Were not revealed
Till after him?
Have ye no understanding?

٦٥- يٰٓاَهْلَ الْكِتٰبِ لِمَ تُحَآجُّوْنَ فِيْٓ اِبْرٰهِيْمَ وَمَآ اُنْزِلَتِ التَّوْرٰىةُ وَالْاِنْجِيْلُ اِلَّا مِنْۢ بَعْدِهٖ ۚ اَفَلَا تَعْقِلُوْنَ ۝

66. Ah! Ye are those
Who fell to disputing
(Even) in matters of which
Ye had some knowledge!
But why dispute ye
In matters of which
Ye have no knowledge?
It is Allah Who knows,
And ye who know not!

٦٦ـ هَآ أَنْتُمْ هٰؤُلَآءِ حَاجَجْتُمْ
فِيْمَا لَكُمْ بِهٖ عِلْمٌ
فَلِمَ تُحَآجُّوْنَ فِيْمَا
لَيْسَ لَكُمْ بِهٖ عِلْمٌ
وَاللّٰهُ يَعْلَمُ وَأَنْتُمْ لَا تَعْلَمُوْنَ ۰

67. Abraham was not a Jew
Nor yet a Christian;
But he was true in Faith,
And bowed his will to Allah's,
(Which is Islam),
And he joined not gods with
Allah.

٦٧ـ مَا كَانَ إِبْرٰهِيْمُ يَهُوْدِيًّا
وَّلَا نَصْرَانِيًّا
وَّلٰكِنْ كَانَ حَنِيْفًا مُّسْلِمًا ؕ
وَمَا كَانَ مِنَ الْمُشْرِكِيْنَ ۰

68. Without a doubt, among men,
The nearest of kin to Abraham,
Are those who follow him,
As are also this Prophet
And those who believe:
And Allah is the Protector
Of those who have faith.

٦٨ـ إِنَّ أَوْلَى النَّاسِ بِإِبْرٰهِيْمَ
لَلَّذِيْنَ اتَّبَعُوْهُ وَهٰذَا النَّبِيُّ
وَالَّذِيْنَ اٰمَنُوْا ؕ
وَاللّٰهُ وَلِيُّ الْمُؤْمِنِيْنَ ۰

69. It is the wish of a section
Of the People of the Book
To lead you astray.
But they shall lead astray
(Not you), but themselves,
And they do not perceive!

٦٩ـ وَدَّتْ طَّآئِفَةٌ مِّنْ أَهْلِ الْكِتٰبِ
لَوْ يُضِلُّوْنَكُمْ ۚ وَمَا يُضِلُّوْنَ إِلَّا أَنْفُسَهُمْ
وَمَا يَشْعُرُوْنَ ۰

70. Ye People of the Book!
Why reject ye
The Signs of Allah,
Of which ye are
(Yourselves) witnesses?

٧٠ـ يَآأَهْلَ الْكِتٰبِ لِمَ تَكْفُرُوْنَ بِاٰيٰتِ اللّٰهِ
وَأَنْتُمْ تَشْهَدُوْنَ ۰

71. Ye People of the Book!
Why do ye clothe
Truth with falsehood,
And conceal the Truth,
While ye have knowledge?

٧١ـ يَآأَهْلَ الْكِتٰبِ لِمَ تَلْبِسُوْنَ
الْحَقَّ بِالْبَاطِلِ
وَتَكْتُمُوْنَ الْحَقَّ وَأَنْتُمْ تَعْلَمُوْنَ ۠ع

SECTION 8.

72. A section of the People
Of the Book say:
"Believe in the morning

٧٢ـ وَقَالَتْ طَّآئِفَةٌ مِّنْ أَهْلِ الْكِتٰبِ
اٰمِنُوْا بِالَّذِيْ

What is revealed
To the Believers,
But reject it at the end
Of the day; perchance
They may (themselves)
Turn back;

أُنْزِلَ عَلَى الَّذِيْنَ
اٰمَنُوْا وَجْهَ النَّهَارِ
وَاكْفُرُوْۤا اٰخِرَهٗ لَعَلَّهُمْ يَرْجِعُوْنَ ۚ

73. "And believe no one
Unless he follows
Your religion."
Say: "True guidance
Is the guidance of Allah;
(Fear ye) lest a revelation[407]
Be sent to someone (else)
Like unto that which was sent
Unto you? Or that those
(Receiving such revelation)
Should engage you in argument
Before your Lord?"
Say: "All bounties
Are in the hand of Allah:
He granteth them
To whom He pleaseth:
And Allah careth for all,
And He knoweth all things."

٧٣ - وَلَا تُؤْمِنُوْۤا
إِلَّا لِمَنْ تَبِعَ دِيْنَكُمْ ۗ
قُلْ إِنَّ الْهُدٰى هُدَى اللّٰهِ ۙ
أَنْ يُّؤْتٰۤى أَحَدٌ
مِّثْلَ مَاۤ أُوْتِيْتُمْ
أَوْ يُحَاۤجُّوْكُمْ عِنْدَ رَبِّكُمْ ۗ
قُلْ إِنَّ الْفَضْلَ بِيَدِ اللّٰهِ ۚ
يُؤْتِيْهِ مَنْ يَّشَاۤءُ ۗ
وَاللّٰهُ وَاسِعٌ عَلِيْمٌ ۚ

74. For His Mercy He specially
                 chooseth
Whom He pleaseth;
For Allah is the Lord
Of bounties unbounded.

٧٤ - يَخْتَصُّ بِرَحْمَتِهٖ مَنْ يَّشَاۤءُ ۗ
وَاللّٰهُ ذُو الْفَضْلِ الْعَظِيْمِ ۧ

75. Among the People of the Book
Are some who, if entrusted
With a hoard of gold,
Will (readily) pay it back;
Others, who, if entrusted
With a single silver coin,
Will not repay it unless
Thou constantly stoodest
Demanding, because,
They say, "there is no call
On us (to keep faith)
With these ignorant (Pagans)."
But they tell a lie against Allah
And (well) they know it.

٧٥ - وَمِنْ أَهْلِ الْكِتٰبِ مَنْ إِنْ تَأْمَنْهُ
بِقِنْطَارٍ يُّؤَدِّهٖۤ إِلَيْكَ ۚ
وَمِنْهُمْ مَّنْ إِنْ تَأْمَنْهُ بِدِيْنَارٍ
لَّا يُؤَدِّهٖۤ إِلَيْكَ إِلَّا مَا دُمْتَ عَلَيْهِ قَاۤئِمًا ۗ
ذٰلِكَ بِأَنَّهُمْ قَالُوْا لَيْسَ عَلَيْنَا
فِى الْأُمِّيِّيْنَ سَبِيْلٌ ۚ
وَيَقُوْلُوْنَ عَلَى اللّٰهِ الْكَذِبَ وَهُمْ يَعْلَمُوْنَ ۞

76. Nay—those that keep
Their plighted faith

٧٦ - بَلٰى مَنْ أَوْفٰى بِعَهْدِهٖ

And act aright—verily
Allah loves those
Who act aright.

77. As for those who sell
The faith they owe to Allah
And their own plighted word
For a small price,
They shall have no portion
In the Hereafter:
Nor will Allah
(Deign to) speak to them
Or look at them
On the Day of Judgement,
Nor will He cleanse them
(Of sin): they shall have
A grievous Penalty.

78. There is among them
A section who distort
The Book with their tongues:
(As they read) you would think
It is a part of the Book,
But it is no part
Of the Book; and they say,
"That is from Allah,"
But it is not from Allah:
It is they who tell
A lie against Allah,
And (well) they know it!

79. It is not (possible)
That a man, to whom
Is given the Book,
And Wisdom,
And the Prophetic Office,
Should say to people:
"Be ye my worshippers
Rather than Allah's":
On the contrary
(He would say):
"Be ye worshippers
Of Him Who is truly
The Cherisher of all:
For ye have taught
The Book and ye
Have studied it earnestly."

80. Nor would he instruct you

To take angels and prophets
For Lords and Patrons.
What! would he bid you
To unbelief after ye have
Bowed your will
(To Allah in Islam)?

SECTION 9.

81. Behold! Allah took
The Covenant of the Prophets,
Saying: "I give you
A Book and Wisdom;
Then comes to you
A Messenger, confirming
What is with you;
Do you believe in him
And render him help."
Allah said: "Do ye agree,
And take this my Covenant
As binding on you?"
They said: "We agree."
He said: "Then bear witness,
And I am with you
Among the witnesses."

82. If any turn back
After this, they are
Perverted transgressors.

83. Do they seek
For other than the Religion
Of Allah?—while all creatures
In the heavens and on earth
Have, willing or unwilling,
Bowed to His Will
(Accepted Islam),
And to Him shall they
All be brought back.

84. Say: "We believe
In Allah, and in what
Has been revealed to us
And what was revealed
To Abraham, Ismā'īl;
Isaac, Jacob, and the Tribes,
And in (the Books)
Given to Moses, Jesus,

And the Prophets,
From their Lord:
We make no distinction
Between one and another
Among them, and to Allah do we
Bow our will (in Islam)."

وَالنَّبِيُّوْنَ
مِنْ رَّبِّهِمْ لَا نُفَرِّقُ
بَيْنَ اَحَدٍ مِّنْهُمْ
وَنَحْنُ لَهُ مُسْلِمُوْنَ ۝

85. If anyone desires
A religion other than
Islam (submission to Allah),
Never will it be accepted
Of him; and in the Hereafter
He will be in the ranks
Of those who have lost
(All spiritual good).

٨٥- وَمَنْ يَّبْتَغِ
غَيْرَ الْاِسْلَامِ دِيْنًا
فَلَنْ يُّقْبَلَ مِنْهُ ۚ
وَهُوَ فِي الْاٰخِرَةِ
مِنَ الْخٰسِرِيْنَ ۝

86. How shall Allah
Guide those who reject
Faith after they accepted it
And bore witness
That the Messenger was true
And that Clear Signs
Had come unto them?
But Allah guides not
A people unjust.

٨٦- كَيْفَ يَهْدِى اللّٰهُ قَوْمًا
كَفَرُوْا بَعْدَ اِيْمَانِهِمْ
وَشَهِدُوْٓا اَنَّ الرَّسُوْلَ حَقٌّ
وَّجَآءَهُمُ الْبَيِّنٰتُ ۚ
وَاللّٰهُ لَا يَهْدِى الْقَوْمَ الظّٰلِمِيْنَ ۝

87. Of such the reward
Is that on them (rests)
The curse of Allah,
Of His angels,
And of all mankind—

٨٧- اُولٰٓئِكَ جَزَآؤُهُمْ
اَنَّ عَلَيْهِمْ لَعْنَةَ اللّٰهِ
وَالْمَلٰٓئِكَةِ وَالنَّاسِ اَجْمَعِيْنَ ۝

88. In that will they dwell;
Nor will their penalty
Be lightened, nor respite
Be their (lot);

٨٨- خٰلِدِيْنَ فِيْهَا ۚ لَا يُخَفَّفُ
عَنْهُمُ الْعَذَابُ وَلَا هُمْ يُنْظَرُوْنَ ۝

89. Except for those that repent
(Even) after that,
And make amends;
For verily Allah
Is Oft-Forgiving,
Most Merciful.

٨٩- اِلَّا الَّذِيْنَ تَابُوْا
مِنْ بَعْدِ ذٰلِكَ
وَاَصْلَحُوْا ۗ
فَاِنَّ اللّٰهَ غَفُوْرٌ رَّحِيْمٌ ۝

90. But those who reject
Faith after they accepted it,
And then go on adding
To their defiance of Faith—

٩٠- اِنَّ الَّذِيْنَ كَفَرُوْا بَعْدَ اِيْمَانِهِمْ
ثُمَّ ازْدَادُوْا كُفْرًا

Never will their repentance
Be accepted; for they
Are those who have
(Of set purpose) gone astray.

لَن تُقْبَلَ تَوْبَتُهُمْ ۚ
وَأُولَٰئِكَ هُمُ الضَّآلُّونَ ۝

91. As to those who reject
Faith, and die rejecting—
Never would be accepted
From any such as much
Gold as the earth contains,
Though they should offer it
For ransom. For such
Is (in store) a penalty grievous,
And they will find no helpers.

٩١- إِنَّ الَّذِينَ كَفَرُوا وَمَاتُوا وَهُمْ كُفَّارٌ
فَلَن يُقْبَلَ مِنْ أَحَدِهِم
مِّلْءُ الْأَرْضِ ذَهَبًا وَّلَوِ افْتَدَىٰ بِهِ ۚ
أُولَٰئِكَ لَهُمْ عَذَابٌ أَلِيمٌ
وَّمَا لَهُم مِّن نَّاصِرِينَ ۝

SECTION 10.

92. By no means shall ye
Attain righteousness unless
Ye give (freely) of that
Which ye love; and whatever
Ye give, of a truth
Allah knoweth it well.

٩٢- لَن تَنَالُوا الْبِرَّ حَتَّىٰ تُنفِقُوا مِمَّا تُحِبُّونَ ۚ
وَمَا تُنفِقُوا مِن شَيْءٍ
فَإِنَّ اللَّهَ بِهِ عَلِيمٌ ۝

93. All food was lawful
To the Children of Israel,
Except what Israel
Made unlawful for itself,
Before the Law (of Moses)
Was revealed. Say:
"Bring ye the Law
And study it,
If ye be men of truth."

٩٣- كُلُّ الطَّعَامِ كَانَ حِلًّا لِّبَنِي إِسْرَآئِيلَ
إِلَّا مَا حَرَّمَ إِسْرَآئِيلُ عَلَىٰ نَفْسِهِ
مِن قَبْلِ أَن تُنَزَّلَ التَّوْرَىٰةُ ۗ
قُلْ فَأْتُوا بِالتَّوْرَىٰةِ فَاتْلُوهَآ
إِن كُنتُمْ صَٰدِقِينَ ۝

94. If any, after this, invent
A lie and attribute it
To Allah, they are indeed
Unjust wrongdoers.

٩٤- فَمَنِ افْتَرَىٰ عَلَى اللَّهِ الْكَذِبَ مِنۢ بَعْدِ
ذَٰلِكَ فَأُولَٰئِكَ هُمُ الظَّٰلِمُونَ ۝

95. Say: "Allah speaketh
The Truth: follow
The religion of Abraham,
The sane in faith; he
Was not of the Pagans."

٩٥- قُلْ صَدَقَ اللَّهُ ۗ
فَاتَّبِعُوا مِلَّةَ إِبْرَٰهِيمَ حَنِيفًا ۖ
وَمَا كَانَ مِنَ الْمُشْرِكِينَ ۝

96. The first House (of worship)
Appointed for men
Was that at Bakka;
Full of blessing

٩٦- إِنَّ أَوَّلَ بَيْتٍ وُضِعَ لِلنَّاسِ
لَلَّذِي بِبَكَّةَ مُبَارَكًا

And of guidance
For all kinds of beings:

وَهُدًى لِّلْعَالَمِينَ ۞

97. In it are Signs
Manifest; (for example),
The Station of Abraham;
Whoever enters it
Attains security;
Pilgrimage thereto is a duty
Men owe to Allah—
Those who can afford
The journey; but if any
Deny faith, Allah stands not
In need of any of His creatures.

٩٧- فِيهِ آيَاتٌ بَيِّنَاتٌ مَّقَامُ إِبْرَٰهِيمَ ۖ
وَمَن دَخَلَهُ كَانَ آمِنًا ۗ
وَلِلَّهِ عَلَى النَّاسِ حِجُّ الْبَيْتِ
مَنِ اسْتَطَاعَ إِلَيْهِ سَبِيلًا ۚ
وَمَن كَفَرَ
فَإِنَّ اللَّهَ غَنِيٌّ عَنِ الْعَالَمِينَ ۞

98. Say: "O People of the Book!
Why reject ye the Signs
Of Allah, when Allah
Is Himself witness
To all ye do?"

٩٨- قُلْ يَا أَهْلَ الْكِتَابِ
لِمَ تَكْفُرُونَ بِآيَاتِ اللَّهِ ۖ
وَاللَّهُ شَهِيدٌ عَلَىٰ مَا تَعْمَلُونَ ۞

99. Say: "O ye People of the Book!
Why obstruct ye
Those who believe,
From the Path of Allah,
Seeking to make it crooked,
While ye were yourselves
Witnesses (to Allah's Covenant)?
But Allah is not unmindful
Of all that ye do."

٩٩- قُلْ يَا أَهْلَ الْكِتَابِ
لِمَ تَصُدُّونَ عَن سَبِيلِ اللَّهِ
مَنْ آمَنَ تَبْغُونَهَا عِوَجًا
وَأَنتُمْ شُهَدَاءُ ۗ
وَمَا اللَّهُ بِغَافِلٍ عَمَّا تَعْمَلُونَ ۞

100. O ye who believe!
If ye listen
To a faction
Among the People of the Book,
They would (indeed)
Render you apostates
After ye have believed!

١٠٠- يَا أَيُّهَا الَّذِينَ آمَنُوا
إِن تُطِيعُوا فَرِيقًا
مِّنَ الَّذِينَ أُوتُوا الْكِتَابَ
يَرُدُّوكُم بَعْدَ إِيمَانِكُمْ كَافِرِينَ ۞

101. And how would ye
Deny Faith while unto you
Are rehearsed the Signs
Of Allah, and among you
Lives the Messenger?
Whoever holds
Firmly to Allah
Will be shown
A Way that is straight.

١٠١- وَكَيْفَ تَكْفُرُونَ
وَأَنتُمْ تُتْلَىٰ عَلَيْكُمْ آيَاتُ اللَّهِ وَفِيكُمْ
رَسُولُهُ ۗ وَمَن يَعْتَصِم بِاللَّهِ
فَقَدْ هُدِيَ إِلَىٰ صِرَاطٍ مُّسْتَقِيمٍ ۞

SECTION 11.

102. O ye who believe!
Fear Allah as He should be
Feared, and die not
Except in a state
Of Islam.

١٠٢ - يَا أَيُّهَا الَّذِينَ أَمَنُوا
اتَّقُوا اللهَ حَقَّ تُقَاتِهِ وَلَا تَمُوتُنَّ
إِلَّا وَأَنْتُمْ مُسْلِمُونَ ۞

103. And hold fast,
All together, by the Rope
Which Allah (stretches out
For you), and be not divided
Among yourselves;
And remember with gratitude
Allah's favour on you;
For ye were enemies
And He joined your hearts
In love, so that by His Grace,
Ye became brethren;
And ye were on the brink
Of the Pit of Fire,
And He saved you from it.
Thus doth Allah make
His Signs clear to you:
That ye may be guided.

١٠٣ - وَاعْتَصِمُوا بِحَبْلِ اللهِ جَمِيعًا
وَلَا تَفَرَّقُوا وَاذْكُرُوا نِعْمَتَ اللهِ عَلَيْكُمْ
إِذْ كُنْتُمْ أَعْدَاءً فَأَلَّفَ بَيْنَ قُلُوبِكُمْ
فَأَصْبَحْتُمْ بِنِعْمَتِهِ إِخْوَانًا ۚ
وَكُنْتُمْ عَلَى شَفَا
حُفْرَةٍ مِنَ النَّارِ فَأَنْقَذَكُمْ مِنْهَا ۗ
كَذَلِكَ يُبَيِّنُ اللهُ لَكُمْ اٰيٰتِهِ
لَعَلَّكُمْ تَهْتَدُونَ ۞

104. Let there arise out of you
A band of people
Inviting to all that is good,
Enjoining what is right,
And forbidding what is wrong:
They are the ones
To attain felicity.

١٠٤ - وَلْتَكُنْ مِنْكُمْ أُمَّةٌ يَدْعُونَ إِلَى الْخَيْرِ
وَيَأْمُرُونَ بِالْمَعْرُوفِ
وَيَنْهَوْنَ عَنِ الْمُنْكَرِ ۗ
وَأُولَئِكَ هُمُ الْمُفْلِحُونَ ۞

105. Be not like those
Who are divided
Amongst themselves
And fall into disputations
After receiving
Clear Signs:
For them
Is a dreadful Penalty—

١٠٥ - وَلَا تَكُونُوا كَالَّذِينَ تَفَرَّقُوا
وَاخْتَلَفُوا
مِنْ بَعْدِ مَا جَاءَهُمُ الْبَيِّنَاتُ ۚ
وَأُولَئِكَ لَهُمْ عَذَابٌ عَظِيمٌ ۞

106. On the Day when
Some faces will be (lit up
With) white, and some faces
Will be (in the gloom of) black:
To those whose faces
Will be black, (will be said):

١٠٦ - يَوْمَ تَبْيَضُّ وُجُوهٌ وَتَسْوَدُّ وُجُوهٌ ۚ
فَأَمَّا الَّذِينَ اسْوَدَّتْ وُجُوهُهُمْ
أَكَفَرْتُمْ بَعْدَ إِيمَانِكُمْ

"Did ye reject Faith
After accepting it?
Taste then the Penalty
For rejecting Faith."

فَذُوقُوا الْعَذَابَ
بِمَا كُنتُمْ تَكْفُرُونَ ۝

107. But those whose faces
Will be (lit with) white—
They will be in (the Light
Of) Allah's mercy; therein
To dwell (forever).

١٠٧- وَأَمَّا الَّذِينَ ابْيَضَّتْ وُجُوهُهُمْ
فَفِي رَحْمَةِ اللّٰهِ
هُمْ فِيهَا خَالِدُونَ ۝

108. These are the Signs
Of Allah: We rehearse them
To thee in Truth;
And Allah means
No injustice to any
Of His creatures.

١٠٨- تِلْكَ آيَاتُ اللّٰهِ
نَتْلُوهَا عَلَيْكَ بِالْحَقِّ
وَمَا اللّٰهُ يُرِيدُ ظُلْمًا لِّلْعَالَمِينَ ۝

109. To Allah belongs all
That is in the heavens
And on earth; to Him
Do all questions
Go back (for decision).

١٠٩- وَلِلّٰهِ مَا فِي السَّمٰوٰتِ
وَمَا فِي الْأَرْضِ
وَإِلَى اللّٰهِ تُرْجَعُ الْأُمُورُ ۝

SECTION 12.

110. Ye are the best
Of Peoples, evolved
For mankind,
Enjoining what is right,
Forbidding what is wrong,
And believing in Allah.
If only the People of the Book
Had faith, it were best
For them: among them
Are some who have faith,
But most of them
Are perverted transgressors.

١١٠- كُنتُمْ خَيْرَ أُمَّةٍ أُخْرِجَتْ لِلنَّاسِ
تَأْمُرُونَ بِالْمَعْرُوفِ وَتَنْهَوْنَ عَنِ الْمُنكَرِ
وَتُؤْمِنُونَ بِاللّٰهِ
وَلَوْ آمَنَ أَهْلُ الْكِتَابِ لَكَانَ خَيْرًا لَّهُمْ
مِنْهُمُ الْمُؤْمِنُونَ
وَأَكْثَرُهُمُ الْفَاسِقُونَ ۝

111. They will do you no harm,
Barring a trifling annoyance;
If they come out to fight you,
They will show you their backs,
And no help shall they get.

١١١- لَن يَضُرُّوكُمْ إِلَّا أَذًى وَإِن يُقَاتِلُوكُمْ
يُوَلُّوكُمُ الْأَدْبَارَ ثُمَّ لَا يُنصَرُونَ ۝

112. Shame is pitched over them
(Like a tent) wherever
They are found,

١١٢- ضُرِبَتْ عَلَيْهِمُ الذِّلَّةُ أَيْنَ مَا ثُقِفُوا

Except when under a covenant
(Of protection) from Allah
And from men; they draw
On themselves wrath from
        Allah,
And pitched over them
Is (the tent of) destitution.
This because they rejected
The Signs of Allah, and slew
The Prophets in defiance of
        right;
This because they rebelled
And transgressed beyond
        bounds.

113. Not all of them are alike:
Of the People of the Book
Are a portion that stand
(For the right); they rehearse
The Signs of Allah all night
        long,
And they prostrate themselves
In adoration.

114. They believe in Allah
And the Last Day;
They enjoin what is right,
And forbid what is wrong;
And they hasten (in emulation)
In (all) good works:
They are in the ranks
Of the righteous.

115. Of the good that they do,
Nothing will be rejected
Of them; for Allah knoweth well
Those that do right.

116. Those who reject Faith—
Neither their possessions
Nor their (numerous) progeny
Will avail them aught against
        Allah:
They will be Companions
Of the Fire—dwelling
Therein (forever).

117. What they spend
In the life

Of this (material) world
May be likened to a Wind
Which brings a nipping frost:
It strikes and destroys the harvest
Of men who have wronged
Their own souls; it is not Allah
That hath wronged them, but
They wrong themselves.

118. O ye who believe!
Take not into your intimacy
Those outside your ranks:
They will not fail
To corrupt you. They
Only desire your ruin:
Rank hatred has already
Appeared from their mouths:
What their hearts conceal
Is far worse.
We have made plain
To you the Signs,
If ye have wisdom.

119. Ah! ye are those
Who love them,
But they love you not—
Though ye believe
In the whole of the Book,
When they meet you,
They say, "We believe":
But when they are alone,
They bite off the very tips
Of their fingers at you
In their rage. Say:
"Perish in your rage;
Allah knoweth well
All the secrets of the heart."

120. If aught that is good
Befalls you, it grieves them;
But if some misfortune
Overtakes you, they rejoice
At it. But if ye are constant
And do right,
Not the least harm
Will their cunning
Do to you; for Allah
Compasseth round about
All that they do.

SECTION 13.

121. **R**emember that morning
Thou didst leave
Thy household (early)
To post the Faithful
At their stations for battle;
And Allah heareth
And knoweth all things:

١٢١- وَإِذْ غَدَوْتَ مِنْ أَهْلِكَ
تُبَوِّئُ الْمُؤْمِنِينَ
مَقَاعِدَ لِلْقِتَالِ ۗ
وَاللّٰهُ سَمِيعٌ عَلِيمٌ ۙ

122. Remember two of your parties
Meditated cowardice;
But Allah was their protector,
And in Allah should the
                    Faithful
(Ever) put their trust.

١٢٢- إِذْ هَمَّتْ طَّآئِفَتَانِ مِنْكُمْ
أَنْ تَفْشَلَا ۙ وَاللّٰهُ وَلِيُّهُمَا ۗ
وَعَلَى اللّٰهِ فَلْيَتَوَكَّلِ الْمُؤْمِنُونَ ○

123. Allah had helped you
At Badr, when ye were
A contemptible little force;
Then fear Allah; thus
May ye show your gratitude.

١٢٣- وَلَقَدْ نَصَرَكُمُ اللّٰهُ بِبَدْرٍ
وَأَنْتُمْ أَذِلَّةٌ ۚ
فَاتَّقُوا اللّٰهَ لَعَلَّكُمْ تَشْكُرُونَ ○

124. Remember thou saidst
To the Faithful: "Is it not enough
For you that Allah should help you
With three thousand angels
(Specially) sent down?

١٢٤- إِذْ تَقُولُ لِلْمُؤْمِنِينَ أَلَنْ يَكْفِيَكُمْ
أَنْ يُمِدَّكُمْ رَبُّكُمْ
بِثَلَاثَةِ آلَافٍ مِنَ الْمَلَائِكَةِ مُنْزَلِينَ ○

125. "Yea—if ye remain firm,
And act aright, even if
The enemy should rush here
On you in hot haste,
Your Lord would help you
With five thousand angels
Making a terrific onslaught."

١٢٥- بَلَى ۚ إِنْ تَصْبِرُوا وَتَتَّقُوا
وَيَأْتُوكُمْ مِنْ فَوْرِهِمْ هٰذَا يُمْدِدْكُمْ
رَبُّكُمْ بِخَمْسَةِ آلَافٍ
مِنَ الْمَلَائِكَةِ مُسَوِّمِينَ ○

126. Allah made it but a message
Of hope for you, and an assurance
To your hearts: (in any case)
There is no help
Except from Allah,
The Exalted, the Wise:

١٢٦- وَمَا جَعَلَهُ اللّٰهُ إِلَّا بُشْرَى لَكُمْ
وَلِتَطْمَئِنَّ قُلُوبُكُمْ بِهِ ۗ
وَمَا النَّصْرُ إِلَّا مِنْ عِنْدِ اللّٰهِ
الْعَزِيزِ الْحَكِيمِ ۙ

127. That He might cut off
A fringe of the Unbelievers
Or expose them to infamy,

١٢٧- لِيَقْطَعَ طَرَفًا
مِنَ الَّذِينَ كَفَرُوا

And they should then
Be turned back,
Frustrated of their purpose.

اَوۡ یَکۡبِتَہُمۡ فَیَنۡقَلِبُوۡا خَآئِبِیۡنَ ۟

128. Not for thee, (but for Allah),
Is the decision:
Whether He turn in mercy
To them, or punish them;
For they are indeed wrong-
　　　　　　　　　doers.

۱۲۸ لَیۡسَ لَکَ مِنَ الۡاَمۡرِ شَیۡءٌ
اَوۡ یَتُوۡبَ عَلَیۡہِمۡ
اَوۡ یُعَذِّبَہُمۡ فَاِنَّہُمۡ ظٰلِمُوۡنَ ۟

129. To Allah belongeth all
That is in the heavens
And on earth.
He forgiveth whom He pleaseth
And punisheth whom He pleaseth;
But Allah is Oft-Forgiving,
Most Merciful.

۱۲۹ وَلِلّٰہِ مَا فِی السَّمٰوٰتِ
وَمَا فِی الۡاَرۡضِ ۟ یَغۡفِرُ لِمَنۡ یَّشَآءُ
وَیُعَذِّبُ مَنۡ یَّشَآءُ ۟
وَاللّٰہُ غَفُوۡرٌ رَّحِیۡمٌ ۠ؔ

SECTION 14.

130. O ye who believe!
Devour not Usury,
Doubled and multiplied;
But fear Allah;that
Ye may (really) prosper.

۱۳۰ یٰۤاَیُّہَا الَّذِیۡنَ اٰمَنُوۡا لَا تَاۡکُلُوا الرِّبٰۤوا
اَضۡعَافًا مُّضٰعَفَۃً ۪
وَاتَّقُوا اللّٰہَ لَعَلَّکُمۡ تُفۡلِحُوۡنَ ۚ

131. Fear the Fire, which is prepared
For those who reject Faith;

۱۳۱ وَاتَّقُوا النَّارَ
الَّتِیۡۤ اُعِدَّتۡ لِلۡکٰفِرِیۡنَ ۚ

132. And obey Allah
And the Messenger;
That ye may obtain mercy.

۱۳۲ وَاَطِیۡعُوا اللّٰہَ وَ الرَّسُوۡلَ
لَعَلَّکُمۡ تُرۡحَمُوۡنَ ۚ

133. Be quick in the race
For forgiveness from your Lord,
And for a Garden whose width
Is that (of the whole)
Of the heavens
And of the earth,
Prepared for the righteous—

۱۳۳ وَسَارِعُوۡۤا اِلٰی مَغۡفِرَۃٍ مِّنۡ رَّبِّکُمۡ
وَجَنَّۃٍ
عَرۡضُہَا السَّمٰوٰتُ وَالۡاَرۡضُ ۙ
اُعِدَّتۡ لِلۡمُتَّقِیۡنَ ۚ

134. Those who spend (freely),
Whether in prosperity,
Or in adversity;
Who restrain anger,
And pardon (all) men—
For Allah loves those

۱۳۴ الَّذِیۡنَ یُنۡفِقُوۡنَ فِی السَّرَّآءِ
وَالضَّرَّآءِ وَالۡکٰظِمِیۡنَ الۡغَیۡظَ
وَالۡعَافِیۡنَ عَنِ النَّاسِ ۟

Who do good—

135. And those who,
Having done something
To be ashamed of,
Or wronged their own souls,
Earnestly bring Allah to mind,
And ask for forgiveness
For their sins—
And who can forgive
Sins except Allah?—
And are never obstinate
In persisting knowingly
In (the wrong) they have done.

136. For such the reward
Is forgiveness from their Lord,
And Gardens with rivers
Flowing underneath—
An eternal dwelling:
How excellent a recompense
For those who work (and strive)!

137. Many were the Ways of Life
That have passed away
Before you: travel through
The earth, and see what was
The end of those
Who rejected Truth.

138. Here is a plain statement
To men, a guidance
And instruction to those
Who fear Allah!

139. So lose not heart,
Nor fall into despair:
For ye must gain mastery
If ye are true in Faith.

140. If a wound hath touched you,
Be sure a similar wound
Hath touched the others.
Such days (of varying fortunes)
We give to men and men
By turns: that Allah may know
Those that believe,
And that He may take

To Himself from your ranks
Martyr-witnesses (to Truth).
And Allah loveth not
Those that do wrong.

وَيَتَّخِذَ مِنْكُمْ شُهَدَآءَ
وَاللهُ لَا يُحِبُّ الظَّالِمِيْنَ ۟

141. Allah's object also is to purge
Those that are true in Faith
And to deprive of blessing
Those that resist Faith.

١٤١- وَلِيُمَحِّصَ اللهُ الَّذِيْنَ اٰمَنُوْا
وَيَمْحَقَ الْكٰفِرِيْنَ ۟

142. Did ye think that ye
Would enter Heaven
Without Allah testing
Those of you who fought hard
(In His Cause) and
Remained steadfast?

١٤٢- اَمْ حَسِبْتُمْ اَنْ تَدْخُلُوا الْجَنَّةَ
وَلَمَّا يَعْلَمِ اللهُ الَّذِيْنَ جٰهَدُوْا مِنْكُمْ
وَيَعْلَمَ الصّٰبِرِيْنَ ۟

143. Ye did indeed
Wish for Death
Before ye met Him:
Now ye have seen Him
With your own eyes,
(And ye flinch!)

١٤٣- وَلَقَدْ كُنْتُمْ تَمَنَّوْنَ الْمَوْتَ
مِنْ قَبْلِ اَنْ تَلْقَوْهُ ۖ
فَقَدْ رَاَيْتُمُوْهُ وَاَنْتُمْ تَنْظُرُوْنَ ۟

SECTION 15.

144. **M**uḥammad is no more
Than a Messenger: many
Were the Messengers that
         passed away
Before him. If he died
Or were slain, will ye then
Turn back on your heels?
If any did turn back
On his heels, not the least
Harm will he do to Allah;
But Allah (on the other hand)
Will swiftly reward those
Who (serve him) with
         gratitude.

١٤٤- وَمَا مُحَمَّدٌ اِلَّا رَسُوْلٌ ۚ
قَدْ خَلَتْ مِنْ قَبْلِهِ الرُّسُلُ ۗ اَفَاۡئِنْ مَّاتَ
اَوْ قُتِلَ
انْقَلَبْتُمْ عَلٰۤى اَعْقَابِكُمْ ۗ
وَمَنْ يَّنْقَلِبْ عَلٰى عَقِبَيْهِ
فَلَنْ يَّضُرَّ اللهَ شَيْئًا ۗ
وَسَيَجْزِى اللهُ الشّٰكِرِيْنَ ۟

145. Nor can a soul die
Except by Allah's leave,
The term being fixed
As by writing. If any
Do desire a reward
In this life, We shall give it
To him; and if any
Do desire a reward
In the Hereafter, We shall

١٤٥- وَمَا كَانَ لِنَفْسٍ اَنْ تَمُوْتَ اِلَّا بِاِذْنِ اللهِ
كِتٰبًا مُّؤَجَّلًا ۗ
وَمَنْ يُّرِدْ
ثَوَابَ الدُّنْيَا نُؤْتِهٖ مِنْهَا ۚ
وَمَنْ يُّرِدْ ثَوَابَ الْاٰخِرَةِ

Give it to him.
And swiftly shall We reward
Those that (serve us with)
                    gratitude.

نُؤْتِهِ مِنْهَا
وَسَنَجْزِى الشَّكِرِينَ ۝

146. How many of the Prophets
Fought (in Allah's way),
And with them (fought)
Large bands of godly men?
But they never lost heart
If they met with disaster
In Allah's way, nor did
They weaken (in will)
Nor give in. And Allah
Loves those who are
Firm and steadfast.

١٤٦- وَكَأَيِّنْ مِّنْ نَّبِيٍّ قَاتَلَ مَعَهُ
رِبِّيُّونَ كَثِيرٌ فَمَا وَهَنُوا
لِمَا أَصَابَهُمْ
فِى سَبِيلِ اللهِ وَمَا ضَعُفُوا
وَمَا اسْتَكَانُوا
وَاللهُ يُحِبُّ الصَّبِرِينَ ۝

147. All that they said was:
"Our Lord! forgive us
Our sins and anything
We may have done
That transgressed our duty:
Establish our feet firmly,
And help us against
Those that resist
Faith."

١٤٧- وَمَا كَانَ قَوْلَهُمْ إِلَّا أَنْ قَالُوا
رَبَّنَا اغْفِرْ لَنَا
ذُنُوبَنَا وَإِسْرَافَنَا فِى أَمْرِنَا
وَثَبِّتْ أَقْدَامَنَا
وَانْصُرْنَا عَلَى الْقَوْمِ الْكَفِرِينَ ۝

148. And Allah gave them
A reward in this world,
And the excellent reward
Of the Hereafter. For Allah
Loveth those who do good.

١٤٨- فَآتَاهُمُ اللهُ ثَوَابَ الدُّنْيَا وَحُسْنَ
ثَوَابِ الْآخِرَةِ وَاللهُ يُحِبُّ الْمُحْسِنِينَ ۝

SECTION 16.

149. O ye who believe!
If ye obey the Unbelievers,
They will drive you back
On your heels, and ye
Will turn back (from Faith)
To your own loss.

١٤٩- يَا أَيُّهَا الَّذِينَ آمَنُوا إِنْ تُطِيعُوا الَّذِينَ
كَفَرُوا يَرُدُّوكُمْ عَلَى أَعْقَابِكُمْ
فَتَنْقَلِبُوا خَاسِرِينَ ۝

150. Nay, Allah is your Protector,
And He is the best of helpers.

١٥٠- بَلِ اللهُ مَوْلَكُمْ وَهُوَ خَيْرُ النَّاصِرِينَ ۝

151. Soon shall We cast terror
Into the hearts of the
                    Unbelievers,
For that they joined companions
With Allah, for which He had sent

١٥١- سَنُلْقِى فِى قُلُوبِ الَّذِينَ كَفَرُوا الرُّعْبَ
بِمَا أَشْرَكُوا بِاللهِ
مَا لَمْ يُنَزِّلْ بِهِ سُلْطَانًا

No authority; their abode
Will be the Fire; and evil
Is the home of the wrongdoers!

وَمَأْوَاهُمُ النَّارُ
وَبِئْسَ مَثْوَى الظَّالِمِينَ ٠

152. Allah did indeed fulfil
His promise to you
When ye with His permission
Were about to annihilate
Your enemy—until ye flinched
And fell to disputing
About the order,
And disobeyed it
After He brought you in sight
(Of the Booty) which ye covet.
Among you are some
That hanker after this world
And some that desire
The Hereafter. Then did He
Divert you from your foes
In order to test you.
But He forgave you:
For Allah is full of grace
To those who believe.

١٥٢- وَلَقَدْ صَدَقَكُمُ اللهُ وَعْدَهُ إِذْ
تَحُسُّونَهُم بِإِذْنِهِ حَتَّى إِذَا فَشِلْتُمْ
وَتَنَازَعْتُمْ فِي الْأَمْرِ
وَعَصَيْتُم مِّنۢ بَعْدِ مَا أَرَاكُم مَّا
تُحِبُّونَ
مِنكُم مَّن يُرِيدُ الدُّنْيَا
وَمِنكُم مَّن يُرِيدُ الْآخِرَةَ
ثُمَّ صَرَفَكُمْ
عَنْهُمْ لِيَبْتَلِيَكُمْ وَلَقَدْ عَفَا عَنكُمْ
وَاللهُ ذُو فَضْلٍ عَلَى الْمُؤْمِنِينَ ٠

153. Behold! ye were climbing up
The high ground, without even
Casting a side glance
At anyone, and the Messenger
In your rear was calling you
Back. There did Allah give you
One distress after another
By way of requital,
To teach you not to grieve
For (the booty) that had escaped
                              you
And for (the ill) that had befallen
                              you.
For Allah is well aware
Of all that ye do.

١٥٣- إِذْ تُصْعِدُونَ
وَلَا تَلْوُونَ عَلَى أَحَدٍ وَالرَّسُولُ
يَدْعُوكُمْ فِي أُخْرَاكُمْ
فَأَثَابَكُمْ غَمًّا بِغَمٍّ
لِكَيْلَا تَحْزَنُوا
عَلَى مَا فَاتَكُمْ
وَلَا مَا أَصَابَكُمْ
وَاللهُ خَبِيرٌ بِمَا تَعْمَلُونَ ٠

154. After (the excitement)
Of the distress, He sent down
Calm on a band of you
Overcome with slumber,
While another band
Was stirred to anxiety
By their own feelings,
Moved by wrong suspicions

١٥٤- ثُمَّ أَنزَلَ عَلَيْكُم مِّنۢ بَعْدِ الْغَمِّ
أَمَنَةً نُّعَاسًا يَغْشَى طَائِفَةً مِّنكُمْ
وَطَائِفَةٌ قَدْ أَهَمَّتْهُمْ أَنفُسُهُمْ
يَظُنُّونَ بِاللهِ غَيْرَ الْحَقِّ ظَنَّ الْجَاهِلِيَّةِ

Of Allah—suspicions due
To Ignorance. They said:
"What affair is this of ours?"
Say thou: "Indeed, this affair
Is wholly Allah's." They hide
In their minds what they
Dare not reveal to thee.
They say (to themselves):
"If we had had anything
To do with this affair,
We should not have been
In the slaughter here."
Say: "Even if you had remained
In your homes, those
For whom death was decreed
Would certainly have gone
                                    forth
To the place of their death";
But (all this was)
That Allah might test
What is in your breasts
And purge what is
In your hearts.

For Allah knoweth well
The secrets of your hearts.

يَقُولُونَ هَلْ لَنَا مِنَ الْأَمْرِ مِنْ شَيْءٍ

قُلْ إِنَّ الْأَمْرَ

كُلَّهُ لِلَّهِ يُخْفُونَ فِي أَنْفُسِهِمْ

مَا لَا يُبْدُونَ لَكَ يَقُولُونَ

لَوْ كَانَ لَنَا مِنَ الْأَمْرِ شَيْءٌ

مَا قُتِلْنَا هٰهُنَا قُلْ لَوْ كُنْتُمْ

فِي بُيُوتِكُمْ

لَبَرَزَ الَّذِينَ كُتِبَ عَلَيْهِمُ

الْقَتْلُ إِلَى مَضَاجِعِهِمْ

وَلِيَبْتَلِيَ اللهُ مَا فِي صُدُورِكُمْ

وَلِيُمَحِّصَ مَا فِي قُلُوبِكُمْ

وَاللهُ عَلِيمٌ بِذَاتِ الصُّدُورِ ۝

155. Those of you
Who turned back
On the day the two hosts
Met—it was Satan
Who caused them to fail,
Because of some (evil)
They had done. But Allah
Has blotted out (their fault):
For Allah is Oft-Forgiving,
Most Forbearing.
        SECTION 17.

١٥٥- إِنَّ الَّذِينَ تَوَلَّوْا مِنْكُمْ يَوْمَ الْتَقَى

الْجَمْعَانِ إِنَّمَا اسْتَزَلَّهُمُ الشَّيْطَانُ

بِبَعْضِ مَا كَسَبُوا

وَلَقَدْ عَفَا اللهُ عَنْهُمْ

إِنَّ اللهَ غَفُورٌ حَلِيمٌ ۝

156. O ye who believe!
Be not like the Unbelievers,
Who say of their brethren,
When they are travelling
Through the earth or engaged
In fighting: "If they had
                                    stayed
With us, they would not
Have died, or been slain."
This that Allah may make it

١٥٦- يَا أَيُّهَا الَّذِينَ آمَنُوا لَا تَكُونُوا كَالَّذِينَ

كَفَرُوا وَقَالُوا لِإِخْوَانِهِمْ

إِذَا ضَرَبُوا فِي الْأَرْضِ أَوْ كَانُوا غُزًّى

لَوْ كَانُوا عِنْدَنَا مَا مَاتُوا وَمَا قُتِلُوا

لِيَجْعَلَ اللهُ ذٰلِكَ حَسْرَةً فِي قُلُوبِهِمْ

A cause of sighs and regrets
In their hearts. It is Allah
That gives Life and Death,
And Allah sees well
All that ye do.

157. And if ye are slain, or die,
In the way of Allah,
Forgiveness and mercy
From Allah are far better
Than all they could amass.

158. And if ye die, or are slain,
Lo! it is unto Allah
That ye are brought together.

159. It is part of the Mercy
Of Allah that thou dost deal
Gently with them.
Wert thou severe
Or harsh-hearted,
They would have broken away
From about thee: so pass over
(Their faults), and ask
For (Allah's) forgiveness
For them; and consult
Them in affairs (of moment).
Then, when thou hast
Taken a decision,
Put thy trust in Allah.
For Allah loves those
Who put their trust (in Him).

160. If Allah helps you,
None can overcome you:
If He forsakes you,
Who is there, after that,
That can help you?
In Allah, then,
Let Believers put their trust.

161. No prophet could (ever)
Be false to his trust.
If any person is so false,
He shall, on the Day
Of Judgement, restore

وَاللهُ يُحْيٖ وَيُمِيتُ ۗ
وَاللهُ بِمَا تَعْمَلُوْنَ بَصِيْرٌ ۞

١٥٧- وَلَئِنْ قُتِلْتُمْ فِيْ سَبِيْلِ اللهِ
اَوْ مُتُّمْ لَمَغْفِرَةٌ مِّنَ اللهِ
وَرَحْمَةٌ خَيْرٌ مِّمَّا يَجْمَعُوْنَ ۞

١٥٨- وَلَئِنْ مُّتُّمْ اَوْ قُتِلْتُمْ
لَاِلَى اللهِ تُحْشَرُوْنَ ۞

١٥٩- فَبِمَا رَحْمَةٍ مِّنَ اللهِ لِنْتَ لَهُمْ ۚ
وَلَوْ كُنْتَ فَظًّا غَلِيْظَ الْقَلْبِ
لَا نْفَضُّوْا مِنْ حَوْلِكَ ۖ
فَاعْفُ عَنْهُمْ
وَاسْتَغْفِرْ لَهُمْ
وَشَاوِرْهُمْ فِى الْاَمْرِ ۚ
فَاِذَا عَزَمْتَ فَتَوَكَّلْ عَلَى اللهِ ۚ
اِنَّ اللهَ يُحِبُّ الْمُتَوَكِّلِيْنَ ۞

١٦٠- اِنْ يَّنْصُرْكُمُ اللهُ فَلَا غَالِبَ لَكُمْ ۚ
وَاِنْ يَّخْذُلْكُمْ
فَمَنْ ذَا الَّذِيْ يَنْصُرُكُمْ مِّنْ بَعْدِهٖ ۗ
وَعَلَى اللهِ فَلْيَتَوَكَّلِ الْمُؤْمِنُوْنَ ۞

١٦١- وَمَا كَانَ لِنَبِيٍّ اَنْ يَّغُلَّ ۚ
وَمَنْ يَّغْلُلْ
يَأْتِ بِمَا غَلَّ يَوْمَ الْقِيٰمَةِ ۚ

What he misappropriated;
Then shall every soul
Receive its due,
Whatever it earned—
And none shall be
Dealt with unjustly.

162. Is the man who follows
The good pleasure of Allah
Like the man who draws
On himself the wrath
Of Allah, and whose abode
Is in Hell?—
A woeful refuge!

163. They are in varying grades
In the sight of Allah,
And Allah sees well,
All that they do.

164. Allah did confer
A great favour
On the Believers
When He sent among them
A Messenger from among
Themselves, rehearsing
Unto them the Signs
Of Allah, sanctifying them,
And instructing them
In Scripture and Wisdom,
While, before that,
They had been
In manifest error.

165. What! When a single
Disaster smites you,
Although ye smote (your
                enemies)
With one twice as great,
Do ye say?—
"Whence is this?"
Say (to them):
"It is from yourselves:
For Allah hath power
Over all things."

166. What ye suffered
On the day the two armies

Met, was with the leave
Of Allah, in order that
He might test[475] the Believers—

فَبِإِذْنِ اللّٰهِ
وَلِيَعْلَمَ الْمُؤْمِنِيْنَ ۙ

167. And the Hypocrites also.
These were told: "Come,
Fight in the way of Allah,
Or (at least) drive
(The foe from your city)."
They said: "Had we known
There would be a fight, we
                              should
Certainly have followed you."
They were that day
Nearer to Unbelief
Than to Faith,
Saying with their lips
What was not in their hearts.
But Allah hath full knowledge
Of all they conceal.

١٦٧- وَلِيَعْلَمَ الَّذِيْنَ نَافَقُوْا ۖ وَقِيْلَ لَهُمْ
تَعَالَوْا قَاتِلُوْا فِيْ سَبِيْلِ اللّٰهِ
أَوِ ادْفَعُوْا ۖ
قَالُوْا لَوْ نَعْلَمُ قِتَالًا لَّاتَّبَعْنٰكُمْ ۚ
هُمْ لِلْكُفْرِ يَوْمَئِذٍ أَقْرَبُ مِنْهُمْ لِلْإِيْمَانِ ۚ
يَقُوْلُوْنَ بِأَفْوَاهِهِمْ
مَّا لَيْسَ فِيْ قُلُوْبِهِمْ ۗ
وَاللّٰهُ أَعْلَمُ بِمَا يَكْتُمُوْنَ ۚ

168. (They are) the ones that say,
(Of their brethren slain),
While they themselves
Sit (at ease): "If only
They had listened to us,
They would not have been slain."
Say: "Avert death
From your own selves,
If ye speak the truth."

١٦٨- اَلَّذِيْنَ قَالُوْا لِإِخْوَانِهِمْ
وَقَعَدُوْا لَوْ أَطَاعُوْنَا مَا قُتِلُوْا ۗ
قُلْ فَادْرَءُوْا عَنْ أَنْفُسِكُمُ الْمَوْتَ
إِنْ كُنْتُمْ صٰدِقِيْنَ ۝

169. Think not of those
Who are slain in Allah's way
As dead. Nay, they live,
Finding their sustenance
In the Presence of their Lord;

١٦٩- وَلَا تَحْسَبَنَّ الَّذِيْنَ قُتِلُوْا فِيْ سَبِيْلِ
اللّٰهِ أَمْوَاتًا ۗ
بَلْ أَحْيَاءٌ عِنْدَ رَبِّهِمْ يُرْزَقُوْنَ ۙ

170. They rejoice in the Bounty
Provided by Allah:
And with regard to those
Left behind, who have not
Yet joined them (in their bliss),
The (Martyrs) glory in the fact
That on them is no fear,
Nor have they (cause to) grieve.

١٧٠- فَرِحِيْنَ بِمَا آتَاهُمُ اللّٰهُ مِنْ فَضْلِهِ ۙ
وَيَسْتَبْشِرُوْنَ
بِالَّذِيْنَ لَمْ يَلْحَقُوْا بِهِمْ مِّنْ خَلْفِهِمْ ۙ
أَلَّا خَوْفٌ عَلَيْهِمْ وَلَا هُمْ يَحْزَنُوْنَ ۝

171. They glory in the Grace
And the Bounty from Allah,

١٧١- يَسْتَبْشِرُوْنَ بِنِعْمَةٍ مِّنَ اللّٰهِ وَفَضْلٍ ۙ

And in the fact that
Allah suffereth not
The reward of the Faithful
To be lost (in the least).

وَأَنَّ اللَّهَ
لَا يُضِيعُ أَجْرَ الْمُؤْمِنِينَ ۝

SECTION 18.

172. ❂f those who answered
The call of Allah
And the Messenger,
Even after being wounded,
Those who do right
And refrain from wrong
Have a great reward—

١٧٢- الَّذِينَ اسْتَجَابُوا لِلَّهِ
وَالرَّسُولِ مِنْ بَعْدِ مَا أَصَابَهُمُ الْقَرْحُ ۚ
لِلَّذِينَ أَحْسَنُوا مِنْهُمْ وَاتَّقَوْا
أَجْرٌ عَظِيمٌ ۝

173. Men said to them:
"A great army is gathering
Against you, so fear them":
But it (only) increased
Their Faith; they said:
"For us Allah sufficeth,
And He is the best
Disposer of affairs."

١٧٣- الَّذِينَ قَالَ لَهُمُ النَّاسُ
إِنَّ النَّاسَ قَدْ جَمَعُوا لَكُمْ
فَاخْشَوْهُمْ
فَزَادَهُمْ إِيمَانًا ۖ
وَقَالُوا حَسْبُنَا اللَّهُ وَنِعْمَ الْوَكِيلُ ۝

174. And they returned
With Grace and Bounty
From Allah; no harm
Ever touched them:
For they followed
The good pleasure of Allah:
And Allah is the Lord
Of bounties unbounded.

١٧٤- فَانْقَلَبُوا بِنِعْمَةٍ مِنَ اللَّهِ وَفَضْلٍ
لَمْ يَمْسَسْهُمْ سُوءٌ ۙ
وَاتَّبَعُوا رِضْوَانَ اللَّهِ ۗ
وَاللَّهُ ذُو فَضْلٍ عَظِيمٍ ۝

175. ❂t is only the Evil One
That suggests to you
The fear of his votaries:
Be ye not afraid
Of them, but fear Me,
If ye have Faith.

١٧٥- إِنَّمَا ذَٰلِكُمُ الشَّيْطَانُ يُخَوِّفُ أَوْلِيَاءَهُ ۖ
فَلَا تَخَافُوهُمْ
وَخَافُونِ إِنْ كُنْتُمْ مُؤْمِنِينَ ۝

176. Let not those grieve thee
Who rush headlong
Into Unbelief:
Not the least harm
Will they do to Allah:
Allah's Plan is that He
Will give them no portion
In the Hereafter.

١٧٦- وَلَا يَحْزُنْكَ الَّذِينَ يُسَارِعُونَ فِي
الْكُفْرِ ۚ إِنَّهُمْ لَنْ يَضُرُّوا اللَّهَ شَيْئًا ۗ
يُرِيدُ اللَّهُ
أَلَّا يَجْعَلَ لَهُمْ حَظًّا فِي الْآخِرَةِ ۖ

But a severe punishment.

وَلَهُمْ عَذَابٌ عَظِيمٌ ۝

177. Those who purchase
Unbelief at the price
Of faith—
Not the least harm
Will they do to Allah,
But they will have
A grievous punishment.

١٧٧ـ إِنَّ الَّذِينَ اشْتَرَوُا
الْكُفْرَ بِالْإِيمَانِ
لَنْ يَضُرُّوا اللهَ شَيْئًا ۚ
وَلَهُمْ عَذَابٌ أَلِيمٌ ۝

178. Let not the Unbelievers
Think that Our respite
To them is good for themselves:
We grant them respite
That they may grow[480]
In their iniquity:
But they will have
A shameful punishment.

١٧٨ـ وَلَا يَحْسَبَنَّ الَّذِينَ كَفَرُوا
أَنَّمَا نُمْلِي لَهُمْ خَيْرٌ لِأَنْفُسِهِمْ ۚ
إِنَّمَا نُمْلِي لَهُمْ لِيَزْدَادُوا إِثْمًا ۚ
وَلَهُمْ عَذَابٌ مُهِينٌ ۝

179. Allah will not leave
The Believers in the state
In which ye are now,
Until He separates
What is evil
From what is good.
Nor will Allah disclose
To you the secrets
Of the Unseen,
But He chooses
Of His Messengers
(For the purpose)
Whom He pleases.
So believe in Allah
And His Messengers;
And if ye believe
And do right,
Ye have a reward
Without measure.

١٧٩ـ مَا كَانَ اللهُ لِيَذَرَ الْمُؤْمِنِينَ
عَلَى مَا أَنْتُمْ عَلَيْهِ
حَتَّى يَمِيزَ الْخَبِيثَ مِنَ الطَّيِّبِ ۗ
وَمَا كَانَ اللهُ
لِيُطْلِعَكُمْ عَلَى الْغَيْبِ وَلَكِنَّ اللهَ
يَجْتَبِي مِنْ رُسُلِهِ مَنْ يَشَاءُ ۖ
فَآمِنُوا بِاللهِ وَرُسُلِهِ ۚ
وَإِنْ تُؤْمِنُوا
وَتَتَّقُوا فَلَكُمْ أَجْرٌ عَظِيمٌ ۝

180. And let not those
Who covetously withheld
Of the gifts which Allah
Hath given them of His Grace,
Think that it is good for them:
Nay, it will be the worse
For them; soon shall the things
Which they covetously withheld

١٨٠ـ وَلَا يَحْسَبَنَّ الَّذِينَ
يَبْخَلُونَ بِمَا آتَاهُمُ اللهُ مِنْ فَضْلِهِ
هُوَ خَيْرًا لَهُمْ ۖ
بَلْ هُوَ شَرٌّ لَهُمْ ۚ سَيُطَوَّقُونَ

Be tied to their necks
Like a twisted collar,
On the Day of Judgement.
To Allah belongs the heritage
Of the heavens and the earth;
And Allah is well-acquainted
With all that ye do.

SECTION 19.

181. Allah hath heard
The taunt of those
Who say: "Truly, Allah
Is indigent and we
Are rich!"—We shall
Certainly record their word
And (their act) of slaying
The Prophets in defiance
Of right, and We shall say:
"Taste ye the Penalty
Of the Scorching Fire!

182. "This is because
Of the (unrighteous deeds)
Which your hands
Sent on before ye;
For Allah never harms
Those who serve Him."

183. They (also) said: "Allah took
Our promise not to believe
In a messenger unless
He showed us a sacrifice
Consumed by fire
(From heaven)." Say:
"There came to you
Messengers before me,
With Clear Signs
And even with what
Ye ask for: why then
Did ye slay them,
If ye speak the truth?"

184. Then if they reject thee,
So were rejected messengers
Before thee, who came
With Clear Signs,
And the Scriptures,
And the Book of

مَا بَخِلُوا بِهِ يَوْمَ الْقِيَامَةِ ۗ
وَلِلَّهِ مِيرَاثُ السَّمَوَاتِ وَالْأَرْضِ ۗ
وَاللَّهُ بِمَا تَعْمَلُونَ خَبِيرٌ ۞

١٨١- لَقَدْ سَمِعَ اللَّهُ قَوْلَ الَّذِينَ
قَالُوا إِنَّ اللَّهَ فَقِيرٌ
وَّنَحْنُ أَغْنِيَاءُ ۘ سَنَكْتُبُ مَا قَالُوا
وَقَتْلَهُمُ الْأَنْبِيَاءَ
بِغَيْرِ حَقٍّ ۙ
وَّنَقُولُ ذُوقُوا عَذَابَ الْحَرِيقِ ○

١٨٢- ذَٰلِكَ بِمَا قَدَّمَتْ أَيْدِيكُمْ
وَأَنَّ اللَّهَ
لَيْسَ بِظَلَّامٍ لِلْعَبِيدِ ۞

١٨٣- الَّذِينَ قَالُوا إِنَّ اللَّهَ عَهِدَ إِلَيْنَا
أَلَّا نُؤْمِنَ لِرَسُولٍ
حَتَّى يَأْتِيَنَا بِقُرْبَانٍ تَأْكُلُهُ النَّارُ ۗ
قُلْ قَدْ جَاءَكُمْ رُسُلٌ مِنْ قَبْلِي
بِالْبَيِّنَاتِ وَبِالَّذِي قُلْتُمْ
فَلِمَ قَتَلْتُمُوهُمْ
إِنْ كُنْتُمْ صَادِقِينَ ○

١٨٤- فَإِنْ كَذَّبُوكَ فَقَدْ كُذِّبَ رُسُلٌ
مِنْ قَبْلِكَ جَاءُوا بِالْبَيِّنَاتِ
وَالزُّبُرِ وَالْكِتَابِ

Enlightenment.

المُنِيرُ ٥

185. Every soul shall have
A taste of death:
And only on the Day
Of Judgement shall you
Be paid your full recompense.
Only he who is saved
Far from the Fire
And admitted to the Garden
Will have attained
The object (of Life):
For the life of this world
Is but goods and chattels
Of deception.

١٨٥- كُلُّ نَفْسٍ ذَآئِقَةُ الْمَوْتِ
وَإِنَّمَا تُوَفَّوْنَ أُجُوْرَكُمْ يَوْمَ الْقِيٰمَةِ
فَمَنْ زُحْزِحَ عَنِ النَّارِ
وَأُدْخِلَ الْجَنَّةَ فَقَدْ فَازَ
وَمَا الْحَيٰوةُ الدُّنْيَآ
إِلَّا مَتَاعُ الْغُرُوْرِ ٥

186. Ye shall certainly
Be tried and tested
In your possessions
And in your personal selves;
And ye shall certainly
Hear much that will grieve you,
From those who received
The Book before you
And from those who
Worship many gods.
But if ye persevere
Patiently, and guard
Against evil—then
That will be
A determining factor
In all affairs.

١٨٦- لَتُبْلَوُنَّ فِيْ أَمْوَالِكُمْ وَأَنْفُسِكُمْ
وَلَتَسْمَعُنَّ مِنَ الَّذِيْنَ
أُوْتُوا الْكِتٰبَ مِنْ قَبْلِكُمْ
وَمِنَ الَّذِيْنَ
أَشْرَكُوْا أَذًى كَثِيْرًا
وَإِنْ تَصْبِرُوْا
وَتَتَّقُوْا
فَإِنَّ ذٰلِكَ مِنْ عَزْمِ الْأُمُوْرِ ٥

187. And remember
Allah took a Covenant
From the People of the Book,
To make it known
And clear to mankind,
And not to hide it;
But they threw it away
Behind their backs,
And purchased with it
Some miserable gain!
And vile was the bargain
They made!

١٨٧- وَإِذْ أَخَذَ اللهُ مِيْثَاقَ
الَّذِيْنَ أُوْتُوا الْكِتٰبَ
لَتُبَيِّنُنَّهُ لِلنَّاسِ وَلَا تَكْتُمُوْنَهُ
فَنَبَذُوْهُ وَرَآءَ ظُهُوْرِهِمْ
وَاشْتَرَوْا بِهِ ثَمَنًا قَلِيْلًا
فَبِئْسَ مَا يَشْتَرُوْنَ ٥

188. Think not that those
Who exult in what they
Have brought about, and love

١٨٨- لَا تَحْسَبَنَّ الَّذِيْنَ يَفْرَحُوْنَ بِمَآ أَتَوْا
وَيُحِبُّوْنَ أَنْ يُحْمَدُوْا

To be praised for what
They have not done—
Think not that they
Can escape the Penalty.
For them is a Penalty
Grievous indeed.

١٨٩. وَلِلّٰهِ
189. To Allah belongeth
The dominion
Of the heavens
And the earth;
And Allah hath power
Over all things.

مُلْكُ السَّمٰوٰتِ وَالْأَرْضِ
وَاللّٰهُ عَلٰى كُلِّ شَيْءٍ قَدِيْرٌ

SECTION 20.

190. Behold! In the creation
Of the heavens and the earth,
And the alternation
Of Night and Day—
There are indeed Signs
For men of understanding—

١٩٠. إِنَّ فِيْ خَلْقِ السَّمٰوٰتِ وَالْأَرْضِ
وَاخْتِلَافِ الَّيْلِ وَالنَّهَارِ
لَأيٰتٍ لِّأُولِى الْأَلْبَابِ

191. Men who celebrate
The praises of Allah,
Standing, sitting,
And lying down on their
                    sides,
And contemplate
The (wonders of) creation
In the heavens and the earth,
(With the thought):
"Our Lord! not for naught
Hast Thou created (all) this!
Glory to Thee! Give us[499]
Salvation from the Penalty
Of the Fire.

١٩١. الَّذِيْنَ يَذْكُرُوْنَ اللّٰهَ قِيٰمًا
وَّقُعُوْدًا وَّعَلٰى جُنُوْبِهِمْ
وَيَتَفَكَّرُوْنَ فِيْ خَلْقِ
السَّمٰوٰتِ وَالْأَرْضِ
رَبَّنَا مَا خَلَقْتَ هٰذَا بَاطِلًا
سُبْحٰنَكَ
فَقِنَا عَذَابَ النَّارِ

192. "Our Lord! any whom Thou
Dost admit to the Fire,
Truly Thou coverest with shame,
And never will wrongdoers
Find any helpers!

١٩٢. رَبَّنَا إِنَّكَ مَنْ تُدْخِلِ النَّارَ
فَقَدْ أَخْزَيْتَهُ
وَمَا لِلظّٰلِمِيْنَ مِنْ أَنْصَارٍ

193. "Our Lord! we have heard
The call of one calling
(Us) to Faith, 'Believe ye
In the Lord,' and we
Have believed. Our Lord!

١٩٣. رَبَّنَا إِنَّنَا سَمِعْنَا
مُنَادِيًا يُّنَادِيْ لِلْإِيْمَانِ
أَنْ أٰمِنُوْا بِرَبِّكُمْ فَأٰمَنَّا

Forgive us our sins,
Blot out from us
Our iniquities, and take
To Thyself our souls
In the company of the righteous.

194. "Our Lord! Grant us
What Thou didst promise
Unto us through Thy Messengers,
And save us from shame
On the Day of Judgment;
For Thou never breakest
Thy promise."

195. And their Lord hath accepted
Of them, and answered them:
"Never will I suffer to be lost
The work of any of you,
Be he male or female:
Ye are members, one of
                 another;
Those who have left their homes,
And were driven out therefrom,
And suffered harm in My Cause,
And fought and were slain—
Verily, I will blot out
From them their iniquities,
And admit them into Gardens
With rivers flowing beneath—
A reward from the Presence
Of Allah, and from His Presence
Is the best of rewards."

196. Let not the strutting about
Of the Unbelievers
Through the land
Deceive thee:

197. Little is it for enjoyment:
Their ultimate abode
Is Hell; what an evil bed
(To lie on)!

198. On the other hand, for those
Who fear their Lord,
Are Gardens, with rivers
Flowing beneath; therein
Are they to dwell (forever)—
A gift from the Presence

Of Allah; and that which is
In the Presence of Allah
Is the best (bliss)
For the righteous.

نُزُلاً مِّنْ عِنْدِ اللَّهِ
وَمَا عِنْدَ اللَّهِ خَيْرٌ لِّلْأَبْرَارِ

199. And there are, certainly,
Among the People of the Book,
Those who believe in Allah,
In the revelation to you,
And in the revelation to them,
Bowing in humility to Allah:
They will not sell
The Signs of Allah
For a miserable gain!
For them is a reward
With their Lord,
And Allah is swift in account.

١٩٩- وَإِنَّ مِنْ أَهْلِ الْكِتَابِ
لَمَنْ يُّؤْمِنُ بِاللَّهِ وَمَآ أُنْزِلَ إِلَيْكُمْ
وَمَآ أُنْزِلَ إِلَيْهِمْ
خَاشِعِيْنَ لِلَّهِ لَا يَشْتَرُوْنَ بِآيَاتِ اللَّهِ
ثَمَنًا قَلِيْلاً أُولٰئِكَ لَهُمْ
أَجْرُهُمْ عِنْدَ رَبِّهِمْ
إِنَّ اللَّهَ سَرِيْعُ الْحِسَابِ ٠

200. O ye who believe!
Persevere in patience
And constancy; vie
In such perseverance;
Strengthen each other;
And fear Allah;
That ye may prosper.

٢٠٠- يَا أَيُّهَا الَّذِيْنَ آمَنُوا اصْبِرُوْا
وَصَابِرُوْا
وَرَابِطُوْا
وَاتَّقُوا اللَّهَ لَعَلَّكُمْ تُفْلِحُوْنَ ٠

INTRODUCTION TO SURA IV (Nisāa) — 176 Verses

    This Sūra is closely connected chronologically with Sūra III. Its subject-matter deals with the social problems which the Muslim community had to face immediately after Uḥud. While the particular occasion made the necessity urgent, the principles laid down have permanently governed Muslim Law and social practice.

    Broadly speaking, the Sūra consists of two parts: (1) that dealing with women, orphans, inheritance, marriage, and family rights generally, and (2) that dealing with the recalcitrants in the larger family, the community at Medina, viz., the Hypocrites and their accomplices.

Al Nisā' (The Women)

In the name of Allah, Most Gracious,
Most Merciful.

بِسْمِ اللهِ الرَّحْمٰنِ الرَّحِيْمِ ۝

1. **O** mankind! reverence
Your Guardian-Lord,
Who created you
From a single Person,
Created, of like nature,
His mate, and from them twain
Scattered (like seeds)
Countless men and women—
Fear Allah, through Whom
Ye demand your mutual (rights),
And (reverence) the wombs
(That bore you): for Allah
Ever watches over you.

١- يٰۤاَيُّهَا النَّاسُ اتَّقُوْا رَبَّكُمُ
الَّذِيْ خَلَقَكُمْ مِّنْ نَفْسٍ وَّاحِدَةٍ
وَّخَلَقَ مِنْهَا زَوْجَهَا وَبَثَّ مِنْهُمَا
رِجَالًا كَثِيْرًا وَّنِسَآءً ۚ
وَاتَّقُوا اللهَ الَّذِيْ تَسَآءَلُوْنَ بِهٖ
وَالْاَرْحَامَ ۚ
اِنَّ اللهَ كَانَ عَلَيْكُمْ رَقِيْبًا ۝

2. **T**o orphans restore their property
(When they reach their age),
Nor substitute (your) worthless
        things
For (their) good ones; and
        devour not
Their substance (by mixing it
        up)
With your own. For this is
Indeed a great sin.

٢- وَاٰتُوا الْيَتٰمٰۤى اَمْوَالَهُمْ
وَلَا تَتَبَدَّلُوا الْخَبِيْثَ بِالطَّيِّبِ ۠
وَلَا تَأْكُلُوْۤا اَمْوَالَهُمْ
اِلٰۤى اَمْوَالِكُمْ ۗ اِنَّهٗ كَانَ حُوْبًا كَبِيْرًا ۝

3. **I**f ye fear that ye shall not
Be able to deal justly
With the orphans,
Marry women of your choice,

٣- وَاِنْ خِفْتُمْ اَلَّا تُقْسِطُوْا فِى الْيَتٰمٰى
فَانْكِحُوْا مَا طَابَ لَكُمْ مِّنَ النِّسَآءِ

Two, or three, or four;
But if ye fear that ye shall not
Be able to deal justly (with them),
Then only one, or (a captive)
That your right hands possess.
That will be more suitable,
To prevent you
From doing injustice.

مَثْنَىٰ وَثُلَٰثَ وَرُبَٰعَ ۖ
فَإِنْ خِفْتُمْ أَلَّا تَعْدِلُوا فَوَاحِدَةً
أَوْ مَا مَلَكَتْ أَيْمَانُكُمْ ۚ
ذَٰلِكَ أَدْنَىٰ أَلَّا تَعُولُوا ۞

4. And give the women
(On marriage) their dower
As a free gift; but if they,
Of their own good pleasure,
Remit any part of it to you,
Take it and enjoy it
With right good cheer.

٤ - وَآتُوا النِّسَاءَ صَدُقَاتِهِنَّ نِحْلَةً ۚ
فَإِنْ طِبْنَ لَكُمْ عَنْ شَيْءٍ
مِنْهُ نَفْسًا
فَكُلُوهُ هَنِيئًا مَرِيئًا ۞

5. To those weak of understanding
Make not over your property,
Which Allah hath made
A means of support for you,
But feed and clothe them
Therewith, and speak to them
Words of kindness and justice.

٥ - وَلَا تُؤْتُوا السُّفَهَاءَ
أَمْوَالَكُمُ الَّتِي جَعَلَ اللَّهُ لَكُمْ قِيَامًا
وَارْزُقُوهُمْ فِيهَا وَاكْسُوهُمْ
وَقُولُوا لَهُمْ قَوْلًا مَعْرُوفًا

6. Make trial of orphans
Until they reach the age
Of marriage; if then ye find
Sound judgement in them,
Release their property to them;
But consume it not wastefully,
Nor in haste against their growing
up.
If the guardian is well-off,
Let him claim no remuneration,
But if he is poor, let him
Have for himself what is
Just and reasonable.
When ye release their property
To them, take witnesses
In their presence:
But all-sufficient
Is Allah in taking account.

٦ - وَابْتَلُوا الْيَتَامَىٰ حَتَّىٰ إِذَا بَلَغُوا النِّكَاحَ ۖ
فَإِنْ آنَسْتُمْ مِنْهُمْ رُشْدًا
فَادْفَعُوا إِلَيْهِمْ أَمْوَالَهُمْ ۖ
وَلَا تَأْكُلُوهَا إِسْرَافًا وَبِدَارًا أَنْ يَكْبَرُوا ۚ
وَمَنْ كَانَ غَنِيًّا فَلْيَسْتَعْفِفْ ۖ
وَمَنْ كَانَ فَقِيرًا فَلْيَأْكُلْ بِالْمَعْرُوفِ ۚ
فَإِذَا دَفَعْتُمْ إِلَيْهِمْ أَمْوَالَهُمْ
فَأَشْهِدُوا عَلَيْهِمْ ۚ
وَكَفَىٰ بِاللَّهِ حَسِيبًا ۞

7. From what is left by parents
And those nearest related
There is a share for men
And a share for women,

٧ - لِلرِّجَالِ نَصِيبٌ مِمَّا تَرَكَ الْوَالِدَانِ
وَالْأَقْرَبُونَ وَلِلنِّسَاءِ نَصِيبٌ مِمَّا تَرَكَ

Whether the property be small
Or large—a determinate share.

الْوَالِدَانِ وَالْأَقْرَبُوْنَ مِمَّا قَلَّ مِنْهُ أَوْ كَثُرَ ۚ
نَصِيْبًا مَّفْرُوْضًا ۟

8. But if at the time of division
Other relatives, or orphans,
Or poor, are present,
Feed them out of the (property),
And speak to them
Words of kindness and justice.

٨ ۔ وَإِذَا حَضَرَ الْقِسْمَةَ أُولُوا الْقُرْبٰى وَ
الْيَتٰمٰى وَالْمَسٰكِيْنُ فَارْزُقُوْهُمْ مِّنْهُ
وَقُوْلُوْا لَهُمْ قَوْلًا مَّعْرُوْفًا ۟

9. Let those (disposing of an estate)
Have the same fear in their minds
As they would have for their own
If they had left a helpless
                    family behind:
Let them fear Allah, and speak
Words of appropriate
                    (comfort).

٩ ۔ وَلْيَخْشَ الَّذِيْنَ لَوْ تَرَكُوْا مِنْ خَلْفِهِمْ
ذُرِّيَّةً ضِعٰفًا خَافُوْا عَلَيْهِمْ ۖ
فَلْيَتَّقُوا اللّٰهَ وَلْيَقُوْلُوْا قَوْلًا سَدِيْدًا ۟

10. Those who unjustly
Eat up the property
Of orphans, eat up
A Fire into their own
Bodies: they will soon
Be enduring a blazing Fire!

١٠ ۔ إِنَّ الَّذِيْنَ يَأْكُلُوْنَ أَمْوَالَ الْيَتٰمٰى ظُلْمًا
إِنَّمَا يَأْكُلُوْنَ فِيْ بُطُوْنِهِمْ نَارًا ۚ
وَسَيَصْلَوْنَ سَعِيْرًا ۟ ۖ

SECTION 2.

11. Allah (thus) directs you
As regards your children's
(Inheritance): to the male,
A portion equal to that
Of two females: if only
Daughters, two or more,
Their share is two-thirds
Of the inheritance;
If only one, her share
Is a half.

For parents, a sixth share
Of the inheritance to each,
If the deceased left children;
If no children, and the parents
Are the (only) heirs, the mother
Has a third; if the deceased
Left brothers (or sisters)
The mother has a sixth.
(The distribution in all cases

١١ ۔ يُوْصِيْكُمُ اللّٰهُ فِيْ أَوْلَادِكُمْ ۖ
لِلذَّكَرِ مِثْلُ حَظِّ الْأُنْثَيَيْنِ ۚ
فَإِنْ كُنَّ نِسَاءً فَوْقَ اثْنَتَيْنِ
فَلَهُنَّ ثُلُثَا مَا تَرَكَ ۚ وَإِنْ كَانَتْ وَاحِدَةً
فَلَهَا النِّصْفُ ۚ وَلِأَبَوَيْهِ
لِكُلِّ وَاحِدٍ مِّنْهُمَا السُّدُسُ
مِمَّا تَرَكَ إِنْ كَانَ لَهُ وَلَدٌ ۚ فَإِنْ لَمْ يَكُنْ لَّهُ
وَلَدٌ وَّوَرِثَهُ أَبَوَاهُ فَلِأُمِّهِ الثُّلُثُ ۚ
فَإِنْ كَانَ لَهُ إِخْوَةٌ
فَلِأُمِّهِ السُّدُسُ مِنْ بَعْدِ وَصِيَّةٍ
يُّوْصِيْ بِهَا أَوْ دَيْنٍ ۗ

Is) after the payment
Of legacies and debts.
Ye know not whether
Your parents or your children
Are nearest to you
In benefit. These are
Settled portions ordained
By Allah; and Allah is
All-Knowing, All-Wise.

12. In what your wives leave,
Your share is a half,
If they leave no child;
But if they leave a child,
Ye get a fourth; after payment
Of legacies and debts.
In what ye leave,
Their share is a fourth,
If ye leave no child;
But if ye leave a child,
They get an eighth; after
                              payment
Of legacies and debts.

If the man or woman
Whose inheritance is in
                              question,
Has left neither ascendants nor
                              descendants,
But has left a brother[521]
Or a sister, each one of the two
Gets a sixth; but if more
Than two, they share in a third;
After payment of legacies
And debts; so that no loss
Is caused (to anyone).
Thus is it ordained by Allah;
And Allah is All-Knowing,
Most Forbearing.

13. Those are limits
Set by Allah; those who
Obey Allah and His Messenger
Will be admitted to Gardens
With rivers flowing beneath,
To abide therein (forever)
And that will be
The Supreme achievement.

14. But those who disobey
Allah and His Messenger
And transgress His limits
Will be admitted
To a Fire, to abide therein:
And they shall have
A humiliating punishment.

SECTION 3.

15. If any of your women
Are guilty of lewdness,
Take the evidence of four
(Reliable) witnesses from
               amongst you
Against them; and if they
               testify,
Confine them to houses until
Death do claim them,
Or Allah ordain for them
Some (other) way.

16. If two men among you
Are guilty of lewdness,
Punish them both.
If they repent and amend,
Leave them alone; for Allah
Is Oft-Returning, Most
               Merciful.

17. Allah accepts the repentance
Of those who do evil
In ignorance and repent
Soon afterwards; to them
Will Allah turn in mercy:
For Allah is full of knowledge
And wisdom.

18. Of no effect is the repentance
Of those who continue
To do evil, until Death
Faces one of them, and he says,
"Now have I repented indeed;"
Nor of those who die
Rejecting Faith; for them
Have we prepared
A punishment most grievous.

19. O ye who believe!
Ye are forbidden to inherit

Women against their will.
Nor should ye treat them
With harshness, that ye may
Take away part of the dower
Ye have given them — except
Where they have been guilty
Of open lewdness;
On the contrary live with them
On a footing of kindness and
equity.
If ye take a dislike to them
It may be that ye dislike
A thing, and Allah brings about
Through it a great deal of good.

لَا يَحِلُّ لَكُمْ أَنْ تَرِثُوا النِّسَاءَ كَرْهاً

وَلَا تَعْضُلُوهُنَّ لِتَذْهَبُوا بِبَعْضِ

مَا آتَيْتُمُوهُنَّ

إِلَّا أَنْ يَأْتِينَ بِفَاحِشَةٍ مُبَيِّنَةٍ

وَعَاشِرُوهُنَّ بِالْمَعْرُوفِ

فَإِنْ كَرِهْتُمُوهُنَّ فَعَسَى أَنْ تَكْرَهُوا شَيْئاً

وَيَجْعَلَ اللهُ فِيهِ خَيْراً كَثِيراً ۝

20. But if ye decide to take
One wife in place of another,
Even if ye had given the latter
A whole treasure   for dower,
Take not the least bit of it back;
Would ye take it by slander
And a manifest wrong?

٢٠- وَإِنْ أَرَدْتُمُ اسْتِبْدَالَ زَوْجٍ مَكَانَ

زَوْجٍ وَآتَيْتُمْ إِحْدَاهُنَّ قِنْطَاراً

فَلَا تَأْخُذُوا مِنْهُ شَيْئاً

أَتَأْخُذُونَهُ بُهْتَاناً وَإِثْماً مُبِيناً ۝

21. And how could ye take it
When ye have gone in
Unto each other, and they have
Taken from you a solemn
covenant?

٢١- وَكَيْفَ تَأْخُذُونَهُ

وَقَدْ أَفْضَى بَعْضُكُمْ إِلَى بَعْضٍ

وَأَخَذْنَ مِنْكُمْ مِيثَاقاً غَلِيظاً ۝

22. And marry not women
Whom your fathers married —
Except what is past:
It was shameful and odious —
An abominable custom indeed.

٢٢- وَلَا تَنْكِحُوا مَا نَكَحَ آبَاؤُكُمْ مِنَ

النِّسَاءِ إِلَّا مَا قَدْ سَلَفَ

إِنَّهُ كَانَ فَاحِشَةً وَمَقْتاً وَسَاءَ سَبِيلاً ۝

SECTION 4.

23. Prohibited to you
(For marriage) are —
Your mothers, daughters,
Sisters; father's sisters,
Mother's sisters; brother's
daughters,
Sister's daughters;
foster-mothers
(Who gave you suck),
foster-sisters;

٢٣- حُرِّمَتْ عَلَيْكُمْ أُمَّهَاتُكُمْ وَبَنَاتُكُمْ

وَأَخَوَاتُكُمْ وَعَمَّاتُكُمْ وَخَالَاتُكُمْ وَبَنَاتُ

الْأَخِ وَبَنَاتُ الْأُخْتِ

وَأُمَّهَاتُكُمُ اللَّاتِي أَرْضَعْنَكُمْ

وَأَخَوَاتُكُمْ مِنَ الرَّضَاعَةِ

وَأُمَّهَاتُ نِسَائِكُمْ وَرَبَائِبُكُمُ اللَّاتِي

Your wives' mothers;
Your step-daughters under your
Guardianship, born of your wives
To whom ye have gone in—
No prohibition if ye have not gone
          in—
(Those who have been)
Wives of your sons   proceeding
From your loins;
And two sisters in wedlock
At one and the same time,
Except for what is past;
For Allah is Oft-Forgiving,
Most Merciful—

في حُجُورِكُم مِّن نِّسَآئِكُمُ الَّتِي
دَخَلْتُم بِهِنَّ فَإِن لَّمْ تَكُونُوا
دَخَلْتُم بِهِنَّ فَلَا جُنَاحَ عَلَيْكُمْ
وَحَلَائِلُ أَبْنَآئِكُمُ الَّذِينَ مِنْ أَصْلَابِكُمْ
وَأَن تَجْمَعُوا بَيْنَ الْأُخْتَيْنِ
إِلَّا مَا قَدْ سَلَفَ
إِنَّ اللّهَ كَانَ غَفُورًا رَّحِيمًا ۩

24. Also (prohibited are)
Women already married,
Except those
Whom your right hands
         possess:
Thus hath Allah ordained
(Prohibitions) against you:
Except for these, all others
Are lawful, provided
Ye seek (them in marriage)
With gifts from your property—
Desiring chastity, not lust.
Seeing that ye derive
Benefit from them, give them
Their dowers (at least)
As prescribed; but if,
After a dower is prescribed, ye
Mutually (to vary it),   agree
There is no blame on you,
And Allah is All-Knowing,
All-Wise.

٢٤ - وَالْمُحْصَنَاتُ مِنَ النِّسَآءِ
إِلَّا مَا مَلَكَتْ أَيْمَانُكُمْ
كِتَابَ اللّهِ عَلَيْكُمْ
وَأُحِلَّ لَكُم مَّا وَرَآءَ ذَلِكُمْ
أَن تَبْتَغُوا بِأَمْوَالِكُم
مُّحْصِنِينَ غَيْرَ مُسَافِحِينَ
فَمَا اسْتَمْتَعْتُم بِهِ مِنْهُنَّ
فَآتُوهُنَّ أُجُورَهُنَّ فَرِيضَةً
وَلَا جُنَاحَ عَلَيْكُمْ
فِيمَا تَرَاضَيْتُم بِهِ مِن بَعْدِ الْفَرِيضَةِ
إِنَّ اللّهَ كَانَ عَلِيمًا حَكِيمًا ۩

25. If any of you have not
The means wherewith
To wed free believing women,
They may wed believing
Girls from among those
Whom your right hands
         possess:
And Allah hath full knowledge
About your Faith.

٢٥ - وَمَن لَّمْ يَسْتَطِعْ مِنكُمْ
طَوْلًا أَن يَنكِحَ الْمُحْصَنَاتِ الْمُؤْمِنَاتِ
فَمِن مَّا مَلَكَتْ أَيْمَانُكُم
مِّن فَتَيَاتِكُمُ الْمُؤْمِنَاتِ
وَاللّهُ أَعْلَمُ بِإِيمَانِكُم بَعْضُكُم مِّن بَعْضٍ

Ye are one from another:
Wed them with the leave
Of their owners, and give them
Their dowers, according to what
Is reasonable: they should be
Chaste, not lustful, nor taking
Paramours: when they
Are taken in wedlock,
If they fall into shame,
Their punishment is half
That for free women.
This (permission) is for those
Among you who fear sin;
But is better for you
That ye practise self-restraint.
And Allah is Oft-Forgiving,
Most Merciful.

فَانْكِحُوهُنَّ بِإِذْنِ أَهْلِهِنَّ
وَآتُوهُنَّ أُجُورَهُنَّ
بِالْمَعْرُوفِ مُحْصَنَاتٍ غَيْرَ مُسَافِحَاتٍ
وَلَا مُتَّخِذَاتِ أَخْدَانٍ
فَإِذَا أُحْصِنَّ فَإِنْ أَتَيْنَ بِفَاحِشَةٍ
فَعَلَيْهِنَّ نِصْفُ مَا عَلَى الْمُحْصَنَاتِ مِنَ
الْعَذَابِ ذَلِكَ لِمَنْ خَشِيَ الْعَنَتَ مِنْكُمْ
وَأَنْ تَصْبِرُوا خَيْرٌ لَكُمْ
وَاللهُ غَفُورٌ رَحِيمٌ ۞

SECTION 5.

26. Allah doth wish
To make clear to you
And to show you
The ordinances of those
Before you; and (He
Doth wish to) turn to you
(In Mercy); and Allah
Is All-Knowing, All-Wise.

٢٦ - يُرِيدُ اللهُ لِيُبَيِّنَ لَكُمْ
وَيَهْدِيَكُمْ سُنَنَ الَّذِينَ مِنْ قَبْلِكُمْ
وَيَتُوبَ عَلَيْكُمْ
وَاللهُ عَلِيمٌ حَكِيمٌ ۞

27. Allah doth wish
To turn to you,
But the wish of those
Who follow their lusts
Is that ye should turn
Away (from Him)—
Far, far away.

٢٧ - وَاللهُ يُرِيدُ أَنْ يَتُوبَ عَلَيْكُمْ
وَيُرِيدُ الَّذِينَ
يَتَّبِعُونَ الشَّهَوَاتِ
أَنْ تَمِيلُوا مَيْلاً عَظِيمًا ۞

28. Allah doth wish
To lighten your (difficulties):
For man was created
Weak (in flesh).

٢٨ - يُرِيدُ اللهُ أَنْ يُخَفِّفَ عَنْكُمْ
وَخُلِقَ الْإِنْسَانُ ضَعِيفًا ۞

29. O ye who believe!
Eat not up your property
Among yourselves in vanities;
But let there be amongst you
Traffic and trade
By mutual good will:

٢٩ - يَا أَيُّهَا الَّذِينَ آمَنُوا لَا تَأْكُلُوا أَمْوَالَكُمْ
بَيْنَكُمْ بِالْبَاطِلِ
إِلَّا أَنْ تَكُونَ تِجَارَةً عَنْ تَرَاضٍ مِنْكُمْ

Nor kill (or destroy)
Yourselves: for verily
Allah hath been to you
Most Merciful!

وَلَا تَقْتُلُوا أَنْفُسَكُمْ ۚ
إِنَّ اللّٰهَ كَانَ بِكُمْ رَحِيمًا ۝

30. If any do that
In rancour and injustice—
Soon shall We cast them
Into the Fire: and easy
It is for Allah.

٣٠ ـ وَمَنْ يَّفْعَلْ ذٰلِكَ عُدْوَانًا وَّظُلْمًا
فَسَوْفَ نُصْلِيهِ نَارًا ۚ
وَكَانَ ذٰلِكَ عَلَى اللّٰهِ يَسِيرًا ۝

31. If ye (but) eschew
The most heinous
Of the things
Which ye are forbidden to do,
We shall expel
Out of you
All the evil in you,
And admit you to a Gate
Of great honour.

٣١ ـ إِنْ تَجْتَنِبُوا كَبَائِرَ
مَا تُنْهَوْنَ عَنْهُ
نُكَفِّرْ عَنْكُمْ سَيِّئَاتِكُمْ
وَنُدْخِلْكُمْ مُّدْخَلًا كَرِيمًا ۝

32. And in nowise covet
Those things in which Allah
Hath bestowed His gifts
More freely on some of you
Than on others: to men
Is allotted what they earn,
And to women what they earn:
But ask Allah of His bounty.
For Allah hath full knowledge
Of all things.

٣٢ ـ وَلَا تَتَمَنَّوْا مَا فَضَّلَ اللّٰهُ بِهِ بَعْضَكُمْ
عَلَى بَعْضٍ ۚ لِلرِّجَالِ نَصِيبٌ مِّمَّا اكْتَسَبُوا
وَلِلنِّسَاءِ نَصِيبٌ مِّمَّا اكْتَسَبْنَ ۚ
وَسْئَلُوا اللّٰهَ مِنْ فَضْلِهِ ۚ
إِنَّ اللّٰهَ كَانَ بِكُلِّ شَيْءٍ عَلِيمًا ۝

33. To (benefit) every one,
We have appointed
Sharers and heirs
To property left
By parents and relatives.
To those, also, to whom
Your right hand was pledged,
Give their due portion.
For truly Allah is witness
To all things.

٣٣ ـ وَلِكُلٍّ جَعَلْنَا مَوَالِيَ
مِمَّا تَرَكَ الْوَالِدَانِ وَالْأَقْرَبُونَ ۚ
وَالَّذِينَ عَقَدَتْ أَيْمَانُكُمْ
فَآتُوهُمْ نَصِيبَهُمْ ۚ
إِنَّ اللّٰهَ كَانَ عَلَى كُلِّ شَيْءٍ شَهِيدًا ۝

SECTION 6.

34. Men are the protectors
And maintainers of women,
Because Allah has given
The one more (strength)
Than the other, and because

٣٤ ـ اَلرِّجَالُ قَوَّامُونَ عَلَى النِّسَاءِ
بِمَا فَضَّلَ اللّٰهُ بَعْضَهُمْ عَلَى بَعْضٍ

They support them
From their means.
Therefore the righteous women
Are devoutly obedient, and
           guard
In (the husband's) absence
What Allah would have them
           guard.
As to those women
On whose part ye fear
Disloyalty and ill-conduct,
Admonish them (first),
(Next), refuse to share their
           beds,
(And last) beat them (lightly);
But if they return to obedience,
Seek not against them
Means (of annoyance):
For Allah is Most High,
Great (above you all).

35. If ye fear a breach
Between them twain,
Appoint (two) arbiters,
One from his family,
And the other from hers;
If they wish for peace,
Allah will cause
Their reconciliation:
For Allah hath full knowledge,
And is acquainted
With all things.

36. Serve Allah, and join not
Any partners with Him;
And do good—
To parents, kinsfolk,
Orphans, those in need,
Neighbours who are near
Neighbours who are strangers,
The Companion by your side,
The wayfarer (ye meet),
And what your right hands
           possess:
For Allah loveth not
The arrogant, the
           vainglorious—

وَبِمَآ أَنْفَقُوا مِنْ أَمْوَالِهِمْ ۚ
فَالصَّالِحَاتُ قَانِتَاتٌ حَافِظَاتٌ لِلْغَيْبِ
بِمَا حَفِظَ اللَّهُ ۚ
وَالَّاتِي تَخَافُونَ نُشُوزَهُنَّ فَعِظُوهُنَّ
وَاهْجُرُوهُنَّ فِي الْمَضَاجِعِ
وَاضْرِبُوهُنَّ ۖ
فَإِنْ أَطَعْنَكُمْ
فَلَا تَبْغُوا عَلَيْهِنَّ سَبِيلًا ۗ
إِنَّ اللَّهَ كَانَ عَلِيًّا كَبِيرًا ۝

٣٥- وَإِنْ خِفْتُمْ شِقَاقَ بَيْنِهِمَا
فَابْعَثُوا حَكَمًا مِنْ أَهْلِهِ
وَحَكَمًا مِنْ أَهْلِهَا ۚ
إِنْ يُرِيدَا إِصْلَاحًا
يُوَفِّقِ اللَّهُ بَيْنَهُمَا ۗ
إِنَّ اللَّهَ كَانَ عَلِيمًا خَبِيرًا ۝

٣٦- وَاعْبُدُوا اللَّهَ وَلَا تُشْرِكُوا بِهِ شَيْئًا
وَبِالْوَالِدَيْنِ إِحْسَانًا
وَبِذِي الْقُرْبَى وَالْيَتَامَى وَالْمَسَاكِينِ
وَالْجَارِ ذِي الْقُرْبَى وَالْجَارِ الْجُنُبِ
وَالصَّاحِبِ بِالْجَنْبِ وَابْنِ السَّبِيلِ ۙ
وَمَا مَلَكَتْ أَيْمَانُكُمْ ۗ
إِنَّ اللَّهَ لَا يُحِبُّ
مَنْ كَانَ مُخْتَالًا فَخُورًا ۝

37. (Nor) those who are niggardly,
Or enjoin niggardliness on others,
Or hide the bounties
Which Allah hath bestowed
On them; for We have prepared,
For those who resist Faith,
A Punishment that steeps
Them in contempt—

٣٧ - اَلَّذِيْنَ يَبْخَلُوْنَ
وَيَأْمُرُوْنَ النَّاسَ بِالْبُخْلِ
وَيَكْتُمُوْنَ مَاۤ اٰتٰهُمُ اللّٰهُ مِنْ فَضْلِهٖ
وَاَعْتَدْنَا لِلْكٰفِرِيْنَ عَذَابًا مُّهِيْنًا ۚ

38. Nor those who spend
Of their substance, to be seen
Of men, but have no faith
In Allah and the Last Day:
If any take the Evil One
For their intimate,
What a dreadful intimate he is!

٣٨ - وَالَّذِيْنَ يُنْفِقُوْنَ اَمْوَالَهُمْ رِئَآءَ النَّاسِ
وَلَا يُؤْمِنُوْنَ بِاللّٰهِ وَلَا بِالْيَوْمِ الْاٰخِرِ ۚ
وَمَنْ يَّكُنِ الشَّيْطٰنُ لَهٗ قَرِيْنًا فَسَآءَ
قَرِيْنًا ۚ

39. And what burden
Were it on them if they
Had faith in Allah
And in the Last Day,
And they spent
Out of what Allah hath
Given them for sustenance?
For Allah hath full
Knowledge of them.

٣٩ - وَمَاذَا عَلَيْهِمْ لَوْ اٰمَنُوْا بِاللّٰهِ
وَالْيَوْمِ الْاٰخِرِ
وَاَنْفَقُوْا مِمَّا رَزَقَهُمُ اللّٰهُ ۚ
وَكَانَ اللّٰهُ بِهِمْ عَلِيْمًا ۚ

40. Allah is never unjust
In the least degree:
If there is any good (done),
He doubleth it,
And giveth from His own
Presence a great reward.

٤٠ - اِنَّ اللّٰهَ لَا يَظْلِمُ مِثْقَالَ ذَرَّةٍ ۚ
وَاِنْ تَكُ حَسَنَةً يُّضٰعِفْهَا
وَيُؤْتِ مِنْ لَّدُنْهُ اَجْرًا عَظِيْمًا ۚ

41. How then if We brought
From each People a witness,
And We brought thee
As a witness against
These People!

٤١ - فَكَيْفَ اِذَا جِئْنَا مِنْ كُلِّ اُمَّةٍ بِشَهِيْدٍ
وَّجِئْنَا بِكَ عَلٰى هٰۤؤُلَآءِ شَهِيْدًا ۚ

42. On that day
Those who reject Faith
And disobey the Messenger
Will wish that the earth
Were made one with them:
But never will they hide
A single fact from Allah!

٤٢ - يَوْمَئِذٍ يَّوَدُّ الَّذِيْنَ كَفَرُوْا
وَعَصَوُا الرَّسُوْلَ
لَوْ تُسَوّٰى بِهِمُ الْاَرْضُ ۚ
وَلَا يَكْتُمُوْنَ اللّٰهَ حَدِيْثًا ۚ

SECTION 7.

43. O ye who believe!
Approach not prayers
With a mind befogged,
Until ye can understand
All that ye say—
Nor in a state
Of ceremonial impurity
(Except when travelling on the
                    road),
Until after washing
Your whole body.
If ye are ill,
Or on a journey,
Or one of you cometh
From offices of nature,
Or ye have been
In contact with women,
And ye find no water,
Then take for yourselves
Clean sand or earth,
And rub therewith
Your faces and hands.
For Allah doth blot out sins
And forgive again and again.

٤٣- يَٰأَيُّهَا الَّذِينَ ءَامَنُوا لَا تَقْرَبُوا الصَّلَوٰةَ
وَأَنْتُمْ سُكَٰرَىٰ
حَتَّىٰ تَعْلَمُوا مَا تَقُولُونَ
وَلَا جُنُبًا إِلَّا عَابِرِى سَبِيلٍ
حَتَّىٰ تَغْتَسِلُوا ۚ وَإِنْ كُنْتُمْ مَرْضَىٰ
أَوْ عَلَىٰ سَفَرٍ
أَوْ جَآءَ أَحَدٌ مِنْكُمْ مِنَ الْغَآئِطِ
أَوْ لَٰمَسْتُمُ النِّسَآءَ
فَلَمْ تَجِدُوا مَآءً
فَتَيَمَّمُوا صَعِيدًا طَيِّبًا
فَامْسَحُوا بِوُجُوهِكُمْ وَأَيْدِيكُمْ
إِنَّ اللَّهَ كَانَ عَفُوًّا غَفُورًا ۝

44. Hast thou not turned
Thy vision to those
Who were given a portion
Of the Book? They traffic
In error, and wish that ye
Should lose the right path.

٤٤- أَلَمْ تَرَ إِلَى الَّذِينَ أُوتُوا نَصِيبًا مِنَ
الْكِتَٰبِ يَشْتَرُونَ الضَّلَٰلَةَ
وَيُرِيدُونَ أَنْ تَضِلُّوا السَّبِيلَ ۝

45. But Allah hath full knowledge
Of your enemies:
Allah is enough for a Protector,
And Allah is enough for a Helper.

٤٥- وَاللَّهُ أَعْلَمُ بِأَعْدَآئِكُمْ
وَكَفَىٰ بِاللَّهِ وَلِيًّا ۚ وَكَفَىٰ بِاللَّهِ نَصِيرًا ۝

46. Of the Jews there are those
Who displace words
From their (right) places,
And say: "We hear
And we disobey";
And "Hear, may you not
Hear;" and "*Rā'inā*";
With a twist of their tongues
And a slander to Faith.
If only they had said:
"We hear and we obey";

٤٦- مِنَ الَّذِينَ هَادُوا يُحَرِّفُونَ الْكَلِمَ
عَنْ مَوَاضِعِهِ
وَيَقُولُونَ سَمِعْنَا وَعَصَيْنَا
وَاسْمَعْ غَيْرَ مُسْمَعٍ وَرَاعِنَا لَيًّا بِأَلْسِنَتِهِمْ
وَطَعْنًا فِي الدِّينِ ۚ وَلَوْ أَنَّهُمْ قَالُوا سَمِعْنَا
وَأَطَعْنَا وَاسْمَعْ

And "Do hear";
And "Do look at us":
It would have been better
For them, and more proper;
But Allah hath cursed them
For their Unbelief; and but few
Of them will believe.

وَانْظُرْنَا لَكَانَ خَيْرًا لَّهُمْ وَاَقْوَمَ ۙ

وَلَٰكِنْ لَّعَنَهُمُ اللّٰهُ

بِكُفْرِهِمْ فَلَا يُؤْمِنُوْنَ اِلَّا قَلِيْلًا ۟

47. Ⓞ ye People of the Book!
Believe in what We
Have (now) revealed, confirming
What was (already) with you,
Before We change the face and
                        fame
Of some (of you) beyond all
                        recognition,
And turn them hindwards,
Or curse them as We cursed
The Sabbath-breakers,
For the decision of Allah
Must be carried out.

٤٧- يٰۤاَيُّهَا الَّذِيْنَ اُوْتُوا الْكِتٰبَ اٰمِنُوْا
بِمَا نَزَّلْنَا مُصَدِّقًا لِّمَا مَعَكُمْ
مِّنْ قَبْلِ اَنْ نَّطْمِسَ وُجُوْهًا
فَنَرُدَّهَا عَلٰۤى اَدْبَارِهَاۤ
اَوْ نَلْعَنَهُمْ كَمَا لَعَنَّاۤ اَصْحٰبَ السَّبْتِ ۚ
وَكَانَ اَمْرُ اللّٰهِ مَفْعُوْلًا

48. Allah forgiveth not
That partners should be set up
With Him; but He forgiveth
Anything else, to whom
He pleaseth; to set up
Partners with Allah
Is to devise a sin
Most heinous indeed.

٤٨- اِنَّ اللّٰهَ لَا يَغْفِرُ اَنْ يُّشْرَكَ بِهٖ
وَيَغْفِرُ مَا دُوْنَ ذٰلِكَ لِمَنْ يَّشَآءُ ۚ
وَمَنْ يُّشْرِكْ بِاللّٰهِ
فَقَدِ افْتَرٰۤى اِثْمًا عَظِيْمًا ۟

49. Ⓗast thou not turned
Thy vision to those
Who claim sanctity
For themselves?
Nay—but Allah
Doth sanctify
Whom He pleaseth.
But never will they
Fail to receive justice
In the least little thing.

٤٩- اَلَمْ تَرَ اِلَى الَّذِيْنَ
يُزَكُّوْنَ اَنْفُسَهُمْ ۗ
بَلِ اللّٰهُ يُزَكِّيْ مَنْ يَّشَآءُ
وَلَا يُظْلَمُوْنَ فَتِيْلًا

50. Behold! how they invent
A lie against Allah!
But that by itself
Is a manifest sin!

SECTION 8.

٥٠- اُنْظُرْ كَيْفَ يَفْتَرُوْنَ عَلَى اللّٰهِ الْكَذِبَ ۗ
وَكَفٰى بِهٖۤ اِثْمًا مُّبِيْنًا ۟

51. Ⓗast thou not turned

٥١- اَلَمْ تَرَ اِلَى الَّذِيْنَ اُوْتُوْا

Thy vision to those
Who were given a portion
Of the Book? They believe
In Sorcery and Evil,
And say to the Unbelievers
That they are better guided
In the (right) way
Than the Believers!

نَصِيبًا مِّنَ الْكِتٰبِ
يُؤْمِنُونَ بِالْجِبْتِ وَالطَّاغُوتِ
وَيَقُولُونَ لِلَّذِينَ كَفَرُوا هٰؤُلَاءِ
أَهْدٰى مِنَ الَّذِينَ اٰمَنُوا سَبِيلًا

52. They are (men) whom
Allah hath cursed:
And those whom Allah
Hath cursed, thou wilt find,
Have no one to help.

٥٢- أُولٰئِكَ الَّذِينَ لَعَنَهُمُ اللهُ
وَمَنْ يَلْعَنِ اللهُ
فَلَنْ تَجِدَ لَهُ نَصِيرًا ۚ

53. Have they a share
In dominion or power?
Behold, they give not a farthing
To their fellow-men?

٥٣- أَمْ لَهُمْ نَصِيبٌ مِّنَ الْمُلْكِ
فَإِذًا لَّا يُؤْتُونَ النَّاسَ نَقِيرًا ۙ

54. Or do they envy mankind
For what Allah hath given them
Of His bounty? But We
Had already given the people
Of Abraham the Book
And Wisdom, and conferred
Upon them a great kingdom.

٥٤- أَمْ يَحْسُدُونَ النَّاسَ
عَلٰى مَا اٰتٰهُمُ اللهُ مِنْ فَضْلِهِ
فَقَدْ اٰتَيْنَا اٰلَ إِبْرٰهِيمَ الْكِتٰبَ
وَالْحِكْمَةَ وَاٰتَيْنٰهُمْ مُّلْكًا عَظِيمًا ۙ

55. Some of them believed,
And some of them averted
Their faces from him; and enough
Is Hell for a burning fire.

٥٥- فَمِنْهُمْ مَّنْ اٰمَنَ بِهِ وَمِنْهُمْ مَّنْ
صَدَّ عَنْهُ ۚ وَكَفٰى بِجَهَنَّمَ سَعِيرًا ۗ

56. Those who reject
Our Signs, We shall soon
Cast into the Fire;
As often as their skins
Are roasted through,
We shall change them
For fresh skins,
That they may taste
The Penalty: for Allah
Is Exalted in Power, Wise.

٥٦- إِنَّ الَّذِينَ كَفَرُوا بِاٰيٰتِنَا
سَوْفَ نُصْلِيهِمْ نَارًا ۚ
كُلَّمَا نَضِجَتْ جُلُودُهُمْ بَدَّلْنٰهُمْ جُلُودًا
غَيْرَهَا لِيَذُوقُوا الْعَذَابَ ۗ
إِنَّ اللهَ كَانَ عَزِيزًا حَكِيمًا ۗ

57. But those who believe
And do deeds of righteousness,
We shall soon admit to Gardens,
With rivers flowing beneath—

٥٧- وَالَّذِينَ اٰمَنُوا وَعَمِلُوا الصّٰلِحٰتِ
سَنُدْخِلُهُمْ جَنّٰتٍ تَجْرِى

Their eternal home;
Therein shall they have
Companions pure and holy:
We shall admit them
To shades, cool and ever
           deepening.

مِنْ تَحْتِهَا الْأَنْهَارُ خٰلِدِيْنَ فِيْهَآ أَبَدًا ۖ
لَهُمْ فِيْهَآ أَزْوَاجٌ مُّطَهَّرَةٌ ۖ
وَّنُدْخِلُهُمْ ظِلًّا ظَلِيْلًا ۝

58. Allah doth command you
To render back your Trusts
To those to whom they are due;
And when ye judge
Between man and man,
That ye judge with justice:
Verily how excellent
Is the teaching which He giveth
           you!
For Allah is He Who heareth
And seeth all things.

٥٨ـ إِنَّ اللّٰهَ يَأْمُرُكُمْ أَنْ تُؤَدُّوا الْأَمٰنٰتِ
إِلٰى أَهْلِهَا ۙ وَإِذَا حَكَمْتُمْ بَيْنَ النَّاسِ
أَنْ تَحْكُمُوْا بِالْعَدْلِ ۚ
إِنَّ اللّٰهَ نِعِمَّا يَعِظُكُمْ بِهٖ ۗ
إِنَّ اللّٰهَ كَانَ سَمِيْعًا بَصِيْرًا ۝

59. O ye who believe!
Obey Allah, and obey the
           Messenger,
And those charged
With authority among you.
If ye differ in anything
Among yourselves, refer it
To Allah and His Messenger,
If ye do believe in Allah
And the Last Day:
That is best, and most suitable
For final determination.

       SECTION 9.

٥٩ـ يٰٓأَيُّهَا الَّذِيْنَ اٰمَنُوْٓا
أَطِيْعُوا اللّٰهَ وَأَطِيْعُوا الرَّسُوْلَ وَأُولِي الْأَمْرِ
مِنْكُمْ ۚ فَإِنْ تَنَازَعْتُمْ فِيْ شَيْءٍ
فَرُدُّوْهُ إِلَى اللّٰهِ وَالرَّسُوْلِ
إِنْ كُنْتُمْ تُؤْمِنُوْنَ بِاللّٰهِ وَالْيَوْمِ الْاٰخِرِ ۚ
ذٰلِكَ خَيْرٌ وَّأَحْسَنُ تَأْوِيْلًا ۝ ۞

60. Hast thou not turned
Thy vision to those[581]
Who declare that they believe
In the revelations
That have come to thee
And to those before thee?
Their (real) wish is
To resort together for judgement
(In their disputes)
To the Evil One,
Though they were ordered
To reject him.
But Satan's wish
Is to lead them astray
Far away (from the Right).

٦٠ـ أَلَمْ تَرَ إِلَى الَّذِيْنَ
يَزْعُمُوْنَ أَنَّهُمْ اٰمَنُوْا بِمَآ أُنْزِلَ إِلَيْكَ
وَمَآ أُنْزِلَ مِنْ قَبْلِكَ
يُرِيْدُوْنَ أَنْ يَّتَحَاكَمُوْٓا
إِلَى الطَّاغُوْتِ
وَقَدْ أُمِرُوْٓا أَنْ يَّكْفُرُوْا بِهٖ ۖ
وَيُرِيْدُ الشَّيْطٰنُ
أَنْ يُّضِلَّهُمْ ضَلٰلًا بَعِيْدًا ۝

61. When it is said to them:
"Come to what Allah hath
revealed,
And to the Messenger.":
Thou seest the Hypocrites avert
Their faces from thee in disgust.

٦١- وَإِذَا قِيْلَ لَهُمْ تَعَالَوْا إِلَى مَاۤ أَنْزَلَ اللّٰهُ
وَإِلَى الرَّسُوْلِ رَأَيْتَ الْمُنٰفِقِيْنَ يَصُدُّوْنَ
عَنْكَ صُدُوْدًا ۚ

62. How then, when they are
Seized by misfortune,
Because of the deeds
Which their hands have sent forth?
Then they come to thee,
Swearing by Allah:
"We meant no more
Than goodwill and conciliation!"

٦٢- فَكَيْفَ إِذَاۤ أَصَابَتْهُمْ مُّصِيْبَةٌۢ
بِمَا قَدَّمَتْ أَيْدِيْهِمْ
ثُمَّ جَآءُوْكَ يَحْلِفُوْنَ ۖ
بِاللّٰهِ إِنْ أَرَدْنَاۤ إِلَّاۤ إِحْسَانًا وَّتَوْفِيْقًا ۞

63. Those men—Allah knows
What is in their hearts;
So keep clear of them,
But admonish them,
And speak to them a word
To reach their very souls.

٦٣- أُولٰٓئِكَ الَّذِيْنَ يَعْلَمُ اللّٰهُ مَا فِيْ قُلُوْبِهِمْ
فَأَعْرِضْ عَنْهُمْ وَعِظْهُمْ
وَقُلْ لَّهُمْ فِيْ أَنْفُسِهِمْ قَوْلًاۢ بَلِيْغًا ۞

64. We sent not a Messenger,
But to be obeyed, in accordance
With the Will of Allah.
If they had only,
When they were unjust
To themselves,
Come unto thee
And asked Allah's forgiveness,
And the Messenger had asked
Forgiveness for them,
They would have found
Allah indeed Oft-Returning,
Most Merciful.

٦٤- وَمَاۤ أَرْسَلْنَا مِنْ رَّسُوْلٍ
إِلَّا لِيُطَاعَ بِإِذْنِ اللّٰهِ ۚ
وَلَوْ أَنَّهُمْ إِذْ ظَّلَمُوْۤا أَنْفُسَهُمْ
جَآءُوْكَ فَاسْتَغْفَرُوا اللّٰهَ
وَاسْتَغْفَرَ لَهُمُ الرَّسُوْلُ
لَوَجَدُوا اللّٰهَ تَوَّابًا رَّحِيْمًا ۞

65. But no, by the Lord,
They can have
No (real) Faith,
Until they make thee judge
In all disputes between them,
And find in their souls
No resistance against
Thy decisions, but accept
Them with the fullest
conviction.

٦٥- فَلَا وَرَبِّكَ لَا يُؤْمِنُوْنَ
حَتّٰى يُحَكِّمُوْكَ فِيْمَا شَجَرَ بَيْنَهُمْ
ثُمَّ لَا يَجِدُوْا فِيْۤ أَنْفُسِهِمْ
حَرَجًا مِّمَّا قَضَيْتَ وَيُسَلِّمُوْا تَسْلِيْمًا ۞

66. If We had ordered them
To sacrifice their lives
Or to leave their homes,
Very few of them
Would have done it:
But if they had done
What they were (actually) told,
It would have been best
For them, and would have gone
Farthest to strengthen their (faith);

٦٦ـ وَلَوْ أَنَّا كَتَبْنَا عَلَيْهِمْ أَنِ اقْتُلُوْا أَنْفُسَكُمْ أَوِ اخْرُجُوْا مِنْ دِيَارِكُمْ مَّا فَعَلُوْهُ إِلَّا قَلِيْلٌ مِّنْهُمْ وَلَوْ أَنَّهُمْ فَعَلُوْا مَا يُوْعَظُوْنَ بِهِ لَكَانَ خَيْرًا لَّهُمْ وَأَشَدَّ تَثْبِيْتًا ۙ

67. And We should then have
Given them from Our Presence
A great reward;

٦٧ـ وَّإِذًا لَّآتَيْنَاهُمْ مِّنْ لَّدُنَّا أَجْرًا عَظِيْمًا ۙ

68. And We should have
Shown them the Straight Way.

٦٨ـ وَّلَهَدَيْنَاهُمْ صِرَاطًا مُّسْتَقِيْمًا ۙ

69. All who obey Allah
And the Messenger
Are in the Company
Of those on whom
Is the Grace of Allah—
Of the Prophets (who teach),
The Sincere (lovers of Truth),
The Witnesses (who testify),
And the Righteous (who do good):
Ah! what a beautiful Fellowship!

٦٩ـ وَمَنْ يُّطِعِ اللّٰهَ وَالرَّسُوْلَ فَأُولٰٓئِكَ مَعَ الَّذِيْنَ أَنْعَمَ اللّٰهُ عَلَيْهِمْ مِّنَ النَّبِيِّيْنَ وَالصِّدِّيْقِيْنَ وَالشُّهَدَآءِ وَالصّٰلِحِيْنَ ۚ وَحَسُنَ أُولٰٓئِكَ رَفِيْقًا ۙ

70. Such is the Bounty
From Allah; and sufficient
Is it that Allah knoweth all.

٧٠ـ ذٰلِكَ الْفَضْلُ مِنَ اللّٰهِ وَكَفٰى بِاللّٰهِ عَلِيْمًا ۙ

SECTION 10.

71. O ye who believe!
Take your precautions,
And either go forth in parties
Or go forth all together.

٧١ـ يٰٓأَيُّهَا الَّذِيْنَ آمَنُوْا خُذُوْا حِذْرَكُمْ فَانْفِرُوْا ثُبَاتٍ أَوِ انْفِرُوْا جَمِيْعًا ۙ

72. There are certainly among you
Men who would tarry behind;
If a misfortune befalls you,
They say: "Allah did favour us
In that we were not
Present among them."

٧٢ـ وَإِنَّ مِنْكُمْ لَمَنْ لَّيُبَطِّئَنَّ ۚ فَإِنْ أَصَابَتْكُمْ مُّصِيْبَةٌ قَالَ قَدْ أَنْعَمَ اللّٰهُ عَلَيَّ إِذْ لَمْ أَكُنْ مَّعَهُمْ شَهِيْدًا ۙ

73. But if good fortune comes to
you

٧٣ـ وَلَئِنْ أَصَابَكُمْ فَضْلٌ مِّنَ اللّٰهِ

From Allah, they would be sure
To say—as if there had never
been
Ties of affection between you
and them—
"Oh! I wish I had been with
them;
A fine thing should I then
Have made of it!"

74. Let those fight
In the cause of Allah
Who sell the life of this world
For the Hereafter.
To him who fighteth
In the cause of Allah—
Whether he is slain
Or gets victory—
Soon shall We give him
A reward of great (value).

٧٤- فَلْيُقَاتِلْ فِي سَبِيلِ اللهِ
الَّذِينَ يَشْرُونَ الْحَيٰوةَ الدُّنْيَا بِالْاٰخِرَةِ ۗ
وَمَنْ يُّقَاتِلْ فِي سَبِيلِ اللهِ
فَيُقْتَلْ اَوْ يَغْلِبْ
فَسَوْفَ نُؤْتِيهِ اَجْرًا عَظِيمًا ۝

75. And why should ye not
Fight in the cause of Allah
And of those who, being
weak,
Are ill-treated (and
oppressed)?—
Men, women, and children,
Whose cry is: "Our Lord!
Rescue us from this town,
Whose people are oppressors;
And raise for us trom Thee
One who will protect;
And raise for us from Thee
One who will help!"

٧٥- وَمَا لَكُمْ لَا تُقَاتِلُوْنَ فِي سَبِيلِ اللهِ
وَالْمُسْتَضْعَفِيْنَ مِنَ الرِّجَالِ وَالنِّسَاءِ وَ
الْوِلْدَانِ الَّذِينَ يَقُوْلُوْنَ رَبَّنَا اَخْرِجْنَا مِنْ
هٰذِهِ الْقَرْيَةِ الظَّالِمِ اَهْلُهَا ۚ
وَاجْعَلْ لَّنَا مِنْ لَّدُنْكَ وَلِيًّا ۙ
وَّاجْعَلْ لَّنَا مِنْ لَّدُنْكَ نَصِيرًا ۝

76. Those who believe
Fight in the cause of Allah,
And those who reject Faith
Fight in the cause of Evil:
So fight ye against the
Friends of Satan: feeble indeed
Is the cunning of Satan.

SECTION 11.

٧٦- اَلَّذِينَ اٰمَنُوْا يُقَاتِلُوْنَ فِي سَبِيلِ اللهِ
وَالَّذِينَ كَفَرُوْا يُقَاتِلُوْنَ فِي سَبِيلِ
الطَّاغُوتِ فَقَاتِلُوْا اَوْلِيَاءَ الشَّيْطٰنِ ۚ
اِنَّ كَيْدَ الشَّيْطٰنِ كَانَ ضَعِيْفًا ۝

77. Hast thou not turned
Thy vision to those
Who were told to hold back
Their hands (from fight)

٧٧- اَلَمْ تَرَ اِلَى الَّذِينَ
قِيْلَ لَهُمْ كُفُّوْا اَيْدِيَكُمْ

But establish regular prayers
And spend in regular Charity?
When (at length) the order
For fighting was issued to them,
Behold! a section of them
Feared men as—
Or even more than—
They should have feared Allah:
They said: "Our Lord!
Why hast Thou ordered us
To fight? Wouldst Thou not
Grant us respite
To our (natural) term,
Near (enough)?" Say: "Short
Is the enjoyment of this world:
The Hereafter is the best
For those who do right;
Never will ye be
Dealt with unjustly
In the very least!

78. "Wherever ye are,
Death will find you out,
Even if ye are in towers
Built up strong and high!"

If some good befalls them,
They say, "This is from Allah";
But if evil, they say,
"This is from thee" (O Prophet).
Say: "All things are from Allah."
But what hath come
To these people,
That they fail
To understand
A single fact?

79. Whatever good, (O man!)
Happens to thee, is from Allah;
But whatever evil happens
To thee, is from thy (own) soul.
And We have sent thee
As a Messenger
To (instruct) mankind.
And enough is Allah
For a witness.

80. He who obeys
The Messenger, obeys Allah;

But if any turn away,
We have not sent thee
To watch over
Their (evil deeds).

81. They have "Obedience"
On their lips; but
When they leave thee,
A section of them
Meditate all night
On things very different
From what thou tellest them.
But Allah records
Their nightly (plots):
So keep clear of them,
And put thy trust in Allah,
And enough is Allah
As a disposer of affairs.

وَمَن تَوَلَّىٰ
فَمَآ أَرْسَلْنَاكَ عَلَيْهِمْ حَفِيظًا

٨١- وَيَقُولُونَ طَاعَةٌ
فَإِذَا بَرَزُوا مِنْ عِنْدِكَ بَيَّتَ طَآئِفَةٌ مِنْهُم
غَيْرَ الَّذِى تَقُولُ
وَاللَّهُ يَكْتُبُ مَا يُبَيِّتُونَ
فَأَعْرِضْ عَنْهُمْ
وَتَوَكَّلْ عَلَى اللَّهِ وَكَفَىٰ بِاللَّهِ وَكِيلًا

82. Do they not consider
The Qur'ān (with care)?
Had it been from other
Than Allah, they would surely
Have found therein
Much discrepancy.

٨٢- أَفَلَا يَتَدَبَّرُونَ الْقُرْآنَ
وَلَوْ كَانَ مِنْ عِنْدِ غَيْرِ اللَّهِ
لَوَجَدُوا فِيهِ اخْتِلَافًا كَثِيرًا

83. When there comes to them
Some matter touching
(Public) safety or fear,
They divulge it.
If they had only referred it
To the Messenger or to those
Charged with authority
Among them, the proper
Investigators would have
Tested it from them (direct).
Were it not for the Grace
And Mercy of Allah unto you,
All but a few of you
Would have followed Satan.

٨٣- وَإِذَا جَآءَهُمْ
أَمْرٌ مِنَ الْأَمْنِ أَوِ الْخَوْفِ أَذَاعُوا بِهِ
وَلَوْ رَدُّوهُ إِلَى الرَّسُولِ وَإِلَىٰ
أُولِي الْأَمْرِ مِنْهُمْ
لَعَلِمَهُ الَّذِينَ يَسْتَنْبِطُونَهُ مِنْهُمْ
وَلَوْلَا فَضْلُ اللَّهِ عَلَيْكُمْ وَرَحْمَتُهُ
لَاتَّبَعْتُمُ الشَّيْطَانَ إِلَّا قَلِيلًا

84. Then fight in Allah's cause—
Thou art held responsible
Only for thyself—
And rouse the Believers.
It may be that Allah
Will restrain the fury
Of the Unbelievers;

٨٤- فَقَاتِلْ فِى سَبِيلِ اللَّهِ
لَا تُكَلَّفُ إِلَّا نَفْسَكَ وَحَرِّضِ الْمُؤْمِنِينَ
عَسَى اللَّهُ أَنْ يَكُفَّ بَأْسَ
الَّذِينَ كَفَرُوا

For Allah is the strongest
In might and in punishment.

وَاللَّهُ أَشَدُّ بَأْسًا وَّأَشَدُّ تَنْكِيلًا ۝

85. Whoever recommends
And helps a good cause
Becomes a partner therein:
And whoever recommends
And helps an evil cause,
Shares in its burden:
And Allah hath power
Over all things.

٨٥- مَنْ يَّشْفَعْ شَفَاعَةً حَسَنَةً يَّكُنْ لَّهُ
نَصِيبٌ مِّنْهَا ۚ وَمَنْ يَّشْفَعْ شَفَاعَةً سَيِّئَةً
يَّكُنْ لَّهُ كِفْلٌ مِّنْهَا ۗ
وَكَانَ اللَّهُ عَلَى كُلِّ شَيْءٍ مُّقِيتًا ۝

86. When a (courteous) greeting
Is offered you, meet it
With a greeting still more
Courteous, or (at least)
Of equal courtesy.
Allah takes careful account
Of all things.

٨٦- وَإِذَا حُيِّيتُمْ بِتَحِيَّةٍ
فَحَيُّوا بِأَحْسَنَ مِنْهَا
أَوْ رُدُّوهَا ۗ
إِنَّ اللَّهَ كَانَ عَلَى كُلِّ شَيْءٍ حَسِيبًا ۝

87. Allah! There is no god
But He: of a surety
He will gather together
Against the Day of Judgement,
About which there is no doubt.
And whose word can be
Truer than Allah's?

SECTION 12.

٨٧- اللَّهُ لَا إِلَهَ إِلَّا هُوَ ۚ
لَيَجْمَعَنَّكُمْ إِلَى يَوْمِ الْقِيَامَةِ
لَا رَيْبَ فِيهِ ۗ
وَمَنْ أَصْدَقُ مِنَ اللَّهِ حَدِيثًا ۝

88. Why should ye be
Divided into two parties
About the Hypocrites?
Allah hath upset them
For their (evil) deeds.
Would ye guide those
Whom Allah hath thrown
Out of the Way? For those
Whom Allah hath thrown
Out of the Way, never
Shalt thou find the Way.

٨٨- فَمَا لَكُمْ فِي الْمُنَافِقِينَ فِئَتَيْنِ
وَاللَّهُ أَرْكَسَهُمْ بِمَا كَسَبُوا ۚ
أَتُرِيدُونَ أَنْ تَهْدُوا مَنْ أَضَلَّ اللَّهُ ۗ
وَمَنْ يُّضْلِلِ اللَّهُ
فَلَنْ تَجِدَ لَهُ سَبِيلًا ۝

89. They but wish that ye
Should reject Faith,
As they do, and thus be
On the same footing (as they):
So take not friends
From their ranks

٨٩- وَدُّوا لَوْ تَكْفُرُونَ كَمَا كَفَرُوا
فَتَكُونُونَ سَوَاءً ۖ
فَلَا تَتَّخِذُوا مِنْهُمْ أَوْلِيَاءَ

Until they flee[607]
In the way of Allah
(From what is forbidden).
But if they turn renegades,
Seize them and slay them
Wherever ye find them;
And (in any case) take
No friends or helpers
From their ranks—

حَتّٰى يُهَاجِرُوْا فِىْ سَبِيْلِ اللّٰهِ
فَاِنْ تَوَلَّوْا
فَخُذُوْهُمْ وَاقْتُلُوْهُمْ حَيْثُ وَجَدْتُّمُوْهُمْ
وَلَا تَتَّخِذُوْا مِنْهُمْ وَلِيًّا وَّلَا نَصِيْرًا ۙ

90. Except those who join
A group between whom
And you there is a treaty
(Of peace), or those who
           approach
You with hearts restraining
Them from fighting you
As well as fighting their own
People. If Allah had pleased,
He could have given them
Power over you, and they
Would have fought you:
Therefore if they withdraw
From you but fight you not,
And (instead) send you
(Guarantees of) peace, then Allah
Hath opened no way
For you (to war against them).

٩٠ ـ اِلَّا الَّذِيْنَ يَصِلُوْنَ اِلٰى قَوْمٍ بَيْنَكُمْ
وَبَيْنَهُمْ مِّيْثَاقٌ
اَوْ جَآءُوْكُمْ حَصِرَتْ صُدُوْرُهُمْ
اَنْ يُّقَاتِلُوْكُمْ اَوْ يُقَاتِلُوْا قَوْمَهُمْ ۚ
وَلَوْ شَآءَ اللّٰهُ لَسَلَّطَهُمْ عَلَيْكُمْ فَلَقَاتَلُوْكُمْ ۚ
فَاِنِ اعْتَزَلُوْكُمْ فَلَمْ يُقَاتِلُوْكُمْ
وَاَلْقَوْا اِلَيْكُمُ السَّلَمَ ۙ
فَمَا جَعَلَ اللّٰهُ
لَكُمْ عَلَيْهِمْ سَبِيْلًا

91. Others you will find
That wish to gain
Your confidence as well
As that of their people:
Every time they are sent back
To temptation, they succumb
Thereto; if they withdraw not
From you nor give you
           (guarantees)

Of peace besides
Restraining their hands,
Seize them and slay them
Wherever ye get them;
In their case
We have provided you
With a clear argument
Against them.

٩١ ـ سَتَجِدُوْنَ اٰخَرِيْنَ
يُرِيْدُوْنَ اَنْ يَّأْمَنُوْكُمْ وَيَأْمَنُوْا قَوْمَهُمْ ۚ
كُلَّمَا رُدُّوْا اِلَى الْفِتْنَةِ اُرْكِسُوْا فِيْهَا ۚ
فَاِنْ لَّمْ يَعْتَزِلُوْكُمْ
وَيُلْقُوْا اِلَيْكُمُ السَّلَمَ وَيَكُفُّوْا اَيْدِيَهُمْ
فَخُذُوْهُمْ وَاقْتُلُوْهُمْ حَيْثُ ثَقِفْتُمُوْهُمْ ۚ
وَاُولٰئِكُمْ جَعَلْنَا لَكُمْ عَلَيْهِمْ سُلْطٰنًا
مُّبِيْنًا ۟

SECTION 13.

92. Never should a Believer
Kill a Believer; but
(If it so happens) by mistake,
(Compensation is due);
If one (so) kills a Believer,
It is ordained that he
Should free a believing slave,
And pay compensation
To the deceased's family,
Unless they remit it freely.
If the deceased belonged
To a people at war with you,
And he was a Believer,
The freeing of a believing slave
(Is enough). If he belonged
To a people with whom
Ye have. a treaty of mutual
Alliance, compensation should
Be paid to his family,
And a believing slave be freed.
For those who find this
Beyond their means, (is
           prescribed)
A fast for two months
Running: by way of repentance
To Allah; for Allah hath
All knowledge and all wisdom.

٩٢- وَمَا كَانَ لِمُؤْمِنٍ اَنْ يَّقْتُلَ مُؤْمِنًا اِلَّا خَطَأً وَمَنْ قَتَلَ مُؤْمِنًا خَطَأً فَتَحْرِيْرُ رَقَبَةٍ مُّؤْمِنَةٍ وَّدِيَةٌ مُّسَلَّمَةٌ اِلَى اَهْلِهِ اِلَّا اَنْ يَّصَّدَّقُوْا فَاِنْ كَانَ مِنْ قَوْمٍ عَدُوٍّ لَّكُمْ وَهُوَ مُؤْمِنٌ فَتَحْرِيْرُ رَقَبَةٍ مُّؤْمِنَةٍ وَاِنْ كَانَ مِنْ قَوْمٍ بَيْنَكُمْ وَبَيْنَهُمْ مِّيْثَاقٌ فَدِيَةٌ مُّسَلَّمَةٌ اِلَى اَهْلِهِ وَتَحْرِيْرُ رَقَبَةٍ مُّؤْمِنَةٍ فَمَنْ لَّمْ يَجِدْ فَصِيَامُ شَهْرَيْنِ مُتَتَابِعَيْنِ تَوْبَةً مِّنَ اللّٰهِ وَكَانَ اللّٰهُ عَلِيْمًا حَكِيْمًا

93. If a man kills a Believer
Intentionally, his recompense
Is Hell, to abide therein
(Forever): and the wrath
And the curse of Allah
Are upon him, and
A dreadful penalty
Is prepared for him.

٩٣- وَمَنْ يَّقْتُلْ مُؤْمِنًا مُّتَعَمِّدًا فَجَزَاؤُهُ جَهَنَّمُ خَالِدًا فِيْهَا وَغَضِبَ اللّٰهُ عَلَيْهِ وَلَعَنَهُ وَاَعَدَّ لَهُ عَذَابًا عَظِيْمًا

94. O ye who believe!
When ye go abroad
In the cause of Allah,
Investigate carefully,
And say not to anyone
Who offers you a salutation:
"Thou art none of a Believer!"
Coveting the perishable goods
Of this life: with Allah
Are profits and spoils abundant.

٩٤- يَاَيُّهَا الَّذِيْنَ اٰمَنُوْا اِذَا ضَرَبْتُمْ فِيْ سَبِيْلِ اللّٰهِ فَتَبَيَّنُوْا وَلَا تَقُوْلُوْا لِمَنْ اَلْقَى اِلَيْكُمُ السَّلٰمَ لَسْتَ مُؤْمِنًا تَبْتَغُوْنَ عَرَضَ الْحَيٰوةِ الدُّنْيَا فَعِنْدَ اللّٰهِ مَغَانِمُ كَثِيْرَةٌ

Even thus were ye yourselves
Before, till Allah conferred
On you His favours: therefore
Carefully investigate.
For Allah is well aware
Of all that ye do.

كَذٰلِكَ كُنْتُمْ مِّنْ قَبْلُ
فَمَنَّ اللّٰهُ عَلَيْكُمْ فَتَبَيَّنُوْا ؕ
اِنَّ اللّٰهَ كَانَ بِمَا تَعْمَلُوْنَ خَبِيْرًا ۝

95. Not equal are those
Believers who sit (at home)
And receive no hurt,
And those who strive
And fight in the cause
Of Allah with their goods
And their persons.
Allah hath granted
A grade higher to those
Who strive and fight
With their goods and persons
Than to those who sit (at home).
Unto all (in Faith)
Hath Allah promised good:
But those who strive and fight
Hath He distinguished
Above those who sit (at home)
By a special reward—

٩٥۔ لَا يَسْتَوِى الْقَاعِدُوْنَ مِنَ الْمُؤْمِنِيْنَ
غَيْرُ أُولِى الضَّرَرِ وَالْمُجَاهِدُوْنَ فِى سَبِيْلِ
اللّٰهِ بِأَمْوَالِهِمْ وَأَنْفُسِهِمْ ؕ
فَضَّلَ اللّٰهُ الْمُجَاهِدِيْنَ
بِأَمْوَالِهِمْ وَأَنْفُسِهِمْ
عَلَى الْقَاعِدِيْنَ دَرَجَةً ؕ
وَكُلًّا
وَعَدَ اللّٰهُ الْحُسْنٰى ؕ
وَفَضَّلَ اللّٰهُ الْمُجَاهِدِيْنَ
عَلَى الْقَاعِدِيْنَ أَجْرًا عَظِيْمًا ۝

96. Ranks specially bestowed
By Him and Forgiveness
And Mercy, For Allah is
Oft-Forgiving, Most Merciful.

٩٦۔ دَرَجٰتٍ مِّنْهُ وَمَغْفِرَةً وَّرَحْمَةً ؕ
وَكَانَ اللّٰهُ غَفُوْرًا رَّحِيْمًا ۝

SECTION 14.

97. When angels take
The souls of those
Who die in sin
Against their souls,
They say: "In what (plight)
Were ye?" They reply:
"Weak and oppressed
Were we in the earth."
They say: "Was not
The earth of Allah
Spacious enough for you
To move yourselves away
(From evil)?" Such men
Will find their abode
In Hell—What an evil
Refuge!—

٩٧۔ اِنَّ الَّذِيْنَ تَوَفّٰهُمُ الْمَلٰٓئِكَةُ
ظَالِمِىْ أَنْفُسِهِمْ
قَالُوْا فِيْمَ كُنْتُمْ ؕ
قَالُوْا كُنَّا مُسْتَضْعَفِيْنَ فِى الْأَرْضِ ؕ
قَالُوْٓا أَلَمْ تَكُنْ أَرْضُ اللّٰهِ وَاسِعَةً
فَتُهَاجِرُوْا فِيْهَا ؕ
فَأُولٰٓئِكَ مَأْوَاهُمْ جَهَنَّمُ ؕ
وَسَاءَتْ مَصِيْرًا ۝

98. Except those who are
(Really) weak and oppressed—
Men, women, and children
Who have no means
In their power, nor (a guide
post)
To direct their way.

٩٨- إِلَّا الْمُسْتَضْعَفِيْنَ مِنَ الرِّجَالِ وَ
النِّسَاءِ وَالْوِلْدَانِ لَا يَسْتَطِيْعُوْنَ حِيْلَةً
وَّلَا يَهْتَدُوْنَ سَبِيْلًا ۙ۞

99. For these, there is hope
That Allah will forgive:
For Allah doth blot out (sins)
And forgive again and again.

٩٩- فَأُولٰٓئِكَ عَسَى اللّٰهُ أَنْ يَّعْفُوَ عَنْهُمْ ؕ
وَكَانَ اللّٰهُ عَفُوًّا غَفُوْرًا

100. He who forsakes his home
In the cause of Allah,
Finds in the earth
Many a refuge,
Wide and spacious:
Should he die
As a refugee from home
For Allah and His Messenger,
His reward becomes due
And sure with Allah:
And Allah is Oft-Forgiving,
Most Merciful.

١٠٠- وَمَنْ يُّهَاجِرْ فِيْ سَبِيْلِ اللّٰهِ
يَجِدْ فِي الْأَرْضِ مُرَاغَمًا كَثِيْرًا وَّسَعَةً ؕ
وَمَنْ يَّخْرُجْ مِنْ بَيْتِهِ مُهَاجِرًا إِلَى اللّٰهِ
وَرَسُوْلِهِ ثُمَّ يُدْرِكْهُ الْمَوْتُ
فَقَدْ وَقَعَ أَجْرُهُ عَلَى اللّٰهِ ؕ
وَكَانَ اللّٰهُ غَفُوْرًا رَّحِيْمًا ۞

SECTION 15.

101. When ye travel
Through the earth,
There is no blame on you
If ye shorten your prayers,
For fear the Unbelievers
May attack you:
For the Unbelievers are
Unto you open enemies.

١٠١- وَإِذَا ضَرَبْتُمْ فِي الْأَرْضِ
فَلَيْسَ عَلَيْكُمْ جُنَاحٌ أَنْ تَقْصُرُوْا مِنَ
الصَّلٰوةِ ۖ إِنْ خِفْتُمْ أَنْ يَّفْتِنَكُمُ الَّذِيْنَ كَفَرُوْا ؕ
إِنَّ الْكٰفِرِيْنَ كَانُوْا لَكُمْ عَدُوًّا مُّبِيْنًا

102. When thou (O Messenger)
Art with them, and standest
To lead them in prayer,
Let one party of them
Stand up (in prayer) with thee,
Taking their arms with them;
When they finish
Their prostrations, let them
Take their position in the rear.
And let the other party come up
Which hath not yet prayed—
And let them pray with thee,
Taking all precautions,

١٠٢- وَإِذَا كُنْتَ فِيْهِمْ فَأَقَمْتَ لَهُمُ الصَّلٰوةَ
فَلْتَقُمْ طَائِفَةٌ مِّنْهُمْ مَّعَكَ
وَلْيَأْخُذُوْا أَسْلِحَتَهُمْ ۙ فَإِذَا سَجَدُوْا
فَلْيَكُوْنُوْا مِنْ وَّرَائِكُمْ ۖ
وَلْتَأْتِ طَائِفَةٌ
أُخْرٰى لَمْ يُصَلُّوْا فَلْيُصَلُّوْا مَعَكَ
وَلْيَأْخُذُوْا حِذْرَهُمْ وَأَسْلِحَتَهُمْ ۚ

And bearing arms:
The Unbelievers wish,
If ye were negligent
Of your arms and your baggage,
To assault you in a single rush.
But there is no blame on you
If ye put away your arms
Because of the inconvenience
Of rain or because ye are ill;
But take (every) precaution
For yourselves. For the
              Unbelievers
Allah hath prepared
A humiliating punishment.

103. When ye pass
(Congregational) prayers,
Celebrate Allah's praises,
Standing, sitting down,
Or lying down on your sides;
But when ye are free
From danger, set up
Regular Prayers:
For such prayers
Are enjoined on Believers
At stated times.

104. And slacken not
In following up the enemy:
If ye are suffering hardships,
They are suffering similar
Hardships; but ye have
Hope from Allah, while they
Have none. And Allah
Is full of knowledge and wisdom.

SECTION 16.

105. We have sent down
To thee the Book in truth,
That thou mightest judge
Between men, as guided
By Allah: so be not (used)
As an advocate by those
Who betray their trust;

106. But seek the forgiveness

Of Allah; for Allah is
Oft-Forgiving, Most Merciful.

إِنَّ اللَّهَ كَانَ غَفُورًا رَحِيمًا ۞

107. Contend not on behalf
Of such as betray
Their own souls;
For Allah loveth not
One given to perfidy
And crime;

١٠٧ـ وَلَا تُجَادِلْ عَنِ الَّذِينَ يَخْتَانُونَ
أَنْفُسَهُمْ ۚ إِنَّ اللَّهَ لَا يُحِبُّ
مَنْ كَانَ خَوَّانًا أَثِيمًا ۞

108. They may hide
(Their crimes) from men,
But they cannot hide
(Them) from Allah, seeing that
He is with them
When they plot by night,
In words that He cannot
Approve; and Allah
Doth compass round
All that they do.

١٠٨ـ يَسْتَخْفُونَ مِنَ النَّاسِ
وَلَا يَسْتَخْفُونَ مِنَ اللَّهِ
وَهُوَ مَعَهُمْ إِذْ يُبَيِّتُونَ مَا لَا يَرْضَىٰ
مِنَ الْقَوْلِ ۚ
وَكَانَ اللَّهُ بِمَا يَعْمَلُونَ مُحِيطًا ۞

109. Ah! these are the sort
Of men on whose behalf
Ye may contend in this world;
But who will contend with Allah
On their behalf on the Day
Of Judgement, or who
Will carry their affairs through?

١٠٩ـ هَا أَنْتُمْ هَٰؤُلَاءِ
جَادَلْتُمْ عَنْهُمْ فِي الْحَيَاةِ الدُّنْيَا
فَمَنْ يُجَادِلُ اللَّهَ عَنْهُمْ يَوْمَ الْقِيَامَةِ
أَمْ مَنْ يَكُونُ عَلَيْهِمْ وَكِيلًا ۞

110. If anyone does evil
Or wrongs his own soul
But afterwards seeks
Allah's forgiveness, he will find
Allah Oft-Forgiving,
Most Merciful.

١١٠ـ وَمَنْ يَعْمَلْ سُوءًا أَوْ يَظْلِمْ نَفْسَهُ
ثُمَّ يَسْتَغْفِرِ اللَّهَ
يَجِدِ اللَّهَ غَفُورًا رَحِيمًا ۞

111. And if any one earns
Sin, he earns it against
His own soul: for Allah
Is full of knowledge and wisdom.

١١١ـ وَمَنْ يَكْسِبْ
إِثْمًا فَإِنَّمَا يَكْسِبُهُ
عَلَىٰ نَفْسِهِ ۚ وَكَانَ اللَّهُ عَلِيمًا حَكِيمًا ۞

112. But if anyone earns
A fault or a sin
And throws it on to one
That is innocent,
He carries (on himself)
(Both) a falsehood
And a flagrant sin.

١١٢ـ وَمَنْ يَكْسِبْ خَطِيئَةً أَوْ إِثْمًا
ثُمَّ يَرْمِ بِهِ بَرِيئًا
فَقَدِ احْتَمَلَ بُهْتَانًا
وَإِثْمًا مُبِينًا ۞

SECTION 17.

113. But for the Grace of Allah
To thee and His Mercy,
A party of them would
Certainly have plotted
To lead thee astray.
But (in fact) they will only
Lead their own souls astray,
And to thee they can do
No harm in the least.
For Allah hath sent down
To thee the Book and Wisdom
And taught thee what thou
Knewest not (before):
And great is the Grace
Of Allah unto thee.

١١٣- وَلَوْلَا فَضْلُ اللهِ عَلَيْكَ
وَرَحْمَتُهُ
لَهَمَّتْ طَّآئِفَةٌ مِّنْهُمْ أَنْ يُضِلُّوكَ
وَمَا يُضِلُّونَ إِلَّا أَنْفُسَهُمْ
وَمَا يَضُرُّونَكَ مِنْ شَيْءٍ
وَأَنْزَلَ اللهُ عَلَيْكَ الْكِتَبَ وَالْحِكْمَةَ
وَعَلَّمَكَ مَا لَمْ تَكُنْ تَعْلَمُ
وَكَانَ فَضْلُ اللهِ عَلَيْكَ عَظِيْمًا

114. In most of their secret talks
There is no good; but if
One exhorts to a deed
Of charity or justice
Or conciliation between men,
(Secrecy is permissible):
To him who does this,
Seeking the good pleasure
Of Allah, We shall soon give
A reward of the highest (value).

١١٤- لَا خَيْرَ فِيْ كَثِيْرٍ مِّنْ نَّجْوٰهُمْ
إِلَّا مَنْ أَمَرَ بِصَدَقَةٍ أَوْ مَعْرُوْفٍ
أَوْ إِصْلَاحٍ بَيْنَ النَّاسِ
وَمَنْ يَفْعَلْ ذٰلِكَ ابْتِغَآءَ مَرْضَاتِ
اللهِ فَسَوْفَ نُؤْتِيْهِ أَجْرًا عَظِيْمًا

115. If anyone contends with
The Messenger even after
Guidance has been plainly
Conveyed to him, and follows
A path other than that
Becoming to men of Faith,
We shall leave him
In the path he has chosen,
And land him in Hell—
What an evil refuge!

١١٥- وَمَنْ يُّشَاقِقِ الرَّسُوْلَ
مِنْ بَعْدِ مَا تَبَيَّنَ لَهُ الْهُدٰى
وَيَتَّبِعْ غَيْرَ سَبِيْلِ الْمُؤْمِنِيْنَ نُوَلِّهِ
مَا تَوَلّٰى وَنُصْلِهِ جَهَنَّمَ
وَسَآءَتْ مَصِيْرًا

SECTION 18.

116. Allah forgiveth not
(The sin of) joining other gods
With Him; but He forgiveth
Whom He pleaseth other sins
Than this: one who joins
Other gods with Allah,
Hath strayed far, far away
(From the Right).

١١٦- إِنَّ اللهَ لَا يَغْفِرُ أَنْ يُّشْرَكَ بِهِ
وَيَغْفِرُ مَا دُوْنَ ذٰلِكَ لِمَنْ يَّشَآءُ
وَمَنْ يُّشْرِكْ بِاللهِ
فَقَدْ ضَلَّ ضَلٰلًا بَعِيْدًا

117. (The Pagans), leaving Him,
Call but upon female deities:
They call but upon Satan
The persistent rebel!

١١٧- اِنْ يَّدْعُونَ مِنْ دُوْنِهِ اِلَّا اِنَاثًا ۚ
وَاِنْ يَّدْعُونَ اِلَّا شَيْطَانًا مَّرِيْدًا ۙ

118. Allah did curse him,
But he said: "I will take
Of Thy servants a portion
Marked off;

١١٨- لَّعَنَهُ اللّٰهُ ۘ وَقَالَ لَاَتَّخِذَنَّ مِنْ
عِبَادِكَ نَصِيْبًا مَّفْرُوْضًا ۙ

119. "I will mislead them,
And I will create
In them false desires; I will
Order them to slit the ears
Of cattle, and to deface
The (fair) nature created
By Allah." Whoever,
Forsaking Allah, takes Satan
For a friend, hath
Of a surety suffered
A loss that is manifest.

١١٩- وَّلَاُضِلَّنَّهُمْ وَلَاُمَنِّيَنَّهُمْ
وَلَاٰمُرَنَّهُمْ فَلَيُبَتِّكُنَّ اٰذَانَ الْاَنْعَامِ
وَلَاٰمُرَنَّهُمْ فَلَيُغَيِّرُنَّ خَلْقَ اللّٰهِ ۚ
وَمَنْ يَّتَّخِذِ الشَّيْطٰنَ وَلِيًّا
مِّنْ دُوْنِ اللّٰهِ
فَقَدْ خَسِرَ خُسْرَانًا مُّبِيْنًا ۙ

120. Satan makes them promises,
And creates in them false desires;
But Satan's promises
Are nothing but deception.

١٢٠- يَعِدُهُمْ وَيُمَنِّيْهِمْ ۚ
وَمَا يَعِدُهُمُ الشَّيْطٰنُ اِلَّا غُرُوْرًا ۙ

121. They (his dupes)
Will have their dwelling
In Hell, and from it
They will find no way
Of escape.

١٢١- اُولٰٓئِكَ مَأْوٰىهُمْ جَهَنَّمُ ۙ
وَلَا يَجِدُوْنَ عَنْهَا مَحِيْصًا ۙ

122. But those who believe
And do deeds of righteousness—
We shall soon admit them
To Gardens, with rivers
Flowing beneath—to dwell
Therein forever.
Allah's promise is the truth,
And whose word can be
Truer than Allah's?

١٢٢- وَالَّذِيْنَ اٰمَنُوْا وَعَمِلُوا الصّٰلِحٰتِ
سَنُدْخِلُهُمْ جَنّٰتٍ تَجْرِيْ مِنْ تَحْتِهَا
الْاَنْهٰرُ خٰلِدِيْنَ فِيْهَآ اَبَدًا ۚ وَعْدَ اللّٰهِ
حَقًّا ۚ وَمَنْ اَصْدَقُ مِنَ اللّٰهِ قِيْلًا ۙ

123. Not your desires, nor those
Of the People of the Book
(Can prevail): whoever
Works evil, will be
Requited accordingly.

١٢٣- لَيْسَ بِاَمَانِيِّكُمْ وَلَا اَمَانِيِّ
اَهْلِ الْكِتٰبِ ۚ مَنْ يَّعْمَلْ سُوْٓءًا يُّجْزَ بِهِ ۙ

Nor will he find, besides Allah,
Any protector or helper.

وَلَا يَجِدُ لَهُ مِنْ دُوْنِ اللهِ وَلِيًّا وَّلَا نَصِيْرًا

124. If any do deeds
Of righteousness —
Be they male or female —
And have faith,
They will enter Heaven,
And not the least injustice
Will be done to them.

١٢٤ـ وَمَنْ يَّعْمَلْ مِنَ الصّٰلِحٰتِ
مِنْ ذَكَرٍ أَوْ أُنْثٰى وَهُوَ مُؤْمِنٌ
فَأُولٰٓئِكَ يَدْخُلُوْنَ الْجَنَّةَ
وَلَا يُظْلَمُوْنَ نَقِيْرًا ۞

125. Who can be better
In religion than one
Who submits his whole self
To Allah, does good,
And follows the way
Of Abraham the true in faith?
For Allah did take
Abraham for a friend.

١٢٥ـ وَمَنْ أَحْسَنُ دِيْنًا
مِّمَّنْ أَسْلَمَ وَجْهَهٗ لِلّٰهِ وَهُوَ مُحْسِنٌ
وَّاتَّبَعَ مِلَّةَ إِبْرٰهِيْمَ حَنِيْفًا
وَاتَّخَذَ اللهُ إِبْرٰهِيْمَ خَلِيْلًا ۞

126. But to Allah belong all things
In the heavens and on earth;
And He it is that
Encompasseth all things.

١٢٦ـ وَلِلّٰهِ مَا فِى السَّمٰوٰتِ وَمَا فِى الْأَرْضِ
وَكَانَ اللهُ بِكُلِّ شَيْءٍ مُّحِيْطًا ۞

SECTION 19.

127. They ask thy instruction
Concerning the Women.
Say: Allah doth
Instruct you about them:
And (remember) what hath
Been rehearsed unto you
In the Book, concerning
The orphans of women to
whom
Ye give not the portions
Prescribed, and yet whom ye
Desire to marry, as also
Concerning the children
Who are weak and oppressed;
That ye stand firm
For justice to orphans.
There is not a good deed
Which ye do, but Allah
Is well-acquainted therewith.

١٢٧ـ وَيَسْتَفْتُوْنَكَ فِى النِّسَاءِ
قُلِ اللهُ يُفْتِيْكُمْ فِيْهِنَّ
وَمَا يُتْلٰى عَلَيْكُمْ فِى الْكِتٰبِ
فِى يَتٰمَى النِّسَاءِ الّٰتِى
لَا تُؤْتُوْنَهُنَّ مَا كُتِبَ لَهُنَّ
وَتَرْغَبُوْنَ أَنْ تَنْكِحُوْهُنَّ
وَالْمُسْتَضْعَفِيْنَ مِنَ الْوِلْدَانِ
وَأَنْ تَقُوْمُوْا لِلْيَتٰمٰى بِالْقِسْطِ
وَمَا تَفْعَلُوْا مِنْ خَيْرٍ
فَإِنَّ اللهَ كَانَ بِهٖ عَلِيْمًا ۞

128. If a wife fears
Cruelty or desertion

١٢٨ـ وَإِنِ امْرَأَةٌ خَافَتْ

On her husband's part,
There is no blame on them
If they arrange
An amicable settlement
Between themselves;
And such settlement is best;
Even though men's souls
Are swayed by greed.
But if ye do good
And practise self-restraint,
Allah is well-acquainted
With all that ye do.

مِنْ بَعْلِهَا نُشُوزًا أَوْ إِعْرَاضًا
فَلَا جُنَاحَ عَلَيْهِمَا
أَنْ يُّصْلِحَا بَيْنَهُمَا صُلْحًا ۚ
وَالصُّلْحُ خَيْرٌ ۗ وَأُحْضِرَتِ الْأَنْفُسُ
الشُّحَّ ۚ وَإِنْ تُحْسِنُوا وَتَتَّقُوا
فَإِنَّ اللّٰهَ كَانَ بِمَا تَعْمَلُونَ خَبِيرًا

129. Ye are never able
To be fair and just
As between women,
Even if it is
Your ardent desire:
But turn not away
(From a woman) altogether,
So as to leave her (as it were)
Hanging (in the air).
If ye come to a friendly
Understanding, and practise
Self-restraint, Allah is
Oft-Forgiving, Most Merciful.

١٢٩- وَلَنْ تَسْتَطِيعُوا
أَنْ تَعْدِلُوا بَيْنَ النِّسَاءِ
وَلَوْ حَرَصْتُمْ
فَلَا تَمِيلُوا كُلَّ الْمَيْلِ
فَتَذَرُوهَا كَالْمُعَلَّقَةِ ۚ
وَإِنْ تُصْلِحُوا وَتَتَّقُوا
فَإِنَّ اللّٰهَ كَانَ غَفُورًا رَّحِيمًا

130. But if they disagree
(And must part), Allah
Will provide abundance
For all from His
All-Reaching bounty:
For Allah is He
That careth for all
And is Wise.

١٣٠- وَإِنْ يَّتَفَرَّقَا
يُغْنِ اللّٰهُ كُلًّا مِّنْ سَعَتِهِ ۚ
وَكَانَ اللّٰهُ وَاسِعًا حَكِيمًا

131. To Allah belong all things
In the heavens and on earth.
Verily We have directed
The People of the Book
Before you, and you (O Muslims)
To fear Allah. But if ye
Deny Him, lo! unto Allah
Belong all things
In the heavens and on earth,
And Allah is free
Of all wants, worthy
Of all praise.

١٣١- وَلِلّٰهِ مَا فِي السَّمٰوٰتِ وَمَا فِي الْأَرْضِ ۗ
وَلَقَدْ وَصَّيْنَا الَّذِينَ أُوتُوا الْكِتٰبَ
مِنْ قَبْلِكُمْ وَإِيَّاكُمْ أَنِ اتَّقُوا اللّٰهَ ۚ
وَإِنْ تَكْفُرُوا
فَإِنَّ لِلّٰهِ مَا فِي السَّمٰوٰتِ وَمَا فِي الْأَرْضِ ۚ
وَكَانَ اللّٰهُ غَنِيًّا حَمِيدًا

132. Yea, unto Allah belong
All things in the heavens
And on earth, and énough
Is Allah to carry through
All affairs.

١٣٢- وَلِلّٰهِ مَا فِى السَّمٰوٰتِ
وَمَا فِى الْأَرْضِ ۗ
وَكَفٰى بِاللّٰهِ وَكِيْلًا ۟

133. If it were His Will,
He could destroy you,
O mankind, and create
Another race; for He
Hath power this to do.

١٣٣- إِنْ يَّشَأْ يُذْهِبْكُمْ أَيُّهَا النَّاسُ
وَيَأْتِ بِأٰخَرِيْنَ ۗ
وَكَانَ اللّٰهُ عَلٰى ذٰلِكَ قَدِيْرًا ۟

134. If anyone desires
A reward in this life,
In Allah's (gift) is the reward
(Both) of this life
And of the Hereafter;
For Allah is He that heareth
And seeth (all things).

١٣٤- مَنْ كَانَ يُرِيْدُ ثَوَابَ الدُّنْيَا
فَعِنْدَ اللّٰهِ ثَوَابُ الدُّنْيَا وَالْأٰخِرَةِ ۗ
وَكَانَ اللّٰهُ سَمِيْعًۢا بَصِيْرًا ۟

SECTION 20.

135. O ye who believe!
Stand out firmly
For justice, as witnesses
To Allah, even as against
Yourselves, or your parents,
Or your kin, and whether
It be (against) rich or poor:
For Allah can best protect both.
Follow not the lusts
(Of your hearts), lest ye
Swerve, and if ye
Distort (justice) or decline
To do justice, verily
Allah is well-acquainted
With all that ye do.

١٣٥- يٰٓأَيُّهَا الَّذِيْنَ اٰمَنُوْا كُوْنُوْا قَوّٰمِيْنَ
بِالْقِسْطِ شُهَدَآءَ لِلّٰهِ
وَلَوْ عَلٰٓى أَنْفُسِكُمْ أَوِ الْوَالِدَيْنِ
وَالْأَقْرَبِيْنَ ۚ إِنْ يَّكُنْ غَنِيًّا أَوْ فَقِيْرًا
فَاللّٰهُ أَوْلٰى بِهِمَا ۖ
فَلَا تَتَّبِعُوا الْهَوٰٓى أَنْ تَعْدِلُوْا ۚ
وَإِنْ تَلْوٗٓا أَوْ تُعْرِضُوْا
فَإِنَّ اللّٰهَ كَانَ بِمَا تَعْمَلُوْنَ خَبِيْرًا ۟

136. O ye who believe!
Believe in Allah
And His Messenger,
And the scripture which He
Hath sent to His Messenger
And the scripture which He sent
To those before (him).
Any who denieth Allah,
His angels, His Books,
His Messengers, and the Day

١٣٦- يٰٓأَيُّهَا الَّذِيْنَ اٰمَنُوْٓا
اٰمِنُوْا بِاللّٰهِ وَرَسُوْلِهٖ
وَالْكِتٰبِ الَّذِيْ نَزَّلَ عَلٰى رَسُوْلِهٖ
وَالْكِتٰبِ الَّذِيْٓ أَنْزَلَ مِنْ قَبْلُ ۗ
وَمَنْ يَّكْفُرْ بِاللّٰهِ
وَمَلٰٓئِكَتِهٖ وَكُتُبِهٖ وَرُسُلِهٖ وَالْيَوْمِ الْٰاخِرِ

Of Judgement, hath gone
Far, far astray.

137. Those who believe,
Then reject Faith,
Then believe (again)
And (again) reject Faith,
And go on increasing
In Unbelief—Allah
Will not forgive them
Nor guide them on the Way.

138. To the Hypocrites give
The glad tidings that
There is for them
(But) a grievous Penalty—

139. Yea, to those who take
For friends Unbelievers
Rather than Believers:
Is it honour they seek
Among them? Nay—
All honour is with Allah.

140. Already has He sent you
Word in the Book, that when
Ye hear the Signs of Allah
Held in defiance and ridicule,
Ye are not to sit with them
Unless they turn to a different
Theme: if ye did, ye would be
Like them. For Allah will
Collect the Hypocrites and those
Who defy Faith—all in Hell—

141. (These are) the ones who
Wait and watch about you:
If ye do gain
A victory from Allah,
They say: "Were we not
With you?"—but if
The Unbelievers gain
A success, they say
(To them): "Did we not
Gain an advantage over you,
And did we not guard
You from the Believers?"
But Allah will judge

١٣٧- إِنَّ الَّذِينَ آمَنُوا ثُمَّ كَفَرُوا
ثُمَّ آمَنُوا ثُمَّ كَفَرُوا ثُمَّ ازْدَادُوا
كُفْرًا لَمْ يَكُنِ اللهُ لِيَغْفِرَ لَهُمْ
وَلَا لِيَهْدِيَهُمْ سَبِيلًا ۟

١٣٨- بَشِّرِ الْمُنَافِقِينَ
بِأَنَّ لَهُمْ عَذَابًا أَلِيمًا ۟

١٣٩- الَّذِينَ يَتَّخِذُونَ الْكَافِرِينَ أَوْلِيَاءَ
مِنْ دُونِ الْمُؤْمِنِينَ ۚ أَيَبْتَغُونَ عِنْدَ
هُمُ الْعِزَّةَ فَإِنَّ الْعِزَّةَ لِلّهِ جَمِيعًا ۟

١٤٠- وَقَدْ نَزَّلَ عَلَيْكُمْ فِي الْكِتَابِ أَنْ إِذَا
سَمِعْتُمْ آيَاتِ اللهِ يُكْفَرُ بِهَا وَيُسْتَهْزَأُ بِهَا
فَلَا تَقْعُدُوا مَعَهُمْ
حَتَّى يَخُوضُوا فِي حَدِيثٍ غَيْرِهِ ۚ
إِنَّكُمْ إِذًا مِثْلُهُمْ ۗ إِنَّ اللهَ جَامِعُ الْمُنَافِقِينَ
وَالْكَافِرِينَ فِي جَهَنَّمَ جَمِيعًا ۟

١٤١- الَّذِينَ يَتَرَبَّصُونَ بِكُمْ
فَإِنْ كَانَ لَكُمْ فَتْحٌ مِّنَ اللهِ
قَالُوا أَلَمْ نَكُنْ مَعَكُمْ ۖ
وَإِنْ كَانَ لِلْكَافِرِينَ نَصِيبٌ ۙ قَالُوا
أَلَمْ نَسْتَحْوِذْ عَلَيْكُمْ
وَنَمْنَعْكُمْ مِّنَ الْمُؤْمِنِينَ ۚ
فَاللهُ يَحْكُمُ بَيْنَكُمْ

Betwixt you on the Day
Of Judgement. And never
Will Allah grant
To the Unbelievers
A way (to triumph)
Over the Believers.

SECTION 21.

142. The Hypocrites—they think
They are over-reaching Allah
But He will over-reach them:
When they stand up to prayer,
They stand without earnestness,
To be seen of men,
But little do they hold
Allah in remembrance;

143. (They are) distracted in mind
Even in the midst of it—
Being (sincerely) for neither
One group nor for another.
Whom Allah leaves straying—
Never wilt thou find
For him the Way.

144. O ye who believe!
Take not for friends
Unbelievers rather than
Believers: do ye wish
To offer Allah an open
Proof against yourselves?

145. The Hypocrites will be
In the lowest depths
Of the Fire; no helper
Wilt thou find for them—

146. Except for those who repent,
Mend (their life), hold fast
To Allah, and purify their religion
As in Allah's sight; if so
They will be (numbered)
With the Believers.
And soon will Allah
Grant to the Believers
A reward of immense value.

147. What can Allah gain
By your punishment,

If ye are grateful
And ye believe?
Nay, it is Allah
That recogniseth[653]
(All good), and knoweth
All things.

148. Allah loveth not that evil
Should be noised abroad
In public speech, except
Where injustice hath been
Done; for Allah
Is He who heareth
And knoweth all things.

149. Whether ye publish
A good deed or conceal it
Or cover evil with pardon,
Verily Allah doth blot out
(Sins) and hath power
(In the judgement of values).

150. Those who deny Allah
And His Messengers, and (those
Who) wish to separate
Allah from His Messengers,
Saying: "We believe in some
But reject others":
And (those who) wish
To take a course midway—

151. They are in truth
(Equally) Unbelievers;
And We have prepared
For Unbelievers a humiliating
Punishment.

152. To those who believe
In Allah and His Messengers
And make no distinction
Between any of the messengers,
We shall soon give
Their (due) rewards:
For Allah is Oft-Forgiving,
Most Merciful.

SECTION 22.

153. The People of the Book

Ask thee to cause
A book to descend to them
From heaven: indeed
They asked Moses
For an even greater
(Miracle), for they said:
"Show us Allah in public,"
But they were dazed
For their presumption,
By thunder and lightning.
Yet they worshipped the calf
Even after Clear Signs
Had come to them;
Even so We forgave them;
And gave Moses manifest
Proofs of authority.

أَنْ تُنَزِّلَ عَلَيْهِمْ كِتَابًا مِّنَ السَّمَاءِ
فَقَدْ سَأَلُوا مُوسَى أَكْبَرَ مِن ذَلِكَ
فَقَالُوا أَرِنَا اللهَ جَهْرَةً
فَأَخَذَتْهُمُ الصَّاعِقَةُ بِظُلْمِهِمْ
ثُمَّ اتَّخَذُوا الْعِجْلَ مِنْ بَعْدِ مَا جَاءَتْهُمُ
الْبَيِّنَاتُ فَعَفَوْنَا عَنْ ذَلِكَ
وَآتَيْنَا مُوسَى سُلْطَانًا مُّبِينًا ۝

154. And for their Covenant
We raised over them
(The towering height)
Of Mount (Sinai);
And (on another occasion)
We said: "Enter the gate
With humility"; and (once again)
We commanded them:
"Transgress not in the matter
Of the Sabbath."
And We took from them
A solemn Covenant.

١٥٤- وَرَفَعْنَا فَوْقَهُمُ الطُّورَ
بِمِيثَاقِهِمْ
وَقُلْنَا لَهُمُ ادْخُلُوا الْبَابَ
سُجَّدًا
وَقُلْنَا لَهُمْ لَا تَعْدُوا فِي السَّبْتِ
وَأَخَذْنَا مِنْهُمْ مِّيثَاقًا غَلِيظًا ۝

155. (They have incurred divine
Displeasure): in that they
Broke their Covenant;
That they rejected the Signs
Of Allah; that they slew
The Messengers in defiance
Of right; that they said,
"Our hearts are the wrappings
(Which preserve Allah's Word;
We need no more)"— nay,
Allah hath set the seal on
their hearts
For their blasphemy,
And little is it they believe—

١٥٥- فَبِمَا نَقْضِهِمْ مِّيثَاقَهُمْ
وَكُفْرِهِم بِآيَاتِ اللهِ
وَقَتْلِهِمُ الْأَنْبِيَاءَ بِغَيْرِ حَقٍّ
وَقَوْلِهِمْ قُلُوبُنَا غُلْفٌ
بَلْ طَبَعَ اللهُ عَلَيْهَا بِكُفْرِهِمْ
فَلَا يُؤْمِنُونَ إِلَّا قَلِيلًا ۝

156. That they rejected Faith;
That they uttered against Mary
A grave false charge;—

١٥٦- وَبِكُفْرِهِمْ وَ قَوْلِهِمْ عَلَى مَرْيَمَ
بُهْتَانًا عَظِيمًا ۙ

157. That they said (in boast),
"We killed Christ Jesus
The son of Mary,
The Messenger of Allah";—
But they killed him not,
Nor crucified him,
But so it was made
To appear to them,
And those who differ
Therein are full of doubts,
With no (certain) knowledge,
But only conjecture to follow,
For of a surety
They killed him not—

١٥٧- وَّ قَوْلِهِمْ إِنَّا قَتَلْنَا الْمَسِيحَ عِيسَى
ابْنَ مَرْيَمَ رَسُولَ اللهِ ۚ
وَمَا قَتَلُوهُ
وَمَا صَلَبُوهُ وَلَكِنْ شُبِّهَ لَهُمْ ۚ
وَإِنَّ الَّذِينَ اخْتَلَفُوا فِيهِ
لَفِي شَكٍّ مِنْهُ ۚ مَا لَهُمْ بِهِ مِنْ عِلْمٍ
إِلَّا اتِّبَاعَ الظَّنِّ ۚ
وَمَا قَتَلُوهُ يَقِينًا ۙ

158. Nay, Allah raised him up
Unto Himself; and Allah
Is Exalted in Power, Wise—

١٥٨- بَلْ رَفَعَهُ اللهُ إِلَيْهِ ۚ
وَكَانَ اللهُ عَزِيزًا حَكِيمًا ۙ

159. And there is none
Of the People of the Book
But must believe in him
Before his death;
And on the Day of Judgement
He will be a witness
Against them—

١٥٩- وَإِنْ مِّنْ أَهْلِ الْكِتَابِ
إِلَّا لَيُؤْمِنَنَّ بِهِ قَبْلَ مَوْتِهِ ۚ
وَيَوْمَ الْقِيَامَةِ
يَكُونُ عَلَيْهِمْ شَهِيدًا ۙ

160. For the iniquity of the Jews
We made unlawful for them
Certain (foods) good and
wholesome
Which had been lawful for
them—
In that they hindered many
From Allah's Way—

١٦٠- فَبِظُلْمٍ مِّنَ الَّذِينَ هَادُوا
حَرَّمْنَا عَلَيْهِمْ طَيِّبَاتٍ
أُحِلَّتْ لَهُمْ
وَبِصَدِّهِمْ عَنْ سَبِيلِ اللهِ كَثِيرًا ۙ

161. That they took usury,
Though they were forbidden;
And that they devoured
Men's substance wrongfully—
We have prepared for those
Among them who reject Faith
A grievous punishment.

١٦١- وَّأَخْذِهِمُ الرِّبَا وَقَدْ نُهُوا عَنْهُ
وَأَكْلِهِمْ أَمْوَالَ النَّاسِ بِالْبَاطِلِ ۚ
وَأَعْتَدْنَا لِلْكَافِرِينَ مِنْهُمْ
عَذَابًا أَلِيمًا ۙ

2. But those among them
Who are well-grounded in
knowledge,
And the Believers,
Believe in what hath been
Revealed to thee and what was
Revealed before thee:
And (especially) those
Who establish regular prayer
And practise regular charity
And believe in Allah
And in the Last Day:
To them shall We soon
Give a great reward.

SECTION 23.

3. We have sent thee
Inspiration, as We sent it
To Noah and the Messengers
After him: We sent
Inspiration to Abraham,
Isma'īl, Isaac, Jacob
And the Tribes, to Jesus,
Job, Jonah, Aaron, and Solomon,
And to David We gave
The Psalms.

4. Of some messengers We have
Already told thee the story;
Of others we have not—
And to Moses Allah spoke
direct—

5. Messengers who gave good news
As well as warning,
That mankind, after (the coming)
Of the messengers, should have
No plea against Allah:
For Allah is Exalted in Power,
Wise.

6. But Allah beareth witness
That what He hath sent
Unto thee He hath sent
From His (own) knowledge,
And the angels bear witness:
But enough is Allah for a witness.

١٧٢- لٰكِنِ الرَّاسِخُونَ فِى الْعِلْمِ مِنْهُمْ
وَالْمُؤْمِنُونَ يُؤْمِنُونَ بِمَا أُنْزِلَ إِلَيْكَ
وَمَا أُنْزِلَ مِنْ قَبْلِكَ
وَالْمُقِيمِينَ الصَّلٰوةَ
وَالْمُؤْتُونَ الزَّكٰوةَ
وَالْمُؤْمِنُونَ بِاللّٰهِ وَالْيَوْمِ الْآخِرِ
أُولٰٓئِكَ سَنُؤْتِيهِمْ أَجْرًا عَظِيمًا ۞

١٧٣- إِنَّا أَوْحَيْنَا إِلَيْكَ
كَمَا أَوْحَيْنَا إِلٰى نُوحٍ وَّالنَّبِيِّنَ مِنْ بَعْدِهِ
وَأَوْحَيْنَا إِلٰى إِبْرٰهِيمَ وَإِسْمٰعِيلَ وَإِسْحٰقَ
وَيَعْقُوبَ وَالْأَسْبَاطِ وَعِيسٰى وَأَيُّوبَ وَ
يُونُسَ وَهٰرُونَ وَسُلَيْمٰنَ وَآتَيْنَا دَاوُدَ زَبُورًا

١٧٤- وَرُسُلًا قَدْ قَصَصْنٰهُمْ عَلَيْكَ مِنْ
قَبْلُ وَرُسُلًا لَّمْ نَقْصُصْهُمْ عَلَيْكَ
وَكَلَّمَ اللّٰهُ مُوسٰى تَكْلِيمًا

١٧٥- رُسُلًا مُّبَشِّرِينَ وَمُنْذِرِينَ لِئَلَّا
يَكُونَ لِلنَّاسِ عَلَى اللّٰهِ حُجَّةٌ
بَعْدَ الرُّسُلِ وَكَانَ اللّٰهُ عَزِيزًا حَكِيمًا

١٧٧- لٰكِنِ اللّٰهُ يَشْهَدُ بِمَا أَنْزَلَ إِلَيْكَ
أَنْزَلَهُ بِعِلْمِهِ وَالْمَلٰئِكَةُ يَشْهَدُونَ
وَكَفٰى بِاللّٰهِ شَهِيدًا

167. Those who reject Faith
And keep off (men)
From the Way of Allah,
Have verily strayed far,
Far away from the Path.

١٦٧- اِنَّ الَّذِيْنَ كَفَرُوْا وَصَدُّوْا عَنْ
سَبِيْلِ اللّٰهِ
قَدْ ضَلُّوْا ضَلٰلًا بَعِيْدًا ۝

168. Those who reject Faith
And do wrong—Allah
Will not forgive them
Nor guide them
To any way—

١٦٨- اِنَّ الَّذِيْنَ كَفَرُوْا وَظَلَمُوْا لَمْ يَكُنِ اللّٰهُ
لِيَغْفِرَ لَهُمْ وَلَا لِيَهْدِيَهُمْ طَرِيْقًا ۝

169. Except the way of Hell,
To dwell therein forever.
And this to Allah is easy.

١٦٩- اِلَّا طَرِيْقَ جَهَنَّمَ خٰلِدِيْنَ فِيْهَآ اَبَدًا ۚ
وَكَانَ ذٰلِكَ عَلَى اللّٰهِ يَسِيْرًا ۝

170. O mankind! the Messenger
Hath come to you in truth
From Allah: believe in him;
It is best for you. But if
Ye reject Faith, to Allah
Belong all things in the heavens
And on earth: and Allah
Is All-Knowing, All-Wise.

١٧٠- يٰٓاَيُّهَا النَّاسُ قَدْ جَآءَكُمُ الرَّسُوْلُ
بِالْحَقِّ مِنْ رَّبِّكُمْ فَاٰمِنُوْا خَيْرًا لَّكُمْ ۚ وَاِنْ
تَكْفُرُوْا فَاِنَّ لِلّٰهِ مَا فِى السَّمٰوٰتِ وَالْاَرْضِ ۚ
وَكَانَ اللّٰهُ عَلِيْمًا حَكِيْمًا ۝

171. O People of the Book!
Commit no excesses
In your religion: nor say
Of Allah aught but the truth.
Christ Jesus the son of Mary
Was (no more than)
A Messenger of Allah,
And His Word,
Which He bestowed on Mary,
And a Spirit proceeding
From Him: so believe
In Allah and His Messengers.
Say not "Trinity": desist:
It will be better for you:
For Allah is One God:
Glory be to Him:
(Far Exalted is He) above
Having a son. To Him
Belong all things in the heavens
And on earth. And enough
Is Allah as a Disposer of affairs.

١٧١- يٰٓاَهْلَ الْكِتٰبِ لَا تَغْلُوْا فِىْ دِيْنِكُمْ
وَلَا تَقُوْلُوْا عَلَى اللّٰهِ اِلَّا الْحَقَّ ۗ
اِنَّمَا الْمَسِيْحُ عِيْسَى ابْنُ مَرْيَمَ
رَسُوْلُ اللّٰهِ وَكَلِمَتُهٗ ۚ
اَلْقٰهَآ اِلٰى مَرْيَمَ وَرُوْحٌ مِّنْهُ ۖ
فَاٰمِنُوْا بِاللّٰهِ وَرُسُلِهٖ ۖ وَلَا تَقُوْلُوْا ثَلٰثَةٌ ۚ
اِنْتَهُوْا خَيْرًا لَّكُمْ ۚ
اِنَّمَا اللّٰهُ اِلٰهٌ وَّاحِدٌ ۚ
سُبْحٰنَهٗ اَنْ يَّكُوْنَ لَهٗ وَلَدٌ ۘ
لَهٗ مَا فِى السَّمٰوٰتِ وَمَا فِى الْاَرْضِ ۗ
وَكَفٰى بِاللّٰهِ وَكِيْلًا ۝

SECTION 24.

172. Christ disdaineth not

١٧٢- لَنْ يَّسْتَنْكِفَ الْمَسِيْحُ

To serve and worship Allah,
Nor do the angels, those
Nearest (to Allah):
Those who disdain
His worship and are arrogant—
He will gather them all
Together unto Himself
To (answer).

73. But to those who believe
And do deeds of righteousness,
He will give their (due)
Rewards—and more,
Out of His bounty:
But those who are
Disdainful and arrogant,
He will punish
With a grievous penalty;
Nor will they find,
Besides Allah, any
To protect or help them.

74. O mankind! Verily
There hath come to you
A convincing proof
From your Lord:
For We have sent unto you
A light (that is) manifest.

75. Then those who believe
In Allah, and hold fast
To Him—soon will He
Admit them to Mercy
And Grace from Himself,
And guide them to Himself
By a straight Way.

76. They ask thee
For a legal decision.
Say: Allah directs (thus)
About those who leave
No descendants or ascendants
As heirs. If it is a man[681]
That dies, leaving a sister
But no child, she shall
Have half the inheritance:

If (such a deceased was)
A woman, who left no child,
Her brother takes her inheritance:
If there are two sisters,
They shall have two-thirds
Of the inheritance
(Between them): if there are
Brothers and sisters, (they share),
The male having twice
The share of the female.
Thus doth Allah make clear
To you (His law), lest
Ye err. And Allah
Hath knowledge of all things.

INTRODUCTION TO SŪRA V (*Mā'ida*) — 120 Verses

This Sūra deals, by way of recapitulation, with the backsliding of the Jews and Christians from their pure religions, to which the coping stone was placed by Islam. It refers particularly to the Christians, and to their solemn Sacrament of the Last Supper, to whose mystic meaning they are declared to have been false.

As a logical corollary to corruption of the earlier religions of God, the practical percepts of Islam, about food, cleanliness, justice, and fidelity are recapitulated.

The fourth verse contains the memorable declaration: "This day have I perfected your religion for you": which was promulgated in 10 H., during the Apostle's last Pilgrimage to Makkah. Chronologically it was the last verse to be revealed.

Al Mā'idah (The Repast)

In the name of Allah, Most Gracious,
Most Merciful.

1. O ye who believe!
   Fulfil (all) obligations.

   Lawful unto you (for food)
   Are all four-footed animals
   With the exceptions named:
   But animals of the chase
   Are forbidden while ye
   Are in the Sacred Precincts
   Or in pilgrim garb:
   For Allah doth command
   According to His Will and Plan.

2. O ye who believe!
   Violate not the sanctity
   Of the Symbols of Allah,
   Nor of the Sacred Month,
   Nor of the animals brought
   For sacrifice, nor the garlands
   That mark out such animals,
   Nor the people resorting
   To the Sacred House,
   Seeking of the bounty
   And good pleasure
   Of their Lord.
   But when ye are clear
   Of the Sacred Precincts
   And of pilgrim garb,
   Ye may hunt

And let not the hatred
Of some people
In (once) shutting you out
Of the Sacred Mosque
Lead you to transgression
(And hostility on your part).
Help ye one another
In righteousness and piety,
But help ye not one another
In sin and rancour:
Fear Allah: for Allah
Is strict in punishment.

عَنِ الْمَسْجِدِ الْحَرَامِ
أَنْ تَعْتَدُوا وَتَعَاوَنُوا عَلَى الْبِرِّ وَالتَّقْوَى
وَلَا تَعَاوَنُوا عَلَى الْإِثْمِ وَالْعُدْوَانِ
وَاتَّقُوا اللَّهَ
إِنَّ اللَّهَ شَدِيدُ الْعِقَابِ ۝

3. Forbidden to you (for food)
Are: dead meat, blood,
The flesh of swine, and that
On which hath been invoked
The name of other than Allah;
That which hath been
Killed by strangling,
Or by a violent blow,
Or by a headlong fall,
Or by being gored to death;
That which hath been (partly)
Eaten by a wild animal;
Unless ye are able
To slaughter it (in due form);
That which is sacrificed
On stone (altars);
(Forbidden) also is the division
(Of meat) by raffling
With arrows: that is impiety.

٣- حُرِّمَتْ عَلَيْكُمُ الْمَيْتَةُ وَالدَّمُ
وَلَحْمُ الْخِنْزِيرِ وَمَا أُهِلَّ لِغَيْرِ اللَّهِ بِهِ
وَالْمُنْخَنِقَةُ
وَالْمَوْقُوذَةُ
وَالْمُتَرَدِّيَةُ
وَالنَّطِيحَةُ
وَمَا أَكَلَ السَّبُعُ إِلَّا مَا ذَكَّيْتُمْ
وَمَا ذُبِحَ عَلَى النُّصُبِ
وَأَنْ تَسْتَقْسِمُوا بِالْأَزْلَامِ
ذَلِكُمْ فِسْقٌ

This day have those who
Reject Faith given up
All hope of your religion:
Yet fear them not
But fear Me.
This day have I
Perfected your religion
For you, completed
My favour upon you,
And have chosen for you
Islām as your religion.

الْيَوْمَ يَئِسَ الَّذِينَ كَفَرُوا مِنْ دِينِكُمْ
فَلَا تَخْشَوْهُمْ وَاخْشَوْنِ
الْيَوْمَ أَكْمَلْتُ لَكُمْ دِينَكُمْ
وَأَتْمَمْتُ عَلَيْكُمْ نِعْمَتِي
وَرَضِيتُ لَكُمُ الْإِسْلَامَ دِينًا

But if any is forced
By hunger, with no inclination
To transgression, Allah is
Indeed Oft-Forgiving,
Most Merciful.

فَمَنِ اضْطُرَّ فِي مَخْمَصَةٍ غَيْرَ مُتَجَانِفٍ
لِإِثْمٍ
فَإِنَّ اللَّهَ غَفُورٌ رَحِيمٌ ۝

4. They ask thee what is
Lawful to them (as food).
Say: Lawful unto you
Are (all) things good and pure:
And what ye have taught
Your trained hunting animals
(To catch) in the manner
Directed to you by Allah:
Eat what they catch for you,
But pronounce the name
Of Allah over it: and fear
Allah; for Allah is swift
In taking account.

٤- يَسْـَلُونَكَ مَاذَآ أُحِلَّ لَهُمْ
قُلْ أُحِلَّ لَكُمُ الطَّيِّبَٰتُ
وَمَا عَلَّمْتُم مِّنَ الْجَوَارِحِ مُكَلِّبِينَ
تُعَلِّمُونَهُنَّ مِمَّا عَلَّمَكُمُ اللَّهُ
فَكُلُوا مِمَّآ أَمْسَكْنَ عَلَيْكُمْ
وَاذْكُرُوا اسْمَ اللَّهِ عَلَيْهِ وَاتَّقُوا اللَّهَ
إِنَّ اللَّهَ سَرِيعُ الْحِسَابِ ۝

5. This day are (all) things
Good and pure made lawful
Unto you. The food
Of the People of the Book
Is lawful unto you
And yours is lawful
Unto them.
(Lawful unto you in marriage)
Are (not only) chaste women
Who are believers, but
Chaste women among
The People of the Book,
Revealed before your time—
When ye give them
Their due dowers, and desire
Chastity, not lewdness,
Nor secret intrigues.
If anyone rejects faith,
Fruitless is his work,
And in the Hereafter
He will be in the ranks
Of those who have lost
(All spiritual good).

٥- الْيَوْمَ أُحِلَّ لَكُمُ الطَّيِّبَٰتُ
وَطَعَامُ الَّذِينَ أُوتُوا الْكِتَٰبَ حِلٌّ
لَّكُمْ
وَطَعَامُكُمْ حِلٌّ لَّهُمْ
وَالْمُحْصَنَٰتُ مِنَ الْمُؤْمِنَٰتِ
وَالْمُحْصَنَٰتُ مِنَ الَّذِينَ أُوتُوا الْكِتَٰبَ
مِن قَبْلِكُمْ إِذَآ ءَاتَيْتُمُوهُنَّ
أُجُورَهُنَّ مُحْصِنِينَ
غَيْرَ مُسَٰفِحِينَ
وَلَا مُتَّخِذِيٓ أَخْدَانٍ
وَمَن يَكْفُرْ بِالْإِيمَٰنِ فَقَدْ حَبِطَ عَمَلُهُ
وَهُوَ فِي الْآخِرَةِ مِنَ الْخَٰسِرِينَ ۝

SECTION 2.

6. ۝ ye who believe!
When ye prepare
For prayer, wash
Your faces, and your hands
(And arms) to the elbows;
Rub your heads (with water);
And (wash) your feet
To the ankles.
If ye are in a state

٦- يَٰٓأَيُّهَا الَّذِينَ ءَامَنُوٓا إِذَا قُمْتُمْ إِلَى الصَّلَوٰةِ
فَاغْسِلُوا وُجُوهَكُمْ وَأَيْدِيَكُمْ
إِلَى الْمَرَافِقِ
وَامْسَحُوا بِرُءُوسِكُمْ وَأَرْجُلَكُمْ إِلَى الْكَعْبَيْنِ
وَإِن كُنتُمْ جُنُبًا فَاطَّهَّرُوا

Of ceremonial impurity,
Bathe your whole body.
But if ye are ill,
Or on a journey,
Or one of you cometh
From offices of nature,
Or ye have been
In contact with women,
And ye find no water,
Then take for yourselves
Clean sand or earth,
And rub therewith
Your faces and hands.
Allah doth not wish
To place you in a difficulty,
But to make you clean,
And to complete
His favour to you,
That ye may be grateful.

7. And call in remembrance
The favour of Allah
Unto you, and His Covenant,
Which He ratified
With you, when ye said:
"We hear and we obey":
And fear Allah, for Allah
Knoweth well
The secrets of your hearts.

8. O ye who believe!
Stand out firmly
For Allah, as witnesses
To fair dealing, and let not
The hatred of others
To you make you swerve
To wrong and depart from
Justice. Be just: that is
Next to Piety: and fear Allah.
For Allah is well-acquainted
With all that ye do.

9. To those who believe
And do deeds of righteousness
Hath Allah promised forgiveness
And a great reward.

10. Those who reject faith
And deny Our Signs
Will be Companions

Of Hell-fire.

11. O ye who believe!
Call! in remembrance
The favour of Allah
Unto you when
Certain men formed the design
To stretch out
Their hands against you,
But (Allah) held back
Their hands from you:
So fear Allah. And on Allah
Let Believers put
(All) their trust.

SECTION 3.

12. Allah did aforetime
Take a Covenant from
The Children of Israel,
And We appointed twelve
Captains among them.
And Allah said: "I am
With you: if ye (but)
Establish regular Prayers,
Practise regular Charity,
Believe in My messengers,
Honour and assist them,
And loan to Allah
A beautiful loan,
Verily I will wipe out
From you your evils,
And admit you to Gardens
With rivers flowing beneath;
But if any of you, after this,
Resisteth faith, he hath truly
Wandered from the path
Of rectitude."

13. But because of their breach
Of their Covenant, We
Cursed them,   and made
Their hearts grow hard:
They change the words
From their (right) places
And forget a good part
Of the Message that was
Sent them, nor wilt thou
Cease to find them—
Barring a few—ever
Bent on (new) deceits:

But forgive them, and overlook
(Their misdeeds): for Allah
Loveth those who are kind.

14. From those, too, who call
Themselves Christians,
We did take a Covenant,
But they forgot a good part
Of the Message that was
Sent them: so We estranged
Them, with enmity and hatred
Between the one and the other,
To the Day of Judgement.
And soon will Allah   show
Them what it is
They have done.

15. O People of the Book!
There hath come to you
Our Messenger, revealing
To you much that ye
Used to hide in the Book,
And passing over much
(That is now unnecessary):

There hath come to you
From Allah a (new) light
And a perspicuous Book—

16. Wherewith Allah guideth all
Who seek His good pleasure
To ways of peace and safety,
And leadeth them out
Of darkness, by His Will,
Unto the light—guideth them
To a Path that is Straight.

17. In blasphemy indeed
Are those that say
That Allah is Christ
The son of Mary.
Say: "Who then
Hath the least power
Against Allah, if His Will
Were to destroy Christ
The son of Mary, his mother,
And all—everyone
That is on the earth?
For to Allah belongeth
The dominion of the heavens

And the earth, and all
That is between. He createth
What He pleaseth. For Allah
Hath power over all things."

وَمَابَيْنَهُمَاۗ يَخْلُقُ مَايَشَآءُ
وَاللّٰهُ عَلٰى كُلِّ شَىْءٍ قَدِيْرٌ ۟

18. (Both) the Jews and the Christians
Say: "We are sons
Of Allah, and His beloved."
Say: "Why then doth He
Punish you for your sins?
Nay, ye are but men—
Of the men He hath created:
He forgiveth whom He pleaseth,
And He punisheth whom He
                                pleaseth:
And to Allah belongeth
The dominion of the heavens
And the earth, and all
That is between:
And unto Him
Is the final goal (of all)."

١٨- وَقَالَتِ الْيَهُوْدُ وَالنَّصٰرٰى
نَحْنُ اَبْنٰۗؤُا اللّٰهِ وَاَحِبَّآؤُهٗۗ
قُلْ فَلِمَ يُعَذِّبُكُمْ بِذُنُوْبِكُمْ ۗ
بَلْ اَنْتُمْ بَشَرٌ مِّمَّنْ خَلَقَ ۗ
يَغْفِرُ لِمَنْ يَّشَآءُ
وَيُعَذِّبُ مَنْ يَّشَآءُ ۗ
وَلِلّٰهِ مُلْكُ السَّمٰوٰتِ وَالْاَرْضِ
وَمَابَيْنَهُمَا ۗ
وَاِلَيْهِ الْمَصِيْرُ ۟

19. O People of the Book!
Now hath come unto you,
Making (things) clear unto you,
Our Messenger, after the break
In (the series of) our messengers,
Lest ye should say:
"There came unto us
No bringer of glad tidings
And no warner (from evil)";
But now hath come
Unto you a bringer
Of glad tidings
And a warner (from evil).
And Allah hath power
Over all things.

١٩- يٰۗاَهْلَ الْكِتٰبِ قَدْ جَآءَكُمْ رَسُوْلُنَا
يُبَيِّنُ لَكُمْ عَلٰى فَتْرَةٍ مِّنَ الرُّسُلِ
اَنْ تَقُوْلُوْا مَاجَآءَنَا مِنْ بَشِيْرٍ
وَّلَا نَذِيْرٍ ۗ
فَقَدْ جَآءَكُمْ بَشِيْرٌ وَّنَذِيْرٌ ۗ
وَاللّٰهُ عَلٰى كُلِّ شَىْءٍ قَدِيْرٌ ۟

SECTION 4.

20. Remember Moses said
To his people: "O my People!
Call in remembrance the favour
Of Allah unto you, when He
Produced prophets among you,
Made you kings,   and gave
You what He had not given
To any other among the peoples.

٢٠- وَاِذْ قَالَ مُوْسٰى لِقَوْمِهٖ
يٰقَوْمِ اذْكُرُوْا نِعْمَةَ اللّٰهِ عَلَيْكُمْ
اِذْ جَعَلَ فِيْكُمْ اَنْۢبِيَآءَ وَجَعَلَكُمْ مُّلُوْكًا ۖ
وَّاٰتٰىكُمْ مَّالَمْ يُؤْتِ اَحَدًا مِّنَ الْعٰلَمِيْنَ

21. "O my people! enter
The holy land which
Allah hath assigned unto you,
And turn not back
Ignominiously, for then
Will ye be overthrown,
To your own ruin."

٢١- يَقَوْمِ ادْخُلُوا الْأَرْضَ الْمُقَدَّسَةَ
الَّتِى كَتَبَ اللهُ لَكُمْ
وَلَا تَرْتَدُّوا عَلَى أَدْبَارِكُمْ
فَتَنْقَلِبُوا خَاسِرِينَ ○

22. They said: "O Moses!
In this land are a people
Of exceeding strength:
Never shall we enter it
Until they leave it:
If (once) they leave,
Then shall we enter."

٢٢- قَالُوا يَمُوسَى إِنَّ فِيهَا قَوْمًا جَبَّارِينَ ۖ
وَإِنَّا لَنْ نَدْخُلَهَا حَتَّى يَخْرُجُوا مِنْهَا ۖ
فَإِنْ يَخْرُجُوا مِنْهَا فَإِنَّا دَاخِلُونَ ○

23. (But) among (their) God-fearing
men
Were two on whom
Allah had bestowed His grace:
They said: "Assault them
At the (proper) Gate:
When once ye are in,
Victory will be yours;

But on Allah put your trust
If ye have faith."

٢٣- قَالَ رَجُلَانِ مِنَ الَّذِينَ يَخَافُونَ
أَنْعَمَ اللهُ
عَلَيْهِمَا ادْخُلُوا عَلَيْهِمُ الْبَابَ ۖ
فَإِذَا دَخَلْتُمُوهُ فَإِنَّكُمْ غَالِبُونَ ۚ
وَعَلَى اللهِ فَتَوَكَّلُوا إِنْ كُنْتُمْ مُؤْمِنِينَ ○

24. They said: "O Moses!
While they remain there,
Never shall we be able
To enter, to the end of time.
Go thou, and thy Lord,
And fight ye two,
While we sit here
(And watch)."

٢٤- قَالُوا يَمُوسَى إِنَّا لَنْ نَدْخُلَهَا أَبَدًا
مَا دَامُوا فِيهَا
فَاذْهَبْ أَنْتَ وَرَبُّكَ فَقَاتِلَا
إِنَّا هَهُنَا قَاعِدُونَ ○

25. He said: "O my Lord!
I have power only
Over myself and my brother:
So separate us from this
Rebellious people!"

٢٥- قَالَ رَبِّ إِنِّي لَا أَمْلِكُ إِلَّا نَفْسِي
وَأَخِي ۖ فَافْرُقْ بَيْنَنَا وَبَيْنَ الْقَوْمِ الْفَاسِقِينَ ○

26. Allah said: "Therefore
Will the land be out
Of their reach for forty years:
In distraction will they
Wander through the land:
But sorrow thou not
Over these rebellious people.

٢٦- قَالَ فَإِنَّهَا
مُحَرَّمَةٌ عَلَيْهِمْ أَرْبَعِينَ
سَنَةً ۚ يَتِيهُونَ فِي الْأَرْضِ ۚ
فَلَا تَأْسَ عَلَى الْقَوْمِ الْفَاسِقِينَ ○

SECTION 5.

27. Recite to them the truth
Of the story of the two sons
Of Adam. Behold! they each
Presented a sacrifice (to Allah):
It was accepted from one,
But not from the other.
Said the latter: "Be sure
I will slay thee." "Surely,"
Said the former, "Allah
Doth accept of the sacrifice
Of those who are righteous.

٢٧- وَاتْلُ عَلَيْهِمْ نَبَأَ ابْنَيْ
اٰدَمَ بِالْحَقِّ ۘ اِذْ قَرَّبَا قُرْبَانًا فَتُقُبِّلَ
مِنْ اَحَدِهِمَا وَلَمْ يُتَقَبَّلْ مِنَ الْاٰخَرِ ۘ
قَالَ لَاَقْتُلَنَّكَ ۘ
قَالَ اِنَّمَا يَتَقَبَّلُ اللّٰهُ مِنَ الْمُتَّقِيْنَ ○

28. "If thou dost stretch thy hand
Against me, to slay me,
It is not for me to stretch
My hand against thee
To slay thee: for I do fear
Allah, the Cherisher of the Worlds.

٢٨- لَئِنْ بَسَطْتَّ اِلَيَّ يَدَكَ لِتَقْتُلَنِيْ
مَاۤ اَنَا بِبَاسِطٍ يَّدِيَ اِلَيْكَ لِاَقْتُلَكَ ۚ
اِنِّيْۤ اَخَافُ اللّٰهَ رَبَّ الْعٰلَمِيْنَ ○

29. "For me, I intend to let
Thee draw on thyself
My sin as well as thine,
For thou wilt be among
The Companions of the Fire,
And that is the reward
Of those who do wrong."

٢٩- اِنِّيْۤ اُرِيْدُ اَنْ تَبُوْۤاَ بِاِثْمِيْ وَاِثْمِكَ
فَتَكُوْنَ مِنْ اَصْحٰبِ النَّارِ ۚ
وَذٰلِكَ جَزٰٓؤُا الظّٰلِمِيْنَ ۚ

30. The (selfish) soul of the other
Led him to the murder
Of his brother: he murdered
Him, and became (himself)
One of the lost ones.

٣٠- فَطَوَّعَتْ لَهُ نَفْسُهُ قَتْلَ اَخِيْهِ
فَقَتَلَهُ فَاَصْبَحَ مِنَ الْخٰسِرِيْنَ ○

31. Then Allah sent a raven,
Who scratched the ground,
To show him how to hide
The shame of his brother.
"Woe is me!" said he;
"Was I not even able
To be as this raven,
And to hide the shame
Of my brother?" Then he became
Full of regrets—

٣١- فَبَعَثَ اللّٰهُ غُرَابًا يَّبْحَثُ فِى الْاَرْضِ
لِيُرِيَهُ كَيْفَ يُوَارِيْ سَوْءَةَ اَخِيْهِ ۚ
قَالَ يٰوَيْلَتٰۤى اَعَجَزْتُ اَنْ اَكُوْنَ مِثْلَ
هٰذَا الْغُرَابِ فَاُوَارِيَ سَوْءَةَ
اَخِيْ ۚ فَاَصْبَحَ مِنَ النّٰدِمِيْنَ ۚ۟

32. On that account: We ordained
For the Children of Israel
That if anyone slew
A person—unless it be
For murder or for spreading

٣٢- مِنْ اَجْلِ ذٰلِكَ ۚ
كَتَبْنَا عَلٰى بَنِيْۤ اِسْرَآءِيْلَ
اَنَّهٗ مَنْ قَتَلَ نَفْسًا

Mischief in the land—
It would be as if
He slew the whole people:
And if anyone saved a life,
It would be as if he saved
The life of the whole people.
Then although there came
To them Our Messengers
With Clear Signs, yet,
Even after that, many
Of them continued to commit
Excesses in the land.

بِغَيْرِ نَفْسٍ أَوْ فَسَادٍ فِى الْأَرْضِ
فَكَأَنَّمَا قَتَلَ النَّاسَ جَمِيعًا ۗ
وَمَنْ أَحْيَاهَا فَكَأَنَّمَا أَحْيَا النَّاسَ جَمِيعًا ۚ
وَلَقَدْ جَاءَتْهُمْ رُسُلُنَا بِالْبَيِّنَاتِ
ثُمَّ إِنَّ كَثِيرًا مِّنْهُمْ
بَعْدَ ذَٰلِكَ فِى الْأَرْضِ لَمُسْرِفُونَ ۝

33. The punishment of those
Who wage war against Allah
And His Messenger, and strive
With might and main
For mischief through the land
Is: execution, or crucifixion,
Or the cutting off of hands
And feet from opposite sides,
Or exile from the land:
That is their disgrace
In this world, and
A heavy punishment is theirs
In the Hereafter;

٣٣- إِنَّمَا جَزَٰٓؤُا الَّذِينَ يُحَارِبُونَ اللَّهَ
وَرَسُولَهُ وَيَسْعَوْنَ فِى الْأَرْضِ فَسَادًا
أَنْ يُقَتَّلُوا أَوْ يُصَلَّبُوا
أَوْ تُقَطَّعَ أَيْدِيهِمْ وَأَرْجُلُهُمْ مِّنْ خِلَافٍ
أَوْ يُنْفَوْا مِنَ الْأَرْضِ ۚ
ذَٰلِكَ لَهُمْ خِزْيٌ فِى الدُّنْيَا
وَلَهُمْ فِى الْآخِرَةِ عَذَابٌ عَظِيمٌ ۝

34. Except for those who repent
Before they fall
Into your power:
In that case, know
That Allah is Oft-Forgiving,
Most Merciful.

٣٤- إِلَّا الَّذِينَ تَابُوا
مِنْ قَبْلِ أَنْ تَقْدِرُوا عَلَيْهِمْ ۖ
فَاعْلَمُوا أَنَّ اللَّهَ غَفُورٌ رَحِيمٌ ۝

SECTION 6.

35. O ye who believe!
Do your duty to Allah,
Seek the means
Of approach unto Him,
And strive with might
And main in His cause:
That ye may prosper.

٣٥- يَا أَيُّهَا الَّذِينَ آمَنُوا اتَّقُوا اللَّهَ
وَابْتَغُوا إِلَيْهِ الْوَسِيلَةَ
وَجَاهِدُوا فِى سَبِيلِهِ
لَعَلَّكُمْ تُفْلِحُونَ ۝

36. As to those who reject
Faith—if they had
Everything on earth,
And twice repeated,
To give as ransom

٣٦- إِنَّ الَّذِينَ كَفَرُوا
لَوْ أَنَّ لَهُمْ مَّا فِى الْأَرْضِ جَمِيعًا

For the penalty of the Day
Of Judgement, it would
Never be accepted of them.
Theirs would be
A grievous Penalty.

37. Their wish will be
To get out of the Fire,
But never will they
Get out therefrom:
Their Penalty will be
One that endures.

38. As to the thief,
Male or female,
Cut off his or her hands:
A punishment by way
Of example, from Allah,
For their crime:
And Allah is Exalted in Power,
Full of Wisdom.

39. But if the thief repents
After his crime,
And amends his conduct,
Allah turneth to him
In forgiveness; for Allah
Is Oft-Forgiving, Most Merciful.

40. Knowest thou not
That to Allah (alone)
Belongeth the dominion
Of the heavens and the earth?
He punisheth whom He pleaseth,
And He forgiveth whom He
                pleaseth:
And Allah hath power
Over all things.

41. O Messenger! let not
Those grieve thee, who race
Each other into Unbelief:
(Whether it be) among those
Who say "We believe"
With their lips but
Whose hearts have no faith;
Or it be among the Jews—

Men who will listen
To any lie—will listen
Even to others who have
Never so much as come[745]
To thee. They change the words
From their (right) times
And places: they say,
"If ye are given this,
Take it, but if not,
Beware!" If anyone's trial
Is intended by Allah, thou hast
No authority in the least
For him against Allah.
For such—it is not
Allah's will to purify
Their hearts. For them
There is disgrace
In this world, and
In the Hereafter
A heavy punishment.

42. (They are fond of) listening
To falsehood, of devouring
Anything forbidden.
If they do come to thee,
Either judge between them,
Or decline to interfere.
If thou decline, they cannot
Hurt thee in the least.
If thou judge, judge
In equity between them.
For Allah loveth those
Who judge in equity.

43. But why do they come
To thee for decision,
When they have (their own)
Law before them?—
Therein is the (plain)
Command of Allah; yet
Even after that, they would
Turn away. For they
Are not (really)
People of Faith.

SECTION 7.

44. It was We who revealed
The Law (to Moses): therein
Was guidance and light.
By its standard have been judged
The Jews, by the Prophets
Who bowed (as in Islam)
To Allah's Will, by the Rabbis
And the Doctors of Law:
For to them was entrusted
The protection of Allah's Book,
And they were witnesses thereto:
Therefore fear not men,
But fear Me, and sell not
My Signs for a miserable price.
If any do fail to judge
By (the light of) what Allah
Hath revealed, they are
(No better than) Unbelievers.

٤٤- ﺍِﻧَّﺎ ﺍَﻧْﺰَﻟْﻨَﺎ ﺍﻟﺘَّﻮْﺭٰﯨﺔَ ﻓِﯿْﮭَﺎ ﮬُﺪًﯼ ﻭَّ ﻧُﻮْﺭٌ ۙ
ﯾَﺤْﻜُﻢُ ﺑِﮭَﺎ ﺍﻟﻨَّﺒِﯿُّﻮْﻥَ ﺍﻟَّﺬِﯾْﻦَ ﺍَﺳْﻠَﻤُﻮْﺍ
ﻟِﻠَّﺬِﯾْﻦَ ﮬَﺎﺩُﻭْﺍ
ﻭَ ﺍﻟﺮَّﺑّٰﻨِﯿُّﻮْﻥَ ﻭَ ﺍﻟْﺎَﺣْﺒَﺎﺭُ
ﺑِﻤَﺎ ﺍﺳْﺘُﺤْﻔِﻈُﻮْﺍ ﻣِﻦْ ﻛِﺘٰﺐِ ﺍﻟﻠﻪِ ﻭَ ﻛَﺎﻧُﻮْﺍ ﻋَﻠَﯿْﻪِ
ﺷُﮭَﺪَﺁﺀَ ۚ ﻓَﻠَﺎ ﺗَﺨْﺸَﻮُﺍ ﺍﻟﻨَّﺎﺱَ ﻭَ ﺍﺧْﺸَﻮْﻥِ
ﻭَ ﻟَﺎ ﺗَﺸْﺘَﺮُﻭْﺍ ﺑِﺎٰﯾٰﺘِﯽْ ﺛَﻤَﻨًﺎ ﻗَﻠِﯿْﻠًﺎ ؕ
ﻭَ ﻣَﻦْ ﻟَّﻢْ ﯾَﺤْﻜُﻢْ ﺑِﻤَﺎ ﺍَﻧْﺰَﻝَ ﺍﻟﻠﻪُ
ﻓَﺎُﻭﻟٰٓﺌِﻚَ ﮬُﻢُ ﺍﻟْﻜٰﻔِﺮُﻭْﻥَ ۟

45. We ordained therein for them:
"Life for life, eye for eye,
Nose for nose, ear for ear,
Tooth for tooth, and wounds
Equal for equal." But if
Anyone remits the retaliation
By way of charity, it is
An act of atonement for himself.
And if any fail to judge
By (the light of) what Allah
Hath revealed, they are
(No better than) wrongdoers.

٤٥- ﻭَ ﻛَﺘَﺒْﻨَﺎ ﻋَﻠَﯿْﮭِﻢْ ﻓِﯿْﮭَﺂ
ﺍَﻥَّ ﺍﻟﻨَّﻔْﺲَ ﺑِﺎﻟﻨَّﻔْﺲِ ۙ ﻭَ ﺍﻟْﻌَﯿْﻦَ ﺑِﺎﻟْﻌَﯿْﻦِ
ﻭَ ﺍﻟْﺎَﻧْﻒَ ﺑِﺎﻟْﺎَﻧْﻒِ ﻭَ ﺍﻟْﺎُﺫُﻥَ ﺑِﺎﻟْﺎُﺫُﻥِ
ﻭَ ﺍﻟﺴِّﻦَّ ﺑِﺎﻟﺴِّﻦِّ ۙ ﻭَ ﺍﻟْﺠُﺮُﻭْﺡَ ﻗِﺼَﺎﺹٌ ؕ
ﻓَﻤَﻦْ ﺗَﺼَﺪَّﻕَ ﺑِﻪٖ ﻓَﮭُﻮَ ﻛَﻔَّﺎﺭَﺓٌ ﻟَّﻪٗ ؕ ﻭَ ﻣَﻦْ ﻟَّﻢْ
ﯾَﺤْﻜُﻢْ ﺑِﻤَﺎ ﺍَﻧْﺰَﻝَ ﺍﻟﻠﻪُ ﻓَﺎُﻭﻟٰٓﺌِﻚَ ﮬُﻢُ ﺍﻟﻈّٰﻠِﻤُﻮْﻥَ ۟

46. And in their footsteps
We sent Jesus the son
Of Mary, confirming
The Law that had come
Before him: We sent him
The Gospel: therein
Was guidance and light,
And confirmation of the Law
That had come before him:
A guidance and an admonition
To those who fear Allah.

٤٦- ﻭَ ﻗَﻔَّﯿْﻨَﺎ ﻋَﻠٰٓﯽ ﺍٰﺛَﺎﺭِﮬِﻢْ ﺑِﻌِﯿْﺴَﯽ ﺍﺑْﻦِ
ﻣَﺮْﯾَﻢَ ﻣُﺼَﺪِّﻗًﺎ
ﻟِّﻤَﺎ ﺑَﯿْﻦَ ﯾَﺪَﯾْﻪِ ﻣِﻦَ ﺍﻟﺘَّﻮْﺭٰﯨﺔِ ۫
ﻭَ ﺍٰﺗَﯿْﻨٰﻪُ ﺍﻟْﺎِﻧْﺠِﯿْﻞَ ﻓِﯿْﻪِ ﮬُﺪًﯼ ﻭَّ ﻧُﻮْﺭٌ ۙ
ﻭَّ ﻣُﺼَﺪِّﻗًﺎ ﻟِّﻤَﺎ ﺑَﯿْﻦَ ﯾَﺪَﯾْﻪِ ﻣِﻦَ ﺍﻟﺘَّﻮْﺭٰﯨﺔِ
ﻭَ ﮬُﺪًﯼ ﻭَّ ﻣَﻮْﻋِﻈَﺔً ﻟِّﻠْﻤُﺘَّﻘِﯿْﻦَ ﻪ۟

47. Let the People of the Gospel
Judge by what Allah hath revealed

٤٧- ﻭَ ﻟْﯿَﺤْﻜُﻢْ ﺍَﮬْﻞُ ﺍﻟْﺎِﻧْﺠِﯿْﻞِ ﺑِﻤَﺎ ﺍَﻧْﺰَﻝَ

Therein. If any do fail
To judge by (the light of)
What Allah hath revealed,
They are (no better than)
Those who rebel.

48. To thee We sent the Scripture
In truth, confirming
The scripture that came
Before it, and guarding it
In safety: so judge
Between them by what
Allah hath revealed,
And follow not their vain
Desires, diverging
From the Truth that hath come
To thee. To each among you
Have We prescribed a Law
And an Open Way.
If Allah had so willed,
He would have made you
A single People, but (His
Plan is) to test you in what
He hath given you; so strive
As in a race in all virtues.
The goal of you all is to Allah;
It is He that will show you
The truth of the matters
In which ye dispute;

49. And this (He commands):
Judge thou between them
By what Allah hath revealed,
And follow not their vain
Desires, but beware of them
Lest they beguile thee
From any of that (teaching)
Which Allah hath sent down
To thee. And if they turn
Away, be assured that
For some of their crimes
It is Allah's purpose to punish
Them. And truly most men
Are rebellious.

50. Do they then seek after
A judgement of (the Days

Of) Ignorance? But who,
For a people whose faith
Is assured, can give
Better judgement than Allah?

SECTION 8.

51. (⊕) ye who believe!
Take not the Jews
And the Christians
For your friends and protectors;
They are but friends and
　　　　　　　protectors
To each other. And he
Amongst you that turns to them
(For friendship) is of them.
Verily Allah guideth not
A people unjust.

52. Those in whose hearts
Is a disease—thou seest
How eagerly they run about
Amongst them, saying:
"We do fear lest a change
Of fortune bring us disaster."
Ah! perhaps Allah will give
(Thee) victory, or a decision
According to His Will.
Then will they repent
Of the thoughts which they secretly
Harboured in their hearts.

53. And those who believe
Will say: "Are these
The men who swore
Their strongest oaths by Allah,
That they were with you?"
All that they do
Will be in vain,
And they will fall
Into (nothing but) ruin.

54. (⊕) ye who believe!
If any from among you
Turn back from his Faith,
Soon will Allah produce
A people whom He will love
As they will love Him—
Lowly with the Believers,
Mighty against the Rejecters,
Fighting in the Way of Allah,

And never afraid
Of the reproaches
Of such as find fault.
That is the Grace of Allah,
Which He will bestow
On whom He pleaseth.
And Allah encompasseth all,
And He knoweth all things.

اَعِزَّةٍ عَلَى الْكٰفِرِیْنَ یُجَاهِدُوْنَ فِیْ سَبِیْلِ
اللّٰهِ وَلَا یَخَافُوْنَ لَوْمَةَ لَائِمٍ ؕ
ذٰلِكَ فَضْلُ اللّٰهِ یُؤْتِیْهِ مَنْ یَّشَآءُ ؕ
وَاللّٰهُ وَاسِعٌ عَلِیْمٌ ۟

55. Your (real) friends are
(No less than) Allah,
His Messenger, and the (Fellowship
Of) Believers—those who
Establish regular prayers
And regular charity,
And they bow
Down humbly (in worship).

٥٥- اِنَّمَا وَلِیُّكُمُ اللّٰهُ وَرَسُوْلُهٗ وَالَّذِیْنَ
اٰمَنُوا
الَّذِیْنَ یُقِیْمُوْنَ الصَّلٰوةَ
وَیُؤْتُوْنَ الزَّكٰوةَ وَهُمْ رَاكِعُوْنَ ۟

56. As to those who turn
(For friendship) to Allah,
His Messenger, and the (Fellowship
Of) Believers—it is
The Fellowship of Allah
That must certainly triumph.

٥٦- وَمَنْ یَّتَوَلَّ اللّٰهَ وَرَسُوْلَهٗ
وَالَّذِیْنَ اٰمَنُوْا
فَاِنَّ حِزْبَ اللّٰهِ هُمُ الْغٰلِبُوْنَ ۟

SECTION 9.

57. O ye who believe!
Take not for friends
And protectors those
Who take your religion
For a mockery or sport—
Whether among those
Who received the Scripture
Before you, or among those
Who reject Faith;
But fear ye Allah,
If ye have Faith (indeed).

٥٧- یٰۤاَیُّهَا الَّذِیْنَ اٰمَنُوْا
لَا تَتَّخِذُوا الَّذِیْنَ اتَّخَذُوْا دِیْنَكُمْ هُزُوًا
وَّلَعِبًا مِّنَ
الَّذِیْنَ اُوْتُوا الْكِتٰبَ مِنْ قَبْلِكُمْ
وَالْكُفَّارَ اَوْلِیَآءَ ۚ
وَاتَّقُوا اللّٰهَ اِنْ كُنْتُمْ مُّؤْمِنِیْنَ ۟

58. When ye proclaim
Your call to prayer,
They take it (but)
As mockery and sport;
That is because they are
A people without understanding.

٥٨- وَاِذَا نَادَیْتُمْ اِلَى الصَّلٰوةِ
اتَّخَذُوْهَا هُزُوًا وَّلَعِبًا ؕ
ذٰلِكَ بِاَنَّهُمْ قَوْمٌ لَّا یَعْقِلُوْنَ ۟

59. Say: "O People of the Book!
Do ye disapprove of us
For no other reason than
That we believe in Allah,

٥٩- قُلْ یٰۤاَهْلَ الْكِتٰبِ
هَلْ تَنْقِمُوْنَ مِنَّاۤ اِلَّاۤ اَنْ اٰمَنَّا بِاللّٰهِ

And the revelation
That hath come to us
And that which came
Before (us), and (perhaps)
That most of you
Are rebellious and disobedient?"

وَمَآ أُنْزِلَ إِلَيْنَا
وَمَآ أُنْزِلَ مِنْ قَبْلُ
وَأَنَّ أَكْثَرَكُمْ فٰسِقُوْنَ ۝

60. Say: "Shall I point out
To you something much worse
Than this, (as judged)
By the treatment it received
From Allah? Those who
Incurred the curse of Allah
And His wrath, those of whom some
He transformed into apes and swine,
Those who worshipped Evil—
These are (many times) worse
In rank, and far more astray
From the even Path!"

۶۰ قُلْ هَلْ أُنَبِّئُكُمْ بِشَرٍّ مِّنْ ذٰلِكَ
مَثُوْبَةً عِنْدَ اللّٰهِ
مَنْ لَّعَنَهُ اللّٰهُ وَغَضِبَ عَلَيْهِ
وَجَعَلَ مِنْهُمُ الْقِرَدَةَ وَالْخَنَازِيْرَ وَعَبَدَ
الطَّاغُوْتَ
أُولٰٓئِكَ شَرٌّ مَّكَانًا
وَّأَضَلُّ عَنْ سَوَآءِ السَّبِيْلِ ۝

61. When they come to thee,
They say: "We believe":
But in fact they enter
With a mind against Faith,
And they go out
With the same.
But Allah knoweth fully
All that they hide.

۶۱ وَإِذَا جَآءُوْكُمْ قَالُوْٓا اٰمَنَّا
وَقَدْ دَّخَلُوْا بِالْكُفْرِ
وَهُمْ قَدْ خَرَجُوْا بِهٖ
وَاللّٰهُ أَعْلَمُ بِمَا كَانُوْا يَكْتُمُوْنَ ۝

62. Many of them dost thou
See, racing each other
In sin and transgression
And their eating of things
Forbidden. Evil indeed
Are the things that they do.

۶۲ وَتَرٰى كَثِيْرًا مِّنْهُمْ يُسَارِعُوْنَ فِى
الْإِثْمِ وَالْعُدْوَانِ وَأَكْلِهِمُ السُّحْتَ
لَبِئْسَ مَا كَانُوْا يَعْمَلُوْنَ ۝

63. Why do not the Rabbis
And the doctors of law forbid
Them from their (habit
Of) uttering sinful words
And eating things forbidden?
Evil indeed are their works.

۶۳ لَوْلَا يَنْهٰهُمُ الرَّبَّانِيُّوْنَ وَالْأَحْبَارُ
عَنْ قَوْلِهِمُ الْإِثْمَ وَأَكْلِهِمُ السُّحْتَ
لَبِئْسَ مَا كَانُوْا يَصْنَعُوْنَ ۝

64. The Jews say: "Allah's hand
Is tied up." Be *their* hands
Tied up and be they accursed
For the (blasphemy) they utter.
Nay, both His hands
Are widely outstretched:
He giveth and spendeth
(Of His bounty) as He pleaseth.
But the revelation that
Cometh to thee from Allah
Increaseth in most of them
Their obstinate rebellion
And blasphemy. Amongst them
We have placed enmity
And hatred till the Day
Of Judgement. Every time
They kindle the fire of war,
Allah doth extinguish it;
But they (ever) strive
To do mischief on earth.
And Allah loveth not
Those who do mischief.

65. If only the People of the Book
Had believed and been
            righteous,
We should indeed have
Blotted out their iniquities
And admitted them
To Gardens of Bliss.

66. If only they had stood fast
By the Law, the Gospel,
And all the revelation that was
            sent
To them from their Lord,
They would have enjoyed
Happiness from every side.
There is from among them
A party on the right course:
But many of them
Follow a course that is evil.

SECTION 10.

67. Messenger! proclaim

The (Message) which hath been
Sent to thee from thy Lord.
If thou didst not, thou
Wouldst not have fulfilled
And proclaimed His Mission.
And Allah will defend thee
From men (who mean
         mischief).

For Allah guideth not
Those who reject Faith.

مَآ أُنزِلَ إِلَيْكَ
مِن رَّبِّكَ ۖ وَإِن لَّمْ تَفْعَلْ
فَمَا بَلَّغْتَ رِسَالَتَهُ ۚ
وَاللَّهُ يَعْصِمُكَ مِنَ النَّاسِ ۗ
إِنَّ اللَّهَ لَا يَهْدِي الْقَوْمَ الْكَافِرِينَ ۞

68. Say: "O People of the Book!
Ye have no ground
To stand upon unless
Ye stand fast by the Law,
The Gospel, and all the
         revelation
That has come to you from
Your Lord." It is the revelation
That cometh to thee from
Thy Lord, that increaseth in
         most
Of them their obstinate
Rebellion and blasphemy.
But sorrow thou not
Over (these) people without
         Faith.

٦٨- قُلْ يَا أَهْلَ الْكِتَابِ لَسْتُمْ عَلَىٰ شَيْءٍ
حَتَّىٰ تُقِيمُوا التَّوْرَاةَ وَالْإِنجِيلَ
وَمَا أُنزِلَ إِلَيْكُم مِّن رَّبِّكُمْ ۚ
وَلَيَزِيدَنَّ كَثِيرًا مِّنْهُم مَّا أُنزِلَ إِلَيْكَ
مِن رَّبِّكَ
طُغْيَانًا وَكُفْرًا ۖ
فَلَا تَأْسَ عَلَى الْقَوْمِ الْكَافِرِينَ ۞

69. Those who believe (in the
         Qur'ān),
Those who follow the Jewish
         (scriptures),
And the Sabians and the
         Christians—
Any who believe in Allah
And the Last Day,
And work righteousness—
On them shall be no fear,
Nor shall they grieve.

٦٩- إِنَّ الَّذِينَ آمَنُوا
وَالَّذِينَ هَادُوا وَالصَّابِئُونَ وَالنَّصَارَىٰ
مَنْ آمَنَ بِاللَّهِ وَالْيَوْمِ الْآخِرِ
وَعَمِلَ صَالِحًا
فَلَا خَوْفٌ عَلَيْهِمْ وَلَا هُمْ يَحْزَنُونَ ۞

70. We took the Covenant
Of the Children of Israel
And sent them Messengers.
Every time there came
To them a Messenger

٧٠- لَقَدْ أَخَذْنَا مِيثَاقَ بَنِي إِسْرَائِيلَ
وَأَرْسَلْنَا إِلَيْهِمْ رُسُلًا ۖ
كُلَّمَا جَاءَهُمْ رَسُولٌ

With what they themselves
Desired not—some
(Of these) they called
Imposters, and some they
(Go so far as to) slay.

بِمَا لَا تَهْوٰى أَنْفُسُهُمْ فَرِيْقًا
كَذَّبُوْا وَفَرِيْقًا يَّقْتُلُوْنَ ۝

71. They thought there would be
No trial (or punishment);
So they became blind and deaf;
Yet Allah (in mercy) turned
To them; yet again many
Of them became blind and deaf.
But Allah sees well
All that they do.

٧١ - وَحَسِبُوْۤا اَلَّا تَكُوْنَ فِتْنَةٌ فَعَمُوْا وَ
صَمُّوْا ثُمَّ تَابَ اللّٰهُ عَلَيْهِمْ
ثُمَّ عَمُوْا وَصَمُّوْا كَثِيْرٌ مِّنْهُمْ ۗ
وَاللّٰهُ بَصِيْرٌ بِمَا يَعْمَلُوْنَ ۝

72. They do blaspheme who say:
"Allah is Christ the son
Of Mary." But said Christ:
"O Children of Israel!
Worship Allah, my Lord
And your Lord." Whoever
Joins other gods with Allah—
Allah will forbid him
The Garden, and the Fire
Will be his abode. There will
For the wrongdoers
Be no one to help.

٧٢ - لَقَدْ كَفَرَ الَّذِيْنَ قَالُوْۤا إِنَّ اللّٰهَ هُوَ
الْمَسِيْحُ ابْنُ مَرْيَمَ ۗ وَقَالَ الْمَسِيْحُ
يٰبَنِيْۤ إِسْرَآءِيْلَ اعْبُدُوا
اللّٰهَ رَبِّيْ وَرَبَّكُمْ ۗ إِنَّهٗ مَنْ يُّشْرِكْ بِاللّٰهِ
فَقَدْ حَرَّمَ اللّٰهُ عَلَيْهِ الْجَنَّةَ
وَمَأْوَاهُ النَّارُ ۗ وَمَا لِلظّٰلِمِيْنَ مِنْ أَنْصَارٍ ۝

73. They do blaspheme who say:
Allah is one of three
In a Trinity: for there is
No god except One God.
If they desist not
From their word (of blasphemy),
Verily a grievous penalty
Will befall the blasphemers
Among them.

٧٣ - لَقَدْ كَفَرَ الَّذِيْنَ قَالُوْۤا إِنَّ اللّٰهَ ثَالِثُ
ثَلٰثَةٍ ۘ وَمَا مِنْ إِلٰهٍ إِلَّاۤ إِلٰهٌ وَّاحِدٌ ۗ
وَإِنْ لَّمْ يَنْتَهُوْا
عَمَّا يَقُوْلُوْنَ لَيَمَسَّنَّ الَّذِيْنَ كَفَرُوْا
مِنْهُمْ عَذَابٌ أَلِيْمٌ ۝

74. Why turn they not to Allah
And seek His forgiveness?
For Allah is Oft-Forgiving,
Most Merciful.

٧٤ - أَفَلَا يَتُوْبُوْنَ إِلَى اللّٰهِ وَيَسْتَغْفِرُوْنَهٗ ۗ
وَاللّٰهُ غَفُوْرٌ رَّحِيْمٌ ۝

75. Christ, the son of Mary,
Was no more than
A Messenger; many were
The Messengers that passed away
Before him. His mother
Was a woman of truth.

٧٥ - مَا الْمَسِيْحُ ابْنُ مَرْيَمَ إِلَّا رَسُوْلٌ ۚ
قَدْ خَلَتْ مِنْ قَبْلِهِ الرُّسُلُ ۗ
وَأُمُّهٗ صِدِّيْقَةٌ ۗ

They had both to eat
Their (daily) food.
See how Allah doth make
His Signs clear to them;
Yet see in what ways
They are deluded
Away from the truth!

76. Say: "Will ye worship,
Besides Allah, something
Which hath no power either
To harm or benefit you?
But Allah—He it is
That heareth and knoweth
All things."

كَانَا يَأْكُلَانِ الطَّعَامَ ۗ
انْظُرْ كَيْفَ نُبَيِّنُ لَهُمُ الْاٰيٰتِ
ثُمَّ انْظُرْ اَنّٰى يُؤْفَكُوْنَ ۝

٧٦- قُلْ اَتَعْبُدُوْنَ مِنْ دُوْنِ اللّٰهِ
مَا لَا يَمْلِكُ لَكُمْ ضَرًّا وَّلَا نَفْعًا ۗ
وَاللّٰهُ هُوَ السَّمِيْعُ الْعَلِيْمُ ۝

77. Say: "O People of the Book!
Exceed not in your religion
The bounds (of what is proper),
Trespassing beyond the truth,
Nor follow the vain desires
Of people who went wrong
In times gone by—who misled
Many, and strayed (themselves)
From the even Way.

SECTION 11.

٧٧- قُلْ يٰٓاَهْلَ الْكِتٰبِ
لَا تَغْلُوْا فِيْ دِيْنِكُمْ غَيْرَ الْحَقِّ
وَلَا تَتَّبِعُوْٓا اَهْوَآءَ قَوْمٍ قَدْ ضَلُّوْا مِنْ قَبْلُ
وَاَضَلُّوْا كَثِيْرًا
وَّضَلُّوْا عَنْ سَوَآءِ السَّبِيْلِ ۩

78. Curses were pronounced
On those among the Children
Of Israel who rejected Faith,
By the tongue of David
And of Jesus, the son of Mary,
Because they disobeyed
And persisted in Excesses.

٧٨- لُعِنَ الَّذِيْنَ كَفَرُوْا مِنْ بَنِيْٓ اِسْرَآءِيْلَ
عَلٰى لِسَانِ دَاوٗدَ وَعِيْسَى ابْنِ مَرْيَمَ ۗ
ذٰلِكَ بِمَا عَصَوْا وَّكَانُوْا يَعْتَدُوْنَ ۝

79. Nor did they (usually)
Forbid one another
The iniquities which they
Committed: evil indeed
Were the deeds which they did.

٧٩- كَانُوْا لَا يَتَنَاهَوْنَ عَنْ مُّنْكَرٍ فَعَلُوْهُ ۗ
لَبِئْسَ مَا كَانُوْا يَفْعَلُوْنَ ۝

80. Thou seest many of them
Turning in friendship
To the Unbelievers.
Evil indeed are (the works) which
Their souls have sent forward
Before them (with the result),
That Allah's wrath
Is on them.

٨٠- تَرٰى كَثِيْرًا مِّنْهُمْ
يَتَوَلَّوْنَ الَّذِيْنَ كَفَرُوْا ۗ
لَبِئْسَ مَا قَدَّمَتْ لَهُمْ اَنْفُسُهُمْ
اَنْ سَخِطَ اللّٰهُ عَلَيْهِمْ

And in torment
Will they abide.

و في العذاب هم خلدون ٥

81. If only they had believed
In Allah, in the Prophet,
And in what hath been
Revealed to him, never
Would they have taken
Them for friends and protectors,
But most of them are
Rebellious wrongdoers.

٨١- ولو كانوا يؤمنون بالله والنبي
وما انزل اليه
ما اتخذوهم اولياء
ولكن كثيرا منهم فسقون ٥

7/30

82. Strongest among men in enmity
To the Believers wilt thou
Find the Jews and Pagans;
And nearest among them in love
To the Believers wilt thou
Find those who say,
"We are Christians":
Because amongst these are
Men devoted to learning
And men who have renounced
The world, and they
Are not arrogant.

٨٢- لتجدن اشد الناس عداوة للذين
امنوا اليهود والذين اشركوا
ولتجدن اقربهم مودة للذين امنوا
الذين قالوا انا نصرى ذلك بان منهم
قسيسين ورهبانا
وانهم لا يستكبرون ٥

83. And when they listen
To the revelation received
By the Messenger, thou wilt
See their eyes overflowing
With tears, for they
Recognise the truth:
They pray: "Our Lord!
We believe; write us
Down among the witnesses.

٨٣- واذا سمعوا ما انزل الى الرسول
ترى اعينهم تفيض من الدمع
مما عرفوا من الحق
يقولون ربنا امنا
فاكتبنا مع الشهدين ٥

84. "What cause can we have
Not to believe in Allah
And the truth which has
Come to us, seeing that
We long for our Lord
To admit us to the company
Of the righteous?"

٨٤- وما لنا لا نؤمن بالله وما جاءنا
من الحق ونطمع ان يدخلنا ربنا
مع القوم الصلحين ٥

85. And for this their prayer
Hath Allah rewarded them
With Gardens, with rivers
Flowing underneath—their
                        eternal
Home. Such is the recompense

٨٥- فاثابهم الله بما قالوا
جنت تجري من تحتها الانهر
خلدين فيها وذلك

Of those who do good.

جَزَآءُ الْمُحْسِنِيْنَ ۞

86. But those who reject Faith
And belie Our Signs—
They shall be Companions
Of Hell-fire.

٨٦ - وَالَّذِيْنَ كَفَرُوْا وَكَذَّبُوْا بِاٰيٰتِنَآ
أُولٰٓئِكَ أَصْحٰبُ الْجَحِيْمِ ۞

SECTION 12.

87. (O) ye who believe!
Make not unlawful
The good things which Allah
Hath made lawful for you,
But commit no excess;
For Allah loveth not
Those given to excess.

٨٧ - يٰٓأَيُّهَا الَّذِيْنَ اٰمَنُوْا لَا تُحَرِّمُوْا
طَيِّبٰتِ مَآ أَحَلَّ اللّٰهُ لَكُمْ
وَلَا تَعْتَدُوْا ۚ
إِنَّ اللّٰهَ لَا يُحِبُّ الْمُعْتَدِيْنَ ۞

88. Eat of the things which
Allah hath provided for you,
Lawful and good; but fear
Allah, in Whom ye believe.

٨٨ - وَكُلُوْا مِمَّا رَزَقَكُمُ اللّٰهُ حَلٰلًا طَيِّبًا ۚ
وَاتَّقُوا اللّٰهَ الَّذِيْ أَنْتُمْ بِهٖ مُؤْمِنُوْنَ ۞

89 Allah will not call you
To account for what is
Futile in your oaths,
But He will call you
To account for your deliberate
Oaths: for expiation, feed
Ten indigent persons,
On a scale of the average
For the food of your families;
Or clothe them; or give
A slave his freedom
If that is beyond your means,
Fast for three days.
That is the expiation
For the oaths ye have sworn.
But keep to your oaths.
Thus doth Allah make clear
To you His Signs, that ye
May be grateful.

٨٩ - لَا يُؤَاخِذُكُمُ اللّٰهُ بِاللَّغْوِ فِيْٓ أَيْمَانِكُمْ
وَلٰكِنْ يُؤَاخِذُكُمْ بِمَا عَقَّدْتُّمُ الْأَيْمَانَ ۚ
فَكَفَّارَتُهٗٓ إِطْعَامُ عَشَرَةِ مَسٰكِيْنَ
مِنْ أَوْسَطِ مَا تُطْعِمُوْنَ أَهْلِيْكُمْ
أَوْ كِسْوَتُهُمْ أَوْ تَحْرِيْرُ رَقَبَةٍ ۚ
فَمَنْ لَّمْ يَجِدْ فَصِيَامُ ثَلٰثَةِ أَيَّامٍ ۚ ذٰلِكَ
كَفَّارَةُ أَيْمَانِكُمْ إِذَا حَلَفْتُمْ ۚ
وَاحْفَظُوْٓا أَيْمَانَكُمْ ۚ
كَذٰلِكَ يُبَيِّنُ اللّٰهُ لَكُمْ اٰيٰتِهٖ
لَعَلَّكُمْ تَشْكُرُوْنَ ۞

90. (O) ye who believe!
Intoxicants and gambling,
(Dedication of) stones,
And (divination by) arrows,
Are an abomination—
Of Satan's handiwork;
Eschew such (abomination),
That ye may prosper.

٩٠ - يٰٓأَيُّهَا الَّذِيْنَ اٰمَنُوْٓا إِنَّمَا الْخَمْرُ وَالْمَيْسِرُ
وَالْأَنْصَابُ وَالْأَزْلَامُ
رِجْسٌ مِّنْ عَمَلِ الشَّيْطٰنِ
فَاجْتَنِبُوْهُ لَعَلَّكُمْ تُفْلِحُوْنَ ۞

91. Satan's plan is (but)
To excite enmity and hatred
Between you, with intoxicants
And gambling, and hinder you
From the remembrance
Of Allah, and from prayer:
Will ye not then abstain?

٩١- اِنَّمَا يُرِيْدُ الشَّيْطٰنُ
اَنْ يُّوْقِعَ بَيْنَكُمُ الْعَدَاوَةَ وَالْبَغْضَآءَ فِى
الْخَمْرِ وَالْمَيْسِرِ وَيَصُدَّكُمْ عَنْ ذِكْرِ اللهِ
وَعَنِ الصَّلٰوةِ ۚ فَهَلْ اَنْتُمْ مُّنْتَهُوْنَ ۰

92. Obey Allah, and obey the
Messenger,
And beware (of evil):
If ye do turn back,
Know ye that it is
Our Messenger's duty
To proclaim (the Message)
In the clearest manner.

٩٢- وَاَطِيْعُوا اللهَ وَاَطِيْعُوا الرَّسُوْلَ
وَاحْذَرُوْا ۚ
فَاِنْ تَوَلَّيْتُمْ فَاعْلَمُوْۤا اَنَّمَا عَلٰى رَسُوْلِنَا
الْبَلٰغُ الْمُبِيْنُ ۰

93. On those who believe
And do deeds of righteousness
There is no blame
For what they ate (in the past),
When they guard themselves
From evil, and believe,
And do deeds of righteousness—
(Or) again, guard themselves
From evil and believe—
(Or) again, guard themselves
From evil and do good.
For Allah loveth those
Who do good.

٩٣- لَيْسَ عَلَى الَّذِيْنَ اٰمَنُوْا وَعَمِلُوا
الصّٰلِحٰتِ
جُنَاحٌ فِيْمَا طَعِمُوْۤا اِذَا مَا اتَّقَوْا
وَّاٰمَنُوْا وَعَمِلُوا الصّٰلِحٰتِ
ثُمَّ اتَّقَوْا وَّاٰمَنُوْا
ثُمَّ اتَّقَوْا وَّاَحْسَنُوْا ۗ
وَاللهُ يُحِبُّ الْمُحْسِنِيْنَ ۰

SECTION 13.

94. O ye who believe!
Allah doth but make a trial of you
In a little matter
Of game well within reach
Of your hands and your lances,
That He may test
Who feareth Him unseen;
Any who transgress
Thereafter, will have
A grievous penalty.

٩٤- يٰۤاَيُّهَا الَّذِيْنَ اٰمَنُوْا لَيَبْلُوَنَّكُمُ اللهُ
بِشَيْءٍ مِّنَ الصَّيْدِ تَنَالُهٗۤ اَيْدِيْكُمْ وَ
رِمَاحُكُمْ لِيَعْلَمَ اللهُ مَنْ يَّخَافُهٗ بِالْغَيْبِ ۚ
فَمَنِ اعْتَدٰى بَعْدَ ذٰلِكَ
فَلَهٗ عَذَابٌ اَلِيْمٌ ۰

95. O ye who believe!
Kill not game
While in the Sacred

٩٥- يٰۤاَيُّهَا الَّذِيْنَ اٰمَنُوْا لَا تَقْتُلُوا الصَّيْدَ

Precincts or in pilgrim garb.
If any of you doth so
Intentionally, the compensation
Is an offering, brought
To the Ka'bah, of a domestic
animal
Equivalent to the one he killed,
As adjudged by two just men
Among you; or by way
Of atonement, the feeding
Of the indigent; or its
Equivalent in fasts; that he
May taste of the penalty
Of his deed. Allah
Forgives what is past:
For repetition Allah will
Exact from him the penalty.
For Allah is Exalted,
And Lord of Retribution.

وَأَنتُمْ حُرُمٌ
وَمَن قَتَلَهُ مِنكُم مُّتَعَمِّدًا
فَجَزَآءٌ مِّثْلُ مَا قَتَلَ مِنَ النَّعَمِ
يَحْكُمُ بِهِ ذَوَا عَدْلٍ مِّنكُمْ هَدْيًا بَٰلِغَ
الْكَعْبَةِ أَوْ كَفَّٰرَةٌ طَعَامُ مَسَٰكِينَ
أَوْ عَدْلُ ذَٰلِكَ صِيَامًا لِّيَذُوقَ وَبَالَ
أَمْرِهِ عَفَا اللَّهُ عَمَّا سَلَفَ
وَمَنْ عَادَ فَيَنتَقِمُ اللَّهُ مِنْهُ
وَاللَّهُ عَزِيزٌ ذُو انتِقَامٍ ٠

96. Lawful to you is the pursuit
Of water-game and its use
For food—for the benefit
Of yourselves and those who
Travel; but forbidden
Is the pursuit of land-game
As long as ye are
In the Sacred Precincts
Or in pilgrim garb.
And fear Allah, to Whom
Ye shall be gathered back.

٩٦- أُحِلَّ لَكُمْ صَيْدُ الْبَحْرِ وَطَعَامُهُ
مَتَٰعًا لَّكُمْ وَلِلسَّيَّارَةِ
وَحُرِّمَ عَلَيْكُمْ صَيْدُ الْبَرِّ
مَا دُمْتُمْ حُرُمًا
وَاتَّقُوا اللَّهَ الَّذِي إِلَيْهِ تُحْشَرُونَ ٠

97. Allah made the Ka'bah,
The Sacred House, an asylum
Of security for men, as
Also the Sacred Months,
The animals for offerings,
And the garlands that mark
         them:
That ye may know
That Allah hath knowledge
Of what is in the heavens
And on earth and that Allah
Is well-acquainted
With all things.

٩٧- جَعَلَ اللَّهُ الْكَعْبَةَ
الْبَيْتَ الْحَرَامَ قِيَٰمًا لِّلنَّاسِ
وَالشَّهْرَ الْحَرَامَ
وَالْهَدْيَ وَالْقَلَٰٓئِدَ
ذَٰلِكَ لِتَعْلَمُوٓا أَنَّ اللَّهَ
يَعْلَمُ مَا فِي السَّمَٰوَٰتِ وَمَا فِي الْأَرْضِ
وَأَنَّ اللَّهَ بِكُلِّ شَيْءٍ عَلِيمٌ ٠

98. Know ye that Allah
Is strict in punishment

٩٨- اعْلَمُوٓا أَنَّ اللَّهَ شَدِيدُ الْعِقَابِ

And that Allah is
Oft-Forgiving, Most Merciful.

وَأَنَّ اللّٰهَ غَفُوْرٌ رَّحِيْمٌ ۟

99. The Messenger's duty is
But to proclaim (the Message).
But Allah knoweth all
That ye reveal and ye conceal.

٩٩- مَا عَلَى الرَّسُوْلِ إِلَّا الْبَلَاغُ ۗ
وَاللّٰهُ يَعْلَمُ مَا تُبْدُوْنَ وَمَا تَكْتُمُوْنَ ۟

100. Say: "Not equal are things
That are bad and things
That are good, even though
The abundance of the bad
May dazzle thee;
So fear Allah, O ye
That understand;
That (so) ye may prosper."

١٠٠- قُلْ لَّا يَسْتَوِى الْخَبِيْثُ
وَالطَّيِّبُ وَلَوْ أَعْجَبَكَ كَثْرَةُ الْخَبِيْثِ ۗ
فَاتَّقُوا اللّٰهَ يَا أُولِى الْأَلْبَابِ
لَعَلَّكُمْ تُفْلِحُوْنَ ۟

SECTION 14.

101. ۞ ye who believe!
Ask not questions
About things which,
If made plain to you,
May cause you trouble.
But if ye ask about things
When the Qur'ān is being
Revealed, they will be
Made plain to you,
Allah will forgive those:
For Allah is Oft-Forgiving,
Most Forbearing.

١٠١- يَا أَيُّهَا الَّذِيْنَ اٰمَنُوْا لَا تَسْأَلُوْا
عَنْ أَشْيَاءَ إِنْ تُبْدَ لَكُمْ تَسُؤْكُمْ ۚ
وَإِنْ تَسْأَلُوْا
عَنْهَا حِيْنَ يُنَزَّلُ الْقُرْاٰنُ تُبْدَ لَكُمْ ۗ
عَفَا اللّٰهُ عَنْهَا ۗ
وَاللّٰهُ غَفُوْرٌ حَلِيْمٌ ۟

102. Some people before you
Did ask such questions,
And on that account
Lost their faith.

١٠٢- قَدْ سَأَلَهَا قَوْمٌ مِّنْ قَبْلِكُمْ
ثُمَّ أَصْبَحُوْا بِهَا كٰفِرِيْنَ ۟

103. It was not Allah
Who instituted (superstitions
Like those of) a slit-ear
She-camel, or a she-camel
Let loose for free pasture,
Or idol sacrifices for
Twin-births in animals,
Or stallion-camels
Freed from work:
It is blasphemers
Who invent a lie
Against Allah; but most
Of them lack wisdom.

١٠٣- مَا جَعَلَ اللّٰهُ
مِنْ بَحِيْرَةٍ وَّلَا سَائِبَةٍ
وَّلَا وَصِيْلَةٍ
وَّلَا حَامٍ ۙ
وَّلٰكِنَّ الَّذِيْنَ كَفَرُوْا
يَفْتَرُوْنَ عَلَى اللّٰهِ الْكَذِبَ ۗ
وَأَكْثَرُهُمْ لَا يَعْقِلُوْنَ ۟

04. When it is said to them:
"Come to what Allah
Hath revealed; come
To the Messenger":
They say: "Enough for us
Are the ways we found
Our fathers following."
What! even though their fathers
Were void of knowledge
And guidance?

١٠٤- وَاِذَا قِيْلَ لَهُمْ تَعَالَوْا اِلٰى مَاۤ اَنْزَلَ
اللّٰهُ وَاِلَى الرَّسُوْلِ
قَالُوْا حَسْبُنَا مَا وَجَدْنَا عَلَيْهِ اٰبَاۤءَنَا
اَوَلَوْ كَانَ اٰبَاۤؤُهُمْ لَا يَعْلَمُوْنَ شَيْئًا
وَّلَا يَهْتَدُوْنَ ۞

05. O ye who believe!
Guard your own souls:
If ye follow (right) guidance,
No hurt can come to you
From those who stray.
The goal of you all
Is to Allah: it is He
That will show you
The truth of all
That ye do.

١٠٥- يَاۤيُّهَا الَّذِيْنَ اٰمَنُوْا عَلَيْكُمْ
اَنْفُسَكُمْ
لَا يَضُرُّكُمْ مَّنْ ضَلَّ اِذَا اهْتَدَيْتُمْ
اِلَى اللّٰهِ مَرْجِعُكُمْ جَمِيْعًا
فَيُنَبِّئُكُمْ بِمَا كُنْتُمْ تَعْمَلُوْنَ۞

06. O ye who believe!
When death approaches
Any of you, (take) witnesses
Among yourselves when making
Bequests—two just men
Of your own (brotherhood)
Or others from outside
If ye are journeying
Through the earth,
And the chance of death
Befalls you (thus).
If ye doubt (their truth),
Detain them both
After prayer, and let them both
Swear by Allah:
"We wish not in this
For any worldly gain,
Even though the (beneficiary)
Be our near relation:
We shall hide not
The evidence before Allah:
If we do, then behold!
The sin be upon us!"

١٠٦- يَاۤيُّهَا الَّذِيْنَ اٰمَنُوْا شَهَادَةُ بَيْنِكُمْ
اِذَا حَضَرَ اَحَدَكُمُ الْمَوْتُ
حِيْنَ الْوَصِيَّةِ اثْنٰنِ ذَوَا عَدْلٍ مِّنْكُمْ
اَوْ اٰخَرٰنِ مِنْ غَيْرِكُمْ
اِنْ اَنْتُمْ ضَرَبْتُمْ فِى الْاَرْضِ
فَاَصَابَتْكُمْ مُّصِيْبَةُ الْمَوْتِ
تَحْبِسُوْنَهُمَا مِنْ بَعْدِ الصَّلٰوةِ
فَيُقْسِمٰنِ بِاللّٰهِ
اِنِ ارْتَبْتُمْ لَا نَشْتَرِيْ بِه ثَمَنًا
وَّلَوْ كَانَ ذَا قُرْبٰى
وَلَا نَكْتُمُ شَهَادَةَ اللّٰهِ
اِنَّاۤ اِذًا لَّمِنَ الْاٰثِمِيْنَ۞

07. But if it gets known

١٠٧- فَاِنْ عُثِرَ عَلٰى

That these two were guilty
Of the sin (of perjury),
Let two others stand forth
In their places—nearest
In kin from among those
Who claim a lawful right:
Let them swear by Allah;
"We affirm that our witness
Is truer than that
Of those two, and that we
Have not trespassed (beyond
The truth): if we did,
Behold! the wrong be
Upon us!"

108. That is most suitable:
That they may give the evidence
In its true nature and shape,
Or else they would fear
That other oaths would be
Taken after their oaths.
But fear Allah, and listen
(To His counsel): for Allah
Guideth not a rebellious people.

SECTION 15.

109. One day will Allah
Gather the Messengers together,
And ask: "What was
The response ye received
(From men to your teaching)?"
They will say: "We
Have no knowledge: it is Thou
Who knowest in full
All that is hidden."

110. Then will Allah say:
"O Jesus the son of Mary!
Recount My favour
To thee and to thy mother.
Behold! I strengthened thee
With the holy spirit,
So that thou didst speak
To the people in childhood
And in maturity.
Behold! I taught thee
The Book and Wisdom,
The Law and the Gospel.

And behold! thou makest
Out of clay, as it were,
The figure of a bird,
By My leave,
And thou breathest into it,
And it becometh a bird
By My leave,
And thou healest those
Born blind, and the lepers,
By My leave.
And behold! thou
Bringest forth the dead
By My leave.
And behold! I did
Restrain the Children of Israel
From (violence to) thee
When thou didst show them
The Clear Signs,
And the unbelievers among them
Said: 'This is nothing
But evident magic.'

وَإِذْ تَخْلُقُ مِنَ الطِّينِ
كَهَيْئَةِ الطَّيْرِ بِإِذْنِي
فَتَنْفُخُ فِيهَا
فَتَكُونُ طَيْرًا بِإِذْنِي
وَتُبْرِئُ الْأَكْمَهَ وَالْأَبْرَصَ بِإِذْنِي
وَإِذْ تُخْرِجُ الْمَوْتَى بِإِذْنِي
وَإِذْ كَفَفْتُ بَنِي إِسْرَآءِيلَ عَنْكَ
إِذْ جِئْتَهُمْ بِالْبَيِّنَاتِ
فَقَالَ الَّذِينَ كَفَرُوا مِنْهُمْ
إِنْ هَذَا إِلَّا سِحْرٌ مُّبِينٌ ۝

111. "And behold! I inspired
The Disciples to have faith
In Me and Mine Messenger;
They said, 'We have faith,
And do thou   bear witness
That we bow to Allah
As Muslims'."

١١١- وَإِذْ أَوْحَيْتُ إِلَى الْحَوَارِيِّنَ
أَنْ آمِنُوا بِي وَبِرَسُولِي
قَالُوا آمَنَّا
وَاشْهَدْ بِأَنَّنَا مُسْلِمُونَ ۝

112. Behold! the Disciples said:
"O Jesus the son of Mary!
Can thy Lord send down to us
A Table set (with viands)
From heaven?" Said Jesus:
"Fear Allah, if ye have faith."

١١٢- إِذْ قَالَ الْحَوَارِيُّونَ يَعِيسَى ابْنَ مَرْيَمَ
هَلْ يَسْتَطِيعُ رَبُّكَ أَنْ يُنَزِّلَ عَلَيْنَا مَآئِدَةً
مِنَ السَّمَآءِ قَالَ اتَّقُوا اللَّهَ إِنْ كُنْتُمْ مُّؤْمِنِينَ ۝

113. They said: "We only wish
To eat thereof and satisfy
Our hearts, and to know
That thou has indeed
Told us the truth; and
That we ourselves may be
Witnesses to the miracle."

١١٣- قَالُوا نُرِيدُ أَنْ نَّأْكُلَ مِنْهَا وَ
تَطْمَئِنَّ قُلُوبُنَا
وَنَعْلَمَ أَنْ قَدْ صَدَقْتَنَا
وَنَكُونَ عَلَيْهَا مِنَ الشَّاهِدِينَ ۝

114. Said Jesus the son of Mary:
"O Allah our Lord!

١١٤- قَالَ عِيسَى ابْنُ مَرْيَمَ اللَّهُمَّ رَبَّنَا

Send us from heaven
A Table set (with viands),
That there may be for us—
For the first and the last of us—
A solemn festival
And a Sign from Thee;
And provide for our sustenance,
For Thou art the best
Sustainer (of our needs)."

أَنْزِلْ عَلَيْنَا مَآئِدَةً مِّنَ السَّمَآءِ
تَكُونُ لَنَا عِيدًا لِّأَوَّلِنَا وَاٰخِرِنَا
وَاٰيَةً مِّنْكَ ۖ
وَارْزُقْنَا وَأَنْتَ خَيْرُ الرّٰزِقِينَ ۞

115. Allah said: "I will
Send it down unto you;
But if any of you
After that resisteth faith,
I will punish him
With a penalty such
As I have not inflicted
On anyone among
All the peoples."

١١٥- قَالَ اللّٰهُ إِنِّي مُنَزِّلُهَا عَلَيْكُمْ ۖ
فَمَنْ يَّكْفُرْ بَعْدُ مِنْكُمْ
فَإِنِّي أُعَذِّبُهٗ عَذَابًا
لَّآ أُعَذِّبُهٗٓ أَحَدًا مِّنَ
الْعٰلَمِينَ ۞

SECTION 16.

116. And behold! Allah will say:
"O Jesus the son of Mary!
Didst thou say unto men,
'Worship me and my mother
As gods in derogation of Allah'?"
He will say: "Glory to Thee!
Never could I say
What I had no right
(To say). Had I said
Such a thing, Thou wouldst
Indeed have known it.
Thou knowest what is
In my heart, though I
Know not what is
In Thine. For Thou
Knowest in full
All that is hidden.

١١٦- وَإِذْ قَالَ اللّٰهُ يٰعِيسَى ابْنَ مَرْيَمَ
ءَأَنْتَ قُلْتَ لِلنَّاسِ اتَّخِذُونِي وَأُمِّيَ
إِلٰهَيْنِ مِنْ دُونِ اللّٰهِ ۖ
قَالَ سُبْحٰنَكَ
مَا يَكُونُ لِيٓ أَنْ أَقُولَ مَا لَيْسَ لِي بِحَقٍّ ۚ
إِنْ كُنْتُ قُلْتُهٗ فَقَدْ عَلِمْتَهٗ ۚ
تَعْلَمُ مَا فِي نَفْسِي
وَلَآ أَعْلَمُ مَا فِي نَفْسِكَ ۚ
إِنَّكَ أَنْتَ عَلَّامُ الْغُيُوبِ ۞

117. "Never said I to them
Aught except what Thou
Didst command me
To say, to wit, 'Worship
Allah, my Lord and your Lord';
And I was a witness
Over them whilst I dwelt
Amongst them; when thou

١١٧- مَا قُلْتُ لَهُمْ إِلَّا مَآ أَمَرْتَنِي بِهٖٓ
أَنِ اعْبُدُوا اللّٰهَ رَبِّي وَرَبَّكُمْ ۚ
وَكُنْتُ عَلَيْهِمْ شَهِيدًا
مَّا دُمْتُ فِيهِمْ ۚ فَلَمَّا تَوَفَّيْتَنِي

Didst take me up
Thou wast the Watcher
Over them, and Thou
Art a witness to all things.

كُنْتَ أَنْتَ الرَّقِيبَ عَلَيْهِمْ وَأَنْتَ عَلَى كُلِّ شَيْءٍ شَهِيدٌ ۝

118. "If Thou dost punish them,
They are Thy servants:
If Thou dost forgive them,
Thou art the Exalted in power,
The Wise."

١١٨- إِنْ تُعَذِّبْهُمْ فَإِنَّهُمْ عِبَادُكَ وَإِنْ تَغْفِرْ لَهُمْ فَإِنَّكَ أَنْتَ الْعَزِيزُ الْحَكِيمُ ۝

119. Allah will say: "This is
A day on which
The truthful will profit
From their truth: theirs
Are Gardens, with rivers
Flowing beneath—their eternal
Home: Allah well-pleased
With them, and they with Allah:
That is the great Salvation.
(The fulfilment of all desires).

١١٩- قَالَ اللهُ هٰذَا يَوْمُ يَنْفَعُ الصَّادِقِينَ صِدْقُهُمْ لَهُمْ جَنَّاتٌ تَجْرِي مِنْ تَحْتِهَا الْأَنْهَارُ خَالِدِينَ فِيهَا أَبَدًا رَضِيَ اللهُ عَنْهُمْ وَرَضُوا عَنْهُ ذٰلِكَ الْفَوْزُ الْعَظِيمُ ۝

120. To Allah doth belong the
                              dominion
Of the heavens and the earth,
And all that is therein,
And it is He who hath power
Over all things.

١٢٠- لِلّٰهِ مُلْكُ السَّمٰوٰتِ وَالْأَرْضِ وَمَا فِيهِنَّ وَهُوَ عَلَى كُلِّ شَيْءٍ قَدِيرٌ ۝

INTRODUCTION TO SŪRA VI (Anʿām) — 165 Verses

This is a Sūra of the late Makkan period. The greater part of it was revealed entire. Its place in the traditional order of arrangement is justified by logical considerations. We have already had the spiritual history of mankind, a discussion of the earlier revelations and how they were lost or corrupted, the regulations for the outer life of the new Community and the points in which the Jews and Christians failed to maintain the central doctrine of Islam— the unity of God. The next step now taken is to expound this doctrine in relation to Pagan Arabia.

Al Anʿām (The Cattle)

In the name of Allah, Most Gracious, Most Merciful.

1. Praise be to Allah,
Who created the heavens
And the earth,
And made the Darkness
And the Light.
Yet those who reject Faith
Hold (others) as equal
With their Guardian-Lord.

2. He it is Who created
You from clay, and then
Decreed a stated term
(For you). And there is
In His Presence another
Determined term; yet
Ye doubt within yourselves!

3. And He is Allah
In the heavens
And on earth.
He knoweth what ye
Hide, and what ye reveal,
And He knoweth
The (recompense) which
Ye earn (by your deeds).

4. But never did a single
One of the Signs
Of their Lord reach them,
But they turned
Away therefrom.

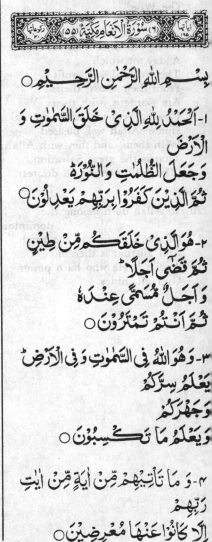

5. And now they reject
The truth when it reaches
Them; but soon shall they
Learn the reality of what
They used to mock at.

٥- فَقَدْ كَذَّبُوا بِالْحَقِّ لَمَّا جَاءَهُمْ ۖ
فَسَوْفَ يَأْتِيهِمْ أَنْبَؤُا
مَا كَانُوا بِهِ يَسْتَهْزِئُونَ ۝

6. See they not how many
Of those before them
We did destroy?—
Generations We had established
On the earth, in strength
Such as We have not given
To you—for whom
We poured out rain
From the skies in abundance,
And gave (fertile) streams
Flowing beneath their (feet):
Yet for their sins
We destroyed them,
And raised in their wake
Fresh generations
(To succeed them).

٦- أَلَمْ يَرَوْا كَمْ أَهْلَكْنَا مِنْ قَبْلِهِمْ
مِنْ قَرْنٍ مَّكَّنَّاهُمْ فِى الْأَرْضِ
مَا لَمْ نُمَكِّنْ لَّكُمْ
وَأَرْسَلْنَا السَّمَاءَ عَلَيْهِمْ مِّدْرَارًا
وَجَعَلْنَا الْأَنْهَارَ تَجْرِى مِنْ تَحْتِهِمْ
فَأَهْلَكْنَاهُمْ
بِذُنُوبِهِمْ
وَأَنْشَأْنَا مِنْ بَعْدِهِمْ قَرْنًا آخَرِينَ ۝

7. If We had sent
Unto thee a written
(Message) on parchment,
So that they could
Touch it with their hands,
The Unbelievers would
Have been sure to say:
"This is nothing but
Obvious magic!"

٧- وَلَوْ نَزَّلْنَا عَلَيْكَ كِتَابًا فِى قِرْطَاسٍ
فَلَمَسُوهُ بِأَيْدِيهِمْ
لَقَالَ الَّذِينَ كَفَرُوا
إِنْ هَذَا إِلَّا سِحْرٌ مُّبِينٌ ۝

8. They say: "Why is not
An angel sent down to him?"
If We did send down
An angel, the matter
Would be settled at once,
And no respite
Would be granted them.

٨- وَقَالُوا لَوْلَا أُنْزِلَ عَلَيْهِ مَلَكٌ
وَلَوْ أَنْزَلْنَا مَلَكًا
لَقُضِيَ الْأَمْرُ
ثُمَّ لَا يُنْظَرُونَ ۝

9. If We had made it
An angel, We should
Have sent him as a man,
And We should certainly
Have caused them confusion
In a matter which they have

٩- وَلَوْ جَعَلْنَاهُ مَلَكًا
لَّجَعَلْنَاهُ رَجُلًا
وَلَلَبَسْنَا عَلَيْهِمْ

Already covered with confusion.

10. Mocked were (many)
Messengers before thee;
But their scoffers
Were hemmed in
By the thing that they mocked.

SECTION 2.

11. Say: "Travel through the earth
And see what was the end
Of those who rejected Truth."

12. Say: "To whom belongeth
All that is in the heavens
And on earth?" Say:
"To Allah. He hath inscribed
For Himself (the rule of) Mercy.
That He will gather you
Together for the Day of Judgment,
There is no doubt whatever.
It is they who have lost
Their own souls, that will
Not believe.

13. To him belongeth all
That dwelleth (or lurketh)
In the Night and the Day.
For He is the One
Who heareth and knoweth
All things."

14. Say: "Shall I take
For my protector
Any other than Allah,
The Maker of the heavens
And the earth?
And He it is that
Feedeth but is not fed."
Say: "Nay! but I am
Commanded to be the first
Of those who bow
To Allah (in Islam),
And be not thou
Of the company of those
Who join gods with Allah."

15. Say: "I would, if I

مَا يَلْبِسُونَ ۝

١٠- وَلَقَدِ اسْتُهْزِئَ بِرُسُلٍ مِّنْ قَبْلِكَ فَحَاقَ بِالَّذِينَ سَخِرُوْا مِنْهُمْ مَّا كَانُوْا بِهِ يَسْتَهْزِءُوْنَ ۝

١١- قُلْ سِيْرُوْا فِي الْأَرْضِ ثُمَّ انْظُرُوْا كَيْفَ كَانَ عَاقِبَةُ الْمُكَذِّبِيْنَ ۝

١٢- قُلْ لِّمَنْ مَّا فِي السَّمٰوٰتِ وَالْأَرْضِ قُلْ لِلّٰهِ كَتَبَ عَلٰى نَفْسِهِ الرَّحْمَةَ لَيَجْمَعَنَّكُمْ إِلٰى يَوْمِ الْقِيٰمَةِ لَا رَيْبَ فِيْهِ الَّذِيْنَ خَسِرُوْا أَنْفُسَهُمْ فَهُمْ لَا يُؤْمِنُوْنَ ۝

١٣- وَلَهُ مَا سَكَنَ فِي الَّيْلِ وَالنَّهَارِ وَهُوَ السَّمِيْعُ الْعَلِيْمُ ۝

١٤- قُلْ أَغَيْرَ اللّٰهِ أَتَّخِذُ وَلِيًّا فَاطِرِ السَّمٰوٰتِ وَالْأَرْضِ وَهُوَ يُطْعِمُ وَلَا يُطْعَمُ قُلْ إِنِّيْ أُمِرْتُ أَنْ أَكُوْنَ أَوَّلَ مَنْ أَسْلَمَ وَلَا تَكُوْنَنَّ مِنَ الْمُشْرِكِيْنَ ۝

١٥- قُلْ إِنِّيْ أَخَافُ

Disobeyed my Lord,
Indeed have fear
Of the Penalty
Of a Mighty Day.

اِنْ عَصَيْتُ
رَبِّىْ عَذَابَ يَوْمٍ عَظِيْمٍ ۞

16. "On that day, if the Penalty
Is averted from any,
It is due to Allah's Mercy;
And that would be (Salvation),
The obvious fulfilment
Of all desire.

١٦- مَنْ يُّصْرَفْ عَنْهُ يَوْمَئِذٍ
فَقَدْ رَحِمَهُ ؕ
وَ ذٰلِكَ الْفَوْزُ الْمُبِيْنُ ۞

17. "If Allah touch thee
With affliction, none
Can remove it but He;
If He touch thee with happiness,
He hath power over all things.

١٧- وَ اِنْ يَّمْسَسْكَ اللّٰهُ بِضُرٍّ فَلَا كَاشِفَ
لَهٗ اِلَّا هُوَ ؕ وَ اِنْ يَّمْسَسْكَ بِخَيْرٍ
فَهُوَ عَلٰى كُلِّ شَىْءٍ قَدِيْرٌ ۞

18. "He is the Irresistible, (watching)
From above over His worshippers;
And He is the Wise,
Acquainted with all things."

١٨- وَ هُوَ الْقَاهِرُ فَوْقَ عِبَادِهٖ ؕ
وَ هُوَ الْحَكِيْمُ الْخَبِيْرُ ۞

19. Say: "What thing is most
Weighty in evidence?"
Say: "Allah is witness
Between me and you;
This Qurʾān hath been
Revealed to me by inspiration.
That I may warn you
And all whom it reaches.
Can ye possibly bear witness
That besides Allah there is
Another God?" Say:
"Nay! I cannot bear witness!"
Say: "But in truth
He is the One God,
And I truly am innocent
Of (your blasphemy of) joining
Others with Him."

١٩- قُلْ اَىُّ شَىْءٍ اَكْبَرُ شَهَادَةً ؕ
قُلِ اللّٰهُ ۟ شَهِيْدٌۢ بَيْنِىْ وَ بَيْنَكُمْ ۟
وَ اُوْحِىَ اِلَىَّ هٰذَا الْقُرْاٰنُ
لِاُنْذِرَكُمْ بِهٖ وَ مَنْۢ بَلَغَ ؕ اَئِنَّكُمْ
لَتَشْهَدُوْنَ اَنَّ مَعَ اللّٰهِ اٰلِهَةً اُخْرٰى ؕ
قُلْ لَّاۤ اَشْهَدُ ۚ
قُلْ اِنَّمَا هُوَ اِلٰهٌ وَّاحِدٌ
وَّ اِنَّنِىْ بَرِىْٓءٌ مِّمَّا تُشْرِكُوْنَ ۞

20. Those to whom
We have given the Book
Know this as they know
Their own sons.
Those who have lost
Their own souls
Refuse therefore to believe.

٢٠- اَلَّذِيْنَ اٰتَيْنٰهُمُ الْكِتٰبَ يَعْرِفُوْنَهٗ
كَمَا يَعْرِفُوْنَ اَبْنَآءَهُمُ ؕ اَلَّذِيْنَ خَسِرُوْٓا
اَنْفُسَهُمْ فَهُمْ لَا يُؤْمِنُوْنَ ۞

SECTION 3.

21. Who doth more wrong
Than he who inventeth
A lie against Allah
Or rejecteth His Signs?
But verily the wrongdoers
Never shall prosper.

22. One day shall We gather
Them all together: We
Shall say to those
Who ascribed partners (to Us):
"Where are the partners
Whom ye (invented
And) talked about!"

23. There will then be (left)
No subterfuge for them
But to say: "By Allah
Our Lord, we were not
Those who joined gods
With Allah."

24. Behold! how they lie
Against their own souls!
But the (lie) which they
Invented will leave them
In the lurch.

25. Of them there are some
Who (pretend to) listen to thee;
But We have thrown
Veils on their hearts,
So they understand it not,
And deafness in their ears;
If they saw every one
Of the Signs, they will
Not believe in them;
In so much that
When they come to thee,
They (but) dispute with thee;
The Unbelievers say:
"These are nothing
But tales of the ancients."

26. Others they keep away from it,
And themselves they keep away;
But they only destroy

٢١- وَمَنْ أَظْلَمُ مِمَّنِ افْتَرَى عَلَى اللهِ كَذِبًا أَوْ كَذَّبَ بِآيَاتِهِ ۗ إِنَّهُ لَا يُفْلِحُ الظَّالِمُونَ ۝

٢٢- وَيَوْمَ نَحْشُرُهُمْ جَمِيعًا ثُمَّ نَقُولُ لِلَّذِينَ أَشْرَكُوا أَيْنَ شُرَكَاؤُكُمُ الَّذِينَ كُنْتُمْ تَزْعُمُونَ ۝

٢٣- ثُمَّ لَمْ تَكُنْ فِتْنَتُهُمْ إِلَّا أَنْ قَالُوا وَاللهِ رَبِّنَا مَا كُنَّا مُشْرِكِينَ ۝

٢٤- أُنْظُرْ كَيْفَ كَذَبُوا عَلَى أَنْفُسِهِمْ وَضَلَّ عَنْهُمْ مَا كَانُوا يَفْتَرُونَ ۝

٢٥- وَمِنْهُمْ مَنْ يَسْتَمِعُ إِلَيْكَ ۖ وَجَعَلْنَا عَلَى قُلُوبِهِمْ أَكِنَّةً أَنْ يَفْقَهُوهُ وَفِي آذَانِهِمْ وَقْرًا ۚ وَإِنْ يَرَوْا كُلَّ آيَةٍ لَا يُؤْمِنُوا بِهَا ۚ حَتَّى إِذَا جَاءُوكَ يُجَادِلُونَكَ يَقُولُ الَّذِينَ كَفَرُوا إِنْ هَذَا إِلَّا أَسَاطِيرُ الْأَوَّلِينَ ۝

٢٦- وَهُمْ يَنْهَوْنَ عَنْهُ وَيَنْأَوْنَ عَنْهُ ۖ وَإِنْ يُهْلِكُونَ

Their own souls,
And they perceive it not.

إِلَّا أَنْفُسَهُمْ وَمَا يَشْعُرُونَ ٥

27. If thou couldst but see
When they are confronted
With the Fire!
They will say:
"Would that we were
But sent back!
Then would we not reject
The Signs of our Lord,
But would be amongst those
Who believe!"

٢٧- وَلَوْ تَرَى إِذْ وُقِفُوا عَلَى النَّارِ
فَقَالُوا يَا لَيْتَنَا نُرَدُّ
وَلَا نُكَذِّبَ
بِآيَاتِ رَبِّنَا
وَنَكُونَ مِنَ الْمُؤْمِنِينَ ٥

28. Yea, in their own (eyes)
Will become manifest
What before they concealed.
But if they were returned,
They would certainly relapse
To the things they were forbidden,
For they are indeed liars.

٢٨- بَلْ بَدَا لَهُمْ مَا كَانُوا يُخْفُونَ مِنْ
قَبْلُ
وَلَوْ رُدُّوا لَعَادُوا
لِمَا نُهُوا عَنْهُ وَإِنَّهُمْ لَكَاذِبُونَ ٥

29. And they (sometimes) say:
"There is nothing except
Our life on this earth,
And never shall we be
Raised up again."

٢٩- وَقَالُوا إِنْ هِيَ إِلَّا حَيَاتُنَا الدُّنْيَا
وَمَا نَحْنُ بِمَبْعُوثِينَ ٥

30. If thou couldst but see
When they are confronted
With their Lord!
He will say:
"Is not this the truth?"
They will say:
"Yea, by our Lord!"
He will say:
"Taste ye then the Penalty,
Because ye rejected Faith."

٣٠- وَلَوْ تَرَى إِذْ وُقِفُوا عَلَى رَبِّهِمْ
قَالَ أَلَيْسَ هَذَا بِالْحَقِّ
قَالُوا بَلَى وَرَبِّنَا
قَالَ فَذُوقُوا الْعَذَابَ
بِمَا كُنْتُمْ تَكْفُرُونَ ٥

SECTION 4.

31. Lost indeed are they
Who treat it as a falsehood
That they must meet Allah—
Until on a sudden
The hour is on them,
And they say: "Ah! woe

٣١- قَدْ خَسِرَ الَّذِينَ كَذَّبُوا بِلِقَاءِ اللَّهِ
حَتَّى إِذَا جَاءَتْهُمُ السَّاعَةُ بَغْتَةً
قَالُوا يَا حَسْرَتَنَا عَلَى مَا فَرَّطْنَا فِيهَا

Unto us that we took
No thought of it";
For they bear their burdens
On their backs,
And evil indeed are
The burdens that they bear.

وَ هُمْ يَحْمِلُونَ أَوْزَارَهُمْ عَلَى
ظُهُورِهِمْ أَلَا سَآءَ مَا يَزِرُونَ۞

32. What is the life of this world
But play and amusement?
But best is the Home
In the Hereafter, for those
Who are righteous.
Will ye not then understand?

٣٢- وَمَا الْحَيٰوةُ الدُّنْيَآ إِلَّا لَعِبٌ وَّلَهْوٌ
وَلَلدَّارُ الْأَخِرَةُ خَيْرٌ
لِّلَّذِيْنَ يَتَّقُوْنَ أَفَلَا تَعْقِلُوْنَ۞

33. We know indeed the grief
Which their words do cause thee:
It is not thee they reject:
It is the Signs of Allah,
Which the wicked condemn.

٣٣- قَدْ نَعْلَمُ إِنَّهُ لَيَحْزُنُكَ الَّذِيْ يَقُوْلُوْنَ
فَإِنَّهُمْ لَا يُكَذِّبُوْنَكَ
وَلٰكِنَّ الظّٰلِمِيْنَ بِأَيٰتِ اللّٰهِ يَجْحَدُوْنَ۞

34. Rejected were the Messengers
Before thee: with patience
And constancy they bore
Their rejection and their wrongs,
Until Our aid did reach
Them: there is none
That can alter the Words
(And Decrees) of Allah.
Already hast thou received
Some account of those Messengers.

٣٤- وَلَقَدْ كُذِّبَتْ رُسُلٌ مِّنْ قَبْلِكَ
فَصَبَرُوْا عَلٰى مَا كُذِّبُوْا
وَأُوْذُوْا حَتّٰى أَتٰىهُمْ نَصْرُنَا
وَلَا مُبَدِّلَ لِكَلِمٰتِ اللّٰهِ
وَلَقَدْ جَآءَكَ مِنْ نَّبَإِى الْمُرْسَلِيْنَ۞

35. If their spurning is hard
On thy mind, yet if
Thou wert able to seek
A tunnel in the ground
Or a ladder to the skies
And bring them a Sign—
(What good?). If it were
Allah's Will, He could
Gather them together
Unto true guidance:
So be not thou
Amongst those who are swayed
By ignorance (and impatience)!

٣٥- وَإِنْ كَانَ كَبُرَ عَلَيْكَ إِعْرَاضُهُمْ
فَإِنِ اسْتَطَعْتَ أَنْ تَبْتَغِيَ نَفَقًا فِى
الْأَرْضِ أَوْ سُلَّمًا فِى السَّمَآءِ
فَتَأْتِيَهُمْ بِأَيَةٍ
وَلَوْ شَآءَ اللّٰهُ لَجَمَعَهُمْ عَلَى الْهُدٰى
فَلَا تَكُوْنَنَّ مِنَ الْجٰهِلِيْنَ۞

36. Those who listen (in truth),
Be sure, will accept:
As to the dead, Allah will

٣٦- إِنَّمَا يَسْتَجِيْبُ الَّذِيْنَ يَسْمَعُوْنَ
وَالْمَوْتٰى يَبْعَثُهُمُ اللّٰهُ

Raise them up; then will they
Be returned unto Him.

ثُمَّ اِلَيْهِ يُرْجَعُوْنَ ۝

37. They say: "Why is not
A Sign sent down
To him from his Lord?"
Say: "Allah hath certainly
Power to send down a Sign:
But most of them
Understand not."

٣٧- وَقَالُوْا لَوْلَا نُزِّلَ عَلَيْهِ اٰيَةٌ
مِّنْ رَّبِّهٖ
قُلْ اِنَّ اللّٰهَ قَادِرٌ عَلٰى اَنْ يُّنَزِّلَ اٰيَةً
وَّلٰكِنَّ اَكْثَرَهُمْ لَا يَعْلَمُوْنَ ۝

38. There is not an animal
(That lives) on the earth,
Nor a being that flies
On its wings, but (forms
Part of) communities like you.
Nothing have We omitted
From the Book, and they (all)
Shall be gathered to their Lord
In the end.

٣٨- وَمَا مِنْ دَآبَّةٍ فِى الْاَرْضِ
وَلَا طٰئِرٍ يَّطِيْرُ بِجَنَاحَيْهِ
اِلَّا اُمَمٌ اَمْثَالُكُمْ
مَا فَرَّطْنَا فِى الْكِتٰبِ مِنْ شَىْءٍ
ثُمَّ اِلٰى رَبِّهِمْ يُحْشَرُوْنَ ۝

39. Those who reject our Signs
Are deaf and dumb—
In the midst of darkness
Profound: whom Allah willeth,
He leaveth to wander;
Whom He willeth, He placeth
On the Way that is Straight.

٣٩- وَالَّذِيْنَ كَذَّبُوْا بِاٰيٰتِنَا صُمٌّ وَّبُكْمٌ
فِى الظُّلُمٰتِ
مَنْ يَّشَاِ اللّٰهُ يُضْلِلْهُ وَمَنْ يَّشَأْ
يَجْعَلْهُ عَلٰى صِرَاطٍ مُّسْتَقِيْمٍ ۝

40. Say: "Think ye to yourselves,
If there come upon you
The Wrath of Allah,
Or the Hour (that ye dread),
Would ye then call upon
Other than Allah?—
(Reply) if ye are truthful!

٤٠- قُلْ اَرَءَيْتَكُمْ
اِنْ اَتٰكُمْ عَذَابُ اللّٰهِ
اَوْ اَتَتْكُمُ السَّاعَةُ اَغَيْرَ اللّٰهِ تَدْعُوْنَ
اِنْ كُنْتُمْ صٰدِقِيْنَ ۝

41. "Nay—On Him would ye
Call, and if it be
His Will, He would remove
(The distress) which occasioned
Your call upon Him,
And ye would forget
(The false gods) which ye
Join with Him!"

٤١- بَلْ اِيَّاهُ تَدْعُوْنَ
فَيَكْشِفُ مَا تَدْعُوْنَ اِلَيْهِ
اِنْ شَآءَ
وَتَنْسَوْنَ مَا تُشْرِكُوْنَ ۝

SECTION 5.

42. Before thee We sent

٤٢- وَلَقَدْ اَرْسَلْنَا اِلٰى اُمَمٍ مِّنْ قَبْلِكَ

(Messengers) to many nations,
And We afflicted the nations
With suffering and adversity,
That they might learn humility.

فَأَخَذْنٰهُمْ بِالْبَأْسَآءِ وَالضَّرَّآءِ
لَعَلَّهُمْ يَتَضَرَّعُوْنَ ۟

43. When the suffering reached
Them from Us, why then
Did they not learn humility?
On the contrary their hearts
Became hardened, and Satan
Made their (sinful) acts
Seem alluring to them.

٤٣- فَلَوْلَاۤ اِذْ جَآءَهُمْ بَأْسُنَا
تَضَرَّعُوْا وَلٰكِنْ قَسَتْ قُلُوْبُهُمْ
وَزَيَّنَ لَهُمُ الشَّيْطٰنُ
مَا كَانُوْا يَعْمَلُوْنَ ۟

44. But when they forgot
The warning they had received,
We opened to them the gates
Of all (good) things,
Until, in the midst
Of their enjoyment
Of Our gifts,
On a sudden, We called
Them to account, when lo!
They were plunged in despair!

٤٤- فَلَمَّا نَسُوْا مَا ذُكِّرُوْا بِهٖ
فَتَحْنَا عَلَيْهِمْ اَبْوَابَ كُلِّ شَيْءٍ ۚ
حَتّٰۤى اِذَا فَرِحُوْا بِمَاۤ اُوْتُوْا
اَخَذْنٰهُمْ بَغْتَةً
فَاِذَا هُمْ مُّبْلِسُوْنَ ۟

45. Of the wrongdoers the last
Remnant was cut off.
Praise be to Allah,
The Cherisher of the Worlds.

٤٥- فَقُطِعَ دَابِرُ الْقَوْمِ الَّذِيْنَ ظَلَمُوْا
وَالْحَمْدُ لِلّٰهِ رَبِّ الْعٰلَمِيْنَ ۟

46. Say: "Think ye, if Allah
Took away your hearing
And your sight, and sealed up
Your hearts, who—a god
Other than Allah—could
Restore them to you?"
See how We explain
The Signs by various (symbols);
Yet they turn aside.

٤٦- قُلْ اَرَءَيْتُمْ اِنْ اَخَذَ اللّٰهُ سَمْعَكُمْ
وَاَبْصَارَكُمْ وَخَتَمَ عَلٰى قُلُوْبِكُمْ
مَّنْ اِلٰهٌ غَيْرُ اللّٰهِ يَأْتِيْكُمْ بِهٖ ۚ
اُنْظُرْ كَيْفَ نُصَرِّفُ الْاٰيٰتِ
ثُمَّ هُمْ يَصْدِفُوْنَ ۟

47. Say: "Think ye, if
The Punishment of Allah
Comes to you,
Whether suddenly or openly,
Will any be destroyed
Except those who do wrong?

٤٧- قُلْ اَرَءَيْتَكُمْ اِنْ اَتٰكُمْ عَذَابُ اللّٰهِ
بَغْتَةً اَوْ جَهْرَةً
هَلْ يُهْلَكُ اِلَّا الْقَوْمُ الظّٰلِمُوْنَ ۟

48. We send the Messengers

٤٨- وَمَا نُرْسِلُ الْمُرْسَلِيْنَ اِلَّا مُبَشِّرِيْنَ

Only to give good news
And to warn: so those
Who believe and mend
(Their lives) — upon them
Shall be no fear,
Nor shall they grieve.

49. But those who reject
Our Signs — them
Shall punishment touch,
For that they ceased not
From transgressing.

50. Say: "I tell you not
That with me
Are the Treasures of Allah,
Nor do I know
What is hidden,
Nor do I tell you I am
An angel. I but follow
What is revealed to me."
Say: "Can the blind
Be held equal to the seeing?"
Will ye then consider not?

SECTION 6.

51. Give this warning to those
In whose (hearts) is the fear
That they will be brought
(To Judgement) before their Lord:
Except for Him
They will have no protector
Nor intercessor;
That they may guard
(Against evil).

52. Send not away those
Who call on their Lord
Morning and evening,
Seeking His Face.
In naught art thou accountable
For them, and in naught are they
Accountable for thee,
That thou shouldst turn
Them away, and thus be
(One) of the unjust.

53. Thus did We try
Some of them by comparison

With others, that they
Should say: "Is it these
Then that Allah hath
Favoured from amongst us?"
Doth not Allah know best
Those who are grateful?

لِّيَقُوْلُوْۤا اَهٰۤؤُلَآءِ مَنَّ اللّٰهُ عَلَيْهِمْ
مِّنْۢ بَيْنِنَا ؕ
اَلَيْسَ اللّٰهُ بِاَعْلَمَ بِالشّٰكِرِيْنَ ۝

54. When those come to thee
Who believe in Our Signs,
Say: "Peace be on you;"
Your Lord hath inscribed
For Himself (the rule
Of) Mercy: verily,
If any of you did evil
In ignorance, and thereafter
Repented, and amended
(His conduct), lo! He is
Oft-Forgiving, Most Merciful.

۵۴- وَاِذَا جَآءَكَ الَّذِيْنَ يُؤْمِنُوْنَ بِاٰيٰتِنَا
فَقُلْ سَلٰمٌ عَلَيْكُمْ
كَتَبَ رَبُّكُمْ عَلٰى نَفْسِهِ الرَّحْمَةَ ۙ
اَنَّهٗ مَنْ عَمِلَ مِنْكُمْ سُوْۤءًۢا بِجَهَالَةٍ ثُمَّ
تَابَ مِنْۢ بَعْدِهٖ وَاَصْلَحَ
فَاَنَّهٗ غَفُوْرٌ رَّحِيْمٌ ۝

55. Thus do We explain
The Signs in detail:
That the way of the sinners
May be shown up.

۵۵- وَكَذٰلِكَ نُفَصِّلُ الْاٰيٰتِ
وَلِتَسْتَبِيْنَ سَبِيْلُ الْمُجْرِمِيْنَ ۟ۙ

SECTION 7.

56. Say: "I am forbidden
To worship those—others
Than Allah—whom ye
Call upon." Say: "I will
Not follow your vain desires:
If I did, I would stray
From the path, and be not
Of the company of those
Who receive guidance."

۵۶- قُلْ اِنِّيْ نُهِيْتُ اَنْ اَعْبُدَ
الَّذِيْنَ تَدْعُوْنَ مِنْ دُوْنِ اللّٰهِ ؕ
قُلْ لَّاۤ اَتَّبِعُ اَهْوَآءَكُمْ ۙ
قَدْ ضَلَلْتُ اِذًا
وَّمَاۤ اَنَا مِنَ الْمُهْتَدِيْنَ ۝

57. Say: "For me, I (work)
On a clear Sign from my Lord,
But ye reject Him. What ye
Would see hastened, is not
In my power. The Command
Rests with none but Allah:
He declares the Truth,
And He is the best of judges."

۵۷- قُلْ اِنِّيْ عَلٰى بَيِّنَةٍ مِّنْ رَّبِّيْ
وَكَذَّبْتُمْ بِهٖ ؕ مَا عِنْدِيْ مَا تَسْتَعْجِلُوْنَ
بِهٖ ؕ اِنِ الْحُكْمُ اِلَّا لِلّٰهِ ؕ
يَقُصُّ الْحَقَّ وَهُوَ خَيْرُ الْفٰصِلِيْنَ ۝

58. Say: "If what ye would see
Hastened were in my power,
The matter would be settled
At once between you and me.
But Allah knoweth best
Those who do wrong."

۵۸- قُلْ لَّوْ اَنَّ عِنْدِيْ مَا تَسْتَعْجِلُوْنَ
بِهٖ لَقُضِيَ الْاَمْرُ بَيْنِيْ وَبَيْنَكُمْ ؕ
وَاللّٰهُ اَعْلَمُ بِالظّٰلِمِيْنَ ۝

59. With Him are the keys
    Of the Unseen, the treasures
    That none knoweth but He.
    He knoweth whatever there is
    On the earth and in the sea.
    Not a leaf doth fall
    But with His knowledge:
    There is not a grain
    In the darkness (or depths)
    Of the earth, nor anything
    Fresh or dry (green or withered),
    But is (inscribed) in a Record
    Clear (to those who can read).

٥٩- وَعِنْدَهٗ مَفَاتِحُ الْغَيْبِ
لَا يَعْلَمُهَا إِلَّا هُوَ ۚ
وَيَعْلَمُ مَا فِى الْبَرِّ وَالْبَحْرِ ۚ
وَمَا تَسْقُطُ مِنْ وَّرَقَةٍ إِلَّا يَعْلَمُهَا
وَلَا حَبَّةٍ فِى ظُلُمَاتِ الْاَرْضِ
وَلَا رَطْبٍ وَّلَا يَابِسٍ
إِلَّا فِى كِتَابٍ مُّبِيْنٍ ۞

60. It is He Who doth take
    Your souls by night,
    And hath knowledge of all
    That ye have done by day;
    By day doth He raise
    You up again; that a term
    Appointed be fulfilled;
    In the end unto Him
    Will be your return;
    Then will He show you
    The truth of all
    That ye did.

٦٠- وَهُوَ الَّذِىْ يَتَوَفّٰىكُمْ بِالَّيْلِ
وَيَعْلَمُ مَا جَرَحْتُمْ بِالنَّهَارِ
ثُمَّ يَبْعَثُكُمْ فِيْهِ لِيُقْضٰى أَجَلٌ مُّسَمًّى ۚ
ثُمَّ إِلَيْهِ مَرْجِعُكُمْ
ثُمَّ يُنَبِّئُكُمْ
بِمَا كُنْتُمْ تَعْمَلُوْنَ ۞

SECTION 8.

61. He is Irresistible, (watching)
    From above over His worshippers,
    And He sets guardians
    Over you. At length,
    When death approaches
    One of you, Our angels
    Take his soul, and they
    Never fail in their duty.

٦١- وَهُوَ الْقَاهِرُ فَوْقَ عِبَادِهٖ
وَيُرْسِلُ عَلَيْكُمْ حَفَظَةً ۚ
حَتّٰى إِذَا جَاءَ أَحَدَكُمُ الْمَوْتُ
تَوَفَّتْهُ رُسُلُنَا وَهُمْ لَا يُفَرِّطُوْنَ ۞

62. Then are men returned
    Unto Allah, their True Protector,
    Surely His is the Command,
    And He is the Swiftest
    In taking account.

٦٢- ثُمَّ رُدُّوْا إِلَى اللّٰهِ مَوْلٰىهُمُ الْحَقِّ ۚ
أَلَا لَهُ الْحُكْمُ ۗ
وَهُوَ أَسْرَعُ الْحَاسِبِيْنَ ۞

63. Say: "Who is it
    That delivereth you
    From the dark recesses
    Of land and sea,
    When ye call upon Him
    In humility

٦٣- قُلْ مَنْ يُّنَجِّيْكُمْ
مِّنْ ظُلُمَاتِ الْبَرِّ وَالْبَحْرِ
تَدْعُوْنَهٗ تَضَرُّعًا وَّخُفْيَةً ۚ

And silent terror:
'If He only delivers us
From these (dangers),
(We vow) we shall truly
Show our gratitude.'?"

لَئِنْ اَنْجَيْتَنَا مِنْ هٰذِهٖ
لَنَكُوْنَنَّ مِنَ الشّٰكِرِيْنَ ۝

64. Say: "It is Allah
That delivereth you
From these and all (other)
Distresses: and yet
Ye worship false gods!"

٦٤- قُلِ اللهُ يُنَجِّيْكُمْ
مِّنْهَا وَمِنْ كُلِّ كَرْبٍ
ثُمَّ اَنْتُمْ تُشْرِكُوْنَ ۝

65. Say: "He hath power
To send calamities
On you, from above
And below, or to cover
You with confusion
In party strife,
Giving you a taste
Of mutual vengeance—
Each from the other."
See how We explain
The Signs by various (symbols);
That they may understand.

٦٥- قُلْ هُوَ الْقَادِرُ عَلٰى اَنْ يَّبْعَثَ
عَلَيْكُمْ عَذَابًا مِّنْ فَوْقِكُمْ
اَوْ مِنْ تَحْتِ اَرْجُلِكُمْ
اَوْ يَلْبِسَكُمْ شِيَعًا وَّيُذِيْقَ بَعْضَكُمْ
بَأْسَ بَعْضٍ ۗ اُنْظُرْ كَيْفَ نُصَرِّفُ
الْاٰيٰتِ لَعَلَّهُمْ يَفْقَهُوْنَ ۝

66. But thy people reject
This, though it is
The Truth. Say: "Not mine
Is the responsibility
For arranging your affairs;

٦٦- وَكَذَّبَ بِهٖ قَوْمُكَ وَهُوَ الْحَقُّ ۗ
قُلْ لَّسْتُ عَلَيْكُمْ بِوَكِيْلٍ ۝

67. For every Message
Is a limit of time,
And soon shall ye
Know it."

٦٧- لِكُلِّ نَبَاٍ مُّسْتَقَرٌّ ۖ
وَّسَوْفَ تَعْلَمُوْنَ ۝

68. When thou seest men
Engaged in vain discourse
About Our Signs, turn
Away from them unless
They turn to a different
Theme. If Satan ever
Makes thee forget, then
After recollection, sit not
Thou in the company
Of those who do wrong.

٦٨- وَاِذَا رَاَيْتَ الَّذِيْنَ يَخُوْضُوْنَ
فِيْٓ اٰيٰتِنَا فَاَعْرِضْ عَنْهُمْ حَتّٰى
يَخُوْضُوْا فِيْ حَدِيْثٍ غَيْرِهٖ ۗ
وَاِمَّا يُنْسِيَنَّكَ الشَّيْطٰنُ فَلَا تَقْعُدْ
بَعْدَ الذِّكْرٰى مَعَ الْقَوْمِ الظّٰلِمِيْنَ ۝

69. On their account
No responsibility
Falls on the righteous,

٦٩- وَمَا عَلَى الَّذِيْنَ يَتَّقُوْنَ مِنْ

But (their duty)
Is to remind them,
That they may (learn
To) fear Allah.

70. Leave alone those
Who take their religion
To be mere play
And amusement,
And are deceived
By the life of this world.
But proclaim (to them)
This (truth): that every soul
Delivers itself to ruin
By its own acts;
It will find for itself
No protector or intercessor
Except Allah; if it offered
Every ransom, (or
Reparation), none
Will be accepted; such is
(The end of) those who
Deliver themselves to ruin
By their own acts:
They will have for drink
(Only) boiling water,
And for punishment,
One most grievous;
For they persisted
In rejecting Allah.

SECTION 9.

71. Say: "Shall we indeed
Call on others besides Allah—
Things that can do us
Neither good nor harm—
And turn on our heels
After receiving guidance
From Allah—like one
Whom the evil ones
Have made into a fool,
Wandering bewildered
Through the earth, his friends
Calling 'Come to us',
(Vainly) guiding him to the Path?"

Say: "Allah's guidance
Is the (only) guidance,
And we have been directed

حِسَابِهِمْ مِّنْ شَيْءٍ وَّلٰكِنْ ذِكْرٰى لَعَلَّهُمْ يَتَّقُوْنَ ۞

٧٠ وَذَرِ الَّذِيْنَ اتَّخَذُوْا دِيْنَهُمْ لَعِبًا وَّلَهْوًا وَّغَرَّتْهُمُ الْحَيٰوةُ الدُّنْيَا وَذَكِّرْ بِهٖ أَنْ تُبْسَلَ نَفْسٌ بِمَا كَسَبَتْ ۖ لَيْسَ لَهَا مِنْ دُوْنِ اللّٰهِ وَلِيٌّ وَّلَا شَفِيْعٌ ۚ وَإِنْ تَعْدِلْ كُلَّ عَدْلٍ لَّا يُؤْخَذْ مِنْهَا ۗ أُولٰٓئِكَ الَّذِيْنَ أُبْسِلُوْا بِمَا كَسَبُوْا ۖ لَهُمْ شَرَابٌ مِّنْ حَمِيْمٍ وَّعَذَابٌ أَلِيْمٌ بِمَا كَانُوْا يَكْفُرُوْنَ ۞

٧١ قُلْ أَنَدْعُوْا مِنْ دُوْنِ اللّٰهِ مَا لَا يَنْفَعُنَا وَلَا يَضُرُّنَا وَنُرَدُّ عَلٰى أَعْقَابِنَا بَعْدَ إِذْ هَدٰىنَا اللّٰهُ كَالَّذِى اسْتَهْوَتْهُ الشَّيٰطِيْنُ فِى الْأَرْضِ حَيْرَانَ ۖ لَهٗٓ أَصْحٰبٌ يَّدْعُوْنَهٗٓ إِلَى الْهُدَى ائْتِنَا ۗ قُلْ إِنَّ هُدَى اللّٰهِ هُوَ الْهُدٰى ۖ

وَأُمِرْنَا لِنُسْلِمَ لِرَبِّ الْعٰلَمِينَ ۞

To submit ourselves
To the Lord of the worlds—

72. "To establish regular prayers
And to fear Allah:
For it is to Him
That we shall be
Gathered together."

٧٢ ـ وَأَنْ أَقِيمُوا الصَّلٰوةَ
وَاتَّقُوهُ ۚ
وَهُوَ الَّذِيٓ إِلَيْهِ تُحْشَرُونَ ۞

73. It is He Who created
The heavens and the earth
In true (proportions):
The day He saith, "Be,"
Behold! it is. His Word
Is the Truth. His will be
The dominion the day
The trumpet will be blown.
He knoweth the Unseen
As well as that which is
Open. For He
Is the Wise, well-acquainted
(With all things).

٧٣ ـ وَهُوَ الَّذِيْ خَلَقَ السَّمٰوٰتِ وَالْأَرْضَ
بِالْحَقِّ ۚ وَيَوْمَ يَقُولُ كُنْ فَيَكُونُ ۚ
قَوْلُهُ الْحَقُّ ۚ وَلَهُ
الْمُلْكُ يَوْمَ يُنْفَخُ فِى الصُّورِ ۚ
عٰلِمُ الْغَيْبِ وَالشَّهَادَةِ ۚ
وَهُوَ الْحَكِيمُ الْخَبِيرُ ۞

74. Lo! Abraham said
To his father Āzar:
"Takest thou idols for gods?
For I see thee
And thy people
In manifest error."

٧٤ ـ وَإِذْ قَالَ إِبْرٰهِيمُ لِأَبِيهِ آزَرَ
أَتَتَّخِذُ أَصْنَامًا آلِهَةً ۚ
إِنِّيٓ أَرٰىكَ وَقَوْمَكَ فِى ضَلٰلٍ مُّبِينٍ ۞

75. So also did We show
Abraham the power
And the laws of the heavens
And the earth, that he
Might (with understanding)
Have certitude.

٧٥ ـ وَكَذٰلِكَ نُرِيٓ
إِبْرٰهِيمَ مَلَكُوتَ السَّمٰوٰتِ وَالْأَرْضِ
وَلِيَكُونَ مِنَ الْمُوقِنِينَ ۞

76. When the night
Covered him over,
He saw a star:
He said: "This is my Lord."
But when it set,
He said: "I love not
Those that set."

٧٦ ـ فَلَمَّا جَنَّ عَلَيْهِ الَّيْلُ
رَأَ كَوْكَبًا ۚ
قَالَ هٰذَا رَبِّى ۚ
فَلَمَّآ أَفَلَ قَالَ لَآ أُحِبُّ الْآفِلِينَ ۞

77. When he saw the moon
Rising in splendour,
He said: "This is my Lord."
But when the moon set,

٧٧ ـ فَلَمَّا رَأَ الْقَمَرَ بَازِغًا
قَالَ هٰذَا رَبِّى ۚ فَلَمَّآ أَفَلَ

He said: "Unless my Lord
Guide me, I shall surely
Be among those
Who go astray."

78. When he saw the sun
Rising in splendour,
He said: "This is my Lord;
This is the greatest (of all)."
But when the sun set,
He said: "O my people!
I am indeed free
From your (guilt)
Of giving partners to Allah.

79. "For me, I have set
My face, firmly and truly,
Towards Him Who created
The heavens and the earth,
And never shall I give
Partners to Allah."

80. His people disputed
With him. He said:
"(Come) ye to dispute
With me, about Allah,
When He (Himself)
Hath guided me?
I fear not (the beings)
Ye associate with Allah:
Unless my Lord willeth,
(Nothing can happen).
My Lord comprehendeth
In His knowledge all things.
Will ye not (yourselves)
Be admonished?

81. "How should I fear
(The beings) ye associate
With Allah, when ye
Fear not to give partners
To Allah without any warrant
Having been given to you?
Which of (us) two parties
Hath more right to security?
(Tell me) if ye know.

82. "It is those who believe
And confuse not their beliefs

With wrong[901-A]—that are
(Truly) in security, for they
Are on (right) guidance."

SECTION 10.

83. That was the reasoning
About Us, which
We gave to Abraham
(To use) against his people:
We raise whom We will,
Degree after degree:
For thy Lord is full
Of wisdom and knowledge.

84. We gave him Isaac
And Jacob: all (three)
We guided:
And before him,
We guided Noah,
And among his progeny,
David, Solomon, Job,
Joseph, Moses, and Aaron:
Thus do We reward
Those who do good:

85. And Zakariyyā and John,
And Jesus and Elias:
All in the ranks
Of the Righteous:

86. And Ismā'īl and Elisha,
And Jonah, and Lot:
And to all We gave
Favour above the nations:

87. (To them) and to their fathers,
And progeny and brethren:
We chose them,
And We guided them
To a straight Way.

88. This is the Guidance
Of Allah: He giveth
That guidance to whom
He pleaseth of His worshippers.
If they were to join
Other gods with Him,
All that they did
Would be vain for them.

٨٩. اُولٰٓئِكَ الَّذِيْنَ اٰتَيْنٰهُمُ الْكِتٰبَ وَ
الْحُكْمَ وَالنُّبُوَّةَ ۚ
فَاِنْ يَّكْفُرْ بِهَا هٰٓؤُلَآءِ فَقَدْ وَكَّلْنَا بِهَا
قَوْمًا لَّيْسُوْا بِهَا بِكٰفِرِيْنَ ۞

89. These were the men
To whom We gave
The Book, and Authority,
And Prophethood: if these
(Their descendants) reject them,
Behold! We shall entrust
Their charge to a new People
Who reject them not.

٩٠. اُولٰٓئِكَ الَّذِيْنَ هَدَى اللّٰهُ
فَبِهُدٰىهُمُ اقْتَدِهْ ۚ
قُلْ لَّاۤ اَسْـَٔلُكُمْ عَلَيْهِ اَجْرًا ۚ
اِنْ هُوَ اِلَّا ذِكْرٰى لِلْعٰلَمِيْنَ ۞

90. Those were the (prophets)
Who received Allah's guidance:
Copy the guidance they received;
Say: "No reward for this
Do I ask of you:
This is no less than
A Message for the nations."

SECTION 11.

٩١. وَمَا قَدَرُوا اللّٰهَ حَقَّ قَدْرِهٖ اِذْ قَالُوْا
مَاۤ اَنْزَلَ اللّٰهُ عَلٰى بَشَرٍ مِّنْ شَيْءٍ ۚ
قُلْ مَنْ اَنْزَلَ الْكِتٰبَ الَّذِيْ جَآءَ بِهٖ
مُوْسٰى نُوْرًا وَّهُدًى لِّلنَّاسِ
تَجْعَلُوْنَهٗ قَرَاطِيْسَ تُبْدُوْنَهَا
وَتُخْفُوْنَ كَثِيْرًا ۚ
وَعُلِّمْتُمْ مَّا لَمْ تَعْلَمُوْۤا اَنْتُمْ وَلَاۤ
اٰبَآؤُكُمْ ۚ قُلِ اللّٰهُ ۙ
ثُمَّ ذَرْهُمْ فِيْ خَوْضِهِمْ يَلْعَبُوْنَ ۞

91. No just estimate of Allah
Do they make when they say:
"Nothing doth Allah send down
To man (by way of revelation)":
Say: "Who then sent down
The Book which Moses brought?—
A light and guidance to man:
But ye make it into
(Separate) sheets for show,
While ye conceal much
(Of its contents): therein
Were ye taught that
Which ye knew not—
Neither ye nor your fathers."
Say: "Allah (sent it down)":
Then leave them to plunge
In vain discourse and trifling.

٩٢. وَهٰذَا كِتٰبٌ اَنْزَلْنٰهُ مُبٰرَكٌ مُّصَدِّقُ
الَّذِيْ بَيْنَ يَدَيْهِ وَلِتُنْذِرَ اُمَّ الْقُرٰى
وَمَنْ حَوْلَهَا ۚ
وَالَّذِيْنَ يُؤْمِنُوْنَ بِالْاٰخِرَةِ
يُؤْمِنُوْنَ بِهٖ
وَهُمْ عَلٰى صَلَاتِهِمْ يُحَافِظُوْنَ ۞

92. And this is a Book
Which We have sent down,
Bringing blessings,   and
     confirming
(The revelations) which came
Before it: that thou
Mayest warn the Mother
Of Cities and all around her.
Those who believe
In the Hereafter,
Believe in this (Book),
And they are constant
In guarding their Prayers.

93. Who can be more wicked
Than one who inventeth
A lie against Allah,
Or said, "I have
Received inspiration,"
When he hath received
None, or (again) who saith,
"I can reveal the like
Of what Allah hath revealed"?
If thou couldst but see
How the wicked (do fare)
In the flood of confusion
At death!—the angels
Stretch forth their hands,
(Saying), "Yield up your souls:
This day shall ye receive
Your reward—a penalty
Of shame, for that ye used
To tell lies against Allah,
And scornfully to reject
Of His Signs!"

٩٣ - وَمَنْ أَظْلَمُ مِمَّنِ
افْتَرَى عَلَى اللهِ كَذِبًا أَوْ قَالَ أُوحِيَ إِلَيَّ
وَلَمْ يُوحَ إِلَيْهِ شَيْءٌ
وَمَنْ قَالَ سَأُنْزِلُ مِثْلَ مَا أَنْزَلَ اللهُ
وَلَوْ تَرَى إِذِ الظَّالِمُونَ
فِي غَمَرَاتِ الْمَوْتِ
وَالْمَلَائِكَةُ بَاسِطُوا أَيْدِيهِمْ
أَخْرِجُوا أَنْفُسَكُمُ
الْيَوْمَ تُجْزَوْنَ عَذَابَ الْهُونِ
بِمَا كُنْتُمْ تَقُولُونَ عَلَى اللهِ غَيْرَ الْحَقِّ
وَكُنْتُمْ عَنْ آيَاتِهِ تَسْتَكْبِرُونَ ۟

94. "And behold! ye come
To Us bare and alone
As We created you
For the first time:
Ye have left behind you
All (the favours) which
We bestowed on you:
We see not with you
Your intercessors
Whom ye thought to be
Partners in your affairs:
So now all relations
Between you have been
Cut off, and your (pet) fancies
Have left you in the lurch!"

٩٤ - وَلَقَدْ جِئْتُمُونَا فُرَادَى
كَمَا خَلَقْنَاكُمْ أَوَّلَ مَرَّةٍ
وَتَرَكْتُمْ مَا خَوَّلْنَاكُمْ وَرَاءَ ظُهُورِكُمْ
وَمَا نَرَى مَعَكُمْ شُفَعَاءَكُمُ الَّذِينَ
زَعَمْتُمْ أَنَّهُمْ فِيكُمْ شُرَكَاءُ
لَقَدْ تَقَطَّعَ بَيْنَكُمْ
وَضَلَّ عَنْكُمْ مَا كُنْتُمْ تَزْعُمُونَ ۟

SECTION 12.

95. It is Allah Who causeth
The seed grain
And the date stone
To split and sprout.
He causeth the living
To issue from the dead,
And He is the One

٩٥ - إِنَّ اللهَ فَالِقُ الْحَبِّ وَالنَّوَى
يُخْرِجُ الْحَيَّ
مِنَ الْمَيِّتِ

To cause the dead
To issue from the living.
That is Allah: then how
Are ye deluded
Away from the truth?

وَ مُخْرِجُ الْمَيِّتِ
مِنَ الْحَيِّ
ذٰلِكُمُ اللّٰهُ فَأَنّٰى تُؤْفَكُوْنَ ۟

96. He it is that cleaveth
The daybreak (from the dark):
He makes the night
For rest and tranquillity,
And the sun and moon
For the reckoning (of time):
Such is the judgement
And ordering of (Him),
The Exalted in Power,
The Omniscient.

٩٦- فَالِقُ الْإِصْبَاحِ ۚ
وَجَعَلَ الَّيْلَ سَكَنًا
وَّ الشَّمْسَ وَ الْقَمَرَ حُسْبَانًا ۚ
ذٰلِكَ تَقْدِيْرُ
الْعَزِيْزِ الْعَلِيْمِ ۟

97. It is He Who maketh
The stars (as beacons) for you,
That ye may guide yourselves,
With their help,
Through the dark spaces
Of land and sea:
We detail Our Signs
For people who know.

٩٧- وَهُوَ الَّذِيْ جَعَلَ لَكُمُ النُّجُوْمَ
لِتَهْتَدُوْا بِهَا
فِيْ ظُلُمٰتِ الْبَرِّ وَ الْبَحْرِ ۚ
قَدْ فَصَّلْنَا الْاٰيٰتِ لِقَوْمٍ يَّعْلَمُوْنَ ۟

98. It is He Who hath
Produced you
From a single Person;
Here is a place of sojourn
And a place of departure:
We detail Our signs
For people who understand.

٩٨- وَهُوَ الَّذِيْ أَنْشَأَكُمْ
مِّنْ نَّفْسٍ وَّاحِدَةٍ
فَمُسْتَقَرٌّ وَّ مُسْتَوْدَعٌ ۚ
قَدْ فَصَّلْنَا الْاٰيٰتِ لِقَوْمٍ يَّفْقَهُوْنَ ۟

99. It is He Who sendeth down
Rain from the skies;
With it We produce
Vegetation of all kinds:
From some We produce
Green (crops), out of which
We produce grain,
Heaped up (at harvest);
Out of the date palm
And its sheaths (or spathes)
(Come) clusters of dates
Hanging low and near:
And (then there are) gardens
Of grapes, and olives,
And pomegranates,

٩٩- وَهُوَ الَّذِيْ أَنْزَلَ مِنَ السَّمَاءِ مَاءً ۚ
فَأَخْرَجْنَا بِهٖ نَبَاتَ كُلِّ شَيْءٍ
فَأَخْرَجْنَا مِنْهُ خَضِرًا
نُّخْرِجُ مِنْهُ حَبًّا مُّتَرَاكِبًا ۚ
وَمِنَ النَّخْلِ مِنْ طَلْعِهَا
قِنْوَانٌ دَانِيَةٌ وَّ جَنّٰتٍ مِّنْ أَعْنَابٍ
وَّ الزَّيْتُوْنَ وَ الرُّمَّانَ مُشْتَبِهًا
وَّ غَيْرَ مُتَشَابِهٍ ۚ

Each similar (in kind)
Yet different (in variety):
When they begin to bear fruit,
Feast your eyes with the fruit
And the ripeness thereof.
Behold! in these things
There are Signs for people
Who believe.

100. Yet they make
The Jinns equals
With Allah, though Allah
Did create the Jinns;

And they falsely,
Having no knowledge,
Attribute to Him
Sons and daughters.
Praise and glory be
To Him! (for He is) above
What they attribute to Him!

SECTION 13.

101. To Him is due
The primal origin
Of the heavens and the earth:
How can He have a son
When He hath no consort?
He created all things,
And He hath full knowledge
Of all things.

102. That is Allah, your Lord!
There is no god but He,
The Creator of all things;
Then worship ye Him;
And He hath power
To dispose of all affairs.

103. No vision can grasp Him.
But His grasp is over
All vision: He is
Above all comprehension,
Yet is acquainted with all things.

104. "Now have come to you,
From your Lord, proofs
(To open your eyes):
If any will see,
It will be for (the good
Of) his own soul;

If any will be blind,
It will be to his own
(Harm): I am not (here)
To watch over your doings."

105. Thus do We explain
The Signs by various
                    (symbols)
That they may say,
"Thou hast learnt this
(From somebody),"
And that We may make
The matter clear
To those who know.

106. Follow what thou art taught
By inspiration from thy Lord:
There is no god but He:
And turn aside from those
Who join gods with Allah.

107. If it had been Allah's Plan,
They would not have taken
False gods: but We
Made thee not one
To watch over their doings,
Nor art thou set
Over them to dispose
Of their affairs.

108. Revile not ye
Those whom they call upon
Besides Allah, lest
They out of spite
Revile Allah
In their ignorance.
Thus have We made
Alluring to each people
Its own doings.
In the end will they
Return to their Lord,
And We shall then
Tell them the truth
Of all that they did.

109. They swear their strongest

وَمَنْ عَمِيَ فَعَلَيْهَا ۚ
وَمَا أَنَا عَلَيْكُمْ بِحَفِيظٍ ۝

١٠٥ - وَكَذٰلِكَ نُصَرِّفُ الْاٰيٰتِ
وَلِيَقُوْلُوْا دَرَسْتَ
وَلِنُبَيِّنَهُ
لِقَوْمٍ يَّعْلَمُوْنَ ۝

١٠٦ - اِتَّبِعْ مَا أُوْحِيَ اِلَيْكَ مِنْ رَّبِّكَ ۚ
لَا اِلٰهَ اِلَّا هُوَ ۚ
وَاَعْرِضْ عَنِ الْمُشْرِكِيْنَ ۝

١٠٧ - وَلَوْ شَاءَ اللّٰهُ
مَا أَشْرَكُوْا ۚ
وَمَا جَعَلْنٰكَ
عَلَيْهِمْ حَفِيْظًا ۚ
وَمَا أَنْتَ عَلَيْهِمْ بِوَكِيْلٍ ۝

١٠٨ - وَلَا تَسُبُّوا الَّذِيْنَ
يَدْعُوْنَ مِنْ دُوْنِ اللّٰهِ
فَيَسُبُّوا اللّٰهَ عَدْوًا
بِغَيْرِ عِلْمٍ ۗ كَذٰلِكَ زَيَّنَّا
لِكُلِّ أُمَّةٍ عَمَلَهُمْ ۗ
ثُمَّ اِلٰى رَبِّهِمْ مَّرْجِعُهُمْ
فَيُنَبِّئُهُمْ بِمَا كَانُوْا يَعْمَلُوْنَ ۝

١٠٩ - وَأَقْسَمُوْا بِاللّٰهِ جَهْدَ أَيْمَانِهِمْ

Oaths by Allah, that if
A (special) Sign came
To them, by it they would
Believe. Say: "Certainly
(All) Signs are in the power
Of Allah: but what will
Make you (Muslims) realise
That (even) if (special) Signs
Came, they will not believe?"

لَبِنْ جَآءَتْهُمْ اٰيَةٌ لَيُؤْمِنُنَّ بِهَا ۚ
قُلْ اِنَّمَا الْاٰيٰتُ عِنْدَ اللهِ
وَمَا يُشْعِرُكُمْ اَنَّهَاۤ اِذَا جَآءَتْ
لَا يُؤْمِنُوْنَ ۚ

110. We (too) shall turn
To (confusion) their hearts
And their eyes, even as they
Refused to believe in this
In the first instance:
We shall leave them
In their trespasses,
To wander in distraction.

١١٠- وَنُقَلِّبُ اَفْئِدَتَهُمْ
وَاَبْصَارَهُمْ كَمَا لَمْ يُؤْمِنُوْا بِهٖۤ
اَوَّلَ مَرَّةٍ وَّنَذَرُهُمْ
فِيْ طُغْيَانِهِمْ يَعْمَهُوْنَ ۚ

SECTION 14.

111. Even if We did send
Unto them angels,
And the dead did speak
Unto them, and We gathered
Together all things before
Their very eyes, they are not
The ones to believe,
Unless it is in Allah's Plan.
But most of them
Ignore (the truth).

١١١- وَلَوْ اَنَّنَا نَزَّلْنَاۤ اِلَيْهِمُ الْمَلٰٓئِكَةَ
وَكَلَّمَهُمُ الْمَوْتٰى
وَحَشَرْنَا عَلَيْهِمْ كُلَّ شَيْءٍ قُبُلًا
مَّا كَانُوْا لِيُؤْمِنُوْۤا اِلَّاۤ اَنْ يَّشَآءَ اللهُ
وَلٰكِنَّ اَكْثَرَهُمْ يَجْهَلُوْنَ ۚ

112. Likewise did We make
For every Messenger
An enemy—evil ones
Among men and Jinns,
Inspiring each other
With flowery discourses
By way of deception.
If thy Lord had so planned,
They would not have
Done it: so leave them
And their inventions alone.

١١٢- وَكَذٰلِكَ جَعَلْنَا لِكُلِّ نَبِيٍّ
عَدُوًّا شَيٰطِيْنَ الْاِنْسِ وَالْجِنِّ
يُوْحِيْ بَعْضُهُمْ اِلٰى بَعْضٍ
زُخْرُفَ الْقَوْلِ غُرُوْرًا ۚ
وَلَوْ شَآءَ رَبُّكَ مَا فَعَلُوْهُ
فَذَرْهُمْ وَمَا يَفْتَرُوْنَ ۚ

113. To such (deceit)
Let the hearts of those
Incline, who have no faith
In the Hereafter: let them
Delight in it, and let them
Earn from it what they may.

١١٣- وَلِتَصْغٰۤى اِلَيْهِ اَفْئِدَةُ الَّذِيْنَ
لَا يُؤْمِنُوْنَ بِالْاٰخِرَةِ وَلِيَرْضَوْهُ
وَلِيَقْتَرِفُوْا مَا هُمْ مُّقْتَرِفُوْنَ ۚ

114. Say: "Shall I seek
For judge other than Allah?—
When He it is
Who hath sent unto you
The Book, explained in detail."
They know full well,
To whom We have given
The Book, that it hath been
Sent down from thy Lord
In truth. Never be then
Of those who doubt.

115. The Word of thy Lord
Doth find its fulfilment
In truth and in justice:
None can change His Words:
For He is the one Who
Heareth and knoweth all.

116. Wert thou to follow
The common run of those
On earth, they will lead
Thee away from the Way
Of Allah. They follow
Nothing but conjecture: they
Do nothing but lie.

117. Thy Lord knoweth best
Who strayeth from His Way:
He knoweth best
Who they are that receive
His guidance.

118. So eat of (meats)
On which Allah's name
Hath been pronounced,
If ye have faith
In His Signs.

119. Why should ye not
Eat of (meats) on which
Allah's name hath been
Pronounced, when He hath
Explained to you in detail
What is forbidden to you—
Except under compulsion
Of necesssity?
But many do mislead (men)
By their appetites unchecked

By knowledge. Thy Lord
Knoweth best those who transgress.

120. Eschew all sin,
Open or secret:
Those who earn sin
Will get due recompense
For their "earnings."

121. Eat not of (meats)
On which Allah's name
Hath not been pronounced:
That would be impiety.
But the evil ones
Ever inspire their friends
To contend with you
If ye were to obey them,
Ye would indeed be Pagans.

SECTION 15.

122. Can he who was dead,
To whom We gave life,
And a Light whereby
He can walk amongst men,
Be like him who is
In the depths of darkness,
From which he can
Never come out?
Thus to those without Faith
Their own deeds seem pleasing.

123. Thus have We placed
Leaders in every town,
Its wicked men, to plot
(And burrow) therein:
But they only plot
Against their own souls,
And they perceive it not.

124. When there comes to them
A Sign (from Allah),
They say: "We shall not
Believe until we receive
One (exactly) like those
Received by Allah's messengers."
Allah knoweth best where
(And how) to carry out
His mission. Soon

إِنَّ رَبَّكَ هُوَ أَعْلَمُ بِالْمُعْتَدِينَ ۝

١٢٠- وَذَرُوا ظَاهِرَ الْإِثْمِ وَبَاطِنَهُ ۖ
إِنَّ الَّذِينَ يَكْسِبُونَ الْإِثْمَ
سَيُجْزَوْنَ بِمَا كَانُوا يَقْتَرِفُونَ ۝

١٢١- وَلَا تَأْكُلُوا
مِمَّا لَمْ يُذْكَرِ اسْمُ اللهِ عَلَيْهِ
وَإِنَّهُ لَفِسْقٌ ۗ وَإِنَّ الشَّيَاطِينَ
لَيُوحُونَ إِلَى أَوْلِيَائِهِمْ لِيُجَادِلُوكُمْ ۖ
وَإِنْ أَطَعْتُمُوهُمْ إِنَّكُمْ لَمُشْرِكُونَ ۝

١٢٢- أَوَمَنْ كَانَ مَيْتًا فَأَحْيَيْنَاهُ
وَجَعَلْنَا لَهُ نُورًا يَمْشِي بِهِ فِي النَّاسِ
كَمَنْ مَثَلُهُ
فِي الظُّلُمَاتِ لَيْسَ بِخَارِجٍ مِنْهَا ۚ
كَذَلِكَ زُيِّنَ لِلْكَافِرِينَ مَا كَانُوا يَعْمَلُونَ ۝

١٢٣- وَكَذَلِكَ جَعَلْنَا فِي كُلِّ قَرْيَةٍ أَكَابِرَ
مُجْرِمِيهَا لِيَمْكُرُوا فِيهَا ۖ
وَمَا يَمْكُرُونَ إِلَّا بِأَنْفُسِهِمْ
وَمَا يَشْعُرُونَ ۝

١٢٤- وَإِذَا جَاءَتْهُمْ آيَةٌ
قَالُوا لَنْ نُؤْمِنَ حَتَّى نُؤْتَى
مِثْلَ مَا أُوتِيَ رُسُلُ اللهِ ۘ
اللهُ أَعْلَمُ حَيْثُ يَجْعَلُ رِسَالَتَهُ ۗ
سَيُصِيبُ الَّذِينَ أَجْرَمُوا صَغَارٌ عِنْدَ

Will the wicked
Be overtaken by
Humiliation before Allah,
And a severe punishment,
For all their plots.

25. Those whom Allah (in His Plan)
Willeth to guide—He openeth
Their breast to Islam;
Those whom He willeth
To leave straying—He maketh
Their breast close and constricted,
As if they had to climb
Up to the skies: thus
Doth Allah (heap) the penalty
On those who refuse to believe.

126. This is the Way
Of thy Lord, leading straight:
We have detailed the Signs
For those who
Receive admonition.

127. For them will be a Home
Of Peace in the presence
Of their Lord: He will be
Their Friend, because
They practised (righteousness).

128. Onc day will He gather
Them all together, (and say);
"O ye assembly of Jinns!
Much (toll) did ye take
Of men." Their friends
Amongst men will say:
"Our Lord! we made profit
From each other: but (alas!)
We reached our term—
Which Thou didst appoint
For us." He will say:
"The Fire be your dwelling place:
You will dwell therein forever,
Except as Allah willeth."
For thy Lord is full
Of wisdom and knowledge.

129. Thus do We make
The wrongdoers turn
To each other, because
Of what they earn.

SECTION 16.

130. "O ye assembly of Jinns
And men! came there not
Unto you messengers from
                    amongst you,
Setting forth unto you
My Signs, and warning you
Of the meeting of this Day
Of yours?" They will say:
"We bear witness against
Ourselves." It was
The life of this world
That deceived them. So
Against themselves will they
Bear witness that they
Rejected Faith.

١٣٠-يَمَعْشَرَ الْجِنِّ وَالْإِنْسِ
لَمْ يَأْتِكُمْ رُسُلٌ مِّنْكُمْ
يَقُصُّونَ عَلَيْكُمْ اٰيٰتِىْ
وَيُنْذِرُوْنَكُمْ لِقَآءَ يَوْمِكُمْ هٰذَا ؕ
قَالُوْا شَهِدْنَا عَلٰٓى اَنْفُسِنَا
وَغَرَّتْهُمُ الْحَيٰوةُ الدُّنْيَا
وَشَهِدُوْا عَلٰٓى اَنْفُسِهِمْ
اَنَّهُمْ كَانُوْا كٰفِرِيْنَ ۝

131. (The messengers were sent) thus,
For thy Lord would not
Destroy, for their wrongdoing
Men's habitations whilst
Their occupants were unwarned.

١٣١-ذٰلِكَ اَنْ لَّمْ يَكُنْ رَّبُّكَ مُهْلِكَ
الْقُرٰى بِظُلْمٍ
وَّاَهْلُهَا غٰفِلُوْنَ ۝

132. To all are degrees (or ranks)
According to their deeds:
For thy Lord
Is not unmindful
Of anything that they do.

١٣٢-وَلِكُلٍّ دَرَجٰتٌ مِّمَّا عَمِلُوْا ؕ
وَمَا رَبُّكَ بِغَافِلٍ
عَمَّا يَعْمَلُوْنَ ۝

133. Thy Lord is Self-sufficient,
Full of Mercy: if it were
His Will, He could destroy
You, and in your place
Appoint whom He will
As your successors, even as
He raised you up
From the posterity
Of other people.

١٣٣-وَرَبُّكَ الْغَنِيُّ ذُو الرَّحْمَةِ ؕ
اِنْ يَّشَأْ يُذْهِبْكُمْ
وَيَسْتَخْلِفْ مِنْ بَعْدِكُمْ
مَّا يَشَآءُ كَمَآ اَنْشَاَكُمْ
مِّنْ ذُرِّيَّةِ قَوْمٍ اٰخَرِيْنَ ؕ

134. All that hath been
Promised unto you
Will come to pass:
Nor can ye frustrate it
(In the least bit).

١٣٤-اِنَّ مَا تُوْعَدُوْنَ لَاٰتٍ ۙ
وَّمَآ اَنْتُمْ بِمُعْجِزِيْنَ ۝

135. Say: "O my people!
Do whatever ye can:
I will do (my part):
Soon will ye know

١٣٥-قُلْ يٰقَوْمِ اعْمَلُوْا عَلٰى مَكَانَتِكُمْ
اِنِّىْ عَامِلٌ ۚ فَسَوْفَ تَعْلَمُوْنَ ۙ

Who it is whose end
Will be (best) in the Hereafter:
Certain it is that
The wrongdoers will not prosper."

مَنْ تَكُونُ لَهُ عَاقِبَةُ الدَّارِ
إِنَّهُ لَا يُفْلِحُ الظَّالِمُونَ ۝

136. Out of what Allah
Hath produced in abundance
In tilth and in cattle,
They assigned Him a share:
They say, according to their
fancies:
"This is for Allah, and this—
For Our 'partners'"!
But the share of their "partners"
Reacheth not Allah, whilst
The share of Allah reacheth
Their "partners"! Evil
(And unjust) is their assignment!

١٣٦ وَجَعَلُوا لِلَّهِ مِمَّا ذَرَأَ مِنَ الْحَرْثِ وَ
الْأَنْعَامِ نَصِيبًا فَقَالُوا هٰذَا لِلَّهِ بِزَعْمِهِمْ
وَهٰذَا لِشُرَكَائِنَا ۚ
فَمَا كَانَ لِشُرَكَائِهِمْ
فَلَا يَصِلُ إِلَى اللَّهِ ۖ وَمَا كَانَ لِلَّهِ فَهُوَ يَصِلُ
إِلَى شُرَكَائِهِمْ ۗ سَاءَ مَا يَحْكُمُونَ ۝

137. Even so, in the eyes
Of most of the Pagans,
Their "partners" made alluring
The slaughter of their children,
In order to lead them
To their own destruction,
And cause confusion
In their religion.
If Allah had willed,
They would not have done so:
But leave alone
Them and their inventions.

١٣٧ وَكَذٰلِكَ زَيَّنَ لِكَثِيرٍ مِنَ الْمُشْرِكِينَ
قَتْلَ أَوْلَادِهِمْ شُرَكَاؤُهُمْ لِيُرْدُوهُمْ
وَلِيَلْبِسُوا عَلَيْهِمْ دِينَهُمْ ۚ
وَلَوْ شَاءَ اللَّهُ
مَا فَعَلُوهُ
فَذَرْهُمْ وَمَا يَفْتَرُونَ ۝

138. And they say that
Such and such cattle and crops
Are taboo, and none should
Eat of them except those
Whom—so they say—We
Wish; further, there are
Cattle forbidden to yoke
Or burden, and cattle
On which, (at slaughter),
The name of Allah is not
Pronounced—inventions
Against Allah's name: soon
Will He requite them
For their inventions.

١٣٨ وَقَالُوا هٰذِهِ أَنْعَامٌ وَحَرْثٌ حِجْرٌ ۗ
لَا يَطْعَمُهَا إِلَّا مَنْ نَشَاءُ
بِزَعْمِهِمْ وَأَنْعَامٌ حُرِّمَتْ ظُهُورُهَا وَ
أَنْعَامٌ
لَا يَذْكُرُونَ اسْمَ اللَّهِ عَلَيْهَا
افْتِرَاءً عَلَيْهِ ۚ
سَيَجْزِيهِمْ بِمَا كَانُوا يَفْتَرُونَ ۝

139. They say: "What is

١٣٩ وَقَالُوا مَا فِي بُطُونِ هٰذِهِ الْأَنْعَامِ

In the wombs of
Such and such cattle
Is specially reserved
(For food) for our men,
And forbidden to our women;
But if it is stillborn,
Then all have shares therein.
For their (false) attribution
(Of superstitions to Allah),
He will soon punish them:
For He is full
Of wisdom and knowledge.

140. Lost are those who slay
Their children, from folly,
Without knowledge, and forbid
Food which Allah hath provided
For them, inventing (lies)
Against Allah. They have
Indeed gone astray
And heeded no guidance.

SECTION 17.

141. It is He who produceth
Gardens, with trellises
And without, and dates,
And tilth with produce
Of all kinds, and olives
And pomegranates,
Similar (in kind)
And different (in variety):
Eat of their fruit
In their season, but render
The dues that are proper
On the day that the harvest
Is gathered. But waste not
By excess: for Allah
Loveth not the wasters.

142. Of the cattle are some
For burden and some for meat:
Eat what Allah hath provided
For you, and follow not
The footsteps of Satan:
For he is to you
An avowed enemy.

143. (Take) eight (head of cattle)
In (four) pairs:

Of sheep a pair,
And of goats a pair;
Say, hath He forbidden
The two males,
Or the two females,
Or (the young) which the wombs
Or the two females enclose?
Tell me with knowledge
If ye are truthful:

144. Of camels a pair,
And of oxen a pair;
Say, hath He forbidden
The two males,
Or the two females,
Or (the young) which the wombs
Of the two females enclose?—
Were ye present when Allah
Ordered you such a thing?
But who doth more wrong
Than one who invents
A lie against Allah,
To lead astray men
Without knowledge?
For Allah guideth not
People who do wrong.

SECTION 18.

145. Say: "I find not
In the Message received
By me by inspiration
Any (meat) forbidden
To be eaten by one
Who wishes to eat it,
Unless it be dead meat,
Or blood poured forth,
Or the flesh of swine—
For it is an abomination—
Or what is impious, (meat)
On which a name has been
Invoked other than Allah's."
But (even so), if a person
Is forced by necessity,
Without willful disobedience,
Nor transgressing due limits—
Thy Lord is Oft-Forgiving,
Most Merciful.

وَمِنَ الْمَعْزِ اثْنَيْنِ
قُلْ ءَآلذَّكَرَيْنِ حَرَّمَ
أَمِ الْأُنْثَيَيْنِ
أَمَّا اشْتَمَلَتْ عَلَيْهِ أَرْحَامُ الْأُنْثَيَيْنِ
نَبِّئُونِي بِعِلْمٍ إِنْ كُنْتُمْ صَادِقِينَ ۞

١٤٤- وَمِنَ الْإِبِلِ اثْنَيْنِ
وَمِنَ الْبَقَرِ اثْنَيْنِ
قُلْ ءَآلذَّكَرَيْنِ حَرَّمَ أَمِ الْأُنْثَيَيْنِ
أَمَّا اشْتَمَلَتْ عَلَيْهِ أَرْحَامُ الْأُنْثَيَيْنِ
أَمْ كُنْتُمْ شُهَدَاءَ إِذْ وَصَّاكُمُ اللهُ بِهَذَا
فَمَنْ أَظْلَمُ مِمَّنِ افْتَرَى عَلَى اللهِ كَذِبًا
لِيُضِلَّ النَّاسَ بِغَيْرِ عِلْمٍ
إِنَّ اللهَ لَا يَهْدِي الْقَوْمَ الظَّالِمِينَ ۞

١٤٥- قُلْ لَا أَجِدُ فِي مَا أُوحِيَ
إِلَيَّ مُحَرَّمًا عَلَى طَاعِمٍ
يَطْعَمُهُ إِلَّا أَنْ يَكُونَ مَيْتَةً أَوْ دَمًا
مَسْفُوحًا
أَوْ لَحْمَ خِنْزِيرٍ
فَإِنَّهُ رِجْسٌ أَوْ فِسْقًا
أُهِلَّ لِغَيْرِ اللهِ بِهِ
فَمَنِ اضْطُرَّ غَيْرَ بَاغٍ وَلَا عَادٍ
فَإِنَّ رَبَّكَ غَفُورٌ رَحِيمٌ ۞

146. For those who followed
The Jewish Law, We forbade
Every (animal) with
Undivided hoof,
And We forbade them
The fat of the ox
And the sheep, except
What adheres to their backs
Or their entrails,
Or is mixed up
With a bone:
This in recompense
For their willful disobedience:
For We are True
(In Our ordinances).

147. If they accuse thee
Of falsehood, say:
"Your Lord is Full
Of Mercy, All-Embracing;"
But from people in guilt
Never will His wrath
Be turned back.

148. Those who give partners
(To Allah) will say:
"If Allah had wished,
We should not have
Given partners to Him,
Nor would our fathers:
Nor should we have had
Any taboos." So did
Their ancestors argue
Falsely, until they tasted
Of Our wrath. Say:
"Have ye any (certain)
Knowledge? If so, produce
It before us. Ye follow
Nothing but conjecture:
Ye do nothing but lie."

149. Say: "With Allah is the
argument
That reaches home: if it had
Been His Will, He could
Indeed have guided you all."

150. Say: "Bring forward your
witnesses

١٤٦- وَعَلَى الَّذِينَ هَادُوا حَرَّمْنَا كُلَّ ذِي ظُفُرٍ ۚ وَمِنَ الْبَقَرِ وَالْغَنَمِ حَرَّمْنَا عَلَيْهِمْ شُحُومَهُمَا إِلَّا مَا حَمَلَتْ ظُهُورُهُمَا أَوِ الْحَوَايَا أَوْ مَا اخْتَلَطَ بِعَظْمٍ ۚ ذَٰلِكَ جَزَيْنَاهُمْ بِبَغْيِهِمْ ۖ وَإِنَّا لَصَادِقُونَ ۝

١٤٧- فَإِنْ كَذَّبُوكَ فَقُلْ رَبُّكُمْ ذُو رَحْمَةٍ وَاسِعَةٍ ۖ وَلَا يُرَدُّ بَأْسُهُ عَنِ الْقَوْمِ الْمُجْرِمِينَ ۝

١٤٨- سَيَقُولُ الَّذِينَ أَشْرَكُوا لَوْ شَاءَ اللَّهُ مَا أَشْرَكْنَا وَلَا آبَاؤُنَا وَلَا حَرَّمْنَا مِنْ شَيْءٍ ۚ كَذَٰلِكَ كَذَّبَ الَّذِينَ مِنْ قَبْلِهِمْ حَتَّى ذَاقُوا بَأْسَنَا ۗ قُلْ هَلْ عِنْدَكُمْ مِنْ عِلْمٍ فَتُخْرِجُوهُ لَنَا ۖ إِنْ تَتَّبِعُونَ إِلَّا الظَّنَّ وَإِنْ أَنْتُمْ إِلَّا تَخْرُصُونَ ۝

١٤٩- قُلْ فَلِلَّهِ الْحُجَّةُ الْبَالِغَةُ ۖ فَلَوْ شَاءَ لَهَدَاكُمْ أَجْمَعِينَ ۝

١٥٠- قُلْ هَلُمَّ شُهَدَاءَكُمُ

To prove that Allah did
Forbid so and so." If they
Bring such witnesses,
Be not thou amongst 'them:
Nor follow thou the vain
Desires of such as treat
Our Signs as falsehoods,
And such as believe not
In the Hereafter: for they
Hold others as equal
With their Guardian-Lord.

SECTION 19.

151. **S**ay: "Come, I will rehearse
What Allah hath (really)
Prohibited you from": join not
Anything as equal with Him;
Be good to your parents;
Kill not your children
On a plea of want—We
Provide sustenance for you
And for them—come not
Nigh to shameful deeds,
Whether open or secret;
Take not life, which Allah
Hath made sacred, except
By way of justice and law:
Thus doth He command you,
That ye may learn wisdom.

152. And come not nigh
To the orphan's property,
Except to improve it,
Until he attains the age
Of full strength; give measure
And weight with (full) justice—
No burden do We place
On any soul, but that
Which it can bear—
Whenever ye speak, speak justly,
Even if a near relative
Is concerned; and fulfil
The Covenant of Allah:
Thus doth He command you,
That ye may remember.

153. Verily, this is My Way
Leading straight: follow it;
Follow not (other) paths:

الَّذِينَ يَشْهَدُونَ اَنَّ اللهَ حَرَّمَ هٰذَا
فَاِنْ شَهِدُوا فَلَا تَشْهَدْ مَعَهُمْ
وَلَا تَتَّبِعْ اَهْوَآءَ الَّذِينَ كَذَّبُوا بِاٰيٰتِنَا
وَالَّذِينَ لَا يُؤْمِنُونَ
بِالْاٰخِرَةِ وَهُمْ بِرَبِّهِمْ يَعْدِلُونَ ۞

151. قُلْ تَعَالَوْا اَتْلُ مَا حَرَّمَ رَبُّكُمْ عَلَيْكُمْ
اَلَّا تُشْرِكُوا بِهِ شَيْئًا
وَّبِالْوَالِدَيْنِ اِحْسَانًا
وَلَا تَقْتُلُوا اَوْلَادَكُمْ مِّنْ اِمْلَاقٍ
نَحْنُ نَرْزُقُكُمْ وَاِيَّاهُمْ وَلَا تَقْرَبُوا
الْفَوَاحِشَ مَا ظَهَرَ مِنْهَا وَمَا بَطَنَ
وَلَا تَقْتُلُوا النَّفْسَ الَّتِي حَرَّمَ اللهُ اِلَّا بِالْحَقِّ
ذٰلِكُمْ وَصّٰكُمْ بِهِ لَعَلَّكُمْ تَعْقِلُونَ ۞

152. وَلَا تَقْرَبُوا مَالَ الْيَتِيمِ
اِلَّا بِالَّتِي هِيَ اَحْسَنُ حَتّٰى يَبْلُغَ اَشُدَّهُ
وَاَوْفُوا الْكَيْلَ وَالْمِيزَانَ بِالْقِسْطِ
لَا نُكَلِّفُ نَفْسًا اِلَّا وُسْعَهَا
وَاِذَا قُلْتُمْ فَاعْدِلُوا
وَلَوْ كَانَ ذَا قُرْبٰى
وَبِعَهْدِ اللهِ اَوْفُوا
ذٰلِكُمْ وَصّٰكُمْ بِهِ لَعَلَّكُمْ تَذَكَّرُونَ ۞

153. وَاَنَّ هٰذَا صِرَاطِي مُسْتَقِيمًا فَاتَّبِعُوهُ
وَلَا تَتَّبِعُوا السُّبُلَ فَتَفَرَّقَ بِكُمْ عَنْ

They will scatter you about
From His (great) Path;
Thus doth He command you,
That ye may be righteous.

154. Moreover, We gave Moses
The Book, completing
(Our favour) to those
Who would do right,
And explaining all things
In detail—and a guide
And a mercy, that they
Might believe in the meeting
With their Lord.

SECTION 20.

155. And this is a Book
Which We have revealed
As a blessing: so follow it
And be righteous, that ye
May receive mercy;

156. Lest ye should say:
"The Book was sent down
To two Peoples before us,
And for our part, we
Remained unacquainted
With all that they learned
By assiduous study;"

157. Or lest ye should say:
"If the Book had only
Been sent down to us,
We should have followed
Its guidance better than they."
Now then hath come
Unto you a Clear (Sign)
From your Lord—and a guide
And a mercy: then who
Could do more wrong
Than one who rejecteth
Allah's Signs, and turneth
Away therefrom? In good time
Shall We requite those
Who turn away from Our Signs,
With a dreadful penalty,
For their turning away.

سَبِيلِهِ ذٰلِكُمْ وَصّٰكُمْ بِهِ لَعَلَّكُمْ تَتَّقُوْنَ ۝

١٥٤- ثُمَّ اٰتَيْنَا مُوْسَى الْكِتٰبَ تَمَامًا عَلَى الَّذِيْ اَحْسَنَ وَتَفْصِيْلًا لِّكُلِّ شَيْءٍ وَّهُدًى وَّرَحْمَةً لَّعَلَّهُمْ بِلِقَاءِ رَبِّهِمْ يُؤْمِنُوْنَ ۝

١٥٥- وَهٰذَا كِتٰبٌ اَنْزَلْنٰهُ مُبٰرَكٌ فَاتَّبِعُوْهُ وَاتَّقُوْا لَعَلَّكُمْ تُرْحَمُوْنَ ۝

١٥٦- اَنْ تَقُوْلُوْٓا اِنَّمَآ اُنْزِلَ الْكِتٰبُ عَلٰى طَآئِفَتَيْنِ مِنْ قَبْلِنَا وَاِنْ كُنَّا عَنْ دِرَاسَتِهِمْ لَغٰفِلِيْنَ ۝

١٥٧- اَوْ تَقُوْلُوْا لَوْ اَنَّآ اُنْزِلَ عَلَيْنَا الْكِتٰبُ لَكُنَّآ اَهْدٰى مِنْهُمْ فَقَدْ جَآءَكُمْ بَيِّنَةٌ مِّنْ رَّبِّكُمْ وَهُدًى وَّرَحْمَةٌ فَمَنْ اَظْلَمُ مِمَّنْ كَذَّبَ بِاٰيٰتِ اللّٰهِ وَصَدَفَ عَنْهَا سَنَجْزِي الَّذِيْنَ يَصْدِفُوْنَ عَنْ اٰيٰتِنَا سُوْءَ الْعَذَابِ بِمَا كَانُوْا يَصْدِفُوْنَ ۝

158. Are they waiting to see
If the angels come to them,
Or thy Lord (Himself),
Or certain of the Signs
Of thy Lord!
The day that certain
Of the Signs of thy Lord
Do come, no good
Will it do to a soul
To believe in them then,
If it believed not before
Nor earned righteousness
Through its Faith. Say:
"Wait ye: we too
Are waiting."

١٥٨- هَلْ يَنْظُرُوْنَ إِلَّا أَنْ تَأْتِيَهُمُ
الْمَلَائِكَةُ أَوْ يَأْتِيَ رَبُّكَ
أَوْ يَأْتِيَ بَعْضُ اٰيٰتِ رَبِّكَ
يَوْمَ يَأْتِيْ بَعْضُ اٰيٰتِ رَبِّكَ
لَا يَنْفَعُ نَفْسًا اِيْمَانُهَا
لَمْ تَكُنْ اٰمَنَتْ مِنْ قَبْلُ
أَوْ كَسَبَتْ فِيْ اِيْمَانِهَا خَيْرًا ۗ
قُلِ انْتَظِرُوْا اِنَّا مُنْتَظِرُوْنَ ۠

159. As for those who divide
Their religion and break up
Into sects, thou hast
No part in them in the least:
Their affair is with Allah:
He will in the end
Tell them the truth
Of all that they did.

١٥٩- اِنَّ الَّذِيْنَ فَرَّقُوْا دِيْنَهُمْ وَكَانُوْا شِيَعًا
لَسْتَ مِنْهُمْ فِيْ شَيْءٍ ۗ
اِنَّمَا اَمْرُهُمْ اِلَى اللّٰهِ
ثُمَّ يُنَبِّئُهُمْ بِمَا كَانُوْا يَفْعَلُوْنَ ۠

160. He that doeth good
Shall have ten times
As much to his credit:
He that doeth evil
Shall only be recompensed
According to his evil:
No wrong shall be done
Unto (any of) them.

١٦٠- مَنْ جَاءَ بِالْحَسَنَةِ فَلَهُ عَشْرُ اَمْثَالِهَا ۚ
وَمَنْ جَاءَ بِالسَّيِّئَةِ
فَلَا يُجْزٰى اِلَّا مِثْلَهَا
وَهُمْ لَا يُظْلَمُوْنَ ۠

161. Say: "Verily, my Lord
Hath guided me to
A Way that is straight—
A religion of right—
The Path (trod) by Abraham
The true in faith,
And he (certainly)
Joined not gods with Allah."

١٦١- قُلْ اِنَّنِيْ هَدٰىنِيْ رَبِّيْ اِلٰى صِرَاطٍ
مُسْتَقِيْمٍ ۚ دِيْنًا قِيَمًا
مِلَّةَ اِبْرٰهِيْمَ حَنِيْفًا ۚ
وَمَا كَانَ مِنَ الْمُشْرِكِيْنَ ۠

162. Say: "Truly, my prayer
And my service of sacrifice,
My life and my death,
Are (all) for Allah,
The Cherisher of the Worlds;

١٦٢- قُلْ اِنَّ صَلَاتِيْ وَنُسُكِيْ
وَمَحْيَايَ وَمَمَاتِيْ
لِلّٰهِ رَبِّ الْعٰلَمِيْنَ ۙ

163. No partner hath He:
This am I commanded,
And I am the first
Of those who bow
To His Will.

١٦٣-لَا شَرِيكَ لَهُ ۚ
بِذٰلِكَ أُمِرْتُ
وَأَنَا أَوَّلُ الْمُسْلِمِينَ ۝

164. Say: "Shall I seek
For (my) Cherisher
Other than Allah,
When He is the Cherisher
Of all things (that exist)?
Every soul draws the meed
Of its acts on none
But itself: no bearer
Of burdens can bear
The burden of another.
Your goal in the end
Is towards Allah: He will tell
You the truth of the things
Wherein ye disputed."

١٦٤- قُلْ أَغَيْرَ اللّٰهِ أَبْغِى رَبًّا
وَهُوَ رَبُّ كُلِّ شَىْءٍ ۚ
وَلَا تَكْسِبُ كُلُّ نَفْسٍ إِلَّا عَلَيْهَا ۚ
وَلَا تَزِرُ وَازِرَةٌ وِزْرَ أُخْرٰى ۚ
ثُمَّ إِلٰى رَبِّكُمْ مَّرْجِعُكُمْ
فَيُنَبِّئُكُمْ بِمَا كُنْتُمْ فِيهِ تَخْتَلِفُونَ ۝

165. It is He Who hath made
You (His) agents, inheritors
Of the earth: He hath raised
You in ranks, some above
Others: that He may try you
In the gifts He hath given you:
For thy Lord is quick
In punishment: yet He
Is indeed Oft-Forgiving,
Most Merciful.

١٦٥- وَهُوَ الَّذِى جَعَلَكُمْ خَلٰٓئِفَ الْأَرْضِ
وَرَفَعَ بَعْضَكُمْ فَوْقَ بَعْضٍ دَرَجٰتٍ
لِّيَبْلُوَكُمْ فِى مَآ اٰتٰكُمْ ۚ
إِنَّ رَبَّكَ سَرِيعُ الْعِقَابِ ۖ
وَإِنَّهُ لَغَفُورٌ رَّحِيمٌ ۝

INTRODUCTION TO SŪRA VII (A'rāf) — 206 Verses

This Sūra is closely connected, both chronologically and in respect of the argument, with the previous Sūra. But it expounds the doctrine of revelation and man's spiritual history by illustrations from Adam onwards, through various Prophets, and the details of Moses's struggles, to the time of the Apostle Muhammad, in whom God's revelation in completed.

Al A'rāf (The Heights)

In the name of Allah, Most Gracious, Most Merciful.

بِسْمِ اللهِ الرَّحْمٰنِ الرَّحِيْمِ ۝

1. Alif Lām Mīm Ṣād.

١ـ الٓمٓصٓ ۝

2. A Book revealed unto thee—
So let thy heart be oppressed
No more by any difficulty
On that account—
That with it thou mightest
Warn (the erring) and teach
The Believers.

٢ـ كِتَابٌ أُنْزِلَ إِلَيْكَ
فَلَا يَكُنْ فِيْ صَدْرِكَ حَرَجٌ مِّنْهُ
لِتُنْذِرَ بِهٖ
وَذِكْرٰى لِلْمُؤْمِنِيْنَ ۝

3. Follow (O men!) the revelation
Given unto you from your Lord,
And follow not, as friends
Or protectors, other than Him.
Little it is ye remember
Of admonition.

٣ـ اِتَّبِعُوْا مَآ أُنْزِلَ إِلَيْكُمْ مِّنْ رَّبِّكُمْ
وَلَا تَتَّبِعُوْا مِنْ دُوْنِهٖ أَوْلِيَآءَ
قَلِيْلًا مَّا تَذَكَّرُوْنَ ۝

4. How many towns have We
Destroyed (for their sins)?
Our punishment took them
On a sudden by night
Or while they slept
For their afternoon rest.

٤ـ وَكَمْ مِّنْ قَرْيَةٍ أَهْلَكْنٰهَا
فَجَآءَهَا بَأْسُنَا بَيَاتًا
أَوْ هُمْ قَآئِلُوْنَ ۝

5. When (thus) Our punishment
Took them, no cry
Did they utter but this:
"Indeed we did wrong."

٥ـ فَمَا كَانَ دَعْوٰىهُمْ إِذْ جَآءَهُمْ بَأْسُنَآ
اِلَّا أَنْ قَالُوْا إِنَّا كُنَّا ظٰلِمِيْنَ ۝

6. Then shall We question

٦ـ فَلَنَسْـَٔلَنَّ الَّذِيْنَ

Those to whom Our Message
Was sent and those by whom
We sent it.

7. And verily We shall recount
Their whole story
With knowledge, for We
Were never absent
(At any time or place).

أُرْسِلَ إِلَيْهِمْ وَلَنَسْـَٔلَنَّ الْمُرْسَلِيْنَ ۙ

٧- فَلَنَقُصَّنَّ عَلَيْهِمْ بِعِلْمٍ
وَّمَا كُنَّا غَآئِبِيْنَ ۟

8. The balance that day
Will be true (to a nicety):
Those whose scale (of good)
Will be heavy, will prosper:

٨- وَالْوَزْنُ يَوْمَئِذِ ِۨالْحَقُّ ۚ فَمَنْ ثَقُلَتْ
مَوَازِيْنُهٗ فَأُولٰٓئِكَ هُمُ الْمُفْلِحُوْنَ ۟

9. Those whose scale will be light,
Will find their souls
In perdition, for that they
Wrongfully treated Our Signs.

٩- وَمَنْ خَفَّتْ مَوَازِيْنُهٗ فَأُولٰٓئِكَ الَّذِيْنَ
خَسِرُوْٓا أَنْفُسَهُمْ بِمَا كَانُوْا بِاٰيٰتِنَا يَظْلِمُوْنَ ۟

10. It is We Who have
Placed you with authority
On earth, and provided
You therein with means
For the fulfilment of your life:
Small are the thanks
That ye give!

١٠- وَلَقَدْ مَكَّنّٰكُمْ فِى الْأَرْضِ
وَجَعَلْنَا لَكُمْ فِيْهَا مَعَايِشَ ۗ
قَلِيْلًا مَّا تَشْكُرُوْنَ ۟ ۙ ع

SECTION 2.

11. It is We Who created you
And gave you shape;
Then We bade the angels
Bow down to Adam, and they
Bowed down; not so Iblīs;
He refused to be of those
Who bow down.

١١- وَلَقَدْ خَلَقْنٰكُمْ ثُمَّ صَوَّرْنٰكُمْ
ثُمَّ قُلْنَا لِلْمَلٰٓئِكَةِ اسْجُدُوْا لِاٰدَمَ ۗ
فَسَجَدُوْٓا إِلَّا إِبْلِيْسَ ۗ
لَمْ يَكُنْ مِّنَ السّٰجِدِيْنَ ۟

12. (Allah) said: "What prevented
Thee from bowing down
When I commanded thee?"
He said: "I am better
Than he: Thou didst create
Me from fire, and him from
clay."

١٢- قَالَ مَا مَنَعَكَ أَلَّا تَسْجُدَ إِذْ أَمَرْتُكَ ۗ
قَالَ أَنَا خَيْرٌ مِّنْهُ ۚ
خَلَقْتَنِيْ مِنْ نَّارٍ وَّخَلَقْتَهٗ مِنْ طِيْنٍ ۟

13. (Allah) said: "Get thee down
From this: it is not
For thee to be arrogant
Here: get out, for thou

١٣- قَالَ فَاهْبِطْ مِنْهَا
فَمَا يَكُوْنُ لَكَ أَنْ تَتَكَبَّرَ فِيْهَا

Art of the meanest (of
creatures)."

فَاخْرُجْ إِنَّكَ مِنَ الصَّغِرِينَ ۞

14. He said: "Give me respite
Till the day they are
Raised up."

١٤- قَالَ أَنْظِرْنِيٓ
إِلَىٰ يَوْمِ يُبْعَثُونَ ۞

15. (Allah) said: "Be thou
Amongst those who have
respite."

١٥- قَالَ إِنَّكَ مِنَ الْمُنْظَرِينَ ۞

16. He said: "Because Thou
Hast thrown me out[1001]
Of the Way, lo! I will
Lie in wait for them
On Thy Straight Way:

١٦- قَالَ فَبِمَا أَغْوَيْتَنِي
لَأَقْعُدَنَّ لَهُمْ صِرَاطَكَ الْمُسْتَقِيمَ ۞

17. "Then will I assault them
From before them and behind
them,
From their right and their left:
Nor wilt Thou find,
In most of them,
Gratitude (for Thy mercies)."

١٧- ثُمَّ لَأَتِيَنَّهُمْ مِنْ بَيْنِ أَيْدِيهِمْ وَ
مِنْ خَلْفِهِمْ وَعَنْ أَيْمَانِهِمْ وَعَنْ
شَمَائِلِهِمْ وَلَا تَجِدُ أَكْثَرَهُمْ شَكِرِينَ ۞

18. (Allah) said: "Get out
From this, disgraced
And expelled. If any
Of them follow thee—
Hell will I fill
With you all.

١٨- قَالَ اخْرُجْ مِنْهَا مَذْءُومًا مَدْحُورًا
لَمَنْ تَبِعَكَ مِنْهُمْ
لَأَمْلَأَنَّ جَهَنَّمَ مِنْكُمْ أَجْمَعِينَ ۞

19. "O Adam! dwell thou
And thy wife in the Garden,
And enjoy   (its good things)
As ye wish: but approach not
This tree, or ye run
Into harm and transgression."

١٩- وَيَا آدَمُ اسْكُنْ أَنْتَ وَزَوْجُكَ الْجَنَّةَ
فَكُلَا مِنْ حَيْثُ شِئْتُمَا وَلَا تَقْرَبَا هَٰذِهِ
الشَّجَرَةَ فَتَكُونَا مِنَ الظَّالِمِينَ ۞

20. Then began Satan   to whisper
Suggestions to them,
In order to reveal to them
Their shame
That was hidden from them
(Before): he said: "Your Lord
Only forbade you this tree,
Lest ye should become angels
Or such beings as live forever."

٢٠- فَوَسْوَسَ لَهُمَا الشَّيْطَانُ لِيُبْدِيَ
لَهُمَا مَا وُورِيَ عَنْهُمَا مِنْ سَوْآتِهِمَا
وَقَالَ مَا نَهَاكُمَا رَبُّكُمَا عَنْ هَٰذِهِ
الشَّجَرَةِ إِلَّا أَنْ تَكُونَا مَلَكَيْنِ أَوْ تَكُونَا
مِنَ الْخَالِدِينَ ۞

21. And he swore to them

٢١- وَقَاسَمَهُمَا إِنِّي

Both, that he was
Their sincere adviser.

لَكُمَا لَمِنَ النَّاصِحِيْنَ ۝

22. So by deceit he brought about
Their fall: when they
Tasted of the tree,
Their shame became manifest
To them, and they began
To sew together the leaves
Of the Garden over their
bodies.
And their Lord called
Unto them: "Did I not
Forbid you that tree,
And tell you that Satan
Was an avowed
Enemy unto you?"

٢٢- فَدَلّٰىهُمَا بِغُرُوْرٍ ۚ فَلَمَّا ذَاقَا الشَّجَرَةَ
بَدَتْ لَهُمَا سَوْاٰتُهُمَا
وَطَفِقَا يَخْصِفٰنِ عَلَيْهِمَا مِنْ وَّرَقِ
الْجَنَّةِ ۚ
وَنَادٰىهُمَا رَبُّهُمَا
اَلَمْ اَنْهَكُمَا عَنْ تِلْكُمَا الشَّجَرَةِ وَاَقُلْ
لَّكُمَا اِنَّ الشَّيْطٰنَ لَكُمَا عَدُوٌّ مُّبِيْنٌ ۝

23. They said: "Our Lord!
We have wronged our own
souls:
If Thou forgive us not
And bestow not upon us
Thy Mercy, we shall
Certainly be lost."

٢٣- قَالَا رَبَّنَا ظَلَمْنَا اَنْفُسَنَا
وَاِنْ لَّمْ تَغْفِرْ لَنَا وَتَرْحَمْنَا
لَنَكُوْنَنَّ مِنَ الْخٰسِرِيْنَ ۝

24. (Allah) said: "Get ye down,
With enmity between yourselves.
On earth will be your
dwelling-place
And your means of livelihood—
For a time."

٢٤- قَالَ اهْبِطُوْا بَعْضُكُمْ لِبَعْضٍ عَدُوٌّ ۚ
وَلَكُمْ فِى الْاَرْضِ مُسْتَقَرٌّ
وَّمَتَاعٌ اِلٰى حِيْنٍ ۝

25. He said: "Therein shall ye
Live, and therein shall ye
Die; but from it shall ye
Be taken out (at last)."
SECTION 3.

٢٥- قَالَ فِيْهَا تَحْيَوْنَ وَفِيْهَا
تَمُوْتُوْنَ وَمِنْهَا تُخْرَجُوْنَ ۞

26. O ye Children of Adam!
We have bestowed raiment
Upon you to cover
Your shame, as well as
To be an adornment to you.
But the raiment of
That is the best. righteousness—
Such are among the Signs
Of Allah, that they
May receive admonition!

٢٦- يٰبَنِيْ اٰدَمَ قَدْ اَنْزَلْنَا عَلَيْكُمْ لِبَاسًا
يُّوَارِىْ سَوْاٰتِكُمْ وَرِيْشًا ۚ
وَلِبَاسُ التَّقْوٰى ۙ ذٰلِكَ خَيْرٌ ۚ
ذٰلِكَ مِنْ اٰيٰتِ اللّٰهِ
لَعَلَّهُمْ يَذَّكَّرُوْنَ ۝

27. O ye Children of Adam!
Let not Satan seduce you,
In the same manner as
He got your parents out
Of the Garden, stripping them
Of their raiment, to expose
Their shame: for he
And his tribe watch you
From a position where ye
Cannot see them: We made
The Evil Ones friends
(Only) to those without Faith.

٢٧- يَبَنِىٓ اٰدَمَ لَا يَفْتِنَنَّكُمُ الشَّيْطٰنُ
كَمَآ اَخْرَجَ اَبَوَيْكُمْ مِّنَ الْجَنَّةِ
يَنْزِعُ عَنْهُمَا لِبَاسَهُمَا لِيُرِيَهُمَا سَوْاٰتِهِمَا ؕ
اِنَّهٗ يَرٰىكُمْ هُوَ وَقَبِيْلُهٗ مِنْ حَيْثُ لَا
تَرَوْنَهُمْ ؕ اِنَّا جَعَلْنَا الشَّيٰطِيْنَ اَوْلِيَآءَ
لِلَّذِيْنَ لَا يُؤْمِنُوْنَ ۞

28. When they do aught
That is shameful, they say:
"We found our fathers
Doing so"; and "Allah
Commanded us thus;"
Say: "Nay, Allah never
Commands what is shameful:
Do ye say of Allah
What ye know not?"

٢٨- وَاِذَا فَعَلُوْا فَاحِشَةً
قَالُوْا وَجَدْنَا عَلَيْهَآ اٰبَآءَنَا وَاللّٰهُ اَمَرَنَا
بِهَا ؕ قُلْ اِنَّ اللّٰهَ لَا يَأْمُرُ بِالْفَحْشَآءِ ؕ
اَتَقُوْلُوْنَ عَلَى اللّٰهِ مَا لَا تَعْلَمُوْنَ ۞

29. Say: "My Lord hath commanded
Justice; and that ye set
Your whole selves (to Him)
At every time and place
Of prayer, and call upon Him,
Making your devotion sincere
As in His sight:
Such as He created you
In the beginning, so
Shall ye return."

٢٩- قُلْ اَمَرَ رَبِّىْ بِالْقِسْطِ ۟
وَاَقِيْمُوْا وُجُوْهَكُمْ
عِنْدَ كُلِّ مَسْجِدٍ
وَّادْعُوْهُ مُخْلِصِيْنَ لَهُ الدِّيْنَ ؕ
كَمَا بَدَاَكُمْ تَعُوْدُوْنَ ؕ

30. Some He hath guided:
Others have (by their choice)
Deserved the loss of their way;
In that they took
The Evil Ones, in preference
To Allah, for their friends
And protectors, and think
That they receive guidance.

٣٠- فَرِيْقًا هَدٰى وَفَرِيْقًا حَقَّ عَلَيْهِمُ
الضَّلٰلَةُ ؕ اِنَّهُمُ اتَّخَذُوا الشَّيٰطِيْنَ
اَوْلِيَآءَ مِنْ دُوْنِ اللّٰهِ
وَيَحْسَبُوْنَ اَنَّهُمْ مُّهْتَدُوْنَ ۞

31. O Children of Adam!
Wear your beautiful apparel
At every time and place
Of prayer: eat and drink:
But waste not by excess,
For Allah loveth not the wasters.

٣١- يَبَنِىٓ اٰدَمَ خُذُوْا زِيْنَتَكُمْ عِنْدَ
كُلِّ مَسْجِدٍ وَّكُلُوْا وَاشْرَبُوْا وَلَا تُسْرِفُوْا ؕ
اِنَّهٗ لَا يُحِبُّ الْمُسْرِفِيْنَ ۞

SECTION 4.

32. Say: Who hath forbidden
The beautiful (gifts) of Allah,
Which He hath produced
For His servants,
And the things, clean and pure,
(Which He hath provided)
For sustenance?
Say: They are, in the life
Of this world, for those
Who believe, (and) purely
For them on the Day
Of Judgement. Thus do We
Explain the Signs in detail
For those who understand.

٣٢ـ قُلْ مَنْ حَرَّمَ زِيْنَةَ اللّٰهِ
الَّتِيْٓ اَخْرَجَ لِعِبَادِهٖ
وَالطَّيِّبٰتِ مِنَ الرِّزْقِ
قُلْ هِيَ لِلَّذِيْنَ اٰمَنُوْا فِى الْحَيٰوةِ
الدُّنْيَا
خَالِصَةً يَّوْمَ الْقِيٰمَةِ
كَذٰلِكَ نُفَصِّلُ الْاٰيٰتِ لِقَوْمٍ يَّعْلَمُوْنَ ۝

33. Say: The things that my Lord
Hath indeed forbidden are:
Shameful deeds, whether open
Or secret; sins and trespasses
Against truth or reason; assigning
Of partners to Allah, for which
He hath given no authority;
And saying things about Allah
Of which ye have no knowledge.

٣٣ـ قُلْ اِنَّمَا حَرَّمَ رَبِّيَ الْفَوَاحِشَ مَا ظَهَرَ
مِنْهَا وَمَا بَطَنَ وَالْاِثْمَ وَالْبَغْيَ
بِغَيْرِ الْحَقِّ وَاَنْ تُشْرِكُوْا بِاللّٰهِ
مَا لَمْ يُنَزِّلْ بِهٖ سُلْطٰنًا
وَاَنْ تَقُوْلُوْا عَلَى اللّٰهِ مَا لَا تَعْلَمُوْنَ ۝

34. To every People is a term
Appointed: when their term
Is reached, not an hour
Can they cause delay,
Nor (an hour) can they
Advance (it in anticipation).

٣٤ـ وَلِكُلِّ اُمَّةٍ اَجَلٌ فَاِذَا جَاۤءَ اَجَلُهُمْ
لَا يَسْتَأْخِرُوْنَ سَاعَةً
وَّلَا يَسْتَقْدِمُوْنَ ۝

35. O ye Children of Adam!
Whenever there come to you
Messengers from amongst you,
Rehearsing My Signs unto you—
Those who are righteous
And mend (their lives)—
On them shall be no fear
Nor shall they grieve.

٣٥ـ يٰبَنِيْٓ اٰدَمَ اِمَّا يَأْتِيَنَّكُمْ رُسُلٌ مِّنْكُمْ
يَقُصُّوْنَ عَلَيْكُمْ اٰيٰتِيْ فَمَنِ اتَّقٰى وَاَصْلَحَ
فَلَا خَوْفٌ عَلَيْهِمْ
وَلَا هُمْ يَحْزَنُوْنَ ۝

36. But those who reject
Our Signs and treat them
With arrogance—they
Are Companions of the Fire,
To dwell therein (forever).

٣٦ـ وَالَّذِيْنَ كَذَّبُوْا بِاٰيٰتِنَا
وَاسْتَكْبَرُوْا عَنْهَآ اُولٰٓئِكَ اَصْحٰبُ النَّارِ
هُمْ فِيْهَا خٰلِدُوْنَ ۝

37. Who is more unjust
Than one who invents

٣٧ـ فَمَنْ اَظْلَمُ مِمَّنِ افْتَرٰى عَلَى اللّٰهِ

A lie against Allah
Or rejects His Signs?
For such, their portion
Appointed must reach them
From the Book (of Decrees):
Until, when Our messengers
(Of death) arrive and take
Their souls, they say:
"Where are the things
That ye used to invoke
Besides Allah?"
They will reply, "They
Have left us in the lurch,"
And they will bear witness
Against themselves, that they
Had rejected Allah.

38. He will say: "Enter ye
In the company of
The Peoples who passed away
Before you—men and Jinns—
Into the Fire. Every time
A new People enters,
It curses its sister-People
(That went before), until
They follow each other, all
Into the Fire. Saith the last
About the first: "Our Lord!
It is these that misled us:
So give them a double
Penalty in the Fire."
He will say: "Doubled
For all": but this
Ye do not understand.

39. Then the first will say
To the last: "See then!
No advantage have ye
Over us; so taste ye
Of the Penalty for all
That ye did!"

SECTION 5.

40. To those who reject
Our Signs and treat them
With arrogance, no opening
Will there be of the gates

كَذِبًا أَوْ كَذَّبَ بِأَيْتِهِ
أُولَٰئِكَ يَنَالُهُمْ نَصِيبُهُمْ مِنَ الْكِتَابِ
حَتَّىٰ إِذَا جَاءَتْهُمْ رُسُلُنَا يَتَوَفَّوْنَهُمْ
قَالُوا أَيْنَ مَا كُنْتُمْ تَدْعُونَ مِنْ
دُونِ اللَّهِ
قَالُوا
ضَلُّوا عَنَّا وَشَهِدُوا عَلَىٰ أَنْفُسِهِمْ
أَنَّهُمْ كَانُوا كَافِرِينَ ۝

٣٨- قَالَ ادْخُلُوا فِي أُمَمٍ قَدْ خَلَتْ مِنْ
قَبْلِكُمْ مِنَ الْجِنِّ وَالْإِنْسِ
فِي النَّارِ
كُلَّمَا دَخَلَتْ أُمَّةٌ لَعَنَتْ أُخْتَهَا
حَتَّىٰ إِذَا ادَّارَكُوا فِيهَا جَمِيعًا
قَالَتْ أُخْرَاهُمْ لِأُولَاهُمْ
رَبَّنَا هَٰؤُلَاءِ أَضَلُّونَا
فَآتِهِمْ عَذَابًا ضِعْفًا مِنَ النَّارِ
قَالَ لِكُلٍّ ضِعْفٌ وَلَٰكِنْ لَا تَعْلَمُونَ ۝

٣٩- وَقَالَتْ أُولَاهُمْ لِأُخْرَاهُمْ
فَمَا كَانَ لَكُمْ عَلَيْنَا مِنْ فَضْلٍ
فَذُوقُوا الْعَذَابَ بِمَا كُنْتُمْ تَكْسِبُونَ ۝

٤٠- إِنَّ الَّذِينَ كَذَّبُوا بِأَيَاتِنَا وَاسْتَكْبَرُوا
عَنْهَا لَا تُفَتَّحُ لَهُمْ أَبْوَابُ

Of heaven, nor will they
Enter the Garden, until
The camel can pass
Through the eye of the needle:
Such is Our reward
For those in sin.

41. For them there is
Hell, as a couch
(Below) and folds and folds
Of covering above: such
Is Our requital of those
Who do wrong.

42. But those who believe
And work righteousness—
No burden do We place
On any soul, but that
Which it can bear—
They will be Companions
Of the Garden, therein
To dwell (forever).

43. And We shall remove
From their hearts any
Lurking sense of injury—
Beneath them will be
Rivers flowing—and they
Shall say: "Praise be to Allah,
Who hath guided us
To this (felicity): never
Could we have found
Guidance, had it not been
For the guidance of Allah:
Indeed it was the truth
That the Messengers of our Lord
Brought unto us." And they
Shall hear the cry:
"Behold! the Garden before you!
Ye have been made
Its inheritors, for your
Deeds (of righteousness)."

44. The Companions of the Garden
Will call out to the Companions
Of the Fire: "We have
Indeed found the promises
Of our Lord to us true:

Have you also found
Your Lord's promises true?"
They shall say, "Yes"; but
A Crier shall proclaim·
Between them: "The curse
Of Allah is on the wrongdoers—

قَالُوْا نَعَمْ ۚ
فَاَذَّنَ مُؤَذِّنٌ
بَيْنَهُمْ اَنْ لَّعْنَةُ اللهِ عَلَى الظّٰلِمِيْنَ ۙ

45. "Those who would hinder (men)
From the path of Allah
And would seek in it
Something crooked:
They were those who
Denied the Hereafter."

٤٥- الَّذِيْنَ يَصُدُّوْنَ عَنْ سَبِيْلِ اللهِ
وَيَبْغُوْنَهَا عِوَجًا ۚ
وَهُمْ بِالْاٰخِرَةِ كٰفِرُوْنَ ۟

46. Between them shall be
A veil, and on the Heights
Will be men
Who would know everyone
By his marks: they will call
Out to the Companions
Of the Garden, "Peace on you"·
They will not have entered,
But they will have
An assurance (thereof).

٤٦- وَبَيْنَهُمَا حِجَابٌ ۚ وَعَلَى الْاَعْرَافِ
رِجَالٌ يَّعْرِفُوْنَ كُلًّا بِسِيْمٰهُمْ ۚ
وَنَادَوْا اَصْحٰبَ الْجَنَّةِ
اَنْ سَلٰمٌ عَلَيْكُمْ ۗ لَمْ يَدْخُلُوْهَا
وَهُمْ يَطْمَعُوْنَ ۟

47. When their eyes   shall be turned
Towards the Companions
Of the Fire, they will say:
"Our Lord! send us not
To the company
Of the wrongdoers."

٤٧- وَاِذَا صُرِفَتْ اَبْصَارُهُمْ
تِلْقَآءَ اَصْحٰبِ النَّارِ ۙ قَالُوْا رَبَّنَا لَا تَجْعَلْنَا
مَعَ الْقَوْمِ الظّٰلِمِيْنَ ۟

SECTION 6.

48. The men on the Heights
Will call to certain men
Whom they will know
From their marks, saying:
"Of what profit to you
Were your hoards and your
Arrogant ways?

٤٨- وَنَادٰى اَصْحٰبُ الْاَعْرَافِ رِجَالًا
يَّعْرِفُوْنَهُمْ بِسِيْمٰهُمْ
قَالُوْا مَاۤ اَغْنٰى عَنْكُمْ جَمْعُكُمْ
وَمَا كُنْتُمْ تَسْتَكْبِرُوْنَ ۟

49. "Behold! are these not
The men whom you swore
That Allah with His Mercy
Would never bless?
Enter ye the Garden:
No fear shall be on you,
Nor shall ye grieve."

٤٩- اَهٰۤؤُلَآءِ الَّذِيْنَ اَقْسَمْتُمْ
لَا يَنَالُهُمُ اللهُ بِرَحْمَةٍ ۗ اُدْخُلُوا الْجَنَّةَ
لَا خَوْفٌ عَلَيْكُمْ وَلَاۤ اَنْتُمْ تَحْزَنُوْنَ ۟

50. The Companions of the Fire

٥٠- وَنَادٰۤى اَصْحٰبُ النَّارِ اَصْحٰبَ الْجَنَّةِ

Will call to the Companions
Of the Garden: "Pour down
To us water or anything
That Allah doth provide
For your sustenance."
They will say: "Both
These things hath Allah forbidden
To those who rejected Him—

51. "Such as took their religion
To be mere amusement
And play, and were deceived
By the life of the world."
That day shall We forget them
As they forgot the meeting
Of this day of theirs,
And as they were wont
To reject Our Signs.

52. For We had certainly
Sent unto them a Book,
Based on knowledge,
Which We explained
In detail—a guide
And a mercy
To all who believe.

53. Do they just wait
For the final fulfilment
Of the event? On the day
The event is finally fulfilled,
Those who disregarded it
Before will say: "The Messengers
Of our Lord did indeed
Bring true (tidings). Have we
No intercessors now to intercede
On our behalf? Or could we
Be sent back? Then should we
Behave differently from our
Behaviour in the past."
In fact they will have lost
Their souls, and the things
They invented will leave
Them in the lurch.

SECTION 7.

54. Your Guardian-Lord
Is Allah, Who created
The heavens and the earth[1031]

اَنْ اَفِيضُوْا عَلَيْنَا مِنَ الْمَآءِ اَوْ مِمَّا
رَزَقَكُمُ اللّٰهُ ۖ قَالُوْٓا اِنَّ اللّٰهَ حَرَّمَهُمَا
عَلَى الْكٰفِرِيْنَ ﴾

٥١- الَّذِيْنَ اتَّخَذُوْا دِيْنَهُمْ لَهْوًا
وَّلَعِبًا وَّغَرَّتْهُمُ الْحَيٰوةُ الدُّنْيَا ۚ
فَالْيَوْمَ نَنْسٰهُمْ
كَمَا نَسُوْا لِقَآءَ يَوْمِهِمْ هٰذَا ۙ
وَمَا كَانُوْا بِاٰيٰتِنَا يَجْحَدُوْنَ ۝

٥٢- وَلَقَدْ جِئْنٰهُمْ بِكِتٰبٍ
فَصَّلْنٰهُ عَلٰى عِلْمٍ هُدًى
وَّرَحْمَةً لِّقَوْمٍ يُّؤْمِنُوْنَ ۝

٥٣- هَلْ يَنْظُرُوْنَ اِلَّا تَأْوِيْلَهٗ ۗ
يَوْمَ يَأْتِيْ تَأْوِيْلُهٗ
يَقُوْلُ الَّذِيْنَ نَسُوْهُ مِنْ قَبْلُ
قَدْ جَآءَتْ رُسُلُ رَبِّنَا بِالْحَقِّ ۚ فَهَلْ لَّنَا
مِنْ شُفَعَآءَ فَيَشْفَعُوْا لَنَآ اَوْ نُرَدُّ
فَنَعْمَلَ غَيْرَ الَّذِيْ كُنَّا نَعْمَلُ ۚ
قَدْ خَسِرُوْٓا اَنْفُسَهُمْ وَضَلَّ عَنْهُمْ
مَّا كَانُوْا يَفْتَرُوْنَ ۝

٥٤- اِنَّ رَبَّكُمُ اللّٰهُ الَّذِيْ خَلَقَ

In six Days, then He
Established Himself on the
                Throne
(Of authority): He draweth
The night as a veil
O'er the day, each seeking
The other in rapid succession:
He created the sun,
The moon, and the stars,
(All) governed by laws
Under His Command.
Is it not His to create
And to govern? Blessed
Be Allah, the Cherisher
And Sustainer of the Worlds!

السَّمَوتِ وَالأَرْضَ
فِى سِتَّةِ أَيَّامٍ
ثُمَّ اسْتَوَى عَلَى الْعَرْشِ
يُغْشِى الَّيْلَ النَّهَارَ يَطْلُبُهُ حَثِيثًا
وَالشَّمْسَ وَالْقَمَرَ وَالنُّجُومَ
مُسَخَّرَاتٍ بِأَمْرِهِ
أَلَا لَهُ الْخَلْقُ وَالأَمْرُ
تَبَارَكَ اللهُ رَبُّ الْعَلَمِينَ ۝

55. Call on your Lord
With humility and in private:
For Allah loveth not
Those who trespass beyond
                bounds.

٥٥- اُدْعُوا رَبَّكُمْ تَضَرُّعًا وَخُفْيَةً
إِنَّهُ لَا يُحِبُّ الْمُعْتَدِينَ ۝

56. Do no mischief on the earth,
After it hath been
Set in order, but call
On Him with fear
And longing (in your hearts):
For the Mercy of Allah
Is (always) near
To those who do good.

٥٦- وَلَا تُفْسِدُوا فِى الأَرْضِ
بَعْدَ إِصْلَاحِهَا
وَادْعُوهُ خَوْفًا وَطَمَعًا إِنَّ رَحْمَتَ اللهِ
قَرِيبٌ مِّنَ الْمُحْسِنِينَ ۝

57. It is He Who sendeth
The Winds like heralds
Of glad tidings, going before
His Mercy: when they have
Carried the heavy-laden
Clouds, We drive them
To a land that is dead,
Make rain to descend thereon,
And produce every kind
Of harvest therewith: thus
Shall We raise up the dead:
Perchance ye may remember.

٥٧- وَهُوَ الَّذِى يُرْسِلُ الرِّيَحَ
بُشْرًا بَيْنَ يَدَىْ رَحْمَتِهِ
حَتَّى إِذَا أَقَلَّتْ سَحَابًا ثِقَالًا سُقْنَهُ
لِبَلَدٍ مَّيِّتٍ فَأَنْزَلْنَا بِهِ الْمَاءَ فَأَخْرَجْنَا
بِهِ مِنْ كُلِّ الثَّمَرَتِ
كَذَلِكَ نُخْرِجُ الْمَوْتَى لَعَلَّكُمْ تَذَكَّرُونَ ۝

58. From the land that is clean
And good, by the Will
Of its Cherisher, springs up
Produce, (rich) after its kind:

٥٨- وَالْبَلَدُ الطَّيِّبُ
يَخْرُجُ نَبَاتُهُ بِإِذْنِ رَبِّهِ

But from the land that is
Bad, springs up nothing
But that which is niggardly:
Thus do we explain the Signs
By various (symbols) to those
Who are grateful.

وَالَّذِى خَبُثَ لَا يَخْرُجُ إِلَّا نَكِدًا
كَذَلِكَ نُصَرِّفُ الْآيَاتِ
لِقَوْمٍ يَشْكُرُونَ ۞

SECTION 8.

59. We sent Noah to his people.
He said: "O my people!
Worship Allah! ye have
No other god but Him.
I fear for you the Punishment
Of a dreadful Day!

٥- لَقَدْ أَرْسَلْنَا نُوحًا إِلَى قَوْمِهِ
فَقَالَ يَا قَوْمِ اعْبُدُوا اللهَ
مَا لَكُمْ مِنْ إِلَهٍ غَيْرُهُ إِنِّى أَخَافُ
عَلَيْكُمْ عَذَابَ يَوْمٍ عَظِيمٍ ۞

60. The leaders of his people
Said: "Ah! we see thee
Evidently wandering (in mind)."

٦٠- قَالَ الْمَلَأُ مِنْ قَوْمِهِ
إِنَّا لَنَرَاكَ فِى ضَلَالٍ مُبِينٍ ۞

61. He said: "O my people!
No wandering is there
In my (mind): on the contrary
I am a messenger from
The Lord and Cherisher
Of the Worlds!

٦١- قَالَ يَا قَوْمِ لَيْسَ بِى ضَلَالَةٌ
وَلَكِنِّى رَسُولٌ
مِنْ رَبِّ الْعَالَمِينَ ۞

62. "I but fulfil towards you
The duties of my Lord's mission:
Sincere is my advice to you,
And I know from Allah
Something that ye know not.

٦٢- أُبَلِّغُكُمْ رِسَالَاتِ رَبِّى
وَأَنْصَحُ لَكُمْ
وَأَعْلَمُ مِنَ اللهِ مَا لَا تَعْلَمُونَ ۞

63. "Do ye wonder that
There hath come to you
A message from your Lord,
Through a man of your own
People, to warn you—
So that ye may fear Allah
And haply receive His Mercy?"

٦٣- أَوَعَجِبْتُمْ أَنْ جَاءَكُمْ
ذِكْرٌ مِنْ رَبِّكُمْ
عَلَى رَجُلٍ مِنْكُمْ لِيُنْذِرَكُمْ
وَلِتَتَّقُوا وَلَعَلَّكُمْ تُرْحَمُونَ ۞

64. But they rejected him,
And We delivered him,
And those with him
In the Ark:
But We overwhelmed
In the Flood those
Who rejected Our Signs.
They were indeed
A blind people!

٦٤- فَكَذَّبُوهُ فَأَنْجَيْنَاهُ
وَالَّذِينَ مَعَهُ فِى الْفُلْكِ
وَأَغْرَقْنَا الَّذِينَ كَذَّبُوا بِآيَاتِنَا
إِنَّهُمْ كَانُوا قَوْمًا عَمِينَ ۞

SECTION 9.

65. To the 'Ad people,
(We sent) Hūd, one
Of their (own) brethren:
He said: "O my people!
Worship Allah! ye have
No other god but Him.
Will ye not fear (Allah)?"

٦٥- وَإِلَى عَادٍ أَخَاهُمْ هُوْدًا
قَالَ يٰقَوْمِ اعْبُدُوا اللهَ
مَا لَكُمْ مِنْ إِلٰهٍ غَيْرُهُ
أَفَلَا تَتَّقُوْنَ ۝

66. The leaders of the unbelievers
Among his people said:
"Ah! we see thou art
An imbecile!" and "We think
Thou art a liar!"

٦٦- قَالَ الْمَلَأُ الَّذِيْنَ كَفَرُوْا مِنْ قَوْمِهٖ
إِنَّا لَنَرٰىكَ فِيْ سَفَاهَةٍ
وَّإِنَّا لَنَظُنُّكَ مِنَ الْكٰذِبِيْنَ ۝

67. He said "O my people!
I am no imbecile, but
(I am) a messenger from
The Lord and Cherisher
Of the Worlds!

٦٧- قَالَ يٰقَوْمِ لَيْسَ بِيْ سَفَاهَةٌ
وَّلٰكِنِّيْ رَسُوْلٌ
مِنْ رَّبِّ الْعٰلَمِيْنَ ۝

68. "I but fulfil towards you
The duties of my Lord's mission:
I am to you a sincere
And trustworthy adviser.

٦٨- أُبَلِّغُكُمْ رِسٰلٰتِ رَبِّيْ
وَأَنَا لَكُمْ نَاصِحٌ أَمِيْنٌ ۝

69. "Do ye wonder that
There hath come to you
A message from your Lord
Through a man of your own
People, to warn you?
Call in remembrance
That He made you
Inheritors after the people
Of Noah, and gave you
A stature tall among the nations.
Call in remembrance
The benefits (ye have received)
From Allah: that so
Ye may prosper."

٦٩- أَوَعَجِبْتُمْ أَنْ جَآءَكُمْ
ذِكْرٌ مِنْ رَّبِّكُمْ عَلٰى رَجُلٍ مِّنْكُمْ
لِيُنْذِرَكُمْ
وَاذْكُرُوْا إِذْ جَعَلَكُمْ
خُلَفَآءَ مِنْ بَعْدِ قَوْمِ نُوْحٍ
وَّزَادَكُمْ فِي الْخَلْقِ بَصْطَةً
فَاذْكُرُوْا آلَآءَ اللهِ لَعَلَّكُمْ تُفْلِحُوْنَ ۝

70. They said: "Comest thou
To us, that we may worship
Allah alone, and give up
The cult of our fathers?
Bring us what thou
Threatenest us with,
If so be that thou
Tellest the truth!"

٧٠- قَالُوْا أَجِئْتَنَا لِنَعْبُدَ اللهَ وَحْدَهٗ
وَنَذَرَ مَا كَانَ يَعْبُدُ آبَآؤُنَا
فَأْتِنَا بِمَا تَعِدُنَا
إِنْ كُنْتَ مِنَ الصّٰدِقِيْنَ ۝

71. He said: "Punishment
And wrath have already
Come upon you from your Lord:
Dispute ye with me
Over names which ye
Have devised—ye
And your fathers—
Without authority from Allah?
Then wait: I am
Amongst you, also waiting."

٧١- قَالَ قَدْ وَقَعَ عَلَيْكُمْ مِّنْ رَّبِّكُمْ رِجْسٌ وَغَضَبٌ ۖ أَتُجَادِلُوْنَنِيْ فِيْٓ أَسْمَآءٍ سَمَّيْتُمُوْهَآ أَنْتُمْ وَآبَآؤُكُمْ مَّا نَزَّلَ اللّٰهُ بِهَا مِنْ سُلْطٰنٍ ۚ فَانْتَظِرُوْٓا إِنِّيْ مَعَكُمْ مِّنَ الْمُنْتَظِرِيْنَ ۞

72. We saved him and those
Who adhered to him,
By Our Mercy and We
Cut off the roots of those
Who rejected Our Signs
And did not believe.

٧٢- فَأَنْجَيْنٰهُ وَالَّذِيْنَ مَعَهٗ بِرَحْمَةٍ مِّنَّا وَقَطَعْنَا دَابِرَ الَّذِيْنَ كَذَّبُوْا بِاٰيٰتِنَا ۖ وَمَا كَانُوْا مُؤْمِنِيْنَ ۞

SECTION 10.

73. To the Thamūd people
(We sent) Ṣāliḥ, one
Of their own brethren:
He said: "O my people!
Worship Allah; ye have
No other god but Him.
Now hath come unto you
A clear (Sign) from your Lord!
This she-camel of Allah
Is a Sign unto you:
So leave her to graze

In Allah's earth, and let her
Come to no harm,
Or ye shall be seized
With a grievous punishment.

٧٣- وَإِلٰى ثَمُوْدَ أَخَاهُمْ صٰلِحًا ۗ قَالَ يٰقَوْمِ اعْبُدُوا اللّٰهَ مَا لَكُمْ مِّنْ إِلٰهٍ غَيْرُهٗ ۖ قَدْ جَآءَتْكُمْ بَيِّنَةٌ مِّنْ رَّبِّكُمْ ۖ هٰذِهٖ نَاقَةُ اللّٰهِ لَكُمْ اٰيَةً فَذَرُوْهَا تَأْكُلْ فِيْٓ أَرْضِ اللّٰهِ وَلَا تَمَسُّوْهَا بِسُوْٓءٍ فَيَأْخُذَكُمْ عَذَابٌ أَلِيْمٌ ۞

74. "And remember how He
Made you inheritors
After the 'Ād people
And gave you habitations
In the land: ye build
For yourselves palaces and castles
In (open) plains, and carve out
Homes in the mountains;
So bring to remembrance
The benefits (ye have received)
From Allah, and refrain
From evil and mischief
On the earth."

٧٤- وَاذْكُرُوْٓا إِذْ جَعَلَكُمْ خُلَفَآءَ مِنْ بَعْدِ عَادٍ وَّبَوَّأَكُمْ فِي الْأَرْضِ تَتَّخِذُوْنَ مِنْ سُهُوْلِهَا قُصُوْرًا وَّتَنْحِتُوْنَ الْجِبَالَ بُيُوْتًا ۖ فَاذْكُرُوْٓا اٰلَآءَ اللّٰهِ وَلَا تَعْثَوْا فِي الْأَرْضِ مُفْسِدِيْنَ ۞

5. The leaders of the arrogant
Party among his people said
To those who were reckoned
Powerless—those among them
Who believed: "Know ye
Indeed that Ṣāliḥ is
A messenger from his Lord?"
They said: "We do indeed
Believe in the revelation
Which hath been sent
Through him."

٧٥ـ قَالَ الْمَلَأُ الَّذِينَ اسْتَكْبَرُوا
مِنْ قَوْمِهِ لِلَّذِينَ اسْتُضْعِفُوا
لِمَنْ آمَنَ مِنْهُمْ
أَتَعْلَمُونَ أَنَّ صَالِحًا مُّرْسَلٌ مِّنْ رَّبِّهِ
قَالُوا إِنَّا بِمَا أُرْسِلَ بِهِ مُؤْمِنُونَ ٠

76. The arrogant party said:
"For our part, we reject
What ye believe in."

٧٦ـ قَالَ الَّذِينَ اسْتَكْبَرُوا
إِنَّا بِالَّذِي آمَنتُم بِهِ كَافِرُونَ ٠

77. Then they hamstrung
The she-camel, and insolently
Defied the order of their Lord,
Saying: "O Ṣāliḥ! bring about
Thy threats, if thou art
A messenger (of Allah)!"

٧٧ـ فَعَقَرُوا النَّاقَةَ وَعَتَوْا عَنْ أَمْرِ رَبِّهِمْ
وَقَالُوا يَا صَالِحُ ائْتِنَا بِمَا تَعِدُنَا
إِن كُنتَ مِنَ الْمُرْسَلِينَ ٠

78. So the earthquake took them
Unawares, and they lay
Prostrate in their homes
In the morning!

٧٨ـ فَأَخَذَتْهُمُ الرَّجْفَةُ
فَأَصْبَحُوا فِي دَارِهِمْ جَاثِمِينَ ٠

79. So Ṣāliḥ left them,
Saying: "O my people!
I did indeed convey to you
The message for which
I was sent by my Lord:
I gave you good counsel,
But ye love not good counsellors!"

٧٩ـ فَتَوَلَّى عَنْهُمْ وَقَالَ يَا قَوْمِ لَقَدْ
أَبْلَغْتُكُمْ رِسَالَةَ رَبِّي وَنَصَحْتُ لَكُمْ
وَلَكِن لَّا تُحِبُّونَ النَّاصِحِينَ ٠

80. We also (sent) Luṭ:
He said to his people:
"Do ye commit lewdness
Such as no people
In creation (ever) committed
Before you?

٨٠ـ وَلُوطًا إِذْ قَالَ لِقَوْمِهِ
أَتَأْتُونَ الْفَاحِشَةَ مَا سَبَقَكُم بِهَا مِنْ
أَحَدٍ مِّنَ الْعَالَمِينَ ٠

81. "For ye practise your lusts
On men in preference
To women: ye are indeed
A people transgressing
Beyond bounds."

٨١ـ إِنَّكُمْ لَتَأْتُونَ الرِّجَالَ
شَهْوَةً مِّن دُونِ
النِّسَاءِ بَلْ أَنتُمْ قَوْمٌ مُّسْرِفُونَ ٠

82. And his people gave
    No answer but this:
    They said, "Drive them out
    Of your city: these are
    Indeed men who want
    To be clean and pure!"

٨٢۔ وَمَا كَانَ جَوَابَ قَوْمِهِ إِلَّا
أَن قَالُوا أَخْرِجُوهُم مِّن قَرْيَتِكُمْ ۖ
إِنَّهُمْ أُنَاسٌ يَتَطَهَّرُونَ ۝

83. But We saved him
    And his family, except
    His wife: she was
    Of those who lagged behind

٨٣۔ فَأَنجَيْنَاهُ وَأَهْلَهُ إِلَّا امْرَأَتَهُ ۖ
كَانَتْ مِنَ الْغَابِرِينَ ۝

84. And we rained down on them
    A shower (of brimstone):
    Then see what was the end
    Of those who indulged
    In sin and crime!

٨٤۔ وَأَمْطَرْنَا عَلَيْهِم مَّطَرًا ۖ
فَانظُرْ كَيْفَ كَانَ عَاقِبَةُ الْمُجْرِمِينَ ۝

SECTION 11.

85. To the Madyan people
    We sent Shu'ayb, one
    Of their own brethren: he said:
    "O my people! worship Allah;
    Ye have no other god
    But Him. Now hath come
    Unto you a clear (Sign)
    From your Lord! Give just
    Measure and weight, nor
                        withhold
    From the people the things
    That are their due; and do
    No mischief on the earth
    After it has been set
    In order: that will be best
    For you, if ye have Faith.

٨٥۔ وَإِلَىٰ مَدْيَنَ أَخَاهُمْ شُعَيْبًا ۗ
قَالَ يَا قَوْمِ اعْبُدُوا اللَّهَ
مَا لَكُم مِّنْ إِلَٰهٍ غَيْرُهُ ۖ
قَدْ جَاءَتْكُم بَيِّنَةٌ مِّن رَّبِّكُمْ ۖ
فَأَوْفُوا الْكَيْلَ وَالْمِيزَانَ
وَلَا تَبْخَسُوا النَّاسَ أَشْيَاءَهُمْ وَلَا تُفْسِدُوا
فِي الْأَرْضِ بَعْدَ إِصْلَاحِهَا ۚ
ذَٰلِكُمْ خَيْرٌ لَّكُمْ إِن كُنتُم مُّؤْمِنِينَ ۝

86. "And squat not on every road,
    Breathing threats, hindering
    From the path of Allah
    Those who believe in Him,
    And seeking in it
    Something crooked;
    But remember how ye were
    Little, and He gave you
                        increase.
    And hold in your mind's eye
    What was the end

٨٦۔ وَلَا تَقْعُدُوا بِكُلِّ صِرَاطٍ تُوعِدُونَ
وَتَصُدُّونَ عَن سَبِيلِ اللَّهِ
مَنْ آمَنَ بِهِ وَتَبْغُونَهَا عِوَجًا ۚ
وَاذْكُرُوا إِذْ كُنتُمْ قَلِيلًا فَكَثَّرَكُمْ ۖ
وَانظُرُوا كَيْفَ كَانَ عَاقِبَةُ

Of those who did mischief.

87. "And if there is a party
Among you who believes
In the Message with which
I have been sent, and a party
Which does not believe,
Hold yourselves in patience
Until Allah doth decide
Between us: for He
Is the best to decide."

المُفْسِدِيْنَ ۝

٨٧- وَاِنْ كَانَ طَآئِفَةٌ مِّنْكُمْ اٰمَنُوْا
بِالَّذِيْٓ اُرْسِلْتُ بِهٖ وَطَآئِفَةٌ لَّمْ يُؤْمِنُوْا
فَاصْبِرُوْا حَتّٰى يَحْكُمَ اللّٰهُ بَيْنَنَا ۚ
وَهُوَ خَيْرُ الْحٰكِمِيْنَ ۝

88. The leaders, the arrogant
Party among his people, said:
O Shu'ayb! we shall
Certainly drive thee out
Of our city—(thee) and those
Who believe with thee;
Or else ye (thou and they)
Shall have to return
To our ways and religion."
He said: "What! even
Though we do detest (them)?

٨٨- قَالَ الْمَلَاُ الَّذِيْنَ اسْتَكْبَرُوْا
مِنْ قَوْمِهٖ لَنُخْرِجَنَّكَ يٰشُعَيْبُ
وَالَّذِيْنَ اٰمَنُوْا مَعَكَ مِنْ قَرْيَتِنَا
اَوْ لَتَعُوْدُنَّ فِيْ مِلَّتِنَا ۚ
قَالَ اَوَلَوْ كُنَّا كَارِهِيْنَ ۝

89 "We should indeed invent
A lie against Allah,
If we returned to your ways
After Allah hath rescued
Us therefrom; nor could we
By any manner of means
Return thereto unless it be
As in the will and plan of Allah,
Our Lord. Our Lord
Can reach out to the utmost
Recesses of things by His
                              knowledge.
In Allah is our trust.
Our Lord! Decide thou
Between us and our people
In truth, for thou
Art the best to decide."

٨٩- قَدِ افْتَرَيْنَا عَلَى اللّٰهِ كَذِبًا
اِنْ عُدْنَا فِيْ مِلَّتِكُمْ
بَعْدَ اِذْ نَجّٰنَا اللّٰهُ مِنْهَا ۚ
وَمَا يَكُوْنُ لَنَآ اَنْ نَعُوْدَ فِيْهَآ
اِلَّآ اَنْ يَّشَآءَ اللّٰهُ رَبُّنَا ۚ
وَسِعَ رَبُّنَا كُلَّ شَيْءٍ عِلْمًا ۚ
عَلَى اللّٰهِ تَوَكَّلْنَا ۚ
رَبَّنَا افْتَحْ بَيْنَنَا وَبَيْنَ قَوْمِنَا
بِالْحَقِّ وَاَنْتَ خَيْرُ الْفَاتِحِيْنَ ۝

90. The leaders, the Unbelievers
Among his people, said:
"If ye follow Shu'ayb,
Be sure then ye are ruined!"

٩٠- وَقَالَ الْمَلَاُ الَّذِيْنَ كَفَرُوْا مِنْ قَوْمِهٖ
لَئِنِ اتَّبَعْتُمْ شُعَيْبًا اِنَّكُمْ اِذًا لَّخٰسِرُوْنَ ۝

91. But the earthquake took them
Unawares, and they lay

٩١- فَاَخَذَتْهُمُ الرَّجْفَةُ

Prostrate in their homes
Before the morning!

92. The men who rejected
Shu'ayb became as if
They had never been
In the homes where they
Had flourished: the men
Who rejected Shu'ayb—
It was they who were ruined!

93. So Shu'ayb left them,
Saying: "O my people!
I did indeed convey to you
The Messages for which
I was sent by my Lord:
I gave you good counsel,
But how shall I lament
Over a people who refuse
To believe!"

SECTION 12.

94. Whenever We sent a prophet
To a town, We took up
Its people in suffering

And adversity, in order
That they might learn humility.

95. Then We changed their suffering
Into prosperity, until they grew
And multiplied, and began
To say: "Our fathers (too)
Were touched by suffering
And affluence"... Behold!
We called them to account
Of a sudden, while they
Realised not (their peril).

96. If the people of the towns
Had but believed and feared
Allah, We should indeed
Have opened out to them
(All kinds of) blessings
From heaven and earth;
But they rejected (the truth),
And We brought them
To book for their misdeeds.

97. Did the people of the towns

Feel secure against the coming
Of Our wrath by night
While they were asleep?

اَنْ يَّأْتِيَهُمْ بَأْسُنَا بَيَاتًا وَّهُمْ نَآئِمُوْنَ ۞

98. Or else did they feel
Secure against its coming
In broad daylight while they
Played about (carefree)?

٩٨- اَوَ اَمِنَ اَهْلُ الْقُرَى اَنْ يَّأْتِيَهُمْ
بَأْسُنَا ضُحًى وَّهُمْ يَلْعَبُوْنَ ۞

99. Did they then feel secure
Against the Plan of Allah?—
But no one can feel
Secure from the Plan
Of Allah, except those
(Doomed) to ruin!

٩٩- اَفَاَمِنُوْا مَكْرَ اللهِ ۚ فَلَا يَأْمَنُ
مَكْرَ اللهِ إِلَّا الْقَوْمُ الْخَسِرُوْنَ ۞

SECTION 13.

100. To those who inherit
The earth in succession
To its (previous) possessors,
Is it not a guiding (lesson)
That, if We so willed,
We could punish them (too)
For their sins, and seal up
Their hearts so that they
Could not hear?

١٠٠- اَوَلَمْ يَهْدِ لِلَّذِيْنَ يَرِثُوْنَ الْأَرْضَ
مِنْ بَعْدِ اَهْلِهَا اَنْ لَّوْ نَشَآءُ اَصَبْنَاهُمْ بِذُنُوْبِهِمْ ۚ
وَنَطْبَعُ عَلَى قُلُوْبِهِمْ
فَهُمْ لَا يَسْمَعُوْنَ ۞

101. Such were the towns
Whose story We (thus)
Relate unto thee:
There came indeed to them
Their Messengers with clear
(Signs):
But they would not believe
What they had rejected before.
Thus doth Allah seal up
The hearts of those
Who reject Faith.

١٠١- تِلْكَ الْقُرَى
نَقُصُّ عَلَيْكَ مِنْ اَنْبَآئِهَا ۚ
وَلَقَدْ جَآءَتْهُمْ رُسُلُهُمْ بِالْبَيِّنَاتِ ۚ
فَمَا كَانُوْا لِيُؤْمِنُوْا بِمَا كَذَّبُوْا مِنْ قَبْلُ ۚ
كَذٰلِكَ يَطْبَعُ اللهُ
عَلَى قُلُوْبِ الْكَافِرِيْنَ ۞

102. Most of them We found not
Men (true) to their covenant:
But most of them We found
Rebellious and disobedient.

١٠٢- وَمَا وَجَدْنَا لِاَكْثَرِهِمْ مِنْ عَهْدٍ ۚ
وَإِنْ وَّجَدْنَا اَكْثَرَهُمْ لَفَسِقِيْنَ ۞

103. Then after them We sent
Moses with Our Signs
To Pharaoh and his chiefs,
But they wrongfully rejected them:

١٠٣- ثُمَّ بَعَثْنَا مِنْ بَعْدِهِمْ مُّوْسَى بِآيَاتِنَا
إِلَى فِرْعَوْنَ وَمَلَائِهِ فَظَلَمُوْا بِهَا ۚ

So see what was the end
Of those who made mischief.

فَانْظُرْ كَيْفَ كَانَ عَاقِبَةُ الْمُفْسِدِيْنَ ٥

104. Moses[1071] said: "O Pharaoh!
I am a messenger from
The Lord of the Worlds—

١٠٤ـ وَقَالَ مُوْسَى يٰفِرْعَوْنُ
اِنِّىْ رَسُوْلٌ مِّنْ رَّبِّ الْعٰلَمِيْنَ ٥

105. "One for whom it is right
To say nothing but truth
About Allah. Now have I
Come unto you (people), from
Your Lord, with a clear (Sign):
So let the Children of Israel
Depart along with me."

١٠٥ـ حَقِيْقٌ عَلٰى اَنْ لَّآ اَقُوْلَ
عَلَى اللّٰهِ اِلَّا الْحَقَّ
قَدْ جِئْتُكُمْ بِبَيِّنَةٍ مِّنْ رَّبِّكُمْ
فَاَرْسِلْ مَعِىَ بَنِىْ اِسْرَآءِيْلَ ٥

106. (Pharaoh) said: "If indeed
Thou hast come with a Sign,
Show it forth—
If thou tellest the truth."

١٠٦ـ قَالَ اِنْ كُنْتَ جِئْتَ بِاٰيَةٍ
فَأْتِ بِهَآ اِنْ كُنْتَ مِنَ الصّٰدِقِيْنَ ٥

107. Then (Moses) threw his rod,
And behold! it was
A serpent, plain (for all to see)!

١٠٧ـ فَاَلْقٰى عَصَاهُ
فَاِذَا هِىَ ثُعْبَانٌ مُّبِيْنٌ ٥

108. And he drew out his hand,
And behold! it was white
To all beholders!

١٠٨ـ وَّنَزَعَ يَدَهُ
فَاِذَا هِىَ بَيْضَآءُ لِلنّٰظِرِيْنَ ٥

SECTION 14.

109. Said the Chiefs of the people
Of Pharaoh: "This is indeed
A sorcerer well-versed.

١٠٩ـ قَالَ الْمَلَأُ مِنْ قَوْمِ فِرْعَوْنَ
اِنَّ هٰذَا لَسٰحِرٌ عَلِيْمٌ ٥

110. "His plan is to get you out
Of your land: then
What is it ye counsel?"

١١٠ـ يُّرِيْدُ اَنْ يُّخْرِجَكُمْ مِّنْ اَرْضِكُمْ
فَمَاذَا تَأْمُرُوْنَ ٥

111. They said: "Keep him
And his brother in suspense
(For awhile); and send
To the cities men to collect—

١١١ـ قَالُوْۤا اَرْجِهْ وَاَخَاهُ
وَاَرْسِلْ فِى الْمَدَآئِنِ حٰشِرِيْنَ ٥

112. And bring up to thee
All (our) sorcerers well-versed."

١١٢ـ يَأْتُوْكَ بِكُلِّ سٰحِرٍ عَلِيْمٍ ٥

113. So there came
The sorcerers to Pharaoh:
They said, "Of course

١١٣ـ وَجَآءَ السَّحَرَةُ فِرْعَوْنَ قَالُوْۤا اِنَّ

We shall have a (suitable)
Reward if we win!"

لَنَا لَاَجْرًا اِنْ كُنَّا نَحْنُ الْغٰلِبِيْنَ ۞

114. He said: "Yea, (and more)—
For ye shall in that case
Be (raised to posts)
Nearest (to my person)."

١١٤- قَالَ نَعَمْ
وَاِنَّكُمْ لَمِنَ الْمُقَرَّبِيْنَ ۞

115. They said: "O Moses!
Wilt thou throw (first),
Or shall we have
The (first) throw?"

١١٥- قَالُوْا يٰمُوْسٰۤى اِمَّاۤ اَنْ تُلْقِىَ
وَاِمَّاۤ اَنْ نَّكُوْنَ نَحْنُ الْمُلْقِيْنَ ۞

116. Said Moses: "Throw ye (first)."
So when they threw,
They bewitched the eyes
Of the people, and struck
Terror into them: for they
Showed a great (feat of) magic.

١١٦- قَالَ اَلْقُوْا ۚ
فَلَمَّاۤ اَلْقَوْا سَحَرُوْۤا اَعْيُنَ النَّاسِ
وَاسْتَرْهَبُوْهُمْ وَجَاۤءُوْ بِسِحْرٍ عَظِيْمٍ ۞

117. We put it into Moses's mind
By inspiration: "Throw (now)
Thy rod": and behold!
It swallows up straightway
All the falsehoods
Which they fake!

١١٧- وَاَوْحَيْنَاۤ اِلٰى مُوْسٰۤى
اَنْ اَلْقِ عَصَاكَ ۚ
فَاِذَا هِىَ تَلْقَفُ مَا يَاْفِكُوْنَ ۚ

118. Thus truth was confirmed.
And all that they did
Was made of no effect.

١١٨- فَوَقَعَ الْحَقُّ
وَبَطَلَ مَا كَانُوْا يَعْمَلُوْنَ ۚ

119. So the (great ones) were vanquished
There and then, and were
Made to look small.

١١٩- فَغُلِبُوْا هُنَالِكَ
وَانْقَلَبُوْا صٰغِرِيْنَ ۚ

120. But the sorcerers fell down
Prostrate in adoration.

١٢٠- وَاُلْقِىَ السَّحَرَةُ سٰجِدِيْنَ ۚ

121. Saying: "We believe
In the Lord of the Worlds.

١٢١- قَالُوْۤا اٰمَنَّا بِرَبِّ الْعٰلَمِيْنَ ۚ

122. "The Lord of Moses and Aaron."

١٢٢- رَبِّ مُوْسٰى وَهٰرُوْنَ ۞

123. Said Pharaoh: "Believe ye
In Him before I give
You permission? Surely
This is a trick which ye

١٢٣- قَالَ فِرْعَوْنُ اٰمَنْتُمْ بِهٖ
قَبْلَ اَنْ اٰذَنَ لَكُمْ ۚ اِنَّ هٰذَا لَمَكْرٌ

Have planned in the City
To drive out its people:
But soon shall ye know
(The consequences).

124 "Be sure I will cut off
Your hands and your feet
On opposite sides, and I
Will cause you all
To die on the cross."

125. They said: "For us,
We are but sent back
Unto our Lord:

126. "But thou dost wreak
Thy vengeance on us
Simply because we believed
In the Signs of our Lord
When they reached us!
Our Lord! pour out on us
Patience and constancy, and take
Our souls unto Thee
As Muslims (who bow
To Thy Will)!"

SECTION 15.

127. Said the chiefs of Pharaoh's
People: "Wilt thou leave
Moses and his people,
To spread mischief in the land,
And to abandon thee
And thy gods?" He said
"Their male children will we
Slay; (only) their females
Will we save alive;
And we have over them
(Power) irresistible."

128. Said Moses to his people:
"Pray for help from Allah,"
And (wait) in patience and
constancy:
For the earth is Allah's,
To give as a heritage
To such of His servants
As He pleaseth; and the end
Is (best) for the righteous.

مَكَرْتُمُوْهُ فِى الْمَدِيْنَةِ
لِتُخْرِجُوْا مِنْهَا اَهْلَهَا ۚ فَسَوْفَ تَعْلَمُوْنَ ۝

١٢٤- لَاُقَطِّعَنَّ اَيْدِيَكُمْ وَاَرْجُلَكُمْ
مِّنْ خِلَافٍ
ثُمَّ لَاُصَلِّبَنَّكُمْ اَجْمَعِيْنَ ۝

١٢٥- قَالُوْٓا
اِنَّآ اِلٰى رَبِّنَا مُنْقَلِبُوْنَ ۚ

١٢٦- وَمَا تَنْقِمُ مِنَّآ
اِلَّآ اَنْ اٰمَنَّا بِاٰيٰتِ رَبِّنَا
لَمَّا جَآءَتْنَا ۭ
رَبَّنَآ اَفْرِغْ عَلَيْنَا صَبْرًا
وَّ تَوَفَّنَا مُسْلِمِيْنَ ۝

١٢٧- وَقَالَ الْمَلَاُ مِنْ قَوْمِ فِرْعَوْنَ
اَتَذَرُ مُوْسٰى وَقَوْمَهٗ لِيُفْسِدُوْا فِى الْاَرْضِ
وَيَذَرَكَ وَاٰلِهَتَكَ ۭ
قَالَ سَنُقَتِّلُ اَبْنَآءَهُمْ
وَنَسْتَحْيٖ نِسَآءَهُمْ ۚ وَاِنَّا فَوْقَهُمْ
قَاهِرُوْنَ ۝
١٢٨- قَالَ مُوْسٰى لِقَوْمِهِ اسْتَعِيْنُوْا بِاللّٰهِ
وَاصْبِرُوْا ۚ اِنَّ الْاَرْضَ لِلّٰهِ ۙ
يُوْرِثُهَا مَنْ يَّشَآءُ مِنْ عِبَادِهٖ ۭ
وَالْعَاقِبَةُ لِلْمُتَّقِيْنَ ۝

129. They said: "We have had
(Nothing but) trouble, both before
And after thou camest
To us." He said:
"It may be that your Lord
Will destroy your enemy
And make you inheritors
In the earth; that so
He may try you
By your deeds."

SECTION 16.

130. We punished the people
Of Pharaoh with years
(Of drought) and shortness
Of crops; that they might
Receive admonition.

131. But when good (times) came,
They said, "This is due
To us;" when gripped
By calamity, they ascribed it
To evil omens connected
With Moses and those with him!
Behold! in truth the omens
Of evil are theirs
In Allah's sight, but most
Of them do not understand!

132. They said (to Moses):
"Whatever be the Signs
Thou bringest, to work
Therewith thy sorcery on us,
We shall never believe
In thee."

133. So We sent (plagues) on them:
Wholesale Death,
Locusts, Lice, Frogs,
And Blood: Signs openly
Self-explained: but they
Were steeped in arrogance,
A people given to sin.

134. Every time the Penalty
Fell on them, they said:
"O Moses! on our behalf
Call on thy Lord in virtue
Of His promise to thee:

١٢٩- قَالُوا أُوذِينَا مِنْ قَبْلِ أَنْ تَأْتِيَنَا
وَمِنْ بَعْدِ مَا جِئْتَنَا ۚ
قَالَ عَسَى رَبُّكُمْ أَنْ يُهْلِكَ عَدُوَّكُمْ
وَيَسْتَخْلِفَكُمْ
فِي الْأَرْضِ فَيَنْظُرَ كَيْفَ تَعْمَلُونَ ۩

١٣٠- وَلَقَدْ أَخَذْنَا آلَ فِرْعَوْنَ بِالسِّنِينَ
وَنَقْصٍ مِنَ الثَّمَرَاتِ
لَعَلَّهُمْ يَذَّكَّرُونَ ○

١٣١- فَإِذَا جَاءَتْهُمُ الْحَسَنَةُ
قَالُوا لَنَا هَٰذِهِ ۖ وَإِنْ تُصِبْهُمْ سَيِّئَةٌ
يَطَّيَّرُوا بِمُوسَى وَمَنْ مَعَهُ ۗ
أَلَا إِنَّمَا طَائِرُهُمْ عِنْدَ اللَّهِ
وَلَٰكِنَّ أَكْثَرَهُمْ لَا يَعْلَمُونَ ○

١٣٢- وَقَالُوا مَهْمَا تَأْتِنَا بِهِ مِنْ آيَةٍ
لِتَسْحَرَنَا بِهَا ۙ
فَمَا نَحْنُ لَكَ بِمُؤْمِنِينَ ○

١٣٣- فَأَرْسَلْنَا عَلَيْهِمُ الطُّوفَانَ
وَالْجَرَادَ وَالْقُمَّلَ وَالضَّفَادِعَ
وَالدَّمَ آيَاتٍ مُفَصَّلَاتٍ ۚ
فَاسْتَكْبَرُوا وَكَانُوا قَوْمًا مُجْرِمِينَ ○

١٣٤- وَلَمَّا وَقَعَ عَلَيْهِمُ الرِّجْزُ قَالُوا
يَا مُوسَى ادْعُ لَنَا رَبَّكَ
بِمَا عَهِدَ عِنْدَكَ

If thou wilt remove
The Penalty from us,
We shall truly believe in thee,
And we shall send away
The Children of Israel
With thee."

لَئِنْ كَشَفْتَ عَنَّا الرِّجْزَ
لَنُؤْمِنَنَّ لَكَ
وَلَنُرْسِلَنَّ مَعَكَ بَنِيْ اِسْرَآءِيْلَ ۚ

135. But every time We removed
The Penalty from them
According to a fixed term
Which they had to fulfil—
Behold! they broke their word!

١٣٥- فَلَمَّا كَشَفْنَا عَنْهُمُ الرِّجْزَ
اِلٰى اَجَلٍ
هُمْ بَالِغُوْهُ اِذَا هُمْ يَنْكُثُوْنَ ۟

136. So We exacted retribution
From them: We drowned them
In the sea, because they
Rejected Our Signs, and failed
To take warning from them.

١٣٦- فَانْتَقَمْنَا مِنْهُمْ فَاَغْرَقْنٰهُمْ فِي الْيَمِّ
بِاَنَّهُمْ كَذَّبُوْا بِاٰيٰتِنَا
وَكَانُوْا عَنْهَا غٰفِلِيْنَ ۟

137. And We made a people,
Considered weak (and of no
account),
Inheritors of lands
In both East and West—
Lands whereon We sent
Down Our blessings.
The fair promise of thy Lord
Was fulfilled for the Children
Of Israel, because they had
Patience and constancy,
And We levelled to the ground
The Great Works and fine
Buildings
Which Pharaoh and His people
Erected (with such pride).

١٣٧- وَاَوْرَثْنَا الْقَوْمَ الَّذِيْنَ كَانُوْا
يُسْتَضْعَفُوْنَ
مَشَارِقَ الْاَرْضِ
وَمَغَارِبَهَا الَّتِيْ بٰرَكْنَا فِيْهَا ۚ
وَتَمَّتْ كَلِمَتُ رَبِّكَ الْحُسْنٰى
عَلٰى بَنِيْ اِسْرَآءِيْلَ ۙ۬ ۟
بِمَا صَبَرُوْا ۚ
وَدَمَّرْنَا مَا كَانَ يَصْنَعُ فِرْعَوْنُ وَ
قَوْمُهُ وَمَا كَانُوْا يَعْرِشُوْنَ ۟

138. We took the Children of Israel
(With safety) across the sea.
They came upon a people
Devoted entirely to some idols
They had. They said:
"O Moses! fashion for us
A god like unto the gods
They have." He said:
"Surely ye are a people
Without knowledge.

١٣٨- وَجَاوَزْنَا بِبَنِيْ اِسْرَآءِيْلَ الْبَحْرَ
فَاَتَوْا عَلٰى قَوْمٍ يَّعْكُفُوْنَ عَلٰى اَصْنَامٍ
لَّهُمْ ۚ قَالُوْا يٰمُوْسَى اجْعَلْ لَّنَا
اِلٰهًا كَمَا لَهُمْ اٰلِهَةٌ ۚ قَالَ
اِنَّكُمْ قَوْمٌ تَجْهَلُوْنَ ۟

139. "As to these folk—
The cult they are in
Is (but) a fragment of a ruin,
And vain is the (worship)
Which they practise."

١٣٩- اِنَّ هٰؤُلَاءِ
مُتَبَّرٌ مَّا هُمْ فِيْهِ
وَبٰطِلٌ مَّا كَانُوْا يَعْمَلُوْنَ ٥

140. He said: "Shall I seek for you
A god other than the (true)
God, when it is Allah
Who hath endowed you
With gifts above the nations?"

١٤٠- قَالَ اَغَيْرَ اللّٰهِ
اَبْغِيْكُمْ اِلٰهًا
وَّهُوَ فَضَّلَكُمْ عَلَى الْعٰلَمِيْنَ ٥

141. And remember We rescued you
From Pharaoh's people,
Who afflicted you with
The worst of penalties,
Who slew your male children
And saved alive your females:
In that was a momentous
Trial from your Lord.

١٤١- وَاِذْ اَنْجَيْنٰكُمْ مِّنْ اٰلِ فِرْعَوْنَ
يَسُوْمُوْنَكُمْ سُوْءَ الْعَذَابِ ۚ
يُقَتِّلُوْنَ اَبْنَاءَكُمْ وَيَسْتَحْيُوْنَ نِسَاءَكُمْ ۚ
وَفِيْ ذٰلِكُمْ بَلَاءٌ مِّنْ رَّبِّكُمْ عَظِيْمٌ ۞

SECTION 17.

142. We appointed for Moses
Thirty nights, and completed
(The period) with ten (more):
Thus was completed the term
(Of communion) with his Lord,
Forty nights. And Moses
Had charged his brother Aaron
(Before he went up):
"Act for me amongst my people.
Do right, and follow not
The way of those
Who do mischief."

١٤٢- وَوٰعَدْنَا مُوْسٰى ثَلٰثِيْنَ لَيْلَةً
وَّاَتْمَمْنٰهَا بِعَشْرٍ
فَتَمَّ مِيْقَاتُ رَبِّهِ اَرْبَعِيْنَ لَيْلَةً ۚ
وَقَالَ مُوْسٰى لِاَخِيْهِ هٰرُوْنَ
اخْلُفْنِيْ فِيْ قَوْمِيْ وَاَصْلِحْ
وَلَا تَتَّبِعْ سَبِيْلَ الْمُفْسِدِيْنَ ٥

143. When Moses came
To the place appointed by Us,
And his Lord addressed him,
He said: "O my Lord!
Show (Thyself) to me,
That I may look upon Thee."
Allah said: "By no means
Canst thou see Me (direct);
But look upon the mount;
If it abide
In its place, then
Shalt thou see Me."
When his Lord manifested

١٤٣- وَلَمَّا جَاءَ مُوْسٰى لِمِيْقَاتِنَا
وَكَلَّمَهُ رَبُّهُ ۙ قَالَ رَبِّ
اَرِنِيْ اَنْظُرْ اِلَيْكَ ۚ قَالَ لَنْ تَرٰنِيْ
وَلٰكِنِ انْظُرْ اِلَى الْجَبَلِ
فَاِنِ اسْتَقَرَّ مَكَانَهُ فَسَوْفَ تَرٰنِيْ ۚ
فَلَمَّا تَجَلّٰى رَبُّهُ لِلْجَبَلِ
جَعَلَهُ دَكًّا

His glory on the Mount,
He made it as dust,
And Moses fell down
In a swoon. When he
Recovered his senses he said:
"Glory be to Thee! To Thee
I turn in repentance, and I
Am the first to believe."

وَخَرَّ مُوسَى صَعِقًا
فَلَمَّا أَفَاقَ
قَالَ سُبْحَانَكَ تُبْتُ إِلَيْكَ
وَأَنَا أَوَّلُ الْمُؤْمِنِينَ ٠

144. (Allah) said: "O Moses!
I have chosen thee
Above (other) men,
By the mission I (have
Given thee) and the words
I (have spoken to thee):
Take then the (revelation)
Which I give thee,
And be of those
Who give thanks."

١٤٤- قَالَ يَا مُوسَى
إِنِّي اصْطَفَيْتُكَ عَلَى النَّاسِ
بِرِسَالَاتِي وَبِكَلَامِي
فَخُذْ مَا آتَيْتُكَ
وَكُنْ مِنَ الشَّاكِرِينَ ٠

145. And We ordained laws
For him in the Tablets
In all matters, both
Commanding and explaining
All things, (and said):
"Take and hold these
With firmness, and enjoin
Thy people to hold fast
By the best in the precepts:
Soon shall I show you
The homes of the wicked—
(How they lie desolate)."

١٤٥- وَكَتَبْنَا لَهُ فِي الْأَلْوَاحِ
مِنْ كُلِّ شَيْءٍ مَوْعِظَةً
وَتَفْصِيلًا لِكُلِّ شَيْءٍ
فَخُذْهَا بِقُوَّةٍ
وَأْمُرْ قَوْمَكَ يَأْخُذُوا بِأَحْسَنِهَا
سَأُورِيكُمْ دَارَ الْفَاسِقِينَ ٠

146. Those who behave arrogantly
On the earth in defiance
Of right—them will I
Turn away from My Signs:
Even if they see all the Signs,
They will not believe in them;
And if they see the way
Of right conduct, they will
Not adopt it as the Way;
But if they see the way
Of error, that is
The Way they will adopt.
For they have rejected[1111]
Our Signs, and failed
To take warning from them.

١٤٦- سَأَصْرِفُ عَنْ آيَاتِيَ الَّذِينَ يَتَكَبَّرُونَ
فِي الْأَرْضِ بِغَيْرِ الْحَقِّ
وَإِنْ يَرَوْا كُلَّ آيَةٍ لَا يُؤْمِنُوا بِهَا
وَإِنْ يَرَوْا سَبِيلَ الرُّشْدِ
لَا يَتَّخِذُوهُ سَبِيلًا
وَإِنْ يَرَوْا سَبِيلَ الْغَيِّ يَتَّخِذُوهُ سَبِيلًا
ذَلِكَ بِأَنَّهُمْ كَذَّبُوا
بِآيَاتِنَا وَكَانُوا عَنْهَا غَافِلِينَ ٠

147. Those who reject Our Signs
And the Meeting in the
                    Hereafter—
Vain are their deeds:
Can they expect to be rewarded
Except as they have wrought?

SECTION 18.

148. The people of Moses made,
In his absence, out of their
                    ornaments,
The image of a calf,
              (for worship):
It seemed to low: did they
Not see that it could
Neither speak to them, nor
Show them the Way?
They took it for worship
And they did wrong.

149. When they repented, and saw
That they had erred,
They said: "If our Lord
Have not mercy upon us
And forgive us, we shall
Indeed be of those who perish."

150. When Moses came back
To his people, angry and grieved,
He said: "Evil it is that ye
Have done in my place
In my absence: did ye
Make haste to bring on
The judgement of your Lord?"
He put down the Tablets,
Seized his brother by (the hair
Of) his head, and dragged him
To him. Aaron said:
"Son of my mother! The people
Did indeed reckon me
As naught, and went near
To slaying me! Make not
The enemies rejoice over
My misfortune, nor count thou
Me amongst the people
Of sin."

151. Moses prayed: "O my Lord!

١٤٧- وَالَّذِيْنَ كَذَّبُوْا بِاٰيٰتِنَا وَلِقَاءِ الْاٰخِرَةِ
حَبِطَتْ اَعْمَالُهُمْ هَلْ يُجْزَوْنَ
اِلَّا مَا كَانُوْا يَعْمَلُوْنَ ۞

١٤٨- وَاتَّخَذَ قَوْمُ مُوْسٰى
مِنْ بَعْدِهٖ مِنْ حُلِيِّهِمْ
عِجْلًا جَسَدًا لَّهٗ خُوَارٌ
اَلَمْ يَرَوْا اَنَّهٗ لَا يُكَلِّمُهُمْ
وَلَا يَهْدِيْهِمْ سَبِيْلًا
اِتَّخَذُوْهُ وَكَانُوْا ظٰلِمِيْنَ ۞

١٤٩- وَلَمَّا سُقِطَ فِيْٓ اَيْدِيْهِمْ وَرَاَوْا اَنَّهُمْ
قَدْ ضَلُّوْا قَالُوْا لَئِنْ لَّمْ يَرْحَمْنَا رَبُّنَا
وَيَغْفِرْ لَنَا لَنَكُوْنَنَّ مِنَ الْخٰسِرِيْنَ ۞

١٥٠- وَلَمَّا رَجَعَ مُوْسٰٓى اِلٰى قَوْمِهٖ غَضْبَانَ
اَسِفًا ۙ قَالَ بِئْسَمَا خَلَفْتُمُوْنِيْ مِنْۢ بَعْدِيْ ۚ
اَعَجِلْتُمْ اَمْرَ رَبِّكُمْ ۚ
وَاَلْقَى الْاَلْوَاحَ
وَاَخَذَ بِرَاْسِ اَخِيْهِ يَجُرُّهٗٓ اِلَيْهِ ۗ
قَالَ ابْنَ اُمَّ
اِنَّ الْقَوْمَ اسْتَضْعَفُوْنِيْ
وَكَادُوْا يَقْتُلُوْنَنِيْ ۖ
فَلَا تُشْمِتْ بِيَ الْاَعْدَاءَ
وَلَا تَجْعَلْنِيْ مَعَ الْقَوْمِ الظّٰلِمِيْنَ ۞

١٥١- قَالَ رَبِّ اغْفِرْ لِيْ وَلِاَخِيْ

Forgive me and my brother![1119]
Admit us to Thy mercy!
For Thou art the Most Merciful
Of those who show mercy!"
SECTION 19.

وَاَدْخِلْنَا فِى رَحْمَتِكَ ۚ
وَاَنْتَ اَرْحَمُ الرّٰحِمِيْنَ ۟

152. **T**hose who took the calf
(For worship) will indeed
Be overwhelmed with wrath
From their Lord, and with
Shame in this life:
Thus do We recompense
Those who invent (falsehoods).

١٥٢- اِنَّ الَّذِيْنَ اتَّخَذُوا الْعِجْلَ
سَيَنَالُهُمْ غَضَبٌ مِّنْ رَّبِّهِمْ
وَذِلَّةٌ فِى الْحَيٰوةِ الدُّنْيَا ۚ
وَكَذٰلِكَ نَجْزِى الْمُفْتَرِيْنَ ۟

153. But those who do wrong
But repent thereafter and
(Truly) believe—verily
Thy Lord is thereafter
Oft-Forgiving, Most Merciful.

١٥٣- وَالَّذِيْنَ عَمِلُوا السَّيِّاٰتِ
ثُمَّ تَابُوْا مِنْۢ بَعْدِهَا وَاٰمَنُوْا ۚ اِنَّ رَبَّكَ
مِنْۢ بَعْدِهَا لَغَفُوْرٌ رَّحِيْمٌ ۟

154. When the anger of Moses
Was appeased, he took up
The Tablets: in the writing
Thereon was Guidance and
                    Mercy
For such as fear their Lord.

١٥٤- وَلَمَّا سَكَتَ عَنْ مُّوْسَى الْغَضَبُ
اَخَذَ الْاَلْوَاحَ ۚ وَفِىْ نُسْخَتِهَا هُدًى وَّ
رَحْمَةٌ لِّلَّذِيْنَ هُمْ لِرَبِّهِمْ يَرْهَبُوْنَ ۟

155. **A**nd Moses chose seventy
Of his people for Our place
Of meeting: when they
Were seized with violent
                    quaking,
He prayed: "O my Lord!
If it had been Thy Will
Thou couldst have destroyed,
Long before, both them
And me: wouldst Thou
Destroy us for the deeds
Of the foolish ones among us?
This is no more than
Thy trial: by it Thou causest
Whom Thou wilt to stray,
And Thou leadest whom
Thou wilt into the right path.
Thou art our Protector:
So forgive us and give us
Thy mercy; for Thou art
The Best of those who forgive.

١٥٥- وَاخْتَارَ مُوْسٰى قَوْمَهٗ سَبْعِيْنَ رَجُلًا
لِّمِيْقَاتِنَا ۚ فَلَمَّا اَخَذَتْهُمُ الرَّجْفَةُ
قَالَ رَبِّ
لَوْ شِئْتَ اَهْلَكْتَهُمْ مِّنْ قَبْلُ وَاِيَّايَ ۚ
اَتُهْلِكُنَا بِمَا فَعَلَ السُّفَهَاءُ مِنَّا ۚ
اِنْ هِىَ اِلَّا
فِتْنَتُكَ ۚ تُضِلُّ بِهَا مَنْ تَشَاءُ
وَتَهْدِىْ مَنْ تَشَاءُ ۚ
اَنْتَ وَلِيُّنَا فَاغْفِرْ لَنَا وَارْحَمْنَا
وَاَنْتَ خَيْرُ الْغَافِرِيْنَ ۟

156. "And ordain for us

١٥٦- وَاكْتُبْ لَنَا فِىْ هٰذِهِ الدُّنْيَا حَسَنَةً

That which is good,
In this life
And in the Hereafter:
For we have turned unto Thee."
He said: "With My Punishment
I visit whom I will;
But My Mercy extendeth
To all things. That (Mercy)
I shall ordain for those
Who do right, and practise
Regular charity, and those
Who believe in Our Signs—

وَفِى الْاٰخِرَةِ
اِنَّا هُدْنَا اِلَيْكَ قَالَ عَذَابِىْ
اُصِيْبُ بِهٖ مَنْ اَشَاءُ وَرَحْمَتِىْ وَسِعَتْ
كُلَّ شَىْءٍ فَسَاَكْتُبُهَا لِلَّذِيْنَ يَتَّقُوْنَ
وَيُؤْتُوْنَ الزَّكٰوةَ
وَالَّذِيْنَ هُمْ بِاٰيٰتِنَا يُؤْمِنُوْنَ ۚ

157. "Those who follow the Messenger,
The unlettered Prophet,
Whom they find mentioned
In their own (Scriptures)—
In the Law and the Gospel—
For he commands them
What is just and forbids them
What is evil; he allows
Them as lawful what is good
(And pure) and prohibits them
From what is bad (and impure);
He releases them
From their heavy burdens
And from the yokes
That are upon them.
So it is those who believe
In him, honour him,
Help him, and follow the Light
Which is sent down with him—
It is they who will prosper."

١٥٧- اَلَّذِيْنَ يَتَّبِعُوْنَ الرَّسُوْلَ
النَّبِىَّ الْاُمِّىَّ الَّذِىْ يَجِدُوْنَهٗ مَكْتُوْبًا
عِنْدَهُمْ فِى التَّوْرٰىةِ وَالْاِنْجِيْلِ
يَأْمُرُهُمْ بِالْمَعْرُوْفِ وَيَنْهٰهُمْ عَنِ الْمُنْكَرِ
وَيُحِلُّ لَهُمُ الطَّيِّبٰتِ
وَيُحَرِّمُ عَلَيْهِمُ
الْخَبٰٓئِثَ وَيَضَعُ عَنْهُمْ
اِصْرَهُمْ وَالْاَغْلٰلَ الَّتِىْ كَانَتْ عَلَيْهِمْ
فَالَّذِيْنَ اٰمَنُوْا بِهٖ وَعَزَّرُوْهُ وَنَصَرُوْهُ
وَاتَّبَعُوا النُّوْرَ الَّذِىْٓ اُنْزِلَ مَعَهٗٓ
اُولٰٓئِكَ هُمُ الْمُفْلِحُوْنَ ۚ

SECTION 20.

158. Say: "O men! I am sent
Unto you all, as the Messenger
Of Allah, to Whom belongeth
The dominion of the heavens
And the earth: there is no god
But He: it is He that giveth
Both life and death. So believe
In Allah and His Messenger,
The unlettered Prophet,
Who believeth in Allah
And His Words: follow him
That (so) ye may be guided."

١٥٨- قُلْ يٰٓاَيُّهَا النَّاسُ اِنِّىْ رَسُوْلُ اللّٰهِ
اِلَيْكُمْ جَمِيْعًا الَّذِىْ لَهٗ مُلْكُ السَّمٰوٰتِ وَ
الْاَرْضِ لَآ اِلٰهَ اِلَّا هُوَ يُحْىٖ وَيُمِيْتُ
فَاٰمِنُوْا بِاللّٰهِ وَرَسُوْلِهِ
النَّبِىِّ الْاُمِّىِّ
الَّذِىْ يُؤْمِنُ بِاللّٰهِ وَكَلِمٰتِهٖ
وَاتَّبِعُوْهُ لَعَلَّكُمْ تَهْتَدُوْنَ ۚ

159. Of the people of Moses
There is a section
Who guide and do justice
In the light of truth.

١٥٩- وَمِنْ قَوْمِ مُوسَى
أُمَّةٌ يَهْدُونَ بِالْحَقِّ وَبِهِ يَعْدِلُونَ ۞

160. We divided them into twelve
Tribes
Or nations. We directed
Moses by inspiration,
When his (thirsty) people asked
Him for water: "Strike the rock
With thy staff": out of it
There gushed forth twelve springs:
Each group knew its own place
For water. We gave them
The shade of clouds, and sent
Down to them manna and quails,
(Saying): "Eat of the good things
We have provided for you":
(But they rebelled); to Us
They did no harm, but
They harmed their own souls.

١٦٠- وَقَطَّعْنَاهُمُ اثْنَتَيْ عَشْرَةَ أَسْبَاطًا
أُمَمًا ۚ وَأَوْحَيْنَا إِلَى مُوسَى إِذِ اسْتَسْقَاهُ
قَوْمُهُ أَنِ اضْرِبْ بِعَصَاكَ الْحَجَرَ ۖ
فَانْبَجَسَتْ مِنْهُ اثْنَتَا عَشْرَةَ عَيْنًا ۖ
قَدْ عَلِمَ كُلُّ أُنَاسٍ مَشْرَبَهُمْ ۚ
وَظَلَّلْنَا عَلَيْهِمُ الْغَمَامَ
وَأَنْزَلْنَا عَلَيْهِمُ الْمَنَّ وَالسَّلْوَى ۖ
كُلُوا مِنْ طَيِّبَاتِ مَا رَزَقْنَاكُمْ ۚ وَمَا ظَلَمُونَا
وَلَٰكِنْ كَانُوا أَنْفُسَهُمْ يَظْلِمُونَ ۞

161. And remember it was
Said to them:
"Dwell in this town
And eat   therein as ye wish,
But say the word of humility
And enter the gate
In a posture of humility:
We shall forgive you
Your faults; We shall increase
(The portion of) those who do
good."

١٦١- وَإِذْ قِيلَ لَهُمُ اسْكُنُوا هَٰذِهِ الْقَرْيَةَ
وَكُلُوا مِنْهَا حَيْثُ شِئْتُمْ
وَقُولُوا حِطَّةٌ وَادْخُلُوا الْبَابَ
سُجَّدًا نَغْفِرْ لَكُمْ خَطِيئَاتِكُمْ ۚ
سَنَزِيدُ الْمُحْسِنِينَ ۞

162. But the transgressors among them
Changed the word from that
Which had been given them
So we sent on them
A plague from heaven.
For that they repeatedly
transgressed.

SECTION 21.

١٦٢- فَبَدَّلَ الَّذِينَ ظَلَمُوا مِنْهُمْ
قَوْلًا غَيْرَ الَّذِي
قِيلَ لَهُمْ فَأَرْسَلْنَا عَلَيْهِمْ رِجْزًا مِنَ
السَّمَاءِ بِمَا كَانُوا يَظْلِمُونَ ۞

163. Ask them concerning the town
Standing close by the sea.
Behold! they transgressed
In the matter of the Sabbath.
For on the day of their Sabbath
Their fish did come to them,

١٦٣- وَسْأَلْهُمْ عَنِ الْقَرْيَةِ الَّتِي كَانَتْ
حَاضِرَةَ الْبَحْرِ إِذْ يَعْدُونَ فِي السَّبْتِ
إِذْ تَأْتِيهِمْ حِيتَانُهُمْ يَوْمَ سَبْتِهِمْ شُرَّعًا

Openly holding up their heads,
But on the day they had
No Sabbath, they came not:
Thus did We make a trial
Of them, for they were
Given to transgression.

وَّيَوْمَ لَا يَسْبِتُونَ لَا تَأْتِيهِمْ
كَذَلِكَ نَبْلُوهُمْ
بِمَا كَانُوا يَفْسُقُونَ ٥

164. When some of them said:
"Why do ye preach
To a people whom Allah
Will destroy or visit
With a terrible punishment?"¹¹³⁸
Said the preachers: "To discharge
Our duty to your Lord,
And perchance they may fear
Him."

١٦٤- وَإِذْ قَالَتْ أُمَّةٌ مِّنْهُمْ
لِمَ تَعِظُونَ قَوْمًا ۙ اللَّهُ مُهْلِكُهُمْ
أَوْ مُعَذِّبُهُمْ عَذَابًا شَدِيدًا ۖ
قَالُوا مَعْذِرَةً
إِلَى رَبِّكُمْ وَلَعَلَّهُمْ يَتَّقُونَ ٥

165. When they disregarded the
warnings
That had been given them,
We rescued those who forbade
Evil; but We visited
The wrongdoers with a
Grievous punishment, because
They were given to transgression.

١٦٥- فَلَمَّا نَسُوا مَا ذُكِّرُوا بِهِ
أَنْجَيْنَا الَّذِينَ يَنْهَوْنَ عَنِ السُّوءِ
وَأَخَذْنَا الَّذِينَ ظَلَمُوا
بِعَذَابٍ بَئِيسٍ بِمَا كَانُوا يَفْسُقُونَ ٥

166. When in their insolence
They transgressed (all)
prohibitions,
We said to them:
"Be ye apes.
Despised and rejected."¹¹³⁹

١٦٦- فَلَمَّا عَتَوْا عَنْ مَا نُهُوا عَنْهُ
قُلْنَا لَهُمْ
كُونُوا قِرَدَةً خَاسِئِينَ ٥

167. Behold! thy Lord did declare¹¹⁴⁰
That He would send
Against them, to the Day
Of Judgement, those who would
Afflict them with grievous
Penalty. Thy Lord is quick
In retribution, but He is also
Oft-Forgiving, Most Merciful.

١٦٧- وَإِذْ تَأَذَّنَ رَبُّكَ لَيَبْعَثَنَّ عَلَيْهِمْ
إِلَى يَوْمِ الْقِيَامَةِ مَنْ يَّسُومُهُمْ سُوءَ
الْعَذَابِ ۗ إِنَّ رَبَّكَ لَسَرِيعُ الْعِقَابِ ۖ
وَإِنَّهُ لَغَفُورٌ رَّحِيمٌ ٥

168. We broke them up
Into sections on this earth.¹¹⁴¹
There are among them some
That are the righteous, and some
That are the opposite.
We have tried them
With both prosperity and
adversity:

١٦٨- وَقَطَّعْنَاهُمْ فِي الْأَرْضِ أُمَمًا ۚ
مِنْهُمُ الصَّالِحُونَ
وَمِنْهُمْ دُونَ ذَلِكَ ۖ
وَبَلَوْنَاهُمْ بِالْحَسَنَاتِ

In order that they
Might turn (to Us).

وَالسَّيِّاٰتِ لَعَلَّهُمْ يَرْجِعُوْنَ ۟

169. After them succeeded
An (evil) generation: they
Inherited the Book, but
They chose (for themselves)
The vanities of this world,
Saying (for excuse): "(Everything)
Will be forgiven us."
(Even so), if similar vanities
Came their way, they would
(Again) seize them.
Was not the Covenant
Of the Book taken from them,
That they would not
Ascribe to Allah anything
But the truth? And they
Study what is in the Book.
But best for the righteous
Is the Home in the Hereafter.
Will ye not understand?

١٦٩ـ فَخَلَفَ مِنْۢ بَعْدِهِمْ خَلْفٌ
وَّرِثُوا الْكِتٰبَ
يَأْخُذُوْنَ عَرَضَ هٰذَا الْاَدْنٰى
وَيَقُوْلُوْنَ سَيُغْفَرُ لَنَا ۚ
وَاِنْ يَّأْتِهِمْ عَرَضٌ مِّثْلُهٗ يَأْخُذُوْهُ ۗ
اَلَمْ يُؤْخَذْ عَلَيْهِمْ مِّيْثَاقُ الْكِتٰبِ
اَنْ لَّا يَقُوْلُوْا عَلَى اللّٰهِ
اِلَّا الْحَقَّ وَدَرَسُوْا مَا فِيْهِ ۗ
وَالدَّارُ الْاٰخِرَةُ خَيْرٌ لِّلَّذِيْنَ يَتَّقُوْنَ ۗ
اَفَلَا تَعْقِلُوْنَ ۟

170. As to those who hold fast
By the Book and establish
Regular Prayer—never
Shall We suffer the reward
Of the righteous to perish.

١٧٠ـ وَالَّذِيْنَ يُمَسِّكُوْنَ بِالْكِتٰبِ
وَاَقَامُوا الصَّلٰوةَ ۗ
اِنَّا لَا نُضِيْعُ اَجْرَ الْمُصْلِحِيْنَ ۟

171. When We shook the Mount
Over them, as if it had been
A canopy, and they thought
It was going to fall on them
(We said): "Hold firmly
To what We have given you,
And bring (ever) to remembrance
What is therein;
Perchance ye may fear Allah."

١٧١ـ وَاِذْ نَتَقْنَا الْجَبَلَ فَوْقَهُمْ
كَاَنَّهٗ ظُلَّةٌ وَّظَنُّوْا اَنَّهٗ وَاقِعٌۢ بِهِمْ ۚ
خُذُوْا مَا اٰتَيْنٰكُمْ بِقُوَّةٍ
وَّاذْكُرُوْا مَا فِيْهِ
لَعَلَّكُمْ تَتَّقُوْنَ ۟

SECTION 22.

172. When thy Lord drew forth
From the Children of Adam
From their loins—
Their descendants, and made
them
Testify concerning themselves,
(saying):
"Am I not your Lord
(Who cherishes and sustains
you?"—

١٧٢ـ وَاِذْ اَخَذَ رَبُّكَ مِنْۢ بَنِيْۤ اٰدَمَ
مِنْ ظُهُوْرِهِمْ ذُرِّيَّتَهُمْ
وَاَشْهَدَهُمْ عَلٰۤى اَنْفُسِهِمْ ۚ
اَلَسْتُ بِرَبِّكُمْ ۗ
قَالُوْا بَلٰى ۚ شَهِدْنَا ۚ

They said: "Yea!
We do testify!"   (This), lest
Ye should say on the Day
Of Judgement: "Of this we
Were never mindful."

اَنْ تَقُوْلُوْا يَوْمَ الْقِيٰمَةِ
اِنَّا كُنَّا عَنْ هٰذَا غٰفِلِيْنَ ۙ

173. Or lest ye should say:
"Our fathers before us
May have taken false gods,
But we are (their) descendants
After them: wilt Thou then
Destroy us because of the deeds
Of men who were futile?"

١٧٣- اَوْ تَقُوْلُوْا
اِنَّمَا اَشْرَكَ اٰبَآؤُنَا مِنْ قَبْلُ
وَكُنَّا ذُرِّيَّةً مِّنْ بَعْدِهِمْ ۚ
اَفَتُهْلِكُنَا بِمَا فَعَلَ الْمُبْطِلُوْنَ

174. Thus do We explain
The Signs in detail;
And perchance they may turn
(Unto Us).

١٧٤- وَكَذٰلِكَ نُفَصِّلُ الْاٰيٰتِ
وَلَعَلَّهُمْ يَرْجِعُوْنَ ۟

175. Relate to them the story
Of the man to whom
We sent Our Signs,
But he passed them by:
So Satan followed him up,
And he went astray.

١٧٥- وَاتْلُ عَلَيْهِمْ نَبَاَ الَّذِيْٓ اٰتَيْنٰهُ
اٰيٰتِنَا فَانْسَلَخَ مِنْهَا
فَاَتْبَعَهُ الشَّيْطٰنُ فَكَانَ مِنَ الْغٰوِيْنَ ۟

176. If it had been Our Will,
We should have elevated him
With Our Signs; but he
Inclined to the earth,
And followed his own vain
               desires.
His similitude is that
Of a dog: if you attack
Him, he lolls out his tongue,
Or if you leave him alone,
He (still) lolls out his tongue.
That is the similitude
Of those who reject Our Signs;
So relate the story;
Perchance they may reflect.

١٧٦- وَلَوْ شِئْنَا لَرَفَعْنٰهُ بِهَا
وَلٰكِنَّهٗٓ اَخْلَدَ اِلَى الْاَرْضِ
وَاتَّبَعَ هَوٰىهُ ۚ
فَمَثَلُهٗ كَمَثَلِ الْكَلْبِ ۚ
اِنْ تَحْمِلْ عَلَيْهِ يَلْهَثْ
اَوْ تَتْرُكْهُ يَلْهَثْ ذٰلِكَ مَثَلُ الْقَوْمِ
الَّذِيْنَ كَذَّبُوْا بِاٰيٰتِنَا ۚ
فَاقْصُصِ الْقَصَصَ لَعَلَّهُمْ يَتَفَكَّرُوْنَ ۟

177. Evil as an example are
People who reject Our Signs
And wrong their own souls.

١٧٧- سَآءَ مَثَلًا ۨ الْقَوْمُ الَّذِيْنَ كَذَّبُوْا
بِاٰيٰتِنَا وَاَنْفُسَهُمْ كَانُوْا يَظْلِمُوْنَ ۟

178. Whom Allah doth guide—
He is on the right path:

١٧٨- مَنْ يَّهْدِ اللّٰهُ فَهُوَ الْمُهْتَدِيْ ۚ

Whom He rejects from His
                    guidance—
Such are the persons who perish.

179. Many are the Jinns and men
We have made for Hell:
They have hearts wherewith they
Understand not, eyes wherewith
They see not, and ears wherewith
They hear not. They are
Like cattle—nay more
Misguided: for they
Are heedless (of warning).

180. The most beautiful names
Belong to Allah:
So call on him by them;
But shun such men as
Use profanity in His names:
For what they do, they will
Soon be requited.

181. Of those We have created
Are people who direct
(Others) with truth,
And dispense justice therewith.

SECTION 23.

182. Those who reject Our Signs,
We shall gradually visit
With punishment, in ways
They perceive not;

183. Respite will I grant
Unto them: for My scheme
Is strong (and unfailing).

184. Do they not reflect?
Their Companion is not seized
With madness: he is but
A perspicuous warner.

185. Do they see nothing
In the government of the heavens
And the earth and all
That Allah hath created?
(Do they not see) that
It may well be that
Their term is nigh

Drawing to an end?
In what Message after this
Will they then believe?

فَبِأَيِّ حَدِيثٍ
بَعْدَهُ يُؤْمِنُونَ ٥

186. To such as Allah rejects
From His guidance, there can be
No guide: He will
Leave them in their trespasses,
Wandering in distraction.

١٨٦- مَنْ يُضْلِلِ اللهُ
فَلَا هَادِيَ لَهُ ۚ
وَيَذَرُهُمْ فِي طُغْيَانِهِمْ يَعْمَهُونَ ٥

187. They ask thee about
The (final) Hour—when
Will be its appointed time?
Say: "The knowledge thereof
Is with my Lord (alone):
None but He can reveal
As to when it will occur.
Heavy were its burden through

The heavens and the earth.
Only, all of a sudden
Will it come to you."
They ask thee as if thou
Wert eager in search thereof:
Say: "The knowledge thereof
Is with Allah (alone),
But most men know not."

١٨٧- يَسْأَلُونَكَ عَنِ السَّاعَةِ
أَيَّانَ مُرْسَاهَا ۚ قُلْ إِنَّمَا عِلْمُهَا
عِنْدَ رَبِّي ۚ لَا يُجَلِّيهَا لِوَقْتِهَا
إِلَّا هُوَ ۚ ثَقُلَتْ
فِي السَّمَاوَاتِ وَالْأَرْضِ ۚ
لَا تَأْتِيكُمْ إِلَّا بَغْتَةً ۗ يَسْأَلُونَكَ كَأَنَّكَ
حَفِيٌّ عَنْهَا ۗ قُلْ إِنَّمَا عِلْمُهَا عِنْدَ اللهِ
وَلَكِنَّ أَكْثَرَ النَّاسِ لَا يَعْلَمُونَ ٥

188. Say: "I have no power
Over any good or harm
To myself except as Allah
Willeth. If I had knowledge
Of the unseen, I should have
Multiplied all good, and no evil
Should have touched me:
I am but a warner,
And a bringer of glad tidings
To those who have faith."

SECTION 24.

١٨٨- قُلْ لَا أَمْلِكُ لِنَفْسِي نَفْعًا وَّلَا
ضَرًّا إِلَّا مَا شَاءَ اللهُ ۚ وَلَوْ كُنْتُ أَعْلَمُ الْغَيْبَ
لَاسْتَكْثَرْتُ مِنَ الْخَيْرِ ۛ
وَمَا مَسَّنِيَ السُّوءُ ۚ إِنْ أَنَا إِلَّا نَذِيرٌ
وَّبَشِيرٌ لِقَوْمٍ يُؤْمِنُونَ ۟

189. It is He Who created
You from a single person,
And made his mate
Of like nature,   in order
That he might dwell with her
(In love). When they are
United, she bears a light
Burden and carries it about
(Unnoticed). When she grows

١٨٩- هُوَ الَّذِي خَلَقَكُمْ مِنْ نَفْسٍ وَّاحِدَةٍ
وَّجَعَلَ مِنْهَا زَوْجَهَا لِيَسْكُنَ إِلَيْهَا ۖ
فَلَمَّا تَغَشَّاهَا
حَمَلَتْ حَمْلًا خَفِيفًا
فَمَرَّتْ بِهِ ۖ

Heavy, they both pray
To Allah their Lord, (saying):
"If Thou givest us
A goodly child,
We vow we shall
(Ever) be grateful."

فَلَمَّا أَثْقَلَت دَّعَوَا اللّٰهَ رَبَّهُمَا لَئِنْ اٰتَيْتَنَا صَالِحًا لَّنَكُوْنَنَّ مِنَ الشّٰكِرِيْنَ ۝

190. But when He giveth them
A goodly child, they ascribe
To others a share in the gift
They have received:
But Allah is exalted
High above the partners
They ascribe to Him.

١٩٠۔ فَلَمَّا اٰتٰهُمَا صَالِحًا جَعَلَا لَهٗ شُرَكَآءَ فِيْمَا اٰتٰهُمَا ۚ فَتَعٰلَى اللّٰهُ عَمَّا يُشْرِكُوْنَ ۝

191. Do they indeed ascribe
To Him as partners things
That can create nothing,
But are themselves created?

١٩١۔ اَيُشْرِكُوْنَ مَا لَا يَخْلُقُ شَيْئًا وَّهُمْ يُخْلَقُوْنَ ۝

192. No aid can they give them,
Nor can they aid themselves!

١٩٢۔ وَلَا يَسْتَطِيْعُوْنَ لَهُمْ نَصْرًا وَّلَآ اَنْفُسَهُمْ يَنْصُرُوْنَ ۝

193. If ye call them to guidance,
They will not obey:
For you it is the same
Whether ye call them
Or ye hold your peace!

١٩٣۔ وَاِنْ تَدْعُوْهُمْ اِلَى الْهُدٰى لَا يَتَّبِعُوْكُمْ ۚ سَوَآءٌ عَلَيْكُمْ اَدَعَوْتُمُوْهُمْ اَمْ اَنْتُمْ صَامِتُوْنَ ۝

194. Verily those whom ye
Call upon besides Allah
Are servants like unto you:
Call upon them, and let them
Listen to your prayer,
If ye are (indeed) truthful!

١٩٤۔ اِنَّ الَّذِيْنَ تَدْعُوْنَ مِنْ دُوْنِ اللّٰهِ عِبَادٌ اَمْثَالُكُمْ فَادْعُوْهُمْ فَلْيَسْتَجِيْبُوْا لَكُمْ اِنْ كُنْتُمْ صٰدِقِيْنَ ۝

195. Have they feet to walk with?
Or hands to lay hold with?
Or eyes to see with?
Or ears to hear with?
Say: "Call your 'god-partners',
Scheme (your worst) against me,
And give me no respite!

١٩٥۔ اَلَهُمْ اَرْجُلٌ يَّمْشُوْنَ بِهَآ اَمْ لَهُمْ اَيْدٍ يَّبْطِشُوْنَ بِهَآ اَمْ لَهُمْ اَعْيُنٌ يُّبْصِرُوْنَ بِهَآ اَمْ لَهُمْ اٰذَانٌ يَّسْمَعُوْنَ بِهَا ۗ قُلِ ادْعُوْا شُرَكَآءَكُمْ ثُمَّ كِيْدُوْنِ فَلَا تُنْظِرُوْنَ ۝

196. "For my Protector is Allah,
Who revealed the Book
(From time to time),
And He will choose
And befriend the righteous.

١٩٦۔ اِنَّ وَلِيِّـۧ اللّٰهُ الَّذِيْ نَزَّلَ الْكِتٰبَ ۖ وَهُوَ يَتَوَلَّى الصّٰلِحِيْنَ ۝

197. "But those ye call upon
Besides Him, are unable
To help you, and indeed
To help themselves."

١٩٧- وَالَّذِينَ تَدْعُونَ مِنْ دُونِهِ لَا
يَسْتَطِيعُونَ نَصْرَكُمْ وَلَا أَنْفُسَهُمْ يَنْصُرُونَ ۝

198. If thou callest them
To guidance, they hear not.
Thou wilt see them
Looking at thee, but
They see not.

١٩٨- وَإِنْ تَدْعُوهُمْ إِلَى الْهُدَى
لَا يَسْمَعُوا وَتَرَاهُمْ يَنْظُرُونَ إِلَيْكَ
وَهُمْ لَا يُبْصِرُونَ ۝

199. Hold to forgiveness;
Command what is right;
But turn away from the
ignorant.

١٩٩- خُذِ الْعَفْوَ وَأْمُرْ بِالْعُرْفِ
وَأَعْرِضْ عَنِ الْجَاهِلِينَ ۝

200. If a suggestion from Satan
Assail thy (mind),
Seek refuge with Allah;
For He heareth and knoweth
(All things).

٢٠٠- وَإِمَّا يَنْزَغَنَّكَ مِنَ الشَّيْطَانِ نَزْغٌ
فَاسْتَعِذْ بِاللهِ إِنَّهُ سَمِيعٌ عَلِيمٌ ۝

201. Those who fear Allah,
When a thought of evil
From Satan assaults them,
Bring Allah to remembrance,
When lo! they see (aright)!

٢٠١- إِنَّ الَّذِينَ اتَّقَوْا
إِذَا مَسَّهُمْ طَائِفٌ مِنَ الشَّيْطَانِ
تَذَكَّرُوا فَإِذَا هُمْ مُبْصِرُونَ ۝

202. But their brethren (the evil
ones)
Plunge them deeper into error,
And never relax (their efforts).

٢٠٢- وَإِخْوَانُهُمْ يَمُدُّونَهُمْ فِي الْغَيِّ
ثُمَّ لَا يُقْصِرُونَ ۝

203. If thou bring them not
A revelation, they say:
"Why hast thou not
Got it together?"
Say: "I but follow
What is revealed to me
From my Lord:
This is (nothing but)
Lights from your Lord,
And Guidance, and Mercy,
For any who have Faith."

٢٠٣- وَإِذَا لَمْ تَأْتِهِمْ بِآيَةٍ
قَالُوا لَوْلَا اجْتَبَيْتَهَا
قُلْ إِنَّمَا أَتَّبِعُ مَا يُوحَى إِلَيَّ مِنْ رَبِّي
هَذَا بَصَائِرُ مِنْ رَبِّكُمْ
وَهُدًى وَرَحْمَةٌ
لِقَوْمٍ يُؤْمِنُونَ ۝

204. When the Qur'ān is read,

٢٠٤- وَإِذَا قُرِئَ الْقُرْآنُ فَاسْتَمِعُوا لَهُ

Listen to it with attention,
And hold your peace:
That ye may receive Mercy.

وَأَنْصِتُوا لَعَلَّكُمْ تُرْحَمُونَ ۞

205. And do thou (O reader!)
Bring thy Lord to remembrance
In thy (very) soul,
With humility and in reverence,
Without loudness in words,
In the mornings and evenings;
And be not thou
Of those who are unheedful.

٢٠٥ ـ وَاذْكُرْ رَّبَّكَ فِي نَفْسِكَ تَضَرُّعًا وَّ
خِيفَةً وَّدُونَ الْجَهْرِ مِنَ الْقَوْلِ
بِالْغُدُوِّ وَالْأَصَالِ
وَلَا تَكُنْ مِّنَ الْغَافِلِينَ ۞

206. Those who are near
To thy Lord, disdain not
To do Him worship:
They celebrate His praises,
And bow down before Him.

٢٠٦ ـ إِنَّ الَّذِينَ عِنْدَ رَبِّكَ
لَا يَسْتَكْبِرُونَ عَنْ عِبَادَتِهِ
وَيُسَبِّحُونَهُ وَلَهُ يَسْجُدُونَ ۩

INTRODUCTION TO SŪRA VIII *(Anfāl)* — 75 Verses

In the previous introductions to the Sūras we have shown how each Sūra is a step or gradation in the teaching of the Qur-ān. The first seven Sūras, comprising a little less than one-third of the Qur-ān, form a gradation, sketching the early spiritual history of man and leading up to the formation of the new Ummat or Community of the Holy Apostle. Now we begin another gradation, consolidating that Ummat and directing us as to various phases in our new collective life.

In this chapter we have the lessons of the battle of Badr enforced in their larger aspect: (1) the question of war booty; (2) the true virtues necessary for fighting the good fight; (3) victory against odds; (4) clemency and consideration for one's own and for outers in the hour of victory.

As regards booty taken in battle, the first point to note is that that should never be our aim in war. It is only an adventitious circumstance, a sort of windfall. Secondly, no soldier or troop has any inherent right to it. A righteous war is a community affair and any accessions resulting from it belong to God, or the community or Cause. Thirdly, certain equitable principles of division should be laid down to check human greed and selfishness. A fifth share goes to the Commander, and he can use it at his discretion, for his own expenses, and for the relief of the poor and suffering, and the orphans and widows (viii. 41). The remainder was divided, according to the Prophet's practice, not only among those who were actually in the fight physically, but all who were in the enterprise, young and old, provided they loyally did some duty assigned to them. Fourthly, there should be no disputes, as they interfere with internal discipline and harmony.

These principles are followed in the best modern practice of civilised nations. All acquisitions of war belong absolutely to the Sovereign as representing the commonwealth. In the distribution of booty not only the actual captors but also the "joint captors" and 'the "constructive captors" share. See Sir R. Phillimore's *International Law* (1885), vol. 3, pp, 206-10, 221-24.

As regards the military virtues, which are the types of virtues throughout life, we are shown by an analysis of the incidents of Badr how, against the greatest odds, God's help will give the victory if men are fighting not for themselves but for the sacred Cause of God. And directions are given for the treatment of prisoners and for maintaining the solidarity of the Muslim community.

The date of this Sūra is shortly after the battle of Badr, which was fought on Friday, the 17th of Ramadhān in the second year of the Hijra. A short account of the battle is given in n. 352 to iii. 13 ——————————

Al Anfāl (The Spoils of War)

In the name of Allah, Most Gracious, Most Merciful.

1. They ask thee   concerning
(Things taken as) spoils of war.
Say: "(Such) spoils are
At the disposal of Allah
And the Messenger: so fear
Allah, and keep straight
The relations between yourselves:
Obey Allah and His Messenger,
If ye do believe."

2. For, Believers are those
Who, when Allah is mentioned,
Feel a tremor in their hearts,
And when they hear
His Signs rehearsed, find
Their faith strengthened,
And put (all) their trust
In their Lord;

١- إِنَّمَا الْمُؤْمِنُونَ الَّذِينَ إِذَا ذُكِرَ اللّٰهُ
وَجِلَتْ قُلُوبُهُمْ وَإِذَا تُلِيَتْ عَلَيْهِمْ
اٰيٰتُهُ زَادَتْهُمْ إِيمَانًا
وَعَلٰى رَبِّهِمْ يَتَوَكَّلُونَ ۞

3. Who establish regular prayers
And spend (freely) out of
The gifts We have given
Them for sustenance:

٢- الَّذِينَ يُقِيمُونَ الصَّلٰوةَ
وَمِمَّا رَزَقْنٰهُمْ يُنْفِقُونَ ۞

4. Such in truth are the Believers:
They have grades of dignity
With their Lord, and forgiveness,
And generous sustenance:

٣- أُولٰٓئِكَ هُمُ الْمُؤْمِنُونَ حَقًّا لَهُمْ دَرَجٰتٌ
عِنْدَ رَبِّهِمْ وَمَغْفِرَةٌ وَرِزْقٌ كَرِيمٌ ۞

5. Just as thy Lord ordered thee
Out of thy house in truth,
Even though a party among
The Believers disliked it,

٥- كَمَآ أَخْرَجَكَ رَبُّكَ مِنْ بَيْتِكَ بِالْحَقِّ
وَإِنَّ فَرِيقًا مِنَ الْمُؤْمِنِينَ لَكٰرِهُونَ ۞

6. Disputing with thee concerning
The truth after it was made
Manifest, as if they were
Being driven to death
And they (actually) saw it.

٦- يُجَادِلُونَكَ فِي الْحَقِّ بَعْدَ مَا
تَبَيَّنَ كَأَنَّمَا يُسَاقُونَ إِلَى الْمَوْتِ
وَهُمْ يَنْظُرُونَ ۞

7. Behold! Allah promised you
One of the two (enemy) parties,
That it should be yours:
Ye wished that the one
Unarmed should be yours,
But Allah willed
To justify the Truth
According to His words,
And to cut off the roots
Of the Unbelievers—

٧- وَإِذْ يَعِدُكُمُ اللّٰهُ إِحْدَى الطَّآئِفَتَيْنِ
أَنَّهَا لَكُمْ وَتَوَدُّونَ أَنَّ غَيْرَ ذَاتِ
الشَّوْكَةِ تَكُونُ لَكُمْ
وَيُرِيدُ اللّٰهُ أَنْ يُحِقَّ الْحَقَّ بِكَلِمٰتِهِ
وَيَقْطَعَ دَابِرَ الْكٰفِرِينَ ۞

8. That He might justify Truth
And prove Falsehood false,
Distasteful though it be
To those in guilt.

٨- لِيُحِقَّ الْحَقَّ وَيُبْطِلَ الْبَاطِلَ
وَلَوْ كَرِهَ الْمُجْرِمُونَ ۞

9. Remember ye implored
The assistance of your Lord,
And He answered you:

٩- إِذْ تَسْتَغِيثُونَ رَبَّكُمْ فَاسْتَجَابَ لَكُمْ

"I will assist you
With a thousand of the angels,
Ranks on ranks."

10. Allah made it but a message
Of hope, and an assurance
To your hearts: (in any case)
There is no help
Except from Allah:
And Allah is Exalted in Power,
Wise.

SECTION 2.

11. Remember He covered you
With a sort of drowsiness,
To give you calm as from
Himself, and he caused
Rain to descend on you
From heaven, to clean you
Therewith, to remove from you
The stain of Satan,
To strengthen your hearts,
And to plant your feet
Firmly therewith.

12. Remember thy Lord inspired
The angels (with the message):
"I am with you: give
Firmness to the Believers:
I will instil terror
Into the hearts of the Unbelievers:
Smite ye above their necks
And smite all their
Finger tips off them."

13. This because they contended
Against Allah and His Messenger:
If any contend against Allah
And His Messenger, Allah
Is strict in punishment.

14. Thus (will it be said): "Taste ye
Then of the (punishment):
For those who resist Allah,
Is the penalty of the Fire."

15. O ye who believe!
When ye meet

The Unbelievers
In hostile array,
Never turn your backs
To them.

16. If any do turn his back
To them on such a day—
Unless it be in a stratagem
Of war, or to retreat
To a troop (of his own)—
He draws on himself
The wrath of Allah,
And his abode is Hell—
An evil refuge (indeed)!

إِذَا لَقِيتُمُ الَّذِينَ كَفَرُوا زَحْفًا
فَلَا تُوَلُّوهُمُ الْأَدْبَارَ ۞

١٦- وَمَنْ يُوَلِّهِمْ يَوْمَئِذٍ دُبُرَهُ
إِلَّا مُتَحَرِّفًا لِقِتَالٍ أَوْ مُتَحَيِّزًا إِلَى فِئَةٍ
فَقَدْ بَاءَ بِغَضَبٍ مِّنَ اللهِ
وَمَأْوَاهُ جَهَنَّمُ
وَبِئْسَ الْمَصِيرُ ۝

17. It is not ye who
Slew them; it was Allah:
When thou threwest (a handful
Of dust), it was not
Thy act, but Allah's:
In order that He might
Test the Believers
By a gracious trial
From Himself: for Allah
Is He Who heareth
And knoweth (all things).

١٧- فَلَمْ تَقْتُلُوهُمْ وَلَكِنَّ اللهَ قَتَلَهُمْ
وَمَا رَمَيْتَ إِذْ رَمَيْتَ
وَلَكِنَّ اللهَ رَمَى
وَلِيُبْلِيَ الْمُؤْمِنِينَ مِنْهُ بَلَاءً حَسَنًا
إِنَّ اللهَ سَمِيعٌ عَلِيمٌ ۝

18. That, and also because
Allah is He Who makes feeble
The Plans and stratagems
Of the Unbelievers.

١٨- ذَلِكُمْ وَأَنَّ اللهَ
مُوهِنُ كَيْدِ الْكَافِرِينَ ۝

19. (O Unbelievers!) if ye prayed
For victory and judgement,
Now hath the judgement
Come to you: if ye desist
(From wrong), it will be
Best for you: if ye return
(To the attack), so shall We.
Not the least good
Will your forces be to you
Even if they were multiplied:
For verily Allah
Is with those who believe!

SECTION 3.

١٩- إِنْ تَسْتَفْتِحُوا فَقَدْ جَاءَكُمُ الْفَتْحُ
وَإِنْ تَنْتَهُوا فَهُوَ خَيْرٌ لَّكُمْ
وَإِنْ تَعُودُوا نَعُدْ
وَلَنْ تُغْنِيَ عَنْكُمْ فِئَتُكُمْ شَيْئًا
وَلَوْ كَثُرَتْ
وَأَنَّ اللهَ مَعَ الْمُؤْمِنِينَ ۝

20. O ye who believe!

٢٠- يَا أَيُّهَا الَّذِينَ آمَنُوا أَطِيعُوا اللهَ وَرَسُولَهُ

Obey Allah and His Messenger,
And turn not away from him
When ye hear (him speak).

وَلَا تَوَلَّوْا عَنْهُ وَأَنْتُمْ تَسْمَعُوْنَ ۞

21. Nor be like those who say,
"We hear," but listen not:

٢١- وَلَا تَكُوْنُوْا كَالَّذِيْنَ قَالُوْا سَمِعْنَا وَ
هُمْ لَا يَسْمَعُوْنَ ۞

22. For the worst of beasts
In the sight of Allah
Are the deaf and the dumb—
Those who understand not.

٢٢- إِنَّ شَرَّ الدَّوَابِّ عِنْدَ اللهِ الصُّمُّ
الْبُكْمُ الَّذِيْنَ لَا يَعْقِلُوْنَ ۞

23. If Allah had found in them
Any good, He would indeed
Have made them listen:
(As it is), if He had made them
Listen, they would but have
Turned back and declined (faith).

٢٣- وَلَوْ عَلِمَ اللهُ فِيْهِمْ
خَيْرًا لَّأَسْمَعَهُمْ ۗ
وَلَوْ أَسْمَعَهُمْ لَتَوَلَّوْا وَّهُمْ مُّعْرِضُوْنَ ۞

24. O ye who believe!
Give your response to Allah
And His Messenger, when He
Calleth you to that which
Will give you life;
And know that Allah
Cometh in between a man
And his heart, and that
It is He to Whom
Ye shall (all) be gathered.

٢٤- يَآأَيُّهَا الَّذِيْنَ أٰمَنُوا
اسْتَجِيْبُوْا لِلهِ وَلِلرَّسُوْلِ
إِذَا دَعَاكُمْ لِمَا يُحْيِيْكُمْ ۚ
وَاعْلَمُوْا أَنَّ اللهَ يَحُوْلُ بَيْنَ الْمَرْءِ
وَقَلْبِهٖ وَأَنَّهٗٓ إِلَيْهِ تُحْشَرُوْنَ ۞

25. And fear tumult or oppression,
Which affecteth not in particular
(Only) those of you who do wrong
And know that Allah
Is strict in punishment.

٢٥- وَاتَّقُوْا فِتْنَةً
لَّا تُصِيْبَنَّ الَّذِيْنَ ظَلَمُوْا مِنْكُمْ خَاصَّةً ۚ
وَاعْلَمُوْا أَنَّ اللهَ شَدِيْدُ الْعِقَابِ ۞

26. Call to mind when ye
Were a small (band),
Despised through the land,
And afraid that men might
Despoil and kidnap you;
But He provided a safe asylum
For you, strengthened you
With His aid, and gave you
Good things for sustenance:
That ye might be grateful.

٢٦- وَاذْكُرُوْا إِذْ أَنْتُمْ قَلِيْلٌ
مُسْتَضْعَفُوْنَ فِى الْأَرْضِ
تَخَافُوْنَ أَنْ يَتَخَطَّفَكُمُ النَّاسُ
فَأٰوَاكُمْ وَأَيَّدَكُمْ بِنَصْرِهٖ
وَرَزَقَكُمْ مِّنَ الطَّيِّبَاتِ لَعَلَّكُمْ تَشْكُرُوْنَ ۞

27. O ye that believe!
Betray not the trust
Of Allah and the Messenger,
Nor misappropriate knowingly
Things entrusted to you.

٢٧- يَاۤيُّهَا الَّذِيۡنَ اٰمَنُوۡا لَا تَخُوۡنُوا اللّٰهَ
وَالرَّسُوۡلَ وَتَخُوۡنُوۡۤا اَمٰنٰتِكُمۡ
وَاَنۡتُمۡ تَعۡلَمُوۡنَ ۝

28. And know ye
That your possessions
And your progeny
Are but a trial;
And that it is Allah
With whom lies
Your highest reward.

٢٨- وَاعۡلَمُوۡۤا اَنَّمَاۤ اَمۡوَالُكُمۡ
وَاَوۡلَادُكُمۡ فِتۡنَةٌ ۙ
وَاَنَّ اللّٰهَ عِنۡدَهٗۤ اَجۡرٌ عَظِيۡمٌ ۝ ۶

SECTION 4.

29. O ye who believe!
If ye fear Allah,
He will grant you a Criterion
(To judge between right and
wrong),
Remove from you (all) evil
(That may afflict) you,
And forgive you:
For Allah is the Lord
Of grace unbounded.

٢٩- يَاۤيُّهَا الَّذِيۡنَ اٰمَنُوۡۤا اِنۡ تَتَّقُوا اللّٰهَ
يَجۡعَلۡ لَّكُمۡ فُرۡقَانًا
وَّيُكَفِّرۡ عَنۡكُمۡ سَيِّاٰتِكُمۡ
وَيَغۡفِرۡ لَكُمۡ ۗ
وَاللّٰهُ ذُو الۡفَضۡلِ الۡعَظِيۡمِ ۝

30. Remember how the Unbelievers
Plotted against thee, to keep
Thee in bonds, or slay thee,
Or get thee out (of thy home).
They plot and plan,
And Allah too plans,
But the best of planners
Is Allah.

٣٠- وَاِذۡ يَمۡكُرُ بِكَ الَّذِيۡنَ كَفَرُوۡا
لِيُثۡبِتُوۡكَ اَوۡ يَقۡتُلُوۡكَ اَوۡ يُخۡرِجُوۡكَ ۚ
وَيَمۡكُرُوۡنَ وَيَمۡكُرُ اللّٰهُ ۗ
وَاللّٰهُ خَيۡرُ الۡمَاكِرِيۡنَ ۝

31. When Our Signs are rehearsed
To them, they say: "We
Have heard this (before):
If we wished, we could
Say (words) like these:
These are nothing
But tales of the ancients."

٣١- وَاِذَا تُتۡلٰى عَلَيۡهِمۡ اٰيٰتُنَا قَالُوۡا قَدۡ
سَمِعۡنَا لَوۡ نَشَاۤءُ لَقُلۡنَا مِثۡلَ هٰذَاۤ ۙ
اِنۡ هٰذَاۤ اِلَّاۤ اَسَاطِيۡرُ الۡاَوَّلِيۡنَ ۝

32. Remember how they said:
"O Allah! if this is indeed
The Truth from Thee,
Rain down on us a shower
Of stones from the sky,
Or send us a grievous Penalty."

٣٢- وَاِذۡ قَالُوا اللّٰهُمَّ اِنۡ كَانَ هٰذَا هُوَ
الۡحَقَّ مِنۡ عِنۡدِكَ فَاَمۡطِرۡ عَلَيۡنَا حِجَارَةً
مِّنَ السَّمَاۤءِ اَوِ ائۡتِنَا بِعَذَابٍ اَلِيۡمٍ ۝

33. But Allah was not going
To send them a Penalty
Whilst thou wast amongst them;
Nor was He going to send it
Whilst they could ask for pardon.

٣٣- وَمَا كَانَ اللّٰهُ لِيُعَذِّبَهُمْ وَأَنْتَ فِيهِمْ ۚ وَمَا كَانَ اللّٰهُ مُعَذِّبَهُمْ وَهُمْ يَسْتَغْفِرُوْنَ ۝

34. But what plea have they
That Allah should not punish
Them, when they keep out
(Men) from the Sacred Mosque—
And they are not its guardians?
No men can be its guardians
Except the righteous; but most
Of them do not understand.

٣٤- وَمَا لَهُمْ اَلَّا يُعَذِّبَهُمُ اللّٰهُ وَهُمْ يَصُدُّوْنَ عَنِ الْمَسْجِدِ الْحَرَامِ وَمَا كَانُوْٓا اَوْلِيَآءَهُ ۚ اِنْ اَوْلِيَآؤُهُ اِلَّا الْمُتَّقُوْنَ وَلٰكِنَّ اَكْثَرَهُمْ لَا يَعْلَمُوْنَ ۝

35. Their prayer at the House
(Of Allah) is nothing but
Whistling and clapping of hands:
(Its only answer can be),
"Taste ye the Penalty
Because ye blasphemed."

٣٥- وَمَا كَانَ صَلَاتُهُمْ عِنْدَ الْبَيْتِ اِلَّا مُكَآءً وَّتَصْدِيَةً ۚ فَذُوْقُوا الْعَذَابَ بِمَا كُنْتُمْ تَكْفُرُوْنَ ۝

36. The Unbelievers spend their
wealth
To hinder (men) from the path
Of Allah, and so will they
Continue to spend; but
In the end they will have
(Only) regrets and sighs;
At length they will be overcome:
And the Unbelievers will be
Gathered together to Hell—

٣٦- اِنَّ الَّذِيْنَ كَفَرُوْا يُنْفِقُوْنَ اَمْوَالَهُمْ لِيَصُدُّوْا عَنْ سَبِيْلِ اللّٰهِ ۚ فَسَيُنْفِقُوْنَهَا ثُمَّ تَكُوْنُ عَلَيْهِمْ حَسْرَةً ثُمَّ يُغْلَبُوْنَ ۚ وَالَّذِيْنَ كَفَرُوْٓا اِلٰى جَهَنَّمَ يُحْشَرُوْنَ ۝

37. In order that Allah may
separate
The impure from the pure,
Put the impure, one on another,
Heap them together, and cast them
Into Hell. They will be
The ones to have lost.

٣٧- لِيَمِيْزَ اللّٰهُ الْخَبِيْثَ مِنَ الطَّيِّبِ وَيَجْعَلَ الْخَبِيْثَ بَعْضَهُ عَلٰى بَعْضٍ فَيَرْكُمَهُ جَمِيْعًا فَيَجْعَلَهُ فِيْ جَهَنَّمَ ۚ اُولٰٓئِكَ هُمُ الْخٰسِرُوْنَ ۝

SECTION 5.

38. Say to the Unbelievers,
If (now) they desist (from
Unbelief),
Their past would be forgiven
them;

٣٨- قُلْ لِّلَّذِيْنَ كَفَرُوْٓا اِنْ يَّنْتَهُوْا يُغْفَرْ لَهُمْ مَّا قَدْ سَلَفَ ۚ وَاِنْ يَّعُوْدُوْا فَقَدْ

But if they persist, the punishment
Of those before them is already
(A matter of warning for them).

مَضَتْ سُنَّتُ الْأَوَّلِيْنَ ٥

39. And fight them on
Until there is no more
Tumult or oppression,
And there prevails
Justice and faith in Allah
Altogether and everywhere;
But if they cease, verily Allah
Doth see all that they do.

٣٩- وَقَاتِلُوْهُمْ حَتّٰى لَا تَكُوْنَ فِتْنَةٌ
وَّيَكُوْنَ الدِّيْنُ كُلُّهٗ لِلّٰهِ ۚ
فَإِنِ انْتَهَوْا
فَإِنَّ اللّٰهَ بِمَا يَعْمَلُوْنَ بَصِيْرٌ ٥

40. If they refuse, be sure
That Allah is your Protector—
The Best to protect
And the Best to help.

٤٠- وَإِنْ تَوَلَّوْا فَاعْلَمُوْا أَنَّ اللّٰهَ مَوْلٰكُمْ ۚ
نِعْمَ الْمَوْلٰى وَنِعْمَ النَّصِيْرُ ٥

41. And know that out of
All the booty that ye
May acquire (in war),
A fifth share is assigned
To Allah—and to the Messenger,
And to near relatives,
Orphans, the needy,
And the wayfarer—
If ye do believe in Allah
And in the revelation
We sent down to our Servant
On the Day of Testing—
The Day of the meeting
Of the two forces.
For Allah hath power
Over all things.

٤١- وَاعْلَمُوْا أَنَّمَا غَنِمْتُمْ مِّنْ شَيْءٍ
فَأَنَّ لِلّٰهِ خُمُسَهٗ وَلِلرَّسُوْلِ
وَلِذِى الْقُرْبٰى وَالْيَتٰمٰى وَالْمَسٰكِيْنِ
وَابْنِ السَّبِيْلِ ۙ
إِنْ كُنْتُمْ اٰمَنْتُمْ بِاللّٰهِ
وَمَا أَنْزَلْنَا عَلٰى عَبْدِنَا يَوْمَ الْفُرْقَانِ
يَوْمَ الْتَقَى الْجَمْعٰنِ ۚ
وَاللّٰهُ عَلٰى كُلِّ شَيْءٍ قَدِيْرٌ ٥

42. Remember ye were
On the hither side
Of the valley, and they
On the farther side,
And the caravan
On lower ground than ye.
Even if ye had made
A mutual appointment
To meet, ye would certainly
Have failed in the appointment:
But (thus ye met),
That Allah might accomplish
A matter already enacted;
That those who died might

٤٢- إِذْ أَنْتُمْ بِالْعُدْوَةِ الدُّنْيَا
وَهُمْ بِالْعُدْوَةِ الْقُصْوٰى
وَالرَّكْبُ أَسْفَلَ مِنْكُمْ ۚ
وَلَوْ تَوَاعَدْتُّمْ
لَاخْتَلَفْتُمْ فِى الْمِيْعٰدِ ۙ
وَلٰكِنْ لِّيَقْضِىَ اللّٰهُ أَمْرًا
كَانَ مَفْعُوْلًا ۙ ﮪ

Die after a clear Sign
(Had been given), and those who
    lived
Might live after a Clear Sign
(Had been given). And verily
Allah is He who heareth
And knoweth (all things).

لِّيَهْلِكَ مَنْ هَلَكَ عَنْ بَيِّنَةٍ
وَّيَحْيَى مَنْ حَيَّ عَنْ بَيِّنَةٍ ۚ
وَإِنَّ اللّٰهَ لَسَمِيعٌ عَلِيمٌ ۞

43. Remember in thy dream
Allah showed them to thee
As few: if He had shown
Them to thee as many,
Ye would surely have been
Discouraged, and ye would
Surely have disputed
In (your) decision: but Allah
Saved (you) for He knoweth
Well the (secrets) of (all) hearts.

٤٣- إِذْ يُرِيكَهُمُ اللّٰهُ فِي مَنَامِكَ قَلِيلًا ۖ
وَلَوْ أَرَاكَهُمْ كَثِيرًا لَّفَشِلْتُمْ
وَلَتَنَازَعْتُمْ فِي الْأَمْرِ
وَلٰكِنَّ اللّٰهَ سَلَّمَ ۚ
إِنَّهُ عَلِيمٌ بِذَاتِ الصُّدُورِ ۞

44. And remember when ye met,
He showed them to you
As few in your eyes,
And He made you appear
As contemptible in their eyes:
That Allah might accomplish
A matter already enacted.
For to Allah do all questions
Go back (for decision).

٤٤- وَإِذْ يُرِيكُمُوهُمْ
إِذِ الْتَقَيْتُمْ فِي أَعْيُنِكُمْ قَلِيلًا
وَّيُقَلِّلُكُمْ فِي أَعْيُنِهِمْ
لِيَقْضِيَ اللّٰهُ أَمْرًا كَانَ مَفْعُولًا ۚ
وَإِلَى اللّٰهِ تُرْجَعُ الْأُمُورُ ۞

SECTION 6.

45. O ye who believe!
When ye meet a force,
Be firm, and call Allah
In remembrance much (and
    often);
That ye may prosper:

٤٥- يَا أَيُّهَا الَّذِينَ آمَنُوا إِذَا لَقِيتُمْ فِئَةً
فَاثْبُتُوا وَاذْكُرُوا اللّٰهَ كَثِيرًا
لَّعَلَّكُمْ تُفْلِحُونَ ۞

46. And obey Allah and His
    Messenger;
And fall into no disputes,
Lest ye lose heart
And your power depart;
And be patient and persevering:
For Allah is with those
Who patiently persevere:

٤٦- وَأَطِيعُوا اللّٰهَ وَرَسُولَهُ وَلَا تَنَازَعُوا
فَتَفْشَلُوا وَتَذْهَبَ رِيحُكُمْ وَ
اصْبِرُوا ۚ
إِنَّ اللّٰهَ مَعَ الصَّابِرِينَ ۞

47. And be not like those
Who started from their homes
Insolently and to be seen of men,

٤٧- وَلَا تَكُونُوا كَالَّذِينَ خَرَجُوا
مِنْ دِيَارِهِمْ بَطَرًا وَّرِئَاءَ النَّاسِ

And to hinder (men)
From the path of Allah:
For Allah compasseth round about
All that they do.

وَيَصُدُّوْنَ عَنْ سَبِيْلِ اللّٰهِ
وَاللّٰهُ بِمَا يَعْمَلُوْنَ مُحِيْطٌ ٥

48. Remember Satan made
Their (sinful) acts seem
Alluring to them, and said:
"No one among men
Can overcome you this day,
While I am near to you":
But when the two forces
Came in sight of each other,
He turned on his heels,
And said: "Lo! I am clear
Of you; lo! I see
What ye see not;
Lo! I fear Allah; for Allah
Is strict in punishment."

٤٨- وَاِذْ زَيَّنَ لَهُمُ الشَّيْطٰنُ اَعْمَالَهُمْ
وَقَالَ لَا غَالِبَ لَكُمُ الْيَوْمَ مِنَ النَّاسِ
وَاِنِّىْ جَارٌ لَّكُمْ ۚ فَلَمَّا تَرَآءَتِ الْفِئَتٰنِ
نَكَصَ عَلٰى عَقِبَيْهِ وَقَالَ اِنِّىْ بَرِىْٓءٌ
مِّنْكُمْ اِنِّىْٓ اَرٰى مَا لَا تَرَوْنَ
اِنِّىْٓ اَخَافُ اللّٰهَ
وَاللّٰهُ شَدِيْدُ الْعِقَابِ ٥

SECTION 7.

49. Lo! the Hypocrites say, and those
In whose hearts is a disease:
"These people—their religion
Has misled them." But
If any trust in Allah, behold!
Allah is Exalted in might, Wise.

٤٩- اِذْ يَقُوْلُ الْمُنٰفِقُوْنَ
وَالَّذِيْنَ فِىْ قُلُوْبِهِمْ مَّرَضٌ
غَرَّ هٰٓؤُلَاءِ دِيْنُهُمْ ۗ وَمَنْ يَّتَوَكَّلْ عَلَى اللّٰهِ
فَاِنَّ اللّٰهَ عَزِيْزٌ حَكِيْمٌ ٥

50. If thou couldst see,
When the angels take the souls
Of the Unbelievers (at death),
(How) they smite their faces
And their backs, (saying):
"Taste the Penalty of the blazing
Fire—

٥٠- وَلَوْ تَرٰٓى اِذْ يَتَوَفَّى الَّذِيْنَ كَفَرُوا
الْمَلٰٓئِكَةُ يَضْرِبُوْنَ وُجُوْهَهُمْ وَاَدْبَارَهُمْ ۚ
وَذُوْقُوْا عَذَابَ الْحَرِيْقِ ٥

51. "Because of (the deeds) which
Your (own) hands sent forth:
For Allah is never unjust
To His servants:

٥١- ذٰلِكَ بِمَا قَدَّمَتْ اَيْدِيْكُمْ
وَاَنَّ اللّٰهَ لَيْسَ بِظَلَّامٍ لِّلْعَبِيْدِ ٥

52. "(Deeds) after the manner
Of the People of Pharaoh
And of those before them:
They rejected the Signs of Allah,
And Allah punished them
For their crimes: for Allah
Is Strong, and Strict in
punishment:

٥٢- كَدَأْبِ اٰلِ فِرْعَوْنَ وَالَّذِيْنَ مِنْ
قَبْلِهِمْ ۚ كَفَرُوْا بِاٰيٰتِ اللّٰهِ
فَاَخَذَهُمُ اللّٰهُ بِذُنُوْبِهِمْ ۗ
اِنَّ اللّٰهَ قَوِيٌّ شَدِيْدُ الْعِقَابِ ٥

53. "Because Allah will never
       change
 The Grace which He hath
       bestowed
 On a people until they change
 What is in their (own) souls:
 And verily Allah is He
 Who heareth and knoweth (all
       things)."

٥٣- ذٰلِكَ بِاَنَّ اللّٰهَ لَمْ يَكُ مُغَيِّرًا
نِّعْمَةً اَنْعَمَهَا عَلٰى قَوْمٍ حَتّٰى يُغَيِّرُوْا
مَا بِاَنْفُسِهِمْ ۙ
وَاَنَّ اللّٰهَ سَمِيْعٌ عَلِيْمٌ ۙ

54. "(Deeds) after the manner
 Of the People of the Pharaoh
 And those before them":
 They treated as false the Signs
 Of their Lord: so We
 Destroyed them for their crimes,
 And We drowned the People
 Of Pharaoh: for they were all
 Oppressors and wrongdoers.

٥٤- كَدَاْبِ اٰلِ فِرْعَوْنَ ۙ
وَالَّذِيْنَ مِنْ قَبْلِهِمْ ۘ
كَذَّبُوْا بِاٰيٰتِ
رَبِّهِمْ فَاَهْلَكْنٰهُمْ بِذُنُوْبِهِمْ وَاَغْرَقْنَآ
اٰلَ فِرْعَوْنَ ۚ وَكُلٌّ كَانُوْا ظٰلِمِيْنَ ٥

55. For the worst of beasts
 In the sight of Allah
 Are those who reject Him:
 They will not believe.

٥٥- اِنَّ شَرَّ الدَّوَآبِّ عِنْدَ اللّٰهِ
الَّذِيْنَ كَفَرُوْا فَهُمْ لَا يُؤْمِنُوْنَ ۙ

56. They are those with whom
 Thou didst make a covenant,
 But they break their covenant
 Every time, and they have not
 The fear (of Allah).

٥٦- الَّذِيْنَ عَاهَدْتَّ مِنْهُمْ
ثُمَّ يَنْقُضُوْنَ عَهْدَهُمْ
فِيْ كُلِّ مَرَّةٍ وَّهُمْ لَا يَتَّقُوْنَ ٥

57. If ye gain the mastery
 Over them in war,
 Disperse, with them, those
 Who follow them,
 That they may remember.

٥٧- فَاِمَّا تَثْقَفَنَّهُمْ فِى الْحَرْبِ
فَشَرِّدْ بِهِمْ مَّنْ خَلْفَهُمْ
لَعَلَّهُمْ يَذَّكَّرُوْنَ ٥

58. If thou fearest treachery
 From any group, throw back
 (Their Covenant) to them, (so as
 To be) on equal terms:
 For Allah loveth not the
       treacherous.

٥٨- وَاِمَّا تَخَافَنَّ مِنْ قَوْمٍ خِيَانَةً
فَانْۢبِذْ اِلَيْهِمْ عَلٰى سَوَآءٍ ۭ
اِنَّ اللّٰهَ لَا يُحِبُّ الْخَآئِنِيْنَ ٥

SECTION 8.

59. Let not the Unbelievers
 Think that they can
 Get the better (of the godly):
 They will never frustrate (them).

٥٩- وَلَا يَحْسَبَنَّ الَّذِيْنَ كَفَرُوْا
سَبَقُوْا ۭ اِنَّهُمْ لَا يُعْجِزُوْنَ ٥

60. Against them make ready
Your strength to the utmost
Of your power, including
Steeds of war, to strike terror
Into (the hearts of) the enemies,
Of Allah and your enemies,
And others besides, whom
Ye may not know, but whom
Allah doth know. Whatever
Ye shall spend in the Cause
Of Allah, shall be repaid
Unto you, and ye shall not
Be treated unjustly.

٦٠- وَاَعِدُّوْا لَهُمْ مَّا اسْتَطَعْتُمْ مِّنْ قُوَّةٍ
وَمِنْ رِّبَاطِ الْخَيْلِ تُرْهِبُوْنَ بِهِ
عَدُوَّ اللّٰهِ وَعَدُوَّكُمْ
وَاٰخَرِيْنَ مِنْ دُوْنِهِمْ ۚ
لَا تَعْلَمُوْنَهُمْ ۚ اَللّٰهُ يَعْلَمُهُمْ ۚ
وَمَا تُنْفِقُوْا مِنْ شَيْءٍ فِيْ سَبِيْلِ اللّٰهِ
يُوَفَّ اِلَيْكُمْ وَاَنْتُمْ لَا تُظْلَمُوْنَ ۟

61. But if the enemy
Incline towards peace,
Do thou (also) incline
Towards peace, and trust
In Allah: for He is the One
That heareth and knoweth
(All things).

٦١- وَاِنْ جَنَحُوْا لِلسَّلْمِ
فَاجْنَحْ لَهَا
وَتَوَكَّلْ عَلَى اللّٰهِ
اِنَّهُ هُوَ السَّمِيْعُ الْعَلِيْمُ ۟

62. Should they intend
To deceive thee—verily Allah
Sufficeth thee: He it is
That hath strengthened thee
With His aid and
With (the company of)
The Believers;

٦٢- وَاِنْ يُّرِيْدُوْا اَنْ يَّخْدَعُوْكَ
فَاِنَّ حَسْبَكَ اللّٰهُ ۚ
هُوَ الَّذِيْ اَيَّدَكَ بِنَصْرِهِ
وَبِالْمُؤْمِنِيْنَ ۙ

63. And (moreover) He hath put
Affection between their hearts:
Not if thou hadst spent
All that is in the earth,
Couldst thou have produced
That affection, but Allah
Hath done it: for He
Is Exalted in might, Wise.

٦٣- وَاَلَّفَ بَيْنَ قُلُوْبِهِمْ ۚ
لَوْ اَنْفَقْتَ مَا فِي الْاَرْضِ جَمِيْعًا
مَّا اَلَّفْتَ بَيْنَ قُلُوْبِهِمْ وَلٰكِنَّ اللّٰهَ
اَلَّفَ بَيْنَهُمْ ۚ اِنَّهُ عَزِيْزٌ حَكِيْمٌ ۟

64. O Prophet! Sufficient
Unto thee is Allah—
(Unto thee) and unto those
Who follow thee
Among the Believers.

٦٤- يٰاَيُّهَا النَّبِيُّ حَسْبُكَ اللّٰهُ
وَمَنِ اتَّبَعَكَ مِنَ الْمُؤْمِنِيْنَ ۟ ۢ

SECTION 9.

65. O Prophet! rouse the Believers

٦٥- يٰاَيُّهَا النَّبِيُّ حَرِّضِ الْمُؤْمِنِيْنَ عَلَى

To the fight. If there are
Twenty amongst you, patient
And persevering, they will
Vanquish two hundred: if a
                    hundred,
They will vanquish a thousand
Of the Unbelievers: for these
Are a people without
                    understanding.

القِتَالِ ۚ اِنْ يَّكُنْ مِّنْكُمْ عِشْرُوْنَ صَابِرُوْنَ يَغْلِبُوْا مِائَتَيْنِ ۚ وَاِنْ يَّكُنْ مِّنْكُمْ مِّائَةٌ يَّغْلِبُوْٓا اَلْفًا مِّنَ الَّذِيْنَ كَفَرُوْا بِاَنَّهُمْ قَوْمٌ لَّا يَفْقَهُوْنَ ۟

66. For the present, Allah
Hath lightened your (task),
For He knoweth that there is
A weak spot in you:
But (even so), if there are
A hundred of you, patient
And persevering, they will
Vanquish two hundred, and if
A thousand, they will vanquish
Two thousand, with the leave
Of Allah: for Allah is with those
Who patiently persevere.

٦٦ ـ اَلْـٰٔنَ خَفَّفَ اللّٰهُ عَنْكُمْ وَعَلِمَ اَنَّ فِيْكُمْ ضَعْفًا ۚ فَاِنْ يَّكُنْ مِّنْكُمْ مِّائَةٌ صَابِرَةٌ يَّغْلِبُوْا مِائَتَيْنِ ۚ وَاِنْ يَّكُنْ مِّنْكُمْ اَلْفٌ يَّغْلِبُوْٓا اَلْفَيْنِ بِاِذْنِ اللّٰهِ ۚ وَاللّٰهُ مَعَ الصّٰبِرِيْنَ ۟

67. It is not fitting
For a Prophet
That he should have
Prisoners of war until
He hath thoroughly subdued
The land. Ye look
For the temporal goods
Of this world; but Allah
Looketh to the Hereafter:
And Allah is Exalted in might,
                    Wise.

٦٧ ـ مَا كَانَ لِنَبِيٍّ اَنْ يَّكُوْنَ لَهٗٓ اَسْرٰى حَتّٰى يُثْخِنَ فِى الْاَرْضِ ۚ تُرِيْدُوْنَ عَرَضَ الدُّنْيَا ۖ وَاللّٰهُ يُرِيْدُ الْاٰخِرَةَ ۚ وَاللّٰهُ عَزِيْزٌ حَكِيْمٌ ۟

68. Had it not been for
A previous ordainment
From Allah, a severe penalty
Would have reached you
For the (ransom) that ye took.

٦٨ ـ لَوْلَا كِتَابٌ مِّنَ اللّٰهِ سَبَقَ لَمَسَّكُمْ فِيْمَآ اَخَذْتُمْ عَذَابٌ عَظِيْمٌ ۟

69. But (now) enjoy   what ye took
In war, lawful and good:
But fear Allah: for Allah
Is Oft-Forgiving, Most Merciful.
        SECTION 10.

٦٩ ـ فَكُلُوْا مِمَّا غَنِمْتُمْ حَلَالًا طَيِّبًا ۚ وَّاتَّقُوا اللّٰهَ ۚ اِنَّ اللّٰهَ غَفُوْرٌ رَّحِيْمٌ ۟

70. ⊕ Prophet! say to those

٧٠ ـ يٰٓاَيُّهَا النَّبِيُّ قُلْ لِّمَنْ فِيْٓ اَيْدِيْكُمْ مِّنَ

Who are captives in your hands:
"If Allah findeth any good[1237]
In your hearts, He will
Give you something better
Than what has been taken
From you, and He will
Forgive you: for Allah
Is Oft-Forgiving, Most Merciful."

الْأَسْرَى
إِنْ يَعْلَمِ اللهُ فِى قُلُوبِكُمْ خَيْرًا
يُّؤْتِكُمْ خَيْرًا مِّمَّا أُخِذَ مِنْكُمْ
وَيَغْفِرْ لَكُمْ ۗ وَاللهُ غَفُورٌ رَّحِيمٌ ۟

71. But if they have
Treacherous designs against thee,
(O Messenger!), they have already
Been in treason against Allah,
And so hath He given
(Thee) power over them.
And Allah is He who hath
(Full) knowledge and wisdom.

٧١- وَإِنْ يُّرِيدُوا خِيَانَتَكَ
فَقَدْ خَانُوا اللهَ مِنْ قَبْلُ
فَأَمْكَنَ مِنْهُمْ ۗ
وَاللهُ عَلِيمٌ حَكِيمٌ ۟

72. Those who believed,
And adopted exile,
And fought for the Faith,
With their property
And their persons,
In the cause of Allah,
As well as those
Who gave (them) asylum
And aid—these are (all)
Friends and protectors,
One of another.
As to those who believed
But came not into exile;
Ye owe no duty
Of protection to them
Until they come into exile;
But if they seek
Your aid in religion,
It is your duty
To help them,
Except against a people
With whom ye have
A treaty of mutual alliance.
And (remember) Allah
Seeth all that ye do.

٧٢- إِنَّ الَّذِينَ آمَنُوا وَهَاجَرُوا
وَجَاهَدُوا بِأَمْوَالِهِمْ
وَأَنْفُسِهِمْ فِى سَبِيلِ اللهِ
وَالَّذِينَ آوَوْا وَّنَصَرُوا
أُولَٰئِكَ بَعْضُهُمْ أَوْلِيَاءُ بَعْضٍ ۗ
وَالَّذِينَ آمَنُوا وَلَمْ يُهَاجِرُوا
مَا لَكُمْ مِنْ وَّلَايَتِهِمْ مِنْ شَىْءٍ
حَتَّى يُهَاجِرُوا ۗ
وَإِنِ اسْتَنْصَرُوكُمْ فِى الدِّينِ
فَعَلَيْكُمُ النَّصْرُ
إِلَّا عَلَى قَوْمٍ بَيْنَكُمْ
وَبَيْنَهُمْ مِّيثَاقٌ ۗ
وَاللهُ بِمَا تَعْمَلُونَ بَصِيرٌ ۟

73. The Unbelievers are
Protectors, one of another:
Unless ye do this,

٧٣- وَالَّذِينَ كَفَرُوا بَعْضُهُمْ أَوْلِيَاءُ
بَعْضٍ ۚ إِلَّا تَفْعَلُوهُ

(Protect each other),
There would be
Tumult and oppression
On earth, and great mischief.

تَكُنْ فِتْنَةٌ فِى الْأَرْضِ وَفَسَادٌ كَبِيْرٌ

74. Those who believe,
And adopt exile,
And fight for the Faith,
In the cause of Allah,
As well as those
Who give (them) asylum
And aid — these are (all)
In very truth the Believers:
For them is the forgiveness
Of sins and a provision
Most generous.

٧٤ ـ وَالَّذِيْنَ اٰمَنُوْا وَهَاجَرُوْا
وَجَاهَدُوْا فِىْ سَبِيْلِ اللّٰهِ
وَالَّذِيْنَ اٰوَوْا وَّنَصَرُوْۤا
أُولٰٓئِكَ هُمُ الْمُؤْمِنُوْنَ حَقًّا
لَهُمْ مَّغْفِرَةٌ
وَّرِزْقٌ كَرِيْمٌ

75. And those who
Accept Faith subsequently,
And adopt exile,
And fight for the Faith
In your company —
They are of you.
But kindred by blood
Have prior rights
Against each other
In the Book of Allah.
Verily Allah is well-acquainted
With all things

٧٥ ـ وَالَّذِيْنَ اٰمَنُوْا مِنْ بَعْدُ وَهَاجَرُوْا
وَجَاهَدُوْا مَعَكُمْ
فَأُولٰٓئِكَ مِنْكُمْ وَأُولُوا الْأَرْحَامِ
بَعْضُهُمْ أَوْلٰى بِبَعْضٍ
فِىْ كِتٰبِ اللّٰهِ
إِنَّ اللّٰهَ بِكُلِّ شَىْءٍ عَلِيْمٌ

INTRODUCTION TO SŪRA IX: — 129 Verses

Tauba (Repentance) or *Barāat* (Immunity)

Logically this Sūra follows up the argument of the last Sūra (VIII) and indeed may be considered a part of it, although chronologically the two are separated by an interval of seven years.

We saw that Sūra VIII, dealt with the larger questions arising at the outset of the life of a new Ummat or organised nation: questions of defence under attack, distribution of war acquisitions after victory, the virtues needed for concerted action, and clemency and consideration for one's own and for enemies in the hour of victory. We pass on in this Sūra to deal with the question: what is to be done if the enemy breaks faith and is guilty of treachery? No nation can go on with a treaty if the other party violates it at will; but it is laid down that a period of four months should be allowed by way of notice after denunciation of the treaty; that due protection should be accorded in the intervening period; that there would always be open the door to repentance and reunion with the people of God; and that if all these fail, and war must be undertaken, it must be pushed with utmost vigour.

These are the general principles deducible from the Sūra. The immediate occasion for their promulgation may be considered in connection with the chronological place of the Sūra.

Chronologically, verses 1-29 were a notable declaration of State policy promulgated about the month of Shawwāl, A.H. 9, and read out by Hadhrat 'Alī at the Pilgrimage two months later in order to give the policy the widest publicity possible. The remainder of the Sūra, verses 30-129, was revealed a little earlier, say about the month of Ramadhān, A.H. 9 and sums up the lessons of the Apostle's Tabūk expedition in the summer of A.H. 9 (say October 630).

Tabūk is a place near the frontier of Arabia, quite close to what was then Byzantine territory in the Province of Syria (which includes Palestine). It is on the Hijāz Railway, about 350 miles north-west of Medina, and 150 miles south of Ma'ān. It had a fort and a spring of sweet water. In consequence of strong and persistent rumours that the Byzantines (Romans) were preparing to invade Arabia and that the Byzantine Emperor himself had arrived near the frontier for the purpose, the Apostle collected as large a force as he could, and marched to Tabūk. The Byzantine invasion did not come off. But the Apostle took the opportunity of consolidating the Muslim position in that direction and making treaties of alliance with certain Christian and Jewish tribes near the Gulf of 'Aqaba. On his return to Medina he considered the situation. During his absence the Hypocrites had played, as always, a double game, and the policy hitherto followed, of free access to the sacred centre of Islam, to Muslims and Pagans alike, was now altered, as it had been abused by the enemies of Islam.

This is the only Sūra to which the usual formula of *Bismillāh* is not prefixed. It was among the last of the Sūras revealed, and though the Apostle had directed that it should follow Sūra VIII, it was not clear whether it was to form a separate Sūra or only a part of Sūra VIII. It is now treated as a separate Sūra, but the *Bismillāh* is not prefixed to it, as there is no warrant for supposing that the Apostle used the *Bismillāh* before it in his recitation of the Qur-ān. The Sūra is known under many names: the two most commonly used are: (1) *Tauba* (Repentance), with reference to ix. 104 and (2) *Barāat* (Immunity), the opening words of the Sūra.

Al Tawbah (The Repentance) or
    Barā'ah (The Disavowel)

بِسْمِ اللَّهِ الرَّحْمَٰنِ الرَّحِيمِ

1. A (declaration) of immunity
From Allah and His Messenger,
To those of the Pagans
With whom ye have contracted
Mutual alliances—

2. Go ye, then, for four months,
Backwards and forwards,
(As ye will), throughout the land,
But know ye that ye cannot
Frustrate Allah (by your falsehood)
But that Allah will cover
With shame those who reject Him.

3. And an announcement from Allah
And His Messenger, to the people
(Assembled) on the day
Of the Great Pilgrimage—
That Allah and His Messenger
Dissolve (treaty) obligations
With the Pagans.
If, then, ye repent,
It were best for you;
But if ye turn away,
Know ye that ye cannot
Frustrate Allah. And proclaim
A grievous penalty to those
Who reject Faith.

4. (But the treaties are) not
            dissolved
With those Pagans with whom
Ye have entered into alliance
And who have not subsequently
Failed you in aught,
Nor aided anyone against you.
So fulfil your engagements
With them to the end
Of their term: for Allah
Loveth the righteous.

5. But when the forbidden
            months
Are past, then fight and slay

١- بَرَآءَةٌ مِّنَ اللَّهِ وَرَسُوْلِهِ إِلَى الَّذِيْنَ عَاهَدْتُّمْ مِّنَ الْمُشْرِكِيْنَ ۗ

٢- فَسِيْحُوْا فِي الْأَرْضِ أَرْبَعَةَ أَشْهُرٍ وَّاعْلَمُوْا أَنَّكُمْ غَيْرُ مُعْجِزِي اللَّهِ ۙ وَأَنَّ اللَّهَ مُخْزِي الْكَافِرِيْنَ ○

٣- وَأَذَانٌ مِّنَ اللَّهِ وَرَسُوْلِهِ إِلَى النَّاسِ يَوْمَ الْحَجِّ الْأَكْبَرِ أَنَّ اللَّهَ بَرِيْٓءٌ مِّنَ الْمُشْرِكِيْنَ ۙ وَرَسُوْلُهُ ۚ فَإِنْ تُبْتُمْ فَهُوَ خَيْرٌ لَّكُمْ ۚ وَإِنْ تَوَلَّيْتُمْ فَاعْلَمُوْا أَنَّكُمْ غَيْرُ مُعْجِزِي اللَّهِ ۗ وَبَشِّرِ الَّذِيْنَ كَفَرُوْا بِعَذَابٍ أَلِيْمٍ ۙ

٤- إِلَّا الَّذِيْنَ عَاهَدْتُّمْ مِّنَ الْمُشْرِكِيْنَ ثُمَّ لَمْ يَنْقُصُوْكُمْ شَيْئًا وَّلَمْ يُظَاهِرُوْا عَلَيْكُمْ أَحَدًا فَأَتِمُّوْا إِلَيْهِمْ عَهْدَهُمْ إِلَى مُدَّتِهِمْ ۚ إِنَّ اللَّهَ يُحِبُّ الْمُتَّقِيْنَ ○

٥- فَإِذَا انْسَلَخَ الْأَشْهُرُ الْحُرُمُ

The Pagans wherever ye find
them,
And seize them, beleaguer them,
And lie in wait for them
In every stratagem (of war);
But if they repent,
And establish regular prayers
And practise regular charity,
Then open the way for them:
For Allah is Oft-Forgiving,
Most Merciful.

فَاقْتُلُوا الْمُشْرِكِيْنَ حَيْثُ وَجَدْتُّمُوْهُمْ
وَخُذُوْهُمْ وَاحْصُرُوْهُمْ
وَاقْعُدُوْا لَهُمْ كُلَّ مَرْصَدٍ ۚ
فَاِنْ تَابُوْا وَاَقَامُوا الصَّلٰوةَ
وَاٰتَوُا الزَّكٰوةَ فَخَلُّوْا سَبِيْلَهُمْ ۚ
اِنَّ اللّٰهَ غَفُوْرٌ رَّحِيْمٌ ۟

6. If one amongst the Pagans
Ask thee for asylum,
Grant it to him,
So that he may hear the Word
Of Allah; and then escort him
To where he can be secure.
That is because they are
Men without knowledge.

٦ۭ وَاِنْ اَحَدٌ مِّنَ الْمُشْرِكِيْنَ اسْتَجَارَكَ
فَاَجِرْهُ حَتّٰى يَسْمَعَ كَلٰمَ اللّٰهِ
ثُمَّ اَبْلِغْهُ مَاْمَنَهٗ ۚ
ذٰلِكَ بِاَنَّهُمْ قَوْمٌ لَّا يَعْلَمُوْنَ ۟ ؏

SECTION 2.

7. How can there be a league,
Before Allah and His Messenger,
With the Pagans, except those
With whom ye made a treaty
Near the Sacred Mosque?
As long as these stand true
To you, stand ye true to them:
For Allah doth love the righteous.

٧ۭ كَيْفَ يَكُوْنُ لِلْمُشْرِكِيْنَ عَهْدٌ عِنْدَ
اللّٰهِ وَعِنْدَ رَسُوْلِهٖٓ اِلَّا الَّذِيْنَ عَاهَدْتُّمْ
عِنْدَ الْمَسْجِدِ الْحَرَامِ ۚ فَمَا اسْتَقَامُوْا لَكُمْ
فَاسْتَقِيْمُوْا لَهُمْ ۚ اِنَّ اللّٰهَ يُحِبُّ الْمُتَّقِيْنَ ۟

8. How (can there be such a
league),
Seeing that if they get an
advantage
Over you, they respect not
In you the ties either of kinship
Or of covenant? With (fair words
From) their mouths they entice
you,
But their hearts are averse
From you; and most of them
Are rebellious and wicked.

٨ۭ كَيْفَ وَاِنْ يَّظْهَرُوْا عَلَيْكُمْ
لَا يَرْقُبُوْا فِيْكُمْ اِلًّا
وَّلَا ذِمَّةً ۚ يُرْضُوْنَكُمْ بِاَفْوَاهِهِمْ
وَتَاْبٰى قُلُوْبُهُمْ ۚ
وَاَكْثَرُهُمْ فٰسِقُوْنَ ۟

9. The Signs of Allah have they sold
For a miserable price,
And (many) have they hindered
From His Way: evil indeed
Are the deeds they have done.

٩ۭ اِشْتَرَوْا بِاٰيٰتِ اللّٰهِ ثَمَنًا قَلِيْلًا فَصَدُّوْا
عَنْ سَبِيْلِهٖ ۚ اِنَّهُمْ سَآءَ
مَا كَانُوْا يَعْمَلُوْنَ ۟

10. In a Believer they respect not
The ties either of kinship
Or of covenant! It is they
Who have transgressed all
              bounds.

١٠ـ لَا يَرْقُبُوْنَ فِيْ مُؤْمِنٍ إِلًّا وَّلَا ذِمَّةً ۚ
وَأُولٰٓئِكَ هُمُ الْمُعْتَدُوْنَ ۞

11. But (even so), if they repent,
Establish regular prayers,
And practise regular charity—
They are your brethren in Faith:
(Thus) do We explain the Signs
In detail, for those who
           understand.

١١ـ فَإِنْ تَابُوْا وَأَقَامُوا الصَّلٰوةَ
وَأَتَوُا الزَّكٰوةَ فَإِخْوَانُكُمْ فِي الدِّيْنِ ۚ
وَنُفَصِّلُ الْأٰيٰتِ لِقَوْمٍ يَّعْلَمُوْنَ ۞

12. But if they violate their oaths
After their covenant,
And taunt you for your Faith—
Fight ye the chiefs of Unfaith:
For their oaths are nothing to
             them:
That thus they may be restrained.

١٢ـ وَإِنْ نَّكَثُوْا أَيْمَانَهُمْ مِّنْ بَعْدِ عَهْدِهِمْ
وَطَعَنُوْا فِيْ دِيْنِكُمْ
فَقَاتِلُوْا أَئِمَّةَ الْكُفْرِ ۙ
إِنَّهُمْ لَا أَيْمَانَ لَهُمْ لَعَلَّهُمْ يَنْتَهُوْنَ ۞

13. Will ye not fight people
Who violated their oaths,
Plotted to expel the Messenger,
And took the aggressive
By being the first (to assault) you?
Do ye fear them? Nay,
It is Allah Whom ye should
More justly fear, if ye believe!

١٣ـ أَلَا تُقَاتِلُوْنَ قَوْمًا نَّكَثُوْا أَيْمَانَهُمْ
وَهَمُّوْا بِإِخْرَاجِ الرَّسُوْلِ وَهُمْ بَدَءُوْكُمْ
أَوَّلَ مَرَّةٍ ۚ أَتَخْشَوْنَهُمْ ۚ
فَاللّٰهُ أَحَقُّ أَنْ تَخْشَوْهُ إِنْ كُنْتُمْ مُّؤْمِنِيْنَ ۞

14. Fight them, and Allah will
Punish them by your hands,
Cover them with shame,
Help you (to victory) over them,
Heal the breasts of Believers,

١٤ـ قَاتِلُوْهُمْ يُعَذِّبْهُمُ اللّٰهُ بِأَيْدِيْكُمْ
وَيُخْزِهِمْ وَيَنْصُرْكُمْ عَلَيْهِمْ
وَيَشْفِ صُدُوْرَ قَوْمٍ مُّؤْمِنِيْنَ ۙ

15. And still the indignation of their
             hearts.
For Allah will turn (in mercy)
To whom He will; and Allah
Is All-Knowing, All-Wise.

١٥ـ وَيُذْهِبْ غَيْظَ قُلُوْبِهِمْ ۚ
وَيَتُوْبُ اللّٰهُ عَلٰى مَنْ يَّشَاءُ ۚ
وَاللّٰهُ عَلِيْمٌ حَكِيْمٌ ۞

16. Or think ye that ye
Shall be abandoned,
As though Allah did not know
Those among you who strive
With might and main, and take

١٦ـ أَمْ حَسِبْتُمْ أَنْ تُتْرَكُوْا
وَلَمَّا يَعْلَمِ اللّٰهُ الَّذِيْنَ جَاهَدُوْا مِنْكُمْ

None for friends and protectors
Except Allah, His Messenger,
And the (community of) Believers?
But Allah is well-acquainted
With (all) that ye do.

SECTION 3.

17. It is not for such
As join gods with Allah,
To visit or maintain
The mosques of Allah
While they witness
Against their own souls
To infidelity. The works
Of such bear no fruit:
In Fire shall they dwell.

18. The mosques of Allah
Shall be visited and maintained
By such as believe in Allah
And the Last Day, establish
Regular prayers, and practise
Regular charity, and fear
None (at all) except Allah.
It is they who are expected
To be on true guidance.

19. Do ye make the giving
Of drink to pilgrims,
Or the maintenance of
The Sacred Mosque, equal
To (the pious service of) those
Who believe in Allah
And the Last Day, and strive
With might and main
In the cause of Allah?
They are not comparable
In the sight of Allah:
And Allah guides not
Those who do wrong.

20. Those who believe, and suffer
Exile and strive with might
And main, in Allah's cause,
With their goods and their
                  persons,
Have the highest rank
In the sight of Allah:
They are the people
Who will achieve (salvation).

وَلَمْ يَتَّخِذُوا مِنْ دُوْنِ اللّٰهِ وَلَا رَسُوْلِهٖ
وَلَا الْمُؤْمِنِيْنَ وَلِيْجَةً ؕ
وَاللّٰهُ خَبِيْرٌۢ بِمَا تَعْمَلُوْنَ ۟ ۚ ع

١٧- مَا كَانَ لِلْمُشْرِكِيْنَ اَنْ يَّعْمُرُوْا
مَسٰجِدَ اللّٰهِ شٰهِدِيْنَ عَلٰۤى اَنْفُسِهِمْ
بِالْكُفْرِ ؕ اُولٰٓئِكَ حَبِطَتْ اَعْمَالُهُمْ ۚ
وَفِى النَّارِ هُمْ خٰلِدُوْنَ ۟

١٨- اِنَّمَا يَعْمُرُ مَسٰجِدَ اللّٰهِ
مَنْ اٰمَنَ بِاللّٰهِ وَالْيَوْمِ الْاٰخِرِ
وَاَقَامَ الصَّلٰوةَ وَاٰتَى الزَّكٰوةَ
وَلَمْ يَخْشَ اِلَّا اللّٰهَ ۫ فَعَسٰۤى اُولٰٓئِكَ
اَنْ يَّكُوْنُوْا مِنَ الْمُهْتَدِيْنَ ۟

١٩- اَجَعَلْتُمْ سِقَايَةَ الْحَاجِّ
وَعِمَارَةَ الْمَسْجِدِ الْحَرَامِ كَمَنْ اٰمَنَ
بِاللّٰهِ وَالْيَوْمِ الْاٰخِرِ وَجَاهَدَ
فِيْ سَبِيْلِ اللّٰهِ ؕ
لَا يَسْتَوٗنَ عِنْدَ اللّٰهِ ؕ
وَاللّٰهُ لَا يَهْدِى الْقَوْمَ الظّٰلِمِيْنَ ۟ ۘ

٢٠- اَلَّذِيْنَ اٰمَنُوْا وَهَاجَرُوْا وَجَاهَدُوْا فِيْ
سَبِيْلِ اللّٰهِ بِاَمْوَالِهِمْ وَاَنْفُسِهِمْ ۙ
اَعْظَمُ دَرَجَةً عِنْدَ اللّٰهِ ؕ
وَاُولٰٓئِكَ هُمُ الْفَآئِزُوْنَ ۟

1. Their Lord doth give them
Glad tidings of a Mercy
From Himself, of His good
              pleasure,
And of Gardens for them,
Wherein are delights
That endure:

٢١- يُبَشِّرُهُمْ رَبُّهُمْ بِرَحْمَةٍ مِّنْهُ
وَرِضْوَانٍ وَّجَنّٰتٍ لَّهُمْ
فِيْهَا نَعِيْمٌ مُّقِيْمٌ ۙ

2. They will dwell therein
Forever. Verily in Allah's presence
Is a reward, the greatest (of all).

٢٢- خٰلِدِيْنَ فِيْهَاۤ اَبَدًا ۭ
اِنَّ اللّٰهَ عِنْدَهٗۤ اَجْرٌ عَظِيْمٌ ۙ

3. O ye who believe! Take not
For protectors your fathers
And your brothers if they love
Infidelity above Faith:
If any of you do so,
They do wrong.

٢٣- يٰۤاَيُّهَا الَّذِيْنَ اٰمَنُوْا لَا تَتَّخِذُوْۤا اٰبَآءَكُمْ
وَاِخْوَانَكُمْ اَوْلِيَآءَ اِنِ اسْتَحَبُّوا الْكُفْرَ عَلَى
الْاِيْمَانِ ۭ وَمَنْ يَّتَوَلَّهُمْ مِّنْكُمْ فَاُولٰٓئِكَ
هُمُ الظّٰلِمُوْنَ ۩

4. Say: If it be that your fathers,
Your sons, your brothers,
Your mates, or your kindred;
The wealth that ye have gained;
The commerce in which ye fear
A decline; or the dwellings
In which ye delight—
Are dearer to you than Allah,
Or His Messenger, or the striving
In His cause—then wait
Until Allah brings about
His Decision: and Allah
Guides not the rebellious.

٢٤- قُلْ اِنْ كَانَ اٰبَآؤُكُمْ وَاَبْنَآؤُكُمْ وَ
اِخْوَانُكُمْ وَاَزْوَاجُكُمْ وَعَشِيْرَتُكُمْ
وَاَمْوَالُ ۨاقْتَرَفْتُمُوْهَا وَتِجَارَةٌ تَخْشَوْنَ
كَسَادَهَا وَمَسٰكِنُ تَرْضَوْنَهَاۤ اَحَبَّ اِلَيْكُمْ
مِّنَ اللّٰهِ وَرَسُوْلِهٖ وَجِهَادٍ فِيْ سَبِيْلِهٖ
فَتَرَبَّصُوْا حَتّٰى يَاْتِيَ اللّٰهُ بِاَمْرِهٖ ۭ وَاللّٰهُ
لَا يَهْدِى الْقَوْمَ الْفٰسِقِيْنَ ۩

SECTION 4.

5. Assuredly Allah did help you
In many battlefields
And on the day of Ḥunayn:
Behold! your great numbers
Elated you, but they availed
You naught: the land,
For all that it is wide,
Did constrain you, and ye
Turned back in retreat.

٢٥- لَقَدْ نَصَرَكُمُ اللّٰهُ فِيْ مَوَاطِنَ كَثِيْرَةٍ ۙ
وَّيَوْمَ حُنَيْنٍ ۙ اِذْ اَعْجَبَتْكُمْ كَثْرَتُكُمْ
فَلَمْ تُغْنِ عَنْكُمْ شَيْئًا
وَّضَاقَتْ عَلَيْكُمُ الْاَرْضُ بِمَا رَحُبَتْ
ثُمَّ وَلَّيْتُمْ مُّدْبِرِيْنَ ۙ

6. But Allah did pour His calm
On the Messenger and on the
              Believers,
And sent down forces which ye
Saw not: He punished

٢٦- ثُمَّ اَنْزَلَ اللّٰهُ سَكِيْنَتَهٗ عَلٰى رَسُوْلِهٖ
وَعَلَى الْمُؤْمِنِيْنَ وَاَنْزَلَ جُنُوْدًا لَّمْ
تَرَوْهَا ۚ وَعَذَّبَ الَّذِيْنَ كَفَرُوْا

The Unbelievers: thus doth He
Reward those without Faith.

وَذٰلِكَ جَزَاءُ الْكٰفِرِيْنَ ۟

27. Again will Allah, after this,
Turn (in mercy) to whom
He will: for Allah
Is Oft-Forgiving, Most Merciful.

٢٧- ثُمَّ يَتُوْبُ اللّٰهُ مِنْ بَعْدِ ذٰلِكَ عَلٰى
مَنْ يَّشَاءُ ۗ وَاللّٰهُ غَفُوْرٌ رَّحِيْمٌ ۟

28. O ye who believe! Truly
The Pagans are unclean;
So let them not,
After this year of theirs,
Approach the Sacred Mosque.
And if ye fear poverty,
Soon will Allah enrich you,
If He wills, out of His bounty,
For Allah is All-Knowing,
　　　　　　All-Wise.

٢٨- يٰۤاَيُّهَا الَّذِيْنَ اٰمَنُوْۤا اِنَّمَا الْمُشْرِكُوْنَ
نَجَسٌ فَلَا يَقْرَبُوا
الْمَسْجِدَ الْحَرَامَ بَعْدَ عَامِهِمْ هٰذَا ۚ وَاِنْ
خِفْتُمْ عَيْلَةً فَسَوْفَ يُغْنِيْكُمُ اللّٰهُ مِنْ
فَضْلِهٖۤ اِنْ شَاءَ ۗ اِنَّ اللّٰهَ عَلِيْمٌ حَكِيْمٌ ۟

29. Fight those who believe not
In Allah nor the Last Day,
Nor hold that forbidden
Which hath been forbidden
By Allah and His Messenger,
Nor acknowledge the Religion
Of Truth, from among
The People of the Book,
Until they pay the *Jizyah*
With willing submission,
And feel themselves subdued.

٢٩- قَاتِلُوا الَّذِيْنَ لَا يُؤْمِنُوْنَ بِاللّٰهِ وَلَا
بِالْيَوْمِ الْاٰخِرِ وَلَا يُحَرِّمُوْنَ مَا حَرَّمَ
اللّٰهُ وَرَسُوْلُهٗ وَلَا يَدِيْنُوْنَ دِيْنَ الْحَقِّ
مِنَ الَّذِيْنَ اُوْتُوا الْكِتٰبَ
حَتّٰى يُعْطُوا الْجِزْيَةَ عَنْ يَّدٍ
وَّهُمْ صَاغِرُوْنَ ۟ ۍ

SECTION 5.

30. The Jews call 'Uzayr a son
Of God, and the Christians
Call Christ the Son of God.
That is a saying from their mouth;
(In this) they but imitate
What the Unbelievers of old
Used to say. Allah's curse
Be on them: how they are deluded
Away from the Truth!

٣٠- وَقَالَتِ الْيَهُوْدُ عُزَيْرُ ابْنُ اللّٰهِ
وَقَالَتِ النَّصٰرَى الْمَسِيْحُ ابْنُ اللّٰهِ ۗ
ذٰلِكَ قَوْلُهُمْ بِاَفْوَاهِهِمْ ۚ
يُضَاهِئُوْنَ قَوْلَ الَّذِيْنَ كَفَرُوْا مِنْ قَبْلُ ۗ
قَاتَلَهُمُ اللّٰهُ ۗ اَنّٰى يُؤْفَكُوْنَ ۟

31. They take their priests
And their anchorites to be
Their lords in derogation of
　　　　　　Allah,
And (they take as their Lord)
Christ, the son of Mary;
Yet they were commanded
To worship but One God:

٣١- اِتَّخَذُوْۤا اَحْبَارَهُمْ وَرُهْبَانَهُمْ
اَرْبَابًا مِّنْ دُوْنِ اللّٰهِ
وَالْمَسِيْحَ ابْنَ مَرْيَمَ ۚ
وَمَاۤ اُمِرُوْۤا اِلَّا لِيَعْبُدُوْۤا اِلٰهًا وَّاحِدًا ۚ

There is no god but He.
Praise and glory to Him:
(Far is He) from having
The partners they associate
(With Him).

لَاۤ اِلٰهَ اِلَّا هُوَ ۚ
سُبْحٰنَهٗ عَمَّا يُشْرِكُوْنَ ۞

32. Fain would they extinguish
Allah's Light with their mouths,
But Allah will not allow
But that His Light should be
Perfected, even though the
                              Unbelievers
May detest (it).

٣٢۔ يُرِيْدُوْنَ اَنْ يُّطْفِـُٔوْا نُوْرَ اللّٰهِ
بِاَفْوَاهِهِمْ
وَيَاۡبَى اللّٰهُ اِلَّاۤ اَنْ يُّتِمَّ نُوْرَهٗ
وَلَوْ كَرِهَ الْكٰفِرُوْنَ ۞

33. It is He Who hath sent
His Messenger with Guidance
And the Religion of Truth,
To proclaim it
Over all religion,
Even though the Pagans
May detest (it).

٣٣۔ هُوَ الَّذِيۤ اَرْسَلَ رَسُوْلَهٗ بِالْهُدٰى
وَدِيْنِ الْحَقِّ
لِيُظْهِرَهٗ عَلَى الدِّيْنِ كُلِّهٖ ۙ
وَلَوْ كَرِهَ الْمُشْرِكُوْنَ ۞

34. O ye who believe! There are
Indeed many among the priests
And anchorites, who in
                              falsehood
Devour the substance of men
And hinder (them) from the Way
Of Allah. And there are those
Who bury gold and silver
And spend it not in the Way
Of Allah! announce unto them
A most grievous penalty—

٣٤۔ يٰۤاَيُّهَا الَّذِيْنَ اٰمَنُوْۤا اِنَّ كَثِيْرًا مِّنَ
الْاَحْبَارِ وَالرُّهْبَانِ لَيَاۡكُلُوْنَ اَمْوَالَ النَّاسِ
بِالْبَاطِلِ وَيَصُدُّوْنَ عَنْ سَبِيْلِ اللّٰهِ ۗ وَ
الَّذِيْنَ يَكْنِزُوْنَ الذَّهَبَ وَالْفِضَّةَ وَلَا يُنْفِقُوْنَهَا
فِيْ سَبِيْلِ اللّٰهِ ۙ فَبَشِّرْهُمْ بِعَذَابٍ اَلِيْمٍ ۞

35. On the Day when heat
Will be produced out of
That (wealth) in the fire
Of Hell, and with it will be
Branded their foreheads,
Their flanks, and their backs—
"This is the (treasure) which ye
Buried for yourselves: taste ye,
Then, the (treasures) ye buried!"

٣٥۔ يَّوْمَ يُحْمٰى عَلَيْهَا فِيْ نَارِ جَهَنَّمَ
فَتُكْوٰى بِهَا جِبَاهُهُمْ وَجُنُوْبُهُمْ وَ
ظُهُوْرُهُمْ ۖ
هٰذَا مَا كَنَزْتُمْ لِاَنْفُسِكُمْ
فَذُوْقُوْا مَا كُنْتُمْ تَكْنِزُوْنَ ۞

36. The number of months
In the sight of Allah
Is twelve (in a year)—
So ordained by Him

٣٦۔ اِنَّ عِدَّةَ الشُّهُوْرِ عِنْدَ اللّٰهِ اثْنَا عَشَرَ
شَهْرًا فِيْ كِتٰبِ اللّٰهِ يَوْمَ خَلَقَ السَّمٰوٰتِ

The day He created
The heavens and the earth;
Of them four are sacred:
That is the straight usage.
So wrong not yourselves
Therein, and fight the Pagans
All together as they
Fight you all together.
But know that Allah
Is with those who restrain
Themselves.

وَالْأَرْضِ مِنْهَآ أَرْبَعَةٌ حُرُمٌ
ذٰلِكَ الدِّيْنُ الْقَيِّمُ فَلَا تَظْلِمُوْا فِيْهِنَّ
أَنْفُسَكُمْ وَقَاتِلُوا الْمُشْرِكِيْنَ
كَآفَّةً كَمَا يُقَاتِلُوْنَكُمْ كَآفَّةً
وَاعْلَمُوْا أَنَّ اللّٰهَ
مَعَ الْمُتَّقِيْنَ ۟

37. Verily the transposing
(Of a prohibited month)
Is an addition to Unbelief:
The Unbelievers are led
To wrong thereby: for they make
It lawful one year,
And forbidden another year,
In order to adjust the number
Of months forbidden by Allah
And make such forbidden ones
Lawful. The evil of their course
Seems pleasing to them.
But Allah guideth not
Those who reject Faith.

٣٧۔ اِنَّمَا النَّسِيْٓءُ زِيَادَةٌ فِي الْكُفْرِ
يُضَلُّ بِهِ الَّذِيْنَ كَفَرُوْا
يُحِلُّوْنَهُ عَامًا وَّيُحَرِّمُوْنَهُ عَامًا
لِّيُوَاطِئُوْا عِدَّةَ مَا حَرَّمَ اللّٰهُ
فَيُحِلُّوْا مَا حَرَّمَ اللّٰهُ ۚ
زُيِّنَ لَهُمْ سُوْٓءُ أَعْمَالِهِمْ ۗ
وَاللّٰهُ لَا يَهْدِى الْقَوْمَ الْكٰفِرِيْنَ ۟

SECTION 6.

38. O ye who believe! what
Is the matter with you,
That, when ye are asked
To go forth in the Cause of Allah,
Ye cling heavily to the earth?
Do ye prefer the life
Of this world to the Hereafter?
But little is the comfort
Of this life, as compared
With the Hereafter.

٣٨۔ يٰٓأَيُّهَا الَّذِيْنَ اٰمَنُوْا مَا لَكُمْ
اِذَا قِيْلَ لَكُمُ انْفِرُوْا فِيْ سَبِيْلِ اللّٰهِ
اثَّاقَلْتُمْ اِلَى الْأَرْضِ ۗ أَرَضِيْتُمْ بِالْحَيٰوةِ الدُّنْيَا
مِنَ الْاٰخِرَةِ ۚ فَمَا مَتَاعُ الْحَيٰوةِ الدُّنْيَا فِي
الْاٰخِرَةِ اِلَّا قَلِيْلٌ ۟

39. Unless ye go forth,
He will punish you
With a grievous penalty,
And put others in your place;
But Him ye would not harm
In the least. For Allah
Hath power over all things.

٣٩۔ اِلَّا تَنْفِرُوْا يُعَذِّبْكُمْ عَذَابًا اَلِيْمًا ۙ
وَّيَسْتَبْدِلْ قَوْمًا غَيْرَكُمْ
وَلَا تَضُرُّوْهُ شَيْئًا ۗ
وَاللّٰهُ عَلٰى كُلِّ شَيْءٍ قَدِيْرٌ ۟

0. If ye help not (your Leader),
   (It is no matter): for Allah
   Did indeed help him,
   When the Unbelievers
   Drove him out: he had
   No more than one companion:
   The two were in the Cave,
   And he said to his companion,
   "Have no fear for Allah
   Is with us": then Allah
   Sent down His peace upon him,
   And strengthened him with forces
   Which ye saw not, and
            humbled
   To the depths the word
   Of the Unbelievers.
   But the word of Allah
   Is exalted to the heights:
   For Allah is Exalted in might,
            Wise

٤٠- اِلَّا تَنْصُرُوْهُ فَقَدْ نَصَرَهُ اللّٰهُ
اِذْ اَخْرَجَهُ الَّذِيْنَ كَفَرُوْا
ثَانِيَ اثْنَيْنِ اِذْ هُمَا فِى الْغَارِ
اِذْ يَقُوْلُ لِصَاحِبِهٖ
لَا تَحْزَنْ اِنَّ اللّٰهَ مَعَنَا ۚ
فَاَنْزَلَ اللّٰهُ سَكِيْنَتَهٗ عَلَيْهِ
وَ اَيَّدَهٗ بِجُنُوْدٍ لَّمْ تَرَوْهَا
وَجَعَلَ كَلِمَةَ الَّذِيْنَ كَفَرُوا السُّفْلٰى ۗ
وَكَلِمَةُ اللّٰهِ هِيَ الْعُلْيَا ۗ
وَاللّٰهُ عَزِيْزٌ حَكِيْمٌ ۞

41. Go ye forth, (whether
             equipped)
    Lightly or heavily, and strive
    And struggle, with your goods
    And your persons, in the Cause
    Of Allah. That is best
    For you, if ye (but) knew.

٤١- اِنْفِرُوْا خِفَافًا وَّثِقَالًا
وَّجَاهِدُوْا بِاَمْوَالِكُمْ وَاَنْفُسِكُمْ فِى سَبِيْلِ
اللّٰهِ ۚ ذٰلِكُمْ خَيْرٌ لَّكُمْ اِنْ كُنْتُمْ تَعْلَمُوْنَ ۞

42. If there had been
    Immediate gain (in sight),
    And the journey easy,
    They would (all) without doubt
    Have followed thee, but
    The distance was long,
    (And weighed) on them.
    They would indeed swear
    By Allah, "If we only could,
    We should certainly
    Have come out with you:"
    They would destroy their
             own souls;
    For Allah doth know
    That they are certainly lying.

٤٢- لَوْ كَانَ عَرَضًا قَرِيْبًا
وَّسَفَرًا قَاصِدًا لَّاتَّبَعُوْكَ
وَلٰكِنْ بَعُدَتْ
عَلَيْهِمُ الشُّقَّةُ ؕ
وَسَيَحْلِفُوْنَ بِاللّٰهِ
لَوِ اسْتَطَعْنَا لَخَرَجْنَا مَعَكُمْ ۚ
يُهْلِكُوْنَ اَنْفُسَهُمْ ۚ
وَاللّٰهُ يَعْلَمُ اِنَّهُمْ لَكٰذِبُوْنَ ۞

SECTION 7.

43. Allah give thee grace!   Why
Didst thou grant them exemption
Until those who told the truth
Were seen by thee in a clear light,
And thou hadst proved the liars?

٤٣۔ عَفَا اللهُ عَنْكَ ۚ
لِمَ اَذِنْتَ لَهُمْ حَتّٰى يَتَبَيَّنَ لَكَ الَّذِيْنَ
صَدَقُوْا وَتَعْلَمَ الْكٰذِبِيْنَ ۟

44. Those who believe in Allah
And the Last Day ask thee
For no exemption from fighting
With their goods and persons.
And Allah knoweth well
Those who do their duty.

٤٤۔ لَا يَسْتَاْذِنُكَ الَّذِيْنَ يُؤْمِنُوْنَ بِاللهِ وَ
يَوْمِ الْاٰخِرِ اَنْ يُّجَاهِدُوْا بِاَمْوَالِهِمْ وَ
اَنْفُسِهِمْ ۗ وَاللهُ عَلِيْمٌۢ بِالْمُتَّقِيْنَ ۟

45. Only those ask thee for exemption
Who believe not in Allah
And the Last Day, and
Whose hearts are in doubt,
So that they are tossed
In their doubts to and fro.

٤٥۔ اِنَّمَا يَسْتَاْذِنُكَ الَّذِيْنَ لَا يُؤْمِنُوْنَ
بِاللهِ وَالْيَوْمِ الْاٰخِرِ وَارْتَابَتْ قُلُوْبُهُمْ
فَهُمْ فِيْ رَيْبِهِمْ يَتَرَدَّدُوْنَ ۟

46. If they had intended
To come out, they would
Certainly have made
Some preparation therefor;
But Allah was averse
To their being sent forth;
So He made them lag behind,
And they were told,
"Sit ye among those
Who sit (inactive)."

٤٦۔ وَلَوْ اَرَادُوا الْخُرُوْجَ
لَاَعَدُّوْا لَهٗ عُدَّةً
وَّلٰكِنْ كَرِهَ اللهُ انْبِعَاثَهُمْ فَثَبَّطَهُمْ
وَقِيْلَ اقْعُدُوْا
مَعَ الْقٰعِدِيْنَ ۟

47. If they had come out
With you, they would not
Have added to your (strength)
But only (made for) disorder,
Hurrying to and fro in your
                              midst
And sowing sedition among you,
And there would have been
Some among you
Who would have listened to them.
But Allah knoweth well
Those who do wrong.

٤٧۔ لَوْ خَرَجُوْا فِيْكُمْ مَّا زَادُوْكُمْ
اِلَّا خَبَالًا
وَّلَاَ اَوْضَعُوْا خِلَالَكُمْ
يَبْغُوْنَكُمُ الْفِتْنَةَ ۚ
وَفِيْكُمْ سَمّٰعُوْنَ لَهُمْ ۗ
وَاللهُ عَلِيْمٌۢ بِالظّٰلِمِيْنَ ۟

48. Indeed they had plotted
Sedition before, and upset
Matters for thee—until

٤٨۔ لَقَدِ ابْتَغَوُا الْفِتْنَةَ مِنْ قَبْلُ وَقَلَّبُوْا
لَكَ الْاُمُوْرَ حَتّٰى جَآءَ الْحَقُّ وَظَهَرَ

The Truth arrived, and the Decree
Of Allah became manifest,
Much to their disgust.

أَمْرُ اللّٰهِ وَهُمْ كٰرِهُوْنَ ۟

49. Among them is (many) a man
Who says: "Grant me exemption
And draw me not
Into trial." Have they not
Fallen into trial already?
And indeed Hell surrounds
The Unbelievers (on all sides).

٤٩- وَمِنْهُمْ مَّنْ يَّقُوْلُ ائْذَنْ لِّيْ وَ
لَا تَفْتِنِّيْ ۗ اَلَا فِى الْفِتْنَةِ سَقَطُوْا ۗ
وَاِنَّ جَهَنَّمَ لَمُحِيْطَةٌ ۢ بِالْكٰفِرِيْنَ ۟

50. If good befalls thee,
It grieves them; but if
A misfortune befalls thee,
They say, "We took indeed
Our precautions beforehand,"
And they turn away rejoicing.

٥٠- اِنْ تُصِبْكَ حَسَنَةٌ تَسُؤْهُمْ ۚ وَاِنْ
تُصِبْكَ مُصِيْبَةٌ
يَّقُوْلُوْا قَدْ اَخَذْنَا اَمْرَنَا مِنْ قَبْلُ
وَيَتَوَلَّوْا وَّهُمْ فَرِحُوْنَ ۟

51. Say: "Nothing will happen to us
Except what Allah has decreed
For us: He is our Protector":
And on Allah let the Believers
Put their trust.

٥١- قُلْ لَّنْ يُّصِيْبَنَآ اِلَّا مَا كَتَبَ اللّٰهُ لَنَا ۚ
هُوَ مَوْلٰىنَا ۚ
وَعَلَى اللّٰهِ فَلْيَتَوَكَّلِ الْمُؤْمِنُوْنَ ۟

52. Say: "Can you expect for us
(Any fate) other than one
Of two glorious things—
(Martyrdom or victory)?
But we can expect for you
Either that Allah will send
His punishment from Himself,
Or by your hands. So wait
(Expectant); we too
Will wait with you."

٥٢- قُلْ هَلْ تَرَبَّصُوْنَ بِنَآ اِلَّا اِحْدَى
الْحُسْنَيَيْنِ ۗ وَنَحْنُ نَتَرَبَّصُ بِكُمْ
اَنْ يُّصِيْبَكُمُ اللّٰهُ بِعَذَابٍ مِّنْ عِنْدِهٖٓ
اَوْ بِاَيْدِيْنَا ۖ فَتَرَبَّصُوْا
اِنَّا مَعَكُمْ مُّتَرَبِّصُوْنَ ۟

53. Say: "Spend (for the Cause)
Willingly or unwillingly:
Not from you will it be
Accepted: for ye are indeed
A people rebellious and wicked."

٥٣- قُلْ اَنْفِقُوْا طَوْعًا اَوْ كَرْهًا
لَّنْ يُّتَقَبَّلَ مِنْكُمْ ۗ
اِنَّكُمْ كُنْتُمْ قَوْمًا فٰسِقِيْنَ ۟

54. The only reasons why
Their contributions are not
Accepted are: that they reject
Allah and His Messenger;
That they come to prayer
Without earnestness; and that

٥٤- وَمَا مَنَعَهُمْ اَنْ تُقْبَلَ مِنْهُمْ
نَفَقٰتُهُمْ اِلَّآ اَنَّهُمْ كَفَرُوْا بِاللّٰهِ وَبِرَسُوْلِهٖ
وَلَا يَأْتُوْنَ الصَّلٰوةَ اِلَّا وَهُمْ كُسَالٰى

They offer contributions
unwillingly.

وَلَا يُنْفِقُوْنَ إِلَّا وَهُمْ كٰرِهُوْنَ ۟

55. Let not their wealth
Nor their (following in) sons
Dazzle thee: in reality
Allah's Plan is to punish them
With these things in this life,
And that their souls may perish
In their (very) denial of Allah.

٥٥- فَلَا تُعْجِبْكَ اَمْوَالُهُمْ وَلَا اَوْلَادُهُمْ ۗ اِنَّمَا
يُرِيْدُ اللّٰهُ لِيُعَذِّبَهُمْ بِهَا فِى الْحَيٰوةِ الدُّنْيَا
وَتَزْهَقَ اَنْفُسُهُمْ وَهُمْ كٰفِرُوْنَ ۟

56. They swear by Allah
That they are indeed
Of you; but they are not
Of you: yet they are afraid
(To appear in their true colours).

٥٦- وَيَحْلِفُوْنَ بِاللّٰهِ اِنَّهُمْ لَمِنْكُمْ ۗ
وَمَا هُمْ مِّنْكُمْ
وَلٰكِنَّهُمْ قَوْمٌ يَّفْرَقُوْنَ ۟

57. If they could find
A place to flee to,
Or caves, or a place
Of concealment, they would
Turn straightway thereto,
With an obstinate rush.

٥٧- لَوْ يَجِدُوْنَ مَلْجَأً اَوْ مَغٰرٰتٍ
اَوْ مُدَّخَلًا لَّوَلَّوْا اِلَيْهِ
وَهُمْ يَجْمَحُوْنَ ۟

58. And among them are men
Who slander thee in the matter
Of (the distribution of) the alms.
If they are given part thereof,
They are pleased, but if not,
Behold! they are indignant!

٥٨- وَمِنْهُمْ مَّنْ يَّلْمِزُكَ فِى الصَّدَقٰتِ ۚ
فَاِنْ اُعْطُوْا مِنْهَا رَضُوْا وَاِنْ لَّمْ يُعْطَوْا
مِنْهَا اِذَا هُمْ يَسْخَطُوْنَ ۟

59. If only they had been content
With what Allah and His
Messenger
Gave them, and had said,
"Sufficient unto us is Allah!
Allah and His Messenger will soon
Give us of His bounty:
To Allah do we turn our hopes!"
(That would have been the right
course).

٥٩- وَلَوْ اَنَّهُمْ رَضُوْا
مَا اٰتٰىهُمُ اللّٰهُ وَرَسُوْلُهُ ۙ
وَقَالُوْا حَسْبُنَا اللّٰهُ
سَيُؤْتِيْنَا اللّٰهُ مِنْ فَضْلِهِ وَرَسُوْلُهُ ٓ ۙ
اِنَّا اِلَى اللّٰهِ رٰغِبُوْنَ ۟ ۞

SECTION 8.

60. Alms are for the poor
And the needy, and those
Employed to administer the
(funds);
For those whose hearts
Have been (recently) reconciled

٦٠- اِنَّمَا الصَّدَقٰتُ لِلْفُقَرَآءِ وَالْمَسٰكِيْنِ
وَالْعٰمِلِيْنَ عَلَيْهَا وَالْمُؤَلَّفَةِ قُلُوْبُهُمْ
وَفِى الرِّقَابِ وَالْغٰرِمِيْنَ

(To the Truth); for those in
bondage
And in debt; in the cause
Of Allah; and for the
wayfarer:
(Thus is it) ordained by Allah,
And Allah is full of knowledge
And wisdom.

وَفِي سَبِيْلِ اللهِ وَابْنِ السَّبِيْلِ
فَرِيْضَةً مِّنَ اللهِ
وَاللهُ عَلِيْمٌ حَكِيْمٌ ۞

61. Among them are men
Who molest the Prophet
And say, "He is (all) ear."
Say, "He listens to what is
Best for you: he believes
In Allah, has faith
In the Believers, and is a Mercy
To those of you who believe."
But those who molest the Prophet
Will have a grievous penalty.

٦١ - وَمِنْهُمُ الَّذِيْنَ يُؤْذُوْنَ النَّبِيَّ
وَيَقُوْلُوْنَ هُوَ اُذُنٌ قُلْ اُذُنُ خَيْرٍ لَّكُمْ
يُؤْمِنُ بِاللهِ وَيُؤْمِنُ لِلْمُؤْمِنِيْنَ وَرَحْمَةٌ
لِّلَّذِيْنَ اٰمَنُوْا مِنْكُمْ وَالَّذِيْنَ يُؤْذُوْنَ
رَسُوْلَ اللهِ لَهُمْ عَذَابٌ اَلِيْمٌ ۞

62. To you they swear by Allah.
In order to please you:
But it is more fitting
That they should please
Allah and His Messenger,
If they are Believers.

٦٢ - يَحْلِفُوْنَ بِاللهِ لَكُمْ لِيُرْضُوْكُمْ
وَاللهُ وَرَسُوْلُهُ اَحَقُّ اَنْ يُّرْضُوْهُ
اِنْ كَانُوْا مُؤْمِنِيْنَ ۞

63. Know they not that for those
Who oppose Allah and His
Messenger,
Is the Fire of Hell?—
Wherein they shall dwell.
That is the supreme disgrace.

٦٣ - اَلَمْ يَعْلَمُوْا اَنَّهُ مَنْ يُّحَادِدِ اللهَ وَ
رَسُوْلَهُ فَاَنَّ لَهُ نَارَ جَهَنَّمَ خَالِدًا فِيْهَا
ذٰلِكَ الْخِزْيُ الْعَظِيْمُ ۞

64. The Hypocrites are afraid
Lest a Sūrah should be sent down
About them, showing them what
Is (really passing) in their hearts.
Say: "Mock ye! But verily
Allah will bring to light all
That ye fear (should be revealed)."

٦٤ - يَحْذَرُ الْمُنٰفِقُوْنَ اَنْ تُنَزَّلَ عَلَيْهِمْ
سُوْرَةٌ تُنَبِّئُهُمْ بِمَا فِيْ قُلُوْبِهِمْ
قُلِ اسْتَهْزِءُوْا اِنَّ اللهَ
مُخْرِجٌ مَّا تَحْذَرُوْنَ ۞

65. If thou dost question them,
They declare (with emphasis):
"We were only talking idly
And in play." Say: "Was it
At Allah, and His Signs,
And His Messenger, that ye
Were mocking?"

٦٥ - وَلَئِنْ سَاَلْتَهُمْ
لَيَقُوْلُنَّ اِنَّمَا كُنَّا نَخُوْضُ وَنَلْعَبُ
قُلْ اَبِاللهِ وَاٰيٰتِهِ وَرَسُوْلِهِ
كُنْتُمْ تَسْتَهْزِءُوْنَ ۞

66. Make ye no excuses:
Ye have rejected Faith
After ye had accepted it.
If We pardon some of you,
We will punish others amongst
you,
For that they are in sin.

SECTION 9.

٦٦ـ لَا تَعْتَذِرُوا قَدْ كَفَرْتُمْ بَعْدَ إِيْمَانِكُمْ
إِنْ نَّعْفُ عَنْ طَآئِفَةٍ مِّنْكُمْ نُعَذِّبْ
طَآئِفَةً بِأَنَّهُمْ كَانُوْا مُجْرِمِيْنَ ۞

67. The Hypocrites, men and women,
(Have an understanding) with
each other:
They enjoin evil, and forbid
What is just, and are close
With their hands. They have
Forgotten Allah; so He
Hath forgotten them. Verily
The Hypocrites are rebellious
And perverse.

٦٧ـ اَلْمُنٰفِقُوْنَ وَالْمُنٰفِقٰتُ بَعْضُهُمْ
مِّنْ بَعْضٍ ۛ يَأْمُرُوْنَ بِالْمُنْكَرِ وَيَنْهَوْنَ
عَنِ الْمَعْرُوْفِ وَيَقْبِضُوْنَ
أَيْدِيَهُمْ ۚ نَسُوا اللّٰهَ فَنَسِيَهُمْ ۗ
إِنَّ الْمُنٰفِقِيْنَ هُمُ الْفٰسِقُوْنَ ۞

68. Allah hath promised the
Hypocrites
Men and women, and the
rejecters,
Of Faith, the fire of Hell:
Therein shall they dwell:
Sufficient is it for them:
For them is the curse of Allah,
And an enduring punishment—

٦٨ـ وَعَدَ اللّٰهُ الْمُنٰفِقِيْنَ وَالْمُنٰفِقٰتِ وَ
الْكُفَّارَ نَارَ جَهَنَّمَ خٰلِدِيْنَ فِيْهَا ۗ
هِيَ حَسْبُهُمْ ۚ وَلَعَنَهُمُ اللّٰهُ ۚ
وَلَهُمْ عَذَابٌ مُّقِيْمٌ ۞

69. As in the case of those
Before you: they were
Mightier than you in power,
And more flourishing in wealth
And children. They had
Their enjoyment of their portion:
And ye have of yours, as did
Those before you; and ye
Indulge in idle talk
As they did. They!—
Their works are fruitless
In this world and in the Hereafter,
And they will lose
(All spiritual good).

٦٩ـ كَالَّذِيْنَ مِنْ قَبْلِكُمْ كَانُوْا أَشَدَّ
مِنْكُمْ قُوَّةً وَّأَكْثَرَ أَمْوَالًا وَّأَوْلَادًا ۗ
فَاسْتَمْتَعُوْا بِخَلَاقِهِمْ فَاسْتَمْتَعْتُمْ
بِخَلَاقِكُمْ كَمَا اسْتَمْتَعَ الَّذِيْنَ مِنْ قَبْلِكُمْ
بِخَلَاقِهِمْ وَخُضْتُمْ كَالَّذِيْ خَاضُوْا ۚ
أُولٰٓئِكَ حَبِطَتْ أَعْمَالُهُمْ فِى الدُّنْيَا
وَالْاٰخِرَةِ ۚ وَأُولٰٓئِكَ هُمُ الْخٰسِرُوْنَ ۞

70. Hath not the story reached them
Of those before them?—
The people of Noah, and 'Ād,
And Thamūd; the people

٧٠ـ اَلَمْ يَأْتِهِمْ نَبَأُ الَّذِيْنَ مِنْ قَبْلِهِمْ
قَوْمِ نُوْحٍ وَّعَادٍ وَّثَمُوْدَ ۛ وَقَوْمِ

Of Abraham, the men
Of Midian, and the Cities
            overthrown.
To them came their messengers
With Clear Signs. It is
Not Allah Who wrongs them,
But they wrong their own souls.

اِبْرٰهِيْمَ وَاَصْحٰبِ مَدْيَنَ وَالْمُؤْتَفِكٰتِ ۚ
اَتَتْهُمْ رُسُلُهُمْ بِالْبَيِّنٰتِ ۚ فَمَا كَانَ اللّٰهُ
لِيَظْلِمَهُمْ وَلٰكِنْ كَانُوْٓا اَنْفُسَهُمْ يَظْلِمُوْنَ ۟

71. The Believers, men
And women, are protectors,
One of another: they enjoin
What is just, and forbid
What is evil: they observe
Regular prayers, practice
Regular charity, and obey
Allah and His Messenger.
On them will Allah pour
His Mercy: for Allah
Is Exalted in power, Wise.

٧١ - وَالْمُؤْمِنُوْنَ وَالْمُؤْمِنٰتُ بَعْضُهُمْ
اَوْلِيَاءُ بَعْضٍ ۚ يَأْمُرُوْنَ بِالْمَعْرُوْفِ
وَيَنْهَوْنَ عَنِ الْمُنْكَرِ
وَيُقِيْمُوْنَ الصَّلٰوةَ وَيُؤْتُوْنَ الزَّكٰوةَ
وَيُطِيْعُوْنَ اللّٰهَ وَرَسُوْلَهٗ ۚ اُولٰٓئِكَ سَيَرْحَمُهُمُ
اللّٰهُ ۗ اِنَّ اللّٰهَ عَزِيْزٌ حَكِيْمٌ ۟

72. Allah hath promised to Believers—
Men and women—Gardens
Under which rivers flow,
To dwell therein,
And beautiful mansions
In Gardens of everlasting bliss.
But the greatest bliss
Is the Good Pleasure of Allah:
That is the supreme felicity.

٧٢ - وَعَدَ اللّٰهُ الْمُؤْمِنِيْنَ وَالْمُؤْمِنٰتِ جَنّٰتٍ
تَجْرِيْ مِنْ تَحْتِهَا الْاَنْهٰرُ خٰلِدِيْنَ فِيْهَا
وَمَسٰكِنَ طَيِّبَةً فِيْ جَنّٰتِ عَدْنٍ ۚ
وَرِضْوَانٌ مِّنَ اللّٰهِ اَكْبَرُ ۚ
ذٰلِكَ هُوَ الْفَوْزُ الْعَظِيْمُ ۟ ۞

SECTION 10.

73. O Prophet! strive hard against
The Unbelievers and the
            Hypocrites,
And be firm against them.
Their abode is Hell—
An evil refuge indeed.

٧٣ - يٰٓاَيُّهَا النَّبِيُّ جَاهِدِ الْكُفَّارَ وَ
الْمُنٰفِقِيْنَ وَاغْلُظْ عَلَيْهِمْ ۚ
وَمَأْوٰىهُمْ جَهَنَّمُ ۚ وَبِئْسَ الْمَصِيْرُ ۟

74. They swear by Allah that they
Said nothing (evil), but indeed
They uttered blasphemy,
And they did it after accepting
Islam; and they meditated
A plot which they were unable
To carry out: this revenge
Of theirs was (their) only return
For the bounty with which
Allah and His Messenger had
            enriched

٧٤ - يَحْلِفُوْنَ بِاللّٰهِ مَا قَالُوْا ۚ
وَلَقَدْ قَالُوْا كَلِمَةَ الْكُفْرِ وَكَفَرُوْا بَعْدَ
اِسْلَامِهِمْ
وَهَمُّوْا بِمَا لَمْ يَنَالُوْا ۚ وَمَا نَقَمُوْٓا اِلَّآ
اَنْ اَغْنٰىهُمُ اللّٰهُ وَرَسُوْلُهٗ مِنْ فَضْلِهٖ ۚ
فَاِنْ يَّتُوْبُوْا يَكُ خَيْرًا لَّهُمْ ۚ

Them! If they repent,
It will be best for them;
But if they turn back
(To their evil ways),
Allah will punish them
With a grievous penalty
In this life and in the Hereafter:
They shall have none on earth
To protect or help them.

75. Amongst them are men
Who made a Covenant with Allah,
That if He bestowed on them
Of His bounty, they would give
(Largely) in charity, and be truly
Amongst those who are righteous.

76. But when He did bestow
Of His bounty, they became
Covetous, and turned back
(From their Covenant), averse
(From its fulfilment).

77. So He hath put as a
consequence
Hypocrisy into their hearts,
(To last) till the Day whereon
They shall meet Him: because
They broke their Covenant
With Allah, and because they
Lied (again and again).

78. Know they not that Allah
Doth know their secret (thoughts)
And their secret counsels,
And that Allah knoweth well
All things unseen?

79. Those who slander such
Of the Believers as give themselves
Freely to (deeds of) charity,
As well as such as can find
Nothing to give except
The fruits of their labour—
And throw ridicule on them—
Allah will throw back
Their ridicule on them:
And they shall have
A grievous penalty.

وَإِن يَتَوَلَّوْا يُعَذِّبْهُمُ اللَّهُ
عَذَابًا أَلِيمًا فِى الدُّنْيَا وَالْآخِرَةِ ۚ
وَمَا لَهُمْ فِى الْأَرْضِ
مِن وَلِيٍّ وَلَا نَصِيرٍ ۝

٧٥- وَمِنْهُم مَّنْ عَاهَدَ اللَّهَ
لَئِنْ آتَانَا مِن فَضْلِهِ لَنَصَّدَّقَنَّ
وَلَنَكُونَنَّ مِنَ الصَّالِحِينَ ۝

٧٦- فَلَمَّا آتَاهُم مِّن فَضْلِهِ
بَخِلُوا بِهِ وَتَوَلَّوْا
وَّهُم مُّعْرِضُونَ ۝

٧٧- فَأَعْقَبَهُمْ نِفَاقًا فِى قُلُوبِهِمْ
إِلَىٰ يَوْمِ يَلْقَوْنَهُ
بِمَا أَخْلَفُوا اللَّهَ مَا وَعَدُوهُ
وَبِمَا كَانُوا يَكْذِبُونَ ۝

٧٨- أَلَمْ يَعْلَمُوا أَنَّ اللَّهَ يَعْلَمُ سِرَّهُمْ
وَنَجْوَاهُمْ
وَأَنَّ اللَّهَ عَلَّامُ الْغُيُوبِ ۝

٧٩- الَّذِينَ يَلْمِزُونَ الْمُطَّوِّعِينَ مِنَ
الْمُؤْمِنِينَ فِى الصَّدَقَاتِ
وَالَّذِينَ لَا يَجِدُونَ إِلَّا جُهْدَهُمْ
فَيَسْخَرُونَ مِنْهُمْ ۖ سَخِرَ اللَّهُ
مِنْهُمْ وَلَهُمْ عَذَابٌ أَلِيمٌ ۝

80. Whether thou ask
For their forgiveness,
Or not, (their sin is unforgivable):
If thou ask seventy times
For their forgiveness, Allah
Will not forgive them:
Because they have rejected
Allah and His Messenger; and
               Allah
Guideth not those
Who are perversely rebellious.

SECTION 11.

81. Those who were left behind
(In the Tabūk expedition)
Rejoiced in their inaction
Behind the back of the Messenger
Of Allah: they hated to strive
And fight, with their goods
And their persons, in the Cause
Of Allah: they said,
"Go not forth in the heat."
Say, "The fire of Hell
Is fiercer in heat." If
Only they could understand!

82. Let them laugh a little:
Much will they weep:
A recompense for the (evil)
That they do.

83. If, then, Allah bring thee back
To any of them, and they ask
Thy permission to come out
(With thee), say: "Never shall ye
Come out with me, nor fight
An enemy with me:
For ye preferred to sit
Inactive on the first occasion:
Then sit ye (now)
With those who lag behind."

84. Nor do thou ever pray
For any of them that dies,
Nor stand at his grave;
For they rejected Allah
And His Messenger, and died
In a state of perverse rebellion.

٨٠- اِسْتَغْفِرْ لَهُمْ
اَوْ لَا تَسْتَغْفِرْ لَهُمْ ۭ
اِنْ تَسْتَغْفِرْ لَهُمْ سَبْعِيْنَ مَرَّةً
فَلَنْ يَّغْفِرَ اللّٰهُ لَهُمْ ۭ
ذٰلِكَ بِاَنَّهُمْ كَفَرُوْا بِاللّٰهِ وَرَسُوْلِهٖ ۭ
وَاللّٰهُ لَا يَهْدِى الْقَوْمَ الْفٰسِقِيْنَ ۞

٨١- فَرِحَ الْمُخَلَّفُوْنَ بِمَقْعَدِهِمْ خِلٰفَ
رَسُوْلِ اللّٰهِ وَكَرِهُوْٓا اَنْ يُّجَاهِدُوْا
بِاَمْوَالِهِمْ وَاَنْفُسِهِمْ فِىْ سَبِيْلِ اللّٰهِ
وَقَالُوْا
لَا تَنْفِرُوْا فِى الْحَرِّ ۭ قُلْ نَارُ جَهَنَّمَ اَشَدُّ
حَرًّا ۭ لَوْ كَانُوْا يَفْقَهُوْنَ ۞

٨٢- فَلْيَضْحَكُوْا قَلِيْلًا وَّلْيَبْكُوْا كَثِيْرًا ۚ
جَزَاۗءً بِمَا كَانُوْا يَكْسِبُوْنَ ۞

٨٣- فَاِنْ رَّجَعَكَ اللّٰهُ اِلٰى طَاۗئِفَةٍ مِّنْهُمْ
فَاسْتَاْذَنُوْكَ لِلْخُرُوْجِ فَقُلْ لَّنْ تَخْرُجُوْا
مَعِيَ اَبَدًا وَّلَنْ تُقَاتِلُوْا مَعِيَ عَدُوًّا ۭ
اِنَّكُمْ رَضِيْتُمْ بِالْقُعُوْدِ اَوَّلَ مَرَّةٍ
فَاقْعُدُوْا مَعَ الْخٰلِفِيْنَ ۞

٨٤- وَلَا تُصَلِّ عَلٰٓى اَحَدٍ مِّنْهُمْ مَّاتَ
اَبَدًا وَّلَا تَقُمْ عَلٰى قَبْرِهٖ ۭ اِنَّهُمْ كَفَرُوْا
بِاللّٰهِ وَرَسُوْلِهٖ وَمَاتُوْا وَهُمْ فٰسِقُوْنَ ۞

85. Nor let their wealth
Nor their (following in) sons
Dazzle thee: Allah's Plan
Is to punish them
With these things in this world,
And that their souls may perish
In their (very) denial of Allah.

٨٥- وَلَا تُعْجِبْكَ أَمْوَالُهُمْ وَأَوْلَادُهُمْ
إِنَّمَا يُرِيدُ اللّٰهُ أَنْ يُّعَذِّبَهُمْ بِهَا فِى الدُّنْيَا
وَتَزْهَقَ أَنْفُسُهُمْ وَهُمْ كٰفِرُوْنَ ۞

86. When a Sūrah comes down,
Enjoining them to believe
In Allah and to strive and fight
Along with His Messenger,
Those with wealth and influence
Among them ask thee
For exemption, and say:
"Leave us (behind): we
Would be with those
Who sit (at home)."

٨٦- وَإِذَآ أُنْزِلَتْ سُوْرَةٌ أَنْ أٰمِنُوْا
بِاللّٰهِ وَجَاهِدُوْا مَعَ رَسُوْلِهِ
اسْتَأْذَنَكَ أُولُوا الطَّوْلِ مِنْهُمْ
وَقَالُوْا ذَرْنَا نَكُنْ مَّعَ الْقٰعِدِيْنَ ۞

87. They prefer to be with
(the women),
Who remain behind (at home):
Their hearts are sealed
And so they understand not.

٨٧- رَضُوْا بِأَنْ يَّكُوْنُوْا مَعَ الْخَوَالِفِ
وَطُبِعَ عَلٰى قُلُوْبِهِمْ فَهُمْ لَا يَفْقَهُوْنَ ۞

88. But the Messenger, and those
Who believe with him,
Strive and fight with their wealth
And their persons: for them
Are (all) good things:
And it is they
Who will prosper.

٨٨- لٰكِنِ الرَّسُوْلُ وَالَّذِيْنَ أٰمَنُوْا
مَعَهُ جَاهَدُوْا بِأَمْوَالِهِمْ وَأَنْفُسِهِمْ
وَأُولٰٓئِكَ لَهُمُ الْخَيْرٰتُ
وَأُولٰٓئِكَ هُمُ الْمُفْلِحُوْنَ ۞

89. Allah hath prepared for them
Gardens under which rivers flow,
To dwell therein:
That is the supreme felicity.

٨٩- أَعَدَّ اللّٰهُ لَهُمْ جَنّٰتٍ تَجْرِيْ مِنْ
تَحْتِهَا الْأَنْهٰرُ خٰلِدِيْنَ فِيْهَا
ذٰلِكَ الْفَوْزُ الْعَظِيْمُ ۞

SECTION 12.

90. And there were, among
The desert Arabs (also),
Men who made excuses
And came to claim exemption;
And those who were false
To Allah and His Messenger
(Merely) sat inactive.
Soon will a grievous penalty
Seize the Unbelievers
Among them.

٩٠- وَجَآءَ الْمُعَذِّرُوْنَ مِنَ الْأَعْرَابِ
لِيُؤْذَنَ لَهُمْ
وَقَعَدَ الَّذِيْنَ كَذَبُوا اللّٰهَ وَرَسُوْلَهُ
سَيُصِيْبُ الَّذِيْنَ كَفَرُوْا مِنْهُمْ
عَذَابٌ أَلِيْمٌ ۞

91. There is no blame
On those who are infirm,
Or ill, or who find
No resources to spend
(On the Cause), if they
Are sincere (in duty) to Allah
And his Messenger:
No ground (of complaint)
Can there be against such
As do right: and Allah
Is Oft-Forgiving, Most Merciful.

٩١- لَيۡسَ عَلَى الضُّعَفَآءِ وَلَا عَلَى الۡمَرۡضٰى وَلَا عَلَى الَّذِيۡنَ لَا يَجِدُوۡنَ مَا يُنۡفِقُوۡنَ حَرَجٌ اِذَا نَصَحُوۡا لِلّٰهِ وَرَسُوۡلِهٖ مَا عَلَى الۡمُحۡسِنِيۡنَ مِنۡ سَبِيۡلٍ وَاللّٰهُ غَفُوۡرٌ رَّحِيۡمٌ ۖ

92. Nor (is there blame)
On those who came to thee
To be provided with mounts,
And when thou saidst,
"I can find no mounts
For you," they turned back,
Their eyes streaming with tears
Of grief that they had
No resources wherewith
To provide the expenses.

٩٢- وَّلَا عَلَى الَّذِيۡنَ اِذَا مَآ اَتَوۡكَ لِتَحۡمِلَهُمۡ قُلۡتَ لَاۤ اَجِدُ مَاۤ اَحۡمِلُكُمۡ عَلَيۡهِ ۖ تَوَلَّوۡا وَّاَعۡيُنُهُمۡ تَفِيۡضُ مِنَ الدَّمۡعِ حَزَنًا اَلَّا يَجِدُوۡا مَا يُنۡفِقُوۡنَ ۞

93. The ground (of complaint)
Is against such as claim
Exemption while they are rich.
They prefer to stay
With the (women) who remain
Behind: Allah hath sealed
Their hearts; so they know not
(What they miss).

٩٣- اِنَّمَا السَّبِيۡلُ عَلَى الَّذِيۡنَ يَسۡتَاۡذِنُوۡنَكَ وَهُمۡ اَغۡنِيَآءُ ۚ رَضُوۡا بِاَنۡ يَّكُوۡنُوۡا مَعَ الۡخَوَالِفِ ۙ وَطَبَعَ اللّٰهُ عَلٰى قُلُوۡبِهِمۡ فَهُمۡ لَا يَعۡلَمُوۡنَ ۞

94. They will present their excuses
To you when ye return
To them. Say thou: "Present
No excuses: we shall not
Believe you: Allah hath already
Informed us of the true state
Of matters concerning you:
It is your actions that Allah
And His Messenger will observe:
In the end will ye
Be brought back to Him
Who knoweth what is hidden
And what is open:
Then will He show you
The truth of all
That ye did."

٩٤- يَعۡتَذِرُوۡنَ اِلَيۡكُمۡ اِذَا رَجَعۡتُمۡ اِلَيۡهِمۡ ۚ قُلۡ لَّا تَعۡتَذِرُوۡا لَنۡ نُّؤۡمِنَ لَكُمۡ قَدۡ نَبَّاَنَا اللّٰهُ مِنۡ اَخۡبَارِكُمۡ وَسَيَرَى اللّٰهُ عَمَلَكُمۡ وَرَسُوۡلُهٗ ثُمَّ تُرَدُّوۡنَ اِلٰى عٰلِمِ الۡغَيۡبِ وَالشَّهَادَةِ فَيُنَبِّئُكُمۡ بِمَا كُنۡتُمۡ تَعۡمَلُوۡنَ ۞

95. They will swear to you by Allah,
When ye return to them,
That ye may leave them alone.
So leave them alone:
For they are an abomination,
And Hell is their dwelling place—
A fitting recompense
For the (evil) that they did.

٩٥ ـ سَيَحْلِفُوْنَ بِاللّٰهِ لَكُمْ اِذَا انْقَلَبْتُمْ
اِلَيْهِمْ لِتُعْرِضُوْا عَنْهُمْ ۖ فَاَعْرِضُوْا عَنْهُمْ ۖ
اِنَّهُمْ رِجْسٌ ۖ وَّمَاْوٰىهُمْ جَهَنَّمُ ۚ
جَزَآءً بِمَا كَانُوْا يَكْسِبُوْنَ ۞

96. They will swear unto you,
That ye may be pleased with them.
But if ye are pleased with them,
Allah is not pleased
With those who disobey.

٩٦ ـ يَحْلِفُوْنَ لَكُمْ لِتَرْضَوْا عَنْهُمْ ۖ فَاِنْ
تَرْضَوْا عَنْهُمْ فَاِنَّ اللّٰهَ لَا يَرْضٰى عَنِ
الْقَوْمِ الْفٰسِقِيْنَ ۞

97. The Arabs of the desert
Are the worst in unbelief
And hypocrisy, and most fitted
To be in ignorance
Of the command which Allah
Hath sent down to His Messenger
But Allah is All-Knowing,
All-Wise.

٩٧ ـ اَلْاَعْرَابُ اَشَدُّ كُفْرًا
وَّنِفَاقًا وَّاَجْدَرُ اَلَّا يَعْلَمُوْا
حُدُوْدَ مَاۤ اَنْزَلَ اللّٰهُ عَلٰى رَسُوْلِهٖ ۗ
وَاللّٰهُ عَلِيْمٌ حَكِيْمٌ ۞

98. Some of the desert Arabs
Look upon their payments
As a fine, and watch
For disasters for you: on them
Be the disaster of Evil:
For Allah is He that heareth
And knoweth (all things).

٩٨ ـ وَمِنَ الْاَعْرَابِ مَنْ يَّتَّخِذُ مَا يُنْفِقُ
مَغْرَمًا وَّيَتَرَبَّصُ بِكُمُ الدَّوَآئِرَ ۚ
عَلَيْهِمْ دَآئِرَةُ السَّوْءِ ۗ
وَاللّٰهُ سَمِيْعٌ عَلِيْمٌ ۞

99. But some of the desert Arabs
Believe in Allah and the Last Day,
And look on their payments
As pious gifts bringing them
Nearer to Allah and obtaining
The prayers of the Messenger.
Aye, indeed they bring them
Nearer (to Him): soon will Allah
Admit them to His Mercy:
For Allah is Oft-Forgiving,
Most Merciful.

٩٩ ـ وَمِنَ الْاَعْرَابِ مَنْ يُّؤْمِنُ بِاللّٰهِ وَ
الْيَوْمِ الْاٰخِرِ وَيَتَّخِذُ مَا يُنْفِقُ
قُرُبٰتٍ عِنْدَ اللّٰهِ وَصَلَوٰتِ الرَّسُوْلِ ۚ
اَلَاۤ اِنَّهَا قُرْبَةٌ لَّهُمْ ۚ سَيُدْخِلُهُمُ اللّٰهُ فِيْ
رَحْمَتِهٖ ۗ اِنَّ اللّٰهَ غَفُوْرٌ رَّحِيْمٌ ۞

SECTION 13.

100. The vanguard (of Islam)—

١٠٠ ـ وَالسّٰبِقُوْنَ الْاَوَّلُوْنَ

The first of those who forsook
(Their homes) and of those
Who gave them aid, and (also)
Those who follow them
In (all) good deeds—
Well-pleased is Allah with them,
As are they with Him:
For them hath He prepared
Gardens under which rivers
flow,
To dwell therein forever:
That is the supreme Felicity.

مِنَ الْمُهَاجِرِينَ وَالْأَنْصَارِ
وَالَّذِينَ اتَّبَعُوهُمْ بِإِحْسَانٍ
رَّضِيَ اللّٰهُ عَنْهُمْ وَرَضُوا عَنْهُ
وَأَعَدَّ لَهُمْ جَنَّاتٍ تَجْرِى تَحْتَهَا الْأَنْهَارُ
خَالِدِينَ فِيهَا أَبَدًا ذٰلِكَ الْفَوْزُ الْعَظِيمُ ۝

101. Certain of the desert Arabs
Round about you are Hypocrites,
As well as (desert Arabs) among
The Madīnah folk: they are
Obstinate in hypocrisy: thou
Knowest them not. We know them:
Twice shall We punish them:
And in addition shall they be
Sent to a grievous Penalty.

١٠١- وَمِمَّنْ حَوْلَكُمْ مِّنَ الْأَعْرَابِ مُنَافِقُونَ
وَمِنْ أَهْلِ الْمَدِينَةِ مَرَدُوا عَلَى النِّفَاقِ
لَا تَعْلَمُهُمْ نَحْنُ نَعْلَمُهُمْ
سَنُعَذِّبُهُمْ مَّرَّتَيْنِ
ثُمَّ يُرَدُّونَ إِلَى عَذَابٍ عَظِيمٍ ۝

102. Others (there are who) have
Acknowledged their wrongdoings:
They have mixed an act
That was good with another
That was evil. Perhaps Allah
Will turn unto them (in mercy):
For Allah is Oft-Forgiving,
Most Merciful.

١٠٢- وَآخَرُونَ اعْتَرَفُوا بِذُنُوبِهِمْ
خَلَطُوا عَمَلًا صَالِحًا وَآخَرَ
سَيِّئًا عَسَى اللّٰهُ أَنْ يَتُوبَ عَلَيْهِمْ
إِنَّ اللّٰهَ غَفُورٌ رَّحِيمٌ ۝

103. Of their goods take alms,
That so thou mightest
Purify and sanctify them;
And pray on their behalf,
Verily thy prayers are a source
Of security for them:
And Allah is One
Who heareth and knoweth.

١٠٣- خُذْ مِنْ أَمْوَالِهِمْ صَدَقَةً
تُطَهِّرُهُمْ وَتُزَكِّيهِمْ بِهَا وَصَلِّ عَلَيْهِمْ
إِنَّ صَلَوٰتَكَ سَكَنٌ لَّهُمْ
وَاللّٰهُ سَمِيعٌ عَلِيمٌ ۝

104. Know they not that Allah
Doth accept repentance from
His votaries and receives
Their gifts of charity, and that
Allah is verily He,
The Oft-Returning, Most
Merciful?

١٠٤- أَلَمْ يَعْلَمُوا أَنَّ اللّٰهَ هُوَ يَقْبَلُ التَّوْبَةَ
عَنْ عِبَادِهِ وَيَأْخُذُ الصَّدَقَاتِ
وَأَنَّ اللّٰهَ هُوَ التَّوَّابُ الرَّحِيمُ ۝

105. And say: "Work
　　　　　(righteousness):
　　Soon will Allah observe your work,
　　And His Messenger, and the
　　　　　　　Believers:
　　Soon will ye be brought back
　　To the Knower of what is
　　Hidden and what is open:
　　Then will He show you
　　The truth of all that ye did."

١٠٥۔ وَقُلِ اعْمَلُوْا فَسَيَرَى اللّٰهُ عَمَلَكُمْ
وَرَسُوْلُهٗ وَالْمُؤْمِنُوْنَ
وَسَتُرَدُّوْنَ اِلٰى عٰلِمِ الْغَيْبِ وَالشَّهَادَةِ
فَيُنَبِّئُكُمْ
بِمَا كُنْتُمْ تَعْمَلُوْنَ ۞

106. There are (yet) others,
　　Held in suspense for the command
　　Of Allah, whether He will
　　Punish them, or turn in mercy
　　To them: and Allah
　　Is All-Knowing, Wise.

١٠٦۔ وَاٰخَرُوْنَ مُرْجَوْنَ لِاَمْرِ اللّٰهِ
اِمَّا يُعَذِّبُهُمْ وَاِمَّا يَتُوْبُ عَلَيْهِمْ
وَاللّٰهُ عَلِيْمٌ حَكِيْمٌ ۞

107. And there are those
　　Who put up a mosque
　　By way of mischief and infidelity—
　　To disunite the Believers—
　　And in preparation for one
　　Who warred against Allah
　　And His Messenger aforetime.
　　They will indeed swear
　　That their intention is nothing
　　But good; but Allah doth declare
　　That they are certainly liars.

١٠٧۔ وَالَّذِيْنَ اتَّخَذُوْا مَسْجِدًا
ضِرَارًا وَّكُفْرًا وَّتَفْرِيْقًا بَيْنَ الْمُؤْمِنِيْنَ
وَاِرْصَادًا لِّمَنْ حَارَبَ اللّٰهَ وَرَسُوْلَهٗ مِنْ
قَبْلُ وَلَيَحْلِفُنَّ اِنْ اَرَدْنَا اِلَّا الْحُسْنٰى
وَاللّٰهُ يَشْهَدُ
اِنَّهُمْ لَكٰذِبُوْنَ ۞

108. Never stand thou forth therein.
　　There is a mosque whose
　　　　　　　foundation
　　Was laid from the first day
　　On piety; it is more worthy
　　Of thy standing forth (for prayer)
　　Therein. In it are men who
　　Love to be purified; and Allah
　　Loveth those who make
　　　　　　themselves pure.

١٠٨۔ لَا تَقُمْ فِيْهِ اَبَدًا
لَمَسْجِدٌ اُسِّسَ عَلَى التَّقْوٰى مِنْ اَوَّلِ
يَوْمٍ اَحَقُّ اَنْ تَقُوْمَ فِيْهِ
فِيْهِ رِجَالٌ يُّحِبُّوْنَ اَنْ يَّتَطَهَّرُوْا
وَاللّٰهُ يُحِبُّ الْمُطَّهِّرِيْنَ ۞

109. Which then is best?—he that
　　Layeth his foundation
　　On piety to Allah
　　And His Good Pleasure?—or he
　　That layeth his foundation
　　On an undermined sand cliff
　　Ready to crumble to pieces?
　　And it doth crumble to pieces

١٠٩۔ اَفَمَنْ اَسَّسَ بُنْيَانَهٗ عَلٰى
تَقْوٰى مِنَ اللّٰهِ وَرِضْوَانٍ
خَيْرٌ اَمْ مَّنْ اَسَّسَ بُنْيَانَهٗ
عَلٰى شَفَا جُرُفٍ هَارٍ

With him, into the fire
Of Hell. And Allah guideth not
People that do wrong.

0. The foundation of those
Who so build is never free
From suspicion and shakiness
In their hearts, until
Their hearts are cut to pieces.
And Allah is All-Knowing, Wise.

SECTION 14.

1. Allah hath purchased of the
Believers
Their persons and their goods;
For theirs (in return)
Is the Garden (of Paradise):
They fight in His Cause,
And slay and are slain:
A promise binding on Him
In Truth, through the Law,
The Gospel, and the Qur'ān:
And who is more faithful
To his Covenant than Allah?
Then rejoice in the bargain
Which ye have concluded:
That is the achievement supreme.

2. Those that turn (to Allah)
In repentance; that serve Him,
And praise Him; that wander
In devotion to the Cause of Allah;
That bow down and prostrate
themselves
In prayer; that enjoin good
And forbid evil; and observe
The limits set by Allah —
(These do rejoice). So proclaim
The glad tidings to the Believers.

13. It is not fitting,
For the Prophet and those
Who believe, that they should
Pray for forgiveness
For Pagans, even though
They be of kin, after it is

Clear to them that they
Are companions of the Fire.

لَهُمْ أَنَّهُمْ أَصْحَابُ الْجَحِيمِ ۝

114. And Abraham prayed
For his father's forgiveness
Only because of a promise
He had made to him.
But when it became clear
To him that he was
An enemy to Allah, he
Dissociated himself from him:
For Abraham was most
Tender-hearted, forbearing.

١١٤- وَمَا كَانَ اسْتِغْفَارُ إِبْرَاهِيمَ لِأَبِيهِ
إِلَّا عَنْ مَوْعِدَةٍ وَعَدَهَا إِيَّاهُ ۚ
فَلَمَّا تَبَيَّنَ لَهُ أَنَّهُ عَدُوٌّ لِلّٰهِ
تَبَرَّأَ مِنْهُ ۚ
إِنَّ إِبْرَاهِيمَ لَأَوَّاهٌ حَلِيمٌ ۝

115. And Allah will not mislead
A people after He hath
Guided them, in order that
He may make clear to them
What to fear (and avoid)—
For Allah hath knowledge
Of all things.

١١٥- وَمَا كَانَ اللّٰهُ لِيُضِلَّ قَوْمًا بَعْدَ إِذْ
هَدَاهُمْ حَتّٰى يُبَيِّنَ لَهُمْ مَا يَتَّقُونَ ۚ
إِنَّ اللّٰهَ بِكُلِّ شَيْءٍ عَلِيمٌ ۝

116. Unto Allah belongeth
The dominion of the heavens
And the earth. He giveth life
And He taketh it. Except for Him
Ye have no protector
Nor helper.

١١٦- إِنَّ اللّٰهَ لَهُ مُلْكُ السَّمَاوَاتِ وَالْأَرْضِ
يُحْيِ وَيُمِيتُ ۚ وَمَا لَكُمْ مِنْ دُونِ اللّٰهِ
مِنْ وَلِيٍّ وَلَا نَصِيرٍ ۝

117. Allah turned with favour
To the Prophet, the Muhājirs,
And the Ansār— who followed
Him in a time of distress,
After that the hearts of a part
Of them had nearly swerved
(From duty); but He turned
To them (also): for He is
Unto them Most Kind,
Most Merciful.

١١٧- لَقَدْ تَابَ اللّٰهُ عَلَى النَّبِيِّ وَالْمُهَاجِرِينَ
وَالْأَنْصَارِ الَّذِينَ اتَّبَعُوهُ فِي سَاعَةِ
الْعُسْرَةِ مِنْ بَعْدِ مَا كَادَ يَزِيغُ قُلُوبُ
فَرِيقٍ مِنْهُمْ ثُمَّ تَابَ عَلَيْهِمْ ۚ
إِنَّهُ بِهِمْ رَءُوفٌ رَحِيمٌ ۝

118. (He turned in mercy also)
To the three who were left
Behind; (they felt guilty)
To such a degree that the earth
Seemed constrained to them,
For all its spaciousness,

١١٨- وَعَلَى الثَّلَاثَةِ الَّذِينَ خُلِّفُوا ۚ
حَتّٰى إِذَا ضَاقَتْ عَلَيْهِمُ الْأَرْضُ
بِمَا رَحُبَتْ وَضَاقَتْ عَلَيْهِمْ أَنْفُسُهُمْ

And their (very) Souls seemed
Straitened to them—
And they perceived that
There is no fleeing from Allah
(And no refuge) but to Himself.
Then He turned to them,
That they might repent:
For Allah is Oft-Returning,
Most Merciful.

SECTION 15.

9. O ye who believe! Fear Allah
And be with those
Who are true (in word and deed).

20. It was not fitting
For the people of Madīnah
And the Bedouin Arabs
Of the neighbourhood, to refuse
To follow Allah's Messenger,
Nor to prefer their own lives
To his: because nothing
Could they suffer or do,
But was reckoned to their credit
As a deed of righteousness—
Whether they suffered thirst,
Or fatigue, or hunger, in the Cause
Of Allah, or trod paths
To raise the ire of the Unbelievers,
Or received any injury
Whatever from an enemy:
For Allah suffereth not
The reward to be lost
Of those who do good—

21. Nor could they spend anything
(For the Cause)—small or great—
Nor cut across a valley,
But the deed is inscribed
To their credit; that Allah
May requite their deed
With the best (possible reward).

22. Nor should the Believers
All go forth together:
If a contingent
From every expedition
Remained behind,

وَظَنُّوٓا اَنْ لَّا مَلْجَاَ مِنَ اللّٰهِ
اِلَّآ اِلَيْهِ ؕ
ثُمَّ تَابَ عَلَيْهِمْ لِيَتُوْبُوْا ؕ
اِنَّ اللّٰهَ هُوَ التَّوَّابُ الرَّحِيْمُ ۟ ۜ

١١٩- يٰٓاَيُّهَا الَّذِيْنَ اٰمَنُوا اتَّقُوا اللّٰهَ
وَكُوْنُوْا مَعَ الصّٰدِقِيْنَ ۟

١٢٠- مَا كَانَ لِاَهْلِ الْمَدِيْنَةِ
وَمَنْ حَوْلَهُمْ مِّنَ الْاَعْرَابِ
اَنْ يَّتَخَلَّفُوْا عَنْ رَّسُوْلِ اللّٰهِ
وَلَا يَرْغَبُوْا بِاَنْفُسِهِمْ عَنْ نَّفْسِهٖ ؕ
ذٰلِكَ بِاَنَّهُمْ لَا يُصِيْبُهُمْ
ظَمَاٌ وَّلَا نَصَبٌ وَّلَا مَخْمَصَةٌ فِيْ سَبِيْلِ
اللّٰهِ وَلَا يَطَئُوْنَ مَوْطِئًا يَّغِيْظُ الْكُفَّارَ
وَلَا يَنَالُوْنَ مِنْ عَدُوٍّ نَّيْلًا
اِلَّا كُتِبَ لَهُمْ بِهٖ عَمَلٌ صَالِحٌ ؕ
اِنَّ اللّٰهَ لَا يُضِيْعُ اَجْرَ الْمُحْسِنِيْنَ ۟

١٢١- وَلَا يُنْفِقُوْنَ نَفَقَةً صَغِيْرَةً وَّلَا
كَبِيْرَةً
وَّلَا يَقْطَعُوْنَ وَادِيًا اِلَّا كُتِبَ لَهُمْ
لِيَجْزِيَهُمُ اللّٰهُ اَحْسَنَ مَا كَانُوْا يَعْمَلُوْنَ۟

١٢٢- وَمَا كَانَ الْمُؤْمِنُوْنَ لِيَنْفِرُوْا كَآفَّةً ؕ
فَلَوْلَا نَفَرَ مِنْ كُلِّ فِرْقَةٍ مِّنْهُمْ طَآئِفَةٌ

They could devote themselves
To studies in religion,
And admonish the people
When they return to them—
That thus they (may learn)
To guard themselves (against evil).

SECTION 16.

123. O ye who believe! Fight
The Unbelievers who gird you
about,
And let them find firmness
In you: and know that Allah
Is with those who fear Him.

124. Whenever there cometh down
A Sūrah, some of them say:
"Which of you has had
His faith increased by it?"
Yea, those who believe—
Their faith is increased,
And they do rejoice.

125. But those in whose hearts
Is a disease—it will add doubt
To their doubt, and they will die
In a state of Unbelief.

126. See they not that they
Are tried every year
Once or twice? Yet they
Turn not in repentance,
And they take no heed.

127. Whenever there cometh down
A Sūrah, they look at each other,
(Saying), "Doth anyone see you?"
Then they turn aside:
Allah hath turned their hearts
(From the light); for they
Are a people that understand not.

128. Now hath come unto you
A Messenger from amongst
Yourselves: it grieves him

١٢٣- يَتَفَقَّهُوْا فِى الدِّيْنِ
وَلِيُنْذِرُوْا قَوْمَهُمْ اِذَا رَجَعُوْا اِلَيْهِمْ
لَعَلَّهُمْ يَحْذَرُوْنَ ۞

١٢٣- يٰاَيُّهَا الَّذِيْنَ اٰمَنُوْا قَاتِلُوا الَّذِيْنَ
يَلُوْنَكُمْ مِّنَ الْكُفَّارِ وَلْيَجِدُوْا فِيْكُمْ غِلْظَةً ۚ
وَاعْلَمُوْا اَنَّ اللّٰهَ مَعَ الْمُتَّقِيْنَ ۞

١٢٤- وَاِذَا مَآ اُنْزِلَتْ سُوْرَةٌ فَمِنْهُمْ مَّنْ
يَّقُوْلُ اَيُّكُمْ زَادَتْهُ هٰذِهٖٓ اِيْمَانًا ۚ
فَاَمَّا الَّذِيْنَ اٰمَنُوْا فَزَادَتْهُمْ اِيْمَانًا
وَّهُمْ يَسْتَبْشِرُوْنَ ۞

١٢٥- وَاَمَّا الَّذِيْنَ فِيْ قُلُوْبِهِمْ مَّرَضٌ فَزَادَتْهُمْ
رِجْسًا اِلٰى رِجْسِهِمْ وَمَاتُوْا وَهُمْ كٰفِرُوْنَ ۞

١٢٦- اَوَلَا يَرَوْنَ اَنَّهُمْ يُفْتَنُوْنَ فِيْ كُلِّ
عَامٍ مَّرَّةً اَوْ مَرَّتَيْنِ ثُمَّ لَا يَتُوْبُوْنَ
وَلَا هُمْ يَذَّكَّرُوْنَ ۞

١٢٧- وَاِذَا مَآ اُنْزِلَتْ سُوْرَةٌ نَّظَرَ بَعْضُهُمْ
اِلٰى بَعْضٍ ۚ هَلْ يَرٰىكُمْ مِّنْ
اَحَدٍ ثُمَّ انْصَرَفُوْا ۚ صَرَفَ اللّٰهُ قُلُوْبَهُمْ
بِاَنَّهُمْ قَوْمٌ لَّا يَفْقَهُوْنَ ۞

١٢٨- لَقَدْ جَآءَكُمْ رَسُوْلٌ مِّنْ

That ye should perish:
Ardently anxious is he
Over you: to the Believers
Is he most kind and merciful.

اَنْفُسِكُمْ عَزِيزٌ عَلَيْهِ مَا عَنِتُّمْ حَرِيصٌ
عَلَيْكُمْ بِالْمُؤْمِنِينَ رَؤُوفٌ رَّحِيمٌ ۝

129. But if they turn away,
Say: "Allah sufficeth me:
There is no god but He:
On Him is my trust
He the Lord of the Throne
(Of Glory) Supreme!"

١٢٩- فَاِنْ تَوَلَّوْا فَقُلْ حَسْبِيَ اللّٰهُ ۖ
لَا اِلٰهَ اِلَّا هُوَ عَلَيْهِ تَوَكَّلْتُ وَهُوَ رَبُّ
الْعَرْشِ الْعَظِيمِ ۝

INTRODUCTION TO SŪRA X: *(Yūnas)* — 109 Verses

Chronologically this Sūra and the five that follow (Sūras xi, xii, xiii, xiv., and xv) are closely connected, and were revealed in the later Meccan period, as the great event of the Hijrat was gradually approaching down the stream of Time. But their chronology has no particular significance.

On the other hand their arrangement in the gradation of Quranic teaching fits in with the subject-matter. S.viii, and S.ix. were mainly concerned with the first questions that arose on the formation of the new and organised Community of Islam in its conflict with those who wished to suppress or destroy it or use force to prevent its growth and the consolidation of its ideals. See Introduction to those Sūras. The present group leads us to the questions that face us when external hostility has been met, and our relations to God have to be considered from a higher standpoint than that of self-preservation. How does revelation work? What is the meaning of divine grace and its withdrawal? How do the Messengers of God deliver their Message? How should we receive it?

All these questions revolve round the revelation of the Qur-ān and each Sūra of this group except the 13th has the abbreviated Letters A. L.,R. attached to it. S. xiii. has the letters A. L. M. R. and we shall discuss this variation when we come to S.xiii.

As shown in Appendix I (Sīpāra 3), the Abbreviated Letters are mystic symbols, about whose meaning there is no authoritative explanation. If the theory advanced in n. 25 to ii. I has any validity, and the present group A. L. R. is cognate to the group A.L.M., we have to consider and form some idea in our minds as to the probable meaning of the variation. We took A. L. M. to be a symbol of those Sūras that deal with the beginning, the middle, and the end of man's spiritual history,— the origin, the present position, and the things to come in the Last Days (eschatology, to use a theological term). We took A. L. to stand as symbols of the first two, and M. of the last. In the present group of Sūras we find hardly any eschatological matter, and therefore we can understand the absence of M, the symbol standing for such matter. In its place comes R, which is phonetically allied to L. L is produced by the impact of the tongue to the front of the palate, and R to the middle of the palate. In many languages the letters L and R are interchangeable; e.g., in Arabic, *al-Raḥmān* becomes *ar-Raḥmān*, and R in imperfect enunciation becomes, L, as in Chinese lallation. If L is a symbol of present-day things looking to the future, we may take R as a symbol of present-day things looking within i.e, into the interior of the organisation of the Ummat. And this symbolism fits in with the subject-matter of the Sūras in question. But no one should be dogmatic in speculation about mystic Symbols.

Let us now consider Sūra x, alone. The central theme is that God's wonderful Creation must not be viewed by us as a creation of material things only, once made and finished with. Most wonderful of all is how He reveals Himself to men through Apostles and Scriptures; how Apostles are rejected by men, and the Message disbelieved until it is too late for repentance; and how, as in the case of Yūnus (Jonah) and his people, even the rejection (when repentance supervenes) does not prevent God's grace and mercy from working, and how for that working is beyond man's comprehension.

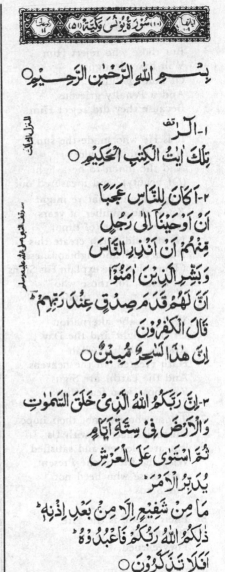

Yunus, (Jonah)

In the name of Allah, Most Gracious,
Most Merciful

1. Alif Lām Rā'
   These are the Ayāt
   Of the Book of Wisdom.

2. Is it a matter
   Of wonderment to men
   That We have sent
   Our inspiration to a man
   From among themselves?—
   That he should warn mankind
   (Of their danger), and give
   The good news to the Believers
   That they have before their Lord
   The lofty rank of Truth.
   (But) say the Unbelievers:
   "This is indeed
   An evident sorcerer!"

3. Verily your Lord is Allah,
   Who created the heavens
   And the earth in six Days,
   Then He established Himself
   On the Throne (of authority),
   Regulating and governing all
            things.
   No intercessor (can plead with
            Him)
   Except after His leave
   (Hath been obtained). This
   Is Allah your Lord; Him therefore
   Serve ye: will yet not
   Receive admonition?

4. To Him will be your return—
   Of all of you. The promise
   Of Allah is true and sure.
   It is He who beginneth
   The process of Creation,
   And repeateth it, that He

May reward with justice
Those who believe
And work righteousness;
But those who reject Him
Will have draughts
Of boiling fluids,
And a Penalty grievous,
Because they did reject Him.

لِيَجْزِىَ الَّذِيْنَ اٰمَنُوْا وَعَمِلُوا الصّٰلِحٰتِ بِالْقِسْطِ ۚ وَالَّذِيْنَ كَفَرُوْا لَهُمْ شَرَابٌ مِّنْ حَمِيْمٍ وَّعَذَابٌ اَلِيْمٌۢ بِمَا كَانُوْا يَكْفُرُوْنَ ۞

5. It is He who made the sun
To be a shining glory
And the moon to be a light
(Of beauty), and measured out
Stages for it; that ye might
Know the number of years
And the count (of time).
Nowise did Allah create this
But in truth and righteousness.
(Thus) doth He explain His Signs
In detail, for those who
understand.

٥- هُوَ الَّذِىْ جَعَلَ الشَّمْسَ ضِيَآءً وَّالْقَمَرَ نُوْرًا وَّقَدَّرَهٗ مَنَازِلَ لِتَعْلَمُوْا عَدَدَ السِّنِيْنَ وَالْحِسَابَ ۚ مَا خَلَقَ اللّٰهُ ذٰلِكَ اِلَّا بِالْحَقِّ ۚ يُفَصِّلُ الْاٰيٰتِ لِقَوْمٍ يَّعْلَمُوْنَ ۞

6. Verily, in the alternation
Of the Night and the Day,
And in all that Allah
Hath created, in the heavens
And the earth, are Signs
For those who fear Him.

٦- اِنَّ فِى اخْتِلَافِ الَّيْلِ وَالنَّهَارِ وَمَا خَلَقَ اللّٰهُ فِى السَّمٰوٰتِ وَالْاَرْضِ لَاٰيٰتٍ لِّقَوْمٍ يَّتَّقُوْنَ ۞

7. Those who rest not their hope
On their meeting with Us,
But are pleased and satisfied
With the life of the Present,
And those who heed not
Our Signs—

٧- اِنَّ الَّذِيْنَ لَا يَرْجُوْنَ لِقَآءَنَا وَرَضُوْا بِالْحَيٰوةِ الدُّنْيَا وَاطْمَاَنُّوْا بِهَا وَالَّذِيْنَ هُمْ عَنْ اٰيٰتِنَا غٰفِلُوْنَ ۞

8. Their abode is the Fire,
Because of the (evil)
They earned.

٨- اُولٰٓئِكَ مَأْوٰىهُمُ النَّارُ بِمَا كَانُوْا يَكْسِبُوْنَ ۞

9. Those who believe,
And work righteousness—
Their Lord will guide them
Because of their Faith:
Beneath them will flow
Rivers in Gardens of Bliss.

٩- اِنَّ الَّذِيْنَ اٰمَنُوْا وَعَمِلُوا الصّٰلِحٰتِ يَهْدِيْهِمْ رَبُّهُمْ بِاِيْمَانِهِمْ ۚ تَجْرِىْ مِنْ تَحْتِهِمُ الْاَنْهٰرُ فِىْ جَنّٰتِ النَّعِيْمِ ۞

10. (This will be) their cry therein:
"Glory to Thee, O Allah!"

١٠- دَعْوٰىهُمْ فِيْهَا سُبْحٰنَكَ اللّٰهُمَّ

And "Peace" will be their
            greeting therein!
And the close of their cry
Will be: "Praise be to Allah,
The Cherisher and Sustainer
Of the Worlds!"

SECTION 2.

11. If Allah were to hasten for men
The ill (they have earned)
As they would fain hasten on
The good—then would
Their respite be settled at once.
But We leave those
Who rest not their hope
On their meeting with Us,
In their trespasses, wandering
In distraction to and fro.

12. When trouble toucheth a man,
He crieth unto Us
(In all postures)—lying down
On his side, or sitting,
Or standing. But when We
Have solved his trouble,
He passeth on his way as if
He had never cried to Us
For a trouble that touched him!
Thus do the deeds of transgressors
Seem fair in their eyes!

13. Generations before you
We destroyed when they
Did wrong: their Messengers
Came to them with Clear Signs,
But they would not believe!
Thus do We requite
Those who sin!

14. Then We made you heirs
In the land after them,
To see how ye would behave!

15. But when Our Clear Signs
Are rehearsed unto them,
Those who rest not their hope
On their meeting with Us,
Say: "Bring us a Reading

اتِ بِقُرْانٍ غَيْرِ هٰذَآ اَوْ بَدِّلْهُ ۚ

Other than this, or change this,"
Say: "It is not for me,
Of my own accord,
To change it: I follow
Naught but what is revealed
Unto me: if I were
To disobey my Lord,
I should myself fear the Penalty
Of a Great Day (to come)."

قُلْ مَا يَكُوْنُ لِيْ
اَنْ اُبَدِّلَهٗ مِنْ تِلْقَآئِ نَفْسِيْ ۚ
اِنْ اَتَّبِعُ اِلَّا مَا يُوْحٰٓى اِلَيَّ ۚ اِنِّيْٓ اَخَافُ
اِنْ عَصَيْتُ رَبِّيْ عَذَابَ يَوْمٍ عَظِيْمٍ ۟

16. Say: "If Allah had so willed,
I should not have rehearsed it
To you, or would He
Have made it known to you.
A whole lifetime before this
Have I tarried amongst you:
Will ye not then understand?"

١٦- قُلْ لَّوْ شَآءَ اللّٰهُ مَا تَلَوْتُهٗ
عَلَيْكُمْ وَلَاۤ اَدْرٰىكُمْ بِهٖ ۖ
فَقَدْ لَبِثْتُ فِيْكُمْ عُمُرًا مِّنْ قَبْلِهٖ ۚ
اَفَلَا تَعْقِلُوْنَ ۟

17. Who doth more wrong
Than such as forge a lie
Against Allah, or deny
His Signs? But never
Will prosper those who sin.

١٧- فَمَنْ اَظْلَمُ مِمَّنِ افْتَرٰى
عَلَى اللّٰهِ كَذِبًا اَوْ كَذَّبَ بِاٰيٰتِهٖ ۚ
اِنَّهٗ لَا يُفْلِحُ الْمُجْرِمُوْنَ ۟

18. They serve, besides Allah,
Things that hurt them not
Nor profit them, and they say:
"These are our intercessors
With Allah." Say: "Do ye
Indeed inform Allah of something
He knows not, in the heavens
Or on earth?—Glory to Him!
And far is He above the partners
They ascribe (to Him)!"

١٨- وَيَعْبُدُوْنَ مِنْ دُوْنِ اللّٰهِ مَا لَا
يَضُرُّهُمْ وَلَا يَنْفَعُهُمْ وَيَقُوْلُوْنَ هٰٓؤُلَآءِ
شُفَعَآؤُنَا عِنْدَ اللّٰهِ ۚ قُلْ اَتُنَبِّـُٔوْنَ اللّٰهَ
بِمَا لَا يَعْلَمُ فِى السَّمٰوٰتِ وَلَا فِى الْاَرْضِ ۚ
سُبْحٰنَهٗ وَتَعٰلٰى عَمَّا يُشْرِكُوْنَ ۟

19. Mankind was but one nation,
But differed (later). Had it not
Been for a Word
That went forth before
From thy Lord, their differences
Would have been settled
Between them.

١٩- وَمَا كَانَ النَّاسُ اِلَّاۤ اُمَّةً وَّاحِدَةً
فَاخْتَلَفُوْا ۚ
وَلَوْلَا كَلِمَةٌ سَبَقَتْ مِنْ رَّبِّكَ
لَقُضِيَ بَيْنَهُمْ فِيْمَا فِيْهِ يَخْتَلِفُوْنَ ۟

20. They say: "Why is not
A Sign sent down to him
From his Lord?" Say:
"The Unseen is only
For Allah (to know).

٢٠- وَيَقُوْلُوْنَ لَوْلَاۤ اُنْزِلَ عَلَيْهِ اٰيَةٌ مِّنْ
رَّبِّهٖ ۚ فَقُلْ اِنَّمَا الْغَيْبُ لِلّٰهِ فَانْتَظِرُوْا ۚ

Then wait ye: I too
Will wait with you."

SECTION 3.

21. When We make mankind
Taste of some mercy after
Adversity hath touched them,
Behold! they take to plotting
Against Our Signs! Say:
"Swifter to plan is Allah!"
Verily, Our messengers record
All the plots that ye make!

22. He it is who enableth you
To traverse through land
And sea; so that ye even board
Ships—they sail with them
With a favourable wind,
And they rejoice thereat;
Then comes a stormy wind
And the waves come to them
From all sides, and they think
They are being overwhelmed:
They cry unto Allah, sincerely
Offering (their) duty unto Him,
Saying, "If Thou dost deliver us
From this, we shall truly
Show our gratitude!"

23. But when he delivereth them,
Behold! they transgress
Insolently through the earth
In defiance of right!
O mankind! your insolence
Is against your own souls—
An enjoyment of the life
Of the Present: in the end,
To Us is your return,
And We shall show you
The truth of all that ye did.

24. The likeness of the life
Of the Present is
As the rain which We
Send down from the skies:
By its mingling arises
The produce of the earth—

Which provides food
For men and animals:
(It grows) till the earth
Is clad with its golden
Ornaments and is decked out
(In beauty): the people to whom
It belongs think they have
All powers of disposal over it:
There reaches it Our command
By night or by day,
And We make it
Like a harvest clean-mown,
As if it had not flourished
Only the day before!
Thus do We explain
The Signs in detail
For those who reflect.

25. But Allah doth call
To the Home of Peace:
He doth guide whom He pleaseth
To a Way that is straight.

26. To those who do right
Is a goodly (reward)—
Yea, more (than in measure)!
No darkness nor shame
Shall cover their faces!
They are Companions of the
                Garden;
They will abide therein
(For aye)!

27. But those who have earned
Evil will have a reward
Of like evil: ignominy
Will cover their (faces):
No defender will they have
From (the wrath of) Allah:
Their faces will be covered,
As it were, with pieces
From the depth of the darkness
Of Night: they are Companions
Of the Fire: they will
Abide therein (for aye)!

28. One Day shall We gather them

All together. Then shall We say
To those who joined gods (with
Us):
"To your place! ye and those
Ye joined as 'partners'."
We shall separate them,
And their "partners" shall say:
"It was not us
That ye worshipped!"1418

لِلَّذِيْنَ
اَشْرَكُوْا مَكَانَكُمْ اَنْتُمْ وَشُرَكَآؤُكُمْ
فَزَيَّلْنَا بَيْنَهُمْ وَقَالَ شُرَكَآؤُهُمْ
مَّا كُنْتُمْ اِيَّانَا تَعْبُدُوْنَ ۝

29. "Enough is Allah for a witness
Between us and you: we
Certainly knew nothing
Of your worship of us!"

۲۹۔ فَكَفٰى بِاللهِ شَهِيْدًا بَيْنَنَا وَبَيْنَكُمْ
اِنْ كُنَّا عَنْ عِبَادَتِكُمْ لَغٰفِلِيْنَ ۝

30. There will every soul prove
(The fruits of) the deeds
It sent before   : they will
Be brought back to Allah
Their rightful Lord,
And their invented falsehoods
Will leave them in the lurch.

۳۰۔ هُنَالِكَ تَبْلُوْا كُلُّ نَفْسٍ مَّا اَسْلَفَتْ وَ
رُدُّوْا اِلَى اللهِ مَوْلٰىهُمُ الْحَقِّ
وَضَلَّ عَنْهُمْ مَّا كَانُوْا يَفْتَرُوْنَ ۝

SECTION 4.

31. Say: "Who is it that
Sustains you (in life)
From the sky and from the
earth?
Or who is it that
Has power over hearing
And sight? And who
Is it that brings out
The living from the dead
And the dead from the living?
And who is it that
Rules and regulates all affairs?"
They will soon say, "Allah".
Say, "Will ye not then
Show piety (to Him)?"

۳۱۔ قُلْ مَنْ يَّرْزُقُكُمْ مِّنَ السَّمَآءِ وَ
الْاَرْضِ
اَمَّنْ يَّمْلِكُ السَّمْعَ وَالْاَبْصَارَ
وَمَنْ يُّخْرِجُ الْحَيَّ مِنَ الْمَيِّتِ
وَيُخْرِجُ الْمَيِّتَ مِنَ الْحَيِّ
وَمَنْ يُّدَبِّرُ الْاَمْرَ فَسَيَقُوْلُوْنَ اللهُ
فَقُلْ اَفَلَا تَتَّقُوْنَ ۝

32. Such is Allah, your real
Cherisher and Sustainer:
Apart from Truth,
What (remains) but error?
How then are ye turned away?

۳۲۔ فَذٰلِكُمُ اللهُ رَبُّكُمُ الْحَقُّ
فَمَاذَا بَعْدَ الْحَقِّ اِلَّا الضَّلٰلُ
فَاَنّٰى تُصْرَفُوْنَ ۝

33. Thus is the Word
Of thy Lord proved true

۳۳۔ كَذٰلِكَ حَقَّتْ كَلِمَتُ رَبِّكَ عَلٰى

Against those who rebel:
Verily they will not believe.

الَّذِيْنَ فَسَقُوْا اَنَّهُمْ لَا يُؤْمِنُوْنَ ۝

34. Say: "Of your 'partners',
Can any originate creation
And repeat it?" Say:
"It is Allah Who originates
Creation and repeats it:
Then how are ye deluded
Away (from the truth)?"

٣٤- قُلْ هَلْ مِنْ شُرَكَآئِكُمْ مَّنْ يَّبْدَؤُا
الْخَلْقَ ثُمَّ يُعِيْدُهٗ ۚ
قُلِ اللّٰهُ يَبْدَؤُا الْخَلْقَ
ثُمَّ يُعِيْدُهٗ فَاَنّٰى تُؤْفَكُوْنَ ۝

35. Say: "Of your 'partners'
Is there any that
Can give any guidance
Towards Truth?" Say: "It is Allah
Who gives guidance
Towards Truth. Is then He
Who gives guidance to Truth
More worthy to be followed,
Or he who finds not guidance
(Himself) unless he is guided?
What then is the matter
With you? How judge ye?"

٣٥- قُلْ هَلْ مِنْ شُرَكَآئِكُمْ مَّنْ
يَّهْدِيْ إِلَى الْحَقِّ ۚ قُلِ اللّٰهُ يَهْدِيْ لِلْحَقِّ
اَفَمَنْ يَّهْدِيْ إِلَى الْحَقِّ
اَحَقُّ اَنْ يُّتَّبَعَ اَمَّنْ لَّا يَهِدِّيْ
اِلَّا اَنْ يُّهْدٰى ۚ
فَمَا لَكُمْ ۚ كَيْفَ تَحْكُمُوْنَ ۝

36. But most of them follow
Nothing but fancy: truly
Fancy can be of no avail
Against Truth. Verily Allah
Is well aware of all
That they do.

٣٦- وَمَا يَتَّبِعُ اَكْثَرُهُمْ اِلَّا ظَنًّا ۚ
اِنَّ الظَّنَّ لَا يُغْنِيْ مِنَ الْحَقِّ شَيْئًا ۚ
اِنَّ اللّٰهَ عَلِيْمٌ بِمَا يَفْعَلُوْنَ ۝

37. This Qur'ān is not such
As can be produced
By other than Allah;
On the contrary it is
A confirmation of (revelations)
That went before it,
And a fuller explanation
Of the Book—wherein
There is no doubt—
From the Lord of the Worlds.

٣٧- وَمَا كَانَ هٰذَا الْقُرْاٰنُ
اَنْ يُّفْتَرٰى مِنْ دُوْنِ اللّٰهِ
وَلٰكِنْ تَصْدِيْقَ الَّذِيْ بَيْنَ يَدَيْهِ
وَتَفْصِيْلَ الْكِتٰبِ
لَا رَيْبَ فِيْهِ مِنْ رَّبِّ الْعٰلَمِيْنَ ۝

38. Or do they say,
"He forged it"?
Say: "Bring then
A Sūrah like unto it,
And call (to your aid)
Anyone you can,

٣٨- اَمْ يَقُوْلُوْنَ افْتَرٰىهُ ۚ
قُلْ فَأْتُوْا بِسُوْرَةٍ مِّثْلِهٖ
وَ ادْعُوْا مَنِ اسْتَطَعْتُمْ مِّنْ دُوْنِ اللّٰهِ

Besides Allah, if it be
Ye speak the truth!"

اِنْ كُنْتُمْ صٰدِقِيْنَ ۞

9. Nay, they charge with falsehood
That whose knowledge they
Cannot compass, even before
The elucidation thereof
Hath reached them: thus
Did those before them
Make charges of falsehood:
But see what was the end
Of those who did wrong!

٣٩- بَلْ كَذَّبُوْا بِمَا لَمْ يُحِيْطُوْا بِعِلْمِهٖ
وَلَمَّا يَأْتِهِمْ تَأْوِيْلُهٗ ۚ
كَذٰلِكَ كَذَّبَ الَّذِيْنَ مِنْ قَبْلِهِمْ
فَانْظُرْ كَيْفَ كَانَ عَاقِبَةُ الظّٰلِمِيْنَ ۞

0. Of them there are some
Who believe therein,
And some who do not:
And thy Lord knoweth best
Those who are out for mischief.

٤٠- وَمِنْهُمْ مَّنْ يُّؤْمِنُ بِهٖ
وَمِنْهُمْ مَّنْ لَّا يُؤْمِنُ بِهٖ ۚ
وَرَبُّكَ أَعْلَمُ بِالْمُفْسِدِيْنَ ۞

SECTION 5.

1. If they charge thee
With falsehood, say:
"My work to me,
And yours to you!
Ye are free from responsibility
For what I do and I
For what ye do!"

٤١- وَاِنْ كَذَّبُوْكَ فَقُلْ لِّيْ عَمَلِيْ وَلَكُمْ
عَمَلُكُمْ ۚ أَنْتُمْ بَرِيْٓـُٔوْنَ مِمَّآ أَعْمَلُ
وَأَنَا بَرِيْٓءٌ مِّمَّا تَعْمَلُوْنَ ۞

42. Among them are some who
(Pretend to) listen to thee:
But canst thou make the deaf
To hear—even though
They are without
       understanding?

٤٢- وَمِنْهُمْ مَّنْ يَّسْتَمِعُوْنَ اِلَيْكَ ۚ
أَفَأَنْتَ تُسْمِعُ الصُّمَّ
وَلَوْ كَانُوْا لَا يَعْقِلُوْنَ ۞

43. And among them are some
Who look at thee:
But canst thou guide
The blind—even though
They will not see?

٤٣- وَمِنْهُمْ مَّنْ يَّنْظُرُ اِلَيْكَ ۚ
أَفَأَنْتَ تَهْدِى الْعُمْىَ
وَلَوْ كَانُوْا لَا يُبْصِرُوْنَ ۞

44. Verily Allah will not deal
Unjustly with man in aught:
It is man that wrongs
His own soul.

٤٤- اِنَّ اللّٰهَ لَا يَظْلِمُ النَّاسَ شَيْئًا
وَّلٰكِنَّ النَّاسَ أَنْفُسَهُمْ يَظْلِمُوْنَ ۞

45. One day He will
Gather them together:

٤٥- وَيَوْمَ يَحْشُرُهُمْ كَأَنْ لَّمْ يَلْبَثُوْا

(It will be) as if
They had tarried
But an hour of a day:
They will recognise each other:
Assuredly those will be lost
Who denied the meeting
With Allah and refused
To receive true guidance.

46. Whether We show thee
(Realised in thy lifetime)
Some part of what We
Promise them—or We
Take thy soul (to Our Mercy)
(Before that)—in any case,
To Us is their return:
Ultimately Allah is witness
To all that they do.

47. To every people (was sent)
A Messenger: when their
                  Messenger
Comes (before them), the matter
Will be judged between them
With justice, and they
Will not be wronged.

48. They say: "When
Will this promise
Come to pass—
If ye speak the truth?"

49. Say: "I have no power
Over any harm or profit
To myself except as Allah
Willeth. To every People
Is a term appointed:
When their term is reached,
Not an hour can they cause
Delay, nor (an hour) can they
Advance (it in anticipation)."

50. Say: "Do ye see—
If His punishment should come
To you by night or by day,

What portion of it
Would the Sinners
Wish to hasten?

أَوْ نَهَارًا مَّا ذَا يَسْتَعْجِلُ مِنْهُ الْمُجْرِمُوْنَ ۝

1. "Would ye then believe in it
At last, when it actually cometh
To pass? (It will then be said:)
'Ah! now? and ye wanted
(Aforetime) to hasten it on!'

٥١ - أَثُمَّ إِذَا مَا وَقَعَ اٰمَنْتُمْ بِهٖ ۚ
اٰلْـٰٔنَ وَقَدْ كُنْتُمْ بِهٖ تَسْتَعْجِلُوْنَ ۝

2. "At length will be said
To the wrongdoers: 'Taste ye
The enduring punishment!
Ye get but the recompense
Of what ye earned!'"

٥٢ - ثُمَّ قِيْلَ لِلَّذِيْنَ ظَلَمُوْا ذُوْقُوْا
عَذَابَ الْخُلْدِ ۚ
هَلْ تُجْزَوْنَ إِلَّا بِمَا كُنْتُمْ تَكْسِبُوْنَ ۝

3. They seek to be informed
By thee: "Is that true?"
Say: "Aye! by my Lord!
It is the very truth!
And ye cannot frustrate it!"

٥٣ - وَيَسْتَنْۢبِـُٔوْنَكَ أَحَقٌّ هُوَ ۚ
قُلْ إِيْ وَرَبِّيْٓ إِنَّهٗ لَحَقٌّ ۚ
وَمَآ أَنْتُمْ بِمُعْجِزِيْنَ ۝

SECTION 6.

4. Every soul that hath sinned,
If it possessed all
That is on earth,
Would fain give it in ransom:
They would declare (their)
                repentance
When they see the Penalty:
But the judgement between them
Will be with justice,
And no wrong will be done
Unto them.

٥٤ - وَلَوْ أَنَّ لِكُلِّ نَفْسٍ ظَلَمَتْ
مَا فِى الْأَرْضِ لَافْتَدَتْ بِهٖ ۗ
وَأَسَرُّوا النَّدَامَةَ لَمَّا رَأَوُا الْعَذَابَ ۚ
وَقُضِيَ بَيْنَهُمْ بِالْقِسْطِ
وَهُمْ لَا يُظْلَمُوْنَ ۝

5. Is it not (the case) that to Allah
Belongeth whatever is
In the heavens and on earth?
Is it not (the case) that
Allah's promise is assuredly true?
Yet most of them understand not.

٥٥ - أَلَآ إِنَّ لِلّٰهِ مَا فِى السَّمٰوٰتِ وَالْأَرْضِ ۗ
أَلَآ إِنَّ وَعْدَ اللّٰهِ حَقٌّ
وَلٰكِنَّ أَكْثَرَهُمْ لَا يَعْلَمُوْنَ ۝

56. It is He who giveth life
And who taketh it,
And to Him shall ye
All be brought back.

٥٦ - هُوَ يُحْيٖ وَيُمِيْتُ
وَإِلَيْهِ تُرْجَعُوْنَ ۝

57. O mankind! there hath come

٥٧ - يٰٓأَيُّهَا النَّاسُ قَدْ جَآءَتْكُمْ مَّوْعِظَةٌ

To you a direction from your Lord
And a healing for the (diseases)
In your hearts—and for those
Who believe, a Guidance
And a Mercy.

58. Say: "In the Bounty of Allah.
And in His Mercy—in that
Let them rejoice": that is better
Than the (wealth) they hoard.

59. Say: "See ye what things
Allah hath sent down to you
For sustenance? Yet ye
Hold forbidden some things
Thereof and (some things) lawful."
Say: "Hath Allah indeed
Permitted you, or do ye invent
(Things) to attribute to Allah?"

60. And what think those
Who invent lies against Allah,
Of the Day of Judgement?
Verily Allah is full of Bounty
To mankind, but most
Of them are ungrateful.

SECTION 7.

61. In whatever business thou
Mayest be, and whatever portion
Thou mayest be reciting
From the Qur'ān—and whatever
Deed ye (mankind) may be
               doing—
We are Witnesses thereof
When ye are deeply engrossed
Therein. Nor is hidden
From the Lord (so much as)
The weight of an atom
On the earth or in heaven.
And not the least
And not the greatest
Of these things but are recorded
In a clear Record.

62. Behold! verily on the friends
Of Allah there is no fear,
Nor shall they grieve;

3. Those who believe
And (constantly) guard
Against evil—

٦٣- اَلَّذِيۡنَ اٰمَنُوۡا وَكَانُوۡا يَتَّقُوۡنَ ۚ

4. For them are Glad Tidings,
In the life of the Present
And in the Hereafter:
No change can there be
In the Words of Allah.
This is indeed
The supreme Felicity.

٦٤- لَهُمُ الۡبُشۡرٰى فِى الۡحَيٰوةِ الدُّنۡيَا
وَفِى الۡاٰخِرَةِ ۚ
لَا تَبۡدِيۡلَ لِكَلِمٰتِ اللّٰهِ ۚ
ذٰلِكَ هُوَ الۡفَوۡزُ الۡعَظِيۡمُ ۚ

5. Let not their speech
Grieve thee: for all power
And honour belong to Allah:
It is He Who heareth
And knoweth (all things).

٦٥- وَلَا يَحۡزُنۡكَ قَوۡلُهُمۡ ۘ
اِنَّ الۡعِزَّةَ لِلّٰهِ جَمِيۡعًا ۚ
هُوَ السَّمِيۡعُ الۡعَلِيۡمُ ۞

6. Behold! verily to Allah
Belong all creatures,
In the heavens and on earth.
What do they follow
Who worship as His "partners"
Other than Allah? They follow
Nothing but fancy, and
They do nothing but lie.

٦٦- أَلَا اِنَّ لِلّٰهِ مَنۡ فِى السَّمٰوٰتِ وَمَنۡ
فِى الۡاَرۡضِ ۚ وَمَا يَتَّبِعُ الَّذِيۡنَ يَدۡعُوۡنَ
مِنۡ دُوۡنِ اللّٰهِ شُرَكَاءَ ۚ اِنۡ يَّتَّبِعُوۡنَ اِلَّا
الظَّنَّ وَاِنۡ هُمۡ اِلَّا يَخۡرُصُوۡنَ ۞

67. He it is that hath
Made you the Night
That ye may rest therein,
And the Day to make
Things visible (to you).
Verily in this are Signs
For those who listen
(To His Message).

٦٧- هُوَ الَّذِيۡ جَعَلَ لَكُمُ الَّيۡلَ
لِتَسۡكُنُوۡا فِيۡهِ وَالنَّهَارَ مُبۡصِرًا ۚ
اِنَّ فِىۡ ذٰلِكَ لَاٰيٰتٍ
لِّقَوۡمٍ يَّسۡمَعُوۡنَ ۞

68. They say, "Allah hath begotten
A son!"—Glory be to Him!
He is Self-Sufficient! His
Are all things in the heavens
And on earth! No warrant
Have ye for this! Say ye
About Allah what ye know not?

٦٨- قَالُوا اتَّخَذَ اللّٰهُ وَلَدًا سُبۡحٰنَهٗ ۚ
هُوَ الۡغَنِىُّ ۚ لَهٗ مَا فِى السَّمٰوٰتِ وَمَا فِى
الۡاَرۡضِ ۚ اِنۡ عِنۡدَكُمۡ مِّنۡ سُلۡطٰنٍ بِهٰذَا ۚ
اَتَقُوۡلُوۡنَ عَلَى اللّٰهِ مَا لَا تَعۡلَمُوۡنَ ۞

69. Say: "Those who invent

٦٩- قُلۡ اِنَّ الَّذِيۡنَ يَفۡتَرُوۡنَ

A lie against Allah
Will never prosper."

70. A little enjoyment
In this world!—
And then, to Us
Will be their return.
Then shall We make them
Taste the severest Penalty
For their blasphemies.

SECTION 8.

71. Relate to them the story
Of Noah. Behold! he said
To his People: "O my People,
If it be hard on your (mind)
That I should stay (with you)
And commemorate the Signs
Of Allah—yet I put
My trust in Allah.
Get ye then an agreement
About your plan and among
Your Partners, so your plan
Be not to you dark and dubious.
Then pass your sentence on me,
And give me no respite.

72. "But if ye turn back, (consider):
No reward have I asked
Of you: my reward is only
Due from Allah, and I
Have been commanded to be
Of those who submit
To Allah's Will (in Islam)."

73. They rejected him,
But We delivered him,
And those with him,
In the Ark, and We made
Them inherit (the earth),
While We overwhelmed
In the Flood those
Who rejected Our Signs.
Then see what was the end

Of those who were warned
(But heeded not)!

عَاقِبَةُ الْمُنْذَرِيْنَ ۞

74. Then after him We sent
(Many) messengers to their
Peoples:
They brought them Clear Signs,
But they would not believe
What they had already rejected
Beforehand. Thus do We seal
The hearts of the transgressors.

٧٤- ثُمَّ بَعَثْنَا مِنْ بَعْدِهٖ رُسُلًا اِلٰى قَوْمِهِمْ
فَجَآءُوْهُمْ بِالْبَيِّنٰتِ
فَمَا كَانُوْا لِيُؤْمِنُوْا بِمَا كَذَّبُوْا بِهٖ مِنْ
قَبْلُ ۚ كَذٰلِكَ نَطْبَعُ عَلٰى قُلُوْبِ الْمُعْتَدِيْنَ ۞

75. Then after them sent We
Moses and Aaron to Pharaoh
And his chiefs with Our Signs.
But they were arrogant:
They were a people in sin.

٧٥- ثُمَّ بَعَثْنَا مِنْ بَعْدِهِمْ مُّوْسٰى وَ
هٰرُوْنَ اِلٰى فِرْعَوْنَ وَمَلَا۟ئِهٖ بِاٰيٰتِنَا
فَاسْتَكْبَرُوْا وَكَانُوْا قَوْمًا مُّجْرِمِيْنَ ۞

76. When the Truth did come
To them from Us, they said:
"This is indeed evident sorcery!"

٧٦- فَلَمَّا جَآءَهُمُ الْحَقُّ مِنْ عِنْدِنَا
قَالُوْۤا اِنَّ هٰذَا لَسِحْرٌ مُّبِيْنٌ ۞

77. Said Moses: "Say ye (this)
About the Truth when
It hath (actually) reached you?
Is sorcery (like) this?
But sorcerers will not prosper."

٧٧- قَالَ مُوْسٰۤى اَتَقُوْلُوْنَ لِلْحَقِّ لَمَّا جَآءَكُمْ
اَسِحْرٌ هٰذَا ۚ
وَلَا يُفْلِحُ السّٰحِرُوْنَ ۞

78. They said: "Hast thou
Come to us to turn us
Away from the ways
We found our fathers following—
In order that thou and thy brother
May have greatness in the land?
But not we shall believe in you!"

٧٨- قَالُوْۤا اَجِئْتَنَا لِتَلْفِتَنَا عَمَّا وَجَدْنَا عَلَيْهِ
اٰبَآءَنَا وَتَكُوْنَ لَكُمَا الْكِبْرِيَآءُ فِى
الْاَرْضِ ۖ
وَمَا نَحْنُ لَكُمَا بِمُؤْمِنِيْنَ ۞

79. Said Pharaoh: "Bring me
Every sorcerer well-versed."

٧٩- وَقَالَ فِرْعَوْنُ ائْتُوْنِيْ بِكُلِّ سٰحِرٍ عَلِيْمٍ

80. When the sorcerers came,
Moses said to them:
"Throw ye what ye (wish)
To throw!"

٨٠- فَلَمَّا جَآءَ السَّحَرَةُ قَالَ لَهُمْ مُّوْسٰۤى
اَلْقُوْا مَاۤ اَنْتُمْ مُّلْقُوْنَ ۞

81. When they had had their throw,
Moses said: "What ye
Have brought is sorcery:

٨١- فَلَمَّاۤ اَلْقَوْا قَالَ مُوْسٰى
مَا جِئْتُمْ بِهِ السِّحْرُ

Allah will surely make it
Of no effect: for Allah
Prospereth not the work
Of those who make mischief.

82. "And Allah by His Words
Doth prove and establish
His Truth, however much
The Sinners may hate it!"

SECTION 9.

83. But none believed in Moses
Except some children of his
           People,
Because of the fear of Pharaoh
And his chiefs, lest they
Should persecute them; and
           certainly
Pharaoh was mighty on the earth
And one who transgressed all
           bounds.

84. Moses said: "O my People!
If ye do (really) believe
In Allah, then in Him
Put your trust if ye
Submit (your will to His)."

85. They said: "In Allah
Do we put our trust.
Our Lord! make us not
A trial for those
Who practise oppression;

86. "And deliver us by Thy Mercy
From those who reject (Thee)."

87. We inspired Moses and his brother
With this Message: "Provide
Dwellings for your People
In Egypt, make your dwellings
Into places of worship,
And establish regular prayers:
And give Glad Tidings
To those who believe!"

88. Moses prayed: "Our Lord!
Thou hast indeed bestowed
On Pharaoh and his Chiefs

إِنَّ اللّٰهَ سَيُبْطِلُهُ ۗ إِنَّ اللّٰهَ
لَا يُصْلِحُ عَمَلَ الْمُفْسِدِيْنَ ۟

٨٢- وَيُحِقُّ اللّٰهُ الْحَقَّ بِكَلِمٰتِهٖ
وَلَوْ كَرِهَ الْمُجْرِمُوْنَ ۟ؕع

٨٣- فَمَآ اٰمَنَ لِمُوْسٰۤى اِلَّا ذُرِّيَّةٌ مِّنْ
قَوْمِهٖ عَلٰى خَوْفٍ مِّنْ فِرْعَوْنَ وَمَلَا۟ئِهِمْ
اَنْ يَّفْتِنَهُمْ ؕ
وَاِنَّ فِرْعَوْنَ لَعَالٍ فِى الْاَرْضِ ۚ
وَاِنَّهٗ لَمِنَ الْمُسْرِفِيْنَ ۟

٨٤- وَقَالَ مُوْسٰى يٰقَوْمِ اِنْ كُنْتُمْ اٰمَنْتُمْ
بِاللّٰهِ فَعَلَيْهِ
تَوَكَّلُوْۤا اِنْ كُنْتُمْ مُّسْلِمِيْنَ ۟

٨٥- فَقَالُوْا عَلَى اللّٰهِ تَوَكَّلْنَا ۚ
رَبَّنَا لَا تَجْعَلْنَا فِتْنَةً لِّلْقَوْمِ الظّٰلِمِيْنَ ۟

٨٦- وَنَجِّنَا بِرَحْمَتِكَ مِنَ الْقَوْمِ الْكٰفِرِيْنَ ۟

٨٧- وَاَوْحَيْنَآ اِلٰى مُوْسٰى وَاَخِيْهِ
اَنْ تَبَوَّاٰ لِقَوْمِكُمَا بِمِصْرَ بُيُوْتًا وَّاجْعَلُوْا
بُيُوْتَكُمْ قِبْلَةً وَّاَقِيْمُوا الصَّلٰوةَ ؕ
وَبَشِّرِ الْمُؤْمِنِيْنَ ۟

٨٨- وَقَالَ مُوْسٰى رَبَّنَآ اِنَّكَ اٰتَيْتَ
فِرْعَوْنَ وَمَلَاَهٗ زِيْنَةً وَّاَمْوَالًا فِى الْحَيٰوةِ

Splendour and wealth in the life
Of the Present, and so,
Our Lord, they mislead (men)
From Thy Path. Deface,
Our Lord, the features of their
        wealth,
And send hardness to their hearts,
So they will not believe
Until they see
The grievous Penalty."

89. Allah said: "Accepted is
Your prayer (O Moses and Aaron)!
So stand ye straight,
And follow not the path
Of those who know not."

90. We took the Children
Of Israel across the sea:
Pharaoh and his hosts followed
        them
In insolence and spite.
At length, when overwhelmed
With the flood, he said:
"I believe that there is no god
Except Him Whom the Children
Of Israel believe in:
I am of those who submit
(To Allah in Islam)."

91. (It was said to him:)
"Ah now!—But a little while
Before, wast thou in rebellion!—
And thou didst mischief (and
        violence)!

92. "This day shall We save thee
In thy body, that thou
Mayest be a Sign to those
Who come after thee!
But verily, many among mankind
Are heedless of Our Signs!"

SECTION 10.

93. We settled the Children
Of Israel in a beautiful
Dwelling place, and provided
For them sustenance of the best;
It was after knowledge had been

الدُّنْيَا ۚ

رَبَّنَا لِيُضِلُّوا عَنْ سَبِيلِكَ ۖ

رَبَّنَا اطْمِسْ عَلَى أَمْوَالِهِمْ

وَاشْدُدْ عَلَى قُلُوبِهِمْ فَلَا يُؤْمِنُوا

حَتَّى يَرَوُا الْعَذَابَ الْأَلِيمَ ۝

٨٩- قَالَ قَدْ أُجِيبَتْ دَعْوَتُكُمَا فَاسْتَقِيمَا

وَلَا تَتَّبِعَانِّ سَبِيلَ الَّذِينَ لَا يَعْلَمُونَ ۝

٩٠- وَجَاوَزْنَا بِبَنِي إِسْرَآئِيلَ الْبَحْرَ

فَأَتْبَعَهُمْ فِرْعَوْنُ وَجُنُودُهُ بَغْيًا وَعَدْوًا ۗ

حَتَّى إِذَآ أَدْرَكَهُ الْغَرَقُ

قَالَ آمَنْتُ أَنَّهُ لَا إِلَهَ إِلَّا

الَّذِيٓ آمَنَتْ بِهِ بَنُوٓا إِسْرَآئِيلَ

وَأَنَا مِنَ الْمُسْلِمِينَ ۝

٩١- آلْآنَ وَقَدْ عَصَيْتَ قَبْلُ

وَكُنْتَ مِنَ الْمُفْسِدِينَ ۝

٩٢- فَالْيَوْمَ نُنَجِّيكَ بِبَدَنِكَ لِتَكُونَ

لِمَنْ خَلْفَكَ آيَةً ۚ وَإِنَّ كَثِيرًا مِنَ

النَّاسِ عَنْ آيَاتِنَا لَغَافِلُونَ ۝

٩٣- وَلَقَدْ بَوَّأْنَا بَنِي إِسْرَآئِيلَ

مُبَوَّأَ صِدْقٍ وَرَزَقْنَاهُمْ مِنَ الطَّيِّبَاتِ ۚ

Granted to them, that they
Fell into schisms. Verily
Allah will judge between them
As to the schisms amongst them
On the Day of Judgement.

94. If thou wert in doubt
As to what We have revealed
Unto thee, then ask those
Who have been reading
The Book from before thee:
The Truth hath indeed come
To thee from thy Lord:
So be in nowise
Of those in doubt.

95. Nor be of those who reject
The Signs of Allah,
Or thou shalt be of those
Who perish.

96. Those against whom the Word
Of thy Lord hath been verified
Would not believe—

97. Even if every Sign was brought
Unto them—until they see
(For themselves) the Grievous
Penalty.

98. Why was there not
A single township (among those
We warned), which believed—
So its Faith should have
Profited it—except the People
Of Jonah? When they believed,
We removed from them
The Penalty of Ignominy
In the life of the Present,
And permitted them to enjoy
(Their life) for awhile.

99. If it had been the Lord's Will,
They would all have believed—
All who are on earth!
Wilt thou then compel mankind,
Against their will, to believe!

100. No soul can believe, except

By the Will of Allah,
And He will place Doubt
(Or obscurity) on those
Who will not understand.

101. Say: "Behold all that is
In the heavens and on earth";
But neither Signs nor Warners
Profit those who believe not.

102. Do they then expect
(Anything) but (what happened
In) the days of the men
Who passed away before them?
Say: "Wait ye then:
For I, too, will wait with you."

103. In the end We deliver
Our messengers and those who
believe:
Thus is it fitting on Our part
That We should deliver
Those who believe!

SECTION 11.

104. Say: "O ye men!
If ye are in doubt
As to my religion, (behold!)
I worship not what ye
Worship other than Allah!
But I worship Allah—
Who will take your souls
(At death): I am commanded
To be (in the ranks)
Of the Believers,¹⁴⁸⁸

105. "And further (thus): 'set thy face
Towards Religion with true piety,
And never in anywise
Be of the Unbelievers;

106. "'Nor call on any,
Other than Allah—
Such will neither profit thee
Nor hurt thee: if thou dost,
Behold! thou shalt certainly
Be of those who do wrong.'"

107. If Allah do touch thee

With hurt, there is none
Can remove it but He:
If He do design some benefit
For thee, there is none
Can keep back His favour:
He causeth it to reach
Whomsoever of His servants
He pleaseth. And He is
The Oft-Forgiving, Most
Merciful.

لَهُ إِلَّا هُوَ وَإِنْ يُّرِدْكَ بِخَيْرٍ
فَلَا رَآدَّ لِفَضْلِهِ
يُصِيبُ بِهِ مَنْ يَّشَآءُ مِنْ عِبَادِهِ
وَهُوَ الْغَفُوْرُ الرَّحِيْمُ ۝

108. Say: "O ye men! Now
Truth hath reached you
From your Lord! Those who
receive
Guidance, do so for the good
Of their own souls; those
Who stray, do so to their own loss:
And I am not (set) over you
To arrange your affairs."

١٠٨ۧۧ قُلْ يَآأَيُّهَا النَّاسُ قَدْ جَآءَكُمُ الْحَقُّ
مِنْ رَّبِّكُمْ فَمَنِ اهْتَدٰى
فَإِنَّمَا يَهْتَدِيْ لِنَفْسِهِ
وَمَنْ ضَلَّ فَإِنَّمَا يَضِلُّ عَلَيْهَا
وَمَآ أَنَا عَلَيْكُمْ بِوَكِيْلٍ ۝

109. Follow thou the inspiration
Sent unto thee, and be
Patient and constant, till Allah
Doth decide: for He
Is the Best to decide.

١٠٩ وَاتَّبِعْ مَا يُوْحٰى إِلَيْكَ
وَاصْبِرْ حَتّٰى يَحْكُمَ اللّٰهُ
وَهُوَ خَيْرُ الْحٰكِمِيْنَ ۝ ع

INTRODUCTION TO SŪRA XI.*(Hūd)* — 123 Verses

For the chronological place of the Sūra and this general arguments of Sūras x. to xv., see Introduction to S.x.

In subject matter this Sūra supplements the preceding one. In the last Sūra stress was laid on that side of God's dealings with man which leans to Mercy: here stress is laid on the side which deals with justice and the punishment of Sin when all Grace is resisted.

Hūd (The Prophet Hūd)

In the name of Allah, Most Gracious, Most Merciful.

بِسْمِ اللهِ الرَّحْمٰنِ الرَّحِيمِ

1. Alif Lām Rā'.
   (This is) a Book,
   With verses basic or
                   fundamental
   (Of established meaning)—
   Further explained in detail
   From One Who is Wise
   And Well-Acquainted (with all
                        things):

١- الرّ كِتَابٌ أُحْكِمَتْ آيَاتُهُ ثُمَّ فُصِّلَتْ مِنْ لَدُنْ حَكِيمٍ خَبِيرٍ ۝

2. (It teacheth) that ye should
   Worship none but Allah.
   (Say:) "Verily I am
   (Sent) unto you from Him
   To warn and to bring
   Glad tidings:

٢- أَلَّا تَعْبُدُوا إِلَّا اللهَ إِنَّنِي لَكُمْ مِنْهُ نَذِيرٌ وَبَشِيرٌ ۝

3. "(And to preach thus), 'Seek ye
   The forgiveness of your Lord,
   And turn to Him in repentance;
   That He may grant you
   Enjoyment, good (and true),
   For a term appointed,
   And bestow His abounding grace
   On all who abound in merit!¹⁴⁹⁵
   But if ye turn away,
   Then I fear for you
   The Penalty of a Great Day:

٣- وَأَنِ اسْتَغْفِرُوا رَبَّكُمْ ثُمَّ تُوبُوا إِلَيْهِ يُمَتِّعْكُمْ مَتَاعًا حَسَنًا إِلَى أَجَلٍ مُسَمًّى وَيُؤْتِ كُلَّ ذِي فَضْلٍ فَضْلَهُ وَإِنْ تَوَلَّوْا فَإِنِّي أَخَافُ عَلَيْكُمْ عَذَابَ يَوْمٍ كَبِيرٍ ۝

4. "'To Allah is your return
   And He hath power
   Over all things.'"

٤- إِلَى اللهِ مَرْجِعُكُمْ وَهُوَ عَلَى كُلِّ شَيْءٍ قَدِيرٌ ۝

5. Behold! they fold up
Their hearts, that they may lie
Hid from Him! Ah! even
When they cover themselves
With their garments, He knoweth
What they conceal, and what
They reveal: for He knoweth
Well the (inmost secrets)
Of the hearts.

6. There is no moving creature
On earth but its sustenance
Dependeth on Allah: He knoweth
The time and place of its
Definite abode and its
Temporary deposit:
All is in a clear Record.

7. He it is Who created
The heavens and the earth
In six Days   — and His Throne
Was over the Waters—
That He might try you,
Which of you is best
In conduct. But if
Thou wert to say to them,
"Ye shall indeed be raised up
After death," the Unbelievers
Would be sure to say,
"This is nothing but
Obvious sorcery!"

8. If We delay the penalty
For them for a definite term,
They are sure to say,
"What keeps it back?"
Ah! On the day it (actually)
Reaches them, nothing will
Turn it away from them,
And they will be completely
Encircled by that which
They used to mock at!

SECTION 2.

9. If We give man a taste
Of mercy from Ourselves,
And then withdraw it from him,
Behold! he is in despair
And (falls into) blasphemy.

٥ اَلَاۤ اِنَّهُمۡ یَثۡنُوۡنَ صُدُوۡرَهُمۡ لِیَسۡتَخۡفُوۡا
مِنۡهُ ؕ اَلَا حِیۡنَ یَسۡتَغۡشُوۡنَ ثِیَابَهُمۡ ۙ
یَعۡلَمُ مَا یُسِرُّوۡنَ وَمَا یُعۡلِنُوۡنَ ۚ
اِنَّهٗ عَلِیۡمٌۢ بِذَاتِ الصُّدُوۡرِ ۟

٦ وَمَا مِنۡ دَآبَّةٍ فِی الۡاَرۡضِ اِلَّا
عَلَی اللّٰهِ رِزۡقُهَا وَیَعۡلَمُ مُسۡتَقَرَّهَا وَ
مُسۡتَوۡدَعَهَا ؕ
کُلٌّ فِیۡ کِتٰبٍ مُّبِیۡنٍ ۟

٧ وَهُوَ الَّذِیۡ خَلَقَ السَّمٰوٰتِ وَالۡاَرۡضَ
فِیۡ سِتَّةِ اَیَّامٍ وَّکَانَ عَرۡشُهٗ عَلَی الۡمَآءِ
لِیَبۡلُوَکُمۡ اَیُّکُمۡ اَحۡسَنُ عَمَلًا ؕ
وَلَئِنۡ قُلۡتَ اِنَّکُمۡ مَّبۡعُوۡثُوۡنَ مِنۡۢ بَعۡدِ
الۡمَوۡتِ لَیَقُوۡلَنَّ الَّذِیۡنَ کَفَرُوۡۤا
اِنۡ هٰذَاۤ اِلَّا سِحۡرٌ مُّبِیۡنٌ ۟

٨ وَلَئِنۡ اَخَّرۡنَا عَنۡهُمُ الۡعَذَابَ اِلٰۤی
اُمَّةٍ مَّعۡدُوۡدَةٍ لَّیَقُوۡلُنَّ مَا یَحۡبِسُهٗ ؕ
اَلَا یَوۡمَ یَاۡتِیۡهِمۡ لَیۡسَ مَصۡرُوۡفًا عَنۡهُمۡ
وَحَاقَ بِهِمۡ
مَّا کَانُوۡا بِهٖ یَسۡتَهۡزِءُوۡنَ ۟

٩ وَلَئِنۡ اَذَقۡنَا الۡاِنۡسَانَ مِنَّا رَحۡمَةً
ثُمَّ نَزَعۡنٰهَا مِنۡهُ ۚ اِنَّهٗ لَیَـُٔوۡسٌ کَفُوۡرٌ ۟

10. But if We give him a taste
Of (Our) favours after
Adversity hath touched him,
He is sure to say,
"All evil has departed from
me;"
Behold! he falls into exultation
And pride.

١٠- وَلَئِنْ أَذَقْنٰهُ نَعْمَآءَ
بَعْدَ ضَرَّآءَ مَسَّتْهُ
لَيَقُوْلَنَّ ذَهَبَ السَّيِّاٰتُ عَنِّيْ ۗ
اِنَّهٗ لَفَرِحٌ فَخُوْرٌ ۙ

11. Not so do those who show
Patience and constancy, and
work
Righteousness; for them
Is forgiveness (of sins)
And a great reward.

١١- اِلَّا الَّذِيْنَ صَبَرُوْا وَعَمِلُوا الصّٰلِحٰتِ ۗ
اُولٰٓئِكَ لَهُمْ مَغْفِرَةٌ
وَّاَجْرٌ كَبِيْرٌ ○

12. Perchance thou mayest (feel
The inclination) to give up
A part of what is revealed
Unto thee, and thy heart
Feeleth straitened lest they say,
"Why is not a treasure sent down
Unto him, or why does not
An angel come down with him?"
But thou art there only to warn!
It is Allah that arrangeth
All affairs!

١٢- فَلَعَلَّكَ تَارِكٌۢ
بَعْضَ مَا يُوْحٰىٓ اِلَيْكَ وَضَآئِقٌۢ بِهٖ
صَدْرُكَ اَنْ يَّقُوْلُوْا لَوْلَآ اُنْزِلَ عَلَيْهِ كَنْزٌ
اَوْ جَآءَ مَعَهٗ مَلَكٌ ۗ اِنَّمَآ اَنْتَ نَذِيْرٌ ۗ
وَاللّٰهُ عَلٰى كُلِّ شَيْءٍ وَّكِيْلٌ ○

13. Or they may say, "He forged it."
Say, "Bring ye then ten Sūrahs
Forged, like unto it, and call
(To your aid) whomsoever
Ye can, other than Allah!—
If ye speak the truth!

١٣- اَمْ يَقُوْلُوْنَ افْتَرٰىهُ ۗ قُلْ فَأْتُوْا بِعَشْرِ سُوَرٍ
مِّثْلِهٖ مُفْتَرَيٰتٍ وَّادْعُوْا مَنِ اسْتَطَعْتُمْ
مِّنْ دُوْنِ اللّٰهِ اِنْ كُنْتُمْ صٰدِقِيْنَ ○

14. "If then they (your false gods)
Answer not your (call),
Know ye that this Revelation
Is sent down (replete) with the
knowledge
Of Allah, and that there is
No god but He! Will ye
Even then submit (to Islam)?"

١٤- فَاِلَّمْ يَسْتَجِيْبُوْا لَكُمْ
فَاعْلَمُوْٓا اَنَّمَآ اُنْزِلَ بِعِلْمِ اللّٰهِ
وَاَنْ لَّآ اِلٰهَ اِلَّا هُوَ ۚ
فَهَلْ اَنْتُمْ مُّسْلِمُوْنَ ○

15. Those who desire
The life of the Present
And its glitter—to them
We shall pay (the price

١٥- مَنْ كَانَ يُرِيْدُ الْحَيٰوةَ الدُّنْيَا
وَزِيْنَتَهَا نُوَفِّ اِلَيْهِمْ اَعْمَالَهُمْ فِيْهَا

Of) their deeds therein—
Without diminution.

وَهُمْ فِيْهَا لَا يُبْخَسُوْنَ ۞

16. They are those for whom
There is nothing in the Hereafter
But the Fire: vain
Are the designs they frame therein,
And of no effect
Are the deeds that they do!

١٦- اُولٰٓئِكَ الَّذِيْنَ لَيْسَ لَهُمْ فِي الْاٰخِرَةِ اِلَّا النَّارُ ۖ وَحَبِطَ مَا صَنَعُوْا فِيْهَا وَبٰطِلٌ مَّا كَانُوْا يَعْمَلُوْنَ ۞

17. Can they be (like) those
Who accept a Clear (Sign)
From their Lord, and whom
A witness from Himself
Doth teach, as did the Book
Of Moses before it—a guide
And a mercy? They believe
Therein; but those of the Sects
That reject it—the Fire
Will be their promised
Meeting place. Be not then
In doubt thereon: for it is
The Truth from thy Lord:
Yet many among men
Do not believe!

١٧- اَفَمَنْ كَانَ عَلٰى بَيِّنَةٍ مِّنْ رَّبِّهٖ وَيَتْلُوْهُ شَاهِدٌ مِّنْهُ وَمِنْ قَبْلِهٖ كِتٰبُ مُوْسٰۤى اِمَامًا وَّرَحْمَةً ۚ اُولٰٓئِكَ يُؤْمِنُوْنَ بِهٖ ۚ وَمَنْ يَّكْفُرْ بِهٖ مِنَ الْاَحْزَابِ فَالنَّارُ مَوْعِدُهٗ ۚ فَلَا تَكُ فِيْ مِرْيَةٍ مِّنْهُ ۗ اِنَّهُ الْحَقُّ مِنْ رَّبِّكَ وَلٰكِنَّ اَكْثَرَ النَّاسِ لَا يُؤْمِنُوْنَ ۞

18. Who doth more wrong
Than those who invent a lie
Against Allah? They will be
Turned back to the presence
Of their Lord, and the witnesses
Will say, "There are the ones
Who lied against their Lord!
Behold! the Curse of Allah
Is on those who do wrong!—

١٨- وَمَنْ اَظْلَمُ مِمَّنِ افْتَرٰى عَلَى اللّٰهِ كَذِبًا ۚ اُولٰٓئِكَ يُعْرَضُوْنَ عَلٰى رَبِّهِمْ وَيَقُوْلُ الْاَشْهَادُ هٰٓؤُلَاۤءِ الَّذِيْنَ كَذَبُوْا عَلٰى رَبِّهِمْ ۚ اَلَا لَعْنَةُ اللّٰهِ عَلَى الظّٰلِمِيْنَ ۞

19. "Those who would hinder (men)
From the path of Allah
And would seek in it
Something crooked: these were
They who denied the
                    Hereafter!"

١٩- الَّذِيْنَ يَصُدُّوْنَ عَنْ سَبِيْلِ اللّٰهِ وَيَبْغُوْنَهَا عِوَجًا ۚ وَهُمْ بِالْاٰخِرَةِ هُمْ كٰفِرُوْنَ ۞

20. They will in nowise
Frustrate (His design) on earth,
Nor have they protectors
Besides Allah! Their penalty
Will be doubled! They lost
The power to hear,

٢٠- اُولٰٓئِكَ لَمْ يَكُوْنُوْا مُعْجِزِيْنَ فِي الْاَرْضِ وَمَا كَانَ لَهُمْ مِّنْ دُوْنِ اللّٰهِ مِنْ اَوْلِيَاۤءَ ۘ يُضٰعَفُ لَهُمُ الْعَذَابُ مَا كَانُوْا يَسْتَطِيْعُوْنَ

And they did not see!

21. They are the ones who
Have lost their own souls:
And the (fancies) they invented
Have left them in the lurch!

22. Without a doubt, these
Are the very ones who
Will lose most in the Hereafter!

23. But those who believe
And work righteousness,
And humble themselves
Before their Lord—
They will be Companions
Of the Garden, to dwell
Therein for aye!

24. These two kinds (of men)
May be compared to
The blind and deaf,
And those who can see
And hear well. Are they
Equal when compared?
Will ye not then take heed?

SECTION 3.

25. We sent Noah to his People
(With a mission): "I have come
To you with a Clear Warning:

26. "That ye serve none but Allah:
Verily I do fear for you
The Penalty of a Grievous
Day."

27. But the Chiefs of the
Unbelievers
Among his People said:
"We see (in) thee nothing
But a man like ourselves
Nor do we see that any
Follow thee but the meanest
Among us, in judgement
immature:
Nor do we see in you (all)
Any merit above us:
In fact we think ye are
liars!"

28. He said: "O my People!
    See ye if (it be that)
    I have a Clear Sign
    From my Lord, and that He
    Hath sent Mercy unto me
    From His own Presence, but
    That the Mercy hath been
    Obscured from your sight?
    Shall we compel you
    To accept it when ye
    Are averse to it?

٢٨- قَالَ يَقَوْمِ أَرَءَيْتُمْ
إِنْ كُنْتُ عَلَى بَيِّنَةٍ مِّنْ رَّبِّي
وَاٰتَنِى رَحْمَةً مِّنْ عِنْدِهِ
فَعُمِّيَتْ عَلَيْكُمْ
أَنُلْزِمُكُمُوهَا وَأَنْتُمْ لَهَا كَارِهُونَ ٠

29. "And O my People!
    I ask you for no wealth
    In return: my reward
    Is from none but Allah:
    But I will not drive away
    (In contempt) those who believe:
    For verily they are
    To meet their Lord, and ye,
    I see, are the ignorant ones!

٢٩- وَيَقَوْمِ لَا أَسْئَلُكُمْ عَلَيْهِ مَالًا
إِنْ أَجْرِيَ إِلَّا عَلَى اللّٰهِ
وَمَآ أَنَا بِطَارِدِ الَّذِيْنَ اٰمَنُوْا
إِنَّهُمْ مُّلَاقُوْا رَبِّهِمْ
وَلٰكِنِّى أَرٰكُمْ قَوْمًا تَجْهَلُوْنَ ٠

30. "And O my People!
    Who would help me against Allah
    If I drove them away?
    Will ye not then take heed?

٣٠- وَيَقَوْمِ مَنْ يَّنْصُرُنِى مِنَ اللّٰهِ
إِنْ طَرَدْتُّهُمْ أَفَلَا تَذَكَّرُوْنَ ٠

31, "I tell you not that
    With me are the Treasures
    Of Allah, nor do I know
    What is hidden,
    Nor claim I to be
    An angel. Nor yet
    Do I say, of those whom
    Your eyes do despise
    That Allah will not grant them
    (All) that is good:
    Allah knoweth best
    What is in their souls:
    I should, if I did,
    Indeed be a wrongdoer."

٣١- وَلَا أَقُوْلُ لَكُمْ عِنْدِى خَزَآئِنُ اللّٰهِ
وَلَا أَعْلَمُ الْغَيْبَ
وَلَا أَقُوْلُ إِنِّى مَلَكٌ
وَلَا أَقُوْلُ لِلَّذِيْنَ تَزْدَرِى أَعْيُنُكُمْ
لَنْ يُّؤْتِيَهُمُ اللّٰهُ خَيْرًا
اللّٰهُ أَعْلَمُ بِمَا فِى أَنْفُسِهِمْ
إِنِّى إِذًا لَّمِنَ الظّٰلِمِيْنَ ٠

32. They said: "O Noah!
    Thou hath disputed with us,
    And (much) hast thou prolonged
    The dispute with us: now
    Bring upon us what thou
    Threatenest us with, if thou
    Speakest the truth!?"

٣٢- قَالُوْا يَنُوْحُ قَدْ جَادَلْتَنَا
فَأَكْثَرْتَ جِدَالَنَا
فَأْتِنَا بِمَا تَعِدُنَآ
إِنْ كُنْتَ مِنَ الصّٰدِقِيْنَ ٠

33. He said: "Truly, Allah
Will bring it on you
If He wills—and then,
Ye will not be able
To frustrate it!

34. "Of no profit will be
My counsel to you,
Much as I desire
To give you (good) counsel,
If it be that Allah
Willeth to leave you astray:
He is your Lord!
And to Him will ye return!"

35. Or do they say,
"He has forged it?" Say:
"If I had forged it,
On me were my sin!
And I am free
Of the sins of which
Ye are guilty!"

SECTION 4.

36. It was revealed to Noah:
"None of thy People will believe
Except those who have believed
Already! So grieve no longer
Over their (evil) deeds.

37. "But construct an Ark
Under Our eyes and Our
Inspiration, and address Me
No (further) on behalf
Of those who are in sin:
For they are about to be
Overwhelmed (in the Flood)."

38. Forthwith he (starts)
Constructing the Ark:
Every time that the Chiefs
Of his People passed by him,
They threw ridicule on him.
He said: "If ye ridicule
Us now, we (in our turn)
Can look down on you
With ridicule likewise!

39. "But soon will ye know

٣٣- قَالَ إِنَّمَا يَأْتِيكُمْ بِهِ اللّٰهُ
إِنْ شَآءَ
وَمَآ أَنْتُمْ بِمُعْجِزِيْنَ ۞

٣٤- وَلَا يَنْفَعُكُمْ نُصْحِيْ
إِنْ أَرَدْتُّ أَنْ أَنْصَحَ لَكُمْ
إِنْ كَانَ اللّٰهُ يُرِيْدُ أَنْ يُّغْوِيَكُمْ
هُوَ رَبُّكُمْ ۖ وَإِلَيْهِ تُرْجَعُوْنَ ۞

٣٥- أَمْ يَقُوْلُوْنَ افْتَرٰىهُ
قُلْ إِنِ افْتَرَيْتُهُ فَعَلَيَّ إِجْرَامِيْ
وَأَنَا بَرِيٓءٌ مِّمَّا تُجْرِمُوْنَ ۞

٣٦- وَأُوْحِيَ إِلٰى نُوْحٍ أَنَّهُ لَنْ يُّؤْمِنَ مِنْ
قَوْمِكَ إِلَّا مَنْ قَدْ اٰمَنَ
فَلَا تَبْتَئِسْ بِمَا كَانُوْا يَفْعَلُوْنَ ۞

٣٧- وَاصْنَعِ الْفُلْكَ
بِأَعْيُنِنَا وَوَحْيِنَا
وَلَا تُخَاطِبْنِيْ فِى الَّذِيْنَ ظَلَمُوْا
إِنَّهُمْ مُّغْرَقُوْنَ ۞

٣٨- وَيَصْنَعُ الْفُلْكَ
وَكُلَّمَا مَرَّ عَلَيْهِ مَلَأٌ مِّنْ قَوْمِهِ سَخِرُوْا
مِنْهُ ۚ قَالَ إِنْ تَسْخَرُوْا مِنَّا فَإِنَّا
نَسْخَرُ مِنْكُمْ كَمَا تَسْخَرُوْنَ ۞

٣٩- فَسَوْفَ تَعْلَمُوْنَ

Who it is on whom
Will descend a Penalty
That will cover them
With shame—on whom will be
Unloosed a Penalty lasting:"

40. At length, behold!
There came Our Command,
And the fountains of the
                    earth
Gushed forth! We said:
"Embark therein, of each kind
Two, male and female,
And your family—except
Those against whom the Word
Has already gone forth—
And the Believers."
But only a few
Believed with him.

41. So he said: "Embark ye
On the Ark
In the name of Allah,
Whether it move
Or be at rest!
For my Lord is, be sure,
Oft-Forgiving, Most Merciful!"

42. So the Ark floated
With them on the waves
(Towering) like mountains,
And Noah called out
To his son, who had
Separated himself (from the
                    rest):
"O my son! embark
With us, and be not
With the Unbelievers!"

43. The son replied: "I will
Betake myself to some
                    mountain:
It will save me from
The water." Noah said:
"This day nothing can save,
From the Command of Allah,
Any but those on whom
He hath mercy!"—
And the waves came

مَنْ يَأْتِيهِ عَذَابٌ

نُخْزِيهِ وَيَحِلُّ عَلَيْهِ عَذَابٌ مُقِيمٌ ۟

٤٠- حَتّىٰ إِذَا جَاءَ أَمْرُنَا

وَفَارَ التَّنُّوْرُ ۙ

قُلْنَا احْمِلْ فِيهَا مِنْ كُلٍّ زَوْجَيْنِ

اثْنَيْنِ وَأَهْلَكَ إِلَّا مَنْ سَبَقَ عَلَيْهِ

الْقَوْلُ وَمَنْ اٰمَنَ ۚ

وَمَا اٰمَنَ مَعَهُ إِلَّا قَلِيلٌ ۟

٤١- وَقَالَ ارْكَبُوْا فِيهَا

بِسْمِ اللّٰهِ مَجْرٖىهَا وَمُرْسٰىهَا ۚ

إِنَّ رَبِّيْ لَغَفُوْرٌ رَّحِيْمٌ ۟

٤٢- وَهِيَ تَجْرِيْ بِهِمْ فِيْ مَوْجٍ كَالْجِبَالِ

وَنَادٰى نُوْحُ ﹰابْنَهُ

وَكَانَ فِيْ مَعْزِلٍ

يّٰبُنَيَّ ارْكَبْ مَّعَنَا

وَلَا تَكُنْ مَّعَ الْكٰفِرِيْنَ ۟

٤٣- قَالَ سَاٰوِيْٓ إِلٰى جَبَلٍ

يَّعْصِمُنِيْ مِنَ الْمَاءِ ۚ

قَالَ لَا عَاصِمَ الْيَوْمَ

مِنْ أَمْرِ اللّٰهِ إِلَّا مَنْ رَّحِمَ ۚ

وَحَالَ بَيْنَهُمَا الْمَوْجُ

Between them, and the son
Was among those
Overwhelmed in the Flood.

فَكَانَ مِنَ الْمُغْرَقِينَ ۝

44. Then the word went forth:
"O earth! swallow up
Thy water, and O sky!
Withhold (thy rain)!"
And the water abated,
And the matter was ended.
The Ark rested on Mount
Jūdī, and the word
Went forth: "Away
With those who do wrong!"

٤٤- وَقِيلَ يَا أَرْضُ ابْلَعِي
مَاءَكِ وَيَا سَمَاءُ
أَقْلِعِي وَغِيضَ الْمَاءُ وَقُضِيَ الْأَمْرُ
وَاسْتَوَتْ عَلَى الْجُودِيِّ
وَقِيلَ بُعْدًا لِلْقَوْمِ الظَّالِمِينَ ۝

45. And Noah called upon
His Lord, and said:
"O my Lord! surely
My son is of my family!
And Thy promise is true,
And Thou art
The Justest of Judges!"

٤٥- وَنَادَى نُوحٌ رَبَّهُ فَقَالَ
رَبِّ إِنَّ ابْنِي مِنْ أَهْلِي
وَإِنَّ وَعْدَكَ الْحَقُّ
وَأَنْتَ أَحْكَمُ الْحَاكِمِينَ ۝

46. He said: "O Noah!
He is not of thy family:
For his conduct is unrighteous.
So ask not of Me
That of which thou
Hast no knowledge!
I give thee counsel, lest
Thou act like the ignorant!"

٤٦- قَالَ يَا نُوحُ إِنَّهُ لَيْسَ مِنْ أَهْلِكَ
إِنَّهُ عَمَلٌ غَيْرُ صَالِحٍ
فَلَا تَسْأَلْنِ مَا لَيْسَ لَكَ بِهِ عِلْمٌ
إِنِّي أَعِظُكَ أَنْ تَكُونَ مِنَ الْجَاهِلِينَ ۝

47. Noah said: "O my Lord!
I do seek refuge with Thee,
Lest I ask Thee for that
Of which I have no knowledge.
And unless Thou forgive me
And have Mercy on me,
I should indeed be lost!"

٤٧- قَالَ رَبِّ إِنِّي أَعُوذُ بِكَ
أَنْ أَسْأَلَكَ مَا لَيْسَ لِي بِهِ عِلْمٌ
وَإِلَّا تَغْفِرْ لِي وَتَرْحَمْنِي أَكُنْ
مِنَ الْخَاسِرِينَ ۝

48. The word came: "O Noah!
Come down (from the Ark)
With Peace from Us,
And Blessing on thee
And on some of the Peoples
(Who will spring) from those
With thee: but (there will be
Other) Peoples to whom We

٤٨- قِيلَ يَا نُوحُ اهْبِطْ
بِسَلَامٍ مِنَّا وَبَرَكَاتٍ عَلَيْكَ
وَعَلَى أُمَمٍ مِمَّنْ مَعَكَ
وَأُمَمٌ سَنُمَتِّعُهُمْ

Shall grant their pleasures
(For a time), but in the end
Will a grievous Penalty
Reach them from Us."

ثُمَّ يَمَسُّهُمْ مِّنَّا
عَذَابٌ اَلِيْمٌ ۟

49. Such are some of the stories
Of the Unseen, which We
Have revealed unto thee:
Before this, neither thou
Nor thy People knew them.
So persevere patiently:
For the End is for those
Who are righteous.

۴۹- تِلْكَ مِنْ اَنْۢبَآءِ الْغَيْبِ
نُوْحِيْهَآ اِلَيْكَ ۚ مَا كُنْتَ تَعْلَمُهَآ اَنْتَ
وَلَا قَوْمُكَ مِنْ قَبْلِ هٰذَا ۚ فَاصْبِرْ ۚ
اِنَّ الْعَاقِبَةَ لِلْمُتَّقِيْنَ ۟

SECTION 5.

50. To the 'Ād People
(We sent) Hūd, one
Of their own brethren.
He said: "O my people!
Worship Allah! ye have
No other god but Him.
(Your other gods) ye do nothing
But invent!

۵۰- وَاِلٰى عَادٍ اَخَاهُمْ هُوْدًا ۚ
قَالَ يٰقَوْمِ اعْبُدُوا اللّٰهَ
مَا لَكُمْ مِّنْ اِلٰهٍ غَيْرُهٗ ۚ
اِنْ اَنْتُمْ اِلَّا مُفْتَرُوْنَ ۟

51. "O my people! I ask of you
No reward for this (Message).
My reward is from none
But Him who created me:
Will ye not then understand?

۵۱- يٰقَوْمِ لَا اَسْـَٔلُكُمْ عَلَيْهِ اَجْرًا ۚ
اِنْ اَجْرِيَ اِلَّا عَلَى الَّذِيْ فَطَرَنِيْ ۚ
اَفَلَا تَعْقِلُوْنَ ۟

52. "And O my people! Ask
Forgiveness of your Lord,
And turn to Him (in
　　　　　repentance):
He will send you the skies
Pouring abundant rain,
And add strength
To your strength:
So turn ye not back
In sin!"

۵۲- وَيٰقَوْمِ اسْتَغْفِرُوْا رَبَّكُمْ
ثُمَّ تُوْبُوْٓا اِلَيْهِ يُرْسِلِ السَّمَآءَ عَلَيْكُمْ
مِّدْرَارًا
وَّيَزِدْكُمْ قُوَّةً اِلٰى قُوَّتِكُمْ
وَلَا تَتَوَلَّوْا مُجْرِمِيْنَ ۟

53. They said: "O Hūd!
No Clear (Sign) hast thou
Brought us, and we are not
The ones to desert our gods
On thy word! Nor shall we
Believe in thee!

۵۳- قَالُوْا يٰهُوْدُ مَا جِئْتَنَا بِبَيِّنَةٍ
وَّمَا نَحْنُ بِتَارِكِيْٓ اٰلِهَتِنَا عَنْ
قَوْلِكَ وَمَا نَحْنُ لَكَ بِمُؤْمِنِيْنَ ۟

54. "We say nothing but that

۵۴- اِنْ نَّقُوْلُ اِلَّا

(Perhaps) some of our gods
May have seized thee
With imbecility." He said:
"I call Allah to witness,
And do ye bear witness,
That I am free from the sin
Of ascribing, to Him.

اعْتَرَاكَ بَعْضُ الِهَتِنَا بِسُوْٓءٍ ۖ
قَالَ اِنِّىٓ اُشْهِدُ اللّٰهَ وَ اشْهَدُوْۤا
اَنِّىْ بَرِىْٓءٌ مِّمَّا تُشْرِكُوْنَ ۙ

55. "Other gods as partners!
So scheme (your worst) against me,
All of you, and give me
No respite.

۵۵- مِنْ دُوْنِهٖ فَكِيْدُوْنِىْ
جَمِيْعًا ثُمَّ لَا تُنْظِرُوْنِ ۟

56. "I put my trust in Allah,
My Lord and your Lord!
There is not a moving
Creature, but He hath
Grasp of its forelock.
Verily, it is my Lord
That is on a straight Path.

۵۶- اِنِّىْ تَوَكَّلْتُ عَلَى اللّٰهِ رَبِّىْ وَ رَبِّكُمْ ۚ
مَا مِنْ دَآبَّةٍ اِلَّا هُوَ اٰخِذٌۢ بِنَاصِيَتِهَا ؕ
اِنَّ رَبِّىْ عَلٰى صِرَاطٍ مُّسْتَقِيْمٍ ۟

57. "If ye turn away —
I (at least) have conveyed
The Message with which I
Was sent to you. My Lord
Will make another People
To succeed you, and you
Will not harm Him
In the least. For my Lord
Hath care and watch
Over all things."

۵۷- فَاِنْ تَوَلَّوْا فَقَدْ اَبْلَغْتُكُمْ
مَّاۤ اُرْسِلْتُ بِهٖۤ اِلَيْكُمْ ؕ
وَ يَسْتَخْلِفُ رَبِّىْ قَوْمًا
غَيْرَكُمْ ۚ وَ لَا تَضُرُّوْنَهٗ شَيْئًا ؕ
اِنَّ رَبِّىْ عَلٰى كُلِّ شَىْءٍ حَفِيْظٌ ۟

58. So when Our decree
Issued, We saved Hūd
And those who believed
With him, by (special) Grace
From Ourselves: We saved them
From a severe Penalty.

۵۸- وَ لَمَّا جَآءَ اَمْرُنَا نَجَّيْنَا هُوْدًا
وَّ الَّذِيْنَ اٰمَنُوْا مَعَهٗ بِرَحْمَةٍ مِّنَّا ۚ
وَ نَجَّيْنٰهُمْ مِّنْ عَذَابٍ غَلِيْظٍ ۟

59. Such were the 'Ād People:
They rejected the Signs
Of their Lord and Cherisher;
Disobeyed His Messengers;
And followed the command
Of every powerful, obstinate
Transgressor.

۵۹- وَ تِلْكَ عَادٌ ۟ جَحَدُوْا بِاٰيٰتِ
رَبِّهِمْ وَ عَصَوْا رُسُلَهٗ
وَ اتَّبَعُوْۤا اَمْرَ كُلِّ جَبَّارٍ عَنِيْدٍ ۟

60. And they were pursued
By a Curse in this Life —

۶۰- وَ اُتْبِعُوْا فِىْ هٰذِهِ الدُّنْيَا لَعْنَةً

And on the Day of Judgement.
Ah! Behold! For the 'Ad
Rejected their Lord and Cherisher!
Ah! Behold! Removed (from sight)
Were 'Ad, the People of Hūd!

SECTION 6.

61. To the Thamūd People
(We sent) Ṣāliḥ, one
Of their own brethren.
He said: "O my People!
Worship Allah: ye have
No other god but Him.
It is He Who hath produced
                                    you
From the earth and settled you
Therein: then ask forgiveness
Of Him, and turn to Him
(In repentance): for my Lord
Is (always) near, ready
To answer."

62. They said: "O Ṣāliḥ!
Thou hast been of us!—
A centre of our hopes
Hitherto! Dost thou (now)
Forbid us the worship
Of what our fathers worshipped?
But we are really
In suspicious (disquieting)
Doubt as to that to which
Thou invitest us."

63. He said: "O my people!
Do ye see?—If I have
A Clear (Sign) from my Lord
And He hath sent Mercy
Unto me from Himself—who
Then can help me
Against Allah if I were
To disobey Him? What
Then would ye add
To my (portion) but perdition?

64. "And O my people!
This she-camel of Allah is
A symbol to you:
Leave her to feed
On Allah's (free) earth,

And inflict no harm
On her, or a swift Penalty
Will seize you!"

فَيَأْخُذَكُمْ عَذَابٌ قَرِيبٌ ۝

65. But they did hamstring her.
So he said: "Enjoy yourselves
In your homes for three days:
(Then will be your ruin):
(Behold) there a promise
Not to be belied!"

٦٥- فَعَقَرُوهَا فَقَالَ تَمَتَّعُوا فِي
دَارِكُمْ ثَلَاثَةَ أَيَّامٍ ۚ
ذٰلِكَ وَعْدٌ غَيْرُ مَكْذُوبٍ ۝

66. When Our Decree issued,
We saved Ṣāliḥ and those
Who believed with him,
By (special) Grace from
             Ourselves—
And from the Ignominy
Of that Day. For thy Lord—
He is the Strong One, and Able
To enforce His Will.

٦٦- فَلَمَّا جَاءَ أَمْرُنَا نَجَّيْنَا صَالِحًا
وَالَّذِينَ آمَنُوا مَعَهُ بِرَحْمَةٍ مِّنَّا
وَمِنْ خِزْيِ يَوْمِئِذٍ ۗ
إِنَّ رَبَّكَ هُوَ الْقَوِيُّ الْعَزِيزُ ۝

67. The (mighty) Blast   overtook
The wrongdoers, and they
Lay prostrate in their homes
Before the morning—

٦٧- وَأَخَذَ الَّذِينَ ظَلَمُوا الصَّيْحَةُ
فَأَصْبَحُوا فِي دِيَارِهِمْ جَاثِمِينَ ۙ

68. As if they had never
Dwelt and flourished there.
Ah! Behold! For the Thamūd
Rejected their Lord and Cherisher!
Ah! Behold! Removed
(From sight) were the Thamūd!

٦٨- كَأَنْ لَّمْ يَغْنَوْا فِيهَا ۗ
أَلَا إِنَّ ثَمُودَا كَفَرُوا رَبَّهُمْ ۗ
أَلَا بُعْدًا لِّثَمُودَ ۝

SECTION 7.

69. There came Our Messengers
To Abraham with glad tidings.
They said, "Peace!" He answered,
"Peace!" and hastened
To entertain them
With a roasted calf.

٦٩- وَلَقَدْ جَاءَتْ رُسُلُنَا إِبْرَاهِيمَ بِالْبُشْرَى
قَالُوا سَلَامًا ۖ قَالَ سَلَامٌ ۖ فَمَا لَبِثَ
أَنْ جَاءَ بِعِجْلٍ حَنِيذٍ ۝

70. But when he saw
Their hands went not
Towards the (meal), he felt
Some mistrust of them,
And conceived a fear of
            them.
They said: "Fear not:

٧٠- فَلَمَّا رَأَى أَيْدِيَهُمْ لَا تَصِلُ إِلَيْهِ نَكِرَهُمْ
وَأَوْجَسَ مِنْهُمْ خِيفَةً ۚ
قَالُوا لَا تَخَفْ

We have been sent
Against the people of Lūṭ."

اِنَّآ اُرْسِلْنَآ اِلٰی قَوْمِ لُوْطٍ ۞

71. And his wife was standing
(There), and she laughed:
But We gave her
Glad tidings of Isaac,
And after him, of Jacob.

٧١- وَامْرَاَتُهٗ قَآئِمَةٌ فَضَحِكَتْ
فَبَشَّرْنٰهَا بِاِسْحٰقَ ۙ
وَمِنْ وَّرَآءِ اِسْحٰقَ يَعْقُوْبَ ۞

72. She said: "Alas for me!
Shall I bear a child,
Seeing I am an old woman,
And my husband here
Is an old man?
That would indeed
Be a wonderful thing!"

٧٢- قَالَتْ يٰوَيْلَتٰٓی ءَاَلِدُ وَاَنَا عَجُوْزٌ
وَّهٰذَا بَعْلِیْ شَیْخًا ۗ
اِنَّ هٰذَا لَشَیْءٌ عَجِیْبٌ ۞

73. They said: "Dost thou
Wonder at Allah's decree?
The grace of Allah
And His blessings on you,
O ye people of the house!
For He is indeed
Worthy of all praise,
Full of all glory!"

٧٣- قَالُوْٓا اَتَعْجَبِیْنَ مِنْ اَمْرِ اللّٰهِ
رَحْمَتُ اللّٰهِ وَبَرَكٰتُهٗ عَلَیْكُمْ
اَهْلَ الْبَیْتِ ۗ
اِنَّهٗ حَمِیْدٌ مَّجِیْدٌ ۞

74. When fear had passed
From (the mind of) Abraham
And the glad tidings
Had reached him, he
Began to plead with Us
For Lūṭ's people.

٧٤- فَلَمَّا ذَهَبَ عَنْ اِبْرٰهِیْمَ الرَّوْعُ
وَجَآءَتْهُ الْبُشْرٰی
یُجَادِلُنَا فِیْ قَوْمِ لُوْطٍ ۞

75. For Abraham was,
Without doubt, forbearing
(Of faults), compassionate,
And given to look to Allah.

٧٥- اِنَّ اِبْرٰهِیْمَ لَحَلِیْمٌ
اَوَّاهٌ مُّنِیْبٌ ۞

76. O Abraham! Seek not this.
The decree of thy Lord
Hath gone forth: for them
There cometh a Penalty
That cannot be turned back!

٧٦- یٰٓاِبْرٰهِیْمُ اَعْرِضْ عَنْ هٰذَا ۚ اِنَّهٗ قَدْ
جَآءَ اَمْرُ رَبِّكَ ۚ وَاِنَّهُمْ اٰتِیْهِمْ عَذَابٌ
غَیْرُ مَرْدُوْدٍ ۞

77. When Our Messengers
Came to Lūṭ, he was
Grieved on their account

٧٧- وَلَمَّا جَآءَتْ رُسُلُنَا لُوْطًا

And felt himself powerless
(To protect) them. He said:
"This is a distressful day."

78. And his people came
Rushing towards him,
And they had been long
In the habit of practising
Abominations. He said:
"O my people! Here are
My daughters: they are purer
For you (if ye marry)!
Now fear Allah, and cover me not
With shame about my guests!
Is there not among you
A single right-minded man?"

79. They said: "Well dost thou
Know we have no need
Of thy daughters: indeed
Thou knowest quite well
What we want!"

80. He said: "Would that I
Had power to suppress you
Or that I could betake
Myself to some powerful
support."

81. (The Messengers) said: "O Lūṭ!
We are Messengers from thy Lord!
By no means shall they
Reach thee! Now travel
With thy family while yet
A part of the night remains,
And let not any of you
Look back: but thy wife
(Will remain behind):
To her will happen
What happens to the people.
Morning is their time appointed:
Is not the morning nigh?"

82. When Our decree issued,
We turned (the cities)
Upside down, and rained down
On them brimstones
Hard as baked clay,
Spread, layer on layer—

سِىءَ بِهِمْ وَضَاقَ بِهِمْ ذَرْعًا
وَّقَالَ هٰذَا يَوْمٌ عَصِيْبٌ ۟

٧٨ وَجَاءَهُ قَوْمُهُ يُهْرَعُوْنَ اِلَيْهِ
وَمِنْ قَبْلُ كَانُوْا يَعْمَلُوْنَ السَّيِّاٰتِ
قَالَ يٰقَوْمِ هٰٓؤُلَاءِ بَنَاتِيْ هُنَّ اَطْهَرُ لَكُمْ
فَاتَّقُوا اللّٰهَ
وَلَا تُخْزُوْنِ فِيْ ضَيْفِيْ
اَلَيْسَ مِنْكُمْ رَجُلٌ رَّشِيْدٌ ۟

٧٩ قَالُوْا لَقَدْ عَلِمْتَ مَا لَنَا
فِيْ بَنٰتِكَ مِنْ حَقٍّ ۚ
وَاِنَّكَ لَتَعْلَمُ مَا نُرِيْدُ ۟

٨٠ قَالَ لَوْ اَنَّ لِيْ بِكُمْ قُوَّةً
اَوْ اٰوِيْ اِلٰى رُكْنٍ شَدِيْدٍ ۟

٨١ قَالُوْا يٰلُوْطُ اِنَّا رُسُلُ رَبِّكَ
لَنْ يَّصِلُوْٓا اِلَيْكَ
فَاَسْرِ بِاَهْلِكَ بِقِطْعٍ مِّنَ الَّيْلِ
وَلَا يَلْتَفِتْ مِنْكُمْ اَحَدٌ اِلَّا امْرَاَتَكَ ؕ
اِنَّهُ مُصِيْبُهَا مَاۤ اَصَابَهُمْ ؕ
اِنَّ مَوْعِدَهُمُ الصُّبْحُ ؕ
اَلَيْسَ الصُّبْحُ بِقَرِيْبٍ ۟

٨٢ فَلَمَّا جَاۤءَ اَمْرُنَا
جَعَلْنَا عَالِيَهَا سَافِلَهَا وَاَمْطَرْنَا عَلَيْهَا
حِجَارَةً مِّنْ سِجِّيْلٍ ۙ مَّنْضُوْدٍ ۟

83. Marked as from thy Lord:
Nor are they　ever far
From those who do wrong!

SECTION 8.

84. To the Madyan people
(We sent) Shu'ayb, one
Of their own brethren: he said:
"O my people! worship Allah:
Ye have no other god
But Him. And give not
Short measure or weight:
I see you in prosperity,
But I fear for you
The Penalty of a Day
That will compass (you) all round.

85. "And O my people! give
Just measure and weight,
Nor withhold from the people
The things that are their due:
Commit not evil in the land
With intent to do mischief.

86. "That which is left you
By Allah is best for you,
If ye (but) believed!
But I am not set
Over you to keep watch!"

87. They said: "O Shu'ayb!
Does thy (religion of) prayer
Command thee that we
Leave off the worship which
Our fathers practised, or
That we leave off doing
What we like with our property?
Truly, thou art the one
That forbeareth with faults
And is right-minded!"

88. He said: "O my people!
See ye whether I have
A Clear (Sign) from my Lord,
And He hath given me
Sustenance (pure and) good
As from Himself? I wish not,
In opposition to you, to do
That which I forbid you to do.

٨٣- مُّسَوَّمَةً عِنْدَ رَبِّكَ ۚ وَمَا هِىَ مِنَ الظّٰلِمِيْنَ بِبَعِيْدٍ ۚ ۝

٨٤- وَاِلٰى مَدْيَنَ اَخَاهُمْ شُعَيْبًا ۚ قَالَ يٰقَوْمِ اعْبُدُوا اللّٰهَ مَا لَكُمْ مِّنْ اِلٰهٍ غَيْرُهٗ ۚ وَلَا تَنْقُصُوا الْمِكْيَالَ وَالْمِيْزَانَ اِنِّىْٓ اَرٰىكُمْ بِخَيْرٍ وَّاِنِّىْٓ اَخَافُ عَلَيْكُمْ عَذَابَ يَوْمٍ مُّحِيْطٍ ۝

٨٥- وَيٰقَوْمِ اَوْفُوا الْمِكْيَالَ وَالْمِيْزَانَ بِالْقِسْطِ وَلَا تَبْخَسُوا النَّاسَ اَشْيَاءَهُمْ وَلَا تَعْثَوْا فِى الْاَرْضِ مُفْسِدِيْنَ ۝

٨٦- بَقِيَّتُ اللّٰهِ خَيْرٌ لَّكُمْ اِنْ كُنْتُمْ مُّؤْمِنِيْنَ ۚ وَمَآ اَنَا عَلَيْكُمْ بِحَفِيْظٍ ۝

٨٦- قَالُوْا يٰشُعَيْبُ اَصَلٰوتُكَ تَأْمُرُكَ اَنْ نَّتْرُكَ مَا يَعْبُدُ اٰبَآؤُنَآ اَوْ اَنْ نَّفْعَلَ فِىْٓ اَمْوَالِنَا مَا نَشٰٓؤُا ۚ اِنَّكَ لَاَنْتَ الْحَلِيْمُ الرَّشِيْدُ ۝

٨٨- قَالَ يٰقَوْمِ اَرَءَيْتُمْ اِنْ كُنْتُ عَلٰى بَيِّنَةٍ مِّنْ رَّبِّىْ وَرَزَقَنِىْ مِنْهُ رِزْقًا حَسَنًا ۚ وَمَآ اُرِيْدُ اَنْ اُخَالِفَكُمْ اِلٰى مَآ اَنْهٰكُمْ

I only desire (your) betterment
To the best of my power;
And my success (in my task)
Can only come from Allah.
In Him I trust,
And unto Him I look.

عَنْهُ إِنْ أُرِيدُ إِلَّا الْإِصْلَاحَ مَا اسْتَطَعْتُ وَمَا تَوْفِيقِي إِلَّا بِاللَّهِ عَلَيْهِ تَوَكَّلْتُ وَإِلَيْهِ أُنِيبُ ٠

89. "And O my people!
Let not my dissent (from you)
Cause you to sin,
Lest ye suffer
A fate similar to that
Of the people of Noah
Or of Hūd or of Ṣāliḥ,
Nor are the people of Lūṭ
Far off from you!

٨٩- وَيَقَوْمِ لَا يَجْرِمَنَّكُمْ شِقَاقِي أَنْ يُصِيبَكُم مِّثْلُ مَا أَصَابَ قَوْمَ نُوحٍ أَوْ قَوْمَ هُودٍ أَوْ قَوْمَ صَالِحٍ وَمَا قَوْمُ لُوطٍ مِّنكُم بِبَعِيدٍ ٠

90. "But ask forgiveness
Of your Lord, and turn
Unto Him (in repentance):
For my Lord is indeed
Full of mercy and loving-kindness."

٩٠- وَاسْتَغْفِرُوا رَبَّكُمْ ثُمَّ تُوبُوا إِلَيْهِ إِنَّ رَبِّي رَحِيمٌ وَدُودٌ ٠

91. They said: "O Shu'ayb!
Much of what thou sayest
We do not understand!
In fact, among us we see
That thou hast no strength!
Were it not for thy family,
We should certainly
Have stoned thee!
For thou hast among us
No great position!"

٩١- قَالُوا يَا شُعَيْبُ مَا نَفْقَهُ كَثِيرًا مِّمَّا تَقُولُ وَإِنَّا لَنَرَاكَ فِينَا ضَعِيفًا وَلَوْلَا رَهْطُكَ لَرَجَمْنَاكَ وَمَا أَنتَ عَلَيْنَا بِعَزِيزٍ ٠

92. He said: "O my people!
Is then my family
Of more consideration with you
Than Allah? For ye cast Him
Away behind your backs
(With contempt). But verily
My Lord encompasseth
On all sides
All that ye do!

٩٢- قَالَ يَا قَوْمِ أَرَهْطِي أَعَزُّ عَلَيْكُم مِّنَ اللَّهِ وَاتَّخَذْتُمُوهُ وَرَاءَكُمْ ظِهْرِيًّا إِنَّ رَبِّي بِمَا تَعْمَلُونَ مُحِيطٌ ٠

93. "And O my people
Do whatever ye can:
I will do (my part):
Soon will ye know

٩٣- وَيَا قَوْمِ اعْمَلُوا عَلَىٰ مَكَانَتِكُمْ إِنِّي عَامِلٌ

Who it is on whom
Descends the Penalty
Of ignominy, and who
Is a liar!
And watch ye!
For I too am watching
With you!"

سَوْفَ تَعْلَمُوْنَ مَنْ يَّأْتِيْهِ عَذَابٌ يُّخْزِيْهِ وَمَنْ هُوَ كَاذِبٌ ۗ وَارْتَقِبُوْا اِنِّيْ مَعَكُمْ رَقِيْبٌ ۞

94. When Our decree issued,
We saved Shu'ayb and those
Who believed with him,
By (special) Mercy from
        Ourselves:
But the (mighty) Blast did seize
The wrongdoers, and they
Lay prostrate in their homes
By the morning—

٩٤- وَلَمَّا جَآءَ اَمْرُنَا نَجَّيْنَا شُعَيْبًا وَّالَّذِيْنَ اٰمَنُوْا مَعَهٗ بِرَحْمَةٍ مِّنَّا ۚ وَاَخَذَتِ الَّذِيْنَ ظَلَمُوا الصَّيْحَةُ فَاَصْبَحُوْا فِيْ دِيَارِهِمْ جٰثِمِيْنَ ۙ

95. As if they had never
Dwelt and flourished there!
Ah! Behold! How the Madyan
Were removed (from sight)
As were removed the Thamūd!

٩٥- كَاَنْ لَّمْ يَغْنَوْا فِيْهَا ۗ اَلَا بُعْدًا لِّمَدْيَنَ كَمَا بَعِدَتْ ثَمُوْدُ ۞ ع

SECTION 9.

96. And we sent Moses,
With our Clear (signs)
And an authority manifest,

٩٦- وَلَقَدْ اَرْسَلْنَا مُوْسٰى بِاٰيٰتِنَا وَسُلْطٰنٍ مُّبِيْنٍ ۙ

97. Unto Pharaoh and his Chiefs:
But they followed the
           command
Of Pharaoh, and the command
Of Pharaoh was no right (guide).

٩٧- اِلٰى فِرْعَوْنَ وَمَلَا۟ئِهٖ فَاتَّبَعُوْا اَمْرَ فِرْعَوْنَ ۚ وَمَآ اَمْرُ فِرْعَوْنَ بِرَشِيْدٍ ۞

98. He will go before his people
On the Day of Judgement,
And lead them into the Fire
(As cattle are led to water):
But woeful indeed will be
The place to which they are led!

٩٨- يَقْدُمُ قَوْمَهٗ يَوْمَ الْقِيٰمَةِ فَاَوْرَدَهُمُ النَّارَ ۚ وَبِئْسَ الْوِرْدُ الْمَوْرُوْدُ ۞

99. And they are followed
By a curse in this (life)
And on the Day of Judgement:
And woeful is the gift
Which shall be given
(Unto them)!

٩٩- وَاُتْبِعُوْا فِيْ هٰذِهٖ لَعْنَةً وَّيَوْمَ الْقِيٰمَةِ ۚ بِئْسَ الرِّفْدُ الْمَرْفُوْدُ ۞

100. These are some of the stories

١٠٠- ذٰلِكَ مِنْ اَنْۢبَآءِ الْقُرٰى

Of communities which We
Relate unto thee: of them
Some are standing,   and some
Have been mown down
(By the sickle of time).

نَقُصُّهُ عَلَيْكَ مِنْهَا قَآئِمٌ وَّحَصِيْدٌ ۟

101. It was not We that wronged them:
They wronged their own souls:
The deities, other than Allah,
Whom they invoked, profited them
No whit when there issued
The decree of thy Lord:
Nor did they add aught
(To their lot) but perdition!

١٠١- وَمَا ظَلَمْنٰهُمْ وَلٰكِنْ ظَلَمُوْۤا اَنْفُسَهُمْ فَمَاۤ اَغْنَتْ عَنْهُمْ اٰلِهَتُهُمُ الَّتِيْ يَدْعُوْنَ مِنْ دُوْنِ اللّٰهِ مِنْ شَيْءٍ لَّمَّا جَآءَ اَمْرُ رَبِّكَ ۚ وَمَا زَادُوْهُمْ غَيْرَ تَتْبِيْبٍ ۟

102. Such is the chastisement
Of thy Lord when He chastises
Communities in the midst of
Their wrong: grievous, indeed,
And severe is His chastisement.

١٠٢- وَكَذٰلِكَ اَخْذُ رَبِّكَ اِذَاۤ اَخَذَ الْقُرٰى وَهِيَ ظَالِمَةٌ ۚ اِنَّ اَخْذَهٗۤ اَلِيْمٌ شَدِيْدٌ ۟

103. In that is a Sign
For those who fear
The Penalty of the Hereafter:
That is a Day for which mankind
Will be gathered together:
That will be a Day
Of Testimony.

١٠٣- اِنَّ فِيْ ذٰلِكَ لَاٰيَةً لِّمَنْ خَافَ عَذَابَ الْاٰخِرَةِ ۚ ذٰلِكَ يَوْمٌ مَّجْمُوْعٌ ۙ لَّهُ النَّاسُ وَذٰلِكَ يَوْمٌ مَّشْهُوْدٌ ۟

104. Nor shall We delay it
But for a term appointed.

١٠٤- وَمَا نُؤَخِّرُهٗۤ اِلَّا لِاَجَلٍ مَّعْدُوْدٍ ۟

105. The day it arrives,
No soul shall speak
Except by His leave:
Of those (gathered) some
Will be wretched and some
Will be blessed.

١٠٥- يَوْمَ يَأْتِ لَا تَكَلَّمُ نَفْسٌ اِلَّا بِاِذْنِهٖ ۚ فَمِنْهُمْ شَقِيٌّ وَّسَعِيْدٌ ۟

106. Those who are wretched
Shall be in the Fire:
There will be for them
Therein (nothing but) the heaving
Of sighs and sobs:

١٠٦- فَاَمَّا الَّذِيْنَ شَقُوْا فَفِي النَّارِ لَهُمْ فِيْهَا زَفِيْرٌ وَّشَهِيْقٌ ۟

107. They will dwell therein
For all the time that
The heavens and the earth

١٠٧- خٰلِدِيْنَ فِيْهَا مَا دَامَتِ السَّمٰوٰتُ وَالْاَرْضُ

Endure, except as thy Lord
Willeth: for thy Lord
Is the (sure) Accomplisher
Of what He planneth.

إِلَّا مَا شَاءَ رَبُّكَ ۚ إِنَّ رَبَّكَ
فَعَّالٌ لِّمَا يُرِيدُ ۞

108. And those who are blessed
Shall be in the Garden:
They will dwell therein
For all the time that
The heavens and the earth
Endure, except as thy Lord
Willeth: a gift without break.

١٠٨- وَأَمَّا الَّذِيْنَ سُعِدُوْا فَفِي الْجَنَّةِ
خٰلِدِيْنَ فِيْهَا مَا دَامَتِ
السَّمٰوٰتُ وَالْأَرْضُ
إِلَّا مَا شَاءَ رَبُّكَ ۚ عَطَاءً غَيْرَ مَجْذُوْذٍ ۞

SECTION 10.

109. Be not then in doubt
As to what these men
Worship. They worship nothing
But what their fathers worshipped
Before (them): but verily
We shall pay them back
(In full) their portion
Without (the least) abatement.

١٠٩- فَلَا تَكُ فِيْ مِرْيَةٍ مِّمَّا يَعْبُدُ هٰؤُلَاءِ ۚ
مَا يَعْبُدُوْنَ إِلَّا
كَمَا يَعْبُدُ اٰبَآؤُهُمْ مِّنْ قَبْلُ ۚ وَإِنَّا
لَمُوَفُّوْهُمْ نَصِيْبَهُمْ غَيْرَ مَنْقُوْصٍ ۞

110. We certainly gave the Book
To Moses, but differences
Arose therein: had it not been
That a Word had gone forth
Before from thy Lord, the matter
Would have been decided
Between them: but they
Are in suspicious doubt
Concerning it.

١١٠- وَلَقَدْ اٰتَيْنَا مُوْسَى الْكِتٰبَ فَاخْتُلِفَ
فِيْهِ ۚ
وَلَوْ لَا كَلِمَةٌ
سَبَقَتْ مِنْ رَّبِّكَ لَقُضِيَ بَيْنَهُمْ ۚ
وَإِنَّهُمْ لَفِيْ شَكٍّ مِّنْهُ مُرِيْبٍ ۞

111. And, of a surety, to all
Will your Lord pay back
(In full the recompense)
Of their deeds: for He
Knoweth well all that they do.

١١١- وَإِنَّ كُلًّا لَّمَّا لَيُوَفِّيَنَّهُمْ رَبُّكَ أَعْمَالَهُمْ ۚ
إِنَّهُ بِمَا يَعْمَلُوْنَ خَبِيْرٌ ۞

112. Therefore stand firm (in the
straight
Path) as thou art commanded—
Thou and those who with thee
Turn (unto Allah); and transgress
not
(From the Path); for He seeth
Well all that ye do.

١١٢- فَاسْتَقِمْ كَمَا أُمِرْتَ
وَمَنْ تَابَ مَعَكَ وَلَا تَطْغَوْا ۚ
إِنَّهُ بِمَا تَعْمَلُوْنَ بَصِيْرٌ ۞

113. And incline not to those

١١٣- وَلَا تَرْكَنُوْا إِلَى الَّذِيْنَ ظَلَمُوْا فَتَمَسَّكُمُ

Who do wrong, or the Fire
Will seize you; and ye have
No protectors other than Allah,
Nor shall ye be helped.

النَّارُ وَمَا لَكُمْ مِّنْ دُوْنِ اللّٰهِ مِنْ اَوْلِيَآءَ
ثُمَّ لَا تُنْصَرُوْنَ ۟

114. And establish regular prayers
At the two ends of the day
And at the approaches of
                    the night:
For those things that are good
Remove those that are evil:
Be that the word of remembrance
To those who remember
                    (their Lord):

١١٤- وَاَقِمِ الصَّلٰوةَ طَرَفَيِ النَّهَارِ
وَزُلَفًا مِّنَ الَّيْلِ ؕ
اِنَّ الْحَسَنٰتِ يُذْهِبْنَ السَّيِّاٰتِ ؕ
ذٰلِكَ ذِكْرٰى لِلذّٰكِرِيْنَ ۟

115. And be steadfast in patience;
For verily Allah will not suffer
The reward of the righteous
To perish.

١١٥- وَاصْبِرْ
فَاِنَّ اللّٰهَ لَا يُضِيْعُ اَجْرَ الْمُحْسِنِيْنَ ۟

116. Why were there not,
Among the generations before you,
Persons possessed of balanced
Good sense, prohibiting (men)
From mischief in the earth—
Except a few among them
Whom We saved (from harm)?
But the wrongdoers pursued
The enjoyment of the good things
Of life which were given them,
And persisted in sin.

١١٦- فَلَوْلَا كَانَ مِنَ الْقُرُوْنِ مِنْ قَبْلِكُمْ
اُولُوْا بَقِيَّةٍ يَّنْهَوْنَ
عَنِ الْفَسَادِ فِى الْاَرْضِ اِلَّا قَلِيْلًا
مِّمَّنْ اَنْجَيْنَا مِنْهُمْ ؕ
وَاتَّبَعَ الَّذِيْنَ ظَلَمُوْا مَا اُتْرِفُوْا فِيْهِ
وَكَانُوْا مُجْرِمِيْنَ ۟

117. Nor would thy Lord be
The One to destroy
Communities for a single
                    wrongdoing
If its members were likely
To mend.

١١٧- وَمَا كَانَ رَبُّكَ لِيُهْلِكَ
الْقُرٰى بِظُلْمٍ
وَّاَهْلُهَا مُصْلِحُوْنَ ۟

118. If thy Lord had so willed,
He could have made mankind
One People: but they
Will not cease to dispute,

١١٨- وَلَوْ شَآءَ رَبُّكَ لَجَعَلَ النَّاسَ اُمَّةً
وَّاحِدَةً وَّلَا يَزَالُوْنَ مُخْتَلِفِيْنَ ۟

119. Except those on whom thy Lord
Hath bestowed His Mercy:
And for this did He create

١١٩- اِلَّا مَنْ رَّحِمَ رَبُّكَ ؕ
وَلِذٰلِكَ خَلَقَهُمْ ؕ وَتَمَّتْ كَلِمَةُ رَبِّكَ

Them: and the Word
Of thy Lord shall be fulfilled:
"I will fill Hell with jinns
And men all together."

لَاَمْلَأَنَّ جَهَنَّمَ مِنَ الْجِنَّةِ
وَالنَّاسِ أَجْمَعِينَ ۝

120. All that we relate to thee
Of the stories of the
               messengers—
With it We make firm
Thy heart: in them there
               cometh
To thee the Truth, as well as
An exhortation and a message
Of remembrance to those who
               believe.

١٢٠- وَكُلًّا نَّقُصُّ عَلَيْكَ مِنْ أَنْبَآءِ الرُّسُلِ
مَا نُثَبِّتُ بِهِ فُؤَادَكَ ۚ
وَجَآءَكَ فِي هٰذِهِ الْحَقُّ
وَمَوْعِظَةٌ وَّذِكْرٰى لِلْمُؤْمِنِينَ ۝

121. Say to those who do not
Believe: "Do whatever ye can:
We shall do our part;

١٢١- وَقُلْ لِّلَّذِينَ لَا يُؤْمِنُونَ اعْمَلُوا
عَلٰى مَكَانَتِكُمْ إِنَّا عَامِلُونَ ۝

122. "And wait ye!
We too shall wait."

١٢٢- وَانْتَظِرُوا إِنَّا مُنْتَظِرُونَ ۝

123. To Allah do belong
The unseen (secrets)
Of the heavens and the earth,
And to Him goeth back
Every affair (for decision):
Then worship Him,
And put thy trust in Him:
And thy Lord is not
Unmindful of aught
That ye do.

١٢٣- وَلِلّٰهِ غَيْبُ السَّمٰوٰتِ وَالْأَرْضِ
وَإِلَيْهِ يُرْجَعُ الْأَمْرُ
كُلُّهُ فَاعْبُدْهُ
وَتَوَكَّلْ عَلَيْهِ ۚ
وَمَا رَبُّكَ بِغَافِلٍ عَمَّا تَعْمَلُونَ ۝ ۚ ۏ

INTRODUCTION TO SŪRA XII.*(Yūsuf)* — 111 Verses

For the chronological place of this Sūra and the general argument of Sūras x. to xv. see Introduction to Sūra X.

In Subject-matter this Sūra is entirely taken up with the story (recapitulated rather than told) of Joseph, the youngest (but one) of the twelve sons of the patriarch Jacob. The story is called the most beautiful of stories (xii.3) for many reasons: (1) it is the most detailed of any in the Qur-ān (2) it is full of human vicissitudes, and has therefore deservedly appealed to men and women of all classes; (3) it paints in vivid colours, with their spiritual implications, the most varied aspects of life— the patriarch's old age and the confidence between him and his little best-beloved son, the elder brother's jealousy of this little son, their plot and their father's grief, the sale of the father's darling into slavery for a miserable little price, carnal love contrasted with purity and chastity, false charges, prison, the interpretation of dreams, low life and high life, Innocence raised to honour; the sweet "revenge" of Forgiveness and Benevolence, high matters of State and administration, humility, in exaltation, filial love, and the beauty of Piety and Truth.

The story is similar to but not identical with the Biblical story; but the atmosphere is wholly different. The Biblical story is like a folk-tale in which morality has no place. Its tendency is to exalt the clever and financially-minded Jew against the Egyptian, and to explain certain ethnic and tribal peculiarities in later Jewish history. Joseph is shown as buying up all the cattle and the land of the poor Egyptians for the State under the stress of famine conditions, and making the Israelites "rulers" over Pharaoh's cattle. The Quranic story, on the other hand, is less a narrative than a highly spiritual sermon or allegory explaining the seeming contradictions in life, the enduring nature of virtue in a world full of flux and change, and the marvellous working of God's eternal purpose in His Plan as unfolded to us on the wide canvas of history. This aspect of the matter has been a favourite with Muslim poets and Ṣūfī exegetists, and is further referred to in Appendix VI. (at the end of this Sūra), in connection with Jāmī's great Persian masterpiece, *Yūsuf-o-Zulaikhā*.

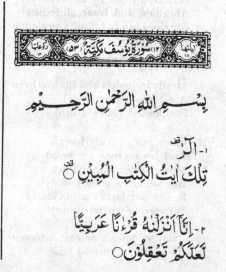

Yūsuf (Joseph)

In the name of Allah, Most Gracious,
Most Merciful.

1. Alif Lām Rā'.[1627] These are
The Symbols[1628] (or Verses)
Of the Perspicuous Book.

2. We have sent it down
As an Arabic Qur'ān,
In order that ye may
Learn wisdom.

3. We do relate unto thee
The most beautiful of stories,
In that We reveal to thee
This (portion of the) Qur'ān:
Before this, thou too
Was among those
Who knew it not.

٣ـ نَحْنُ نَقُصُّ عَلَيْكَ أَحْسَنَ الْقَصَصِ بِمَا أَوْحَيْنَا إِلَيْكَ هٰذَا الْقُرْاٰنَ ۚ وَإِنْ كُنْتَ مِنْ قَبْلِهِ لَمِنَ الْغٰفِلِيْنَ ۞

4. Behold, Joseph said
To his father: "O my father!
I did see eleven stars
And the sun and the moon:
I saw them prostrate themselves
To me!"

٤ـ إِذْ قَالَ يُوْسُفُ لِأَبِيْهِ يٰأَبَتِ إِنِّيْ رَأَيْتُ أَحَدَ عَشَرَ كَوْكَبًا وَّالشَّمْسَ وَالْقَمَرَ رَأَيْتُهُمْ لِيْ سٰجِدِيْنَ ۞

5. Said (the father):
"My (dear) little son!
Relate not thy vision
To thy brothers, lest they
Concoct a plot against thee:
For Satan is to man
An avowed enemy!

٥ـ قَالَ يٰبُنَيَّ لَا تَقْصُصْ رُؤْيَاكَ عَلٰى إِخْوَتِكَ فَيَكِيْدُوْا لَكَ كَيْدًا ۚ إِنَّ الشَّيْطٰنَ لِلْإِنْسَانِ عَدُوٌّ مُّبِيْنٌ ۞

6. "Thus will thy Lord
Choose thee and teach thee
The interpretation of stories
(and events)
And perfect His favour
To thee and to the posterity
Of Jacob—even as He
Perfected it to thy fathers
Abraham and Isaac aforetime!
For thy Lord is full of knowledge
And wisdom."

٦ـ وَكَذٰلِكَ يَجْتَبِيْكَ رَبُّكَ وَيُعَلِّمُكَ مِنْ تَأْوِيْلِ الْأَحَادِيْثِ وَيُتِمُّ نِعْمَتَهٗ عَلَيْكَ وَعَلٰى اٰلِ يَعْقُوْبَ كَمَا أَتَمَّهَا عَلٰى أَبَوَيْكَ مِنْ قَبْلُ إِبْرٰهِيْمَ وَإِسْحٰقَ ۚ إِنَّ رَبَّكَ عَلِيْمٌ حَكِيْمٌ ۞

SECTION 2.

7. Verily in Joseph and his brethren
Are Signs (or Symbols)
For Seekers (after Truth).

٧ـ لَقَدْ كَانَ فِيْ يُوْسُفَ وَإِخْوَتِهِ اٰيٰتٌ لِّلسَّائِلِيْنَ ۞

8. They said: "Truly Joseph
And his brother are loved
More by our father than we:
But we are a goodly body!
Really our father is obviously
Wandering (in his mind)!

٨ـ إِذْ قَالُوْا لَيُوْسُفُ وَأَخُوْهُ أَحَبُّ إِلٰى أَبِيْنَا مِنَّا وَنَحْنُ عُصْبَةٌ ۚ إِنَّ أَبَانَا لَفِيْ ضَلٰلٍ مُّبِيْنٍ ۞

9. "Slay ye Joseph or cast him out
To some (unknown) land,

٩ـ اقْتُلُوْا يُوْسُفَ أَوِ اطْرَحُوْهُ أَرْضًا

That so the favour
Of your father may be
Given to you alone:
(There will be time enough)
For you to be righteous after
that!"

١٠. Said one of them: "Slay not
Joseph, but if ye must
Do something, throw him down
To the bottom of the well:
He will be picked up
By some caravan of travellers."

١١. They said: "O our father!
Why dost thou not
Trust us with Joseph—
Seeing we are indeed
His sincere well-wishers?

١٢. "Send him with us tomorrow
To enjoy himself and play,
And we shall take
Every care of him."

13. (Jacob) said: "Really
It saddens me that ye
Should take him away:
I fear lest the wolf
Should devour him
While ye attend not
To him."

14. They said: "If the wolf
Were to devour him
While we are (so large) a party,
Then should we indeed
(First) have perished ourselves!"

15. So they did take him away,
And they all agreed
To throw him down
To the bottom of the well:
And We put into his heart
(This Message): 'Of a surety
Thou shalt (one day)
Tell them the truth
Of this their affair
While they know (thee) not.'"

16. Then they came
To their father
In the early part
Of the night,
Weeping.

17. They said: "O our father!
We went racing with one
another,
And left Joseph with our things;
And the wolf devoured him...
But thou wilt never believe us
Even though we tell the truth."

18. They stained his shirt
With false blood. He said:
"Nay, but your minds
Have made up a tale
(That may pass) with you.
(For me) patience is most fitting:
Against that which ye assert,
It is Allah (alone)
Whose help can be sought.". . .

19. Then there came a caravan
Of travellers: they sent
Their water-carrier (for water),
And he let down his bucket
(Into the well)...He said:
"Ah there! Good news!
Here is a (fine) young man!"
So they concealed him
As a treasure! But Allah
Knoweth well all that they do!

20. The (Brethren) sold him
For a miserable price—
For a few dirhams   counted out:
In such low estimation
Did they hold him!

SECTION 3.

21. The man in Egypt
Who bought him, said
To his wife: "Make his stay
(Among us) honourable:
Maybe he will bring us
Much good, or we shall
Adopt him as a son."

١- وَجَآءُوٓ أَبَاهُمْ عِشَآءً يَبْكُونَ ۟

١٧- قَالُوا يَٰٓأَبَانَآ إِنَّا ذَهَبْنَا نَسْتَبِقُ وَتَرَكْنَا يُوسُفَ عِندَ مَتَاعِنَا فَأَكَلَهُ الذِّئْبُ ۖ وَمَآ أَنتَ بِمُؤْمِنٍ لَّنَا وَلَوْ كُنَّا صَٰدِقِينَ ۟

١٨- وَجَآءُو عَلَىٰ قَمِيصِهِ بِدَمٍ كَذِبٍ ۚ قَالَ بَلْ سَوَّلَتْ لَكُمْ أَنفُسُكُمْ أَمْرًا ۖ فَصَبْرٌ جَمِيلٌ ۖ وَٱللَّهُ ٱلْمُسْتَعَانُ عَلَىٰ مَا تَصِفُونَ ۟

١٩- وَجَآءَتْ سَيَّارَةٌ فَأَرْسَلُوا وَارِدَهُمْ فَأَدْلَىٰ دَلْوَهُ ۖ قَالَ يَٰبُشْرَىٰ هَٰذَا غُلَٰمٌ ۚ وَأَسَرُّوهُ بِضَٰعَةً ۚ وَٱللَّهُ عَلِيمٌ بِمَا يَعْمَلُونَ ۟

٢٠- وَشَرَوْهُ بِثَمَنٍ بَخْسٍ دَرَٰهِمَ مَعْدُودَةٍ وَكَانُوا فِيهِ مِنَ ٱلزَّٰهِدِينَ ۟

٢١- وَقَالَ ٱلَّذِى ٱشْتَرَىٰهُ مِن مِّصْرَ لِٱمْرَأَتِهِ أَكْرِمِى مَثْوَىٰهُ عَسَىٰٓ أَن يَنفَعَنَآ أَوْ نَتَّخِذَهُ وَلَدًا ۚ

Thus did We establish
Joseph in the land,
That We might teach him
The interpretation of stories
(And events). And Allah
Hath full power and control
Over His affairs; but most
Among mankind know it not.

وَكَذٰلِكَ مَكَّنَّا لِيُوسُفَ فِي الْأَرْضِ
وَلِنُعَلِّمَهُ مِنْ تَأْوِيلِ الْأَحَادِيثِ ۚ
وَاللّٰهُ غَالِبٌ عَلَى أَمْرِهٖ
وَلٰكِنَّ أَكْثَرَ النَّاسِ لَا يَعْلَمُونَ ۞

22. When Joseph attained
His full manhood, We gave him
Power and knowledge: thus do We
Reward those who do right.

٢٢- وَلَمَّا بَلَغَ أَشُدَّهُ آتَيْنٰهُ حُكْمًا وَّعِلْمًا ۚ
وَكَذٰلِكَ نَجْزِي الْمُحْسِنِينَ ۞

23. But she in whose house
He was, sought to seduce him
From his (true) self: she fastened
The doors, and said:
"Now come, thou (dear one)!"
He said: "Allah forbid!
Truly (thy husband) is
My lord! he made
My sojourn agreeable!
Truly to no good
Come those who do wrong!

٢٣- وَرَاوَدَتْهُ الَّتِي هُوَ فِي بَيْتِهَا عَنْ
نَفْسِهٖ
وَغَلَّقَتِ الْأَبْوَابَ
وَقَالَتْ هَيْتَ لَكَ ۚ
قَالَ مَعَاذَ اللّٰهِ إِنَّهُ رَبِّي أَحْسَنَ مَثْوَايَ
إِنَّهُ لَا يُفْلِحُ الظّٰلِمُونَ ۞

24. And (with passion) did she
Desire him, and he would
Have desired her, but that
He saw the evidence
Of his Lord: thus
(Did We order) that We
Might turn away from him
(All) evil and shameful deeds:
For he was one of Our servants,
Sincere and purified.

٢٤- وَلَقَدْ هَمَّتْ بِهٖ ۚ وَهَمَّ بِهَا
لَوْلَا أَنْ رَّا بُرْهَانَ
رَبِّهٖ ۚ كَذٰلِكَ لِنَصْرِفَ عَنْهُ
السُّوءَ وَالْفَحْشَاءَ ۚ
إِنَّهُ مِنْ عِبَادِنَا الْمُخْلَصِينَ ۞

25. So they both raced each other
To the door, and she
Tore his shirt from the back:
They both found her lord
Near the door. She said:
"What is the (fitting) punishment
For one who formed
An evil design against
Thy wife, but prison
Or a grievous chastisement?"

٢٥- وَاسْتَبَقَا الْبَابَ
وَقَدَّتْ قَمِيصَهُ مِنْ دُبُرٍ
وَّأَلْفَيَا سَيِّدَهَا لَدَى الْبَابِ ۚ
قَالَتْ مَا جَزَاءُ مَنْ أَرَادَ بِأَهْلِكَ سُوءًا
إِلَّا أَنْ يُّسْجَنَ أَوْ عَذَابٌ أَلِيمٌ ۞

26. He said: "It was she
That sought to seduce me—

٢٦- قَالَ هِيَ رَاوَدَتْنِي عَنْ نَفْسِي

From my (true) self." And one
Of her household saw (this)
And bore witness, (thus)—
"If it be that his shirt
Is rent from the front, then
Is her tale true,
And he is a liar!

وَشَهِدَ شَاهِدٌ مِّنْ أَهْلِهَا ۚ
إِنْ كَانَ قَمِيْصُهُ قُدَّ مِنْ قُبُلٍ
فَصَدَقَتْ
وَهُوَ مِنَ الْكٰذِبِيْنَ ۟

27. "But if it be that his shirt
Is torn from the back,
Then is she the liar,
And he is telling the truth!"

٢٧- وَإِنْ كَانَ قَمِيْصُهُ قُدَّ مِنْ دُبُرٍ
فَكَذَبَتْ وَهُوَ مِنَ الصّٰدِقِيْنَ ۟

28. So when he saw his shirt—
That it was torn at the back—
(Her husband) said: "Behold!
It is a snare of you women!
Truly, mighty is your snare!

٢٨- فَلَمَّا رَأَى قَمِيْصَهُ قُدَّ مِنْ دُبُرٍ
قَالَ إِنَّهُ مِنْ كَيْدِكُنَّ ۚ
إِنَّ كَيْدَكُنَّ عَظِيْمٌ ۟

29. "O Joseph, pass this over!
(O wife), ask forgiveness
For thy sin, for truly
Thou hast been at fault!"

٢٩- يُوْسُفُ أَعْرِضْ عَنْ هٰذَا ۚ وَاسْتَغْفِرِىْ
لِذَنْبِكِ ۖ إِنَّكِ كُنْتِ مِنَ الْخٰطِئِيْنَ ۟ ۚ ۖ

SECTION 4.

30. Ladies said in the City:
"The wife of the (great) 'Azīz
Is seeking to seduce her slave
From his (true) self:
Truly hath he inspired her
With violent love: we see
She is evidently going astray."

٣٠- وَقَالَ نِسْوَةٌ فِى الْمَدِيْنَةِ امْرَأَتُ الْعَزِيْزِ
تُرَاوِدُ فَتٰهَا عَنْ نَفْسِهٖ ۚ قَدْ شَغَفَهَا
حُبًّا ۖ إِنَّا لَنَرٰىهَا فِىْ ضَلٰلٍ مُّبِيْنٍ ۟

31. When she heard
Of their malicious talk,
She sent for them
And prepared a banquet
For them: she gave
Each of them a knife:
And she said (to Joseph),
"Come out before them."
When they saw him,
They did extol him,
And (in their amazement)
Cut their hands: they said,
"Allah preserve us! no mortal
Is this! This is none other
Than a noble angel!"

٣١- فَلَمَّا سَمِعَتْ بِمَكْرِهِنَّ أَرْسَلَتْ إِلَيْهِنَّ
وَأَعْتَدَتْ لَهُنَّ مُتَّكَأً
وَآتَتْ كُلَّ وَاحِدَةٍ مِّنْهُنَّ سِكِّيْنًا
وَقَالَتِ اخْرُجْ عَلَيْهِنَّ ۖ فَلَمَّا رَأَيْنَهُ أَكْبَرْنَهُ
وَقَطَّعْنَ أَيْدِيَهُنَّ
وَقُلْنَ حَاشَ لِلّٰهِ مَا هٰذَا بَشَرًا ۖ
إِنْ هٰذَا إِلَّا مَلَكٌ كَرِيْمٌ ۟

32. She said: "There before you

٣٢- قَالَتْ فَذٰلِكُنَّ الَّذِىْ

Is the man about whom
Ye did blame me!
I did seek to seduce him from
His (true) self but he did
Firmly save himself guiltless! ...
And now, if he doth not
My bidding, he shall certainly
Be cast into prison,
And (what is more)
Be of the company of the vilest!"

33. He said: "O my Lord!
The prison is more
To my liking than that
To which they invite me:
Unless Thou turn away
Their snare from me,
I should (in my youthful folly)
Feel inclined towards them
And join the ranks of the
　　　　　　　　　　ignorant."

34. So his Lord hearkened to him
(In his prayer) and turned
Away from him their snare:
Verily He heareth and knoweth
(All things).

35. Then it occurred to the men
After they had seen the Signs,
(That it was best)
To imprison him
For a time.

SECTION 5.

36. Now with him there came
Into the prison two young men.
Said one of them: "I see
Myself (in a dream)
Pressing wine." Said the other:
"I see myself (in a dream)
Carrying bread on my head,
And birds are eating thereof."
"Tell us" (they said) "the truth
And meaning thereof: for we
See thou art one
That doth good (to all)."

37. He said: "Before any food
Comes (in due course)
To feed either of you
I will surely reveal
To you the truth
And meaning of this
Ere it befall you.
That is part of the (Duty)
Which my Lord hath taught
                    me.

    I have (I assure you)
Abandoned the ways
Of a people that believe not
In Allah and that (even)
Deny the Hereafter.

٣٧- قَالَ لَا يَأْتِيكُمَا طَعَامٌ تُرْزَقَانِهِ
إِلَّا نَبَّأْتُكُمَا بِتَأْوِيلِهِ
قَبْلَ أَنْ يَأْتِيَكُمَا ۚ
ذٰلِكُمَا مِمَّا عَلَّمَنِى رَبِّىۗ إِنِّى
تَرَكْتُ مِلَّةَ قَوْمٍ لَّا يُؤْمِنُوْنَ بِاللّٰهِ وَهُمْ
بِالْاٰخِرَةِ هُمْ كٰفِرُوْنَ ۟

38. "And I follow the ways
Of my fathers—Abraham,
Isaac, and Jacob; and never
Could we attribute any partners
Whatever to Allah: that (comes)
Of the grace of Allah to us
And to mankind: yet
Most men are not grateful.

٣٨- وَاتَّبَعْتُ مِلَّةَ اٰبَآئِى إِبْرٰهِيمَ وَإِسْحٰقَ
وَيَعْقُوْبَ ۚ مَا كَانَ لَنَآ أَنْ نُّشْرِكَ بِاللّٰهِ
مِنْ شَىْءٍ ۚ ذٰلِكَ مِنْ فَضْلِ اللّٰهِ عَلَيْنَا وَ
عَلَى النَّاسِ وَلٰكِنَّ أَكْثَرَ النَّاسِ لَا يَشْكُرُوْنَ ۟

39. "O my two companions
Of the prison! (I ask you):
Are many lords differing
Among themselves better,
Or Allah, the One,
Supreme and Irresistible?

٣٩- يٰصَاحِبَىِ السِّجْنِ
ءَأَرْبَابٌ مُّتَفَرِّقُوْنَ خَيْرٌ
أَمِ اللّٰهُ الْوَاحِدُ الْقَهَّارُ ۟

40. "If not Him, ye worship nothing
But names which ye have
                named—
Ye and your fathers—
For which Allah hath sent down
No authority: the Command
Is for none but Allah: He
Hath commanded that ye worship
None but Him: that is
The right religion, but
Most men understand not...

٤٠- مَا تَعْبُدُوْنَ مِنْ دُوْنِهِ إِلَّا أَسْمَآءً
سَمَّيْتُمُوْهَآ
أَنْتُمْ وَاٰبَآؤُكُمْ مَّا أَنْزَلَ اللّٰهُ بِهَا مِنْ
سُلْطٰنٍ ۚ إِنِ الْحُكْمُ إِلَّا لِلّٰهِ ۚ
أَمَرَ أَلَّا تَعْبُدُوْا إِلَّا إِيَّاهُ ۚ ذٰلِكَ الدِّيْنُ
الْقَيِّمُ وَلٰكِنَّ أَكْثَرَ النَّاسِ لَا يَعْلَمُوْنَ ۟

41. "O my two companions
Of the prison! As to one

٤١- يٰصَاحِبَىِ السِّجْنِ أَمَّآ أَحَدُكُمَا

Of you, he will pour out
The wine for his lord to drink:
As for the other, he will
Hang from the cross, and the birds
Will eat from off his head.
(So) hath been decreed
That matter whereof
Ye twain do enquire"...

فَيَسْقِى رَبَّهُ خَمْرًا ۚ

وَأَمَّا الْآخَرُ فَيُصْلَبُ

فَتَأْكُلُ الطَّيْرُ مِنْ رَأْسِهِ ۚ

قُضِيَ الْأَمْرُ الَّذِى فِيهِ تَسْتَفْتِيَانِ ۝

42. And of the two,
To that one whom he considered
About to be saved, he said:
"Mention me to thy lord."
But Satan made him forget
To mention him to his lord:
And (Joseph) lingered in prison
A few (more) years.

٤٢- وَقَالَ لِلَّذِى ظَنَّ أَنَّهُ

نَاجٍ مِّنْهُمَا اذْكُرْنِى عِنْدَ رَبِّكَ

فَأَنْسَاهُ الشَّيْطَانُ ذِكْرَ رَبِّهِ

فَلَبِثَ فِى السِّجْنِ بِضْعَ سِنِينَ ۝

SECTION 6.

43. The king (of Egypt) said:
"I do see (in a vision)
Seven fat kine, whom seven
Lean ones devour—and seven
Green ears of corn, and seven
                    (others)
Withered. O ye chiefs!
Expound to me my vision,
If it be that ye can
Interpret visions."

٤٣- وَقَالَ الْمَلِكُ إِنِّى أَرَى سَبْعَ بَقَرَاتٍ

سِمَانٍ يَأْكُلُهُنَّ سَبْعٌ عِجَافٌ

وَسَبْعَ سُنْبُلَاتٍ خُضْرٍ وَأُخَرَ يَابِسَاتٍ ۖ

يَا أَيُّهَا الْمَلَأُ أَفْتُونِى فِى رُؤْيَايَ

إِنْ كُنْتُمْ لِلرُّؤْيَا تَعْبُرُونَ ۝

44. They said: "A confused medley
Of dreams: and we are not
Skilled in the interpretation
Of dreams."

٤٤- قَالُوا أَضْغَاثُ أَحْلَامٍ ۖ وَمَا نَحْنُ

بِتَأْوِيلِ الْأَحْلَامِ بِعَالِمِينَ ۝

45. But the man who had been
Released, one of the two
(Who had been in prison)
And who now bethought him
After (so long) a space of time,
Said: "I will tell you
The truth of its interpretation:
Send ye me (therefor)."

٤٥- وَقَالَ الَّذِى نَجَا مِنْهُمَا

وَادَّكَرَ بَعْدَ أُمَّةٍ

أَنَا أُنَبِّئُكُمْ

بِتَأْوِيلِهِ فَأَرْسِلُونِ ۝

46. "O Joseph!" (he said).
"O man of truth! Expound
To us (the dream)
Of seven fat kine
Whom seven lean ones

٤٦- يُوسُفُ أَيُّهَا الصِّدِّيقُ

أَفْتِنَا فِى سَبْعِ بَقَرَاتٍ سِمَانٍ

يَأْكُلُهُنَّ سَبْعٌ عِجَافٌ

Devour, and of seven
Green ears of corn
And (seven) others withered:
That I may return
To the people, and that
They may understand."

وَسَبْعِ سُنْبُلَاتٍ خُضْرٍ وَّأُخَرَ يَبِسَتٍ
لَّعَلِّي أَرْجِعُ إِلَى النَّاسِ
لَعَلَّهُمْ يَعْلَمُونَ ۝

47. (Joseph) said: "For seven years
Shall ye diligently sow
As is your wont:
And the harvests that ye reap,
Ye shall leave them in the ear—
Except a little, of which
Ye shall eat.

٤٧۔ قَالَ تَزْرَعُونَ سَبْعَ سِنِينَ دَأَبًا ۚ
فَمَا حَصَدْتُّمْ فَذَرُوهُ فِي سُنْبُلِهِ
إِلَّا قَلِيلًا مِّمَّا تَأْكُلُونَ ۝

48. "Then will come
After that (period)
Seven dreadful (years),
Which will devour
What ye shall have laid by
In advance for them—
(All) except a little
Which ye shall have
(Specially) guarded.

٤٨۔ ثُمَّ يَأْتِي مِنْ بَعْدِ ذَلِكَ
سَبْعٌ شِدَادٌ
يَأْكُلْنَ مَا قَدَّمْتُمْ لَهُنَّ
إِلَّا قَلِيلًا
مِّمَّا تُحْصِنُونَ ۝

49. "Then will come
After that (period) a year
In which the people will have
Abundant water, and in which
They will press (wine and oil)."

٤٩۔ ثُمَّ يَأْتِي مِنْ بَعْدِ ذَلِكَ عَامٌ
فِيهِ يُغَاثُ النَّاسُ
وَفِيهِ يَعْصِرُونَ ۝ ع

SECTION 7.

50. So the king said:
"Bring ye him unto me."
But when the messenger
Came to him, (Joseph) said:
"Go thou back to thy lord,
And ask him, 'What is
The state of mind
Of the ladies
Who cut their hands'?
For my Lord is
Certainly well aware
Of their snare."

٥٠۔ وَقَالَ الْمَلِكُ ائْتُونِي بِهِ ۚ
فَلَمَّا جَاءَهُ الرَّسُولُ قَالَ ارْجِعْ إِلَى رَبِّكَ
فَسْأَلْهُ مَا بَالُ النِّسْوَةِ الَّتِي
قَطَّعْنَ أَيْدِيَهُنَّ ۚ
إِنَّ رَبِّي بِكَيْدِهِنَّ عَلِيمٌ ۝

51. (The king) said (to the ladies):
"What was your affair
When ye did seek to seduce

٥١۔ قَالَ مَا خَطْبُكُنَّ

Joseph from his (true) self?"
The ladies said: "Allah
Preserve us! no evil
Know we against him!"
Said the 'Azīz's wife:
"Now is the truth manifest
(To all): it was I
Who sought to seduce him
From his (true) self:
He is indeed of those
Who are (ever) true (and
                 virtuous).

إِذْ رَاوَدْتُّنَّ يُوسُفَ عَنْ نَّفْسِهٖ ۚ

قُلْنَ حَاشَ لِلّٰهِ مَا عَلِمْنَا عَلَيْهِ مِنْ سُوْءٍ ۚ

قَالَتِ امْرَاَتُ الْعَزِيْزِ الْـٰٔنَ حَصْحَصَ

الْحَقُّ ۖ اَنَا رَاوَدْتُّهٗ عَنْ نَّفْسِهٖ

وَاِنَّهٗ لَمِنَ الصّٰدِقِيْنَ ۞

52. "This (say I), in order that
He may know that I
Have never been false
To him in his absence,
And that Allah will never
Guide the snare of the false
                ones.

٥٢- ذٰلِكَ لِيَعْلَمَ اَنِّيْ

لَمْ اَخُنْهُ بِالْغَيْبِ

وَاَنَّ اللّٰهَ لَا يَهْدِيْ كَيْدَ الْخَآئِنِيْنَ ۞

53. "Nor do I absolve my own self
(Of blame): the (human) soul
Is certainly prone to evil,[1712 A]
Unless my Lord do bestow
His Mercy: but surely
My Lord is Oft-Forgiving,
Most Merciful."

٥٣- وَمَاۤ اُبَرِّئُ نَفْسِيْ ۚ

اِنَّ النَّفْسَ لَاَمَّارَةٌۢ بِالسُّوْءِ

اِلَّا مَا رَحِمَ رَبِّيْ ۚ

اِنَّ رَبِّيْ غَفُوْرٌ رَّحِيْمٌ ۞

54. So the king said:
"Bring him unto me;
I will take him specially
To serve about my own person."
Therefore when he had spoken
To him, he said:
"Be assured this day,
Thou art, before our own
                Presence,
With rank firmly established.
And fidelity fully proved!"

٥٤- وَقَالَ الْمَلِكُ ائْتُوْنِيْ بِهٖۤ

اَسْتَخْلِصْهُ لِنَفْسِيْ ۚ

فَلَمَّا كَلَّمَهٗ قَالَ

اِنَّكَ الْيَوْمَ لَدَيْنَا

مَكِيْنٌ اَمِيْنٌ ۞

55. (Joseph) said: "Set me
Over the storehouses
Of the land: I will
Indeed guard them,
As one that knows
(Their importance)."

٥٥- قَالَ اجْعَلْنِيْ

عَلٰى خَزَآئِنِ الْاَرْضِ ۚ

اِنِّيْ حَفِيْظٌ عَلِيْمٌ ۞

56. Thus did we give

٥٦- وَكَذٰلِكَ مَكَّنَّا لِيُوْسُفَ

Established power to Joseph
In the land, to take possession
Therein as, when, or where
He pleased. We bestow
Of Our mercy on whom
We please, and We suffer not,
To be lost, the reward
Of those who do good.

في الْأَرْضِ يَتَبَوَّأُ مِنْهَا حَيْثُ يَشَاءُ
نُصِيبُ بِرَحْمَتِنَا مَنْ نَشَاءُ
وَلَا نُضِيعُ أَجْرَ الْمُحْسِنِينَ ۝

57. But verily the reward
Of the Hereafter
Is the best, for those
Who believe, and are constant
In righteousness.

٥٧- وَلَأَجْرُ الْآخِرَةِ خَيْرٌ لِلَّذِينَ آمَنُوا
وَكَانُوا يَتَّقُونَ ۝

SECTION 8.

58. Then came Joseph's brethren:
They entered his presence,
And he knew them,
But they knew him not.

٥٨- وَجَاءَ إِخْوَةُ يُوسُفَ فَدَخَلُوا عَلَيْهِ
فَعَرَفَهُمْ وَهُمْ لَهُ مُنْكِرُونَ ۝

59. And when he had furnished
Them forth with provisions
(Suitable) for them, he said:
"Bring unto me a brother
Ye have, of the same father
As yourselves, (but a different
                    mother):
See ye not that I pay out
Full measure, and that I
Do provide the best hospitality?

٥٩- وَلَمَّا جَهَّزَهُمْ بِجَهَازِهِمْ
قَالَ ائْتُونِي بِأَخٍ
لَكُمْ مِنْ أَبِيكُمْ
أَلَا تَرَوْنَ أَنِّي أُوفِي الْكَيْلَ
وَأَنَا خَيْرُ الْمُنْزِلِينَ ۝

60. "Now if ye bring him not
To me, ye shall have
No measure (of corn) from me,
Nor shall ye (even) come
Near me."

٦٠- فَإِنْ لَمْ تَأْتُونِي بِهِ
فَلَا كَيْلَ لَكُمْ عِنْدِي
وَلَا تَقْرَبُونِ ۝

61. They said: "We shall
Certainly seek to get
Our wish about him
From his father:
Indeed we shall do it."

٦١- قَالُوا سَنُرَاوِدُ عَنْهُ
أَبَاهُ وَإِنَّا لَفَاعِلُونَ ۝

62. And (Joseph) told his servants
To put their stock in trade
(With which they have bartered)

٦٢- وَقَالَ لِفِتْيَانِهِ اجْعَلُوا بِضَاعَتَهُمْ فِي
رِحَالِهِمْ

Into their saddlebags,
So they should know it only
When they returned to their
people,
In order that they
Might come back.

لَعَلَّهُمْ يَعْرِفُوْنَهَا
اِذَا انْقَلَبُوْا اِلٰۤى اَهْلِهِمْ
لَعَلَّهُمْ يَرْجِعُوْنَ ۟

63. Now when they returned
To their father, they said:
"O our father! No more
Measure of grain shall we get
(Unless we take our brother):
So send our brother with us,
That we may get our measure;
And we will indeed
Take every care of him."

٦٣ـ فَلَمَّا رَجَعُوْۤا اِلٰۤى اَبِيْهِمْ قَالُوْا
يٰۤاَبَانَا مُنِعَ مِنَّا الْكَيْلُ
فَاَرْسِلْ مَعَنَاۤ اَخَانَا نَكْتَلْ
وَاِنَّا لَهٗ لَحٰفِظُوْنَ ۟

64. He said: "Shall I trust you
With him with any result
Other than when I trusted you
With his brother aforetime?
But Allah is the best
To take care (of him),
And He is the Most Merciful
Of those who show mercy!"

٦٤ـ قَالَ هَلْ اٰمَنُكُمْ عَلَيْهِ اِلَّا
كَمَاۤ اَمِنْتُكُمْ عَلٰۤى اَخِيْهِ مِنْ قَبْلُ ۖ
فَاللّٰهُ خَيْرٌ حٰفِظًا ۖ
وَّهُوَ اَرْحَمُ الرّٰحِمِيْنَ ۟

65. Then when they opened
Their baggage, they found
Their stock in trade had been
Returned to them. They said:
"O our father! What (more)
Can we desire? This our
Stock in trade has been
returned
To us: so we shall get
(More) food for our family;
We shall take care of our brother;
And add (at the same time)
A full camel's load (of grain
To our provisions).
This is but a small quantity.

٦٥ـ وَلَمَّا فَتَحُوْا مَتَاعَهُمْ وَجَدُوْا
بِضَاعَتَهُمْ رُدَّتْ اِلَيْهِمْ ۖ
قَالُوْا يٰۤاَبَانَا مَا نَبْغِيْ ۖ
هٰذِهٖ بِضَاعَتُنَا رُدَّتْ اِلَيْنَا ۚ
وَنَمِيْرُ اَهْلَنَا وَنَحْفَظُ اَخَانَا
وَنَزْدَادُ كَيْلَ بَعِيْرٍ ۖ
ذٰلِكَ كَيْلٌ يَّسِيْرٌ ۟

66. (Jacob) said: "Never will I
Send him with you until
Ye swear a solemn oath to me,
In Allah's name, that ye

٦٦ـ قَالَ لَنْ اُرْسِلَهٗ مَعَكُمْ حَتّٰى
تُؤْتُوْنِ مَوْثِقًا مِّنَ اللّٰهِ

Will be sure to bring him back
To me unless ye are yourselves
Hemmed in (and made
                    powerless).
And when they had sworn
Their solemn oath,
He said: "Over all
That we say, be Allah
The Witness and Guardian!"

لَتَأْتُنَّنِى بِهِ
إِلَّا أَن يُحَاطَ بِكُمْ
فَلَمَّا آتَوْهُ مَوْثِقَهُمْ
قَالَ اللّٰهُ عَلَىٰ مَا نَقُولُ وَكِيلٌ ۝

67. Further he said:
"O my sons! enter not
All by one gate: enter ye
By different gates. Not that
I can profit you aught
Against Allah (with my advice):
None can command except Allah:
On Him do I put my trust:
And let all that trust
Put their trust on Him."

٦٧ـ وَقَالَ يَـٰبَنِىَّ لَا تَدْخُلُوا
مِنۢ بَابٍ وَاحِدٍ وَّادْخُلُوا مِنْ أَبْوَابٍ مُّتَفَرِّقَةٍ
وَمَآ أُغْنِى عَنكُم مِّنَ اللّٰهِ مِن شَىْءٍ
إِنِ الْحُكْمُ إِلَّا لِلّٰهِ عَلَيْهِ تَوَكَّلْتُ وَعَلَيْهِ
فَلْيَتَوَكَّلِ الْمُتَوَكِّلُونَ ۝

68. And when they entered
In the manner their father
Had enjoined, it did not
Profit them in the least
Against (the Plan of) Allah:
It was but a necessity
Of Jacob's soul, which he
Discharged. For he was,
By Our instruction, full
Of knowledge (and experience):
But most men know not.

٦٨ـ وَلَمَّا دَخَلُوا مِنْ حَيْثُ أَمَرَهُمْ أَبُوهُم
مَّا كَانَ يُغْنِى عَنْهُم مِّنَ اللّٰهِ مِن شَىْءٍ
إِلَّا حَاجَةً فِى نَفْسِ يَعْقُوبَ قَضَاهَا
وَإِنَّهُ لَذُو عِلْمٍ لِّمَا عَلَّمْنَاهُ
وَلَـٰكِنَّ أَكْثَرَ النَّاسِ لَا يَعْلَمُونَ ۝

SECTION 9.

69. Now when they came
Into Joseph's presence,
He received his (full) brother
To stay with him. He said
(To him): "Behold! I am thy (own)
Brother; so grieve not
At aught of their doings."

٦٩ـ وَلَمَّا دَخَلُوا عَلَىٰ يُوسُفَ
آوَىٰ إِلَيْهِ أَخَاهُ
قَالَ إِنِّىٓ أَنَا أَخُوكَ
فَلَا تَبْتَئِسْ بِمَا كَانُوا يَعْمَلُونَ ۝

70. At length when he had furnished
Them forth with provisions
(Suitable) for them, he put
The drinking cup into
His brother's saddlebag.
Then shouted out a Crier:

٧٠ـ فَلَمَّا جَهَّزَهُم بِجَهَازِهِمْ
جَعَلَ السِّقَايَةَ فِى رَحْلِ أَخِيهِ
ثُمَّ أَذَّنَ مُؤَذِّنٌ

"O ye (in) the Caravan!
Behold! ye are thieves,
Without doubt!"

اَيَّتُهَا الْعِيْرُ اِنَّكُمْ لَسَارِقُوْنَ ۝

71. They said, turning towards them:
"What is it that ye miss?"

٧١- قَالُوْا وَاَقْبَلُوْا عَلَيْهِمْ مَّاذَا تَفْقِدُوْنَ ۝

72. They said: "We miss
The great beaker of the king;
For him who produces it,
Is (the reward of)
A camel load; I
Will be bound by it."

٧٢- قَالُوْا نَفْقِدُ صُوَاعَ الْمَلِكِ
وَلِمَنْ جَآءَ بِهِ حِمْلُ بَعِيْرٍ
وَّاَنَا بِهِ زَعِيْمٌ ۝

73. (The brothers) said: "By Allah!
Well ye know that we
Came not to make mischief
In the land, and we are
No thieves!"

٧٣- قَالُوْا تَاللّٰهِ لَقَدْ عَلِمْتُمْ مَّا جِئْنَا
لِنُفْسِدَ فِى الْاَرْضِ
وَمَا كُنَّا سَارِقِيْنَ ۝

74. (The Egyptians) said: "What then
Shall be the penalty of this,
If ye are (proved) to have lied?"

٧٤- قَالُوْا فَمَا جَزَآؤُهٗ
اِنْ كُنْتُمْ كٰذِبِيْنَ ۝

75. They said: "The penalty
Should be that he
In whose saddlebag
It is found, should be held
(As bondman) to atone
For the (crime). Thus it is
We punish the wrongdoers!"

٧٥- قَالُوْا جَزَآؤُهٗ مَنْ وُّجِدَ فِىْ رَحْلِهٖ
فَهُوَ جَزَآؤُهٗ ۚ
كَذٰلِكَ نَجْزِى الظّٰلِمِيْنَ ۝

76. So he　　began (the search)
With their baggage,
Before (he came to) the baggage
Of his brother: at length
He brought it　　out of his
Brother's baggage. Thus did We
Plan for Joseph. He could not
Take his brother by the law
Of the king except that Allah
Willed it (so). We raise
To degrees (of wisdom) whom
We please: but over all
Endued with knowledge is One,
The All-Knowing.

٧٦- فَبَدَاَ بِاَوْعِيَتِهِمْ
قَبْلَ وِعَآءِ اَخِيْهِ
ثُمَّ اسْتَخْرَجَهَا مِنْ وِّعَآءِ اَخِيْهِ ۚ
كَذٰلِكَ كِدْنَا لِيُوْسُفَ ۚ مَا كَانَ لِيَاْخُذَ
اَخَاهُ فِىْ دِيْنِ الْمَلِكِ اِلَّاۤ اَنْ يَّشَآءَ اللّٰهُ ۚ
نَرْفَعُ دَرَجٰتٍ مَّنْ نَّشَآءُ ۗ
وَفَوْقَ كُلِّ ذِىْ عِلْمٍ عَلِيْمٌ ۝

77. They said: "If he steals,

٧٧- قَالُوْا اِنْ يَّسْرِقْ فَقَدْ سَرَقَ اَخٌ

There was a brother of his
Who did steal before (him)."
But these things did Joseph
Keep locked in his heart,
Revealing not the secrets to
           them.
He (simply) said (to himself):
"Ye are the worse situated;
And Allah knoweth best
The truth of what ye assert!"

78. They said: "O exalted one!
Behold! he has a father,
Aged and venerable, (who will
Grieve for him); so take
One of us in his place;
For we see that thou art
(Gracious) in doing good."

79. He said: "Allah forbid
That we take other than him
With whom we found
Our property: indeed
(If we did so), we should
Be acting wrongfully."

       SECTION 10.

80. Now when they saw
No hope of his (yielding),
They held a conference in private.
The leader among them said:
"Know ye not that your father
Did take an oath from you
In Allah's name, and how
Before this, ye did fail
In your duty with Joseph?
Therefore will I not leave
This land until my father
Permits me, or Allah
Commands me; and He
Is the best to command.

81. "Turn ye back to your father,
And say, 'O our father!
Behold! thy son committed theft!
We bear witness only to what
We know, and we could not
Well guard against the unseen!

82. "'Ask at the town where
We have been and the caravan
In which we returned,
And (you will find) we are
Indeed telling the truth.'"

٨٢- وَسْئَلِ الْقَرْيَةَ الَّتِي كُنَّا فِيهَا
وَالْعِيرَ الَّتِي اَقْبَلْنَا فِيهَا
وَاِنَّا لَصٰدِقُوْنَ ۟

83. Jacob said: "Nay, but ye
Have yourselves contrived
A story (good enough) for you.
So patience is most fitting
(For me). Maybe Allah will
Bring them (back) all
To me (in the end).
For He is indeed full
Of knowledge and wisdom."

٨٣- قَالَ بَلْ سَوَّلَتْ لَكُمْ اَنْفُسُكُمْ اَمْرًا
فَصَبْرٌ جَمِيلٌ
عَسَى اللهُ اَنْ يَّاْتِيَنِيْ بِهِمْ جَمِيْعًا
اِنَّهٗ هُوَ الْعَلِيْمُ الْحَكِيْمُ ۟

84. And he turned away from them,
And said: "How great
Is my grief for Joseph!"
And his eyes became white
With sorrow, and he fell
Into silent melancholy.

٨٤- وَتَوَلّٰى عَنْهُمْ وَقَالَ يٰاَسَفٰى عَلٰى يُوْسُفَ
وَابْيَضَّتْ عَيْنٰهُ مِنَ الْحُزْنِ
فَهُوَ كَظِيْمٌ ۟

85. They said: "By Allah!
(Never) wilt thou cease
To remember Joseph
Until thou reach the last
Extremity of illness,
Or until thou die!"?

٨٥- قَالُوْا تَاللهِ تَفْتَؤُا
تَذْكُرُ يُوْسُفَ حَتّٰى تَكُوْنَ حَرَضًا اَوْ تَكُوْنَ
مِنَ الْهٰلِكِيْنَ ۟

86. He said: "I only complain
Of my distraction and anguish
To Allah, and I know from
                    Allah
That which ye know not...

٨٦- قَالَ اِنَّمَا اَشْكُوْا بَثِّيْ وَحُزْنِيْ اِلَى اللهِ
وَاَعْلَمُ مِنَ اللهِ مَا لَا تَعْلَمُوْنَ ۟

87. "O my sons! go ye
And enquire about Joseph
And his brother, and never
Give up hope of Allah's
Soothing Mercy: truly
No one despairs of Allah's
Soothing Mercy, except
Those who have no faith."

٨٧- يٰبَنِيَّ اذْهَبُوْا فَتَحَسَّسُوْا مِنْ يُّوْسُفَ
وَاَخِيْهِ وَلَا تَايْــَٔسُوْا مِنْ رَّوْحِ اللهِ
اِنَّهٗ لَا يَايْــَٔسُ مِنْ رَّوْحِ اللهِ
اِلَّا الْقَوْمُ الْكٰفِرُوْنَ ۟

88. Then, when they came
(Back) into (Joseph's) presence
They said: "O exalted one!

٨٨- فَلَمَّا دَخَلُوْا عَلَيْهِ
قَالُوْا يٰاَيُّهَا الْعَزِيْزُ مَسَّنَا

Distress has seized us
And our family: we have
(Now) brought but scanty capital:
So pay us full measure,
(We pray thee), and treat it
As charity to us: for Allah
Doth reward the charitable."

89. He said: "Know ye
How ye dealt with Joseph
And his brother, not knowing
(What ye were doing)?"

90. They said: "Art thou indeed
Joseph?" He said, "I am
Joseph, and this is my brother:
Allah has indeed been gracious
To us (all): behold, he that is
Righteous and patient—never
Will Allah suffer the reward
To be lost, of those
Who do right."

91. They said: "By Allah! Indeed
Has Allah preferred thee
Above us, and we certainly
Have been guilty of sin!"

92. He said: "This day
Let no reproach be (cast)
On you: Allah will forgive you,
And He is the Most Merciful
Of those who show mercy!

93. "Go with this my shirt,
And cast it over the face
Of my father: he will
Come to see (clearly). Then come
Ye (here) to me together
With all your family."

SECTION 11.

94. When the Caravan left (Egypt),
Their father said: "I do indeed
Scent the presence of Joseph:
Nay, think me not a dotard."

95. They[1771] said: "By Allah!
Truly thou art in
Thine old wandering mind."

٩٥ ـ قَالُوا تَاللّٰهِ إِنَّكَ لَفِي ضَلٰلِكَ الْقَدِيمِ ۞

96. Then when the bearer
Of the good news came,
He cast (the shirt)
Over his face, and he
Forthwith   regained clear
           sight.
He said: "Did I not say
To you, 'I know from Allah
That which ye know not?'"

٩٦ ـ فَلَمَّا أَنْ جَاءَ الْبَشِيرُ أَلْقَاهُ عَلٰى وَجْهِهِ
فَارْتَدَّ بَصِيرًا ۖ
قَالَ أَلَمْ أَقُلْ لَكُمْ
إِنِّي أَعْلَمُ مِنَ اللّٰهِ
مَا لَا تَعْلَمُونَ ۞

97. They said: "O our father!
Ask for us forgiveness
For our sins, for we
Were truly at fault."

٩٧ ـ قَالُوا يَا أَبَانَا اسْتَغْفِرْ لَنَا ذُنُوبَنَا
إِنَّا كُنَّا خَاطِئِينَ ۞

98. He said: "Soon   will I
Ask my Lord for forgiveness
For you: for He is indeed
Oft-Forgiving, Most Merciful."

٩٨ ـ قَالَ سَوْفَ أَسْتَغْفِرُ لَكُمْ رَبِّي ۖ
إِنَّهُ هُوَ الْغَفُورُ الرَّحِيمُ ۞

99. Then when they entered
The presence of Joseph,
He provided a home
For his parents with himself,
And said: "Enter ye
Egypt (all) in safety
If it please Allah."

٩٩ ـ فَلَمَّا دَخَلُوا عَلٰى يُوسُفَ
آوَى إِلَيْهِ أَبَوَيْهِ
وَقَالَ ادْخُلُوا مِصْرَ إِنْ شَاءَ اللّٰهُ
آمِنِينَ ۞

100. And he raised his parents
High on the throne (of dignity),
And they fell down in prostration,
(All) before him.   He said:
"O my father! this is
The fulfilment of my vision
Of old! Allah hath made it
Come true! He was indeed
Good to me when He
Took me out of prison
And brought you (all here)
Out of the desert,

١٠٠ ـ وَرَفَعَ أَبَوَيْهِ عَلَى الْعَرْشِ
وَخَرُّوا لَهُ سُجَّدًا ۖ وَقَالَ
يَا أَبَتِ هٰذَا تَأْوِيلُ رُؤْيَايَ
مِنْ قَبْلُ قَدْ جَعَلَهَا رَبِّي حَقًّا ۖ وَقَدْ
أَحْسَنَ بِي إِذْ أَخْرَجَنِي مِنَ السِّجْنِ
وَجَاءَ بِكُمْ مِنَ الْبَدْوِ
مِنْ بَعْدِ أَنْ نَزَغَ الشَّيْطٰنُ بَيْنِي وَبَيْنَ

(Even) after Satan had sown
Enmity between me and my
                    brothers.
Verily my Lord understandeth
Best the mysteries of all
That he planneth to do.
For verily He is full
Of knowledge and wisdom.

خُوَتِیْ
اِنَّ رَبِّیْ لَطِیْفٌ لِّمَا یَشَآءُ ؕ
اِنَّهٗ هُوَ الْعَلِیْمُ الْحَکِیْمُ ۟

101. "O my Lord! Thou hast
Indeed bestowed on me
Some power, and taught me
Something of the interpretation
Of dreams and events—O thou
Creator of the heavens
And the earth! Thou art
My Protector in this world
And in the Hereafter.
Take Thou my soul (at death)
As one submitting to Thy Will
(As a Muslim), and unite me
With the righteous."

۱۰۱۔ رَبِّ قَدْ اٰتَیْتَنِیْ
مِنَ الْمُلْکِ وَ عَلَّمْتَنِیْ مِنْ تَاْوِیْلِ
الْاَحَادِیْثِ ۚ
فَاطِرَ السَّمٰوٰتِ وَالْاَرْضِ ۟
اَنْتَ وَلِیّٖ فِی الدُّنْیَا وَالْاٰخِرَةِ ۚ
تَوَفَّنِیْ مُسْلِمًا
وَّ اَلْحِقْنِیْ بِالصّٰلِحِیْنَ ۟

102. Such is one of the stories
Of what happened unseen,
Which We reveal by inspiration
Unto thee: nor wast thou
(Present) with them when they
Concerted their plans together
In the process of weaving their
                    plots.

۱۰۲۔ ذٰلِکَ مِنْ اَنْۢبَآءِ الْغَیْبِ
نُوْحِیْهِ اِلَیْکَ ۚ
وَمَا کُنْتَ لَدَیْهِمْ
اِذْ اَجْمَعُوْۤا اَمْرَهُمْ وَهُمْ یَمْکُرُوْنَ ۟

103. Yet no faith will
The greater part of mankind
Have, however ardently
Thou dost desire it.

۱۰۳۔ وَمَاۤ اَکْثَرُ النَّاسِ
وَلَوْ حَرَصْتَ بِمُؤْمِنِیْنَ ۟

104. And no reward dost thou ask
Of them for this: it is
No less than a Message
For all creatures.

۱۰۴۔ وَمَا تَسْـَٔلُهُمْ عَلَیْهِ مِنْ اَجْرٍ ؕ
اِنْ هُوَ اِلَّا ذِکْرٌ لِّلْعٰلَمِیْنَ ۟ۙ

SECTION 12.

105. And how many Signs
In the heavens and the earth
Do they pass by? Yet they
Turn (their faces) away
                    from them!

۱۰۵۔ وَکَاَیِّنْ مِّنْ اٰیَةٍ فِی السَّمٰوٰتِ وَالْاَرْضِ
یَمُرُّوْنَ عَلَیْهَا وَهُمْ عَنْهَا مُعْرِضُوْنَ ۟

106. And most of them
Believe not in Allah
Without associating (others
As partners) with Him!

١٠٦- وَمَا يُؤْمِنُ أَكْثَرُهُمْ بِاللّٰهِ
إِلَّا وَهُمْ مُّشْرِكُوْنَ ۝

107. Do they then feel secure
From the coming against them
Of the covering veil
Of the wrath of Allah—
Or of the coming against them
Of the (final) Hour
All of a sudden
While they perceive not?

١٠٧- أَفَأَمِنُوْا أَنْ تَأْتِيَهُمْ
غَاشِيَةٌ مِّنْ عَذَابِ اللّٰهِ
أَوْ تَأْتِيَهُمُ السَّاعَةُ بَغْتَةً
وَّهُمْ لَا يَشْعُرُوْنَ ۝

108. Say thou: "This is my Way:
I do invite unto Allah—
On evidence clear as
The seeing with one's eyes—
I and whoever follows me.
Glory to Allah! and never
Will I join gods with Allah!"

١٠٨- قُلْ هٰذِهٖ سَبِيْلِيْ أَدْعُوْا إِلَى اللّٰهِ
عَلٰى بَصِيْرَةٍ أَنَا وَمَنِ اتَّبَعَنِيْ
وَسُبْحَانَ اللّٰهِ وَمَا أَنَا مِنَ الْمُشْرِكِيْنَ ۝

109. Nor did We send before thee
(As Messengers) any but men,
Whom We did inspire—
(Men) living in human habitations.
Do they not travel
Through the earth, and see
What was the end
Of those before them?
But the home of the Hereafter
Is best, for those who do right.
Will ye not then understand?

١٠٩- وَمَا أَرْسَلْنَا مِنْ قَبْلِكَ إِلَّا رِجَالًا
نُّوْحِيْ إِلَيْهِمْ مِّنْ أَهْلِ الْقُرٰى
أَفَلَمْ يَسِيْرُوْا فِي الْأَرْضِ فَيَنْظُرُوْا كَيْفَ
كَانَ عَاقِبَةُ الَّذِيْنَ مِنْ قَبْلِهِمْ
وَلَدَارُ الْآخِرَةِ خَيْرٌ لِّلَّذِيْنَ اتَّقَوْا
أَفَلَا تَعْقِلُوْنَ ۝

110. (Respite will be granted)
Until, when the messengers
Give up hope (of their people)
And (come to) think that they
Were treated as liars,
There reaches them Our help,
And those whom We will
Are delivered into safety.
But never will be warded off
Our punishment from those
Who are in sin.

١١٠- حَتّٰى إِذَا اسْتَيْئَسَ الرُّسُلُ
وَظَنُّوْا أَنَّهُمْ قَدْ كُذِبُوْا
جَاءَهُمْ نَصْرُنَا فَنُجِّيَ مَنْ نَّشَاءُ
وَلَا يُرَدُّ بَأْسُنَا
عَنِ الْقَوْمِ الْمُجْرِمِيْنَ ۝

111. There is, in their stories,

١١١- لَقَدْ كَانَ فِيْ قَصَصِهِمْ عِبْرَةٌ لِّأُولِي

Instruction for men endued
With understanding. It is not
A tale invented, but a
　　　　　　　confirmation

Of what went before it —
A detailed exposition
Of all things, and a Guide
And a Mercy to any such
As believe.

الْأَلْبَابِ مَا كَانَ حَدِيثًا يُفْتَرَى
وَلَٰكِن تَصْدِيقَ
الَّذِي بَيْنَ يَدَيْهِ وَتَفْصِيلَ كُلِّ شَيْءٍ
وَهُدًى وَرَحْمَةً لِّقَوْمٍ يُؤْمِنُونَ ۝

INTRODUCTION TO SŪRA XIII. *(Ra'd)* — 43 Verses

The chronological place of this Sūra and the general argument of Sūras v. to xv. has been described in the Introduction to S.x.

The special argument of this Sūra deals with that aspect of God's revelation of Himself to man and His dealings with him, which is concerned with certain contrasts which are here pointed out. There is the revelation to the Prophets, which comes in spoken words adapted to the language of the various men and groups of men to whom it comes; and there is the parallel revelation or Signs in the constant laws of external nature, on this earth and in the visible heavens. There is the contrast between recurring life and death already in the external world: why should men disbelieve in the life after death? They mock at the idea of punishment because it is deferred: but can they not see God's power and glory in thunder and the forces of Nature? All creation praises Him: it is good that endures and the evil that is swept away like froth or scum. Not only in miracles, but in the normal working of the world, are shown God's power and mercy. What is Punishment in this world, compared to that in the life to come? Even here there are Signs of the working of His law: plot or plan as men will, it is God's Will that must prevail. This is illustrated in Joseph's story in the preceding Sūra.

Al Ra'd (The Thunder)

In the name of Allah, Most Gracious, Most Merciful.

1. **Alif Lām Mīm Rā**. These are
The Signs (or Verses)
Of the Book: that which
Hath been revealed unto thee
From thy Lord is the Truth;
But most men believe not.

2. Allah is He Who raised
The heavens without any
pillars
That ye can see;
Then He established Himself
On the Throne (of Authority);
He has subjected the sun
And the moon (to his Law)!
Each one runs (its course)
For a term appointed.

He doth regulate all affairs,
Explaining the Signs in detail,
That ye may believe with certainty
In the meeting with your Lord.

لَعَلَّكُمْ بِلِقَآءِ رَبِّكُمْ تُوْقِنُوْنَ ٢

3. And it is He Who spread out
The earth, and set thereon
Mountains standing firm,
And (flowing) rivers: and fruit
Of every kind He made
In pairs, two and two:
He draweth the Night as a veil
O'er the Day. Behold, verily
In these things there are Signs
For those who consider!

٣ـ وَهُوَ الَّذِىْ مَدَّ الْاَرْضَ وَجَعَلَ فِيْهَا
رَوَاسِىَ وَاَنْهٰرًا ۖ وَمِنْ كُلِّ الثَّمَرٰتِ جَعَلَ فِيْهَا زَوْجَيْنِ
اثْنَيْنِ يُغْشِى الَّيْلَ النَّهَارَ ۚ
اِنَّ فِىْ ذٰلِكَ لَاٰيٰتٍ لِقَوْمٍ يَتَفَكَّرُوْنَ ٢

4. And in the earth are tracts
(Diverse though) neighbouring,
And gardens of vines
And fields sown with corn,
And palm trees—growing
Out of single roots or otherwise:
Watered with the same water,
Yet some of them We make
More excellent than others to
eat.
Behold, verily in these things
There are Signs for those
Who understand!

٤ـ وَفِى الْاَرْضِ قِطَعٌ مُّتَجٰوِرٰتٌ وَّجَنّٰتٌ مِنْ
اَعْنَابٍ وَّزَرْعٌ وَّنَخِيْلٌ صِنْوَانٌ وَّغَيْرُ
صِنْوَانٍ
يُّسْقٰى بِمَآءٍ وَّاحِدٍ ۗ
وَنُفَضِّلُ بَعْضَهَا عَلٰى بَعْضٍ فِى الْاُكُلِ ۗ
اِنَّ فِىْ ذٰلِكَ لَاٰيٰتٍ لِقَوْمٍ يَعْقِلُوْنَ ٢

5. If thou dost marvel
(At their want of faith),
Strange is their saying:
"When we are (actually) dust,
Shall we indeed then be
In a creation renewed?" They are
Those who deny their Lord! They
Are those round whose necks
Will be yokes (of servitude):
They will be Companions
Of the Fire, to dwell therein
(For aye)!

٥ـ وَاِنْ تَعْجَبْ فَعَجَبٌ قَوْلُهُمْ
ءَاِذَا كُنَّا تُرٰبًا
ءَاِنَّا لَفِىْ خَلْقٍ جَدِيْدٍ ۗ
اُولٰٓئِكَ الَّذِيْنَ كَفَرُوْا بِرَبِّهِمْ ۚ
وَاُولٰٓئِكَ الْاَغْلٰلُ فِىْ اَعْنَاقِهِمْ ۚ وَاُولٰٓئِكَ
اَصْحٰبُ النَّارِ ۖ هُمْ فِيْهَا خٰلِدُوْنَ ٢

6. They ask thee to hasten on
The evil in preference to the
good:
Yet have come to pass,
Before them, (many) exemplary

٦ـ وَيَسْتَعْجِلُوْنَكَ بِالسَّيِّئَةِ قَبْلَ الْحَسَنَةِ
وَقَدْ خَلَتْ مِنْ قَبْلِهِمُ الْمَثُلٰتُ ۗ

Punishments! But verily
Thy Lord is full of forgiveness
For mankind for their
                wrongdoing.
And verily thy Lord
Is (also) strict in punishment.

وَاِنَّ رَبَّكَ لَذُوْ مَغْفِرَةٍ
لِّلنَّاسِ عَلٰى ظُلْمِهِمْ ۚ
وَاِنَّ رَبَّكَ لَشَدِيْدُ الْعِقَابِ ۝

7. And the Unbelievers say:
"Why is not a Sign sent down
To him from his Lord?"
But thou art truly
A warner, and to every people
A guide.

٧۔ وَيَقُوْلُ الَّذِيْنَ كَفَرُوْا لَوْلَاۤ اُنْزِلَ عَلَيْهِ
اٰيَةٌ مِّنْ رَّبِّهٖ ۗ اِنَّمَاۤ اَنْتَ
مُنْذِرٌ ۖ وَّلِكُلِّ قَوْمٍ هَادٍ ۝

SECTION 2.

8. Allah doth know what
Every female (womb) doth bear,
By how much the wombs
Fall short (of their time
Or number) or do exceed.
Every single thing is before
His sight, in (due) proportion.

٨۔ اَللّٰهُ يَعْلَمُ مَا تَحْمِلُ كُلُّ اُنْثٰى
وَمَا تَغِيْضُ الْاَرْحَامُ وَمَا تَزْدَادُ ۗ
وَكُلُّ شَيْءٍ عِنْدَهٗ بِمِقْدَارٍ ۝

9. He knoweth the Unseen
And that which is open:
He is the Great,
The most High.

٩۔ عٰلِمُ الْغَيْبِ وَالشَّهَادَةِ
الْكَبِيْرُ الْمُتَعَالِ ۝

10. It is the same (to Him)
Whether any of you
Conceal his speech or
Declare it openly;
Whether he lie hid by night
Or walk forth freely by day.

١٠۔ سَوَآءٌ مِّنْكُمْ
مَّنْ اَسَرَّ الْقَوْلَ وَمَنْ جَهَرَ بِهٖ وَمَنْ
هُوَ مُسْتَخْفٍ بِالَّيْلِ وَسَارِبٌ بِالنَّهَارِ ۝

11. For each (such person)
There are (angels) in succession.
Before and behind him:
They guard him by command
Of Allah. Verily never
Will Allah change the condition
Of a people until they
Change it themselves
(With their own souls).
But when (once) Allah willeth
A people's punishment,
There can be no
Turning it back, nor

١١۔ لَهٗ مُعَقِّبٰتٌ مِّنْۢ بَيْنِ يَدَيْهِ وَمِنْ
خَلْفِهٖ يَحْفَظُوْنَهٗ مِنْ اَمْرِ اللّٰهِ ۗ
اِنَّ اللّٰهَ لَا يُغَيِّرُ مَا بِقَوْمٍ
حَتّٰى يُغَيِّرُوْا مَا بِاَنْفُسِهِمْ ۗ
وَاِذَاۤ اَرَادَ اللّٰهُ بِقَوْمٍ سُوْٓءًا
فَلَا مَرَدَّ لَهٗ ۚ
وَمَا لَهُمْ

Will they find, besides Him,
Any to protect.

12. It is He Who doth show you
The lightning, by way
Both of fear and of hope:
It is He Who doth raise up
The clouds, heavy
With (fertilising) rain!

13. Nay, thunder repeateth His
praises,
And so do the angels, with awe:
He flingeth the loud-voiced
Thunderbolts, and therewith
He striketh whomsoever He
will...
Yet these (are the men)
Who (dare to) dispute
About Allah, with the strength
Of His power (supreme)!

14. For Him (alone) is prayer
In Truth: any others that they
Call upon besides Him hear them
No more than if they were
To stretch forth their hands
For water to reach their mouths
But it reaches them not:
For the prayer of those
Without Faith is nothing
But (futile) wandering (in the
mind).

15. Whatever beings there are
In the heavens and the earth
Do prostrate themselves to
Allah
(Acknowledging subjection)—with
goodwill
Or in spite of themselves:
So do their shadows
In the mornings and evenings.

16. Say: "Who is the Lord and
Sustainer
Of the heavens and the earth?"
Say: "(It is) Allah."
Say: "Do ye then take

(For worship) protectors other
Than Him, such as have
No power either for good
Or for harm to themselves?"
Say: "Are the blind equal
With those who see?
Or the depths of darkness
Equal with Light?"
Or do they assign to Allah
Partners who have created
(Anything) as He has created,
So that the creation seemed
To them similar?
Say: "Allah is the Creator
Of all things: He is
The One, the Supreme and
           Irresistible."

لَا يَمْلِكُونَ لِأَنْفُسِهِمْ
نَفْعًا وَلَا ضَرًّا ۚ
قُلْ هَلْ يَسْتَوِى الْأَعْمَى وَالْبَصِيرُ ۙ
أَمْ هَلْ تَسْتَوِى الظُّلُمَاتُ وَالنُّورُ ۙ
أَمْ جَعَلُوا لِلَّهِ شُرَكَاءَ خَلَقُوا
كَخَلْقِهِ فَتَشَابَهَ الْخَلْقُ عَلَيْهِمْ ۚ
قُلِ اللَّهُ خَالِقُ كُلِّ شَيْءٍ
وَهُوَ الْوَاحِدُ الْقَهَّارُ ۝

17. He sends down water
From the skies, and the channels
Flow, each according to its
           measure:
But the torrent bears away
The foam that mounts up
To the surface. Even so,
From that (ore) which they heat
In the fire, to make ornaments
Or utensils therewith,
There is a scum likewise.
Thus doth Allah (by parables)
Show forth Truth and Vanity.
For the scum disappears
Like froth cast out;
While that which is for the good
Of mankind remains
On the earth. Thus doth Allah
Set forth parables.

١٧- أَنْزَلَ مِنَ السَّمَاءِ مَاءً
فَسَالَتْ أَوْدِيَةٌ بِقَدَرِهَا
فَاحْتَمَلَ السَّيْلُ زَبَدًا رَابِيًا ۚ
وَمِمَّا يُوقِدُونَ عَلَيْهِ فِى النَّارِ ابْتِغَاءَ
حِلْيَةٍ أَوْ مَتَاعٍ زَبَدٌ مِثْلُهُ ۚ
كَذَٰلِكَ يَضْرِبُ اللَّهُ الْحَقَّ وَالْبَاطِلَ ۚ
فَأَمَّا الزَّبَدُ فَيَذْهَبُ جُفَاءً ۖ
وَأَمَّا مَا يَنْفَعُ النَّاسَ فَيَمْكُثُ فِى الْأَرْضِ ۚ
كَذَٰلِكَ يَضْرِبُ اللَّهُ الْأَمْثَالَ ۝

18. For those who respond
To their Lord, are (all)
Good things. But those
Who respond not to Him—
Even if they had all
That is in the heavens
And on earth, and as much more,
(In vain) would they offer it
For ransom. For them
Will the reckoning be terrible:

١٨- لِلَّذِينَ اسْتَجَابُوا لِرَبِّهِمُ الْحُسْنَى ۚ
وَالَّذِينَ لَمْ يَسْتَجِيبُوا لَهُ
لَوْ أَنَّ لَهُمْ مَا فِى الْأَرْضِ جَمِيعًا
وَمِثْلَهُ مَعَهُ لَافْتَدَوْا بِهِ ۚ
أُولَٰئِكَ لَهُمْ سُوءُ الْحِسَابِ ۙ

Their abode will be Hell—
What a bed of misery!
SECTION 3.

وَمَأْوٰىهُمْ جَهَنَّمُ وَبِئْسَ الْمِهَادُ ۞

19. Is then one who doth know
That that which hath been
Revealed unto thee
From thy Lord is the Truth,
Like one who is blind?
It is those who are
Endued with understanding
That receive admonition—

١٩۔ اَفَمَنْ يَّعْلَمُ اَنَّمَآ
اُنْزِلَ اِلَيْكَ مِنْ رَّبِّكَ الْحَقُّ
كَمَنْ هُوَ اَعْمٰى ۚ
اِنَّمَا يَتَذَكَّرُ اُولُوا الْاَلْبَابِ ۞

20. Those who fulfil the Covenant
Of Allah and fail not
In their plighted word;

٢٠۔ اَلَّذِيْنَ يُوْفُوْنَ بِعَهْدِ اللّٰهِ
وَلَا يَنْقُضُوْنَ الْمِيْثَاقَ ۞

21. Those who join together
Those things which Allah
Hath commanded to be joined,
Hold their Lord in awe,
And fear the terrible reckoning;

٢١۔ وَالَّذِيْنَ يَصِلُوْنَ مَآ اَمَرَ اللّٰهُ
بِهٖۤ اَنْ يُّوْصَلَ وَيَخْشَوْنَ رَبَّهُمْ
وَيَخَافُوْنَ سُوْٓءَ الْحِسَابِ ۞

22. Those who patiently persevere,
Seeking the countenance of
their Lord;
Establish regular prayers; spend,
Out of (the gifts) We have
bestowed
For their sustenance, secretly
And openly; and turn off Evil
With good: for such there is
The final attainment
Of the (Eternal) Home—

٢٢۔ وَالَّذِيْنَ صَبَرُوا ابْتِغَآءَ وَجْهِ رَبِّهِمْ
وَاَقَامُوا الصَّلٰوةَ وَاَنْفَقُوْا مِمَّا رَزَقْنٰهُمْ
سِرًّا وَّعَلَانِيَةً
وَّيَدْرَءُوْنَ بِالْحَسَنَةِ السَّيِّئَةَ
اُولٰٓئِكَ لَهُمْ عُقْبَى الدَّارِ ۞

23. Gardens of perpetual bliss:
They shall enter there,
As well as the righteous
Among their fathers, their spouses,
And their offspring:
And angels shall enter unto them
From every gate
(with the salutation):

٢٣۔ جَنّٰتُ عَدْنٍ يَّدْخُلُوْنَهَا
وَمَنْ صَلَحَ مِنْ اٰبَآئِهِمْ وَاَزْوَاجِهِمْ
وَذُرِّيّٰتِهِمْ وَالْمَلٰٓئِكَةُ
يَدْخُلُوْنَ عَلَيْهِمْ مِّنْ كُلِّ بَابٍ ۞

24. "Peace unto you for that ye
Persevered in patience! Now
How excellent is the final Home!"

٢٤۔ سَلٰمٌ عَلَيْكُمْ بِمَا صَبَرْتُمْ فَنِعْمَ
عُقْبَى الدَّارِ ۞

25. But those who break

٢٥۔ وَالَّذِيْنَ يَنْقُضُوْنَ عَهْدَ اللّٰهِ مِنْ

The Covenant of Allah, after
Having plighted their word
thereto,
And cut asunder those things
Which Allah has commanded
To be joined, and work mischief
In the land—on them
Is the Curse; for them
Is the terrible Home!

26. Allah doth enlarge, or grant
By (strict) measure, the
Sustenance
(Which He giveth) to whom so
He pleaseth. (The worldly) rejoice
In the life of this world:
But the life of this world
Is but little comfort
In the Hereafter.

SECTION 4.

27. The Unbelievers say: "Why
Is not a Sign sent down
To him from his Lord?"
Say: "Truly Allah leaveth.
To stray, whom He will;
But He guideth to Himself
Those who turn to Him
In penitence—

28. "Those who believe, and whose
hearts
Find satisfaction in the
remembrance
Of Allah: for without doubt
In the remembrance of Allah
Do hearts find satisfaction.

29. "For those who believe
And work righteousness,
Is (every) blessedness,
And a beautiful place
Of (final) return."

30. Thus have We sent thee
Amongst a People before whom
(Long since) have (other) Peoples
(Gone and) passed away;
In order that thou mightest
Rehearse unto them what We

بَعْدِ مِيْثَاقِهٖ

وَيَقْطَعُوْنَ مَآ اَمَرَ اللّٰهُ بِهٖۤ اَنْ يُّوْصَلَ

وَيُفْسِدُوْنَ فِى الْاَرْضِ

اُولٰٓئِكَ لَهُمُ اللَّعْنَةُ وَلَهُمْ سُوْٓءُ الدَّارِ ۟

٢٦- اَللّٰهُ يَبْسُطُ الرِّزْقَ لِمَنْ يَّشَآءُ وَيَقْدِرُ

وَفَرِحُوْا بِالْحَيٰوةِ الدُّنْيَا

وَمَا الْحَيٰوةُ الدُّنْيَا فِى الْاٰخِرَةِ

اِلَّا مَتَاعٌ ۟ ؏

٢٧- وَيَقُوْلُ الَّذِيْنَ كَفَرُوْا

لَوْلَاۤ اُنْزِلَ عَلَيْهِ اٰيَةٌ مِّنْ رَّبِّهٖ

قُلْ اِنَّ اللّٰهَ يُضِلُّ مَنْ يَّشَآءُ

وَيَهْدِيْۤ اِلَيْهِ مَنْ اَنَابَ ۖ

٢٨- اَلَّذِيْنَ اٰمَنُوْا وَتَطْمَئِنُّ قُلُوْبُهُمْ

بِذِكْرِ اللّٰهِ

اَلَا بِذِكْرِ اللّٰهِ تَطْمَئِنُّ الْقُلُوْبُ ۟

٢٩- اَلَّذِيْنَ اٰمَنُوْا وَعَمِلُوا الصّٰلِحٰتِ

طُوْبٰى لَهُمْ وَحُسْنُ مَاٰبٍ ۟

٣٠- كَذٰلِكَ اَرْسَلْنٰكَ فِيْۤ اُمَّةٍ

قَدْ خَلَتْ مِنْ قَبْلِهَاۤ اُمَمٌ

لِّتَتْلُوَا۟ عَلَيْهِمُ الَّذِيْۤ اَوْحَيْنَاۤ اِلَيْكَ

Send down unto thee by
                inspiration;
Yet do they reject (Him),
The Most Gracious!
Say: "He is my Lord!
There is no god but He!
On Him is my trust,
And to Him do I turn!"

31. If there were a Qur'ān
With which mountains were
                moved,
Or the earth were cloven asunder,
Or the dead were made to speak,
(This would be the one!)
But, truly, the Command is
With Allah in all things!
Do not the Believers know,
That, had Allah (so) willed,
He could have guided
All mankind (to the Right)?

But the Unbelievers—never
Will disaster cease to seize
Them for their (ill) deeds,
Or to settle close to their homes,
Until the Promise of Allah
Come to pass, for, verily,
Allah will not fail
In His promise.

SECTION 5.

32. Mocked were (many)
                Messengers
Before thee: but I granted
Respite to the Unbelievers,
And finally I punished them:
Then how (terrible) was My
                requital!

33. Is then He Who standeth
Over every soul (and knoweth)
All that it doth,
(Like any others)? And yet
They ascribe partners to Allah.
Say: "But name them!
Is it that ye will
Inform Him of something
He knoweth not on earth,

وَهُمْ يَكْفُرُونَ بِالرَّحْمٰنِ
قُلْ هُوَ رَبِّي لَا إِلٰهَ إِلَّا هُوَ
عَلَيْهِ تَوَكَّلْتُ وَإِلَيْهِ مَتَابِ ۝

٣١- وَلَوْ أَنَّ قُرْآنًا سُيِّرَتْ بِهِ الْجِبَالُ
أَوْ قُطِّعَتْ بِهِ الْأَرْضُ
أَوْ كُلِّمَ بِهِ الْمَوْتٰى
بَلْ لِلّٰهِ الْأَمْرُ جَمِيعًا
أَفَلَمْ يَايْئَسِ الَّذِينَ آمَنُوا
أَنْ لَوْ يَشَاءُ اللّٰهُ لَهَدَى النَّاسَ جَمِيعًا

وَلَا يَزَالُ الَّذِينَ كَفَرُوا تُصِيبُهُمْ
بِمَا صَنَعُوا قَارِعَةٌ أَوْ تَحُلُّ قَرِيبًا مِنْ
دَارِهِمْ حَتّٰى يَأْتِيَ وَعْدُ اللّٰهِ
إِنَّ اللّٰهَ لَا يُخْلِفُ الْمِيعَادَ ۝ ع

٣٢- وَلَقَدِ اسْتُهْزِئَ بِرُسُلٍ مِنْ قَبْلِكَ
فَأَمْلَيْتُ لِلَّذِينَ كَفَرُوا
ثُمَّ أَخَذْتُهُمْ فَكَيْفَ كَانَ عِقَابِ ۝

٣٣- أَفَمَنْ هُوَ قَائِمٌ عَلٰى كُلِّ نَفْسٍ بِمَا
كَسَبَتْ وَجَعَلُوا لِلّٰهِ شُرَكَاءَ
قُلْ سَمُّوهُمْ
أَمْ تُنَبِّئُونَهُ بِمَا لَا يَعْلَمُ فِي الْأَرْضِ
أَمْ بِظَاهِرٍ

Or is it (just) a show
Of words?" Nay! to those
Who believe not, their pretence
Seems pleasing, but they are
Kept back (thereby) from the Path.
And those whom Allah leaves
To stray, no one can guide.

مِنَ الْقَوْلِ بَلْ زُيِّنَ لِلَّذِيْنَ كَفَرُوْا
مَكْرُهُمْ وَصُدُّوْا عَنِ السَّبِيْلِ
وَمَنْ يُّضْلِلِ اللّٰهُ فَمَا لَهٗ مِنْ هَادٍ ۞

34. For them is a Penalty
In the life of this world,
But harder, truly, is the Penalty
Of the Hereafter: and defender
Have they none against Allah.

٣٤- لَهُمْ عَذَابٌ فِى الْحَيٰوةِ الدُّنْيَا
وَلَعَذَابُ الْاٰخِرَةِ اَشَقُّ ۚ
وَمَا لَهُمْ مِّنَ اللّٰهِ مِنْ وَّاقٍ ۞

35. The parable of the Garden
Which the righteous are
                    promised!—
Beneath it flow rivers:
Perpetual is the enjoyment
                    thereof
And the shade therein:
Such is the End
Of the Righteous; and the End
Of Unbelievers is the Fire.

٣٥- مَثَلُ الْجَنَّةِ الَّتِىْ وُعِدَ الْمُتَّقُوْنَ ۗ
تَجْرِىْ مِنْ تَحْتِهَا الْاَنْهٰرُ ۗ
اُكُلُهَا دَآئِمٌ وَّظِلُّهَا ۗ
تِلْكَ عُقْبَى الَّذِيْنَ اتَّقَوْا ۖ
وَّعُقْبَى الْكٰفِرِيْنَ النَّارُ ۞

36. Those to whom We have
Given the Book   rejoice
At what hath been revealed
Unto thee: but there are
Among the clans   those who
                    reject
A part thereof. Say:
"I am commanded to worship
Allah, and not to join partners
With Him. Unto him
Do I call, and
Unto Him is my return."

٣٦- وَالَّذِيْنَ اٰتَيْنٰهُمُ الْكِتٰبَ يَفْرَحُوْنَ
بِمَا اُنْزِلَ اِلَيْكَ
وَمِنَ الْاَحْزَابِ مَنْ يُّنْكِرُ بَعْضَهٗ ۗ
قُلْ اِنَّمَا اُمِرْتُ
اَنْ اَعْبُدَ اللّٰهَ وَلَا اُشْرِكَ بِهٖ ۗ
اِلَيْهِ اَدْعُوْا وَاِلَيْهِ مَاٰبِ ۞

37. Thus have We revealed it
To be a judgement of authority
In Arabic. Wert thou to follow
Their (vain) desires after the
                    knowledge
Which hath reached thee,
Then wouldst thou find
Neither protector nor defender
Against Allah.

٣٧- وَكَذٰلِكَ اَنْزَلْنٰهُ حُكْمًا عَرَبِيًّا ۗ
وَلَئِنِ اتَّبَعْتَ اَهْوَآءَهُمْ
بَعْدَ مَا جَآءَكَ مِنَ الْعِلْمِ ۙ
مَا لَكَ مِنَ اللّٰهِ مِنْ وَّلِيٍّ وَّلَا وَاقٍ ۞ ع

SECTION 6.

38. We did send messengers
Before thee, and appointed
For them wives and children:
And it was never the part
Of a messenger to bring a Sign
Except as Allah permitted
(Or commanded). For each period
Is a Book (revealed).

٣- وَلَقَدْ أَرْسَلْنَا رُسُلًا مِّنْ قَبْلِكَ وَ
جَعَلْنَا لَهُمْ أَزْوَاجًا وَّذُرِّيَّةً
وَمَا كَانَ لِرَسُولٍ أَنْ يَّأْتِيَ بِاٰيَةٍ
إِلَّا بِإِذْنِ اللّٰهِ ۚ لِكُلِّ أَجَلٍ كِتَابٌ ۞

39. Allah doth blot out
Or confirm what He pleaseth:
With Him is
The Mother of the Book.

٣- يَمْحُوا اللّٰهُ مَا يَشَاءُ وَيُثْبِتُ ۖ
وَعِنْدَهٗ أُمُّ الْكِتَابِ ۞

40. Whether We shall show thee
(Within thy lifetime)
Part of what We promised them
Or take to Ourselves thy soul
(Before it is all accomplished),
Thy duty is to make
(The Message) reach them:
It is Our part
To call them to account.

٤- وَإِنْ مَّا نُرِيَنَّكَ بَعْضَ الَّذِيْ نَعِدُهُمْ
وَنَتَوَفَّيَنَّكَ
فَإِنَّمَا عَلَيْكَ الْبَلَاغُ
وَعَلَيْنَا الْحِسَابُ ۞

41. See they not that We
Gradually reduce the land
(In their control) from its
Outlying border?   (Where)
                    Allah
Commands, there is none
To put back His command:
And He is Swift
In calling to account.

٤- أَوَلَمْ يَرَوْا أَنَّا نَأْتِي الْأَرْضَ
نَنْقُصُهَا مِنْ أَطْرَافِهَا ۚ
وَاللّٰهُ يَحْكُمُ لَا مُعَقِّبَ لِحُكْمِهٖ ۚ
وَهُوَ سَرِيعُ الْحِسَابِ ۞

42. Those before them did (also)
Devise plots; but in all things
The master-planning is Allah's.
He knoweth the doings
Of every soul; and soon
Will the Unbelievers know
Who gets home in the End.

٤- وَقَدْ مَكَرَ الَّذِيْنَ مِنْ قَبْلِهِمْ
فَلِلّٰهِ الْمَكْرُ جَمِيعًا ۖ
يَعْلَمُ مَا تَكْسِبُ كُلُّ نَفْسٍ ۚ
وَسَيَعْلَمُ الْكُفَّارُ لِمَنْ عُقْبَى الدَّارِ ۞

43. The Unbelievers say: "No
                    messenger
Art thou." Say: "Enough
For a witness between me
And you is Allah, and such
As have knowledge of the
                    Book."

٤- وَيَقُوْلُ الَّذِيْنَ كَفَرُوْا لَسْتَ مُرْسَلًا ۚ
قُلْ كَفَى بِاللّٰهِ شَهِيدًا بَيْنِي وَبَيْنَكُمْ ۙ
وَمَنْ عِنْدَهٗ عِلْمُ الْكِتَابِ ۞

INTRODUCTION TO SURA XIV. *(Ibrahim)* — 52 Verses

For the chronology and the general argument of this Sura, in the series, Suras x. to xv., see Introduction to S.x.

The special subject-matter of this Sura is a continuation of the concluding portion of the last Sura, which explained how God's revelation gains ground in spite of selfish men's opposition. Here illustrations are given from the story of Moses and Abraham, and Abraham's Prayer for Mecca forms the core of the Sura.

Ibrahim (Abraham)

In the name of Allah, Most Gracious, Most Merciful.

1. Alif Lam Ra. A Book
Which We have revealed
Unto thee, in order that
Thou mightest lead mankind
Out of the depths of darkness
Into light—by the leave
Of their Lord—to the Way
Of (Him) the Exalted in Power,
Worthy of all Praise!—

2. Of Allah, to Whom do belong
All things in the heavens
And on earth!
But alas for the Unbelievers
For a terrible Penalty
(Their Unfaith will bring
them)!—

3. Those who love the life
Of this world more than
The Hereafter, who hinder
(men)
From the Path of Allah
And seek therein something
crooked:
They are astray
By a long distance.

4. We sent not a messenger
Except (to teach) in the
language
Of his (own) people, in order

To make (things) clear to them.
Now Allah leaves straying
Those whom He pleases
And guides whom He pleases:
And He is Exalted in Power,
Full of Wisdom.

فَيُضِلُّ اللّٰهُ مَنْ يَشَآءُ
وَيَهْدِىْ مَنْ يَشَآءُ ؕ
وَهُوَ الْعَزِيْزُ الْحَكِيْمُ ۝

5. We sent Moses with Our Signs
(And the command). "Bring out
Thy people from the depths
Of darkness into light,
And teach them to remember
The Days of Allah." Verily
In this there are Signs
For such as are firmly patient
And constant—grateful and
appreciative.

٥- وَلَقَدْ اَرْسَلْنَا مُوْسٰى بِاٰيٰتِنَآ
اَنْ اَخْرِجْ قَوْمَكَ مِنَ الظُّلُمٰتِ اِلَى النُّوْرِ ۙ۬
وَذَكِّرْهُمْ بِاَيّٰمِ اللّٰهِ ؕ
اِنَّ فِىْ ذٰلِكَ لَاٰيٰتٍ
لِّكُلِّ صَبَّارٍ شَكُوْرٍ ۝

6. Remember! Moses said
To his people: "Call to mind
The favour of Allah to you
When He delivered you
From the people of Pharaoh:
They set you hard tasks
And punishments, slaughtered
Your sons, and let your womenfolk
Live; therein was
A tremendous trial from your
Lord."

٦- وَاِذْ قَالَ مُوْسٰى لِقَوْمِهِ اذْكُرُوْا
نِعْمَةَ اللّٰهِ عَلَيْكُمْ اِذْ اَنْجٰكُمْ مِّنْ اٰلِ
فِرْعَوْنَ يَسُوْمُوْنَكُمْ سُوْٓءَ الْعَذَابِ وَيُذَبِّحُوْنَ
اَبْنَآءَكُمْ وَيَسْتَحْيُوْنَ نِسَآءَكُمْ ؕ
وَفِىْ ذٰلِكُمْ بَلَآءٌ مِّنْ رَّبِّكُمْ عَظِيْمٌ ۠ۚ

SECTION 2.

7. And remember! your Lord
Caused to be declared (publicly):
"If ye are grateful, I will
Add more (favours) unto you;
But if ye show ingratitude,
Truly My punishment
Is terrible indeed."

٧- وَاِذْ تَاَذَّنَ رَبُّكُمْ
لَئِنْ شَكَرْتُمْ لَاَزِيْدَنَّكُمْ
وَلَئِنْ كَفَرْتُمْ
اِنَّ عَذَابِىْ لَشَدِيْدٌ ۝

8. And Moses said: "If ye
Show ingratitude, ye and all
On earth together—yet
Is Allah Free of all wants,
Worthy of all praise.

٨- وَقَالَ مُوْسٰى اِنْ تَكْفُرُوْا
اَنْتُمْ وَمَنْ فِى الْاَرْضِ جَمِيْعًا ۙ
فَاِنَّ اللّٰهَ لَغَنِىٌّ حَمِيْدٌ ۝

9. Has not the story
Reached you, (O people!), of those
Who (went) before you?—
Of the People of Noah,
And 'Ād, and Thamūd?—

٩- اَلَمْ يَاْتِكُمْ نَبَؤُا الَّذِيْنَ مِنْ قَبْلِكُمْ
قَوْمِ نُوْحٍ وَّعَادٍ وَّثَمُوْدَ ۛۚ

And of those who (came)
After them? None knows them
But Allah. To them came
Messengers with Clear (Signs);
But they put their hands
Up to their mouths, and said:
"We do deny (the mission)
On which ye have been sent,
And we are really
In suspicious (disquieting)
               doubt
As to that to which
Ye invite us."

وَالَّذِينَ مِنْ بَعْدِهِمْ لَا يَعْلَمُهُمْ إِلَّا اللَّهُ
جَاءَتْهُمْ رُسُلُهُمْ بِالْبَيِّنَاتِ
فَرَدُّوٓا أَيْدِيَهُمْ فِيٓ أَفْوَاهِهِمْ
وَقَالُوٓا إِنَّا كَفَرْنَا
بِمَآ أُرْسِلْتُم بِهِۦ وَإِنَّا
لَفِى شَكٍّ مِّمَّا تَدْعُونَنَآ إِلَيْهِ مُرِيبٍ ۞

10. Their messengers said: "Is there
A doubt about Allah,
The Creator of the heavens
And the earth." It is He
Who invites you, in order
That He may forgive you
Your sins and give you
Respite for a term appointed!"
They said: "Ah! ye are
No more than human,
Like ourselves! Ye wish
To turn us away from
The (gods) our fathers
Used to worship: then
Bring us some clear authority."

١٠- قَالَتْ رُسُلُهُمْ أَفِى اللَّهِ شَكٌّ
فَاطِرِ السَّمَٰوَٰتِ وَالْأَرْضِ
يَدْعُوكُمْ لِيَغْفِرَ لَكُم مِّن ذُنُوبِكُمْ
وَيُؤَخِّرَكُمْ إِلَىٰٓ أَجَلٍ مُّسَمًّى
قَالُوٓا إِنْ أَنتُمْ إِلَّا بَشَرٌ مِّثْلُنَا
تُرِيدُونَ أَن تَصُدُّونَا عَمَّا كَانَ يَعْبُدُ
ءَابَآؤُنَا فَأْتُونَا بِسُلْطَٰنٍ مُّبِينٍ ۝

11. Their messengers said to them:
"True, we are human
Like yourselves, but Allah
Doth grant His grace
To such of His servants
As He pleases. It is not
For us to bring you
An authority except as Allah
Permits. And on Allah
Let all men of faith
Put their trust.

١١- قَالَتْ لَهُمْ رُسُلُهُمْ إِن نَّحْنُ إِلَّا بَشَرٌ
مِّثْلُكُمْ وَلَٰكِنَّ اللَّهَ يَمُنُّ عَلَىٰ
مَن يَشَآءُ مِنْ عِبَادِهِۦ
وَمَا كَانَ لَنَآ أَن نَّأْتِيَكُم بِسُلْطَٰنٍ
إِلَّا بِإِذْنِ اللَّهِ
وَعَلَى اللَّهِ فَلْيَتَوَكَّلِ الْمُؤْمِنُونَ ۝

12. "No reason have we why
We should not put our trust
On Allah. Indeed He
Has guided us to the Ways
We (follow). We shall certainly

١٢- وَمَا لَنَآ أَلَّا نَتَوَكَّلَ عَلَى اللَّهِ
وَقَدْ هَدَىٰنَا سُبُلَنَا

Bear with patience all
The hurt you may cause us.
For those who put their trust
Should put their trust on Allah."

SECTION 3.

13. And the Unbelievers said
To their messengers: "Be sure
We shall drive you out
Of our land, or ye shall
Return to our religion."
But their Lord inspired
(This Message) to them:
"Verily We shall cause
The wrongdoers to perish!

14. "And verily We shall
Cause you to abide
In the land, and succeed them.
This for such as fear
The Time when they shall stand
Before My tribunal—such
As fear the Punishment
                    denounced."

15. But they sought victory and
                    decision
(There and then), and frustration
Was the lot of every
Powerful obstinate transgressor.

16. In front of such a one
Is Hell, and he is given
For drink, boiling fetid water.

17. In gulps will he sip it,
But never will he be near
Swallowing it down his throat:
Death will come to him
From every quarter, yet
Will he not die: and
In front of him will be
A chastisement unrelenting.

18. The parable of those who
Reject their Lord is that
Their works are as ashes,
On which the wind blows
Furiously on a tempestuous day:

No power have they over
Aught that they have earned:
That is the straying
Far, far (from the goal).

لَا يَقْدِرُوْنَ مِمَّا كَسَبُوْا عَلٰى شَىْءٍ ۗ ذٰلِكَ هُوَ الضَّلٰلُ الْبَعِيْدُ ۝

19. Seest thou not that Allah
Created the heavens and the earth
In Truth? If He so will,
He can remove you
And put (in your place)
A new Creation?

١٩- اَلَمْ تَرَ اَنَّ اللّٰهَ خَلَقَ السَّمٰوٰتِ وَالْاَرْضَ بِالْحَقِّ ۗ اِنْ يَّشَأْ يُذْهِبْكُمْ وَيَأْتِ بِخَلْقٍ جَدِيْدٍ ۙ

20. Nor is that for Allah
Any great matter.

٢٠- وَّمَا ذٰلِكَ عَلَى اللّٰهِ بِعَزِيْزٍ ۝

21. They will all be marshalled
Before Allah together: then
Will the weak say to those
Who were arrogant: "For us,
We but followed you; can ye
Then avail us at all
Against the Wrath of Allah?"
They will reply, "If we
Had received the guidance
Of Allah, we should have
Given it to you: to us
It makes no difference (now)
Whether we rage, or bear
(These torments) with patience:
For ourselves there is no way
Of escape."

٢١- وَبَرَزُوْا لِلّٰهِ جَمِيْعًا فَقَالَ الضُّعَفٰٓؤُا لِلَّذِيْنَ اسْتَكْبَرُوْٓا اِنَّا كُنَّا لَكُمْ تَبَعًا فَهَلْ اَنْتُمْ مُّغْنُوْنَ عَنَّا مِنْ عَذَابِ اللّٰهِ مِنْ شَىْءٍ ۗ قَالُوْا لَوْ هَدٰىنَا اللّٰهُ لَهَدَيْنٰكُمْ ۗ سَوَآءٌ عَلَيْنَآ اَجَزِعْنَآ اَمْ صَبَرْنَا مَا لَنَا مِنْ مَّحِيْصٍ ۞

SECTION 4.

22. And Satan will say
When the matter is decided:
"It was Allah Who gave you
A promise of Truth: I too
Promised, but I failed
In my promise to you.
I had no authority over you
Except to call you, but ye
Listened to me: then
Reproach not me, but reproach
Your own souls. I cannot listen
To your cries, nor can ye
Listen to mine. I reject
Your former act in associating

٢٢- وَقَالَ الشَّيْطٰنُ لَمَّا قُضِيَ الْاَمْرُ اِنَّ اللّٰهَ وَعَدَكُمْ وَعْدَ الْحَقِّ وَوَعَدْتُّكُمْ فَاَخْلَفْتُكُمْ ۗ وَمَا كَانَ لِيَ عَلَيْكُمْ مِّنْ سُلْطٰنٍ اِلَّآ اَنْ دَعَوْتُكُمْ فَاسْتَجَبْتُمْ لِيْ ۚ فَلَا تَلُوْمُوْنِيْ وَلُوْمُوْٓا اَنْفُسَكُمْ ۗ مَآ اَنَا بِمُصْرِخِكُمْ وَمَآ اَنْتُمْ بِمُصْرِخِيَّ ۗ اِنِّيْ كَفَرْتُ بِمَآ اَشْرَكْتُمُوْنِ مِنْ قَبْلُ ۗ

Me with Allah.
For wrongdoers there must be
A Grievous Penalty."

إِنَّ الظَّٰلِمِينَ لَهُمْ عَذَابٌ أَلِيمٌ ۝

23. But those who believe
And work righteousness
Will be admitted to Gardens
Beneath which rivers flow—
To dwell therein for aye
With the leave of their Lord.
Their greeting therein
Will be: "Peace!"

٢٣- وَأُدْخِلَ الَّذِينَ آمَنُوا وَعَمِلُوا الصَّٰلِحَٰتِ
جَنَّٰتٍ تَجْرِي مِن تَحْتِهَا الْأَنْهَٰرُ
خَٰلِدِينَ فِيهَا بِإِذْنِ رَبِّهِمْ
تَحِيَّتُهُمْ فِيهَا سَلَٰمٌ ۝

24. Seest thou not how
Allah sets forth a parable?—
A goodly Word
Like a goodly tree,
Whose root is firmly fixed,
And its branches (reach)
To the heavens—

٢٤- أَلَمْ تَرَ كَيْفَ ضَرَبَ اللَّهُ مَثَلًا
كَلِمَةً طَيِّبَةً كَشَجَرَةٍ طَيِّبَةٍ
أَصْلُهَا ثَابِتٌ وَفَرْعُهَا فِي السَّمَاءِ ۝

25. It brings forth its fruit
At all times, by the leave
Of its Lord.
So Allah sets forth parables
For men, in order that
They may receive admonition.

٢٥- تُؤْتِي أُكُلَهَا كُلَّ حِينٍ بِإِذْنِ
رَبِّهَا وَيَضْرِبُ اللَّهُ الْأَمْثَالَ
لِلنَّاسِ لَعَلَّهُمْ يَتَذَكَّرُونَ ۝

26. And the parable
Of an evil Word
Is that of any evil tree:
It is torn up by the root
From the surface of the earth:
It has no stability.

٢٦- وَمَثَلُ كَلِمَةٍ خَبِيثَةٍ كَشَجَرَةٍ خَبِيثَةٍ
اجْتُثَّتْ مِن فَوْقِ الْأَرْضِ مَا لَهَا مِن
قَرَارٍ ۝

27. Allah will establish in strength
Those who believe, with the Word
That stands firm, in this world
And in the Hereafter; but Allah
Will leave, to stray, those
Who do wrong: Allah doeth
What he willeth.

SECTION 5.

٢٧- يُثَبِّتُ اللَّهُ الَّذِينَ آمَنُوا بِالْقَوْلِ
الثَّابِتِ فِي الْحَيَوٰةِ الدُّنْيَا وَفِي الْآخِرَةِ
وَيُضِلُّ اللَّهُ الظَّٰلِمِينَ
وَيَفْعَلُ اللَّهُ مَا يَشَاءُ ۝

28. Hast thou not turned
Thy vision to those who
Have changed the favour of Allah
Into blasphemy and caused
Their people to descend
To the House of Perdition?—

٢٨- أَلَمْ تَرَ إِلَى الَّذِينَ
بَدَّلُوا نِعْمَتَ اللَّهِ كُفْرًا
وَأَحَلُّوا قَوْمَهُمْ دَارَ الْبَوَارِ ۝

29. Into Hell? They will burn
Therein — an evil place
To stay in!

٢٩ ـ جَهَنَّمَ ۚ يَصْلَوْنَهَا ۖ وَبِئْسَ الْقَرَارُ ○

30. And they set up (idols)
As equal to Allah, to mislead
(Men) from the Path! Say:
"Enjoy (your brief power)!
But verily ye are making
Straightway for Hell!"

٣٠ ـ وَجَعَلُوا لِلَّهِ أَنْدَادًا لِّيُضِلُّوا
عَن سَبِيلِهِ ۗ قُلْ تَمَتَّعُوا
فَإِنَّ مَصِيرَكُمْ إِلَى النَّارِ ○

31. Speak to my servants
Who have believed,
That they may establish
Regular prayers, and spend
(In charity) out of the
              Sustenance
We have given them,
Secretly and openly, before
The coming of a Day
In which there will be
Neither mutual bargaining
Nor befriending.

٣١ ـ قُل لِّعِبَادِيَ الَّذِينَ آمَنُوا
يُقِيمُوا الصَّلَوٰةَ وَيُنفِقُوا مِمَّا
رَزَقْنَاهُمْ سِرًّا وَّعَلَانِيَةً
مِّن قَبْلِ أَن يَّأْتِيَ يَوْمٌ
لَّا بَيْعٌ فِيهِ وَلَا خِلَالٌ ○

32. It is Allah Who hath created
The heavens and the earth
And sendeth down rain
From the skies, and with it
Bringeth out fruits wherewith
To feed you. It is He
Who hath made the ships subject
To you, that they may sail
Through the sea by His
              Command;
And the rivers (also)
Hath He made subject to you.

٣٢ ـ اللَّهُ الَّذِي خَلَقَ السَّمَاوَاتِ وَالْأَرْضَ
وَأَنزَلَ مِنَ السَّمَاءِ مَاءً
فَأَخْرَجَ بِهِ مِنَ الثَّمَرَاتِ رِزْقًا لَّكُمْ ۖ
وَسَخَّرَ لَكُمُ الْفُلْكَ
لِتَجْرِيَ فِي الْبَحْرِ بِأَمْرِهِ ۖ
وَسَخَّرَ لَكُمُ الْأَنْهَارَ ○

33. And He hath made subject
To you the sun and the moon,
Both diligently pursuing
Their courses: and the Night
And the Day hath He (also)
Made subject to you.

٣٣ ـ وَسَخَّرَ لَكُمُ
الشَّمْسَ وَالْقَمَرَ دَائِبَيْنِ ۖ
وَسَخَّرَ لَكُمُ الَّيْلَ وَالنَّهَارَ ○

34. And he giveth you
Of all that ye ask for.
But if ye count the favours

٣٤ ـ وَآتَاكُم مِّن كُلِّ مَا سَأَلْتُمُوهُ ۚ

Of Allah, never will ye
Be able to number them.
Verily, man is given up
To injustice and ingratitude.

SECTION 6.

35. Remember Abraham said:
"O my Lord! make this city
One of peace and security:
And preserve me and my sons
From worshipping idols.

وَإِنْ تَعُدُّوْا نِعْمَتَ اللهِ لَا تُحْصُوْهَا ۚ
اِنَّ الْإِنْسَانَ لَظَلُوْمٌ كَفَّارٌ ۝

٣٥ - وَإِذْ قَالَ اِبْرٰهِيْمُ رَبِّ اجْعَلْ
هٰذَا الْبَلَدَ اٰمِنًا وَّاجْنُبْنِيْ
وَبَنِيَّ اَنْ نَّعْبُدَ الْاَصْنَامَ ۝

36. "O my Lord! they have indeed
Led astray many among mankind;
He then who follows my (ways)
Is of me, and he that
Disobeys me—but Thou
Art indeed Oft-Forgiving,
Most Merciful.

٣٦ - رَبِّ اِنَّهُنَّ اَضْلَلْنَ كَثِيْرًا مِّنَ
النَّاسِ ۚ فَمَنْ تَبِعَنِيْ فَاِنَّهُ مِنِّيْ ۚ
وَمَنْ عَصَانِيْ
فَاِنَّكَ غَفُوْرٌ رَّحِيْمٌ ۝

37. "O our Lord! I have made
Some of my offspring to dwell
In a valley without cultivation,
By Thy Sacred House;
In order, O our Lord, that they
May establish regular Prayer:
So fill the hearts of some
Among men with love towards
             them,
And feed them with Fruits:
So that they may give thanks.

٣٧ - رَبَّنَا اِنِّيْ اَسْكَنْتُ مِنْ ذُرِّيَّتِيْ
بِوَادٍ غَيْرِ ذِيْ زَرْعٍ عِنْدَ بَيْتِكَ الْمُحَرَّمِ ۙ
رَبَّنَا لِيُقِيْمُوا الصَّلٰوةَ فَاجْعَلْ اَفْئِدَةً
مِّنَ النَّاسِ تَهْوِيْ اِلَيْهِمْ
وَارْزُقْهُمْ مِّنَ الثَّمَرٰتِ لَعَلَّهُمْ يَشْكُرُوْنَ ۝

38. "O our Lord! truly Thou
Dost know what we conceal
And what we reveal:
For nothing whatever is hiddden
From Allah, whether on earth
Or in heaven.

٣٨ - رَبَّنَا اِنَّكَ تَعْلَمُ مَا نُخْفِيْ
وَمَا نُعْلِنُ ۗ وَمَا يَخْفٰى عَلَى اللهِ مِنْ شَيْءٍ
فِى الْاَرْضِ وَلَا فِى السَّمَاءِ ۝

39. "Praise be to Allah. Who hath
Granted unto me in old age
Ismā'īl and Isaac: for truly
My Lord is He, the Hearer
Of Prayer!

٣٩ - اَلْحَمْدُ لِلهِ الَّذِيْ وَهَبَ لِيْ عَلَى الْكِبَرِ
اِسْمٰعِيْلَ وَاِسْحٰقَ ۗ
اِنَّ رَبِّيْ لَسَمِيْعُ الدُّعَاءِ ۝

40. "O my Lord! make me
One who establishes regular
                 Prayer,
And also (raise such)
Among my offspring

٤٠ - رَبِّ اجْعَلْنِيْ مُقِيْمَ الصَّلٰوةِ
وَمِنْ ذُرِّيَّتِيْ ۚ

O our Lord!
And accept Thou my Prayer.

رَبَّنَا وَتَقَبَّلْ دُعَآءِ ٥

41. "O our Lord!   cover (us)
With Thy Forgiveness—me,
My parents,   and (all) Believers,
On the Day that the Reckoning
Will be established!"

٤١ ۔ رَبَّنَا اغْفِرْلِيْ
وَلِوَالِدَيَّ وَلِلْمُؤْمِنِيْنَ يَوْمَ يَقُوْمُ
الْحِسَابُ ٥

SECTION 7.

42. Think not that Allah
Doth not heed the deeds
Of those who do wrong.
He but giveth them respite
Against a Day when
The eyes will fixedly stare
In horror—

٤٢ ۔ وَلَا تَحْسَبَنَّ اللّٰهَ غَافِلًا
عَمَّا يَعْمَلُ الظّٰلِمُوْنَ ۬
اِنَّمَا يُؤَخِّرُهُمْ لِيَوْمٍ
تَشْخَصُ فِيْهِ الْاَبْصَارُ ٥

43. They are running forward
With necks outstretched,
Their heads uplifted, their gaze
Returning not towards them,
And their hearts a (gaping)
void!

٤٣ ۔ مُهْطِعِيْنَ مُقْنِعِيْ رُءُوْسِهِمْ
لَا يَرْتَدُّ اِلَيْهِمْ طَرْفُهُمْ ۚ
وَاَفْئِدَتُهُمْ هَوَآءٌ ٥

44. So warn mankind
Of the Day when the Wrath
Will reach them: then will
The wrongdoers say: "Our Lord!
Respite us (if only)
For a short Term: we will
Answer Thy Call, and follow
The messengers!"
"What! were ye not wont
To swear aforetime that ye
Should suffer no decline?

٤٤ ۔ وَاَنْذِرِ النَّاسَ يَوْمَ يَاْتِيْهِمُ الْعَذَابُ
فَيَقُوْلُ الَّذِيْنَ ظَلَمُوْا رَبَّنَا
اَخِّرْنَا اِلٰى اَجَلٍ قَرِيْبٍ ۙ
نُّجِبْ دَعْوَتَكَ وَنَتَّبِعِ الرُّسُلَ ؕ
اَوَلَمْ تَكُوْنُوْا اَقْسَمْتُمْ مِّنْ قَبْلُ
مَا لَكُمْ مِّنْ زَوَالٍ ٥

45. "And ye dwelt in the dwellings
Of men who wronged their own
Souls; ye were clearly shown
How We dealt with them;
And We put forth (many) Parables
In your behalf!"

٤٥ ۔ وَّسَكَنْتُمْ فِيْ مَسٰكِنِ الَّذِيْنَ ظَلَمُوْا
اَنْفُسَهُمْ وَتَبَيَّنَ لَكُمْ كَيْفَ فَعَلْنَا بِهِمْ
وَضَرَبْنَا لَكُمُ الْاَمْثَالَ ٥

46. Mighty indeed were the plots
Which they made, but their plots
Were (well) within the sight
Of Allah, even though they were
Such as to shake the hills!

٤٦ ۔ وَقَدْ مَكَرُوْا مَكْرَهُمْ وَعِنْدَ اللّٰهِ
مَكْرُهُمْ ؕ وَاِنْ كَانَ مَكْرُهُمْ
لِتَزُوْلَ مِنْهُ الْجِبَالُ ٥

47. Never think that Allah would fail
His messengers in His promise:
For Allah is Exalted in Power—
The Lord of Retribution.

٤٧- فَلَا تَحْسَبَنَّ اللّٰهَ مُخْلِفَ وَعْدِهٖ
رُسُلَهٗ ۚ إِنَّ اللّٰهَ عَزِيزٌ ذُو انْتِقَامٍ ۙ

48. One day the Earth will be
Changed to a different Earth,
And so will be the Heavens,
And (men) will be marshalled
Forth, before Allah, the One,
The Irresistible;

٤٨- يَوْمَ تُبَدَّلُ الْأَرْضُ غَيْرَ الْأَرْضِ
وَالسَّمٰوٰتُ وَبَرَزُوا لِلّٰهِ
الْوَاحِدِ الْقَهَّارِ

49. And thou wilt see
The Sinners that day
Bound together in fetters—

٤٩- وَتَرَى الْمُجْرِمِينَ يَوْمَئِذٍ
مُّقَرَّنِينَ فِي الْأَصْفَادِ ۖ

50. Their garments of liquid
  pitch,
And their faces covered with Fire;

٥٠- سَرَابِيلُهُمْ مِّنْ قَطِرَانٍ
وَّتَغْشٰى وُجُوهَهُمُ النَّارُ ۙ

51. That Allah may requite
Each soul according
To its deserts;
And verily Allah is Swift
In calling to account.

٥١- لِيَجْزِيَ اللّٰهُ كُلَّ نَفْسٍ مَّا كَسَبَتْ ۚ
إِنَّ اللّٰهَ سَرِيعُ الْحِسَابِ ۞

52. Here is a Message for mankind:
Let them take warning therefrom,
And let them know that He
Is (no other than) One God:
Let men of understanding
Take heed.

٥٢- هٰذَا بَلَاغٌ لِّلنَّاسِ وَلِيُنْذَرُوا بِهٖ
وَلِيَعْلَمُوا أَنَّمَا هُوَ إِلٰهٌ وَّاحِدٌ
وَّلِيَذَّكَّرَ أُولُوا الْأَلْبَابِ ۞

INTRODUCTION TO SŪRA XV. (*Ḥijr*) — 99 Verses

This is the last of the six Sūras of the A. L. M. series (x. to xv.). Its place in chronology is the late Meccan period, probably somewhere near the middle of that period. See Introduction to S.x., where will be found also an indication of the general subject-matter of the whole series in the gradation of Quranic teaching.

The special subject-matter of this Sūra is the protection of God's Revelation and God's Truth. Evil arose from Pride and the warping of man's will, but God's Mercy is the antidote, as was proved in the case of Abraham and Lot, and might have been proved by the people of the Aika and the Ḥijr if they had only attended to God's "Signs". The Qur-ān, beginning with the Seven Oft-repeated Verses, is the precious vehicle for the praises of God.

Al Ḥijr

In the name of Allah, Most Gracious, Most Merciful.

1. Alif Lām Ra. These are
The Ayāt of Revelation—
Of a Qur'ān
That makes things clear.

2. Again and again will those
Who disbelieve, wish that they
Had bowed (to Allah's Will)
In Islam.

3. Leave them alone, to enjoy
(The good things of this life)
And to please themselves:
Let (false) Hope amuse them: soon
Will knowledge (undeceive
them).

4. Never did We destroy
A population that had not
A term decreed and assigned
Beforehand.

5. Neither can a people anticipate
Its Term, nor delay it.

6. They say: "O thou to whom
The Message is being revealed!

Truly thou art mad
   (or possessed)!

إِنَّكَ لَمَجْنُونٌ ۝

7. "Why bringest thou not
Angels to us if it be
That thou hast the Truth?"

٧- لَوْ مَا تَأْتِينَا بِالْمَلَائِكَةِ
إِنْ كُنْتَ مِنَ الصَّادِقِينَ ۝

8. We send not the angels
Down except for just cause:
If they came (to the ungodly),
Behold! no respite would they
     have!

٨- مَا نُنَزِّلُ الْمَلَائِكَةَ إِلَّا بِالْحَقِّ
وَمَا كَانُوا إِذًا مُنْظَرِينَ ۝

9. We have, without doubt,
Sent down the Message;
And We will assuredly
Guard it (from corruption).

٩- إِنَّا نَحْنُ نَزَّلْنَا الذِّكْرَ
وَإِنَّا لَهُ لَحَافِظُونَ ۝

10. We did send messengers before
      thee
Amongst the religious sects
Of old:

١٠- وَلَقَدْ أَرْسَلْنَا مِنْ قَبْلِكَ فِي شِيَعِ
الْأَوَّلِينَ ۝

11. But never came a messenger
To them but they mocked him.

١١- وَمَا يَأْتِيهِمْ مِنْ رَسُولٍ إِلَّا كَانُوا بِهِ
يَسْتَهْزِئُونَ ۝

12. Even so do We let it creep
Into the hearts of the sinners—

١٢- كَذَلِكَ نَسْلُكُهُ فِي قُلُوبِ الْمُجْرِمِينَ ۝

13. That they should not believe
In the (Message); but the ways
Of the ancients have passed
      away.

١٣- لَا يُؤْمِنُونَ بِهِ وَقَدْ
خَلَتْ سُنَّةُ الْأَوَّلِينَ ۝

14. Even if We opened out to them
A gate from heaven,
And they were to continue
(All day) ascending therein,

١٤- وَلَوْ فَتَحْنَا عَلَيْهِمْ بَابًا مِنَ السَّمَاءِ
فَظَلُّوا فِيهِ يَعْرُجُونَ ۝

15. They would only say:
"Our eyes have been intoxicated:
Nay, we have been bewitched
By sorcery."
  SECTION 2.

١٥- لَقَالُوا إِنَّمَا سُكِّرَتْ أَبْصَارُنَا
بَلْ نَحْنُ قَوْمٌ مَسْحُورُونَ ۝

16. It is We Who have set out
The Zodiacal Signs[1950] in the
      heavens,

١٦- وَلَقَدْ جَعَلْنَا فِي السَّمَاءِ بُرُوجًا

And made them fair-seeming
To (all) beholders;

وَزَيَّنَّاهَا لِلنَّاظِرِينَ ۞

17. And (moreover) We have guarded
them
From every evil spirit accursed:

١٧- وَحَفِظْنَاهَا مِنْ كُلِّ شَيْطَانٍ رَجِيمٍ ۞

18. But any that gains a hearing
By stealth, is pursued
By a flaming fire, bright (to
see).

١٨- إِلَّا مَنِ اسْتَرَقَ السَّمْعَ
فَأَتْبَعَهُ شِهَابٌ مُبِينٌ ۞

19. And the earth We have spread
out
(Like a carpet); set thereon
Mountains firm and immovable;
And produced therein all kinds
Of things in due balance.

١٩- وَالْأَرْضَ مَدَدْنَاهَا
وَأَلْقَيْنَا فِيهَا رَوَاسِيَ
وَأَنْبَتْنَا فِيهَا مِنْ كُلِّ شَيْءٍ مَوْزُونٍ ۞

20. And We have provided therein
Means of subsistence—for you
And for those for whose sustenance
Ye are not responsible.

٢٠- وَجَعَلْنَا لَكُمْ فِيهَا مَعَايِشَ
وَمَنْ لَسْتُمْ لَهُ بِرَازِقِينَ ۞

21. And there is not a thing
But its (sources and) treasures
(Inexhaustible) are with Us;
But We only send down
Thereof in due and ascertainable
measures.

٢١- وَإِنْ مِنْ شَيْءٍ إِلَّا عِنْدَنَا خَزَائِنُهُ
وَمَا نُنَزِّلُهُ
إِلَّا بِقَدَرٍ مَعْلُومٍ ۞

22. And We send the fecundating
winds,
Then cause the rain to descend
From the sky, therewith providing
You with water (in abundance),
Though ye are not the
guardians
Of its stores.

٢٢- وَأَرْسَلْنَا الرِّيَاحَ لَوَاقِحَ
فَأَنْزَلْنَا مِنَ السَّمَاءِ مَاءً
فَأَسْقَيْنَاكُمُوهُ
وَمَا أَنْتُمْ لَهُ بِخَازِنِينَ ۞

23. And verily, it is We
Who give life, and Who give
Death: it is We Who remain
Inheritors
(After all else passes away).

٢٣- وَإِنَّا لَنَحْنُ نُحْيِي وَنُمِيتُ
وَنَحْنُ الْوَارِثُونَ ۞

24. To Us are known those of you
Who hasten forward, and those
Who lag behind.

٢٤- وَلَقَدْ عَلِمْنَا الْمُسْتَقْدِمِينَ مِنْكُمْ
وَلَقَدْ عَلِمْنَا الْمُسْتَأْخِرِينَ ۞

25. Assuredly it is thy Lord
Who will gather them together:
For He is Perfect in Wisdom
And Knowledge.

SECTION 3.

26. We created man from sounding
clay,
From mud moulded into shape;

27. And the Jinn race, We had
Created before, from the fire
Of a scorching wind.

28. Behold! thy Lord said
To the angels: "I am about
To create man, from sounding clay
From mud moulded into shape;

29. "When I have fashioned him
(In due proportion) and breathed
Into him of My spirit,
Fall ye down in obeisance
Unto him."

30. So the angels prostrated
themselves,
All of them together:

31. Not so   Iblīs: he refused to be
Among those who prostrated
themselves.

32. (Allah) said: "O Iblīs!
What is your reason
For not being among those
Who prostrated themselves?"

33. (Iblīs) said: "I am not one
To prostrate myself to man,
Whom Thou didst create
From sounding clay, from mud
Moulded into shape."

34. (Allah) said: "Then get thee out
From here: for thou art
Rejected, accursed.

35. "And the Curse shall be

٢٥- وَإِنَّ رَبَّكَ هُوَ يَحْشُرُهُمْ ۚ
اِنَّهٗ حَكِيمٌ عَلِيمٌ ۞

٢٦- وَلَقَدْ خَلَقْنَا الْاِنْسَانَ مِنْ صَلْصَالٍ
مِّنْ حَمَاٍ مَّسْنُوْنٍ ۚ

٢٧- وَالْجَآنَّ خَلَقْنٰهُ مِنْ قَبْلُ مِنْ
نَّارِ السَّمُوْمِ ۞

٢٨- وَاِذْ قَالَ رَبُّكَ لِلْمَلٰٓئِكَةِ اِنِّيْ خَالِقٌۢ
بَشَرًا مِّنْ صَلْصَالٍ مِّنْ حَمَاٍ مَّسْنُوْنٍ

٢٩- فَاِذَا سَوَّيْتُهٗ
وَنَفَخْتُ فِيْهِ مِنْ رُّوْحِيْ
فَقَعُوْا لَهٗ سٰجِدِيْنَ ۞

٣٠- فَسَجَدَ الْمَلٰٓئِكَةُ كُلُّهُمْ اَجْمَعُوْنَ ۞

٣١- اِلَّآ اِبْلِيْسَ ۗ
اَبٰٓى اَنْ يَّكُوْنَ مَعَ السّٰجِدِيْنَ ۞

٣٢- قَالَ يٰٓاِبْلِيْسُ مَا لَكَ
اَلَّا تَكُوْنَ مَعَ السّٰجِدِيْنَ ۞

٣٣- قَالَ لَمْ اَكُنْ لِّاَسْجُدَ لِبَشَرٍ
خَلَقْتَهٗ مِنْ صَلْصَالٍ
مِّنْ حَمَاٍ مَّسْنُوْنٍ ۞

٣٤- قَالَ فَاخْرُجْ مِنْهَا فَاِنَّكَ رَجِيْمٌ ۙ

٣٥- وَّاِنَّ عَلَيْكَ

On thee till the Day of
           Judgement."

اللَّعْنَةَ اِلٰى يَوْمِ الدِّيْنِ ۞

36. (Iblīs) said: "O my Lord!
Give me then respite
Till the Day
The (dead) are raised."

٣٦- قَالَ رَبِّ فَاَنْظِرْنِيْۤ
اِلٰى يَوْمِ يُبْعَثُوْنَ ۞

37. (Allah) said: "Respite
Is granted thee—

٣٧- قَالَ فَاِنَّكَ مِنَ الْمُنْظَرِيْنَ ۙ

38. "Till the Day
Of the Time Appointed."

٣٨- اِلٰى يَوْمِ الْوَقْتِ الْمَعْلُوْمِ ۞

39. (Iblīs) said: "O my Lord!
Because Thou hast put me
In the wrong, I will
Make (wrong) fair-seeming
To them on the earth,
And I will put them
All in the wrong—

٣٩- قَالَ رَبِّ بِمَاۤ اَغْوَيْتَنِيْ
لَاُزَيِّنَنَّ لَهُمْ فِى الْاَرْضِ
وَلَاُغْوِيَنَّهُمْ اَجْمَعِيْنَ ۙ

40. "Except Thy servants among
           them,
Sincere and purified
(By Thy grace)."

٤٠- اِلَّا عِبَادَكَ مِنْهُمُ
الْمُخْلَصِيْنَ ۞

41. (Allah) said: "This (Way
Of My sincere servants) is
Indeed a Way that leads
Straight to Me.

٤١- قَالَ هٰذَا صِرَاطٌ
عَلَيَّ مُسْتَقِيْمٌ ۞

42. "For over My servants
No authority shalt thou
Have, except such as
Put themselves in the wrong
And follow thee."

٤٢- اِنَّ عِبَادِيْ لَيْسَ لَكَ عَلَيْهِمْ سُلْطٰنٌ
اِلَّا مَنِ اتَّبَعَكَ مِنَ الْغٰوِيْنَ ۞

43. And verily, Hell
Is the promised abode
For them all!

٤٣- وَاِنَّ جَهَنَّمَ
لَمَوْعِدُهُمْ اَجْمَعِيْنَ ۙ

44. To it are seven Gates:
For each of those Gates
Is a (special) class
(Of sinners) assigned.

SECTION 4.

٤٤- لَهَا سَبْعَةُ اَبْوَابٍ
لِكُلِّ بَابٍ مِّنْهُمْ جُزْءٌ مَّقْسُوْمٌ ۞

45. The righteous (will be)
Amid Gardens

٤٥- اِنَّ الْمُتَّقِيْنَ فِيْ جَنّٰتٍ

And fountains
(Of clear-flowing water).

وَّعُيُوْنٍ ۟

46. (Their greeting will· be):
"Enter ye here
In Peace and Security."

٤٦- اُدْخُلُوْهَا بِسَلٰمٍ اٰمِنِيْنَ ۟

47. And We shall remove
From their hearts any
Lurking sense of injury:
(They will be) brothers
(Joyfully) facing each other
On thrones (of dignity).

٤٧- وَنَزَعْنَا مَا فِيْ صُدُوْرِهِمْ
مِّنْ غِلٍّ
اِخْوَانًا عَلٰى سُرُرٍ مُّتَقٰبِلِيْنَ ۟

48. There no sense of fatigue
Shall touch them,
Nor shall they (ever)
Be asked to leave.

٤٨- لَا يَمَسُّهُمْ فِيْهَا نَصَبٌ
وَّمَا هُمْ مِّنْهَا بِمُخْرَجِيْنَ ۟

49. Tell My servants
That I am indeed
The Oft-Forgiving,
Most Merciful;

٤٩- نَبِّئْ عِبَادِيْٓ
اَنِّيْٓ اَنَا الْغَفُوْرُ الرَّحِيْمُ ۟

50. And that my Penalty
Will be indeed
The most grievous Penalty.

٥٠- وَاَنَّ عَذَابِيْ هُوَ الْعَذَابُ الْاَلِيْمُ ۟

51. Tell them about
The guests of Abraham.

٥١- وَنَبِّئْهُمْ عَنْ ضَيْفِ اِبْرٰهِيْمَ ۟

52. When they entered his presence
And said, "Peace!"
He said, "We feel
Afraid of you!"

٥٢- اِذْ دَخَلُوْا عَلَيْهِ فَقَالُوْا سَلٰمًا ۟
قَالَ اِنَّا مِنْكُمْ وَجِلُوْنَ ۟

53. They said: "Fear not!
We give thee glad tidings
Of a son endowed
With wisdom."

٥٣- قَالُوْا لَا تَوْجَلْ اِنَّا نُبَشِّرُكَ
بِغُلٰمٍ عَلِيْمٍ ۟

54. He said: "Do you give me
Glad tidings that old age
Has seized me? Of what
Then, is your good news?"

٥٤- قَالَ اَبَشَّرْتُمُوْنِيْ عَلٰٓى اَنْ مَّسَّنِيَ الْكِبَرُ
فَبِمَ تُبَشِّرُوْنَ ۟

55. They said: "We give thee
Glad tidings in truth:
Be not then in despair!"

٥٥- قَالُوْا بَشَّرْنٰكَ بِالْحَقِّ
فَلَا تَكُنْ مِّنَ الْقٰنِطِيْنَ ۟

56. He said: "And who
Despairs of the mercy
Of his Lord, but such
As go astray?"

٥٦- قَالَ وَمَنْ يَّقْنَطُ مِنْ رَّحْمَةِ رَبِّهٖۤ اِلَّا الضَّآلُّوْنَ ۞

57. Abraham said: "What then
Is the business of which
Ye (have come), O ye
Messengers (of Allah)?"

٥٧- قَالَ فَمَا خَطْبُكُمْ اَيُّهَا الْمُرْسَلُوْنَ ۞

58. They said: "We have been
Sent to a people
(Deep) in sin.

٥٨- قَالُوْۤا اِنَّاۤ اُرْسِلْنَاۤ اِلٰى قَوْمٍ مُّجْرِمِيْنَ ۞

59. "Excepting the adherents
Of Lūṭ: them we are certainly
(Charged) to save (from
                    harm)—
All—

٥٩- اِلَّاۤ اٰلَ لُوْطٍ ۭ اِنَّا لَمُنَجُّوْهُمْ اَجْمَعِيْنَ ۞

60. "Except his wife, who,
We have ascertained,
Will be among those
Who lag behind."

٦٠- اِلَّا امْرَاَتَهٗ قَدَّرْنَاۤ اِنَّهَا لَمِنَ الْغٰبِرِيْنَ ۞

SECTION 5.

61. At length when the messengers
Arrived among the adherents
Of Lūṭ,

٦١- فَلَمَّا جَآءَ اٰلَ لُوْطِ ﹾالْمُرْسَلُوْنَ ۞

62. He said: "Ye appear
To be uncommon folk."

٦٢- قَالَ اِنَّكُمْ قَوْمٌ مُّنْكَرُوْنَ ۞

63. They said: "Yea
We have come to thee
To accomplish that
Of which they doubt.

٦٣- قَالُوْا بَلْ جِئْنٰكَ بِمَا كَانُوْا فِيْهِ يَمْتَرُوْنَ ۞

64. "We have brought to thee
That which is inevitably
Due, and assuredly
We tell the truth.

٦٤- وَاَتَيْنٰكَ بِالْحَقِّ وَاِنَّا لَصٰدِقُوْنَ ۞

65. "Then travel by night
With thy household,
When a portion of the night
(Yet remains), and do thou
Bring up the rear:
Let no one amongst you

٦٥- فَاَسْرِ بِاَهْلِكَ بِقِطْعٍ مِّنَ الَّيْلِ وَاتَّبِعْ اَدْبَارَهُمْ وَلَا يَلْتَفِتْ مِنْكُمْ اَحَدٌ

Look back, but pass on
Whither ye are ordered."

وَامْضُوا حَيْثُ تُؤْمَرُونَ ۞

66. And We made known
This decree to him,
That the last remnants
Of those (sinners) should be
Cut off by the morning.

٦٦ ـ وَقَضَيْنَآ إِلَيْهِ ذٰلِكَ الْأَمْرَ أَنَّ دَابِرَ هٰؤُلَآءِ مَقْطُوعٌ مُّصْبِحِينَ ۞

67. The inhabitants of the City
Came in (mad) joy
(At news of the young men).

٦٧ ـ وَجَآءَ أَهْلُ الْمَدِينَةِ يَسْتَبْشِرُونَ ۞

68. Lūt said: "These are
My guests: disgrace me not:

٦٨ ـ قَالَ إِنَّ هٰؤُلَآءِ ضَيْفِي فَلَا تَفْضَحُونِ ۞

69. "But fear Allah
And shame me not."

٦٩ ـ وَاتَّقُوا اللّٰهَ وَلَا تُخْزُونِ ۞

70. They said: "Did we not
Forbid thee (to speak)
For all and sundry?"

٧٠ ـ قَالُوٓا أَوَلَمْ نَنْهَكَ عَنِ الْعٰلَمِينَ ۞

71. He said: "There are
My daughters (to marry),
If ye must act (so)."

٧١ ـ قَالَ هٰؤُلَآءِ بَنٰتِي إِنْ كُنْتُمْ فٰعِلِينَ ۞

72. Verily, by thy life (O Prophet),
In their wild intoxication,
They wander in distraction,
To and fro.

٧٢ ـ لَعَمْرُكَ إِنَّهُمْ لَفِي سَكْرَتِهِمْ يَعْمَهُونَ ۞

73. But the (mighty) Blast
Overtook them before morning,

٧٣ ـ فَأَخَذَتْهُمُ الصَّيْحَةُ مُشْرِقِينَ ۞

74. And We turned (the Cities)
Upside down, and rained down
On them brimstones
Hard as baked clay.

٧٤ ـ فَجَعَلْنَا عَالِيَهَا سَافِلَهَا وَأَمْطَرْنَا عَلَيْهِمْ حِجَارَةً مِّنْ سِجِّيلٍ ۞

75. Behold! in this are Signs
For those who by tokens
Do understand.

٧٥ ـ إِنَّ فِي ذٰلِكَ لَأيٰتٍ لِّلْمُتَوَسِّمِينَ ۞

76. And the (Cities were)
Right on the highroad.

٧٦ ـ وَإِنَّهَا لَبِسَبِيلٍ مُّقِيمٍ ۞

77. Behold! in this
Is a Sign

٧٧ ـ إِنَّ فِي ذٰلِكَ لَأيَةً

For those who believe!   لِلْمُؤْمِنِيْنَ ۞

8. And the Companions of the
Wood
Were also wrongdoers;

٧٨- وَاِنْ كَانَ اَصْحٰبُ الْاَيْكَةِ لَظٰلِمِيْنَ ۞

79. So We exacted retribution
From them. They were both
On an open highway,
Plain to see.

٧٩- فَانْتَقَمْنَا مِنْهُمْ ۚ
وَاِنَّهُمَا لَبِاِمَامٍ مُبِيْنٍ ۞

SECTION 6.

80. The Companions of the Rocky
Tract
Also rejected the messengers:

٨٠- وَلَقَدْ كَذَّبَ اَصْحٰبُ الْحِجْرِ الْمُرْسَلِيْنَ ۞

81. We sent them Our Signs,
But they persisted
In turning away from them.

٨١- وَاٰتَيْنٰهُمْ اٰيٰتِنَا
فَكَانُوْا عَنْهَا مُعْرِضِيْنَ ۞

82. Out of mountains
Did they hew (their) edifices,
(Feeling themselves) secure.

٨٢- وَكَانُوْا يَنْحِتُوْنَ مِنَ الْجِبَالِ بُيُوْتًا
اٰمِنِيْنَ ۞

83. But the (mighty) Blast
Seized them of a morning,

٨٣- فَاَخَذَتْهُمُ الصَّيْحَةُ مُصْبِحِيْنَ ۞

84. And of no avail to them
Was all that they did
(With such art and care)!

٨٤- فَمَا اَغْنٰى عَنْهُمْ مَا كَانُوْا يَكْسِبُوْنَ ۞

85. We created not the heavens,
The earth, and all between them,
But for just ends.
And the Hour is surely
Coming (when this will be
manifest).
So overlook (any human faults)
With gracious forgiveness.

٨٥- وَمَا خَلَقْنَا السَّمٰوٰتِ وَالْاَرْضَ وَمَا بَيْنَهُمَا
اِلَّا بِالْحَقِّ ۗ
وَاِنَّ السَّاعَةَ لَاٰتِيَةٌ
فَاصْفَحِ الصَّفْحَ الْجَمِيْلَ ۞

86. For verily it is thy Lord
Who is the Master-Creator,
Knowing all things.

٨٦- اِنَّ رَبَّكَ هُوَ الْخَلّٰقُ الْعَلِيْمُ ۞

87. And We have bestowed
Upon thee the Seven
Oft-repeated (Verses)
And the Grand Qur'ān.

٨٧- وَلَقَدْ اٰتَيْنٰكَ سَبْعًا
مِنَ الْمَثَانِيْ وَالْقُرْاٰنَ الْعَظِيْمَ ۞

88. Strain not thine eyes,
    (Wistfully) at what We
    Have betowed on certain classes
    Of them, nor grieve over them:
    But lower thy wings (in
                      gentleness)
    To the Believers.

٨٨- لَا تَمُدَّنَّ عَيْنَيْكَ
إِلَى مَا مَتَّعْنَا بِهِ أَزْوَاجًا مِّنْهُمْ
وَلَا تَحْزَنْ عَلَيْهِمْ
وَاخْفِضْ جَنَاحَكَ لِلْمُؤْمِنِينَ ٠

89. And say: "I am indeed he
    That warneth openly
    And without ambiguity"—

٨٩- وَقُلْ إِنِّيْ أَنَا النَّذِيْرُ الْمُبِيْنُ ٥

90. (Of just such wrath)
    As We sent down
    On those who divided
    (Scripture into arbitrary
                        parts)—

٩٠- كَمَا أَنْزَلْنَا
عَلَى الْمُقْتَسِمِينَ ٥

91. (So also on such)
    As have made the Qur'ān
    Into shreds (as they please).

٩١- الَّذِيْنَ جَعَلُوا الْقُرْآنَ عِضِيْنَ ٥

92. Therefore, by thy Lord,
    We will, of a surety,
    Call them to account,

٩٢- فَوَرَبِّكَ لَنَسْئَلَنَّهُمْ أَجْمَعِيْنَ ٥

93. For all their deeds.

٩٣- عَمَّا كَانُوا يَعْمَلُوْنَ ٥

94. Therefore expound openly
    What thou art commanded,
    And turn away from those
    Who join false gods with Allah.

٩٤- فَاصْدَعْ بِمَا تُؤْمَرُ
وَأَعْرِضْ عَنِ الْمُشْرِكِيْنَ ٥

95. For sufficient are We
    Unto thee against those
    Who scoff—

٩٥- إِنَّا كَفَيْنَاكَ الْمُسْتَهْزِئِيْنَ ٥

96. Those who adopt, with Allah,
    Another god: but soon
    Will they come to know.

٩٦- الَّذِيْنَ يَجْعَلُوْنَ مَعَ اللهِ إِلَهًا آخَرَ
فَسَوْفَ يَعْلَمُوْنَ ٥

97. We do indeed know
    How thy heart is distressed
    At what they say.

٩٧- وَلَقَدْ نَعْلَمُ أَنَّكَ يَضِيْقُ صَدْرُكَ
بِمَا يَقُوْلُوْنَ ٥

98. But celebrate the praises
Of thy Lord, and be of those
Who prostrate themselves
In adoration.

٩٨ ـ فَسَبِّحْ بِحَمْدِ رَبِّكَ
وَكُنْ مِنَ السَّاجِدِينَ ۝

99. And serve thy Lord
Until there come unto thee
The Hour that is Certain.

٩٩ ـ وَاعْبُدْ رَبَّكَ
حَتَّى يَأْتِيَكَ الْيَقِينُ ۝

INTRODUCTION TO SŪRA XVI. *(Nahl)* — 128 Verses

　　Chronologically this Sūra, like the six which preceded it, belongs to the late Meccan period, except perhaps verse 110 and some of the verses that follow. But the chronology has no significance. In subject-matter it sums up, from a new point of view, the arguments on the great questions of God's dealings with man, His Self-revelation to man, and how the Messengers and the Message are writ large in every phase of God's Creation and the life of Man. The new point of view is that Nature points to Nature's God.

Al Nahl (Bees)

In the name of Allah, Most Gracious,
Most Merciful.

1. (Inevitably) cometh (to pass)
   The Command of Allah:
   Seek ye not then
   To hasten it: glory to Him,
   And far is He above
   Having the partners
   They ascribe unto Him!

2. He doth send down His angels
   With inspiration of His
   　　　　　　　Command,
   To such of His servants
   As He pleaseth, (saying):
   "Warn (Man) that there is
   No god but I: so do
   Your duty unto Me."

3. He has created the heavens
   And the earth for just ends:
   Far is He above having
   The partners they ascribe to Him!

4. He has created man
   From a sperm-drop
   And behold this same (man)
   Becomes an open disputer!

5. And cattle He has created[2023]
   For you (men): from them
   Ye derive warmth,
   And numerous benefits,
   And of their (meat) ye eat.

6. And ye have a sense
Of pride and beauty in them
As ye drive them home
In the evening, and as ye
Lead them forth to pasture
In the morning.

٦- وَلَكُمْ فِيهَا جَمَالٌ
حِينَ تُرِيحُونَ
وَحِينَ تَسْرَحُونَ ۝

7. And they carry your heavy loads
To lands that you could not
(Otherwise) reach except with
Souls distressed: for your Lord
Is indeed Most Kind, Most
                Merciful.

٧- وَتَحْمِلُ أَثْقَالَكُمْ إِلَى بَلَدٍ لَّمْ تَكُونُوا
بَالِغِيهِ إِلَّا بِشِقِّ الْأَنْفُسِ ۚ
إِنَّ رَبَّكُمْ لَرَءُوفٌ رَّحِيمٌ ۝

8. And (He has created) horses,
Mules, and donkeys, for you
To ride and use for show;
And He has created (other) things
Of which ye have no
                knowledge.

٨- وَالْخَيْلَ وَالْبِغَالَ وَالْحَمِيرَ
لِتَرْكَبُوهَا وَزِينَةً ۚ
وَيَخْلُقُ مَا لَا تَعْلَمُونَ ۝

9. And unto Allah leads straight
The Way, but there are ways
That turn aside: if Allah
Had willed, He could have
Guided all of you.

٩- وَعَلَى اللَّهِ قَصْدُ السَّبِيلِ
وَمِنْهَا جَائِرٌ ۚ
وَلَوْ شَاءَ لَهَدَاكُمْ أَجْمَعِينَ ۝ ع

SECTION 2.

10. It is He Who sends down
Rain from the sky.
From it ye drink,
And out of it (grows)
The vegetation on which
Ye feed your cattle.

١٠- هُوَ الَّذِي أَنْزَلَ مِنَ السَّمَاءِ مَاءً
لَّكُمْ مِنْهُ شَرَابٌ
وَمِنْهُ شَجَرٌ فِيهِ تُسِيمُونَ ۝

11. With it He produces
For you corn, olives,
Date palms, grapes,
And every kind of fruit:
Verily in this is a Sign
For those who give thought.

١١- يُنْبِتُ لَكُمْ بِهِ الزَّرْعَ وَالزَّيْتُونَ وَ
النَّخِيلَ وَالْأَعْنَابَ وَمِنْ كُلِّ الثَّمَرَاتِ ۚ
إِنَّ فِي ذَلِكَ لَآيَةً لِّقَوْمٍ يَتَفَكَّرُونَ ۝

12. He has made subject to you
The Night and the Day;
The Sun and the Moon;
And the Stars are in subjection
By His Command: verily

١٢- وَسَخَّرَ لَكُمُ الَّيْلَ وَالنَّهَارَ ۙ
وَالشَّمْسَ وَالْقَمَرَ وَالنُّجُومُ مُسَخَّرَاتٌ
بِأَمْرِهِ ۗ إِنَّ فِي

In this are signs
For men who are wise.

ذٰلِكَ لَاٰيٰتٍ لِّقَوْمٍ يَّعْقِلُوْنَ ۞

13. And the things on this earth
Which He has multiplied
In varying colours (and
           qualities):
Verily in this is a Sign
For men who celebrate
The praises of Allah
       (in gratitude).

١٣- وَمَا ذَرَاَ لَكُمْ فِى الْاَرْضِ
مُخْتَلِفًا اَلْوَانُهٗ ؕ
اِنَّ فِىْ ذٰلِكَ لَاٰيَةً
لِّقَوْمٍ يَّذَّكَّرُوْنَ ۞

14. It is He Who has made
The sea subject, that ye
May eat thereof flesh
That is fresh and tender,
And that ye may extract
Therefrom ornaments to wear,
And thou seest the ships
Therein that plough the waves,
That ye may seek (thus)
Of the bounty of Allah
And that ye may be grateful.

١٤- وَهُوَ الَّذِىْ سَخَّرَ الْبَحْرَ
لِتَأْكُلُوْا مِنْهُ لَحْمًا طَرِيًّا
وَّتَسْتَخْرِجُوْا مِنْهُ حِلْيَةً تَلْبَسُوْنَهَا
وَتَرَى الْفُلْكَ مَوَاخِرَ فِيْهِ
وَلِتَبْتَغُوْا مِنْ فَضْلِهٖ
وَلَعَلَّكُمْ تَشْكُرُوْنَ ۞

15. And He has set up
On the earth mountains
Standing firm, lest it should
Shake with you; and rivers
And roads; that ye
May guide yourselves,

١٥- وَاَلْقٰى فِى الْاَرْضِ رَوَاسِىَ اَنْ
تَمِيْدَ بِكُمْ وَاَنْهٰرًا
وَّسُبُلًا لَّعَلَّكُمْ تَهْتَدُوْنَ ۙ

16. And marks and signposts;
And by the stars
(Men) guide themselves.

١٦- وَعَلٰمٰتٍ ؕ وَبِالنَّجْمِ هُمْ يَهْتَدُوْنَ ۞

17. Is then He Who creates
Like one that creates not?
Will ye not receive admonition?

١٧- اَفَمَنْ يَّخْلُقُ كَمَنْ لَّا يَخْلُقُ ؕ
اَفَلَا تَذَكَّرُوْنَ ۞

18. If ye would count up
The favours of Allah,
Never would ye be able
To number them; for Allah
Is Oft-Forgiving, Most
           Merciful.

١٨- وَاِنْ تَعُدُّوْا نِعْمَةَ اللّٰهِ
لَا تُحْصُوْهَا ؕ
اِنَّ اللّٰهَ لَغَفُوْرٌ رَّحِيْمٌ ۞

19. And Allah doth know
What ye conceal,
And what ye reveal.

١٩- وَاللّٰهُ يَعْلَمُ مَا تُسِرُّوْنَ
وَمَا تُعْلِنُوْنَ ۞

20. Those whom they invoke
Besides Allah create nothing
And are themselves created.

٢٠- وَالَّذِيْنَ يَدْعُوْنَ مِنْ دُوْنِ اللّٰهِ لَا يَخْلُقُوْنَ شَيْئًا وَّهُمْ يُخْلَقُوْنَ ۞

21. (They are things) dead,
Lifeless: nor do they know
When they will be raised up.

٢١- اَمْوَاتٌ غَيْرُ اَحْيَآءٍ ۚ وَمَا يَشْعُرُوْنَ ۙ اَيَّانَ يُبْعَثُوْنَ ۞ ؏

SECTION 3.

22. Your God is One God:
As to those who believe not
In the Hereafter, their hearts
Refuse to know, and they
Are arrogant.

٢٢- اِلٰهُكُمْ اِلٰهٌ وَّاحِدٌ ۚ فَالَّذِيْنَ لَا يُؤْمِنُوْنَ بِالْاٰخِرَةِ قُلُوْبُهُمْ مُّنْكِرَةٌ وَّهُمْ مُّسْتَكْبِرُوْنَ ۞

23. Undoubtedly, Allah doth know
What they conceal,
And what they reveal:
Verily He loveth not the arrogant

٢٣- لَا جَرَمَ اَنَّ اللّٰهَ يَعْلَمُ مَا يُسِرُّوْنَ وَمَا يُعْلِنُوْنَ ۚ اِنَّهٗ لَا يُحِبُّ الْمُسْتَكْبِرِيْنَ ۞

24. When it is said to them,
"What is it that your Lord
Has revealed?" they say,
"Tales of the ancients!"

٢٤- وَاِذَا قِيْلَ لَهُمْ مَّاذَآ اَنْزَلَ رَبُّكُمْ ۙ قَالُوْۤا اَسَاطِيْرُ الْاَوَّلِيْنَ ۞

25. Let them bear, on the Day
Of Judgement, their own burdens
In full, and also (something)
Of the burdens of those
Without knowledge, whom they
Misled. Alas, how grievous
The burdens they will bear!

٢٥- لِيَحْمِلُوْۤا اَوْزَارَهُمْ كَامِلَةً يَّوْمَ الْقِيٰمَةِ ۙ وَمِنْ اَوْزَارِ الَّذِيْنَ يُضِلُّوْنَهُمْ بِغَيْرِ عِلْمٍ ۗ اَلَا سَآءَ مَا يَزِرُوْنَ ۞ ؏

SECTION 4

26. Those before them did also
Plot (against Allah's Way):
But Allah took their structures
From their foundations, and
        the roof
Fell down on them from above;
And the Wrath seized them
From directions they did not
        perceive.

٢٦- قَدْ مَكَرَ الَّذِيْنَ مِنْ قَبْلِهِمْ فَاَتَى اللّٰهُ بُنْيَانَهُمْ مِّنَ الْقَوَاعِدِ فَخَرَّ عَلَيْهِمُ السَّقْفُ مِنْ فَوْقِهِمْ وَاَتَاهُمُ الْعَذَابُ مِنْ حَيْثُ لَا يَشْعُرُوْنَ ۞

27. Then, on the Day of Judgement,
He will cover them
With shame, and say:
"Where are My 'partners'
Concerning whom ye used
To dispute (with the godly)?"

٢٧- ثُمَّ يَوْمَ الْقِيٰمَةِ يُخْزِيْهِمْ وَيَقُوْلُ اَيْنَ شُرَكَآءِيَ الَّذِيْنَ كُنْتُمْ تُشَآقُّوْنَ فِيْهِمْ

Those endued with knowledge
Will say: "This Day, indeed,
Are the Unbelievers covered
With Shame and Misery—

قَالَ الَّذِينَ أُوتُوا الْعِلْمَ اِنَّ الْخِزْيَ الْيَوْمَ وَالسُّوْٓءَ عَلَى الْكٰفِرِينَ ۙ

28. "(Namely) those whose lives the
angels
Take in a state of wrongdoing
To their own souls.
Then would they offer submission
(With the pretence), 'We did
No evil (knowingly).'" (The angels
Will reply), "Nay, but verily
Allah knoweth all that ye did;

٢٨- الَّذِينَ تَتَوَفّٰىهُمُ الْمَلٰٓئِكَةُ ظَالِمِىٓ اَنْفُسِهِمْ ۖ فَاَلْقَوُا السَّلَمَ مَا كُنَّا نَعْمَلُ مِنْ سُوْٓءٍ ۚ بَلٰىٓ اِنَّ اللّٰهَ عَلِيْمٌۢ بِمَا كُنْتُمْ تَعْمَلُوْنَ ۟

29. "So enter the gates of Hell,
To dwell therein.
Thus evil indeed
Is the abode of the arrogant."

٢٩- فَادْخُلُوٓا اَبْوَابَ جَهَنَّمَ خٰلِدِينَ فِيْهَا ۖ فَلَبِئْسَ مَثْوَى الْمُتَكَبِّرِينَ ۟

30. To the righteous
(When) it is said, "What
Is it that your Lord
Has revealed?" they say,
"All that is good." To those
Who do good, there is good
In this world, and the Home
Of the Hereafter is even better
And excellent indeed is the Home
Of the righteous—

٣٠- وَقِيْلَ لِلَّذِينَ اتَّقَوْا مَاذَآ اَنْزَلَ رَبُّكُمْ ۙ قَالُوْا خَيْرًا ۗ لِلَّذِينَ اَحْسَنُوْا فِىْ هٰذِهِ الدُّنْيَا حَسَنَةٌ ۗ وَلَدَارُ الْاٰخِرَةِ خَيْرٌ ۗ وَلَنِعْمَ دَارُ الْمُتَّقِيْنَ ۟

31. Gardens of Eternity which they
Will enter: beneath them
Flow (pleasant) rivers: they
Will have therein all
That they wish: thus doth
Allah reward the righteous—

٣١- جَنّٰتُ عَدْنٍ يَّدْخُلُوْنَهَا تَجْرِىْ مِنْ تَحْتِهَا الْاَنْهٰرُ لَهُمْ فِيْهَا مَا يَشَآءُوْنَ ۗ كَذٰلِكَ يَجْزِى اللّٰهُ الْمُتَّقِيْنَ ۟

32. (Namely) those whose lives
The angels take in a state
Of purity, saying (to them),
"Peace be on you; enter ye
The Garden, because of (the good)
Which ye did (in the world)."

٣٢- الَّذِينَ تَتَوَفّٰىهُمُ الْمَلٰٓئِكَةُ طَيِّبِيْنَ ۙ يَقُوْلُوْنَ سَلٰمٌ عَلَيْكُمُ ادْخُلُوا الْجَنَّةَ بِمَا كُنْتُمْ تَعْمَلُوْنَ ۟

33. Do the (ungodly) wait until
The angels come to them,
Or there comes the Command
Of thy Lord (for their doom)?

٣٣- هَلْ يَنْظُرُوْنَ اِلَّآ اَنْ تَأْتِيَهُمُ الْمَلٰٓئِكَةُ اَوْ يَأْتِيَ اَمْرُ رَبِّكَ ۚ

So did those who went
Before them. But Allah
Wronged them not: nay,
They wronged their own souls.

كَذٰلِكَ فَعَلَ الَّذِيْنَ مِنْ قَبْلِهِمْ وَمَا ظَلَمَهُمُ
اللّٰهُ وَلٰكِنْ كَانُوْا اَنْفُسَهُمْ يَظْلِمُوْنَ ۟

34. But the evil results
Of their deeds overtook them,
And that very (Wrath)
At which they had scoffed
Hemmed them in.

٣٤- فَاَصَابَهُمْ سَيِّاٰتُ مَا عَمِلُوْا
وَحَاقَ بِهِمْ
مَّا كَانُوْا بِهٖ يَسْتَهْزِءُوْنَ ۟ ۣ

SECTION 5.

35. The worshippers of false gods
Say: "If Allah had so willed,
We should not have worshipped
Aught but Him — neither we
Nor our fathers — nor should
We have prescribed
                    prohibitions
Other than His." So did those
Who went before them.
But what is the mission
Of messengers but to preach
The Clear Message?

٣٥- وَقَالَ الَّذِيْنَ اَشْرَكُوْا لَوْ شَآءَ اللّٰهُ
مَا عَبَدْنَا مِنْ دُوْنِهٖ مِنْ شَيْءٍ نَّحْنُ
وَلَاۤ اٰبَآؤُنَا وَلَا
حَرَّمْنَا مِنْ دُوْنِهٖ مِنْ شَيْءٍ ؕ
كَذٰلِكَ فَعَلَ الَّذِيْنَ مِنْ قَبْلِهِمْ ۚ
فَهَلْ عَلَى الرُّسُلِ اِلَّا الْبَلٰغُ الْمُبِيْنُ ۟

36. For We assuredly sent
Amongst every People a
                    messenger,
(With the Command), "Serve
Allah, and eschew Evil":
Of the poeple were some whom
Allah guided, and some
On whom Error became
Inevitably (established). So travel
Through the earth, and see
What was the end of those
Who denied (the Truth).

٣٦- وَلَقَدْ بَعَثْنَا فِيْ كُلِّ اُمَّةٍ رَّسُوْلًا
اَنِ اعْبُدُوا اللّٰهَ وَاجْتَنِبُوا الطَّاغُوْتَ ۚ
فَمِنْهُمْ مَّنْ هَدَى اللّٰهُ
وَمِنْهُمْ مَّنْ حَقَّتْ عَلَيْهِ الضَّلٰلَةُ ؕ
فَسِيْرُوْا فِى الْاَرْضِ
فَانْظُرُوْا كَيْفَ كَانَ عَاقِبَةُ الْمُكَذِّبِيْنَ ۟

37. If thou art anxious
For their guidance, yet
Allah guideth not such
As He leaves to stray.
And there is none
To help them.

٣٧- اِنْ تَحْرِصْ عَلٰى هُدٰىهُمْ
فَاِنَّ اللّٰهَ لَا يَهْدِيْ مَنْ يُّضِلُّ
وَمَا لَهُمْ مِّنْ نّٰصِرِيْنَ ۟

38. They swear their strongest
                    oath
By Allah, that Allah will not

٣٨- وَاَقْسَمُوْا بِاللّٰهِ جَهْدَ اَيْمَانِهِمْ ۙ لَا
يَبْعَثُ اللّٰهُ مَنْ يَّمُوْتُ ؕ

Raise up those who die;
Nay, but it is a promise
(Binding) on Him in truth:
But most among mankind
Realise it not.

39. (They must be raised up),
In order that He may manifest
To them the truth of that
Wherein they differ, and that
The rejecters of Truth
May realise that they had
Indeed (surrendered to)
　　　　　　　　Falsehood.

40. For to anything which We
Have willed, We but say
The Word, "Be", and it is.
　　　SECTION 6.

41. To those who leave
Their homes in the cause
Of Allah, after suffering
　　　　　　oppression —
We will assuredly give
A goodly home in this world:
But truly the reward
Of the Hereafter will be greater.
If they only realised (this)!

42. (They are) those who persevere
In patience, and put
Their trust on their Lord.

43. And before thee also
The messengers We sent
Were but men,　　to whom
We granted inspiration: if ye
Realise this not, ask of those
Who possess the Message.

44. (We sent them) with Clear Signs
And Scriptures
And We have sent down
Unto thee (also) the Message;
That thou mayest explain clearly
To men what is sent

For them, and that they
May give thought.

وَلَعَلَّهُمْ يَتَفَكَّرُوْنَ ۞

45. Do then those who devise
Evil (plots) feel secure
That Allah will not cause
The earth to swallow them up,
Or that the Wrath will not
Seize them from directions
They little perceive?—

٤٥- أَفَأَمِنَ الَّذِيْنَ مَكَرُوا السَّيِّاٰتِ
اَنْ يَّخْسِفَ اللّٰهُ بِهِمُ الْاَرْضَ
اَوْ يَأْتِيَهُمُ الْعَذَابُ
مِنْ حَيْثُ لَا يَشْعُرُوْنَ ۞

46. Or that He may not
Call them to account
In the midst of their goings
To and fro, without a chance
Of their frustrating Him?—

٤٦- اَوْ يَأْخُذَهُمْ
فِيْ تَقَلُّبِهِمْ فَمَا هُمْ بِمُعْجِزِيْنَ ۞

47. Or that He may not
Call them to account
By a process of slow wastage—
For thy Lord is indeed
Full of kindness and mercy.

٤٧- اَوْ يَأْخُذَهُمْ
عَلٰى تَخَوُّفٍ ۗ فَإِنَّ رَبَّكُمْ
لَرَءُوْفٌ رَّحِيْمٌ ۞

48. Do they not look
At Allah's creation, (even)
Among (inanimate) things—
How their (very) shadows
Turn round, from the right
And the left, prostrating
Themselves to Allah, and that
In the humblest manner?

٤٨- اَوَلَمْ يَرَوْا اِلٰى مَا خَلَقَ اللّٰهُ مِنْ شَيْءٍ
يَّتَفَيَّؤُا ظِلٰلُهٗ
عَنِ الْيَمِيْنِ وَالشَّمَآئِلِ سُجَّدًا لِّلّٰهِ
وَهُمْ دَاخِرُوْنَ ۞

49. And to Allah doth obeisance
All that is in the heavens
And on earth, whether
Moving (living) creatures
Or the angels: for none
Are arrogant (before their Lord).

٤٩- وَلِلّٰهِ يَسْجُدُ مَا فِى السَّمٰوٰتِ وَمَا فِى
الْاَرْضِ مِنْ دَآبَّةٍ وَّالْمَلٰئِكَةُ
وَهُمْ لَا يَسْتَكْبِرُوْنَ ۞

50. They all revere their Lord,
High above them, and they do
All that they are commanded.

٥٠- يَخَافُوْنَ رَبَّهُمْ مِّنْ فَوْقِهِمْ
وَيَفْعَلُوْنَ مَا يُؤْمَرُوْنَ ۞

SECTION 7.

51. Allah has said: "Take not
(For worship) two gods:
For He is just One God:
Then fear Me (and Me alone)."

٥١- وَقَالَ اللّٰهُ لَا تَتَّخِذُوْا اِلٰهَيْنِ اثْنَيْنِ ۗ
اِنَّمَا هُوَ اِلٰهٌ وَّاحِدٌ ۚ فَإِيَّايَ فَارْهَبُوْنِ ۞

52. To Him belongs whatever
Is in the heavens and on earth.
And to Him is duty due always:
Then will ye fear other
Than Allah?

٥٢- وَلَهُ مَا فِى السَّمٰوٰتِ وَالْأَرْضِ
وَلَهُ الدِّيْنُ وَاصِبًا ۚ
أَفَغَيْرَ اللّٰهِ تَتَّقُوْنَ ۞

53. And ye have no good thing
But is from Allah: and moreover,
When ye are touched by distress,
Unto Him ye cry with groans;

٥٣- وَمَا بِكُمْ مِّنْ نِّعْمَةٍ فَمِنَ اللّٰهِ ثُمَّ
إِذَا مَسَّكُمُ الضُّرُّ فَإِلَيْهِ تَجْـَٔرُوْنَ ۞

54. Yet, when He removes
The distress from you, behold!
Some of you turn to other gods
To join with their Lord—

٥٤- ثُمَّ إِذَا كَشَفَ الضُّرَّ عَنْكُمْ
إِذَا فَرِيْقٌ مِّنْكُمْ بِرَبِّهِمْ يُشْرِكُوْنَ ۙ

55. (As if) to show their ingratitude
For the favours We have
Bestowed on them! Then enjoy
(Your brief day); but soon
Will ye know (your folly)!

٥٥- لِيَكْفُرُوْا بِمَا آتَيْنٰهُمْ
فَتَمَتَّعُوْا ۚ فَسَوْفَ تَعْلَمُوْنَ ۞

56. And they (even) assign,
To things they do not know,
A portion out of that
Which We have bestowed
For their sustenance!
By Allah, ye shall certainly
Be called to account
For your false inventions.

٥٦- وَيَجْعَلُوْنَ لِمَا لَا يَعْلَمُوْنَ
نَصِيْبًا مِّمَّا رَزَقْنٰهُمْ ۗ
تَاللّٰهِ لَتُسْـَٔلُنَّ
عَمَّا كُنْتُمْ تَفْتَرُوْنَ ۞

57. And they assign daughters
For Allah!—Glory be to Him!—
And for themselves (sons—
The issue) they desire!

٥٧- وَيَجْعَلُوْنَ لِلّٰهِ الْبَنٰتِ سُبْحٰنَهُ ۙ
وَلَهُمْ مَّا يَشْتَهُوْنَ ۞

58. When news is brought
To one of them, of (the birth
Of) a female (child), his face
Darkens, and he is filled
With inward grief!

٥٨- وَإِذَا بُشِّرَ أَحَدُهُمْ بِالْأُنْثٰى
ظَلَّ وَجْهُهُ مُسْوَدًّا وَّهُوَ كَظِيْمٌ ۞

59. With shame does he hide
Himself from his people,
Because of the bad news
He has had!
Shall he retain it
On (sufferance and) contempt,

٥٩- يَتَوٰرٰى مِنَ الْقَوْمِ مِنْ سُوْءِ
مَا بُشِّرَ بِهٖ ۗ
أَيُمْسِكُهُ عَلٰى هُوْنٍ أَمْ يَدُسُّهُ

Or bury it in the dust?
Ah! what an evil (choice)
They decide on?

فِى التُّرَابِ ۗ اَلَا سَآءَ مَا يَحْكُمُوْنَ ۞

60. To those who believe not
In the Hereafter, applies
The similitude of evil:
To Allah applies the highest
Similitude: for He is
The Exalted in Power,
Full of Wisdom.

٦٠۔ لِلَّذِيْنَ لَا يُؤْمِنُوْنَ بِالْاٰخِرَةِ مَثَلُ السَّوْءِ ۚ وَلِلّٰهِ الْمَثَلُ الْاَعْلٰى ۗ وَهُوَ الْعَزِيْزُ الْحَكِيْمُ ۞

SECTION 8.

61. If Allah were to punish
Men for their wrongdoing,
He would not leave, on the (earth),
A single living creature:
But He gives them respite
For a stated Term:
When their Term expires,
They would not be able
To delay (the punishment)
For a single hour, just as
They would not be able
To anticipate it (for a single
                    hour).

٦١۔ وَلَوْ يُؤَاخِذُ اللّٰهُ النَّاسَ بِظُلْمِهِمْ مَّا تَرَكَ عَلَيْهَا مِنْ دَآبَّةٍ وَّلٰكِنْ يُّؤَخِّرُهُمْ اِلٰٓى اَجَلٍ مُّسَمًّى ۚ فَاِذَا جَآءَ اَجَلُهُمْ لَا يَسْتَأْخِرُوْنَ سَاعَةً وَّ لَا يَسْتَقْدِمُوْنَ ۞

62. They attribute to Allah
What they hate (for
                themselves).
And their tongues assert
The falsehood that all good
                        things
Are for themselves: without doubt
For them is the Fire, and they
Will be the first to be
Hastened on into it!

٦٢۔ وَيَجْعَلُوْنَ لِلّٰهِ مَا يَكْرَهُوْنَ وَتَصِفُ اَلْسِنَتُهُمُ الْكَذِبَ اَنَّ لَهُمُ الْحُسْنٰى ۚ لَا جَرَمَ اَنَّ لَهُمُ النَّارَ وَاَنَّهُمْ مُّفْرَطُوْنَ ۞

63. By Allah, We (also) sent
(Our prophets) to Peoples
Before thee: but Satan
Made, (to the wicked),
Their own acts seem alluring:
He is also their patron today,
But they shall have
A most grievous penalty.

٦٣۔ تَاللّٰهِ لَقَدْ اَرْسَلْنَآ اِلٰٓى اُمَمٍ مِّنْ قَبْلِكَ فَزَيَّنَ لَهُمُ الشَّيْطٰنُ اَعْمَالَهُمْ فَهُوَ وَلِيُّهُمُ الْيَوْمَ وَلَهُمْ عَذَابٌ اَلِيْمٌ ۞

64. And We sent down the Book
To thee for the express purpose,
That thou shouldst make clear
To them those things in which

٦٤۔ وَمَآ اَنْزَلْنَا عَلَيْكَ الْكِتٰبَ اِلَّا لِتُبَيِّنَ لَهُمُ الَّذِى اخْتَلَفُوْا فِيْهِ ۙ

They differ, and that it should be
A guide and a mercy
To those who believe.

65. And Allah sends down rain
From the skies, and gives therewith
Life to the earth after its death:
Verily in this is a Sign
For those who listen.

SECTION 9.

66. And verily in cattle (too)
Will ye find an instructive Sign.
From what is within their
                        bodies,
Between excretions and blood,
We produce, for your drink,
Milk, pure and agreeable
To those who drink it.

67. And from the fruit
Of the date palm and the vine,
Ye get out wholesome drink,
And food: behold, in this
Also is a Sign
For those who are wise.

68. And thy Lord taught the Bee
To build its cells in hills,
On trees, and in (men's)
                        habitations;

69. Then to eat of all
The produce (of the earth),
And find with skill the spacious
Paths of its Lord: there issues
From within their bodies
A drink of varying colours,
Wherein is healing for men:
Verily in this is a Sign
For those who give thought.

70. It is Allah Who creates you
And takes your souls at death;
And of you there are
Some who are sent back
To a feeble age, so that
They know nothing after
Having known (much):
For Allah is All-Knowing,
All-Powerful.

SECTION 10.

71. Allah has bestowed His gifts
Of sustenance more freely on some
Of you than on others: those
More favoured are not going
To throw back their gifts
To those whom their right hands
Possess, so as to be equal
In that respect. Will they then
Deny the favours of Allah?

٧١ـ وَاللّٰهُ فَضَّلَ بَعْضَكُمْ عَلٰى بَعْضٍ فِى الرِّزْقِ فَمَا الَّذِيْنَ فُضِّلُوْا بِرَآدِّىْ رِزْقِهِمْ عَلٰى مَا مَلَكَتْ اَيْمَانُهُمْ فَهُمْ فِيْهِ سَوَآءٌ ۚ اَفَبِنِعْمَةِ اللّٰهِ يَجْحَدُوْنَ ۟

72. And Allah has made for you
Mates (and Companions) of your
own nature,
And made for you, out of them,
Sons and daughters and
grandchildren.
And provided for your sustenance
Of the best: will they
Then believe in vain things,
And be ungrateful for Allah's
favours?—

٧٢ـ وَاللّٰهُ جَعَلَ لَكُمْ مِّنْ اَنْفُسِكُمْ اَزْوَاجًا وَّجَعَلَ لَكُمْ مِّنْ اَزْوَاجِكُمْ بَنِيْنَ وَحَفَدَةً وَّرَزَقَكُمْ مِّنَ الطَّيِّبٰتِ ۚ اَفَبِالْبَاطِلِ يُؤْمِنُوْنَ وَبِنِعْمَتِ اللّٰهِ هُمْ يَكْفُرُوْنَ ۙ

73. And worship others than Allah—
Such as have no power
Of providing them, for
sustenance,
With anything in the heavens or
earth,
And cannot possibly have Such
power?

٧٣ـ وَيَعْبُدُوْنَ مِنْ دُوْنِ اللّٰهِ مَا لَا يَمْلِكُ لَهُمْ رِزْقًا مِّنَ السَّمٰوٰتِ وَالْاَرْضِ شَيْئًا وَّلَا يَسْتَطِيْعُوْنَ ۟

74. Invent not similitudes
For Allah: for Allah knoweth,
And ye know not.

٧٤ـ فَلَا تَضْرِبُوْا لِلّٰهِ الْاَمْثَالَ ۚ اِنَّ اللّٰهَ يَعْلَمُ وَاَنْتُمْ لَا تَعْلَمُوْنَ ۟

75. Allah sets forth the Parable
(Of two men: one) a slave
Under the dominion of
another;
He has no power of any sort;
And (the other) a man
On whom We have bestowed
Goodly favours from Ourselves.
And he spends thereof (freely),
Privately and publicly:
Are the two equal? (By no means;)
Praise be to Allah. But
Most of them understand not.

٧٥ـ ضَرَبَ اللّٰهُ مَثَلًا عَبْدًا مَّمْلُوْكًا لَّا يَقْدِرُ عَلٰى شَيْءٍ وَّمَنْ رَّزَقْنٰهُ مِنَّا رِزْقًا حَسَنًا فَهُوَ يُنْفِقُ مِنْهُ سِرًّا وَّجَهْرًا ۚ هَلْ يَسْتَوٗنَ ۚ اَلْحَمْدُ لِلّٰهِ ۚ بَلْ اَكْثَرُهُمْ لَا يَعْلَمُوْنَ ۟

76. Allah sets forth (another) Parable
Of two men: one of them
Dumb, with no power
Of any sort: a wearisome burden
Is he to his master;
Whichever way he directs him,
He brings no good:
Is such a man equal
With one who commands
Justice, and is on
A Straight Way?

SECTION 11.

77. To Allah belongeth the
Mystery
Of the heavens and the earth.
And the Decision of the Hour
(Of Judgement) is as
The twinkling of any eye,
Or even quicker:
For Allah hath power
Over all things.

78. It is He Who brought you
Forth from the wombs
Of your mothers when
Ye knew nothing; and He
Gave you hearing and sight
And intelligence and affection:
That ye may give thanks
(To Allah).

79. Do they not look at
The birds, held poised
In the midst of (the air
And) the sky? Nothing
Holds them up but (the power
Of) Allah. Verily in this
Are Signs for those who believe.

80. It is Allah Who made your
habitations
Homes of rest and quiet
For you; and made for you,
Out of the skins of animals,
(Tents for) dwellings, which
Ye find so light (and handy)
When ye travel and when
Ye stop (in your travels),

And out of their wool,
And their soft fibres
(Between wool and hair),
And their hair, rich stuff
And articles of convenience
(To serve you) for a time.

وَأَشْعَارِهَآ أَثَاثًا
وَّمَتَاعًا اِلٰى حِيْنٍ ۟

81. It is Allah Who made
Out of the things He created,
Some things to give you shade;
Of the hills He made some
For your shelter; He made you
Garments to protect you
From heat, and coats of mail
To protect you from
Your (mutual) violence.
Thus does He complete
His favours on you, that
Ye may bow to His Will
(In Islam).

٨١- وَاللّٰهُ جَعَلَ لَكُمْ مِّمَّا خَلَقَ
ظِلَالًا وَّجَعَلَ لَكُمْ مِّنَ الْجِبَالِ
اَكْنَانًا وَّجَعَلَ لَكُمْ سَرَابِيْلَ
تَقِيْكُمُ الْحَرَّ
وَسَرَابِيْلَ تَقِيْكُمْ بَأْسَكُمْ ۚ كَذٰلِكَ يُتِمُّ
نِعْمَتَهٗ عَلَيْكُمْ لَعَلَّكُمْ تُسْلِمُوْنَ ۟

82. But if they turn away,
Thy duty is only to preach
The Clear Message.

٨٢- فَاِنْ تَوَلَّوْا
فَاِنَّمَا عَلَيْكَ الْبَلٰغُ الْمُبِيْنُ ۟

83. They recognise the favours
Of Allah; then they deny them;
And most of them
Are (creatures) ungrateful.

٨٣- يَعْرِفُوْنَ نِعْمَتَ اللّٰهِ ثُمَّ يُنْكِرُوْنَهَا
وَأَكْثَرُهُمُ الْكٰفِرُوْنَ ۟

SECTION 12.

84. One day we shall raise
From all Peoples a Witness:
Then will no excuse be accepted
From Unbelievers, nor will they
Receive any favours.

٨٤- وَيَوْمَ نَبْعَثُ مِنْ كُلِّ اُمَّةٍ شَهِيْدًا
ثُمَّ لَا يُؤْذَنُ لِلَّذِيْنَ كَفَرُوْا وَلَا هُمْ
يُسْتَعْتَبُوْنَ ۟

85. When the wrongdoers
(Actually) see the Penalty,
Then will it in no way
Be mitigated, nor will they
Then receive respite.

٨٥- وَاِذَا رَاَ الَّذِيْنَ ظَلَمُوا الْعَذَابَ
فَلَا يُخَفَّفُ عَنْهُمْ وَلَا هُمْ
يُنْظَرُوْنَ ۟

86. When those who gave partners
To Allah will see their "partners",
They will say: "Our Lord!
These are our 'partners', those

٨٦- وَاِذَا رَاَ الَّذِيْنَ اَشْرَكُوْا شُرَكَآءَهُمْ
قَالُوْا رَبَّنَا هٰٓؤُلَآءِ شُرَكَآؤُنَا الَّذِيْنَ

Whom we used to invoke
Besides Thee." But they will
Throw back their word at them
(And say): "Indeed ye are liars!"

كُنَّا نَدْعُوا مِنْ دُوْنِكَ ۚ
فَأَلْقَوْا إِلَيْهِمُ الْقَوْلَ إِنَّكُمْ لَكٰذِبُوْنَ ۞

87. That day shall they (openly)
show
(Their) submission to Allah: and
all
Their inventions shall leave
Them in the lurch.

٨٧ـ وَأَلْقَوْا إِلَى اللهِ يَوْمَئِذِ ٱلسَّلَمَ
وَضَلَّ عَنْهُمْ
مَّا كَانُوْا يَفْتَرُوْنَ ۞

88. Those who reject Allah
And hinder (men) from the Path
Of Allah—for them
Will We add Penalty
To Penalty; for that they
Used to spread mischief.

٨٨ـ اَلَّذِيْنَ كَفَرُوْا وَصَدُّوْا عَنْ سَبِيْلِ
اللهِ زِدْنٰهُمْ عَذَابًا فَوْقَ
الْعَذَابِ بِمَا كَانُوْا يُفْسِدُوْنَ ۞

89. One day We shall raise
From all Peoples a witness
Against them, from amongst
themselves:
And We shall bring thee
As a witness against these
(Thy people): and We have sent
down
To thee a Book explaining
All things, a Guide, a Mercy,
And Glad Tidings to Muslims.

٨٩ـ وَيَوْمَ نَبْعَثُ فِيْ كُلِّ أُمَّةٍ شَهِيْدًا
عَلَيْهِمْ مِّنْ أَنْفُسِهِمْ
وَجِئْنَا بِكَ شَهِيْدًا عَلٰى هٰؤُلَاءِ ۚ
وَنَزَّلْنَا عَلَيْكَ الْكِتٰبَ تِبْيَانًا لِّكُلِّ شَيْءٍ
وَّهُدًى وَّرَحْمَةً وَّبُشْرٰى لِلْمُسْلِمِيْنَ ۞

SECTION 13.

90. Allah commands justice, the
doing
Of good, and liberality to kith
And kin, and He forbids
All shameful deeds, and injustice
And rebellion: He instructs you,
That ye may receive
admonition.

٩٠ـ اِنَّ اللهَ يَأْمُرُ بِالْعَدْلِ وَالْاِحْسَانِ وَ
اِيْتَآئِ ذِى الْقُرْبٰى وَيَنْهٰى عَنِ الْفَحْشَاءِ
وَالْمُنْكَرِ وَالْبَغْيِ ۚ يَعِظُكُمْ لَعَلَّكُمْ تَذَكَّرُوْنَ ۞

91. Fulfil the Covenant of Allah
When ye have entered into it,
And break not your oaths
After ye have confirmed them:
Indeed ye have made
Allah your surety; for Allah
Knoweth all that ye do.

٩١ـ وَأَوْفُوْا بِعَهْدِ اللهِ إِذَا عٰهَدْتُّمْ
وَلَا تَنْقُضُوا الْأَيْمَانَ بَعْدَ تَوْكِيْدِهَا
وَقَدْ جَعَلْتُمُ اللهَ عَلَيْكُمْ كَفِيْلًا ۚ
اِنَّ اللهَ يَعْلَمُ مَا تَفْعَلُوْنَ ۞

92. And be not like a woman
Who breaks into untwisted strands
The yarn she has spun
After it has become strong.
Nor[2130] take your oaths to practise
Deception between yourselves,
Lest one party should be
More numerous than another:
For Allah will test you by this;
And on the Day of Judgement
He will certainly make clear
To you (the truth of) that
Wherein ye disagree.

٩٢ - وَلَا تَكُوْنُوْا كَالَّتِيْ نَقَضَتْ
غَزْلَهَا مِنْۢ بَعْدِ قُوَّةٍ اَنْكَاثًا ۗ
تَتَّخِذُوْنَ اَيْمَانَكُمْ دَخَلًۢا بَيْنَكُمْ
اَنْ تَكُوْنَ اُمَّةٌ هِيَ اَرْبٰى مِنْ اُمَّةٍ ۗ
اِنَّمَا يَبْلُوْكُمُ اللّٰهُ بِهٖ ۗ وَلَيُبَيِّنَنَّ لَكُمْ يَوْمَ
الْقِيٰمَةِ مَا كُنْتُمْ فِيْهِ تَخْتَلِفُوْنَ ۝

93. If Allah so willed, He
Could make you all one People:
But He leaves straying
Whom He pleases, and He guides
Whom He pleases: but ye
Shall certainly be called to account
For all your actions.

٩٣ - وَلَوْ شَاءَ اللّٰهُ لَجَعَلَكُمْ اُمَّةً وَّاحِدَةً
وَّلٰكِنْ يُّضِلُّ مَنْ يَّشَاءُ وَيَهْدِيْ
مَنْ يَّشَاءُ ۗ وَلَتُسْـَٔلُنَّ
عَمَّا كُنْتُمْ تَعْمَلُوْنَ ۝

94. And take not your oaths,
To practise deception between
                         yourselves,
With the result that someone's foot
May slip after it was
Firmly planted, and ye may
Have to taste the evil
                         (consequences)
Of having hindered (men)
From the Path of Allah,
And a mighty Wrath
Descend on you.

٩٤ - وَلَا تَتَّخِذُوْۤا اَيْمَانَكُمْ
دَخَلًۢا بَيْنَكُمْ
فَتَزِلَّ قَدَمٌۢ بَعْدَ ثُبُوْتِهَا
وَتَذُوْقُوا السُّوْٓءَ
بِمَا صَدَدْتُّمْ عَنْ سَبِيْلِ اللّٰهِ ۚ
وَلَكُمْ عَذَابٌ عَظِيْمٌ ۝

95. Nor sell the Covenant of Allah
For a miserable price:
For with Allah is (a prize)
Far better for you,
If ye only knew.

٩٥ - وَلَا تَشْتَرُوْا بِعَهْدِ اللّٰهِ ثَمَنًا قَلِيْلًا ۗ
اِنَّمَا عِنْدَ اللّٰهِ هُوَ خَيْرٌ لَّكُمْ
اِنْ كُنْتُمْ تَعْلَمُوْنَ ۝

96. What is with you must vanish:
What is with Allah will endure.
And We will certainly bestow,
On those who patiently persevere,
Their reward according to
The best of their actions.

٩٦ - مَا عِنْدَكُمْ يَنْفَدُ وَمَا عِنْدَ اللّٰهِ بَاقٍ ۗ
وَلَنَجْزِيَنَّ الَّذِيْنَ صَبَرُوْۤا
اَجْرَهُمْ بِاَحْسَنِ مَا كَانُوْا يَعْمَلُوْنَ ۝

97. Whoever works righteousness,
Man or woman, and has Faith,

٩٧ - مَنْ عَمِلَ صَالِحًا مِّنْ ذَكَرٍ اَوْ اُنْثٰى

Verily, to him will We give
A new Life, and life
That is good and pure, and We
Will bestow on such their reward
According to the best
Of their actions.

وَهُوَ مُؤْمِنٌ فَلَنُحْيِيَنَّهُ حَيٰوةً طَيِّبَةً
وَلَنَجْزِيَنَّهُمْ اَجْرَهُمْ بِاَحْسَنِ
مَا كَانُوْا يَعْمَلُوْنَ ۟

98. When thou does read
The Qur'ān, seek Allah's
protection
From Satan the Rejected One.

٩٨ ـ فَاِذَا قَرَاْتَ الْقُرْاٰنَ فَاسْتَعِذْ بِاللّٰهِ
مِنَ الشَّيْطٰنِ الرَّجِيْمِ ۟

99. No authority has he over those
Who believe and put their trust
In their Lord.

٩٩ ـ اِنَّهٗ لَيْسَ لَهٗ سُلْطٰنٌ عَلَى الَّذِيْنَ
اٰمَنُوْا وَعَلٰى رَبِّهِمْ يَتَوَكَّلُوْنَ ۟

100. His authority is over those
Only, who take him as patron
And who join partners with Allah.

١٠٠ ـ اِنَّمَا سُلْطٰنُهٗ عَلَى الَّذِيْنَ يَتَوَلَّوْنَهٗ
وَالَّذِيْنَ هُمْ بِهٖ مُشْرِكُوْنَ ۟

SECTION 14.

101. When We substitute one
revelation
For another—and Allah knows
best
What He reveals (in stages)—
They say, "Thou art but a forger":
But most of them understand not.

١٠١ ـ وَاِذَا بَدَّلْنَا اٰيَةً مَّكَانَ اٰيَةٍ وَّاللّٰهُ
اَعْلَمُ
بِمَا يُنَزِّلُ قَالُوْا اِنَّمَا اَنْتَ مُفْتَرٍ
بَلْ اَكْثَرُهُمْ لَا يَعْلَمُوْنَ ۟

102. Say, the Holy Spirit²¹⁴¹ has brought
The revelation from thy Lord
In Truth, in order to strengthen
Those who believe,   and as a
Guide
And Glad Tidings to Muslims.

١٠٢ ـ قُلْ نَزَّلَهٗ رُوْحُ الْقُدُسِ مِنْ رَّبِّكَ
بِالْحَقِّ لِيُثَبِّتَ الَّذِيْنَ اٰمَنُوْا وَهُدًى
وَّبُشْرٰى لِلْمُسْلِمِيْنَ ۟

103. We know indeed that they
Say, "It is a man that
Teaches him." The tongue
Of him they wickedly point to
Is notably foreign, while this
Is Arabic, pure and clear.

١٠٣ ـ وَلَقَدْ نَعْلَمُ اَنَّهُمْ يَقُوْلُوْنَ اِنَّمَا يُعَلِّمُهٗ
بَشَرٌ لِسَانُ الَّذِيْ يُلْحِدُوْنَ اِلَيْهِ اَعْجَمِيٌّ
وَّهٰذَا لِسَانٌ عَرَبِيٌّ مُّبِيْنٌ ۟

104. Those who believe not
In the Signs of Allah—
Allah will not guide them,
And theirs will be
A grievous Penalty.

١٠٤ ـ اِنَّ الَّذِيْنَ لَا يُؤْمِنُوْنَ بِاٰيٰتِ اللّٰهِ
لَا يَهْدِيْهِمُ اللّٰهُ وَلَهُمْ عَذَابٌ اَلِيْمٌ ۟

105. It is those who believe not

١٠٥ ـ اِنَّمَا يَفْتَرِي الْكَذِبَ الَّذِيْنَ لَا يُؤْمِنُوْنَ

بِاٰيٰتِ اللهِ وَاُولٰٓئِكَ هُمُ الْكٰذِبُوْنَ ۞

In the Signs of Allah,
That forge falsehood:
It is they who lie!

106. Anyone who, after accepting
Faith in Allah, utters
            Unbelief—
Except under compulsion,
His heart remaining firm
In Faith—but such as
Open their breast to Unbelief—
On them is Wrath from Allah,
And theirs will be
A dreadful Penalty.

١٠٦ـ مَنْ كَفَرَ بِاللهِ مِنْ بَعْدِ اِيْمَانِهٖٓ اِلَّا مَنْ اُكْرِهَ وَقَلْبُهٗ مُطْمَئِنٌّۢ بِالْاِيْمَانِ وَلٰكِنْ مَّنْ شَرَحَ بِالْكُفْرِ صَدْرًا فَعَلَيْهِمْ غَضَبٌ مِّنَ اللهِ ۚ وَلَهُمْ عَذَابٌ عَظِيْمٌ ۞

107. This because they love
The life of this world
Better than the Hereafter:
And Allah will not guide
Those who reject Faith.

١٠٧ـ ذٰلِكَ بِاَنَّهُمُ اسْتَحَبُّوا الْحَيٰوةَ الدُّنْيَا عَلَى الْاٰخِرَةِ ۙ وَاَنَّ اللهَ لَا يَهْدِى الْقَوْمَ الْكٰفِرِيْنَ ۞

108. Those are they whose hearts,
Ears, and eyes Allah has
            sealed up
And they take no heed.

١٠٨ـ اُولٰٓئِكَ الَّذِيْنَ طَبَعَ اللهُ عَلٰى قُلُوْبِهِمْ وَسَمْعِهِمْ وَاَبْصَارِهِمْ ۚ وَاُولٰٓئِكَ هُمُ الْغٰفِلُوْنَ ۞

109. Without doubt, in the Hereafter
They will perish.

١٠٩ـ لَا جَرَمَ اَنَّهُمْ فِى الْاٰخِرَةِ هُمُ الْخٰسِرُوْنَ ۞

110. But verily thy Lord—
To those who leave their homes
After trials and persecutions—
And who thereafter strive
And fight for the Faith
And patiently persevere—
Thy Lord, after all this
Is Oft-Forgiving, Most Merciful.

١١٠ـ ثُمَّ اِنَّ رَبَّكَ لِلَّذِيْنَ هَاجَرُوْا مِنْۢ بَعْدِ مَا فُتِنُوْا ثُمَّ جٰهَدُوْا وَصَبَرُوْا ۙ اِنَّ رَبَّكَ مِنْۢ بَعْدِهَا لَغَفُوْرٌ رَّحِيْمٌ ۞

SECTION 15.

111. One Day every soul
Will come up struggling
For itself, and every soul
Will be recompensed (fully)
For all its actions, and none
Will be unjustly dealt with.

١١١ـ يَوْمَ تَأْتِيْ كُلُّ نَفْسٍ تُجَادِلُ عَنْ نَّفْسِهَا وَتُوَفّٰى كُلُّ نَفْسٍ مَّا عَمِلَتْ وَهُمْ لَا يُظْلَمُوْنَ ۞

112. Allah sets forth a Parable:
A city enjoying security
And quiet, abundantly supplied
With sustenance from every place:

١١٢ـ وَضَرَبَ اللهُ مَثَلًا قَرْيَةً كَانَتْ اٰمِنَةً مُّطْمَئِنَّةً يَّأْتِيْهَا رِزْقُهَا رَغَدًا مِّنْ كُلِّ

Yet was it ungrateful
For the favours of Allah:
So Allah made it taste
Of hunger and terror (in extremes)
(Closing in on it) like a garment
(From every side), because
Of the (evil) which
(Its people) wrought.

مَكَانٍ فَكَفَرَتْ بِأَنْعُمِ اللّٰهِ
فَأَذَاقَهَا اللّٰهُ
لِبَاسَ الْجُوْعِ وَالْخَوْفِ
بِمَا كَانُوْا يَصْنَعُوْنَ ۞

113. And there came to them
A Messenger from among
                themselves,
But they falsely rejected him;
So the Wrath seized them
Even in the midst
Of their iniquities.

١١٣- وَلَقَدْ جَاءَهُمْ رَسُوْلٌ مِّنْهُمْ
فَكَذَّبُوْهُ فَأَخَذَهُمُ الْعَذَابُ
وَهُمْ ظٰلِمُوْنَ ۞

114. So eat of the sustenance
Which Allah has provided
For you, lawful and good;
And be grateful for the favours
Of Allah, if it is He
Whom ye serve.

١١٤- فَكُلُوْا مِمَّا رَزَقَكُمُ اللّٰهُ
حَلٰلًا طَيِّبًا ۖ وَّ اشْكُرُوْا نِعْمَتَ اللّٰهِ
اِنْ كُنْتُمْ اِيَّاهُ تَعْبُدُوْنَ ۞

115. He has only forbidden you
Dead meat, and blood,
And the flesh of swine,
And any (food) over which
The name of other than Allah
Has been invoked.
But if one is forced by necessity,
Without willful disobedience,
Nor transgressing due limits—
Then Allah is Oft-Forgiving,
Most Merciful.

١١٥- اِنَّمَا حَرَّمَ عَلَيْكُمُ الْمَيْتَةَ وَالدَّمَ
وَلَحْمَ الْخِنْزِيْرِ وَمَآ اُهِلَّ لِغَيْرِ اللّٰهِ بِهٖ ۚ
فَمَنِ اضْطُرَّ غَيْرَ بَاغٍ
وَّلَا عَادٍ
فَاِنَّ اللّٰهَ غَفُوْرٌ رَّحِيْمٌ ۞

116. But say not—for any false thing
That your tongues may put
                forth—
"This is lawful, and this
Is forbidden," so as to ascribe
False things to Allah. For those
Who ascribe false things
To Allah, will never prosper.

١١٦- وَلَا تَقُوْلُوْا لِمَا تَصِفُ اَلْسِنَتُكُمُ
الْكَذِبَ هٰذَا حَلٰلٌ وَّهٰذَا حَرَامٌ لِّتَفْتَرُوْا
عَلَى اللّٰهِ الْكَذِبَ ۚ اِنَّ الَّذِيْنَ يَفْتَرُوْنَ
عَلَى اللّٰهِ الْكَذِبَ لَا يُفْلِحُوْنَ ۞

117. In such falsehood
Is but a paltry profit;
But they will have
A most grievous Penalty.

١١٧- مَتَاعٌ قَلِيْلٌ ۖ
وَّلَهُمْ عَذَابٌ اَلِيْمٌ ۞

118. To the Jews We prohibited
Such things as We have
Mentioned to thee before:
We did them no wrong,
But they were used to
Doing wrong to themselves.

١١٨- وَعَلَى الَّذِينَ هَادُوا حَرَّمْنَا
مَا قَصَصْنَا عَلَيْكَ مِنْ قَبْلُ وَمَا ظَلَمْنَهُمْ
وَلَكِنْ كَانُوا أَنْفُسَهُمْ يَظْلِمُونَ ٥

119. But verily thy Lord—
To those who do wrong
In ignorance, but who
Thereafter repent and make
                    amends—
Thy Lord, after all this,
Is Oft-Forgiving, Most
                    Merciful.

١١٩- ثُمَّ إِنَّ رَبَّكَ لِلَّذِينَ عَمِلُوا السُّوءَ
بِجَهَالَةٍ ثُمَّ تَابُوا مِنْ بَعْدِ ذَلِكَ وَأَصْلَحُوا
إِنَّ رَبَّكَ مِنْ بَعْدِهَا
لَغَفُورٌ رَحِيمٌ ٥

SECTION 16.

120. Abraham was indeed a model.
Devoutly obedient to Allah,
(And) true in faith, and he
Joined not gods with Allah.

١٢٠- إِنَّ إِبْرَاهِيمَ كَانَ أُمَّةً قَانِتًا لِلَّهِ
حَنِيفًا وَلَمْ يَكُ مِنَ الْمُشْرِكِينَ ٥

121. He showed his gratitude
For the favours of Allah,
Who chose him, and guided him
To a Straight Way.

١٢١- شَاكِرًا لِأَنْعُمِهِ
اجْتَبَاهُ وَهَدَاهُ إِلَى صِرَاطٍ مُسْتَقِيمٍ ٥

122. And We gave him Good
In this world, and he will be,
In the Hereafter, in the ranks
Of the Righteous.

١٢٢- وَآتَيْنَاهُ فِي الدُّنْيَا حَسَنَةً وَإِنَّهُ
فِي الْآخِرَةِ لَمِنَ الصَّالِحِينَ ٥

123. So We have taught thee
The inspired (message),
"Follow the ways of Abraham
The True in Faith, and he
Joined not gods with Allah."

١٢٣- ثُمَّ أَوْحَيْنَا إِلَيْكَ
أَنِ اتَّبِعْ مِلَّةَ إِبْرَاهِيمَ حَنِيفًا
وَمَا كَانَ مِنَ الْمُشْرِكِينَ ٥

124. The Sabbath was only made
(Strict) for those who disagreed
(As to its observance);
But Allah will judge between them
On the Day of Judgement,
As to their differences.

١٢٤- إِنَّمَا جُعِلَ السَّبْتُ عَلَى الَّذِينَ اخْتَلَفُوا
فِيهِ وَإِنَّ رَبَّكَ لَيَحْكُمُ بَيْنَهُمْ يَوْمَ الْقِيَامَةِ
فِيمَا كَانُوا فِيهِ يَخْتَلِفُونَ ٥

125. Invite (all) to the Way
Of thy Lord with wisdom
And beautiful preaching;
And argue with them

١٢٥- ادْعُ إِلَى سَبِيلِ رَبِّكَ بِالْحِكْمَةِ
وَالْمَوْعِظَةِ الْحَسَنَةِ

In ways that are best
And most gracious:
For thy Lord knoweth best,
Who have strayed from His Path,
And who receive guidance.

وَجَادِلْهُمْ بِالَّتِيْ هِيَ أَحْسَنُ إِنَّ رَبَّكَ
هُوَ أَعْلَمُ بِمَنْ ضَلَّ عَنْ سَبِيْلِهِ
وَهُوَ أَعْلَمُ بِالْمُهْتَدِيْنَ ۝

126. And if ye do catch them out,
Catch them out no worse
Than they catch you out:
But if ye show patience,
That is indeed the best (course)
For those who are patient.

١٢٦- وَإِنْ عَاقَبْتُمْ فَعَاقِبُوْا
بِمِثْلِ مَا عُوْقِبْتُمْ بِهِ
وَلَئِنْ صَبَرْتُمْ لَهُوَ خَيْرٌ لِّلصَّابِرِيْنَ ۝

127. And do thou be patient,
For thy patience is but
From Allah; nor grieve over them:
And distress not thyself
Because of their plots.

١٢٧- وَاصْبِرْ وَمَا صَبْرُكَ
إِلَّا بِاللّٰهِ وَلَا تَحْزَنْ عَلَيْهِمْ
وَلَا تَكُ فِيْ ضَيْقٍ مِّمَّا يَمْكُرُوْنَ ۝

128. For Allah is with those
Who restrain themselves,
And those who do good.

١٢٨- إِنَّ اللّٰهَ مَعَ الَّذِيْنَ اتَّقَوْا
وَّالَّذِيْنَ هُمْ مُّحْسِنُوْنَ ۝

INTRODUCTION TO SŪRA XVII. *(Banī Isrā-īl)* — 111 Verses

In the gradation of spiritual teaching (see Introduction to Sūra viii), we saw that the first seven Sūras sketched the early spiritual history of man, and led up to the formation of the new Ummat of Islam. Sūras viii. to xvi. formed another series dealing with the formation of the new Ummat and its consolidation, and God's dealing with man taken as an Ummat and considered in his social relations in organised communities (see Introduction to Sūras viii, x., and xvi). We now come to a fresh series, (Suras xvii xxix), which may be considered in three parts, Suras xvii-xxi, begin with an allusion to the *Mi'raj* (of which more later), and proceed to spiritual history as touching individuals rather than nations. The old prophets and stories of the past are now referred to from this point of view. Suras xxii-xxv. refer to Hajj (pilgrimage), worship and prayer, chastity, privacy, etc, as related to a man's individual spiritual growth. Sūras xxvi.xxix. go back to the old prophets and stories of the past, as illustrating the growth of the individual soul in its reactions against the lives of the communities and the reactions of the communities to the lives of its great individual souls.

Let us now consider S xvii. by itself. It opens with the mystic Vision of the Ascension of the Holy Prophet: he was transported from the Sacred Mosque (of Mecca) to the Farthest Mosque (of Jerusalem) in a night and shown some of the Signs of God. The majority of Commentators take this Night Journey literally, but allow that there were other occasions on which a spiritual Journey of Vision occurred. Even on the supposition of a miraculous bodily Journey, it is conceded that the body was almost transformed into a spiritual fineness. The Ḥadīth literature gives details of this Journey and its study helps to elucidate its mystic meaning. The Holy Prophet was first transported to the seat of the earlier revelations in Jerusalem, and then taken through the seven heavens, even to the Sublime Throne, and initiated into the spiritual mysteries of the human soul struggling in Space and Time. The Spaniard, Miguel Asin, Arabic Professor in the University of Madrid, has shown that his Mi'raj literature had a great influence on the Mediaeval literature of Europe, and especially on the great Italian poem, the *Divine Comedy* (or Drama) of Dante, which towers like a landmark in Mediaeval European literature.

The reference to this great mystic story of the Mi'raj is a fitting prelude to the journey of the human soul in its spiritual growth, in life. The first steps in such growth must be through moral conduct—the reciprocal rights of parents and children, kindness to our fellow-men, courage and firmness in the hour of danger, a sense of personal responsibility, and a sense of God's Presence through prayer and praise.

The Mir'rāj is usually dated to the 27th night of the month of Rajab (through other dates, e.g., 17th of Rabī' I, are also given) in the year before the Hijrah. This fixes the date of the opening verse of the Sūra, though portions of the Sūra may have been a little earlier.

Al Isrā' (The Night Journey), or
Banī Isrā'īl (The Children of Israel)

In the name of Allah, Most Gracious,
Most Merciful.

بِسْمِ اللهِ الرَّحْمٰنِ الرَّحِيْمِ

1. Glory to (Allah)
   Who did take His Servant
   For a Journey by night
   From the Sacred Mosque
   To the Farthest Mosque,
   Whose precincts We did
   Bless—in order that We
   Might show him some
   Of Our Signs: for He
   Is the One Who heareth
   And seeth (all things).

١- سُبْحٰنَ الَّذِيْٓ اَسْرٰى بِعَبْدِهٖ
لَيْلًا مِّنَ الْمَسْجِدِ الْحَرَامِ
اِلَى الْمَسْجِدِ الْاَقْصَا
الَّذِيْ بٰرَكْنَا حَوْلَهٗ لِنُرِيَهٗ
مِنْ اٰيٰتِنَا ۗ
اِنَّهٗ هُوَ السَّمِيْعُ الْبَصِيْرُ ۝

2. We gave Moses the Book,
   And made it a Guide
   To the Children of Israel,
   (Commanding): "Take not
   Other than Me
   As Disposer of (your) affairs."

٢- وَاٰتَيْنَا مُوْسَى الْكِتٰبَ وَجَعَلْنٰهُ هُدًى
لِّبَنِيْٓ اِسْرَآءِيْلَ اَلَّا تَتَّخِذُوْا
مِنْ دُوْنِيْ وَكِيْلًا ۝

3. O ye that are sprung
   From those whom We carried
   (In the Ark) with Noah!
   Verily he was a devotee
   Most grateful.

٣- ذُرِّيَّةَ مَنْ حَمَلْنَا مَعَ نُوْحٍ
اِنَّهٗ كَانَ عَبْدًا شَكُوْرًا ۝

4. And We gave (clear) warning
   To the Children of Israel
   In the Book, that twice
   Would they do mischief
   On the earth and be elated
   With mighty arrogance
   (And twice would they be
            punished)!

٤- وَقَضَيْنَآ اِلٰى بَنِيْٓ اِسْرَآءِيْلَ
فِى الْكِتٰبِ لَتُفْسِدُنَّ فِى الْاَرْضِ مَرَّتَيْنِ
وَلَتَعْلُنَّ عُلُوًّا كَبِيْرًا ۝

5. When the first of the warnings
   Came to pass, We sent
   Against you Our servants
   Given to terrible warfare.
   They entered the very inmost

٥- فَاِذَا جَآءَ وَعْدُ اُوْلٰىهُمَا بَعَثْنَا
عَلَيْكُمْ عِبَادًا لَّنَآ اُولِيْ بَأْسٍ شَدِيْدٍ
فَجَاسُوْا خِلٰلَ الدِّيَارِ

Parts of your homes;
And it was a warning
(Completely) fulfilled.

6. Then did we grant you
The Return as against them:
We gave you increase
In resources and sons,
And made you
The more numerous
In manpower.

٦- ثُمَّ رَدَدْنَا لَكُمُ الْكَرَّةَ عَلَيْهِمْ
وَأَمْدَدْنَكُمْ بِأَمْوَالٍ وَبَنِينَ
وَجَعَلْنَكُمْ أَكْثَرَ نَفِيرًا ٥

7. If ye did well,
Ye did well for yourselves;
If ye did evil,
(Ye did it) against yourselves.
So when the second
Of the warnings came to pass,
(We permitted your enemies)
To disfigure your faces,
And to enter your Temple
As they had entered it before,
And to visit with destruction
All that fell into their power.

٧- إِنْ أَحْسَنتُمْ أَحْسَنتُمْ لِأَنفُسِكُمْ
وَإِنْ أَسَأْتُمْ فَلَهَا
فَإِذَا جَاءَ وَعْدُ الْآخِرَةِ
لِيَسُوءُوا وُجُوهَكُمْ
وَلِيَدْخُلُوا الْمَسْجِدَ كَمَا دَخَلُوهُ أَوَّلَ مَرَّةٍ
وَلِيُتَبِّرُوا مَا عَلَوْا تَتْبِيرًا ٥

8. It may be that your Lord
May (yet) show Mercy
Unto you; but if ye
Revert (to your sins)
We shall revert
(To Our punishments):
And We have made Hell
A prison for those who
Reject (all Faith).

٨- عَسَى رَبُّكُمْ أَن يَرْحَمَكُمْ وَإِنْ
عُدتُّمْ عُدْنَا
وَجَعَلْنَا جَهَنَّمَ
لِلْكَافِرِينَ حَصِيرًا ٥

9. Verily this Qur'ān
Doth guide to that
Which is most right (or stable),
And giveth the glad tidings
To the Believers who work
Deeds of righteousness,
That they shall have
A magnificent reward;

٩- إِنَّ هَذَا الْقُرْآنَ يَهْدِى لِلَّتِى
هِيَ أَقْوَمُ وَيُبَشِّرُ
الْمُؤْمِنِينَ الَّذِينَ يَعْمَلُونَ الصَّالِحَاتِ
أَنَّ لَهُمْ أَجْرًا كَبِيرًا ٥

10. And to those who believe not
In the Hereafter, (it announceth)
That We have prepared
For them a Penalty
Grievous (indeed).

١٠- وَأَنَّ الَّذِينَ لَا يُؤْمِنُونَ بِالْآخِرَةِ
أَعْتَدْنَا لَهُمْ عَذَابًا أَلِيمًا ٥

SECTION 2.

11. The prayer that man
Should make for good,
He maketh for evil;
For man is given to
Hasty (deeds).

١١- وَيَدْعُ الْإِنْسَانُ بِالشَّرِّ دُعَاءَهُ بِالْخَيْرِ
وَكَانَ الْإِنْسَانُ عَجُولًا ۞

12. We have made the Night
And the Day as two
(Of Our) Signs: the Sign
Of the Night have We obscured,
While the Sign of the Day
We have made to enlighten
You; that ye may seek
Bounty from your Lord,
And that ye may know
The number and count
Of the years: all things
Have We explained in detail.

١٢- وَجَعَلْنَا الَّيْلَ وَالنَّهَارَ آيَتَيْنِ
فَمَحَوْنَا آيَةَ الَّيْلِ
وَجَعَلْنَا آيَةَ النَّهَارِ مُبْصِرَةً
لِتَبْتَغُوا فَضْلًا مِّن رَّبِّكُمْ
وَلِتَعْلَمُوا عَدَدَ السِّنِينَ وَالْحِسَابَ
وَكُلَّ شَيْءٍ فَصَّلْنَاهُ تَفْصِيلًا ۞

13. Every man's fate
We have fastened
On his own neck:
On the Day of Judgement
We shall bring out
For him a scroll,
Which he will see
Spread open.

١٣- وَكُلَّ إِنْسَانٍ أَلْزَمْنَاهُ
طَائِرَهُ فِي عُنُقِهِ
وَنُخْرِجُ لَهُ يَوْمَ الْقِيَامَةِ كِتَابًا
يَلْقَاهُ مَنْشُورًا ۞

14. (It will be said to him:)
"Read thine (own) record;
Sufficient is thy soul
This day to make out
An account against thee."

١٤- اِقْرَأْ كِتَابَكَ
كَفَى بِنَفْسِكَ الْيَوْمَ عَلَيْكَ حَسِيبًا ۞

15. Who receiveth guidance,
Receiveth it for his own
Benefit: who goeth astray
Doth so to his own loss:
No bearer of burdens
Can bear the burden[2191]
Of another: nor would We
Visit with Our Wrath
Until We had sent
A messenger (to give warning).

١٥- مَنِ اهْتَدَى فَإِنَّمَا يَهْتَدِي لِنَفْسِهِ
وَمَن ضَلَّ فَإِنَّمَا يَضِلُّ عَلَيْهَا
وَلَا تَزِرُ وَازِرَةٌ وِزْرَ أُخْرَى
وَمَا كُنَّا مُعَذِّبِينَ
حَتَّى نَبْعَثَ رَسُولًا ۞

16. When We decide to destroy
A population, We (first) send
A definite order to those

١٦- وَإِذَا أَرَدْنَا أَن نُّهْلِكَ قَرْيَةً أَمَرْنَا

Among them who are given
The good things of this life
And yet transgress; so that
The word is proved true
Against them: then
We destroy them utterly.

17. How many generations
Have We destroyed after Noah?
And enough is thy Lord
To note and see
The sins of His servants.

18. If any do wish
For the transitory things
(Of this life), We readily
Grant them—such things
As We will, to such persons
As We will: in the end
Have We provided Hell
For them: they will burn
Therein, disgraced and
　　　　　　rejected.

19. Those who do wish
For the (things of) the
　　　　　　Hereafter,
And strive therefor
With all due striving,
And have Faith—
They are the ones
Whose striving is acceptable
(To Allah).

20. Of the bounties of thy Lord
We bestow freely on all—
These as well as those:
The bounties of thy Lord
Are not closed (to anyone).

21. See how We have bestowed
More on some than on others;
But verily the Hereafter
Is more in rank and gradation
And more in excellence.

22. Take not with Allah
Another object of worship;
Or thou (O man!) wilt sit

مُتْرَفِيهَا فَفَسَقُوا فِيهَا
فَحَقَّ عَلَيْهَا الْقَوْلُ
فَدَمَّرْنَاهَا تَدْمِيرًا ۞

١٧- وَكَمْ أَهْلَكْنَا مِنَ الْقُرُونِ مِنْ بَعْدِ
نُوحٍ ۗ وَكَفٰى بِرَبِّكَ بِذُنُوبِ عِبَادِهِ
خَبِيرًا بَصِيرًا ۞

١٨- مَنْ كَانَ يُرِيدُ الْعَاجِلَةَ عَجَّلْنَا
لَهُ فِيهَا مَا نَشَاءُ لِمَنْ نُرِيدُ
ثُمَّ جَعَلْنَا لَهُ جَهَنَّمَ ۚ
يَصْلَاهَا مَذْمُومًا مَدْحُورًا ۞

١٩- وَمَنْ أَرَادَ الْآخِرَةَ
وَسَعٰى لَهَا سَعْيَهَا
وَهُوَ مُؤْمِنٌ فَأُولَٰئِكَ
كَانَ سَعْيُهُمْ مَشْكُورًا ۞

٢٠- كُلًّا نُمِدُّ هٰؤُلَاءِ وَهٰؤُلَاءِ مِنْ عَطَاءِ
رَبِّكَ ۚ
وَمَا كَانَ عَطَاءُ رَبِّكَ مَحْظُورًا ۞

٢١- انْظُرْ كَيْفَ فَضَّلْنَا بَعْضَهُمْ عَلٰى بَعْضٍ
وَلَلْآخِرَةُ أَكْبَرُ دَرَجَاتٍ وَأَكْبَرُ تَفْضِيلًا ۞

٢٢- لَا تَجْعَلْ مَعَ اللَّهِ إِلٰهًا آخَرَ فَتَقْعُدَ

In disgrace and destitution.

SECTION 3.

23. Thy Lord hath decreed
That ye worship none but Him,
And that ye be kind
To parents. Whether one
Or both of them attain
Old age in thy life,
Say not to them a word
Of contempt, nor repel them,
But address them
In terms of honour.

24. And, out of kindness,
Lower to them the wing
Of humility, and say:
"My Lord! bestow on them
Thy Mercy even as they
Cherished me in childhood."

25. Your Lord knoweth best
What is in your hearts:
If ye do deeds of righteousness,
Verily He is Most Forgiving
To those who turn to Him
Again and again
(in true penitence).

26. And render to the kindred
Their due rights, as (also)
To those in want,
And to the wayfarer:
But squander not (your wealth)
In the manner of a spendthrift.

27. Verily spendthrifts are brothers
Of the Evil Ones
And the Evil One
Is to his Lord (Himself)
Ungrateful.

28. And even if thou hast
To turn away from them
In pursuit of the Mercy
From thy Lord which thou
Dost expect, yet speak
To them a word
Of easy kindness.

 نْدُمُومَّا مَّحْذُولاً ۞

٢- وَقَضَى رَبُّكَ أَلَّا تَعْبُدُوا إِلَّا إِيَّاهُ
بِالْوَالِدَيْنِ إِحْسَانًا
تَمَا يَبْلُغَنَّ عِنْدَكَ الْكِبَرَ أَحَدُهُمَا
وَكِلَاهُمَا فَلَا تَقُلْ لَهُمَا أُفٍّ وَلَا تَنْهَرْهُمَا
وَقُلْ لَهُمَا قَوْلًا كَرِيمًا ۞

٢٤- وَاخْفِضْ لَهُمَا جَنَاحَ الذُّلِّ مِنَ
الرَّحْمَةِ وَقُلْ
بِّ ارْحَمْهُمَا كَمَا رَبَّيَانِي صَغِيرًا ۞

٢٥- رَبُّكُمْ أَعْلَمُ بِمَا فِي نُفُوسِكُمْ
بِنْ تَكُونُوا صَالِحِينَ
فَإِنَّهُ كَانَ لِلْأَوَّابِينَ غَفُورًا ۞

٢٦- وَآتِ ذَا الْقُرْبَى حَقَّهُ
وَالْمِسْكِينَ وَابْنَ السَّبِيلِ
وَلَا تُبَذِّرْ تَبْذِيرًا ۞

٢٧- إِنَّ الْمُبَذِّرِينَ كَانُوا إِخْوَانَ الشَّيَاطِينِ
وَكَانَ الشَّيْطَانُ لِرَبِّهِ كَفُورًا ۞

٢٨- وَإِمَّا تُعْرِضَنَّ عَنْهُمُ ابْتِغَاءَ رَحْمَةٍ
مِّن رَّبِّكَ تَرْجُوهَا
فَقُلْ لَهُمْ قَوْلًا مَيْسُورًا ۞

29. Make not thy hand tied
(Like a niggard's) to thy neck,
Nor stretch it forth
To its utmost reach,
So that thou become
Blameworthy and destitute.

٢٩- وَلَا تَجْعَلْ يَدَكَ مَغْلُوْلَةً إِلٰى عُنُقِكَ
وَلَا تَبْسُطْهَا كُلَّ الْبَسْطِ
فَتَقْعُدَ مَلُوْمًا مَّحْسُوْرًا ۞

30. Verily thy Lord doth provide
Sustenance in abundance
For whom He pleaseth, and He
Provideth in a just measure,
For He doth know
And regard all His servants.

٣٠- إِنَّ رَبَّكَ يَبْسُطُ الرِّزْقَ
لِمَنْ يَّشَاءُ وَيَقْدِرُ
إِنَّهُ كَانَ بِعِبَادِهِ خَبِيْرًا بَصِيْرًا ۞

SECTION 4.

31. Kill not your children
For fear of want: We shall
Provide sustenance for them
As well as for you.
Verily the killing of them
Is a great sin.

٣١- وَلَا تَقْتُلُوْا أَوْلَادَكُمْ خَشْيَةَ إِمْلَاقٍ
نَحْنُ نَرْزُقُهُمْ وَإِيَّاكُمْ
إِنَّ قَتْلَهُمْ كَانَ خِطْأً كَبِيْرًا ۞

32. Nor come nigh to adultery:
For it is a shameful (deed)

And an evil, opening the road
(To other evils).

٣٢- وَلَا تَقْرَبُوا الزِّنٰى إِنَّهُ كَانَ فَاحِشَةً
وَسَاءَ سَبِيْلًا ۞

33. Nor take life—which Allah
Has made sacred—except
For just cause. And if
Anyone is slain wrongfully,
We have given his heir
Authority (to demand Qiṣāṣ
Or to forgive): but let him
Not exceed bounds in the matter
Of taking life: for he
Is helped (by the Law).

٣٣- وَلَا تَقْتُلُوا النَّفْسَ الَّتِيْ حَرَّمَ اللهُ
إِلَّا بِالْحَقِّ وَمَنْ قُتِلَ مَظْلُوْمًا
فَقَدْ جَعَلْنَا لِوَلِيِّهِ سُلْطَانًا
فَلَا يُسْرِفْ فِّي الْقَتْلِ
إِنَّهُ كَانَ مَنْصُوْرًا ۞

34. Come not nigh
To the orphan's property
Except to improve it,
Until he attains the age
Of full strength: and fulfil
(Every) engagement,
For (every) engagement
Will be enquired into
(On the Day of Reckoning).

٣٤- وَلَا تَقْرَبُوْا مَالَ الْيَتِيْمِ إِلَّا بِالَّتِيْ
هِيَ أَحْسَنُ
حَتّٰى يَبْلُغَ أَشُدَّهُ
وَأَوْفُوْا بِالْعَهْدِ
إِنَّ الْعَهْدَ كَانَ مَسْؤُوْلًا ۞

35. Give full measure when ye
Measure, and weigh
With a balance that is straight:
That is the most fitting
And the most advantageous
In the final determination.

٣٥ ـ وَأَوْفُوا الْكَيْلَ إِذَا كِلْتُمْ وَزِنُوْا
بِالْقِسْطَاسِ الْمُسْتَقِيْمِ ۚ
ذٰلِكَ خَيْرٌ وَّأَحْسَنُ تَأْوِيْلًا ۞

36. And pursue not that
Of which thou hast
No knowledge; for
Every act of hearing,
Or of seeing,
Or of (feeling in) the heart
Will be enquired into
(On the Day of Reckoning).

٣٦ ـ وَلَا تَقْفُ مَا لَيْسَ لَكَ بِهٖ عِلْمٌ ۚ
إِنَّ السَّمْعَ وَالْبَصَرَ
وَالْفُؤَادَ كُلُّ
أُولٰٓئِكَ كَانَ عَنْهُ مَسْئُوْلًا ۞

37. Nor walk on the earth
With insolence: for thou
Canst not rend the earth
Asunder, nor reach
The mountains in height.

٣٧ ـ وَلَا تَمْشِ فِي الْأَرْضِ مَرَحًا ۚ إِنَّكَ
لَنْ تَخْرِقَ الْأَرْضَ
وَلَنْ تَبْلُغَ الْجِبَالَ طُوْلًا ۞

38. Of all such things
The evil is hateful
In the sight of thy Lord.

٣٨ ـ كُلُّ ذٰلِكَ كَانَ سَيِّئُهٗ
عِنْدَ رَبِّكَ مَكْرُوْهًا ۞

39. These are among the (precepts
Of) wisdom, which thy Lord
Has revealed to thee.
Take not, with Allah,
Another object of worship,
Lest thou shouldst be thrown
Into Hell, blameworthy and
rejected.

٣٩ ـ ذٰلِكَ مِمَّا أَوْحٰى إِلَيْكَ
رَبُّكَ مِنَ الْحِكْمَةِ ۚ
وَلَا تَجْعَلْ مَعَ اللّٰهِ إِلٰهًا اٰخَرَ فَتُلْقٰى
فِيْ جَهَنَّمَ مَلُوْمًا مَّدْحُوْرًا ۞

40. Has then your Lord,
(O Pagans!) preferred for you
Sons, and taken for Himself
Daughters among the angels?
Truly ye utter
A most dreadful saying!

٤٠ ـ أَفَأَصْفٰكُمْ رَبُّكُمْ بِالْبَنِيْنَ
وَاتَّخَذَ مِنَ الْمَلٰٓئِكَةِ إِنَاثًا ۚ
إِنَّكُمْ لَتَقُوْلُوْنَ قَوْلًا عَظِيْمًا ۞

SECTION 5.

41. We have explained (things)
In various (ways) in this Qur'ān,
In order that they may receive
Admonition, but it only increases
Their flight (from the Truth)!

٤١ ـ وَلَقَدْ صَرَّفْنَا فِيْ هٰذَا الْقُرْاٰنِ لِيَذَّكَّرُوْا ۚ
وَمَا يَزِيْدُهُمْ إِلَّا نُفُوْرًا ۞

42. Say: if there had been
(Other) gods with Him—
As they say—behold,
They would certainly have
Sought out a way
To the Lord of the Throne!

٤٢ـ قُل لَّوْ كَانَ مَعَهُ آلِهَةٌ
كَمَا يَقُولُونَ إِذًا لَّابْتَغَوْا
إِلَى ذِى الْعَرْشِ سَبِيلًا ۝

43. Glory to Him! He is high
Above all that they say!—
Exalted and Great (beyond
measure)!

٤٣ـ سُبْحَانَهُ وَتَعَالَى عَمَّا يَقُولُونَ
عُلُوًّا كَبِيرًا ۝

44. The seven heavens and the earth,
And all beings therein,
Declare His glory:
There is not a thing
But celebrates His praise:
And yet ye understand not
How they declare His glory!
Verily He is Oft-Forbearing,
Most Forgiving!

٤٤ـ تُسَبِّحُ لَهُ السَّمَاوَاتُ السَّبْعُ وَالْأَرْضُ
وَمَن فِيهِنَّ ۚ
وَإِن مِّن شَىْءٍ إِلَّا يُسَبِّحُ بِحَمْدِهِ
وَلَٰكِن لَّا تَفْقَهُونَ تَسْبِيحَهُمْ
إِنَّهُ كَانَ حَلِيمًا غَفُورًا ۝

45. When thou dost recite
The Qur'ān, We put,
Between thee and those who
Believe not in the Hereafter,
A veil invisible:

٤٥ـ وَإِذَا قَرَأْتَ الْقُرْآنَ جَعَلْنَا
بَيْنَكَ وَبَيْنَ الَّذِينَ لَا يُؤْمِنُونَ بِالْآخِرَةِ
حِجَابًا مَسْتُورًا ۝

46. And We put coverings
Over their hearts (and minds)
Lest they should understand
The Qur'ān, and deafness
Into their ears; when thou
Dost commemorate thy Lord—
And Him alone—in the Qur'ān,
They turn on their backs,
Fleeing (from the Truth).

٤٦ـ وَجَعَلْنَا عَلَى قُلُوبِهِمْ
أَكِنَّةً أَن يَفْقَهُوهُ وَفِى آذَانِهِمْ وَقْرًا
وَإِذَا ذَكَرْتَ رَبَّكَ فِى الْقُرْآنِ وَحْدَهُ
وَلَّوْا عَلَى أَدْبَارِهِمْ نُفُورًا ۝

47. We know best why it is
They listen, when they listen
To thee; and when they
Meet in private conference,
Behold, the wicked say,
"Ye follow none other than
A man bewitched!"

٤٧ـ نَّحْنُ أَعْلَمُ بِمَا يَسْتَمِعُونَ بِهِ إِذْ
يَسْتَمِعُونَ إِلَيْكَ وَإِذْ هُمْ نَجْوَى
إِذْ يَقُولُ الظَّالِمُونَ
إِن تَتَّبِعُونَ إِلَّا رَجُلًا مَّسْحُورًا ۝

48. See what similes they strike
For thee; but they have gone
Astray, and never can they
Find a way.

انظر كيف ضربوا لك الأمثال فضلوا فلا يستطيعون سبيلا ۞

49. They say: "What!
When we are reduced
To bones and dust,
Should we really be raised up
(To be) a new creation?"

وقالوا ءاذا كنا عظاما ورفاتا ءانا لمبعوثون خلقا جديدا ۞

50. Say: "(Nay!) be ye
Stones or iron,

قل كونوا حجارة أو حديدا ۞

51. "Or created matter
Which, in your minds,
Is hardest (to be raised up)—
(Yet shall ye be raised up)!"
Then will they say:
"Who will cause us
To return?" Say: "He
Who created you first!"
Then will they wag
Their heads towards thee,
And say, "When will
That be?" Say, "Maybe
It will be quite soon!"

أو خلقا مما يكبر في صدوركم فسيقولون من يعيدنا قل الذي فطركم أول مرة فسينغضون إليك رءوسهم ويقولون متى هو قل عسى أن يكون قريبا ۞

52. "It will be on a Day
When He will call you,
And ye will answer
(His call) with (words
Of) His praise, and ye
Will think that ye tarried
But a little while!"

يوم يدعوكم فتستجيبون بحمده وتظنون إن لبثتم إلا قليلا ۞

SECTION 6.

53. Say to My servants
That they should (only) say
Those things that are best:
For Satan doth sow
Dissensions among them:
For Satan is to man
An avowed enemy.

وقل لعبادي يقولوا التي هي أحسن إن الشيطن ينزغ بينهم إن الشيطن كان للإنسان عدوا مبينا ۞

54. It is your Lord
That knoweth you best;
If He please, He granteth
You mercy, or if He please,

ربكم أعلم بكم إن يشأ يرحمكم أو إن يشأ يعذبكم

Punishment: We have not sent
Thee to be a disposer
Of their affairs for them.

وَمَآ أَرْسَلْنَاكَ عَلَيْهِمْ وَكِيلًا ۝

55. And it is your Lord
That knoweth best all beings
That are in the heavens
And on earth: We
Did bestow on some Prophets
More (and other) gifts
Than on others: and We gave
To David (the gift
Of) the Psalms.

٥٥ ۔ وَرَبُّكَ أَعْلَمُ بِمَنْ فِي السَّمَاوَاتِ وَالْأَرْضِ ۗ وَلَقَدْ فَضَّلْنَا بَعْضَ النَّبِيِّنَ عَلَى بَعْضٍ ۖ وَآتَيْنَا دَاوُدَ زَبُورًا ۝

56. Say: "Call on those—
Besides Him—whom ye fancy:
They have neither the power
To remove your troubles
From you nor to change them."

٥٦ ۔ قُلِ ادْعُوا الَّذِينَ زَعَمْتُمْ مِنْ دُونِهِ فَلَا يَمْلِكُونَ كَشْفَ الضُّرِّ عَنْكُمْ وَلَا تَحْوِيلًا ۝

57. Those whom they call upon
Do desire (for themselves) means
Of access to their Lord—
Even those who are nearest:
They hope for His Mercy
And fear His Wrath:
For the Wrath of thy Lord
Is something to take heed of.

٥٧ ۔ أُولَٰئِكَ الَّذِينَ يَدْعُونَ يَبْتَغُونَ إِلَى رَبِّهِمُ الْوَسِيلَةَ أَيُّهُمْ أَقْرَبُ وَيَرْجُونَ رَحْمَتَهُ وَيَخَافُونَ عَذَابَهُ ۚ إِنَّ عَذَابَ رَبِّكَ كَانَ مَحْذُورًا ۝

58. There is not a population
But We shall destroy it
Before the Day of Judgement
Or punish it with
A dreadful Penalty:
That is written
In the (eternal) Record.

٥٨ ۔ وَإِنْ مِنْ قَرْيَةٍ إِلَّا نَحْنُ مُهْلِكُوهَا قَبْلَ يَوْمِ الْقِيَامَةِ أَوْ مُعَذِّبُوهَا عَذَابًا شَدِيدًا ۚ كَانَ ذَٰلِكَ فِي الْكِتَابِ مَسْطُورًا ۝

59. And We refrain from sending
The Signs, only because
The men of former generations
Treated them as false:
We sent the She-camel
To the Thamūd to open
Their eyes, but they
Treated her wrongfully:
We only sent the Signs
By way of terror
(And warning from evil).

٥٩ ۔ وَمَا مَنَعَنَا أَنْ نُرْسِلَ بِالْآيَاتِ إِلَّا أَنْ كَذَّبَ بِهَا الْأَوَّلُونَ ۚ وَآتَيْنَا ثَمُودَ النَّاقَةَ مُبْصِرَةً فَظَلَمُوا بِهَا ۚ وَمَا نُرْسِلُ بِالْآيَاتِ إِلَّا تَخْوِيفًا ۝

60. Behold! We told thee
That thy Lord doth encompass
Mankind round about:
We granted the Vision
Which We showed thee,
But as a trial for men—
As also the Cursed Tree
(Mentioned) in the Qur'ān:
We put terror (and warning)
Into them, but it only
Increases their inordinate
            transgression!

٦٠ ـ وَإِذْ قُلْنَا لَكَ إِنَّ رَبَّكَ أَحَاطَ بِالنَّاسِ
وَمَا جَعَلْنَا الرُّؤْيَا الَّتِىٓ أَرَيْنَٰكَ
إِلَّا فِتْنَةً لِّلنَّاسِ
وَالشَّجَرَةَ الْمَلْعُونَةَ فِى الْقُرْءَانِ ۚ
وَنُخَوِّفُهُمْ فَمَا يَزِيدُهُمْ
إِلَّا طُغْيَانًا كَبِيرًا ۝

SECTION 7.

61. Behold! We said to the angels:
"Bow down unto Adam'"
They bowed down except Iblīs:
He said: "Shall I bow down
To one whom Thou didst create
From clay?"

٦١ ـ وَإِذْ قُلْنَا لِلْمَلَٰٓئِكَةِ اسْجُدُوا لِآدَمَ
فَسَجَدُوٓا إِلَّآ إِبْلِيسَ ۗ
قَالَ ءَأَسْجُدُ لِمَنْ خَلَقْتَ طِينًا ۝

62. He said: "Seest Thou? This is
The one whom Thou hast
            honoured
Above me! If Thou wilt but
Respite me to the Day
Of Judgement, I will surely
Bring his descendants
Under my sway—
All but a few!"

٦٢ ـ قَالَ أَرَءَيْتَكَ هَٰذَا الَّذِى كَرَّمْتَ
عَلَىَّ لَئِنْ أَخَّرْتَنِ إِلَىٰ يَوْمِ
الْقِيَٰمَةِ لَأَحْتَنِكَنَّ ذُرِّيَّتَهُ
إِلَّا قَلِيلًا ۝

63. (Allah) said: "Go thy way;
If any of them follow thee,
Verily Hell will be
The recompense of you (all)—
An ample recompense.

٦٣ ـ قَالَ اذْهَبْ فَمَن تَبِعَكَ مِنْهُمْ
فَإِنَّ جَهَنَّمَ جَزَآؤُكُمْ جَزَآءً
مَّوْفُورًا ۝

64. "Lead to destruction those
Whom thou canst among
            them,
With thy (seductive) voice,
Make assaults on them
With thy cavalry and thy
Infantry; mutually share
With them wealth and
            children;
And make promises to them.
But Satan promises them
Nothing but deceit.

٦٤ ـ وَاسْتَفْزِزْ مَنِ اسْتَطَعْتَ مِنْهُم
بِصَوْتِكَ وَأَجْلِبْ عَلَيْهِم
بِخَيْلِكَ وَرَجِلِكَ وَشَارِكْهُمْ
فِى الْأَمْوَالِ وَالْأَوْلَادِ وَعِدْهُمْ ۚ
وَمَا يَعِدُهُمُ الشَّيْطَٰنُ إِلَّا غُرُورًا ۝

65. "As for My servants,
No authority shalt thou
Have over them."
Enough is thy Lord
For a Disposer of affairs.

٦٥- اِنَّ عِبَادِى لَيْسَ لَكَ عَلَيْهِمْ سُلْطٰنٌ ۚ وَكَفٰى بِرَبِّكَ وَكِيْلًا ۟

66. Your Lord is He
That maketh the Ship
Go smoothly for you
Through the sea, in order that
Ye may seek of His Bounty.
For He is unto you
Most Merciful.

٦٦- رَبُّكُمُ الَّذِىْ يُزْجِىْ لَكُمُ الْفُلْكَ فِى الْبَحْرِ لِتَبْتَغُوْا مِنْ فَضْلِهٖ ۚ اِنَّهٗ كَانَ بِكُمْ رَحِيْمًا ۟

67. When distress seizes you
At sea, those that ye
Call upon – besides Himself –
Leave you in the lurch!
But when He brings you back
Safe to land, ye turn
Away (from Him), Most
             ungrateful
Is man!

٦٧- وَاِذَا مَسَّكُمُ الضُّرُّ فِى الْبَحْرِ ضَلَّ مَنْ تَدْعُوْنَ اِلَّآ اِيَّاهُ ۚ فَلَمَّا نَجّٰىكُمْ اِلَى الْبَرِّ اَعْرَضْتُمْ ۚ وَكَانَ الْاِنْسَانُ كَفُوْرًا ۟

68. Do ye then feel secure
That He will not cause you
To be swallowed up
Beneath the earth
When ye are on land,
Or that He will not send
Against you a violent tornado
(With showers of stones)
So that ye shall find
No one to carry out
Your affairs for you?

٦٨- اَفَاَمِنْتُمْ اَنْ يَّخْسِفَ بِكُمْ جَانِبَ الْبَرِّ اَوْ يُرْسِلَ عَلَيْكُمْ حَاصِبًا ثُمَّ لَا تَجِدُوْا لَكُمْ وَكِيْلًا ۟ۙ

69. Or do ye feel secure
That He will not send you
Back a second time
To sea and send against you
A heavy gale to drown you
Because of your ingratitude,
So that ye find no helper
Therein against Us?

٦٩- اَمْ اَمِنْتُمْ اَنْ يُّعِيْدَكُمْ فِيْهِ تَارَةً اُخْرٰى فَيُرْسِلَ عَلَيْكُمْ قَاصِفًا مِّنَ الرِّيْحِ فَيُغْرِقَكُمْ بِمَا كَفَرْتُمْ ۙ ثُمَّ لَا تَجِدُوْا لَكُمْ عَلَيْنَا بِهٖ تَبِيْعًا ۟

70. We have honoured the sons
Of Adam; provided them
With transport on land and sea;
Given them for sustenance things
Good and pure; and conferred

٧٠- وَلَقَدْ كَرَّمْنَا بَنِىْ اٰدَمَ وَحَمَلْنٰهُمْ فِى الْبَرِّ وَالْبَحْرِ وَرَزَقْنٰهُمْ مِّنَ الطَّيِّبٰتِ وَفَضَّلْنٰهُمْ

On them special favours,
Above a great part
Of Our Creation.

SECTION 8.

71. One day We shall call
Together all human beings
With their (respective) Imāms:
Those who are given their record
In their right hand
Will read it (with pleasure),
And they will not be
Dealt with unjustly
In the least.

عَلٰى كَثِيْرٍ مِّمَّنْ خَلَقْنَا تَفْضِيْلًا ۝

١٧۔ يَوْمَ نَدْعُوْا كُلَّ أُنَاسٍ بِإِمَامِهِمْ ۚ
فَمَنْ أُوْتِيَ كِتٰبَهٗ بِيَمِيْنِهٖ
فَأُولٰٓئِكَ يَقْرَءُوْنَ كِتٰبَهُمْ
وَلَا يُظْلَمُوْنَ فَتِيْلًا ۝

72. But those who were blind
In this world, will be
Blind in the Hereafter,
And most astray
From the Path.

٧٢۔ وَمَنْ كَانَ فِيْ هٰذِهٖٓ أَعْمٰى
فَهُوَ فِى الْاٰخِرَةِ أَعْمٰى
وَأَضَلُّ سَبِيْلًا ۝

73. And their purpose was
To tempt thee away
From that which We
Had revealed unto thee,
To substitute in Our name
Something quite different:
(In that case), behold!
They would certainly have
Made thee (their) friend!

٧٣۔ وَإِنْ كَادُوْا لَيَفْتِنُوْنَكَ عَنِ الَّذِيْٓ
أَوْحَيْنَآ إِلَيْكَ لِتَفْتَرِيَ عَلَيْنَا
غَيْرَهٗ ۖ
وَإِذًا لَّاتَّخَذُوْكَ خَلِيْلًا ۝

74. And had We not
Given thee strength
Thou wouldst nearly
Have inclined to them
A little.

٧٤۔ وَلَوْلَآ أَنْ ثَبَّتْنٰكَ
لَقَدْ كِدْتَّ تَرْكَنُ إِلَيْهِمْ شَيْئًا قَلِيْلًا ۝

75. In that case We should
Have made thee taste
An equal portion (of punishment)
In this life, and an equal
portion
In death: and moreover
Thou wouldst have found
None to help thee against Us!

٧٥۔ إِذًا لَّأَذَقْنٰكَ
ضِعْفَ الْحَيٰوةِ وَضِعْفَ الْمَمَاتِ
ثُمَّ لَا تَجِدُ لَكَ عَلَيْنَا نَصِيْرًا ۝

76. Their purpose was to scare
Thee off the land,
In order to expel thee:
But in that case they

٧٦۔ وَإِنْ كَادُوْا لَيَسْتَفِزُّوْنَكَ مِنَ الْأَرْضِ
لِيُخْرِجُوْكَ مِنْهَا وَإِذًا لَّا يَلْبَثُوْنَ

Would not have stayed
(Therein) after thee,
Except for a little while.

خَلْفَكَ إِلَّا قَلِيْلًا ۞

77. (This was Our) way
With the messengers We sent
Before thee: thou wilt find
No change in Our ways.

٧٧ـ سُنَّةَ مَنْ قَدْ اَرْسَلْنَا قَبْلَكَ مِنْ
رُّسُلِنَا وَلَا تَجِدُ لِسُنَّتِنَا تَحْوِيْلًا ۞

SECTION 9.

78. Establish regular prayers—
At the sun's decline
Till the darkness of the night,
And the morning prayer
And reading: for the prayer
And reading in the morning
Carry their testimony.

٧٨ـ اَقِمِ الصَّلٰوةَ لِدُلُوْكِ الشَّمْسِ
اِلٰى غَسَقِ الَّيْلِ وَ قُرْاٰنَ الْفَجْرِ
اِنَّ قُرْاٰنَ الْفَجْرِ كَانَ مَشْهُوْدًا ۞

79. And pray in the small watches
Of the morning: (it would be)
An additional prayer
(Or spiritual profit)
For thee: soon will thy Lord
Raise thee to a Station
Of Praise and Glory!

٧٩ـ وَمِنَ الَّيْلِ فَتَهَجَّدْ بِهٖ
نَافِلَةً لَّكَ ۖ
عَسٰى اَنْ يَّبْعَثَكَ رَبُّكَ مَقَامًا
مَّحْمُوْدًا ۞

80. Say: "O my Lord!
Let my entry be
By the Gate of Truth
And Honour, and likewise
My exit by the Gate
Of Truth and Honour;
And grant me
From Thy Presence
An authority to aid (me)."

٨٠ـ وَقُلْ رَّبِّ اَدْخِلْنِيْ
مُدْخَلَ صِدْقٍ
وَّاَخْرِجْنِيْ مُخْرَجَ صِدْقٍ
وَّاجْعَلْ لِّيْ مِنْ لَّدُنْكَ سُلْطٰنًا
نَّصِيْرًا ۞

81. And say: "Truth has (now)
Arrived, and Falsehood perished:
For Falsehood is (by its nature)
Bound to perish."

٨١ـ وَقُلْ جَآءَ الْحَقُّ وَزَهَقَ الْبَاطِلُ
اِنَّ الْبَاطِلَ كَانَ زَهُوْقًا ۞

82. We send down (stage by stage)
In the Qur'ān that which
Is a healing and a mercy
To those who believe:
To the unjust it causes
Nothing but loss after loss.

٨٢ـ وَنُنَزِّلُ مِنَ الْقُرْاٰنِ
مَا هُوَ شِفَآءٌ وَّرَحْمَةٌ لِّلْمُؤْمِنِيْنَ ۙ
وَلَا يَزِيْدُ الظّٰلِمِيْنَ اِلَّا خَسَارًا ۞

83. Yet when We bestow
Our favours on man,

٨٣ـ وَاِذَآ اَنْعَمْنَا عَلَى الْاِنْسَانِ

He turns away and becomes
Remote on his side (instead
Of coming to Us), and when
Evil siezes him he
Gives himself up to despair!

84. Say: "Everyone acts
According to his own disposition:
But your Lord knows best
Who it is that is
Best guided on the Way."

SECTION 10.

85. They ask thee concerning
The Spirit (of inspiration).
Say: "The Spirit (cometh)
By command of my Lord:
Of knowledge it is only
A little that is communicated
To you, (O men!)"

86. If it were Our Will,
We could take away
That which We have
Sent thee by inspiration:
Then wouldst thou find
None to plead thy affair
In that matter as against Us—

87. Except for Mercy from thy
Lord:
For His Bounty is
To thee (indeed) great.

88. Say: 'If the whole
Of mankind and Jinns
Were to gather together
To produce the like
Of this Qur'ān they
Could not produce
The like thereof, even if
They backed up each other
With help and support.

89. And We have explained
To man, in this Qur'ān,
Every kind of similitude:
Yet the greater part of men

Refuse (to receive it)
Except with ingratitude!

النَّاسِ إِلَّا كُفُوراً ۞

90. They say: 'We shall not
Believe in thee, until thou
Cause a spring to gush
Forth for us from the earth,

٩٠- وَقَالُوا لَنْ نُؤْمِنَ لَكَ حَتَّى
تَفْجُرَ لَنَا مِنَ الْأَرْضِ يَنْبُوعًا ۞

91. 'Or (until) thou have
A garden of date trees
And vines, and cause rivers
To gush forth in their midst,
Carrying abundant water,

٩١- أَوْ تَكُونَ لَكَ جَنَّةٌ مِّن نَّخِيلٍ
وَعِنَبٍ فَتُفَجِّرَ الْأَنْهَارَ خِلَالَهَا تَفْجِيرًا ۞

92. 'Or thou cause the sky
To fall in pieces, as thou
Sayest (will happen), against us,
Or thou bring Allah·
And the angels before (us)
Face to face;

٩٢- أَوْ تُسْقِطَ السَّمَاءَ كَمَا
زَعَمْتَ عَلَيْنَا كِسَفًا
أَوْ تَأْتِيَ بِاللهِ وَالْمَلَائِكَةِ قَبِيلًا ۞

93. "Or thou have a house
Adorned with gold,
Or thou mount a ladder
Right into the skies.
No, we shall not even believe
In thy mounting until thou
Send down to us a book
That we can read."
Say: "Glory to my Lord!
Am I aught but a man—
A messenger?"

٩٣- أَوْ يَكُونَ لَكَ بَيْتٌ مِّن زُخْرُفٍ
أَوْ تَرْقَى فِي السَّمَاءِ
وَلَن نُّؤْمِنَ لِرُقِيِّكَ حَتَّى
تُنَزِّلَ عَلَيْنَا كِتَابًا نَّقْرَؤُهُ
قُلْ سُبْحَانَ رَبِّي
هَلْ كُنتُ إِلَّا بَشَرًا رَّسُولًا ۞

SECTION 11.

94. What kept men back
From Belief when Guidance
Came to them, was nothing
But this: they said.
"Has Allah sent a man
(Like us) to be (His) Messenger?"

٩٤- وَمَا مَنَعَ النَّاسَ أَن يُؤْمِنُوا إِذْ جَاءَهُمُ
الْهُدَى إِلَّا أَن قَالُوا
أَبَعَثَ اللهُ بَشَرًا رَّسُولًا ۞

95. Say, "If there were settled,
On earth, angels walking about
In peace and quiet, We should
Certainly have sent them
Down from the heavens
An angel for a messenger."

٩٥- قُل لَّوْ كَانَ فِي الْأَرْضِ مَلَائِكَةٌ
يَمْشُونَ مُطْمَئِنِّينَ لَنَزَّلْنَا عَلَيْهِم
مِّنَ السَّمَاءِ مَلَكًا رَّسُولًا ۞

96. Say: "Enough is Allah

٩٦- قُلْ كَفَى بِاللهِ

For a witness between me
And you: for He is
Well-acquainted with His servants,
And He sees (all things)."

شَهِيدًا بَيْنِى وَبَيْنَكُمْ
إِنَّهُ كَانَ بِعِبَادِهٖ خَبِيرًۢا بَصِيرًا ۝

97. It is he whom Allah guides,
That is on true guidance;
But he whom He leaves
Astray—for such wilt thou
Find no protector besides Him.
On the Day of Judgement
We shall gather them together,
Prone on their faces,
Blind, dumb, and deaf:
Their abode will be Hell:
Every time it shows abatement,
We shall increase for them
The fierceness of the Fire.

٩٧ ۔ وَمَنْ يَّهْدِ اللهُ فَهُوَ الْمُهْتَدِ ۚ
وَمَنْ يُّضْلِلْ فَلَنْ تَجِدَ لَهُمْ أَوْلِيَآءَ
مِنْ دُوْنِهٖ ۚ
وَنَحْشُرُهُمْ يَوْمَ الْقِيٰمَةِ عَلٰى وُجُوْهِهِمْ
عُمْيًا وَّبُكْمًا وَّصُمًّا ۗ
مَأْوٰىهُمْ جَهَنَّمُ ۗ
كُلَّمَا خَبَتْ زِدْنٰهُمْ سَعِيرًا ۝

98. That is their recompense,
Because they rejected Our Signs.
And said, "When we are reduced
To bones and broken dust,
Should we really be raised up
(To be) a new Creation?"

٩٨ ۔ ذٰلِكَ جَزَآؤُهُمْ بِأَنَّهُمْ كَفَرُوْا بِاٰيٰتِنَا
وَقَالُوْۤا ءَاِذَا كُنَّا عِظَامًا وَّرُفَاتًا
ءَاِنَّا لَمَبْعُوْثُوْنَ خَلْقًا جَدِيْدًا ۝

99. See they not that Allah,
Who created the heavens
And the earth, has power
To create the like of them
(Anew)? Only He has
Decreed a term appointed,
Of which there is no doubt.
But the unjust refuse
(To receive it) except
With ingratitude.

٩٩ ۔ أَوَلَمْ يَرَوْا أَنَّ اللهَ الَّذِى خَلَقَ السَّمٰوٰتِ
وَالْأَرْضَ قَادِرٌ عَلٰۤى أَنْ يَّخْلُقَ مِثْلَهُمْ
وَجَعَلَ لَهُمْ أَجَلًا
لَّا رَيْبَ فِيْهِ ۗ
فَأَبَى الظّٰلِمُوْنَ إِلَّا كُفُوْرًا ۝

100. Say: "If ye had
Control of the Treasures
Of the Mercy of my Lord,
Behold, ye would keep them
Back, for fear of spending
Them: for man
Is (ever) niggardly!"

١٠٠ ۔ قُلْ لَّوْ أَنْتُمْ تَمْلِكُوْنَ خَزَآئِنَ
رَحْمَةِ رَبِّيْ
إِذًا لَّأَمْسَكْتُمْ خَشْيَةَ الْإِنْفَاقِ ۗ
وَكَانَ الْإِنْسَانُ قَتُوْرًا ۞

SECTION 12

101. To Moses We did give

١٠١ ۔ وَلَقَدْ اٰتَيْنَا مُوْسٰى تِسْعَ اٰيٰتٍ

Nine Clear Signs:
Ask the Children of Israel:
When he came to them,
Pharaoh said to him:
"O Moses! I consider thee,
Indeed, to have been
Worked upon by sorcery!

بَيِّنَٰتٍ فَسْـَٔلْ بَنِىٓ إِسْرَآءِيلَ إِذْ جَآءَهُمْ
فَقَالَ لَهُ فِرْعَوْنُ إِنِّى لَأَظُنُّكَ يَٰمُوسَىٰ
مَسْحُورًا ۟

102. Moses said, "Thou knowest
Well that these things
Have been sent down by none
But the Lord of the heavens
And the earth as eye-opening
Evidence: and I consider thee
Indeed, O Pharaoh, to be
One doomed to destruction!"

١٠٢۔ قَالَ لَقَدْ عَلِمْتَ مَآ أَنزَلَ
هَٰٓؤُلَآءِ إِلَّا رَبُّ السَّمَٰوَٰتِ
وَالْأَرْضِ بَصَآئِرَ ۚ
وَإِنِّى لَأَظُنُّكَ يَٰفِرْعَوْنُ مَثْبُورًا ۟

103. So he resolved to remove them
From the face of the earth:
But We did drown him
And all who were with him.

١٠٣۔ فَأَرَادَ أَن يَسْتَفِزَّهُم مِّنَ الْأَرْضِ
فَأَغْرَقْنَٰهُ وَمَن مَّعَهُ جَمِيعًا ۟

104. And We said thereafter
To The Children of Israel,
"Dwell securely in the land
(Of promise)": but when
The second of the warnings came
To pass, We gathered you
Together in a mingled crowd

١٠٤۔ وَقُلْنَا مِنۢ بَعْدِهِۦ لِبَنِىٓ إِسْرَآءِيلَ
اسْكُنُوا الْأَرْضَ فَإِذَا جَآءَ وَعْدُ الْآخِرَةِ
جِئْنَا بِكُمْ لَفِيفًا ۟

105. We sent down the (Qur'ān)
In Truth, and in Truth
Has it descended: and We sent
Thee but to give Glad
Tidings and to warn (sinners).

١٠٥۔ وَبِالْحَقِّ أَنزَلْنَٰهُ وَبِالْحَقِّ نَزَلَ ۗ
وَمَآ أَرْسَلْنَٰكَ إِلَّا مُبَشِّرًا وَنَذِيرًا ۟

106. (It is) a Qur'ān
Which We have divided
(Into parts from time to time),
In order that thou mightest
Recite it to men
At intervals: We have
Revealed it by stages.

١٠٦۔ وَقُرْءَانًا فَرَقْنَٰهُ لِتَقْرَأَهُۥ عَلَى النَّاسِ
عَلَىٰ مُكْثٍ
وَنَزَّلْنَٰهُ تَنزِيلًا ۟

107. Say: "Whether ye believe
In it or not, it is true
That those who were given

١٠٧۔ قُلْ ءَامِنُوا بِهِۦٓ أَوْ لَا تُؤْمِنُوٓا ۚ
إِنَّ الَّذِينَ أُوتُوا الْعِلْمَ مِن قَبْلِهِۦٓ إِذَا

Knowledge beforehand, when
It is recited to them,
Fall down on their faces
In humble prostration,

108. And they say: "Glory
To our Lord! Truly
Has the promise of our Lord
Been fulfilled!"

109. They fall down on their faces
In tears, and it increases
Their (earnest) humility.

110. Say: "Call upon Allah, or
Call upon Raḥmān:
By whatever name ye call
Upon Him, (it is well):
For to Him belong
The Most Beautiful Names.
Neither speak thy Prayer aloud,
Nor speak it in a low tone,
But seek a middle course
Between."

111. Say: "Praise be to Allah,
Who begets no son,
And has no partner
In (His) dominion:
Nor (needs) He any
To protect Him from
                    humiliation:
Yea, magnify Him
For His greatness and glory!"

يُتْلَىٰ عَلَيْهِمْ
يَخِرُّونَ لِلْأَذْقَانِ سُجَّدًا ۩

١٠٨- وَيَقُولُونَ سُبْحَانَ رَبِّنَا إِن
كَانَ وَعْدُ رَبِّنَا لَمَفْعُولًا ○

١٠٩- وَيَخِرُّونَ لِلْأَذْقَانِ يَبْكُونَ وَيَزِيدُهُمْ
خُشُوعًا ○ ۩

١١٠- قُلِ ادْعُوا اللَّهَ أَوِ ادْعُوا الرَّحْمَٰنَ
أَيًّا مَا تَدْعُوا
فَلَهُ الْأَسْمَاءُ الْحُسْنَىٰ
وَلَا تَجْهَرْ بِصَلَاتِكَ وَلَا تُخَافِتْ بِهَا
وَابْتَغِ بَيْنَ ذَٰلِكَ سَبِيلًا ○

١١١- وَقُلِ الْحَمْدُ لِلَّهِ الَّذِي لَمْ يَتَّخِذْ
وَلَدًا وَلَمْ يَكُنْ لَهُ شَرِيكٌ فِي الْمُلْكِ
وَلَمْ يَكُنْ لَهُ وَلِيٌّ مِنَ الذُّلِّ
وَكَبِّرْهُ تَكْبِيرًا ○

INTRODUCTION TO SŪRA XVIII. *(Kahf)* — 110 Verses

It has been explained in the Introduction to S.xvii, how the five Sūras xvii. to xxi. develop the theme of the individual soul's spiritual history, and how they fit into the general scheme of exposition.

This particular Meccan Sūra may be called a lesson on the brevity and mystery of Life. First there is the story of the Companions of the Cave who slept therein for a long period, and yet thought they had been there only a day or less. Then there is the story of the mysterious Teacher who shows Moses how Life itself is a parable. And further there is the story of Zul-qarnain, the two-horned one, the powerful ruler of west and east, who made an iron wall to protect the weak against the strong. The parables refer to the brevity, uncertainty, and vanity of this life; to the many paradoxes in it, which can only be understood by patience and the fulness to knowledge; and to the need of guarding our spiritual gains against the incursions of evil.

Al Kahf (The Cave)

In the name of Allah, Most Gracious, Most Merciful.

1. Praise be to Allah,
   Who hath sent to His Servant
   The Book, and hath allowed
   Therein no Crookedness:

2. (He hath made it) Straight
   (And Clear) in order that
   He may warn (the godless)
   Of a terrible Punishment
   From Him, and that He
   May give Glad Tidings
   To the Believers who work
   Righteous deeds, that they
   Shall have a goodly Reward.

3. Wherein they shall
   Remain forever:

4. Further, that He may warn
   Those (also) who say,
   "Allah hath begotten a son":

5. No knowledge have they
   Of such a thing, nor
   Had their fathers. It is
   A grievous thing that issues

From their mouths as a saying.
What they say is nothing
But falsehood!

نْ يَقُولُونَ إِلَّا كَذِبًا ۝

6. ℭhou wouldst only, perchance,
Fret thyself to death,
Following after them, in grief,
If they believe not
In this Message.

فَلَعَلَّكَ بَاخِعٌ نَفْسَكَ عَلَى آثَارِهِمْ
نْ لَمْ يُؤْمِنُوا بِهَذَا الْحَدِيثِ أَسَفًا ۝

7. That which is on earth
We have made but as
A glittering show for the earth,
In order that We may test
Them — as to which of them
Are best in conduct.

إِنَّا جَعَلْنَا مَا عَلَى الْأَرْضِ
زِينَةً لَهَا لِنَبْلُوَهُمْ
أَيُّهُمْ أَحْسَنُ عَمَلًا ۝

8. Verily what is on earth
We shall make but as
Dust and dry soil
(Without growth or herbage).

وَإِنَّا لَجَاعِلُونَ مَا عَلَيْهَا
صَعِيدًا جُرُزًا ۝

9. ℭr dost thou reflect
That the Companions of the
                              Cave
And of the Inscription
Were wonders among Our Signs?

أَمْ حَسِبْتَ أَنَّ أَصْحَابَ الْكَهْفِ
وَالرَّقِيمِ كَانُوا مِنْ آيَاتِنَا عَجَبًا ۝

10. Behold, the youths betook
                              themselves
To the Cave: they said,
"Our Lord! bestow on us
Mercy from Thyself,
And dispose of our affair
For us in the right way!

إِذْ أَوَى الْفِتْيَةُ
إِلَى الْكَهْفِ فَقَالُوا رَبَّنَا آتِنَا
مِنْ لَدُنْكَ رَحْمَةً
وَهَيِّئْ لَنَا مِنْ أَمْرِنَا رَشَدًا ۝

11. Then We drew (a veil)
Over their ears, for a number
Of years, in the Cave,
(So that they heard not):

فَضَرَبْنَا عَلَى آذَانِهِمْ
فِي الْكَهْفِ سِنِينَ عَدَدًا ۝

12. Then We roused them,
In order to test which
Of the two parties was best
At calculating the term
Of years they had tarried!
SECTION 2.

ثُمَّ بَعَثْنَاهُمْ لِنَعْلَمَ
أَيُّ الْحِزْبَيْنِ أَحْصَى لِمَا لَبِثُوا أَمَدًا ۝

13. 𝔚e relate to thee their story
In truth: they were youths

نَحْنُ نَقُصُّ عَلَيْكَ نَبَأَهُمْ بِالْحَقِّ ۝

Who believed in their Lord,
And We advanced them
In guidance:

إِنَّهُمْ فِتْيَةٌ امَنُوْا بِرَبِّهِمْ وَزِدْنٰهُمْ
هُدًى ۝

14. We gave strength to their
                            hearts:
Behold, they stood up
And said: "Our Lord is
The Lord of the heavens
And of the earth: never
Shall we call upon any god
Other than Him: if we
Did, we should indeed
Have uttered an enormity!"

١٤- وَرَبَطْنَا عَلٰى قُلُوْبِهِمْ
إِذْ قَامُوْا فَقَالُوْا رَبُّنَا
رَبُّ السَّمٰوٰتِ وَالْأَرْضِ لَنْ
نَّدْعُوَا مِنْ دُوْنِهٖ إِلٰهًا لَّقَدْ
قُلْنَا إِذًا شَطَطًا ۝

15. "These our people have taken
For worship gods other
Than Him: why do they
Not bring forward an authority
Clear (and convincing)
For what they do?
Who doth more wrong
Than such as invent
A falsehood against Allah?

١٥- هٰؤُلَآءِ قَوْمُنَا اتَّخَذُوْا
مِنْ دُوْنِهٖ الِهَةً
لَوْ لَا يَأْتُوْنَ عَلَيْهِمْ بِسُلْطٰنٍ بَيِّنٍ
فَمَنْ اَظْلَمُ مِمَّنِ افْتَرٰى
عَلَى اللّٰهِ كَذِبًا ۝

16. "When ye turn away
From them and the things
They worship other than Allah
Betake yourself to the Cave:
Your Lord will shower
His mercies on you
And dispose of your affair
Towards comfort and ease."

١٦- وَإِذِ اعْتَزَلْتُمُوْهُمْ وَمَا يَعْبُدُوْنَ اِلَّا
اللّٰهَ فَأْوُۤا اِلَى الْكَهْفِ
يَنْشُرْ لَكُمْ رَبُّكُمْ مِنْ رَّحْمَتِهٖ
وَيُهَيِّئْ لَكُمْ مِنْ اَمْرِكُمْ مِّرْفَقًا ۝

17. Thou wouldst have seen
The sun, when it rose,
Declining to the right
From their Cave, and when
It set, turning away
From them to the left,
While they lay in the open
Space in the midst
Of the Cave. Such are
Among the signs of Allah:
He whom Allah guides
Is rightly guided; but he

١٧- وَتَرَى الشَّمْسَ إِذَا طَلَعَتْ
تَّزٰوَرُ عَنْ كَهْفِهِمْ ذَاتَ الْيَمِيْنِ وَإِذَا
غَرَبَتْ تَّقْرِضُهُمْ ذَاتَ الشِّمَالِ
وَهُمْ فِيْ فَجْوَةٍ مِّنْهُ
ذٰلِكَ مِنْ ايٰتِ اللّٰهِ
مَنْ يَّهْدِ اللّٰهُ فَهُوَ الْمُهْتَدِ

Whom Allah leaves to stray—
For him wilt thou find
No protector to lead him
To the Right Way.

        Section 3.

18. Thou wouldst have deemed
                them
    Awake, whilst they were asleep,
    And We turned them
    On their right and on
    Their left sides: their dog
    Stretching forth his two forelegs
    On the threshold: if thou
    Hadst come up on to them,
    Thou wouldst have certainly
    Turned back from them in flight,
    And wouldst certainly have been
    Filled with terror of them.

19. Such (being their state),
    We raised them up (from sleep).
    That they might question
    Each other. Said one of them,
    "How long have ye stayed (here)?"
    They said, "We have stayed
    (Perhaps) a day, or part
    Of a day." (At length)
    They (all) said, "Allah (alone)
    Knows best how long
    Ye have stayed here...
    Now send ye then one of you
    With this money of yours
    To the town: let him
    Find out which is the best
    Food (to be had) and bring some
    To you, that (ye may)
    Satisfy your hunger therewith:
    And let him behave
    With care and courtesy,
    And let him not inform
    Any one about you.

20. "For if they should
    Come upon you, they would
    Stone you or force you
    To return to their cult,
    And in that case ye would
    Never attain prosperity."

مَنْ يُّضْلِلْ فَلَنْ تَجِدَ لَهٗ وَلِيًّا مُّرْشِدًا ۝

١٨- وَتَحْسَبُهُمْ اَيْقَاظًا وَّهُمْ رُقُوْدٌ ۖ وَّنُقَلِّبُهُمْ ذَاتَ الْيَمِيْنِ وَذَاتَ الشِّمَالِ ۖ وَكَلْبُهُمْ بَاسِطٌ ذِرَاعَيْهِ بِالْوَصِيْدِ ۚ وَاطَّلَعْتَ عَلَيْهِمْ لَوَلَّيْتَ مِنْهُمْ فِرَارًا وَّلَمُلِئْتَ مِنْهُمْ رُعْبًا ۝

١٩- وَكَذٰلِكَ بَعَثْنَاهُمْ لِيَتَسَآءَلُوْا بَيْنَهُمْ ۚ قَالَ قَآئِلٌ مِّنْهُمْ كَمْ لَبِثْتُمْ ۗ قَالُوْا لَبِثْنَا يَوْمًا اَوْ بَعْضَ يَوْمٍ ۗ قَالُوْا رَبُّكُمْ اَعْلَمُ بِمَا لَبِثْتُمْ ۚ فَابْعَثُوْا اَحَدَكُمْ بِوَرِقِكُمْ هٰذِهٖٓ اِلَى الْمَدِيْنَةِ فَلْيَنْظُرْ اَيُّهَآ اَزْكٰى طَعَامًا فَلْيَأْتِكُمْ بِرِزْقٍ مِّنْهُ وَلْيَتَلَطَّفْ وَلَا يُشْعِرَنَّ بِكُمْ اَحَدًا ۝

٢٠- اِنَّهُمْ اِنْ يَّظْهَرُوْا عَلَيْكُمْ يَرْجُمُوْكُمْ اَوْ يُعِيْدُوْكُمْ فِيْ مِلَّتِهِمْ وَلَنْ تُفْلِحُوْٓا اِذًا اَبَدًا ۝

21. Thus did We make
Their case known to the people,
That they might know
That the promise of Allah
Is true, and that there can
Be no doubt about the Hour
Of Judgement. Behold,
They dispute among themselves
As to their affair. (Some) said,
"Construct a building over them":
Their Lord knows best
About them: those who prevailed
Over their affair said,
"Let us surely build a place
Of worship over them."

٢١- وَكَذَلِكَ أَعْثَرْنَا عَلَيْهِمْ
لِيَعْلَمُوا أَنَّ وَعْدَ اللهِ
حَقٌّ وَّأَنَّ السَّاعَةَ لَا رَيْبَ فِيهَا ۚ
إِذْ يَتَنَازَعُونَ بَيْنَهُمْ أَمْرَهُمْ فَقَالُوا
ابْنُوا عَلَيْهِمْ بُنْيَانًا ۚ رَبُّهُمْ أَعْلَمُ بِهِمْ ۚ
قَالَ الَّذِينَ غَلَبُوا عَلَى أَمْرِهِمْ
لَنَتَّخِذَنَّ عَلَيْهِمْ مَّسْجِدًا ۝

22. (Some) say they were three,
The dog being the fourth
Among them; (others) say
They were five, the dog
Being the sixth—doubtfully
Guessing at the unknown;
(Yet others) say they were
Seven, the dog being the eighth.
Say thou; "My Lord
Knoweth best their number;
It is but few that know
Their (real case)." Enter not,
Therefore, into controversies
Concerning them, except
On a matter that is clear,
Nor consult any of them
About (the affair of) the
Sleepers.

٢٢- سَيَقُولُونَ ثَلَاثَةٌ رَّابِعُهُمْ كَلْبُهُمْ ۚ
وَيَقُولُونَ خَمْسَةٌ سَادِسُهُمْ كَلْبُهُمْ
رَجْمًا بِالْغَيْبِ ۖ وَيَقُولُونَ سَبْعَةٌ
وَّثَامِنُهُمْ كَلْبُهُمْ ۚ
قُلْ رَّبِّي أَعْلَمُ بِعِدَّتِهِمْ
مَّا يَعْلَمُهُمْ إِلَّا قَلِيلٌ ۗ
فَلَا تُمَارِ فِيهِمْ
إِلَّا مِرَاءً ظَاهِرًا ۖ
وَّلَا تَسْتَفْتِ فِيهِمْ مِّنْهُمْ أَحَدًا ۝

SECTION 4.

23. Nor say of anything,
"I shall be sure to do
So and so tomorrow"—

٢٣- وَلَا تَقُولَنَّ لِشَايْءٍ
إِنِّي فَاعِلٌ ذَلِكَ غَدًا ۝

24: Without adding, "So please
Allah!"
And call thy Lord to mind
When thou forgetest, and say,
"I hope that my Lord
Will guide me ever closer
(Even) than this
To the right road."

٢٤- إِلَّا أَنْ يَشَاءَ اللهُ ۚ وَاذْكُرْ رَّبَّكَ
إِذَا نَسِيتَ وَقُلْ
عَسَى أَنْ يَهْدِيَنِ رَبِّي
لِأَقْرَبَ مِنْ هَذَا رَشَدًا ۝

25. So they stayed in their Cave
Three hundred years, and (some)
Add nine (more).

٢٥- وَلَبِثُوا فِى كَهْفِهِمْ ثَلَثَ مِائَةٍ
سِنِينَ وَازْدَادُوا تِسْعًا ۝

26. Say: "Allah knows best
How long they stayed:
With Him is (the knowledge
Of) the secrets of the heavens
And the earth: how clearly
He sees, how finely He hears
(Everything)! They have no
                    protector
Other than Him; nor does
He share His Command
With any person whatsoever.

٢٦- قُلِ اللهُ أَعْلَمُ بِمَا لَبِثُوا ۖ
لَهُ غَيْبُ السَّمٰوٰتِ وَالْأَرْضِ ۖ
أَبْصِرْ بِهِ وَأَسْمِعْ ۚ
مَا لَهُمْ مِنْ دُونِهِ مِنْ وَلِيٍّ ۖ
وَلَا يُشْرِكُ فِى حُكْمِهِ أَحَدًا ۝

27. And recite (and teach)
What has been revealed
To thee of the Book
Of thy Lord: none
Can change His Words,
And none wilt thou find
As a refuge other than Him.

٢٧- وَاتْلُ مَا أُوحِىَ
إِلَيْكَ مِنْ كِتَابِ رَبِّكَ ۖ
لَا مُبَدِّلَ لِكَلِمٰتِهِ ۚ
وَلَنْ تَجِدَ مِنْ دُونِهِ مُلْتَحَدًا ۝

28. And keep thy soul content
With those who call
On their Lord morning
And evening, seeking
His Face; and let not
Thine eyes pass beyond them,
Seeking the pomp and glitter
Of this Life; nor obey
Any whose heart We
Have permitted to neglect
The remembrance of Us,
One who follows his own
Desires, whose case has
Gone beyond all bounds.

٢٨- وَاصْبِرْ نَفْسَكَ مَعَ الَّذِينَ يَدْعُونَ
رَبَّهُمْ بِالْغَدٰوةِ وَالْعَشِىِّ
يُرِيدُونَ وَجْهَهُ ۖ وَلَا تَعْدُ عَيْنَاكَ عَنْهُمْ ۚ
تُرِيدُ زِينَةَ الْحَيٰوةِ الدُّنْيَا ۖ
وَلَا تُطِعْ مَنْ أَغْفَلْنَا قَلْبَهُ
عَنْ ذِكْرِنَا وَاتَّبَعَ
هَوٰهُ وَكَانَ أَمْرُهُ فُرُطًا ۝

29. Say, "The Truth is
From your Lord":
Let him who will,
Believe, and let him
Who will, reject (it):

For the wrongdoers We
Have prepared a Fire
Whose (smoke and flames),
Like the walls and roof

٢٩- وَقُلِ الْحَقُّ مِنْ رَبِّكُمْ ۖ
فَمَنْ شَاءَ فَلْيُؤْمِنْ
وَمَنْ شَاءَ فَلْيَكْفُرْ ۚ
إِنَّا أَعْتَدْنَا لِلظّٰلِمِينَ نَارًا
أَحَاطَ بِهِمْ سُرَادِقُهَا ۚ

Of a tent, will hem
Them in: if they implore
Relief they will be granted
Water like melted brass
That will scald their faces.
How dreadful the drink!
How uncomfortable a couch
To recline on!

وَاِنْ يَّسْتَغِيْثُوْا يُغَاثُوْا
بِمَآءٍ كَالْمُهْلِ يَشْوِى الْوُجُوْهَ
بِئْسَ الشَّرَابُ
وَسَآءَتْ مُرْتَفَقًا ۞

30. As to those who believe
And work righteousness,
Verily We shall not suffer
To perish the reward
Of any who do
A (single) righteous deed.

٣٠ ـ اِنَّ الَّذِيْنَ اٰمَنُوْا وَعَمِلُوا الصّٰلِحٰتِ
اِنَّا لَا نُضِيْعُ اَجْرَ
مَنْ اَحْسَنَ عَمَلًا ۖ

31. For them will be Gardens
Of Eternity; beneath them
Rivers will flow: they will
Be adorned therein
With bracelets of gold,
And they will wear
Green garments   of fine silk
And heavy brocade;
They will recline therein
On raised thrones.
How good the recompense!
How beautiful a couch
To recline on!

٣١ ـ اُولٰٓئِكَ لَهُمْ جَنّٰتُ عَدْنٍ
تَجْرِىْ مِنْ تَحْتِهِمُ الْاَنْهٰرُ يُحَلَّوْنَ فِيْهَا
مِنْ اَسَاوِرَ مِنْ ذَهَبٍ وَّيَلْبَسُوْنَ
ثِيَابًا خُضْرًا مِّنْ سُنْدُسٍ وَّاِسْتَبْرَقٍ
مُّتَّكِئِيْنَ فِيْهَا عَلَى الْاَرَآئِكِ
نِعْمَ الثَّوَابُ
وَحَسُنَتْ مُرْتَفَقًا ۞

SECTION 5.

32. Set forth to them
The parable of two men:
For one of them We provided
Two gardens of grapevines

And surrounded them
With date palms:
In between the two
We placed cornfields.

٣٢ ـ وَاضْرِبْ لَهُمْ مَّثَلًا رَّجُلَيْنِ
جَعَلْنَا لِاَحَدِهِمَا جَنَّتَيْنِ مِنْ اَعْنَابٍ
وَّحَفَفْنٰهُمَا بِنَخْلٍ
وَّجَعَلْنَا بَيْنَهُمَا زَرْعًا ۞

33. Each of those gardens
Brought forth its produce,
And failed not in the least
Therein: in the midst
Of them We caused
A river to flow.

٣٣ ـ كِلْتَا الْجَنَّتَيْنِ اٰتَتْ اُكُلَهَا
وَلَمْ تَظْلِمْ مِّنْهُ شَيْئًا
وَّفَجَّرْنَا خِلٰلَهُمَا نَهَرًا ۞

34. (Abundant) was the produce
This man had: he said

٣٤ ـ وَّكَانَ لَهُ ثَمَرٌ فَقَالَ

To his companion, in the course
Of a mutual argument:
"More wealth have I
Than you, and more honour
And power in (my following
Of) men."

لِصَاحِبِهٖ وَهُوَ يُحَاوِرُهٗ
اَنَا اَكْثَرُ مِنْكَ مَالًا
وَّ اَعَزُّ نَفَرًا ۟

35. He went into his garden
In a state (of mind)
Unjust to his soul:
He said, "I deem not
That this will ever perish.

٣٥- وَدَخَلَ جَنَّتَهٗ وَهُوَ ظَالِمٌ لِّنَفْسِهٖ ۚ
قَالَ مَاۤ اَظُنُّ اَنْ تَبِيْدَ هٰذِهٖۤ اَبَدًا ۟

36. "Nor do I deem
That the Hour (of Judgement)
Will (ever) come:
Even if I am brought back
To my Lord, I shall
Surely find (there)
Something better in exchange.

٣٦- وَّمَاۤ اَظُنُّ السَّاعَةَ قَائِمَةً ۙ
وَّلَئِنْ رُّدِدْتُّ اِلٰى رَبِّيْ
لَاَجِدَنَّ خَيْرًا مِّنْهَا مُنْقَلَبًا ۟

37. His companion said to him,
In the course of the argument
With him: "Dost thou deny
Him Who created thee
Out of the dust, then out of
A sperm-drop, then fashioned
Thee into a man?

٣٧- قَالَ لَهٗ صَاحِبُهٗ وَهُوَ يُحَاوِرُهٗۤ
اَكَفَرْتَ بِالَّذِيْ خَلَقَكَ مِنْ تُرَابٍ
ثُمَّ مِنْ
نُّطْفَةٍ ثُمَّ سَوّٰىكَ رَجُلًا ۟

38. "But (I think) for my part
That He is Allah,
My Lord, and none shall I
Associate with my Lord.

٣٨- لٰكِنَّا۟ هُوَ اللّٰهُ
رَبِّيْ وَلَاۤ اُشْرِكُ بِرَبِّيْۤ اَحَدًا ۟

39. "Why didst thou not,
As thou wentest into
Thy garden, say: 'Allah's Will
(Be done)! There is no power
But with Allah!' If thou
Dost see me less than
Thee in wealth and sons,

٣٩- وَلَوْلَاۤ اِذْ دَخَلْتَ جَنَّتَكَ قُلْتَ مَا
شَاۤءَ اللّٰهُ ۙ لَا قُوَّةَ اِلَّا بِاللّٰهِ ۚ اِنْ
تَرَنِ اَنَا۟ اَقَلَّ مِنْكَ مَالًا وَّوَلَدًا ۟

40. "It may be that my Lord
Will give me something
Better than thy garden,
And that He will send
On thy garden thunderbolts
(By way of reckoning)

٤٠- فَعَسٰى رَبِّيْۤ اَنْ يُّؤْتِيَنِ
خَيْرًا مِّنْ جَنَّتِكَ وَيُرْسِلَ
عَلَيْهَا حُسْبَانًا

From heaven, making it
(But) slippery sand!

قِمْنَ السَّمَآءِ فَتُصْبِحَ صَعِيدًا زَلَقًا ۝

41. "Or the water of the garden
Will run off underground
So that thou wilt never
Be able to find it.

۝ اَوْ يُصْبِحَ مَآؤُهَا غَوْرًا
فَلَنْ تَسْتَطِيعَ لَهٗ طَلَبًا ۝

42. So his fruits (and enjoyment)
Were encompassed (with ruin),
And he remained twisting
And turning his hands
Over what he had spent
On his property, which had
(Now) tumbled to pieces
To its very foundations,
And he could only say,
"Woe is me! Would I had
Never ascribed partners
To my Lord and Cherisher!"

۝ وَاُحِيطَ بِثَمَرِهٖ
فَاَصْبَحَ يُقَلِّبُ كَفَّيْهِ
عَلٰى مَآ اَنْفَقَ فِيهَا
وَهِيَ خَاوِيَةٌ عَلٰى عُرُوشِهَا
وَيَقُوْلُ يٰلَيْتَنِيْ
لَمْ اُشْرِكْ بِرَبِّيْ اَحَدًا ۝

43. Nor had he numbers
To help him against Allah,
Nor was he able
To deliver himself.

۝ وَلَمْ تَكُنْ لَّهٗ فِئَةٌ يَّنْصُرُوْنَهٗ مِنْ
دُوْنِ اللّٰهِ وَمَا كَانَ مُنْتَصِرًا ۝

44. There, the (only) protection comes
From Allah, the True One.
He is the Best to reward,
And the Best to give success.

۝ هُنَالِكَ الْوَلَايَةُ لِلّٰهِ الْحَقِّ
هُوَ خَيْرٌ ثَوَابًا وَّخَيْرٌ عُقْبًا ۝

SECTION 6.

45. Set forth to them
The similitude of the life
Of this world: it is like
The rain which We send
Down from the skies:
The earth's vegetation absorbs it.
But soon it becomes
Dry stubble, which the winds
Do scatter: it is (only) Allah
Who prevails over all things.

۝ وَاضْرِبْ لَهُمْ مَّثَلَ الْحَيٰوةِ الدُّنْيَا
كَمَآءٍ اَنْزَلْنٰهُ مِنَ السَّمَآءِ
فَاخْتَلَطَ بِهٖ نَبَاتُ الْاَرْضِ
فَاَصْبَحَ هَشِيْمًا تَذْرُوْهُ الرِّيٰحُ
وَكَانَ اللّٰهُ عَلٰى كُلِّ شَيْءٍ مُّقْتَدِرًا ۝

46. Wealth and sons are allurements
Of the life of this world:
But the things that endure,
Good Deeds, are best
In the sight of thy Lord,

۝ اَلْمَالُ وَالْبَنُوْنَ زِيْنَةُ الْحَيٰوةِ الدُّنْيَا
وَالْبٰقِيٰتُ الصّٰلِحٰتُ خَيْرٌ

As rewards, and best
As (the foundation for) hopes.

عِنْدَ رَبِّكَ ثَوَابًا وَّخَيْرٌ أَمَلًا ۟

47. One Day We shall
Remove the mountains, and thou
Wilt see the earth
As a level stretch,
And We shall gather them,
All together, nor shall We
Leave out any one of them.

۴۷- وَيَوْمَ نُسَيِّرُ الْجِبَالَ وَ
تَرَى الْأَرْضَ بَارِزَةً ۙ
وَّحَشَرْنٰهُمْ فَلَمْ نُغَادِرْ مِنْهُمْ أَحَدًا ۟

48. And they will be marshalled
Before thy Lord in ranks,
(With the announcement),
"Now have ye come to Us
(Bare) as We created you
First: aye, ye thought
We shall not fulfil
The appointment made to you
To meet (Us)!"·

۴۸- وَعُرِضُوْا عَلٰى رَبِّكَ صَفًّا ۙ
لَقَدْ جِئْتُمُوْنَا كَمَا خَلَقْنٰكُمْ
أَوَّلَ مَرَّةٍ ۢ بَلْ زَعَمْتُمْ
أَلَّنْ نَّجْعَلَ لَكُمْ مَّوْعِدًا ۟

49. And the Book (of Deeds)
Will be placed (before you);
And thou wilt see
The sinful in great terror
Because of what is (recorded)
Therein; they will say,
"Ah! woe to us!
What a book is this!
It leaves out nothing
Small or great, but
Takes account thereof!"
They will find all that they
Did, placed before them:
And not one will thy Lord
Treat with injustice.

۴۹- وَوُضِعَ الْكِتٰبُ
فَتَرَى الْمُجْرِمِيْنَ مُشْفِقِيْنَ
مِمَّا فِيْهِ وَيَقُوْلُوْنَ يٰوَيْلَتَنَا
مَالِ هٰذَا الْكِتٰبِ لَا يُغَادِرُ
صَغِيْرَةً وَّلَا كَبِيْرَةً
إِلَّا أَحْصٰهَا ۚ
وَوَجَدُوْا مَا عَمِلُوْا حَاضِرًا ۗ
وَلَا يَظْلِمُ رَبُّكَ أَحَدًا ۟

SECTION 7.

50. Behold! We said
To the angels, "Bow down
To Adam": they bowed down
Except Iblīs. He was
One of the Jinns,   and he
Broke the Command
Of his Lord.
Will ye then take him
And his progeny   as protectors
Rather than Me? And they

۵۰- وَإِذْ قُلْنَا لِلْمَلٰٓئِكَةِ اسْجُدُوْا
لِاٰدَمَ فَسَجَدُوْا إِلَّا إِبْلِيْسَ ۗ كَانَ
مِنَ الْجِنِّ فَفَسَقَ عَنْ أَمْرِ رَبِّهِ ۗ
أَفَتَتَّخِذُوْنَهُ وَذُرِّيَّتَهُ أَوْلِيَآءَ
مِنْ دُوْنِيْ وَهُمْ لَكُمْ عَدُوٌّ ۗ

Are enemies to you!
Evil would be the exchange
For the wrongdoers!

بِئْسَ لِلظّٰلِمِيْنَ بَدَلًا ۰

51. I called them not
To witness the creation
Of the heavens and the earth,
Nor (even) their own creation:
Nor is it for Me
To take as helpers
Such as lead (men) astray!

۵۱- مَآ اَشْهَدْتُّهُمْ خَلْقَ
السَّمٰوٰتِ وَالْاَرْضِ وَلَا خَلْقَ اَنْفُسِهِمْ ۪
وَمَا كُنْتُ مُتَّخِذَ الْمُضِلِّيْنَ عَضُدًا۰

52. One Day He will say,
"Call on those whom ye
Thought to be My partners,"
And they will call on them,
But they will not listen
To them; and We shall
Make for them a place
Of common perdition.

۵۲- وَيَوْمَ يَقُوْلُ نَادُوْا
شُرَكَآءِيَ الَّذِيْنَ زَعَمْتُمْ فَدَعَوْهُمْ
فَلَمْ يَسْتَجِيْبُوْا لَهُمْ
وَجَعَلْنَا بَيْنَهُمْ مَّوْبِقًا۰

53. And the Sinful shall see
The Fire and apprehend
That they have to fall
Therein: no means will they
Find to turn away therefrom.

۵۳- وَرَاَ الْمُجْرِمُوْنَ النَّارَ فَظَنُّوْۤا اَنَّهُمْ
مُّوَاقِعُوْهَا
وَلَمْ يَجِدُوْا عَنْهَا مَصْرِفًا ۪۰

SECTION 8.

54. We have explained
In detail in this Qur'ān,
For the benefit of mankind,
Every kind of similitude:
But man is, in most things,
Contentious.

۵۴- وَلَقَدْ صَرَّفْنَا فِيْ هٰذَا الْقُرْاٰنِ
لِلنَّاسِ مِنْ كُلِّ مَثَلٍ ۪
وَكَانَ الْاِنْسَانُ اَكْثَرَ شَيْءٍ جَدَلًا۰

55. And what is there
To keep back men
From believing, now that
Guidance has come to them,
Nor from praying for forgiveness
From their Lord, but that
(They ask that) the ways
Of the ancients be repeated
With them, or the Wrath
Be brought to them
Face to face?

۵۵- وَمَا مَنَعَ النَّاسَ اَنْ
يُّؤْمِنُوْۤا اِذْ جَآءَهُمُ الْهُدٰى
وَيَسْتَغْفِرُوْا رَبَّهُمْ اِلَّاۤ اَنْ
تَأْتِيَهُمْ سُنَّةُ الْاَوَّلِيْنَ
اَوْ يَأْتِيَهُمُ الْعَذَابُ قُبُلًا۰

56. We only send the Messengers
To give glad tidings

۵۶- وَمَا نُرْسِلُ الْمُرْسَلِيْنَ اِلَّا مُبَشِّرِيْنَ

And to give warnings:
But the Unbelievers dispute
With vain argument, in order
Therewith to weaken the truth,
And they treat My Signs
As a jest, as also the fact
That they are warned!

57. And who doth more wrong
Than one who is reminded
Of the Signs of his Lord,
But turns away from them,
Forgetting the (deeds) which his
                              hands
Have sent forth? Verily We
Have set veils over their hearts
Lest they should understand this,
And over their ears, deafness.
If thou callest them
To guidance, even then
Will they never accept guidance.

58. But your Lord is Most Forgiving,
Full of Mercy. If He were
To call them (at once) to account
For what they have earned,
Then surely He would
Have hastened their Punishment:
But they have their appointed
Time, beyond which   they
Will find no refuge.

59. Such were the populations
We destroyed when they
Committed iniquities; but
We fixed an appointed time
For their destruction.
      SECTION 9.

60. Behold, Moses said
To his attendant, "I will not
Give up until I reach
The junction of the two
Seas or (until) I spend
Years and years in travel."

وَمُنذِرِينَ ۚ وَيُجَٰدِلُ ٱلَّذِينَ كَفَرُوا۟
بِٱلْبَٰطِلِ لِيُدْحِضُوا۟ بِهِ ٱلْحَقَّ
وَٱتَّخَذُوٓا۟ ءَايَٰتِى
وَمَآ أُنذِرُوا۟ هُزُوًا ۞

٥٧ ـ وَمَنْ أَظْلَمُ مِمَّن ذُكِّرَ
بِـَٔايَٰتِ رَبِّهِۦ فَأَعْرَضَ عَنْهَا
وَنَسِىَ مَا قَدَّمَتْ يَدَاهُ
إِنَّا جَعَلْنَا عَلَىٰ قُلُوبِهِمْ
أَكِنَّةً أَن يَفْقَهُوهُ وَفِىٓ ءَاذَانِهِمْ وَقْرًا
وَإِن تَدْعُهُمْ إِلَى ٱلْهُدَىٰ
فَلَن يَهْتَدُوٓا۟ إِذًا أَبَدًا ۞

٥٨ ـ وَرَبُّكَ ٱلْغَفُورُ ذُو ٱلرَّحْمَةِ ۖ لَوْ
يُؤَاخِذُهُم بِمَا كَسَبُوا۟ لَعَجَّلَ لَهُمُ ٱلْعَذَابَ ۚ
بَل لَّهُم مَّوْعِدٌ
لَّن يَجِدُوا۟ مِن دُونِهِۦ مَوْئِلًا ۞

٥٩ ـ وَتِلْكَ ٱلْقُرَىٰٓ أَهْلَكْنَٰهُمْ لَمَّا
ظَلَمُوا۟ وَجَعَلْنَا لِمَهْلِكِهِم مَّوْعِدًا ۞ ع

٦٠ ـ وَإِذْ قَالَ مُوسَىٰ لِفَتَىٰهُ لَآ
أَبْرَحُ حَتَّىٰٓ أَبْلُغَ مَجْمَعَ
ٱلْبَحْرَيْنِ أَوْ أَمْضِىَ حُقُبًا ۞

61. But when they reached
The Junction,   they forgot
(About) their Fish,   which took
Its course through the sea
(Straight) as in a tunnel.

٦١- فَلَمَّا بَلَغَا مَجْمَعَ بَيْنِهِمَا نَسِيَا حُوْتَهُمَا
فَاتَّخَذَ سَبِيلَهُ فِى الْبَحْرِ سَرَبًا ۟

62. When they had passed on
(Some distance). Moses said
To his attendant: "Bring us
Our early meal; truly
We have suffered much fatigue
At this (stage of) our journey."

٦٢- فَلَمَّا جَاوَزَا قَالَ
لِفَتَٰهُ اٰتِنَا غَدَآءَنَا لَقَدْ
لَقِينَا مِنْ سَفَرِنَا هٰذَا نَصَبًا ۟

63. He replied: "Sawest thou
(What happened) when we
Betook ourselves to the rock?
I did indeed forget
(About) the Fish: none but
Satan made me forget
To tell (you) about it:
It took its course through
The sea in a marvellous way!"

٦٣- قَالَ اَرَءَيْتَ اِذْ اَوَيْنَا
اِلَى الصَّخْرَةِ فَاِنِّى نَسِيتُ الْحُوْتَ ۚ
وَمَا اَنْسَٰنِيهُ اِلَّا الشَّيْطٰنُ اَنْ اَذْكُرَهُ ۚ
وَاتَّخَذَ سَبِيلَهُ فِى الْبَحْرِ ۖ عَجَبًا ۟

64. Moses said: "That was what
We were seeking after:"
So they went back
On their footsteps, following
(The path they had come).

٦٤- قَالَ ذٰلِكَ مَا كُنَّا نَبْغِ ۖ فَارْتَدَّا
عَلٰى اٰثَارِهِمَا قَصَصًا ۟

65. So they found one
Of Our servants,
On whom We had bestowed
Mercy from Ourselves
And whom We had taught
Knowledge from Our own
Presence.

٦٥- فَوَجَدَا عَبْدًا مِّنْ عِبَادِنَآ
اٰتَيْنٰهُ رَحْمَةً مِّنْ عِنْدِنَا
وَعَلَّمْنٰهُ مِنْ لَّدُنَّا عِلْمًا ۟

66. Moses said to him:
"May I follow thee,
On the footing that
Thou teach me something
Of the (Higher) Truth
Which thou hast been taught?"

٦٦- قَالَ لَهُ مُوْسٰى هَلْ اَتَّبِعُكَ
عَلٰى اَنْ تُعَلِّمَنِ
مِمَّا عُلِّمْتَ رُشْدًا ۟

67. (The other) said: "Verily
Thou wilt not be able
To have patience with me!

٦٧- قَالَ اِنَّكَ لَنْ تَسْتَطِيعَ مَعِىَ
صَبْرًا ۟

68. "And how canst thou

٦٨- وَكَيْفَ تَصْبِرُ

Have patience about things
About which thy understanding
Is not complete?"

على مَا لَمْ تُحِطْ بِهِ خُبْرًا ۞

69. Moses said: "Thou wilt
Find me, if Allah so will,
(Truly) patient: nor shall I
Disobey thee in aught."

٦٩- قَالَ سَتَجِدُنِيْ إِنْ شَاءَ اللهُ
صَابِرًا وَّلَا أَعْصِيْ لَكَ أَمْرًا ۞

70. The other said: "If then
Thou wouldst follow me,
Ask me no questions
About anything until I
Myself speak to thee
Concerning it."

٧٠- قَالَ فَإِنِ اتَّبَعْتَنِيْ
فَلَا تَسْئَلْنِيْ عَنْ شَيْءٍ حَتّٰى
أُحْدِثَ لَكَ مِنْهُ ذِكْرًا ۞

SECTION 10.

71. So they both proceeded:
Until, when they were
In the boat, he scuttled it.
Said Moses: "Hast thou
Scuttled it in order
To drown those in it?
Truly a strange thing
Hast thou done!"

٧١- فَانْطَلَقَا حَتّٰى إِذَا
رَكِبَا فِي السَّفِيْنَةِ خَرَقَهَا
قَالَ أَخَرَقْتَهَا لِتُغْرِقَ أَهْلَهَا
لَقَدْ جِئْتَ شَيْئًا إِمْرًا ۞

72. He answered: "Did I not
Tell thee that thou canst
Have no patience with me?"

٧٢- قَالَ أَلَمْ أَقُلْ إِنَّكَ لَنْ تَسْتَطِيْعَ
مَعِيَ صَبْرًا ۞

73. Moses said: "Rebuke me not
For forgetting, nor grieve me
By raising difficulties
In my case."

٧٣- قَالَ لَا تُؤَاخِذْنِيْ بِمَا نَسِيْتُ وَ
لَا تُرْهِقْنِيْ مِنْ أَمْرِيْ عُسْرًا ۞

74. Then they proceeded:
Until, when they met
A young man, he slew him.
Moses said: "Hast thou
Slain an innocent person
Who had slain none?
Truly a foul (unheard-of) thing
Hast thou done!"

٧٤- فَانْطَلَقَا حَتّٰى إِذَا لَقِيَا
غُلَامًا فَقَتَلَهُ قَالَ
أَقَتَلْتَ نَفْسًا زَكِيَّةً بِغَيْرِ نَفْسٍ
لَقَدْ جِئْتَ شَيْئًا نُكْرًا ۞

75. He answered: "Did I not
Tell thee that thou canst
Have no patience with me?"

٧٥- قَالَ أَلَمْ أَقُلْ لَكَ إِنَّكَ لَنْ
تَسْتَطِيْعَ مَعِيَ صَبْرًا ۞

76. (Moses) said: "If ever I

٧٦- قَالَ إِنْ سَأَلْتُكَ

Ask thee about anything
After this, keep me not
In thy company: then wouldst
Thou have received (full) excuse
From my side."

77. Then they proceeded:
Until, when they came
To the inhabitants of a town,
They asked them for food,
But they refused them
Hospitality. They found there
A wall on the point of
Falling down, but he
Set it up straight.
(Moses) said: "If thou
Hadst wished, surely thou
Couldst have exacted some
Recompense for it!"

78. He answered: "This is
The parting between me
And thee: now will I
Tell thee the interpretation
Of (those things) over which
Thou wast unable
To hold patience.

79. As for the boat,
It belonged to certain
Men in dire want:
They plied on the water:
I but wished to render it
Unserviceable, for there was
After them a certain king
Who seized on every boat
By force.

80. "As for the youth,
His parents were people
Of Faith, and we feared
That he would grieve them
By obstinate rebellion
And ingratitude (to Allah and
man).

81. "So we desired that
Their Lord would give them
In exchange (a son)

Better in purity (of conduct)
And closer in affection.

خَيْرًا مِّنْهُ زَكٰوةً وَّ اَقْرَبَ رُحْمًا ۟

82. "As for the wall,
It belonged to two youths,
Orphans, in the Town;
There was, beneath it,
A buried treasure, to which
They were entitled: their father
Had been a righteous man:
So thy Lord desired that
They should attain their age
Of full strength and get out
Their treasure—a mercy
(And favour) from thy Lord.
I did it not of my own
Accord. Such is the interpretation
Of (those things) over which
Thou wast unable
To hold patience."

٨٢- وَ اَمَّا الْجِدَارُ فَكَانَ لِغُلٰمَيْنِ
يَتِيْمَيْنِ فِى الْمَدِيْنَةِ وَكَانَ تَحْتَهٗ
كَنْزٌ لَّهُمَا وَكَانَ اَبُوْهُمَا صَالِحًا ۚ
فَاَرَادَ رَبُّكَ اَنْ يَّبْلُغَا
اَشُدَّهُمَا وَيَسْتَخْرِجَا كَنْزَهُمَا ۖ
رَحْمَةً مِّنْ رَّبِّكَ ۚ
وَمَا فَعَلْتُهٗ عَنْ اَمْرِىْ ۚ ذٰلِكَ تَاْوِيْلُ
مَا لَمْ تَسْطِعْ عَّلَيْهِ صَبْرًا ۟

SECTION 11.

83. They ask thee concerning
Dhu al Qarnayn.   Say,
"I will rehearse to you
Something of his story."

٨٣- وَيَسْـَٔلُوْنَكَ عَنْ ذِى الْقَرْنَيْنِ ۚ قُلْ
سَاَتْلُوْا عَلَيْكُمْ مِّنْهُ ذِكْرًا ۟

84. Verily We established his power
On earth, and We gave him
The ways and the means
To all ends.

٨٤- اِنَّا مَكَّنَّا لَهٗ فِى الْاَرْضِ وَ اٰتَيْنٰهُ
مِنْ كُلِّ شَىْءٍ سَبَبًا ۟

85. One (such) way he followed,

٨٥- فَاَتْبَعَ سَبَبًا ۟

86. Until, when he reached
The setting of the sun,
He found it set
In a spring of murky water:
Near it he found a People:
We said: "O Dhu al Qarnayn!
(Thou hast authority,) either
To punish them, or
To treat them with kindness."

٨٦- حَتّٰى إِذَا بَلَغَ مَغْرِبَ الشَّمْسِ
وَجَدَهَا تَغْرُبُ فِىْ عَيْنٍ حَمِئَةٍ
وَّوَجَدَ عِنْدَهَا قَوْمًا ۖ قُلْنَا يٰذَا الْقَرْنَيْنِ
اِمَّا اَنْ تُعَذِّبَ وَ اِمَّا اَنْ تَتَّخِذَ فِيْهِمْ
حُسْنًا ۟

87. He said: "Whoever doth wrong,
Him shall we punish; then
Shall he be sent back
To his Lord; and He will

٨٧- قَالَ اَمَّا مَنْ ظَلَمَ فَسَوْفَ نُعَذِّبُهٗ
ثُمَّ يُرَدُّ اِلٰى رَبِّهٖ

Punish him with a punishment
Unheard-of (before).

فَيُعَذِّبُهُ عَذَابًا نُّكْرًا ۟

88. "But whoever believes,
And works righteousness
He shall have a goodly
Reward, and easy will be
His task as we order it
By our command."

٨٨- وَأَمَّا مَنْ اٰمَنَ وَعَمِلَ صَالِحًا فَلَهُ جَزَآءَ الْحُسْنٰى ۚ وَسَنَقُوْلُ لَهُ مِنْ أَمْرِنَا يُسْرًا ۟

89. Then followed he (another) way.

٨٩- ثُمَّ أَتْبَعَ سَبَبًا ۟

90. Until, when he came
To the rising of the sun,
He found it rising
On a people for whom
We had provided
No covering protection
Against the sun.

٩٠- حَتّٰى إِذَا بَلَغَ مَطْلِعَ الشَّمْسِ وَجَدَهَا تَطْلُعُ عَلٰى قَوْمٍ لَّمْ نَجْعَلْ لَّهُمْ مِّنْ دُوْنِهَا سِتْرًا ۟

91. (He left them) as they were:
We completely understood
What was before him.

٩١- كَذٰلِكَ ۚ وَقَدْ أَحَطْنَا بِمَا لَدَيْهِ خُبْرًا ۟

92. Then followed he (another) way,

٩٢- ثُمَّ أَتْبَعَ سَبَبًا ۟

93. Until, when he reached
(A tract) between two
mountains,
He found, beneath them, a people
Who scarcely understood a
word.

٩٣- حَتّٰى إِذَا بَلَغَ بَيْنَ السَّدَّيْنِ وَجَدَ مِنْ دُوْنِهِمَا قَوْمًا ۟ لَّا يَكَادُوْنَ يَفْقَهُوْنَ قَوْلًا ۟

94. They said: "O Dhu al Qarnayn!
The Gog and Magog (people)
Do great mischief on earth:
Shall we then render thee
Tribute in order that
Thou mightest erect a barrier
Between us and them?

٩٤- قَالُوْا يٰذَا الْقَرْنَيْنِ إِنَّ يَأْجُوْجَ وَمَأْجُوْجَ مُفْسِدُوْنَ فِى الْأَرْضِ فَهَلْ نَجْعَلُ لَكَ خَرْجًا عَلٰى أَنْ تَجْعَلَ بَيْنَنَا وَبَيْنَهُمْ سَدًّا ۟

95. He said: "(The power) in which
My Lord had established me
Is better (than tribute):
Help me therefore with strength
(And labour): I will
Erect a stronger barrier
Between you and them:

٩٥- قَالَ مَا مَكَّنِّىْ فِيْهِ رَبِّىْ خَيْرٌ فَأَعِيْنُوْنِىْ بِقُوَّةٍ أَجْعَلْ بَيْنَكُمْ وَبَيْنَهُمْ رَدْمًا ۟

96. "Bring me blocks of iron."
    At length, when he had
    Filled up the space between
    The two steep mountainsides,
    He said, "Blow (with your
                   bellows)"
    Then, when he had made
    It (red) as fire, he said:
    "Bring me, that I may
    Pour over it, molten lead."

97. Thus were they made
    Powerless to scale it
    Or to dig through it.

98. He said: "This is
    A mercy from my Lord:
    But when the promise
    Of my Lord comes to pass,
    He will make it into dust;
    And the promise of
    My Lord is true."

99. On that day We shall
    Leave them to surge
    Like waves on one another;
    The trumpet will be blown,
    And We shall collect them
    All together.

100. And We shall present
    Hell that day for Unbelievers
    To see, all spread out—

101. (Unbelievers) whose eyes
    Had been under a veil
    From Remembrance of Me,
    And who had been unable
    Even to hear.

SECTION 12.

102. Do the Unbelievers think
    That they can take
    My servants as protectors
    Besides Me? Verily We
    Have prepared Hell
    For the Unbelievers
    For (their) entertainment.

103. Say: "Shall we tell you
Of those who lose most
In respect of their deeds?—"

١٠٣- قُلْ هَلْ نُنَبِّئُكُمْ بِالْأَخْسَرِينَ
أَعْمَالًا ۚ

104. "Those whose efforts have
Been wasted in this life,
While they thought that
They were acquiring good
By their works?"

١٠٤- اَلَّذِينَ ضَلَّ سَعْيُهُمْ فِي الْحَيٰوةِ
الدُّنْيَا وَهُمْ يَحْسَبُونَ أَنَّهُمْ يُحْسِنُونَ
صُنْعًا ۝

105. They are those who deny
The Signs of their Lord
And the fact of their
Having to meet Him
(In the Hereafter): vain
Will be their works,
Nor shall We, on the Day
Of Judgement, give them
Any Weight.

١٠٥- أُولٰٓئِكَ الَّذِينَ كَفَرُوا بِاٰيٰتِ رَبِّهِمْ
وَلِقَآئِهِ
فَحَبِطَتْ أَعْمَالُهُمْ
فَلَا نُقِيمُ لَهُمْ يَوْمَ الْقِيٰمَةِ وَزْنًا ۝

106. That is their reward,
Hell; because they rejected
Faith, and took My Signs
And My Messengers
By way of jest.

١٠٦- ذٰلِكَ جَزَآؤُهُمْ جَهَنَّمُ بِمَا
كَفَرُوا وَاتَّخَذُوٓا اٰيٰتِي وَرُسُلِي هُزُوًا ۝

107. As to those who believe
And work righteous deeds,
They have, for their
                    entertainment,
The Gardens of Paradise,

١٠٧- إِنَّ الَّذِينَ اٰمَنُوا وَعَمِلُوا الصّٰلِحٰتِ
كَانَتْ لَهُمْ جَنّٰتُ الْفِرْدَوْسِ نُزُلًا ۝

108. Wherein they shall dwell
(For aye): no change
Will they wish for themselves.

١٠٨- خٰلِدِينَ فِيهَا لَا يَبْغُونَ عَنْهَا
حِوَلًا ۝

109. Say: "If the ocean were
Ink (wherewith to write out)
The words of my Lord,
Sooner would the ocean be
Exhausted than would the words
Of my Lord, even if we
Added another ocean
Like it, for its aid."

١٠٩- قُلْ لَوْ كَانَ الْبَحْرُ مِدَادًا لِّكَلِمٰتِ
رَبِّي لَنَفِدَ الْبَحْرُ
قَبْلَ أَنْ تَنْفَدَ كَلِمٰتُ رَبِّي
وَلَوْ جِئْنَا بِمِثْلِهِ مَدَدًا ۝

110. Say: "I am but a man
Like yourselves, (but)
The inspiration has come
To me, that your God is
One God: whoever expects
To meet his Lord, let him
Work righteousness, and,
In the worship of his Lord,
Admit no one as partner."

١١٠۔ قُلْ إِنَّمَآ أَنَا بَشَرٌ مِّثْلُكُمْ
يُوحَىٰ إِلَيَّ أَنَّمَآ إِلَٰهُكُمْ إِلَٰهٌ
وَاحِدٌ ۖ فَمَن كَانَ يَرْجُوا لِقَآءَ رَبِّهِ
فَلْيَعْمَلْ عَمَلًا صَالِحًا
وَلَا يُشْرِكْ بِعِبَادَةِ رَبِّهِ أَحَدًا ۞

INTRODUCTION TO SURA XIX. *(Maryam)* — 98 Verses

   The spiritual growth of man as an individual soul having been explained in S.xvii: as beginning with the first principles of moral conduct and in S.xviii. as being dependent upon our realisation of the brevity and mystery of this life and the true use of power as in the story of Zul qarnain, we now pass on to the story of individual Messengers of God in their personal relations with their environment,— Yahyā with his father Zakarīya Jesus with his mother Mary, Abraham with his unbelieving father, Moses with his brother Aaron, Ismā'īl with his family, and Idrīs in the high station to which he was called. Seeing how these great ones fitted into the scheme of life, man is condemend for his what of faith, or for degrading his faith to superstition, and warned of the Hereafter.

   In chronology, it was revealed before the first resort of the batch of Muslims to Abyssinia say seven years before the Hijrat.

Maryam (Mary)

In the name of Allah, Most Gracious, Most Merciful.

1. Kaf Hā Yā 'Ayn Sād.

2. (This is) a recital
Of the Mercy of thy Lord
To His Servant Zakarīya.

3. Behold! he cried
To his Lord in secret,

4. Praying: "O my Lord!
Infirm indeed are my bones,
And the hair of my head
Doth glisten with grey:
But never am I unblest,
O my Lord, in my prayer
To Thee!

5. "Now I fear (what)
My relatives (and colleagues)
(Will do) after me:
But my wife is barren:
So give me an heir
As from Thyself—

6. "(One that) will (truly)

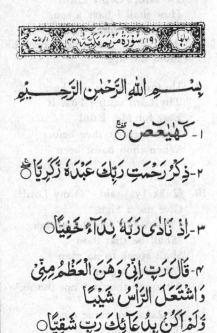

Represent me, and represent
The posterity of Jacob;
And make him, O my Lord!
One with whom Thou art
Well-pleased!"

7. (His prayer was answered):
"O Zakariyyā We give thee
Good news of a son:
His name shall be Yaḥyā:
On none by that name
Have We conferred distinction
before."

8. He said: "O my Lord!
How shall I have a son,
When my wife is barren
And I have grown quite decrepit
From old age?"

9. He said: "So (it will be):
Thy Lord saith, 'That is
Easy for Me: I did
Indeed create thee before,
When thou hadst been
nothing!'"

10. (Zakarīya) said: "O my Lord!
Give me a Sign."
"Thy Sign," was the answer,
"Shall be that thou
Shalt speak to no man
For three nights,
Although thou art not dumb."

11. So Zakarīya came out
To his people
From his chamber:
He told them by signs
To celebrate Allah's praises
In the morning
And in the evening.

12. (To his son came the
command):
"O Yaḥyā! take hold
Of the Book with might":

And We gave him Wisdom
Even as a youth.

وَاٰتَيْنٰهُ الْحُكْمَ صَبِيًّا ۟

13. And pity (for all creatures)
As from Us, and purity:
He was devout,

١٣- وَّ حَنَانًا مِّنْ لَّدُنَّا وَزَكٰوةً ۖ
وَكَانَ تَقِيًّا ۟

14. And kind to his parents,
And he was not overbearing
Or rebellious.

١٤- وَّبَرًّا بِوَالِدَيْهِ
وَلَمْ يَكُنْ جَبَّارًا عَصِيًّا ۟

15. So Peace on him
The day he was born
The day that he dies,
And the day that he
Will be raised up
To life (again)!

١٥- وَسَلٰمٌ عَلَيْهِ يَوْمَ وُلِدَ
وَيَوْمَ يَمُوْتُ
وَيَوْمَ يُبْعَثُ حَيًّا ۟

SECTION 2.

16. Relate in the Book
(The story of) Mary,
When she withdrew
From her family
To a place in the East.

١٦- وَاذْكُرْ فِى الْكِتٰبِ مَرْيَمَ ۘ
اِذِ انْتَبَذَتْ مِنْ اَهْلِهَا مَكَانًا شَرْقِيًّا ۟

17. She placed a screen
(To screen herself) from them;
Then We sent to her
Our angel, and he appeared
Before her as a man
In all respects.

١٧- فَاتَّخَذَتْ مِنْ دُوْنِهِمْ حِجَابًا ۖ
فَاَرْسَلْنَآ اِلَيْهَا رُوْحَنَا
فَتَمَثَّلَ لَهَا بَشَرًا سَوِيًّا ۟

18. She said: "I seek refuge
From thee to (Allah)
Most Gracious: (come not near)
If thou dost fear Allah."

١٨- قَالَتْ اِنِّيْٓ اَعُوْذُ
بِالرَّحْمٰنِ مِنْكَ اِنْ كُنْتَ تَقِيًّا ۟

19. He said: "Nay, I am only
A messenger from thy Lord,
(To announce) to thee
The gift of a holy son."

١٩- قَالَ اِنَّمَآ اَنَا رَسُوْلُ رَبِّكِ ۖ
لِاَهَبَ لَكِ غُلٰمًا زَكِيًّا ۟

20. She said: "How shall I
Have a son, seeing that
No man has touched me,
And I am not unchaste?"

٢٠- قَالَتْ اَنّٰى يَكُوْنُ لِيْ غُلٰمٌ
وَّلَمْ يَمْسَسْنِيْ بَشَرٌ وَّلَمْ اَكُ بَغِيًّا ۟

21. He said: "So (it will be):

٢١- قَالَ كَذٰلِكِ ۚ قَالَ رَبُّكِ

Thy Lord saith, 'That is
Easy for Me: and (We
Wish) to appoint him
As a Sign unto men
And a Mercy from Us':
It is a matter
(So) decreed."

هُوَ عَلَيَّ هَيِّنٌ ۚ وَلِنَجْعَلَهُ
ءَايَةً لِّلنَّاسِ وَرَحْمَةً مِّنَّا ۚ
وَكَانَ أَمْرًا مَّقْضِيًّا ۝

22. So she conceived him,
And she retired with him
To a remote place.

٢٢ فَحَمَلَتْهُ فَانتَبَذَتْ بِهِۦ مَكَانًا قَصِيًّا ۝

23. And the pains of childbirth
Drove her to the trunk
Of a palm tree:
She cried (in her anguish):
"Ah! would that I had
Died before this! would that
I had been a thing
Forgotten and out of sight!"

٢٣ فَأَجَآءَهَا الْمَخَاضُ
إِلَىٰ جِذْعِ النَّخْلَةِ
قَالَتْ يَٰلَيْتَنِي مِتُّ قَبْلَ هَٰذَا
وَكُنتُ نَسْيًا مَّنسِيًّا ۝

24. But (a voice) cried to her
From beneath the (palm tree):
"Grieve not! for thy Lord
Hath provided a rivulet
Beneath thee;

٢٣ فَنَادَىٰهَا مِن تَحْتِهَآ
أَلَّا تَحْزَنِي قَدْ جَعَلَ رَبُّكِ تَحْتَكِ سَرِيًّا ۝

25. "And shake towards thyself
The trunk of the palm tree;
It will let fall
Fresh ripe dates upon thee.

٢٥ وَهُزِّي إِلَيْكِ بِجِذْعِ النَّخْلَةِ
تُسَٰقِطْ عَلَيْكِ رُطَبًا جَنِيًّا ۝

26. "So eat and drink
And cool (thine) eye.
And if thou dost see
Any man, say, 'I have
Vowed a fast to (Allah)
Most Gracious, and this day
Will I enter into no talk
With any human being'"

٢٦ فَكُلِي وَاشْرَبِي وَقَرِّي عَيْنًا ۖ فَإِمَّا تَرَيِنَّ
مِنَ الْبَشَرِ أَحَدًا فَقُولِي إِنِّي
نَذَرْتُ لِلرَّحْمَٰنِ صَوْمًا
فَلَنْ أُكَلِّمَ الْيَوْمَ إِنسِيًّا ۝

27. At length she brought
The (babe) to her people,
Carrying him (in her arms).
They said: "O Mary!
Truly an amazing thing

٢٧ فَأَتَتْ بِهِۦ قَوْمَهَا تَحْمِلُهُۥ ۖ
قَالُوا يَٰمَرْيَمُ

Hast thou brought!

28. "O sister of Aaron!
Thy father was not
A man of evil, nor thy
Mother a woman unchaste!"

29. But she pointed to the babe.
They said: "How can we
Talk to one who is
A child in the cradle?"

30. He said: "I am indeed
A servant of Allah:
He hath given me
Revelation and made me
A prophet;

31. "And He hath made me
Blessed wheresoever I be,
And hath enjoined on me
Prayer and Charity as long
As I live:

92. "(He) hath made me kind
To my mother, and not
Overbearing or miserable;

33. "So Peace is on me
The day I was born,
The day that I die,
And the Day that I
Shall be raised up
To life (again)"!

34. Such (was) Jesus the son
Of Mary: (it is) a statement
Of truth, about which
They (vainly) dispute.

35. It is not befitting
To (the majesty of) Allah
That He should beget
A son. Glory be to Him!
When He determines
A matter, He only says
To it, "Be," and it is.

36. Verily Allah is my Lord

لَقَدۡ جِئۡتِ شَيۡئًا فَرِيًّا ۝

٢٨ ـ يٰۤاُخۡتَ هٰرُوۡنَ مَا كَانَ اَبُوۡكِ امۡرَاَ سَوۡءٍ وَّ مَا كَانَتۡ اُمُّكِ بَغِيًّا ۚ

٢٩ ـ فَاَشَارَتۡ اِلَيۡهِ ؕ قَالُوۡا كَيۡفَ نُكَلِّمُ مَنۡ كَانَ فِى الۡمَهۡدِ صَبِيًّا ۝

٣٠ ـ قَالَ اِنِّىۡ عَبۡدُ اللّٰهِ ۚ اٰتٰنِىَ الۡكِتٰبَ وَجَعَلَنِىۡ نَبِيًّا ۝

٣١ ـ وَّجَعَلَنِىۡ مُبٰرَكًا اَيۡنَ مَا كُنۡتُ ۖ وَاَوۡصٰنِىۡ بِالصَّلٰوةِ وَالزَّكٰوةِ مَا دُمۡتُ حَيًّا ۚ

٣٢ ـ وَّبَرًّا بِوَالِدَتِىۡ ۖ وَلَمۡ يَجۡعَلۡنِىۡ جَبَّارًا شَقِيًّا ۝

٣٣ ـ وَالسَّلٰمُ عَلَىَّ يَوۡمَ وُلِدۡتُّ وَيَوۡمَ اَمُوۡتُ وَيَوۡمَ اُبۡعَثُ حَيًّا ۝

٣٤ ـ ذٰلِكَ عِيۡسَى ابۡنُ مَرۡيَمَ ۚ قَوۡلَ الۡحَقِّ الَّذِىۡ فِيۡهِ يَمۡتَرُوۡنَ ۝

٣٥ ـ مَا كَانَ لِلّٰهِ اَنۡ يَّتَّخِذَ مِنۡ وَّلَدٍ ۙ سُبۡحٰنَهٗ ؕ اِذَا قَضٰٓى اَمۡرًا فَاِنَّمَا يَقُوۡلُ لَهٗ كُنۡ فَيَكُوۡنُ ۝

٣٦ ـ وَاِنَّ اللّٰهَ رَبِّىۡ وَرَبُّكُمۡ

And your Lord: Him
Therefore serve ye: this is
A Way that is straight.

فَاعْبُدُوهُ هٰذَا صِرَاطٌ مُّسْتَقِيمٌ ۝

37. But the sects differ
Among themselves: and woe
To the Unbelievers because
Of the (coming) Judgement
Of a momentous Day!

۳۷ـ فَاخْتَلَفَ الْأَحْزَابُ مِنْ بَيْنِهِمْ فَوَيْلٌ لِّلَّذِينَ كَفَرُوا مِنْ مَّشْهَدِ يَوْمٍ عَظِيمٍ ۝

38. How plainly will they see
And hear, the Day that
They will appear before Us!
But the unjust today
Are in error manifest!

۳۸ـ أَسْمِعْ بِهِمْ وَأَبْصِرْ يَوْمَ يَأْتُونَنَا لٰكِنِ الظّٰلِمُونَ الْيَوْمَ فِى ضَلٰلٍ مُّبِينٍ ۝

39. But warn them of the Day
Of Distress, when
The matter will be determined:
For (behold,) they are negligent
And they do not believe!

۳۹ـ وَأَنْذِرْهُمْ يَوْمَ الْحَسْرَةِ إِذْ قُضِيَ الْأَمْرُ وَهُمْ فِى غَفْلَةٍ وَهُمْ لَا يُؤْمِنُونَ ۝

40. It is We Who will inherit
The earth, and all beings
Thereon: to Us will they
All be returned.

۴۰ـ إِنَّا نَحْنُ نَرِثُ الْأَرْضَ وَمَنْ عَلَيْهَا وَإِلَيْنَا يُرْجَعُونَ ۝

SECTION 3.

41. (Also) mention in the Book
(The story of) Abraham:
He was a man of Truth.
A prophet.

۴۱ـ وَاذْكُرْ فِى الْكِتٰبِ إِبْرٰهِيمَ إِنَّهُ كَانَ صِدِّيقًا نَّبِيًّا ۝

42. Behold, he said to his father:
"O my father! why
Worship that which heareth not
And seeth not, and can
Profit thee nothing?

۴۲ـ إِذْ قَالَ لِأَبِيهِ يٰأَبَتِ لِمَ تَعْبُدُ مَا لَا يَسْمَعُ وَلَا يُبْصِرُ وَلَا يُغْنِى عَنْكَ شَيْئًا ۝

43. "O my father! to me
Hath come knowledge which
Hath not reached thee:
So follow me: I will guide
Thee to a Way that
Is even and straight.

۴۳ـ يٰأَبَتِ إِنِّى قَدْ جَاءَنِى مِنَ الْعِلْمِ مَا لَمْ يَأْتِكَ فَاتَّبِعْنِى أَهْدِكَ صِرَاطًا سَوِيًّا ۝

44. "O my father! serve not
Satan: for Satan is
A rebel against (Allah)

۴۴ـ يٰأَبَتِ لَا تَعْبُدِ الشَّيْطٰنَ إِنَّ الشَّيْطٰنَ كَانَ

Most Gracious.   لِلرَّحْمٰنِ عَصِيًّا ۝

45. "O my father! I fear
Lest a Penalty afflict thee
From (Allah) Most Gracious,
So that thou become
To Satan a friend."

٤٥- يٰٓاَبَتِ اِنِّىۡ اَخَافُ اَنۡ يَّمَسَّكَ عَذَابٌ مِّنَ الرَّحۡمٰنِ فَتَكُوۡنَ لِلشَّيۡطٰنِ وَلِيًّا ۝

46. (The father) replied: "Dost thou
Hate my gods, O Abraham?
If thou forbear not, I will
Indeed stone thee:
Now get away from me
For a good long while!"

٤٦- قَالَ اَرَاغِبٌ اَنۡتَ عَنۡ اٰلِهَتِىۡ يٰٓاِبۡرٰهِيۡمُ ۚ لَئِنۡ لَّمۡ تَنۡتَهِ لَاَرۡجُمَنَّكَ وَاهۡجُرۡنِىۡ مَلِيًّا ۝

47. Abraham said: "Peace be
On thee: I pray
To my Lord for thy
                    forgiveness:
For He is to me
Most Gracious.

٤٧- قَالَ سَلٰمٌ عَلَيۡكَ ۚ سَاَسۡتَغۡفِرُ لَكَ رَبِّىۡ ؕ اِنَّهٗ كَانَ بِىۡ حَفِيًّا ۝

48. "And I will turn away
From you (all) and from those
Whom ye invoke besides Allah:
I will call on my Lord:
Perhaps, by my prayer to my
                        Lord,
I shall be not unblest!"

٤٨- وَاَعۡتَزِلُكُمۡ وَمَا تَدۡعُوۡنَ مِنۡ دُوۡنِ اللّٰهِ وَاَدۡعُوۡا رَبِّىۡ ۖ عَسٰىٓ اَلَّا اَكُوۡنَ بِدُعَآءِ رَبِّىۡ شَقِيًّا ۝

49. When he had turned away
From them and from those
Whom they worshipped besides
Allah, We bestowed on him
Isaac and Jacob, and each one
Of them We made a
                        prophet.

٤٩- فَلَمَّا اعۡتَزَلَهُمۡ وَمَا يَعۡبُدُوۡنَ مِنۡ دُوۡنِ اللّٰهِ ۙ وَهَبۡنَا لَهٗٓ اِسۡحٰقَ وَيَعۡقُوۡبَ ؕ وَكُلًّا جَعَلۡنَا نَبِيًّا ۝

50. And We bestowed
Of Our Mercy on them,
And We granted them
Lofty honour on the tongue
Of truth.
SECTION 4.

٥٠- وَوَهَبۡنَا لَهُمۡ مِّنۡ رَّحۡمَتِنَا وَجَعَلۡنَا لَهُمۡ لِسَانَ صِدۡقٍ عَلِيًّا ۝

51. Also mention in the Book
(The story of) Moses:
For he was specially chosen,

٥١- وَاذۡكُرۡ فِى الۡكِتٰبِ مُوۡسٰىٓ ۖ اِنَّهٗ كَانَ مُخۡلَصًا

And he was a messenger
And a prophet.

وَكَانَ رَسُوْلًا نَّبِيًّا ۞

52. And We called him
From the right side
Of Mount (Sinai), and made
Him draw near to Us,
For mystic (converse).

٥٢- وَنَادَيْنَهُ مِنْ جَانِبِ الطُّوْرِ الْاَيْمَنِ
وَقَرَّبْنَهُ نَجِيًّا ۞

53. And, out of Our Mercy,
We gave him his brother
Aaron, (also) a prophet.

٥٣- وَوَهَبْنَا لَهُ مِنْ رَّحْمَتِنَا
اَخَاهُ هُرُوْنَ نَبِيًّا ۞

54. Also mention in the Book
(The story of) Ismā'īl:
He was (strictly) true
To what he promised,
And he was a messenger
(And) a prophet.

٥٤- وَاذْكُرْ فِي الْكِتَبِ اِسْمَعِيْلَ
اِنَّهُ كَانَ صَادِقَ الْوَعْدِ
وَكَانَ رَسُوْلًا نَّبِيًّا ۞

55. He used to enjoin
On his people Prayer
And Charity, and he was
Most acceptable in the sight
Of his Lord.

٥٥- وَكَانَ يَأْمُرُ اَهْلَهُ بِالصَّلٰوةِ وَالزَّكٰوةِ
وَكَانَ عِنْدَ رَبِّهٖ مَرْضِيًّا ۞

56. Also mention in the Book
The case of Idrīs:
He was a man of truth
(And sincerity), (and) a prophet:

٥٦- وَاذْكُرْ فِي الْكِتَبِ اِدْرِيْسَ
اِنَّهُ كَانَ صِدِّيْقًا نَّبِيًّا ۞

57. And We raised him
To a lofty station.

٥٧- وَّرَفَعْنَهُ مَكَانًا عَلِيًّا ۞

58. Those were some
Of the prophets on whom
Allah did bestow His Grace—
Of the posterity of Adam,
And of those whom We
Carried (in the Ark)
With Noah, and of
The posterity of Abraham
And Israel—of those
Whom We guided and chose;
Whenever the Signs
Of (Allah) Most Gracious
Were rehearsed to them,

٥٨- اُولٰٓئِكَ الَّذِيْنَ اَنْعَمَ اللّٰهُ
عَلَيْهِمْ مِّنَ النَّبِيّٖنَ مِنْ ذُرِّيَّةِ اٰدَمَ
وَمِمَّنْ حَمَلْنَا مَعَ نُوْحٍ
وَمِنْ ذُرِّيَّةِ اِبْرٰهِيْمَ
وَاِسْرَآءِيْلَ وَمِمَّنْ هَدَيْنَا وَاجْتَبَيْنَا
اِذَا تُتْلٰى عَلَيْهِمْ
اٰيٰتُ الرَّحْمٰنِ

They would fall down
In prostrate adoration
And in tears.

خَرُّوْا سُجَّدًا وَّ بُكِيًّا ۩

59. But after them there followed
A posterity who missed
Prayers and followed after lusts:
Soon, then, will they
Face Destruction—

٥٩ - فَخَلَفَ مِنْ بَعْدِهِمْ خَلْفٌ اَضَاعُوا الصَّلٰوةَ وَاتَّبَعُوا الشَّهَوٰتِ فَسَوْفَ يَلْقَوْنَ غَيًّا ۞

60. Except those who repent
And believe, and work
Righteousness: for these
Will enter the Garden
And will not be wronged
In the least—

٦٠ - اِلَّا مَنْ تَابَ وَاٰمَنَ وَعَمِلَ صَالِحًا فَاُولٰٓئِكَ يَدْخُلُوْنَ الْجَنَّةَ وَلَا يُظْلَمُوْنَ شَيْئًا ۞

61. Gardens of Eternity, those
Which (Allah) Most Gracious
Has promised to His servants
In the Unseen: for His promise
Must (necessarily) come to pass.

٦١ - جَنّٰتِ عَدْنِ الَّتِيْ وَعَدَ الرَّحْمٰنُ عِبَادَه بِالْغَيْبِ ۚ اِنَّه كَانَ وَعْدُه مَأْتِيًّا ۞

62. They will not there hear
Any vain discourse, but
Only salutations of Peace:
And they will have therein
Their sustenance,   morning
And evening.

٦٢ - لَا يَسْمَعُوْنَ فِيْهَا لَغْوًا اِلَّا سَلٰمًا ۚ وَلَهُمْ رِزْقُهُمْ فِيْهَا بُكْرَةً وَّعَشِيًّا ۞

63. Such is the Garden which
We give as an inheritance
To those of Our Servants
Who guard against evil.

٦٣ - تِلْكَ الْجَنَّةُ الَّتِيْ نُوْرِثُ مِنْ عِبَادِنَا مَنْ كَانَ تَقِيًّا ۞

64. (The angels say:)
"We descend not but
By command of thy Lord:
To Him belongeth what is
Before us, and what is
Behind us, and what is
Between: and thy Lord
Never doth forget"—

٦٤ - وَمَا نَتَنَزَّلُ اِلَّا بِاَمْرِ رَبِّكَ ۚ لَه مَا بَيْنَ اَيْدِيْنَا وَمَا خَلْفَنَا وَمَا بَيْنَ ذٰلِكَ ۚ وَمَا كَانَ رَبُّكَ نَسِيًّا ۞

65. "Lord of the heavens
And of the earth,
And of all that is
Between them: so worship Him,

٦٥ - رَبُّ السَّمٰوٰتِ وَالْاَرْضِ وَمَا بَيْنَهُمَا فَاعْبُدْهُ

And be constant and patient
In His worship: knowest thou
Of any who is worthy
Of the same Name as He?"

SECTION 5.

66. Man says: "What!
When I am dead, shall I
Then be raised up alive?"

67. But does not man
Call to mind that We
Created him before
Out of nothing?

68. So, by thy Lord,
Without doubt, We shall gather
Them together, and (also)
The Evil Ones (with them);
Then shall We bring them
Forth on their knees
Round about Hell;

69. Then shall We certainly
Drag out from every sect
All those who were worst
In obstinate rebellion
Against (Allah) Most Gracious.

70. And certainly We know best
Those who are most worthy
Of being burned therein.

71. Not one of you but will
Pass over it: this is,
With thy Lord, a Decree
Which must be accomplished.

72. But We shall save those
Who guarded against evil,
And We shall leave
The wrongdoers therein,
(Humbled) to their knees.

73. When Our Clear Signs
Are rehearsed to them,
The Unbelievers say to those
Who believe, "Which of the two

Sides is best in point of
Position? which makes the best
Show in Council?"

74. But how many (countless)
Generations before them
Have We destroyed,
Who were even better
In equipment and in glitter
To the eye?

75. Say: "If any man go
Astray, (Allah) Most Gracious
Extends (the rope) to them.
Until, when they see
The warning of Allah (being
Fulfilled)—either in punishment
Or in (the approach of)
The Hour—they will
At length realise who is
Worst in position, and (who)
Weaker in forces!

76. "And Allah doth advance
In guidance those who seek
Guidance: and the things
That endure, Good Deeds,
Are best in the sight
Of thy Lord, as rewards,
And best in respect of
(Their) eventual returns."

77. Hast thou then seen
The (sort of) man who
Rejects Our Signs, yet
Says: "I shall certainly
Be given wealth and children?"

78. Has he penetrated to
The Unseen, or has he
Taken a contract with
(Allah) Most Gracious?

79. Nay! We shall record
What he says, and We
Shall add and add
To his punishment.

الْفَرِيقَيْنِ خَيْرٌ مَّقَامًا وَّ أَحْسَنُ نَدِيًّا ۟

٧٤ ـ وَكَمْ أَهْلَكْنَا قَبْلَهُمْ مِّنْ قَرْنٍ هُمْ أَحْسَنُ أَثَاثًا وَّ رِءْيًا ۟

٧٥ ـ قُلْ مَنْ كَانَ فِى الضَّلٰلَةِ فَلْيَمْدُدْ لَهُ الرَّحْمٰنُ مَدًّا ۚ حَتّٰى إِذَا رَأَوْا مَا يُوعَدُونَ إِمَّا الْعَذَابَ وَإِمَّا السَّاعَةَ ۚ فَسَيَعْلَمُونَ مَنْ هُوَ شَرٌّ مَّكَانًا وَّ أَضْعَفُ جُنْدًا ۟

٧٦ ـ وَيَزِيدُ اللّٰهُ الَّذِينَ اهْتَدَوْا هُدًى وَ الْبٰقِيٰتُ الصّٰلِحٰتُ خَيْرٌ عِنْدَ رَبِّكَ ثَوَابًا وَّ خَيْرٌ مَّرَدًّا ۟

٧٧ ـ أَفَرَأَيْتَ الَّذِى كَفَرَ بِآيٰتِنَا وَقَالَ لَأُوتَيَنَّ مَالًا وَّ وَلَدًا ۟

٧٨ ـ أَطَّلَعَ الْغَيْبَ أَمِ اتَّخَذَ عِنْدَ الرَّحْمٰنِ عَهْدًا ۟

٧٩ ـ كَلَّا سَنَكْتُبُ مَا يَقُولُ وَ نَمُدُّ لَهُ مِنَ الْعَذَابِ مَدًّا ۟

80. To Us shall return
All that he talks of,
And he shall appear
Before Us bare and alone.

٨٠ - وَّنَرِثُهُ مَا يَقُوْلُ
وَيَأْتِيْنَا فَرْدًا ۝

81. And they have taken
(For worship) gods other than
Allah, to give them
Power and glory!

٨١ - وَاتَّخَذُوْا مِنْ دُوْنِ اللّٰهِ اٰلِهَةً
لِّيَكُوْنُوْا لَهُمْ عِزًّا ۝

82. Instead, they shall reject
Their worship, and become
Adversaries against them.

٨٢ - كَلَّا سَيَكْفُرُوْنَ بِعِبَادَتِهِمْ وَيَكُوْنُوْنَ
عَلَيْهِمْ ضِدًّا ۝

SECTION 6.

83. Seest thou not that We
Have set the Evil Ones on
Against the Unbelievers,
To incite them with fury?

٨٣ - اَلَمْ تَرَ اَنَّا اَرْسَلْنَا الشَّيٰطِيْنَ
عَلَى الْكٰفِرِيْنَ تَؤُزُّهُمْ اَزًّا ۝

84. So make no haste
Against them, for We
But count out to them
A (limited) number (of days).

٨٤ - فَلَا تَعْجَلْ عَلَيْهِمْ ۗ
اِنَّمَا نَعُدُّ لَهُمْ عَدًّا ۝

85. The day We shall gather
The righteous to (Allah)
Most Gracious, like a band
Presented before a king for
honours.

٨٥ - يَوْمَ نَحْشُرُ الْمُتَّقِيْنَ
اِلَى الرَّحْمٰنِ وَفْدًا ۝

86. And We shall drive
The sinners to hell,
Like thirsty cattle
Driven down to water—

٨٦ - وَّنَسُوْقُ الْمُجْرِمِيْنَ اِلٰى جَهَنَّمَ
وِرْدًا ۝

87. None shall have the power
Of intercession, but such a one
As has received permission
(or promise)
From (Allah) Most Gracious.

٨٧ - لَا يَمْلِكُوْنَ الشَّفَاعَةَ اِلَّا مَنِ
اتَّخَذَ عِنْدَ الرَّحْمٰنِ عَهْدًا ۝

88. They say: "(Allah) Most
Gracious
Has begotten a son!

٨٨ - وَقَالُوا اتَّخَذَ الرَّحْمٰنُ وَلَدًا ۝

89. Indeed ye have put forth
A thing most monstrous!

٨٩ - لَقَدْ جِئْتُمْ شَيْئًا اِدًّا ۝

90. As if the skies are ready

٩٠ - تَكَادُ السَّمٰوٰتُ يَتَفَطَّرْنَ مِنْهُ

To burst, the earth
To split asunder, and
The mountains to fall down
In utter ruin.

وَتَنْشَقُّ الْأَرْضُ
وَتَخِرُّ الْجِبَالُ هَدًّا ۟

91. That they should invoke
A son for (Allah) Most
Gracious.

٩١- أَن دَعَوْا لِلرَّحْمَٰنِ وَلَدًا ۟

92. For it is not consonant
With the majesty of (Allah)
Most Gracious that He
Should beget a son.

٩٢- وَمَا يَنْبَغِي لِلرَّحْمَٰنِ
أَن يَتَّخِذَ وَلَدًا ۟

93. Not one of the beings
In the heavens and the earth
But must come to (Allah)
Most Gracious as a servant.

٩٣- إِن كُلُّ مَن فِي السَّمَٰوَٰتِ وَالْأَرْضِ
إِلَّا آتِي الرَّحْمَٰنِ عَبْدًا ۟

94. He does take an account
Of them (all), and hath
Numbered them (all)
exactly.

٩٤- لَّقَدْ أَحْصَىٰهُمْ وَعَدَّهُمْ عَدًّا ۟

95. And every one of them
Will come to Him singly
On the day of Judgement.

٩٥- وَكُلُّهُمْ آتِيهِ يَوْمَ الْقِيَٰمَةِ فَرْدًا ۟

96. On those who believe
And work deeds of
righteousness,
Will (Allah) Most Gracious
Bestow Love.

٩٦- إِنَّ الَّذِينَ آمَنُوا وَعَمِلُوا الصَّٰلِحَٰتِ
سَيَجْعَلُ لَهُمُ الرَّحْمَٰنُ وُدًّا ۟

97. So have We made
The (Qur'ān) easy
In thine own tongue,
That with it thou mayest give
Glad tidings to the righteous,
And warnings to people
Given to contention.

٩٧- فَإِنَّمَا يَسَّرْنَٰهُ بِلِسَانِكَ
لِتُبَشِّرَ بِهِ الْمُتَّقِينَ وَتُنذِرَ بِهِ قَوْمًا
لُّدًّا ۟

98. But how many (countless)
Generations before them
Have We destroyed? Canst thou
Find a single one of them
(Now) or hear (so much
As) a whisper of them?

٩٨- وَكَمْ أَهْلَكْنَا قَبْلَهُم مِّن قَرْنٍ
هَلْ تُحِسُّ مِنْهُم مِّنْ أَحَدٍ
أَوْ تَسْمَعُ لَهُمْ رِكْزًا ۟

INTRODUCTION TO SŪRA XX. (*Ṭā-Hā*) — 135 Verses

The chronology of this Sūra has some significance: it has some relation to the spiritual lessons which it teaches.

It was used with great effect in that remarkable scene which resulted in Ḥadḥrat 'Umar's conversion, and which took place about the seventh year before the Hijrat.

The scene is described with dramatic details by Ibn Hishām. 'Umar had previously been one of the greatest enemies and persecutors of Islam. Like his blood-thirsty kinsmen the Quraish, he meditated slaying the Prophet, when it was suggested to him that there were near relations of his that had embraced Islam. His sister Fāṭima and her husband Sa'īd were Muslims but in those days of persecution they had kept their faith secret. When 'Umar went to their house, he heard them reciting this Sūra from a written copy they had. For a while they concealed the copy. 'Umar attacked his sister and her husband, but they bore the attack with exemplary patience, and declared their Faith. 'Umar was so struck with their sincerity and fortitude that he asked to see the leaf from which they had been reading. It was given to him: his soul was touched and he not only came into the Faith but became one of its strongest supporters and champions.

The leaf contained some portion of this Sūra, perhaps the introductory portion. The mystic letters *Ṭā-hā* are prefixed to this Sūra. What do they mean? The earliest tradition is that they denote a dialectical interjection meaning "O man!" If so, the title is particularly appropriate in two ways, (1) It was a direct and personal address to a man in a high state of excitement, tempted by his temper to do grievous wrong, but called by God's Grace, as by a personal appeal, to face the realities, for God knew his inmost secret thoughts (xx. 7): the revelation was sent by God most Gracious, out of His Grace and Mercy (xx. 5). (2) It takes up the story from the last Sūra, of man as a spiritual being and illustrates it in further details. It tells the story of Moses in the crisis of his life when he received God's Commission and in his personal relations with his mother, and how he came to be brought up in the Pharaoh's house to learn all the wisdom of the Egyptians, for use in God's service, and in his personal relations with Pharaoh, whom we take to be his adoptive father (xxviii. 9). It further tells the story of a fallen soul who misled the Israelites into idolatry, and recalls how man's Arch-enemy Satan caused his fall. Prayer and praise are necessary to man to cure his spiritual blindness and enable him to appreciate God's revelations.

Ṭā Hā[2534]

In the name of Allah, Most Gracious, Most Merciful.

1. Ṭā Hā.

2. We have not sent down
   The Qur'ān to thee to be
   (An occasion) for thy distress,

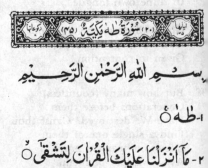

3. But only as an admonition
To those who fear (Allah)—

٣- إِلَّا تَذْكِرَةً لِّمَنْ يَخْشَى ۟

4. A revelation from Him
Who created the earth
And the heavens on high.

٤- تَنْزِيلًا مِّمَّنْ خَلَقَ الْأَرْضَ
وَالسَّمٰوٰتِ الْعُلَى ۟

5. (Allah) Most Gracious
Is firmly established
On the throne (of authority).

٥- اَلرَّحْمٰنُ عَلَى الْعَرْشِ اسْتَوَى ۟

6. To Him belongs what is
In the heavens and on earth,
And all between them,
And all beneath the soil.

٦- لَهٗ مَا فِى السَّمٰوٰتِ وَمَا فِى الْأَرْضِ
وَمَا بَيْنَهُمَا وَمَا تَحْتَ الثَّرَى ۟

7. If thou pronounce the word
Aloud, (it is no matter):
For verily he knoweth
What is secret and what
Is yet more hidden.

٧- وَإِنْ تَجْهَرْ بِالْقَوْلِ فَإِنَّهٗ يَعْلَمُ
السِّرَّ وَأَخْفَى ۟

8. Allah! there is no god
But He! To Him belong
The Most Beautiful Names.

٨- اَللّٰهُ لَا إِلٰهَ إِلَّا هُوَ
لَهُ الْأَسْمَاءُ الْحُسْنَى ۟

9. Has the story of Moses
Reached thee?

٩- وَهَلْ أَتَاكَ حَدِيثُ مُوسَى ۟

10. Behold, he saw a fire:
So he said to his family,
"Tarry ye; I perceive
A fire; perhaps I can
Bring you some burning brand
Therefrom, or find some guidance
At the fire."

١٠- إِذْ رَأَى نَارًا فَقَالَ لِأَهْلِهِ
امْكُثُوا إِنِّي أَنَسْتُ نَارًا
لَعَلِّي آتِيكُمْ مِنْهَا بِقَبَسٍ
أَوْ أَجِدُ عَلَى النَّارِ هُدًى ۟

11. But when he came
To the fire, a voice
Was heard: "O Moses!

١١- فَلَمَّا أَتَاهَا نُودِيَ يٰمُوسَى ۟

12. "Verily I am thy Lord!
Therefore (in My presence)
Put off thy shoes: thou art
In the sacred valley Tuwa.

١٢- إِنِّي أَنَا رَبُّكَ فَاخْلَعْ نَعْلَيْكَ إِنَّكَ
بِالْوَادِ الْمُقَدَّسِ طُوًى ۟

13. "I have chosen thee:
Listen, then to the inspiration
(Sent to thee).

١٣- وَأَنَا اخْتَرْتُكَ فَاسْتَمِعْ لِمَا يُوحَى ۟

14. "Verily, I am Allah:
There is no god but I:
So serve thou Me (only),
And establish regular prayer
For celebrating My praise.

١٤- إِنَّنِي أَنَا اللّٰهُ لَآ إِلٰهَ إِلَّا
أَنَا فَاعْبُدْنِي ۙ
وَأَقِمِ الصَّلٰوةَ لِذِكْرِيْ ۝

15. "Verily the Hour is coming—
My design is to keep it
Hidden—　　　for every soul
To receive its reward
By the measure of
Its Endeavour.

١٥- إِنَّ السَّاعَةَ اٰتِيَةٌ أَكَادُ
أُخْفِيْهَا لِتُجْزٰى كُلُّ نَفْسٍ
بِمَا تَسْعٰى ۝

16. "Therefore let not such as
Believe not therein
But follow their own
Lusts, divert thee therefrom,
Lest thou perish!"

١٦- فَلَا يَصُدَّنَّكَ عَنْهَا مَنْ لَّا يُؤْمِنُ بِهَا
وَاتَّبَعَ هَوٰىهُ فَتَرْدٰى ۝

17. "And what is that
In thy right hand,
O Moses?"

١٧- وَمَا تِلْكَ بِيَمِيْنِكَ يٰمُوْسٰى ۝

18. He said, "It is
My rod: on it
I lean; with it
I beat down fodder
For my flocks; and
In it I find
Other uses."

١٨- قَالَ هِيَ عَصَايَ ۚ أَتَوَكَّؤُا عَلَيْهَا
وَأَهُشُّ بِهَا عَلٰى غَنَمِيْ
وَلِيَ فِيْهَا مَاٰرِبُ أُخْرٰى ۝

19. (Allah) said, "Throw it,
O Moses!"

١٩- قَالَ أَلْقِهَا يٰمُوْسٰى ۝

20. He threw it, and behold!
It was a snake,
Active in motion.

٢٠- فَأَلْقٰهَا فَإِذَا هِيَ حَيَّةٌ تَسْعٰى ۝

21. (Allah) said, "Seize it
And fear not: We
Shall return it at once
To its former condition"...

٢١- قَالَ خُذْهَا وَلَا تَخَفْ ۗ
سَنُعِيْدُهَا سِيْرَتَهَا الْأُوْلٰى ۝

22. "Now draw thy hand
Close to thy side:
It shall come forth white
(And shining), without harm
(Or stain)—as another Sign—

٢٢- وَاضْمُمْ يَدَكَ إِلٰى جَنَاحِكَ تَخْرُجْ
بَيْضَاءَ مِنْ غَيْرِ سُوْٓءٍ اٰيَةً أُخْرٰى ۙ

23. "In order that We
May show thee
(Two) of Our Greater Signs.

٢٣- لِنُرِيَكَ مِنْ اٰيٰتِنَا الْكُبْرَىٰ ۚ

24. "Go thou to Pharaoh,
For he had indeed
Transgressed all bounds."

٢٤- اِذْهَبْ اِلٰى فِرْعَوْنَ اِنَّهٗ طَغٰى ۚ

SECTION 2.

25. (Moses) said: "O my Lord!
Expand me my breast;"

٢٥- قَالَ رَبِّ اشْرَحْ لِيْ صَدْرِيْ ۙ

26. "Ease my task for me;

٢٦- وَيَسِّرْ لِيْٓ اَمْرِيْ ۙ

27. "And remove the impediment
From my speech.

٢٧- وَاحْلُلْ عُقْدَةً مِّنْ لِّسَانِيْ ۙ

28. "So they may understand
What I say:

٢٨- يَفْقَهُوْا قَوْلِيْ ۪ۙ

29. "And give me a Minister
From my family,

٢٩- وَاجْعَلْ لِّيْ وَزِيْرًا مِّنْ اَهْلِيْ ۙ

30. "Aaron, my brother;

٣٠- هٰرُوْنَ اَخِى ۙ

31. "Add to my strength
Through him,

٣١- اشْدُدْ بِهٖٓ اَزْرِيْ ۙ

32. "And make him share
My task:

٣٢- وَاَشْرِكْهُ فِيْٓ اَمْرِيْ ۙ

33. "That we may celebrate
Thy praise without stint,

٣٣- كَيْ نُسَبِّحَكَ كَثِيْرًا ۙ

34. "And remember Thee
Without stint:

٣٤- وَّنَذْكُرَكَ كَثِيْرًا ۙ

35. "For Thou art He
That (ever) regardeth us."

٣٥- اِنَّكَ كُنْتَ بِنَا بَصِيْرًا

36. (Allah) said: "Granted
Is thy prayer, O Moses!"

٣٦- قَالَ قَدْ اُوْتِيْتَ سُؤْلَكَ يٰمُوْسٰى

37. "And indeed We conferred
A favour on thee
Another time (before).

٣٧- وَلَقَدْ مَنَنَّا عَلَيْكَ مَرَّةً اُخْرٰىٓ ۙ

38. "Behold! We sent
    To thy mother, by inspiration,
    The message:

٣٨- اِذْ اَوْحَيْنَا اِلَى اُمِّكَ مَا يُوحَى ۞

39. "'Throw (the child)
    Into the chest, and throw
    (The chest) into the river:
    The river will cast him
    Up on the bank, and he
    Will be taken up by one
    Who is an enemy to Me
    And an enemy to him':
    But I cast (the garment
    Of) love over thee from Me:
    And (this) in order that
    Thou mayest be reared
    Under Mine eye."

٣٩- اَنِ اقْذِفِيهِ فِى التَّابُوتِ
فَاقْذِفِيهِ فِى الْيَمِّ
فَلْيُلْقِهِ الْيَمُّ بِالسَّاحِلِ
يَاْخُذْهُ عَدُوٌّ لِّى وَعَدُوٌّ لَّهُ ۚ
وَاَلْقَيْتُ عَلَيْكَ مَحَبَّةً مِّنِّى ۚ
وَلِتُصْنَعَ عَلَى عَيْنِى ۞

40. "Behold! thy sister goeth forth
    And saith. 'Shall I show you
    One who will nurse
    And rear the (child)?'
    So We brought thee back
    To thy mother, that her eye
    Might be cooled and she
    Should not grieve.
    Then thou didst slay
    A man, but We saved thee
    From trouble, and We tried
    Thee in various ways.
    Then didst thou tarry
    A number of years
    With the people of Midian.
    Then didst thou come hither
    As ordained, O Moses!

٤٠- اِذْ تَمْشِىٓ اُخْتُكَ فَتَقُولُ هَلْ اَدُلُّكُمْ
عَلَى مَنْ يَّكْفُلُهُ ۚ
فَرَجَعْنَاكَ اِلَى اُمِّكَ
كَىْ تَقَرَّ عَيْنُهَا وَلَا تَحْزَنَ ۚ
وَقَتَلْتَ نَفْسًا فَنَجَّيْنَاكَ
مِنَ الْغَمِّ وَفَتَنَّاكَ فُتُونًا ۚ
فَلَبِثْتَ سِنِينَ فِىٓ اَهْلِ مَدْيَنَ ۚ
ثُمَّ جِئْتَ عَلَى قَدَرٍ يَّا مُوسَى ۞

41. "And I have prepared thee
    For Myself (for service)"...

٤١- وَاصْطَنَعْتُكَ لِنَفْسِى ۞

42. "Go, thou and thy brother.
    With My signs,
    And slacken not,
    Either of you, in keeping
    Me in remembrance.

٤٢- اِذْهَبْ اَنْتَ وَاَخُوكَ بِاٰيٰتِى
وَلَا تَنِيَا فِى ذِكْرِى ۞

43. "Go, both of you, to Pharaoh,
    For he has indeed
    Transgressed all bounds;

٤٣- اِذْهَبَآ اِلَى فِرْعَوْنَ اِنَّهُ طَغَى ۞

44. "But speak to him mildly;
Perchance he may take
Warning or fear (Allah)."

٤٤- فَقُوْلَا لَهُ قَوْلًا لَيِّنًا لَعَلَّهُ يَتَذَكَّرُ اَوْ يَخْشٰى ۟

45. They (Moses and Aaron) said:
"Our Lord! We fear lest
He hasten with insolence
Against us, or lest he
Transgress all bounds."

٤٥- قَالَا رَبَّنَا اِنَّنَا نَخَافُ اَنْ يَّفْرُطَ عَلَيْنَا اَوْ اَنْ يَّطْغٰى ۟

46. He said: "Fear not:
For I am with you:
I hear and see (everything).

٤٦- قَالَ لَا تَخَافَا اِنَّنِيْ مَعَكُمَا اَسْمَعُ وَاَرٰى ۟

47. "So go ye both to him,
And say, 'Verily we are
Messengers sent by thy Lord·
Send forth, therefore, the Children
Of Israel with us, and
Afflict them not:
With a Sign, indeed,
Have we come from thy Lord!
And Peace to all
Who follow guidance!

٤٧- فَأْتِيٰهُ فَقُوْلَا اِنَّا رَسُوْلَا رَبِّكَ فَأَرْسِلْ مَعَنَا بَنِيْ اِسْرَآءِيْلَ ۙ وَلَا تُعَذِّبْهُمْ ۚ قَدْ جِئْنٰكَ بِاٰيَةٍ مِّنْ رَّبِّكَ ۖ وَالسَّلٰمُ عَلٰى مَنِ اتَّبَعَ الْهُدٰى ۟

48. "'Verily it has been revealed
To us that the Penalty
(Awaits) those who reject
And turn away.'"

٤٨- اِنَّا قَدْ اُوْحِيَ اِلَيْنَا اَنَّ الْعَذَابَ عَلٰى مَنْ كَذَّبَ وَتَوَلّٰى ۟

49. (When this message was
delivered),
(Pharaoh) said: "Who then,
O Moses, is the Lord
Of you two?"

٤٩- قَالَ فَمَنْ رَّبُّكُمَا يٰمُوْسٰى ۟

50. He said: "Our Lord is
He Who gave to each
(Created) thing its form
And nature, and further,
Gave (it) guidance."

٥٠- قَالَ رَبُّنَا الَّذِيْ اَعْطٰى كُلَّ شَيْءٍ خَلْقَهُ ثُمَّ هَدٰى ۟

51. (Pharaoh) said: "What then
Is the condition
Of previous generations?"

٥١- قَالَ فَمَا بَالُ الْقُرُوْنِ الْاُوْلٰى ۟

52. He replied: "The knowledge
Of that is with my Lord,

٥٢- قَالَ عِلْمُهَا عِنْدَ رَبِّيْ

Duly recorded: my Lord
Never errs, nor forgets—

فِىْ كِتٰبٍ ۚ لَا يَضِلُّ رَبِّىْ وَلَا يَنْسَى ۟

53. "He Who has made for you
The earth like a carpet
Spread out; has enabled you
To go about therein by roads
(And channels); and has sent
Down water from the sky."
With it have We produced
Diverse pairs of plants
Each separate from the others.

٥٣- الَّذِىْ جَعَلَ لَكُمُ الْاَرْضَ مَهْدًا
وَّسَلَكَ لَكُمْ فِيْهَا سُبُلًا
وَّاَنْزَلَ مِنَ السَّمَآءِ مَآءً ۚ
فَاَخْرَجْنَا بِهٖۤ اَزْوَاجًا مِّنْ نَّبَاتٍ شَتّٰى ۟

54. Eat (for yourselves) and pasture
Your cattle: verily, in this
Are Signs, for men
Endued with understanding.

٥٤- كُلُوْا وَارْعَوْا اَنْعَامَكُمْ ۗ
اِنَّ فِىْ ذٰلِكَ لَاٰيٰتٍ لِّاُولِى النُّهٰى ۟ ع

SECTION 3.

55. From the (earth) did We
Create you, and into it
Shall We return you,
And from it shall We
Bring you out once again.

٥٥- مِنْهَا خَلَقْنٰكُمْ وَفِيْهَا نُعِيْدُكُمْ
وَمِنْهَا نُخْرِجُكُمْ تَارَةً اُخْرٰى ۟

56. And We showed Pharaoh
All Our Signs, but he
Did reject and refuse.

٥٦- وَلَقَدْ اَرَيْنٰهُ اٰيٰتِنَا كُلَّهَا
فَكَذَّبَ وَاَبٰى ۟

57. He said: "Hast thou come
To drive us out
Of our land with thy magic
O Moses?

٥٧- قَالَ اَجِئْتَنَا لِتُخْرِجَنَا
مِنْ اَرْضِنَا بِسِحْرِكَ يٰمُوْسٰى ۟

58. "But we can surely produce
Magic to match thine!
So make a tryst
Between us and thee,
Which we shall not fail
To keep—neither we nor thou—
In a place where both
Shall have even chances."

٥٨- فَلَنَاْتِيَنَّكَ بِسِحْرٍ مِّثْلِهٖ
فَاجْعَلْ بَيْنَنَا وَبَيْنَكَ مَوْعِدًا
لَّا نُخْلِفُهٗ نَحْنُ
وَلَاۤ اَنْتَ مَكَانًا سُوًى ۟

59. Moses said: "Your tryst
Is the Day of the Festival,
And let the people be assembled
When the sun is well up."

٥٩- قَالَ مَوْعِدُكُمْ يَوْمُ الزِّيْنَةِ
وَاَنْ يُّحْشَرَ النَّاسُ ضُحًى ۟

60. So Pharaoh withdrew:
    He concerted his plan,
    And then came (back).

٦٠ ـ فَتَوَلّٰى فِرْعَوْنُ فَجَمَعَ كَيْدَهُ ثُمَّ اَتٰى ۞

61. Moses said to them:
    "Woe to you! Forge not
    Ye a lie against Allah,
    Lest He destroy you (at once)
    Utterly by chastisement:
    The forger must suffer
    Frustration!"

٦١ ـ قَالَ لَهُمْ مُّوْسٰى وَيْلَكُمْ لَا تَفْتَرُوْا عَلَى اللّٰهِ كَذِبًا فَيُسْحِتَكُمْ بِعَذَابٍ وَقَدْ خَابَ مَنِ افْتَرٰى ۞

62. So they disputed, one with
    Another, over their affair,
    But they kept their talk secret.

٦٢ ـ فَتَنَازَعُوْٓا اَمْرَهُمْ بَيْنَهُمْ وَاَسَرُّوا النَّجْوٰى ۞

63. They said: "These two
    Are certainly (expert) magicians:
    Their object is to drive you
    Out from your land
    With their magic, and
    To do away with your
    Most cherished institutions.

٦٣ ـ قَالُوْٓا اِنْ هٰذٰنِ لَسٰحِرٰنِ يُرِيْدٰنِ اَنْ يُّخْرِجٰكُمْ مِّنْ اَرْضِكُمْ بِسِحْرِهِمَا وَيَذْهَبَا بِطَرِيْقَتِكُمُ الْمُثْلٰى ۞

64. "Therefore concert your plan,
    And then assemble
    In (serried) ranks:
    He wins (all along) today
    Who gains the upper hand."

٦٤ ـ فَاَجْمِعُوْا كَيْدَكُمْ ثُمَّ ائْتُوْا صَفًّا وَقَدْ اَفْلَحَ الْيَوْمَ مَنِ اسْتَعْلٰى ۞

65. They said: "O Moses!
    Whether wilt thou
    That thou throw (first)
    Or that we be the first
    To throw?"

٦٥ ـ قَالُوْا يٰمُوْسٰى اِمَّآ اَنْ تُلْقِيَ وَاِمَّآ اَنْ تَكُوْنَ اَوَّلَ مَنْ اَلْقٰى ۞

66. He said, "Nay, throw ye
    First!" Then behold
    Their ropes and their rods—
    So it seemed to him
    On account of their magic—
    Began to be in lively motion!

٦٦ ـ قَالَ بَلْ اَلْقُوْا فَاِذَا حِبَالُهُمْ وَعِصِيُّهُمْ يُخَيَّلُ اِلَيْهِ مِنْ سِحْرِهِمْ اَنَّهَا تَسْعٰى ۞

67. So Moses conceived
    In his mind
    A (sort of) fear.

٦٧ ـ فَاَوْجَسَ فِيْ نَفْسِهٖ خِيْفَةً مُّوْسٰى ۞

68. We said, "Fear not!

٦٨ ـ قُلْنَا لَا تَخَفْ

For thou hast indeed
The upper hand:

اِنَّكَ اَنْتَ الْاَعْلٰى ٠

69. "Throw that which is
In thy right hand:
Quickly will it swallow up
That which they have faked:
What they have faked
Is but a magician's trick:
And the magician thrives not,
(No matter) where he goes."

٦٩ۛ وَاَلْقِ مَا فِيْ يَمِيْنِكَ
تَلْقَفْ مَا صَنَعُوْا ؕ اِنَّمَا صَنَعُوْا كَيْدُ سٰحِرٍ ؕ
وَلَا يُفْلِحُ السَّاحِرُ حَيْثُ اَتٰى ٠

70. So the magicians were
Thrown down to prostration:
They said, "We believe
In the Lord of Aaron and
Moses".

٧٠ۛ فَاُلْقِيَ السَّحَرَةُ سُجَّدًا
قَالُوْٓا اٰمَنَّا بِرَبِّ هٰرُوْنَ وَمُوْسٰى ٠

71. (Pharaoh) said: "Believe ye
In Him before I give
You permission? Surely
This must be your leader,
Who has taught you magic!
Be sure I will cut off
Your hands and feet
On opposite sides, and I
Will have you crucified
On trunks of palm trees:
So shall ye know for certain
Which of us can give
The more severe and the more
Lasting Punishment!"

٧١ۛ قَالَ اٰمَنْتُمْ لَهٗ قَبْلَ اَنْ اٰذَنَ لَكُمْ ؕ
اِنَّهٗ لَكَبِيْرُكُمُ
الَّذِيْ عَلَّمَكُمُ السِّحْرَ ۚ فَلَاُقَطِّعَنَّ
اَيْدِيَكُمْ وَاَرْجُلَكُمْ مِّنْ خِلَافٍ
وَّلَاُصَلِّبَنَّكُمْ فِيْ جُذُوْعِ النَّخْلِ ۫
وَلَتَعْلَمُنَّ اَيُّنَآ اَشَدُّ
عَذَابًا وَّاَبْقٰى ٠

72. They said: "Never shall we
Regard thee as more than
The Clear Signs   that have
Come to us or than
Him Who created us!
So decree whatever thou
Desirest to decree: for thou
Canst only decree (touching)
The life of this world.

٧٢ۛ قَالُوْا لَنْ نُّؤْثِرَكَ عَلٰى
مَا جَآءَنَا مِنَ الْبَيِّنٰتِ
وَالَّذِيْ فَطَرَنَا
فَاقْضِ مَآ اَنْتَ قَاضٍ ؕ
اِنَّمَا تَقْضِيْ هٰذِهِ الْحَيٰوةَ الدُّنْيَا ٠

73. "For us, we have believed
In our Lord: may He
Forgive us our faults,
And the magic to which
Thou didst compel us:

٧٣ۛ اِنَّآ اٰمَنَّا بِرَبِّنَا
لِيَغْفِرَ لَنَا خَطٰيٰنَا وَمَآ اَكْرَهْتَنَا عَلَيْهِ
مِنَ السِّحْرِ

For Allah is Best
And Most Abiding."

وَاللّٰهُ خَيْرٌ وَّأَبْقٰى ۝

74. Verily he who comes
To his Lord as a sinner
(At Judgement)—for him
Is Hell; therein shall he
Neither die nor live.

٧٤۔ اِنَّهٗ مَنْ يَّاْتِ رَبَّهٗ مُجْرِمًا فَاِنَّ لَهٗ
جَهَنَّمَ لَا يَمُوْتُ فِيْهَا وَلَا يَحْيٰى ۝

75. But such as comes
To Him as Believers
Who have worked righteous
             deeds—
For them are ranks exalted—

٧٥۔ وَمَنْ يَّاْتِهٖ مُؤْمِنًا قَدْ عَمِلَ الصّٰلِحٰتِ
فَاُولٰٓئِكَ لَهُمُ الدَّرَجٰتُ الْعُلٰى ۙ

76. Gardens of Eternity,
Beneath which flow rivers:
They will dwell therein
For aye: such is the reward
Of those who purify
Themselves (from evil).

٧٦۔ جَنّٰتُ عَدْنٍ تَجْرِيْ مِنْ تَحْتِهَا الْاَنْهٰرُ
خٰلِدِيْنَ فِيْهَا ۚ
وَذٰلِكَ جَزٰٓؤُا مَنْ تَزَكّٰى ۝

SECTION 4.

77. We sent an inspiration
To Moses: "Travel by night
With My servants, and strike
A dry path for them
Through the sea, without fear
Of being overtaken (by Pharaoh)
And without (any other) fear."

٧٧۔ وَلَقَدْ اَوْحَيْنَآ اِلٰى مُوْسٰٓى اَنْ اَسْرِ
بِعِبَادِيْ فَاضْرِبْ لَهُمْ طَرِيْقًا
فِى الْبَحْرِ يَبَسًا ۚ
لَّا تَخٰفُ دَرَكًا وَّلَا تَخْشٰى ۝

78. Then Pharaoh pursued them
With his forces, but
The waters completely
            overwhelmed
Them and covered them up.

٧٨۔ فَاَتْبَعَهُمْ فِرْعَوْنُ بِجُنُوْدِهٖ
فَغَشِيَهُمْ مِّنَ الْيَمِّ مَا غَشِيَهُمْ ۚ

79. Pharaoh led his people astray
Instead of leading them aright.

٧٩۔ وَاَضَلَّ فِرْعَوْنُ قَوْمَهٗ وَمَا هَدٰى ۝

80. O ye Children of Israel!
We delivered you from
Your enemy, and We
Made a Covenant with you
On the right side of
Mount (Sinai), and We sent
Down to you Manna
And quails:

٨٠۔ يٰبَنِيْٓ اِسْرَآءِيْلَ قَدْ اَنْجَيْنٰكُمْ مِّنْ
عَدُوِّكُمْ وَوٰعَدْنٰكُمْ
جَانِبَ الطُّوْرِ الْاَيْمَنَ
وَنَزَّلْنَا عَلَيْكُمُ الْمَنَّ وَالسَّلْوٰى ۝

81. (Saying): "Eat of the good
Things We have provided
For your sustenance, but
Commit no excess therein,
Lest My Wrath should justly
Descend on you: and those
On whom descends My Wrath
Do perish indeed!

٨١- كُلُوا مِنْ طَيِّبٰتِ مَا رَزَقْنٰكُمْ وَلَا تَطْغَوْا فِيهِ فَيَحِلَّ عَلَيْكُمْ غَضَبِىْ وَمَنْ يَحْلِلْ عَلَيْهِ غَضَبِىْ فَقَدْ هَوٰى ۝

82. "But, without doubt, I am
(Also) He that forgives
Again and again, to those
Who repent, believe,
And do right—who,
In fine, are ready to receive
True guidance."

٨٢- وَإِنِّىْ لَغَفَّارٌ لِمَنْ تَابَ وَاٰمَنَ وَعَمِلَ صَالِحًا ثُمَّ اهْتَدٰى ۝

83. (When Moses was up on the
Mount, Allah said): "What made thee
Hasten in advance of thy people,
O Moses?"

٨٣- وَمَا أَعْجَلَكَ عَنْ قَوْمِكَ يٰمُوْسٰى ۝

84. He replied: "Behold, they are
Close on my footsteps:
I hastened to Thee,
O my Lord,
To please Thee."

٨٤- قَالَ هُمْ أُولَاءِ عَلٰى أَثَرِىْ وَعَجِلْتُ إِلَيْكَ رَبِّ لِتَرْضٰى ۝

85. (Allah) said: "We have tested
Thy people in thy absence:
The Sāmirī has led them
Astray."

٨٥- قَالَ فَإِنَّا قَدْ فَتَنَّا قَوْمَكَ مِنْ بَعْدِكَ وَأَضَلَّهُمُ السَّامِرِىُّ ۝

86. So Moses returned to his people
In a state of indignation
And sorrow. He said:
"O my people! did not
Your Lord make a handsome
Promise to you? Did then
The promise seem to you
Long (in coming)? Or did ye
Desire that Wrath should
Descend from your Lord on you,
And so ye broke your promise
To me?"

٨٦- فَرَجَعَ مُوْسٰى إِلٰى قَوْمِهِ غَضْبَانَ أَسِفًا قَالَ يٰقَوْمِ أَلَمْ يَعِدْكُمْ رَبُّكُمْ وَعْدًا حَسَنًا أَفَطَالَ عَلَيْكُمُ الْعَهْدُ أَمْ أَرَدْتُمْ أَنْ يَحِلَّ عَلَيْكُمْ غَضَبٌ مِنْ رَبِّكُمْ فَأَخْلَفْتُمْ مَوْعِدِىْ ۝

87. They said: "We broke not
The promise to thee, as far

٨٧- قَالُوا مَا أَخْلَفْنَا مَوْعِدَكَ بِمَلْكِنَا

As lay in our power:
But we were made to carry
The weight of the ornaments
Of the (whole) people, and we
Threw them (into the fire),
And that was what
The Sāmirī suggested.

وَلَكِنَّا حُمِّلْنَا
أَوْزَارًا مِّن زِينَةِ الْقَوْمِ فَقَذَفْنَاهَا
فَكَذَلِكَ أَلْقَى السَّامِرِيُّ ۞

88. "Then he brought out
(Of the fire) before the (people)
The image of a calf:
It seemed to low:
So they said: 'This is
Your god, and the god
Of Moses, but (Moses)
Has forgotten!'"

٨٨ ـ فَأَخْرَجَ لَهُمْ
عِجْلًا جَسَدًا لَّهُ خُوَارٌ
فَقَالُوا هَذَا إِلَهُكُمْ
وَإِلَهُ مُوسَى فَنَسِيَ ۞

89. Could they not see that
It could not return them
A word (for answer), and that
It had not power either
To harm them or
To do them good?

٨٩ ـ أَفَلَا يَرَوْنَ أَلَّا يَرْجِعُ إِلَيْهِمْ قَوْلًا
وَلَا يَمْلِكُ لَهُمْ
ضَرًّا وَلَا نَفْعًا ۞

SECTION 5.

90. Aaron had already, before this
Said to them: "O my people!
Ye are being tested in this:
For verily your Lord is (Allah)
Most Gracious: so follow me
And obey my command."

٩٠ ـ وَلَقَدْ قَالَ لَهُمْ هَارُونُ مِن قَبْلُ
يَقَوْمِ إِنَّمَا فُتِنتُم بِهِ وَإِنَّ رَبَّكُمُ
الرَّحْمَنُ فَاتَّبِعُونِي وَأَطِيعُوا أَمْرِي ۞

91. They had said: "We will not
Abandon this cult, but we
Will devote ourselves to it
Until Moses returns to us."

٩١ ـ قَالُوا لَن نَّبْرَحَ عَلَيْهِ
عَاكِفِينَ حَتَّى يَرْجِعَ إِلَيْنَا مُوسَى ۞

92. (Moses) said: "O Aaron!
What kept thee back, when
Thou sawest them going wrong,

٩٢ ـ قَالَ يَهَارُونُ مَا مَنَعَكَ
إِذْ رَأَيْتَهُمْ ضَلُّوا ۞

93. "From following me? Didst thou
Then disobey my order?"

٩٣ ـ أَلَّا تَتَّبِعَنِ أَفَعَصَيْتَ أَمْرِي ۞

94. (Aaron) replied: "O son
Of my mother! Sieze (me) not
By my beard nor by
(The hair of) my head!

٩٤ ـ قَالَ يَبْنَؤُمَّ لَا تَأْخُذْ
بِلِحْيَتِي وَلَا بِرَأْسِي

Truly I feared lest thou
Shouldst say, 'Thou hast caused
A division among the Children
Of Israel, and thou didst not
Respect my word!'"

اِنِّیْ خَشِیْتُ اَنْ تَقُوْلَ
فَرَّقْتَ بَیْنَ بَنِیْۤ اِسْرَآءِیْلَ
وَلَمْ تَرْقُبْ قَوْلِیْ ۟

95. (Moses) said: "What then
Is thy case. O Sāmirī?"

۹۵ قَالَ فَمَا خَطْبُكَ یٰسَامِرِیُّ ۟

96. He replied: "I saw what
They saw not, so I took
A handful (of dust) from
The footprint of the Messenger,
And threw it (into the calf):
Thus did my soul suggest
To me."

۹۶ قَالَ بَصُرْتُ بِمَا لَمْ یَبْصُرُوْا بِهٖ فَقَبَضْتُ
قَبْضَةً مِّنْ اَثَرِ الرَّسُوْلِ
فَنَبَذْتُهَا وَكَذٰلِكَ سَوَّلَتْ لِیْ نَفْسِیْ ۟

97. (Moses) said: "Get thee gone!
But thy (punishment) in this life
Will be that thou wilt say,
'Touch me not'; and moreover
(For a future penalty) thou hast
A promise that will not fail:
Now look at thy god,
Of whom thou hast become
A devoted worshipper:
We will certainly (melt) it
In a blazing fire and scatter
It broadcast in the sea!"

۹۷ قَالَ فَاذْهَبْ فَاِنَّ لَكَ فِی الْحَیٰوةِ
اَنْ تَقُوْلَ لَا مِسَاسَ
وَاِنَّ لَكَ مَوْعِدًا لَّنْ تُخْلَفَهٗ ۚ
وَانْظُرْ اِلٰۤى اِلٰهِكَ الَّذِیْ
ظَلْتَ عَلَیْهِ عَاكِفًا ؕ
لَنُحَرِّقَنَّهٗ ثُمَّ لَنَنْسِفَنَّهٗ فِی الْیَمِّ نَسْفًا ۟

98. But the God of you all
Is Allah: there is
No god but He: all things
He comprehends in His
knowledge.

۹۸ اِنَّمَاۤ اِلٰهُكُمُ اللّٰهُ الَّذِیْ لَاۤ اِلٰهَ اِلَّا
هُوَ ؕ وَسِعَ كُلَّ شَیْءٍ عِلْمًا ۟

99. Thus do We relate to thee
Some stories of what happened
Before: for We have sent
Thee a Message from
Our own Presence.

۹۹ كَذٰلِكَ نَقُصُّ عَلَیْكَ مِنْ اَنْبَآءِ مَا
قَدْ سَبَقَ ۚ وَقَدْ اٰتَیْنٰكَ
مِنْ لَّدُنَّا ذِكْرًا ۖ

100. If any do turn away
Therefrom, verily they will
Bear a burden
On the Day of Judgement;

۱۰۰ مَنْ اَعْرَضَ عَنْهُ فَاِنَّهٗ
یَحْمِلُ یَوْمَ الْقِیٰمَةِ وِزْرًا ۟

101. They will abide in this (state):
And grievous will the burden
Be to them on that Day—

١٠١- خٰلِدِيْنَ فِيْهِ
وَسَآءَ لَهُمْ يَوْمَ الْقِيٰمَةِ حِمْلًا ۟

102. The Day when the Trumpet
Will be sounded: that Day,
We shall gather the sinful,
Blear-eyed (with terror),

١٠٢- يَوْمَ يُنْفَخُ فِى الصُّوْرِ
وَنَحْشُرُ الْمُجْرِمِيْنَ يَوْمَئِذٍ زُرْقًا ۖ

103. In whispers will they consult
Each other: "Ye tarried not
Longer than ten (Days);"

١٠٣- يَتَخَافَتُوْنَ بَيْنَهُمْ اِنْ لَبِثْتُمْ
اِلَّا عَشْرًا

104. We know best what they
Will say, when their leader
Most eminent in Conduct
Will say: "Ye tarried not
Longer than a day!"

١٠٤- نَحْنُ اَعْلَمُ بِمَا يَقُوْلُوْنَ اِذْ يَقُوْلُ اَمْثَلُهُمْ
طَرِيْقَةً اِنْ لَبِثْتُمْ اِلَّا يَوْمًا ۟ ۚ

SECTION 6.

105. They ask thee concerning
The Mountains: say, "My Lord
Will uproot them and scatter
Them as dust;"

١٠٥- وَيَسْئَلُوْنَكَ عَنِ الْجِبَالِ فَقُلْ
يَنْسِفُهَا رَبِّيْ نَسْفًا ۟

106. "He will leave them as plains
Smooth and level;"

١٠٦- فَيَذَرُهَا قَاعًا صَفْصَفًا ۟

107. "Nothing crooked or curved
Wilt thou see in their place."

١٠٧- لَا تَرٰى فِيْهَا عِوَجًا وَّلَا اَمْتًا ۟

108. On that Day will they follow
The Caller (straight): no
crookedness
(Can they show) him: all sounds
Shall humble themselves in
The Presence of (Allah) Most
Gracious:
Nothing shalt thou hear
But the tramp of their feet
(As they march).

١٠٨- يَوْمَئِذٍ يَّتَّبِعُوْنَ الدَّاعِىَ لَا عِوَجَ لَهٗ ۚ
وَخَشَعَتِ الْاَصْوَاتُ
لِلرَّحْمٰنِ
فَلَا تَسْمَعُ
اِلَّا هَمْسًا ۟

109. On that Day shall no
Intercession avail
Except for those for whom
Permission has been granted
By (Allah) Most Gracious
And whose word is
Acceptable to Him.

١٠٩- يَوْمَئِذٍ لَّا تَنْفَعُ الشَّفَاعَةُ
اِلَّا مَنْ اَذِنَ لَهُ الرَّحْمٰنُ
وَرَضِىَ لَهٗ قَوْلًا ۟

110. He knows what (appears
To His creatures as) before
Or after or behind them:
But they shall not compass it
With their knowledge.

١١٠- يَعْلَمُ مَا بَيْنَ أَيْدِيْهِمْ
وَمَا خَلْفَهُمْ
وَلَا يُحِيْطُوْنَ بِهِ عِلْمًا ○

111. (All) faces shall be humbled
Before (Him)— the Living,
The Self Subsisting, Eternal:
Hopeless indeed will be
The man that carries
Iniquity (on his back).

١١١- وَعَنَتِ الْوُجُوْهُ
لِلْحَيِّ الْقَيُّوْمِ
وَقَدْ خَابَ مَنْ حَمَلَ ظُلْمًا ○

112. But he who works deeds
Of righteousness, and has faith,
Will have no fear of harm
Nor of any curtailment
(Of what is his due).

١١٢- وَمَنْ يَعْمَلْ مِنَ الصّٰلِحٰتِ وَهُوَ
مُؤْمِنٌ
فَلَا يَخَافُ ظُلْمًا وَّلَا هَضْمًا ○

113. Thus have We sent this
Down— an Arabic Qur'ān—
And explained therein in detail
Some of the warnings,
In order that they may
Fear Allah, or that it may
Cause their remembrance
                      (of Him).

١١٣- وَكَذٰلِكَ أَنْزَلْنٰهُ قُرْاٰنًا عَرَبِيًّا
وَّصَرَّفْنَا فِيْهِ مِنَ الْوَعِيْدِ
لَعَلَّهُمْ يَتَّقُوْنَ
أَوْ يُحْدِثُ لَهُمْ ذِكْرًا ○

114. High above all is Allah,
The King, the Truth!
Be not in haste
With the Qur'ān before
Its revelation to thee
Is completed, but say,
"O my Lord! advance me
In knowledge

١١٤- فَتَعٰلَى اللّٰهُ الْمَلِكُ الْحَقُّ ۚ
وَلَا تَعْجَلْ بِالْقُرْاٰنِ مِنْ قَبْلِ
أَنْ يُّقْضٰى إِلَيْكَ وَحْيُهُ وَقُلْ
رَّبِّ زِدْنِيْ عِلْمًا ○

115. We had already, beforehand,
Taken the covenant of Adam,
But he forgot: and We found
On his part no firm resolve.
        SECTION 7.

١١٥- وَلَقَدْ عَهِدْنَا إِلٰى اٰدَمَ مِنْ قَبْلُ
فَنَسِيَ وَلَمْ نَجِدْ لَهُ عَزْمًا ۚ ○

116. When We said to the angels,
"Prostrate yourselves to Adam",
They prostrated themselves, but
                        not
Iblīs: he refused.

١١٦- وَإِذْ قُلْنَا لِلْمَلٰئِكَةِ اسْجُدُوْا لِاٰدَمَ
فَسَجَدُوْا إِلَّا إِبْلِيْسَ ؕ أَبٰى ○

117. Then We said: "O Adam!
Verily, this is an enemy
To thee and thy wife:
So let him not get you
Both out of the Garden,
So that thou are landed
In misery.

١١٧- فَقُلْنَا يَا آدَمُ إِنَّ هٰذَا عَدُوٌّ لَّكَ وَلِزَوْجِكَ فَلَا يُخْرِجَنَّكُمَا مِنَ الْجَنَّةِ فَتَشْقَى ۝

118. "There is therein (enough
provision)
For thee not to go hungry
Nor to go naked,"

١١٨- إِنَّ لَكَ أَلَّا تَجُوعَ فِيهَا وَلَا تَعْرَى ۝

119. "Nor to suffer from thirst,
Nor from the sun's heat."

١١٩- وَأَنَّكَ لَا تَظْمَأُ فِيهَا وَلَا تَضْحَى ۝

120. But Satan whispered evil
To him: he said, "O Adam!
Shall I lead thee to
The Tree of Eternity
And to a kingdom
That never decays?"

١٢٠- فَوَسْوَسَ إِلَيْهِ الشَّيْطَنُ قَالَ يَا آدَمُ هَلْ أَدُلُّكَ عَلَى شَجَرَةِ الْخُلْدِ وَمُلْكٍ لَا يَبْلَى ۝

121. In the result, they both
Ate of the tree, and so
Their nakedness appeared
To them: they began to sew
Together, for their covering,
Leaves from the Garden:
Thus did Adam disobey
His Lord, and allow himself
To be seduced.

١٢١- فَأَكَلَا مِنْهَا فَبَدَتْ لَهُمَا سَوْآتُهُمَا وَطَفِقَا يَخْصِفَانِ عَلَيْهِمَا مِنْ وَرَقِ الْجَنَّةِ وَعَصَى آدَمُ رَبَّهُ فَغَوَى ۝

122. But his Lord chose him
(For His Grace): He turned
To him, and gave him guidance.

١٢٢- ثُمَّ اجْتَبَاهُ رَبُّهُ فَتَابَ عَلَيْهِ وَهَدَى ۝

123. He said: "Get ye down,
Both of you—all together,
From the Garden, with enmity
One to another: but if,
As is sure, there comes to you
Guidance from Me, whosoever
Follows My guidance, will not
Lose his way, nor fall
Into misery.

١٢٣- قَالَ اهْبِطَا مِنْهَا جَمِيعًا بَعْضُكُمْ لِبَعْضٍ عَدُوٌّ فَإِمَّا يَأْتِيَنَّكُمْ مِنِّي هُدًى فَمَنِ اتَّبَعَ هُدَايَ فَلَا يَضِلُّ وَلَا يَشْقَى ۝

124. "But whosoever turns away
From My Message, verily

١٢٤- وَمَنْ أَعْرَضَ عَنْ ذِكْرِي

For him is a life narrowed
Down, and We shall raise
Him up blind on the Day
Of Judgement."

فَاِنَّ لَهٗ مَعِيشَةً ضَنْكًا وَّنَحْشُرُهٗ
يَوْمَ الْقِيٰمَةِ اَعْمٰى ۝

125. He will say: "O my Lord!
Why hast thou raised me
Up blind, while I had
Sight (before)?"

١٢٥- قَالَ رَبِّ لِمَ حَشَرْتَنِىْ
اَعْمٰى وَقَدْ كُنْتُ بَصِيْرًا ۝

126. (Allah) will say: "Thus
Didst thou, when Our Signs
Came unto thee, disregard
Them: so wilt thou,
This day, be disregarded."

١٢٦- قَالَ كَذٰلِكَ اَتَتْكَ اٰيٰتُنَا فَنَسِيْتَهَا ۚ
وَكَذٰلِكَ الْيَوْمَ تُنْسٰى ۝

127. And thus do We recompense
Him who transgresses beyond
                        bounds
And believes not in the Signs
Of his Lord: and the Penalty
Of the Hereafter is far more
Grievous and more enduring.

١٢٧- وَكَذٰلِكَ نَجْزِىْ مَنْ اَسْرَفَ
وَلَمْ يُؤْمِنْ بِاٰيٰتِ رَبِّهٖ ۚ
وَلَعَذَابُ الْاٰخِرَةِ اَشَدُّ وَاَبْقٰى ۝

128. Is it not a warning to such
Men (to call to mind)
How many generations before
                        them
We destroyed, in whose haunts
They (now) move? Verily,
In this are Signs for men
Endued with understanding,

SECTION 8.

١٢٨- اَفَلَمْ يَهْدِ لَهُمْ
كَمْ اَهْلَكْنَا قَبْلَهُمْ مِّنَ الْقُرُوْنِ
يَمْشُوْنَ فِىْ مَسٰكِنِهِمْ ۚ
اِنَّ فِىْ ذٰلِكَ لَاٰيٰتٍ لِّاُولِى النُّهٰى ۞

129. Had it not been
For a Word that went forth
Before from thy Lord,
(Their punishment) must
                        necessarily
Have come; but there is
A term appointed (for respite).

١٢٩- وَلَوْ لَا كَلِمَةٌ سَبَقَتْ
مِنْ رَّبِّكَ لَكَانَ لِزَامًا
وَّاَجَلٌ مُّسَمًّى ۝

130. Therefore be patient with what
They say, and celebrate
                        (constantly)
The praises of thy Lord
Before the rising of the sun,
And before its setting;
Yea, celebrate them
For part of the hours

١٣٠- فَاصْبِرْ عَلٰى مَا يَقُوْلُوْنَ وَسَبِّحْ
بِحَمْدِ رَبِّكَ قَبْلَ طُلُوْعِ الشَّمْسِ
وَقَبْلَ غُرُوْبِهَا ۚ
وَمِنْ اٰنَآئِ الَّيْلِ

Of the night, and at the sides
Of the day: that thou
Mayest have (spiritual) joy.

فَسَبِّحْ وَأَطْرَافَ النَّهَارِ لَعَلَّكَ تَرْضَىٰ ۝

131. Nor strain thine eyes in longing
For the things We have given
For enjoyment to parties
Of them, the splendour
Of the life of this world,
Through which We test them:
But the provision of thy Lord
Is better and more enduring.

١٣١- وَلَا تَمُدَّنَّ عَيْنَيْكَ إِلَىٰ مَا مَتَّعْنَا بِهِ
أَزْوَاجًا مِّنْهُمْ زَهْرَةَ
الْحَيَاةِ الدُّنْيَا لِنَفْتِنَهُمْ فِيهِ
وَرِزْقُ رَبِّكَ خَيْرٌ وَّأَبْقَىٰ ۝

132. Enjoin prayer on thy people,
And be constant therein.
We ask thee not to provide
Sustenance: We provide it
For thee. But the (fruit of)
The Hereafter is for Righteousness.

١٣٢- وَأْمُرْ أَهْلَكَ بِالصَّلَاةِ وَاصْطَبِرْ عَلَيْهَا
لَا نَسْأَلُكَ رِزْقًا نَّحْنُ نَرْزُقُكَ
وَالْعَاقِبَةُ لِلتَّقْوَىٰ ۝

133. They say: "Why does he not
Bring us a Sign from
His Lord?" Has not
A Clear Sign come to them
Of all that was
In the former Books
Of revelation?

١٣٣- وَقَالُوا لَوْلَا
يَأْتِينَا بِآيَةٍ مِّنْ رَّبِّهِ
أَوَلَمْ تَأْتِهِم بَيِّنَةُ
مَا فِي الصُّحُفِ الْأُولَىٰ ۝

134. And if We had inflicted
On them a penalty before this,
They would have said:
"Our Lord! If only Thou
Hadst sent us a messenger,
We should certainly have followed
Thy Signs before we were
Humbled and put to shame."

١٣٤- وَلَوْ أَنَّا أَهْلَكْنَاهُم بِعَذَابٍ مِّن
قَبْلِهِ لَقَالُوا رَبَّنَا لَوْلَا أَرْسَلْتَ
إِلَيْنَا رَسُولًا فَنَتَّبِعَ
آيَاتِكَ مِن قَبْلِ أَن نَّذِلَّ وَنَخْزَىٰ ۝

135. Say: "Each one (of us)
Is waiting: wait ye,
             therefore,
And soon shall ye know
Who it is that is
On the straight and
             even
Way, and who it is
That has received
             guidance."

١٣٥- قُلْ كُلٌّ مُّتَرَبِّصٌ فَتَرَبَّصُوا
فَسَتَعْلَمُونَ مَنْ
أَصْحَابُ الصِّرَاطِ السَّوِيِّ
وَمَنِ اهْتَدَىٰ ۝

INTRODUCTION TO SURA XXI. *(Anbiyāa)* — 112 Verses

The last Sūra dealt with the individual story (spiritual) of Moses and Aaron, and contrasted it with the growth of evil in individuals like Pharaoh and the Sāmirī, and ended with a warning against evil, and an exhortation to the purification of the soul with prayer and praise. This Sūra begins with the external obstacles placed by Evil against such purification, and gives the assurance of God's power to defend men, illustrating this with reference to Abraham's fight against idolatry, Lot's fight against unnatural wickedness, Noah's against unbelief, that of David and Solomon against injustice and failure to proclaim God's glory by making full use of man's God-given faculties and powers, that of Job against impatience and want of self-confidence, that of Ismā'īl, Idris, and Zul-kifl against want of steady perseverance, that of Zun-nūn against hasty anger, that of Zakarīyā against spiritual isolation, and that of Mary against the lusts of this world. In each illusion there is a special point about the souls purification. The common point is that the Prophets were not, as the vulgar suppose, just irresistible men. They had to win their ground inch by inch against all kinds of resistance from evil.

The chronology of this Sūra has no significance. It probably dates from the middle of the Meccan period of inspiration.

Al Anbiyā' (The Prophets)

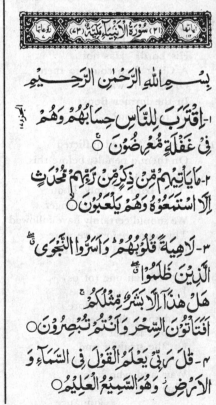

In the Name of Allah, Most Gracious, Most Merciful.

1. **C**loser and closer to mankind
   Comes their Reckoning: yet they
   Heed not and they turn away.

2. Never comes (aught) to them
   Of a renewed Message
   From their Lord, but they
   Listen to it as in jest—

3. Their hearts toying as with
   Trifles. The wrongdoers conceal
   Their private counsels, (saying),
   "Is this (one) more than
   A man like yourselves?
   Will ye go to witchcraft
   With your eyes open?"

4. Say: "My Lord
   Knoweth (every) word (spoken)
   In the heavens and on earth:
   He is the One that heareth
   And knoweth (all things)."

17/30

. "Nay," they say, "(these are)
Medleys of dreams!—Nay,
He forged it!—Nay,
He is (but) a poet!
Let him then bring us
A Sign like the ones
That were sent to
(Prophets) of old!"

٥- بَلْ قَالُوٓا أَضْغَاثُ أَحْلَامٍ
بَلِ افْتَرَىٰهُ بَلْ هُوَ شَاعِرٌ
فَلْيَأْتِنَا بِآيَةٍ كَمَآ
أُرْسِلَ الْأَوَّلُونَ ۞

6. (As to those) before them,
Not one of the populations
Which We destroyed believed:
Will these believe?

٦- مَآ ءَامَنَتْ قَبْلَهُم مِّن قَرْيَةٍ
أَهْلَكْنَاهَا أَفَهُمْ يُؤْمِنُونَ ۞

7. Before thee, also, the messengers
We sent were but men,
To whom We granted inspiration:
If ye realise this not, ask
Of those who possess the
                    Message.

٧- وَمَآ أَرْسَلْنَا قَبْلَكَ إِلَّا رِجَالًا
نُّوحِيٓ إِلَيْهِمْ فَسْـَٔلُوٓا أَهْلَ الذِّكْرِ إِن
كُنتُمْ لَا تَعْلَمُونَ ۞

8. Nor did We give them
Bodies that ate no food,
Nor were they exempt from
                    death.

٨- وَمَا جَعَلْنَاهُمْ جَسَدًا لَّا يَأْكُلُونَ
الطَّعَامَ وَمَا كَانُوا خَالِدِينَ ۞

9. In the end We fulfilled
To them Our promise,
And We saved them
And those whom We pleased,
But We destroyed those
Who transgressed beyond
                    bounds.

٩- ثُمَّ صَدَقْنَاهُمُ الْوَعْدَ فَأَنجَيْنَاهُمْ وَمَن
نَّشَآءُ
وَأَهْلَكْنَا الْمُسْرِفِينَ ۞

10. We have revealed for you
(O men!) a book in which
Is a Message for you:
Will ye not then understand?

SECTION 2.

١٠- لَقَدْ أَنزَلْنَآ إِلَيْكُمْ كِتَابًا فِيهِ
ذِكْرُكُمْ أَفَلَا تَعْقِلُونَ ۞

11. How many were the populations
We utterly destroyed because
Of their iniquities, setting up
In their places other peoples?

١١- وَكَمْ قَصَمْنَا مِن قَرْيَةٍ كَانَتْ ظَالِمَةً وَ
أَنشَأْنَا بَعْدَهَا قَوْمًا ءَاخَرِينَ ۞

12. Yet, when they felt
Our Punishment (coming),
Behold, they (tried to) flee
From it.

١٢- فَلَمَّآ أَحَسُّوا بَأْسَنَآ
إِذَا هُم مِّنْهَا يَرْكُضُونَ ۞

13. Flee not, but return to
    The good things of this life
    Which were given you,
    And to your homes,
    In order that ye may
    Be called to account.

١٣- لَا تَرْكُضُوْا وَارْجِعُوْٓا اِلٰى مَآ
اُتْرِفْتُمْ فِيْهِ وَمَسٰكِنِكُمْ
لَعَلَّكُمْ تُسْـَٔلُوْنَ ۞

14. They said: "Ah! woe to us!
    We were indeed wrongdoers!"

١٤- قَالُوْا يٰوَيْلَنَآ اِنَّا كُنَّا ظٰلِمِيْنَ ۞

15. And that cry of theirs
    Ceased not, till We made
    Them as a field
    That is mown, as ashes
    Silent and quenched.

١٥- فَمَا زَالَتْ تِّلْكَ دَعْوٰىهُمْ حَتّٰى جَعَلْنٰهُمْ
حَصِيْدًا خٰمِدِيْنَ ۞

16. Not for (idle) sport did We
    Create the heavens and the earth
    And all that is between!

١٦- وَمَا خَلَقْنَا السَّمَآءَ وَالْاَرْضَ
وَمَا بَيْنَهُمَا لٰعِبِيْنَ ۞

17. If it had been Our wish
    To take (just) a pastime,
    We should surely have taken
    It from the things nearest
    To Us, if We would
    Do (such a thing)!

١٧- لَوْ اَرَدْنَآ اَنْ نَّتَّخِذَ لَهْوًا
لَّاتَّخَذْنٰهُ مِنْ لَّدُنَّآ ۖ
اِنْ كُنَّا فٰعِلِيْنَ ۞

18. Nay, We hurl the Truth
    Against falsehood, and it knocks
    Out its brain, and behold,
    Falsehood doth perish!
    Ah! woe be to you
    For the (false) things
    Ye ascribe (to Us).

١٨- بَلْ نَقْذِفُ بِالْحَقِّ عَلَى الْبَاطِلِ
فَيَدْمَغُهُ فَاِذَا هُوَ زَاهِقٌ ۖ
وَلَكُمُ الْوَيْلُ مِمَّا تَصِفُوْنَ ۞

19. To Him belong all (creatures)
    In the heavens and on earth:
    Even those who are in His
    (Very) Presence are not
    Too proud to serve Him.
    Nor are they (ever) weary
    (Of His service):

١٩- وَلَهٗ مَنْ فِى السَّمٰوٰتِ وَالْاَرْضِ ۖ
وَمَنْ عِنْدَهٗ لَا يَسْتَكْبِرُوْنَ عَنْ عِبَادَتِهٖ
وَلَا يَسْتَحْسِرُوْنَ ۞

20. They celebrate His praises
    Night and day, nor do they
    Ever flag or intermit.

٢٠- يُسَبِّحُوْنَ الَّيْلَ وَالنَّهَارَ
لَا يَفْتُرُوْنَ ۞

21. Or have they taken
    (For worship) gods from the
            earth

٢١- اَمِ اتَّخَذُوْٓا اٰلِهَةً مِّنَ الْاَرْضِ

Who can raise (the dead)?

22. If there were, in the heavens
And the earth, other gods
Besides Allah, there would
Have been confusion in both!
But glory to Allah,
The Lord of the Throne:
(High is He) above
What they attribute to Him!

23. He cannot be questioned
For His acts, but they
Will be questioned (for theirs).

24. Or have they taken
For worship (other) gods
Besides Him? Say, "Bring
Your convincing proof: this
Is the Message of those
With me and the Message
Of those before me."
But most of them know not
The Truth, and so turn away.

25. Not a messenger did We
Send before thee without
This inspiration sent by Us
To him: that there is
No god but I; therefore
Worship and serve Me.

26. And they say: "(Allah)
Most Gracious has begotten
Offspring."Glory to Him!
They are (but) servants raised
To honour.

27. They speak not before
He speaks, and they act
(In all things) by His command.

28. He knows what is before them,
And what is behind them,
And they offer no intercession
Except for those who are
Acceptable, and they stand
In awe and reverence
Of His (glory).

هُمْ يُنْشِرُونَ ۟

٢٢- لَوْ كَانَ فِيهِمَا آلِهَةٌ إِلَّا اللهُ لَفَسَدَتَا ۚ فَسُبْحَانَ اللهِ رَبِّ الْعَرْشِ عَمَّا يَصِفُونَ ۟

٢٣- لَا يُسْأَلُ عَمَّا يَفْعَلُ وَهُمْ يُسْأَلُونَ ۟

٢٤- أَمِ اتَّخَذُوا مِنْ دُونِهِ آلِهَةً ۘ قُلْ هَاتُوا بُرْهَانَكُمْ ۚ هَذَا ذِكْرُ مَنْ مَعِيَ وَذِكْرُ مَنْ قَبْلِي ۗ بَلْ أَكْثَرُهُمْ لَا يَعْلَمُونَ الْحَقَّ فَهُمْ مُعْرِضُونَ ۟

٢٥- وَمَا أَرْسَلْنَا مِنْ قَبْلِكَ مِنْ رَسُولٍ إِلَّا نُوحِي إِلَيْهِ أَنَّهُ لَا إِلَهَ إِلَّا أَنَا فَاعْبُدُونِ ۟

٢٦- وَقَالُوا اتَّخَذَ الرَّحْمَنُ وَلَدًا سُبْحَانَهُ ۚ بَلْ عِبَادٌ مُكْرَمُونَ ۟

٢٧- لَا يَسْبِقُونَهُ بِالْقَوْلِ وَهُمْ بِأَمْرِهِ يَعْمَلُونَ ۟

٢٨- يَعْلَمُ مَا بَيْنَ أَيْدِيهِمْ وَمَا خَلْفَهُمْ وَلَا يَشْفَعُونَ إِلَّا لِمَنِ ارْتَضَى وَهُمْ مِنْ خَشْيَتِهِ مُشْفِقُونَ ۟

29. If any of them should say,
"I am a god besides Him",
Such a one We should
Reward with Hell: thus
Do We reward those
Who do wrong.

SECTION 3.

30. Do not the Unbelievers see
That the heavens and the earth
Were joined together (as one
Unit of Creation), before
We clove them asunder?
We made from water
Every living thing. Will they
Not then believe?

31. And We have set on the earth
Mountains standing firm,
Lest it should shake with them,
And We have made therein
Broad highways (between
                    mountains)
For them to pass through:
That they may receive
                    guidance.

32. And We have made
The heavens as a canopy
Well guarded: yet do they
Turn away from the Signs
Which these things (point to)!

33. It is He Who created
The Night and the Day,
And the sun and the moon:
All (the celestial bodies)
Swim along, each in its
Rounded course.

34. We granted not to any man
Before thee permanent life
(Here): if then thou shouldst die,
Would they live permanently?

35. Every soul shall have
A taste of death:

٢٩- وَمَنْ يَقُلْ مِنْهُمْ إِنِّيْ إِلٰهٌ مِّنْ دُوْنِهٖ فَذٰلِكَ نَجْزِيْهِ جَهَنَّمَ ۚ كَذٰلِكَ نَجْزِى الظّٰلِمِيْنَ ۞

٣٠- أَوَلَمْ يَرَ الَّذِيْنَ كَفَرُوْا أَنَّ السَّمٰوٰتِ وَالْأَرْضَ كَانَتَا رَتْقًا فَفَتَقْنٰهُمَا ۚ وَجَعَلْنَا مِنَ الْمَآءِ كُلَّ شَيْءٍ حَيٍّ ۗ أَفَلَا يُؤْمِنُوْنَ ۞

٣١- وَجَعَلْنَا فِي الْأَرْضِ رَوَاسِيَ أَنْ تَمِيْدَ بِهِمْ ۖ وَجَعَلْنَا فِيْهَا فِجَاجًا سُبُلًا لَّعَلَّهُمْ يَهْتَدُوْنَ ۞

٣٢- وَجَعَلْنَا السَّمَآءَ سَقْفًا مَّحْفُوْظًا ۚ وَّهُمْ عَنْ اٰيٰتِهَا مُعْرِضُوْنَ ۞

٣٣- وَهُوَ الَّذِيْ خَلَقَ الَّيْلَ وَالنَّهَارَ وَالشَّمْسَ وَالْقَمَرَ ۚ كُلٌّ فِيْ فَلَكٍ يَّسْبَحُوْنَ ۞

٣٤- وَمَا جَعَلْنَا لِبَشَرٍ مِّنْ قَبْلِكَ الْخُلْدَ ۚ أَفَإِنْ مِّتَّ فَهُمُ الْخٰلِدُوْنَ ۞

٣٥- كُلُّ نَفْسٍ ذَآئِقَةُ الْمَوْتِ ۗ

And We test you
By evil and by good
By way of trial.
To Us must ye return.

36. When the Unbelievers see thee,
They treat thee not except
With ridicule. "Is this,"
(They say), "The one who talks
Of your gods?" And they
Blaspheme at the mention
Of (Allah) Most Gracious!

37. Man is a creature of haste:
Soon (enough) will I show
You My Signs; then
Ye will not ask Me
To hasten them!

38. They say: "When will this
Promise come to pass,
If ye are telling the truth?"

39. If only the Unbelievers
Knew (the time) when they
Will not be able
To ward off the Fire
From their faces, nor yet
From their backs, and (when)
No help can reach them!

40. Nay, it may come to them
All of a sudden and confound
Them: no power will they
Have then to avert it,
Nor will they (then)
Get respite.

41. Mocked were (many)
Messengers before thee;
But their scoffers
Were hemmed in
By the thing that they mocked.

SECTION 4.

42. Say: "Who can keep
You safe by night and by day
From (the Wrath of) (Allah)
Most Gracious?" Yet they

Turn away from the mention
Of their Lord.

عَنْ ذِكْرِ رَبِّهِمْ مُّعْرِضُوْنَ ۟

43. Or have they gods that
Can guard them from Us?
They have no power to aid
Themselves, nor can they
Be defended from us.

٤٣- اَمْ لَهُمْ اٰلِهَةٌ تَمْنَعُهُمْ مِّنْ دُوْنِنَا ۚ
لَا يَسْتَطِيْعُوْنَ نَصْرَ اَنْفُسِهِمْ
وَلَا هُمْ مِّنَّا يُصْحَبُوْنَ ۟

44. Nay, We gave the good things
Of this life to these men
And their fathers until
The period   grew long for them;
See they not that We
Gradually reduce the land
(In their control) from
Its outlying borders? Is it
Then they who will win?

٤٤- بَلْ مَتَّعْنَا هٰؤُلَاءِ وَاٰبَاءَهُمْ
حَتّٰى طَالَ عَلَيْهِمُ الْعُمُرُ ؕ
اَفَلَا يَرَوْنَ اَنَّا نَأْتِى الْاَرْضَ
نَنْقُصُهَا مِنْ اَطْرَافِهَا ؕ
اَفَهُمُ الْغٰلِبُوْنَ ۟

45. Say, "I do but warn you
According to revelation";
But the deaf will not hear
The call, (even) when
They are warned!

٤٥- قُلْ اِنَّمَا اَنْذِرُكُمْ بِالْوَحْيِ ۖ ۚ
وَلَا يَسْمَعُ الصُّمُّ الدُّعَاءَ
اِذَا مَا يُنْذَرُوْنَ ۟

46. If but a breath of the Wrath
Of thy Lord do touch them,
They will then say, "Woe
To us! we did wrong indeed!"

٤٦- وَلَئِنْ مَّسَّتْهُمْ نَفْحَةٌ مِّنْ عَذَابِ
رَبِّكَ لَيَقُوْلُنَّ يٰوَيْلَنَا اِنَّا كُنَّا ظٰلِمِيْنَ ۟

47. We shall set up scales
Of justice for the day
Of Judgement, so that
Not a soul will be dealt with
Unjustly in the least.
And if there be
(No more than) the weight
Of a mustard seed,
We will bring it (to account):
And enough are We
To take account.

٤٧- وَنَضَعُ الْمَوَازِيْنَ الْقِسْطَ لِيَوْمِ الْقِيٰمَةِ
فَلَا تُظْلَمُ نَفْسٌ شَيْئًا ؕ
وَاِنْ كَانَ مِثْقَالَ حَبَّةٍ
مِّنْ خَرْدَلٍ اَتَيْنَا بِهَا ؕ
وَكَفٰى بِنَا حٰسِبِيْنَ ۟

48. In the past We granted
To Moses and Aaron
The Criterion (for judgement),
And a Light and a Message
For those who would do right—

٤٨- وَلَقَدْ اٰتَيْنَا مُوْسٰى وَهٰرُوْنَ
الْفُرْقَانَ وَضِيَاءً وَّذِكْرًا لِّلْمُتَّقِيْنَ ۙ

49. Those who fear their Lord
In their most secret thoughts,

٤٩- الَّذِيْنَ يَخْشَوْنَ رَبَّهُمْ بِالْغَيْبِ

And who hold the Hour
(Of Judgement) in awe.

وَهُمْ مِّنَ السَّاعَةِ مُشْفِقُوْنَ ۟

50. And this is a blessed
Message which We have
Sent down: will ye then
Reject it?
SECTION 5.

٥٠- وَهٰذَا ذِكْرٌ مُّبٰرَكٌ اَنْزَلْنٰهُ ۗ
اَفَاَنْتُمْ لَهٗ مُنْكِرُوْنَ ۟ ع

51. We bestowed aforetime
On Abraham his rectitude
Of conduct, and well were We
Acquainted with him.

٥١- وَلَقَدْ اٰتَيْنَا اِبْرٰهِيْمَ رُشْدَهٗ مِنْ قَبْلُ
وَكُنَّا بِهٖ عٰلِمِيْنَ ۟

52. Behold! he said
To his father and his people
"What are these images,
To which ye are
(So assiduously) devoted?"

٥٢- اِذْ قَالَ لِاَبِيْهِ وَقَوْمِهٖ
مَا هٰذِهِ التَّمَاثِيْلُ الَّتِيْ
اَنْتُمْ لَهَا عٰكِفُوْنَ ۟

53. They said, "We found
Our fathers worshipping them."

٥٣- قَالُوْا وَجَدْنَا اٰبَاءَنَا لَهَا عٰبِدِيْنَ ۟

54. He said, "Indeed ye
Have been in manifest
Error—ye and your fathers."

٥٤- قَالَ لَقَدْ كُنْتُمْ
اَنْتُمْ وَاٰبَاؤُكُمْ فِيْ ضَلٰلٍ مُّبِيْنٍ ۟

55. They said, "Have you
Brought us the Truth,
Or are you one
Of those who jest?"

٥٥- قَالُوْا اَجِئْتَنَا بِالْحَقِّ
اَمْ اَنْتَ مِنَ اللّٰعِبِيْنَ ۟

56. He said, "Nay, your Lord
Is the Lord of the heavens
And the earth. He Who
Created them (from nothing):
And I am a witness
To this (truth).

٥٦- قَالَ بَلْ رَّبُّكُمْ رَبُّ السَّمٰوٰتِ وَالْاَرْضِ
الَّذِيْ فَطَرَهُنَّ ۖ
وَاَنَا عَلٰى ذٰلِكُمْ مِّنَ الشّٰهِدِيْنَ ۟

57. "And by Allah, I have
A plan for your idols—
After ye go away
And turn your backs"…

٥٧- وَتَاللّٰهِ لَاَكِيْدَنَّ اَصْنَامَكُمْ
بَعْدَ اَنْ تُوَلُّوْا مُدْبِرِيْنَ ۟

58. So he broke them to pieces,
(All) but the biggest of them,
That they might turn
(And address themselves) to it.

٥٨- فَجَعَلَهُمْ جُذٰذًا اِلَّا كَبِيْرًا لَّهُمْ
لَعَلَّهُمْ اِلَيْهِ يَرْجِعُوْنَ ۟

59. They said, "Who has
Done this to our gods?
He must indeed be
Some man of impiety!"

٥٩- قَالُوْا مَنْ فَعَلَ هٰذَا بِالِهَتِنَآ
اِنَّهُ لَمِنَ الظَّلِمِيْنَ ٥

60. They said, "We heard
A youth talk of them:
He is called Abraham."

٦٠- قَالُوْا سَمِعْنَا فَتًى يَذْكُرُهُمْ
يُقَالُ لَهُ اِبْرٰهِيْمُ ٥

61. They said, "Then bring him
Before the eyes of the people,
That they may bear witness:"

٦١- قَالُوْا فَأْتُوْا بِهِ عَلٰى اَعْيُنِ النَّاسِ
لَعَلَّهُمْ يَشْهَدُوْنَ ٥

62. They said, "Art thou
The one that did this
With our gods, O Abraham?"

٦٢- قَالُوْا ءَاَنْتَ فَعَلْتَ هٰذَا
بِالِهَتِنَا يَاِبْرٰهِيْمُ ٥

63. He said: "Nay, this
Was done by—
This is their biggest one!
Ask them, if they
Can speak intelligently!"

٦٣- قَالَ بَلْ فَعَلَهُ
كَبِيْرُهُمْ هٰذَا
فَسْـَٔلُوْهُمْ اِنْ كَانُوْا يَنْطِقُوْنَ ٥

64. So they turned to themselves
And said, "Surely ye
Are the ones in the wrong!"

٦٤- فَرَجَعُوْا اِلٰى اَنْفُسِهِمْ
فَقَالُوْا اِنَّكُمْ اَنْتُمُ الظَّلِمُوْنَ ٥

65. Then were they confounded
With shame: (they said)
"Thou knowest full well that
These (idols) do not speak!"

٦٥- ثُمَّ نُكِسُوْا عَلٰى رُءُوْسِهِمْ
لَقَدْ عَلِمْتَ مَا هٰؤُلَاءِ يَنْطِقُوْنَ ٥

66. (Abraham) said, "Do ye then
Worship, besides Allah,
Things that can neither
Be of any good to you
Nor do you harm?

٦٦- قَالَ اَفَتَعْبُدُوْنَ مِنْ دُوْنِ اللهِ
مَا لَا يَنْفَعُكُمْ شَيْئًا وَّلَا يَضُرُّكُمْ ٥

67. "Fie upon you, and upon
The things that ye worship
Besides Allah! Have ye
No sense?". . .

٦٧- اُفٍّ لَّكُمْ وَلِمَا تَعْبُدُوْنَ
مِنْ دُوْنِ اللهِ اَفَلَا تَعْقِلُوْنَ ٥

68. They said, "Burn him
And protect your gods,
If ye do (anything at all)!"

٦٨- قَالُوْا حَرِّقُوْهُ وَانْصُرُوْا الِهَتَكُمْ
اِنْ كُنْتُمْ فٰعِلِيْنَ ٥

69. We said, "O Fire!

٦٩- قُلْنَا يٰنَارُ كُوْنِيْ بَرْدًا

Be thou cool,
And (a means of) safety
For Abraham!"

وَسَلَامًا عَلَىٰٓ إِبْرَٰهِيمَ ۞

70. Then they sought a stratagem
Against him: but We
Made them the ones
That lost most!

٧٠۔ وَأَرَادُوا بِهِۦ كَيْدًا
فَجَعَلْنَٰهُمُ ٱلْأَخْسَرِينَ ۞

71. But We delivered him
And (his nephew) Lūṭ
(And directed them) to the land
Which We have blessed
For the nations.

٧١۔ وَنَجَّيْنَٰهُ وَلُوطًا إِلَى ٱلْأَرْضِ
ٱلَّتِى بَٰرَكْنَا فِيهَا لِلْعَٰلَمِينَ ۞

72. And We bestowed on him Isaac
And, as an additional gift,
(A grandson), Jacob, and We
Made righteous men of every one
(Of them).

٧٢۔ وَوَهَبْنَا لَهُۥٓ إِسْحَٰقَ ۗ وَيَعْقُوبَ
نَافِلَةً ۖ وَكُلًّا جَعَلْنَا صَٰلِحِينَ ۞

73. And We made them
Leaders, guiding (men) by
Our Command, and We
Sent them inspiration
To do good deeds,
To establish regular prayers,
And to practise regular charity;
And they constantly served
Us (and Us only).

٧٣۔ وَجَعَلْنَٰهُمْ أَئِمَّةً يَهْدُونَ بِأَمْرِنَا
وَأَوْحَيْنَآ إِلَيْهِمْ فِعْلَ ٱلْخَيْرَٰتِ
وَإِقَامَ ٱلصَّلَوٰةِ وَإِيتَآءَ ٱلزَّكَوٰةِ ۖ
وَكَانُوا لَنَا عَٰبِدِينَ ۞

74. And to Lūṭ, too,
We gave Judgement and
             Knowledge,
And We saved him
From the town which practised
Abominations: truly they were
A people given to Evil,
A rebellious people.

٧٤۔ وَلُوطًا ءَاتَيْنَٰهُ حُكْمًا وَعِلْمًا
وَنَجَّيْنَٰهُ مِنَ ٱلْقَرْيَةِ ٱلَّتِى
كَانَت تَّعْمَلُ ٱلْخَبَٰٓئِثَ ۗ
إِنَّهُمْ كَانُوا قَوْمَ سَوْءٍ فَٰسِقِينَ ۞

75. And We admitted him
To Our Mercy: for he
Was one of the Righteous.

٧٥۔ وَأَدْخَلْنَٰهُ فِى رَحْمَتِنَآ ۖ
إِنَّهُۥ مِنَ ٱلصَّٰلِحِينَ ۞ ع

SECTION 6.

76. (Remember) Noah, when
He cried (to Us) aforetime:
We listened to his (prayer)

٧٦۔ وَنُوحًا إِذْ نَادَىٰ مِن قَبْلُ
فَٱسْتَجَبْنَا لَهُۥ

And delivered him and his
Family from great distress.

فَنَجَّيْنَاهُ وَأَهْلَهُ مِنَ الْكَرْبِ الْعَظِيمِ ۚ

77. We helped him against
People who rejected Our Signs:
Truly they were a people
Given to Evil: so We
Drowned them (in the Flood)
All together.

٧٧- وَنَصَرْنَاهُ مِنَ الْقَوْمِ الَّذِينَ كَذَّبُوا بِآيَاتِنَا ۗ إِنَّهُمْ كَانُوا قَوْمَ سَوْءٍ فَأَغْرَقْنَاهُمْ أَجْمَعِينَ ۞

78. And remember David
And Solomon, when they
Give judgement in the matter
Of the field into which
The sheep of certain people
Had strayed by night:
We did witness their judgement.

٧٨- وَدَاوُدَ وَسُلَيْمَانَ إِذْ يَحْكُمَانِ فِي الْحَرْثِ إِذْ نَفَشَتْ فِيهِ غَنَمُ الْقَوْمِ ۚ وَكُنَّا لِحُكْمِهِمْ شَاهِدِينَ ۞

79. To Solomon We inspired
The (right) understanding
Of the matter: to each
(Of them) We gave Judgement
And Knowledge; it was
Our power that made
The hills and the birds
Celebrate Our praises.
With David: it was We
Who did (all these things).

٧٩- فَفَهَّمْنَاهَا سُلَيْمَانَ ۚ وَكُلًّا آتَيْنَا حُكْمًا وَعِلْمًا ۚ وَسَخَّرْنَا مَعَ دَاوُدَ الْجِبَالَ يُسَبِّحْنَ وَالطَّيْرَ ۚ وَكُنَّا فَاعِلِينَ ۞

80. It was We Who taught him
The making of coats of mail
For your benefit, to guard
You from each other's violence:
Will ye then be grateful?

٨٠- وَعَلَّمْنَاهُ صَنْعَةَ لَبُوسٍ لَكُمْ لِتُحْصِنَكُمْ مِنْ بَأْسِكُمْ ۖ فَهَلْ أَنْتُمْ شَاكِرُونَ ۞

81. (It was Our power that
Made) the violent (unruly)
Wind flow (tamely) for
                    Solomon,
To his order, to the land
Which We had blessed:
For We do know all things.

٨١- وَلِسُلَيْمَانَ الرِّيحَ عَاصِفَةً تَجْرِي بِأَمْرِهِ إِلَى الْأَرْضِ الَّتِي بَارَكْنَا فِيهَا ۚ وَكُنَّا بِكُلِّ شَيْءٍ عَالِمِينَ ۞

82. And of the evil ones,

٨٢- وَمِنَ الشَّيَاطِينِ مَنْ يَغُوصُونَ لَهُ

Were some who dived
For him, and did other work
Besides; and it was We
Who guarded them.

٨٣- وَأَيُّوبَ إِذْ نَادَى رَبَّهُ

83. And (remember) Job, when
He cried to his Lord,
"Truly distress has seized me.
But Thou are the Most
Merciful of those that are
Merciful."

أَنِّي مَسَّنِيَ الضُّرُّ وَأَنْتَ
أَرْحَمُ الرَّاحِمِينَ ۞

84. So We listened to him:
We removed the distress
That was on him,
And We restored his people
To him, and doubled
Their number—as a Grace
From Ourselves, and a thing
For commemoration, for all
Who serve Us.

٨٤- فَاسْتَجَبْنَا لَهُ فَكَشَفْنَا مَا بِهِ مِنْ ضُرٍّ
وَآتَيْنَاهُ أَهْلَهُ وَمِثْلَهُمْ مَعَهُمْ
رَحْمَةً مِنْ عِنْدِنَا
وَذِكْرَى لِلْعَابِدِينَ ۞

85. And (remember) Isma'il,
Idris, and Dhu al Kifl, all
(Men) of constancy and patience;

٨٥- وَإِسْمَاعِيلَ وَإِدْرِيسَ وَذَا الْكِفْلِ
كُلٌّ مِنَ الصَّابِرِينَ ۞

86. We admitted them to
Our Mercy: for they
Were of the Righteous ones.

٨٦- وَأَدْخَلْنَاهُمْ فِي رَحْمَتِنَا
إِنَّهُمْ مِنَ الصَّالِحِينَ ۞

87. And remember Dhu al Nūn,
When he departed in wrath:
He imagined that We
Had no power over him!
But he cried through the depths
Of darkness, "There is
No god but Thou:
Glory to Thee: I was
Indeed wrong!"

٨٧- وَذَا النُّونِ إِذْ ذَهَبَ مُغَاضِبًا
فَظَنَّ أَنْ لَنْ نَقْدِرَ عَلَيْهِ
فَنَادَى فِي الظُّلُمَاتِ
أَنْ لَا إِلَهَ إِلَّا أَنْتَ سُبْحَانَكَ
إِنِّي كُنْتُ مِنَ الظَّالِمِينَ ۞

88. So We listened to him:
And delivered him from
Distress: and thus do We
Deliver those who have faith.

٨٨- فَاسْتَجَبْنَا لَهُ وَنَجَّيْنَاهُ مِنَ الْغَمِّ
وَكَذَلِكَ نُنْجِي الْمُؤْمِنِينَ ۞

89. And (remember) Zakarīyā,
When he cried to his Lord:

٨٩- وَزَكَرِيَّا إِذْ نَادَى رَبَّهُ

"O my Lord! leave me not
Without offspring, though Thou
Art the best of inheritors."

رَبِّ لَا تَذَرْنِي فَرْدًا
وَأَنْتَ خَيْرُ الْوَارِثِينَ ۝

90. So We listened to him:
And We granted him
Yahyā: We cured his wife's
(Barrenness) for him. These
                    (three)
Were ever quick in emulation
In good works; they used
To call on Us with love
And reverence, and humble
                    themselves
Before Us.

٩٠- فَاسْتَجَبْنَا لَهُ وَوَهَبْنَا لَهُ
يَحْيَى وَأَصْلَحْنَا لَهُ زَوْجَهُ
إِنَّهُمْ كَانُوا يُسَارِعُونَ فِي الْخَيْرَاتِ
وَيَدْعُونَنَا رَغَبًا وَرَهَبًا
وَكَانُوا لَنَا خَاشِعِينَ ۝

91. And (remember) her who
Guarded her chastity:
We breathed into her
Of Our Spirit, and We
Made her and her son
A Sign for all peoples.

٩١- وَالَّتِي أَحْصَنَتْ فَرْجَهَا
فَنَفَخْنَا فِيهَا مِنْ رُوحِنَا
وَجَعَلْنَاهَا وَابْنَهَا آيَةً لِلْعَالَمِينَ ۝

92. Verily, this Brotherhood
Of yours is a single
                    Brotherhood,
And I am your Lord
And Cherisher: therefore
Serve Me (and no other).

٩٢- إِنَّ هَذِهِ أُمَّتُكُمْ أُمَّةً وَاحِدَةً
وَأَنَا رَبُّكُمْ فَاعْبُدُونِ ۝

93. But (later generations) cut off
Their affairs (of unity),
One from another: (yet)
Will they all return to Us.

٩٣- وَتَقَطَّعُوا أَمْرَهُمْ بَيْنَهُمْ
كُلٌّ إِلَيْنَا رَاجِعُونَ ۝

SECTION 7.

94. Whoever works any act
Of Righteousness and has Faith—
His endeavour will not
Be rejected: We shall
Record it in his favour.

٩٤- فَمَنْ يَعْمَلْ مِنَ الصَّالِحَاتِ وَهُوَ مُؤْمِنٌ
فَلَا كُفْرَانَ لِسَعْيِهِ
وَإِنَّا لَهُ كَاتِبُونَ ۝

95. But there is a ban
On any population which
We have destroyed: that they
Shall not return.

٩٥- وَحَرَامٌ عَلَى قَرْيَةٍ
أَهْلَكْنَاهَا أَنَّهُمْ لَا يَرْجِعُونَ ۝

96. Until the Gog and Magog
                    (people)
Are let through (their barrier),

٩٦- حَتَّى إِذَا فُتِحَتْ يَأْجُوجُ وَمَأْجُوجُ

And they swiftly swarm
From every hill.

وَهُمْ مِّنْ كُلِّ حَدَبٍ يَنْسِلُوْنَ ۞

97. Then will the True Promise
Draw nigh (of fulfilment):
Then behold! the eyes
Of the Unbelievers will
Fixedly stare in horror: "Ah!
Woe to us! we were indeed
Heedless of this; nay; we
Truly did wrong!"

۹۷ ـ وَاقْتَرَبَ الْوَعْدُ الْحَقُّ
فَاِذَا هِىَ شَاخِصَةٌ اَبْصَارُ الَّذِيْنَ كَفَرُوْا
يٰوَيْلَنَا قَدْ كُنَّا فِىْ غَفْلَةٍ مِّنْ هٰذَا
بَلْ كُنَّا ظٰلِمِيْنَ ۞

98. Verily ye, (Unbelievers),
And the (false) gods that
Ye worship besides Allah,
Are (but) fuel for Hell!
To it will ye (surely) come!

۹۸ ـ اِنَّكُمْ وَمَا تَعْبُدُوْنَ مِنْ دُوْنِ اللّٰهِ
حَصَبُ جَهَنَّمَ ؕ
اَنْتُمْ لَهَا وٰرِدُوْنَ ۞

99. If these had been gods,
They would not have got
there!
But each one will abide
Therein.

۹۹ ـ لَوْ كَانَ هٰٓؤُلَاۤءِ اٰلِهَةً مَّا وَرَدُوْهَا ؕ
وَكُلٌّ فِيْهَا خٰلِدُوْنَ ۞

100. There, sobbing will be
Their lot, nor will they
There hear (aught else).

۱۰۰ ـ لَهُمْ فِيْهَا زَفِيْرٌ
وَّهُمْ فِيْهَا لَا يَسْمَعُوْنَ ۞

101. Those for whom
The Good (Record) from Us
Has gone before, will be
Removed far therefrom.

۱۰۱ ـ اِنَّ الَّذِيْنَ سَبَقَتْ لَهُمْ مِّنَّا الْحُسْنٰىٓ
اُولٰٓئِكَ عَنْهَا مُبْعَدُوْنَ ۞

102. Not the slightest sound
Will they hear of Hell:
What their souls desired,
In that will they dwell.

۱۰۲ ـ لَا يَسْمَعُوْنَ حَسِيْسَهَا ۚ وَهُمْ فِىْ مَا
اشْتَهَتْ اَنْفُسُهُمْ خٰلِدُوْنَ ۞

103. The Great Terror will
Bring them no grief:
But the angels will meet them
(With mutual greetings):
"This is your Day—
(The Day) that ye were promised."

۱۰۳ ـ لَا يَحْزُنُهُمُ الْفَزَعُ الْاَكْبَرُ
وَتَتَلَقّٰهُمُ الْمَلٰٓئِكَةُ ؕ
هٰذَا يَوْمُكُمُ الَّذِىْ كُنْتُمْ تُوْعَدُوْنَ ۞

104. The Day that We roll up
The heavens like a scroll

۱۰۴ ـ يَوْمَ نَطْوِى السَّمَآءَ كَطَىِّ السِّجِلِّ لِلْكُتُبِ ؕ

Rolled up for books
        (completed)—
Even as We produced
The first Creation, so
Shall We produce
A new one: a promise
We have undertaken:
Truly shall We fulfil it.

كَمَا بَدَأْنَا أَوَّلَ خَلْقٍ
نُّعِيْدُهُ ۚ وَعْدًا عَلَيْنَا ۚ
اِنَّا كُنَّا فٰعِلِيْنَ ۝

105. Before this We wrote
In the Psalms,   after the
                Message
(Given to Moses):   "My servants,
The righteous, shall inherit
The earth."

١٠٥- وَلَقَدْ كَتَبْنَا فِي الزَّبُوْرِ
مِنْ بَعْدِ الذِّكْرِ
اَنَّ الْاَرْضَ يَرِثُهَا عِبَادِيَ الصّٰلِحُوْنَ ۝

106. Verily in this (Qur'ān)
Is a Message for people
Who would (truly) worship
                Allah.

١٠٦- اِنَّ فِيْ هٰذَا لَبَلٰغًا
لِّقَوْمٍ عٰبِدِيْنَ ۝

107. We sent thee not, but
As a mercy for all creatures.

١٠٧- وَمَا اَرْسَلْنٰكَ اِلَّا رَحْمَةً لِّلْعٰلَمِيْنَ ۝

108. Say: "What has come to me
By inspiration is that
Your God is One God:
Will ye therefore bow
To His Will (in Islām)?"

١٠٨- قُلْ اِنَّمَا يُوْحٰى اِلَيَّ اَنَّمَا
اِلٰهُكُمْ اِلٰهٌ وَّاحِدٌ ۚ
فَهَلْ اَنْتُمْ مُّسْلِمُوْنَ ۝

109. But if they turn back,
Say: "I have proclaimed
The Message to you all alike
And in truth; but I
Know not whether that
Which ye are promised
Is near or far.

١٠٩- فَاِنْ تَوَلَّوْا فَقُلْ اٰذَنْتُكُمْ
عَلٰى سَوَآءٍ ۚ وَاِنْ اَدْرِيْ اَقَرِيْبٌ
اَمْ بَعِيْدٌ مَّا تُوْعَدُوْنَ ۝

110. "It is He Who knows
What is open in speech
And what ye hide
(In your hearts).

١١٠- اِنَّهُ يَعْلَمُ الْجَهْرَ مِنَ الْقَوْلِ
وَيَعْلَمُ مَا تَكْتُمُوْنَ ۝

111. "I know not but that
It may be a trial
For you, and a grant
Of (worldly) livelihood
(To you) for a time."

١١١- وَاِنْ اَدْرِيْ لَعَلَّهُ فِتْنَةٌ
لَّكُمْ وَمَتَاعٌ اِلٰى حِيْنٍ ۝

112. Say: "O my Lord!
Judge Thou in truth!"
"Our Lord Most Gracious
Is the One Whose assistance
Should be sought against
The blasphemies ye utter!"

١١٢ـ قُلْ رَبِّ احْكُم بِالْحَقِّ
وَرَبُّنَا الرَّحْمَنُ الْمُسْتَعَانُ
عَلَى مَا تَصِفُونَ ٥

INTRODUCTION TO SŪRA XXII. *(Ḥajj)* — 78 Verses

We now come to a new series of four Sūras, dealing with the environments and methods contributing to our spiritual progress, as the last five Sūras dealt with the Messengers who came in various ways to proclaim the Truth and conquer evil. See Introduction to S. xvii.

The subject-matter of this particular Sūra is concerned mainly with the spiritual implications of the Sacred House, the Pilgrimage, the Sacrifices, Striving and Fighting in defence of Truth when attacked, and other acts that make for Unselfishness and uproot Falsehood.

On the chronology of this Sūra, opinion is divided. Some parts were probably revealed in the later Meccan period, and some in Medina. But the chronological question has no significance here.

Al Ḥajj (The Pilgrimage)

In the name of Allah, Most Gracious,
Most Merciful.

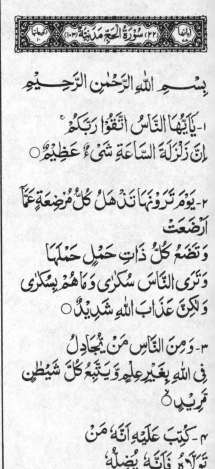

1. ❂ mankind! Fear your Lord!
   For the convulsion of the Hour
   (Of Judgement) will be
   A thing terrible!

2. The Day ye shall see it,
   Every mother giving suck
   Shall forget her suckling babe,
   And every pregnant female
   Shall drop her load (unformed):
   Thou shall see mankind
   As in a drunken riot,
   Yet not drunk: but dreadful
   Will be the Wrath of Allah.

3. And yet among men
   There are such as dispute
   About Allah, without knowledge,
   And follow every evil one
   Obstinate in rebellion!

4. About the (Evil One)
   It is decreed that whoever
   Turns to him for friendship,
   Him will he lead astray,

And he will guide him
To the Penalty of the Fire.

وَيَهْدِيهِ إِلَىٰ عَذَابِ السَّعِيرِ ۝

5. ⓘ mankind! if ye have
A doubt about the
                Resurrection,
(Consider) that We created you
Out of dust, then out of
Sperm, then out of a leech-like
Clot, then out of a morsel
Of flesh, partly formed
And partly unformed, in order
That We may manifest
(Our Power) to you;
And We cause whom We will
To rest in the wombs
For an appointed term,
Then do We bring you out
As babes, then (foster you)
That ye may reach your age
Of full strength; and some
Of you are called to die,
And some are sent back
To the feeblest old age,
So that they know nothing
After having known (much).
And (further), thou seest
The earth barren and lifeless,
But when We pour down
Rain on it, it is stirred
(To life), it swells,
And it puts forth every kind
Of beautiful growth in pairs.

يَا أَيُّهَا النَّاسُ إِن كُنتُمْ فِي رَيْبٍ مِّنَ الْبَعْثِ
فَإِنَّا خَلَقْنَاكُم مِّن تُرَابٍ
ثُمَّ مِن نُّطْفَةٍ ثُمَّ مِنْ عَلَقَةٍ
ثُمَّ مِن مُّضْغَةٍ مُّخَلَّقَةٍ
وَغَيْرِ مُخَلَّقَةٍ لِّنُبَيِّنَ لَكُمْ
وَنُقِرُّ فِي الْأَرْحَامِ مَا نَشَاءُ إِلَىٰ أَجَلٍ مُّسَمًّى
ثُمَّ نُخْرِجُكُمْ طِفْلًا ثُمَّ لِتَبْلُغُوا أَشُدَّكُمْ
وَمِنكُم مَّن يُتَوَفَّىٰ
وَمِنكُم مَّن يُرَدُّ إِلَىٰ أَرْذَلِ الْعُمُرِ
لِكَيْلَا يَعْلَمَ مِنْ بَعْدِ عِلْمٍ شَيْئًا
وَتَرَى الْأَرْضَ هَامِدَةً
فَإِذَا أَنزَلْنَا عَلَيْهَا الْمَاءَ
اهْتَزَّتْ وَرَبَتْ
وَأَنبَتَتْ مِن كُلِّ زَوْجٍ بَهِيجٍ ۝

6. This is so, because Allah
Is the Reality: it is He
Who gives life to the dead,
And it is He Who has
Power over all things.

ذَٰلِكَ بِأَنَّ اللَّهَ هُوَ الْحَقُّ
وَأَنَّهُ يُحْيِي الْمَوْتَىٰ
وَأَنَّهُ عَلَىٰ كُلِّ شَيْءٍ قَدِيرٌ ۝

7. And verily the Hour will come:
There can be no doubt
About it, or about (the fact)
That Allah will raise up
All who are in the graves.

وَأَنَّ السَّاعَةَ آتِيَةٌ لَّا رَيْبَ فِيهَا
وَأَنَّ اللَّهَ يَبْعَثُ مَن فِي الْقُبُورِ

8. Yet there is among men
Such a one as disputes
About Allah, without knowledge,
Without guidance, and without
A Book of Enlightenment—

٨- وَمِنَ النَّاسِ مَنْ يُّجَادِلُ فِى اللّٰهِ بِغَيْرِ عِلْمٍ وَّلَا هُدًى وَّلَا كِتَبٍ مُّنِيْرٍ ۙ

9. (Disdainfully) bending his side,
In order to lead (men) astray
From the Path of Allah:
For him there is disgrace
In this life, and on the Day
Of Judgement We shall
Make him taste the Penalty
Of burning (Fire).

٩- ثَانِىَ عِطْفِهٖ لِيُضِلَّ عَنْ سَبِيْلِ اللّٰهِ ۖ لَهٗ فِى الدُّنْيَا خِزْيٌ وَّنُذِيْقُهٗ يَوْمَ الْقِيٰمَةِ عَذَابَ الْحَرِيْقِ ۟

10. (It will be said): "This is
Because of the deeds which
Thy hands sent forth,
For verily Allah is not
Unjust to His servants."

١٠- ذٰلِكَ بِمَا قَدَّمَتْ يَدٰكَ وَاَنَّ اللّٰهَ لَيْسَ بِظَلَّامٍ لِّلْعَبِيْدِ ۟ ۚ

SECTION 2.

11. There are among men
Some who serve Allah,
As it were, on the verge:
If good befalls them, they are,
Therewith, well content; but
If a trial comes to them,
They turn on their faces:
They lose both this world
And the Hereafter: that
Is loss for all to see!

١١- وَمِنَ النَّاسِ مَنْ يَّعْبُدُ اللّٰهَ عَلٰى حَرْفٍ ۚ فَاِنْ اَصَابَهٗ خَيْرُ ‌ۨاطْمَاَنَّ بِهٖ ۚ وَاِنْ اَصَابَتْهُ فِتْنَةُ ‌ۨانْقَلَبَ عَلٰى وَجْهِهٖ ۟ خَسِرَ الدُّنْيَا وَالْاٰخِرَةَ ۚ ذٰلِكَ هُوَ الْخُسْرَانُ الْمُبِيْنُ ۟

12. They call on such deities,
Besides Allah, as can neither
Hurt nor profit them:
That is straying far indeed
(From the Way)!

١٢- يَدْعُوْا مِنْ دُوْنِ اللّٰهِ مَا لَا يَضُرُّهٗ وَمَا لَا يَنْفَعُهٗ ۚ ذٰلِكَ هُوَ الضَّلٰلُ الْبَعِيْدُ ۚ

13. (Perhaps) they call on one
Whose hurt is nearer
Than his profit: evil, indeed,
Is the patron, and evil
The companion (for help)!

١٣- يَدْعُوْا لَمَنْ ضَرُّهٗ اَقْرَبُ مِنْ نَّفْعِهٖ ۚ لَبِئْسَ الْمَوْلٰى وَلَبِئْسَ الْعَشِيْرُ ۟

14. Verily Allah will admit
Those who believe and work
Righteous deeds, to Gardens,
Beneath which rivers flow:

١٤- اِنَّ اللّٰهَ يُدْخِلُ الَّذِيْنَ اٰمَنُوْا وَعَمِلُوا الصّٰلِحٰتِ جَنّٰتٍ تَجْرِيْ مِنْ تَحْتِهَا الْاَنْهٰرُ

For Allah carries out
All that He plans.[2785]

إن الله يفعل ما يريد ○

15. If any think that Allah
Will not help him
(His Messenger) in this world
And the Hereafter, let him
Stretch out a rope
To the ceiling and cut (himself)
Off: then let him see
Whether his plan will remove
That which enrages (him)!

١٥- من كان يظن أن لن ينصره الله
في الدنيا والآخرة
فليمدد بسبب إلى السماء ثم ليقطع
فلينظر هل يذهبن كيده ما يغيظ ○

16. Thus have We sent down
Clear Signs: and verily
Allah doth guide whom
He will!

١٦- وكذلك أنزلناه آيات بينات
وأن الله يهدي من يريد ○

17. Those who believe (in the Qur'ān),
Those who follow the Jewish
(scriptures),
And the Sabians, Christians,
Magians, and Polytheists—
Allah will judge between them
On the Day of Judgement:
For Allah is witness
Of all things.

١٧- إن الذين آمنوا والذين هادوا
والصابئين والنصارى والمجوس والذين
أشركوا إن الله يفصل بينهم
يوم القيامة إن الله على كل شيء
شهيد ○

18. Seest thou not that
To Allah bow down in worship
All things that are
In the heavens and on earth—
The sun, the moon, the stars;
The hills, the trees, the animals;
And a great number among
Mankind? But a great number
Are (also) such as are
Fit for Punishment: and such
As Allah shall disgrace—
None can raise to honour:
For Allah carries out
All that He wills.

١٨- ألم تر أن الله يسجد له
من في السموات ومن في الأرض
والشمس والقمر والنجوم والجبال والشجر
والدواب وكثير من الناس وكثير
حق عليه العذاب
ومن يهن الله فما له من مكرم
إن الله يفعل ما يشاء ۩ ○

19. These two antagonists dispute
With each other about their Lord:
But those who deny (their Lord)—
For them will be cut out
A garment of Fire:
Over their heads will be

١٩- هذان خصمان اختصموا في ربهم
فالذين كفروا قطعت لهم
ثياب من نار يصب من فوق

Poured out boiling water.

20. With it will be scalded
What is within their bodies,
As well as (their) skins.

٢٠- يُصْهَرُ بِهِ مَا فِيْ بُطُوْنِهِمْ وَالْجُلُوْدُۗ

21. In addition there will be
Maces of iron (to punish) them.

٢١- وَلَهُمْ مَّقَامِعُ مِنْ حَدِيْدٍ۟

22. Every time they wish
To get away therefrom,
From anguish, they will be
Forced back therein, and
(It will be said), "Taste ye
The Penalty of Burning!"

٢٢- كُلَّمَآ اَرَادُوْٓا اَنْ يَّخْرُجُوْا مِنْهَا
مِنْ غَمٍّ اُعِيْدُوْا فِيْهَاۤ
وَذُوْقُوْا عَذَابَ الْحَرِيْقِۗ

SECTION 3.

23. Allah will admit those
Who believe and work righteous
deeds.
To Gardens beneath which
Rivers flow: they shall be
Adorned therein with bracelets
Of gold and pearls; and
Their garments there
Will be of silk.

٢٣- اِنَّ اللّٰهَ يُدْخِلُ الَّذِيْنَ اٰمَنُوْا وَعَمِلُوا
الصّٰلِحٰتِ جَنّٰتٍ تَجْرِيْ مِنْ تَحْتِهَا
الْاَنْهٰرُ يُحَلَّوْنَ فِيْهَا مِنْ اَسَاوِرَ مِنْ
ذَهَبٍ وَّ لُؤْلُؤًا ۚ وَلِبَاسُهُمْ فِيْهَا حَرِيْرٌ۟

24. For they have been guided
(In this life) to the purest
Of speeches; they have been
Guided to the Path of Him
Who is Worthy of (all) Praise.

٢٤- وَهُدُوْٓا اِلَى الطَّيِّبِ مِنَ الْقَوْلِ ۖ
وَهُدُوْٓا اِلٰى صِرَاطِ الْحَمِيْدِ۟

25. As to those who have rejected
(Allah), and would keep back
(men)
From the Way of Allah, and
From the Sacred Mosque, which
We have made (open) to (all)
men—
Equal is the dweller there
And the visitor from the country—
And any whose purpose therein
Is profanity or wrongdoing—
Them will We cause to taste
Of a most grievous Penalty.

٢٥- اِنَّ الَّذِيْنَ كَفَرُوْا وَيَصُدُّوْنَ عَنْ
سَبِيْلِ اللّٰهِ
وَالْمَسْجِدِ الْحَرَامِ الَّذِيْ جَعَلْنٰهُ لِلنَّاسِ
سَوَآءَ ۨالْعَاكِفُ فِيْهِ وَالْبَادِ ۚ
وَمَنْ يُّرِدْ فِيْهِ بِاِلْحَادٍ بِظُلْمٍ
نُّذِقْهُ مِنْ عَذَابٍ اَلِيْمٍ۟

SECTION 4.

26. Behold! We gave the site,

٢٦- وَاِذْ بَوَّاْنَا لِاِبْرٰهِيْمَ

To Abraham, of the (Sacred)
House,
(Saying): "Associate not anything
(In worship) with Me;
And sanctify My House
For those who compass it
round,
Or stand up,
Or bow, or prostrate themselves
(Therein in prayer).

27. "And proclaim the Pilgrimage
Among men: they will come
To thee on foot and (mounted)
On every kind of camel,
Lean on account of journeys
Through deep and distant
Mountain highways;

28. "That they may witness
The benefits (provided) for
them,
And celebrate the name
Of Allah, through the Days
Appointed, over the cattle
Which He has provided for them
(For sacrifice): then eat ye
Thereof and feed the distressed
Ones in want.

29. "Then let them complete
The rites prescribed
For them, perform their vows,
And (again) circumambulate
The Ancient House."

30. Such (is the Pilgrimage):
Whoever honours the sacred
Rites of Allah, for him
It is good in the sight
Of his Lord. Lawful to you
(For food in Pilgrimage) are cattle,
Except those mentioned to you
(As exceptions): but shun
The abomination of idols,
And shun the word
That is false —

31. Being true in faith to Allah,
And never assigning partners

To Him: if anyone assigns
Partners to Allah, he is
As if he had fallen
From heaven and been snatched
up
By birds, or the wind
Had swooped (like a bird
On its prey) and thrown him
Into a far-distant place.

بِهِ ۚ وَمَنْ يُشْرِكْ بِاللّٰهِ
فَكَأَنَّمَا خَرَّ مِنَ السَّمَآءِ
فَتَخْطَفُهُ الطَّيْرُ
اَوْ تَهْوِىْ بِهِ الرِّيْحُ فِىْ مَكَانٍ سَحِيْقٍ ۝

32. Such (is his state): and
Whoever holds in honour
The Symbols of Allah,
(In the sacrifice of animals),
Such (honour) should come truly
From piety of heart.

٣٢- ذٰلِكَ ۚ وَمَنْ يُّعَظِّمْ
شَعَآئِرَ اللّٰهِ
فَاِنَّهَا مِنْ تَقْوَى الْقُلُوْبِ ۝

33. In them   ye have benefits
For a term appointed:
In the end their place
Of sacrifice is near
The Ancient House.

٣٣- لَكُمْ فِيْهَا مَنَافِعُ اِلٰٓى اَجَلٍ مُّسَمًّى
ثُمَّ مَحِلُّهَا اِلَى الْبَيْتِ الْعَتِيْقِ ۝

SECTION 5.

34. To every people did We
Appoint rites (of sacrifice),
That they might celebrate
The name of Allah over
The sustenance He gave them
From animals (fit for food),
But your God is One God:
Submit then your wills to Him
(In Islam): and give thou
The good news   to those
Who humble themselves—

٣٤- وَلِكُلِّ اُمَّةٍ جَعَلْنَا مَنْسَكًا
لِّيَذْكُرُوا اسْمَ اللّٰهِ عَلٰى مَا رَزَقَهُمْ
مِّنْ بَهِيْمَةِ الْاَنْعَامِ ۗ
فَاِلٰهُكُمْ اِلٰهٌ وَّاحِدٌ فَلَهٗٓ اَسْلِمُوْا ۗ
وَبَشِّرِ الْمُخْبِتِيْنَ ۝

35. To those whose hearts,
When Allah is mentioned,
Are filled with fear,
Who show patient perseverance
Over their afflictions, keep up
Regular prayer, and spend
(In charity) out of what
We have bestowed upon them.

٣٥- الَّذِيْنَ اِذَا ذُكِرَ اللّٰهُ وَجِلَتْ قُلُوْبُهُمْ
وَالصّٰبِرِيْنَ عَلٰى مَآ اَصَابَهُمْ
وَالْمُقِيْمِى الصَّلٰوةِ ۙ
وَمِمَّا رَزَقْنٰهُمْ يُنْفِقُوْنَ ۝

36. The sacrificial camels
We have made for you

٣٦- وَالْبُدْنَ جَعَلْنٰهَا لَكُمْ

As among the Symbols from
Allah: in them is (much)
Good for you: then pronounce
The name of Allah over them
As they line up (for sacrifice):
When they are down
On their sides (after slaughter),
Eat ye thereof, and feed
Such as (beg not but)
Live in contentment,
And such as beg
With due humility: thus have
We made animals subject
To you, that ye
May be grateful.

مِنْ شَعَآئِرِ اللّٰهِ
لَكُمْ فِيْهَا خَيْرٌ ۖ
فَاذْكُرُوا اسْمَ اللّٰهِ عَلَيْهَا صَوَآفَّ ۚ
فَإِذَا وَجَبَتْ جُنُوْبُهَا
فَكُلُوْا مِنْهَا وَأَطْعِمُوا
الْقَانِعَ وَالْمُعْتَرَّ ۚ كَذٰلِكَ
سَخَّرْنٰهَا لَكُمْ لَعَلَّكُمْ تَشْكُرُوْنَ ۞

37. It is not their meat
Nor their blood, that reaches
Allah: it is your piety
That reaches Him: He
Has thus made them subject
To you, that ye may glorify
Allah for His guidance to you:
And proclaim the Good News
To all who do right.

٣٧ ـ لَنْ يَّنَالَ اللّٰهَ لُحُوْمُهَا وَلَا دِمَآؤُهَا
وَلٰكِنْ يَّنَالُهُ التَّقْوٰى مِنْكُمْ ۚ
كَذٰلِكَ سَخَّرَهَا لَكُمْ
لِتُكَبِّرُوا اللّٰهَ عَلٰى مَا هَدٰىكُمْ ۚ
وَبَشِّرِ الْمُحْسِنِيْنَ ۞

38. Verily Allah will defend
(From ill) those who believe:
Verily, Allah loveth not
Any that is a traitor
To faith, or shows ingratitude.

٣٨ ـ إِنَّ اللّٰهَ يُدٰفِعُ عَنِ الَّذِيْنَ اٰمَنُوْا ۗ
إِنَّ اللّٰهَ لَا يُحِبُّ كُلَّ خَوَّانٍ كَفُوْرٍ ۞

SECTION 6.

39. To those against whom
War is made, permission
Is given (to fight), because
They are wronged—and verily,
Allah is Most Powerful
For their aid—

٣٩ ـ أُذِنَ لِلَّذِيْنَ
يُقٰتَلُوْنَ بِأَنَّهُمْ ظُلِمُوْا ۚ
وَإِنَّ اللّٰهَ عَلٰى نَصْرِهِمْ لَقَدِيْرٌ ۙ ۞

40. (They are) those who have
Been expelled from their homes
In defiance of right—
(For no cause) except
That they say, "Our Lord
Is Allah". Did not Allah
Check one set of people
By means of another
There would surely have been

٤٠ ـ الَّذِيْنَ أُخْرِجُوْا مِنْ دِيَارِهِمْ
بِغَيْرِ حَقٍّ
إِلَّا أَنْ يَّقُوْلُوْا رَبُّنَا
اللّٰهُ ۗ وَلَوْلَا دَفْعُ اللّٰهِ النَّاسَ
بَعْضَهُمْ بِبَعْضٍ

Pulled down monasteries,
                    churches,
Synagogues, and mosques, in
                    which
The name of Allah is
                    commemorated
In abundant measure. Allah will
Certainly aid those who
Aid His (cause)—for verily
Allah is Full of Strength,
Exalted in Might,
(Able to enforce His Will).

لَّهُدِّمَتْ صَوَامِعُ
وَبِيَعٌ وَصَلَوَاتٌ وَمَسَاجِدُ
يُذْكَرُ فِيهَا اسْمُ اللّٰهِ كَثِيرًا
وَلَيَنْصُرَنَّ اللّٰهُ مَنْ يَنْصُرُهُ
إِنَّ اللّٰهَ لَقَوِيٌّ عَزِيزٌ ۝

41. (They are) those who,
If We establish them
In the land, establish
Regular prayer and give
Regular charity, enjoin
The right and forbid wrong:
With Allah rests the end
(And decision) of (all) affairs.

٤١- اَلَّذِيْنَ اِنْ مَّكَّنَّاهُمْ فِى الْاَرْضِ
اَقَامُوا الصَّلَوٰةَ وَاٰتَوُا الزَّكَوٰةَ
وَاَمَرُوْا بِالْمَعْرُوْفِ وَنَهَوْا عَنِ الْمُنْكَرِ
وَلِلّٰهِ عَاقِبَةُ الْاُمُوْرِ ۝

42. If they treat thy (mission)
As false, so did the Peoples
Before them (with their
                    Prophets)—
The People of Noah,
The 'Ād and Thamūd;

٤٢- وَاِنْ يُّكَذِّبُوْكَ فَقَدْ كَذَّبَتْ
قَبْلَهُمْ قَوْمُ نُوْحٍ
وَّعَادٌ وَّثَمُوْدُ ۝

43. Those of Abraham and Lūṭ;

٤٣- وَقَوْمُ اِبْرٰهِيْمَ وَقَوْمُ لُوْطٍ ۝

44. And the Companions
Of the Madyan people;
And Moses was rejected
(In the same way). But I
Granted respite to the Unbelievers,
And (only) after that
Did I punish them:
But how (terrible) was
My rejection (of them)!

٤٤- وَاَصْحَابُ مَدْيَنَ
وَكُذِّبَ مُوْسٰى
فَاَمْلَيْتُ لِلْكَافِرِيْنَ
ثُمَّ اَخَذْتُهُمْ
فَكَيْفَ كَانَ نَكِيْرِ ۝

45. How many populations have We
Destroyed, which were given
To wrongdoing? They tumbled
                    down
On their roofs. And how many
Wells are lying idle and
                    neglected,
And castles lofty and well-built?

٤٥- فَكَاَيِّنْ مِّنْ قَرْيَةٍ اَهْلَكْنٰهَا
وَهِىَ ظَالِمَةٌ فَهِىَ خَاوِيَةٌ
عَلٰى عُرُوْشِهَا
وَبِئْرٍ مُّعَطَّلَةٍ وَّقَصْرٍ مَّشِيْدٍ ۝

46. Do they not travel
Through the land, so that
Their hearts (and minds)
May thus learn wisdom
And their ears may
Thus learn to hear?
Truly it is not their eyes
That are blind, but their
Hearts which are
In their breasts.

47. Yet they ask thee
To hasten on the Punishment!
But Allah will not fail
In His promise. Verily
A Day in the sight of thy Lord
Is like a thousand years
Of your reckoning.

48. And to how many populations
Did I give respite, which
Were given to wrongdoing?
In the end I punished them.
To Me is the destination (of all).

SECTION 7.

49. Say: "O men! I am
(Sent) to you only to give
A clear warning:

50. "Those who believe and work
Righteousness, for them
Is forgiveness and a sustenance
Most generous.

51. "But those who strive
Against Our Signs, to frustrate
Them—they will be
Companions of the Fire."

52. Never did We send
A messenger or a prophet
Before thee, but, when he
Framed a desire, Satan
Threw some (vanity)
Into his desire: but Allah
Will cancel anything (vain)
That Satan throws in,

٤٦- اَفَلَمْ يَسِيْرُوْا فِى الْاَرْضِ
فَتَكُوْنَ لَهُمْ قُلُوْبٌ يَّعْقِلُوْنَ بِهَآ
اَوْ اٰذَانٌ يَّسْمَعُوْنَ بِهَا ۚ
فَاِنَّهَا لَا تَعْمَى الْاَبْصَارُ
وَلٰكِنْ تَعْمَى الْقُلُوْبُ الَّتِىْ فِى الصُّدُوْرِ ۝

٤٧- وَيَسْتَعْجِلُوْنَكَ بِالْعَذَابِ
وَلَنْ يُّخْلِفَ اللّٰهُ وَعْدَهٗ ۚ
وَاِنَّ يَوْمًا عِنْدَ رَبِّكَ كَاَلْفِ سَنَةٍ مِّمَّا
تَعُدُّوْنَ ۝

٤٨- وَكَاَيِّنْ مِّنْ قَرْيَةٍ اَمْلَيْتُ لَهَا
وَهِىَ ظَالِمَةٌ ثُمَّ اَخَذْتُهَا ۚ
وَاِلَىَّ الْمَصِيْرُ ۝

٤٩- قُلْ يٰۤاَيُّهَا النَّاسُ اِنَّمَاۤ اَنَا لَكُمْ
نَذِيْرٌ مُّبِيْنٌ ۚ

٥٠- فَالَّذِيْنَ اٰمَنُوْا وَعَمِلُوا الصّٰلِحٰتِ
لَهُمْ مَّغْفِرَةٌ وَّرِزْقٌ كَرِيْمٌ ۝

٥١- وَالَّذِيْنَ سَعَوْا فِىْۤ اٰيٰتِنَا مُعٰجِزِيْنَ
اُولٰٓئِكَ اَصْحٰبُ الْجَحِيْمِ ۝

٥٢- وَمَاۤ اَرْسَلْنَا مِنْ قَبْلِكَ مِنْ رَّسُوْلٍ
وَّلَا نَبِىٍّ اِلَّاۤ اِذَا تَمَنّٰۤى
اَلْقَى الشَّيْطٰنُ فِىْۤ اُمْنِيَّتِهٖ ۚ
فَيَنْسَخُ اللّٰهُ مَا يُلْقِى الشَّيْطٰنُ

And Allah will confirm
(And establish) His Signs:
For Allah is full of knoweldge
And wisdom:

53. That He may make
The suggestions thrown in
By Satan, but a trial
For those in whose hearts
Is a disease and who are
Hardened of heart: verily
The wrongdoers are in a schism
Far (from the Truth):

54. And that those on whom
Knowledge has been bestowed
　　　　　　　　may learn
That the (Qur'ān) is the Truth
From thy Lord, and that they
May believe therein, and their
　　　　　　　　hearts
May be made humbly (open)
To it: for verily Allah is
The Guide of those who believe,
To the Straight Way.

55. Those who reject Faith
Will not cease to be
In doubt concerning (Revelation)
Until the Hour (of Judgement)
Comes suddenly upon them,
Or there comes to them
The Penalty of a Day of Disaster.

56. On that Day the Dominion
Will be that of Allah:
He will judge between them:
So those who believe
And work righteous deeds will be
In Gardens of Delight.

57. And for those who reject Faith
And deny Our Signs,
There will be a humiliating
Punishment.
　　　　SECTION 8.

58. Those who leave their homes

In the cause of Allah,
And are then slain or die—
On them will Allah bestow verily
A goodly Provision:
Truly Allah is He Who
Bestows the best Provision.

59. Verily He will admit them
To a place with which
They shall be well pleased;
For Allah is All-Knowing,
Most Forbearing.

60. That (is so). And if one
Has retaliated to no greater
Extent than the injury he received,
And is again set upon
Inordinately, Allah will help
Him: for Allah is One
That blots out (sins)
And forgives (again and again)

61. That is because Allah merges
Night into Day, and He
Merges Day into Night, and
Verily it is Allah Who hears
And sees (all things).

62. That is because Allah—He
Is the Reality; and those
Besides Him whom they invoke—
They are but vain Falsehood:
Verily Allah is He, Most High,
Most Great.

63. Seest thou not that Allah
Sends down rain from the sky,
And forthwith the earth
Becomes clothed with green?
For Allah is He Who
                    understands
The finest mysteries, and
Is well-acquainted (with them).

64. To Him belongs all that is
In the heavens and on earth:

For verily Allah—He is
Free of all wants,
Worthy of all praise.

SECTION 9.

65. Seest thou not that Allah
Has made subject to you (men)
All that is on the earth,
And the ships that sail
Through the sea by His command?
He withholds the sky (rain)
From falling on the earth
Except by His leave:
For Allah is Most Kind
And Most Merciful to man.

66. It is He Who gave you life,
Will cause you to die,
And will again give you
Life: truly man is
A most ungrateful creature!

67. To every People have We
Appointed rites and ceremonies
Which they must follow:
Let them not then dispute
With thee on the matter,
But do thou invite (them)
To thy Lord: for thou art
Assuredly on the Right Way.

68. If they do wrangle with thee,
Say, "Allah knows best
What it is ye are doing."

69. "Allah will judge between you
On the Day of Judgement
Concerning the matters in which
Ye differ."

70. Knowest thou not that
Allah knows all that is
In heaven and on earth?
Indeed it is all
In a record, and that
Is easy for Allah.

71. Yet they worship, besides Allah,

وَاِنَّ اللّٰهَ لَهُوَ الْغَنِيُّ الْحَمِيْدُ ۞

٦٥- اَلَمْ تَرَ اَنَّ اللّٰهَ سَخَّرَ لَكُمْ
مَّا فِي الْاَرْضِ وَالْفُلْكَ تَجْرِيْ فِي الْبَحْرِ
بِاَمْرِهٖ ۚ وَيُمْسِكُ السَّمَآءَ اَنْ تَقَعَ عَلَى
الْاَرْضِ اِلَّا بِاِذْنِهٖ ۗ
اِنَّ اللّٰهَ بِالنَّاسِ لَرَءُوْفٌ رَّحِيْمٌ ۞

٦٦- وَهُوَ الَّذِيْٓ اَحْيَاكُمْ ثُمَّ يُمِيْتُكُمْ
ثُمَّ يُحْيِيْكُمْ ۗ
اِنَّ الْاِنْسَانَ لَكَفُوْرٌ ۞

٦٧- لِكُلِّ اُمَّةٍ جَعَلْنَا مَنْسَكًا
هُمْ نَاسِكُوْهُ فَلَا يُنَازِعُنَّكَ فِي الْاَمْرِ
وَادْعُ اِلٰى رَبِّكَ ۗ
اِنَّكَ لَعَلٰى هُدًى مُّسْتَقِيْمٍ ۞

٦٨- وَاِنْ جَادَلُوْكَ
فَقُلِ اللّٰهُ اَعْلَمُ بِمَا تَعْمَلُوْنَ ۞

٦٩- اَللّٰهُ يَحْكُمُ بَيْنَكُمْ يَوْمَ الْقِيٰمَةِ
فِيْمَا كُنْتُمْ فِيْهِ تَخْتَلِفُوْنَ ۞

٧٠- اَلَمْ تَعْلَمْ اَنَّ اللّٰهَ يَعْلَمُ مَا فِي السَّمَآءِ
وَالْاَرْضِ ۗ اِنَّ ذٰلِكَ فِيْ كِتٰبٍ ۗ
اِنَّ ذٰلِكَ عَلَى اللّٰهِ يَسِيْرٌ ۞

٧١- وَيَعْبُدُوْنَ مِنْ دُوْنِ اللّٰهِ

Things for which no authority
Has been sent down to them,
And of which they have
(Really) no knowledge:
For those that do wrong
There is no helper.

مَا لَمْ يُنَزِّلْ بِهِ سُلْطٰنًا

وَّ مَا لَيْسَ لَهُمْ بِهٖ عِلْمٌ ۗ

وَ مَا لِلظّٰلِمِيْنَ مِنْ نَّصِيْرٍ ۝

72. When Our Clear Signs
Are rehearsed to them,
Thou wilt notice a denial
On the faces of the Unbelievers!
They nearly attack with violence
Those who rehearse Our Signs
To them. Say, "Shall I
Tell you of something
(Far) worse than these Signs?
It is the Fire (of Hell)!
Allah has promised it
To the Unbelievers!
And evil is that destination!"

٧٢ۛ وَ اِذَا تُتْلٰى عَلَيْهِمْ اٰيٰتُنَا بَيِّنٰتٍ

تَعْرِفُ فِيْ وُجُوْهِ الَّذِيْنَ كَفَرُوا الْمُنْكَرَ ۗ

يَكَادُوْنَ يَسْطُوْنَ بِالَّذِيْنَ

يَتْلُوْنَ عَلَيْهِمْ اٰيٰتِنَا ۗ قُلْ اَفَاُنَبِّئُكُمْ

بِشَرٍّ مِّنْ ذٰلِكُمْ ۗ اَلنَّارُ ۗ

وَعَدَهَا اللّٰهُ الَّذِيْنَ كَفَرُوْا ۗ

وَ بِئْسَ الْمَصِيْرُ ۝

SECTION 10.

73. O men! Here is
A parable set forth!
Listen to it! Those
On whom, besides Allah,
Ye call, cannot create
(Even) a fly, if they all
Met together for the purpose!
And if the fly should snatch
Away anything from them,
They would have no power
To release it from the fly.
Feeble are those who petition
And those whom they petition!

٧٣ۛ يٰۤاَيُّهَا النَّاسُ ضُرِبَ مَثَلٌ

فَاسْتَمِعُوْا لَهٗ ۗ اِنَّ الَّذِيْنَ تَدْعُوْنَ مِنْ

دُوْنِ اللّٰهِ

لَنْ يَّخْلُقُوْا ذُبَابًا وَّ لَوِ اجْتَمَعُوْا لَهٗ ۗ

وَ اِنْ يَّسْلُبْهُمُ الذُّبَابُ شَيْئًا

لَّا يَسْتَنْقِذُوْهُ مِنْهُ ۗ

ضَعُفَ الطَّالِبُ وَ الْمَطْلُوْبُ ۝

74. No just estimate have they
Made of Allah: for Allah
Is He Who is strong
And able to carry out
His Will.

٧٤ۛ مَا قَدَرُوا اللّٰهَ حَقَّ قَدْرِهٖ ۗ

اِنَّ اللّٰهَ لَقَوِيٌّ عَزِيْزٌ ۝

75. Allah chooses Messengers
From angels and from men
For Allah is He Who hears
And sees (all things).

٧٥ۛ اَللّٰهُ يَصْطَفِيْ مِنَ الْمَلٰٓئِكَةِ رُسُلًا وَّ

مِنَ النَّاسِ ۗ اِنَّ اللّٰهَ سَمِيْعٌۢ بَصِيْرٌ ۝

76. He knows what is before them
And what is behind them:

٧٦ۛ يَعْلَمُ مَا بَيْنَ اَيْدِيْهِمْ وَ مَا خَلْفَهُمْ ۗ

And to Allah go back
All questions (for decision).

وَإِلَى اللهِ تُرْجَعُ الْأُمُورُ ۝

77. ۝ ye who believe!
Bow down, prostrate yourselves,
And adore your Lord;
And do good;
That ye may prosper.

٧٧ـ يَٰٓأَيُّهَا الَّذِينَ آمَنُوا ارْكَعُوا وَاسْجُدُوا
وَاعْبُدُوا رَبَّكُمْ وَافْعَلُوا الْخَيْرَ
لَعَلَّكُمْ تُفْلِحُونَ ۩ ۝

78. And strive in His cause
As ye ought to strive,
(With sincerity and under
discipline).
He has chosen you, and has
Imposed no difficulties on you
In religion; it is the cult
Of your father Abraham.
It is He Who has named
You Muslims, both before
And in this (Revelation);
That the Messenger may be
A witness for you, and ye
Be witnesses for mankind!
So establish regular Prayer,
Give regular Charity,
And hold fast to Allah!
He is your Protector—
The best to protect
And the Best to help!

٧٨ـ وَجَاهِدُوا فِي اللهِ حَقَّ جِهَادِهِ
هُوَ اجْتَبَاكُمْ وَمَا جَعَلَ عَلَيْكُمْ فِي
الدِّينِ مِنْ حَرَجٍ
مِلَّةَ أَبِيكُمْ إِبْرَاهِيمَ
هُوَ سَمَّاكُمُ الْمُسْلِمِينَ مِنْ قَبْلُ وَ
فِي هَٰذَا لِيَكُونَ الرَّسُولُ شَهِيدًا عَلَيْكُمْ
وَتَكُونُوا شُهَدَاءَ عَلَى النَّاسِ
فَأَقِيمُوا الصَّلَاةَ وَآتُوا الزَّكَاةَ
وَاعْتَصِمُوا بِاللهِ هُوَ مَوْلَاكُمْ
فَنِعْمَ الْمَوْلَى وَنِعْمَ النَّصِيرُ ۝

INTRODUCTION TO SŪRA XXIII. *(Mu-minūn)* — 118 Verses

This Sūra deals with the virtues which are the seed-bed of Faith, especially in an environment in which Truth is denied and its votaries insulted and persecuted, But Truth is One and must prevail. Those who do wrong will be filled with vain regrets when it is too late for repentance.

It belongs to the late Meccan period.

Al Mu'minūn (The Believers)

In the name of Allah, Most Gracious, Most Merciful.

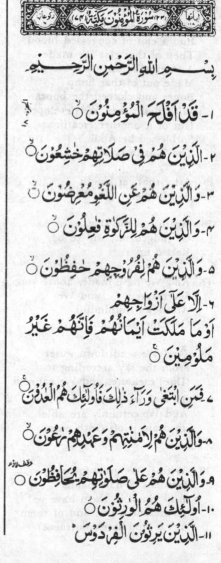

1. The Believers must (Eventually) win through

2. Those who humble themselves In their prayers;

3. Who avoid vain talk:

4. Who are active in deeds Of charity;

5. Who abstain from sex,

6. Except with those joined To them in the marriage bond, Or (the captives) whom Their right hands possess— For (in their case) they are Free from blame,

7. But those whose desires exceed Those limits are transgressors—

8. Those who faithfully observe Their trusts and covenants;

9. And who (strictly) guard Their prayers—

10. These will be the heirs,

11. Who will inherit Paradise:

They will dwell therein
(Forever).

هُمْ فِيهَا خَلِدُوْنَ ۝

12. Man We did create
From a quintessence (of clay);

١٢- وَلَقَدْ خَلَقْنَا الْإِنْسَانَ مِنْ سُلٰلَةٍ مِّنْ طِيْنٍ ۝

13. Then We placed him
As (a drop of) sperm
In a place of rest,
Firmly fixed;

١٣- ثُمَّ جَعَلْنٰهُ نُطْفَةً فِيْ قَرَارٍ مَّكِيْنٍ ۝

14. Then We made the sperm
Into a clot of congealed blood;
Then of that clot We made
A (foetus) lump; then We
Made out of that lump
Bones and clothed the bones
With flesh; then We developed
Out of it another creature.
So blessed be Allah,
The Best to create!

١٤- ثُمَّ خَلَقْنَا النُّطْفَةَ عَلَقَةً فَخَلَقْنَا الْعَلَقَةَ مُضْغَةً فَخَلَقْنَا الْمُضْغَةَ عِظٰمًا فَكَسَوْنَا الْعِظٰمَ لَحْمًا ثُمَّ أَنْشَأْنٰهُ خَلْقًا اٰخَرَ فَتَبٰرَكَ اللّٰهُ أَحْسَنُ الْخٰلِقِيْنَ ۝

15. After that, at length
Ye will die.

١٥- ثُمَّ إِنَّكُمْ بَعْدَ ذٰلِكَ لَمَيِّتُوْنَ ۝

16. Again, on the Day
Of Judgement, will ye be
Raised up.

١٦- ثُمَّ إِنَّكُمْ يَوْمَ الْقِيٰمَةِ تُبْعَثُوْنَ ۝

17. And We have made, above you,
Seven tracts;　　and We
Are never unmindful
Of (Our) Creation.

١٧- وَلَقَدْ خَلَقْنَا فَوْقَكُمْ سَبْعَ طَرَآئِقَ ۖ وَمَا كُنَّا عَنِ الْخَلْقِ غٰفِلِيْنَ ۝

18. And We send down water
From the sky according to
(Due) measure, and We cause it

To soak in the soil;
And We certainly are able
To drain it off (with ease).

١٨- وَأَنْزَلْنَا مِنَ السَّمَآءِ مَآءً بِقَدَرٍ فَأَسْكَنّٰهُ فِي الْأَرْضِ ۖ وَإِنَّا عَلٰى ذَهَابٍ بِهٖ لَقٰدِرُوْنَ ۝

19. With it We grow for you
Gardens of date palms
And vines; in them have ye
Abundant fruits: and of them
Ye eat (and have enjoyment)—

١٩- فَأَنْشَأْنَا لَكُمْ بِهٖ جَنّٰتٍ مِّنْ نَّخِيْلٍ وَّأَعْنَابٍ ۘ لَكُمْ فِيْهَا فَوَاكِهُ كَثِيْرَةٌ وَّمِنْهَا تَأْكُلُوْنَ ۝

20. Also a tree springing
Out of Mount Sinai,
Which produces oil,
And relish for those
Who use it for food.

٢٠- وَشَجَرَةً تَخْرُجُ مِنْ طُوْرِ سَيْنَآءَ
تَنْبُتُ بِالدُّهْنِ وَصِبْغٍ لِّلْاٰكِلِيْنَ ۞

21. And in cattle (too) ye
Have an instructive example:
From within their bodies
We produce (milk) for you
To drink; there are, in them,
(Besides), numerous (other)
Benefits for you;
And of their (meat) ye eat;

٢١- وَإِنَّ لَكُمْ فِى الْاَنْعَامِ لَعِبْرَةً ؕ
نُسْقِيْكُمْ مِّمَّا فِىْ بُطُوْنِهَا
وَلَكُمْ فِيْهَا مَنَافِعُ كَثِيْرَةٌ
وَّمِنْهَا تَاْكُلُوْنَ ۞

22. And on them, as well as
In ships, ye ride.

٢٢- وَعَلَيْهَا وَعَلَى الْفُلْكِ تُحْمَلُوْنَ ۞

SECTION 2

23. (Further, We sent a long line
Of prophets for your
            instruction).
We sent Noah to his people:
He said, "O my people!
Worship Allah! Ye have
No other god but Him.
Will ye not hear (Him)?"

٢٣- وَلَقَدْ اَرْسَلْنَا نُوْحًا اِلٰى قَوْمِهٖ
فَقَالَ يٰقَوْمِ اعْبُدُوا اللّٰهَ
مَا لَكُمْ مِّنْ اِلٰهٍ غَيْرُهٗ ؕ
اَفَلَا تَتَّقُوْنَ ۞

24. The chiefs of the Unbelievers
Among his people said:
"He is no more than a man
Like yourselves: his wish is
To assert his superiority
Over you: if Allah had wished
(To send messengers),
He could have sent down
Angels: never did we hear
Such a thing (as he says),
Among our ancestors of old."

٢٤- فَقَالَ الْمَلَؤُا الَّذِيْنَ كَفَرُوْا مِنْ قَوْمِهٖ
مَا هٰذَا اِلَّا بَشَرٌ مِّثْلُكُمْ ۙ يُرِيْدُ
اَنْ يَّتَفَضَّلَ عَلَيْكُمْ ؕ وَلَوْ شَآءَ اللّٰهُ
لَاَنْزَلَ مَلٰٓئِكَةً ۖ
مَّا سَمِعْنَا بِهٰذَا فِىْۤ اٰبَآئِنَا الْاَوَّلِيْنَ ۞

25. (And some said): "He is
Only a man possessed:
Wait (and have patience)
With him for a time."

٢٥- اِنْ هُوَ اِلَّا رَجُلٌۢ بِهٖ جِنَّةٌ
فَتَرَبَّصُوْا بِهٖ حَتّٰى حِيْنٍ ۞

26. (Noah) said: "O my Lord!
Help me; for that they
Accuse me of falsehood!"

٢٦- قَالَ رَبِّ انْصُرْنِيْ بِمَا كَذَّبُوْنَ ۞

27. So We inspired him
(With this message); "Construct
The Ark within Our sight
And under Our guidance: then
When comes Our command,
And the fountains of the earth
Gush forth, take thou on board
Pairs of every species, male
And female, and thy family—
Except those of them
Against whom the Word
Has already gone forth;
And address Me not
In favour of the wrongdoers:
For they shall be drowned
(In the Flood).

٢٧- فَأَوْحَيْنَا إِلَيْهِ أَنِ اصْنَعِ
الْفُلْكَ بِأَعْيُنِنَا وَوَحْيِنَا
فَإِذَا جَاءَ أَمْرُنَا وَفَارَ التَّنُّورُ ۙ
فَاسْلُكْ فِيهَا مِنْ كُلٍّ زَوْجَيْنِ اثْنَيْنِ
وَأَهْلَكَ
إِلَّا مَنْ سَبَقَ عَلَيْهِ الْقَوْلُ مِنْهُمْ ۖ
وَلَا تُخَاطِبْنِي فِي الَّذِينَ ظَلَمُوا ۚ
إِنَّهُمْ مُغْرَقُونَ ۝

28. And when thou hast embarked
On the Ark—thou and those
With thee—say: "Praise be
To Allah, Who has saved us
From the people who do wrong."

٢٨- فَإِذَا اسْتَوَيْتَ أَنْتَ وَمَنْ مَعَكَ عَلَى
الْفُلْكِ فَقُلِ الْحَمْدُ لِلَّهِ الَّذِي
نَجَّانَا مِنَ الْقَوْمِ الظَّالِمِينَ ۝

29. And say: "O my Lord!
Enable me to disembark
With Thy blessing: for Thou
Art the Best to enable (us)
To disembark."

٢٩- وَقُلْ رَبِّ أَنْزِلْنِي مُنْزَلًا مُبَارَكًا
وَأَنْتَ خَيْرُ الْمُنْزِلِينَ ۝

30. Verily in this there are
Signs (for men to understand);
(Thus) do We try (men).

٣٠- إِنَّ فِي ذَلِكَ لَآيَاتٍ
وَإِنْ كُنَّا لَمُبْتَلِينَ ۝

31. Then We raised after them
Another generation.

٣١- ثُمَّ أَنْشَأْنَا مِنْ بَعْدِهِمْ قَرْنًا آخَرِينَ ۝

32. And We sent to them
A messenger from among
themselves,
(Saying), "Worship Allah!
Ye have no other god
But Him. Will ye not
Fear (Him)?"

SECTION 3.

٣٢- فَأَرْسَلْنَا فِيهِمْ رَسُولًا مِنْهُمْ
أَنِ اعْبُدُوا اللَّهَ مَا لَكُمْ مِنْ إِلَهٍ غَيْرُهُ ۚ
أَفَلَا تَتَّقُونَ ۝ ع

33. And the chiefs
Of his people, who disbelieved

٣٣- وَقَالَ الْمَلَأُ مِنْ قَوْمِهِ الَّذِينَ كَفَرُوا

And denied the Meeting
In the Hereafter, and on whom
We had bestowed the good things
Of this life, said: "He is
No more than a man
Like yourselves: he eats
Of that of which ye eat,
And drinks of what ye drink.

وَكَذَّبُوا بِلِقَآءِ الْاٰخِرَةِ وَأَتْرَفْنٰهُمْ فِى
الْحَيٰوةِ الدُّنْيَا مَا هٰذَآ إِلَّا بَشَرٌ مِّثْلُكُمْ
يَأْكُلُ مِمَّا تَأْكُلُونَ مِنْهُ
وَيَشْرَبُ مِمَّا تَشْرَبُونَ ۟

34. "If ye obey a man
Like yourselves, behold,
It is certain ye will be lost.

٣٤- وَلَئِنْ أَطَعْتُمْ بَشَرًا مِّثْلَكُمْ
إِنَّكُمْ إِذًا لَّخٰسِرُونَ ۟

35. "Does he promise that
When ye die and become dust
And bones, ye shall be
Brought forth (again)?

٣٥- أَيَعِدُكُمْ أَنَّكُمْ إِذَا مِتُّمْ وَكُنْتُمْ تُرَابًا
وَّعِظَامًا أَنَّكُمْ مُّخْرَجُونَ ۟

36. "Far, very far is that
Which ye are promised!

٣٦- هَيْهَاتَ هَيْهَاتَ لِمَا تُوعَدُونَ ۟

37. "There is nothing but
Our life in this world!
We shall die and we live!
But we shall never
Be raised up again!

٣٧- إِنْ هِيَ إِلَّا حَيَاتُنَا الدُّنْيَا
نَمُوتُ وَنَحْيَا
وَمَا نَحْنُ بِمَبْعُوثِينَ ۟

38. "He is only a man
Who invents a lie
Against Allah, but we
Are not the ones
To believe in him!"

٣٨- إِنْ هُوَ إِلَّا رَجُلٌ افْتَرٰى عَلَى اللهِ
كَذِبًا وَّمَا نَحْنُ لَهُ بِمُؤْمِنِينَ ۟

39. (The prophet) said:
"O my Lord! help me:
For that they accuse me
Of falsehood."

٣٩- قَالَ رَبِّ انْصُرْنِي
بِمَا كَذَّبُونِ ۟

40. (Allah) said: "In but
A little while, they
Are sure to be sorry!"

٤٠- قَالَ عَمَّا قَلِيلٍ
لَّيُصْبِحُنَّ نٰدِمِينَ ۟

41. Then the Blast   overtook them
With justice, and We made them
As rubbish of dead leaves
(Floating on the stream of Time)!
So away with the people
Who do wrong!

٤١- فَأَخَذَتْهُمُ الصَّيْحَةُ بِالْحَقِّ
فَجَعَلْنٰهُمْ غُثَآءً
فَبُعْدًا لِّلْقَوْمِ الظّٰلِمِينَ ۟

42. Then We raised after them
Other generations.

٤٢- ثُمَّ أَنْشَأْنَا مِنْ بَعْدِهِمْ قُرُونًا اٰخَرِيْنَ ۚ

43. No people can hasten
Their term, nor can they
Delay (it).

٤٣- مَا تَسْبِقُ مِنْ أُمَّةٍ أَجَلَهَا وَمَا يَسْتَأْخِرُوْنَ ۚ

44. Then sent We Our messengers
In succession: every time
There came to a people
Their messenger, they accused him
Of falsehood: so We made
Them follow each other
(In punishment): We made them
As a tale (that is told):
So away with a people
That will not believe!

٤٤- ثُمَّ أَرْسَلْنَا رُسُلَنَا تَتْرَا ۚ كُلَّمَا جَاءَ أُمَّةً رَّسُوْلُهَا كَذَّبُوْهُ فَأَتْبَعْنَا بَعْضَهُمْ بَعْضًا وَّجَعَلْنٰهُمْ أَحَادِيْثَ ۚ فَبُعْدًا لِّقَوْمٍ لَّا يُؤْمِنُوْنَ ۚ

45. Then We sent Moses
And his brother Aaron,
With Our Signs and
Authority manifest,

٤٥- ثُمَّ أَرْسَلْنَا مُوْسٰى وَأَخَاهُ هٰرُوْنَ ۚ بِاٰيٰتِنَا وَسُلْطٰنٍ مُّبِيْنٍ ۚ

46. To Pharaoh and his Chiefs:
But these behaved insolently:
They were an arrogant people.

٤٦- إِلٰى فِرْعَوْنَ وَمَلَائِهِ فَاسْتَكْبَرُوْا وَكَانُوْا قَوْمًا عَالِيْنَ ۚ

47. They said: "Shall we believe
In two men like ourselves?
And their people are subject
To us!"

٤٧- فَقَالُوْا أَنُؤْمِنُ لِبَشَرَيْنِ مِثْلِنَا وَقَوْمُهُمَا لَنَا عٰبِدُوْنَ ۚ

48. So they accused them
Of falsehood, and they became
Of those who were destroyed.

٤٨- فَكَذَّبُوْهُمَا فَكَانُوْا مِنَ الْمُهْلَكِيْنَ ۚ

49. And We gave Moses
The Book, in order that
They might receive guidance.

٤٩- وَلَقَدْ اٰتَيْنَا مُوْسَى الْكِتٰبَ لَعَلَّهُمْ يَهْتَدُوْنَ ۚ

50. And We made
The son of Mary
And his mother
As a sign:
We gave them both
Shelter on high ground,
Affording rest and security
And furnished with springs.

٥٠- وَجَعَلْنَا ابْنَ مَرْيَمَ وَأُمَّهُ اٰيَةً وَّاٰوَيْنٰهُمَا إِلٰى رَبْوَةٍ ذَاتِ قَرَارٍ وَّمَعِيْنٍ ۚ

SECTION 4.

51. O ye messengers! enjoy
(All) things good and pure,
And work righteousness:
For I am well-acquainted
With (all) that ye do.

٥١- يَاأَيُّهَا الرُّسُلُ كُلُوا مِنَ الطَّيِّبٰتِ
وَاعْمَلُوا صَالِحًا ۖ
إِنِّي بِمَا تَعْمَلُونَ عَلِيمٌ ۞

52. And verily this Brotherhood
Of yours is a single
Brotherhood.
And I am your Lord
And Cherisher: therefore
Fear Me (and no other).

٥٢- وَإِنَّ هٰذِهٖ أُمَّتُكُمْ أُمَّةً وَاحِدَةً
وَأَنَا رَبُّكُمْ فَاتَّقُونِ ۞

53. But people have cut off
Their affair (of unity),
Between them, into sects:
Each party rejoices in that
Which is with itself.

٥٣- فَتَقَطَّعُوا أَمْرَهُمْ بَيْنَهُمْ زُبُرًا ۖ
كُلُّ حِزْبٍ بِمَا لَدَيْهِمْ فَرِحُونَ ۞

54. But leave them
In their confused ignorance
For a time.

٥٤- فَذَرْهُمْ فِي غَمْرَتِهِمْ حَتّٰى حِينٍ ۞

55. Do they think that because
We have granted them abundance
Of wealth and sons,

٥٥- أَيَحْسَبُونَ أَنَّمَا نُمِدُّهُمْ بِهٖ
مِنْ مَالٍ وَبَنِينَ ۙ

56. We would hasten them
On in every good? Nay
They do not understand.

٥٦- نُسَارِعُ لَهُمْ فِي الْخَيْرٰتِ ۚ
بَلْ لَا يَشْعُرُونَ ۞

57. Verily those who live
In awe for fear of their Lord;

٥٧- إِنَّ الَّذِينَ هُمْ مِنْ خَشْيَةِ رَبِّهِمْ مُشْفِقُونَ ۞

58. Those who believe
In the Signs of their Lord;

٥٨- وَالَّذِينَ هُمْ بِآيٰتِ رَبِّهِمْ يُؤْمِنُونَ ۞

59. Those who join not (in worship)
Partners with their Lord;

٥٩- وَالَّذِينَ هُمْ بِرَبِّهِمْ لَا يُشْرِكُونَ ۞

60. And those who dispense
Their charity with their hearts
Full of fear, because
They will return to their Lord—

٦٠- وَالَّذِينَ يُؤْتُونَ مَا آتَوْا وَقُلُوبُهُمْ وَجِلَةٌ
أَنَّهُمْ إِلٰى رَبِّهِمْ رَاجِعُونَ ۞

61. It is these who hasten

٦١- أُولٰئِكَ يُسَارِعُونَ

In every good work,
And these who are
Foremost in them.

فِى الْخَيْرَاتِ وَهُمْ لَهَا سَابِقُونَ ۟

62. On no soul do We
Place a burden greater
Than it can bear:
Before Us is a record
Which clearly shows the truth.
They will never be wronged.

٦٢ ـ وَلَا نُكَلِّفُ نَفْسًا إِلَّا وُسْعَهَا
وَلَدَيْنَا كِتَابٌ يَنْطِقُ بِالْحَقِّ
وَهُمْ لَا يُظْلَمُونَ ۟

63. But their hearts are
In confused ignorance
Of this; and there are,
Besides that, deeds of theirs,
Which they will (continue)
To do—

٦٣ ـ بَلْ قُلُوبُهُمْ فِى غَمْرَةٍ مِّنْ هَٰذَا
وَلَهُمْ أَعْمَالٌ مِّنْ دُونِ ذَٰلِكَ
هُمْ لَهَا عَامِلُونَ ۟

64. Until, when We seize
In Punishment those of them
Who received the good things
Of this world, behold,
They will groan in supplication!

٦٤ ـ حَتَّىٰ إِذَا أَخَذْنَا مُتْرَفِيهِمْ بِالْعَذَابِ
إِذَا هُمْ يَجْأَرُونَ ۟

65. (It will be said):
"Groan not in supplication
This day; for ye shall
Certainly not be helped by Us.

٦٥ ـ لَا تَجْأَرُوا الْيَوْمَ ۖ
إِنَّكُمْ مِّنَّا لَا تُنْصَرُونَ ۟

66. "My Signs used to be
Rehearsed to you, but ye
Used to turn back
On your heels—

٦٦ ـ قَدْ كَانَتْ آيَاتِى تُتْلَىٰ عَلَيْكُمْ
فَكُنْتُمْ عَلَىٰ أَعْقَابِكُمْ تَنْكِصُونَ ۟

67. "In arrogance: talking nonsense
About the (Qur'ān), like one
Telling fables by night."

٦٧ ـ مُسْتَكْبِرِينَ ۙ
بِهِ سَامِرًا تَهْجُرُونَ ۟

68. Do they not ponder over
The Word (of Allah), or
Has anything (new) come
To them that did not
Come to their fathers of old?

٦٨ ـ أَفَلَمْ يَدَّبَّرُوا الْقَوْلَ
أَمْ جَاءَهُمْ مَّا لَمْ يَأْتِ آبَاءَهُمُ الْأَوَّلِينَ ۟

69. Or do they not recognise
Their Messenger, that they
Deny him?

٦٩ ـ أَمْ لَمْ يَعْرِفُوا رَسُولَهُمْ
فَهُمْ لَهُ مُنْكِرُونَ ۟

70. Or do they say, "he is

٧٠ ـ أَمْ يَقُولُونَ بِهِ جِنَّةٌ ۚ

Possessed"? Nay, he has
Brought them the Truth,
But most of them
Hate the Truth.

بَلْ جَاءَهُمْ بِالْحَقِّ
وَأَكْثَرُهُمْ لِلْحَقِّ كَارِهُونَ ۝

71. If the Truth had been
In accord with their desires,
Truly the heavens and the earth,
And all beings therein
Would have been in confusion
And corruption! Nay, We
Have sent them their admonition,
But they turn away
From their admonition.

۷۱ـ وَلَوِ اتَّبَعَ الْحَقُّ أَهْوَاءَهُمْ
لَفَسَدَتِ السَّمٰوٰتُ وَالْأَرْضُ وَمَنْ
فِيهِنَّ ۚ
بَلْ أَتَيْنٰهُمْ بِذِكْرِهِمْ
فَهُمْ عَنْ ذِكْرِهِمْ مُّعْرِضُونَ ۝

72. Or is it that thou
Askest them for some
Recompense? But the recompense
Of thy Lord is best:
He is the Best of those
Who give sustenance.

۷۲ـ أَمْ تَسْأَلُهُمْ
خَرْجًا فَخَرَاجُ رَبِّكَ خَيْرٌ ۖ
وَهُوَ خَيْرُ الرّٰزِقِينَ ۝

73. But verily thou callest them
To the Straight Way;

۷۳ـ وَإِنَّكَ لَتَدْعُوهُمْ إِلٰى صِرَاطٍ مُّسْتَقِيمٍ ۝

74. And verily those who
Believe not in the Hereafter
Are deviating from that Way.

۷۴ـ وَإِنَّ الَّذِينَ لَا يُؤْمِنُونَ بِالْآخِرَةِ
عَنِ الصِّرَاطِ لَنَاكِبُونَ ۝

75. If We had mercy on them
And removed the distress
Which is on them, they
Would obstinately persist
In their transgression,
Wandering in distraction
To and fro.

۷۵ـ وَلَوْ رَحِمْنٰهُمْ وَكَشَفْنَا مَا بِهِمْ مِّنْ
ضُرٍّ
لَلَجُّوا فِي طُغْيَانِهِمْ
يَعْمَهُونَ ۝

76. We inflicted Punishment
On them, but they
Humbled not themselves
To their Lord, nor do they
Submissively entreat (Him)! —

۷۶ـ وَلَقَدْ أَخَذْنٰهُمْ بِالْعَذَابِ
فَمَا اسْتَكَانُوا لِرَبِّهِمْ
وَمَا يَتَضَرَّعُونَ ۝

77. Until We open on them
A gate leading to
A severe Punishment: then
Lo! they will be plunged
In despair therein!

۷۷ـ حَتّٰى إِذَا فَتَحْنَا عَلَيْهِمْ بَابًا
ذَا عَذَابٍ شَدِيدٍ
إِذَا هُمْ فِيهِ مُبْلِسُونَ ۝

SECTION 5.

78. It is He Who has created
For you (the faculties of)
Hearing, sight, feeling
And understanding: little thanks
It is ye give!

٧٨ ـ وَهُوَ الَّذِيٓ أَنْشَأَ لَكُمُ
السَّمْعَ وَالْأَبْصَارَ وَالْأَفْئِدَةَ ۚ
قَلِيلًا مَّا تَشْكُرُونَ ۝

79. And He has multiplied you
Through the earth, and to Him
Shall ye be gathered back.

٧٩ ـ وَهُوَ الَّذِي ذَرَأَكُمْ فِي الْأَرْضِ
وَإِلَيْهِ تُحْشَرُونَ ۝

80. It is He Who gives
Life and death, and to Him
(Is due) the alternation
Of Night and Day:
Will ye not then understand?

٨٠ ـ وَهُوَ الَّذِي يُحْيِي وَيُمِيتُ
وَلَهُ اخْتِلَافُ الَّيْلِ وَالنَّهَارِ ۚ
أَفَلَا تَعْقِلُونَ ۝

81. On the contrary they say
Things similar to what
The ancients said.

٨١ ـ بَلْ قَالُوا مِثْلَ مَا قَالَ الْأَوَّلُونَ ۝

82. They say: "What! When we
Die and become dust and bones,
Could we really be
Raised up again?

٨٢ ـ قَالُوٓا أَءِذَا مِتْنَا وَكُنَّا تُرَابًا وَعِظَامًا
أَءِنَّا لَمَبْعُوثُونَ ۝

83. "Such things have been promised
To us and to our fathers
Before! They are nothing
But tales of the ancients!"

٨٣ ـ لَقَدْ وُعِدْنَا نَحْنُ وَآبَاؤُنَا هَٰذَا مِنْ
قَبْلُ إِنْ هَٰذَآ إِلَّآ أَسَاطِيرُ الْأَوَّلِينَ ۝

84. Say: "To whom belong
The earth and all beings therein?
(Say) if ye know!"

٨٤ ـ قُلْ لِمَنِ الْأَرْضُ وَمَنْ فِيهَآ
إِنْ كُنْتُمْ تَعْلَمُونَ ۝

85. They will say, "To Allah!"
Say: "Yet will ye not
Receive admonition?"

٨٥ ـ سَيَقُولُونَ لِلَّهِ ۚ قُلْ
أَفَلَا تَذَكَّرُونَ ۝

86. Say: "Who is the Lord
Of the seven heavens,
And the Lord of the Throne
(Of Glory) Supreme?"

٨٦ ـ قُلْ مَنْ رَبُّ السَّمَٰوَٰتِ السَّبْعِ
وَرَبُّ الْعَرْشِ الْعَظِيمِ ۝

87. They will say, "(They belong)
To Allah." Say: "Will ye not
Then be filled with awe?"

٨٧ ـ سَيَقُولُونَ لِلَّهِ ۚ
قُلْ أَفَلَا تَتَّقُونَ ۝

88. Say: "Who is it in whose
Hands is the governance

٨٨ ـ قُلْ مَنْ بِيَدِهِ مَلَكُوتُ كُلِّ شَيْءٍ

Of all things—Who protects
(All), but is not protected
(Of any)? (Say) if ye know."

وَهُوَ يُجِيرُ وَلَا يُجَارُ عَلَيْهِ
إِنْ كُنْتُمْ تَعْلَمُونَ ۟

89. They will say, "(It belongs)
To Allah," Say: "Then how
Are ye deluded?"

٨٩- سَيَقُولُونَ لِلّٰهِ
قُلْ فَأَنّٰى تُسْحَرُونَ ۟

90. We have sent them the Truth:
But they indeed practise
Flasehood!

٩٠- بَلْ أَتَيْنٰهُمْ بِالْحَقِّ
وَإِنَّهُمْ لَكٰذِبُونَ ۟

91. No son did Allah beget,
Nor is there any god
Along with Him: (if there were
Many gods), behold, each god
Would have taken away
What he had created,
And some would have
Lorded it over others!
Glory to Allah! (He is free)
From the (sort of) things
They attribute to Him!

٩١- مَا اتَّخَذَ اللّٰهُ مِنْ وَلَدٍ
وَّ مَا كَانَ مَعَهُ مِنْ إِلٰهٍ
إِذًا لَّذَهَبَ كُلُّ إِلٰهٍ بِمَا خَلَقَ
وَلَعَلَا بَعْضُهُمْ عَلٰى بَعْضٍ
سُبْحٰنَ اللّٰهِ عَمَّا يَصِفُونَ ۟

92. He knows what is hidden
And what is open: too high
Is He for the partners
They attribute to Him!

٩٢- عٰلِمِ الْغَيْبِ وَالشَّهَادَةِ
فَتَعٰلٰى عَمَّا يُشْرِكُونَ ۟ ۽

SECTION 6.

93. Say: "O my Lord!
If Thou wilt show me
(In my lifetime) that which
They are warned against—

٩٣- قُلْ رَّبِّ
إِمَّا تُرِيَنِّي مَا يُوعَدُونَ ۟

94. "Then, O my Lord! put me not
Amongst the people
Who do wrong!"

٩٤- رَبِّ فَلَا تَجْعَلْنِي فِي الْقَوْمِ
الظّٰلِمِينَ ۟

95. And We are certainly able
To show thee (in fulfilment)
That against which they are
warned.

٩٥- وَإِنَّا عَلٰى أَنْ نُّرِيَكَ
مَا نَعِدُهُمْ لَقٰدِرُونَ ۟

96. Repel evil with that
Which is best: We are
Well-acquainted with
The things they say.

٩٦- اِدْفَعْ بِالَّتِي هِيَ أَحْسَنُ السَّيِّئَةَ
نَحْنُ أَعْلَمُ بِمَا يَصِفُونَ ۟

97. And say "O my Lord!
I seek refuge with Thee
From the suggestions
Of the Evil Ones.

٩٧- وَقُل رَّبِّ أَعُوذُ بِكَ
مِنْ هَمَزَاتِ الشَّيَاطِينِ ۝

98. "And I seek refuge with Thee
O my Lord! lest they
Should come near me."

٩٨- وَأَعُوذُ بِكَ رَبِّ أَن يَحْضُرُونِ ۝

99. (In Falsehood will they be)
Until, when death comes
To one of them, he says:
"O my Lord! send me back
(To life)—

٩٩- حَتَّى إِذَا جَاءَ أَحَدَهُمُ الْمَوْتُ
قَالَ رَبِّ ارْجِعُونِ ۝

100. "In order that I may
Work righteousness in the
                                things
I neglected"—"By no means!
It is but a word he says"—
Before them is a Partition
Till the Day they are
Raised up.

١٠٠- لَعَلِّي أَعْمَلُ صَالِحًا فِيمَا تَرَكْتُ
كَلَّا إِنَّهَا كَلِمَةٌ هُوَ قَائِلُهَا
وَمِن وَرَائِهِم بَرْزَخٌ
إِلَى يَوْمِ يُبْعَثُونَ ۝

101. Then when the Trumpet
Is blown, there will be
No more relationships
Between them that day,
Nor will one ask after another!

١٠١- فَإِذَا نُفِخَ فِي الصُّورِ
فَلَا أَنسَابَ بَيْنَهُمْ يَوْمَئِذٍ
وَلَا يَتَسَاءَلُونَ ۝

102. Then those whose balance
(Of good deeds) is heavy—
They will attain salvation:

١٠٢- فَمَن ثَقُلَتْ مَوَازِينُهُ
فَأُولَئِكَ هُمُ الْمُفْلِحُونَ ۝

103. But those whose balance
Is light, will be those
Who have lost their souls;
In Hell will they abide.

١٠٣- وَمَنْ خَفَّتْ مَوَازِينُهُ فَأُولَئِكَ الَّذِينَ
خَسِرُوا أَنفُسَهُمْ فِي جَهَنَّمَ خَالِدُونَ ۝

104. The Fire will burn their faces,
And they will therein
Grin, with their lips displaced.

١٠٤- تَلْفَحُ وُجُوهَهُمُ النَّارُ
وَهُمْ فِيهَا كَالِحُونَ ۝

105. "Were not My Signs rehearsed
To you, and ye did but
Treat them as falsehoods?"

١٠٥- أَلَمْ تَكُنْ آيَاتِي تُتْلَى عَلَيْكُمْ
فَكُنتُم بِهَا تُكَذِّبُونَ ۝

106. They will say: "Our Lord!
Our misfortune overwhelmed
                                us,

١٠٦- قَالُوا رَبَّنَا غَلَبَتْ عَلَيْنَا شِقْوَتُنَا

And we became a people
Astray!

وَكُنَّا قَوْمًا ضَالِّينَ ٥

107. "Our Lord! Bring us out
Of this: if ever we return
('To evil), then shall we be
Wrongdoers indeed!"

١٠٧- رَبَّنَا أَخْرِجْنَا مِنْهَا
فَإِنْ عُدْنَا فَإِنَّا ظَالِمُونَ ٥

108. He will say: "Be ye
Driven into it (with ignominy)!
And speak ye not to Me!

١٠٨- قَالَ اخْسَئُوا فِيهَا
وَلَا تُكَلِّمُونِ ٥

109. "A part of My servants
There was, who used to pray,
'Our Lord! we believe;
Then do Thou forgive us,
And have mercy upon us:
For Thou art the Best
Of those who show mercy!'

١٠٩- إِنَّهُ كَانَ فَرِيقٌ مِنْ عِبَادِي يَقُولُونَ
رَبَّنَا آمَنَّا فَاغْفِرْ لَنَا وَارْحَمْنَا
وَأَنْتَ خَيْرُ الرَّاحِمِينَ ۖ

110. "But ye treated them
With ridicule, so much so
That (ridicule of) them made
you
Forget My Message while
Ye were laughing at them!

١١٠- فَاتَّخَذْتُمُوهُمْ سِخْرِيًّا
حَتَّى أَنْسَوْكُمْ ذِكْرِي
وَكُنْتُمْ مِنْهُمْ تَضْحَكُونَ ٥

111: "I have rewarded them
This day for their patience
And constancy; they are indeed
The ones that have achieved
Bliss...'

١١١- إِنِّي جَزَيْتُهُمُ الْيَوْمَ بِمَا صَبَرُوا
أَنَّهُمْ هُمُ الْفَائِزُونَ ٥

112. He will say: "What number
Of years did ye stay
On earth?"

١١٢- قُلْ كَمْ لَبِثْتُمْ فِي الْأَرْضِ عَدَدَ
سِنِينَ ٥

113. They will say: "We stayed
A day or part of a day:
But ask those who
Keep account."

١١٣- قَالُوا لَبِثْنَا يَوْمًا أَوْ بَعْضَ يَوْمٍ
فَاسْأَلِ الْعَادِّينَ ٥

114. He will say: "Ye stayed
Not but a little—
If ye had only known!

١١٤- قُلْ إِنْ لَبِثْتُمْ إِلَّا قَلِيلًا
لَوْ أَنَّكُمْ كُنْتُمْ تَعْلَمُونَ ٥

115. "Did ye then think
That We had created you
In jest, and that ye

١١٥- أَفَحَسِبْتُمْ أَنَّمَا خَلَقْنَاكُمْ

Would not be brought back
To Us (for account)?"

عَبَثًا وَّ أَنَّكُمْ إِلَيْنَا لَا تُرْجَعُونَ ۟

116. Therefore exalted be Allah,
The King, the Reality:
There is no god but He,
The Lord of the Throne
Of Honour!

١١٦- فَتَعَلَى اللهُ الْمَلِكُ الْحَقُّ ۚ
لَا إِلٰهَ إِلَّا هُوَ ۚ
رَبُّ الْعَرْشِ الْكَرِيْمِ ۟

117. If anyone invokes, besides Allah,
Any other god, he has
No authority therefor;
And his reckoning will be
Only with his Lord!
And verily the Unbelievers
Will fail to win through!

١١٧- وَمَنْ يَّدْعُ مَعَ اللهِ إِلٰهًا اٰخَرَ ۙ
لَا بُرْهَانَ لَهٗ بِهٖ ۙ
فَإِنَّمَا حِسَابُهٗ عِنْدَ رَبِّهٖ ۗ
إِنَّهٗ لَا يُفْلِحُ الْكٰفِرُوْنَ ۟

118. So say: "O my Lord!
Grant Thou forgiveness and mercy!
For Thou art the Best
Of those who show mercy!"

١١٨- وَقُلْ رَّبِّ اغْفِرْ وَارْحَمْ
وَأَنْتَ خَيْرُ الرّٰحِمِيْنَ ۟ ۧ

INTRODUCTION TO SŪRA XXIV. (*Nūr*) — 64 Verses

The environment and social influence which most frequently wreck our spiritual ideals have to do with sex, and especially with its misuse, whether in the form of unregulated behaviour, of false charges or scandals, of breach of the refined conventions of personal or domestic privacy. Our complete conquest of all pitfalls in such matters enables us to rise to the higher regions of Light and of God-created Nature, about which a mystic doctrine is suggested. This subject is continued in the next Sūra.

As the reprobation of false slanders about women (xxiv. 11-20) is connected with an incident that happened to Ḥaḍhrat 'Ā'isha in A.H. 5-6, that fixes the chronological place of this Medina Sura.

Al Nūr (The Light)

In the name of Allah, Most Gracious,
Most Merciful.

بِسْمِ اللهِ الرَّحْمٰنِ الرَّحِيْمِ

1. A Sūrah which We
Have sent down and
Which We have ordained:
In it have We sent down
Clear Signs, in order that
Ye may receive admonition.

١- سُوْرَةٌ اَنْزَلْنٰهَا وَفَرَضْنٰهَا
وَاَنْزَلْنَا فِيْهَآ اٰيٰتٍ بَيِّنٰتٍ
لَّعَلَّكُمْ تَذَكَّرُوْنَ ٥

2. The woman and the man
Guilty of adultery or
        fornication—
Flog each of them
With a hundred stripes:
Let not compassion move you
In their case, in a matter
Prescribed by Allah, if ye believe
In Allah and the Last Day:
And let a party
Of the Believers
Witness their punishment.

٢- اَلزَّانِيَةُ وَالزَّانِيْ
فَاجْلِدُوْا كُلَّ وَاحِدٍ مِّنْهُمَا مِائَةَ جَلْدَةٍ
وَّلَا تَأْخُذْكُمْ بِهِمَا رَأْفَةٌ
فِيْ دِيْنِ اللهِ اِنْ كُنْتُمْ
تُؤْمِنُوْنَ بِاللهِ وَالْيَوْمِ الْاٰخِرِ وَلْيَشْهَدْ
عَذَابَهُمَا طَآئِفَةٌ مِّنَ الْمُؤْمِنِيْنَ ٥

3. Let no man guilty of
Adultery or fornication marry
Any but a woman
Similarly guilty, or an Unbeliever:
Nor let any but such a man
Or an Unbeliever
Marry such a woman:

٣- اَلزَّانِيْ لَا يَنْكِحُ اِلَّا زَانِيَةً اَوْ مُشْرِكَةً
وَّالزَّانِيَةُ لَا يَنْكِحُهَآ
اِلَّا زَانٍ اَوْ مُشْرِكٌ
وَحُرِّمَ ذٰلِكَ

To the Believers such a thing
Is forbidden.

4. And those who launch
A charge against chaste women,
And produce not four witnesses
(To support their allegations)—
Flog them with eighty stripes;
And reject their evidence
Ever after: for such men
Are wicked transgressors—

5. Unless they repent thereafter
And mend (their conduct);
For Allah is Oft-Forgiving,
Most Merciful.

6. And for those who launch
A charge against their spouses,
And have (in support)
No evidence but their own—
Their solitary evidence
(Can be received) if they
Bear witness four times
(With an oath) by Allah
That they are solemnly
Telling the truth;

7. And the fifth (oath)
(Should be) that they solemnly
Invoke the curse of Allah
On themselves if they
Tell a lie.

8. But it would avert
The punishment from the wife,
If she bears witness
Four times (with an oath)
By Allah, that (her husband)
Is telling a lie;

9. And the fifth (oath)
Should be that she solemnly
Invokes the wrath of Allah
On herself if (her accuser)
Is telling the truth.

10. If it were not
For Allah's grace and mercy

On you, and that Allah
Is Oft-Returning,
Full of Wisdom—
(Ye would be ruined indeed).
SECTION 2.

11. Those who brought forward
The lie are a body
Among yourselves: think it not
To be an evil to you;
On the contrary it is good
For you: to every man
Among them (will come
The punishment) of the sin
That he earned, and to him
Who took on himself the lead
Among them, will be
A Penalty grievous.

١١ ـ اِنَّ الَّذِيْنَ جَآءُوْ بِالْاِفْكِ عُصْبَةٌ
مِّنْكُمْ ۚ لَا تَحْسَبُوْهُ شَرًّا لَّكُمْ ۖ
بَلْ هُوَ خَيْرٌ لَّكُمْ ۚ
لِكُلِّ امْرِئٍ مِّنْهُمْ مَّا اكْتَسَبَ مِنَ الْاِثْمِ ۚ
وَالَّذِيْ تَوَلّٰى كِبْرَهٗ مِنْهُمْ
لَهٗ عَذَابٌ عَظِيْمٌ ۝

12. Why did not the Believers—
Men and women   when ye
Heard of the affair—put
The best construction on it
In their own minds
And say, "This (charge)
Is an obvious lie"?

١٢ ـ لَوْلَا اِذْ سَمِعْتُمُوْهُ
ظَنَّ الْمُؤْمِنُوْنَ وَالْمُؤْمِنٰتُ بِاَنْفُسِهِمْ
خَيْرًا ۙ
وَّ قَالُوْا هٰذَآ اِفْكٌ مُّبِيْنٌ ۝

13. Why did they not bring
Four witnesses to prove it?
When they have not brought
The witnesses, such men,
In the sight of Allah
(Stand forth) themselves as liars!

١٣ ـ لَوْلَا جَآءُوْ عَلَيْهِ بِاَرْبَعَةِ شُهَدَآءَ ۚ
فَاِذْ لَمْ يَأْتُوْا بِالشُّهَدَآءِ
فَاُولٰٓئِكَ عِنْدَ اللّٰهِ هُمُ الْكٰذِبُوْنَ ۝

14. Were it not for the grace
And mercy of Allah on you,
In this world and the Hereafter,
A grievous penalty would have
Seized you in that ye rushed
Glibly into this affair.

١٤ ـ وَلَوْلَا فَضْلُ اللّٰهِ عَلَيْكُمْ وَرَحْمَتُهٗ
فِى الدُّنْيَا وَالْاٰخِرَةِ
لَمَسَّكُمْ فِيْ مَآ اَفَضْتُمْ فِيْهِ عَذَابٌ عَظِيْمٌ ۝

15. Behold, ye received it
On your tongues.
And said out of your mouths
Things of which ye had
No knowledge; and ye thought
It to be a light matter,
While it was most serious
In the sight of Allah.

١٥ ـ اِذْ تَلَقَّوْنَهٗ بِاَلْسِنَتِكُمْ
وَتَقُوْلُوْنَ بِاَفْوَاهِكُمْ مَّا لَيْسَ لَكُمْ بِهٖ
عِلْمٌ وَّ تَحْسَبُوْنَهٗ هَيِّنًا ۖ
وَّ هُوَ عِنْدَ اللّٰهِ عَظِيْمٌ ۝

16. And why did ye not
When ye heard it, say?—
"It is not right of us
To speak of this:
Glory to Thee (our Lord) this is
A most serious slander!"

١٦- وَلَوْلَا إِذْ سَمِعْتُمُوهُ قُلْتُمْ
مَّا يَكُونُ لَنَا أَنْ نَتَكَلَّمَ بِهَذَا
سُبْحَانَكَ هَذَا بُهْتَانٌ عَظِيمٌ ۝

17. Allah doth admonish you,
That ye may never repeat
Such (conduct), if ye
Are (true) Believers.

١٧- يَعِظُكُمُ اللهُ أَنْ تَعُودُوا لِمِثْلِهِ أَبَدًا
إِنْ كُنْتُمْ مُّؤْمِنِينَ ۝

18. And Allah makes the Signs
Plain to you: for Allah
Is full of knowledge and wisdom.

١٨- وَيُبَيِّنُ اللهُ لَكُمُ الْآيَاتِ
وَاللهُ عَلِيمٌ حَكِيمٌ ۝

19. Those who love (to see)
Scandal published broadcast
Among the Believers, will have
A grievous Penalty in this life
And in the Hereafter: Allah
Knows, and ye know not.

١٩- إِنَّ الَّذِينَ يُحِبُّونَ أَنْ تَشِيعَ الْفَاحِشَةُ
فِي الَّذِينَ آمَنُوا لَهُمْ عَذَابٌ أَلِيمٌ فِي
الدُّنْيَا وَالْآخِرَةِ وَاللهُ يَعْلَمُ وَأَنْتُمْ لَا تَعْلَمُونَ ۝

20. Were it not for the grace
And mercy of Allah on you,
And that Allah is
Full of kindness and mercy,
(Ye would be ruined indeed).

٢٠- وَلَوْلَا فَضْلُ اللهِ عَلَيْكُمْ وَرَحْمَتُهُ
وَأَنَّ اللهَ رَءُوفٌ رَحِيمٌ ۝

SECTION 3.

21. O ye who believe!
Follow not Satan's footsteps:
If any will follow the footsteps
Of Satan, he will (but) command
What is shameful and wrong:
And were it not for the grace
And mercy of Allah on you,
Not one of you would ever
Have been pure: but Allah
Doth purify whom He pleases:
And Allah is One Who
Hears and knows (all things).

٢١- يَا أَيُّهَا الَّذِينَ آمَنُوا لَا تَتَّبِعُوا خُطُوَاتِ
الشَّيْطَانِ وَمَنْ يَتَّبِعْ خُطُوَاتِ الشَّيْطَانِ
فَإِنَّهُ يَأْمُرُ بِالْفَحْشَاءِ وَالْمُنْكَرِ وَلَوْلَا
فَضْلُ اللهِ عَلَيْكُمْ وَرَحْمَتُهُ مَا زَكَى
مِنْكُمْ مِنْ أَحَدٍ أَبَدًا وَلَكِنَّ اللهَ
يُزَكِّي مَنْ يَشَاءُ وَاللهُ سَمِيعٌ عَلِيمٌ ۝

22. Let not those among you
Who are endued with grace
And amplitude of means
Resolve by oath against helping
Their kinsmen, those in want,

٢٢- وَلَا يَأْتَلِ أُولُوا الْفَضْلِ مِنْكُمْ
وَالسَّعَةِ أَنْ يُؤْتُوا
أُولِي الْقُرْبَى وَالْمَسَاكِينَ

And those who have left
Their homes in Allah's cause:
Let them forgive and overlook,
Do you not wish
That Allah should forgive you?
For Allah is Oft-Forgiving,
Most Merciful.

وَالْمُهٰجِرِيْنَ فِيْ سَبِيْلِ اللّٰهِ وَلْيَعْفُوْا وَلْيَصْفَحُوْا ۗ اَلَا تُحِبُّوْنَ اَنْ يَّغْفِرَ اللّٰهُ لَكُمْ ۗ وَاللّٰهُ غَفُوْرٌ رَّحِيْمٌ ۟

23. Those who slander chaste women,
Indiscreet but believing,
Are cursed in this life
And in the Hereafter:
For them is a grievous Penalty—

٢٣- اِنَّ الَّذِيْنَ يَرْمُوْنَ الْمُحْصَنٰتِ الْغٰفِلٰتِ الْمُؤْمِنٰتِ لُعِنُوْا فِي الدُّنْيَا وَالْاٰخِرَةِ ۖ وَلَهُمْ عَذَابٌ عَظِيْمٌ ۟

24. On the Day when their tongues,
Their hands, and their feet
Will bear witness against them
As to their actions.

٢٤- يَّوْمَ تَشْهَدُ عَلَيْهِمْ اَلْسِنَتُهُمْ وَاَيْدِيْهِمْ وَاَرْجُلُهُمْ بِمَا كَانُوْا يَعْمَلُوْنَ ۟

25. On that Day Allah
Will pay them back
(All) their just dues,
And they will realise
That Allah is
The (very) Truth,
That makes all things manifest.

٢٥- يَوْمَئِذٍ يُّوَفِّيْهِمُ اللّٰهُ دِيْنَهُمُ الْحَقَّ وَيَعْلَمُوْنَ اَنَّ اللّٰهَ هُوَ الْحَقُّ الْمُبِيْنُ ۟

26. Women impure are for men
impure,
And men impure for women
impure,
And women of purity
Are for men of purity,
And men of purity
Are for women of purity:
These are not affected
By what people say:
For them there is forgiveness,
And a provision honourable.

٢٦- اَلْخَبِيْثٰتُ لِلْخَبِيْثِيْنَ وَالْخَبِيْثُوْنَ لِلْخَبِيْثٰتِ ۚ وَالطَّيِّبٰتُ لِلطَّيِّبِيْنَ وَالطَّيِّبُوْنَ لِلطَّيِّبٰتِ ۚ اُولٰٓئِكَ مُبَرَّءُوْنَ مِمَّا يَقُوْلُوْنَ ۖ لَهُمْ مَّغْفِرَةٌ وَّرِزْقٌ كَرِيْمٌ ۟ ‏ع

SECTION 4.

27. ⓞ ye who believe!
Enter not houses other than
Your own, until ye have
Asked permission and saluted
Those in them: that is

٢٧- يٰٓاَيُّهَا الَّذِيْنَ اٰمَنُوْا لَا تَدْخُلُوْا بُيُوْتًا غَيْرَ بُيُوْتِكُمْ حَتّٰى تَسْتَأْنِسُوْا وَتُسَلِّمُوْا عَلٰٓى اَهْلِهَا ۗ

Best for you, in order that
Ye may heed (what is seemly).

28. If ye find no one
In the house, enter not
Until permission is given
To you: if ye are asked
To go back, go back:
That makes for greater purity
For yourselves: and Allah
Knows well all that ye do.

29. It is no fault on your part
To enter houses not used
For living in, which serve
Some (other) use for you:
And Allah has knowledge
Of what ye reveal
And what ye conceal.

30. Say to the believing men
That they should lower
Their gaze and guard
Their modesty: that will make
For greater purity for them:
And Allah is well acquainted
With all that they do.

31. And say to the believing women
That they should lower
Their gaze and guard
Their modesty; that they
Should not display their
Beauty and ornaments   except
What (must ordinarily) appear
Thereof; that they should
Draw their veils over
Their bosoms and not display
Their beauty except
To their husbands, their fathers,
Their husbands' fathers, their
sons,
Their husbands' sons,
Their brothers or their brothers'
Or their sisters' sons,   sons,
Or their women, or the slaves
Whom their right hands
Possess, or male servants
Free of physical needs,

Or small children who
Have no sense of the shame
Of sex; and that they
Should not strike their feet
In order to draw attention
To their hidde ornaments.
And O ye Believers!
Turn ye all together
Towards Allah, that ye
May attain Bliss.

مِنَ الرِّجَالِ اَوِ الطِّفْلِ الَّذِيْنَ لَمْ يَظْهَرُوْا
عَلٰى عَوْرٰتِ النِّسَآءِ ۖ وَ لَا يَضْرِبْنَ
بِاَرْجُلِهِنَّ لِيُعْلَمَ مَا يُخْفِيْنَ مِنْ زِيْنَتِهِنَّ ۚ
وَ تُوْبُوْٓا اِلَى اللّٰهِ جَمِيْعًا اَيُّهَ الْمُؤْمِنُوْنَ
لَعَلَّكُمْ تُفْلِحُوْنَ ۞

32. **M**arry those among you
Who are single,   or
The virtuous ones among
Your slaves, male or female:
If they are in poverty,
Allah will give them
Means out of His grace:
For Allah encompasseth all,
And He knoweth all things.

٣٢- وَ اَنْكِحُوا الْاَيَامٰى مِنْكُمْ
وَ الصّٰلِحِيْنَ مِنْ عِبَادِكُمْ وَ اِمَآئِكُمْ ۚ
اِنْ يَّكُوْنُوْا فُقَرَآءَ يُغْنِهِمُ اللّٰهُ مِنْ فَضْلِهٖ ۗ
وَ اللّٰهُ وَاسِعٌ عَلِيْمٌ ۞

33. Let those who find not
The wherewithal for marriage
Keep themselves chaste, until
Allah gives them means
Out of His grace.
And if any of your slaves
Ask for a deed in writing
(To enable them to earn
Their freedom for a certain sum),
Give them such a deed
If ye know any good
In them; yea, give them
Something yourselves
Out of the means which
Allah has given to you.
But force not your maids
To prostitution when   they desire
Chastity, in order that ye
May make a gain
In the goods of this life.
But if anyone compels them,
Yet, after such compulsion,
Is Allah Oft-Forgiving,
Most Merciful (to them).

٣٣- وَ لْيَسْتَعْفِفِ الَّذِيْنَ لَا يَجِدُوْنَ
نِكَاحًا حَتّٰى
يُغْنِيَهُمُ اللّٰهُ مِنْ فَضْلِهٖ ۗ
وَ الَّذِيْنَ يَبْتَغُوْنَ الْكِتٰبَ
مِمَّا مَلَكَتْ اَيْمَانُكُمْ
فَكَاتِبُوْهُمْ اِنْ عَلِمْتُمْ فِيْهِمْ خَيْرًا ۖ
وَّ اٰتُوْهُمْ مِّنْ مَّالِ اللّٰهِ الَّذِيْۤ اٰتٰكُمْ ۗ
وَ لَا تُكْرِهُوْا فَتَيٰتِكُمْ عَلَى الْبِغَآءِ
اِنْ اَرَدْنَ تَحَصُّنًا
لِّتَبْتَغُوْا عَرَضَ الْحَيٰوةِ الدُّنْيَا ۚ
وَ مَنْ يُّكْرِهْهُّنَّ
فَاِنَّ اللّٰهَ مِنْۢ بَعْدِ اِكْرَاهِهِنَّ
غَفُوْرٌ رَّحِيْمٌ ۞

34. **W**e have already sent down
To you verses making things

٣٤- وَ لَقَدْ اَنْزَلْنَآ اِلَيْكُمْ اٰيٰتٍ مُّبَيِّنٰتٍ

Clear, an illustration from (the
story

Of) people who passed away
Before you, and an admonition
For those who fear (Allah).

SECTION 5.

35. Allah is the Light
Of the heavens and the earth.
The parable of His Light
Is as if there were a Niche
And within it a Lamp:
The Lamp enclosed in Glass;
The glass as it were
A brilliant star:
Lit from a blessed Tree,
An Olive, neither of the East
Nor of the West,
Whose Oil is well-nigh
Luminous,
Though fire scarce touched it:
Light upon Light!
Allah doth set forth Parables
For men: and Allah
Doth know all things.

36. (Lit is such a light)
In houses, which Allah
Hath permitted to be raised
To honour; for the celebration,
In them, of His name:
In them is He glorified.
In the mornings and
In the evenings, (again and
again)—

37. By men whom neither
Traffic nor merchandise
Can divert from the
Remembrance
Of Allah, nor from regular Prayer,
Nor from the practice
Of regular Charity:
Their (only) fear is
For the Day when
Hearts and eyes
Will be transformed
(In a world wholly new)—

وَّ مَثَلًا مِّنَ الَّذِيْنَ خَلَوْا مِنْ قَبْلِكُمْ وَمَوْعِظَةً لِّلْمُتَّقِيْنَ ۟

٣٥ۭ اَللّٰهُ نُوْرُ السَّمٰوٰتِ وَالْاَرْضِ ۭ مَثَلُ نُوْرِهٖ كَمِشْكٰوةٍ فِيْهَا مِصْبَاحٌ ۭ اَلْمِصْبَاحُ فِيْ زُجَاجَةٍ ۭ اَلزُّجَاجَةُ كَاَنَّهَا كَوْكَبٌ دُرِّيٌّ يُّوْقَدُ مِنْ شَجَرَةٍ مُّبٰرَكَةٍ زَيْتُوْنَةٍ لَّا شَرْقِيَّةٍ وَّلَا غَرْبِيَّةٍ ۙ يَّكَادُ زَيْتُهَا يُضِيْٓءُ وَلَوْ لَمْ تَمْسَسْهُ نَارٌ ۭ نُوْرٌ عَلٰى نُوْرٍ ۭ يَهْدِى اللّٰهُ لِنُوْرِهٖ مَنْ يَّشَاءُ ۭ وَيَضْرِبُ اللّٰهُ الْاَمْثَالَ لِلنَّاسِ ۭ وَاللّٰهُ بِكُلِّ شَيْءٍ عَلِيْمٌ ۟

٣٦ۭ فِيْ بُيُوْتٍ اَذِنَ اللّٰهُ اَنْ تُرْفَعَ وَيُذْكَرَ فِيْهَا اسْمُهٗ ۙ يُسَبِّحُ لَهٗ فِيْهَا بِالْغُدُوِّ وَالْاٰصَالِ ۟

٣٧ۭ رِجَالٌ ۙ لَّا تُلْهِيْهِمْ تِجَارَةٌ وَّلَا بَيْعٌ عَنْ ذِكْرِ اللّٰهِ وَاِقَامِ الصَّلٰوةِ وَاِيْتَاءِ الزَّكٰوةِ ۙ يَخَافُوْنَ يَوْمًا تَتَقَلَّبُ فِيْهِ الْقُلُوْبُ وَالْاَبْصَارُ ۟

38. That Allah may reward them
According to the best
Of their deeds, and add
Even more for them
Out of His Grace:
For Allah doth provide
For those whom He will,
Without measure.

٣٨ - لِيَجْزِيَهُمُ اللهُ أَحْسَنَ مَا عَمِلُوا
وَيَزِيدَهُمْ مِّنْ فَضْلِهِ ۚ
وَاللهُ يَرْزُقُ مَنْ يَّشَاءُ
بِغَيْرِ حِسَابٍ ۟

39. But the Unbelievers —
Their deeds are like a mirage
In sandy deserts, which
The man parched with thirst
Mistakes for water; until
When he comes up to it,
He finds it to be nothing:
But he finds Allah
(Ever) with him, and Allah
Will pay him his account:
And Allah is swift
In taking account.

٣٩ - وَالَّذِينَ كَفَرُوا أَعْمَالُهُمْ كَسَرَابٍ
بِقِيعَةٍ يَّحْسَبُهُ الظَّمْآنُ مَآءً ۗ
حَتّٰى إِذَا جَآءَهُ
لَمْ يَجِدْهُ شَيْئًا
وَّوَجَدَ اللهَ عِنْدَهُ فَوَفّٰهُ حِسَابَهُ ۗ
وَاللهُ سَرِيعُ الْحِسَابِ ۟

40. Or (the Unbelievers' state)
Is like the depths of darkness
In a vast deep ocean,
Overwhelmed with billow
Topped by billow,
Topped by (dark) clouds:
Depths of darkness, one
Above another: if a man
Stretches out his hand,
He can hardly see it!
For any to whom Allah
Giveth not light,
There is no light!

٤٠ - أَوْ كَظُلُمٰتٍ فِي بَحْرٍ
لُّجِّيٍّ يَّغْشٰهُ مَوْجٌ مِّنْ فَوْقِهِ
مَوْجٌ مِّنْ فَوْقِهِ سَحَابٌ ۚ
ظُلُمٰتٌ بَعْضُهَا فَوْقَ بَعْضٍ ۗ
إِذَا أَخْرَجَ يَدَهُ لَمْ يَكَدْ يَرٰهَا ۗ
وَمَنْ لَّمْ يَجْعَلِ اللهُ لَهُ نُورًا
فَمَا لَهُ مِنْ نُّورٍ ۟

SECTION 6.

41. Seest thou not that it is
Allah Whose praises all beings
In the heavens and on earth
Do celebrate, and the birds
(Of the air) with wings
Outspread? Each one knows
Its own (mode of) prayer
And praise. And Allah
Knows well all that they do.

٤١ - أَلَمْ تَرَ أَنَّ اللهَ يُسَبِّحُ
لَهُ مَنْ فِي السَّمٰوٰتِ وَالْأَرْضِ وَالطَّيْرُ
صَآفّٰتٍ ۗ كُلٌّ قَدْ عَلِمَ صَلَاتَهُ
وَتَسْبِيحَهُ ۗ وَاللهُ عَلِيمٌ بِمَا يَفْعَلُونَ ۟

42. Yea, to Allah belongs
The dominion of the heavens

٤٢ - وَلِلّٰهِ مُلْكُ السَّمٰوٰتِ

And the earth; and to Allah
Is the final goal (of all).

وَالْأَرْضِ وَإِلَى اللهِ الْمَصِيرُ ۞

43. Seest thou not that Allah
Makes the clouds move
Gently, then joins them
Together, then makes them
Into a heap?—then wilt thou
See rain issue forth
From their midst. And He
Sends down from the sky
Mountain masses (of clouds)
Wherein is hail: He strikes
Therewith whom He pleases
And He turns it away
From whom He pleases.
The vivid flash of His lightning
Well-nigh blinds the sight.

٤٣ - أَلَمْ تَرَ أَنَّ اللهَ يُزْجِى سَحَابًا
ثُمَّ يُؤَلِّفُ بَيْنَهُ
ثُمَّ يَجْعَلُهُ رُكَامًا
فَتَرَى الْوَدْقَ يَخْرُجُ مِنْ خِلَالِهِ وَيُنَزِّلُ
مِنَ السَّمَاءِ مِنْ جِبَالٍ فِيهَا مِنْ بَرَدٍ
فَيُصِيبُ بِهِ مَنْ يَشَاءُ
وَيَصْرِفُهُ عَنْ مَنْ يَشَاءُ
يَكَادُ سَنَا بَرْقِهِ يَذْهَبُ بِالْأَبْصَارِ ۞

44. Is it Allah Who alternates
The Night and the Day:
Verily in these things
Is an instructive example
For those who have vision!

٤٤ - يُقَلِّبُ اللهُ الَّيْلَ وَالنَّهَارَ
إِنَّ فِى ذَلِكَ لَعِبْرَةً لِأُولِى الْأَبْصَارِ ۞

45. And Allah has created
Every animal from water:
Of them there are some
That creep on their bellies;
Some that walk on two legs;
And some that walk on four.
Allah creates what He wills;
For verily Allah has power
Over all things.

٤٥ - وَاللهُ خَلَقَ كُلَّ دَآبَّةٍ مِنْ مَآءٍ
فَمِنْهُمْ مَنْ يَمْشِى عَلَى بَطْنِهِ
وَمِنْهُمْ مَنْ يَمْشِى عَلَى رِجْلَيْنِ وَمِنْهُمْ
مَنْ يَمْشِى عَلَى أَرْبَعٍ يَخْلُقُ اللهُ مَا يَشَاءُ
إِنَّ اللهَ عَلَى كُلِّ شَيْءٍ قَدِيرُ ۞

46. We have indeed sent down
Signs that make things manifest:
And Allah guides whom He wills
To a Way that is straight.

٤٦ - لَقَدْ أَنْزَلْنَا آيَاتٍ مُبَيِّنَاتٍ وَاللهُ
يَهْدِى مَنْ يَشَاءُ إِلَى صِرَاطٍ مُسْتَقِيمٍ ۞

47. They say, "We believe
In Allah and in the Messenger,
And we obey": but
Even after that, some of them
Turn away: they are not
(Really) Believers.

٤٧ - وَيَقُولُونَ آمَنَّا بِاللهِ وَبِالرَّسُولِ وَ
أَطَعْنَا ثُمَّ يَتَوَلَّى فَرِيقٌ مِنْهُمْ مِنْ بَعْدِ
ذَلِكَ وَمَا أُولَئِكَ بِالْمُؤْمِنِينَ ۞

48. When they are summoned
To Allah and His Messenger,

٤٨ - وَإِذَا دُعُوا إِلَى اللهِ وَرَسُولِهِ لِيَحْكُمَ

In order that He may judge
Between them, behold, some
Of them decline (to come).

بَيْنَهُمْ اِذَا فَرِيْقٌ مِّنْهُمْ مُّعْرِضُوْنَ ۞

49. But if the right is
On their side, they come
To him with all submission.

۴۹- وَاِنْ يَّكُنْ لَّهُمُ الْحَقُّ
يَاْتُوْۤا اِلَيْهِ مُذْعِنِيْنَ ؕ

50. Is it that there is
A disease in their hearts?
Or do they doubt,
Or are they in fear,
That Allah and His Messenger
Will deal unjustly with them?
Nay, it is they themselves
Who do wrong.
SECTION 7.

۵۰- اَفِیْ قُلُوْبِهِمْ مَّرَضٌ
اَمِ ارْتَابُوْۤا اَمْ يَخَافُوْنَ
اَنْ يَّحِيْفَ اللّٰهُ عَلَيْهِمْ وَرَسُوْلُهٗ ؕ
بَلْ اُولٰٓئِكَ هُمُ الظّٰلِمُوْنَ ۞

51. The answer of the Believers,
When summoned to Allah
And His Messenger, in order
That he may judge between them,
Is no other than this:
They say, "We hear and we
    obey":
It is such as these
That will attain felicity.

۵۱- اِنَّمَا كَانَ قَوْلَ الْمُؤْمِنِيْنَ اِذَا دُعُوْۤا
اِلَى اللّٰهِ وَرَسُوْلِهٖ لِيَحْكُمَ بَيْنَهُمْ
اَنْ يَّقُوْلُوْا سَمِعْنَا وَاَطَعْنَا ؕ
وَاُولٰٓئِكَ هُمُ الْمُفْلِحُوْنَ ۞

52. It is such as obey
Allah and His Messenger,
And fear Allah and do
Right, that will win
(In the end).

۵۲- وَمَنْ يُّطِعِ اللّٰهَ وَرَسُوْلَهٗ
وَيَخْشَ اللّٰهَ وَيَتَّقْهِ
فَاُولٰٓئِكَ هُمُ الْفَآئِزُوْنَ ۞

53. They swear their strongest oaths
By Allah that, if only thou
Wouldst command them, they
Would leave (their homes).
Say: "Swear ye not;
Obedience is (more) reasonable;
Verily, Allah is well acquainted
With all that ye do."

۵۳- وَاَقْسَمُوْا بِاللّٰهِ جَهْدَ اَيْمَانِهِمْ لَئِنْ
اَمَرْتَهُمْ لَيَخْرُجُنَّ ؕ
قُلْ لَّا تُقْسِمُوْا ۚ طَاعَةٌ مَّعْرُوْفَةٌ ؕ
اِنَّ اللّٰهَ خَبِيْرٌۢ بِمَا تَعْمَلُوْنَ ۞

54. Say: "Obey Allah, and obey
The Messenger: but if ye turn
Away, he is only responsible
For the duty placed on him
And ye for that placed
On you. If ye obey him,
Ye shall be on right guidance.

۵۴- قُلْ اَطِيْعُوا اللّٰهَ وَاَطِيْعُوا الرَّسُوْلَ ۚ
فَاِنْ تَوَلَّوْا فَاِنَّمَا عَلَيْهِ مَا حُمِّلَ
وَعَلَيْكُمْ مَّا حُمِّلْتُمْ ؕ
وَاِنْ تُطِيْعُوْهُ تَهْتَدُوْا ؕ

The Messenger's duty is only
To preach the clear (Message).

55. Allah has promised, to those
Among you who believe
And work righteous deeds, that
He
Will, of a surety, grant them
In the land, inheritance
(Of power), as He granted it
To those before them; that
He will establish in authority
Their religion—the one
Which He has chosen for them;
And that He will change
(Their state), after the fear
In which they (lived), to one
Of security and peace:
'They will worship Me (alone)
And not associate aught with Me.'
If any do reject Faith
After this, they are
Rebellious and wicked.

56. So establish regular Prayer
And give regular Charity;
And obey the Messenger;
That ye may receive mercy.

57. Never think thou
That the Unbelievers
Are going to frustrate
(Allah's Plan) on earth:
Their abode is the Fire—
And it is indeed
An evil refuge!

SECTION 8.

58. O ye who believe!
Let those whom your right
hands
Possess, and the (children) among
you
Who have not come of age
Ask your permission (before
They come to your presence),
On three occasions: before
Morning prayer; the while
Ye doff your clothes

For the noonday heat;
And after the late-night prayer:
These are your three times
Of undress: outside these times
It is not wrong for you
Or for them to move about
Attending to each other:
Thus does Allah make clear
The Signs to you: for Allah
Is full of knowledge and wisdom.

59. But when the children among
                     you
Come of age, let them (also)
Ask for permission, as do those
Senior to them (in age):
Thus does Allah make clear
His Signs to you: for Allah
Is full of knowledge and
                     wisdom.

60. Such elderly women   as are
Past the prospect of marriage—
There is no blame on them
If they lay aside
Their (outer) garments, provided
They make not a wanton display
Of their beauty: but
It is best for them
To be modest: and Allah
Is One Who sees and knows
All things.

61. It is no fault in the blind
Nor in one born lame, nor
In one afflicted with illness,
Nor in yourselves, that ye
Should eat in your own houses,
Or those of your fathers,
Or your mothers, or your brothers,
Or your sisters, or your father's
                     brothers
Or your father's sisters,
Or your mother's brothers,
Or your mother's sisters,
Or in houses of which
The keys are in your possession,

Or in the house of a sincere
Friend of yours: there is
No blame on you, whether
Ye eat in company or
Separately. But if ye
Enter houses, salute each other—
A greeting or blessing
And purity as from Allah,
Thus does Allah make clear
The Signs to you: that ye
May understand.

SECTION 9.

أَنْ تَأْكُلُوا جَمِيعًا أَوْ أَشْتَاتًا ۚ
فَإِذَا دَخَلْتُمْ بُيُوتًا فَسَلِّمُوا عَلَىٰ أَنْفُسِكُمْ
تَحِيَّةً مِنْ عِنْدِ اللَّهِ مُبَارَكَةً طَيِّبَةً ۚ
كَذَٰلِكَ يُبَيِّنُ اللَّهُ لَكُمُ
الْآيَاتِ لَعَلَّكُمْ تَعْقِلُونَ ۝

62. Only those are Believers,
Who believe in Allah and
His Messenger: when they are
With him on a matter
Requiring collective action,
They do not depart until
They have asked for his leave:
Those who ask for thy leave
Are those who believe in Allah
And His Messenger; so when
They ask for thy leave,
For some business of theirs,
Give leave to those of them
Whom thou wilt,   and ask
Allah for their forgiveness:
For Allah is Oft-Forgiving,
Most Merciful.

٦٢- إِنَّمَا الْمُؤْمِنُونَ الَّذِينَ آمَنُوا بِاللَّهِ
وَرَسُولِهِ وَإِذَا كَانُوا مَعَهُ عَلَىٰ أَمْرٍ جَامِعٍ
لَمْ يَذْهَبُوا حَتَّىٰ يَسْتَأْذِنُوهُ ۚ
إِنَّ الَّذِينَ يَسْتَأْذِنُونَكَ
أُولَٰئِكَ الَّذِينَ يُؤْمِنُونَ بِاللَّهِ وَرَسُولِهِ ۚ
فَإِذَا اسْتَأْذَنُوكَ لِبَعْضِ شَأْنِهِمْ
فَأْذَنْ لِمَنْ
شِئْتَ مِنْهُمْ وَاسْتَغْفِرْ لَهُمُ اللَّهَ ۚ
إِنَّ اللَّهَ غَفُورٌ رَحِيمٌ ۝

63. Deem not the summons
Of the Messenger among
yourselves
Like the summons of one
Of you to another: Allah
Doth know those of you
Who slip away under shelter
Of some excuse: then
Let those beware who
Withstand the Messenger's order,
Lest some trial befall them,
Or a grievous Penalty
Be inflicted on them.

٦٣- لَا تَجْعَلُوا دُعَاءَ الرَّسُولِ بَيْنَكُمْ
كَدُعَاءِ بَعْضِكُمْ بَعْضًا ۚ
قَدْ يَعْلَمُ اللَّهُ الَّذِينَ يَتَسَلَّلُونَ مِنْكُمْ
لِوَاذًا ۚ فَلْيَحْذَرِ الَّذِينَ
يُخَالِفُونَ عَنْ أَمْرِهِ أَنْ تُصِيبَهُمْ فِتْنَةٌ
أَوْ يُصِيبَهُمْ عَذَابٌ أَلِيمٌ ۝

64. Be quite sure that
To Allah doth belong

٦٤- أَلَا إِنَّ لِلَّهِ

Whatever is in the heavens
And on earth. Well doth He
Know what ye are intent upon:
And one day they will be
Brought back to Him, and He
Will tell them the truth
Of what they did.
For Allah doth know
All things.

مَا فِى السَّمَوَاتِ وَالْأَرْضِ
قَدْ يَعْلَمُ مَا أَنْتُمْ عَلَيْهِ
وَيَوْمَ يُرْجَعُونَ إِلَيْهِ فَيُنَبِّئُهُمْ بِمَا عَمِلُوا
وَاللّٰهُ بِكُلِّ شَىْءٍ عَلِيمٌ ۝

INTRODUCTION TO SŪRA XXV. *(Furqān)* — 77 Verses

This Sūra further develops the contrast between Light and Darkness, as symbolical of knowledge and ignorance, righteousness and sin, spiritual progress and degradation. It closes with a definition of the deeds by which the righteous are known in the environment of this world.

It is mainly an early Meccan Sūra, but its date has no significance.

Al Furqān (The Criterion)

*In the name of Allah, Most Gracious,
Most Merciful.*

1. Blessed[3052] is He Who
Sent down the Criterion
To His servant, that it
May be an admonition
To all creatures—

2. He to Whom belongs
The dominion of the heavens
And the earth: no son
Has He begotten, nor has He
A partner in His dominion:
It is He Who created
All things, and ordered them
In due proportions.

3. Yet have they taken,
Besides Him, gods that can
Create nothing but are themselves
Created; that have no control
Of hurt or good to themselves;
Nor can they control Death
Nor Life nor Resurrection.

4. But the Misbelievers say:
"Naught is this but a lie
Which he has forged,
And others have helped him
At it." In truth it is they
Who have put forward
An iniquity and a falsehood.

5. And they say: "Tales of
The ancients, which he has caused

To be written: and they
Are dictated before him
Morning and evening."

فَهِيَ تُمْلٰى عَلَيْهِ بُكْرَةً وَّاَصِيْلًا ۟

6. Say: "The (Qur'ān) was sent down
By Him Who knows
The Mystery (that is) in the
           heavens
And the earth: verily He
Is Oft-Forgiving, Most Merciful."

٦- قُلْ اَنْزَلَهُ الَّذِيْ يَعْلَمُ
السِّرَّ فِى السَّمٰوٰتِ وَالْاَرْضِ ۚ
اِنَّهٗ كَانَ غَفُوْرًا رَّحِيْمًا ۟

7. And they say: "What sort
Of a messenger is this,
Who eats foods, and walks
Through the streets? Why
Has not an angel
Been sent down to him
To give admonition with him?

٧- وَ قَالُوْا مَالِ هٰذَا الرَّسُوْلِ
يَأْكُلُ الطَّعَامَ وَيَمْشِيْ فِى الْاَسْوَاقِ ۚ
لَوْ لَاۤ اُنْزِلَ اِلَيْهِ مَلَكٌ
فَيَكُوْنَ مَعَهٗ نَذِيْرًا ۟

8. "Or (why) has not a treasure
Been bestowed on him, or
Why has he (not) a garden
For enjoyment?"   The wicked
Say: "Ye follow none other
Than a man bewitched."

٨- اَوْ يُلْقٰٓى اِلَيْهِ كَنْزٌ اَوْ تَكُوْنُ لَهٗ جَنَّةٌ
يَّأْكُلُ مِنْهَا ۚ وَقَالَ الظّٰلِمُوْنَ اِنْ تَتَّبِعُوْنَ
اِلَّا رَجُلًا مَّسْحُوْرًا ۟

9. See what kinds of companions
They make for thee!
But they have gone astray,
And never a way will they
Be able to find!

٩- اُنْظُرْ كَيْفَ ضَرَبُوْا لَكَ الْاَمْثَالَ
فَضَلُّوْا فَلَا يَسْتَطِيْعُوْنَ سَبِيْلًا ۟ ۼ

SECTION 2.

10. Blessed is He Who,
If that were His Will,
Could give thee better (things)
Than those—Gardens beneath
           which
Rivers flow; and He could
Give thee Palaces (secure
To dwell in).

١٠- تَبٰرَكَ الَّذِيْٓ اِنْ شَآءَ
جَعَلَ لَكَ خَيْرًا
مِّنْ ذٰلِكَ جَنّٰتٍ تَجْرِيْ مِنْ تَحْتِهَا
الْاَنْهٰرُ ۙ وَيَجْعَلْ لَّكَ قُصُوْرًا ۟

11. Nay, they deny the Hour
(Of the Judgement to come):
But We have prepared
A Blazing Fire for such
As deny the Hour:

١١- بَلْ كَذَّبُوْا بِالسَّاعَةِ ۟
وَاَعْتَدْنَا لِمَنْ كَذَّبَ بِالسَّاعَةِ سَعِيْرًا ۟

12. When it sees them

١٢- اِذَا رَاَتْهُمْ مِّنْ مَّكَانٍ

From a place far off,
They will hear its fury
And its raging sigh.

بَعِيْدٍ سَمِعُوْا لَهَا تَغَيُّظًا وَّزَفِيْرًا ٠

13. And when they are cast,
Bound together, into a
Constricted place therein, they
Will plead for destruction
There and then!

١٣- وَاِذَاۤ اُلْقُوْا مِنْهَا مَكَانًا ضَيِّقًا
مُّقَرَّنِيْنَ دَعَوْا هُنَالِكَ ثُبُوْرًا ٠

14. "This day plead not
For a single destruction:
Plead for a destruction oft-
             repeated!"

١٤- لَا تَدْعُوا الْيَوْمَ ثُبُوْرًا وَّاحِدًا
وَّ ادْعُوْا ثُبُوْرًا كَثِيْرًا ٠

15. Say: "Is that best, or
The eternal Garden, promised
To the righteous? For them,
That is a reward as well
As a goal (or attainment).

١٥- قُلْ اَذٰلِكَ خَيْرٌ اَمْ جَنَّةُ الْخُلْدِ
الَّتِيْ وُعِدَ الْمُتَّقُوْنَ كَانَتْ لَهُمْ جَزَآءً
وَّمَصِيْرًا ٠

16. "For them there will be
Therein all that they wish for:
They will dwell (there) for aye:
A promise to be prayed for
From thy Lord."

١٦- لَهُمْ فِيْهَا مَا يَشَآءُوْنَ خٰلِدِيْنَ
كَانَ عَلٰى رَبِّكَ وَعْدًا مَّسْئُوْلًا ٠

17. The Day He will gather
Them together as well as
Those whom they worship
Besides Allah, He will ask
"Was it ye who led
These My servants astray.
Or did they stray
From the Path themselves?"

١٧- وَ يَوْمَ يَحْشُرُهُمْ وَمَا يَعْبُدُوْنَ
مِنْ دُوْنِ اللّٰهِ فَيَقُوْلُ ءَاَنْتُمْ اَضْلَلْتُمْ
عِبَادِيْ هٰٓؤُلَآءِ اَمْ هُمْ
ضَلُّوا السَّبِيْلَ ٠

18. They will say: "Glory to Thee!
Not meet was it for us
That we should take
For protectors others besides
                  Thee:
But Thou didst bestow,
On them and their fathers,
Good things (in life), until
They forgot the Message:
For they were a people
(Worthless and) lost."

١٨- قَالُوْا سُبْحٰنَكَ مَا كَانَ يَنْبَغِيْ لَنَاۤ
اَنْ نَّتَّخِذَ مِنْ دُوْنِكَ مِنْ اَوْلِيَآءَ
وَلٰكِنْ مَّتَّعْتَهُمْ وَاٰبَآءَهُمْ
حَتّٰى نَسُوا الذِّكْرَ ۚ
وَ كَانُوْا قَوْمًۢا بُوْرًا ٠

19. (Allah will say): "Now
Have they proved you liars

١٩- فَقَدْ كَذَّبُوْكُمْ بِمَا تَقُوْلُوْنَ ۙ

In what ye say: so
Ye cannot avert (your penalty)
Nor (get) help." And, whoever
Among you does wrong,
Him shall We cause to taste
Of a grievous Penalty.

فَمَا تَسْتَطِيعُوْنَ صَرْفًا وَّلَا نَصْرًا ۚ
وَمَنْ يَّظْلِمْ مِّنْكُمْ
نُذِقْهُ عَذَابًا كَبِيْرًا ۝

20. And the messengers whom We
Sent before thee were all
(Men) who ate food
And walked through the streets:
We have made some of you
As a trial for others:

Will ye have patience?
For Allah is One Who
Sees (all things).

SECTION 3.

٢٠ وَمَآ اَرْسَلْنَا قَبْلَكَ مِنَ الْمُرْسَلِيْنَ
اِلَّاۤ اِنَّهُمْ لَيَاْكُلُوْنَ الطَّعَامَ وَيَمْشُوْنَ
فِى الْاَسْوَاقِ ۗ وَجَعَلْنَا بَعْضَكُمْ لِبَعْضٍ
فِتْنَةً ۗ اَتَصْبِرُوْنَ ۚ وَكَانَ رَبُّكَ بَصِيْرًا ۝

21. Such as fear not
The meeting with Us
(For Judgement) say:
"Why are not the angels
Sent down to us, or
(Why) do we not see
Our Lord?" Indeed they
Have an arrogant conceit
Of themselves, and mighty
Is the insolence of their impiety!

٢١ وَقَالَ الَّذِيْنَ لَا يَرْجُوْنَ لِقَآءَنَا
لَوْلَاۤ اُنْزِلَ عَلَيْنَا الْمَلٰٓئِكَةُ
اَوْ نَرٰى رَبَّنَا ۗ
لَقَدِ اسْتَكْبَرُوْا فِيْۤ اَنْفُسِهِمْ
وَعَتَوْ عُتُوًّا كَبِيْرًا ۝

22. The Day they see the angels—
No joy will there be
To the sinners that Day.
The (angels) will say:
"There is a barrier
Forbidden (to you) altogether!"

٢٢ يَوْمَ يَرَوْنَ الْمَلٰٓئِكَةَ
لَا بُشْرٰى يَوْمَئِذٍ لِّلْمُجْرِمِيْنَ
وَيَقُوْلُوْنَ حِجْرًا مَّحْجُوْرًا ۝

23. And We shall turn
To whatever deeds they did
(In this life), and We shall
Make such deeds as floating dust
Scattered about.

٢٣ وَقَدِمْنَاۤ اِلٰى مَا عَمِلُوْا مِنْ عَمَلٍ
فَجَعَلْنٰهُ هَبَآءً مَّنْثُوْرًا ۝

24. The Companions of the Garden
Will be well, that Day,
In their abode, and have
The fairest of places for repose.

٢٤ اَصْحٰبُ الْجَنَّةِ يَوْمَئِذٍ خَيْرٌ مُّسْتَقَرًّا
وَّاَحْسَنُ مَقِيْلًا ۝

25. The Day the heaven shall be
Rent asunder with clouds,

٢٥ وَيَوْمَ تَشَقَّقُ السَّمَآءُ بِالْغَمَامِ

And angels shall be sent down,
Descending (in ranks)—

وَنُزِّلَ الْمَلَٰٓئِكَةُ تَنْزِيلًا ۟

26. That Day, the dominion
As of right and truth,
Shall be (wholly) for (Allah)
Most Merciful: it will be
A Day for dire difficulty
For the Misbelievers.

٢٦- اَلْمُلْكُ يَوْمَئِذِ ۨ الْحَقُّ لِلرَّحْمٰنِ ۚ وَكَانَ يَوْمًا عَلَى الْكٰفِرِيْنَ عَسِيْرًا ۟

27. The Day that the wrongdoer
Will bite at his hands,
He will say, "Oh! would that
I had taken a (straight) path
With the Messenger!

٢٧- وَيَوْمَ يَعَضُّ الظَّالِمُ عَلٰى يَدَيْهِ يَقُوْلُ يٰلَيْتَنِى اتَّخَذْتُ مَعَ الرَّسُوْلِ سَبِيْلًا ۟

28. "Ah! woe is me!
Would that I had never
Taken such a one
For a friend!

٢٨- يٰوَيْلَتٰى لَيْتَنِى لَمْ اَتَّخِذْ فُلَانًا خَلِيْلًا ۟

29. "He did lead me astray
From the Message (of Allah)
After it had come to me!
Ah! the Evil One is
But a traitor to man!

٢٩- لَقَدْ اَضَلَّنِى عَنِ الذِّكْرِ بَعْدَ اِذْ جَاۤءَنِىْ ۗ وَكَانَ الشَّيْطٰنُ لِلْاِنْسَانِ خَذُوْلًا ۟

30. Then the Messenger will say:
"O my Lord! Truly
My people took this Qur'ān
For just foolish nonsense."

٣٠- وَقَالَ الرَّسُوْلُ يٰرَبِّ اِنَّ قَوْمِى اتَّخَذُوْا هٰذَا الْقُرْاٰنَ مَهْجُوْرًا ۟

31. Thus have We made
For every prophet an enemy
Among the sinners: but enough
Is thy Lord to guide
And to help.

٣١- وَكَذٰلِكَ جَعَلْنَا لِكُلِّ نَبِىٍّ عَدُوًّا مِّنَ الْمُجْرِمِيْنَ ۗ وَكَفٰى بِرَبِّكَ هَادِيًا وَّنَصِيْرًا ۟

32. Those who reject Faith
Say: "Why is not the Qur'ān
Revealed to him all at once?
Thus (is it revealed), that We
May strengthen thy heart
Thereby, and We have
Rehearsed it to thee in slow,
Well-arranged stages, gradually.

٣٢- وَقَالَ الَّذِيْنَ كَفَرُوْا لَوْلَا نُزِّلَ عَلَيْهِ الْقُرْاٰنُ جُمْلَةً وَّاحِدَةً ۚ كَذٰلِكَ ۛ لِنُثَبِّتَ بِهٖ فُؤَادَكَ وَرَتَّلْنٰهُ تَرْتِيْلًا ۟

33. And no question do they
Bring to thee but We
Reveel to thee the truth
And the best explanation
                    (thereof).

٣٣- وَلَا يَأْتُوْنَكَ بِمَثَلٍ اِلَّا جِئْنٰكَ بِالْحَقِّ وَاَحْسَنَ تَفْسِيْرًا ۚ

34. Those who will be gathered
To Hell (prone) on their
                    faces—
They will be in an evil
Plight, and as to Path,
Most astray.

٣٤- اَلَّذِيْنَ يُحْشَرُوْنَ عَلٰى وُجُوْهِهِمْ اِلٰى جَهَنَّمَ اُولٰٓئِكَ شَرٌّ مَّكَانًا وَّاَضَلُّ سَبِيْلًا ۞

SECTION 4.

35. (Before this), We sent Moses
The Book, and appointed
His brother Aaron with him
As Minister;

٣٥- وَلَقَدْ اٰتَيْنَا مُوْسَى الْكِتٰبَ وَجَعَلْنَا مَعَهٗٓ اَخَاهُ هٰرُوْنَ وَزِيْرًا ۚ

36. And We commanded: "Go ye
Both, to the people who
Have rejectd our Signs:"
And those (people) We destroyed
With utter destruction.

٣٦- فَقُلْنَا اذْهَبَآ اِلَى الْقَوْمِ الَّذِيْنَ كَذَّبُوْا بِاٰيٰتِنَا ۖ فَدَمَّرْنٰهُمْ تَدْمِيْرًا ۚ

37. And the people of Noah—
When they rejected the
                    messengers,
We drowned them,
And We made them
As a Sign for mankind;
And We have prepared
For (all) wrongdoers
A grievous Penalty—

٣٧- وَقَوْمَ نُوْحٍ لَّمَّا كَذَّبُوا الرُّسُلَ اَغْرَقْنٰهُمْ وَجَعَلْنٰهُمْ لِلنَّاسِ اٰيَةً ۖ وَاَعْتَدْنَا لِلظّٰلِمِيْنَ عَذَابًا اَلِيْمًا ۚ

38. And also 'Ad and Thamūd,
And the Companions
Of the *Rass*, and many
A generation between them.

٣٨- وَّعَادًا وَّثَمُوْدَا۟ وَاَصْحٰبَ الرَّسِّ وَقُرُوْنًا بَيْنَ ذٰلِكَ كَثِيْرًا ۚ

39. To each one We set forth
Parables and examples;
And each one We broke
To utter annihilation
(For their sins).

٣٩- وَكُلًّا ضَرَبْنَا لَهُ الْاَمْثَالَ ۖ وَكُلًّا تَبَّرْنَا تَتْبِيْرًا ۚ

40. And the (Unbelievers) must indeed
Have passed by the town
On which was rained
A shower of evil: did they not

٤٠- وَلَقَدْ اَتَوْا عَلَى الْقَرْيَةِ الَّتِيْٓ اُمْطِرَتْ مَطَرَ السَّوْءِ ۚ

Then see it (with their own
Eyes)? But they fear not
The Resurrection.

اَفَلَمْ يَكُوْنُوْا يَرَوْنَهَا ۗ
بَلْ كَانُوْا لَا يَرْجُوْنَ نُشُوْرًا ۟

41. When they see thee,
They treat thee no otherwise
Than in mockery: "Is this
The one whom Allah has sent
As a messenger?"

٤١- وَاِذَا رَاَوْكَ اِنْ يَّتَّخِذُوْنَكَ اِلَّا هُزُوًا ۗ
اَهٰذَا الَّذِيْ بَعَثَ اللّٰهُ رَسُوْلًا ۟

42. "He indeed would well-nigh
Have misled us from
Our gods, had it not been
That we were constant
To them!"—Soon will they
Know, when they see
The Penalty, who it is
That is most misled
In Path!

٤٢- اِنْ كَادَ لَيُضِلُّنَا عَنْ اٰلِهَتِنَا
لَوْلَا اَنْ صَبَرْنَا عَلَيْهَا ۗ
وَسَوْفَ يَعْلَمُوْنَ حِيْنَ يَرَوْنَ الْعَذَابَ
مَنْ اَضَلُّ سَبِيْلًا ۟

43. Seest thou such a one
As taketh for his god
His own passion (or impulse)?
Couldst thou be a disposer
Of affairs for him?

٤٣- اَرَءَيْتَ مَنِ اتَّخَذَ اِلٰهَهٗ هَوٰىهُ ۗ
اَفَاَنْتَ تَكُوْنُ عَلَيْهِ وَكِيْلًا ۟

44. Or thinkest thou that most
Of them listen or understand?
They are only like cattle;—
Nay, they are worse astray
In Path.

SECTION 5.

٤٤- اَمْ تَحْسَبُ اَنَّ اَكْثَرَهُمْ يَسْمَعُوْنَ
اَوْ يَعْقِلُوْنَ ۗ اِنْ هُمْ اِلَّا كَالْاَنْعَامِ
بَلْ هُمْ اَضَلُّ سَبِيْلًا ۟ ع

45. Hast thou not turned
Thy vision to thy Lord?—
How He doth prolong
The Shadow! If He willed,
He could make it stationary!
Then do We make
The sun its guide;

٤٥- اَلَمْ تَرَ اِلٰى رَبِّكَ كَيْفَ مَدَّ الظِّلَّ ۗ
وَلَوْ شَآءَ لَجَعَلَهٗ سَاكِنًا ۗ
ثُمَّ جَعَلْنَا الشَّمْسَ عَلَيْهِ دَلِيْلًا ۟

46. Then We draw it in
Towards Ourselves—
A contraction by easy stages.

٤٦- ثُمَّ قَبَضْنٰهُ اِلَيْنَا قَبْضًا يَّسِيْرًا ۟

47. And He it is Who makes
The Night as a Robe
For you, and Sleep as Repose,
And makes the Day
(As it were) a Resurrection.

٤٧- وَهُوَ الَّذِيْ جَعَلَ لَكُمُ الَّيْلَ لِبَاسًا
وَّالنَّوْمَ سُبَاتًا
وَّجَعَلَ النَّهَارَ نُشُوْرًا ۟

48. And He it is Who sends
The Winds as heralds
Of glad tidings, going before
His Mercy, and We send down
Pure water from the sky

٤٨- وَهُوَ الَّذِيْٓ اَرْسَلَ الرِّيٰحَ بُشْرًۢا بَيْنَ يَدَيْ رَحْمَتِهٖ ۚ وَاَنْزَلْنَا مِنَ السَّمَآءِ مَآءً طَهُوْرًا ۟

49. That with it, We may give
Life to a dead land,
And slake the thirst
Of things We have created—
Cattle and men in great numbers.

٤٩- لِّنُحْيِۦَ بِهٖ بَلْدَةً مَّيْتًا وَّنُسْقِيَهٗ مِمَّا خَلَقْنَآ اَنْعَامًا وَّاَنَاسِيَّ كَثِيْرًا ۟

50. And We have distributed
The (water) amongst them, in
order
That they may celebrate
(Our) praises, but most men
Are averse (to aught) but
(Rank) ingratitude.

٥٠- وَلَقَدْ صَرَّفْنٰهُ بَيْنَهُمْ لِيَذَّكَّرُوْا ۖ فَاَبٰٓى اَكْثَرُ النَّاسِ اِلَّا كُفُوْرًا ۟

51. Had it been Our Will,
We could have sent
A warner to every centre
Of population,

٥١- وَلَوْ شِئْنَا لَبَعَثْنَا فِيْ كُلِّ قَرْيَةٍ نَّذِيْرًا ۖ

52. Therefore listen not
To the Unbelievers, but strive
Against them with the utmost
Strenuousness, with the
(Qur'ān),

٥٢- فَلَا تُطِعِ الْكٰفِرِيْنَ وَجَاهِدْهُمْ بِهٖ جِهَادًا كَبِيْرًا ۟

53. It is He Who has
Let free the two bodies
Of flowing water:
One palpable and sweet,
And the other salt and bitter;
Yet has He
Made a barrier between them,
A partition that is forbidden
To be passed.

٥٣- وَهُوَ الَّذِيْ مَرَجَ الْبَحْرَيْنِ هٰذَا عَذْبٌ فُرَاتٌ وَّهٰذَا مِلْحٌ اُجَاجٌ ۚ وَجَعَلَ بَيْنَهُمَا بَرْزَخًا وَّحِجْرًا مَّحْجُوْرًا ۟

54. It is He Who has
Created man from water:
Then has He established
Relationships of lineage
And marriage: for thy Lord
Has power (over all things).

٥٤- وَهُوَ الَّذِيْ خَلَقَ مِنَ الْمَآءِ بَشَرًا فَجَعَلَهٗ نَسَبًا وَّصِهْرًا ۖ وَكَانَ رَبُّكَ قَدِيْرًا ۟

55. Yet do they worship,

٥٥- وَيَعْبُدُوْنَ مِنْ دُوْنِ اللّٰهِ

Besides Allah, things that can
Neither profit them nor
Harm them: and the Misbeliever
Is a helper (of Evil),
Against his own Lord!

مَا لَا يَنْفَعُهُمْ وَلَا يَضُرُّهُمْ ۖ وَكَانَ الْكَافِرُ عَلَى رَبِّهِ ظَهِيرًا ۝

56. But thee We only sent
To give glad tidings
And admonition.

٥٦ ـ وَمَآ أَرْسَلْنَاكَ إِلَّا مُبَشِّرًا وَنَذِيرًا ۝

57. Say: "No reward do I
Ask of you for it but this:
That each one who will
May take a (straight) Path
To his Lord."

٥٧ ـ قُلْ مَآ أَسْئَلُكُمْ عَلَيْهِ مِنْ أَجْرٍ إِلَّا مَن شَآءَ أَن يَّتَّخِذَ إِلَى رَبِّهِ سَبِيلًا ۝

58. And put thy trust
In Him Who lives
And dies not; and celebrate
His praise; and enough is He
To be acquainted with
The faults of His servants—

٥٨ ـ وَتَوَكَّلْ عَلَى الْحَيِّ الَّذِى لَا يَمُوتُ وَسَبِّحْ بِحَمْدِهِ ۚ وَكَفَى بِهِ بِذُنُوبِ عِبَادِهِ خَبِيرًا ۝

59. He Who created the heavens
And the earth and all
That is between, in six days,
And is firmly established
On the Throne (of authority):
Allah, Most Gracious:
Ask thou, then, about Him
Of any acquainted (with such
things.

٥٩ ـ الَّذِى خَلَقَ السَّمَاوَاتِ وَالْأَرْضَ وَمَا بَيْنَهُمَا فِى سِتَّةِ أَيَّامٍ ثُمَّ اسْتَوَى عَلَى الْعَرْشِ ۚ الرَّحْمَنُ فَسْئَلْ بِهِ خَبِيرًا ۝

60. When it is said to them,
"Adore ye (Allah) Most Gracious!",
They say, "And what is (Allah)
Most Gracious? Shall we adore
That which thou commandest us?"
And it increases their flight
(From the Truth).

٦٠ ـ وَإِذَا قِيلَ لَهُمُ اسْجُدُوا لِلرَّحْمَنِ قَالُوا وَمَا الرَّحْمَنُ أَنَسْجُدُ لِمَا تَأْمُرُنَا وَزَادَهُمْ نُفُورًا ۩ ۝

SECTION 6.

61. Blessed is He Who made
Constellations in the skies,
And placed therein a Lamp
And a Moon giving light;

٦١ ـ تَبَارَكَ الَّذِى جَعَلَ فِى السَّمَآءِ بُرُوجًا وَجَعَلَ فِيهَا سِرَاجًا وَقَمَرًا مُّنِيرًا ۝

62. And it is He Who made
The Night and the Day

٦٢ ـ وَهُوَ الَّذِى جَعَلَ الَّيْلَ وَالنَّهَارَ خِلْفَةً

To follow each other:
For such as have the will
To celebrate His praises
Or to show their gratitude.

لِمَنْ اَرَادَ اَنْ يَّذَّكَّرَ
اَوْ اَرَادَ شُكُوْرًا ۞

63. And the servants of (Allah)
Most Gracious are those
Who walk on the earth
In humility, and when the
              ignorant
Address them, they say,
"Peace!";

٦٢- وَعِبَادُ الرَّحْمٰنِ الَّذِيْنَ
يَمْشُوْنَ عَلَى الْاَرْضِ هَوْنًا
وَّاِذَا خَاطَبَهُمُ الْجَاهِلُوْنَ
قَالُوْا سَلٰمًا ۞

64. Those who spend the night
In adoration of their Lord
Prostrate and standing;

٦٤- وَالَّذِيْنَ يَبِيْتُوْنَ لِرَبِّهِمْ سُجَّدًا وَّ
قِيَامًا ۞

65. Those who say: "Our Lord!
Avert from us the Wrath
Of Hell, for its Wrath
Is indeed an affliction
              grievous—

٦٥- وَالَّذِيْنَ يَقُوْلُوْنَ رَبَّنَا
اصْرِفْ عَنَّا عَذَابَ جَهَنَّمَ ۖ
اِنَّ عَذَابَهَا كَانَ غَرَامًا ۞

66. "Evil indeed is it
As an abode, and as
A place to rest in";

٦٦- اِنَّهَا سَاءَتْ مُسْتَقَرًّا وَّمُقَامًا ۞

67. Those who, when they spend,
Are not extravagant and not
Niggardly, but hold a just
              (balance)
Between those (extremes);

٦٧- وَالَّذِيْنَ اِذَآ اَنْفَقُوْا لَمْ يُسْرِفُوْا وَلَمْ
يَقْتُرُوْا وَكَانَ بَيْنَ ذٰلِكَ قَوَامًا ۞

68. Those who invoke not,
With Allah, any other god,
Nor slay such life as Allah
Has made sacred, except
For just cause, nor commit
Fornication—and any that does
This (not only) meets punishment

٦٨- وَالَّذِيْنَ لَا يَدْعُوْنَ مَعَ اللهِ اِلٰهًا اٰخَرَ
وَلَا يَقْتُلُوْنَ النَّفْسَ الَّتِيْ حَرَّمَ اللهُ اِلَّا
بِالْحَقِّ وَلَا يَزْنُوْنَ ۚ
وَمَنْ يَّفْعَلْ ذٰلِكَ يَلْقَ اَثَامًا ۙ

69. (But) the Penalty on the Day
Of Judgement will be doubled
To him, and he will dwell
Therein in ignominy—

٦٩- يُّضَاعَفْ لَهُ الْعَذَابُ يَوْمَ الْقِيٰمَةِ
وَيَخْلُدْ فِيْهِ مُهَانًا ۙ

70. Unless he repents, believes
And works righteous deeds,
For Allah will change

٧٠- اِلَّا مَنْ تَابَ وَاٰمَنَ وَعَمِلَ عَمَلًا
صَالِحًا فَاُولٰٓئِكَ يُبَدِّلُ اللهُ سَيِّاٰتِهِمْ

The evil of such persons
Into good, and Allah' is
Oft-Forgiving, Most Merciful,

حَسَنٰتٍ ۗ وَكَانَ اللّٰهُ غَفُوْرًا رَّحِيْمًا ۞

71. And whoever repents and does
good
Has truly turned to Allah
With an (acceptable)
conversion—

١٧- وَمَنْ تَابَ وَعَمِلَ صَالِحًا
فَاِنَّهٗ يَتُوْبُ اِلَى اللّٰهِ مَتَابًا ۞

72. Those who witness no falsehood
And, if they pass by futility,
They pass by it
With honourable (avoidance);

٧٢- وَالَّذِيْنَ لَا يَشْهَدُوْنَ الزُّوْرَ ۙ
وَاِذَا مَرُّوْا بِاللَّغْوِ مَرُّوْا كِرَامًا ۞

73. Those who, when they are
Admonished with the Signs
Of their Lord, droop not down
At them as if they were
Deaf or blind;

٧٣- وَالَّذِيْنَ اِذَا ذُكِّرُوْا بِاٰيٰتِ رَبِّهِمْ
لَمْ يَخِرُّوْا عَلَيْهَا صُمًّا وَّعُمْيَانًا ۞

74. And those who pray,
"Our Lord! Grant unto us
Wives and offspring who will be
The comfort of our eyes,
And give us (the grace)
To lead the righteous."

٧٤- وَالَّذِيْنَ يَقُوْلُوْنَ رَبَّنَا هَبْ لَنَا
مِنْ اَزْوَاجِنَا وَذُرِّيّٰتِنَا قُرَّةَ اَعْيُنٍ
وَّاجْعَلْنَا لِلْمُتَّقِيْنَ اِمَامًا ۞

75. Those are the ones who
Will be rewarded with
The highest place in heaven,
Because of their patient constancy:
Therein shall they be met
With salutations and peace,

٧٥- اُولٰٓئِكَ يُجْزَوْنَ
الْغُرْفَةَ بِمَا صَبَرُوْا
وَيُلَقَّوْنَ فِيْهَا تَحِيَّةً وَّسَلٰمًا ۞

76. Dwelling therein—how beautiful
An abode and place of rest!

٧٦- خٰلِدِيْنَ فِيْهَا ۗ حَسُنَتْ مُسْتَقَرًّا وَّمُقَامًا ۞

77. Say (to the Rejecters):
"My Lord is not uneasy
Because of you if ye call not on
Him:
But ye have indeed rejected
(Him), and soon will come
The inevitable (punishment)!"

٧٧- قُلْ مَا يَعْبَؤُا بِكُمْ رَبِّيْ
لَوْلَا دُعَاؤُكُمْ ۚ
فَقَدْ كَذَّبْتُمْ فَسَوْفَ يَكُوْنُ لِزَامًا ۞

INTRODUCTION TO SŪRA XXVI. *(Shu'arāa)* — 227 Verses

This Sūra begins a new series of four Sūras (xxvi, xxix.), which illustrate the contrast between the spirit of Prophecy and spiritual Light and the reactions to it in the communities among whom it appeared, by going back to old Prophets and the stories of the Past, as explained in the Introduction to S. xvii.

In this particular Sūra we have the story of Moses in his fight with Pharaoh and of Pharaoh's discomfiture. Other Prophets mentioned are Abraham, Noah, Hūd, Ṣāliḥ, Lūṭ, and Shu'aib. The lesson is drawn that the Qur-ān is continuation and fulfilment of previous Revelations, and is pure Truth, unlike the poetry of vain poets.

Chronologically the Sūra belongs to the middle Meccan period, when the contact of the Light of Prophecy with the milieu of Pagan Mecca was testing the Meccans in their most arrogant mood.

Al Shu'arā' (The Poets)

In the name of Allah, Most Gracious, Most Merciful.

1. Ṭā' Sīn Mīm.

2. These are Verses of the Book
   That makes (things) clear.

3. It may be thou frettest
   Thy soul with grief, that they
   Do not become Believers.

4. If (such) were Our Will,
   We could send down to them
   From the sky a Sign,
   To which they would bend
   Their necks in humility.

5. But there comes not
   To them a newly-revealed
   Message from (Allah) Most
              Gracious,
   But they turn away therefrom.

6. They have indeed rejected
   (The Message):
   So they will know soon (enough)
   the truth

Of what they mocked at!

بِهٖ يَسۡتَهۡزِءُوۡنَ ۝

7. Do they not look
At the earth—how many
Noble things of all kinds
We have produced therein?

٧- اَوَلَمۡ يَرَوۡا اِلَى الۡاَرۡضِ
كَمۡ اَنۡبَتۡنَا فِيۡهَا مِنۡ كُلِّ زَوۡجٍ كَرِيۡمٍ ۝

8. Verily, in this is a Sign:
But most of them
Do not believe.

٨- اِنَّ فِىۡ ذٰلِكَ لَاٰيَةً ؕ
وَمَا كَانَ اَكۡثَرُهُمۡ مُّؤۡمِنِيۡنَ ۝

9. And verily, thy Lord
Is He, the Exalted in Might,
Most Merciful.

٩- وَاِنَّ رَبَّكَ لَهُوَ الۡعَزِيۡزُ الرَّحِيۡمُ ۚ۬

SECTION 2.

10. Behold, thy Lord called
Moses: "Go to the people
Of iniquity—

١٠- وَاِذۡ نَادٰى رَبُّكَ مُوۡسٰۤى
اَنِ ائۡتِ الۡقَوۡمَ الظّٰلِمِيۡنَ ۙ

11. "The people of Pharaoh:
Will they not fear Allah?"

١١- قَوۡمَ فِرۡعَوۡنَ ؕ اَلَا يَتَّقُوۡنَ ۝

12. He said: "O my Lord!
I do fear that they
Will charge me with falsehood:

١٢- قَالَ رَبِّ
اِنِّىۡۤ اَخَافُ اَنۡ يُّكَذِّبُوۡنِ ۙ

13. "My breast will be straitened.
And my speech may not go
(Smoothly): so send unto Aaron.

١٣- وَيَضِيۡقُ صَدۡرِىۡ وَلَا يَنۡطَلِقُ لِسَانِىۡ
فَاَرۡسِلۡ اِلٰى هٰرُوۡنَ ۝

14. And (further), they have
A charge of crime against me;
And I fear they may
Slay me."

١٤- وَلَهُمۡ عَلَىَّ ذَنۡۢبٌ
فَاَخَافُ اَنۡ يَّقۡتُلُوۡنِ ۚ

15. Allah said: "By no means!
Proceed then, both of you,
With Our Signs; We
Are with you, and will
Listen (to your call).

١٥- قَالَ كَلَّا ۚ فَاذۡهَبَا بِاٰيٰتِنَاۤ
اِنَّا مَعَكُمۡ مُّسۡتَمِعُوۡنَ ۝

16. "So go forth, both of you,
To Pharaoh, and say:
'We have been sent
By the Lord and Cherisher
Of the Worlds;

١٦- فَاۡتِيَا فِرۡعَوۡنَ فَقُوۡلَاۤ
اِنَّا رَسُوۡلُ
رَبِّ الۡعٰلَمِيۡنَ ۙ

17. " 'Send thou with us
The Children of Israel.' "

١٧- أَنْ أَرْسِلْ مَعَنَا بَنِيٓ إِسْرَآءِيلَ ۚ

18. (Pharaoh) said: "Did we not
Cherish thee as a child
Among us, and didst thou not
Stay in our midst
Many years of thy life?

١٨- قَالَ أَلَمْ نُرَبِّكَ فِيْنَا وَلِيْدًا
وَّلَبِثْتَ فِيْنَا مِنْ عُمُرِكَ سِنِيْنَ ۚ

19. "And thou didst a deed
Of thine which (thou knowest)
Thou didst, and thou art
An ungrateful (wretch)!"

١٩- وَفَعَلْتَ فَعْلَتَكَ الَّتِيْ فَعَلْتَ
وَأَنْتَ مِنَ الْكٰفِرِيْنَ ۝

20. Moses said: "I did it
Then, when I was
In error.

٢٠- قَالَ فَعَلْتُهَآ
إِذًا وَّأَنَا مِنَ الضَّآلِّيْنَ ۚ

21. "So I fled from you (all)
When I feared you;
But My Lord has (since)
Invested me with judgement
(And wisdom) and appointed me
As one of the messengers.

٢١- فَفَرَرْتُ مِنْكُمْ لَمَّا خِفْتُكُمْ
فَوَهَبَ لِيْ رَبِّيْ حُكْمًا
وَّجَعَلَنِيْ مِنَ الْمُرْسَلِيْنَ ۝

22. "And this is the favour
With which thou dost
Reproach me—that you
Hast enslaved the Children
Of Israel!"

٢٢- وَتِلْكَ نِعْمَةٌ تَمُنُّهَا عَلَيَّ
أَنْ عَبَّدْتَّ بَنِيٓ إِسْرَآءِيلَ ۚ

23. Pharaoh said: "And what
Is the 'Lord and Cherisher
Of the Worlds?' "

٢٣- قَالَ فِرْعَوْنُ وَمَا رَبُّ الْعٰلَمِيْنَ ۚ

24. (Moses) said: "The Lord
And Cherisher of the heavens
And the earth, and all between—
If ye want to be
Quite sure."

٢٤- قَالَ رَبُّ السَّمٰوٰتِ وَالْأَرْضِ وَمَا
بَيْنَهُمَا ۖ
إِنْ كُنْتُمْ مُّوْقِنِيْنَ ۝

25. (Pharaoh) said to those
Around: "Do ye not listen
(To what he says)?"

٢٥- قَالَ لِمَنْ حَوْلَهُ أَلَا تَسْتَمِعُوْنَ ۝

26. (Moses) said: "Your Lord
And the Lord of your fathers
From the beginning!"

٢٦- قَالَ رَبُّكُمْ وَرَبُّ آبَآئِكُمُ الْأَوَّلِيْنَ ۝

27. (Pharaoh) said: "Truly
Your messenger who has been
Sent to you is
A veritable madman!"

٢٧- قَالَ إِنَّ رَسُولَكُمُ الَّذِىٓ
أُرْسِلَ إِلَيْكُمْ لَمَجْنُونٌ ۝

28. (Moses) said: "Lord of the East
And the West, and all between!
If ye only had sense!"

٢٨- قَالَ رَبُّ الْمَشْرِقِ وَالْمَغْرِبِ وَمَا
بَيْنَهُمَا إِنْ كُنْتُمْ تَعْقِلُونَ ۝

29. (Pharaoh) said: "If thou
Dost put forward any god
Other than me, I will
Certainly put thee in prison!"

٢٩- قَالَ لَئِنِ اتَّخَذْتَ إِلَٰهًا غَيْرِى
لَأَجْعَلَنَّكَ مِنَ الْمَسْجُونِينَ ۝

30. (Moses) said: "Even if I
Showed you something
Clear (and) convincing?"

٣٠- قَالَ أَوَلَوْ جِئْتُكَ بِشَىْءٍ مُّبِينٍ ۝

31. (Pharaoh) said: "Show it then
If thou tellest the truth!"

٣١- قَالَ فَأْتِ بِهِ إِنْ كُنْتَ مِنَ الصَّادِقِينَ ۝

32. So (Moses) threw his rod,
And behold, it was
A serpent, plain (for all to see)!

٣٢- فَأَلْقَىٰ عَصَاهُ فَإِذَا هِىَ ثُعْبَانٌ مُّبِينٌ ۝

33. And he drew out his hand,
And behold, it was white
To all beholders!

٣٣- وَنَزَعَ يَدَهُ فَإِذَا هِىَ بَيْضَاءُ
لِلنَّاظِرِينَ ۝

SECTION 3.

34. (Pharaoh) said to the Chiefs
Around him "This is indeed
A sorcerer well-versed:

٣٤- قَالَ لِلْمَلَإِ حَوْلَهُ
إِنَّ هَٰذَا لَسَاحِرٌ عَلِيمٌ ۝

35. "His plan is to get you out
Of your land by his sorcery;
Then what is it ye counsel?"

٣٥- يُرِيدُ أَنْ يُخْرِجَكُمْ مِنْ أَرْضِكُمْ
بِسِحْرِهِ فَمَاذَا تَأْمُرُونَ ۝

36. They said; "Keep him
And his brother in suspense
(For a while), and dispatch
To the Cities heralds to collect—

٣٦- قَالُوٓا أَرْجِهْ وَأَخَاهُ
وَابْعَثْ فِى الْمَدَائِنِ حَاشِرِينَ ۝

37. "And bring up to thee
All (our) sorcerers well-versed."

٣٧- يَأْتُوكَ بِكُلِّ سَحَّارٍ عَلِيمٍ ۝

38. So the sorcerers were got
Together for the appointment
Of a day well-known,

٣٨- فَجُمِعَ السَّحَرَةُ لِمِيقَاتِ يَوْمٍ مَّعْلُومٍ ۝

39. And the people were told:
"Are ye (now) assembled?—

٣٩- وَقِيلَ لِلنَّاسِ هَلْ أَنْتُمْ مُجْتَمِعُونَ ۟

40. "That we may follow
The sorcerers (in religion)
If they win?"

٤٠- لَعَلَّنَا نَتَّبِعُ السَّحَرَةَ
إِنْ كَانُوا هُمُ الْغَالِبِينَ ۟

41. So when the sorcerers arrived,
They said to Pharaoh:
"Of course—shall we have
A (suitable) reward
If we win?"

٤١- فَلَمَّا جَاءَ السَّحَرَةُ قَالُوا لِفِرْعَوْنَ
أَئِنَّ لَنَا لَأَجْرًا
إِنْ كُنَّا نَحْنُ الْغَالِبِينَ ۟

42. He said: "Yea, (and more)—
For ye shall in that case
Be (raised to posts)
Nearest (to my person)."

٤٢- قَالَ نَعَمْ وَإِنَّكُمْ إِذًا
لَمِنَ الْمُقَرَّبِينَ ۟

43. Moses said to them:
"Throw ye—that which
Ye are about to throw!"

٤٣- قَالَ لَهُمْ مُوسَى أَلْقُوا مَا أَنْتُمْ مُلْقُونَ ۟

44. So they threw their ropes
And their rods, and said:
"By the might of Pharaoh,
It is we who will
Certainly win!"

٤٤- فَأَلْقَوْا حِبَالَهُمْ وَعِصِيَّهُمْ وَقَالُوا
بِعِزَّةِ فِرْعَوْنَ إِنَّا لَنَحْنُ الْغَالِبُونَ ۟

45. Then Moses threw his rod,
When, behold, it straightway
Swallows up all
The falsehoods which they fake!

٤٥- فَأَلْقَى مُوسَى عَصَاهُ
فَإِذَا هِيَ تَلْقَفُ مَا يَأْفِكُونَ ۟

46. Then did the sorcerers
Fall down, prostrate in adoration,

٤٦- فَأُلْقِيَ السَّحَرَةُ سَاجِدِينَ ۟

47. Saying: "We believe
In the Lord of the Worlds,

٤٧- قَالُوا آمَنَّا بِرَبِّ الْعَالَمِينَ ۟

48. "The Lord of Moses and Aaron."

٤٨- رَبِّ مُوسَى وَهَارُونَ ۟

49. Said (Pharaoh): "Believe ye
In Him before I give
You permission? Surely he
Is your leader, who has
Taught you sorcery!
But soon shall ye know!
"Be sure I will cut off

٤٩- قَالَ آمَنْتُمْ لَهُ قَبْلَ أَنْ آذَنَ لَكُمْ
إِنَّهُ لَكَبِيرُكُمُ الَّذِي عَلَّمَكُمُ السِّحْرَ
فَلَسَوْفَ تَعْلَمُونَ
لَأُقَطِّعَنَّ أَيْدِيَكُمْ وَأَرْجُلَكُمْ

Your hands and your feet on
opposite sides,
And I
Will cause you all
To die on the cross!"

مِنْ خِلَافٍ
وَّلَأُوَصِّلِبَنَّكُمْ اَجْمَعِيْنَ ۝

50. They said: "No matter!
For us, we shall but
Return to our Lord!

٥٠ - قَالُوْا لَا ضَيْرَ اِنَّا اِلٰى
رَبِّنَا مُنْقَلِبُوْنَ ۝

51. "Only, our desire is
That our Lord will
Forgive us our faults,
That we may become
Foremost among the Believers!"

٥١ - اِنَّا نَطْمَعُ اَنْ يَّغْفِرَ لَنَا رَبُّنَا خَطٰيٰنَا
اَنْ كُنَّا اَوَّلَ الْمُؤْمِنِيْنَ ۝

SECTION 4.

52. By inspiration We told Moses:
"Travel by night with
My servants; for surely
Ye shall be pursued."

٥٢ - وَاَوْحَيْنَا اِلٰى مُوْسٰى اَنْ اَسْرِ
بِعِبَادِيْۤ اِنَّكُمْ مُّتَّبَعُوْنَ ۝

53. Then Pharaoh sent heralds
To (all) the Cities,

٥٣ - فَاَرْسَلَ فِرْعَوْنُ فِى الْمَدَآئِنِ حٰشِرِيْنَ ۝

54. (Saying): "These (Israelites)
Are but a small band,

٥٤ - اِنَّ هٰۤؤُلَآءِ لَشِرْذِمَةٌ قَلِيْلُوْنَ ۝

55. "And they are raging
Furiously against us;

٥٥ - وَاِنَّهُمْ لَنَا لَغَآئِظُوْنَ ۝

56. "But we are a multitude
Amply forewarned."

٥٦ - وَاِنَّا لَجَمِيْعٌ حٰذِرُوْنَ ۝

57. So We expelled them
From gardens, springs,

٥٧ - فَاَخْرَجْنٰهُمْ مِّنْ جَنّٰتٍ وَّعُيُوْنٍ ۝

58. Treasures, and every kind
Of honourable position;

٥٨ - وَّكُنُوْزٍ وَّمَقَامٍ كَرِيْمٍ ۝

59. Thus it was, but
We made the Children
Of Israel inheritors
Of such things.

٥٩ - كَذٰلِكَ
وَاَوْرَثْنٰهَا بَنِيْۤ اِسْرَآءِيْلَ ۝

60. So they pursued them
At sunrise.

٦٠ - فَاَتْبَعُوْهُمْ مُّشْرِقِيْنَ ۝

61. And when the two bodies
Saw each other, the people
Of Moses said: "We are
Sure to be overtaken."

٦١- فَلَمَّا تَرَاءَ الْجَمْعَنِ
قَالَ اَصْحَبُ مُوسَى إِنَّا لَمُدْرَكُوْنَ ۝

62. (Moses) said: "By no means!
My Lord is with me!
Soon will He guide me!"

٦٢- قَالَ كَلَّا ۚ إِنَّ مَعِيَ رَبِّي سَيَهْدِيْنِ ۝

63. Then We told Moses
By inspiration: "Strike
The sea with thy rod."
So it divided, and each
Separate part became
Like the huge, firm mass
Of a mountain.

٦٣- فَاَوْحَيْنَا إِلَى مُوسَى اَنِ اضْرِبْ
بِعَصَاكَ الْبَحْرَ ۖ
فَانْفَلَقَ فَكَانَ كُلُّ فِرْقٍ
كَالطَّوْدِ الْعَظِيْمِ ۝

64. And We made the other
Party approach thither.

٦٤- وَاَزْلَفْنَا ثَمَّ الْاٰخَرِيْنَ ۝

65. We delivered Moses and all
Who were with him;

٦٥- وَاَنْجَيْنَا مُوسَى وَمَنْ مَعَهُ اَجْمَعِيْنَ ۝

66. But We drowned the others.

٦٦- ثُمَّ اَغْرَقْنَا الْاٰخَرِيْنَ ۝

67. Verily in this is a Sign:
But most of them
Do not believe.

٦٧- إِنَّ فِي ذٰلِكَ لَاٰيَةً ۖ
وَمَا كَانَ اَكْثَرُهُمْ مُّؤْمِنِيْنَ ۝

68. And verily thy Lord
Is He, the Exalted in Might,
Most Merciful.

SECTION 5

٦٨- وَإِنَّ رَبَّكَ لَهُوَ الْعَزِيْزُ الرَّحِيْمُ ۞

69. And rehearse to them
(Something of) Abraham's
story.

٦٩- وَاتْلُ عَلَيْهِمْ نَبَاَ اِبْرٰهِيْمَ ۝

70. Behold, he said
To his father and his people:
"What worship ye?"

٧٠- إِذْ قَالَ لِاَبِيْهِ وَقَوْمِهِ مَا تَعْبُدُوْنَ ۝

71. They said: "We worship
Idols, and we remain constantly
In attendance on them."

٧١- قَالُوْا نَعْبُدُ اَصْنَامًا فَنَظَلُّ لَهَا
عٰكِفِيْنَ ۝

72. He said: "Do they listen
To you when ye call (on them),

٧٢- قَالَ هَلْ يَسْمَعُوْنَكُمْ اِذْ تَدْعُوْنَ ۝

73. Or do you good or harm?"

74. They said: "Nay, but we
Found our fathers doing
Thus (what we do)."

٧٣- اَوَيَنْفَعُوْنَكُمْ اَوْ يَضُرُّوْنَ ۝

٧٤- قَالُوْا بَلْ وَجَدْنَآ اٰبَآءَنَا كَذٰلِكَ يَفْعَلُوْنَ ۝

75. He said: 'Do ye then
See whom ye have been
Worshipping—

٧٥- قَالَ اَفَرَءَيْتُمْ مَّا كُنْتُمْ تَعْبُدُوْنَ ۝

76. "Ye and your fathers before you?—

٧٦- اَنْتُمْ وَاٰبَآؤُكُمُ الْاَقْدَمُوْنَ ۝

77. "For they are enemies to me;
Not so the Lord and Cherisher
Of the Worlds;

٧٧- فَاِنَّهُمْ عَدُوٌّ لِّيْٓ اِلَّا رَبَّ الْعٰلَمِيْنَ ۝

78. "Who created me, and
It is He who guides me;

٧٨- الَّذِيْ خَلَقَنِيْ فَهُوَ يَهْدِيْنِ ۝

79. "Who gives me food and drink,

٧٩- وَالَّذِيْ هُوَ يُطْعِمُنِيْ وَيَسْقِيْنِ ۝

80. "And when I am ill,
It is He who cures me;

٨٠- وَاِذَا مَرِضْتُ فَهُوَ يَشْفِيْنِ ۝

81. "Who will cause me to die,
And then to live (again);

٨١- وَالَّذِيْ يُمِيْتُنِيْ ثُمَّ يُحْيِيْنِ ۝

82. "And who, I hope,
Will forgive me my faults
On the Day of Judgement...

٨٢- وَالَّذِيْٓ اَطْمَعُ اَنْ يَّغْفِرَ لِيْ خَطِيْٓئَتِيْ يَوْمَ الدِّيْنِ ۝

83. "O my Lord! bestow wisdom
On me, and join me
With the righteous;

٨٣- رَبِّ هَبْ لِيْ حُكْمًا وَّاَلْحِقْنِيْ بِالصّٰلِحِيْنَ ۝

84. "Grant me honourable mention
On the tongue of truth
Among the latest (generations);

٨٤- وَاجْعَلْ لِّيْ لِسَانَ صِدْقٍ فِي الْاٰخِرِيْنَ ۝

85. "Make me one of the inheritors
Of the Garden of Bliss;

٨٥- وَاجْعَلْنِيْ مِنْ وَّرَثَةِ جَنَّةِ النَّعِيْمِ ۝

86. "Forgive my father, for that
He is among those astray;

٨٦- وَاغْفِرْ لِاَبِيْٓ اِنَّهٗ كَانَ مِنَ الضَّآلِّيْنَ ۝

87. "And let me not be

٨٧- وَلَا تُخْزِنِيْ

In disgrace on the Day
When (men) will be raised up—

يَوْمَ يُبْعَثُوْنَ ۞

88. "The Day whereon neither
Wealth nor sons will avail,

٨٨- يَوْمَ لَا يَنْفَعُ مَالٌ وَّلَا بَنُوْنَ ۞

89. "But only he (will prosper)
That brings to Allah
A sound heart;

٨٩- إِلَّا مَنْ أَتَى اللّٰهَ بِقَلْبٍ سَلِيْمٍ ۞

90. "To the righteous, the Garden
Will be brought near,

٩٠- وَأُزْلِفَتِ الْجَنَّةُ لِلْمُتَّقِيْنَ ۞

91. "And to those straying in Evil,
The Fire will be placed
In full view;

٩١- وَبُرِّزَتِ الْجَحِيْمُ لِلْغَاوِيْنَ ۞

92. "And it shall be said
To them: 'Where are
The (gods) ye worshipped—

٩٢- وَقِيْلَ لَهُمْ أَيْنَمَا كُنْتُمْ تَعْبُدُوْنَ ۞

93. "Besides Allah? Can they
Help you or help themselves?'

٩٣- مِنْ دُوْنِ اللّٰهِ هَلْ يَنْصُرُوْنَكُمْ أَوْ يَنْتَصِرُوْنَ ۞

94. "Then they will be thrown
Headlong into the (Fire)—
They and those straying
In Evil,

٩٤- فَكُبْكِبُوْا فِيْهَا هُمْ وَالْغَاوُوْنَ ۞

95. "And the whole hosts
Of Iblīs together.

٩٥- وَجُنُوْدُ إِبْلِيْسَ أَجْمَعُوْنَ ۞

96. "They will say there
In their mutual bickerings:

٩٦- قَالُوْا وَهُمْ فِيْهَا يَخْتَصِمُوْنَ ۞

97. "'By Allah, we were truly
In an error manifest,

٩٧- تَاللّٰهِ إِنْ كُنَّا لَفِيْ ضَلَالٍ مُّبِيْنٍ ۞

98. "'When we held you as equals
With the Lord of the Worlds;

٩٨- إِذْ نُسَوِّيْكُمْ بِرَبِّ الْعَالَمِيْنَ ۞

99. "'And our seducers were
Only those who were
Steeped in guilt.

٩٩- وَمَا أَضَلَّنَا إِلَّا الْمُجْرِمُوْنَ ۞

100. "'Now, then, we have none
To intercede (for us),

١٠٠- فَمَا لَنَا مِنْ شَافِعِيْنَ ۞

101. "'Nor a single friend
To feel (for us).

١٠١- وَلَا صَدِيْقٍ حَمِيْمٍ ۞

102. "'Now if we only had
A chance of return,
We shall truly be
Of those who believe!'"

١٠٢- فَلَوْ اَنَّ لَنَا كَرَّةً فَنَكُوْنَ مِنَ الْمُؤْمِنِيْنَ ۞

103. Verily in this is a Sign
But most of them
Do not believe.

١٠٣- اِنَّ فِيْ ذٰلِكَ لَاٰيَةً ۖ وَمَا كَانَ اَكْثَرُهُمْ مُّؤْمِنِيْنَ ۞

104. And verily thy Lord
Is He, the Exalted in Might,
Most Merciful.

١٠٤- وَاِنَّ رَبَّكَ لَهُوَ الْعَزِيْزُ الرَّحِيْمُ ۞

SECTION 6.

105. The people of Noah rejected
The messengers.

١٠٥- كَذَّبَتْ قَوْمُ نُوْحِ �۟الْمُرْسَلِيْنَ ۞

106. Behold, their brother Noah
Said to them: "Will ye not
Fear (Allah)?

١٠٦- اِذْ قَالَ لَهُمْ اَخُوْهُمْ نُوْحٌ اَلَا تَتَّقُوْنَ ۞

107. "I am to you a messenger
Worthy of all trust:

١٠٧- اِنِّيْ لَكُمْ رَسُوْلٌ اَمِيْنٌ ۞

108. "So fear Allah, and obey me.

١٠٨- فَاتَّقُوا اللّٰهَ وَاَطِيْعُوْنِ ۞

109. "No reward do I ask
Of you for it: my reward
Is only from the Lord
Of the Worlds:

١٠٩- وَمَا اَسْئَلُكُمْ عَلَيْهِ مِنْ اَجْرٍ ۖ اِنْ اَجْرِيَ اِلَّا عَلٰى رَبِّ الْعٰلَمِيْنَ ۞

110. "So fear Allah, and obey me."

١١٠- فَاتَّقُوا اللّٰهَ وَاَطِيْعُوْنِ ۞

111. They said: "Shall we
Believe in thee when it is
The meanest that follow thee?"

١١١- قَالُوْٓا اَنُؤْمِنُ لَكَ وَاتَّبَعَكَ الْاَرْذَلُوْنَ ۞

112. He said: "And what
Do I know as to
What they do?

١١٢- قَالَ وَمَا عِلْمِيْ بِمَا كَانُوْا يَعْمَلُوْنَ ۞

113. "Their account is only
With my Lord, if ye
Could (but) understand.

١١٣- اِنْ حِسَابُهُمْ اِلَّا عَلٰى رَبِّيْ لَوْ تَشْعُرُوْنَ ۞

114. "I am not one to drive away
Those who believe.

١١٤- وَمَآ اَنَا بِطَارِدِ الْمُؤْمِنِيْنَ ۞

115. "I am sent only
To warn plainly in public."

١١٥- اِنْ اَنَا اِلَّا نَذِيْرٌ مُّبِيْنٌ ۞

116. They said: "If thou
Desist not, O Noah!
Thou shalt be stoned
(to death)."

١١٦- قَالُوْا لَئِنْ لَّمْ تَنْتَهِ يٰنُوْحُ لَتَكُوْنَنَّ مِنَ الْمَرْجُوْمِيْنَ ۞

117. He said: "O my Lord!
Truly my people have
Rejected me.

١١٧- قَالَ رَبِّ اِنَّ قَوْمِيْ كَذَّبُوْنِ ۞

118. "Judge thou, then, between me
And them openly, and deliver
Me and those of the Believers
Who are with me."

١١٨- فَافْتَحْ بَيْنِيْ وَبَيْنَهُمْ فَتْحًا وَّنَجِّنِيْ وَمَنْ مَّعِيَ مِنَ الْمُؤْمِنِيْنَ ۞

119. So We delivered him
And those with him,
In the Ark filled
(With all creatures).

١١٩- فَاَنْجَيْنٰهُ وَمَنْ مَّعَهٗ فِى الْفُلْكِ الْمَشْحُوْنِ ۞

120. Thereafter We drowned those
Who remained behind.

١٢٠- ثُمَّ اَغْرَقْنَا بَعْدُ الْبٰقِيْنَ ۞

121. Verily in this is a Sign:
But most of them
Do not believe.

١٢١- اِنَّ فِيْ ذٰلِكَ لَاٰيَةً ۖ وَمَا كَانَ اَكْثَرُهُمْ مُّؤْمِنِيْنَ ۞

122. And verily thy Lord
Is He, the Exalted in Might,
Most Merciful.
    SECTION 7.

١٢٢- وَاِنَّ رَبَّكَ لَهُوَ الْعَزِيْزُ الرَّحِيْمُ ۞

123. The 'Ād (people) rejected
The messengers.

١٢٣- كَذَّبَتْ عَادُ الْمُرْسَلِيْنَ ۞

124. Behold, their brother Hūd
Said to them: "Will ye not
Fear (Allah)?

١٢٤- اِذْ قَالَ لَهُمْ اَخُوْهُمْ هُوْدٌ اَلَا تَتَّقُوْنَ ۞

125. "I am to you a messenger
Worthy of all trust:

١٢٥- اِنِّيْ لَكُمْ رَسُوْلٌ اَمِيْنٌ ۞

126. "So fear Allah and obey me.

١٢٦- فَاتَّقُوا اللّٰهَ وَاَطِيْعُوْنِ ۞

127. "No reward do I ask
Of you for it: my reward

١٢٧- وَمَا اَسْـَٔلُكُمْ عَلَيْهِ مِنْ اَجْرٍ ۖ

Is only from the Lord
Of the Worlds.

إِنْ أَجْرِيَ إِلَّا عَلَى رَبِّ الْعَالَمِينَ ۞

128. "Do ye build a landmark
On every high place
To amuse yourselves?

١٢٨- اَتَبْنُونَ بِكُلِّ رِيعٍ اٰيَةً تَعْبَثُونَ ۞

129. "And do ye get for yourselves
Fine buildings in the hope
Of living therein (forever)?

١٢٩- وَتَتَّخِذُونَ مَصَانِعَ لَعَلَّكُمْ تَخْلُدُونَ ۞

130. "And when ye exert
Your strong hand,
Do ye do it like men
Of absolute power?

١٣٠- وَإِذَا بَطَشْتُمْ بَطَشْتُمْ جَبَّارِينَ ۞

131. "Now fear Allah, and obey me.

١٣١- فَاتَّقُوا اللهَ وَأَطِيعُونِ ۞

132. "Yea, fear Him Who
Has bestowed on you
Freely all that ye know.

١٣٢- وَاتَّقُوا الَّذِيَ أَمَدَّكُمْ بِمَا تَعْلَمُونَ ۞

133. "Freely has He bestowed
On you cattle and sons—

١٣٣- أَمَدَّكُمْ بِأَنْعَامٍ وَبَنِينَ ۞

134. "And Gardens and Springs.

١٣٤- وَجَنَّاتٍ وَعُيُونٍ ۞

135. "Truly I fear for you
The Penalty of a Great Day."

١٣٥- إِنِّيَ أَخَافُ عَلَيْكُمْ عَذَابَ يَوْمٍ عَظِيمٍ ۞

136. They said: "It is the same
To us whether thou
Admonish us or be not
Among (our) Admonishers!

١٣٦- قَالُوا سَوَاءٌ عَلَيْنَا أَوَعَظْتَ أَمْ لَمْ تَكُنْ مِنَ الْوَاعِظِينَ ۞

137. "This is no other than
A customary device
Of the ancients,

١٣٧- إِنْ هٰذَا إِلَّا خُلُقُ الْأَوَّلِينَ ۞

138. "And we are not the ones
To receive Pains and Penalties!"

١٣٨- وَمَا نَحْنُ بِمُعَذَّبِينَ ۞

139. So they rejected him,
And We destroyed them.
Verily in this is a Sign:
But most of them
Do not believe.

١٣٩- فَكَذَّبُوهُ فَأَهْلَكْنَاهُمْ إِنَّ فِي ذٰلِكَ لَآيَةً وَمَا كَانَ أَكْثَرُهُمْ مُؤْمِنِينَ ۞

140. And verily thy Lord
Is He, the Exalted in Might,
Most Merciful.

SECTION 8.

141. The Thamūd (people) rejected
The messengers.

142. Behold, their brother Ṣāliḥ
Said to them: "Will you not
Fear (Allah)?

143. "I am to you a messenger
Worthy of all trust.

144. "So fear Allah, and obey me.

145. "No reward do I ask
Of you for it: my reward
Is only from the Lord
Of the Worlds

146. "Will ye be left secure,
In (the enjoyment of) all
That ye have here?—

147. "Gardens and Springs,

148. "And cornfields and date palms
With spathes near breaking
(With the weight of fruit)?

149. "And ye carve houses
Out of (rocky) mountains
With great skill.

150. "But fear Allah and obey me;

151. "And follow not the bidding
Of those who are extravagant—

152. "Who make mischief in the land,
And mend not (their ways)."

153. They said: "Thou art only
One of those bewitched!

١٤٠-وَإِنَّ رَبَّكَ لَهُوَ الْعَزِيزُ الرَّحِيمُ ۞

١٤١-كَذَّبَتْ ثَمُودُ الْمُرْسَلِينَ ۞

١٤٢-إِذْ قَالَ لَهُمْ أَخُوهُمْ صَلِحٌ أَلَا تَتَّقُونَ ۞

١٤٣-إِنِّي لَكُمْ رَسُولٌ أَمِينٌ ۞

١٤٤-فَاتَّقُوا اللَّهَ وَأَطِيعُونِ ۞

١٤٥-وَمَا أَسْـَٔلُكُمْ عَلَيْهِ مِنْ أَجْرٍ إِنْ أَجْرِيَ إِلَّا عَلَى رَبِّ الْعَالَمِينَ ۞

١٤٦-أَتُتْرَكُونَ فِي مَا هَاهُنَا آمِنِينَ ۞

١٤٧-فِي جَنَّاتٍ وَعُيُونٍ ۞

١٤٨-وَزُرُوعٍ وَنَخْلٍ طَلْعُهَا هَضِيمٌ ۞

١٤٩-وَتَنْحِتُونَ مِنَ الْجِبَالِ بُيُوتًا فَارِهِينَ ۞

١٥٠-فَاتَّقُوا اللَّهَ وَأَطِيعُونِ ۞

١٥١-وَلَا تُطِيعُوا أَمْرَ الْمُسْرِفِينَ ۞

١٥٢-الَّذِينَ يُفْسِدُونَ فِي الْأَرْضِ وَلَا يُصْلِحُونَ ۞

١٥٣-قَالُوا إِنَّمَا أَنْتَ مِنَ الْمُسَحَّرِينَ ۞

154. "Thou art no more than
A mortal like us:
Then bring us a Sign,
If thou tellest the truth!"

١٥٤- مَآ أَنتَ إِلَّا بَشَرٌ مِّثْلُنَا ۖ
فَأْتِ بِـَٔايَةٍ إِن كُنتَ مِنَ الصَّـٰدِقِينَ ۞

155. He said: "Here is
A she-camel: she has
A right of watering,
And ye have a right
Of watering, (severally)
On a day appointed.

١٥٥- قَالَ هَـٰذِهِۦ نَاقَةٌ
لَّهَا شِرْبٌ وَلَكُمْ شِرْبُ
يَوْمٍ مَّعْلُومٍ ۞

156. "Touch her not with harm,
Lest the Penalty
Of a Great Day
Sieze you."

١٥٦- وَلَا تَمَسُّوهَا بِسُوٓءٍ
فَيَأْخُذَكُمْ عَذَابُ يَوْمٍ عَظِيمٍ ۞

157. But they hamstrung her:
Then did they become
Full of regrets.

١٥٧- فَعَقَرُوهَا فَأَصْبَحُوا نَـٰدِمِينَ ۞

158. But the Penalty seized them
Verily in this is a Sign:
But most of them
Did not believe.

١٥٨- فَأَخَذَهُمُ الْعَذَابُ ۚ إِنَّ فِى ذَٰلِكَ لَـَٔايَةً
وَمَا كَانَ أَكْثَرُهُم مُّؤْمِنِينَ ۞

159. And verily thy Lord
Is He, the Exalted in Might,
Most Merciful.

١٥٩- وَإِنَّ رَبَّكَ لَهُوَ الْعَزِيزُ الرَّحِيمُ ۞

SECTION 9.

160. The people of Lūṭ rejected
The messengers.

١٦٠- كَذَّبَتْ قَوْمُ لُوطٍ الْمُرْسَلِينَ ۞

161. Behold, their brother Lūṭ
Said to them: "Will ye not
Fear (Allah)?

١٦١- إِذْ قَالَ لَهُمْ أَخُوهُمْ لُوطٌ أَلَا تَتَّقُونَ ۞

162. "I am to you a messenger
Worthy of all trust.

١٦٢- إِنِّى لَكُمْ رَسُولٌ أَمِينٌ ۞

163. "So fear Allah and obey me.

١٦٣- فَاتَّقُوا اللَّهَ وَأَطِيعُونِ ۞

164. "No reward do I ask
Of you for it: my reward
Is only from the Lord
Of the Worlds.

١٦٤- وَمَآ أَسْـَٔلُكُمْ عَلَيْهِ مِنْ أَجْرٍ ۖ
إِنْ أَجْرِىَ إِلَّا عَلَىٰ رَبِّ الْعَـٰلَمِينَ ۞

165. "Of all the creatures

١٦٥- أَتَأْتُونَ

In the world, will ye
Approach males,

الذُّكْرَانَ مِنَ الْعَالَمِينَ ۟

166. "And leave those whom Allah
Has created for you
To be your mates?
Nay, ye are a people
Transgressing (all limits)!"

١٦٦- وَتَذَرُونَ مَا خَلَقَ لَكُمْ رَبُّكُمْ
مِنْ أَزْوَاجِكُمْ ۚ
بَلْ أَنْتُمْ قَوْمٌ عَادُونَ ۟

167. They said. "If thou desist not
O Lūṭ! thou wilt assuredly
Be cast out!"

١٦٧- قَالُوا لَئِنْ لَمْ تَنْتَهِ يَا لُوطُ
لَتَكُونَنَّ مِنَ الْمُخْرَجِينَ ۟

168. He said: "I do detest
Your doings:"

١٦٨- قَالَ إِنِّي لِعَمَلِكُمْ مِنَ الْقَالِينَ ۙ

169. "O my Lord! deliver me
And my family from
Such things as they do!"

١٦٩- رَبِّ نَجِّنِي وَأَهْلِي مِمَّا يَعْمَلُونَ ۟

170. So We delivered him
And his family.—all

١٧٠- فَنَجَّيْنَاهُ وَأَهْلَهُ أَجْمَعِينَ ۙ

171. Except an old woman
Who lingered behind.

١٧١- إِلَّا عَجُوزًا فِي الْغَابِرِينَ ۚ

172. But the rest We destroyed
Utterly.

١٧٢- ثُمَّ دَمَّرْنَا الْآخَرِينَ ۙ

173. We rained down on them
A shower (of brimstone):
And evil was the shower
On those who were admonished
(But heeded not)!

١٧٣- وَأَمْطَرْنَا عَلَيْهِمْ مَطَرًا ۖ
فَسَاءَ مَطَرُ الْمُنْذَرِينَ ۟

174. Verily in this is a Sign:
But most of them
Do not believe.

١٧٤- إِنَّ فِي ذَلِكَ لَآيَةً ۖ
وَمَا كَانَ أَكْثَرُهُمْ مُؤْمِنِينَ ۟

175. And verily thy Lord
Is He, the Exalted in Might,
Most Merciful.

SECTION 10.

١٧٥- وَإِنَّ رَبَّكَ لَهُوَ الْعَزِيزُ الرَّحِيمُ ۟

176. The Companions of the Wood
Rejected the messengers.

١٧٦- كَذَّبَ أَصْحَابُ لْئَيْكَةِ الْمُرْسَلِينَ ۙ

177. Behold, Shu'ayb said to them:
"Will ye not fear (Allah)?

١٧٧- إِذْ قَالَ لَهُمْ شُعَيْبٌ أَلَا تَتَّقُونَ ۙ

178. "I am to you a messenger
Worthy of all trust.

١٦٨ ـ اِنِّى لَكُمْ رَسُوْلٌ اَمِيْنٌ ۙ

179. "So fear Allah and obey me.

١٦٩ ـ فَاتَّقُوا اللّٰهَ وَاَطِيْعُوْنِ ۚ

180. "No reward do I ask
Of you for it: my reward
Is only from the Lord
Of the Worlds.

١٨٠ ـ وَمَآ اَسْئَلُكُمْ عَلَيْهِ مِنْ اَجْرٍ ۚ
اِنْ اَجْرِىَ اِلَّا عَلٰى رَبِّ الْعٰلَمِيْنَ ۙ

181. "Give just measure,
And cause no loss
(To others by fraud).

١٨١ ـ اَوْفُوا الْكَيْلَ وَلَا تَكُوْنُوْا مِنَ
الْمُخْسِرِيْنَ ۙ

182. "And weigh with scales
True and upright.

١٨٢ ـ وَزِنُوْا بِالْقِسْطَاسِ الْمُسْتَقِيْمِ ۚ

183. "And withhold not things
Justly due to men,
Nor do evil in the land,
Working mischief.

١٨٣ ـ وَلَا تَبْخَسُوا النَّاسَ اَشْيَآءَهُمْ
وَلَا تَعْثَوْا فِى الْاَرْضِ مُفْسِدِيْنَ ۚ

184. "And fear Him Who created
You and (Who created)
The generations before (you)"

١٨٤ ـ وَاتَّقُوا الَّذِىْ خَلَقَكُمْ
وَالْجِبِلَّةَ الْاَوَّلِيْنَ ؕ

185. They said: "Thou art only
One of those bewitched!

١٨٥ ـ قَالُوْٓا اِنَّمَآ اَنْتَ مِنَ الْمُسَحَّرِيْنَ ۙ

186. "Thou art no more than
A mortal like us,
And indeed we think
Thou art a liar!

١٨٦ ـ وَمَآ اَنْتَ اِلَّا بَشَرٌ مِّثْلُنَا
وَاِنْ نَّظُنُّكَ لَمِنَ الْكٰذِبِيْنَ ۚ

187. "Now cause a piece
Of the sky to fall on us,
If thou art truthful!"

١٨٧ ـ فَاَسْقِطْ عَلَيْنَا كِسَفًا مِّنَ السَّمَآءِ
اِنْ كُنْتَ مِنَ الصّٰدِقِيْنَ ؕ

188. He said: "My Lord
Knows best what ye do."

١٨٨ ـ قَالَ رَبِّىْٓ اَعْلَمُ بِمَا تَعْمَلُوْنَ ۝

189. But they rejected him.
Then the punishment
Of a day of overshadowing
gloom
Seized them, and that was
The Penalty of a Great Day.

١٨٩ ـ فَكَذَّبُوْهُ
فَاَخَذَهُمْ عَذَابُ يَوْمِ الظُّلَّةِ ؕ
اِنَّهٗ كَانَ عَذَابَ يَوْمٍ عَظِيْمٍ ۝

190. Verily in that is a Sign:
But most of them
Do not believe.

١٩٠ـ اِنَّ فِىْ ذٰلِكَ لَاٰيَةً
وَمَا كَانَ اَكْثَرُهُمْ مُّؤْمِنِيْنَ ۟

191. And verily thy Lord
Is He, the Exalted in Might,
Most Merciful.

١٩١ـ وَاِنَّ رَبَّكَ لَهُوَ الْعَزِيْزُ الرَّحِيْمُ ۟

SECTION 11.

192. Verily this is a Revelation
From the Lord of the Worlds:

١٩٢ـ وَاِنَّهٗ لَتَنْزِيْلُ رَبِّ الْعٰلَمِيْنَ ۟

193. With it came down
The Spirit of Faith and Truth—

١٩٣ـ نَزَلَ بِهِ الرُّوْحُ الْاَمِيْنُ ۟

194. To thy heart and mind,
That thou mayest admonish

١٩٤ـ عَلٰى قَلْبِكَ لِتَكُوْنَ مِنَ الْمُنْذِرِيْنَ ۟

195. In the perspicuous
Arabic tongue.

١٩٥ـ بِلِسَانٍ عَرَبِىٍّ مُّبِيْنٍ ۟

196. Without doubt it is (announced)
In the revealed Books
Of former peoples.

١٩٦ـ وَاِنَّهٗ لَفِىْ زُبُرِ الْاَوَّلِيْنَ ۟

197. Is it not a Sign
To them that the Learned
Of the Children of Israel
Knew it (as true)?

١٩٧ـ اَوَلَمْ يَكُنْ لَّهُمْ اٰيَةً
اَنْ يَّعْلَمَهٗ عُلَمٰٓؤُا بَنِىْٓ اِسْرَآءِيْلَ ۟

198. Had We revealed it
To any of the non-Arabs,

١٩٨ـ وَلَوْ نَزَّلْنٰهُ عَلٰى بَعْضِ الْاَعْجَمِيْنَ ۟

199. And had he recited it
To them, they would not
Have believed in it.

١٩٩ـ فَقَرَاَهٗ عَلَيْهِمْ مَّا كَانُوْا بِهٖ
مُؤْمِنِيْنَ ۟

200. Thus have We caused it
To enter the hearts
Of the Sinners.

٢٠٠ـ كَذٰلِكَ سَلَكْنٰهُ فِىْ قُلُوْبِ الْمُجْرِمِيْنَ ۟

201. They will not believe
In it until they see
The grievous Penalty;

٢٠١ـ لَا يُؤْمِنُوْنَ بِهٖ حَتّٰى يَرَوُا الْعَذَابَ
الْاَلِيْمَ ۟

202. But the (Penalty) will come
To them of a sudden,
While they perceive it not;

٢٠٢ـ فَيَأْتِيَهُمْ بَغْتَةً وَّهُمْ لَا يَشْعُرُوْنَ ۟

203. Then they will say:
"Shall we be respited?"

٢٠٣- فَيَقُولُوا هَلْ نَحْنُ مُنْظَرُونَ ۟

204. Do they then ask
For Our Penalty to be
Hastened on?

٢٠٤- أَفَبِعَذَابِنَا يَسْتَعْجِلُونَ ۟

205. Seest thou? If We do
Let them enjoy (this life)
For a few years,

٢٠٥- أَفَرَءَيْتَ إِنْ مَتَّعْنَاهُمْ سِنِينَ ۟

206. Yet there comes to them
At length the (Punishment)
Which they were promised!

٢٠٦- ثُمَّ جَاءَهُمْ مَا كَانُوا يُوعَدُونَ ۟

207. It will profit them not
That they enjoyed (this life)!

٢٠٧- مَا أَغْنَى عَنْهُمْ مَا كَانُوا يَمْتَعُونَ ۟

208. Never did We destroy
A population, but had
Its warners—

٢٠٨- وَمَا أَهْلَكْنَا مِنْ قَرْيَةٍ إِلَّا لَهَا مُنْذِرُونَ ۙ

209. By way of reminder;
And We never are unjust.

٢٠٩- ذِكْرَى ۚ وَمَا كُنَّا ظَالِمِينَ ۟

210. No evil ones have brought
Down this (Revelation):

٢١٠- وَمَا تَنَزَّلَتْ بِهِ الشَّيَاطِينُ ۟

211. It would neither suit them
Nor would they be able
(To produce it).

٢١١- وَمَا يَنْبَغِي لَهُمْ وَمَا يَسْتَطِيعُونَ ۟

212. Indeed they have been removed
Far from even (a chance of)
Hearing it.

٢١٢- إِنَّهُمْ عَنِ السَّمْعِ لَمَعْزُولُونَ ۟

213. So call not on any
Other god with Allah,
Or thou wilt be among
Those under the Penalty.

٢١٣- فَلَا تَدْعُ مَعَ اللهِ إِلَهًا آخَرَ فَتَكُونَ مِنَ الْمُعَذَّبِينَ ۟

214. And admonish thy nearest
Kinsmen,

٢١٤- وَأَنْذِرْ عَشِيرَتَكَ الْأَقْرَبِينَ ۟

215. And lower thy wing
To the Believers who
Follow thee.

٢١٥- وَاخْفِضْ جَنَاحَكَ لِمَنِ اتَّبَعَكَ مِنَ الْمُؤْمِنِينَ ۟

216. Then if they disobey thee,
Say: "I am free (of responsibility)
For what ye do!"

٢١٦- فَإِنْ عَصَوْكَ فَقُلْ إِنِّي بَرِيٓءٌ مِّمَّا تَعْمَلُونَ ۙ

217. And put thy trust
On the Exalted in Might,
The Merciful—

٢١٧- وَتَوَكَّلْ عَلَى الْعَزِيزِ الرَّحِيمِ ۙ

218. Who seeth thee standing
Forth (in prayer),

٢١٨- الَّذِي يَرَاكَ حِينَ تَقُومُ ۙ

219. And thy movements among
Those who prostrate themselves.

٢١٩- وَتَقَلُّبَكَ فِي السَّاجِدِينَ ۙ

220. For it is He
Who heareth and knoweth
All things.

٢٢٠- إِنَّهُ هُوَ السَّمِيعُ الْعَلِيمُ ۙ

221. Shall I inform you,
(O people!), on whom it is
That the evil ones descend?

٢٢١- هَلْ أُنَبِّئُكُمْ عَلَى مَنْ تَنَزَّلُ الشَّيَاطِينُ ۙ

222. They descend on every
Lying, wicked person,

٢٢٢- تَنَزَّلُ عَلَى كُلِّ أَفَّاكٍ أَثِيمٍ ۙ

223. (Into whose ears) they pour
Hearsay vanities, and most
Of them are liars.

٢٢٣- يُلْقُونَ السَّمْعَ وَأَكْثَرُهُمْ كَاذِبُونَ ۙ

224. And the Poets—
It is those straying in Evil,
Who follow them:

٢٢٤- وَالشُّعَرَاءُ يَتَّبِعُهُمُ الْغَاوُونَ ۙ

225. Seest thou not that they
Wander distractedly in every
Valley?—

٢٢٥- أَلَمْ تَرَ أَنَّهُمْ فِي كُلِّ وَادٍ يَهِيمُونَ ۙ

226. And that they say
What they practise not?—

٢٢٦- وَأَنَّهُمْ يَقُولُونَ مَا لَا يَفْعَلُونَ ۙ

227. Except those who believe,
Work righteousness, engage much
In the remembrance of Allah,
And defend themselves only after
They are unjustly attacked.
And soon will the unjust
Assailants know what vicissitudes
Their affairs will take!

٢٢٧- إِلَّا الَّذِينَ آمَنُوا وَعَمِلُوا الصَّالِحَاتِ وَذَكَرُوا اللَّهَ كَثِيرًا وَانْتَصَرُوا مِنْ بَعْدِ مَا ظُلِمُوا ۚ وَسَيَعْلَمُ الَّذِينَ ظَلَمُوا أَيَّ مُنْقَلَبٍ يَنْقَلِبُونَ ۙ

INTRODUCTION TO SŪRA XXVII. *(Naml)* — 93 Verses

This Sūra is cognate in subject to the one preceding it and the two following it. Its chronological place is also in the same group of four; in the middle Meccan period.

Here there is much mystic symbolism. Wonders in the physical world are types of greater wonders in the spiritual world. The Fire, the White Hand, and the Rod, in the story of Moses; the speech of birds, the crowds of Jinns and men pitted against a humble ant, and the Hoopoe and the Queen of Sheba, in Solomon's story; the defeat of the plot of the nine wicked men in the story of Ṣāliḥ; and the crime of sin with open eyes in the story of Lot;—lead up to lessons of true and false worship and the miracles of God's grace and revelation.

Al Naml (The Ants)

In the Name of Allah, Most Gracious,
Most Merciful.

بِسْمِ اللهِ الرَّحْمٰنِ الرَّحِيْمِ

1. Ṭā Sīn.
   These are verses
   Of the Qur'ān—A Book
   That makes (things) clear;

١- طٰسٓ تِلْكَ اٰيٰتُ الْقُرْاٰنِ وَكِتَابٍ مُّبِيْنٍ ۙ

2. A Guide; and Glad Tidings
   For the Believers—

٢- هُدًى وَّ بُشْرٰى لِلْمُؤْمِنِيْنَ ۙ

3. Those who establish regular
                          prayers
   And give in regular charity,
   And also have (full) assurance
   Of the Hereafter.

٣- الَّذِيْنَ يُقِيْمُوْنَ الصَّلٰوةَ وَيُؤْتُوْنَ الزَّكٰوةَ وَهُمْ بِالْاٰخِرَةِ هُمْ يُوْقِنُوْنَ ۞

4. As to those who believe not
   In the Hereafter, We have
   Made their deeds pleasing
   In their eyes; and so they
   Wander about in distraction.

٤- اِنَّ الَّذِيْنَ لَا يُؤْمِنُوْنَ بِالْاٰخِرَةِ زَيَّنَّا لَهُمْ اَعْمَالَهُمْ فَهُمْ يَعْمَهُوْنَ ۞

5. Such are they for whom
   A grievous Penalty is (waiting):
   And in the Hereafter theirs
   Will be the greatest loss.

٥- اُولٰٓئِكَ الَّذِيْنَ لَهُمْ سُوْٓءُ الْعَذَابِ وَهُمْ فِي الْاٰخِرَةِ هُمُ الْاَخْسَرُوْنَ ۞

6. As to thee, the Qur'ān
   Is bestowed upon thee

٦- وَاِنَّكَ لَتُلَقَّى الْقُرْاٰنَ

From the presence of One
Who is Wise and All-Knowing.

مِن لَّدُنْ حَكِيمٍ عَلِيمٍ ۝

7. Behold! Moses said
To his family: "I perceive
A fire; soon will I bring you
From there some information,
Or I will bring you
A burning brand to light
Our fuel, that ye may
Warm yourselves.

٧- إِذْ قَالَ مُوسَىٰ لِأَهْلِهِ إِنِّي آنَسْتُ نَارًا
سَآتِيكُم مِّنْهَا بِخَبَرٍ
أَوْ آتِيكُم بِشِهَابٍ قَبَسٍ
لَّعَلَّكُمْ تَصْطَلُونَ ۝

8. But when he came
To the (Fire), a voice
Was heard: "Blessed are those
In the Fire and those around:
And Glory to Allah,
The Lord of the Worlds.

٨- فَلَمَّا جَآءَهَا نُودِيَ أَن بُورِكَ
مَن فِي النَّارِ وَمَنْ حَوْلَهَا
وَسُبْحَانَ اللَّهِ رَبِّ الْعَالَمِينَ ۝

9. "O Moses! Verily,
I am Allah, the Exalted
In Might, the Wise!...

٩- يَا مُوسَىٰ إِنَّهُ أَنَا اللَّهُ الْعَزِيزُ الْحَكِيمُ ۝

10. "Now do thou throw they rod!"
But when he saw it
Moving (of its own accord)
As if it had been a snake,
He turned back in retreat,
And retraced not his steps:
"O Moses!" (it was said)
"Fear not: truly, in My presence,
Those called as messengers
Have no fear—

١٠- وَأَلْقِ عَصَاكَ
فَلَمَّا رَآهَا تَهْتَزُّ كَأَنَّهَا جَآنٌّ
وَلَّىٰ مُدْبِرًا وَلَمْ يُعَقِّبْ
يَا مُوسَىٰ لَا تَخَفْ
إِنِّي لَا يَخَافُ لَدَيَّ الْمُرْسَلُونَ ۝

11. "But if any have done wrong
And have thereafter substituted
Good to take the place of evil,
Truly, I am Oft-Forgiving,
Most Merciful.

١١- إِلَّا مَن ظَلَمَ ثُمَّ بَدَّلَ
حُسْنًا بَعْدَ سُوءٍ
فَإِنِّي غَفُورٌ رَّحِيمٌ ۝

12. "Now put thy hand into
Thy bosom, and it will
Come forth white without stain
(Or harm): (these are) among
The nine Signs (thou wilt take)
To Pharaoh and his people:
For they are a people
Rebellious in transgression."

١٢- وَأَدْخِلْ يَدَكَ فِي جَيْبِكَ
تَخْرُجْ بَيْضَآءَ مِنْ غَيْرِ سُوءٍ
فِي تِسْعِ آيَاتٍ إِلَىٰ فِرْعَوْنَ وَقَوْمِهِ
إِنَّهُمْ كَانُوا قَوْمًا فَاسِقِينَ ۝

13. But when Our Signs came
To them, that should have
Opened their eyes, they said:
"This is sorcery manifest!"

١٣- فَلَمَّا جَاءَتْهُمْ اٰيٰتُنَا مُبْصِرَةً
قَالُوا هٰذَا سِحْرٌ مُّبِينٌ ۖ

14. And they rejected those Signs
In iniquity and arrogance,
Though their souls were convinced
Thereof: so see what was
The end of those
Who acted corruptly!

١٤- وَجَحَدُوا بِهَا
وَاسْتَيْقَنَتْهَا أَنْفُسُهُمْ ظُلْمًا وَّعُلُوًّا ۚ
فَانْظُرْ كَيْفَ كَانَ عَاقِبَةُ الْمُفْسِدِينَ ۖ

SECTION 2.

15. We gave (in the past)
Knowledge to David and
                    Solomon:
And they both said:
"Praise be to Allah, Who
Has favoured us above many
Of His servants who believe!"

١٥- وَلَقَدْ اٰتَيْنَا دَاوٗدَ وَسُلَيْمٰنَ عِلْمًا ۚ
وَقَالَا الْحَمْدُ لِلّٰهِ الَّذِيْ
فَضَّلَنَا عَلٰى كَثِيرٍ مِّنْ عِبَادِهِ الْمُؤْمِنِينَ

16. And Solomon was David's heir.
He said: "O ye people!
We have been taught the speech
Of Birds, and on us
Has been bestowed (a little)
Of all things: this is
Indeed Grace manifest (from
                    Allah.)"

١٦- وَوَرِثَ سُلَيْمٰنُ دَاوٗدَ
وَقَالَ يٰأَيُّهَا النَّاسُ عُلِّمْنَا مَنْطِقَ الطَّيْرِ
وَأُوتِينَا مِنْ كُلِّ شَيْءٍ ۖ
إِنَّ هٰذَا لَهُوَ الْفَضْلُ الْمُبِينُ

17. And before Solomon were
                    marshalled
His hosts—of Jinns and men
And birds, and they were all
Kept in order and ranks.

١٧- وَحُشِرَ لِسُلَيْمٰنَ
جُنُودُهُ مِنَ الْجِنِّ وَالْإِنْسِ
وَالطَّيْرِ فَهُمْ يُوزَعُونَ

18. At length, when they came
To a (lowly) valley of ants,
One of the ants said:
"O ye ants, get into
Your habitations, lest Solomon
And his hosts crush you
(Under foot) without knowing
it."

١٨- حَتّٰى إِذَا أَتَوْا عَلٰى وَادِ النَّمْلِ ۙ
قَالَتْ نَمْلَةٌ يٰأَيُّهَا النَّمْلُ ادْخُلُوا
مَسَاكِنَكُمْ لَا يَحْطِمَنَّكُمْ
سُلَيْمٰنُ وَجُنُودُهُ ۙ
وَهُمْ لَا يَشْعُرُونَ

19. So he smiled, amused
At its speech; and he said:
"O my Lord! so order me
That I may be grateful
For Thy favours, which Thou
Hast bestowed on me and
On my parents, and that
I may work the righteousness
That will please Thee:
And admit me, by Thy Grace,
To the ranks of Thy
Righteous Servants."

20. And he took a muster
Of the Birds; and he said:
"Why is it I see not
The Hoopoe? Or is he
Among the absentees?

21. "I will certainly punish him
With a severe penalty,
Or execute him, unless
He bring me a clear reason
(For absence)."

22. But the Hoopoe tarried not
Far: he (came up and) said:
"I have compassed (territory)
Which thou hast not compassed,
And I have come to thee
From Saba' with tidings true.

23. "I found (there) a woman
Ruling over them and provided
With every requisite; and she
Has a magnificent throne.

24. "I found her and her people
Worshipping the sun besides
Allah:
Satan has made their deeds
Seem pleasing to their eyes,
And has kept them away
From the Path—so
They receive no guidance—

١٩- فَتَبَسَّمَ ضَاحِكًا مِّنْ قَوْلِهَا وَقَالَ
رَبِّ أَوْزِعْنِيْ أَنْ أَشْكُرَ
نِعْمَتَكَ الَّتِيْ أَنْعَمْتَ عَلَيَّ
وَعَلَى وَالِدَيَّ وَأَنْ أَعْمَلَ صَالِحًا
تَرْضَاهُ وَأَدْخِلْنِيْ بِرَحْمَتِكَ
فِيْ عِبَادِكَ الصَّالِحِيْنَ ۞

٢٠- وَتَفَقَّدَ الطَّيْرَ فَقَالَ
مَالِيَ لَآ أَرَى الْهُدْهُدَ ۖ
أَمْ كَانَ مِنَ الْغَآئِبِيْنَ ۞

٢١- لَأُعَذِّبَنَّهُ عَذَابًا شَدِيْدًا
أَوْ لَأَاذْبَحَنَّهُ أَوْ لَيَأْتِيَنِّيْ بِسُلْطٰنٍ مُّبِيْنٍ ۞

٢٢- فَمَكَثَ غَيْرَ بَعِيْدٍ فَقَالَ
أَحَطْتُ بِمَا لَمْ تُحِطْ بِهٖ
وَجِئْتُكَ مِنْ سَبَاٍ بِنَبَاٍ يَّقِيْنٍ ۞

٢٣- إِنِّيْ وَجَدْتُّ امْرَأَةً تَمْلِكُهُمْ وَأُوْتِيَتْ
مِنْ كُلِّ شَيْءٍ وَّلَهَا عَرْشٌ عَظِيْمٌ ۞

٢٤- وَجَدْتُّهَا وَقَوْمَهَا يَسْجُدُوْنَ لِلشَّمْسِ
مِنْ دُوْنِ اللهِ وَزَيَّنَ لَهُمُ الشَّيْطٰنُ
أَعْمَالَهُمْ فَصَدَّهُمْ عَنِ السَّبِيْلِ
فَهُمْ لَا يَهْتَدُوْنَ ۙ

25. "(Kept them away from the Path),
That they should not worship
Allah, Who brings to light
What is hidden in the heavens
And the earth, and knows
What ye hide and what
Ye reveal.

٢٥- اَلَّا يَسْجُدُوا لِلّٰهِ الَّذِى
يُخْرِجُ الْخَبْءَ فِى السَّمٰوٰتِ وَالْاَرْضِ
وَيَعْلَمُ مَا تُخْفُوْنَ وَمَا تُعْلِنُوْنَ ۟

26. "Allah!—there is no god
But He!—Lord of the Throne
Supreme!"

٢٦- اَللّٰهُ لَا اِلٰهَ
اِلَّا هُوَ رَبُّ الْعَرْشِ الْعَظِيْمِ ۟

27. (Solomon) said: "Soon shall we
See whether thou hast told
The truth or lied!

٢٧- قَالَ سَنَنْظُرُ اَصَدَقْتَ
اَمْ كُنْتَ مِنَ الْكٰذِبِيْنَ ۟

28. "Go thou, with this letter
Of mine, and deliver it
To them: then draw back
From them, and (wait to) see
What answer they return"...

٢٨- اِذْهَبْ بِّكِتٰبِىْ هٰذَا فَاَلْقِهْ اِلَيْهِمْ
ثُمَّ تَوَلَّ عَنْهُمْ فَانْظُرْ مَاذَا يَرْجِعُوْنَ ۟

29. (The Queen) said: "Ye chiefs!
Here is—delivered to me—
A letter worthy of respect.

٢٩- قَالَتْ يٰٓاَيُّهَا الْمَلَؤُا
اِنِّىْ اُلْقِىَ اِلَىَّ كِتٰبٌ كَرِيْمٌ ۟

30. "It is from Solomon, and is
(As follows): 'In the name
Of Allah, Most Gracious
Most Merciful:

٣٠- اِنَّهٗ مِنْ سُلَيْمٰنَ وَاِنَّهٗ
بِسْمِ اللّٰهِ الرَّحْمٰنِ الرَّحِيْمِ ۟

31. " 'Be ye not arrogant
Against me, but come
To me in submission
(To the true Religion).' "

٣١- اَلَّا تَعْلُوْا عَلَىَّ
وَاْتُوْنِىْ مُسْلِمِيْنَ ۟

SECTION 3.

32. She said: "Ye chiefs!
Advise me in (this)
My affair: no affair
Have I decided
Except in your presence."

٣٢- قَالَتْ يٰٓاَيُّهَا الْمَلَؤُا اَفْتُوْنِىْ فِىْٓ اَمْرِىْ
مَا كُنْتُ قَاطِعَةً اَمْرًا
حَتّٰى تَشْهَدُوْنِ ۟

33. They said: "We are endued
With strength, and given
To vehement war:
But the command is
With thee; so consider
What thou wilt command."

٣٣- قَالُوْا نَحْنُ اُولُوْا قُوَّةٍ
وَّاُولُوْا بَأْسٍ شَدِيْدٍ ۙ وَّالْاَمْرُ اِلَيْكِ
فَانْظُرِىْ مَاذَا تَأْمُرِيْنَ ۟

34. She said: "Kings, when they
Enter a country, despoil it,
And make the noblest
Of its people its meanest
Thus do they behave.

٣٤- قَالَتْ إِنَّ الْمُلُوكَ إِذَا دَخَلُوا قَرْيَةً
أَفْسَدُوهَا وَجَعَلُوا أَعِزَّةَ أَهْلِهَا أَذِلَّةً ۚ
وَكَذَلِكَ يَفْعَلُونَ ۝

35. "But I am going to send
Him a present, and (wait)
To see with what (answer)
Return (my) ambassadors."

٣٥- وَإِنِّي مُرْسِلَةٌ إِلَيْهِمْ بِهَدِيَّةٍ
فَنَاظِرَةٌ بِمَ يَرْجِعُ الْمُرْسَلُونَ ۝

36. Now when (the embassy) came
To Solomon, he said:
"Will ye give me abundance
In wealth? But that which
Allah has given me is better
Than that which He has
Given you! Nay it is ye
Who rejoice in your gift!

٣٦- فَلَمَّا جَاءَ سُلَيْمَانَ قَالَ
أَتُمِدُّونَنِ بِمَالٍ فَمَا
آتَانِيَ اللَّهُ خَيْرٌ مِمَّا آتَاكُمْ ۚ
بَلْ أَنْتُمْ بِهَدِيَّتِكُمْ تَفْرَحُونَ ۝

37. "Go back to them, and be sure
We shall come to them
With such hosts as they
Will never be able to meet:
We shall expel them
From there in disgrace,
And they will feel
Humbled (indeed)."

٣٧- ارْجِعْ إِلَيْهِمْ فَلَنَأْتِيَنَّهُمْ
بِجُنُودٍ لَا قِبَلَ لَهُمْ بِهَا
وَلَنُخْرِجَنَّهُمْ مِنْهَا أَذِلَّةً
وَهُمْ صَاغِرُونَ ۝

38. He said (to his own men):
"Ye Chiefs! which of you
Can bring me her throne
Before they come to me
In submission?"

٣٨- قَالَ يَا أَيُّهَا الْمَلَؤُا أَيُّكُمْ يَأْتِينِي
بِعَرْشِهَا قَبْلَ أَنْ يَأْتُونِي مُسْلِمِينَ ۝

39. Said an 'Ifrīt, of the Jinns:
"I will bring it to thee
Before thou rise from thy
Council: indeed I have
Full strength for the purpose,
And may be trusted."

٣٩- قَالَ عِفْرِيتٌ مِنَ الْجِنِّ أَنَا آتِيكَ بِهِ
قَبْلَ أَنْ تَقُومَ مِنْ مَقَامِكَ ۖ
وَإِنِّي عَلَيْهِ لَقَوِيٌّ أَمِينٌ ۝

40. Said one who had knowledge
Of the Book: "I will
Bring it to thee within
The twinkling of any eye!"
Then when (Solomon) saw it

٤٠- قَالَ الَّذِي عِنْدَهُ عِلْمٌ مِنَ الْكِتَابِ
أَنَا آتِيكَ بِهِ قَبْلَ أَنْ يَرْتَدَّ إِلَيْكَ طَرْفُكَ ۚ
فَلَمَّا رَآهُ مُسْتَقِرًّا عِنْدَهُ

Placed firmly before him,
He said: "This is
By the grace of my Lord!—
To test me whether I am
Grateful or ungrateful!
And if any is grateful,
Truly his gratitude is (a gain)
For his own soul; but if
Any is ungrateful, truly
My Lord is Free of All Needs,
Supreme in Honour!"

قَالَ هٰذَا مِنْ فَضْلِ رَبِّى ۖ
لِيَبْلُوَنِى ءَاَشْكُرُ اَمْ اَكْفُرُ ۖ
وَمَنْ شَكَرَ فَاِنَّمَا يَشْكُرُ لِنَفْسِهِ ۚ
وَمَنْ كَفَرَ
فَاِنَّ رَبِّى غَنِىٌّ كَرِيْمٌ ۝

41. He said: "Transform her throne
Out of all recognition by her:
Let us see whether she
Is guided (to the truth)
Or is one of those who
Receive no guidance."

٤١ - قَالَ نَكِّرُوْا لَهَا عَرْشَهَا
نَنْظُرْ اَتَهْتَدِىٓ
اَمْ تَكُوْنُ مِنَ الَّذِيْنَ لَا يَهْتَدُوْنَ ۝

42. So when she arrived,
She was asked, "Is this
Thy throne?" She said,
It was just like this;
And knowledge was bestowed
On us in advance of this,
And we have submitted
To Allah (in Islam)."

٤٢ - فَلَمَّا جَآءَتْ قِيْلَ اَهٰكَذَا
عَرْشُكِ ۖ قَالَتْ كَاَنَّهٗ هُوَ ۚ
وَاُوْتِيْنَا الْعِلْمَ مِنْ قَبْلِهَا
وَكُنَّا مُسْلِمِيْنَ ۝

43. And he diverted her
From the worship of others
Besides Allah: for she was
(Sprung) of a people
That had no faith.

٤٣ - وَصَدَّهَا مَا كَانَتْ تَعْبُدُ مِنْ
دُوْنِ اللّٰهِ ۖ
اِنَّهَا كَانَتْ مِنْ قَوْمٍ كٰفِرِيْنَ ۝

44. She was asked to enter
The lofty Palace: but
When she saw it, she
Thought it was a lake
Of water, and she (tucked up)
Her skirts), uncovering her legs.
He said: "This is
But a palace paved
Smooth with slabs of glass."
She said: "O my Lord!
I have indeed wronged
My soul: I do (now)
Submit (in Islam), with Solomon,
To the Lord of the Worlds."

٤٤ - قِيْلَ لَهَا ادْخُلِى الصَّرْحَ ۖ
فَلَمَّا رَاَتْهُ حَسِبَتْهُ لُجَّةً
وَّكَشَفَتْ عَنْ سَاقَيْهَا ۚ
قَالَ اِنَّهٗ صَرْحٌ
مُّمَرَّدٌ مِّنْ قَوَارِيْرَ ۚ
قَالَتْ رَبِّ اِنِّى ظَلَمْتُ نَفْسِى
وَاَسْلَمْتُ مَعَ سُلَيْمٰنَ لِلّٰهِ رَبِّ الْعٰلَمِيْنَ ۝ ع

SECTION 4.

45. We sent (aforetime),
    To the Thamūd, their brother
    Ṣāliḥ, saying: "Serve Allah";
    But behold, they became
    Two factions quarrelling
    With each other.

٤٥- وَلَقَدْ اَرْسَلْنَاۤ اِلٰى ثَمُوۡدَ اَخَاهُمْ
صٰلِحًا اَنِ اعۡبُدُوا اللّٰهَ
فَاِذَا هُمْ فَرِيۡقٰنِ يَخۡتَصِمُوۡنَ ۝

46. He said: "O my people!
    Why ask ye to hasten on
    The evil in preference to the
    good?
    If only ye ask Allah for forgiveness,
    Ye may hope to receive mercy."

٤٦- قَالَ يٰقَوۡمِ لِمَ تَسۡتَعۡجِلُوۡنَ
بِالسَّيِّئَةِ قَبۡلَ الۡحَسَنَةِ ۚ
لَوۡلَا تَسۡتَغۡفِرُوۡنَ اللّٰهَ لَعَلَّكُمْ تُرۡحَمُوۡنَ ۝

47. They said: "Ill omen
    Do we augur from thee
    And those that are with thee".
    He said: "Your ill omen
    Is with Allah, yea, ye are
    A people under trial."

٤٧- قَالُوا اطَّيَّرۡنَا بِكَ وَبِمَنۡ مَّعَكَ ۚ
قَالَ طٰٓئِرُكُمۡ عِنۡدَ اللّٰهِ
بَلۡ اَنۡتُمۡ قَوۡمٌ تُفۡتَنُوۡنَ ۝

48. There were in the City
    Nine men of a family
    Who made mischief in the land,
    And would not reform.

٤٨- وَكَانَ فِى الۡمَدِيۡنَةِ تِسۡعَةُ رَهۡطٍ
يُّفۡسِدُوۡنَ فِى الۡاَرۡضِ وَلَا يُصۡلِحُوۡنَ ۝

49. They said: "Swear
    A mutual oath by Allah
    That we shall make
    A secret night attack
    On him and his people,
    And that we shall then
    Say to his heir (when he
    Seeks vengeance): 'We were not
    Present at the slaughter
    Of his people, and we are
    Positively telling the truth.' "

٤٩- قَالُوا تَقَاسَمُوۡا بِاللّٰهِ
لَنُبَيِّتَنَّهٗ وَاَهۡلَهٗ
ثُمَّ لَنَقُوۡلَنَّ لِوَلِيِّهٖ مَا شَهِدۡنَا مَهۡلِكَ
اَهۡلِهٖ
وَاِنَّا لَصٰدِقُوۡنَ ۝

50. They plotted and planned,
    But We too planned,
    Even while they perceived it not.

٥٠- وَمَكَرُوۡا مَكۡرًا وَّمَكَرۡنَا مَكۡرًا
وَّهُمۡ لَا يَشۡعُرُوۡنَ ۝

51. Then see what was the end
    Of their plot!—this,
    That We destroyed them
    And their people, all (of them).

٥١- فَانۡظُرۡ كَيۡفَ كَانَ عَاقِبَةُ مَكۡرِهِمۡ
اَنَّا دَمَّرۡنٰهُمۡ وَقَوۡمَهُمۡ اَجۡمَعِيۡنَ ۝

52. Now such were their houses—
In utter ruin—because
They practised wrongdoing.
Verily in this is a Sign
For people of knowledge.

٥٢ـ فَتِلْكَ بُيُوْتُهُمْ خَاوِيَةً بِمَا ظَلَمُوْا ۗ
اِنَّ فِيْ ذٰلِكَ لَاٰيَةً لِّقَوْمٍ يَّعْلَمُوْنَ ۝

53. And We saved those
Who believed and practised
Righteousness.

٥٣ـ وَاَنْجَيْنَا الَّذِيْنَ اٰمَنُوْا وَكَانُوْا يَتَّقُوْنَ ۝

54. (We also sent) Lūṭ
(As a messenger): behold,
He said to his people,
"Do ye do what is shameful
Though ye see (its iniquity)?

٥٤ـ وَلُوْطًا اِذْ قَالَ لِقَوْمِهٖٓ
اَتَأْتُوْنَ الْفَاحِشَةَ
وَاَنْتُمْ تُبْصِرُوْنَ ۝

55. Would ye really approach men
In your lusts rather than
Women? Nay, ye are
A people (grossly) ignorant!

٥٥ـ اَئِنَّكُمْ لَتَأْتُوْنَ الرِّجَالَ شَهْوَةً مِّنْ
دُوْنِ النِّسَاءِ ۚ بَلْ اَنْتُمْ قَوْمٌ تَجْهَلُوْنَ ۝

56. But his people gave
No other answer but this:
They said, "Drive out
The followers of Lūṭ from
Your city: these are
Indeed men who want
To be clean and pure!"

٥٦ـ فَمَا كَانَ جَوَابَ قَوْمِهٖٓ اِلَّا
اَنْ قَالُوْا اَخْرِجُوْٓا
اٰلَ لُوْطٍ مِّنْ قَرْيَتِكُمْ ۚ
اِنَّهُمْ اُنَاسٌ يَّتَطَهَّرُوْنَ ۝

57. But We saved him
And his family, except
His wife: her We destined
To be of those
Who lagged behind.

٥٧ـ فَاَنْجَيْنٰهُ وَاَهْلَهٗٓ اِلَّا امْرَاَتَهٗ ۖ
قَدَّرْنٰهَا مِنَ الْغٰبِرِيْنَ ۝

58. And We rained down on them
A shower (of brimstone):
And evil was the shower
On those who were admonished
(But heeded not)!

٥٨ـ وَاَمْطَرْنَا عَلَيْهِمْ مَّطَرًا ۚ
فَسَاءَ مَطَرُ الْمُنْذَرِيْنَ ۝

SECTION 5.

59. Say: Praise be to Allah,
And Peace on His servants
Whom He has chosen
(For His Message). (Who)

٥٩ـ قُلِ الْحَمْدُ لِلّٰهِ وَسَلٰمٌ عَلٰى عِبَادِهِ
الَّذِيْنَ اصْطَفٰى ۗ

Is better?—Allah or
The false gods they associate
(With Him)?

آللهُ خَيْرٌ أَمَّا يُشْرِكُونَ ۝

60. Or, who has created
The heavens and the earth,
And who sends you down
Rain from the sky?
Yea, with it We cause
To grow well-planted orchards
Full of beauty and delight:
It is not in your power
To cause the growth
Of the trees in them. (Can there be
Another) god besides Allah?
Nay, they are a people
Who swerve from justice.

٦٠- أَمَّنْ خَلَقَ السَّمٰوٰتِ وَالْأَرْضَ
وَأَنْزَلَ لَكُمْ مِنَ السَّمَاءِ مَاءً ۚ
فَأَنْبَتْنَا بِهِ حَدَائِقَ ذَاتَ بَهْجَةٍ ۚ
مَا كَانَ لَكُمْ أَنْ تُنْبِتُوا شَجَرَهَا ۗ
ءَإِلٰهٌ مَّعَ اللهِ ۚ
بَلْ هُمْ قَوْمٌ يَعْدِلُونَ ۝

61. Or, who has made the earth
Firm to live in; made
Rivers in its midst; set
Thereon mountains
                                    immovable,
And made a separating bar
Between the two bodies
Of flowing water?
(Can there be another) god
Besides Allah? Nay, most
Of them know not.

٦١- أَمَّنْ جَعَلَ الْأَرْضَ قَرَارًا
وَّجَعَلَ خِلٰلَهَا أَنْهٰرًا وَّجَعَلَ لَهَا رَوَاسِيَ
وَجَعَلَ بَيْنَ الْبَحْرَيْنِ حَاجِزًا ۗ
ءَإِلٰهٌ مَّعَ اللهِ ۚ
بَلْ أَكْثَرُهُمْ لَا يَعْلَمُونَ ۝

62. Or, who listens to the (soul)
Distressed when it calls
On Him, and who relieves
Its suffering, and makes you
(Mankind) inheritors of the
                                    earth?
(Can there be another) god
Besides Allah? Little it is
That ye heed!

٦٢- أَمَّنْ يُّجِيبُ الْمُضْطَرَّ إِذَا دَعَاهُ
وَيَكْشِفُ السُّوءَ وَيَجْعَلُكُمْ
خُلَفَاءَ الْأَرْضِ ۗ
ءَإِلٰهٌ مَّعَ اللهِ ۚ
قَلِيلًا مَّا تَذَكَّرُونَ ۝

63. Or, who guides you
Through the depths of darkness
On land and sea, and who
Sends the winds as heralds
Of glad tidings, going before
His mercy? (Can there be
Another) god besides Allah?—

٦٣- أَمَّنْ يَّهْدِيكُمْ فِي ظُلُمٰتِ الْبَرِّ وَالْبَحْرِ
وَمَنْ يُّرْسِلُ الرِّيٰحَ بُشْرًا بَيْنَ يَدَيْ
رَحْمَتِهِ ۗ
ءَإِلٰهٌ مَّعَ اللهِ ۚ

High is Allah above what
They associate with Him!

تَعَلَى اللهُ عَمَّا يُشْرِكُونَ ۝

64. Or, who originates Creation,
Then repeats it,
And who gives you sustenance
From heaven and earth?
(Can there be another) god
Besides Allah? Say, "Bring forth
Your argument, if ye
Are telling the truth!"

٦٤- أَمَّنْ يَبْدَؤُا الْخَلْقَ ثُمَّ يُعِيدُهُ
وَمَنْ يَرْزُقُكُمْ مِّنَ السَّمَآءِ وَالْأَرْضِ
ءَإِلَهٌ مَّعَ اللهِ
قُلْ هَاتُوا بُرْهَانَكُمْ إِنْ كُنْتُمْ صَادِقِينَ ۝

65. Say: None in the heavens
Or on earth, except Allah,
Knows what is hidden:
Nor can they perceive
When they shall be raised
Up (for Judgement).

٦٥- قُلْ لَا يَعْلَمُ مَنْ فِي السَّمَاوَاتِ
وَالْأَرْضِ الْغَيْبَ إِلَّا اللهُ
وَمَا يَشْعُرُونَ أَيَّانَ يُبْعَثُونَ ۝

66. Still less can their knowledge
Comprehend the Hereafter: nay,
They are in doubt and uncertainty
Thereanent; nay, they are blind
Thereunto!
SECTION 6.

٦٦- بَلِ ادَّارَكَ عِلْمُهُمْ فِي الْآخِرَةِ بَلْ
هُمْ فِي شَكٍّ مِّنْهَا
بَلْ هُمْ مِّنْهَا عَمُونَ ۝

67. The Unbelievers say: "What!
When we become dust—
We and our fathers—shall we
Really be raised (from the dead)?

٦٧- وَقَالَ الَّذِينَ كَفَرُوا ءَإِذَا كُنَّا تُرَابًا
وَءَابَآؤُنَا أَئِنَّا لَمُخْرَجُونَ ۝

68. "It is true we were promised
This—we and our fathers
Before (us): these are nothing
But tales of the ancients."

٦٨- لَقَدْ وُعِدْنَا هَذَا نَحْنُ وَءَابَآؤُنَا
مِنْ قَبْلُ إِنْ هَذَا إِلَّا أَسَاطِيرُ الْأَوَّلِينَ ۝

69. Say: "Go ye through the earth
And see what has been
The end of those guilty
(Of sin)."

٦٩- قُلْ سِيرُوا فِي الْأَرْضِ فَانْظُرُوا كَيْفَ
كَانَ عَاقِبَةُ الْمُجْرِمِينَ ۝

70. But grieve not over them,
Nor distress thyself
Because of their plots.

٧٠- وَلَا تَحْزَنْ عَلَيْهِمْ
وَلَا تَكُنْ فِي ضَيْقٍ مِّمَّا يَمْكُرُونَ ۝

71. They also say: "When will
This promise (come to pass)?
(Say) if ye are truthful."

٧١- وَيَقُولُونَ مَتَى هَذَا الْوَعْدُ
إِنْ كُنْتُمْ صَادِقِينَ ۝

72. Say: "It may be that
Some of the events which
Ye wish to hasten on
May be (close) in your pursuit!"

٧٢۔ قُلْ عَسٰۤى اَنْ يَّكُوْنَ رَدِفَ لَكُمْ بَعْضُ الَّذِىْ تَسْتَعْجِلُوْنَ ۟

73. But verily thy Lord is
Full of grace to mankind:
Yet most of them are ungrateful.

٧٣۔ وَاِنَّ رَبَّكَ لَذُوْ فَضْلٍ عَلَى النَّاسِ وَلٰكِنَّ اَكْثَرَهُمْ لَا يَشْكُرُوْنَ ۟

74. And verily thy Lord knoweth
All that their hearts do hide,
As well as all that
They reveal.

٧٤۔ وَاِنَّ رَبَّكَ لَيَعْلَمُ مَا تُكِنُّ صُدُوْرُهُمْ وَمَا يُعْلِنُوْنَ ۟

75. Nor is there aught
Of the Unseen, in heaven
Or earth, but is (recorded)
In a clear record.

٧٥۔ وَمَا مِنْ غَآئِبَةٍ فِى السَّمَآءِ وَالْاَرْضِ اِلَّا فِىْ كِتٰبٍ مُّبِيْنٍ ۟

76. Verily this Qur'ān doth explain
To the Children of Israel
Most of the matters
In which they disagree.

٧٦۔ اِنَّ هٰذَا الْقُرْاٰنَ يَقُصُّ عَلٰى بَنِىْ اِسْرَآئِيْلَ اَكْثَرَ الَّذِىْ هُمْ فِيْهِ يَخْتَلِفُوْنَ ۟

77. And it certainly is
A Guide and a Mercy
To those who believe.

٧٧۔ وَاِنَّهٗ لَهُدًى وَّرَحْمَةٌ لِّلْمُؤْمِنِيْنَ ۟

78. Verily, thy Lord will decide
Between them by His Decree:
And He is Exalted in Might,
All-Knowing.

٧٨۔ اِنَّ رَبَّكَ يَقْضِىْ بَيْنَهُمْ بِحُكْمِهٖ ۚ وَهُوَ الْعَزِيْزُ الْعَلِيْمُ ۟

79. So put thy trust in Allah:
For thou art on (the Path
Of) manifest Truth.

٧٩۔ فَتَوَكَّلْ عَلَى اللّٰهِ ؕ اِنَّكَ عَلَى الْحَقِّ الْمُبِيْنِ ۟

80. Truly thou canst not cause
The Dead to listen, nor
Canst thou cause the Deaf
To hear the call,
(Especially) when they
Turn back in retreat.

٨٠۔ اِنَّكَ لَا تُسْمِعُ الْمَوْتٰى وَلَا تُسْمِعُ الصُّمَّ الدُّعَآءَ اِذَا وَلَّوْا مُدْبِرِيْنَ ۟

81. Nor canst thou be a guide
To the Blind, (to prevent them)
From straying: only those
Wilt thou get to listen

٨١۔ وَمَآ اَنْتَ بِهٰدِى الْعُمْىِ عَنْ ضَلٰلَتِهِمْ ؕ اِنْ تُسْمِعُ اِلَّا

Who believe in Our Signs,
And they will bow in Islam.

مَنْ يُّؤْمِنُ بِاٰيٰتِنَا فَهُمْ مُّسْلِمُوْنَ ۞

82. And when the Word is
Fulfilled against them (the unjust),
We shall produce from the earth
A Beast to (face) them:
He will speak to them,
For that mankind did not
Believe with assurance
In our Signs.

٨٢- وَإِذَا وَقَعَ الْقَوْلُ عَلَيْهِمْ
أَخْرَجْنَا لَهُمْ دَآبَّةً مِّنَ الْأَرْضِ
تُكَلِّمُهُمْ أَنَّ النَّاسَ
كَانُوْا بِاٰيٰتِنَا لَا يُوْقِنُوْنَ ۞

SECTION 7.

83. One Day We shall gather
Together from every people
A troop of those who reject
Our Signs, and they shall
Be kept in ranks—

٨٣- وَيَوْمَ نَحْشُرُ مِنْ كُلِّ أُمَّةٍ
فَوْجًا مِّمَّنْ يُّكَذِّبُ بِاٰيٰتِنَا
فَهُمْ يُوْزَعُوْنَ ۞

84. Until, when they come
(Before the Judgement Seat),
(Allah) will say: "Did ye
Reject My Signs, though ye
Comprehended them not
In knowledge, or what
Was it ye did?"

٨٤- حَتّٰى إِذَا جَآءُوْ
قَالَ أَكَذَّبْتُمْ بِاٰيٰتِيْ وَلَمْ
تُحِيْطُوْا بِهَا عِلْمًا أَمَّا ذَا كُنْتُمْ
تَعْمَلُوْنَ ۞

85. And the Word will be
Fulfilled against them, because
Of their wrongdoing, and they
Will be unable to speak
(In plea).

٨٥- وَوَقَعَ الْقَوْلُ عَلَيْهِمْ بِمَا
ظَلَمُوْا فَهُمْ لَا يَنْطِقُوْنَ ۞

86. See they not that We
Have made the Night
For them to rest in
And the Day to give
Them light? Verily in this
Are Signs for any people
That believe!

٨٦- أَلَمْ يَرَوْا أَنَّا جَعَلْنَا الَّيْلَ
لِيَسْكُنُوْا فِيْهِ وَالنَّهَارَ مُبْصِرًا
إِنَّ فِيْ ذٰلِكَ لَآيٰتٍ لِّقَوْمٍ يُّؤْمِنُوْنَ ۞

87. And the Day that the Trumpet
Will be sounded—then will be
Smitten with terror those
Who are in the heavens,
And those who are on earth,
Except such as Allah will please
(To exempt): and all shall come

٨٧- وَيَوْمَ يُنْفَخُ فِى الصُّوْرِ
فَفَزِعَ مَنْ فِى السَّمٰوٰتِ وَمَنْ فِى
الْأَرْضِ
إِلَّا مَنْ شَآءَ اللهُ

To His (Presence) as beings
Conscious of their lowliness.

وَكُلٌّ أَتَوْهُ دَاخِرِيْنَ ○

88. Thou seest the mountains
And thinkest them firmly fixed:
But they shall pass away
As the clouds pass away:
(Such is) the artistry of Allah,
Who disposes of all things
In perfect order: for He is
Well acquainted with all that ye
do.

٨٨ـ وَتَرَى الْجِبَالَ تَحْسَبُهَا جَامِدَةً وَّهِيَ تَمُرُّ مَرَّ السَّحَابِ ۖ صُنْعَ اللّٰهِ الَّذِيْٓ أَتْقَنَ كُلَّ شَيْءٍ ۗ إِنَّهٗ خَبِيْرٌۢ بِمَا تَفْعَلُوْنَ ○

89. If any do good, good will
(Accrue) to them therefrom;
And they will be secure
From terror that Day.

٨٩ـ مَنْ جَآءَ بِالْحَسَنَةِ فَلَهٗ خَيْرٌ مِّنْهَا ۚ وَهُمْ مِّنْ فَزَعٍ يَّوْمَئِذٍ اٰمِنُوْنَ ○

90. And if any do evil,
Their faces will be thrown
Headlong into the Fire:
"Do ye receive a reward
Other than that which ye
Have earned by your deeds?"

٩٠ـ وَمَنْ جَآءَ بِالسَّيِّئَةِ فَكُبَّتْ وُجُوْهُهُمْ فِى النَّارِ ۗ هَلْ تُجْزَوْنَ إِلَّا مَا كُنْتُمْ تَعْمَلُوْنَ ○

91. "For me, I have been
Commanded to serve the Lord
Of this City, Him Who has
Sactified it and to Whom
(Belong) all things:
And I am commanded
To be of those who bow
In Islam to Allah's Will—

٩١ـ إِنَّمَآ أُمِرْتُ أَنْ أَعْبُدَ رَبَّ هٰذِهِ الْبَلْدَةِ الَّذِيْ حَرَّمَهَا وَلَهٗ كُلُّ شَيْءٍ ۖ وَأُمِرْتُ أَنْ أَكُوْنَ مِنَ الْمُسْلِمِيْنَ ۙ

92. And to rehearse the Qur'ān:
And if any accept guidance,

They do it for the good
Of their own souls,
And if any stray, say:
"I am only a Warner".

٩٢ـ وَأَنْ أَتْلُوَا الْقُرْاٰنَ ۚ فَمَنِ اهْتَدٰى فَإِنَّمَا يَهْتَدِيْ لِنَفْسِهٖ ۚ وَمَنْ ضَلَّ فَقُلْ إِنَّمَآ أَنَا مِنَ الْمُنْذِرِيْنَ ○

93. And say: "Praise be to Allah,
Who will soon show you
His Signs, so that ye
Shall know them"; and thy Lord
Is not unmindful
Of all that ye do.

٩٣ـ وَقُلِ الْحَمْدُ لِلّٰهِ سَيُرِيْكُمْ اٰيٰتِهٖ فَتَعْرِفُوْنَهَا ۗ وَمَا رَبُّكَ بِغَافِلٍ عَمَّا تَعْمَلُوْنَ ۞

INTRODUCTION TO SŪRA XXVIII. *(Qaṣaṣ)* — 88 Verses

This Sūra continues the subject of Revelation and its reception by those to whom it is sent. But it emphasizes new points: how the recipient of inspiration is prepared for his high destiny, even in the growth of his ordinary life, and how the rejection of God's Message by groups of men or by individuals is caused by overweening arrogance or avarice. The plight of those who reject the Truth is contrasted with the reward of the righteous.

With the possible exception of a few verses, it belongs to the late Meccan period, just preceding the Hijrat.

Al Qaṣaṣ (The Narrations)

In the name of Allah, Most Gracious, Most Merciful.

بِسْمِ اللهِ الرَّحْمنِ الرَّحِيمِ

1. 𝔗ā 𝔖īn 𝔐īm.

١- طٰسٓمّٓ ۟

2. These are Verses of the Book
   That makes (things) clear.

٢- تِلْكَ اٰیتُ الْكِتٰبِ الْمُبِيْنِ ۟

3. We rehearse to thee some
   Of the story of Moses
   And Pharaoh in Truth,
   For people who believe.

٣- نَتْلُوْا عَلَيْكَ مِنْ نَّبَاِ مُوْسٰى
وَفِرْعَوْنَ بِالْحَقِّ لِقَوْمٍ يُّؤْمِنُوْنَ ۟

4. 𝔗ruly Pharaoh elated himself
   In the land and broke up
   Its people into sections,
   Depressing a small group
   Among them: their sons he slew,
   But he kept alive their females:
   For he was indeed
   A maker of mischief.

٤- اِنَّ فِرْعَوْنَ عَلَا فِى الْاَرْضِ وَجَعَلَ
اَهْلَهَا شِيَعًا يَّسْتَضْعِفُ طَآئِفَةً
مِّنْهُمْ يُذَبِّحُ اَبْنَآءَهُمْ وَيَسْتَحْيٖ نِسَآءَهُمْ
اِنَّهٗ كَانَ مِنَ الْمُفْسِدِيْنَ ۟

5. And We wished to be
   Gracious to those who were
   Being depressed on the land.
   To make them leaders (in faith)
   And make them heirs,

٥- وَنُرِيْدُ اَنْ نَّمُنَّ عَلَى الَّذِيْنَ
اسْتُضْعِفُوْا فِى الْاَرْضِ وَنَجْعَلَهُمْ اَئِمَّةً
وَّنَجْعَلَهُمُ الْوٰرِثِيْنَ ۟

6. To establish a firm place
   For them in the land,
   And to show Pharaoh, Hāmān,

٦- وَنُمَكِّنَ لَهُمْ فِى الْاَرْضِ
وَنُرِيَ فِرْعَوْنَ وَهَامٰنَ وَجُنُوْدَهُمَا

And their hosts, at their hands,
The very things against which
They were taking precautions.

مِنْهُمْ مَّا كَانُوْا يَحْذَرُوْنَ ۝

7. So We sent this inspiration
To the mother of Moses:
"Suckle (thy child), but when
Thou hast fears about him,
Cast him into the river,
But fear not nor grieve:
For We shall restore him
To thee, and We shall make
Him one of Our messengers."

٧- وَ اَوْحَيْنَا اِلَى اُمِّ مُوْسٰى
اَنْ اَرْضِعِيْهِ ۚ فَاِذَا خِفْتِ عَلَيْهِ
فَاَلْقِيْهِ فِى الْيَمِّ وَلَا تَخَافِىْ وَلَا تَحْزَنِىْ ۚ
اِنَّا رَآدُّوْهُ اِلَيْكِ وَجَاعِلُوْهُ مِنَ
الْمُرْسَلِيْنَ ۝

8. Then the people of Pharaoh
Picked him up (from the river):
(It was intended) that (Moses)
Should be to them an adversary
And a cause of sorrow:
For Pharaoh and Hāmān
And (all) their hosts were
Men of sin.

٨- فَالْتَقَطَهٗٓ اٰلُ فِرْعَوْنَ
لِيَكُوْنَ لَهُمْ عَدُوًّا وَّحَزَنًا ۗ
اِنَّ فِرْعَوْنَ وَهَامٰنَ
وَجُنُوْدَهُمَا كَانُوْا خٰطِئِيْنَ ۝

9. The wife of Pharaoh said:
"(Here is) a joy of the eye,
For me and for thee:
Slay him not. It may be
That he will be of use
To us, or we may adopt
Him as a son." And they
Perceived not (what they
Were doing)!

٩- وَ قَالَتِ امْرَاَتُ فِرْعَوْنَ قُرَّتُ عَيْنٍ
لِّىْ وَلَكَ ۗ لَا تَقْتُلُوْهُ ۖ
عَسٰٓى اَنْ يَّنْفَعَنَآ اَوْ نَتَّخِذَهٗ وَلَدًا
وَّهُمْ لَا يَشْعُرُوْنَ ۝

10. But there came to be
A void in the heart
Of the mother of Moses:
She was going almost to
Disclose his (case), had We
Not strengthened her heart
(With faith), so that she
Might remain a (firm) believer.

١٠- وَاَصْبَحَ فُؤَادُ اُمِّ مُوْسٰى فٰرِغًا ۗ
اِنْ كَادَتْ لَتُبْدِىْ بِهٖ
لَوْلَا اَنْ رَّبَطْنَا عَلٰى قَلْبِهَا
لِتَكُوْنَ مِنَ الْمُؤْمِنِيْنَ ۝

11. And she said to the sister
Of (Moses), "Follow him",
So she (the sister) watched him
In the character of a stranger.
And they knew not.

١١- وَقَالَتْ لِاُخْتِهٖ قُصِّيْهِ ۖ فَبَصُرَتْ بِهٖ
عَنْ جُنُبٍ وَّهُمْ لَا يَشْعُرُوْنَ ۝

12. And We ordained that he

١٢- وَحَرَّمْنَا عَلَيْهِ الْمَرَاضِعَ مِنْ قَبْلُ

Refused suck at first, until
(His sister came up
And) said: "Shall I
Point out to you the people
Of a house that will nourish
And bring him up for you
And be sincerely attached
To him?". . .

فَقَالَتْ هَلْ أَدُلُّكُمْ عَلَىٰ أَهْلِ بَيْتٍ
يَكْفُلُونَهُ لَكُمْ
وَهُمْ لَهُ نَاصِحُونَ ۝

13. Thus did We restore him
To his mother, that her eye
Might be comforted, that she
Might not grieve, and that
She might know that the promise
Of Allah is true; but
Most of them do not
                    understand.

١٣- فَرَدَدْنَاهُ إِلَىٰ أُمِّهِ كَيْ تَقَرَّ عَيْنُهَا وَ
لَا تَحْزَنَ وَلِتَعْلَمَ أَنَّ وَعْدَ
اللَّهِ حَقٌّ وَلَٰكِنَّ أَكْثَرَهُمْ لَا يَعْلَمُونَ ۝

SECTION 2.

14. When he reached full age,
And was firmly established
(In life), We bestowed on him
Wisdom and knowledge: for thus
Do We reward those
Who do good.

١٤- وَلَمَّا بَلَغَ أَشُدَّهُ
وَاسْتَوَىٰ آتَيْنَاهُ حُكْمًا وَعِلْمًا
وَكَذَٰلِكَ نَجْزِي الْمُحْسِنِينَ ۝

15. And he entered the City
At a time when its people
Were not watching: and he
Found there two men fighting—
One of his own people,
And the other, of his foes.
Now the man of his own
People appealed to him
Against his foe, and Moses
Struck him with his fist
And made an end of him.
He said: "This is a work
Of Evil (Satan): for he is
An enemy that manifestly
Misleads!"

١٥- وَدَخَلَ الْمَدِينَةَ عَلَىٰ حِينِ غَفْلَةٍ
مِنْ أَهْلِهَا فَوَجَدَ فِيهَا رَجُلَيْنِ يَقْتَتِلَانِ
هَٰذَا مِنْ شِيعَتِهِ وَهَٰذَا مِنْ عَدُوِّهِ
فَاسْتَغَاثَهُ الَّذِي مِنْ شِيعَتِهِ عَلَى الَّذِي
مِنْ عَدُوِّهِ
فَوَكَزَهُ مُوسَىٰ فَقَضَىٰ عَلَيْهِ
قَالَ هَٰذَا مِنْ عَمَلِ الشَّيْطَانِ
إِنَّهُ عَدُوٌّ مُضِلٌّ مُبِينٌ ۝

16. He prayed: "O my Lord!
I have indeed wronged my soul!
Do Thou then forgive me!"

So (Allah) forgave him: For He
Is the Oft-Forgiving, Most
                    Merciful.

١٦- قَالَ رَبِّ إِنِّي ظَلَمْتُ نَفْسِي
فَاغْفِرْ لِي
فَغَفَرَ لَهُ إِنَّهُ هُوَ الْغَفُورُ الرَّحِيمُ ۝

17. He said: "O my Lord!
   For that Thou hast bestowed
   Thy Grace on me, never
   Shall I be a help
   To those who sin!"

١٧ـ قَالَ رَبِّ بِمَآ اَنْعَمْتَ عَلَيَّ
فَلَنْ اَكُوْنَ ظَهِيْرًا لِّلْمُجْرِمِيْنَ ۟

18. So he saw the morning
   In the City, looking about,
   In a state of fear, when
   Behold, the man who had,
   The day before, sought his help
   Called aloud for his help
   (Again). Moses said to him:
   "Thou art truly, it is clear,
   A quarrelsome fellow!"

١٨ـ فَاَصْبَحَ فِي الْمَدِيْنَةِ خَآئِفًا يَّتَرَقَّبُ
فَاِذَا الَّذِي اسْتَنْصَرَهُ بِالْاَمْسِ
يَسْتَصْرِخُهُ ؕ
قَالَ لَهُ مُوْسٰى
اِنَّكَ لَغَوِيٌّ مُّبِيْنٌ ۟

19. Then, when he decided to lay
   Hold of the man who was
   An enemy to both of them,
   That man said: "O Moses!
   Is it thy intention to slay me
   As thou slewest a man
   Yesterday? Thy intention is
   None other than to become
   A powerful violent man
   In the land, and not to be
   One who sets things right!"

١٩ـ فَلَمَّآ اَنْ اَرَادَ اَنْ يَّبْطِشَ بِالَّذِي
هُوَ عَدُوٌّ لَّهُمَا ۙ
قَالَ يٰمُوْسٰٓى اَتُرِيْدُ اَنْ تَقْتُلَنِيْ
كَمَا قَتَلْتَ نَفْسًۢا بِالْاَمْسِ ۗ اِنْ تُرِيْدُ
اِلَّآ اَنْ تَكُوْنَ جَبَّارًا فِي الْاَرْضِ وَمَا
تُرِيْدُ اَنْ تَكُوْنَ مِنَ الْمُصْلِحِيْنَ ۟

20. And there came a man,
   Running, from the furthest end
   Of the City. He said:
   "O Moses! the Chiefs
   Are taking counsel together
   About thee, to slay thee
   So get thee away, for I
   Do give thee sincere advice."

٢٠ـ وَجَآءَ رَجُلٌ مِّنْ اَقْصَا الْمَدِيْنَةِ يَسْعٰى
قَالَ يٰمُوْسٰٓى اِنَّ الْمَلَاَ يَأْتَمِرُوْنَ بِكَ
لِيَقْتُلُوْكَ فَاخْرُجْ
اِنِّيْ لَكَ مِنَ النّٰصِحِيْنَ ۟

21. He therefore got away
                 therefrom,
   Looking about, in a state
   Of fear. He prayed:
   "O my Lord! save me
   From people given to wrong-
                 doing."

٢١ـ فَخَرَجَ مِنْهَا خَآئِفًا يَّتَرَقَّبُ ۙ
قَالَ رَبِّ نَجِّنِيْ
مِنَ الْقَوْمِ الظّٰلِمِيْنَ ۟ ع

SECTION 3.

22. Then, when he turned his face
   Towards (the land of) Madyan,
   He said: "I do hope

٢٢ـ وَلَمَّا تَوَجَّهَ تِلْقَآءَ مَدْيَنَ
قَالَ عَسٰى رَبِّيْٓ اَنْ

That my Lord will show me
The smooth and straight Path."

يَهۡدِيَنِى سَوَآءَ السَّبِيلِ ۝

23. And when he arrived at
The watering (place) in
                Madyan,
He found there a group
Of men watering (their flocks),
And besides them he found
Two women who were keeping
Back (their flocks). He said:
"What is the matter with you?"
They said: "We cannot water
(Our flocks) until the shepherds
Take back (their flocks):
And our father is
A very old man."

٢٣- وَلَمَّا وَرَدَ مَآءَ مَدۡيَنَ
وَجَدَ عَلَيۡهِ أُمَّةً مِّنَ النَّاسِ يَسۡقُونَ ۬
وَوَجَدَ مِن دُونِهِمُ امۡرَأَتَيۡنِ تَذُودَانِ ۖ
قَالَ
مَا خَطۡبُكُمَا ۖ
قَالَتَا لَا نَسۡقِى حَتَّىٰ يُصۡدِرَ الرِّعَآءُ ۖ
وَأَبُونَا شَيۡخٌ كَبِيرٌ ۝

24. So he watered (their flocks)
For them; then he turned back
To the shade, and said:
"O my Lord!
Truly am I
In (desperate) need
Of any good
That Thou dost send me!". . .

٢٤- فَسَقَىٰ لَهُمَا
ثُمَّ تَوَلَّىٰ إِلَى الظِّلِّ فَقَالَ
رَبِّ إِنِّى لِمَآ أَنزَلۡتَ إِلَىَّ
مِنۡ خَيۡرٍ فَقِيرٌ ۝

25. Afterwards one of the (damsels)
Came (back) to him, walking
Bashfully. She said: "My father
Invites thee that he may
Reward thee for having watered
(Our flocks) for us." So when
He came to him and narrated
The story, he said:
"Fear thou not: (well) hast thou
Escaped from unjust people."

٢٥- فَجَآءَتۡهُ إِحۡدَىٰهُمَا تَمۡشِى عَلَى اسۡتِحۡيَآءٍ
قَالَتۡ إِنَّ أَبِى يَدۡعُوكَ لِيَجۡزِيَكَ أَجۡرَ
مَا سَقَيۡتَ لَنَا ۚ
فَلَمَّا جَآءَهُ وَقَصَّ عَلَيۡهِ الۡقَصَصَ قَالَ
لَا تَخَفۡ ۖ نَجَوۡتَ مِنَ الۡقَوۡمِ الظَّٰلِمِينَ ۝

26. Said one of the (damsels):
"O my (dear) father! engage
Him on wages: truly the best
Of men for thee to employ is
The (man) who is strong and
              trusty" . . .

٢٦- قَالَتۡ إِحۡدَىٰهُمَا يَٰٓأَبَتِ اسۡتَأۡجِرۡهُ ۖ
إِنَّ خَيۡرَ مَنِ اسۡتَأۡجَرۡتَ
الۡقَوِىُّ الۡأَمِينُ ۝

27. He said: "I intend to wed

٢٧- قَالَ إِنِّى أُرِيدُ أَنۡ أُنكِحَكَ إِحۡدَى ابۡنَتَىَّ

One of these my daughters
To thee, on condition that
Thou serve me for eight years;
But if thou complete ten years,
It will be (grace) from thee.
But I intend not to place
Thee under a difficulty:
Thou wilt find me,
Indeed, if Allah wills,
One of the righteous."

هٰتَيْنِ عَلٰى أَنْ تَأْجُرَنِى ثَمٰنِىَ حِجَجٍ ۚ
فَإِنْ أَتْمَمْتَ عَشْرًا فَمِنْ عِنْدِكَ ۚ
وَمَآ أُرِيْدُ أَنْ أَشُقَّ عَلَيْكَ ۚ
سَتَجِدُنِىْ إِنْ شَآءَ اللّٰهُ مِنَ الصّٰلِحِيْنَ ٥

28. He said: 'Be that (the agreement)
Between me and thee:
Whichever of the two terms
I fulfil, let there be
No ill-will to me.
Be Allah a witness
To what we say.'

٢٨۔ قَالَ ذٰلِكَ بَيْنِىْ وَبَيْنَكَ ۖ
أَيَّمَا الْأَجَلَيْنِ قَضَيْتُ فَلَا عُدْوَانَ عَلَىَّ ۚ
وَاللّٰهُ عَلٰى مَا نَقُوْلُ وَكِيْلٌ ٥

SECTION 4.

29. Now when Moses had fulfilled
The term, and was travelling
With his family, he perceived
A fire in the direction
Of Mount Ṭūr. He said
To his family: "Tarry ye;
I perceive a fire; I hope
To bring you from there
Some information, or a burning
Firebrand, that ye may
Warm yourselves."

٢٩۔ فَلَمَّا قَضٰى مُوْسَى الْأَجَلَ وَسَارَ بِأَهْلِهِ
أَنَسَ مِنْ جَانِبِ الطُّوْرِ نَارًا ۚ
قَالَ لِأَهْلِهِ امْكُثُوْا
إِنِّىْ أَنَسْتُ نَارًا لَّعَلِّىْ آتِيْكُمْ مِّنْهَا بِخَبَرٍ
أَوْ جَذْوَةٍ مِّنَ النَّارِ لَعَلَّكُمْ تَصْطَلُوْنَ ٥

30. But when he came
To the (Fire), a voice
Was heard from the right bank
Of the valley, from a tree
In hallowed ground:
"O Moses! Verily
I am Allah, the Lord
Of the Worlds....

٣٠۔ فَلَمَّا أَتَاهَا نُوْدِىَ
مِنْ شَاطِئِ الْوَادِ الْأَيْمَنِ
فِى الْبُقْعَةِ الْمُبَارَكَةِ مِنَ الشَّجَرَةِ
أَنْ يّٰمُوْسٰى إِنِّىْ أَنَا اللّٰهُ رَبُّ الْعٰلَمِيْنَ ٥

31. "Now do thou throw thy rod!"
But when he saw it
Moving (of its own accord)
As if it had been a snake,
He turned back in retreat,
And retraced not his steps:
"O Moses!" (it was said),

٣١۔ وَأَنْ أَلْقِ عَصَاكَ ۚ فَلَمَّا رَآهَا
تَهْتَزُّ كَأَنَّهَا جَآنٌّ
وَلّٰى مُدْبِرًا وَّلَمْ يُعَقِّبْ ۚ
يٰمُوْسٰى أَقْبِلْ وَلَا تَخَفْ ۖ

"Draw near, and fear not:
For thou art of those
Who are secure.

اِنَّكَ مِنَ الْاٰمِنِيْنَ ۟

32. "Move thy hand into
Thy bosom, and it will
Come forth white without stain
(Or harm), and draw thy hand
Close to thy side
(To guard) against fear.
Those are the two credentials
From thy Lord to Pharaoh
And his Chiefs: for truly
They are a people
Rebellious and wicked."

٣٢- اُسْلُكْ يَدَكَ فِيْ جَيْبِكَ
تَخْرُجْ بَيْضَآءَ مِنْ غَيْرِ سُوْٓءٍ ۪
وَّاضْمُمْ اِلَيْكَ جَنَاحَكَ مِنَ الرَّهْبِ
فَذَانِكَ بُرْهَانٰنِ مِنْ رَّبِّكَ اِلٰى فِرْعَوْنَ وَ
مَلَا۟ئِهٖ ؕ
اِنَّهُمْ كَانُوْا قَوْمًا فٰسِقِيْنَ ۟

33. He said: "O my Lord!
I have slain a man
Among them, and I fear
Lest they slay me.

٣٣- قَالَ رَبِّ اِنِّيْ قَتَلْتُ
مِنْهُمْ نَفْسًا فَاَخَافُ اَنْ يَّقْتُلُوْنِ ۟

34. "And my brother Aaron—
He is more eloquent in speech
Than I: so send him
With me as a helper,
To confirm (and strengthen) me:
For I fear that they may
Accuse me of falsehood."

٣٤- وَاَخِيْ هٰرُوْنُ هُوَ اَفْصَحُ مِنِّيْ لِسَانًا
فَاَرْسِلْهُ مَعِيَ رِدْءًا يُّصَدِّقُنِيْٓ ۪
اِنِّيْٓ اَخَافُ اَنْ يُّكَذِّبُوْنِ ۟

35. He said: "We will certainly
Strengthen thy arm through
Thy brother, and invest you both
With authority, so they
Shall not be able to
Touch you: with Our Signs
Shall ye triumph—you two
As well as those
Who follow you."

٣٥- قَالَ سَنَشُدُّ عَضُدَكَ بِاَخِيْكَ
وَنَجْعَلُ لَكُمَا سُلْطٰنًا
فَلَا يَصِلُوْنَ اِلَيْكُمَا ۚ بِاٰيٰتِنَا ۚ
اَنْتُمَا وَمَنِ اتَّبَعَكُمَا الْغٰلِبُوْنَ ۟

36. When Moses came to them
With Our Clear Signs, they said;
"This is nothing but sorcery
Faked up: never did we
Hear the like among our fathers
Of old!"

٣٦- فَلَمَّا جَآءَهُمْ مُّوْسٰى بِاٰيٰتِنَا بَيِّنٰتٍ قَالُوْا
مَا هٰذَآ اِلَّا سِحْرٌ مُّفْتَرًى
وَّمَا سَمِعْنَا بِهٰذَا فِيْٓ اٰبَآئِنَا الْاَوَّلِيْنَ ۟

37. Moses said: "My Lord
Knows best who it is
That comes with guidance
From Him and whose End

٣٧- وَقَالَ مُوْسٰى رَبِّيْٓ اَعْلَمُ
بِمَنْ جَآءَ بِالْهُدٰى مِنْ عِنْدِهٖ

Will be best in the Hereafter:
Certain it is that
The wrongdoers will not
            prosper."

وَمَنْ تَكُونُ لَهُ عَاقِبَةُ الدَّارِ
اِنَّهُ لَا يُفْلِحُ الظَّالِمُونَ ۟

38. Pharaoh said: "O Chiefs!
No god do I know for you
But myself: therefore,
O Hāmān! light me a (kiln
To bake bricks) out of clay,
And build me a loftly
Palace, that I may mount up
To the god of Moses:
But as far as I am concerned,
I think (Moses) is a liar!"

۳۸- وَقَالَ فِرْعَوْنُ يَأَيُّهَا الْمَلَأُ مَا عَلِمْتُ
لَكُمْ مِّنْ اِلَهٍ غَيْرِي ۚ
فَأَوْقِدْ لِي يَهَامَنُ عَلَى الطِّينِ
فَاجْعَلْ لِّي صَرْحًا لَّعَلِّي أَطَّلِعُ اِلَى اِلَهِ مُوسَى
وَاِنِّي لَأَظُنُّهُ مِنَ الْكَاذِبِينَ ۟

39. And he was arrogant and insolent
In the land, beyond reason—
He and his hosts: they thought
That they would not have
To return to Us!

۳۹- وَاسْتَكْبَرَ هُوَ وَجُنُودُهُ فِي الْأَرْضِ
بِغَيْرِ الْحَقِّ
وَظَنُّوا أَنَّهُمْ اِلَيْنَا لَا يُرْجَعُونَ ۟

40. So We seized him
And his hosts, and We
Flung them into the sea:
Now behold what was the End
Of those who did wrong!

۴۰- فَأَخَذْنَاهُ وَجُنُودَهُ فَنَبَذْنَاهُمْ فِي
الْيَمِّ ۖ
فَانْظُرْ كَيْفَ كَانَ عَاقِبَةُ الظَّالِمِينَ ۟

41. And We made them (but)
Leaders inviting to the Fire;
And on the Day of Judgement
No help shall they find.

۴۱- وَجَعَلْنَاهُمْ أَئِمَّةً يَدْعُونَ اِلَى النَّارِ ۖ
وَيَوْمَ الْقِيَامَةِ لَا يُنْصَرُونَ ۟

42. In this world We made
A Curse to follow them:
And on the Day of Judgement
They will be among
The loathed (and despised).

۴۲- وَأَتْبَعْنَاهُمْ فِي هَذِهِ الدُّنْيَا لَعْنَةً ۖ
وَيَوْمَ الْقِيَامَةِ هُمْ مِّنَ الْمَقْبُوحِينَ ۟ ع

SECTION 5.

43. We did reveal to Moses
The Book after We had
Destroyed the earlier generations,
(To give) Insight to men,
And Guidance and Mercy,
That they might receive
         admonition.

۴۳- وَلَقَدْ اَتَيْنَا مُوسَى الْكِتَابَ مِنْ بَعْدِ
مَا أَهْلَكْنَا الْقُرُونَ
الْأُولَى بَصَائِرَ لِلنَّاسِ وَهُدًى وَرَحْمَةً
لَّعَلَّهُمْ يَتَذَكَّرُونَ ۟

44. Thou wast not on the Western

۴۴- وَمَا كُنْتَ بِجَانِبِ الْغَرْبِيِّ اِذْ قَضَيْنَا

Side when We decreed
The commission to Moses,
Nor wast thou a witness
(Of those events).

إِلَى مُوسَى الْأَمْرَ وَمَا كُنْتَ مِنَ الشَّاهِدِينَ ۝

45. But We raised up (new)
Generations, and long were the
                                    ages
That passed over them;
But thou wast not a dweller
Among the people of Madyan,
Rehearsing Our Signs to them;
But it is We Who send
Messengers (with inspiration).

٤٥- وَلَكِنَّا أَنْشَأْنَا قُرُونًا فَتَطَاوَلَ عَلَيْهِمُ الْعُمُرُ ۚ وَمَا كُنْتَ ثَاوِيًا فِي أَهْلِ مَدْيَنَ تَتْلُوا عَلَيْهِمْ آيَاتِنَا وَلَكِنَّا كُنَّا مُرْسِلِينَ ۝

46. Nor wast thou at the side
Of (the Mountain of) Ṭur
When We called (to Moses).
Yet (art thou sent)
As a Mercy from thy Lord,
To give warning to a people
To whom no warner had come
Before thee: in order that
They may receive admonition.

٤٦- وَمَا كُنْتَ بِجَانِبِ الطُّورِ إِذْ نَادَيْنَا وَلَكِنْ رَحْمَةً مِّنْ رَّبِّكَ لِتُنْذِرَ قَوْمًا مَّا أَتَاهُمْ مِّنْ نَّذِيرٍ مِّنْ قَبْلِكَ لَعَلَّهُمْ يَتَذَكَّرُونَ ۝

47. If (We had) not (sent thee
To the Quraysh)—in case
A calamity should seize them
For (the deeds) that their hands
Have sent forth, they might say:
"Our Lord! why didst Thou not
Send us a messenger? We
Should then have followed
The Signs and been amongst
Those who believe!"

٤٧- وَلَوْلَا أَنْ تُصِيبَهُمْ مُصِيبَةٌ بِمَا قَدَّمَتْ أَيْدِيهِمْ فَيَقُولُوا رَبَّنَا لَوْلَا أَرْسَلْتَ إِلَيْنَا رَسُولًا فَنَتَّبِعَ آيَاتِكَ وَنَكُونَ مِنَ الْمُؤْمِنِينَ ۝

48. But (now), when the Truth
Has come to them from Ourselves,
They say, "Why are not
(Signs) sent to him, like
Those which were sent to
                              Moses?"
Do they not then reject
(The Signs) which were formerly
Sent to Moses? They say:
"Two kinds of sorcery,
Each assisting the other?"
And they say: "For us,
We reject all (such things)!"

٤٨- فَلَمَّا جَاءَهُمُ الْحَقُّ مِنْ عِنْدِنَا قَالُوا لَوْلَا أُوتِيَ مِثْلَ مَا أُوتِيَ مُوسَى ۚ أَوَلَمْ يَكْفُرُوا بِمَا أُوتِيَ مُوسَى مِنْ قَبْلُ ۖ قَالُوا سِحْرَانِ تَظَاهَرَا وَقَالُوا إِنَّا بِكُلٍّ كَافِرُونَ ۝

49. Say: "Then bring ye
A Book from Allah,
Which is a better Guide
Than either of them,
That I may follow it!"
(Do), if ye are truthful!"

50. But if they hearken not
To thee, know that they
Only follow their own lusts:
And who is more astray
Than one who follows his own
Lusts, devoid of guidance
From Allah? For Allah guides not
People given to wrongdoing.

SECTION 6.

51. Now have We caused
The Word to reach them
Themselves, in order that
They may receive admonition

52. Those to whom We sent
The Book before this—they
Do believe in this (Revelation);

53. And when it is recited
To them, they say: "We
Believe therein, for it is
The Truth from our Lord:
Indeed we have been Muslims
(Bowing to Allah's Will)
From before this.

54. Twice will they be given
Their reward, for that they
Have persevered, that they avert
Evil with Good, and that
They spend (in charity) out of
What We have given them.

55. And when they hear vain talk,
They turn away therefrom
And say: "To us our deeds,
And to you yours;
Peace be to you: we
Seek not the ignorant."

56. It is true thou wilt not
Be able to guide every one

Whom thou lovest; but Allah
Guides those whom He will
And He knows best those
Who receive guidance.

وَلَٰكِنَّ اللّٰهَ يَهْدِىْ مَنْ يَّشَآءُ ۚ
وَهُوَ أَعْلَمُ بِالْمُهْتَدِيْنَ ۝

57. They say: "If we were
To follow the guidance with thee,
We should be snatched away
From our land." Have We not
Established for them a secure
Sanctuary, to which are brought
As tribute fruits of all kinds—
A provision from Ourselves?
But most of them understand not.

٥٧ وَقَالُوْا إِنْ نَّتَّبِعِ الْهُدَى مَعَكَ
نُتَخَطَّفْ مِنْ أَرْضِنَا ۚ
أَوَلَمْ نُمَكِّنْ لَّهُمْ حَرَمًا أَمِنًا
يُّجْبَى إِلَيْهِ ثَمَرٰتُ كُلِّ شَىْءٍ رِّزْقًا مِّنْ
لَّدُنَّا وَلَٰكِنَّ أَكْثَرَهُمْ لَا يَعْلَمُوْنَ ۝

58. And how many populations
We destroyed, which exulted
In their life (of ease and plenty)!
Now those habitations of theirs,
After them, are deserted—
All but a (miserable) few!
And We are their heirs!

٥٨ وَكَمْ أَهْلَكْنَا مِنْ قَرْيَةٍ بَطِرَتْ
مَعِيْشَتَهَا ۚ
فَتِلْكَ مَسٰكِنُهُمْ لَمْ تُسْكَنْ مِّنْ بَعْدِهِمْ
إِلَّا قَلِيْلًا ۚ وَكُنَّا نَحْنُ الْوٰرِثِيْنَ ۝

59. Nor was thy Lord the one
To destroy a population until
He had sent to its Centre
A messenger, rehearsing to them
Our Signs: nor are We
Going to destroy a population
Except when its members
Practise iniquity.

٥٩ وَمَا كَانَ رَبُّكَ مُهْلِكَ الْقُرٰى
حَتّٰى يَبْعَثَ فِىْ أُمِّهَا رَسُوْلًا يَّتْلُوْا عَلَيْهِمْ
اٰيٰتِنَا ۚ وَمَا كُنَّا مُهْلِكِى الْقُرٰى
إِلَّا وَأَهْلُهَا ظٰلِمُوْنَ ۝

60. The (material) things which
Ye are given are but
The conveniences of this life
And the glitter thereof;
But that which is with Allah
Is better and more enduring:
Will ye not then be wise?

٦٠ وَمَا أُوْتِيْتُمْ مِّنْ شَىْءٍ
فَمَتَاعُ الْحَيٰوةِ الدُّنْيَا وَزِيْنَتُهَا ۚ
وَمَا عِنْدَ اللّٰهِ خَيْرٌ وَّأَبْقٰى ۚ
أَفَلَا تَعْقِلُوْنَ ۝

SECTION 7.

61. Are (these two) alike?—
One to whom We have made
A goodly promise, and who
Is going to reach its (fulfilment),
And one to whom We have
Given the good things of this
Life, but who, on the Day
Of Judgement, is to be among

٦١ أَفَمَنْ وَّعَدْنٰهُ وَعْدًا حَسَنًا
فَهُوَ لَاقِيْهِ كَمَنْ مَّتَّعْنٰهُ
مَتَاعَ الْحَيٰوةِ الدُّنْيَا
ثُمَّ هُوَ يَوْمَ الْقِيٰمَةِ

Those brought up (for
punishment)?

مِنَ الْمُحْضَرِيْنَ ۞

62. That Day (Allah) will
Call to them, and say:
"Where are My 'partners'?—
Whom ye imagined (to be such)?"

٦٢- وَيَوْمَ يُنَادِيْهِمْ فَيَقُوْلُ
اَيْنَ شُرَكَآءِيَ الَّذِيْنَ كُنْتُمْ تَزْعُمُوْنَ ۞

63. Those against whom the charge
Will be proved, will say:
"Our Lord! These are the ones
Whom we led astray:
We led them astray, as we
Were astray ourselves: we free
Ourselves (from them) in Thy
presence:
It was not us they worshipped."

٦٣- قَالَ الَّذِيْنَ حَقَّ عَلَيْهِمُ الْقَوْلُ
رَبَّنَا هٰؤُلَآءِ الَّذِيْنَ اَغْوَيْنَا ۚ
اَغْوَيْنٰهُمْ كَمَا غَوَيْنَا ۚ
تَبَرَّأْنَا اِلَيْكَ مَا كَانُوْا
اِيَّانَا يَعْبُدُوْنَ ۞

64. It will be said (to them):
"Call upon your 'partners'
(For help)": they will call
Upon them, but they will not
Listen to them; and they
Will see the Penalty (before them);
(How they will wish)
'If only they had been
Open to guidance!'

٦٤- وَقِيْلَ ادْعُوْا شُرَكَآءَكُمْ
فَدَعَوْهُمْ فَلَمْ يَسْتَجِيْبُوْا لَهُمْ
وَرَاَوُا الْعَذَابَ ۚ
لَوْ اَنَّهُمْ كَانُوْا يَهْتَدُوْنَ ۞

65. That Day (Allah) will
Call to them, and say:
"What was the answer
Ye gave to the messengers?"

٦٥- وَيَوْمَ يُنَادِيْهِمْ فَيَقُوْلُ
مَاذَا اَجَبْتُمُ الْمُرْسَلِيْنَ ۞

66. Then the (whole) story that day
Will seem obscure to them
(Like light to the blind)
And they will not be able
(Even) to question each other.

٦٦- فَعَمِيَتْ عَلَيْهِمُ الْاَنْبَآءُ يَوْمَئِذٍ
فَهُمْ لَا يَتَسَآءَلُوْنَ ۞

67. But any that (in this life)
Had repented, believed, and
worked
Righteousness, will have hopes
To be among those who
Achieve salvation.

٦٧- فَاَمَّا مَنْ تَابَ وَاٰمَنَ وَعَمِلَ صَالِحًا
فَعَسٰى اَنْ يَّكُوْنَ
مِنَ الْمُفْلِحِيْنَ ۞

68. Thy Lord does create and
choose
As He pleases: no choice

٦٨- وَرَبُّكَ يَخْلُقُ مَا يَشَآءُ وَيَخْتَارُ ۚ
مَا كَانَ لَهُمُ الْخِيَرَةُ ۚ

Have they (in the matter):
Glory to Allah! and far
Is He above the partners
They ascribe (to Him)!

سُبْحٰنَ اللهِ وَتَعٰلٰى عَمَّا يُشْرِكُوْنَ ۝

69. And thy Lord knows all
That their hearts conceal
And all that they reveal.

٦٩ ـ وَرَبُّكَ يَعْلَمُ مَا تُكِنُّ صُدُوْرُهُمْ وَمَا يُعْلِنُوْنَ ۝

70. And He is Allah: there is
No god but He. To Him
Be praise, at the first
And at the last:
For Him is the Command,
And to Him shall ye
(All) be brought back.

٧٠ ـ وَهُوَ اللهُ لَآ اِلٰهَ اِلَّا هُوَ لَهُ الْحَمْدُ فِى الْاُوْلٰى وَالْاٰخِرَةِ وَلَهُ الْحُكْمُ وَاِلَيْهِ تُرْجَعُوْنَ ۝

71. Say: See ye? If Allah
Were to make the Night
Perpetual over you to the Day
Of Judgement, what god
Is there other than Allah,
Who can give you enlightenment?
Will ye not then hearken?

٧١ ـ قُلْ اَرَءَيْتُمْ اِنْ جَعَلَ اللهُ عَلَيْكُمُ الَّيْلَ سَرْمَدًا اِلٰى يَوْمِ الْقِيٰمَةِ مَنْ اِلٰهٌ غَيْرُ اللهِ يَأْتِيْكُمْ بِضِيَآءٍ اَفَلَا تَسْمَعُوْنَ ۝

72. Say: See ye: If Allah
Were to make the Day
Perpetual over you to the Day
Of Judgement, what god
Is there other than Allah
Who can give you a Night
In which ye can rest?
Will ye not then see?

٧٢ ـ قُلْ اَرَءَيْتُمْ اِنْ جَعَلَ اللهُ عَلَيْكُمُ النَّهَارَ سَرْمَدًا اِلٰى يَوْمِ الْقِيٰمَةِ مَنْ اِلٰهٌ غَيْرُ اللهِ يَأْتِيْكُمْ بِلَيْلٍ تَسْكُنُوْنَ فِيْهِ اَفَلَا تُبْصِرُوْنَ ۝

73. It is out of His Mercy
That He has made for you
Night and Day—that ye
May rest therein, and that
Ye may seek of His Grace—
And in order that ye
May be grateful.

٧٣ ـ وَمِنْ رَّحْمَتِهٖ جَعَلَ لَكُمُ الَّيْلَ وَالنَّهَارَ لِتَسْكُنُوْا فِيْهِ وَلِتَبْتَغُوْا مِنْ فَضْلِهٖ وَلَعَلَّكُمْ تَشْكُرُوْنَ ۝

74. The Day that He will³⁴⁰¹
Call on them, He will say:
"Where are my partners?
Whom ye imagined (to be such)?"

٧٤ ـ وَيَوْمَ يُنَادِيْهِمْ فَيَقُوْلُ اَيْنَ شُرَكَآءِىَ الَّذِيْنَ كُنْتُمْ تَزْعُمُوْنَ ۝

75. And from each people

٧٥ ـ وَنَزَعْنَا مِنْ كُلِّ اُمَّةٍ شَهِيْدًا

Shall We draw a witness,
And We shall say: "Produce
Your Proof": then shall they
Know that the Truth is in
Allah (alone), and the (lies)
Which they invented will
Leave them in the lurch.

SECTION 8.

76. Qārūn was doubtless,
Of the people of Moses; but
He acted insolently towards them:
Such were the treasures We
Had bestowed on him, that
Their very keys would
Have been a burden to
A body of strong men:
Behold, his people said to him:
"Exult not, for Allah loveth not
Those who exult (in riches).

77. "But seek, with the (wealth)
Which Allah has bestowed on
thee,
The Home of the Hereafter,
Nor forget thy portion in this
World: but do thou good,
As Allah has been good
To thee, and seek not
(Occasions for) mischief in the
land:
For Allah loves not those
Who do mischief."

78. He said: "This has been given
To me because of a certain
Knowledge which I have."
Did he not know that Allah
Had destroyed, before him
(Whole) generations—which were
Superior to him in strength
And greater in amount
(Of riches) they had collected?
But the wicked are not
Called (immediately) to
account
For their sins.

79. So he went forth among

His people in the (pride
Of his worldly) glitter.
Said those whose aim is
The Life of this World:
"Oh! that we had the like
Of what Qārūn has got!
For he is truly a lord
Of mighty good fortune!"

قَالَ الَّذِيْنَ يُرِيْدُوْنَ
الْحَيٰوةَ الدُّنْيَا يٰلَيْتَ لَنَا مِثْلَ مَآ اُوْتِيَ
قَارُوْنُ ۙ اِنَّهٗ لَذُوْ حَظٍّ عَظِيْمٍ ۞

80. But those who had been granted
(True) knowledge said: "Alas
For you! The reward of Allah
(In the Hereafter) is best
For those who believe
And work righteousness: but this
None shall attain, save those
Who steadfastly presevere
                                (in good)."

٨٠- وَقَالَ الَّذِيْنَ اُوْتُوا الْعِلْمَ
وَيْلَكُمْ ثَوَابُ اللهِ خَيْرٌ
لِّمَنْ اٰمَنَ وَعَمِلَ صَالِحًا ۚ
وَلَا يُلَقّٰهَآ اِلَّا الصّٰبِرُوْنَ ۞

81. Then We caused the earth
To swallow him up and
His house; and he had not
(The least little) party
To help him against Allah,
Nor could he defend himself.

٨١- فَخَسَفْنَا بِهٖ وَبِدَارِهِ الْاَرْضَ ۖ
فَمَا كَانَ لَهٗ مِنْ فِئَةٍ يَّنْصُرُوْنَهٗ مِنْ دُوْنِ
اللهِ ۖ وَمَا كَانَ مِنَ الْمُنْتَصِرِيْنَ ۞

82. And those who had envied
His position the day before
Began to say on the morrow:
"Ah! It is indeed Allah
Who enlarges the provision
Or restricts it, to any
Of His servants He pleases!
Had it not been that Allah
Was gracious to us, He
Could have caused the earth
To swallow us up! Ah!
Those who reject Allah
Will assuredly never prosper."
                SECTION 9.

٨٢- وَاَصْبَحَ الَّذِيْنَ تَمَنَّوْا مَكَانَهٗ
بِالْاَمْسِ يَقُوْلُوْنَ
وَيْكَاَنَّ اللهَ يَبْسُطُ الرِّزْقَ لِمَنْ يَّشَآءُ
مِنْ عِبَادِهٖ وَيَقْدِرُ ۚ
لَوْلَآ اَنْ مَّنَّ اللهُ
عَلَيْنَا لَخَسَفَ بِنَا ۖ
وَيْكَاَنَّهٗ لَا يُفْلِحُ الْكٰفِرُوْنَ ۞ ۏ

83. That House of the Hereafter
We shall give to those
Who intend not high-handedness
Or mischief on earth:
And the End is (best)
For the righteous.

٨٣- تِلْكَ الدَّارُ الْاٰخِرَةُ نَجْعَلُهَا لِلَّذِيْنَ لَا
يُرِيْدُوْنَ عُلُوًّا فِي الْاَرْضِ وَلَا فَسَادًا ۚ
وَالْعَاقِبَةُ لِلْمُتَّقِيْنَ ۞

84. If any does good, the reward
To him is better than

٨٤- مَنْ جَآءَ بِالْحَسَنَةِ فَلَهٗ خَيْرٌ مِّنْهَا ۚ

His deed; but if any
Does evil, the doers of evil
Are only punished (to the extent)
Of their deeds.

وَمَنْ جَاءَ بِالسَّيِّئَةِ فَلَا يُجْزَى الَّذِينَ
عَمِلُوا السَّيِّئَاتِ إِلَّا مَا كَانُوا يَعْمَلُونَ ۝

85. Verily He Who ordained
The Qur'ān for thee, will bring
Thee back to the Place
Of Return. Say: "My Lord
Knows best who it is
That brings true guidance.
And who is in manifest error."

٨٥ـ إِنَّ الَّذِي فَرَضَ عَلَيْكَ الْقُرْآنَ
لَرَادُّكَ إِلَى مَعَادٍ
قُلْ رَبِّي أَعْلَمُ مَنْ جَاءَ
بِالْهُدَى وَمَنْ هُوَ فِي ضَلَالٍ مُبِينٍ ۝

86. And thou hadst not expected
That the Book would be
Sent to thee except as
A Mercy from thy Lord:
Therefore lend not thou support
In any way to those
Who reject (Allah's Message).

٨٦ـ وَمَا كُنْتَ تَرْجُو
أَنْ يُلْقَى إِلَيْكَ الْكِتَابُ
إِلَّا رَحْمَةً مِنْ رَبِّكَ
فَلَا تَكُونَنَّ ظَهِيرًا لِلْكَافِرِينَ ۝

87. And let nothing keep thee
Back from the Signs of Allah
After they have been revealed
To thee: and invite (men)
To thy Lord, and be not
Of the company of those
Who join gods with Allah.

٨٧ـ وَلَا يَصُدُّنَّكَ عَنْ آيَاتِ اللهِ
بَعْدَ إِذْ أُنْزِلَتْ إِلَيْكَ
وَادْعُ إِلَى رَبِّكَ
وَلَا تَكُونَنَّ مِنَ الْمُشْرِكِينَ ۝

88. And call not, besides Allah,
On another god. There is
No god but He. Everything
(That exists) will perish
Except His own Face.
To Him belongs the Command,
And to Him will ye
(All) be brought back.

٨٨ـ وَلَا تَدْعُ مَعَ اللهِ إِلَهًا آخَرَ
لَا إِلَهَ إِلَّا هُوَ
كُلُّ شَيْءٍ هَالِكٌ إِلَّا وَجْهَهُ
لَهُ الْحُكْمُ وَإِلَيْهِ تُرْجَعُونَ ۝

INTRODUCTION TO SŪRA XXIX. (*Ankabūt*) — 69 Verses

This Sūra is the last of the series begun with S. xvii. in which the growth of the spiritual man as an individual is considered, especially illustrated by the way in which the great apostles were prepared for their work and received their mission, and the nature of Revelation in relation to the environments in which it was promulgated. (See Introduction to S. xvii.) It also closes the sub-series beginning with S. xxvi. which is concerned with the spiritual Light, and the reactions to it at certain periods of spiritual history. (See Introduction to S. xxvi.)

The last Sūra closed with a reference to the doctrine of the *Ma'ad*, or final Return of man to God. This theme is further developed here, and as it is continued in the subsequent three Suras all bearing the Abbreviated Letters A.L.M., it forms a connecting link between the present series and those three Sūras.

In particular, emphasis is laid here on the necessity of linking actual conduct with the reception of God's revelation, and reference is again made to the stories of Noah, Abraham, and Lot among the apostles, and the stories of Midian, 'Ād, Thamūd, and Pharaoh among the rejecters of God's Message. This world's life is contrasted with the real Life of the Hereafter.

Chronologically the main Sūra belongs to the late Middle Meccan period, but the chronology has no significance except as showing how clearly the vision of the Future was revealed long before the Hijrat, to the struggling Brotherhood of Islam.

Al 'Ankabūt (The Spider)

In the name of Allah, Most Gracious Most Merciful.

بِسْمِ اللهِ الرَّحْمٰنِ الرَّحِيمِ

1. 𝕬lif 𝕷ām 𝕸īm.

الٓمّٓ ۚ -١

2. 𝕯o men think that
They will be left alone
On saying, "We believe",
And that they will not
Be tested?

٢- اَحَسِبَ النَّاسُ اَنْ يُّتْرَكُوْۤا اَنْ يَّقُوْلُوْۤا اٰمَنَّا وَهُمْ لَا يُفْتَنُوْنَ ۟

3. We did test those
Before them, and Allah will
Certainly know   those who are
True from those who are false.

٣- وَلَقَدْ فَتَنَّا الَّذِيْنَ مِنْ قَبْلِهِمْ فَلَيَعْلَمَنَّ اللهُ الَّذِيْنَ صَدَقُوْا وَلَيَعْلَمَنَّ الْكٰذِبِيْنَ ۟

4. Do those who practise
Evil think that they

٤- اَمْ حَسِبَ الَّذِيْنَ يَعْمَلُوْنَ السَّيِّاٰتِ

Will get the better of Us?
Evil is their judgement!

أَن يَسْبِقُونَا سَآءَ مَا يَحْكُمُونَ ۝

5. For those whose hopes are
In the meeting with Allah
(In the Hereafter, let them strive);
For the Term (appointed)
By Allah is surely coming:
And He hears and knows
(All things).

٥- مَن كَانَ يَرْجُوا لِقَآءَ اللهِ
فَإِنَّ أَجَلَ
اللهِ لَآتٍ ۚ وَهُوَ السَّمِيعُ الْعَلِيمُ ۝

6. And if any strive (with might
And main), they do so
For their own souls:
For Allah is free of all
Needs from all creation.

٦- وَمَن جَاهَدَ فَإِنَّمَا يُجَاهِدُ لِنَفْسِهِ
إِنَّ اللهَ لَغَنِيٌّ عَنِ الْعَٰلَمِينَ ۝

7. Those who believe and work
Righteous deeds—from them
Shall We blot out all evil
(That may be) in them,
And We shall reward
Them according to
The best of their deeds.

٧- وَالَّذِينَ آمَنُوا وَعَمِلُوا الصَّٰلِحَٰتِ
لَنُكَفِّرَنَّ عَنْهُمْ سَيِّـَٔاتِهِمْ
وَلَنَجْزِيَنَّهُمْ أَحْسَنَ الَّذِي كَانُوا
يَعْمَلُونَ ۝

8. We have enjoined on man
Kindness to parents: but if
They (either of them) strive
(To force) thee to join
With Me (in worship)
Anything of which thou hast
No knowledge,   obey them not.
Ye have (all) to return
To Me, and I will
Tell you (the truth)
Of all that ye did.

٨- وَوَصَّيْنَا الْإِنسَانَ بِوَالِدَيْهِ حُسْنًا ۖ
وَإِن جَاهَدَاكَ لِتُشْرِكَ بِي
مَا لَيْسَ لَكَ بِهِ عِلْمٌ فَلَا تُطِعْهُمَا ۚ
إِلَيَّ مَرْجِعُكُمْ
فَأُنَبِّئُكُم بِمَا كُنتُمْ تَعْمَلُونَ ۝

9. And those who believe
And work righteous deeds—
Them shall We admit
To the company of the
Righteous.

٩- وَالَّذِينَ آمَنُوا وَعَمِلُوا الصَّٰلِحَٰتِ
لَنُدْخِلَنَّهُمْ فِي الصَّٰلِحِينَ ۝

10. Then there are among men
Such as say: "We believe
In Allah"; but when they suffer
Affliction in (the cause of) Allah,
They treat men's oppression
As if it were the Wrath

١٠- وَمِنَ النَّاسِ مَن يَقُولُ آمَنَّا
بِاللهِ فَإِذَا أُوذِيَ فِي اللهِ
جَعَلَ فِتْنَةَ النَّاسِ كَعَذَابِ اللهِ

Of Allah! And if help
Comes (to thee) from thy Lord,
They are sure to say,
"We have (always) been
With you!" Does not Allah
Know best all that is
In the hearts of all Creation?!

وَلَئِنْ جَآءَ نَصْرٌ مِّنْ رَّبِّكَ
لَيَقُوْلُنَّ اِنَّا كُنَّا مَعَكُمْ
اَوَلَيْسَ اللّٰهُ بِاَعْلَمَ بِمَا فِیْ صُدُوْرِ
الْعٰلَمِیْنَ ۟

11. And Allah most certainly knows
Those who believe, and as
                    certainly
Those who are Hypocrites.

۱۱- وَلَيَعْلَمَنَّ اللّٰهُ الَّذِیْنَ اٰمَنُوْا
وَلَيَعْلَمَنَّ الْمُنٰفِقِیْنَ ۟

12. And the Unbelievers say
To those who believe:
"Follow our path, and we
Will bear (the consequences)
Of your faults." Never
In the least will they
Bear their faults: in fact
They are liars!

۱۲- وَقَالَ الَّذِیْنَ كَفَرُوْا لِلَّذِیْنَ اٰمَنُوا
اتَّبِعُوْا سَبِیْلَنَا وَلْنَحْمِلْ خَطٰیٰكُمْ
وَمَاهُمْ بِحٰمِلِیْنَ مِنْ خَطٰیٰهُمْ مِّنْ شَیْءٍ
اِنَّهُمْ لَكٰذِبُوْنَ ۟

13. They will bear their own
Burdens, and (other) burdens
Along with their own,
And on the Day of Judgement
They will be called to account
For their falsehoods.

SECTION 2.

۱۳- وَلَيَحْمِلُنَّ اَثْقَالَهُمْ
وَاَثْقَالًا مَّعَ اَثْقَالِهِمْ وَلَيُسْئَلُنَّ یَوْمَ
الْقِیٰمَةِ عَمَّا كَانُوْا يَفْتَرُوْنَ ۟

14. We (once) sent Noah
To his people, and he tarried
Among them a thousand years
Less fifty: but the Deluge
Overwhelmed them while they
(Persisted in) sin.

۱۴- وَلَقَدْ اَرْسَلْنَا نُوْحًا اِلٰى قَوْمِهٖ فَلَبِثَ
فِیْهِمْ اَلْفَ سَنَةٍ اِلَّا خَمْسِیْنَ عَامًا
فَاَخَذَهُمُ الطُّوْفَانُ وَهُمْ ظٰلِمُوْنَ ۟

15. But We saved him
And the Companions
Of the Ark, and We made
The (Ark) a Sign
For all Peoples!

۱۵- فَاَنْجَيْنٰهُ وَاَصْحٰبَ السَّفِیْنَةِ
وَجَعَلْنٰهَا اٰیَةً لِّلْعٰلَمِیْنَ ۟

16. And (We also saved)
Abraham: behold, he said
To his people: "Serve Allah
And fear Him: that
Will be best for you—
If ye understand!

۱۶- وَاِبْرٰهِیْمَ اِذْ قَالَ
لِقَوْمِهِ اعْبُدُوا اللّٰهَ وَاتَّقُوْهُ
ذٰلِكُمْ خَیْرٌ لَّكُمْ اِنْ كُنْتُمْ تَعْلَمُوْنَ ۟

17. "For ye do worship idols
Besides Allah, and ye invent
Falsehood. The things that ye
Worship besides Allah have
No power to give you sustenance:
Then seek ye sustenance
From Allah, serve Him,
And be grateful to Him:
To Him will be your return.

18. "And if ye reject (the Message),
So did generations before you:
And the duty of the messenger
Is only to preach publicly
(And clearly)."

19. See they not how Allah
Originates creation, then
Repeats it: truly that
Is easy for Allah.

20. Say: "Travel through the earth
And see how Allah did
Originate creation; so will
Allah produce a later creation:
For Allah has power
Over all things.

21. "He punishes whom He pleases,
And He grants mercy to whom
He pleases, and towards Him
Are ye turned.

22. "Not on earth nor in heaven
Will ye be able (fleeing)
To frustrate (His Plan),
Nor have ye, besides Allah,
Any protector or helper."

SECTION 3.

23. Those who reject the Signs
Of Allah and the Meeting
With Him (in the Hereafter)—
It is they who shall despair
Of My mercy: it is they
Who will (suffer)
A most grievous Penalty.

24. So naught was the answer
Of (Abraham's) people except
That they said: "Slay him
Or burn him." But Allah
Did save him from the Fire.
Verily in this are Signs
For people who believe.

٢٤ـ فَمَا كَانَ جَوَابَ قَوْمِهِ إِلَّا
أَنْ قَالُوا اقْتُلُوهُ أَوْ حَرِّقُوهُ
فَأَنْجَاهُ اللهُ مِنَ النَّارِ
إِنَّ فِي ذَلِكَ لَآيَاتٍ لِقَوْمٍ يُؤْمِنُونَ ۝

25. And he said: "For you,
Ye have taken (for worship)
Idols besides Allah, out of
Mutual love and regard
Between yourselves in this life;
But on the Day of Judgement
Ye shall disown each other
And curse each other:
And your abode will be
The Fire, and ye shall have
None to help."

٢٥ـ وَقَالَ إِنَّمَا اتَّخَذْتُمْ
مِنْ دُونِ اللهِ أَوْثَانًا مَوَدَّةَ
بَيْنِكُمْ فِي الْحَيَاةِ الدُّنْيَا
ثُمَّ يَوْمَ الْقِيَامَةِ يَكْفُرُ بَعْضُكُمْ بِبَعْضٍ
وَيَلْعَنُ بَعْضُكُمْ بَعْضًا وَمَأْوَاكُمُ
النَّارُ وَمَا لَكُمْ مِنْ نَاصِرِينَ ۝

26. But Lūt had faith in him:
He said: "I will leave
Home for the sake of
My Lord: for He is
Exalted in Might, and Wise."

٢٦ـ فَآمَنَ لَهُ لُوطٌ وَقَالَ إِنِّي
مُهَاجِرٌ إِلَى رَبِّي
إِنَّهُ هُوَ الْعَزِيزُ الْحَكِيمُ ۝

27. And We gave (Abraham)
Isaac and Jacob, and ordained
Among his progeny
            Prophethood
And Revelation, and We
Granted him his reward
In this life; and he was
In the Hereafter (of the company)
Of the Righteous.

٢٧ـ وَوَهَبْنَا لَهُ إِسْحَاقَ وَيَعْقُوبَ وَجَعَلْنَا
فِي ذُرِّيَّتِهِ النُّبُوَّةَ وَالْكِتَابَ
وَآتَيْنَاهُ أَجْرَهُ فِي الدُّنْيَا
وَإِنَّهُ فِي الْآخِرَةِ لَمِنَ الصَّالِحِينَ ۝

28. And (remember) Lūt: behold,
He said to his people:
"Ye do commit lewdness,
Such as no people in Creation
(Ever) committed before you.

٢٨ـ وَلُوطًا إِذْ قَالَ لِقَوْمِهِ
إِنَّكُمْ لَتَأْتُونَ الْفَاحِشَةَ
مَا سَبَقَكُمْ بِهَا مِنْ أَحَدٍ مِنَ الْعَالَمِينَ ۝

29. "Do ye indeed approach men,
And cut off the highway?—
And practise wickedness
(Even) in your councils?"

٢٩ـ أَئِنَّكُمْ لَتَأْتُونَ الرِّجَالَ وَتَقْطَعُونَ
السَّبِيلَ وَتَأْتُونَ فِي نَادِيكُمُ الْمُنْكَرَ

But his people gave no answer
But this: they said:
"Bring us the Wrath of Allah
If thou tellest the truth."

30. He said: "O my Lord!
Help Thou me against people
Who do mischief!"

SECTION 4.

31. When Our Messengers came
To Abraham with the good
news,
They said: "We are indeed
Going to destroy the people
Of this township: for truly
They are (addicted to) crime."

32. He said: "But there is
Lūṭ there." They said:
"Well do we know who
Is there: we will certainly
Save him and his following—
Except his wife: she is
Of those who lag behind!"

33. And when Our Messengers
Came to Lūṭ, he was
Grieved on their account,
And felt himself powerless
(To protect) them: but they said:
"Fear thou not, nor grieve:
We are (here) to save thee
And thy following, except
Thy wife: she is
Of those who lag behind.

34. "For we are going to
Bring down on the people
Of this township a Punishment
From heaven, because they
Have been wickedly rebellious."

35. And We have left thereof
An evident Sign,
For any people who
(Care to) understand.

36. To the Madyan (people)
(We sent) their brother Shu'ayb.

Then he said: "O my people!
Serve Allah, and fear the Last
Day: nor commit evil
On the earth, with intent
To do mischief."

37. But they rejected him:
Then the mighty Blast
Seized them, and they lay
Prostrate in their homes
By the morning.

38. (Remember also) the 'Ād
And the Thamūd (people):
Clearly will appear to you
From (the traces) of their buildings
(Their fate): the Evil One
Made their deeds alluring
To them, and kept them back
From the Path, though they
Were gifted with Intelligence
And Skill.

39. (Remember also) Qārūn,
Pharaoh, and Hāmān: there came
To them Moses with Clear Signs,
But they behaved with insolence
On the earth; yet they
Could not overreach (Us).

40. Each one of them We seized
For his crime: of them,
Against some We sent
A violent tornado (with showers
Of stones); some were caught
By a (mighty) Blast;   some
We caused the earth
To swallow up; and some
We drowned (in the waters):
It was not Allah Who
Injured (or oppressed) them:
They injured (and oppressed)
Their own souls.

41. The parable of those who
Take protectors other than Allah
Is that of the Spider,
Who builds (to itself)
A house; but truly

فَقَالَ يٰقَوْمِ اعْبُدُوا اللّٰهَ وَ ارْجُوا الْيَوْمَ
الْاٰخِرَ وَ لَا تَعْثَوْا فِى الْاَرْضِ مُفْسِدِيْنَ ۟

٣٧- فَكَذَّبُوْهُ فَاَخَذَتْهُمُ الرَّجْفَةُ
فَاَصْبَحُوْا فِىْ دَارِهِمْ جٰثِمِيْنَ ۟

٣٨- وَ عَادًا وَّ ثَمُوْدَا ۫
وَ قَدْ تَّبَيَّنَ لَكُمْ مِّنْ مَّسٰكِنِهِمْ ۫ۖ
وَ زَيَّنَ لَهُمُ الشَّيْطٰنُ اَعْمَالَهُمْ
فَصَدَّهُمْ عَنِ السَّبِيْلِ
وَ كَانُوْا مُسْتَبْصِرِيْنَ ۟

٣٩- وَ قَارُوْنَ وَ فِرْعَوْنَ وَ هَامٰنَ ۫ۖ
وَ لَقَدْ جَآءَهُمْ مُّوْسٰى بِالْبَيِّنٰتِ
فَاسْتَكْبَرُوْا فِى الْاَرْضِ وَ مَا كَانُوْا سٰبِقِيْنَ ۙ

٤٠- فَكُلًّا اَخَذْنَا بِذَنْۢبِهٖ ۚ
فَمِنْهُمْ مَّنْ اَرْسَلْنَا عَلَيْهِ حَاصِبًا ۚ
وَ مِنْهُمْ مَّنْ اَخَذَتْهُ الصَّيْحَةُ ۚ
وَ مِنْهُمْ مَّنْ خَسَفْنَا بِهِ الْاَرْضَ ۚ
وَ مِنْهُمْ مَّنْ اَغْرَقْنَا ۚ
وَ مَا كَانَ اللّٰهُ لِيَظْلِمَهُمْ
وَ لٰكِنْ كَانُوْا اَنْفُسَهُمْ يَظْلِمُوْنَ ۟

٤١- مَثَلُ الَّذِيْنَ اتَّخَذُوْا مِنْ دُوْنِ اللّٰهِ
اَوْلِيَآءَ كَمَثَلِ الْعَنْكَبُوْتِ ۚ اِتَّخَذَتْ
بَيْتًا ۭ وَ اِنَّ اَوْهَنَ الْبُيُوْتِ

The flimsiest of houses
Is the Spider's house—
If they but knew.

42. Verily Allah doth know
Of (every thing) whatever
That they call upon
Besides Him: and He is
Exalted (in power), Wise.

43. And such are the Parables
We set forth for mankind,
But only those understand them
Who have Knowledge.

44. Allah created the heavens
And the earth in true
           (proportions):³⁴⁷⁰
Verily in that is a Sign
For those who believe.

SECTION 5.

45. Recite what is sent
Of the Book by inspiration
To thee, and establish
Regular Prayer: for Prayer
Restrains from shameful
And unjust deeds;
And remembrance of Allah
Is the greatest (thing in life)
Without doubt. And Allah knows
The (deeds) that ye do.

46. And dispute ye not
With the People of the Book,
Except with means better
(Than mere disputation), unless
It be with those of them

Who inflict wrong (and injury);
But say, "We believe
In the Revelation which has
Come down to us and in that
Which came down to you;
Our God and your God
Is One; and it is to Him
We bow (in Islam)."

47. And thus   (it is) that We
    Have sent down the Book
    To thee. So the People
    Of the Book believe therein,
    As also do some of these
    (Pagan Arabs): and none
    But Unbelievers reject Our Signs.

٤٧- وَكَذٰلِكَ اَنْزَلْنَاۤ اِلَيْكَ الْكِتٰبَ ۚ
فَالَّذِيْنَ اٰتَيْنٰهُمُ الْكِتٰبَ يُؤْمِنُوْنَ بِهٖ ۚ
وَمِنْ هٰؤُلَاءِ مَنْ يُّؤْمِنُ بِهٖ ۚ
وَمَا يَجْحَدُ بِاٰيٰتِنَاۤ اِلَّا الْكٰفِرُوْنَ ۟

48. And thou wast not (able)
    To recite a Book before
    This (Book came), nor art thou
    (Able) to transcribe it
    With thy right hand:
    In that case, indeed, would
    The talkers of vanities
    Have doubted.

٤٨- وَمَا كُنْتَ تَتْلُوْا مِنْ قَبْلِهٖ مِنْ
كِتٰبٍ وَّلَا تَخُطُّهٗ
بِيَمِيْنِكَ
اِذًا لَّارْتَابَ الْمُبْطِلُوْنَ ۟

49. Nay, here are Signs
    Self-evident in the hearts
    Of those endowed with
                      knowledge:
    And none but the unjust
    Reject Our Signs.

٤٩- بَلْ هُوَ اٰيٰتٌۢ بَيِّنٰتٌ فِيْ صُدُوْرِ
الَّذِيْنَ اُوْتُوا الْعِلْمَ ۚ
وَمَا يَجْحَدُ بِاٰيٰتِنَاۤ اِلَّا الظّٰلِمُوْنَ ۟

50. Yet they say: "Why
    Are not Signs sent down
    To him from his Lord?"
    Say: "The Signs are indeed
    With Allah: and I am
    Indeed a clear Warner."

٥٠- وَقَالُوْا لَوْلَاۤ اُنْزِلَ عَلَيْهِ اٰيٰتٌ مِّنْ
رَّبِّهٖ ۚ قُلْ اِنَّمَا الْاٰيٰتُ عِنْدَ اللّٰهِ ۚ
وَاِنَّمَاۤ اَنَا نَذِيْرٌ مُّبِيْنٌ ۟

51. And is it not enough
    For them that We have
    Sent down to thee
    The Book which is rehearsed
    To them? Verily, in it
    Is Mercy and a Reminder
    To those who believe.
              SECTION 6.

٥١- اَوَلَمْ يَكْفِهِمْ اَنَّاۤ
اَنْزَلْنَا عَلَيْكَ الْكِتٰبَ يُتْلٰى عَلَيْهِمْ ۚ
اِنَّ فِيْ ذٰلِكَ لَرَحْمَةً وَّذِكْرٰى
لِقَوْمٍ يُّؤْمِنُوْنَ ۟ ع

52. Say: "Enough is Allah
    For a Witness between me
    And you: He knows
    What is in the heavens
    And on earth. And it is
    Those who believe in vanities
    And reject Allah, that

٥٢- قُلْ كَفٰى بِاللّٰهِ بَيْنِيْ
وَبَيْنَكُمْ شَهِيْدًا ۚ يَعْلَمُ مَا فِي السَّمٰوٰتِ وَ
الْاَرْضِ ۚ وَالَّذِيْنَ اٰمَنُوْا بِالْبَاطِلِ وَكَفَرُوْا
بِاللّٰهِ ۙ اُولٰٓئِكَ

Will perish (in the end).

هُمُ الخٰسِرُوْنَ ○

53. They ask thee
To hasten on the Punishment
(For them): had it not been
For a term (of respite)
Appointed, the Punishment
Would certainly have come
To them: and it will
Certainly reach them—
Of a sudden, while they
Perceive not!

٥٣ ۔ وَيَسْتَعْجِلُوْنَكَ بِالْعَذَابِ ۚ
وَلَوْلَاۤ اَجَلٌ مُّسَمًّى
لَّجَآءَهُمُ الْعَذَابُ ۚ
وَلَيَأْتِيَنَّهُمْ بَغْتَةً
وَّهُمْ لَا يَشْعُرُوْنَ ○

54. They ask thee
To hasten on the Punishment:
But, of a surety,
Hell will encompass
The rejecters of Faith!—

٥٤ ۔ يَسْتَعْجِلُوْنَكَ بِالْعَذَابِ ۚ
وَاِنَّ جَهَنَّمَ لَمُحِيْطَةٌ بِالْكٰفِرِيْنَ ۙ○

55. On the Day that
The Punishment shall cover them
From above them and
From below them,
And (a Voice) shall say:
"Taste ye (the fruits)
Of your deeds!"

٥٥ ۔ يَوْمَ يَغْشٰهُمُ الْعَذَابُ
مِنْ فَوْقِهِمْ وَمِنْ تَحْتِ اَرْجُلِهِمْ
وَيَقُوْلُ ذُوْقُوْا مَا كُنْتُمْ تَعْمَلُوْنَ ○

56. O My servants who believe!
Truly, spacious is My Earth:
Therefore serve ye Me—
(And Me alone)!

٥٦ ۔ يٰعِبَادِيَ الَّذِيْنَ اٰمَنُوْۤا اِنَّ اَرْضِىْ
وَاسِعَةٌ فَاِيَّايَ فَاعْبُدُوْنِ ○

57. Every soul shall have
A taste of death:
In the end to Us
Shall ye be brought back.

٥٧ ۔ كُلُّ نَفْسٍ ذَآئِقَةُ الْمَوْتِ ۖ
ثُمَّ اِلَيْنَا تُرْجَعُوْنَ ○

58. But those who believe
And work deeds of righteousness—
To them shall We give
A Home in Heaven—
Lofty mansions beneath which
Flow rivers—to dwell therein
For aye—an excellent reward
For those who do (good)!—

٥٨ ۔ وَالَّذِيْنَ اٰمَنُوْا وَعَمِلُوا الصّٰلِحٰتِ
لَنُبَوِّئَنَّهُمْ مِّنَ الْجَنَّةِ غُرَفًا
تَجْرِىْ مِنْ تَحْتِهَا الْاَنْهٰرُ خٰلِدِيْنَ فِيْهَا ۚ
نِعْمَ اَجْرُ الْعٰمِلِيْنَ ۙ

59. Those who persevere in patience,
And put their trust
In their Lord and Cherisher,

٥٩ ۔ الَّذِيْنَ صَبَرُوْا
وَعَلٰى رَبِّهِمْ يَتَوَكَّلُوْنَ ○

60. How many are the creatures
That carry not their own
Sustenance? It is Allah
Who feeds (both) them and you,
For He hears and knows
(All things).

٦٠- وَكَأَيِّنْ مِّنْ دَآبَّةٍ لَّا تَحْمِلُ
رِزْقَهَا اللّٰهُ يَرْزُقُهَا وَاِيَّاكُمْ ۖ
وَهُوَ السَّمِيْعُ الْعَلِيْمُ ۞

61. If indeed thou ask them
Who has created the heavens
And the earth and subjected
The sun and the moon
(To His Law), they will
Certainly reply, "Allah".
How are they then deluded
Away (from the truth)?

٦١- وَلَئِنْ سَاَلْتَهُمْ مَّنْ خَلَقَ السَّمٰوٰتِ
وَالْاَرْضَ وَسَخَّرَ الشَّمْسَ وَالْقَمَرَ
لَيَقُوْلُنَّ اللّٰهُ ۖ
فَاَنّٰى يُؤْفَكُوْنَ ۞

62. Allah enlarges the sustenance
(Which He gives) to whichever
Of His servants He pleases:
And He (similarly) grants
By (strict) measure, (as He
            pleases):
For Allah has full knowledge
Of all things.

٦٢- اَللّٰهُ يَبْسُطُ الرِّزْقَ
لِمَنْ يَّشَآءُ مِنْ عِبَادِهٖ
وَيَقْدِرُ لَهٗ ۖ
اِنَّ اللّٰهَ بِكُلِّ شَيْءٍ عَلِيْمٌ ۞

63. And if indeed thou ask them
Who it is that sends down
Rain from the sky,
And gives life therewith
To the earth after its death,
They will certainly reply,
"Allah!" Say, "Praise be
To Allah!" but most
Of them understand not.

٦٣- وَلَئِنْ سَاَلْتَهُمْ مَّنْ نَّزَّلَ مِنَ السَّمَآءِ
مَآءً فَاَحْيَا بِهِ الْاَرْضَ مِنْ بَعْدِ مَوْتِهَا
لَيَقُوْلُنَّ اللّٰهُ ۚ قُلِ الْحَمْدُ لِلّٰهِ ۚ
بَلْ اَكْثَرُهُمْ لَا يَعْقِلُوْنَ ۞

SECTION 7.

64. What is the life of this world
But amusement and play?
But verily the Home
In the Hereafter—that is
Life indeed, if they but knew.

٦٤- وَمَا هٰذِهِ الْحَيٰوةُ الدُّنْيَا اِلَّا لَهْوٌ وَّ
لَعِبٌ ۗ وَاِنَّ الدَّارَ الْاٰخِرَةَ لَهِيَ الْحَيَوَانُ ۘ
لَوْ كَانُوْا يَعْلَمُوْنَ ۞

65. Now, if they embark
On a boat, they call
On Allah, making their devotion
Sincerely (and exclusively) to
            Him;
But when He has delivered
Them safely to (dry) land,

٦٥- فَاِذَا رَكِبُوْا فِي الْفُلْكِ
دَعَوُا اللّٰهَ مُخْلِصِيْنَ لَهُ الدِّيْنَ ۚ ة
فَلَمَّا نَجّٰهُمْ اِلَى الْبَرِّ

Behold, they give a share
(Of their worship to others)!—

اِذَا هُمْ يُشْرِكُوْنَ ۞

66. Disdaining ungratefully Our gifts,
And giving themselves up
To (worldly) enjoyment! But soon
Will they know.

٦٦ـ لِيَكْفُرُوْا بِمَاۤ اٰتَيْنٰهُمْ ۙ وَلِيَتَمَتَّعُوْا ۖ
فَسَوْفَ يَعْلَمُوْنَ ۞

67. Do they not then see
That We have made
A Sanctuary secure, and that
Men are being snatched away
From all around them
Then, do they believe in that
Which is vain, and reject
The Grace of Allah!

٦٧ـ اَوَلَمْ يَرَوْا اَنَّا جَعَلْنَا حَرَمًا اٰمِنًا
وَّيُتَخَطَّفُ النَّاسُ مِنْ حَوْلِهِمْ ؕ
اَفَبِالْبَاطِلِ يُؤْمِنُوْنَ
وَبِنِعْمَةِ اللّٰهِ يَكْفُرُوْنَ ۞

68. And who does more wrong
Than he who invents
A lie against Allah
Or rejects the Truth
When it reaches him?
Is there not a home
In Hell for those who
Reject Faith?

٦٨ـ وَمَنْ اَظْلَمُ مِمَّنِ افْتَرٰى عَلَى اللّٰهِ
كَذِبًا اَوْ كَذَّبَ بِالْحَقِّ لَمَّا جَآءَهٗ ؕ
اَلَيْسَ فِيْ جَهَنَّمَ مَثْوًى
لِّلْكٰفِرِيْنَ ۞

69. And those who strive
In Our (Cause)—We will
Certainly guide them
To Our Paths:
For verily Allah
Is with those
Who do right.

٦٩ـ وَالَّذِيْنَ جَاهَدُوْا
فِيْنَا لَنَهْدِيَنَّهُمْ سُبُلَنَا ؕ
وَاِنَّ اللّٰهَ لَمَعَ الْمُحْسِنِيْنَ ۞

INTRODUCTION TO SŪRA XXX. *(Rūm)* — 60 Verses

This Sūra, as remarked in the Introduction to the last Sūra, deals with the question of Mā'ad or the Final End of Things, from various points of view. In the last Sūra, we saw that Revelation was linked up with Life and Conduct, and Time (looking backwards and forwards) figured forth the frailty of this Life. In this Sūra the Time theme and its mystery are brought into relation with human history in the foreground and the evolution of the world in all its aspects in the background. The corruption introduced by man is cleared away by God, Whose Universal Plan points to the Hereafter. We shall see that the next two Sūras (xxxi, and xxxii.) present the theme in other aspects. All four are introduced with the Abbreviated Letters A. L. M. which (without being dogmatic) I have suggested as symbolical of the Past, Present and Future.

The chronology of this Sūra is significant. It was revealed about the 7th or the 6th year *before* the Hijrat, corresponding to 615-16 of the Christian era, when the tide of Persian conquest over the Roman Empire was running strong, as explained in Appendix X (to follow this Sūra). The Christian Empire of Rome had lost Jerusalem to the Persians, and Christianity had been humbled in the dust. At that time it seemed outside the bounds of human possibility, even to one intimately aquainted with the inner resources and conditions of the Persian and Roman armies and empires, that the tables would be turned and the position reversed within the space of eight or nine years. The Pro-Persian Pagan Quraish rejoiced exceedingly, and redoubled their taunts and persecution against The Holy Prophet, whose Message was a renewal of the message of Christ preached in Jerusalem. Then was this passage xxx. 1 - 6 revealed, clearly foreshadowing the final defeat of Persia (Appendix X. 14 - 16) as a prelude to the destruction of the Persian Empire. There is no doubt about the prophecy and its fulfilment. For the exulting Pagans of Mecca laid a heavy wager against the fulfilment of the prophecy with Ḥadhrat Abū Bakr, and they lost it on its fulfilment.

But the rise and fall even of such mighty empires as the Persian and Roman Empires were but small events on the chequer-board of Time, compared to a mightier movement that was taking birth in the promulgation of Islam. In the seventh or sixth year *before* the Hijrat, and for a year or two after the Hijrat, Islam was struggling in the world like the still small voice in the conscience of humanity. It was scarcely heeded, and when it sought to insist upon its divine claim, it was insulted, assaulted, persecuted, boycotted, and (as it seemed) suppressed. The agony of Ṭā-if (two years before Hijrat) and the murder-plot on the eve of the Hijrat were yet to come. But the purpose of God is not to be thwarted. Badr (A.H. 2 = A.D. 624), rightly called the critical Day of Decision, began to redress the balance of outward events in early Islam, in the same year in which Issus (Appendix X. 16) began to redress the balance of outward events in Perso-Roman relations. Mightier events were yet to come. A new inner World was being created through Islam. The spiritual Revolution was of infinitely greater moment in world-history. The toppling down of priestcraft and false worship, the restoration of simplicity in faith and life, the rehabilitation of this life as the first step to the understanding of the Hereafter, the displacement of superstition and hair-splitting theology by a spirit of rational inquiry and knowledge, and the recognition of the divine as covering not merely an isolated thing called "Religion" but the whole way of Life, Thought, and Feeling—this was and is the true message of Islam and its mission. Its struggle— its fight—continues, but it is not without effect, as may be seen it the march of centuries in world-history.

Al Rūm (The Romans)

In the name of Allah, Most Gracious,
Most Merciful.

بِسۡمِ اللّٰهِ الرَّحۡمٰنِ الرَّحِيۡمِ

1. Ⱥlif Ⱡām Mīm.

١- الٓمّٓ ۚ

2. The Roman Empire
Has been defeated—

٢- غُلِبَتِ الرُّوۡمُ ۙ

3. In a land close by:
But they, (even) after
(This) defeat of theirs,
Will soon be victorious—

٣- فِىۡۤ اَدۡنَى الۡاَرۡضِ
وَهُمۡ مِّنۡۢ بَعۡدِ غَلَبِهِمۡ سَيَغۡلِبُوۡنَ ۙ

4. Within a few years.
With Allah is the Decision.
In the Past
And in the Future:
On that Day shall
The Believers rejoice—

٤- فِىۡ بِضۡعِ سِنِيۡنَ ۙ
لِلّٰهِ الۡاَمۡرُ مِنۡ قَبۡلُ وَمِنۡ بَعۡدُ ؕ
وَيَوۡمَئِذٍ يَّفۡرَحُ الۡمُؤۡمِنُوۡنَ ۙ

5. With the help of Allah.
He helps whom He will,
And He is Exalted in Might,
Most Merciful.

٥- بِنَصۡرِ اللّٰهِ ؕ يَنۡصُرُ مَنۡ يَّشَآءُ ؕ
وَهُوَ الۡعَزِيۡزُ الرَّحِيۡمُ ۙ

6. (It is) the promise of Allah.
Never does Allah depart
From His promise:
But most men understand not.

٦- وَعۡدَ اللّٰهِ ؕ لَا يُخۡلِفُ اللّٰهُ وَعۡدَهُ
وَلٰكِنَّ اَكۡثَرَ النَّاسِ لَا يَعۡلَمُوۡنَ ۟

7. They know but the outer
(Things) in the life
Of this world: but
Of the End of things
They are heedless.

٧- يَعۡلَمُوۡنَ ظَاهِرًا مِّنَ الۡحَيٰوةِ الدُّنۡيَا ۖۚ
وَهُمۡ عَنِ الۡاٰخِرَةِ هُمۡ غٰفِلُوۡنَ ۟

8. Ⅾo they not reflect
In their own minds?
Not but for just ends

٨- اَوَلَمۡ يَتَفَكَّرُوۡا فِىۡۤ اَنۡفُسِهِمۡ ۗ
مَا خَلَقَ اللّٰهُ

And for a term appointed,
Did Allah create the heavens
And the earth, and all
Between them: yet are there
Truly many among men
Who deny their meeting
With their Lord
(At the Resurrection)!

السَّمٰوٰتِ وَالْأَرْضَ
وَمَا بَيْنَهُمَا إِلَّا بِالْحَقِّ وَأَجَلٍ مُّسَمًّى ۚ
وَإِنَّ كَثِيْرًا مِّنَ النَّاسِ
بِلِقَآئِ رَبِّهِمْ لَكٰفِرُوْنَ ۝

9. Do they not travel
Through the earth, and see
What was the End
Of those before them?
They were superior to them
In strength: they tilled
The soil and populated it
In greater numbers than these
Have done: there came to them
Their messengers with Clear
(Signs).
(Which they rejected, to their
Own destruction): it was not
Allah who wronged them, but
They wronged their own souls.

٩- أَوَلَمْ يَسِيْرُوْا فِي الْأَرْضِ
فَيَنْظُرُوْا كَيْفَ كَانَ عَاقِبَةُ الَّذِيْنَ مِنْ
قَبْلِهِمْ ۚ كَانُوْا أَشَدَّ مِنْهُمْ قُوَّةً
وَّ أَثَارُوا الْأَرْضَ وَعَمَرُوْهَا أَكْثَرَ مِمَّا
عَمَرُوْهَا وَجَآءَتْهُمْ
رُسُلُهُمْ بِالْبَيِّنٰتِ ۚ
فَمَا كَانَ اللهُ لِيَظْلِمَهُمْ
وَلٰكِنْ كَانُوْا أَنْفُسَهُمْ يَظْلِمُوْنَ ۝

10. In the long run
Evil in the extreme
Will be the End of those
Who do evil; for that
They rejected the Signs
Of Allah, and held them up
To ridicule.

SECTION 2.

١٠- ثُمَّ كَانَ عَاقِبَةَ الَّذِيْنَ أَسَآءُوا السُّوْٓأَى
أَنْ كَذَّبُوْا بِاٰيٰتِ اللهِ
وَكَانُوْا بِهَا يَسْتَهْزِءُوْنَ ۝ ع

11. It is Allah Who begins
(The process of) creation;
Then repeats it; then
Shall ye be brought back
To Him.

١١- اَللهُ يَبْدَؤُا الْخَلْقَ ثُمَّ يُعِيْدُهُ
ثُمَّ إِلَيْهِ تُرْجَعُوْنَ ۝

12. On the Day that
The Hour will be established,
The guilty will be
Struck dumb with despair.

١٢- وَيَوْمَ تَقُوْمُ السَّاعَةُ
يُبْلِسُ الْمُجْرِمُوْنَ ۝

13. No intercessor will they have
Among their "Partners",
And they will (themselves)
Reject their "Partners".

١٣- وَلَمْ يَكُنْ لَّهُمْ مِّنْ شُرَكَآئِهِمْ شُفَعٰٓؤُا
وَكَانُوْا بِشُرَكَآئِهِمْ كٰفِرِيْنَ ۝

14. On the Day that
The Hour will be established—
That Day shall (all men)
Be sorted out.

١٤- وَيَوْمَ تَقُومُ السَّاعَةُ يَوْمَئِذٍ يَتَفَرَّقُونَ ۝

15. Then those who have believed
And worked righteous deeds,
Shall be made happy
In a Mead of Delight.

١٥- فَأَمَّا الَّذِينَ آمَنُوا وَعَمِلُوا الصَّالِحَاتِ فَهُمْ فِي رَوْضَةٍ يُحْبَرُونَ ۝

16. And those who have rejected
Faith and falsely denied
Our Signs and the meeting
Of the Hereafter—such
Shall be brought forth to
Punishment.

١٦- وَأَمَّا الَّذِينَ كَفَرُوا وَكَذَّبُوا بِآيَاتِنَا وَلِقَاءِ الْآخِرَةِ فَأُولَئِكَ فِي الْعَذَابِ مُحْضَرُونَ ۝

17. So (give) glory to Allah,
When ye reach eventide
And when ye rise
In the morning;

١٧- فَسُبْحَانَ اللَّهِ حِينَ تُمْسُونَ وَحِينَ تُصْبِحُونَ ۝

18. Yea, to Him be praise,
In the heavens and on earth;
And in the late afternoon
And when the day
Begins to decline.

١٨- وَلَهُ الْحَمْدُ فِي السَّمَاوَاتِ وَالْأَرْضِ وَعَشِيًّا وَحِينَ تُظْهِرُونَ ۝

19. It is He Who brings out
The living from the dead,
And brings out the dead
From the living, and Who
Gives life to the earth
After it is dead:
And thus shall ye be
Brought out (from the dead).

١٩- يُخْرِجُ الْحَيَّ مِنَ الْمَيِّتِ وَيُخْرِجُ الْمَيِّتَ مِنَ الْحَيِّ وَيُحْيِ الْأَرْضَ بَعْدَ مَوْتِهَا وَكَذَلِكَ تُخْرَجُونَ ۝

SECTION 3.

20. Among His Signs is this,
That He created you
From dust; and then—
Behold, ye are men
Scattered (far and wide)!

٢٠- وَمِنْ آيَاتِهِ أَنْ خَلَقَكُمْ مِنْ تُرَابٍ ثُمَّ إِذَا أَنْتُمْ بَشَرٌ تَنْتَشِرُونَ ۝

21. And among His Signs
Is this, that He created
For you mates from among
Yourselves, that ye may
Dwell in tranquillity with them,

٢١- وَمِنْ آيَاتِهِ أَنْ خَلَقَ لَكُمْ مِنْ أَنْفُسِكُمْ أَزْوَاجًا لِتَسْكُنُوا إِلَيْهَا

And He has put love
And mercy between your (hearts):
Verily in that are Signs
For those who reflect.

وَجَعَلَ بَيْنَكُمْ مَّوَدَّةً وَّرَحْمَةً
اِنَّ فِىْ ذٰلِكَ لَاٰيٰتٍ لِّقَوْمٍ يَّتَفَكَّرُوْنَ ۝

22. And among His Signs
Is the creation of the heavens
And the earth, and the
                        variations
In your languages
And your colours; verily
In that are Signs
For those who know.

٢٢- وَمِنْ اٰيٰتِهٖ خَلْقُ السَّمٰوٰتِ
وَالْاَرْضِ وَاخْتِلَافُ اَلْسِنَتِكُمْ
وَاَلْوَانِكُمْ ۚ
اِنَّ فِىْ ذٰلِكَ لَاٰيٰتٍ لِّلْعٰلِمِيْنَ ۝

23. And among His Signs
Is the sleep that ye take
By night and by day,
And the quest that ye
(Make for livelihood)
Out of His Bounty: verily
In that are Signs
For those who hearken.

٢٣- وَمِنْ اٰيٰتِهٖ مَنَامُكُمْ بِالَّيْلِ وَالنَّهَارِ
وَابْتِغَآؤُكُمْ
مِّنْ فَضْلِهٖ ۚ
اِنَّ فِىْ ذٰلِكَ لَاٰيٰتٍ لِّقَوْمٍ يَّسْمَعُوْنَ ۝

24. And among His Signs,
He shows you the lightning,
By way both of fear
And of hope, and He sends
Down rain from the sky
And with it gives life to
The earth after it is dead:
Verily in that are Signs
For those who are wise.

٢٤- وَمِنْ اٰيٰتِهٖ يُرِيْكُمُ الْبَرْقَ
خَوْفًا وَّطَمَعًا وَّيُنَزِّلُ
مِنَ السَّمَآءِ مَآءً فَيُحْيٖ بِهِ الْاَرْضَ بَعْدَ
مَوْتِهَا ۚ
اِنَّ فِىْ ذٰلِكَ لَاٰيٰتٍ لِّقَوْمٍ يَّعْقِلُوْنَ ۝

25. And among His Signs is this,
That heaven and earth
Stand by His Command:
Then when He calls you,
By a single call, from the earth,
Behold, ye (straightway) come
                        forth.

٢٥- وَمِنْ اٰيٰتِهٖ اَنْ تَقُوْمَ السَّمَآءُ وَالْاَرْضُ
بِاَمْرِهٖ ۚ ثُمَّ اِذَا دَعَاكُمْ دَعْوَةً مِّنَ الْاَرْضِ ۙ
اِذَآ اَنْتُمْ تَخْرُجُوْنَ ۝

26. To Him belongs every being
That is in the heavens
And on earth: all are
Devoutly obedient to Him.

٢٦- وَلَهٗ مَنْ فِى السَّمٰوٰتِ
وَالْاَرْضِ ۚ كُلٌّ لَّهٗ قٰنِتُوْنَ ۝

27. It is He Who begins
(The process of) creation;

٢٧- وَهُوَ الَّذِىْ يَبْدَؤُا الْخَلْقَ ثُمَّ يُعِيْدُهٗ

Then repeats it; and
For Him it is most easy.
To Him belongs the loftiest
Similitude (we can think of)
In the heavens and the earth:
For He is Exalted in Might,
Full of wisdom.

SECTION 4.

28. He does propound
To you a similitude
From your own (experience):
Do ye have partners
Among those whom your right
hands
Possess, to share as equals
In the wealth We have
Bestowed on you? Do ye
Fear them as ye fear
Each other? Thus do We
Explain the Signs in detail
To a people that understand.

29. Nay, the wrongdoers (merely)
Follow their own lusts,
Being devoid of knowledge
But who will guide those
Whom Allah leaves astray?
To them there will be
No helpers.

30. So set thou thy face
Steadily and truly to the Faith:
(Establish) Allah's handiwork
according
To the pattern on which
He has made mankind:
No change (let there be)
In the work (wrought)
By Allah: that is
The standard Religion:
But most among mankind
Understand not.

31. Turn ye back in repentance
To Him, and fear Him:
Establish regular prayers,
And be not ye among those
Who join gods with Allah—

32. Those who split up
Their Religion, and become
(Mere) Sects—each party
Rejoicing in that which
Is with itself!

٣٢- مِنَ الَّذِيْنَ فَرَّقُوْا دِيْنَهُمْ وَكَانُوْا
شِيَعًا ۚ
كُلُّ حِزْبٍ بِمَا لَدَيْهِمْ فَرِحُوْنَ ۞

33. When trouble touches men,
They cry to their Lord,
Turning back to Him
In repentance: but when
He gives them a taste
Of Mercy as from Himself.
Behold, some of them
Pay part-worship to
Other gods besides their Lord—

٣٣- وَإِذَا مَسَّ النَّاسَ ضُرٌّ دَعَوْا رَبَّهُمْ
مُّنِيْبِيْنَ اِلَيْهِ
ثُمَّ اِذَآ اَذَاقَهُمْ
مِّنْهُ رَحْمَةً
اِذَا فَرِيْقٌ مِّنْهُمْ بِرَبِّهِمْ يُشْرِكُوْنَ ۞

34. (As if) to show their ingratitude
For the (favours) We have
Bestowed on them! Then enjoy
(Your brief day); but soon
Will ye know (your folly).

٣٤- لِيَكْفُرُوْا بِمَآ اٰتَيْنٰهُمْ ۗ
فَتَمَتَّعُوْا ۟ فَسَوْفَ تَعْلَمُوْنَ ۞

35. Or have We sent down
Authority to them, which
Points out to them
The things to which
They pay part-worship?

٣٥- اَمْ اَنْزَلْنَا عَلَيْهِمْ سُلْطٰنًا
فَهُوَ يَتَكَلَّمُ بِمَا كَانُوْا بِهٖ يُشْرِكُوْنَ ۞

36. When We give men
A taste of Mercy,
They exult thereat:
And when some evil
Afflicts them because of
What their (own) hands
Have sent forth, behold,
They are in despair!

٣٦- وَإِذَآ اَذَقْنَا النَّاسَ رَحْمَةً فَرِحُوْا بِهَا ۚ
وَاِنْ تُصِبْهُمْ سَيِّئَةٌ
بِمَا قَدَّمَتْ اَيْدِيْهِمْ
اِذَا هُمْ يَقْنَطُوْنَ ۞

37. See they not that Allah
Enlarges the provision and
Restricts it, to whomsoever
He pleases? Verily in that
Are Signs for those who believe.

٣٧- اَوَلَمْ يَرَوْا اَنَّ اللّٰهَ يَبْسُطُ الرِّزْقَ
لِمَنْ يَّشَآءُ وَيَقْدِرُ ۚ
اِنَّ فِيْ ذٰلِكَ لَاٰيٰتٍ لِّقَوْمٍ يُّؤْمِنُوْنَ ۞

38. So give what is due
To kindred, the needy,
And the wayfarer.
That is best for those
Who seek the Countenance,

٣٨- فَاٰتِ ذَا الْقُرْبٰى حَقَّهٗ وَالْمِسْكِيْنَ وَ
ابْنَ السَّبِيْلِ ۗ ذٰلِكَ خَيْرٌ لِّلَّذِيْنَ
يُرِيْدُوْنَ وَجْهَ اللّٰهِ

Of Allah, and it is they
Who will prosper.

وَاُولٰٓئِكَ هُمُ الْمُفْلِحُوْنَ ۟

39. That which ye lay out
For increase through the property
Of (other) people, will have
No increase with Allah:
But that which ye lay out
For charity, seeking
The Countenance of Allah,
(Will increase): it is
These who will get
A recompense multiplied.

٣٩- وَمَآ اٰتَيْتُمْ مِّنْ رِّبًا لِّيَرْبُوَا۟ فِىْٓ اَمْوَالِ النَّاسِ فَلَا يَرْبُوْا عِنْدَ اللّٰهِ ۚ وَمَآ اٰتَيْتُمْ مِّنْ زَكٰوةٍ تُرِيْدُوْنَ وَجْهَ اللّٰهِ فَاُولٰٓئِكَ هُمُ الْمُضْعِفُوْنَ ۟

40. It is Allah who has
Created you: further, He has
Provided for your sustenance;
Then He will cause you
To die; and again He will
Give you life. Are there
Any of your (false) "Partners"
Who can do any single
One of these things?
Glory to Him! and High
Is He above the partners
They attribute (to Him)!

٤٠- اَللّٰهُ الَّذِىْ خَلَقَكُمْ ثُمَّ رَزَقَكُمْ ثُمَّ يُمِيْتُكُمْ ثُمَّ يُحْيِيْكُمْ ۚ هَلْ مِنْ شُرَكَآئِكُمْ مَّنْ يَّفْعَلُ مِنْ ذٰلِكُمْ مِّنْ شَىْءٍ ۚ سُبْحٰنَهٗ وَتَعٰلٰى عَمَّا يُشْرِكُوْنَ ۟

SECTION 5.

41. Mischief has appeared
On land and sea because
Of (the meed) that the hands
Of men have earned.
That (Allah) may give them
A taste of some of their
Deeds: in order that they
May turn back (from Evil).

٤١- ظَهَرَ الْفَسَادُ فِى الْبَرِّ وَالْبَحْرِ بِمَا كَسَبَتْ اَيْدِى النَّاسِ لِيُذِيْقَهُمْ بَعْضَ الَّذِىْ عَمِلُوْا لَعَلَّهُمْ يَرْجِعُوْنَ ۟

42. Say: "Travel through the earth
And see what was the End
Of those before (you):
Most of them worshipped
Others besides Allah."

٤٢- قُلْ سِيْرُوْا فِى الْاَرْضِ فَانْظُرُوْا كَيْفَ كَانَ عَاقِبَةُ الَّذِيْنَ مِنْ قَبْلُ ۚ كَانَ اَكْثَرُهُمْ مُّشْرِكِيْنَ ۟

43. But set thou thy face
To the right Religion,
Before there comes from Allah
The Day which there is
No chance of averting:
On that Day shall men

٤٣- فَاَقِمْ وَجْهَكَ لِلدِّيْنِ الْقَيِّمِ مِنْ قَبْلِ اَنْ يَّاْتِىَ يَوْمٌ لَّا مَرَدَّ لَهٗ مِنَ اللّٰهِ

يَوْمَئِذٍ يَتَصَدَّعُونَ ۝

Be divided (in two).

44. Those who reject Faith
Will suffer from that rejection:
And those who work righteousness
Will spread their couch
(Of repose) for themselves
(In heaven):

٤٤ ـ مَن كَفَرَ فَعَلَيْهِ كُفْرُهُ ۖ وَمَنْ عَمِلَ صَالِحًا فَلِأَنْفُسِهِمْ يَمْهَدُونَ ۝

45. That He may reward those
Who believe and work righteous
Deeds, out of His Bounty.
For He loves not those
Who reject Faith.

٤٥ ـ لِيَجْزِيَ الَّذِينَ آمَنُوا وَعَمِلُوا الصَّالِحَاتِ مِن فَضْلِهِ ۚ إِنَّهُ لَا يُحِبُّ الْكَافِرِينَ ۝

46. Among His Signs is this,
That He sends the Winds,
As heralds of Glad Tidings,
Giving you a taste
Of His (Grace and) Mercy—
That the ships may sail
(Majestically) by His Command
And that ye may seek
Of His Bounty: in order
That ye may be grateful.

٤٦ ـ وَمِنْ آيَاتِهِ أَن يُرْسِلَ الرِّيَاحَ مُبَشِّرَاتٍ وَلِيُذِيقَكُم مِّن رَّحْمَتِهِ وَلِتَجْرِيَ الْفُلْكُ بِأَمْرِهِ وَلِتَبْتَغُوا مِن فَضْلِهِ وَلَعَلَّكُمْ تَشْكُرُونَ ۝

47. We did indeed send,
Before thee, messengers
To their (respective) peoples,
And they came to them
With Clear Signs: then,
To those who transgressed,
We meted out Retribution:
And it was due from Us
To aid those who believed.

٤٧ ـ وَلَقَدْ أَرْسَلْنَا مِن قَبْلِكَ رُسُلًا إِلَىٰ قَوْمِهِمْ فَجَاءُوهُم بِالْبَيِّنَاتِ فَانتَقَمْنَا مِنَ الَّذِينَ أَجْرَمُوا ۖ وَكَانَ حَقًّا عَلَيْنَا نَصْرُ الْمُؤْمِنِينَ ۝

48. It is Allah Who sends
The Winds, and they raise
The Clouds: then does He
Spread them in the sky
As He wills, and break them
Into fragments, until thou seest
Raindrops issue from the midst
Thereof: then when He has
Made them reach such
Of His servants as He wills,

٤٨ ـ اللَّهُ الَّذِي يُرْسِلُ الرِّيَاحَ فَتُثِيرُ سَحَابًا فَيَبْسُطُهُ فِي السَّمَاءِ كَيْفَ يَشَاءُ وَيَجْعَلُهُ كِسَفًا فَتَرَى الْوَدْقَ يَخْرُجُ مِنْ خِلَالِهِ ۖ فَإِذَا أَصَابَ بِهِ مَن يَشَاءُ مِنْ عِبَادِهِ

Behold, they do rejoice!—

اِذَا هُمْ يَسْتَبْشِرُوْنَ ۞

49. Even though, before they received
(The rain)—just before this—
They were dumb with despair!

٤٩ـ وَاِنْ كَانُوْا مِنْ قَبْلِ اَنْ يُّنَزَّلَ
عَلَيْهِمْ مِّنْ قَبْلِهٖ لَمُبْلِسِيْنَ ۞

50. Then contemplate (O man!)
The memorials of Allah's Mercy!—
How He gives life
To the earth after
Its death: verily the Same
Will give life to the men
Who are dead: for He
Has power over all things.

٥٠ـ فَانْظُرْ اِلٰۤى اٰثَارِ رَحْمَتِ اللّٰهِ
كَيْفَ يُحْيِ الْاَرْضَ بَعْدَ مَوْتِهَا ۚ
اِنَّ ذٰلِكَ لَمُحْيِ الْمَوْتٰى ۚ
وَهُوَ عَلٰى كُلِّ شَيْءٍ قَدِيْرٌ ۞

51. And if We (but) send
A Wind from which
They see (their tilth)
Turn yellow—behold,
They become, thereafter,
Ungrateful (Unbelievers)!

٥١ـ وَلَئِنْ اَرْسَلْنَا رِيْحًا
فَرَاَوْهُ مُصْفَرًّا لَّظَلُّوْا مِنْ بَعْدِهٖ
يَكْفُرُوْنَ ۞

52. So verily thou canst not
Make the dead to hear,
Nor canst thou make
The deaf to hear
The call, when they show
Their backs and turn away.

٥٢ـ فَاِنَّكَ لَا تُسْمِعُ الْمَوْتٰى
وَلَا تُسْمِعُ الصُّمَّ الدُّعَاۤءَ
اِذَا وَلَّوْا مُدْبِرِيْنَ ۞

53. Nor canst thou lead back
The blind from their straying:
Only those wilt thou make
To hear, who believe
In Our Signs and submit
(Their wills in Islam).

٥٣ـ وَمَاۤ اَنْتَ بِهٰدِ الْعُمْيِ عَنْ ضَلٰلَتِهِمْ
اِنْ تُسْمِعُ اِلَّا مَنْ يُّؤْمِنُ
بِاٰيٰتِنَا فَهُمْ مُّسْلِمُوْنَ ۞

SECTION 6.

54. It is Allah Who
Created you in a state
Of (helpless) weakness, then
Gave (you) strength after weakness,
Then, after strength, gave (you)
Weakness and a hoary head:
He creates as He wills,—
And it is He Who has
All knowledge and power.

٥٤ـ اَللّٰهُ الَّذِيْ خَلَقَكُمْ مِّنْ ضَعْفٍ
ثُمَّ جَعَلَ مِنْ بَعْدِ ضَعْفٍ قُوَّةً
ثُمَّ جَعَلَ مِنْ بَعْدِ قُوَّةٍ ضَعْفًا وَّشَيْبَةً ۚ
يَخْلُقُ مَا يَشَاۤءُ ۚ وَهُوَ الْعَلِيْمُ الْقَدِيْرُ ۞

55. On the Day that

٥٥ـ وَيَوْمَ تَقُوْمُ

The Hour (of reckoning)
Will be established,
The transgressors will swear
That they tarried not
But an hour: thus were
They used to being deluded!

السَّاعَةُ يُقْسِمُ الْمُجْرِمُوْنَ
مَا لَبِثُوْا غَيْرَ سَاعَةٍ
كَذٰلِكَ كَانُوْا يُؤْفَكُوْنَ ۝

56. But those endued with knowledge
And faith will say:
"Indeed ye did tarry,
Within Allah's Decree,
To the Day of Resurrection,
And this is the Day
Of Resurrection: but ye—
Ye were not aware!"

٥٦- وَقَالَ الَّذِيْنَ أُوْتُوا الْعِلْمَ وَالْإِيْمَانَ
لَقَدْ لَبِثْتُمْ فِيْ كِتٰبِ اللهِ اِلٰى يَوْمِ الْبَعْثِ
فَهٰذَا يَوْمُ الْبَعْثِ
وَلٰكِنَّكُمْ كُنْتُمْ لَا تَعْلَمُوْنَ ۝

57. So on that Day no excuse
Of theirs will
Avail the Transgressors,
Nor will they be invited (then)
To seek grace (by repentance).

٥٧- فَيَوْمَئِذٍ لَّا يَنْفَعُ الَّذِيْنَ ظَلَمُوْا مَعْذِرَتُهُمْ
وَلَا هُمْ يُسْتَعْتَبُوْنَ ۝

58. Verily We have propounded
For men, in this Qur'ān,
Every kind of Parable:
But if thou bring to them
Any Sign, the Unbelievers
Are sure to say, "Ye
Do nothing but talk vanities."

٥٨- وَلَقَدْ ضَرَبْنَا لِلنَّاسِ فِيْ هٰذَا
الْقُرْاٰنِ مِنْ كُلِّ مَثَلٍ وَلَئِنْ جِئْتَهُمْ
بِاٰيَةٍ لَّيَقُوْلَنَّ الَّذِيْنَ كَفَرُوْا اِنْ
اَنْتُمْ اِلَّا مُبْطِلُوْنَ ۝

59. Thus does Allah seal up
The hearts of those
Who understand not.

٥٩- كَذٰلِكَ يَطْبَعُ اللهُ عَلٰى قُلُوْبِ الَّذِيْنَ
لَا يَعْلَمُوْنَ ۝

60. So patiently persevere: for
Verily the promise of Allah
Is true: nor let those
Shake thy firmness, who have
(Themselves) no certainty of faith.

٦٠- فَاصْبِرْ اِنَّ وَعْدَ اللهِ حَقٌّ
وَلَا يَسْتَخِفَّنَّكَ الَّذِيْنَ لَا يُوْقِنُوْنَ ۝ ع

INTRODUCTION TO SŪRA XXXI. (*Luqmān*) — 34 Verses

The argument of the Final End of Things is here continued from another point of view. What is Wisdom?. Where shall she be found? Will she solve the mysteries of Time and Nature, and that world higher than physical Nature, which brings us nearer to God? "Yes," is the answer: "if, as in the advice of Luqmān the Wise, human wisdom looks to God in true worship, ennobles every act of life with true kindness, but avoids the indulgence that infringes the divine law,— and in short follows the golden mean of virtue". And this is indicated by every Sign in nature.

The chronology of this Sūra has no significance. In the main, it belongs to the late Meccan period.

Luqmān

In the name of Allah, Most Gracious,
Most Merciful.

1. Alif Lām Mīm.

2. These are Verses
Of the Wise Book—

3. A Guide and a Mercy
To the Doers of Good—

4. Those who establish regular
Prayer,
And give regular Charity,
And have (in their hearts)
The assurance of the
Hereafter.

5. These are on (true) guidance
From their Lord; and these
Are the ones who will prosper.

6. But there are, among men,
Those who purchase idle tales,
Without knowledge (or meaning),
To mislead (men) from the Path
Of Allah and throw ridicule
(On the Path): for such
There will be a humiliating
Penalty.

7. When Our Signs are rehearsed

To such a one, he turns
Away in arrogance, as if
He heard them not, as if
There were deafness in both
His ears: announce to him
A grievous Penalty.

8. For those who believe
And work righteous deeds,
There will be Gardens
Of Bliss—

9. To dwell therein. The promise
Of Allah is true: and He
Is Exalted in power,   Wise.

10. He created the heavens
Without any pillars that ye
Can see; He set
On the earth mountains
Standing firm, lest it
Should shake with you;
And He scattered through it
Beasts of all kinds.
We send down rain
From the sky, and produce
On the earth every kind
Of noble creature, in pairs.

11. Such is the Creation of Allah:
Now show Me   what is there
That others besides Him
Have created; nay, but
The Transgressors are
In manifest error.

SECTION 2.

12. We bestowed (in the past)
Wisdom on Luqmān:
"Show (thy) gratitude to Allah."
Any who is (so) grateful
Does so to the profit
Of his own soul; but if
Any is ungrateful, verily
Allah is free of all wants,
Worthy of all praise.

13. Behold, Luqmān said
To his son by way of

Instruction: "O my son!
Join not in worship
(Others) with Allah: for
False worship is indeed
The highest wrongdoing."

14. And We have enjoined on man
(To be good) to his parents:
In travail upon travail
Did his mother bear him,
And in years twain
Was his weaning: (hear
The command), "Show gratitude
To Me and to thy parents:
To Me is (thy final) Goal.

15. "But if they strive
To make thee join
In worship with Me
Things of which thou hast
No knowledge, obey them not;
Yet bear them company
In this life with justice
(And consideration), and follow
The way of those who
Turn to Me (in love):
In the End the return
Of you all is to Me,
And I will tell you
The truth (and meaning)
Of all that ye did."

16. "O my son!" (said Luqmān),
"If there be (but) the weight
Of a mustard seed and
It were (hidden) in a rock,
Or (anywhere) in the heavens or
On earth. Allah will bring it
Forth: for Allah understands
The finer mysteries, (and)
Is well-acquainted (with them).

17. "O my son! establish
Regular prayer, enjoin what is
Just, and forbid what is wrong;
And bear with patient constancy
Whate'er betide thee; for this
Is firmness (of purpose)
In (the conduct of) affairs.

18. "And swell not thy cheek
(For pride) at men,
Nor walk in insolence
Through the earth:
For Allah loveth not
Any arrogant boaster.

١٨- وَلَا تُصَعِّرْ خَدَّكَ لِلنَّاسِ
وَلَا تَمْشِ فِى الْأَرْضِ مَرَحًا
إِنَّ اللَّهَ لَا يُحِبُّ كُلَّ مُخْتَالٍ فَخُورٍ

19. "And be moderate
In thy pace, and lower
Thy voice; for the harshest
Of sounds without doubt
Is the braying of the ass."

١٩- وَاقْصِدْ فِى مَشْيِكَ وَاغْضُضْ مِنْ
صَوْتِكَ إِنَّ أَنْكَرَ
الْأَصْوَاتِ لَصَوْتُ الْحَمِيرِ

SECTION 3.

20. Do ye not see
That Allah has subjected
To your (use) all things
In the heavens and on earth,
And has made His bounties
Flow to you in exceeding
Measure, (both) seen and
                      unseen?
Yet there are among men
Those who dispute about Allah,
Without knowledge and without
Guidance, and without a Book.
To enlighten them!

٢٠- أَلَمْ تَرَوْا أَنَّ اللَّهَ سَخَّرَ
لَكُمْ مَا فِى السَّمٰوٰتِ وَمَا فِى الْأَرْضِ
وَأَسْبَغَ عَلَيْكُمْ نِعَمَهُ ظَاهِرَةً وَبَاطِنَةً
وَمِنَ النَّاسِ مَنْ يُجَادِلُ فِى اللَّهِ
بِغَيْرِ عِلْمٍ وَلَا هُدًى
وَلَا كِتٰبٍ مُنِيرٍ

21. When they are told to follow
The (Revelation) that Allah
Has sent down, they say:
"Nay, we shall follow
The ways that we found
Our fathers (following)."
What! even if it is
Satan beckoning them
To the Penalty
Of the (Blazing) Fire?

٢١- وَإِذَا قِيلَ لَهُمُ اتَّبِعُوا مَا أَنْزَلَ اللَّهُ
قَالُوا بَلْ نَتَّبِعُ
مَا وَجَدْنَا عَلَيْهِ آبَاءَنَا
أَوَلَوْ كَانَ الشَّيْطٰنُ يَدْعُوهُمْ
إِلَى عَذَابِ السَّعِيرِ

22. Whoever submits
His whole self to Allah,
And is a doer of good,
Has grasped indeed
The most trustworthy handhold;
And with Allah rests the End
And Decision of (all) affairs.

٢٢- وَمَنْ يُسْلِمْ وَجْهَهُ إِلَى اللَّهِ
وَهُوَ مُحْسِنٌ
فَقَدِ اسْتَمْسَكَ بِالْعُرْوَةِ الْوُثْقٰى
وَإِلَى اللَّهِ عَاقِبَةُ الْأُمُورِ

23. But if any reject Faith,

٢٣- وَمَنْ كَفَرَ فَلَا يَحْزُنْكَ كُفْرُهُ

Let not his rejection
Grieve thee: to Us
Is their Return, and We
Shall tell them the truth
Of their deeds: for Allah
Knows well all that is
In (men's) hearts.

اِلَيْنَا مَرْجِعُهُمْ
فَنُنَبِّئُهُمْ بِمَا عَمِلُوا ۚ
اِنَّ اللّٰهَ عَلِيْمٌ بِذَاتِ الصُّدُوْرِ ۞

24. We grant them their pleasure
For a little while:
In the end shall We
Drive them to
A chastisement unrelenting.

٢٤ ۔ نُمَتِّعُهُمْ قَلِيْلًا
ثُمَّ نَضْطَرُّهُمْ اِلٰى عَذَابٍ غَلِيْظٍ ۞

25. If thou ask them,
Who it is that created
The heavens and the earth,
They will certainly say,
"Allah". Say: "Praise be to
                 Allah."
But most of them
Understand not.

٢٥ ۔ وَلَئِنْ سَاَلْتَهُمْ مَّنْ خَلَقَ
السَّمٰوٰتِ وَالْاَرْضَ لَيَقُوْلُنَّ
اللّٰهُ ۚ قُلِ الْحَمْدُ لِلّٰهِ ۚ
بَلْ اَكْثَرُهُمْ لَا يَعْلَمُوْنَ ۞

26. To Allah belong all things
In heaven and earth: verily
Allah is He (that is)
Free of all wants,
Worthy of all praise.

٢٦ ۔ لِلّٰهِ مَا فِى السَّمٰوٰتِ وَالْاَرْضِ ۚ
اِنَّ اللّٰهَ هُوَ الْغَنِيُّ الْحَمِيْدُ ۞

27. And if all the trees
On earth were pens
And the Ocean (were ink),
With seven Oceans behind it
To add to its (supply),
Yet would not the Words
Of Allah be exhausted
(In the writing): for Allah
Is Exalted in power,
Full of Wisdom.

٢٧ ۔ وَلَوْ اَنَّ مَا فِى الْاَرْضِ مِنْ شَجَرَةٍ
اَقْلَامٌ وَّالْبَحْرُ يَمُدُّهٗ
مِنْ بَعْدِهٖ سَبْعَةُ اَبْحُرٍ
مَا نَفِدَتْ كَلِمٰتُ اللّٰهِ ۗ
اِنَّ اللّٰهَ عَزِيْزٌ حَكِيْمٌ ۞

28. And your creation
Or your resurrection
Is in no wise but
As an individual soul:
For Allah is He Who
Hears and sees (all things).

٢٨ ۔ مَا خَلْقُكُمْ وَلَا بَعْثُكُمْ
اِلَّا كَنَفْسٍ وَّاحِدَةٍ ۗ
اِنَّ اللّٰهَ سَمِيْعٌ بَصِيْرٌ ۞

29. Seest thou not that
Allah merges Night into Day

٢٩ ۔ اَلَمْ تَرَ اَنَّ اللّٰهَ يُوْلِجُ الَّيْلَ فِى النَّهَارِ

And He merges Day into Night;
That He has subjected the sun
And the moon (to His Law),
Each running its course
For a term appointed; and
That Allah is well acquainted
With all that ye do?

وَيُوْلِجُ النَّهَارَ فِى الَّيْلِ
وَسَخَّرَ الشَّمْسَ وَالْقَمَرَ
كُلٌّ يَّجْرِىْ إِلٰى أَجَلٍ مُّسَمًّى
وَأَنَّ اللّٰهَ بِمَا تَعْمَلُوْنَ خَبِيْرٌ ۟

30. That is because Allah is
The (only) Reality, and because
Whatever else they invoke
Besides Him is Falsehood;
And because Allah—He is
The Most High, Most Great.

٣٠- ذٰلِكَ بِأَنَّ اللّٰهَ هُوَ الْحَقُّ
وَأَنَّ مَا يَدْعُوْنَ مِنْ دُوْنِهِ الْبَاطِلُ ۙ
وَأَنَّ اللّٰهَ هُوَ الْعَلِيُّ الْكَبِيْرُ ۟

SECTION 4.

31. Seest thou not that
The ships sail through
The Ocean by the grace
Of Allah?—that He may
Show you of His Signs?
Verily in this are Signs
For all who constantly persevere
And give thanks.

٣١- أَلَمْ تَرَ أَنَّ الْفُلْكَ تَجْرِىْ
فِى الْبَحْرِ بِنِعْمَتِ اللّٰهِ
لِيُرِيَكُمْ مِّنْ اٰيٰتِهٖ
إِنَّ فِىْ ذٰلِكَ لَاٰيٰتٍ لِّكُلِّ صَبَّارٍ شَكُوْرٍ ۟

32. When a wave covers them
Like the canopy (of clouds),
They call to Allah,
Offering Him sincere devotion,
But when He has delivered them
Safely to land, there are
Among them those that halt
Between (right and wrong).
But none reject Our Signs
Except only a perfidious
Ungrateful (wretch)!

٣٢- وَإِذَا غَشِيَهُمْ مَّوْجٌ كَالظُّلَلِ
دَعَوُا اللّٰهَ مُخْلِصِيْنَ لَهُ الدِّيْنَ ۚ
فَلَمَّا نَجّٰهُمْ إِلَى الْبَرِّ فَمِنْهُمْ مُّقْتَصِدٌ ۚ
وَمَا يَجْحَدُ بِاٰيٰتِنَا
إِلَّا كُلُّ خَتَّارٍ كَفُوْرٍ ۟

33. O mankind! do your duty
To your Lord, and fear
(The coming of) a Day
When no father can avail
Aught for his son, nor
A son avail aught
For his father.
Verily, the promise of Allah
Is true: let not then
This present life deceive you,
Nor let the Chief Deceiver
Deceive you about Allah.

٣٣- يٰأَيُّهَا النَّاسُ اتَّقُوْا رَبَّكُمْ وَاخْشَوْا
يَوْمًا لَّا يَجْزِىْ وَالِدٌ عَنْ وَّلَدِهٖ ۚ
وَلَا مَوْلُوْدٌ هُوَ جَازٍ عَنْ وَّالِدِهٖ شَيْئًا ۚ
إِنَّ وَعْدَ اللّٰهِ
حَقٌّ فَلَا تَغُرَّنَّكُمُ الْحَيٰوةُ الدُّنْيَا
وَلَا يَغُرَّنَّكُمْ بِاللّٰهِ الْغَرُوْرُ ۟

34. Verily the knowledge
Of the Hour is
With Allah (alone).
It is He Who sends down
Rain, and He Who knows
What is in the wombs.
Nor does anyone know
What it is that he will
Earn on the morrow;
Nor does anyone know
In what land he is
To die. Verily with Allah
Is full knowledge and He
Is acquainted (with all things).

INTRODUCTION TO SŪRA XXXII. *(Sajda)* — 30 Verses

This short Sūra closes the series of the four A. L. M Sūras, which began with the 29th. Its theme is the mystery of Creation, the mystery of Time and the mystery of the *Ma'ād* (the Final End) as viewed through the light of God's revelation. The contemplation of these mysteries should lead to Faith and the adoration of God. In chronology it belongs to the middle Meccan period and it therefore a little earlier than the last, but its chronology has no significance.

Al Sajdah (The Prostration)

In the name of Allah, Most Gracious,
Most Merciful.

بِسْمِ اللهِ الرَّحْمٰنِ الرَّحِيْمِ

1. Alif Lām Mīm.

١- الٓمّٓ ۚ

2. (This is) the revelation
Of the Book in which
There is no doubt—
From the Lord of the Worlds.

٢- تَنْزِيْلُ الْكِتٰبِ لَا رَيْبَ فِيْهِ
مِنْ رَّبِّ الْعٰلَمِيْنَ ۚ

3. Or   do they say,
"He has forged it"?
Nay, it is the Truth
From thy Lord, that thou
Mayest admonish a people
To whom no warner
Has come before thee:
In order that they
May receive guidance.

٣- اَمْ يَقُوْلُوْنَ افْتَرٰىهُ ۚ
بَلْ هُوَ الْحَقُّ مِنْ رَّبِّكَ
لِتُنْذِرَ قَوْمًا مَّا اَتٰىهُمْ مِنْ نَّذِيْرٍ مِّنْ
قَبْلِكَ
لَعَلَّهُمْ يَهْتَدُوْنَ ۚ

4. It is Allah Who has
Created the heavens
And the earth, and all
Between them, in six Days,
Then He established Himself
On the Throne (of authority);
Ye have none, besides Him,
To protect or intercede (for you):
Will ye not then
Receive admonition?

٤- اَللهُ الَّذِيْ خَلَقَ السَّمٰوٰتِ
وَالْاَرْضَ وَ مَا بَيْنَهُمَا فِيْ سِتَّةِ اَيَّامٍ
ثُمَّ اسْتَوٰى عَلَى الْعَرْشِ ۚ
مَا لَكُمْ مِنْ دُوْنِهِ مِنْ وَّلِيٍّ وَّلَا شَفِيْعٍ ۚ
اَفَلَا تَتَذَكَّرُوْنَ ۚ

5. He rules (all) affairs
From the heavens
To the earth: in the end
Will (all affairs) go up

٥- يُدَبِّرُ الْاَمْرَ مِنَ السَّمَاءِ اِلَى الْاَرْضِ
ثُمَّ يَعْرُجُ اِلَيْهِ فِيْ يَوْمٍ

To Him, on a Day,
The space whereof will be
(As) a thousand years
Of your reckoning.

6. Such is He, the Knower
Of all things, hidden
And open, the Exalted
(In power), the Merciful—

7. He Who has made
Everything which He has
created
Most Good: He began
The creation of man
With (nothing more than) clay,

8. And made his progeny
From a quintessence
Of the nature of
A fluid despised:

9. But He fashioned him
In due proportion, and breathed
Into him something of
His spirit. And He gave
You (the faculties of) hearing
And sight and feeling
(And understanding):
Little thanks do ye give!

10. And they say: "What!
When we lie, hidden
And lost, in the earth,
Shall we indeed be
In a Creation renewed?"
Nay, they deny the Meeting
With their Lord!

11. Say: "The Angel of Death,
Put in charge of you,
Will (duly) take your souls
Then shall ye be brought
Back to your Lord."

SECTION 2.

12. If only thou couldst see
When the guilty ones
Will bend low their heads

كَانَ مِقْدَارُهُ أَلْفَ سَنَةٍ مِّمَّا تَعُدُّوْنَ ۝

٦- ذٰلِكَ عٰلِمُ الْغَيْبِ وَالشَّهَادَةِ الْعَزِيْزُ الرَّحِيْمُ ۝

٧- الَّذِيْ أَحْسَنَ كُلَّ شَيْءٍ خَلَقَهُ وَبَدَأَ خَلْقَ الْإِنْسَانِ مِنْ طِيْنٍ ۝

٨- ثُمَّ جَعَلَ نَسْلَهُ مِنْ سُلٰلَةٍ مِّنْ مَّآءٍ مَّهِيْنٍ ۝

٩- ثُمَّ سَوّٰهُ وَنَفَخَ فِيْهِ مِنْ رُّوْحِهِ وَجَعَلَ لَكُمُ السَّمْعَ وَالْأَبْصَارَ وَالْأَفْئِدَةَ قَلِيْلًا مَّا تَشْكُرُوْنَ ۝

١٠- وَقَالُوْا ءَاِذَا ضَلَلْنَا فِى الْأَرْضِ ءَاِنَّا لَفِيْ خَلْقٍ جَدِيْدٍ بَلْ هُمْ بِلِقَآءِ رَبِّهِمْ كٰفِرُوْنَ ۝

١١- قُلْ يَتَوَفّٰىكُمْ مَّلَكُ الْمَوْتِ الَّذِيْ وُكِّلَ بِكُمْ ثُمَّ اِلٰى رَبِّكُمْ تُرْجَعُوْنَ ۝

١٢- وَلَوْ تَرٰى اِذِ الْمُجْرِمُوْنَ

Before their Lord, (saying:)
"Our Lord! We have seen
And we have heard:
Now then send us back
(To the world): we will
Work righteousness: for we
Do indeed (now) believe."

تَأْكِسُوا رُءُوسِهِمْ عِندَ رَبِّهِمْ
رَبَّنَا أَبْصَرْنَا وَسَمِعْنَا
فَارْجِعْنَا
نَعْمَلْ صَالِحًا إِنَّا مُوقِنُونَ ۞

13. If We had so willed,
We could certainly have
　　　　　　　　　brought
Every soul its true guidance:
But the Word from Me
Will come true, "I will
Fill Hell with Jinns
And men all together."

١٣- وَلَوْ شِئْنَا لَآتَيْنَا كُلَّ نَفْسٍ هُدَاهَا
وَلَٰكِنْ حَقَّ الْقَوْلُ مِنِّي
لَأَمْلَأَنَّ جَهَنَّمَ مِنَ الْجِنَّةِ وَالنَّاسِ
أَجْمَعِينَ ۞

14. "Taste ye then—for ye
Forgot the Meeting
Of this Day of yours.
And We too will
Forget you—taste ye
The penalty of Eternity
For your (evil) deeds!"

١٤- فَذُوقُوا بِمَا نَسِيتُمْ لِقَاءَ يَوْمِكُمْ هَٰذَا
إِنَّا نَسِينَاكُمْ
وَذُوقُوا عَذَابَ الْخُلْدِ
بِمَا كُنتُمْ تَعْمَلُونَ ۞

15. Only those believe
In Our Signs, who, when
They are recited to them
Fall down in adoration,
And celebrate the praises
Of their Lord, nor are they
(Ever) puffed up with pride.

١٥- إِنَّمَا يُؤْمِنُ بِآيَاتِنَا الَّذِينَ إِذَا
ذُكِّرُوا بِهَا خَرُّوا سُجَّدًا وَسَبَّحُوا بِحَمْدِ
رَبِّهِمْ وَهُمْ لَا يَسْتَكْبِرُونَ ۩ ۞

16. Their limbs do forsake
Their beds of sleep, the while
They call on their Lord,
In Fear and Hope:
And they spend (in charity)
Out of the sustenance which
We have bestowed on them.

١٦- تَتَجَافَىٰ جُنُوبُهُمْ عَنِ الْمَضَاجِعِ
يَدْعُونَ رَبَّهُمْ خَوْفًا وَطَمَعًا
وَمِمَّا رَزَقْنَاهُمْ يُنفِقُونَ ۞

17. Now no person knows
What delights of the eye
Are kept hidden (in reserve)
For them—as a reward
For their (good) Deeds.

١٧- فَلَا تَعْلَمُ نَفْسٌ
مَّا أُخْفِيَ لَهُم مِّن قُرَّةِ أَعْيُنٍ
جَزَاءً بِمَا كَانُوا يَعْمَلُونَ ۞

18. Is then the man

١٨- أَفَمَن كَانَ مُؤْمِنًا

Who believes no better
Than the man who is
Rebellious and wicked?
Not equal are they.

19. For those who believe
And do righteous deeds,
Are Gardens as hospitable
Homes, for their (good) deeds.

20. As to those who are
Rebellious and wicked, their
                                    abode
Will be the Fire: every time
They wish to get away
Therefrom, they will be forced
Thereinto, and it will be said
To them: "Taste ye
The Penalty of the Fire,
The which ye were wont
To reject as false."

21. And indeed We will make
Them taste of the Penalty
Of this (life) prior to
The supreme Penalty, in order
That they may (repent and)
                                    return.

22. And who does more wrong
Than one to whom are recited
The Signs of his Lord
And who then turns away
Therefrom? Verily from those
Who transgress We shall exact
(Due) Retribution.
        SECTION 3.

23. We did indeed aforetime
Give the Book to Moses:
Be not then in doubt
Of its reaching (thee):
And We made it
A guide to the Children
Of Israel.

24. And We appointed, from among
Them, Leaders, giving
                                    guidance
Under Our command, so long

١٩- كَمَنْ كَانَ فَاسِقًا ۚ لَا يَسْتَوُنَ ۞

١٩- أَمَّا الَّذِينَ اٰمَنُوْا وَعَمِلُوا الصّٰلِحٰتِ فَلَهُمْ جَنّٰتُ الْمَاْوٰى ۖ نُزُلًا بِمَا كَانُوْا يَعْمَلُوْنَ ۞

٢٠- وَأَمَّا الَّذِينَ فَسَقُوْا فَمَاْوٰىهُمُ النَّارُ ۖ كُلَّمَا أَرَادُوْا أَنْ يَّخْرُجُوْا مِنْهَا أُعِيْدُوْا فِيْهَا وَقِيْلَ لَهُمْ ذُوْقُوْا عَذَابَ النَّارِ الَّذِيْ كُنْتُمْ بِهٖ تُكَذِّبُوْنَ ۞

٢١- وَلَنُذِيْقَنَّهُمْ مِّنَ الْعَذَابِ الْأَدْنٰى دُوْنَ الْعَذَابِ الْأَكْبَرِ لَعَلَّهُمْ يَرْجِعُوْنَ ۞

٢٢- وَمَنْ أَظْلَمُ مِمَّنْ ذُكِّرَ بِاٰيٰتِ رَبِّهٖ ثُمَّ أَعْرَضَ عَنْهَا ۚ إِنَّا مِنَ الْمُجْرِمِيْنَ مُنْتَقِمُوْنَ ۞

٢٣- وَلَقَدْ اٰتَيْنَا مُوْسَى الْكِتٰبَ فَلَا تَكُنْ فِيْ مِرْيَةٍ مِّنْ لِّقَآئِهٖ وَجَعَلْنٰهُ هُدًى لِّبَنِيْ إِسْرَآئِيْلَ ۞

٢٤- وَجَعَلْنَا مِنْهُمْ أَئِمَّةً يَّهْدُوْنَ بِأَمْرِنَا لَمَّا صَبَرُوْا ۖ

As they persevered with patience
And continued to have faith
In Our Signs.

وَكَانُوا بِآيَاتِنَا يُوقِنُونَ ۝

25. Verily thy Lord will judge
Between them on the Day
Of Judgement, in the matters
Wherein they differ
(among themselves)

۲۵ـ إِنَّ رَبَّكَ هُوَ يَفْصِلُ بَيْنَهُمْ يَوْمَ
الْقِيَامَةِ فِيمَا كَانُوا فِيهِ يَخْتَلِفُونَ ۝

26. Does it not teach them
A lesson, how many generations
We destroyed before them,
In whose dwellings they
(Now) go to and fro?
Verily in that are Signs:
Do they not then listen?

۲۶ـ أَوَلَمْ يَهْدِ لَهُمْ كَمْ أَهْلَكْنَا مِنْ قَبْلِهِمْ
مِنَ الْقُرُونِ
يَمْشُونَ فِي مَسَاكِنِهِمْ
إِنَّ فِي ذَٰلِكَ لَآيَاتٍ أَفَلَا يَسْمَعُونَ ۝

27. And do they not see
That We do drive Rain
To parched soil (bare
Of herbage), and produce
therewith
Crops, providing food
For their cattle and themselves?
Have they not the vision?

۲۷ـ أَوَلَمْ يَرَوْا أَنَّا نَسُوقُ الْمَاءَ
إِلَى الْأَرْضِ الْجُرُزِ
فَنُخْرِجُ بِهِ زَرْعًا تَأْكُلُ مِنْهُ أَنْعَامُهُمْ
وَأَنْفُسُهُمْ أَفَلَا يُبْصِرُونَ ۝

28. They say: "When will
This Decision be, if ye
Are telling the truth?"

۲۸ـ وَيَقُولُونَ مَتَىٰ هَٰذَا الْفَتْحُ
إِنْ كُنْتُمْ صَادِقِينَ ۝

29. Say: "On the Day
Of Decision, no profit
Will it be to Unbelievers
If they (then) believe!
Nor will they be granted
A respite."

۲۹ـ قُلْ يَوْمَ الْفَتْحِ لَا يَنْفَعُ
الَّذِينَ كَفَرُوا إِيمَانُهُمْ
وَلَا هُمْ يُنْظَرُونَ ۝

30. So turn away from them,
And wait: they too
Are waiting.

۳۰ـ فَأَعْرِضْ عَنْهُمْ وَانْتَظِرْ
إِنَّهُمْ مُنْتَظِرُونَ ۝

INTRODUCTION TO SŪRA XXXIII. *(Aḥzāb)* — 73 Verses

The series of mystic Sūras beginning with S. xxvi. having been closed with the last Sūra, we now come back to the hard facts of this life. Two questions are mainly considered there, *viz.*, (1) the attempt by violence and brute force to crush the truth, and (2) the attempt, by slander or unseemly conduct, to poison the relations of women with men.

As regards the first, the story of the Aḥzāb or Confederates, who tried to surround and annihilate the Muslim community in Medina, is full of underhand intrigues on the part of such diverse enemies as the Pagan Quraish, the Jews (Banu Nadhīr) who had been already expelled from Medina for their treachery, the Gaṭafān tribe of Bedouin Arabs from the interior, and the Jewish tribe Banū Quraiẓa in Medina. This was the unholy Confederacy against Islam. But though they caused a great deal of anxiety and suffering to the beleaguered Muslims, Islam came triumphantly out of the trial and got more firmly established than ever.

The Quraish in Mecca had tried all sorts of persecution, boycott, insult, and bodily injuries to the Muslims, leading to their partial *hijrat* to Abyssinia and their Hijrat as a body to Medina. The first armed conflict between them and the Muslims took place at Badr in Ramadhān A.H. 2, when the Quraish were signally defeated. (See n. 352 to iii. 13). Next year (Shauwāl A.H. 3) they came to take revenge on Medina. The battle was fought at Uḥud, and though the Muslims suffered severely, Medina was saved and the Meccans had to return to Mecca with their objects frustrated. Then they began to make a network of intrigues and alliances, and besieged Medina with a force of 10,000 men in Shauwal and Ẕul-qaʿd A.H. 5. This is the siege of the Confederates referred to in xxxiii. 9-27, which lasted over two weeks: some accounts give 27 days. It caused much suffering, from hunger, cold, an unceasing shower of arrows, and constant general or concentrated assaults. But it ended in the discomfiture of the Confederates, and established Islam firmer than ever. It was a well-organised and formidable attack, but the Muslims had made preparations to meet it. One of the preparations, which took the enemy by surprise, was the Trench (*Khandaq*) dug round Medina by The Prophet's order and under the supervision of Slamān the Persian. The siege and battle are therefore known as the Battle of the Trench or the Battle of the Confederates.

As regards the position and dignity of the ladies of the Prophet's Household and the Muslim women generally, salutary principles are laid down to safeguard their honour and protect them from slander and insult. The ladies of the Household interested themselves in social work and work of instruction for the Muslim women, and Muslim women were being trained more and more in community service. Two of them (the two Zainabs) devoted themselves to the poor. The nursing of the wounded on or by the battlefield was specially necessary in those days of warfare. The Prophet's daughter Fāṭima, then aged about 19 to 20, lovingly nursed her father's wounds at Uḥud (A.H. 3); Rufaida nursed Saʿd ibn Muʿāz's wounds at the Siege of Medina by the Confederates (A.H. 5); and in the Khaibar expedition (A.H. 7) Muslim women went out from Medina for nursing service.

A portion of this Sūra sums up the lessons of the Battle of the Trench and must have been revealed some time after that Battle (Shauwāl A.H. 5). The marriage with Zainab referred to inverse 37 also took place in the same year. Some portions (e.g., verse 27, see n. 3705) were probably revealed in A.H. 7 after the Khaibar settlement.

Al Aḥzāb (The Confederates)

*In the Name of Allah, Most Gracious,
Most Merciful.*

1. ⊕ Prophet! Fear Allah,
And hearken not
To the Unbelievers
And the Hypocrites:
Verily Allah is full
Of knowledge and wisdom.

2. But follow that which
Comes to thee by inspiration
From thy Lord: for Allah
Is well acquainted
With (all) that ye do.

3. And put thy trust
In Allah, and enough is
              Allah
As a Disposer of affairs.

4. Allah has not made
For any man two hearts
In his (one) body: nor has
He made your wives whom
Ye divorce by Ẓihār
Your mothers: nor has He
Made your adopted sons
Your sons. Such is (only)
Your (manner of) speech
By your mouths. But Allah
Tells (you) the Truth, and He
Shows the (right) Way.

5. Call them by (the names
Of) their fathers: that is
Juster in the sight of Allah.
But if ye know not
Their father's (names, call
Them) your Brothers in faith,
Or your *Mawlās*.
But there is no blame
On ye if ye make
A mistake therein:
(What counts is)

The intention of your hearts:
And Allah is Oft-Forgiving,
Most Merciful.

وَكَانَ اللهُ غَفُورًا رَّحِيمًا ○

6. The Prophet is closer
To the Believers than
Their own selves,
And his wives are
Their mothers. Blood-relations
Among each other have
Closer personal ties,
In the Decree of Allah,
Than (the Brotherhood of)
Believers and Muhājirs:
Nevertheless do ye
What is just to your
Closest friends: such is
The writing of the Decree
(Of Allah).

٦- اَلنَّبِيُّ أَوْلَى بِالْمُؤْمِنِينَ مِنْ
أَنْفُسِهِمْ
وَأَزْوَاجُهُ أُمَّهَاتُهُمْ ۖ
وَأُولُوا الْأَرْحَامِ بَعْضُهُمْ
أَوْلَى بِبَعْضٍ فِي كِتَابِ اللهِ
مِنَ الْمُؤْمِنِينَ وَالْمُهَاجِرِينَ
إِلَّا أَنْ تَفْعَلُوا إِلَى أَوْلِيَائِكُمْ مَعْرُوفًا ۚ
كَانَ ذَٰلِكَ فِي الْكِتَابِ مَسْطُورًا ○

7. And remember We took
From the Prophets their
          Covenant:
As (We did) from thee:
From Noah, Abraham, Moses,
And Jesus the son of Mary:
We took from them
A solemn Covenant:

٧- وَإِذْ أَخَذْنَا مِنَ النَّبِيِّنَ
مِيثَاقَهُمْ وَمِنْكَ وَمِنْ نُوحٍ وَإِبْرَاهِيمَ
وَمُوسَى وَعِيسَى ابْنِ مَرْيَمَ ۖ
وَأَخَذْنَا مِنْهُمْ مِيثَاقًا غَلِيظًا ○

8. That (Allah) may question
The (Custodians) of Truth
          concerning
The Truth they (were charged
          with)
And He has prepared
For the Unbelievers
A grievous Penalty.
      SECTION 2,

٨- لِيَسْأَلَ الصَّادِقِينَ عَنْ
صِدْقِهِمْ ۚ
وَأَعَدَّ لِلْكَافِرِينَ عَذَابًا أَلِيمًا ○

9. O ye who believe!
Remember the Grace of Allah,
(Bestowed) on you, when
There came down on you
Hosts (to overwhelm you):
But We sent against them
A hurricane and forces
That ye saw not:
But Allah sees (clearly)
All that ye do.

٩- يَا أَيُّهَا الَّذِينَ آمَنُوا اذْكُرُوا نِعْمَةَ اللهِ
عَلَيْكُمْ إِذْ جَاءَتْكُمْ
جُنُودٌ فَأَرْسَلْنَا عَلَيْهِمْ
رِيحًا وَجُنُودًا لَمْ تَرَوْهَا ۚ
وَكَانَ اللهُ بِمَا تَعْمَلُونَ بَصِيرًا ○

10. Behold! they came on you
From above you and from
Below you, and behold,
The eyes became dim
And the hearts gaped
Up to the throats,
And ye imagined various
(Vain) thoughts about Allah!

١٠- اِذْ جَآءُوْكُمْ مِّنْ فَوْقِكُمْ وَمِنْ اَسْفَلَ مِنْكُمْ وَاِذْ زَاغَتِ الْاَبْصَارُ وَبَلَغَتِ الْقُلُوْبُ الْحَنَاجِرَ وَتَظُنُّوْنَ بِاللّٰهِ الظُّنُوْنَا ۠

11. In that situation
Were the Believers tried:
They were shaken as by
A tremendous shaking.

١١- هُنَالِكَ ابْتُلِيَ الْمُؤْمِنُوْنَ وَزُلْزِلُوْا زِلْزَالًا شَدِيْدًا ۠

12. And behold! The Hypocrites
And those in whose hearts
Is a disease (even) say: "Allah
And His Messenger promised us
Nothing but delusions!"

١٢- وَاِذْ يَقُوْلُ الْمُنٰفِقُوْنَ وَالَّذِيْنَ فِىْ قُلُوْبِهِمْ مَّرَضٌ مَّا وَعَدَنَا اللّٰهُ وَرَسُوْلُهٗۤ اِلَّا غُرُوْرًا ۠

13. Behold! A party among them
Said: "Ye men of Yathrib!
Ye cannot stand (the attack)!
Therefore go back!"
And a band of them
Ask for leave of the Prophet
Saying, "Truly our houses
Are bare and exposed," though
They were not exposed:
They intended nothing but
To run away.

١٣- وَاِذْ قَالَتْ طَّآئِفَةٌ مِّنْهُمْ يٰۤاَهْلَ يَثْرِبَ لَا مُقَامَ لَكُمْ فَارْجِعُوْا ۚ وَيَسْتَأْذِنُ فَرِيْقٌ مِّنْهُمُ النَّبِيَّ يَقُوْلُوْنَ اِنَّ بُيُوْتَنَا عَوْرَةٌ ۛ وَمَا هِيَ بِعَوْرَةٍ ۛ اِنْ يُّرِيْدُوْنَ اِلَّا فِرَارًا ۠

14. And if an entry had
Been effected to them
From the sides of the (City),
And they had been
Incited to sedition,
They would certainly have
Brought it to pass, with
None but a brief delay!

١٤- وَلَوْ دُخِلَتْ عَلَيْهِمْ مِّنْ اَقْطَارِهَا ثُمَّ سُئِلُوا الْفِتْنَةَ لَاٰتَوْهَا وَمَا تَلَبَّثُوْا بِهَآ اِلَّا يَسِيْرًا ۠

15. And yet they had already
Covenanted with Allah not to turn
Their backs, and a covenant
With Allah must (surely)
Be answered for.

١٥- وَلَقَدْ كَانُوْا عَاهَدُوا اللّٰهَ مِنْ قَبْلُ لَا يُوَلُّوْنَ الْاَدْبَارَ ۚ وَكَانَ عَهْدُ اللّٰهِ مَسْئُوْلًا ۠

16. Say: "Running away will not
Profit you if ye are
Running away from death
Or slaughter: and even if
(Ye do escape), no more
Than a brief (respite)
Will ye be allowed to enjoy!"

17. Say: "Who is it that can
Screen you from Allah
If it be His wish
To give you Punishment
Or to give you Mercy?"
Nor will they find for themselves,
Besides Allah, any protector
Or helper.

18. Verily Allah knows those
Among you who keep back
(Men) and those who say
To their brethren, "Come along
To us", but come not
To the fight except
For just a little while,

19. Covetous over you.
Then when fear comes,
Thou wilt see them looking
To thee, their eyes revolving,
Like (those of) one over whom
Hovers death: but when
The fear is past,
They will smite you
With sharp tongues, covetous
Of goods. Such men have
No faith, and so Allah
Has made their deeds
Of none effect: and that
Is easy for Allah.

20. They think that the Confederates
Have not withdrawn; and if
The Confederates should come
(again),
They would wish they were
In the deserts (wandering)
Among the Bedouins, and
Seeking news about you
(From a safe distance);
And if they were

١٦ـ قُلْ لَّنْ يَّنْفَعَكُمُ الْفِرَارُ اِنْ
فَرَرْتُمْ مِّنَ الْمَوْتِ
اَوِ الْقَتْلِ وَاِذًا لَّا
تُمَتَّعُوْنَ اِلَّا قَلِيْلًا ۝

١٧ـ قُلْ مَنْ ذَا الَّذِيْ يَعْصِمُكُمْ مِّنَ اللهِ
اِنْ اَرَادَ بِكُمْ سُوْءًا
اَوْ اَرَادَ بِكُمْ رَحْمَةً ؕ وَلَا يَجِدُوْنَ لَهُمْ مِّنْ
دُوْنِ اللهِ وَلِيًّا وَّلَا نَصِيْرًا ۝

١٨ـ قَدْ يَعْلَمُ اللهُ الْمُعَوِّقِيْنَ مِنْكُمْ
وَالْقَآئِلِيْنَ لِاِخْوَانِهِمْ
هَلُمَّ اِلَيْنَا ۚ
وَلَا يَأْتُوْنَ الْبَأْسَ اِلَّا قَلِيْلًا ۙ

١٩ـ اَشِحَّةً عَلَيْكُمْ ۚۖ فَاِذَا جَآءَ الْخَوْفُ
رَاَيْتَهُمْ يَنْظُرُوْنَ اِلَيْكَ تَدُوْرُ اَعْيُنُهُمْ
كَالَّذِيْ يُغْشٰى عَلَيْهِ مِنَ الْمَوْتِ ۚ
فَاِذَا ذَهَبَ الْخَوْفُ سَلَقُوْكُمْ بِاَلْسِنَةٍ
حِدَادٍ اَشِحَّةً عَلَى الْخَيْرِ ؕ
اُولٰٓئِكَ لَمْ يُؤْمِنُوْا فَاَحْبَطَ اللهُ اَعْمَالَهُمْ ؕ
وَكَانَ ذٰلِكَ عَلَى اللهِ يَسِيْرًا ۝

٢٠ـ يَحْسَبُوْنَ الْاَحْزَابَ لَمْ يَذْهَبُوْا ۚ
وَاِنْ يَّأْتِ الْاَحْزَابُ
يَوَدُّوْا لَوْ اَنَّهُمْ بَادُوْنَ فِى الْاَعْرَابِ
يَسْاَلُوْنَ عَنْ اَنْبَآئِكُمْ ؕ
وَلَوْ كَانُوْا فِيْكُمْ

In your midst, they
Would fight but little.

SECTION 3.

21. Ye have indeed
In the Messenger of Allah
A beautiful pattern (of
     conduct)
For any one whose hope is
In Allah and the Final Day,
And who engages much
In the praise of Allah.

22. When the Believers saw
The Confederate forces
They said: "This is
What Allah and His
     Messenger
Had promised us, and Allah
And His Messenger told us
What was true." And it
Only added to their faith
And their zeal in obedience.

23. Among the Believers are men
Who have been true to
Their Covenant with Allah:
Of them some have
     completed
Their vow (to the extreme),
And some (still) wait:
But they have never changed
(Their determination) in the
     least:

24. That Allah may reward
The men of Truth for
Their Truth, and punish
The Hypocrites if that be
His Will, or turn to them
In Mercy: for Allah is
Oft-Forgiving, Most Merciful.

25. And Allah turned back
The Unbelievers for (all)
Their fury: no advantage
Did they gain: and enough
Is Allah for the Believers
In their fight. And Allah

ما قاتلوا إلا قليلاً ۝ ع

٢١- لَقَدْ كَانَ لَكُمْ فِيْ رَسُوْلِ اللّٰهِ
أُسْوَةٌ حَسَنَةٌ
لِّمَنْ كَانَ يَرْجُوا اللّٰهَ وَالْيَوْمَ الْآخِرَ
وَذَكَرَ اللّٰهَ كَثِيْرًا ۝

٢٢- وَلَمَّا رَاَ الْمُؤْمِنُوْنَ الْاَحْزَابَ
قَالُوْا هٰذَا مَا وَعَدَنَا اللّٰهُ وَرَسُوْلُهٗ
وَصَدَقَ اللّٰهُ وَرَسُوْلُهٗ
وَمَا زَادَهُمْ إِلَّا إِيْمَانًا
وَّتَسْلِيْمًا ۝

٢٣- مِنَ الْمُؤْمِنِيْنَ رِجَالٌ
صَدَقُوْا مَا عَاهَدُوا اللّٰهَ عَلَيْهِ
فَمِنْهُمْ مَّنْ قَضٰى نَحْبَهٗ وَمِنْهُمْ مَّنْ
يَّنْتَظِرُ ۖ
وَمَا بَدَّلُوْا تَبْدِيْلًا ۝

٢٤- لِيَجْزِيَ اللّٰهُ الصّٰدِقِيْنَ بِصِدْقِهِمْ
وَيُعَذِّبَ الْمُنٰفِقِيْنَ اِنْ
شَاءَ اَوْ يَتُوْبَ عَلَيْهِمْ ۚ
اِنَّ اللّٰهَ كَانَ غَفُوْرًا رَّحِيْمًا ۝

٢٥- وَرَدَّ اللّٰهُ الَّذِيْنَ كَفَرُوْا بِغَيْظِهِمْ
لَمْ يَنَالُوْا خَيْرًا ۚ
وَكَفَى اللّٰهُ الْمُؤْمِنِيْنَ الْقِتَالَ ۚ

Is full of Strength, Able
To enforce His Will.

26. And those of the people
Of the Book who aided
Them—Allah did take them
Down from their strongholds
And cast terror into
Their hearts, (so that)
Some ye slew, and some
Ye made prisoners.

27. And He made you heirs
Of their lands, their houses,
And their goods,
And of a land which
Ye had not frequented
(Before). And Allah has
Power over all things.

SECTION 4.

28. Prophet! say
To thy Consorts:
"If it be that ye desire
The life of this world,
And its glitter,—then come!
I will provide for your
Enjoyment and set you free
In a handsome manner."

29. But if ye seek Allah
And His Messenger, and
The Home of the Hereafter,
Verily Allah has prepared
For the well-doers amongst
you
A great reward.

30. O Consorts of the Prophet
If any of you were guilty
Of evident unseemly
conduct,
The Punishment would be
Doubled to her, and that
Is easy for Allah.

31. But any of you that is
Devout in the service of
Allah and His Messenger,
And works righteousness—

وَكَانَ اللهُ قَوِيًّا عَزِيزًا ۟

٢٦- وَأَنْزَلَ الَّذِيْنَ ظَاهَرُوْهُمْ مِّنْ أَهْلِ الْكِتٰبِ مِنْ صَيَاصِيْهِمْ وَقَذَفَ فِىْ قُلُوْبِهِمُ الرُّعْبَ فَرِيْقًا تَقْتُلُوْنَ وَتَأْسِرُوْنَ فَرِيْقًا ۟

٢٧- وَأَوْرَثَكُمْ أَرْضَهُمْ وَدِيَارَهُمْ وَأَمْوَالَهُمْ وَأَرْضًا لَّمْ تَطَؤُهَا ؕ وَكَانَ اللهُ عَلٰى كُلِّ شَىْءٍ قَدِيْرًا ۟ۛ

٢٨- يٰٓأَيُّهَا النَّبِىُّ قُلْ لِّأَزْوَاجِكَ إِنْ كُنْتُنَّ تُرِدْنَ الْحَيٰوةَ الدُّنْيَا وَزِيْنَتَهَا فَتَعَالَيْنَ أُمَتِّعْكُنَّ وَأُسَرِّحْكُنَّ سَرَاحًا جَمِيْلًا ۟

٢٩- وَإِنْ كُنْتُنَّ تُرِدْنَ اللهَ وَرَسُوْلَهُ وَالدَّارَ الْاٰخِرَةَ فَإِنَّ اللهَ أَعَدَّ لِلْمُحْسِنٰتِ مِنْكُنَّ أَجْرًا عَظِيْمًا ۟

٣٠- يٰنِسَاءَ النَّبِىِّ مَنْ يَّأْتِ مِنْكُنَّ بِفَاحِشَةٍ مُّبَيِّنَةٍ يُّضٰعَفْ لَهَا الْعَذَابُ ضِعْفَيْنِ ؕ وَكَانَ ذٰلِكَ عَلَى اللهِ يَسِيْرًا ۟

٣١- وَمَنْ يَّقْنُتْ مِنْكُنَّ لِلّٰهِ وَرَسُوْلِهِ وَتَعْمَلْ صَالِحًا

To her shall We grant
Her reward twice : and We
Have prepared for her
A generous Sustenance.

32. O Consorts of the Prophet!
Ye are not like any
Of the (other) women:
If ye do fear (Allah),
Be not too complaisant
Of speech, lest one
In whose heart is
A disease should be moved
With desire: but speak ye
A speech (that is) just.

33. And stay quietly in
Your houses, and make not
A dazzling display, like
That of the former Times
Of Ignorance: and establish
Regular Prayer, and give
Regular Charity; and obey
Allah and His Messenger.
And Allah only wishes
To remove all abomination
From you, ye Members
Of the Family, and to make
You pure and spotless.

34. And recite what is
Rehearsed to you in your
Homes, of the Signs of Allah
And His Wisdom:
For Allah understands
The finest mysteries and
Is well-acquainted (with them).

SECTION 5.

35. For Muslim men and
women—
For believing men and women,
For devout men and women,
For true men and women,
For men and women who are
Patient and constant, for men
And women who humble
themselves,
For men and women who give

In charity, for men and women
Who fast (and deny themselves),
For men and women who
Guard their chastity, and
For men and women who
Engage much in Allah's
             praise—
For them has Allah prepared
Forgiveness and great reward.

وَالصَّٰٓئِمٰتِ وَالْحٰفِظِينَ فُرُوجَهُمْ وَ
الْحٰفِظٰتِ وَالذَّٰكِرِينَ اللّٰهَ كَثِيرًا وَّالذَّٰكِرٰتِ
أَعَدَّ اللّٰهُ لَهُمْ مَّغْفِرَةً وَّأَجْرًا عَظِيمًا ۞

36. It is not fitting
For a Believer, man or woman,
When a matter has been decided
By Allah and His Messenger,
To have any option
About their decision:
If anyone disobeys Allah
And His Messenger, he is indeed
On a clearly wrong Path.

٣٦۔ وَمَا كَانَ لِمُؤْمِنٍ وَّلَا مُؤْمِنَةٍ
إِذَا قَضَى اللّٰهُ وَرَسُولُهُ أَمْرًا
أَنْ يَّكُونَ لَهُمُ الْخِيَرَةُ مِنْ أَمْرِهِمْ
وَمَنْ يَّعْصِ اللّٰهَ وَرَسُولَهُ
فَقَدْ ضَلَّ ضَلٰلًا مُّبِينًا ۞

37. Behold! thou didst say
To one who had received
The grace of Allah
And thy favour: "Retain thou
(In wedlock) thy wife,
And fear Allah." But thou
Didst hide in thy heart
That which Allah was about
To make manifest: thou didst
Fear the people, but it is
More fitting that thou
            shouldst
Fear Allah. Then when Zayd
Had dissolved (his marriage)
With her, with the necessary
(Formality), We joined her
In marriage to thee:
In order that (in future)
There may be no difficulty
To the Believers in (the matter
Of) marriage with the wives
Of their adopted sons, when
The latter have dissolved
With the necessary (formality)
(Their marriage) with them.
And Allah's command must
Be fulfilled.

٣٧۔ وَإِذْ تَقُولُ لِلَّذِىٓ
أَنْعَمَ اللّٰهُ عَلَيْهِ وَأَنْعَمْتَ عَلَيْهِ
أَمْسِكْ عَلَيْكَ زَوْجَكَ وَاتَّقِ اللّٰهَ
وَتُخْفِى فِى نَفْسِكَ مَا اللّٰهُ مُبْدِيهِ
وَتَخْشَى النَّاسَ ۚ
وَاللّٰهُ أَحَقُّ أَنْ تَخْشٰهُ ۚ
فَلَمَّا قَضٰى زَيْدٌ مِّنْهَا وَطَرًا
زَوَّجْنٰكَهَا
لِكَىْ لَا
يَكُونَ عَلَى الْمُؤْمِنِينَ حَرَجٌ
فِىٓ أَزْوَاجِ أَدْعِيَآئِهِمْ
إِذَا قَضَوْا مِنْهُنَّ وَطَرًا ۚ
وَكَانَ أَمْرُ اللّٰهِ مَفْعُولًا ۞

38. There can be no difficulty

٣٨۔ مَا كَانَ عَلَى النَّبِىِّ

To the Prophet in what
Allah has indicated to him
As a duty: It was
The practice (approved) of Allah
Amongst those of old
That have passed away,
And the command of Allah
Is a decree determined.

39. (It is the practice of those)
Who preach the Messages
Of Allah, and fear Him,
And fear none but Allah.
And enough is Allah
To call (men) to account.

40. Muḥammad is not
The father of any
Of your men, but (he is)
The Messenger of Allah,
And the Seal of the Prophets:
And Allah has full knowledge
Of all things.

SECTION 6.

41. O ye who believe!
Celebrate the praises of Allah,
And do so often;

42. And glorify Him
Morning and evening.

43. He it is Who sends
Blessings on you, as do
His angels, that He may
Bring you out from the depths
Of Darkness into Light:
And He is Full of Mercy
To the Believers.

44. Their salutation on the Day
They meet Him will be
"Peace!": and He has
Prepared for them
A generous Reward.

45. O Prophet! Truly We
Have sent thee as
A Witness, a Bearer

Of Glad Tidings,
And a Warner—

وَّمُبَشِّرًا وَّنَذِيْرًا ۩

46. And as one who invites
To Allah's (Grace) by His leave,
And as a Lamp
Spreading Light.

٤٦- وَّدَاعِيًا اِلَى اللهِ بِاِذْنِهٖ وَسِرَاجًا مُّنِيْرًا ۩

47. Then give the glad tidings
To the Believers, that
They shall have from Allah
A very great Bounty.

٤٧- وَبَشِّرِ الْمُؤْمِنِيْنَ بِاَنَّ لَهُمْ مِّنَ اللهِ فَضْلًا كَبِيْرًا ۩

48. And obey not (the behests)
Of the Unbelievers
And the Hypocrites,
And heed not their
　　　　　　annoyances,
But put thy trust in Allah.
For enough is Allah
As a Disposer of affairs.

٤٨- وَلَا تُطِعِ الْكٰفِرِيْنَ وَالْمُنٰفِقِيْنَ وَدَعْ اَذٰهُمْ وَتَوَكَّلْ عَلَى اللهِ وَكَفٰى بِاللهِ وَكِيْلًا ۩

49. O ye who believe!
When ye marry believing
　　　　　　women,
And then divorce them
Before ye have touched them,
No period of 'Iddah
Have ye to count
In respect of them:
So give them a present,
And set them free
In a handsome manner.

٤٩- يٰاَيُّهَا الَّذِيْنَ اٰمَنُوْا اِذَا نَكَحْتُمُ الْمُؤْمِنٰتِ ثُمَّ طَلَّقْتُمُوْهُنَّ مِنْ قَبْلِ اَنْ تَمَسُّوْهُنَّ فَمَا لَكُمْ عَلَيْهِنَّ مِنْ عِدَّةٍ تَعْتَدُّوْنَهَا فَمَتِّعُوْهُنَّ وَسَرِّحُوْهُنَّ سَرَاحًا جَمِيْلًا ۩

50. O Prophet! We have
Made lawful to thee
Thy wives to whom thou
Hast paid their dowers;
And those whom thy
Right hand possesses out of
The prisoners of war whom
Allah has assigned to thee;
And daughters of thy paternal
Uncles and aunts, and
　　　　　　daughters
Of thy maternal uncles
And aunts, who migrated

٥٠- يٰاَيُّهَا النَّبِيُّ اِنَّا اَحْلَلْنَا لَكَ اَزْوَاجَكَ الّٰتِيْ اٰتَيْتَ اُجُوْرَهُنَّ وَمَا مَلَكَتْ يَمِيْنُكَ مِمَّا اَفَاءَ اللهُ عَلَيْكَ وَبَنٰتِ عَمِّكَ وَبَنٰتِ عَمّٰتِكَ وَبَنٰتِ خَالِكَ وَبَنٰتِ خٰلٰتِكَ الّٰتِيْ هَاجَرْنَ مَعَكَ وَامْرَاَةً مُّؤْمِنَةً اِنْ وَّهَبَتْ نَفْسَهَا

(From Makkah) with thee;
And any believing woman
Who dedicates her soul
To the Prophet if the
Prophet
Wishes to wed her—this
Only for thee, and not
For the Believers (at large):
We know what We have
Appointed for them as to
Their wives and the captives
Whom their right hands
Possess—in order that
There should be no difficulty
For Thee. And Allah is
Oft-Forgiving, Most Merciful.

لِلنَّبِيِّ إِنْ أَرَادَ النَّبِيُّ أَن يَسْتَنكِحَهَا
خَالِصَةً لَّكَ مِن دُونِ الْمُؤْمِنِينَ
قَدْ عَلِمْنَا مَا فَرَضْنَا عَلَيْهِمْ فِي أَزْوَاجِهِمْ
وَمَا مَلَكَتْ أَيْمَانُهُمْ
لِكَيْلَا يَكُونَ عَلَيْكَ حَرَجٌ
وَكَانَ اللهُ غَفُورًا رَّحِيمًا ○

51. Thou mayest defer (the turn
Of) any of them that thou
Pleasest, and thou mayest receive
Any thou pleasest: and there
Is no blame on thee if
Thou invite one whose (turn)
Thou hadst set aside.
This were nigher to
The cooling of the eyes,
The prevention of their grief,
And their satisfaction—
That of all of them—
With that which thou
Hast to give them:
And Allah knows (all)
That is in your hearts:
And Allah is All-Knowing,
Most Forbearing.

٥١- تُرْجِي مَن تَشَاءُ مِنْهُنَّ
وَتُؤْوِي إِلَيْكَ مَن تَشَاءُ وَمَنِ ابْتَغَيْتَ
مِمَّنْ عَزَلْتَ فَلَا جُنَاحَ عَلَيْكَ
ذَٰلِكَ أَدْنَىٰ أَن تَقَرَّ أَعْيُنُهُنَّ
وَلَا يَحْزَنَّ
وَيَرْضَيْنَ
بِمَا آتَيْتَهُنَّ كُلُّهُنَّ
وَاللهُ يَعْلَمُ مَا فِي قُلُوبِكُمْ
وَكَانَ اللهُ عَلِيمًا حَلِيمًا ○

52. It is not lawful for thee
(To marry more) women
After this, nor to change
Them for (other) wives,
Even though their beauty
Attract thee, except any
Thy right hand should
Possess (as handmaidens):
And Allah doth watch
Over all things.

٥٢- لَا يَحِلُّ لَكَ النِّسَاءُ مِن بَعْدُ
وَلَا أَن تَبَدَّلَ بِهِنَّ مِنْ أَزْوَاجٍ
وَلَوْ أَعْجَبَكَ حُسْنُهُنَّ
إِلَّا مَا مَلَكَتْ يَمِينُكَ
وَكَانَ اللهُ عَلَىٰ كُلِّ شَيْءٍ رَّقِيبًا ○

SECTION 7.

53. O ye who Believe!
Enter not the Prophet's
houses—
Until leave is given you—
For a meal, (and then)
Not (so early as) to wait
For its preparation: but when
Ye are invited, enter;
And when ye have taken
Your meal, disperse,
Without seeking familiar talk.
Such (behaviour) annoys
The Prophet: he is ashamed
To dismiss you, but
Allah is not ashamed
(To tell you) the truth.

And when ye
Ask (his ladies)
For anything ye want
Ask them from before
A screen: that makes
For greater purity for
Your hearts and for theirs.

Nor is it right for you
That ye should annoy
Allah's Messenger, or that
Ye should marry his widows
After him at any time.
Truly such a thing is
In Allah's sight an enormity.

54. Whether ye reveal anything
Or conceal it, verily
Allah has full knowledge
Of all things.

55. There is no blame
(On those ladies if they
Appear) before their fathers
Or their sons, their brothers,
Or their brothers' sons,
Or their sisters' sons,
Or their women,

٥٣ - يَآيُّهَا الَّذِينَ اٰمَنُوا لَا تَدْخُلُوا
بُيُوتَ النَّبِيِّ إِلَّآ أَنْ يُؤْذَنَ لَكُمْ إِلٰى
طَعَامٍ غَيْرَ نٰظِرِينَ اِنٰهُ
وَلٰكِنْ إِذَا دُعِيتُمْ فَادْخُلُوا
فَإِذَا طَعِمْتُمْ فَانْتَشِرُوا
وَلَا مُسْتَأْنِسِينَ لِحَدِيثٍ
إِنَّ ذٰلِكُمْ كَانَ يُؤْذِى النَّبِيَّ فَيَسْتَحْيِ
مِنْكُمْ
وَاللهُ لَا يَسْتَحْيِ مِنَ الْحَقِّ
وَإِذَا سَأَلْتُمُوهُنَّ مَتَاعًا
فَسْئَلُوهُنَّ مِنْ وَّرَآءِ حِجَابٍ
ذٰلِكُمْ أَطْهَرُ لِقُلُوبِكُمْ وَقُلُوبِهِنَّ
وَمَا كَانَ لَكُمْ
أَنْ تُؤْذُوا رَسُولَ اللهِ
وَلَآ أَنْ تَنْكِحُوا أَزْوَاجَهُ مِنْ بَعْدِهِ أَبَدًا
إِنَّ ذٰلِكُمْ كَانَ عِنْدَ اللهِ عَظِيمًا

٥٤ - إِنْ تُبْدُوا شَيْئًا أَوْ تُخْفُوهُ
فَإِنَّ اللهَ كَانَ بِكُلِّ شَيْءٍ عَلِيمًا ۝

٥٥ - لَا جُنَاحَ عَلَيْهِنَّ فِيْ
اٰبَآئِهِنَّ وَلَآ أَبْنَآئِهِنَّ وَلَآ إِخْوَانِهِنَّ
وَلَآ أَبْنَآءِ إِخْوَانِهِنَّ وَلَآ أَبْنَآءِ أَخَوَاتِهِنَّ
وَلَا نِسَآئِهِنَّ وَلَا مَا مَلَكَتْ أَيْمَانُهُنَّ

Or the (slaves) whom
Their right hands possess.
And, (ladies), fear Allah;
For Allah is Witness
To all things.

وَاتَّقِيْنَ اللّٰهَ ۚ
اِنَّ اللّٰهَ كَانَ عَلٰى كُلِّ شَىْءٍ شَهِيْدًا ۟

56. Allah and His Angels
Send blessings on the Prophet:
O ye that believe!
Send ye blessings on him,
And salute him
With all respect.

٥٦ - اِنَّ اللّٰهَ وَمَلٰٓئِكَتَهٗ يُصَلُّوْنَ عَلَى النَّبِىِّ ۚ
يٰٓاَيُّهَا الَّذِيْنَ اٰمَنُوْا صَلُّوْا عَلَيْهِ
وَسَلِّمُوْا تَسْلِيْمًا ۟

57. Those who annoy
Allah and His Messenger—
Allah has cursed them
In this world and
In the Hereafter,
And has prepared for them
A humiliating Punishment.

٥٧ - اِنَّ الَّذِيْنَ يُؤْذُوْنَ اللّٰهَ وَرَسُوْلَهٗ
لَعَنَهُمُ اللّٰهُ فِى الدُّنْيَا وَالْاٰخِرَةِ
وَاَعَدَّ لَهُمْ عَذَابًا مُّهِيْنًا ۟

58. And those who annoy
Believing men and women
Undeservedly, bear (on
                          themselves)
A calumny and a glaring sin.

٥٨ - وَالَّذِيْنَ يُؤْذُوْنَ الْمُؤْمِنِيْنَ وَالْمُؤْمِنٰتِ
بِغَيْرِ مَا اكْتَسَبُوْا
فَقَدِ احْتَمَلُوْا بُهْتَانًا وَّاِثْمًا مُّبِيْنًا ۟ ع

SECTION 8.

59. O Prophet! Tell
Thy wives and daughters,
And the believing women,
That they should cast
Their outer garments over
Their persons (when abroad):
That is most convenient,
That they should be known
(As such) and not molested.
And Allah is Oft-Forgiving,
Most Merciful.

٥٩ - يٰٓاَيُّهَا النَّبِىُّ قُلْ لِّاَزْوَاجِكَ وَبَنٰتِكَ
وَنِسَاءِ الْمُؤْمِنِيْنَ
يُدْنِيْنَ عَلَيْهِنَّ مِنْ جَلَابِيْبِهِنَّ ۚ
ذٰلِكَ اَدْنٰٓى اَنْ يُّعْرَفْنَ
فَلَا يُؤْذَيْنَ ۗ وَكَانَ اللّٰهُ غَفُوْرًا رَّحِيْمًا ۟

60. Truly, if the Hypocrites,
And those in whose hearts
Is a disease, and those who
Stir up sedition in the City,
Desist not, We shall certainly
Stir thee up against them:
Then will they not be
Able to stay in it
As thy neighbours
For any length of time:

٦٠ - لَئِنْ لَّمْ يَنْتَهِ الْمُنٰفِقُوْنَ وَالَّذِيْنَ
فِى قُلُوْبِهِمْ مَّرَضٌ
وَالْمُرْجِفُوْنَ فِى الْمَدِيْنَةِ
لَنُغْرِيَنَّكَ بِهِمْ
ثُمَّ لَا يُجَاوِرُوْنَكَ فِيْهَا اِلَّا قَلِيْلًا ۟

61. They shall have a curse
On them: wherever they
Are found, they shall be
Seized and slain
(Without mercy).

٦١ـ مَلْعُوْنِيْنَ ۛ أَيْنَمَا ثُقِفُوْا
أُخِذُوْا وَ قُتِّلُوْا تَقْتِيْلًا ۞

62. (Such was) the practice
(Approved) of Allah among
those
Who lived aforetime:
No change wilt thou find
In the practice (approved)
Of Allah.

٦٢ـ سُنَّةَ اللهِ فِى الَّذِيْنَ خَلَوْا مِنْ قَبْلُ ۚ
وَلَنْ تَجِدَ
لِسُنَّةِ اللهِ تَبْدِيْلًا ۞

63. Men ask thee concerning
The Hour: say, "The
knowledge
Thereof is with Allah (alone)":
And what will make thee
Understand?—perchance
The Hour is nigh!

٦٣ـ يَسْـَٔلُكَ النَّاسُ عَنِ السَّاعَةِ ۖ
قُلْ إِنَّمَا عِلْمُهَا عِنْدَ اللهِ ۚ
وَمَا يُدْرِيْكَ لَعَلَّ السَّاعَةَ تَكُوْنُ
قَرِيْبًا ۞

64. Verily Allah has cursed
The Unbelievers and prepared
For them a Blazing Fire

٦٤ـ إِنَّ اللهَ لَعَنَ الْكَافِرِيْنَ وَأَعَدَّ
لَهُمْ سَعِيْرًا ۞

65. To dwell therein forever:
No protector will they find,
Nor helper.

٦٥ـ خَالِدِيْنَ فِيْهَا أَبَدًا ۚ
لَا يَجِدُوْنَ وَلِيًّا وَّلَا نَصِيْرًا ۞

66. The Day that their faces
Will be turned upside down
In the Fire, they will say:
"Woe to us! would that
We had obeyed Allah
And obeyed the Messenger!"

٦٦ـ يَوْمَ تُقَلَّبُ وُجُوْهُهُمْ فِى النَّارِ
يَقُوْلُوْنَ يَا لَيْتَنَا
أَطَعْنَا اللهَ وَأَطَعْنَا الرَّسُوْلَا ۞

67. And they would say:
"Our Lord! We obeyed
Our chiefs and our great ones,
And they misled us
As to the (right) path.

٦٧ـ وَقَالُوْا رَبَّنَا إِنَّا أَطَعْنَا
سَادَتَنَا وَكُبَرَاءَنَا
فَأَضَلُّوْنَا السَّبِيْلَا ۞

68. "Our Lord! Give them
Double Penalty
And curse them
With a very great Curse!"

٦٨ـ رَبَّنَا آتِهِمْ ضِعْفَيْنِ مِنَ الْعَذَابِ
وَالْعَنْهُمْ لَعْنًا كَبِيْرًا ۞

SECTION 9.

69. O ye who believe!
Be ye not like those
Who vexed and insulted Moses,
But Allah cleared him
Of the (calumnies) they
Had uttered: and he
Was honourable in Allah's sight.

٦٩- يَاأَيُّهَا الَّذِينَ آمَنُوا لَا تَكُونُوا
كَالَّذِينَ آذَوْا مُوسَى
فَبَرَّأَهُ اللَّهُ مِمَّا قَالُوا
وَكَانَ عِنْدَ اللَّهِ وَجِيهًا ۚ

70. O ye who believe!
Fear Allah, and (always) say
A word directed to the Right:

٧٠- يَاأَيُّهَا الَّذِينَ آمَنُوا اتَّقُوا اللَّهَ
وَقُولُوا قَوْلًا سَدِيدًا ۚ

71. That He may make
Your conduct whole and sound
Anf forgive you your sins:
He that obeys Allah
And His Messenger, has already
Attained the highest
   Achievement.

٧١- يُصْلِحْ لَكُمْ أَعْمَالَكُمْ
وَيَغْفِرْ لَكُمْ ذُنُوبَكُمْ
وَمَنْ يُطِعِ اللَّهَ وَرَسُولَهُ فَقَدْ
فَازَ فَوْزًا عَظِيمًا ۚ

72. We did indeed offer
The Trust To the Heavens
And the Earth
And the Mountains;
But they refused
To undertake it,
Being afraid thereof:
But man undertook it —
He was indeed unjust
And foolish —

٧٢- إِنَّا عَرَضْنَا الْأَمَانَةَ عَلَى السَّمَاوَاتِ
وَالْأَرْضِ وَالْجِبَالِ
فَأَبَيْنَ أَنْ يَحْمِلْنَهَا
وَأَشْفَقْنَ مِنْهَا وَحَمَلَهَا الْإِنْسَانُ إِنَّهُ
كَانَ ظَلُومًا جَهُولًا ۚ

73. (With the result) that
Allah has to punish
The Hypocrites, men and women,
And the Unbelievers, men
And women, and Allah turns
In Mercy to the Believers,
Men and women: for Allah
Is Oft-Forgiving, Most Merciful.

٧٣- لِيُعَذِّبَ اللَّهُ
الْمُنَافِقِينَ وَالْمُنَافِقَاتِ وَالْمُشْرِكِينَ وَالْمُشْرِكَاتِ
وَيَتُوبَ اللَّهُ عَلَى الْمُؤْمِنِينَ وَالْمُؤْمِنَاتِ
وَكَانَ اللَّهُ غَفُورًا رَحِيمًا ۚ

INTRODUCTION TO SŪRA XXXIV. *(Sabā)* — 54 Verses

Now we begin a series of six Sūras, S. xxxiv. to S. xxxix., which recapitulate some of the features of the spiritual world. This Sūra leads off with emphasis on God's Mercy and Power and Truth. Then (in S. xxxv.) we are told how angels manifest the Power of God, and how different is Good from Evil and Truth from Falsehood. S xxxvi. is devoted to the Holy Prophet and the Qur ān that came through him. In S. xxxvii the emphasis is on the snares of the Evil One; in S. xxxviii., on the conquest of evil by wisdom and power as in the case of David and Solomon, and by Patience and Constancy as in the case of Job; and in S. xxxix. on the Final Judgment, which will sort out Faith from Unfaith and give to each its due.

The chronology has here no significance. This Sūra belongs to the early Meccan period.

Saba' (Sheba)[3784-A]

In the name of Allah, Most Gracious,
Most Merciful.

1. Praise be to Allah,
To Whom belong all things
In the heavens and on earth:
To Him be Praise
In the Hereafter:
And He is Full of Wisdom,
Acquainted with all things.

2. He knows all that goes
Into the earth, and all that
Comes out thereof: all that
Comes down from the sky
And all that ascends thereto
And He is the Most Merciful,
The Oft-Forgiving.

3. The Unbelievers say,
"Never to us will come
The Hour": say, "Nay!
But most surely,
By my Lord,   it will come
Upon you — by Him
Who knows the unseen —
From Whom is not hidden
The least little atom
In the Heavens or on earth:

Nor is there anything less
Than that, or greater, but
Is in the Record Perspicuous:

إِلَّا فِى كِتَٰبٍ مُّبِينٍ ۝

4. That He may reward
Those who believe and work
Deeds of righteousness: for such
Is Forgiveness and a
　　　　　　　Sustenance
Most Generous."

٤ـ لِيَجْزِيَ الَّذِينَ ءَامَنُوا وَعَمِلُوا الصَّٰلِحَٰتِ أُولَٰئِكَ لَهُم مَّغْفِرَةٌ وَرِزْقٌ كَرِيمٌ ۝

5. But those who strive
Against Our Signs, to frustrate
Them—for such will be
A Penalty—a Punishment
Most humiliating.

٥ـ وَالَّذِينَ سَعَوْ فِى ءَايَٰتِنَا مُعَٰجِزِينَ أُولَٰئِكَ لَهُمْ عَذَابٌ مِّن رِّجْزٍ أَلِيمٌ ۝

6. And those to whom
Knowledge has come see
That the (Revelation) sent down
To thee from thy Lord—
That is the Truth,
And that it guides
To the Path of the Exalted
(In Might), Worthy
Of all praise.

٦ـ وَيَرَى الَّذِينَ أُوتُوا الْعِلْمَ الَّذِى أُنزِلَ إِلَيْكَ مِن رَّبِّكَ هُوَ الْحَقَّ وَيَهْدِى إِلَىٰ صِرَٰطِ الْعَزِيزِ الْحَمِيدِ ۝

7. The Unbelievers say
(In ridicule): "Shall we
Point out to you a man
That will tell you,
When ye are all scattered
To pieces in disintegration,
That ye shall (then be
Raised) in a New Creation?

٧ـ وَقَالَ الَّذِينَ كَفَرُوا هَلْ نَدُلُّكُمْ عَلَىٰ رَجُلٍ يُنَبِّئُكُمْ إِذَا مُزِّقْتُمْ كُلَّ مُمَزَّقٍ إِنَّكُمْ لَفِى خَلْقٍ جَدِيدٍ ۝

8. "Has he invented a falsehood
Against Allah, or has
A spirit (seized) him?"—
Nay, it is those who
Believe not in the Hereafter,
That are in (real) Penalty,
And in farthest Error.

٨ـ أَفْتَرَىٰ عَلَى اللَّهِ كَذِبًا أَم بِهِ جِنَّةٌ بَلِ الَّذِينَ لَا يُؤْمِنُونَ بِالْءَاخِرَةِ فِى الْعَذَابِ وَالضَّلَٰلِ الْبَعِيدِ ۝

9. See they not what is
Before them and behind them,
Of the sky and the earth?
If We wished, We could
Cause the earth to swallow

٩ـ أَفَلَمْ يَرَوْا إِلَىٰ مَا بَيْنَ أَيْدِيهِمْ وَمَا خَلْفَهُم مِّنَ السَّمَاءِ وَالْأَرْضِ إِن نَّشَأْ نَخْسِفْ بِهِمُ الْأَرْضَ

Them up, or cause a piece
Of the sky to fall upon
            them.
Verily in this is a Sign
For every devotee that
Turns to Allah (in repentance).

SECTION 2.

10. He bestowed Grace aforetime
On David from Ourselves:
"O ye Mountains! sing ye
Back the Praises of Allah
With him! and ye birds
(Also)! And We made
The iron soft for him—

11. (Commanding), "Make thou
Coats of mail, balancing well
The rings of chain armour,
And work ye righteousness:
For be sure I see
(Clearly) all that ye do."

12. And to Solomon (We
Made) the Wind (obedient):
Its early morning (stride)
Was a month's (journey),
And its evening (stride)
Was a month's (journey);
And We made a Font
Of molten brass to flow
For him; and there were
Jinns that worked in front
Of him, by the leave
Of his Lord, and if any
Of them turned aside
From Our command, We
Made him taste
Of the Penalty
Of the Blazing Fire.

13. They worked for him
As he desired, (making)
          Arches,
Images, Basins,
As large as Reservoirs,
And (cooking) Cauldrons fixed
(In their places): "Work ye,
Sons of David, with thanks!

أَوْ نُسْقِطْ عَلَيْهِمْ كِسَفًا مِّنَ السَّمَآءِ

إِنَّ فِى ذٰلِكَ لَآيَةً

لِّكُلِّ عَبْدٍ مُّنِيبٍ ۝

١٠- وَلَقَدْ اٰتَيْنَا دَاوٗدَ مِنَّا فَضْلًا

يٰجِبَالُ أَوِّبِى مَعَهُ وَالطَّيْرَ

وَأَلَنَّا لَهُ الْحَدِيدَ ۝

١١- أَنِ اعْمَلْ سٰبِغٰتٍ وَّقَدِّرْ فِى السَّرْدِ

وَاعْمَلُوْا صَالِحًا

إِنِّى بِمَا تَعْمَلُوْنَ بَصِيْرٌ ۝

١٢- وَلِسُلَيْمٰنَ الرِّيْحَ

غُدُوُّهَا شَهْرٌ

وَّرَوَاحُهَا شَهْرٌ

وَأَسَلْنَا لَهُ عَيْنَ الْقِطْرِ

وَمِنَ الْجِنِّ مَنْ يَّعْمَلُ بَيْنَ يَدَيْهِ

بِإِذْنِ رَبِّهِ

وَمَنْ يَّزِغْ مِنْهُمْ عَنْ أَمْرِنَا

نُذِقْهُ مِنْ عَذَابِ السَّعِيْرِ ۝

١٣- يَعْمَلُوْنَ لَهُ مَا يَشَآءُ مِنْ مَّحَارِيْبَ

وَتَمَاثِيْلَ وَجِفَانٍ كَالْجَوَابِ

وَقُدُوْرٍ رَّاسِيٰتٍ

اعْمَلُوْا اٰلَ دَاوٗدَ شُكْرًا

But few of My servants
Are grateful!"

14. Then, when We decreed
(Solomon's) death, nothing
showed them
His death except a little
Worm of the earth, which
Kept (slowly) gnawing away
At his staff: so when he
Fell down, the Jinns saw
Plainly that if they had
Known the unseen, they
Would not have tarried
In the humiliating Penalty
(Of their Task).

15. There was, for Saba',
Aforetime, a Sign in their
Homeland—two Gardens
To the right and to the left.
Eat of the Sustenance (provided)
By your Lord, and be grateful
To Him: a territory fair and happy,
And a Lord Oft-Forgiving!

16. But they turned away
(From Allah), and We sent
Against them the flood
(Released) from the Dams,
And We converted their two
Garden (rows) into "gardens"
Producing bitter fruit,
And tamarisks, and some few
(Stunted) Lote trees.

17. That was the Requital
We gave them because
They ungratefully rejected
Faith:
And never do We give
(Such) requital except to such
As are ungrateful rejecters.

18. Between them and the Cities
On which We had poured
Our blessings, We had placed
Cities in prominent positions,

وَقَلِيلٌ مِّنْ عِبَادِيَ الشَّكُوْرُ ۞

١٤- فَلَمَّا قَضَيْنَا عَلَيْهِ الْمَوْتَ
مَا دَلَّهُمْ عَلَى مَوْتِهِ
إِلَّا دَابَّةُ الْأَرْضِ
تَأْكُلُ مِنْسَأَتَهُ ۚ
فَلَمَّا خَرَّ تَبَيَّنَتِ الْجِنُّ
أَنْ لَّوْ كَانُوْا يَعْلَمُوْنَ الْغَيْبَ مَا لَبِثُوْا
فِى الْعَذَابِ الْمُهِيْنِ ۞

١٥- لَقَدْ كَانَ لِسَبَإٍ فِيْ مَسْكَنِهِمْ آيَةٌ ۚ
جَنَّتَانِ عَنْ يَّمِيْنٍ وَّشِمَالٍ ۥ
كُلُوْا مِنْ رِّزْقِ رَبِّكُمْ وَاشْكُرُوْا لَهُ ۥ
بَلْدَةٌ طَيِّبَةٌ وَّرَبٌّ غَفُوْرٌ ۞

١٦- فَأَعْرَضُوْا فَأَرْسَلْنَا
عَلَيْهِمْ سَيْلَ الْعَرِمِ
وَبَدَّلْنَاهُمْ بِجَنَّتَيْهِمْ جَنَّتَيْنِ
ذَوَاتَيْ أُكُلٍ خَمْطٍ
وَّأَثْلٍ وَّشَيْءٍ مِّنْ سِدْرٍ قَلِيْلٍ ۞

١٧- ذٰلِكَ جَزَيْنَاهُمْ
بِمَا كَفَرُوْا ۚ
وَهَلْ نُجَازِيْ إِلَّا الْكَفُوْرَ ۞

١٨- وَجَعَلْنَا بَيْنَهُمْ وَبَيْنَ الْقُرَى الَّتِيْ
بَارَكْنَا فِيْهَا قُرًى ظَاهِرَةً

And between them We had
Appointed stages of journey
In due proportion: "Travel therein,
Secure, by night and by day."

وَقَدَّرْنَا فِيهَا السَّيْرَ
سِيرُوا فِيهَا لَيَالِيَ وَأَيَّامًا آمِنِينَ ٠

19. But they said: "Our Lord!
Place longer distances
Between our journey-stages":
But they wronged themselves
               (therein)
At length We made them
As a tale (that is told),
And We dispersed them
All in scattered fragments.
Verily in this are Signs
For every (soul that is)
Patiently constant and grateful.

١٩- فَقَالُوا رَبَّنَا بَاعِدْ بَيْنَ
أَسْفَارِنَا وَظَلَمُوا أَنْفُسَهُمْ
فَجَعَلْنَاهُمْ أَحَادِيثَ
وَمَزَّقْنَاهُمْ كُلَّ مُمَزَّقٍ
إِنَّ فِي ذَلِكَ لَآيَاتٍ
لِكُلِّ صَبَّارٍ شَكُورٍ ٠

20. And on them did Satan
Prove true his idea,
And they followed him, all
But a Party that believed.

٢٠- وَلَقَدْ صَدَّقَ عَلَيْهِمْ إِبْلِيسُ ظَنَّهُ
فَاتَّبَعُوهُ إِلَّا فَرِيقًا مِنَ الْمُؤْمِنِينَ ٠

21. But he had no authority
Over them—except that We
Might test the man who
Believes in the Hereafter
From him who is in doubt
Concerning it: and thy Lord
Doth watch over all things.
      SECTION 3.

٢١- وَمَا كَانَ لَهُ عَلَيْهِمْ مِنْ سُلْطَانٍ
إِلَّا لِنَعْلَمَ مَنْ يُؤْمِنُ بِالْآخِرَةِ
مِمَّنْ هُوَ مِنْهَا فِي شَكٍّ
وَرَبُّكَ عَلَى كُلِّ شَيْءٍ حَفِيظٌ ٠

22. Say: "Call upon other (gods)
Whom ye fancy, besides Allah:
They have no power—
Not the weight of an atom—
In the heavens or on earth:
No (sort of) share have they
Therein, nor is any of them
A helper to Allah.

٢٢- قُلِ ادْعُوا الَّذِينَ زَعَمْتُمْ مِنْ دُونِ
اللَّهِ لَا يَمْلِكُونَ مِثْقَالَ ذَرَّةٍ
فِي السَّمَاوَاتِ وَلَا فِي الْأَرْضِ وَمَا لَهُمْ فِيهِمَا
مِنْ شِرْكٍ وَمَا لَهُ مِنْهُمْ مِنْ ظَهِيرٍ ٠

23. "No intercession can avail
In His Presence, except for
              those
For whom He has granted
Permission. So far (is this
The case) that, when terror
Is removed from their hearts
(At the Day of Judgement, then)

٢٣- وَلَا تَنْفَعُ الشَّفَاعَةُ عِنْدَهُ إِلَّا
لِمَنْ أَذِنَ لَهُ
حَتَّى إِذَا فُزِّعَ عَنْ قُلُوبِهِمْ
قَالُوا مَاذَا قَالَ رَبُّكُمْ

Will they say, 'What is it
That your Lord
             commanded?'
They will say: 'That which is
True and just; and He is
The Most High, Most Great'."

قَالُوا الْحَقَّ
وَهُوَ الْعَلِيُّ الْكَبِيرُ ۝

24. Say: "Who gives you
Sustenance, from the heavens
And the earth?" Say:
"It is Allah; and certain it is
That either we or ye
Are on right guidance
Or in manifest error!"

٢٤- قُلْ مَنْ يَرْزُقُكُمْ مِنَ السَّمَاوَاتِ
وَالْأَرْضِ قُلِ اللَّهُ
وَإِنَّا أَوْ إِيَّاكُمْ لَعَلَى هُدًى
أَوْ فِي ضَلَالٍ مُبِينٍ ۝

25. Say: "Ye shall not be
Questioned as to our sins,
Nor shall we be questioned
As to what ye do."

٢٥- قُلْ لَا تُسْأَلُونَ عَمَّا أَجْرَمْنَا
وَلَا نُسْأَلُ عَمَّا تَعْمَلُونَ ۝

26. Say: "Our Lord will gather us
Together and will in the end
Decide the matter between us
(And you) in truth and
             justice:
And He is the One to decide,
The One Who knows all."

٢٦- قُلْ يَجْمَعُ بَيْنَنَا رَبُّنَا
ثُمَّ يَفْتَحُ بَيْنَنَا بِالْحَقِّ
وَهُوَ الْفَتَّاحُ الْعَلِيمُ ۝

27. Say: "Show me those whom
Ye have joined with Him
As partners: by no means
(Can ye). Nay, He is Allah
The Exalted in Power,
The Wise."

٢٧- قُلْ أَرُونِيَ الَّذِينَ
أَلْحَقْتُمْ بِهِ شُرَكَاءَ كَلَّا
بَلْ هُوَ اللَّهُ الْعَزِيزُ الْحَكِيمُ ۝

28. We have not sent thee
But as a universal
             (Messenger)
To men, giving them
Glad tidings, and warning them
(Against sin), but most men
Understand not.

٢٨- وَمَا أَرْسَلْنَاكَ إِلَّا كَافَّةً
لِلنَّاسِ بَشِيرًا وَنَذِيرًا
وَلَكِنَّ أَكْثَرَ النَّاسِ لَا يَعْلَمُونَ ۝

29. They say: "When will this
Promise (come to pass)
If ye are telling the truth?"

٢٩- وَيَقُولُونَ مَتَى هَذَا الْوَعْدُ
إِنْ كُنْتُمْ صَادِقِينَ ۝

30. Say: "The appointment to you
Is for a Day, which ye

٣٠- قُلْ لَكُمْ مِيعَادُ يَوْمٍ لَا تَسْتَأْخِرُونَ

Cannot put back for an hour
Nor put forward."

SECTION 4.

31. The Unbelievers say:
"We shall neither believe
In this scripture nor in (any)
That (came) before it."
Couldst thou but see when
The wrongdoers will be made
To stand before their Lord,
Throwing back the word
(of blame)
On one another! Those who
Had been despised will say
To the arrogant ones:
"Had it not been for you,
We should certainly
Have been believers!"

32. The arrogant ones will say
To those who had been
despised:
"Was it we who kept you
Back from Guidance after
It reached you? Nay, rather,
It was ye who transgressed."

33. Those who had been despised
Will say to the arrogant ones:
"Nay! it was a plot
(Of yours) by day and by
night:
Behold! ye (constantly) ordered
us
To be ungrateful to Allah
And to attribute equals to
Him!"
They will declare (their)
repentance
When they see the Penalty:
We shall put yokes
On the necks of the
Unbelievers:
It would only be a requital
For their (ill) Deeds.

34. Never did We send
A Warner to a population,

عَنْهُ سَاعَةً وَّلَا يَسْتَقْدِمُوْنَ ۞

٣١- وَقَالَ الَّذِيْنَ كَفَرُوْا لَنْ نُّؤْمِنَ
بِهٰذَا الْقُرْاٰنِ وَلَا بِالَّذِيْ بَيْنَ يَدَيْهِ ۗ
وَلَوْ تَرٰى إِذِ الظّٰلِمُوْنَ مَوْقُوْفُوْنَ عِنْدَ
رَبِّهِمْ ۚ
يَرْجِعُ بَعْضُهُمْ إِلٰى بَعْضٍ ۨالْقَوْلَ ۚ
يَقُوْلُ الَّذِيْنَ اسْتُضْعِفُوا لِلَّذِيْنَ اسْتَكْبَرُوْا
لَوْلَا أَنْتُمْ لَكُنَّا مُؤْمِنِيْنَ ۞

٣٢- قَالَ الَّذِيْنَ اسْتَكْبَرُوا لِلَّذِيْنَ
اسْتُضْعِفُوا أَنَحْنُ صَدَدْنٰكُمْ عَنِ الْهُدٰى
بَعْدَ إِذْ جَاءَكُمْ بَلْ كُنْتُمْ مُّجْرِمِيْنَ ۞

٣٣- وَقَالَ الَّذِيْنَ اسْتُضْعِفُوا لِلَّذِيْنَ
اسْتَكْبَرُوا بَلْ مَكْرُ الَّيْلِ وَالنَّهَارِ
إِذْ تَأْمُرُوْنَنَا أَنْ نَّكْفُرَ بِاللّٰهِ
وَنَجْعَلَ لَهٗ أَنْدَادًا ۗ
وَأَسَرُّوا النَّدَامَةَ لَمَّا رَأَوُا الْعَذَابَ ۚ
وَجَعَلْنَا الْأَغْلٰلَ
فِيْ أَعْنَاقِ الَّذِيْنَ كَفَرُوْا ۚ
هَلْ يُجْزَوْنَ إِلَّا
مَا كَانُوْا يَعْمَلُوْنَ ۞

٣٤- وَمَا أَرْسَلْنَا فِيْ قَرْيَةٍ مِّنْ نَّذِيْرٍ

But the wealthy ones among
them
Said: "We believe not
In the (Message) with which
Ye have been sent."

إِلَّا قَالَ مُتْرَفُوهَا إِنَّا بِمَا أُرْسِلْتُم بِهِ كَفِرُونَ ۝

35. They said: "We have more
In wealth and in sons,
And we cannot be punished."

٣٥- وَقَالُوا نَحْنُ أَكْثَرُ أَمْوَالًا وَأَوْلَادًا وَمَا نَحْنُ بِمُعَذَّبِينَ ۝

36. Say: "Verily my Lord enlarges
And restricts the Provision
To whom He pleases, but
Most men understand not."

٣٦- قُلْ إِنَّ رَبِّي يَبْسُطُ الرِّزْقَ لِمَن يَشَاءُ وَيَقْدِرُ وَلَكِنَّ أَكْثَرَ النَّاسِ لَا يَعْلَمُونَ ۝

SECTION 5.

37. It is not your wealth
Nor your sons, that will
Bring you nearer to Us
In degree: but only
Those who believe and work
Righteousness—these are
The ones for whom there is
A multiplied Reward
For their deeds, while
Secure they (reside)
In the dwellings on high!

٣٧- وَمَا أَمْوَالُكُمْ وَلَا أَوْلَادُكُم بِالَّتِي تُقَرِّبُكُمْ عِندَنَا زُلْفَى إِلَّا مَنْ آمَنَ وَعَمِلَ صَالِحًا فَأُوْلَئِكَ لَهُمْ جَزَاءُ الضِّعْفِ بِمَا عَمِلُوا وَهُمْ فِي الْغُرُفَاتِ آمِنُونَ ۝

38. Those who strive against
Our Signs, to frustrate them,
Will be given over
Into Punishment.

٣٨- وَالَّذِينَ يَسْعَوْنَ فِي آيَاتِنَا مُعَاجِزِينَ أُوْلَئِكَ فِي الْعَذَابِ مُحْضَرُونَ ۝

39. Say: "Verily my Lord enlarges
And restricts the Sustenance
To such of His servants
As He pleases: and nothing
Do ye spend in the least
(In His Cause) but He
Replaces it: for He is
The Best of those who
Grant Sustenance.

٣٩- قُلْ إِنَّ رَبِّي يَبْسُطُ الرِّزْقَ لِمَن يَشَاءُ مِنْ عِبَادِهِ وَيَقْدِرُ لَهُ وَمَا أَنفَقْتُم مِّن شَيْءٍ فَهُوَ يُخْلِفُهُ وَهُوَ خَيْرُ الرَّازِقِينَ ۝

40. One Day He will
Gather them all together,
And say to the angels,
"Was it you that these
Men used to worship?"

٤٠- وَيَوْمَ يَحْشُرُهُمْ جَمِيعًا ثُمَّ يَقُولُ لِلْمَلَائِكَةِ أَهَؤُلَاءِ إِيَّاكُمْ كَانُوا يَعْبُدُونَ ۝

41. They will say, "Glory to Thee!
Our (tie) is with Thee—
As Protector —not with them.
Nay, but they worshipped
The Jinns: most of them
Believed in them."

٤١ ۔ قَالُوا سُبْحٰنَكَ أَنْتَ وَلِيُّنَا
مِنْ دُوْنِهِمْ ۚ بَلْ كَانُوا يَعْبُدُوْنَ
الْجِنَّ ۚ أَكْثَرُهُمْ بِهِمْ مُّؤْمِنُوْنَ ○

42. So on that Day
No power shall they have
Over each other, for profit
Or harm: and We shall
Say to the wrongdoers,
"Taste ye the Penalty
Of the Fire—the which
Ye were wont to deny!"

٤٢ ۔ فَالْيَوْمَ لَا يَمْلِكُ بَعْضُكُمْ لِبَعْضٍ
نَّفْعًا وَّلَا ضَرًّا ۚ
وَنَقُوْلُ لِلَّذِيْنَ ظَلَمُوا ذُوْقُوا عَذَابَ
النَّارِ الَّتِيْ كُنْتُمْ بِهَا تُكَذِّبُوْنَ ○

43. When Our Clear Signs
Are rehearsed to them,
They say, "This is only
A man who wishes
To hinder you from the
(worship)
Which your fathers practised."
And they say,: "This is
Only a falsehood invented!"
And the Unbelievers say
Of the Truth when it comes
To them. "This is nothing
But evident magic!"

٤٣ ۔ وَإِذَا تُتْلٰى عَلَيْهِمْ اٰيَاتُنَا بَيِّنٰتٍ
قَالُوْا مَا هٰذَا إِلَّا رَجُلٌ يُّرِيْدُ أَنْ يَّصُدَّكُمْ
عَمَّا كَانَ يَعْبُدُ اٰبَاؤُكُمْ ۚ
وَقَالُوْا مَا هٰذَا إِلَّا إِفْكٌ مُّفْتَرًى ۚ
وَقَالَ الَّذِيْنَ كَفَرُوا لِلْحَقِّ لَمَّا جَاءَهُمْ ۙ
إِنْ هٰذَا إِلَّا سِحْرٌ مُّبِيْنٌ ○

44. But We had not given
Them Books which they could
Study, nor sent messengers
To them before thee
As Warners.

٤٤ ۔ وَمَا اٰتَيْنٰهُمْ مِّنْ كُتُبٍ يَّدْرُسُوْنَهَا
وَمَا أَرْسَلْنَا إِلَيْهِمْ قَبْلَكَ مِنْ نَّذِيْرٍ ۚ

45. And their predecessors rejected
(The Truth); these have
Not received a tenth
Of what We had granted
To those: yet when they
rejected
My messengers, how (terrible)
Was My rejection (of them)!

٤٥ ۔ وَكَذَّبَ الَّذِيْنَ مِنْ قَبْلِهِمْ ۙ
وَمَا بَلَغُوْا مِعْشَارَ مَا اٰتَيْنٰهُمْ
فَكَذَّبُوْا رُسُلِيْ ۖ
فَكَيْفَ كَانَ نَكِيْرِ ۞

SECTION 6.

46. Say: "I do admonish you
On one point: that ye
Do stand up before Allah—

٤٦ ۔ قُلْ إِنَّمَا أَعِظُكُمْ بِوَاحِدَةٍ ۖ
أَنْ تَقُوْمُوْا لِلّٰهِ مَثْنٰى وَفُرَادٰى

(It may be) in pairs,
Or (it may be) singly—
And reflect (within yourselves):
Your Companion is not
Possessed: he is no less
Than a Warner to you,
In face of a terrible
Penalty."

47. Say: "No reward do I
Ask of you: it is (all)
In your interest: my reward
Is only due from Allah:
And He is Witness
To all things."

48. Say: "Verily my Lord
Doth cast the (mantle
Of) Truth (over His servants)—
He that has full knowledge
Of (all) that is hidden."

49. Say: "The Truth has arrived,
And Falsehood neither creates
Anything new, nor restores
Anything."

50. Say: "If I am astray,
I only stray to the loss
Of my own soul: but if
I receive guidance, it is
Because of the inspiration
Of my Lord to me:
It is He Who hears
All things, and is (ever) near."

51. If thou couldst but see
When they will quake
With terror; but then
There will be no escape
(For them), and they will be
Seized from a position
(Quite) near.

52. And they will say,
"We do believe (now)
In the (Truth)"; but how
Could they receive (Faith)

ثُمَّ تَتَفَكَّرُوْا ۛ
مَا بِصَاحِبِكُمْ مِّنْ جِنَّةٍ ۚ
إِنْ هُوَ إِلَّا نَذِيْرٌ لَّكُمْ
بَيْنَ يَدَيْ عَذَابٍ شَدِيْدٍ ۟

٤٧- قُلْ مَا سَأَلْتُكُمْ مِّنْ أَجْرٍ فَهُوَ لَكُمْ ۚ
إِنْ أَجْرِيَ إِلَّا عَلَى اللّٰهِ ۚ وَهُوَ عَلٰى
كُلِّ شَيْءٍ شَهِيْدٌ ۟

٤٨- قُلْ إِنَّ رَبِّيْ يَقْذِفُ
بِالْحَقِّ ۚ عَلَّامُ الْغُيُوْبِ ۟

٤٩- قُلْ جَاءَ الْحَقُّ
وَمَا يُبْدِئُ الْبَاطِلُ وَمَا يُعِيْدُ ۟

٥٠- قُلْ إِنْ ضَلَلْتُ فَإِنَّمَا أَضِلُّ عَلٰى نَفْسِيْ ۚ
وَإِنِ اهْتَدَيْتُ فَبِمَا يُوْحِيْ إِلَيَّ رَبِّيْ ۚ
إِنَّهُ سَمِيْعٌ قَرِيْبٌ ۟

٥١- وَلَوْ تَرٰى إِذْ فَزِعُوْا
فَلَا فَوْتَ
وَأُخِذُوْا مِنْ مَّكَانٍ قَرِيْبٍ ۟ۙ

٥٢- وَقَالُوْا آمَنَّا بِهٖ ۚ
وَأَنّٰى لَهُمُ التَّنَاوُشُ مِنْ

From a position (so) far off—

تَمَكَانٍ بَعِيدٍ

53. Seeing that they did reject
Faith (entirely) before, and
That they (continually) cast
(Slanders) on the Unseen
From a position far off?

٥٣- وَّقَدْ كَفَرُوْا بِهٖ مِنْ قَبْلُ ۚ
وَيَقْذِفُوْنَ بِالْغَيْبِ مِنْ مَّكَانٍ بَعِيدٍ ۞

54. And between them
And their desires,
Is placed a barrier,
As was done in the past
With their partisans:
For they were indeed
In suspicious (disquieting)
                    doubt.

٥٤- وَحِيْلَ بَيْنَهُمْ وَبَيْنَ مَا يَشْتَهُوْنَ
كَمَا فُعِلَ بِاَشْيَاعِهِمْ مِّنْ قَبْلُ ۚ
اِنَّهُمْ كَانُوْا فِيْ شَكٍّ مُّرِيْبٍ ۞

INTRODUCTION TO SŪRA XXXV. *(Fāṭir)* — 45 Verses

See Introduction to the last Sūra.

This Sūra deals with the mystery of Creation and its maintenance, with various forces typified by the wings of Angels. Whether we look to outer nature or to man, God's Grace proclaims His Glory, and protects His votaries from Evil.

It is an early Meccan Sūra, but its chronology has no significance.

Fāṭir (The Originator of Creation)

In the name of Allah, Most Gracious,
Most Merciful.

1. Praise be to Allah,
Who created (out of nothing)
The heavens and the earth,
Who made the angels
Messengers with wings—
Two, or three, or four (Pairs):
He adds to Creation
As He pleases: for Allah
Has power over all things.

2. What Allah out of His Mercy
Doth bestow on mankind
There is none can withhold:
What He doth withhold,
There is none can grant,
Apart from Him:
And He is the Exalted
In Power, Full of Wisdom.

3. O men! call to mind
The grace of Allah unto you!
Is there a Creator, other
Than Allah, to give you
Sustenance from heaven
Or earth? There is
No god but He: how
Then are ye deluded
Away from the Truth?

4. And if they reject thee,
So were messengers rejected

Before thee: to Allah
Go back for decision
All affairs.

5. O men! certainly
The promise of Allah
Is true. Let not then
This present life deceive you,
Nor let the Chief Deceiver
Deceive you about Allah.

6. Verily Satan is an enemy
To you: so treat him
As an enemy. He only
Invites his adherents,
That they may become
Companions of the Blazing Fire.

7. For those who reject Allah,
Is a terrible Penalty: but
For those who believe
And work righteous deeds,
Is Forgiveness, and
A magnificent Reward.

SECTION 2.

8. Is he, then, to whom
The evil of his conduct
Is made alluring, so
That he looks upon it
As good, (equal to one
Who is rightly guided)?
For Allah leaves to stray
Whom He wills, and guides
Whom He wills. So
Let not thy soul go out
In (vainly) sighing after them:
For Allah knows well
All that they do!

9. It is Allah Who sends
Forth the Winds, so that
They raise up the Clouds,
And We drive them
To a Land that is dead,
And revive the earth therewith
After its death: even so
(Will be) the Resurrection!

10. If any do seek

تَبَّلِكَ ۚ وَإِلَى اللّٰهِ تُرْجَعُ الْأُمُوْرُ ۞

٥ - يٰٓاَيُّهَا النَّاسُ اِنَّ وَعْدَ اللّٰهِ
حَقٌّ فَلَا تَغُرَّنَّكُمُ الْحَيٰوةُ الدُّنْيَا ۖ
وَلَا يَغُرَّنَّكُمْ بِاللّٰهِ الْغَرُوْرُ ۞

٦ - اِنَّ الشَّيْطٰنَ لَكُمْ عَدُوٌّ فَاتَّخِذُوْهُ عَدُوًّا ۚ
اِنَّمَا يَدْعُوْا حِزْبَهٗ
لِيَكُوْنُوْا مِنْ اَصْحٰبِ السَّعِيْرِ ۞

٧ - اَلَّذِيْنَ كَفَرُوْا لَهُمْ عَذَابٌ شَدِيْدٌ ۚ
وَالَّذِيْنَ اٰمَنُوْا وَعَمِلُوا الصّٰلِحٰتِ
لَهُمْ مَّغْفِرَةٌ وَّاَجْرٌ كَبِيْرٌ ۞

٨ - اَفَمَنْ زُيِّنَ لَهٗ سُوْءُ عَمَلِهٖ
فَرَاٰهُ حَسَنًا ۚ
فَاِنَّ اللّٰهَ يُضِلُّ مَنْ يَّشَآءُ
وَيَهْدِيْ مَنْ يَّشَآءُ ۖ
فَلَا تَذْهَبْ نَفْسُكَ عَلَيْهِمْ حَسَرٰتٍ ۚ
اِنَّ اللّٰهَ عَلِيْمٌ بِمَا يَصْنَعُوْنَ ۞

٩ - وَاللّٰهُ الَّذِيْٓ اَرْسَلَ الرِّيٰحَ
فَتُثِيْرُ سَحَابًا
فَسُقْنٰهُ اِلٰى بَلَدٍ مَّيِّتٍ فَاَحْيَيْنَا بِهِ الْاَرْضَ
بَعْدَ مَوْتِهَا ۚ كَذٰلِكَ النُّشُوْرُ ۞

١٠ - مَنْ كَانَ يُرِيْدُ الْعِزَّةَ

For glory and power—
To Allah belong
All glory and power.
To Him mount up
(All) Words of Purity:
It is He Who exalts
Each Deed of Righteousness.
Those that lay Plots
Of Evil—for them
Is a Penalty terrible;
And the plotting of such
Will be void (of result).

فَلِلّٰهِ الْعِزَّةُ جَمِيعًا
إِلَيْهِ يَصْعَدُ الْكَلِمُ الطَّيِّبُ
وَالْعَمَلُ الصَّالِحُ يَرْفَعُهُ
وَالَّذِينَ يَمْكُرُونَ السَّيِّئَاتِ
لَهُمْ عَذَابٌ شَدِيدٌ
وَمَكْرُ أُولٰئِكَ هُوَ يَبُورُ ۝

11. And Allah did create
You from dust;
Then　　from a sperm drop;
Then He made you
In pairs. And no female
Conceives, or lays down
(Her load), but with His
Knowledge. Nor is a man
Long-lived granted length
Of days, nor is a part
Cut off from his life,
But is in a Decree
(Ordained). All this
Is easy for Allah.

١١- وَاللّٰهُ خَلَقَكُمْ مِنْ تُرَابٍ
ثُمَّ مِنْ نُطْفَةٍ ثُمَّ جَعَلَكُمْ أَزْوَاجًا
وَمَا تَحْمِلُ مِنْ أُنْثَى وَلَا تَضَعُ
إِلَّا بِعِلْمِهِ ۚ وَمَا
يُعَمَّرُ مِنْ مُعَمَّرٍ
وَلَا يُنْقَصُ مِنْ عُمُرِهِ إِلَّا فِي كِتَابٍ
إِنَّ ذٰلِكَ عَلَى اللّٰهِ يَسِيرٌ ۝

12. Nor are the two bodies
Of flowing water alike—
The one palatable, sweet,
And pleasant to drink,
And the other, salty
And bitter. Yet from each
(Kind of water) do ye
Eat flesh fresh and tender,
And ye extract ornaments
To wear; and thou seest
The ships therein that plough
The waves, that ye may
Seek (thus) of the Bounty
Of Allah that ye
May be grateful.

١٢- وَمَا يَسْتَوِي الْبَحْرَانِ
هٰذَا عَذْبٌ فُرَاتٌ سَائِغٌ شَرَابُهُ
وَهٰذَا مِلْحٌ أُجَاجٌ
وَمِنْ كُلٍّ تَأْكُلُونَ لَحْمًا طَرِيًّا
وَتَسْتَخْرِجُونَ حِلْيَةً تَلْبَسُونَهَا
وَتَرَى الْفُلْكَ فِيهِ مَوَاخِرَ
لِتَبْتَغُوا مِنْ فَضْلِهِ
وَلَعَلَّكُمْ تَشْكُرُونَ ۝

13. He merges Night into Day,
And He merges Day
Into Night, and He has
Subjected the sun and
The moon (to His Law):

١٣- يُولِجُ اللَّيْلَ فِي النَّهَارِ وَيُولِجُ النَّهَارَ
فِي اللَّيْلِ وَسَخَّرَ الشَّمْسَ وَالْقَمَرَ

Each one runs its course
For a term appointed.
Such is Allah your Lord:
To Him belongs all Dominion.
And those whom ye invoke
Besides Him have not
The least power.

كُلٌّ يَجْرِى لِأَجَلٍ مُّسَمًّى ۚ ذٰلِكُمُ اللّٰهُ رَبُّكُمْ لَهُ الْمُلْكُ ۚ وَالَّذِينَ تَدْعُونَ مِنْ دُونِهِ مَا يَمْلِكُونَ مِنْ قِطْمِيرٍ ۚ

14. If ye invoke them,
They will not listen
To your call, and if
They were to listen,
They cannot answer
Your (prayer). On the Day
Of Judgement they will reject
Your "Partnership". And none,
(O man!) can tell thee
(The Truth) like the One
Who is acquainted with all things.

١٤- إِنْ تَدْعُوهُمْ لَا يَسْمَعُوا دُعَاءَكُمْ ۖ وَلَوْ سَمِعُوا مَا اسْتَجَابُوا لَكُمْ ۖ وَيَوْمَ الْقِيٰمَةِ يَكْفُرُونَ بِشِرْكِكُمْ ۚ وَلَا يُنَبِّئُكَ مِثْلُ خَبِيرٍ ۚ

SECTION 3.

15. O ye men! It is
Ye that have need
Of Allah: but Allah is
The One Free of all wants,
Worthy of all praise.

١٥- يٰأَيُّهَا النَّاسُ أَنْتُمُ الْفُقَرَاءُ إِلَى اللّٰهِ ۖ وَاللّٰهُ هُوَ الْغَنِيُّ الْحَمِيدُ ۚ

16. If He so pleased, He
Could blot you out
And bring in
A New Creation

١٦- إِنْ يَشَأْ يُذْهِبْكُمْ وَيَأْتِ بِخَلْقٍ جَدِيدٍ ۚ

17. Nor is that (at all)
Difficult for Allah.

١٧- وَمَا ذٰلِكَ عَلَى اللّٰهِ بِعَزِيزٍ ۚ

18. Nor can a bearer   of burdens
Bear another's burden.
If one heavily laden should
Call another to (bear) his load,
Not the least portion of it
Can be carried (by the other),
Even though he be nearly
Related. Thou canst but
Admonish such as fear
Their Lord unseen
And establish regular Prayer.
And whoever purifies himself
Does so for the benefit

١٨- وَلَا تَزِرُ وَازِرَةٌ وِزْرَ أُخْرَىٰ ۚ وَإِنْ تَدْعُ مُثْقَلَةٌ إِلَىٰ حِمْلِهَا لَا يُحْمَلْ مِنْهُ شَيْءٌ ۚ وَلَوْ كَانَ ذَا قُرْبَىٰ ۗ إِنَّمَا تُنْذِرُ الَّذِينَ يَخْشَوْنَ رَبَّهُمْ بِالْغَيْبِ وَأَقَامُوا الصَّلٰوةَ ۚ وَمَنْ تَزَكَّىٰ فَإِنَّمَا يَتَزَكَّىٰ لِنَفْسِهِ ۚ

Of his own soul; and
The destination (of all)
Is to Allah.

وَإِلَى اللهِ الْمَصِيرُ ۟

19. The blind and the seeing
Are not alike;

١٩- وَمَا يَسْتَوِى الْأَعْمَى وَالْبَصِيرُ ۙ

20. Nor are the depths
Of Darkness and the Light;

٢٠- وَلَا الظُّلُمَاتُ وَلَا النُّورُ ۙ

21. Nor are the (chilly) shade
And the (genial) heat of the
sun:

٢١- وَلَا الظِّلُّ وَلَا الْحَرُورُ ۚ

22. Nor are alike those
That are living and those
That are dead. Allah can
Make any that He wills
To hear; but thou
Canst not make those
To hear who are
(Buried) in graves.

٢٢- وَمَا يَسْتَوِى الْأَحْيَاءُ وَلَا الْأَمْوَاتُ ۗ
إِنَّ اللهَ يُسْمِعُ مَنْ يَّشَاءُ ۚ
وَمَا أَنْتَ بِمُسْمِعٍ
مَّنْ فِى الْقُبُورِ ۟

23. Thou art no other
Than a warner.

٢٣- إِنْ أَنْتَ إِلَّا نَذِيرٌ ۟

24. Verily We have sent thee
In truth, as a bearer
Of glad tidings,
And as a warner:
And there never was
A people, without a warner
Having lived among them
(In the past).

٢٤- إِنَّا أَرْسَلْنَاكَ بِالْحَقِّ
بَشِيرًا وَّ نَذِيرًا ۚ وَإِنْ مِّنْ أُمَّةٍ
إِلَّا خَلَا فِيهَا نَذِيرٌ ۟

25. And if they reject thee,
So did their predecessors,
To whom came their messengers
With Clear Signs,
Scriptures
And the Book
Of Enlightenment.

٢٥- وَإِنْ يُّكَذِّبُوكَ فَقَدْ كَذَّبَ الَّذِينَ
مِنْ قَبْلِهِمْ ۚ
جَاءَتْهُمْ رُسُلُهُمْ بِالْبَيِّنَاتِ
وَبِالزُّبُرِ وَبِالْكِتَابِ الْمُنِيرِ ۟

26. In the end did I
Punish those who rejected
Faith: and how (terrible)
Was My rejection (of them)!

٢٦- ثُمَّ أَخَذْتُ الَّذِينَ كَفَرُوا ۖ
فَكَيْفَ كَانَ نَكِيرِ ۟ ع

SECTION 4.

27. Seest thou not that

٢٧- أَلَمْ تَرَ أَنَّ اللهَ أَنْزَلَ مِنَ السَّمَاءِ

Allah sends down rain
From the sky? With it
We then bring out produce
Of various colours.
And in the mountains
Are tracts white and red,
Of various shades of colour,
And black intense in hue.

28. And so amongst men
And crawling creatures and
                                    cattle,
Are they of various colours.
Those truly fear Allah,
Among His Servants,
Who have knowledge:
For Allah is Exalted in Might,
Oft-Forgiving.

29. Those who rehearse the Book
Of Allah, establish regular
                                    Prayer,
And send (in Charity)
Out of what We have provided
For them, secretly and openly,
Hope for a Commerce
That will never fail:

30. For He will pay them
Their meed, nay, He will
Give them (even) more
Out of His Bounty:
For He is Oft-Forgiving,
Most Ready to appreciate
                                    (service).

31. That which We have revealed
To thee of the Book
Is the Truth—confirming
What was (revealed) before it:
For Allah is assuredly—
With respect to His servants—
Well acquainted and
Fully-Observant.

32. Then   We have given
The Book for inheritance
To such of Our servants
As We have chosen:

مَآءٌ
فَأَخْرَجْنَا بِهِ ثَمَرٰتٍ مُّخْتَلِفًا اَلْوَانُهَا
وَمِنَ الْجِبَالِ جُدَدٌ بِيْضٌ وَّحُمْرٌ
مُّخْتَلِفٌ اَلْوَانُهَا وَغَرَابِيْبُ سُوْدٌ ۝

٢٨ - وَمِنَ النَّاسِ وَالدَّوَآبِّ وَالْاَنْعَامِ
مُخْتَلِفٌ اَلْوَانُهُ كَذٰلِكَ
اِنَّمَا يَخْشَى اللّٰهَ مِنْ عِبَادِهِ الْعُلَمٰٓؤُا
اِنَّ اللّٰهَ عَزِيْزٌ غَفُوْرٌ ۝

٢٩ - اِنَّ الَّذِيْنَ يَتْلُوْنَ كِتٰبَ اللّٰهِ وَاَقَامُوا
الصَّلٰوةَ وَاَنْفَقُوْا مِمَّا رَزَقْنٰهُمْ
سِرًّا وَّعَلَانِيَةً يَّرْجُوْنَ تِجَارَةً
لَّنْ تَبُوْرَ ۝

٣٠ - لِيُوَفِّيَهُمْ اُجُوْرَهُمْ
وَيَزِيْدَهُمْ مِّنْ فَضْلِهِ
اِنَّهُ غَفُوْرٌ شَكُوْرٌ ۝

٣١ - وَالَّذِيْ اَوْحَيْنَا اِلَيْكَ مِنَ الْكِتٰبِ
هُوَ الْحَقُّ مُصَدِّقًا لِّمَا بَيْنَ يَدَيْهِ
اِنَّ اللّٰهَ بِعِبَادِهِ
لَخَبِيْرٌ بَصِيْرٌ ۝

٣٢ - ثُمَّ اَوْرَثْنَا الْكِتٰبَ الَّذِيْنَ
اصْطَفَيْنَا مِنْ عِبَادِنَا

But there are among them
Some who wrong their own
Souls; some who follow
A middle course; and some
Who are, by Allah's leave,
Foremost in good deeds;
That is the highest Grace.

فَمِنْهُمْ ظَالِمٌ لِنَفْسِهِ
وَمِنْهُمْ مُقْتَصِدٌ
وَمِنْهُمْ سَابِقٌ بِالْخَيْرَاتِ بِإِذْنِ اللهِ
ذَٰلِكَ هُوَ الْفَضْلُ الْكَبِيرُ ۝

33. Gardens of Eternity will they
Enter: therein will they
Be adorned with bracelets
Of gold and pearls;
And their garments there
Will be of silk.

٣٣- جَنَّاتُ عَدْنٍ يَدْخُلُونَهَا
يُحَلَّوْنَ فِيهَا مِنْ أَسَاوِرَ مِنْ ذَهَبٍ وَلُؤْلُؤًا
وَلِبَاسُهُمْ فِيهَا حَرِيرٌ ۝

34. And they will say:
"Praise be to Allah,
Who has removed from us
(All) sorrow: for our Lord
Is indeed Oft-Forgiving
Ready to appreciate (service):

٣٤- وَقَالُوا الْحَمْدُ لِلّٰهِ الَّذِي
أَذْهَبَ عَنَّا الْحَزَنَ
إِنَّ رَبَّنَا لَغَفُورٌ شَكُورٌ ۝

35. "Who has, out of His Bounty,
Settled us in a Home
That will last: no toil
Nor sense of weariness
Shall touch us therein."

٣٥- الَّذِي أَحَلَّنَا دَارَ الْمُقَامَةِ مِنْ فَضْلِهِ
لَا يَمَسُّنَا فِيهَا نَصَبٌ
وَلَا يَمَسُّنَا فِيهَا لُغُوبٌ ۝

36. But those who reject (Allah)—
For them will be
The Fire of Hell:
No term shall be determined
For them, so they should die,
Nor shall its Penalty
Be lightened for them.
Thus do We reward
Every ungrateful one!

٣٦- وَالَّذِينَ كَفَرُوا لَهُمْ نَارُ جَهَنَّمَ
لَا يُقْضَى عَلَيْهِمْ فَيَمُوتُوا
وَلَا يُخَفَّفُ عَنْهُمْ مِنْ عَذَابِهَا
كَذَٰلِكَ نَجْزِي كُلَّ كَفُورٍ ۝

37. Therein will they cry
Aloud (for assistance):
"Our Lord! Bring us out:
We shall work righteousness,
Not the (deeds) we used
To do!"—"Did We not
Give you long enough life
So that he that would
Should receive admonition?
And (moreover) the warner

٣٧- وَهُمْ يَصْطَرِخُونَ فِيهَا
رَبَّنَا أَخْرِجْنَا نَعْمَلْ صَالِحًا
غَيْرَ الَّذِي كُنَّا نَعْمَلُ
أَوَلَمْ نُعَمِّرْكُمْ
مَا يَتَذَكَّرُ فِيهِ مَنْ تَذَكَّرَ

Came to you. So taste ye
(The fruits of your deeds):
For the Wrongdoers
Their is no helper."

SECTION 5.

38. Verily Allah knows
(All) the hidden things
Of the heavens and the
               earth:
Verily He has full knowledge
Of all that is
In (men's) hearts.

٣٨- اِنَّ اللّٰهَ عٰلِمُ غَيْبِ السَّمٰوٰتِ وَالْاَرْضِ ؕ اِنَّهٗ عَلِيْمٌۢ بِذَاتِ الصُّدُوْرِ ۟

39. He it is that has made
You inheritors in the earth:
If, then, any do reject
(Allah), their rejection (works)
Against themselves: their
              rejection
But adds to the odium
For the Unbelievers
In the sight of their Lord:
Their rejection but adds
To (their own) undoing.

٣٩- هُوَ الَّذِيْ جَعَلَكُمْ خَلٰٓئِفَ فِى الْاَرْضِ ؕ فَمَنْ كَفَرَ فَعَلَيْهِ كُفْرُهٗ ؕ وَلَا يَزِيْدُ الْكٰفِرِيْنَ كُفْرُهُمْ عِنْدَ رَبِّهِمْ اِلَّا مَقْتًا ۚ وَلَا يَزِيْدُ الْكٰفِرِيْنَ كُفْرُهُمْ اِلَّا خَسَارًا ۟

40. Say:"Have ye seen
(These) 'Partners' of yours
Whom ye call upon
Besides Allah? Show me
What it is they have created
In the (wide) earth.
Or have they a share
In the heavens? Or
Have We given them a Book
From which they (can derive)
Clear (evidence)?—Nay,
The wrongdoers promise
Each other nothing but
              delusions.

٤٠- قُلْ اَرَءَيْتُمْ شُرَكَآءَكُمُ الَّذِيْنَ تَدْعُوْنَ مِنْ دُوْنِ اللّٰهِ ؕ اَرُوْنِيْ مَاذَا خَلَقُوْا مِنَ الْاَرْضِ اَمْ لَهُمْ شِرْكٌ فِى السَّمٰوٰتِ ۚ اَمْ اٰتَيْنٰهُمْ كِتٰبًا فَهُمْ عَلٰى بَيِّنَتٍ مِّنْهُ ۚ بَلْ اِنْ يَّعِدُ الظّٰلِمُوْنَ بَعْضُهُمْ بَعْضًا اِلَّا غُرُوْرًا ۟

41. It is Allah Who sustains
The heavens and the earth,
Lest they cease (to function):
And if they should fail,
There is none — not one —
Can sustain them thereafter:
Verily He is Most Forbearing,
Oft-Forgiving.

٤١- اِنَّ اللّٰهَ يُمْسِكُ السَّمٰوٰتِ وَالْاَرْضَ اَنْ تَزُوْلَا ۚ وَلَئِنْ زَالَتَآ اِنْ اَمْسَكَهُمَا مِنْ اَحَدٍ مِّنْ بَعْدِهٖ ؕ اِنَّهٗ كَانَ حَلِيْمًا غَفُوْرًا ۟

42. They swore their strongest oaths
By Allah that if a warner
Came to them, they would
Follow his guidance better
Than any (other) of the Peoples:
But when a warner came
To them, it has only
Increased their flight
(From righteousness)—

وَأَقْسَمُوْا بِاللّٰهِ جَهْدَ اَيْمَانِهِمْ
لَئِنْ جَآءَهُمْ نَذِيْرٌ
لَّيَكُوْنُنَّ اَهْدٰى مِنْ اِحْدَى الْاُمَمِ
فَلَمَّا جَآءَهُمْ نَذِيْرٌ
مَّا زَادَهُمْ اِلَّا نُفُوْرًا ۝

43. On account of their arrogance
In the land and their
Plotting of Evil.
But the plotting of Evil
Will hem in only
The authors thereof. Now
Are they but looking for
The way the ancients
Were dealt with? But
No change wilt thou find
In Allah's way (of dealing):
No turning off wilt thou
Find in Allah's way (of dealing).

اِسْتِكْبَارًا فِى الْاَرْضِ وَمَكْرَ السَّيِّئِ
وَلَا يَحِيْقُ الْمَكْرُ السَّيِّئُ
اِلَّا بِاَهْلِهٖ
فَهَلْ يَنْظُرُوْنَ اِلَّا سُنَّتَ الْاَوَّلِيْنَ
فَلَنْ تَجِدَ لِسُنَّتِ اللّٰهِ تَبْدِيْلًا ۚ
وَلَنْ تَجِدَ لِسُنَّتِ اللّٰهِ تَحْوِيْلًا ۝

44. Do they not travel
Through the earth, and see
What was the End
Of those before them—
Though they were superior
To them in strength?
Nor is Allah to be frustrated
By anything whatever
In the heavens
Or on earth: for He
Is All-Knowing, All-Powerful.

اَوَلَمْ يَسِيْرُوْا فِى الْاَرْضِ فَيَنْظُرُوْا
كَيْفَ كَانَ عَاقِبَةُ الَّذِيْنَ مِنْ قَبْلِهِمْ
وَكَانُوْا اَشَدَّ مِنْهُمْ قُوَّةً
وَمَا كَانَ اللّٰهُ لِيُعْجِزَهٗ مِنْ شَىْءٍ
فِى السَّمٰوٰتِ وَلَا فِى الْاَرْضِ
اِنَّهٗ كَانَ عَلِيْمًا قَدِيْرًا ۝

45. If Allah were to punish
Men according to what
They deserve, He would not
Leave on the back
Of the (earth) a single
Living creature: but He
Gives them respite
For a stated Term:

وَلَوْ يُؤَاخِذُ اللّٰهُ النَّاسَ بِمَا كَسَبُوْا
مَا تَرَكَ عَلٰى ظَهْرِهَا مِنْ دَآبَّةٍ
وَّلٰكِنْ يُّؤَخِّرُهُمْ
اِلٰى اَجَلٍ مُّسَمًّى
فَاِذَا جَآءَ اَجَلُهُمْ

When their Term expires,
Verily Allah has in His sight
All His servants.

فَإِنَّ اللّٰهَ كَانَ بِعِبَادِهٖ بَصِيْرًا ۝ ع

INTRODUCTION TO SURA XXXVI. (*Yā-Sin*) — 83 Verses

See introduction to S. xxxiv. This particular Sūra is devoted to the Holy Prophet and the Revelation which he brought. The Abbreviated Letters *Yā-Sin* are usually construed as a title of the Holy Prophet. But it is not permissible to be dogmatic about the meaning of Abbreviated Letters. See Appendix I. after S. ii. This Sūra is considered to be "the heart of The Qur-ān," as it concerns the central figure in the teaching of Islam and the central doctrine of Revelation and the Hereafter. As referring to the Hereafter, it is appropriately read in solemn ceremonies after death.

In chronology it belongs to the middle or early Meccan period.

In S. xxxvii.130 (a cognate Sūra) occurs the word *Il-yā-sin*: see n.4115-A.

Yā Sīn

In the name of Allah, Most Gracious, Most Merciful

بِسْمِ اللهِ الرَّحْمٰنِ الرَّحِيمِ

1. **Yā Sīn.**

يٰسٓ ۚ ١

2. By the Qur'ān, Full of Wisdom —

وَالْقُرْاٰنِ الْحَكِيمِ ۙ ٢

3. Thou art indeed One of the messengers,

اِنَّكَ لَمِنَ الْمُرْسَلِينَ ۙ ٣

4. On a Straight Way.

عَلٰى صِرَاطٍ مُّسْتَقِيمٍ ؕ ٤

5. It is a Revelation Sent down by (Him), The Exalted in Might, Most Merciful,

تَنْزِيلَ الْعَزِيزِ الرَّحِيمِ ۙ ٥

6. In order that thou mayest Admonish a people, Whose fathers had received No admonition, and who Therefore remained heedless (Of the Signs of Allah).

لِتُنْذِرَ قَوْمًا مَّآ اُنْذِرَ اٰبَآؤُهُمْ فَهُمْ غٰفِلُونَ ٦

7. The Word is proved true Against the greater part of them; For they do not believe.

لَقَدْ حَقَّ الْقَوْلُ عَلٰٓى اَكْثَرِهِمْ فَهُمْ لَا يُؤْمِنُونَ ٧

8. We have put yokes
   Round their necks
   Right up to their chins,
   So that their heads are
   Forced up (and they cannot
   see).

٨- اِنَّا جَعَلْنَا فِىۤ اَعْنَاقِهِمْ اَغْلَالًا فَهِىَ اِلَى الْاَذْقَانِ فَهُمْ مُّقْمَحُوْنَ ٥

9. And We have put
   A bar in front of them
   And a bar behind them,
   And further, We have
   Covered them up; so that
   They cannot see.

٩- وَجَعَلْنَا مِنْۢ بَيْنِ اَيْدِيْهِمْ سَدًّا وَّمِنْ خَلْفِهِمْ سَدًّا فَاَغْشَيْنَاهُمْ فَهُمْ لَا يُبْصِرُوْنَ ٥

10. The same is it to them
    Whether thou admonish them
    Or thou do not admonish
    Them: they will not believe.

١٠- وَسَوَاءٌ عَلَيْهِمْ ءَاَنْذَرْتَهُمْ اَمْ لَمْ تُنْذِرْهُمْ لَا يُؤْمِنُوْنَ ٥

11. Thou canst but admonish
    Such a one as follows
    The Message and fears
    The (Lord) Most Gracious,
    unseen:
    Give such a one, therefore,
    Good tidings, of Forgiveness
    And a Reward most generous.

١١- اِنَّمَا تُنْذِرُ مَنِ اتَّبَعَ الذِّكْرَ وَخَشِىَ الرَّحْمٰنَ بِالْغَيْبِ ۚ فَبَشِّرْهُ بِمَغْفِرَةٍ وَّاَجْرٍ كَرِيْمٍ ٥

12. Verily We shall give life
    To the dead, and We record
    That which they sent before
    And that which they leave
    Behind, and of all things
    Have We taken account
    In a clear Book
    (Of evidence).

١٢- اِنَّا نَحْنُ نُحْىِ الْمَوْتٰى وَنَكْتُبُ مَا قَدَّمُوْا وَاٰثَارَهُمْ ۚ وَكُلَّ شَىْءٍ اَحْصَيْنَاهُ فِىۤ اِمَامٍ مُّبِيْنٍ ٥

SECTION 2.

13. Set forth to them,
    By way of a parable,
    The (story of) the Companions
    Of the City. Behold,
    There came messengers to it.

١٣- وَاضْرِبْ لَهُمْ مَّثَلًا اَصْحٰبَ الْقَرْيَةِ ۘ اِذْ جَاءَهَا الْمُرْسَلُوْنَ ٥

14. When We (first) sent
    To them two messengers,
    They rejected them:
    But We strengthened them
    With a third: they said,

١٤- اِذْ اَرْسَلْنَاۤ اِلَيْهِمُ اثْنَيْنِ فَكَذَّبُوْهُمَا فَعَزَّزْنَا بِثَالِثٍ فَقَالُوْۤا

"Truly, we have been sent
On a mission to you."

اِنَّا اِلَيْكُمْ مُرْسَلُوْنَ ۟

15. The (people) said: "Ye are
Only men like ourselves;
And (Allah) Most Gracious
Sends no sort of revelation:
Ye do nothing but lie."

١٥-قَالُوْا مَا اَنْتُمْ اِلَّا بَشَرٌ مِّثْلُنَا ۙ
وَمَا اَنْزَلَ الرَّحْمٰنُ مِنْ شَىْءٍ ۙ
اِنْ اَنْتُمْ اِلَّا تَكْذِبُوْنَ ۟

16. They said: "Our Lord doth
Know that we have beeen sent
On a mission to you:

١٦-قَالُوْا رَبُّنَا يَعْلَمُ ۙ
اِنَّا اِلَيْكُمْ لَمُرْسَلُوْنَ ۟

17. "And our duty is only
To proclaim the clear
Message."

١٧-وَمَا عَلَيْنَا اِلَّا الْبَلٰغُ الْمُبِيْنُ ۟

18. The (people) said "For us,
We augur an evil omen
From you: if ye desist not,
We will certainly stone you,
And a grievous punishment
Indeed will be inflicted
On you by us."

١٨-قَالُوْا اِنَّا تَطَيَّرْنَا بِكُمْ ۚ
لَئِنْ لَّمْ تَنْتَهُوْا لَنَرْجُمَنَّكُمْ
وَلَيَمَسَّنَّكُمْ مِّنَّا عَذَابٌ اَلِيْمٌ ۟

19. They said: "Your evil omens
Are with yourselves:
(Deem ye this an evil omen),
If ye are admonished?
Nay, but ye are a people
Transgressing all bounds!"

١٩-قَالُوْا طَائِرُكُمْ مَّعَكُمْ ۗ
اَئِنْ ذُكِّرْتُمْ ۗ
بَلْ اَنْتُمْ قَوْمٌ مُّسْرِفُوْنَ ۟

20. Then there came running,
From the farthest part
Of the City, a man,
Saying, "O my People
Obey the messengers:

٢٠-وَجَاءَ مِنْ اَقْصَا الْمَدِيْنَةِ
رَجُلٌ يَّسْعٰى قَالَ يٰقَوْمِ
اتَّبِعُوا الْمُرْسَلِيْنَ ۟

21. "Obey those who ask
No reward of you
(For themselves), and who have
Themselves received Guidance.

٢١-اتَّبِعُوْا مَنْ لَّا يَسْـَٔلُكُمْ اَجْرًا
وَّهُمْ مُّهْتَدُوْنَ ۟

22. "It would not be reasonable
In me if I did not
Serve Him Who created me,
And to Whom ye shall
(All) be brought back.

٢٢-وَمَا لِيَ لَا اَعْبُدُ الَّذِيْ
فَطَرَنِيْ
وَاِلَيْهِ تُرْجَعُوْنَ ۟

23. "Shall I take (other) gods
Besides Him? If (Allah)
Most Gracious should
Intend some adversity for me,
Of no use whatever
Will be their intercession
For me, nor can they
Deliver me.

٢٣- ءَاَتَّخِذُ مِنْ دُوْنِهٖٓ اٰلِهَةً
اِنْ يُّرِدْنِ الرَّحْمٰنُ بِضُرٍّ
لَّا تُغْنِ عَنِّيْ شَفَاعَتُهُمْ شَيْئًا
وَّلَا يُنْقِذُوْنِ ۟

24. "I would indeed,
If I were to do so,
Be in manifest Error.

٢٤- اِنِّيْٓ
اِذًا لَّفِيْ ضَلٰلٍ مُّبِيْنٍ ۟

25. "For me, I have faith
In the Lord of you (all):
Listen, then, to me!"

٢٥- اِنِّيْٓ اٰمَنْتُ
بِرَبِّكُمْ فَاسْمَعُوْنِ ۟

26. It was said: "Enter thou
The Garden." He said:
"Ah me! Would that
My People knew (what I know)!—

٢٦- قِيْلَ ادْخُلِ الْجَنَّةَ ۗ قَالَ
يٰلَيْتَ قَوْمِيْ يَعْلَمُوْنَ ۟

27. "For that my Lord
Has granted me Forgiveness
And has enrolled me
Among those held in honour!"

٢٧- بِمَا غَفَرَلِيْ رَبِّيْ
وَجَعَلَنِيْ مِنَ الْمُكْرَمِيْنَ ۟

28. And We sent not down
Against his People, after him,
Any hosts from heaven,
Nor was it needful
For Us so to do.

٢٨- وَمَا اَنْزَلْنَا عَلٰى قَوْمِهٖ مِنْ بَعْدِهٖ
مِنْ جُنْدٍ مِّنَ السَّمَاءِ
وَمَا كُنَّا مُنْزِلِيْنَ ۟

29. It was no more than
A single mighty Blast,
And behold! they were
(like ashes)
Quenched and silent.

٢٩- اِنْ كَانَتْ اِلَّا صَيْحَةً وَّاحِدَةً
فَاِذَا هُمْ خٰمِدُوْنَ ۟

30. Ah! alas for (My) servants!
There comes not a messenger
To them but they mock him!

٣٠- يٰحَسْرَةً عَلَى الْعِبَادِ ۚ مَا يَاْتِيْهِمْ مِّنْ
رَّسُوْلٍ اِلَّا كَانُوْا بِهٖ يَسْتَهْزِءُوْنَ ۟

31. See they not how many
Generations before them
We destroyed? Not to them

٣١- اَلَمْ يَرَوْا كَمْ اَهْلَكْنَا قَبْلَهُمْ مِّنَ
الْقُرُوْنِ اَنَّهُمْ اِلَيْهِمْ

Will they return:

32. But each one of them
All—will be brought
Before Us (for judgement).

SECTION 3.

لَا يَرْجِعُونَ ۝

٣٢- وَإِنْ كُلٌّ لَّمَّا جَمِيعٌ
لَّدَيْنَا مُحْضَرُونَ ۝ ع

33. A Sign for them
Is the earth that is dead:
We do give it life,
And produce grain therefrom,
Of which ye do eat.

٣٣- وَآيَةٌ لَّهُمُ الْأَرْضُ الْمَيْتَةُ ۖ
أَحْيَيْنَاهَا وَأَخْرَجْنَا مِنْهَا حَبًّا
فَمِنْهُ يَأْكُلُونَ ۝

34. And We produce therein
Orchards with date palms
And Vines, and We cause
Springs to gush forth therein:

٣٤- وَجَعَلْنَا فِيهَا جَنَّاتٍ مِّنْ نَّخِيلٍ
وَّأَعْنَابٍ وَّفَجَّرْنَا فِيهَا مِنَ الْعُيُونِ ۝

35. That they may enjoy
The fruits of this (artistry):
It was not their hands
That made this:
Will they not then give thanks?

٣٥- لِيَأْكُلُوا مِنْ ثَمَرِهِ ۙ
وَمَا عَمِلَتْهُ أَيْدِيهِمْ ۖ
أَفَلَا يَشْكُرُونَ ۝

36. Glory to Allah, Who created
In pairs all things that
The earth produces, as well as
Their own (human) kind
And (other) things of which
They have no knowledge.

٣٦- سُبْحَانَ الَّذِي خَلَقَ الْأَزْوَاجَ كُلَّهَا
مِمَّا تُنْبِتُ الْأَرْضُ وَمِنْ أَنْفُسِهِمْ
وَمِمَّا لَا يَعْلَمُونَ ۝

37. And a Sign for them
Is the Night: We withdraw
Therefrom the Day, and behold
They are plunged in darkness;

٣٧- وَآيَةٌ لَّهُمُ اللَّيْلُ نَسْلَخُ مِنْهُ النَّهَارَ
فَإِذَا هُمْ مُّظْلِمُونَ ۝

38. And the Sun
Runs its course
For a period determined
For it; that is
The decree of (Him),
The exalted in Might,
The All-Knowing.

٣٨- وَالشَّمْسُ تَجْرِي
لِمُسْتَقَرٍّ لَّهَا ۚ ذَٰلِكَ
تَقْدِيرُ الْعَزِيزِ الْعَلِيمِ ۝

39. And the Moon—
We have measured for it
Mansions (to traverse)
Till it returns
Like the old (and withered)

٣٩- وَالْقَمَرَ قَدَّرْنَاهُ مَنَازِلَ
حَتَّىٰ عَادَ كَالْعُرْجُونِ

Lower part of a date stalk

القَدِيمِ ۝

40. It is not permitted
To the Sun to catch up
The Moon, nor can
The Night outstrip the Day:
Each (just) swims along
In (its own) orbit
(According to Law).

٤٠ـ لَا الشَّمْسُ يَنْبَغِى لَهَآ اَنْ تُدْرِكَ
الْقَمَرَ وَلَا الَّيْلُ سَابِقُ النَّهَارِ ۚ
وَكُلٌّ فِىْ فَلَكٍ يَّسْبَحُوْنَ ۝

41. And a Sign for them
Is that We bore
Their race (through the Flood)
In the loaded Ark;

٤١ـ وَاٰيَةٌ لَّهُمْ اَنَّا حَمَلْنَا
ذُرِّيَّتَهُمْ فِى الْفُلْكِ الْمَشْحُوْنِ ۝

42. And We have created
For them similar (vessels)
On which they ride.

٤٢ـ وَخَلَقْنَا
لَهُمْ مِّنْ مِّثْلِهٖ مَا يَرْكَبُوْنَ ۝

43. If it were Our Will,
We could drown them:
Then would there be
No helper (to hear
Their cry), nor could
They be delivered

٤٣ـ وَاِنْ نَّشَأْ نُغْرِقْهُمْ
فَلَا صَرِيْخَ لَهُمْ
وَلَا هُمْ يُنْقَذُوْنَ ۝

44. Except by way of Mercy
From Us, and by way
Of (worldly) convenience
(To serve them) for a time,

٤٤ـ اِلَّا رَحْمَةً مِّنَّا وَ
مَتَاعًا اِلٰى حِيْنٍ ۝

45. When they are told,
"Fear ye that which is
Before you and that which
Will be after you, in order
That ye may receive Mercy,"
(They turn back).

٤٥ـ وَاِذَا قِيْلَ لَهُمُ اتَّقُوْا مَا بَيْنَ
اَيْدِيْكُمْ وَمَا خَلْفَكُمْ
لَعَلَّكُمْ تُرْحَمُوْنَ ۝

46. Not a Sign come to them
From among the Signs
Of their Lord, but they
Turn away therefrom.

٤٦ـ وَمَا تَأْتِيْهِمْ مِّنْ اٰيَةٍ مِّنْ اٰيٰتِ
رَبِّهِمْ اِلَّا كَانُوْا عَنْهَا مُعْرِضِيْنَ ۝

47. And when they are told,
"Spend ye of (the bounties)
With which Allah
Has provided you." the Unbelievers

٤٧ـ وَاِذَا قِيْلَ لَهُمْ اَنْفِقُوْا
مِمَّا رَزَقَكُمُ اللّٰهُ ۙ

Say to those who believe:
"Shall we then feed those
Whom, if Allah had so willed,
He would have fed, (Himself)?—
Ye are in nothing
But manifest error."

قَالَ الَّذِيْنَ كَفَرُوْا لِلَّذِيْنَ اٰمَنُوْا اَنُطْعِمُ
مَنْ لَّوْ يَشَآءُ اللّٰهُ اَطْعَمَهٗ ۚ
اِنْ اَنْتُمْ اِلَّا فِيْ ضَلٰلٍ مُّبِيْنٍ ۟

48. Further, they say, "When
Will this promise (come to
                    pass),
If what ye say is true?"

٤٨- وَيَقُوْلُوْنَ مَتٰى هٰذَا الْوَعْدُ
اِنْ كُنْتُمْ صٰدِقِيْنَ ۟

49. They will not (have
To) wait for aught
But a single Blast:
It will seize them while
They are yet disputing
Among themselves!

٤٩- مَا يَنْظُرُوْنَ اِلَّا صَيْحَةً وَّاحِدَةً
تَأْخُذُهُمْ
وَهُمْ يَخِصِّمُوْنَ ۟

50. No (chance) will they then
Have, by will, to dispose
(Of their affairs), nor
To return to their own people!

٥٠- فَلَا يَسْتَطِيْعُوْنَ تَوْصِيَةً
وَّلَا اِلٰى اَهْلِهِمْ يَرْجِعُوْنَ ۟

SECTION 4.

51. The trumpet shall be
Sounded, when behold!
From the sepulchres (men)
Will rush forth
To their Lord!

٥١- وَنُفِخَ فِى الصُّوْرِ
فَاِذَا هُمْ مِّنَ الْاَجْدَاثِ
اِلٰى رَبِّهِمْ يَنْسِلُوْنَ ۟

52. They will say: "Ah!
Woe unto us! Who
Hath raised us up
From our beds of repose?". . .
(A voice will say:)
"This is what (Allah)
Most Gracious had promised,
And true was the word
Of the messengers!"

٥٢- قَالُوْا يٰوَيْلَنَا مَنْ
بَعَثَنَا مِنْ مَّرْقَدِنَا ۟ۚ
هٰذَا مَا وَعَدَ الرَّحْمٰنُ
وَصَدَقَ الْمُرْسَلُوْنَ ۟

53. It will be no more
Than a single Blast,
When lo! they will all
Be brought up before Us!

٥٣- اِنْ كَانَتْ اِلَّا صَيْحَةً وَّاحِدَةً
فَاِذَا هُمْ جَمِيْعٌ لَّدَيْنَا مُحْضَرُوْنَ ۟

54. Then, on that Day,
Not a soul will be
Wronged in the least,

٥٤- فَالْيَوْمَ لَا تُظْلَمُ نَفْسٌ شَيْئًا وَّلَا

And ye shall but
Be repaid the meeds
Of your past Deeds.

تُجْزَوْنَ إِلَّا مَا كُنْتُمْ تَعْمَلُوْنَ ۟

55. Verily the Companions
Of the Garden shall
That Day have joy
In all that they do;

٥٥- إِنَّ أَصْحَابَ الْجَنَّةِ
الْيَوْمَ فِيْ شُغُلٍ فَاكِهُوْنَ ۟

56. They and their associates
Will be in groves
Of (cool) shade, reclining
On Thrones (of dignity);

٥٦- هُمْ وَ أَزْوَاجُهُمْ فِيْ ظِلَالٍ
عَلَى الْأَرَائِكِ مُتَّكِئُوْنَ ۟

57. (Every) fruit (enjoyment)
Will be there for them;
They shall have whatever
They call for;

٥٧- لَهُمْ فِيْهَا فَاكِهَةٌ
وَّلَهُمْ مَّا يَدَّعُوْنَ ۟

58. "Peace!"—a Word
(Of salutation) from a Lord
Most Merciful!

٥٨- سَلَامٌ ۚ قَوْلًا مِّنْ رَّبٍّ رَّحِيْمٍ ۟

59. "And O ye in sin!
Get ye apart this Day!

٥٩- وَ امْتَازُوا الْيَوْمَ أَيُّهَا الْمُجْرِمُوْنَ ۟

60. "Did I not enjoin
On you, O ye children
Of Adam, that ye
Should not worship Satan;
For that he was to you
An enemy avowed?—

٦٠- أَلَمْ أَعْهَدْ إِلَيْكُمْ يَبَنِيْٓ
أٰدَمَ أَنْ لَّا تَعْبُدُوا الشَّيْطٰنَ ۚ
إِنَّهُ لَكُمْ عَدُوٌّ مُّبِيْنٌ ۟

61. "And that ye should
Worship Me, (for that) this
Was the Straight Way?

٦١- وَّ أَنِ اعْبُدُوْنِيْ ۚ
هٰذَا صِرَاطٌ مُّسْتَقِيْمٌ ۟

62. "But he did lead astray
A great multitude of you.
Did ye not, then, understand?

٦٢- وَ لَقَدْ أَضَلَّ مِنْكُمْ جِبِلًّا كَثِيْرًا ۚ
أَفَلَمْ تَكُوْنُوْا تَعْقِلُوْنَ ۟

63. "This is the Hell
Of which ye were
(Repeatedly) warned!

٦٣- هٰذِهِ جَهَنَّمُ
الَّتِيْ كُنْتُمْ تُوْعَدُوْنَ ۟

64. "Embrace ye the (Fire)
This Day, for that ye

٦٤- اِصْلَوْهَا الْيَوْمَ بِمَا

(Persistently) rejected (Truth)."

كُنْتُمْ تَكْفُرُوْنَ ۝

65. That Day shall We set
A seal on their mouths.
But their hands will speak
To Us, and their feet
Bear witness, to all
That they did.

٦٥- اَلْيَوْمَ نَخْتِمُ عَلَى اَفْوَاهِهِمْ
وَتُكَلِّمُنَا اَيْدِيْهِمْ
وَتَشْهَدُ اَرْجُلُهُمْ بِمَا كَانُوْا يَكْسِبُوْنَ ۝

66. If it had been Our Will,
We could surely have
Blotted out their eyes;
Then should they have
Run about groping for the Path,
But how could they have seen?

٦٦- وَلَوْ نَشَآءُ لَطَمَسْنَا عَلَى اَعْيُنِهِمْ
فَاسْتَبَقُوا الصِّرَاطَ
فَاَنّٰى يُبْصِرُوْنَ ۝

67. And if it had been
Our Will, We could
Have transformed them
(To remain) in their places;
Then should they have been
Unable to move about,
Nor could they have returned
(After error).

٦٧- وَلَوْ نَشَآءُ
لَمَسَخْنٰهُمْ عَلَى مَكَانَتِهِمْ
فَمَا اسْتَطَاعُوْا مُضِيًّا
وَّلَا يَرْجِعُوْنَ ۝

SECTION 5.

68. If We grant long life
To any, We cause him
To be reversed in nature:
Will they not then understand?

٦٨- وَمَنْ نُّعَمِّرْهُ نُنَكِّسْهُ فِى الْخَلْقِ
اَفَلَا يَعْقِلُوْنَ ۝

69. We have not instructed
The (Prophet) in Poetry,
Nor is it meet for him:
This is no less than
A Message and a Qur'ān
Making things clear:

٦٩- وَمَا عَلَّمْنٰهُ الشِّعْرَ
وَمَا يَنْبَغِيْ لَهٗ ۗ اِنْ هُوَ اِلَّا
ذِكْرٌ وَّقُرْاٰنٌ مُّبِيْنٌ ۝

70. That it may give admonition
To any (who are) alive,

And that the charge
May be proved against those
Who reject (Truth).

٧٠- لِّيُنْذِرَ مَنْ كَانَ حَيًّا
وَّيَحِقَّ الْقَوْلُ
عَلَى الْكٰفِرِيْنَ ۝

71. See they not that it is
We Who have created
For them—among other things

٧١- اَوَلَمْ يَرَوْا اَنَّا خَلَقْنَا
لَهُمْ مِّمَّا عَمِلَتْ اَيْدِيْنَا

Which our hands have
                    fashioned—
Cattle, which are under
Their dominion?—

أَنْعَامًا فَهُمْ لَهَا مَالِكُونَ ٠

72. And that We have
Subjected them to their (use)?
Of them some do carry them
And some they eat:

٧٢- وَذَلَّلْنَاهَا لَهُمْ فَمِنْهَا
رَكُوبُهُمْ وَمِنْهَا يَأْكُلُونَ ٠

73. And they have (other) profits
From them (besides), and they
Get (milk) to drink.
Will they not then
Be grateful?

٧٣- وَلَهُمْ فِيهَا مَنَافِعُ
وَمَشَارِبُ
أَفَلَا يَشْكُرُونَ ٠

74. Yet they take (for worship)
Gods other than Allah,
(Hoping) that they might
Be helped!

٧٤- وَاتَّخَذُوا مِنْ دُونِ اللهِ آلِهَةً
لَعَلَّهُمْ يُنْصَرُونَ ط

75. They have not the power
To help them: but they
Will be brought up
(Before Our Judgement Seat)
As a troop (to be condemned).

٧٥- لَا يَسْتَطِيعُونَ نَصْرَهُمْ
وَهُمْ لَهُمْ جُنْدٌ مُحْضَرُونَ ٠

76. Let not their speech, then,
Grieve thee. Verily We know
What they hide as well as
What they disclose.

٧٦- فَلَا يَحْزُنْكَ قَوْلُهُمْ إِنَّا نَعْلَمُ
مَا يُسِرُّونَ وَمَا يُعْلِنُونَ ٠

77. Doth not man see
That it is We Who
Created him from sperm?
Yet behold! he (stands forth)
As an open adversary!

٧٧- أَوَلَمْ يَرَ الْإِنْسَانُ أَنَّا
خَلَقْنَاهُ مِنْ نُطْفَةٍ
فَإِذَا هُوَ خَصِيمٌ مُبِينٌ ٠

78. And he makes comparisons
For Us, and forgets his own
(Origin and) Creation:
He says, "Who can give
Life to (dry) bones
And decomposed ones (at that)?"

٧٨- وَضَرَبَ لَنَا مَثَلًا وَنَسِيَ خَلْقَهُ
قَالَ مَنْ يُحْيِ الْعِظَامَ
وَهِيَ رَمِيمٌ ٠

79. Say, "He will give them
Life Who created them

٧٩- قُلْ يُحْيِيهَا الَّذِي أَنْشَأَهَا أَوَّلَ مَرَّةٍ

For the first time!
For He is well-versed
In every kind of creation!—

وَهُوَ بِكُلِّ خَلْقٍ عَلِيمٌ ۞

80. "The same Who produces
For you fire out of
The green tree, when behold!
Ye kindle therewith
(Your own fires)!

٨٠- الَّذِى جَعَلَ لَكُمْ مِنَ الشَّجَرِ الْأَخْضَرِ
نَارًا
فَإِذَا أَنْتُمْ مِنْهُ تُوقِدُونَ ۞

81. "Is not He Who created
The heavens and the earth
Able to create the like
Thereof?"—Yea, indeed!
For He is the Creator Supreme,
Of skill and knowledge (infinite)!

٨١- أَوَلَيْسَ الَّذِى خَلَقَ السَّمَوَاتِ وَالْأَرْضَ
بِقَادِرٍ عَلَى أَنْ يَخْلُقَ مِثْلَهُمْ
بَلَى وَهُوَ الْخَلَّاقُ الْعَلِيمُ ۞

82. Verily, when He intends
A thing, His Command is,
"Be", and it is!

٨٢- إِنَّمَا أَمْرُهُ إِذَا أَرَادَ
شَيْئًا أَنْ يَقُولَ لَهُ كُنْ فَيَكُونُ ۞

83. So glory to Him
In Whose hands is
The dominion of all things:
And to Him will ye
Be all brought back.

٨٣- فَسُبْحَانَ الَّذِى
بِيَدِهِ مَلَكُوتُ كُلِّ شَىْءٍ
وَإِلَيْهِ تُرْجَعُونَ ۞

·INTRODUCTION TO SŪRA XXXVII. (*Ṣāffāt*) — 183 Verses

As explained in the Introduction to S. xxxiv., this is the fourth of a series of Sūras in which the mysteries of the spiritual world are manifested in different ways, tending to the defeat and final extirpation of Evil. The defeat of Evil is throughout connected with Revelation, and here the ranged fight is illustrated by a reference to the angels in heaven and to the earlier Prophets in our earthly history, from Noah of Jonah. In chronology this Sūra belongs to the early middle Meccan period.

Al Ṣāffāt (Those Ranged in Ranks)

In the name of Allah, Most Gracious,
Most Merciful.

1. By⁴⁰³⁰ those who range
   Themselves in ranks,

2. And so are strong
   In repelling (evil),

3. And thus proclaim
   The Message (of Allah)!

4. Verily, verily, your God
   Is One!—

5. Lord of the heavens
   And of the earth,
   And all between them,
   And Lord of every point
   At the rising of the sun!

6. We have indeed decked
   The lower heaven with beauty
   (In) the stars—

7. (For beauty) and for guard
   Against all obstinate
   Rebellious evil spirits,

8. (So) they should not strain
   Their ears in the direction
   Of the Exalted Assembly
   But be cast away
   From every side,

9. Repulsed, for they are
Under a perpetual penalty,

٩- دُحُوْرًا وَّلَهُمْ عَذَابٌ وَّاصِبٌ ۟

10. Except such as snatch away
Something by stealth, and they
Are pursued by a flaming
Fire, of piercing brightness.

١٠- اِلَّا مَنْ خَطِفَ الْخَطْفَةَ
فَاَتْبَعَهٗ شِهَابٌ ثَاقِبٌ ۟

11. ℑust ask their⁴⁰⁴⁰ opinion:
Are they the more difficult
To create, or the (other) beings
We have created?
Them have We created
Out of a sticky clay!

١١- فَاسْتَفْتِهِمْ اَهُمْ اَشَدُّ
خَلْقًا اَمْ مَّنْ خَلَقْنَا ۚ
اِنَّا خَلَقْنٰهُمْ مِّنْ طِيْنٍ لَّازِبٍ ۟

12. Truly dost thou marvel,
While they ridicule,

١٢- بَلْ عَجِبْتَ وَيَسْخَرُوْنَ ۟

13. And, when they are
Admonished, pay no heed—

١٣- وَاِذَا ذُكِّرُوْا لَا يَذْكُرُوْنَ ۟

14. And, when they see
A Sign, turn it
To mockery,

١٤- وَاِذَا رَاَوْا اٰيَةً يَّسْتَسْخِرُوْنَ ۟

15. And say, "This is nothing
But evident sorcery!

١٥- وَقَالُوْا اِنْ هٰذَآ اِلَّا سِحْرٌ مُّبِيْنٌ ۚۖ

16. "What! when we die,
And become dust and bones,
Shall we (then) be
Raised up (again)?

١٦- ءَاِذَا مِتْنَا وَكُنَّا تُرَابًا وَّعِظَامًا
ءَاِنَّا لَمَبْعُوْثُوْنَ ۙ

17. "And also our fathers
Of old?"

١٧- اَوَ اٰبَآؤُنَا الْاَوَّلُوْنَ ۗ

18. Say thou: "Yea, and ye shall
Then be humiliated
(On account of your evil)."

١٨- قُلْ نَعَمْ وَاَنْتُمْ دَاخِرُوْنَ ۚ

19. Then it will be a single
(Compelling) cry;
And behold, they will
Begin to see!

١٩- فَاِنَّمَا هِيَ زَجْرَةٌ وَّاحِدَةٌ
فَاِذَا هُمْ يَنْظُرُوْنَ ۟

20. They will say, "Ah!
Woe to us! this is
The Day of Judgement!"

٢٠- وَقَالُوْا يٰوَيْلَنَا
هٰذَا يَوْمُ الدِّيْنِ ۟

21. (A voice will say,)
"This is the Day[4047]
Of Sorting Out, whose
Truth ye (once) denied!"

SECTION 2.

22. "Bring ye up",
It shall be said,
"The wrongdoers
And their wives,
And the things they worshipped—

٢١- هٰذَا يَوْمُ الْفَصْلِ الَّذِى كُنْتُمْ بِهِ تُكَذِّبُوْنَ ۟

٢٢- اُحْشُرُوا الَّذِيْنَ ظَلَمُوْا وَاَزْوَاجَهُمْ وَمَا كَانُوْا يَعْبُدُوْنَ ۟

23. "Besides Allah,
And lead them to the Way
To the (Fierce) Fire!

٢٣- مِنْ دُوْنِ اللّٰهِ فَاهْدُوْهُمْ اِلٰى صِرَاطِ الْجَحِيْمِ ۟

24. "But stop them,
For they must be asked:

٢٤- وَقِفُوْهُمْ اِنَّهُمْ مَّسْئُوْلُوْنَ ۟

25. "What is the matter
With you that ye
Help not each other?"

٢٥- مَا لَكُمْ لَا تَنَاصَرُوْنَ ۟

26. Nay, but that day they
Shall submit (to Judgement);

٢٦- بَلْ هُمُ الْيَوْمَ مُسْتَسْلِمُوْنَ ۟

27. And they will turn to
One another, and question
One another.

٢٧- وَاَقْبَلَ بَعْضُهُمْ عَلٰى بَعْضٍ يَّتَسَآءَلُوْنَ ۟

28. They will say: "It was ye
Who used to come to us
From the right hand
(Of power and authority)!"

٢٨- قَالُوْا اِنَّكُمْ كُنْتُمْ تَأْتُوْنَنَا عَنِ الْيَمِيْنِ ۟

29. They will reply: "Nay, ye
Yourselves had no Faith!

٢٩- قَالُوْا بَلْ لَّمْ تَكُوْنُوْا مُؤْمِنِيْنَ ۟

30. "Nor had we any authority
Over you. Nay, it was
Ye who were a people
In obstinate rebellion!

٣٠- وَمَا كَانَ لَنَا عَلَيْكُمْ مِّنْ سُلْطٰنٍ بَلْ كُنْتُمْ قَوْمًا طٰغِيْنَ ۟

31. "So now has been proved true,
Against us, the Word
Of our Lord that we
Shall indeed (have to) taste
(The punishment of our sins):

٣١- فَحَقَّ عَلَيْنَا قَوْلُ رَبِّنَآ اِنَّا لَذَآئِقُوْنَ ۟

32. "We led you astray: for truly
We were ourselves astray."

٣٢- فَأَغْوَيْنَكُمْ إِنَّا كُنَّا غَاوِينَ ۞

33. Truly, that Day, they will
(All) share in the Penalty.

٣٣- فَإِنَّهُمْ يَوْمَئِذٍ فِى الْعَذَابِ مُشْتَرِكُونَ ۞

34. Verily that is how We
Shall deal with Sinners.

٣٤- إِنَّا كَذٰلِكَ نَفْعَلُ بِالْمُجْرِمِينَ ۞

35. For they, when they were
Told that there is
No god except Allah, would
Puff themselves up with Pride,

٣٥- إِنَّهُمْ كَانُوا إِذَا قِيلَ لَهُمْ
لَا إِلٰهَ إِلَّا اللهُ يَسْتَكْبِرُونَ ۞

36. And say: "What! Shall we
Give up our gods
For the sake of
A Poet possessed?"

٣٦- وَيَقُولُونَ أَئِنَّا لَتَارِكُوا آلِهَتِنَا
لِشَاعِرٍ مَّجْنُونٍ ۞

37. Nay! he has come
With the (very) Truth,
And he confirms (the Message
Of) the messengers (before
him).

٣٧- بَلْ جَآءَ بِالْحَقِّ
وَصَدَّقَ الْمُرْسَلِينَ ۞

38. Ye shall indeed taste
Of the Grievous Penalty—

٣٨- إِنَّكُمْ لَذَآئِقُوا الْعَذَابِ الْأَلِيمِ ۞

39. But it will be no more
Than the retribution
Of (the Evil) that ye
Have wrought—

٣٩- وَمَا تُجْزَوْنَ
إِلَّا مَا كُنْتُمْ تَعْمَلُونَ ۞

40. But the sincere (and devoted)
Servants of Allah—

٤٠- إِلَّا عِبَادَ اللهِ الْمُخْلَصِينَ ۞

41. For them is a Sustenance
Determined,

٤١- أُولٰئِكَ لَهُمْ رِزْقٌ مَّعْلُومٌ ۞

42. Fruits (Delights);　　and they
(Shall enjoy) honour and dignity,

٤٢- فَوَاكِهُ وَهُمْ مُّكْرَمُونَ ۞

43. In Gardens of Felicity,

٤٣- فِى جَنَّاتِ النَّعِيمِ ۞

44. Facing each other
On Thrones (of dignity):

٤٤- عَلَى سُرُرٍ مُّتَقَابِلِينَ ۞

45. Round will be passed

٤٥- يُطَافُ عَلَيْهِمْ

To them a Cup
From a clear-flowing fountain,

بِكَأْسٍ مِّن مَّعِينٍ ۞

46. Crystal-white, of a taste
Delicious to those
Who drink (thereof),

٤٦- بَيْضَآءَ لَذَّةٍ لِّلشَّارِبِينَ ۞

47. Free from headiness;
Nor will they suffer
Intoxication therefrom.

٤٧- لَا فِيهَا غَوْلٌ
وَّلَا هُمْ عَنْهَا يُنزَفُونَ ۞

48. And besides them will be
Chaste women; restraining
Their glances, with big eyes
(Of wonder and beauty).

٤٨- وَعِندَهُمْ قَاصِرَاتُ
الطَّرْفِ عِينٌ ۞

49. As if they were
(Delicate) eggs closely guarded.

٤٩- كَأَنَّهُنَّ بَيْضٌ مَّكْنُونٌ ۞

50. Then they will turn to
One another and question
One another.

٥٠- فَأَقْبَلَ بَعْضُهُمْ عَلَى بَعْضٍ
يَتَسَآءَلُونَ ۞

51. One of them will start
The talk and say:
"I had an intimate
Companion (on the earth),

٥١- قَالَ قَآئِلٌ مِّنْهُمْ
إِنِّي كَانَ لِي قَرِينٌ ۞

52. "Who used to say,
'What! art thou amongst those
Who bear witness to
The truth (of the Message)?

٥٢- يَقُولُ أَئِنَّكَ
لَمِنَ الْمُصَدِّقِينَ ۞

53. "'When we die and become
Dust and bones, shall we
Indeed receive rewards
And punishments?'"

٥٣- أَءِذَا مِتْنَا وَكُنَّا تُرَابًا وَّعِظَامًا
أَءِنَّا لَمَدِينُونَ ۞

54. (A voice) said: "Would ye
Like to look down?"

٥٤- قَالَ هَلْ أَنتُم مُّطَّلِعُونَ ۞

55. He looked down
And saw him
In the midst of the Fire.

٥٥- فَاطَّلَعَ
فَرَآهُ فِي سَوَآءِ الْجَحِيمِ ۞

56. He said: "By Allah!

٥٦- قَالَ تَاللّٰهِ

Thou wast little short
Of bringing me to perdition!

إِنْ كِدْتَّ لَتُرْدِيْنِ ۟

57. "Had it not been for
The Grace of my Lord,
I should certainly have been
Among those brought (there)!

٥٧- وَلَوْلَا نِعْمَةُ رَبِّيْ لَكُنْتُ مِنَ الْمُحْضَرِيْنَ ۟

58. "Is it (the case) that
We shall not die,

٥٨- أَفَمَا نَحْنُ بِمَيِّتِيْنَ ۟

59. "Except our first death,
And that *we*
Shall not be punished?"

٥٩- إِلَّا مَوْتَتَنَا الْأُوْلٰى وَمَا نَحْنُ بِمُعَذَّبِيْنَ ۟

60. Verily this is
The supreme achievement!

٦٠- إِنَّ هٰذَا لَهُوَ الْفَوْزُ الْعَظِيْمُ ۟

61. For the like of this
Let all strive,
Who wish to strive.

٦١- لِمِثْلِ هٰذَا فَلْيَعْمَلِ الْعٰمِلُوْنَ ۟

62. Is that the better entertainment
Or the Tree of Zaqqūm?

٦٢- أَذٰلِكَ خَيْرٌ نُّزُلًا أَمْ شَجَرَةُ الزَّقُّوْمِ

63. For We have truly
Made it (as) a trial
For the wrongdoers.

٦٣- إِنَّا جَعَلْنٰهَا فِتْنَةً لِّلظّٰلِمِيْنَ ۟

64. For it is a tree
That springs out
Of the bottom of Hellfire:

٦٤- إِنَّهَا شَجَرَةٌ تَخْرُجُ فِيْۤ أَصْلِ الْجَحِيْمِ ۟

65. The shoots of its fruit-stalks
Are like the heads
Of devils:

٦٥- طَلْعُهَا كَأَنَّهٗ رُءُوْسُ الشَّيٰطِيْنِ ۟

66. Truly they will eat thereof
And fill their bellies therewith.

٦٦- فَإِنَّهُمْ لَاٰكِلُوْنَ مِنْهَا فَمَالِئُوْنَ مِنْهَا الْبُطُوْنَ ۟

67. Then on top of that
They will be given
A mixture made of
Boiling water.

٦٧- ثُمَّ إِنَّ لَهُمْ عَلَيْهَا لَشَوْبًا مِّنْ حَمِيْمٍ ۟

68. Then shall their return
Be to the (Blazing) Fire.

٦٨- ثُمَّ إِنَّ مَرْجِعَهُمْ لَإِلَى الْجَحِيْمِ ۟

69. Truly they found their fathers
On the wrong Path;

٦٩ـ اِنَّهُمْ اَلْفَوْا اٰبَآءَهُمْ ضَآلِّيْنَ ۙ

70. So they (too) were rushed
Down on their footsteps!

٧٠ـ فَهُمْ عَلٰٓى اٰثَارِهِمْ يُهْرَعُوْنَ ۞

71. And truly before them,
Many of the ancients
Went astray—

٧١ـ وَلَقَدْ ضَلَّ قَبْلَهُمْ
اَكْثَرُ الْاَوَّلِيْنَ ۙ

72. But We sent aforetime,
Among them, (messengers)
To admonish them—

٧٢ـ وَلَقَدْ اَرْسَلْنَا فِيْهِمْ مُّنْذِرِيْنَ ۞

73. Then see what was
The End of those who
Were admonished
(but heeded not)—

٧٣ـ فَانْظُرْ كَيْفَ
كَانَ عَاقِبَةُ الْمُنْذَرِيْنَ ۙ

74. Except the sincere (and
devoted)
Servants of Allah.

٧٤ـ اِلَّا عِبَادَ اللّٰهِ الْمُخْلَصِيْنَ ۞

SECTION 3.

75. (In the days of old),
Noah cried to Us,
And We are the Best
To hear prayer.

٧٥ـ وَلَقَدْ نَادٰىنَا نُوْحٌ
فَلَنِعْمَ الْمُجِيْبُوْنَ ۙ

76. And We delivered him
And his people from
The Great Calamity,

٧٦ـ وَنَجَّيْنٰهُ وَاَهْلَهُ مِنَ الْكَرْبِ
الْعَظِيْمِ ۙ

77. And made his progeny
To endure (on this earth);

٧٧ـ وَجَعَلْنَا ذُرِّيَّتَهُ هُمُ الْبَاقِيْنَ ۙ

78. And We left (this blessing)
For him among generations
To come in later times:

٧٨ـ وَتَرَكْنَا عَلَيْهِ فِى الْاٰخِرِيْنَ ۙ

79. "Peace and salutation to Noah
Among the nations!"

٧٩ـ سَلٰمٌ عَلٰى نُوْحٍ فِى الْعٰلَمِيْنَ ۞

80. Thus indeed do We reward
Those who do right.

٨٠ـ اِنَّا كَذٰلِكَ نَجْزِى الْمُحْسِنِيْنَ ۞

81. For he was one
Of Our believing Servants.

٨١- اِنَّهُ مِنْ عِبَادِنَا الْمُؤْمِنِينَ ۝

82. Then the rest We overwhelmed
In the Flood.

٨٢- ثُمَّ اَغْرَقْنَا الْاٰخَرِينَ ۝

83. Verily among those
Who followed his Way
Was Abraham.

٨٣- وَاِنَّ مِنْ شِيعَتِهِ لَاِبْرَاهِيمَ ۖ

84. Behold, he approached his Lord
With a sound heart.

٨٤- اِذْ جَآءَ رَبَّهُ بِقَلْبٍ سَلِيمٍ ۝

85. Behold, he said to his father
And to his people, "What
Is that which ye worship?

٨٥- اِذْ قَالَ لِاَبِيهِ وَقَوْمِهِ
مَاذَا تَعْبُدُونَ ۚ

86. "Is it a Falsehood—
Gods other than Allah
That ye desire?

٨٦- اَئِفْكًا
اٰلِهَةً دُونَ اللهِ تُرِيدُونَ ۚ

87. "Then what is your idea
About the Lord of the Worlds?"

٨٧- فَمَا ظَنُّكُمْ بِرَبِّ الْعٰلَمِينَ ۝

88. Then did he cast
A glance at the Stars,

٨٨- فَنَظَرَ نَظْرَةً فِي النُّجُومِ ۝

89. And he said, "I am
Indeed sick (at heart)!"

٨٩- فَقَالَ اِنِّي سَقِيمٌ ۝

90. So they turned away
From him, and departed.

٩٠- فَتَوَلَّوْا عَنْهُ مُدْبِرِينَ ۝

91. Then did he turn
To their gods and said,
"Will ye not eat
(Of the offerings before you)?..

٩١- فَرَاغَ اِلٰى اٰلِهَتِهِمْ فَقَالَ
اَلَا تَأْكُلُونَ ۚ

92. "What is the matter
With you that ye
Speak not (intelligently)?"

٩٢- مَا لَكُمْ لَا تَنْطِقُونَ ۝

93. Then did he turn
Upon them, striking (them)

٩٣- فَرَاغَ عَلَيْهِمْ ضَرْبًا

With the right hand.

بِالْيَمِيْنِ ۞

94. Then came (the worshippers)
With hurried steps,
And faced (him).

٩٤- فَأَقْبَلُوْۤا إِلَيْهِ يَزِفُّوْنَ ۞

95. He said: "Worship ye
That which ye have
(Yourselves) carved?

٩٥- قَالَ أَتَعْبُدُوْنَ مَا تَنْحِتُوْنَ ۞

96. "But Allah has created you
And your handiwork!"

٩٦- وَاللّٰهُ خَلَقَكُمْ وَمَا تَعْمَلُوْنَ ۞

97. They said, "Build him
A furnace, and throw him
Into the blazing fire!"

٩٧- قَالُوا ابْنُوْا لَهٗ بُنْيَانًا فَأَلْقُوْهُ فِى الْجَحِيْمِ ۞

98. (This failing), they then
Sought a stratagem against
him,
But We made them the ones
Most humiliated!

٩٨- فَأَرَادُوْا بِهٖ كَيْدًا فَجَعَلْنٰهُمُ الْأَسْفَلِيْنَ ۞

99. He said: "I will go
To my Lord! He
Will surely guide me!

٩٩- وَقَالَ إِنِّيْ ذَاهِبٌ إِلٰى رَبِّيْ سَيَهْدِيْنِ ۞

100. "O my Lord! grant me
A righteous (son)!"

١٠٠- رَبِّ هَبْ لِيْ مِنَ الصّٰلِحِيْنَ ۞

101. So We gave him
The good news
Of a boy ready
To suffer and forbear.

١٠١- فَبَشَّرْنٰهُ بِغُلٰمٍ حَلِيْمٍ ۞

102. Then, when (the son)
Reached (the age of)
(Serious) work with him,
He said: "O my son!
I see in vision
That I offer thee in sacrifice:
Now see what is
Thy view!" (The son) said:
"O my father! Do
As thou art commanded:

١٠٢- فَلَمَّا بَلَغَ مَعَهُ السَّعْىَ قَالَ يٰبُنَيَّ إِنِّيْۤ أَرٰى فِى الْمَنَامِ أَنِّيْۤ أَذْبَحُكَ فَانْظُرْ مَاذَا تَرٰى قَالَ يٰۤأَبَتِ افْعَلْ مَا تُؤْمَرُ

Thou will find me,
If Allah so wills one
Practising Patience and
　　　　Constancy!"

ۙ سَتَجِدُنِىٓ اِنْ شَآءَ اللّٰهُ
مِنَ الصّٰبِرِيْنَ ۞

103. So when they had both
Submitted their wills (to Allah),
And he had laid him
Prostrate on his forehead
(For sacrifice),

١٠٣ـ فَلَمَّآ اَسْلَمَا وَ تَلَّهٗ
لِلْجَبِيْنِ ۚ

104. We called out to him,
"O Abraham!

١٠٤ـ وَنَادَيْنٰهُ اَنْ يّٰٓاِبْرٰهِيْمُ ۙ

105. "Thou hast already fulfilled
The vision!"—thus indeed
Do We reward
Those who do right.

١٠٥ـ قَدْ صَدَّقْتَ الرُّءْيَا ۚ
اِنَّا كَذٰلِكَ نَجْزِى الْمُحْسِنِيْنَ ۞

106. For this was obviously
A trial—

١٠٦ـ اِنَّ هٰذَا لَهُوَ الْبَلٰٓؤُا الْمُبِيْنُ ۞

107. And We ransomed him
With a momentous sacrifice:

١٠٧ـ وَفَدَيْنٰهُ بِذِبْحٍ عَظِيْمٍ ۞

108. And We left (this blessing)
For him among generations
(To come) in later times:

١٠٨ـ وَتَرَكْنَا عَلَيْهِ فِى الْاٰخِرِيْنَ ۖ ۞

109. "Peace and salutation
To Abraham!"

١٠٩ـ سَلٰمٌ عَلٰٓى اِبْرٰهِيْمَ ۞

110. Thus indeed do We reward
Those who do right

١١٠ـ كَذٰلِكَ نَجْزِى الْمُحْسِنِيْنَ ۞

111. For he was one
Of Our believing Servants.

١١١ـ اِنَّهٗ مِنْ عِبَادِنَا الْمُؤْمِنِيْنَ ۞

112. And We gave him
The good news
Of Isaac—a prophet—
One of the Righteous.

١١٢ـ وَبَشَّرْنٰهُ
بِاِسْحٰقَ نَبِيًّا مِّنَ الصّٰلِحِيْنَ ۞

113. We blessed him and Isaac:
But of their progeny
Are (some) that do right,

١١٣ـ وَبٰرَكْنَا عَلَيْهِ وَعَلٰٓى اِسْحٰقَ ۚ
وَمِنْ ذُرِّيَّتِهِمَا مُحْسِنٌ وَّظَالِمٌ

And (some) that obviously
Do wrong, to their own souls.

لِنَفْسِهٖ مُبِيْنٌ ۙ

SECTION 4.

114. Again, (of old,)
We bestowed Our favour
On Moses and Aaron,

١١٤- وَلَقَدْ مَنَنَّا عَلٰى مُوْسٰى وَهٰرُوْنَ ۚ

115. And We delivered them
And their people from
(Their) Great Calamity;

١١٥- وَنَجَّيْنٰهُمَا
وَقَوْمَهُمَا مِنَ الْكَرْبِ الْعَظِيْمِ ۚ

116. And We helped them,
So they overcame (their
troubles);

١١٦- وَنَصَرْنٰهُمْ فَكَانُوْا هُمُ الْغٰلِبِيْنَ ۚ

117. And We gave them
The Book which helps
To make things clear;

١١٧- وَاٰتَيْنٰهُمَا الْكِتٰبَ الْمُسْتَبِيْنَ ۚ

118. And We guided them
To the Straight Way.

١١٨- وَهَدَيْنٰهُمَا الصِّرَاطَ الْمُسْتَقِيْمَ ۚ

119. And We left (this blessing)
For them among generations
(To come) in later times:

١١٩- وَتَرَكْنَا عَلَيْهِمَا فِى الْاٰخِرِيْنَ ۚ

120. "Peace and salutation
To Moses and Aaron!"

١٢٠- سَلٰمٌ عَلٰى مُوْسٰى وَهٰرُوْنَ ۚ

121. Thus indeed do We reward
Those who do right.

١٢١- اِنَّا كَذٰلِكَ نَجْزِى الْمُحْسِنِيْنَ ۚ

122. For they were two
Of Our believing Servants.

١٢٢- اِنَّهُمَا مِنْ عِبَادِنَا الْمُؤْمِنِيْنَ ۚ

123. So also was Elias
Among those sent (by Us).

١٢٣- وَاِنَّ اِلْيَاسَ لَمِنَ الْمُرْسَلِيْنَ ۚ

124. Behold, he said
To his people,
"Will ye not fear (Allah)?

١٢٤- اِذْ قَالَ لِقَوْمِهٖ
اَلَا تَتَّقُوْنَ ۚ

125. "Will ye call upon Ba'l
And forsake the Best
Of Creators—

١٢٥- اَتَدْعُوْنَ بَعْلًا
وَّتَذَرُوْنَ اَحْسَنَ الْخَالِقِيْنَ ۙ

126. "Allah, your Lord and Cherisher
And the Lord and Cherisher
Of your fathers of old?"

١٢٦- اَللّٰهُ رَبُّكُمْ وَرَبُّ اٰبَآئِكُمُ الْاَوَّلِيْنَ ۟

127. But they rejected him,
And they will certainly
Be called up (for punishment)—

١٢٧- فَكَذَّبُوْهُ فَاِنَّهُمْ لَمُحْضَرُوْنَ ۟

128. Except the sincere and devoted
Servants of Allah (among them).

١٢٨- اِلَّا عِبَادَ اللّٰهِ الْمُخْلَصِيْنَ ۟

129. And We left (this blessing)
For him among generations
(To come) in later times:

١٢٩- وَتَرَكْنَا عَلَيْهِ فِى الْاٰخِرِيْنَ ۟

130. "Peace and salutation
To such as Elias!"

١٣٠- سَلٰمٌ عَلٰٓى اِلْ يَاسِيْنَ ۟

131. Thus indeed do We reward
Those who do right.

١٣١- اِنَّا كَذٰلِكَ نَجْزِى الْمُحْسِنِيْنَ ۟

132. For he was one
Of Our believing Servants.

١٣٢- اِنَّهٗ مِنْ عِبَادِنَا الْمُؤْمِنِيْنَ ۟

133. So also was Lūṭ
Among those sent (by Us).

١٣٣- وَاِنَّ لُوْطًا لَّمِنَ الْمُرْسَلِيْنَ ۟

134. Behold, We delivered him
And his adherents, all

١٣٤- اِذْ نَجَّيْنٰهُ وَاَهْلَهٗٓ اَجْمَعِيْنَ ۟

135. Except an old woman
Who was among those
Who lagged behind:

١٣٥- اِلَّا عَجُوْزًا فِى الْغٰبِرِيْنَ ۟

136. Then We destroyed
The rest.

١٣٦- ثُمَّ دَمَّرْنَا الْاٰخَرِيْنَ ۟

137. Verily, ye pass
By their (sites),
By day—

١٣٧- وَاِنَّكُمْ لَتَمُرُّوْنَ عَلَيْهِمْ مُّصْبِحِيْنَ ۟

138. And by night:
Will ye not understand?

١٣٨- وَبِالَّيْلِ ۗ اَفَلَا تَعْقِلُوْنَ ۟

SECTION 5.

139. So also was Jonah
Among those sent (by Us).

١٣٩- وَإِنَّ يُونُسَ لَمِنَ الْمُرْسَلِينَ ۝

140. When he ran away
(Like a slave from captivity)
To the ship (fully) laden,

١٤٠- إِذْ أَبَقَ إِلَى الْفُلْكِ الْمَشْحُونِ ۝

141. He (agreed to) cast lots,
And he was condemned:

١٤١- فَسَاهَمَ فَكَانَ مِنَ الْمُدْحَضِينَ ۝

142. Then the big Fish
Did swallow him,
And he had done
Acts worthy of blame.

١٤٢- فَالْتَقَمَهُ الْحُوتُ
وَهُوَ مُلِيمٌ ۝

143. Had it not been
That he (repented and)
Glorified Allah,

١٤٣- فَلَوْلَا أَنَّهُ كَانَ مِنَ الْمُسَبِّحِينَ ۝

144. He would certainly have
Remained inside the Fish
Till the Day of Resurrection.

١٤٤- لَلَبِثَ فِي بَطْنِهِ إِلَى يَوْمِ يُبْعَثُونَ ۝

145. But We cast him forth
On the naked shore
In a state of sickness,

١٤٥- فَنَبَذْنَاهُ بِالْعَرَاءِ
وَهُوَ سَقِيمٌ ۝

116. And We caused to grow,
Over him, a spreading plant
Of the Gourd kind,

١٤٦- وَأَنْبَتْنَا عَلَيْهِ شَجَرَةً مِّنْ يَقْطِينٍ ۝

147. And We sent him
(On a mission)
To a hundred thousand
(Men) or more.

١٤٧- وَأَرْسَلْنَاهُ
إِلَى مِائَةِ أَلْفٍ أَوْ يَزِيدُونَ ۝

148. And they believed;
So We permitted them
To enjoy (their life)
For a while.

١٤٨- فَآمَنُوا
فَمَتَّعْنَاهُمْ إِلَى حِينٍ ۝

149. Now ask them their opinion:
Is it that thy Lord
Has (only) daughters, and they
Have sons?—

١٤٩- فَاسْتَفْتِهِمْ
أَلِرَبِّكَ الْبَنَاتُ وَلَهُمُ الْبَنُونَ ۝

150. Or that We created
The angels female, and they
Are witnesses (thereto)?

١٥٠- اَمْ خَلَقْنَا الْمَلَٰئِكَةَ اِنَاثًا وَّهُمْ شٰهِدُوْنَ ۞

151. Is it not that they
Say, from their own invention,

١٥١- اَلَاۤ اِنَّهُمْ مِّنْ اِفْكِهِمْ لَيَقُوْلُوْنَ ۞

152. "Allah has begotten children"?
But they are liars!

١٥٢- وَلَدَ اللّٰهُ وَ اِنَّهُمْ لَكٰذِبُوْنَ ۞

153. Did He (then) choose
Daughters rather than sons?

١٥٣- اَصْطَفَى الْبَنَاتِ عَلَى الْبَنِيْنَ ۞

154. What is the matter
With you? How judge ye?

١٥٤- مَا لَكُمْ كَيْفَ تَحْكُمُوْنَ ۞

155. Will ye not then
Receive admonition?

١٥٥- اَفَلَا تَذَكَّرُوْنَ ۞

156. Or have ye
An authority manifest?

١٥٦- اَمْ لَكُمْ سُلْطٰنٌ مُّبِيْنٌ ۞

157. Then bring ye your Book
(Of authority) if ye be
Truthful!

١٥٧- فَأْتُوْا بِكِتٰبِكُمْ اِنْ كُنْتُمْ صٰدِقِيْنَ ۞

158. And they have invented
A blood-relationship
Between Him and the Jinns:
But the Jinns know
(Quite well) that they
Have indeed to appear
(Before His Judgement Seat)!

١٥٨- وَجَعَلُوْا بَيْنَهٗ وَبَيْنَ الْجِنَّةِ نَسَبًا وَلَقَدْ عَلِمَتِ الْجِنَّةُ اِنَّهُمْ لَمُحْضَرُوْنَ ۞

159. Glory to Allah! (He is free)
From the things they ascribe
(To Him)!

١٥٩- سُبْحٰنَ اللّٰهِ عَمَّا يَصِفُوْنَ ۞

160. Not (so do) the Servants
Of Allah, sincere and devoted.

١٦٠- اِلَّا عِبَادَ اللّٰهِ الْمُخْلَصِيْنَ ۞

161. For, verily, neither ye
Nor those ye worship—

١٦١- فَاِنَّكُمْ وَ مَا تَعْبُدُوْنَ ۞

162. Can lead (any)
Into temptation
Concerning Allah,

١٦٢- مَاۤ أَنتُمۡ عَلَيۡهِ بِفَـٰتِنِينَ ۞

163. Except such as are
(Themselves) going to
The blazing Fire!

١٦٣- إِلَّا مَنۡ هُوَ صَالِ الۡجَحِيمِ ۝

164. (Those ranged in ranks say):
"Not one of us but has
A place appointed;

١٦٤- وَمَا مِنَّاۤ إِلَّا لَهُ مَقَامٌ مَّعۡلُومٌ ۞

165. "And we are verily
Ranged in ranks (for service);

١٦٥- وَّإِنَّا لَنَحۡنُ الصَّآفُّونَ ۞

166. "And we are verily those
Who declare (Allah's) glory!"

١٦٦- وَإِنَّا لَنَحۡنُ الۡمُسَبِّحُونَ ۝

167. And there were those
Who said,

١٦٧- وَإِن كَانُوا لَيَقُولُونَ ۞

168. "If only we had had
Before us a Message
From those of old,

١٦٨- لَوۡ أَنَّ عِندَنَا
ذِكۡرًا مِّنَ الۡأَوَّلِينَ ۞

169. "We should certainly have
Been Servants of Allah,
Sincere (and devoted)!"

١٦٩- لَكُنَّا عِبَادَ اللهِ الۡمُخۡلَصِينَ ۝

170. But (now that the Qur'ān
Has come), they reject it;
But soon will they know!

١٧٠- فَكَفَرُوا بِهِ فَسَوۡفَ يَعۡلَمُونَ ۝

171. Already has Our Word
Been passed before (this)
To Our Servants sent (by Us),

١٧١- وَلَقَدۡ سَبَقَتۡ كَلِمَتُنَا
لِعِبَادِنَا الۡمُرۡسَلِينَ ۖ

172. That they would certainly
Be assisted,

١٧٢- إِنَّهُمۡ لَهُمُ الۡمَنصُورُونَ ۝

173. And that Our forces—
They surely must conquer.

١٧٣- وَإِنَّ جُندَنَا لَهُمُ الۡغَـٰلِبُونَ ۝

174. So turn thou away
From them for a little while,

١٧٤ـ فَتَوَلَّ عَنْهُمْ حَتّٰى حِيْنٍ ۞

175. And watch them (how
They fare), and they soon
Shall see (how thou farest)!

١٧٥ـ وَّ أَبْصِرْهُمْ فَسَوْفَ يُبْصِرُوْنَ ۞

176. Do they wish (indeed)
To hurry on our Punishment?

١٧٦ـ أَفَبِعَذَابِنَا يَسْتَعْجِلُوْنَ ۞

177. But when it descends
Into the open space
Before them, evil will be
The morning for those who
Were warned (and heeded not)!

١٧٧ـ فَإِذَا نَزَلَ بِسَاحَتِهِمْ
فَسَاءَ صَبَاحُ الْمُنْذَرِيْنَ ۞

178. So turn thou away
From them for a little while,

١٧٨ـ وَتَوَلَّ عَنْهُمْ حَتّٰى حِيْنٍ ۞

179. And watch (how they fare)
And they soon shall see
(How thou farest)!

١٧٩ـ وَّ أَبْصِرْ فَسَوْفَ يُبْصِرُوْنَ ۞

180. Glory to thy Lord,
The Lord of Honour
And Power! (He is free)
From what they ascribe
(To Him)!

١٨٠ـ سُبْحٰنَ رَبِّكَ
رَبِّ الْعِزَّةِ
عَمَّا يَصِفُوْنَ ۞

181. And Peace on the Messengers

١٨١ـ وَسَلٰمٌ عَلَى الْمُرْسَلِيْنَ ۞

182. And Praise to Allah,
The Lord and Cherisher
Of the Worlds.

١٨٢ـ وَالْحَمْدُ لِلّٰهِ رَبِّ الْعٰلَمِيْنَ ۞

INTRODUCTION TO SŪRA XXXVIII. (*Ṣād*) — 88 Verses

For the place of this Sūra in the series of six, dealing with some of the mysteries of the spiritual world, see Introduction to S. xxxiv.

This Sūra, both in chronology and subject-matter, is cognate to S. xxxvii., and carries forward the same argument. But here the emphasis is laid on the working of earthly power when combined with spiritual power, and it is pointed out how much more significant (and real) spiritual power is. For this reason the illustrative stories are mainly those of David and Solomon who were kings as well as prophets, and a parallel is suggested with the unfolding public life of our Holy Prophet.

Ṣād

In the name of God, Most Gracious,
Most Merciful.

1. *Ṣād:*
By the Qur'ān,
Full of Admonition:
(This is the Truth).

2. But the Unbelievers
(Are steeped) in Self-glory
And Separatism.

3. How many generations
Before them did We destroy?
In the end they cried
(For mercy)—when
There was no longer time
For being saved!

4. So they wonder
That a Warner has come
To them from among
themselves!
And the Unbelievers say,
"This is a sorcerer
Telling lies!

5. "Has he made the gods
(All) into one God?

Truly this is
A wonderful thing!"

إِنَّ هَذَا لَشَىْءٌ عُجَابٌ ۝

6. And the leaders among them
Go away (impatiently),
               (saying),
"Walk ye away, and remain
Constant to your gods!
For this is truly
A thing designed (against you)!

٦- وَانْطَلَقَ الْمَلَأُ مِنْهُمْ
أَنِ امْشُوا وَاصْبِرُوا عَلَى آلِهَتِكُمْ
إِنَّ هَذَا لَشَىْءٌ يُرَادُ ۝

7. "We never heard (the like)
Of this among the people
Of these latter days:
This is nothing but
A made-up tale!"

٧- مَا سَمِعْنَا بِهَذَا فِى الْمِلَّةِ الْآخِرَةِ
إِنْ هَذَا إِلَّا اخْتِلَاقٌ ۝

8. "What! Has the Message
Been sent to him—
(Of all persons) among us?" . . .
But they are in doubt
Concerning My (own) Message!
Nay, they have not yet
Tasted My Punishment!

٨- أَءُنْزِلَ عَلَيْهِ الذِّكْرُ مِنْ بَيْنِنَا
بَلْ هُمْ فِى شَكٍّ
مِنْ ذِكْرِى ۚ بَلْ لَمَّا يَذُوقُوا عَذَابِ ۝

9. Or have they the Treasures
Of the Mercy of thy Lord—
The Exalted in Power,
The Grantor of Bounties
Without measure?

٩- أَمْ عِنْدَهُمْ خَزَائِنُ
رَحْمَةِ رَبِّكَ الْعَزِيزِ الْوَهَّابِ ۝

10. Or have they the dominion
Of the heavens and the earth
And all between? If so,
Let them mount up
With the ropes and means
(To reach that end)!

١٠- أَمْ لَهُمْ مُلْكُ السَّمَوَاتِ وَالْأَرْضِ
وَمَا بَيْنَهُمَا
فَلْيَرْتَقُوا فِى الْأَسْبَابِ ۝

11. But there—will be
Put to flight even a host
Of confederates.

١١- جُنْدٌ مَا هُنَالِكَ مَهْزُومٌ
مِنَ الْأَحْزَابِ ۝

12. Before them (were many
Who) rejected messengers—
The People of Noah,
And 'Ād, and Pharaoh
The Lord of Stakes,

١٢- كَذَّبَتْ قَبْلَهُمْ قَوْمُ
نُوحٍ وَعَادٌ وَفِرْعَوْنُ ذُو الْأَوْتَادِ ۝

13. And <u>Th</u>amūd, and the People
Of Lūṭ, and the Companions
Of the Wood— such were
The Confederates.

14. Not one (of them) but
Rejected the messengers,
But My Punishment
Came justly and inevitably
(On them).

SECTION 2.

15. These (today) only wait
For a single mighty Blast,
Which (when it comes)
Will brook no delay.

16. They say: "Our Lord!
Hasten to us our sentence
(Even) before the Day
Of Account!"

17. Have patience at what they
Say, and remember Our Servant
David, the man of strength:
For he ever turned (to Allah).

18. It was We that made
The hills declare,
In unison with him,
Our Praises, at eventide
And at break of day,

19. And the birds gathered
(In assemblies): all with him
Did turn (to Allah).

20. We strengthened his kingdom,
And gave him wisdom
And sound judgement
In speech and decision.

21. Has the Story of
The Disputants reached thee?
Behold, they climbed over
The wall of the private chamber;

22. When they entered
The presence of David,

١٣- وَثَمُوْدُ وَقَوْمُ لُوْطٍ وَّأَصْحٰبُ
لْـَٔيْكَةِ ۚ أُولٰٓئِكَ الْأَحْزَابُ ۝

١٤- اِنْ كُلٌّ اِلَّا كَذَّبَ الرُّسُلَ
فَحَقَّ عِقَابِ ۝

١٥- وَمَا يَنْظُرُ هٰٓؤُلَآءِ اِلَّا صَيْحَةً وَّاحِدَةً
مَّا لَهَا مِنْ فَوَاقٍ ۝

١٦- وَقَالُوْا رَبَّنَا عَجِّلْ لَّنَا قِطَّنَا
قَبْلَ يَوْمِ الْحِسَابِ ۝

١٧- اِصْبِرْ عَلٰى مَا يَقُوْلُوْنَ وَاذْكُرْ عَبْدَنَا
دَاوٗدَ ذَا الْأَيْدِ ۚ اِنَّهٗ أَوَّابٌ ۝

١٨- اِنَّا سَخَّرْنَا الْجِبَالَ مَعَهٗ
يُسَبِّحْنَ بِالْعَشِيِّ وَالْإِشْرَاقِ ۝

١٩- وَالطَّيْرَ مَحْشُوْرَةً ۚ
كُلٌّ لَّهٗ أَوَّابٌ ۝

٢٠- وَشَدَدْنَا مُلْكَهٗ وَاٰتَيْنٰهُ الْحِكْمَةَ
وَفَصْلَ الْخِطَابِ ۝

٢١- وَهَلْ أَتٰىكَ نَبَؤُا الْخَصْمِ ۘ
اِذْ تَسَوَّرُوا الْمِحْرَابَ ۝

٢٢- اِذْ دَخَلُوْا عَلٰى دَاوٗدَ

And he was terrified
Of them, they said:
"Fear not: we are two
Disputants, one of whom
Has wronged the other:
Decide now between us
With truth, and treat us not
With injustice, but guide us
To the even Path.

فَفَزِعَ مِنْهُمْ قَالُوا لَا تَخَفْ ۖ
خَصْمَانِ بَغَىٰ بَعْضُنَا عَلَىٰ بَعْضٍ
فَاحْكُم بَيْنَنَا بِالْحَقِّ وَلَا تُشْطِطْ
وَاهْدِنَا إِلَىٰ سَوَاءِ الصِّرَاطِ ۝

23. "This man is my brother:
He has nine and ninety
Ewes, and I have (but) one:
Yet he says, 'Commit her
To my care,' and is (moreover)
Harsh to me in speech."

٢٣ ـ إِنَّ هَٰذَا أَخِي
لَهُ تِسْعٌ وَتِسْعُونَ نَعْجَةً وَلِيَ نَعْجَةٌ وَاحِدَةٌ
فَقَالَ أَكْفِلْنِيهَا وَعَزَّنِي فِي الْخِطَابِ ۝

24. (David) said: "He has
Undoubtedly wronged thee
In demanding thy (single) ewe
To be added to his (flock
Of) ewes; truly many
Are the Partners (in business)
Who wrong each other:
Not so do those who believe
And work deeds of righteousness,
And how few are they?"...
And David gathered that We
Had tried him: he asked
Forgiveness of his Lord,
Fell down, bowing
(In prostration), and turned
(To Allah in repentance)

٢٤ ـ قَالَ لَقَدْ ظَلَمَكَ
بِسُؤَالِ نَعْجَتِكَ إِلَىٰ نِعَاجِهِ ۖ
وَإِنَّ كَثِيرًا مِّنَ الْخُلَطَاءِ لَيَبْغِي بَعْضُهُمْ
عَلَىٰ بَعْضٍ
إِلَّا الَّذِينَ آمَنُوا وَعَمِلُوا الصَّالِحَاتِ
وَقَلِيلٌ مَّا هُمْ ۗ
وَظَنَّ دَاوُودُ أَنَّمَا فَتَنَّاهُ
فَاسْتَغْفَرَ رَبَّهُ وَخَرَّ رَاكِعًا وَأَنَابَ ۩ ۝

25. So We forgave him
This (lapse): he enjoyed,
Indeed, a Near Approach to Us,
And a beautiful Place
Of (final) Return.

٢٥ ـ فَغَفَرْنَا لَهُ ذَٰلِكَ ۖ
وَإِنَّ لَهُ عِندَنَا لَزُلْفَىٰ
وَحُسْنَ مَآبٍ ۝

26. O David! We did indeed
Make thee a vicegerent
On earth: so judge thou
Between men in truth (and
justice):
Nor follow thou the lusts
(Of thy heart), for they will
Mislead thee from the Path

٢٦ ـ يَا دَاوُودُ إِنَّا جَعَلْنَاكَ خَلِيفَةً فِي الْأَرْضِ
فَاحْكُم بَيْنَ النَّاسِ بِالْحَقِّ
وَلَا تَتَّبِعِ الْهَوَىٰ
فَيُضِلَّكَ عَن سَبِيلِ اللَّهِ ۚ

Of Allah: for those who
Wander astray from the Path
Of Allah, is a Penalty Grievous,
For that they forget
The Day of Account.

SECTION 3.

إِنَّ الَّذِيْنَ يَضِلُّوْنَ عَنْ سَبِيْلِ اللّٰهِ
لَهُمْ عَذَابٌ شَدِيْدٌ
بِمَا نَسُوْا يَوْمَ الْحِسَابِ ۩

27. Not without purpose did We
Create heaven and earth
And all between! That
Were the thought of Unbelievers!
But woe to the Unbelievers
Because of the Fire (of Hell)!

٢٧- وَمَا خَلَقْنَا السَّمَآءَ وَالْأَرْضَ وَمَا بَيْنَهُمَا
بَاطِلًا ۗ ذٰلِكَ ظَنُّ الَّذِيْنَ كَفَرُوْا ۚ
فَوَيْلٌ لِّلَّذِيْنَ كَفَرُوْا مِنَ النَّارِ ۩

28. Shall We treat those
Who believe and work deeds
Of righteousness, the same
As those who do mischief
On earth? Shall We treat
Those who guard against evil,
The same as those who
Turn aside from the right?

٢٨- أَمْ نَجْعَلُ الَّذِيْنَ اٰمَنُوْا وَعَمِلُوا الصّٰلِحٰتِ
كَالْمُفْسِدِيْنَ فِى الْأَرْضِ ۖ
أَمْ نَجْعَلُ
الْمُتَّقِيْنَ كَالْفُجَّارِ ۩

29. (Here is) a Book which
We have sent down
Unto thee, full of blessings,
That they may meditate
On its Signs, and that
Men of understanding may
Receive admonition.

٢٩- كِتٰبٌ أَنْزَلْنٰهُ إِلَيْكَ
مُبٰرَكٌ لِّيَدَّبَّرُوْا اٰيٰتِهٖ
وَلِيَتَذَكَّرَ أُولُوا الْأَلْبَابِ ۩

30. To David We gave
Solomon (for a son)—
How excellent in Our service!
Ever did he turn (to Us)!

٣٠- وَوَهَبْنَا لِدَاوٗدَ سُلَيْمٰنَ ۚ
نِعْمَ الْعَبْدُ ۗ إِنَّهٗ أَوَّابٌ ۩

31. Behold, there were brought
Before him, at eventide,
Coursers of the highest breeding,
And swift of foot;

٣١- إِذْ عُرِضَ عَلَيْهِ بِالْعَشِيِّ
الصّٰفِنٰتُ الْجِيَادُ ۩

32. And he said, "Truly
Do I love the love
Of Good, with a view
To the glory of my Lord"—
Until (the sun) was hidden
In the veil (of Night):

٣٢- فَقَالَ إِنِّيْ أَحْبَبْتُ حُبَّ الْخَيْرِ
عَنْ ذِكْرِ رَبِّيْ ۚ
حَتّٰى تَوَارَتْ بِالْحِجَابِ ۩

33. "Bring them back to me."

٣٣- رُدُّوْهَا عَلَيَّ ۖ فَطَفِقَ

Then began he to pass
His hand over (their) legs
And their necks.

مَسْحًا بِالسُّوْقِ وَالْاَعْنَاقِ ۝

34. And We did try
Solomon: We placed
On his throne a body
(Without life): but he did turn
(To Us in true devotion):

٣٤ـ وَلَقَدْ فَتَنَّا سُلَيْمَانَ وَاَلْقَيْنَا عَلٰى كُرْسِيِّهٖ جَسَدًا ثُمَّ اَنَابَ ۝

35. He said: "O my Lord!
Forgive me,   and grant me
A Kingdom which,
(It may be), suits not
Another after me:
For Thou are the Grantor
Of Bounties (without measure).

٣٥ـ قَالَ رَبِّ اغْفِرْ لِيْ وَهَبْ لِيْ مُلْكًا لَّا يَنْبَغِيْ لِاَحَدٍ مِّنْ بَعْدِيْ ۚ اِنَّكَ اَنْتَ الْوَهَّابُ ۝

36. Then We subjected the Wind
To his power, to flow
Gently to his order,
Whithersoever he willed—

٣٦ـ فَسَخَّرْنَا لَهُ الرِّيْحَ تَجْرِيْ بِاَمْرِهٖ رُخَآءً حَيْثُ اَصَابَ ۙ

37. As also the evil ones,
(Including) every kind
Of builder and diver—

٣٧ـ وَالشَّيٰطِيْنَ كُلَّ بَنَّآءٍ وَّغَوَّاصٍ ۙ

38. As also others bound
Together in fetters.

٣٨ـ وَّاٰخَرِيْنَ مُقَرَّنِيْنَ فِى الْاَصْفَادِ ۝

39. "Such are Our Bounties:
Whether thou bestow them
(On others) or withhold them,
No account will be asked."

٣٩ـ هٰذَا عَطَآؤُنَا فَامْنُنْ اَوْ اَمْسِكْ بِغَيْرِ حِسَابٍ ۝

40. And he enjoyed, indeed,
A Near Approach to Us,
And a beautiful Place
Of (final) Return.
         SECTION 4.

٤٠ـ وَاِنَّ لَهٗ عِنْدَنَا لَزُلْفٰى وَحُسْنَ مَاٰبٍ ۞

41. Commemorate Our Servant
         Job.
Behold he cried to his Lord:
"The Evil One has afflicted
Me with distress   and suffering!"

٤١ـ وَاذْكُرْ عَبْدَنَآ اَيُّوْبَ ۘ اِذْ نَادٰى رَبَّهٗٓ اَنِّيْ مَسَّنِيَ الشَّيْطٰنُ بِنُصْبٍ وَّعَذَابٍ ۝

42. (The command was given:)
"Strike with thy foot:
Here is (water) wherein

٤٢ـ اُرْكُضْ بِرِجْلِكَ ۚ هٰذَا مُغْتَسَلٌۢ

To wash, cool and refreshing
And (water) to drink."

بَارِدٌ وَّشَرَابٌ ۟

43. And We gave him (back)
His people and doubled
Their number — as a Grace
From Ourselves, and a thing
For commemoration, for all
Who have Understanding.

٤٣- وَوَهَبْنَا لَهُ أَهْلَهُ
وَمِثْلَهُمْ مَّعَهُمْ رَحْمَةً مِّنَّا
وَذِكْرَى لِأُولِي الْأَلْبَابِ ۟

44. "And take in thy hand
A little grass, and strike
Therewith: and break not
(Thy oath)." Truly We found
Him full of patience and
                          constancy,
How excellent in Our service!
Ever did he turn (to Us)!

٤٤- وَخُذْ بِيَدِكَ ضِغْثًا
فَاضْرِبْ بِّهِ وَلَا تَحْنَثْ
إِنَّا وَجَدْنَاهُ صَابِرًا
نِعْمَ الْعَبْدُ إِنَّهُ أَوَّابٌ ۟

45. And commemorate Our Servants
Abraham, Isaac, and Jacob,
Possessors of Power and Vision.

٤٥- وَاذْكُرْ عِبَادَنَا إِبْرَاهِيمَ وَإِسْحَاقَ وَ
يَعْقُوبَ أُولِي الْأَيْدِي وَالْأَبْصَارِ ۟

46. Verily We did choose them
For a special (purpose) —
Proclaiming the Message
Of the Hereafter.

٤٦- إِنَّا أَخْلَصْنَاهُمْ بِخَالِصَةٍ
ذِكْرَى الدَّارِ ۟

47. They were, in Our sight,
Truly, of the company
Of the Elect and the Good.

٤٧- وَإِنَّهُمْ عِنْدَنَا لَمِنَ
الْمُصْطَفَيْنَ الْأَخْيَارِ ۟

48. And commemorate Ismā'īl,
Elisha, and Dhu al Kifl:
Each of them was
Of the company of the Good.

٤٨- وَاذْكُرْ إِسْمَاعِيلَ وَالْيَسَعَ وَذَا الْكِفْلِ
وَكُلٌّ مِّنَ الْأَخْيَارِ ۟

49. This is a Message
(Of admonition): and verily,
For the Righteous,
Is a beautiful place
Of (final) Return —

٤٩- هٰذَا ذِكْرٌ
وَإِنَّ لِلْمُتَّقِينَ لَحُسْنَ مَآبٍ ۟

50. Gardens of Eternity,
Whose doors will (ever)
Be open to them;

٥٠- جَنَّاتِ عَدْنٍ
مُّفَتَّحَةً لَّهُمُ الْأَبْوَابُ ۟

51. Therein will they
Recline (at ease):

٥١- مُتَّكِئِينَ فِيهَا

Therein can they
Call (at pleasure)
For fruit in abundance,
And (delicious) drink;

يَدْعُوْنَ فِيْهَا بِفَاكِهَةٍ كَثِيْرَةٍ وَّشَرَابٍ ۝

52. And beside them will be
Chaste women restraining
Their glances, (companions)
Of equal age.

٥٢ - وَعِنْدَهُمْ قٰصِرٰتُ الطَّرْفِ اَتْرَابٌ ۝

53. Such is the Promise
Made to you
For the Day of Account!

٥٣ - هٰذَا مَا تُوْعَدُوْنَ لِيَوْمِ الْحِسَابِ ۝

54. Truly such will be
Our Bounty (to you);
It will never fail—

٥٤ - اِنَّ هٰذَا لَرِزْقُنَا مَالَهٗ مِنْ نَّفَادٍ ۝

55. Yea, such! But—
For the wrongdoers
Will be an evil place
Of (final) Return!

٥٥ - هٰذَا ۚ وَاِنَّ لِلطّٰغِيْنَ لَشَرَّ مَاٰبٍ ۝

56. Hell!—they will burn
Therein—an evil bed
(Indeed to lie on)!—

٥٦ - جَهَنَّمَ ۚ يَصْلَوْنَهَا ۚ فَبِئْسَ الْمِهَادُ ۝

57. Yea, such!—Then
Shall they taste it—
A boiling fluid, and a fluid
Dark, murky, intensely cold!—

٥٧ - هٰذَا ۙ فَلْيَذُوْقُوْهُ حَمِيْمٌ وَّغَسَّاقٌ ۝

58. And other Penalties
Of a similar kind,
To match them!

٥٨ - وَّاٰخَرُ مِنْ شَكْلِهٖ اَزْوَاجٌ ۝

59. Here is a troop
Rushing headlong with you!
No welcome for them!
Truly, they shall burn
In the Fire!

٥٩ - هٰذَا فَوْجٌ مُّقْتَحِمٌ مَّعَكُمْ ۚ لَا مَرْحَبًا بِهِمْ ۚ اِنَّهُمْ صَالُوا النَّارِ ۝

60. (The followers shall cry
To the misleaders:)
"Nay, ye (too)! No welcome
For you! It is ye who
Have brought this upon us!

٦٠ - قَالُوْا بَلْ اَنْتُمْ ۚ لَا مَرْحَبًا بِكُمْ ۚ اَنْتُمْ قَدَّمْتُمُوْهُ لَنَا ۚ

Now evil is (this) place
To stay in!"

فَبِئْسَ الْقَرَارُ ۞

61. They will say: "Our Lord!
Whoever brought this upon us—
Add to him a double
Penalty in the Fire!"

٦١ـ قَالُوْا رَبَّنَا مَنْ قَدَّمَ لَنَا هٰذَا
فَزِدْهُ عَذَابًا ضِعْفًا فِى النَّارِ ۞

62. And they will say:
"What has happened to us
That we see not men
Whom we used to number
Among the bad ones?"

٦٢ـ وَقَالُوْا مَا لَنَا لَا نَرٰى رِجَالًا
كُنَّا نَعُدُّهُمْ مِّنَ الْأَشْرَارِ ۞

63. "Did we treat them
(As such) in ridicule,
Or have (our) eyes
Failed to perceive them?"

٦٣ـ أَتَّخَذْنٰهُمْ سِخْرِيًّا
أَمْ زَاغَتْ عَنْهُمُ الْأَبْصَارُ ۞

64. Truly that is just and fitting—
The mutual recriminations
Of the People of the Fire!

٦٤ـ اِنَّ ذٰلِكَ لَحَقٌّ
تَخَاصُمُ أَهْلِ النَّارِ ۞

SECTION 5.

65. Say: "Truly am I
A Warner; no god
Is there but the One
God, Supreme and
                    Irresistible—

٦٥ـ قُلْ اِنَّمَا أَنَا مُنْذِرٌ وَمَا مِنْ اِلٰهٍ اِلَّا
اللّٰهُ الْوَاحِدُ الْقَهَّارُ ۞

66. "The Lord of the heavens
And the earth, and all
Between—Exalted in Might,
Able to enforce His Will,
Forgiving again and again."

٦٦ـ رَبُّ السَّمٰوٰتِ وَالْأَرْضِ
وَمَا بَيْنَهُمَا
الْعَزِيْزُ الْغَفَّارُ ۞

67. Say: "That is a Message
Supreme (above all)—

٦٧ـ قُلْ هُوَ نَبَؤٌا عَظِيْمٌ ۞

68. "From which ye
Do turn away!

٦٨ـ أَنْتُمْ عَنْهُ مُعْرِضُوْنَ ۞

69. "No knowledge have I
Of the Chiefs on high,
When they discuss
(Matters) among themselves.

٦٩ـ مَا كَانَ لِيَ مِنْ عِلْمٍ بِالْمَلَإِ الْأَعْلٰى
اِذْ يَخْتَصِمُوْنَ ۞

70. "Only this has been revealed
To me: that I am

٧٠ـ اِنْ يُوْحٰى اِلَيَّ اِلَّا اَنَّمَا اَنَا

To give warning
Plainly and publicly."

نَذِيرٌ مُّبِينٌ ○

71. Behold, thy Lord said
To the angels: "I am
About to create man
From clay:

٧١ - اِذْ قَالَ رَبُّكَ
لِلْمَلَائِكَةِ اِنِّى خَالِقٌ بَشَرًا مِّن طِينٍ ○

72. "When I have fashioned him
(In due proportion) and
breathed
Into him of My spirit,
Fall ye down in obeisance
Unto him."

٧٢ - فَاِذَا سَوَّيْتُهُ وَ نَفَخْتُ
فِيهِ مِن رُّوحِى
فَقَعُوا لَهُ سٰجِدِينَ ○

73. So the angels prostrated
themselves,
All of them together:

٧٣ - فَسَجَدَ الْمَلَائِكَةُ كُلُّهُمْ اَجْمَعُونَ ۚ

74. Not so Iblīs: he
Was haughty, and became
One of those who reject Faith.

٧٤ - اِلَّا اِبْلِيسَ اسْتَكْبَرَ وَكَانَ
مِنَ الْكٰفِرِينَ ○

75. (Allah) said: "O Iblīs!
What prevents thee from
Prostrating thyself to one
Whom I have created
With My hands?
Art thou haughty?
Or art thou one
Of the high (and mighty)
ones?"

٧٥ - قَالَ يٰٓاِبْلِيسُ مَا مَنَعَكَ
اَن تَسْجُدَ لِمَا خَلَقْتُ بِيَدَىَّ ۗ
اَسْتَكْبَرْتَ
اَمْ كُنتَ مِنَ الْعَالِينَ ○

76. (Iblīs) said: "I am better
Than he: Thou createdst
Me from fire, and him
Thou createdst from clay."

٧٦ - قَالَ اَنَا خَيْرٌ مِّنْهُ ۚ خَلَقْتَنِى
مِن نَّارٍ وَّخَلَقْتَهُ مِن طِينٍ ○

77. (Allah) said: "Then get thee
Out from here: for thou
Art rejected, accursed,

٧٧ - قَالَ فَاخْرُجْ مِنْهَا
فَاِنَّكَ رَجِيمٌ ۖ

78. "And My Curse shall be
On thee till the Day
Of Judgement."

٧٨ - وَاِنَّ عَلَيْكَ لَعْنَتِى
اِلٰى يَوْمِ الدِّينِ ○

79. (Iblīs) said: "O my Lord!

٧٩ - قَالَ رَبِّ فَاَنْظِرْنِى

Give me then respite
Till the Day
The (dead) are raised."

الى يَوْمِ يُبْعَثُونَ ۟

80. (Allah) said: "Respite then
Is granted thee—

٨٠۔قَالَ فَإِنَّكَ مِنَ الْمُنْظَرِينَ ۟ۙ

81. "Till the Day
Of the Time Appointed."

٨١۔إلى يَوْمِ الْوَقْتِ الْمَعْلُومِ ۟

82. (Iblīs) said: "Then,
By Thy Power,   I will
Put them all in the wrong—

٨٢۔قَالَ فَبِعِزَّتِكَ
لَأُغْوِيَنَّهُمْ أَجْمَعِينَ ۟ۙ

83. "Except Thy Servants
Amongst them, sincere
And purified (by Thy grace)."

٨٣۔إلَّا عِبَادَكَ مِنْهُمُ الْمُخْلَصِينَ ۟

84. (Allah) said: "Then
It is just and fitting—
And I say what is
Just and fitting—

٨٤۔قَالَ فَالْحَقُّ ۖ
وَالْحَقَّ أَقُولُ ۟ۚ

85. "That I will certainly fill
Hell with thee
And those who follow thee—
Every one."

٨٥۔لَأَمْلَأَنَّ جَهَنَّمَ مِنْكَ
وَمِمَّنْ تَبِعَكَ مِنْهُمْ أَجْمَعِينَ ۟

86. Say: "No reward do I ask
Of you for this (Qur'ān),
Nor am I a pretender.

٨٦۔قُلْ مَا أَسْأَلُكُمْ عَلَيْهِ مِنْ أَجْرٍ
وَمَا أَنَا مِنَ الْمُتَكَلِّفِينَ ۟

87. "This is no less than
A Message to (all)
The Worlds.

٨٧۔إنْ هُوَ إلَّا ذِكْرٌ لِلْعَالَمِينَ ۟

88. "And ye shall certainly
Know the truth of it (all)
After a while."

٨٨۔وَلَتَعْلَمُنَّ نَبَأَهُ بَعْدَ حِينٍ ۟ۚ

INTRODUCTION TO SŪRA XXXIX. (*Zumar*) — 75 Verses

This is the last of the series of six Sūras beginning with S. xxxiv., which deal with the mysteries of the spiritual world, as leading up to the Ma'ād, or the Hereafter. See Introduction to S. xxxiv.

It subject-matter is how Creation in its great variety is yet sorted out in Groups or Classes, all governed by one Plan, and created and sustained by One God, Who will separate Good from Evil at the Last Day. The word *zumar* occurs in verses 71 and 73.

Its chronology has no significance. It belongs to the latter Meccan period.

Al Zumar (Crowds)

In the name of Allah, Most Gracious, Most Merciful.

بِسْمِ اللهِ الرَّحْمٰنِ الرَّحِيمِ

1. The revelation
Of this Book
Is from Allah,
The Exalted in Power,
Full of Wisdom.

١- تَنْزِيلُ الْكِتٰبِ مِنَ اللهِ الْعَزِيزِ الْحَكِيمِ ۞

2. Verily it is We Who have
Revealed the Book to thee
In Truth: so serve Allah,
Offering Him sincere devotion.

٢- إِنَّا أَنْزَلْنَا إِلَيْكَ الْكِتٰبَ بِالْحَقِّ فَاعْبُدِ اللهَ مُخْلِصًا لَّهُ الدِّينَ ۞

3. Is it not to Allah
That sincere devotion
Is due? But those who
Take for protectors others
Than Allah (say): "We only
Serve them in order that
They may bring us nearer
To Allah." Truly Allah
Will judge between them
In that wherein they differ.
But Allah guides not
Such as are false
And ungrateful.

٣- أَلَا لِلّٰهِ الدِّينُ الْخَالِصُ ۚ وَالَّذِينَ اتَّخَذُوا مِنْ دُونِهٖ أَوْلِيَاءَ ۘ مَا نَعْبُدُهُمْ إِلَّا لِيُقَرِّبُونَا إِلَى اللهِ زُلْفٰى ۚ إِنَّ اللهَ يَحْكُمُ بَيْنَهُمْ فِى مَا هُمْ فِيهِ يَخْتَلِفُونَ ۗ إِنَّ اللهَ لَا يَهْدِى مَنْ هُوَ كٰذِبٌ كَفَّارٌ ۞

4. Had Allah wished
To take to Himself
A son, He could have

٤- لَوْ أَرَادَ اللهُ أَنْ يَتَّخِذَ

Chosen whom He pleased
Out of those whom He
Doth create: but Glory
Be to Him! (He is above
Such things.) He is Allah,
The One, the Irresistible.

5. He created the heavens
And the earth
In true (proportions):
He makes the Night
Overlap the Day, and the Day
Overlap the Night:
He has subjected
The sun and the moon
(To His law):
Each one follows a course
For a time appointed.
Is not He the Exalted
In Power—He Who forgives
Again and again?

6. He created you (all)
From a single Person:
Then created, of like nature,
His mate; and He
Sent down for you eight
             head
Of cattle in pairs:
He makes you,
In the wombs
Of your mothers,
In stages, one after another,
In three veils of darkness.
Such is Allah, your Lord
And Cherisher: to Him belongs
(All) dominion. There is
No god but He: then
How are ye turned away
(From your true Centre)?

7. If ye reject (Allah),
Truly Allah hath no need
Of you; but He liketh not
Ingratitude from His servants:
If ye are grateful, He
Is pleased with you.
No bearer of burdens
Can bear the burden

وَلَدَ الْأَصْطَفَىٰ مِمَّا يَخْلُقُ مَا يَشَآءُ
سُبْحَنَهُ
هُوَ اللَّهُ الْوَاحِدُ الْقَهَّارُ ٥

٥۔ خَلَقَ السَّمَوَاتِ وَالْأَرْضَ بِالْحَقِّ
يُكَوِّرُ الَّيْلَ عَلَى النَّهَارِ
وَيُكَوِّرُ النَّهَارَ عَلَى الَّيْلِ
وَسَخَّرَ الشَّمْسَ وَالْقَمَرَ
كُلٌّ يَجْرِى لِأَجَلٍ مُسَمًّى
أَلَا هُوَ
الْعَزِيزُ الْغَفَّارُ ٥

٦۔ خَلَقَكُمْ مِنْ نَفْسٍ وَاحِدَةٍ
ثُمَّ جَعَلَ مِنْهَا زَوْجَهَا وَ
أَنْزَلَ لَكُمْ مِنَ الْأَنْعَامِ ثَمَانِيَةَ أَزْوَاجٍ
يَخْلُقُكُمْ فِى بُطُونِ
أُمَّهَاتِكُمْ
خَلْقًا مِنْ بَعْدِ خَلْقٍ فِى ظُلُمَاتٍ ثَلَاثٍ
ذَلِكُمُ اللَّهُ رَبُّكُمْ لَهُ الْمُلْكُ
لَا إِلَهَ إِلَّا هُوَ
فَأَنَّى تُصْرَفُونَ ٥

٧۔ إِنْ تَكْفُرُوا فَإِنَّ اللَّهَ غَنِيٌّ عَنْكُمْ
وَلَا يَرْضَى لِعِبَادِهِ الْكُفْرَ
وَإِنْ تَشْكُرُوا يَرْضَهُ لَكُمْ
وَلَا تَزِرُ وَازِرَةٌ وِزْرَ أُخْرَى

Of another. In the End,
To your Lord is your Return,
When He will tell you
The truth of all
That ye did (in this life).
For He knoweth well
All that is in (men's) hearts.

8. When some trouble toucheth
                              man,
He crieth unto his Lord,
Turning to Him in repentance:
But when He bestoweth
A favour upon him
As from Himself, (man)
Doth forget what he cried
And prayed for before,
And he doth set up
Rivals unto Allah,
Thus misleading others
From Allah's Path.
Say, "Enjoy thy blasphemy
For a little while:
Verily thou art (one)
Of the Companions of the Fire!"

9. Is one who worships devoutly
During the hours of the night
Prostrating himself or standing
(In adoration), who takes heed
Of the Hereafter, and who
Places his hope in the Mercy
Of his Lord — (like one
Who does not)? Say:
"Are those equal, those who know
And those who do not know?
It is those who are
Endued with understanding
That receive admonition."

SECTION 2.

10. Say: "O ye
My servants who believe!
Fear your Lord.
Good is (the reward)
For those who do good
In this world.
Spacious is Allah's earth!
Those who patiently persevere

Will truly receive
A reward without measure!"

اِنَّمَا يُوَفَّى الصَّبِرُونَ اَجْرَهُمْ بِغَيْرِ حِسَابٍ ۝

11. Say: "Verily, I am commanded
To serve Allah
With sincere devotion;

١١- قُلْ اِنِّىْ اُمِرْتُ اَنْ اَعْبُدَ اللّٰهَ
مُخْلِصًا لَّهُ الدِّيْنَ ۝

12. "And I am commanded
To be the first
Of those who bow
To Allah in Islam."

١٢- وَاُمِرْتُ
لِاَنْ اَكُوْنَ اَوَّلَ الْمُسْلِمِيْنَ ۝

13. Say: "I would, if I
Disobeyed my Lord,
Indeed have fear
Of the Penalty
Of a Mighty Day."

١٣- قُلْ اِنِّىْ اَخَافُ
اِنْ عَصَيْتُ رَبِّىْ
عَذَابَ يَوْمٍ عَظِيْمٍ ۝

14. Say: "It is Allah I serve,
With my sincere
(And exclusive) devotion:

١٤- قُلِ اللّٰهَ اَعْبُدُ مُخْلِصًا لَّهُ دِيْنِىْ ۝

15. "Serve ye what ye will
Besides Him." Say:
"Truly, those in loss
Are those who lose
Their own souls
And their People
On the Day of Judgement:
Ah! that is indeed
The (real and) evident Loss!"

١٥- فَاعْبُدُوْا مَا شِئْتُمْ مِّنْ دُوْنِهٖ قُلْ
اِنَّ الْخٰسِرِيْنَ الَّذِيْنَ خَسِرُوْا اَنْفُسَهُمْ
وَاَهْلِيْهِمْ يَوْمَ الْقِيٰمَةِ
اَلَا ذٰلِكَ هُوَ الْخُسْرَانُ الْمُبِيْنُ ۝

16. They shall have Layers
Of Fire above them,
And Layers (of Fire)
Below them: with this
Doth Allah warn off
His Servants: "O My Servants!
Then fear ye Me!"

١٦- لَهُمْ مِّنْ فَوْقِهِمْ ظُلَلٌ مِّنَ النَّارِ
وَمِنْ تَحْتِهِمْ ظُلَلٌ
ذٰلِكَ يُخَوِّفُ اللّٰهُ بِهٖ عِبَادَهٗ
يٰعِبَادِ فَاتَّقُوْنِ ۝

17. Those who eschew Evil—
And fall not into
Its worship—and turn
To Allah (in repentance)—
For them is Good News:
So announce the Good News
To My Servants—

١٧- وَالَّذِيْنَ اجْتَنَبُوا الطَّاغُوْتَ اَنْ يَّعْبُدُوْهَا
وَاَنَابُوْا اِلَى اللّٰهِ لَهُمُ الْبُشْرٰى
فَبَشِّرْ عِبَادِ ۝

18. Those who listen

١٨- الَّذِيْنَ يَسْتَمِعُوْنَ الْقَوْلَ

To the Word,
And follow
The best (meaning) in it:
Those are the ones
Whom Allah has guided, and those
Are the ones endued
With understanding.

19. Is, then, one against whom
The decree of Punishment
Is justly due (equal
To one who eschews evil)?
Wouldst thou, then, deliver
One (who is) in the Fire?

20. But it is for those
Who fear their Lord,
That lofty mansions,
One above another,
Have been built:
Beneath them flow
Rivers (of delight): (such is)
The Promise of Allah:
Never doth Allah fail in
(His) promise.

21. Seest thou not that Allah
Sends down rain from
The sky, and leads it
Through springs in the
                    earth?
Then He causes to grow,
Therewith, produce of various
Colours: then it withers;
Thou wilt see it grow yellow;
Then He makes it
Dry up and crumble away.
Truly, in this, is
A Message of remembrance to
Men of understanding.

SECTION 3.

22. Is one whose heart
Allah has opened to Islam,
So that he has received
Enlightenment from Allah,
(No better than one
                    hardhearted)?
Woe to those whose hearts

Are hardened against
                      celebrating
The praises of Allah! They
Are manifestly wandering
(In error)!

قُلُوبُهُمۡ مِّنۡ ذِكۡرِ اللّٰهِ ۚ
أُولٰٓئِكَ فِىۡ ضَلٰلٍ مُّبِيۡنٍ ۞

23. Allah has revealed
(From time to time)
The most beautiful Message
In the form of a Book,
Consistent with itself,
(Yet) repeating (its teaching
In various aspects):
The skins of those who
Fear their Lord tremble
Thereat: then their skins
And their hearts do soften
To the celebration of
Allah's praises. Such is
The guidance of Allah:
He guides therewith
Whom He pleases,   but such
As Allah leaves to stray.
Can have none to guide.

٢٣- اَللّٰهُ نَزَّلَ اَحۡسَنَ الۡحَدِيۡثِ كِتٰبًا
مُّتَشَابِهًا مَّثَانِىَ ۚ
تَقۡشَعِرُّ مِنۡهُ جُلُوۡدُ الَّذِيۡنَ
يَخۡشَوۡنَ رَبَّهُمۡ ۚ
ثُمَّ تَلِيۡنُ جُلُوۡدُهُمۡ وَقُلُوۡبُهُمۡ اِلٰى
ذِكۡرِ اللّٰهِ ۚ ذٰلِكَ هُدَى اللّٰهِ يَهۡدِىۡ بِهٖ
مَنۡ يَّشَاۤءُ ۚ وَمَنۡ يُّضۡلِلِ اللّٰهُ
فَمَا لَهٗ مِنۡ هَادٍ ۞

24. Is, then, one who
Has to fear the brunt
Of the Penalty on the Day
Of Judgement (and receive it)
On his face,   (like one
Guarded therefrom)? It will
Be said to the wrongdoers:
"Taste ye (the fruits
Of) what ye earned!"

٢٤- اَفَمَنۡ يَّتَّقِىۡ
بِوَجۡهِهٖ سُوۡٓءَ الۡعَذَابِ يَوۡمَ الۡقِيٰمَةِ ۚ
وَقِيۡلَ لِلظّٰلِمِيۡنَ
ذُوۡقُوۡا مَا كُنۡتُمۡ تَكۡسِبُوۡنَ ۞

25. Those before them (also)
Rejected (revelation), and so
The Punishment came to them
From directions they did not
Perceive.

٢٥- كَذَّبَ الَّذِيۡنَ مِنۡ قَبۡلِهِمۡ
فَاَتٰهُمُ الۡعَذَابُ
مِنۡ حَيۡثُ لَا يَشۡعُرُوۡنَ ۞

26. So Allah gave them
A taste of humiliation
In the present life,
But greater is the Punishment
Of the Hereafter,
If they only knew!

٢٦- فَاَذَاقَهُمُ اللّٰهُ الۡخِزۡىَ
فِى الۡحَيٰوةِ الدُّنۡيَا ۚ
وَلَعَذَابُ الۡاٰخِرَةِ اَكۡبَرُ ۘ لَوۡ كَانُوۡا يَعۡلَمُوۡنَ ۞

27. We have put forth

٢٧- وَلَقَدۡ ضَرَبۡنَا لِلنَّاسِ

For men, in this Qur'ān
Every kind of Parable,
In order that they
May receive admonition.

فِيْ هٰذَا الْقُرْاٰنِ مِنْ كُلِّ مَثَلٍ
لَّعَلَّهُمْ يَتَذَكَّرُوْنَ ۞

28. (It is) a Qur'ān
In Arabic,   without any
Crookedness (therein):
In order that they
May guard against Evil.

٢٨ ـ قُرْاٰنًا عَرَبِيًّا غَيْرَ ذِيْ عِوَجٍ
لَّعَلَّهُمْ يَتَّقُوْنَ ۞

29. Allah puts forth a Parable—
A man belonging to many
Partners at variance with each
                    other,
And a man belonging entirely
To one master: are those two
Equal in comparision?
Praise be to Allah!
But most of them
Have no knowledge.

٢٩ ـ ضَرَبَ اللّٰهُ مَثَلًا
رَّجُلًا فِيْهِ شُرَكَآءُ مُتَشٰكِسُوْنَ
وَرَجُلًا سَلَمًا لِّرَجُلٍ ؕ
هَلْ يَسْتَوِيٰنِ مَثَلًا ؕ اَلْحَمْدُ لِلّٰهِ ؕ
بَلْ اَكْثَرُهُمْ لَا يَعْلَمُوْنَ ۞

30. Truly thou wilt die
(One day), and truly they
(Too) will die (one day).

٣٠ ـ اِنَّكَ مَيِّتٌ
وَّ اِنَّهُمْ مَّيِّتُوْنَ ۞

31. In the End will ye
(All), on the Day
Of Judgement, settle your
                    disputes
In the presence of your Lord.

SECTION 4.

٣١ ـ ثُمَّ اِنَّكُمْ يَوْمَ الْقِيٰمَةِ
عِنْدَ رَبِّكُمْ تَخْتَصِمُوْنَ ۞

32. Who, then, doth more wrong
Than one who utters
A lie concerning Allah,
And rejects the Truth
When it comes to him!
Is there not in Hell
An abode for blasphemers?

٣٢ ـ فَمَنْ اَظْلَمُ مِمَّنْ كَذَبَ عَلَى اللّٰهِ
وَكَذَّبَ بِالصِّدْقِ اِذْ جَآءَهٗ ؕ
اَلَيْسَ فِيْ جَهَنَّمَ
مَثْوًى لِّلْكٰفِرِيْنَ ۞

33. And he who brings the Truth
And he who confirms
(And supports) it—such are
The men who do right.

٣٣ ـ وَالَّذِيْ جَآءَ بِالصِّدْقِ وَصَدَّقَ بِهٖۤ
اُولٰٓئِكَ هُمُ الْمُتَّقُوْنَ ۞

34. They shall have all
That they wish for,

٣٤ ـ لَهُمْ مَّا يَشَآءُوْنَ عِنْدَ رَبِّهِمْ ؕ

24/30

In the presence of their Lord:
Such is the reward
Of those who do good:

ذٰلِكَ جَزٰٓؤُا الۡمُحۡسِنِیۡنَ ۙ

35. So that Allah will
Turn off from them
(Even) the worst in their
                    deeds
And give them their reward
According to the best
Of what they have done.

۳۵- لِیُکَفِّرَ اللّٰهُ عَنۡهُمۡ اَسۡوَاَ الَّذِیۡ عَمِلُوۡا
وَیَجۡزِیَهُمۡ اَجۡرَهُمۡ بِاَحۡسَنِ الَّذِیۡ
کَانُوۡا یَعۡمَلُوۡنَ ۟

36. Is not Allah enough
For His servant? But
They try to frighten thee
With other (gods) besides Him!
For such as Allah leaves
To stray, there can be
No guide.

۳۶- اَلَیۡسَ اللّٰهُ بِکَافٍ عَبۡدَهٗ ؕ
وَیُخَوِّفُوۡنَکَ بِالَّذِیۡنَ مِنۡ دُوۡنِهٖ ؕ
وَمَنۡ یُّضۡلِلِ اللّٰهُ
فَمَا لَهٗ مِنۡ هَادٍ ۚ

37. And such as Allah doth
Guide there can be
None to lead astray.
Is not Allah Exalted
In Power, (Able to enforce
His Will), Lord of
                    Retribution?

۳۷- وَمَنۡ یَّهۡدِ اللّٰهُ
فَمَا لَهٗ مِنۡ مُّضِلٍّ ؕ
اَلَیۡسَ اللّٰهُ بِعَزِیۡزٍ ذِی انۡتِقَامٍ ۟

38. If indeed thou ask them
Who it is that created
The heavens and the earth,
They would be sure to say,
"Allah". Say: "See ye then?"
The things that ye invoke
Besides Allah—can they,
If Allah wills some Penalty
For me, remove His Penalty?—
Or if He wills some Grace
For me, can they keep back
His Grace?" Say: "Sufficient
Is Allah for me!
In Him trust those
Who put their trust."

۳۸- وَلَئِنۡ سَاَلۡتَهُمۡ مَّنۡ خَلَقَ السَّمٰوٰتِ وَ
الۡاَرۡضَ لَیَقُوۡلُنَّ اللّٰهُ ؕ قُلۡ اَفَرَءَیۡتُمۡ
مَّا تَدۡعُوۡنَ مِنۡ دُوۡنِ اللّٰهِ
اِنۡ اَرَادَنِیَ اللّٰهُ بِضُرٍّ
هَلۡ هُنَّ کٰشِفٰتُ ضُرِّهٖۤ
اَوۡ اَرَادَنِیۡ بِرَحۡمَةٍ هَلۡ هُنَّ مُمۡسِکٰتُ
رَحۡمَتِهٖ ؕ قُلۡ حَسۡبِیَ اللّٰهُ ؕ
عَلَیۡهِ یَتَوَکَّلُ الۡمُتَوَکِّلُوۡنَ ۟

39. Say: "O my people!
Do whatever ye can:
I will do (my part):

۳۹- قُلۡ یٰقَوۡمِ اعۡمَلُوۡا عَلٰی مَکَانَتِکُمۡ
اِنِّیۡ عَامِلٌ ۚ

But soon will ye know—

فَسَوۡفَ تَعۡلَمُوۡنَ ۙ

40. "Who it is to whom
Comes a Penalty
Of ignomINY, and on whom
Descends a Penalty that abides."

۴۰۔مَنۡ یَّاۡتِیۡهِ عَذَابٌ یُّخۡزِیۡهِ
وَیَحِلُّ عَلَیۡهِ عَذَابٌ مُّقِیۡمٌ ۟

41. Verily We have revealed
The Book to thee
In Truth, for (instructing)
           mankind.
He, then, that receives guidance
Benefits his own soul:
But he that strays
Injures his own soul.
Nor art thou set
Over them to dispose
Of their affairs.

۴۱۔اِنَّاۤ اَنۡزَلۡنَا عَلَیۡکَ الۡکِتٰبَ
لِلنَّاسِ بِالۡحَقِّ ۚ
فَمَنِ اهۡتَدٰی فَلِنَفۡسِهٖ ۚ
وَمَنۡ ضَلَّ فَاِنَّمَا یَضِلُّ عَلَیۡهَا ۚ
وَمَاۤ اَنۡتَ عَلَیۡهِمۡ بِوَکِیۡلٍ ۟ ؏

SECTION 5.

42. It is Allah that takes
The souls (of men) at death;
And those that die not
(He takes) during their
           sleep:
Those on whom He
Has passed the decree
Of death, He keeps back
(From returning to life),
But the rest He sends
(To their bodies)
For a term appointed.
Verily in this are Signs
For those who reflect.

۴۲۔اَللّٰهُ یَتَوَفَّی الۡاَنۡفُسَ حِیۡنَ مَوۡتِهَا
وَالَّتِیۡ لَمۡ تَمُتۡ فِیۡ مَنَامِهَا ۚ
فَیُمۡسِکُ الَّتِیۡ قَضٰی عَلَیۡهَا الۡمَوۡتَ
وَیُرۡسِلُ الۡاُخۡرٰۤی
اِلٰۤی اَجَلٍ مُّسَمًّی ؕ
اِنَّ فِیۡ ذٰلِکَ لَاٰیٰتٍ
لِّقَوۡمٍ یَّتَفَکَّرُوۡنَ ۟

43. What! Do they take
For intercessors others
Besides Allah? Say: "Even if
They have no power whatever
And no intelligence?"

۴۳۔اَمِ اتَّخَذُوۡا مِنۡ دُوۡنِ اللّٰهِ شُفَعَآءَ ؕ
قُلۡ اَوَلَوۡ کَانُوۡا لَا یَمۡلِکُوۡنَ شَیۡئًا
وَّلَا یَعۡقِلُوۡنَ ۟

44. Say: "To Allah belongs
Exclusively (the right)
To grant) Intercession:
To Him belongs the dominion
Of the heavens and the earth:
In the End, it is to Him
That ye shall be
Brought back."

۴۴۔قُلۡ لِّلّٰهِ الشَّفَاعَةُ جَمِیۡعًا ؕ
لَهٗ مُلۡکُ
السَّمٰوٰتِ وَالۡاَرۡضِ ؕ
ثُمَّ اِلَیۡهِ تُرۡجَعُوۡنَ ۟

45. When Allah, the One and Only,
    Is mentioned, the hearts
    Of those who believe not
    In the Hereafter are filled
    With disgust and horror;
    But when (gods) other than He
    Are mentioned, behold
    They are filled with joy!

٤٥- وَإِذَا ذُكِرَ اللّٰهُ وَحْدَهُ اشْمَأَزَّتْ قُلُوبُ
الَّذِيْنَ لَا يُؤْمِنُوْنَ بِالْآخِرَةِ ۚ
وَإِذَا ذُكِرَ الَّذِيْنَ مِنْ دُوْنِهٖٓ
إِذَا هُمْ يَسْتَبْشِرُوْنَ ۥ

46. Say: "O Allah!
    Creator of the heavens
    And the earth!
    Knower of all that is
    Hidden and open!
    It is Thou that wilt
    Judge between Thy Servants
    In those matters about which
    They have differed."

٤٦- قُلِ اللّٰهُمَّ فَاطِرَ السَّمٰوٰتِ وَالْأَرْضِ
عٰلِمَ الْغَيْبِ وَالشَّهَادَةِ
أَنْتَ تَحْكُمُ بَيْنَ عِبَادِكَ
فِيْ مَا كَانُوْا فِيْهِ يَخْتَلِفُوْنَ ۥ

47. Even if the wrongdoers
    Had all that there is
    On earth, and as much more,
    (In vain) would they offer it
    For ransom from the pain
    Of the Penalty on the Day
    Of Judgement: but something
    Will confront them from Allah,
    Which they could never
    Have counted upon!

٤٧- وَلَوْ أَنَّ لِلَّذِيْنَ ظَلَمُوْا
مَا فِي الْأَرْضِ جَمِيْعًا وَّمِثْلَهُ مَعَهُ
لَافْتَدَوْا بِهٖ مِنْ سُوْءِ الْعَذَابِ يَوْمَ الْقِيٰمَةِ ۚ
وَبَدَا لَهُمْ مِّنَ اللّٰهِ
مَا لَمْ يَكُوْنُوْا يَحْتَسِبُوْنَ ۥ

48. For the evils of their Deeds
    Will confront them,
    And they will be (completely)
    Encircled by that which
    They used to mock at!

٤٨- وَبَدَا لَهُمْ سَيِّئَاتُ مَا كَسَبُوْا
وَحَاقَ بِهِمْ
مَّا كَانُوْا بِهٖ يَسْتَهْزِءُوْنَ ۥ

49. Now, when trouble touches man,
    He cries to Us:
    But when We bestow
    A favour upon him
    As from Ourselves,
    He says, "This has been
    Given to me because of
    A certain knowledge (I have)!"
    Nay, but this is
    But a trial, but most
    Of them understand not!

٤٩- فَإِذَا مَسَّ الْإِنْسَانَ ضُرٌّ دَعَانَا ۚ
ثُمَّ إِذَا خَوَّلْنٰهُ نِعْمَةً مِّنَّا ۙ
قَالَ إِنَّمَا أُوْتِيْتُهُ عَلٰى عِلْمٍ ۚ
بَلْ هِيَ فِتْنَةٌ
وَّلٰكِنَّ أَكْثَرَهُمْ لَا يَعْلَمُوْنَ ۥ

50. Thus did the (generations)
Before them say! But
All that they did
Was of no profit to them.

٥٠. قَدْ قَالَهَا الَّذِيْنَ مِنْ قَبْلِهِمْ فَمَآ أَغْنٰى عَنْهُمْ مَّا كَانُوْا يَكْسِبُوْنَ ۞

51. Nay, the evil results
Of their deeds overtook them.
And the wrongdoers
Of this (generation)—
The evil results of their deeds
Will soon overtake them (too),
And they will never be
Able to frustrate (Our Plan)!

٥١. فَأَصَابَهُمْ سَيِّاٰتُ مَا كَسَبُوْا ۖ وَالَّذِيْنَ ظَلَمُوْا مِنْ هٰؤُلَاءِ سَيُصِيْبُهُمْ سَيِّاٰتُ مَا كَسَبُوْا ۖ وَمَا هُمْ بِمُعْجِزِيْنَ ۞

52. Know they not that
Allah enlarges the provision
Or restricts it, for any
He pleases? Verily, in this are
Signs for those who believe!

SECTION 6.

٥٢. أَوَلَمْ يَعْلَمُوْٓا أَنَّ اللّٰهَ يَبْسُطُ الرِّزْقَ لِمَنْ يَّشَآءُ وَيَقْدِرُ ۚ إِنَّ فِيْ ذٰلِكَ لَاٰيٰتٍ لِّقَوْمٍ يُّؤْمِنُوْنَ ۞

53. Say: "O my Servants who
Have transgressed against their
souls!
Despair not of the Mercy
Of Allah: for Allah forgives
All sins for He is
Oft-Forgiving, Most Merciful.

٥٣. قُلْ يٰعِبَادِيَ الَّذِيْنَ أَسْرَفُوْا عَلٰٓى أَنْفُسِهِمْ لَا تَقْنَطُوْا مِنْ رَّحْمَةِ اللّٰهِ ۚ إِنَّ اللّٰهَ يَغْفِرُ الذُّنُوْبَ جَمِيْعًا ۚ إِنَّهُ هُوَ الْغَفُوْرُ الرَّحِيْمُ ۞

54. "Turn ye to your Lord
(In repentance) and bow
To His (Will), before
The Penalty comes on you:
After that ye shall not
Be helped.

٥٤. وَأَنِيْبُوْٓا إِلٰى رَبِّكُمْ وَأَسْلِمُوْا لَهُ مِنْ قَبْلِ أَنْ يَّأْتِيَكُمُ الْعَذَابُ ثُمَّ لَا تُنْصَرُوْنَ ۞

55. "And follow the Best
Of (the courses) revealed
To you from your Lord,
Before the Penalty comes
On you—of a sudden,
While ye perceive not!—

٥٥. وَاتَّبِعُوْٓا أَحْسَنَ مَآ أُنْزِلَ إِلَيْكُمْ مِّنْ رَّبِّكُمْ مِّنْ قَبْلِ أَنْ يَّأْتِيَكُمُ الْعَذَابُ بَغْتَةً وَّأَنْتُمْ لَا تَشْعُرُوْنَ ۞

56. "Lest the soul should (then)
Say: 'Ah! woe is me!—
In that I neglected
(My Duty) towards Allah,
And was but among those
Who mocked!'—

٥٦. أَنْ تَقُوْلَ نَفْسٌ يّٰحَسْرَتٰى عَلٰى مَا فَرَّطْتُ فِيْ جَنْبِ اللّٰهِ وَإِنْ كُنْتُ لَمِنَ السّٰخِرِيْنَ ۞

57. "Or (lest) it should say:
'If only Allah had guided
Me, I should certainly
Have been among the righteous!'—

٥٧- اَوْ تَقُوْلَ لَوْ اَنَّ اللّٰهَ هَدٰىنِىْ لَكُنْتُ مِنَ الْمُتَّقِيْنَ ۞

58. "Or (lest) it should say
When it (actually) sees
The Penalty: 'If only
I had another chance,
I should certainly be
Among those who do good!'

٥٨- اَوْ تَقُوْلَ حِيْنَ تَرَى الْعَذَابَ لَوْ اَنَّ لِىْ كَرَّةً فَاَكُوْنَ مِنَ الْمُحْسِنِيْنَ ۞

59. "(The reply will be:) 'Nay,
But there came to thee
My Signs, and thou didst
Reject them: thou wast
Haughty, and became one
Of those who reject Faith!'"

٥٩- بَلٰى قَدْ جَاءَتْكَ اٰيٰتِىْ فَكَذَّبْتَ بِهَا وَاسْتَكْبَرْتَ وَكُنْتَ مِنَ الْكٰفِرِيْنَ ۞

60. On the Day of Judgement
Wilt thou see those
Who told lies against Allah—
Their faces will be turned
Black; is there not
In Hell an abode
For the Haughty?

٦٠- وَيَوْمَ الْقِيٰمَةِ تَرَى الَّذِيْنَ كَذَبُوْا عَلَى اللّٰهِ وُجُوْهُهُمْ مُسْوَدَّةٌ ۚ اَلَيْسَ فِىْ جَهَنَّمَ مَثْوًى لِّلْمُتَكَبِّرِيْنَ ۞

61. But Allah will deliver
The righteous to their place
Of salvation: no evil
Shall touch them,
Nor shall they grieve.

٦١- وَيُنَجِّى اللّٰهُ الَّذِيْنَ اتَّقَوْا بِمَفَازَتِهِمْ ۖ لَا يَمَسُّهُمُ السُّوْءُ وَلَا هُمْ يَحْزَنُوْنَ ۞

62. Allah is the Creator
Of all things, and He
Is the Guardian and Disposer
Of all affairs.

٦٢- اَللّٰهُ خَالِقُ كُلِّ شَىْءٍ ۖ وَّهُوَ عَلٰى كُلِّ شَىْءٍ وَّكِيْلٌ ۞

63. To Him belong the keys
Of the heavens
And the earth:
And those who reject
The Signs of Allah—
It is they who will
Be in loss.

SECTION 7.

٦٣- لَهٗ مَقَالِيْدُ السَّمٰوٰتِ وَالْاَرْضِ ۚ وَالَّذِيْنَ كَفَرُوْا بِاٰيٰتِ اللّٰهِ اُولٰٓئِكَ هُمُ الْخٰسِرُوْنَ ۞

64. Say: "Is it
Someone other than Allah

٦٤- قُلْ اَفَغَيْرَ اللّٰهِ

That ye order me
To worship, O ye
Ignorant ones?"

65. But it has already
Been revealed to thee—
As it was to those
Before thee—"If thou
Wert to join (gods
With Allah), truly fruitless
Will be thy work (in life),
And thou wilt surely
Be in the ranks of those
Who lose (all spiritual good)".

66. Nay, but worship Allah,
And be of those who
Give thanks.

67. No just estimate
Have they made of Allah,
Such as is due to Him:
On the Day of Judgement
The whole of the earth
Will be but His handful,
And the heavens will be
Rolled up in His right hand:
Glory to Him!
High is He above
The Partners they attribute
To Him!

68. The Trumpet will (just)
Be sounded, when all
That are in the heavens
And on earth will swoon,
Except such as it will
Please Allah (to exempt).
Then will a second one
Be sounded, when, behold,
They will be standing
And looking on!

69. And the Earth will shine
With the glory of its Lord:
The Record (of Deeds)
Will be placed (open);
The prophets and the witnesses

Will be brought forward;
And a just decision
Pronounced between them;
And they will not
Be wronged (in the least).

وَقُضِىَ بَيْنَهُم بِالْحَقِّ
وَهُمْ لَا يُظْلَمُونَ ۝

70. And to every soul will be
Paid in full (the fruit)
Of its deeds; and (Allah)
Knoweth best all that
They do.

٧٠ ۔ وَوُفِّيَتْ كُلُّ نَفْسٍ مَّا عَمِلَتْ
وَهُوَ أَعْلَمُ بِمَا يَفْعَلُونَ ۝ ۚ

SECTION 8.

71. The Unbelievers will be
Led to Hell in crowd:⁴³⁴⁷ [4347]
Until, when they arrive there,
Its gates will be opened.
And its Keepers will say,
"Did not messengers come
To you from among yourselves,
Rehearsing to you the Signs
Of your Lord, and warning you
Of the Meeting of this Day
Of yours?" The answer
Will be: "True: but
The Decree of Punishment
Has been proved true⁴³⁴⁹ [4349]
Against the Unbelievers!"

٧١ ۔ وَسِيقَ الَّذِينَ كَفَرُوا إِلَى جَهَنَّمَ زُمَرًا
حَتَّى إِذَا جَاءُوهَا فُتِحَتْ أَبْوَابُهَا
وَقَالَ لَهُمْ خَزَنَتُهَا أَلَمْ يَأْتِكُمْ رُسُلٌ
مِّنكُمْ
يَتْلُونَ عَلَيْكُمْ آيَاتِ رَبِّكُمْ وَيُنذِرُونَكُمْ
لِقَاءَ يَوْمِكُمْ هَٰذَا
قَالُوا بَلَى وَلَٰكِنْ
حَقَّتْ كَلِمَةُ الْعَذَابِ عَلَى الْكَافِرِينَ ۝

72. (To them) will be said:
"Enter ye the gates of Hell,
To dwell therein:
And evil is (this)
Abode of the arrogant!"

٧٢ ۔ قِيلَ ادْخُلُوا أَبْوَابَ جَهَنَّمَ
خَالِدِينَ فِيهَا
فَبِئْسَ مَثْوَى الْمُتَكَبِّرِينَ ۝

73. And those who feared
Their Lord will be led
To the Garden in crowds:
Until behold, they arrive there;
Its gates will be opened;
And its Keepers will say:
"Peace be upon you!
Well have ye done!
Enter ye here,
To dwell therein."

٧٣ ۔ وَسِيقَ الَّذِينَ اتَّقَوْا رَبَّهُمْ إِلَى الْجَنَّةِ
زُمَرًا حَتَّى إِذَا جَاءُوهَا
وَفُتِحَتْ أَبْوَابُهَا وَقَالَ لَهُمْ خَزَنَتُهَا
سَلَامٌ عَلَيْكُمْ طِبْتُمْ
فَادْخُلُوهَا خَالِدِينَ ۝

74. They will say: "Praise be
To Allah, Who has
Truly fulfilled His promise
To us, and has given us

٧٤ ۔ وَقَالُوا الْحَمْدُ لِلَّهِ الَّذِى
صَدَقَنَا وَعْدَهُ وَأَوْرَثَنَا الْأَرْضَ

(This) land in heritage:
We can dwell in the Garden
As we will: how excellent
A reward for those
Who work (righteousness)!"

75. And thou wilt see
The angels surrounding
The Throne (Divine)
On all sides, singing Glory
And Praise to their Lord.
The Decision between them
(At Judgement) will be
In (perfect) justice,
And the cry (on all sides)
Will be, "Praise be to Allah,
The Lord of the Worlds!"

تَبَوَّأُ مِنَ الْجَنَّةِ حَيْثُ نَشَآءُ
فَنِعْمَ أَجْرُ الْعَامِلِينَ ٥

٧٥ ـ وَتَرَى الْمَلَائِكَةَ حَافِّينَ
مِنْ حَوْلِ الْعَرْشِ
يُسَبِّحُونَ بِحَمْدِ رَبِّهِمْ
وَقُضِيَ بَيْنَهُمْ بِالْحَقِّ
وَقِيلَ الْحَمْدُ لِلَّهِ
رَبِّ الْعَالَمِينَ ٥

INTRODUCTION TO SŪRA XL. (*Mū-min*) — 85 Verses

This Sūra is called "The Believer" (*Mū-min*) from the story of the Individual Believer among the people of Pharaoh, who declares his faith and looks to the Future (verses 28-45). It is also called *Gāfir* (He who forgives, see verse 3). In S. xxiii. called *The Believers* (*Mū-minūn*), the argument was about the collective force of Faith and Virtue. Here it is about the Individual's witness to Faith and Virtue, and his triumph in the End.

We now begin a series of seven Sūras (xl. xlvi.) to which are affixed the Abbreviated Letters *Ḥā-Mīm*. Chronologically they all belong to the same period, the later Meccan Period, and they immediately follow the last Sūra in time. About the Abbreviated Letters generally, see Appendix 1. at the end of S. ii. As to the precise meaning of *Ḥā-Mīm* no authoritative explanation is available. It *Mīm* here has a signification similar to *Mīm* in A.L.M. (see n. 25 to ii). it means the End of things, the Last Day, and all these Sūras direct our special attention to that. *Ḥā*, the emphatic guttural, in contrast with the softer breathing of *Alif*, may be meant to suggest that the Beginning (see n. 25 to ii. 1. last paragraph) is only for the End, the Present for the Future, and to emphasise the eschatological element in Faith. But this is mere conjecture, and should be taken for no more than it is worth.

The general theme of the whole series is the relation of Faith to Unfaith, Revelation to Rejection, Goodness to Evil, Truth to Falsehood. It is shown that the first in each of these pairs is the real friend, helper, and protector of man while the second is his enemy. The very word *Ḥamim* in that sense is used in Sūras xl. and xli. (xl. 18 and xli. 34), while in the other Sūras we have words of equivalent import, e.g, *walī* or *naṣīr* (xlii. 8 and 31); *qarīn* (xliii. 36, 38); *maulā* (xliv. 41); *auliyāa* or *nāṣirīn* (xlv. 19, 34); and *auliyāa* (xlvi. 32), Is it permissible to connect the Abbreviated Letters. *Ḥā-Mīm* with these ideas as expressed in the word *Ḥāmīm*?

Another suggestion worthy of consideration is that *Ḥā* stands for *Ḥaiy*, and *Mīm* for Qaiyūm. These are two attributes of God, meaning, (1) the Living, and (2) the Self-Subsisting, Eternal. The one points to Life and Revelation, and the other to the Hereafter and Eternity, and both these matters are specially dealt with in the seven *Ḥā-Mīm* Sūras. The first letter of *Ḥaiy* (*Ḥā*) is appropriate for life, and the last letter of *Qaiyūm* is appropriate for the Last Days, the *Ma'ād*, the Hereafter Again, this is mere conjecture, and should not be taken for more than it is worth.

Ghāfir (Forgiver) or *Al Mu'min*
(The Believer)

In the name of Allah, Most Gracious,
Most Merciful

1. Ḥā Mīm.

2. The revelation

بِسْمِ اللهِ الرَّحْمٰنِ الرَّحِيمِ

١- حٰمٓ ۚ

٢- تَنْزِيلُ

Of this Book
Is from Allah,
Exalted in Power,
Full of Knowledge—

الْكِتٰبِ مِنَ اللّٰهِ
الْعَزِيْزِ الْعَلِيْمِۙ

3 . Who forgiveth Sin,
Accepteth Repentance,
Is Strict in Punishment,
And hath a Long Reach
(In all things).
There is no god
But He: to Him
Is the Final Goal.

٣- غَافِرِ الذَّنْۢبِ وَقَابِلِ التَّوْبِ
شَدِيْدِ الْعِقَابِ ذِى الطَّوْلِۗ
لَآ اِلٰهَ اِلَّا هُوَؕ
اِلَيْهِ الْمَصِيْرُ

4 . None can dispute
About the Signs of Allah
But the Unbelievers.
Let not, then
Their strutting about
Through the land
Deceive thee!

٤- مَا يُجَادِلُ فِىْۤ اٰيٰتِ اللّٰهِ
اِلَّا الَّذِيْنَ كَفَرُوْا
فَلَا يَغْرُرْكَ تَقَلُّبُهُمْ فِى الْبِلَادِ ○

5 . But (there were people) before
them,
Who denied (the Signs)—
The People of Noah,
And the Confederates
(Of Evil) after them;
And every People plotted
Against their prophet,
To seize him, and disputed
By means of vanities,
Therewith to condemn
The Truth: but it was I
That seized them!
And how (terrible)
Was My Requital!

٥- كَذَّبَتْ قَبْلَهُمْ قَوْمُ نُوْحٍ
وَّالْاَحْزَابُ مِنْۢ بَعْدِهِمْ ۪
وَهَمَّتْ كُلُّ اُمَّةٍۭ بِرَسُوْلِهِمْ
لِيَاْخُذُوْهُ وَجَادَلُوْا بِالْبَاطِلِ
لِيُدْحِضُوْا بِهِ الْحَقَّ
فَاَخَذْتُهُمْ ۪
فَكَيْفَ كَانَ عِقَابِ ○

6 . Thus was the Decree
Of thy Lord proved true
Against the Unbelievers;
That truly they are
Companions of the Fire!

٦- وَكَذٰلِكَ حَقَّتْ كَلِمَتُ رَبِّكَ
عَلَى الَّذِيْنَ كَفَرُوْۤا
اَنَّهُمْ اَصْحٰبُ النَّارِۘ

7 . Those who sustain
The Throne (of Allah)
And those around it
Sing Glory and Praise

٧- اَلَّذِيْنَ يَحْمِلُوْنَ الْعَرْشَ
وَمَنْ حَوْلَهٗ يُسَبِّحُوْنَ بِحَمْدِ رَبِّهِمْ وَ

To their Lord; believe
In Him; and implore Forgiveness
For those who believe:
"Our Lord! Thy Reach
Is over all things,
In Mercy and Knowledge.
Forgive, then, those who
Turn in Repentance, and follow
Thy Path; and preserve them
From the Penalty
Of the Blazing Fire!

يُؤْمِنُوْنَ بِهٖ وَيَسْتَغْفِرُوْنَ لِلَّذِيْنَ اٰمَنُوْا ۚ
رَبَّنَا وَسِعْتَ
كُلَّ شَيْءٍ رَّحْمَةً وَّعِلْمًا
فَاغْفِرْ لِلَّذِيْنَ تَابُوْا وَاتَّبَعُوْا سَبِيْلَكَ
وَقِهِمْ عَذَابَ الْجَحِيْمِ ۟

8. "And grant, our Lord!
That they enter
The Gardens of Eternity,
Which Thou hast promised
To them, and to the righteous
Among their fathers,
Their wives, and their posterity!
For Thou art (He),
The Exalted in Might,
Full of Wisdom.

٨- رَبَّنَا وَاَدْخِلْهُمْ جَنّٰتِ عَدْنِۨ الَّتِيْ
وَعَدْتَّهُمْ
وَمَنْ صَلَحَ مِنْ اٰبَآئِهِمْ
وَاَزْوَاجِهِمْ وَذُرِّيّٰتِهِمْ ۚ
اِنَّكَ اَنْتَ الْعَزِيْزُ الْحَكِيْمُ ۟

9. "And preserve them
From (all) ills;
And any whom Thou
Dost preserve from ills
That Day—on them
Wilt Thou have bestowed
Mercy indeed: and that
Will be truly (for them)
The highest Achievement."

٩- وَقِهِمُ السَّيِّاٰتِ ۚ
وَمَنْ تَقِ السَّيِّاٰتِ
يَوْمَئِذٍ فَقَدْ رَحِمْتَهٗ ۚ
وَذٰلِكَ هُوَ الْفَوْزُ الْعَظِيْمُ ۟

SECTION 2.

10. The Unbelievers will be
Addressed: "Greater was
The aversion of Allah to you
Than (is) your aversion
To yourselves, seeing that ye
Were called to the Faith
And ye used to refuse."

١٠- اِنَّ الَّذِيْنَ كَفَرُوْا
يُنَادَوْنَ لَمَقْتُ اللّٰهِ اَكْبَرُ مِنْ مَّقْتِكُمْ
اَنْفُسَكُمْ اِذْ تُدْعَوْنَ اِلَى الْاِيْمَانِ
فَتَكْفُرُوْنَ ۟

11. They will say: "Our Lord!
Twice hast Thou made us
Without life, and twice
Hast Thou given us Life!
Now have we recognised
Our sins: is there
Any way out (of this)?"

١١- قَالُوْا رَبَّنَآ اَمَتَّنَا اثْنَتَيْنِ
وَاَحْيَيْتَنَا اثْنَتَيْنِ
فَاعْتَرَفْنَا بِذُنُوْبِنَا
فَهَلْ اِلٰى خُرُوْجٍ مِّنْ سَبِيْلٍ ۟

12. (The answer will be:)
"This is because, when
Allah was invoked as
The Only (object of worship),
Ye did reject Faith,
But when partners were
Joined to Him, ye believed!
The Command is with Allah,
Most High, Most Great!"

١٢- ذٰلِكُمْ بِاَنَّهٗ اِذَا دُعِيَ اللهُ
وَحْدَهٗ كَفَرْتُمْ ۚ
وَاِنْ يُّشْرَكْ بِهٖ تُؤْمِنُوْا ۗ
فَالْحُكْمُ لِلّٰهِ الْعَلِيِّ الْكَبِيْرِ ۰

13. He it is Who showeth
You His Signs, and sendeth
Down Sustenance for you
From the sky: but only
Those receive admonition
Who turn (to Allah).

١٣- هُوَ الَّذِيْ يُرِيْكُمْ اٰيٰتِهٖ
وَيُنَزِّلُ لَكُمْ مِّنَ السَّمَآءِ رِزْقًا ۗ
وَمَا يَتَذَكَّرُ اِلَّا مَنْ يُّنِيْبُ ۰

14. Call ye, then, upon Allah
With sincere devotion to Him,
Even though the Unbelievers
May detest it.

١٤- فَادْعُوا اللهَ مُخْلِصِيْنَ لَهُ الدِّيْنَ
وَلَوْ كَرِهَ الْكٰفِرُوْنَ۰

15. Raised high above ranks
(Or degrees),
(He is) the Lord
Of the Throne (of authority):
By His Command doth He
Send the spirit (of inspiration)
To any of His servants
He pleases, that it may
Warn (men) of the Day
Of Mutual Meeting—

١٥- رَفِيْعُ الدَّرَجٰتِ ذُو الْعَرْشِ ۚ
يُلْقِى الرُّوْحَ مِنْ اَمْرِهٖ
عَلٰى مَنْ يَّشَآءُ مِنْ عِبَادِهٖ
لِيُنْذِرَ يَوْمَ التَّلَاقِ ۰

16. The Day whereon
They will (all) come forth:
Not a single thing
Concerning them is hidden
From Allah. Whose will be
The Dominion that Day?
That of Allah, the One,
The Irresistible!

١٦- يَوْمَ هُمْ بٰرِزُوْنَ ۚ
لَا يَخْفٰى عَلَى اللهِ مِنْهُمْ شَيْءٌ ۗ
لِمَنِ الْمُلْكُ الْيَوْمَ ۗ
لِلّٰهِ الْوَاحِدِ الْقَهَّارِ۰

17. That Day will every soul
Be requited for what
It earned; no injustice
Will there be that Day,

١٧- اَلْيَوْمَ تُجْزٰى كُلُّ نَفْسٍ بِمَا كَسَبَتْ ۗ
لَا ظُلْمَ الْيَوْمَ ۗ

For Allah is Swift
In taking account.

إِنَّ اللّٰهَ سَرِيعُ الْحِسَابِ ۚ○

18. **W**arn them of the Day
That is (ever) drawing near,
When the Hearts will
(Come) right up to the
            Throats
To choke (them);
No intimate friend
Nor intercessor will the
          wrongdoers
Have, who could be
Listened to.

١٨- وَأَنْذِرْهُمْ يَوْمَ الْأَزِفَةِ
إِذِ الْقُلُوبُ لَدَى الْحَنَاجِرِ كَاظِمِينَ ۚ
مَا لِلظَّالِمِينَ مِنْ حَمِيمٍ
وَّلَا شَفِيعٍ يُّطَاعُ ۚ○

19. (Allah) knows of (the tricks)
That deceive with the eyes,
And all that the hearts
(Of men) conceal.

١٩- يَعْلَمُ خَائِنَةَ الْأَعْيُنِ
وَمَا تُخْفِي الصُّدُورُ ○

20. And Allah will judge
With (Justice and) Truth:
But those whom (men)
Invoke besides Him, will
Not (be in a position)
To judge at all.
Verily it is Allah (alone)
Who hear and sees
(All things).

٢٠- وَاللّٰهُ يَقْضِي بِالْحَقِّ ۚ
وَالَّذِينَ يَدْعُونَ مِنْ دُونِهِ
لَا يَقْضُونَ بِشَيْءٍ ۚ
إِنَّ اللّٰهَ هُوَ السَّمِيعُ الْبَصِيرُ ○

SECTION 3.

21. **D**o they not travel
Through the earth and see
What was the End
Of those before them?
They were even superior
To them in strength,
And in the traces (they
Have left) in the land:
But Allah did call them
To account for their sins,
And none had they
To defend them against Allah.

٢١- أَوَلَمْ يَسِيرُوا فِي الْأَرْضِ فَيَنْظُرُوا
كَيْفَ كَانَ عَاقِبَةُ الَّذِينَ كَانُوا مِنْ قَبْلِهِمْ ۚ
كَانُوا هُمْ أَشَدَّ مِنْهُمْ قُوَّةً
وَّآثَارًا فِي الْأَرْضِ
فَأَخَذَهُمُ اللّٰهُ بِذُنُوبِهِمْ ۚ
وَمَا كَانَ لَهُمْ مِّنَ اللّٰهِ مِنْ وَّاقٍ ○

22. That was because there came
To them their messengers
With Clear (Signs),
But they rejected them:

٢٢- ذٰلِكَ بِأَنَّهُمْ كَانَتْ تَأْتِيهِمْ رُسُلُهُمْ
بِالْبَيِّنَاتِ فَكَفَرُوا

So Allah called them
To account: for He is
Full of Strength,
Strict in Punishment.

فَأَخَذَهُمُ اللّٰهُ
اِنَّهٗ قَوِيٌّ شَدِيْدُ الْعِقَابِ ۟

23. Of old We sent Moses,
With Our Signs
And an Authority manifest,

٢٣- وَلَقَدْ اَرْسَلْنَا مُوْسٰى بِاٰيٰتِنَا
وَسُلْطٰنٍ مُّبِيْنٍ ۟

24. To Pharaoh, Hāmān,
And Qārūn; but they
Called (him) "a sorcerer
Telling lies!". . .

٢٤- اِلٰى فِرْعَوْنَ وَهَامٰنَ وَقَارُوْنَ
فَقَالُوْا سٰحِرٌ كَذَّابٌ ۟

25. Now, when he came to them
In Truth, from Us,
They said, "Slay the sons
Of those who believe
With him, and keep alive
Their females," but the plots
Of Unbelievers (end) in nothing
But errors (and delusions)!. . .

٢٥- فَلَمَّا جَآءَهُمْ بِالْحَقِّ مِنْ عِنْدِنَا
قَالُوا اقْتُلُوْٓا اَبْنَآءَ الَّذِيْنَ اٰمَنُوْا
مَعَهٗ وَاسْتَحْيُوْا نِسَآءَهُمْ ۖ
وَمَا كَيْدُ الْكٰفِرِيْنَ اِلَّا فِيْ ضَلٰلٍ ۟

26. Said Pharaoh: "Leave me
To slay Moses; and let him
Call on his Lord!
What I fear is lest
He should change your
                    religion,
Or lest he should cause
Mischief to appear
In the land!"

٢٦- وَقَالَ فِرْعَوْنُ ذَرُوْنِيْٓ اَقْتُلْ مُوْسٰى
وَلْيَدْعُ رَبَّهٗ ۚ
اِنِّيْٓ اَخَافُ اَنْ يُّبَدِّلَ دِيْنَكُمْ
اَوْ اَنْ يُّظْهِرَ فِى الْاَرْضِ الْفَسَادَ ۟

27. Moses said: "I have indeed
Called upon my Lord
And your Lord
(For protection) from every
Arrogant one who believes not
In the Day of Account!"

٢٧- وَقَالَ مُوْسٰىٓ اِنِّيْ عُذْتُ بِرَبِّيْ
وَرَبِّكُمْ مِّنْ كُلِّ مُتَكَبِّرٍ لَّا يُؤْمِنُ
بِيَوْمِ الْحِسَابِ ۟ ۽

SECTION 4.

28. A Believer, a man
From among the people
Of Pharaoh, who had
                    concealed
His faith, said: "Will ye
Slay a man because he

٢٨- وَقَالَ رَجُلٌ مُّؤْمِنٌ ۙ
مِّنْ اٰلِ فِرْعَوْنَ يَكْتُمُ اِيْمَانَهٗٓ
اَتَقْتُلُوْنَ رَجُلًا اَنْ يَّقُوْلَ رَبِّيَ اللّٰهُ

Says, 'My Lord is Allah'?—
When he has indeed come
To you with Clear (Signs)
From your Lord? And if
He be a liar, on him
Is (the sin of) his lie;
But, if he is telling
The Truth, then will
Fall on you something
Of the (calamity) of which
He warns you: truly
Allah guides not one
Who transgresses and lies!

وَقَدْ جَاءَكُمْ بِالْبَيِّنَاتِ مِنْ رَبِّكُمْ
وَإِنْ يَّكُ كَاذِبًا فَعَلَيْهِ كَذِبُهُ
وَإِنْ يَّكُ صَادِقًا
يُصِبْكُمْ بَعْضُ الَّذِي يَعِدُكُمْ
إِنَّ اللّٰهَ لَا يَهْدِي مَنْ هُوَ
مُسْرِفٌ كَذَّابٌ ٠

29. "O my People! yours
Is the dominion this day:
Ye have the upper hand
In the land: but who
Will help us from
The Punishment of Allah,
Should it befall us?"
Pharaoh said: "I but
Point out to you that
Which I see (myself):
Nor do I guide you
But to the Path of Right!"

٢٩- يٰقَوْمِ لَكُمُ الْمُلْكُ الْيَوْمَ
ظٰهِرِيْنَ فِي الْأَرْضِ
فَمَنْ يَّنْصُرُنَا مِنْ بَأْسِ اللّٰهِ إِنْ جَاءَنَا
قَالَ فِرْعَوْنُ مَا أُرِيكُمْ إِلَّا مَا أَرٰى
وَمَا أَهْدِيكُمْ إِلَّا سَبِيلَ الرَّشَادِ ٠

30. Then said the man
Who believed: "O my People!
Truly I do fear
For you something like
The Day (of disaster)
Of the Confederates (in
sin)!—

٣٠- وَقَالَ الَّذِي أَمَنَ يٰقَوْمِ
إِنِّي أَخَافُ عَلَيْكُمْ مِثْلَ
يَوْمِ الْأَحْزَابِ ٠

31. "Something like the fate
Of the People of Noah,
The 'Ād, and the Thamūd,
And those who came
After them: but Allah
Never wishes injustice
To His Servants.

٣١- مِثْلَ دَأْبِ قَوْمِ نُوحٍ
وَّعَادٍ وَّثَمُودَ وَالَّذِينَ مِنْ بَعْدِهِمْ
وَمَا اللّٰهُ يُرِيدُ ظُلْمًا لِّلْعِبَادِ ٠

32. "And O my People!
I fear for you a Day
When there will be
Mutual calling (and wailing)—

٣٢- وَيٰقَوْمِ إِنِّي أَخَافُ عَلَيْكُمْ
يَوْمَ التَّنَادِ ٠

33. "A Day when ye
Shall turn your backs
And flee: no defender
Shall ye have from Allah:
Any whom Allah leaves
To stray, there is none
To guide...

٣٣- يَوْمَ تُوَلُّونَ مُدْبِرِينَ ۚ
مَا لَكُمْ مِنَ اللهِ مِنْ عَاصِمٍ ۗ
وَمَنْ يُضْلِلِ اللهُ
فَمَا لَهُ مِنْ هَادٍ ۞

34. "And to you there came
Joseph in times gone by,
With Clear Signs, but
Ye ceased not to doubt
Of the (mission) for which
He had come: at length,
When he died, ye said:
'No Messenger will Allah send
After him.' Thus doth Allah
Leave to stray such as
Transgress and live in doubt

٣٤- وَلَقَدْ جَاءَكُمْ يُوسُفُ مِنْ قَبْلُ بِالْبَيِّنَاتِ
فَمَا زِلْتُمْ فِي شَكٍّ
مِمَّا جَاءَكُمْ بِهِ ۖ
حَتَّى إِذَا هَلَكَ قُلْتُمْ
لَنْ يَبْعَثَ اللهُ مِنْ بَعْدِهِ رَسُولًا ۚ
كَذَلِكَ يُضِلُّ اللهُ مَنْ هُوَ مُسْرِفٌ مُرْتَابٌ ۞

35. "(Such) as dispute about
The Signs of Allah,
Without any authority
That hath reached them.
Grievous and odious
(In such conduct)
In the sight of Allah
And of the Believers.
Thus doth Allah seal up
Every heart—of arrogant
And obstinate transgressors."

٣٥- الَّذِينَ يُجَادِلُونَ فِي آيَاتِ اللهِ
بِغَيْرِ سُلْطَانٍ أَتَاهُمْ ۖ
كَبُرَ مَقْتًا
عِنْدَ اللهِ وَعِنْدَ الَّذِينَ آمَنُوا ۚ
كَذَلِكَ يَطْبَعُ اللهُ عَلَى كُلِّ قَلْبِ
مُتَكَبِّرٍ جَبَّارٍ ۞

36. Pharaoh said: "O Hāmān!
Build me a lofty palace,
That I may attain
The ways and means—

٣٦- وَقَالَ فِرْعَوْنُ يَا هَامَانُ ابْنِ لِي صَرْحًا
لَعَلِّي أَبْلُغُ الْأَسْبَابَ ۞

37. "The ways and means
Of (reaching) the heavens,
And that I may mount up
To the God of Moses:
But as far as I am concerned,
I think (Moses) is a liar!"
Thus was made alluring,
In Pharaoh's eyes,
The evil of his deeds,
And he was hindered

٣٧- أَسْبَابَ السَّمَاوَاتِ
فَأَطَّلِعَ إِلَى إِلَهِ مُوسَى
وَإِنِّي لَأَظُنُّهُ كَاذِبًا ۚ
وَكَذَلِكَ زُيِّنَ لِفِرْعَوْنَ سُوءُ عَمَلِهِ
وَصُدَّ عَنِ السَّبِيلِ ۚ

From the Path; and the plot
Of Pharaoh led to nothing
But perdition (for him).

SECTION 5.

وَمَا كَيْدُ فِرْعَوْنَ اِلَّا فِىْ تَبَابٍ ۞

38. The man who believed said
Further: "O my People!
Follow me: I will lead
You to the Path of Right.

٣٨ ـ وَقَالَ الَّذِىْ اٰمَنَ يٰقَوْمِ
اتَّبِعُوْنِ اَهْدِكُمْ سَبِيْلَ الرَّشَادِ ۞

39. "O my People! This life
Of the present is nothing
But (temporary) convenience:
It is the Hereafter
That is the Home
That will last.

٣٩ ـ يٰقَوْمِ اِنَّمَا هٰذِهِ الْحَيٰوةُ الدُّنْيَا مَتَاعٌ ۙ
وَّاِنَّ الْاٰخِرَةَ
هِىَ دَارُ الْقَرَارِ ۞

40. "He that works evil
Will not be requited
But by the like thereof:
And he that works
A righteous deed—whether
Man or woman—and is
A Believer—such will enter
The Garden (of Bliss): therein
Will they have abundance
Without measure.

٤٠ ـ مَنْ عَمِلَ سَيِّئَةً فَلَا يُجْزٰى اِلَّا مِثْلَهَا ۚ
وَمَنْ عَمِلَ صَالِحًا
مِّنْ ذَكَرٍ اَوْ اُنْثٰى وَهُوَ مُؤْمِنٌ
فَاُولٰٓئِكَ يَدْخُلُوْنَ الْجَنَّةَ
يُرْزَقُوْنَ فِيْهَا بِغَيْرِ حِسَابٍ ۞

41. "And O my People!
How (strange) it is
For me to call you
To Salvation while ye
Call me to the Fire!

٤١ ـ وَيٰقَوْمِ
مَا لِىْ اَدْعُوْكُمْ اِلَى النَّجٰوةِ
وَتَدْعُوْنَنِىْ اِلَى النَّارِ ۙ

42. "Ye do call upon me
To blaspheme against Allah,
And to join with Him
Partners of whom I have
No knowledge; and I
Call you to the Exalted
In Power, Who forgives
Again and again!"

٤٢ ـ تَدْعُوْنَنِىْ لِاَكْفُرَ بِاللّٰهِ
وَاُشْرِكَ بِهٖ مَا لَيْسَ لِىْ بِهٖ عِلْمٌ ۙ
وَّاَنَا اَدْعُوْكُمْ اِلَى
الْعَزِيْزِ الْغَفَّارِ ۞

43. "Without doubt ye do call
Me to one who is not
Fit to be called to,
Whether in this world,
Or in the Hereafter;

٤٣ ـ لَا جَرَمَ اَنَّمَا تَدْعُوْنَنِىْ اِلَيْهِ
لَيْسَ لَهٗ دَعْوَةٌ فِى الدُّنْيَا وَلَا فِى الْاٰخِرَةِ

Our Return will be
To Allah; and the Transgressors
Will be Companions
Of the Fire!

وَأَنَّ مَرَدَّنَا إِلَى اللهِ
وَأَنَّ الْمُسْرِفِينَ هُمْ أَصْحَٰبُ النَّارِ ۟

44. "Soon will ye remember
What I say to you (now).
My (own) affair I commit
To Allah: for Allah (ever)
Watches over His Servants."

٤٤- فَسَتَذْكُرُونَ مَا أَقُولُ لَكُمْ
وَأُفَوِّضُ أَمْرِى
إِلَى اللهِ إِنَّ اللهَ بَصِيرٌ بِالْعِبَادِ ۟

45. Then Allah saved him
From (every) ill that they
Plotted (against him),
But the brunt of the Penalty
Encompassed on all sides
The People of Pharaoh.

٤٥- فَوَقَىٰهُ اللهُ سَيِّئَاتِ مَا مَكَرُوا
وَحَاقَ بِآلِ فِرْعَوْنَ
سُوٓءُ الْعَذَابِ ۟

46. In front of the Fire
Will they be brought,
Morning and evening:
And (the Sentence will be)
On the Day that
Judgement will be established:
"Cast ye the People
Of Pharaoh into
The severest Penalty!"

٤٦- النَّارُ يُعْرَضُونَ عَلَيْهَا
غُدُوًّا وَّعَشِيًّا
وَيَوْمَ تَقُومُ السَّاعَةُ
أَدْخِلُوٓا اٰلَ فِرْعَوْنَ
أَشَدَّ الْعَذَابِ ۟

47. Behold, they will dispute
With each other in the Fire!
The weak ones (who followed)
Will say to those who
Had been arrogant, "We but
Followed you: can ye then
Take (on yourselves) from us
Some share of the Fire?"

٤٧- وَإِذْ يَتَحَاجُّونَ فِى النَّارِ
فَيَقُولُ الضُّعَفَٰٓؤُا لِلَّذِينَ اسْتَكْبَرُوٓا
إِنَّا كُنَّا لَكُمْ تَبَعًا فَهَلْ أَنتُم
مُّغْنُونَ عَنَّا نَصِيبًا مِّنَ النَّارِ ۟

48. Those who had been arrogant
Will say: "We are all
In this (Fire)! Truly,
Allah has judged
Between (His) Servants!"

٤٨- قَالَ الَّذِينَ اسْتَكْبَرُوٓا
إِنَّا كُلٌّ فِيهَآ
إِنَّ اللهَ قَدْ حَكَمَ بَيْنَ الْعِبَادِ ۟

49. Those in the Fire will say
To the Keepers of Hell:
"Pray to your Lord

٤٩- وَقَالَ الَّذِينَ فِى النَّارِ لِخَزَنَةِ جَهَنَّمَ
ادْعُوا رَبَّكُمْ يُخَفِّفْ عَنَّا يَوْمًا

To lighten us the Penalty
For a Day (at least)!"

مِنَ الْعَذَابِ ○

50. They will say: "Did there
Not come to you
Your messengers with Clear
Signs?"
They will say: "Yes".
They will reply, "Then
Pray (as ye like)! But
The Prayer of those
Without Faith is nothing
But (futile wandering)
In (mazes of) error!"

٥٠- قَالُوٓا اَوَلَمْ تَكُ تَاْتِيْكُمْ
رُسُلُكُمْ بِالْبَيِّنٰتِ ؕ
قَالُوْا بَلٰى ؕ
قَالُوْا فَادْعُوْا ۚ
وَمَا دُعٰٓؤُا الْكٰفِرِيْنَ اِلَّا فِيْ ضَلٰلٍ ۟ ○

SECTION 6.

51. We will, without doubt,
Help Our messengers and those
Who believe, (both)
In this world's life
And on the Day
When the Witnesses
Will stand forth—

٥١- اِنَّا لَنَنْصُرُ رُسُلَنَا وَالَّذِيْنَ
اٰمَنُوْا فِى الْحَيٰوةِ الدُّنْيَا
وَيَوْمَ يَقُوْمُ الْاَشْهَادُ ۟ ○

52. The Day when no profit
Will it be to Wrongdoers
To present their excuses,
But they will (only) have
The Curse and the Home
Of Misery.

٥٢- يَوْمَ لَا يَنْفَعُ الظّٰلِمِيْنَ مَعْذِرَتُهُمْ
وَلَهُمُ اللَّعْنَةُ
وَلَهُمْ سُوْٓءُ الدَّارِ ○

53. We did aforetime give Moses
The (Book of) Guidance,
And We gave the Book
In inheritance to the Children
Of Israel—

٥٣- وَلَقَدْ اٰتَيْنَا مُوْسَى الْهُدٰى
وَاَوْرَثْنَا بَنِيْٓ اِسْرَآءِيْلَ الْكِتٰبَ ۟ ○

54. A Guide and a Message
To men of understanding.

٥٤- هُدًى وَّذِكْرٰى لِاُولِى الْاَلْبَابِ ○

55. Patiently, then, persevere:
For the Promise of Allah
Is true: and ask forgiveness
For thy fault, and celebrate
The Praises of thy Lord
In the evening
And in the morning.

٥٥- فَاصْبِرْ اِنَّ وَعْدَ اللّٰهِ حَقٌّ
وَّاسْتَغْفِرْ لِذَنْۢبِكَ وَسَبِّحْ
بِحَمْدِ رَبِّكَ بِالْعَشِيِّ وَالْاِبْكَارِ ○

56. Those who dispute

٥٦- اِنَّ الَّذِيْنَ

About the Signs of Allah
Without any authority
Bestowed on them—there is
Nothing in their breasts
But (the quest of) greatness,
Which they shall never
Attain to: seek refuge,
Then, in Allah: it is He
Who hears and sees (all things).

يُجَادِلُونَ فِيَ آيَاتِ اللَّهِ بِغَيْرِ سُلْطَانٍ أَتَاهُمْ

إِن فِيَ صُدُورِهِمْ إِلَّا كِبْرٌ

مَّا هُم بِبَالِغِيهِ فَاسْتَعِذْ بِاللَّهِ

إِنَّهُ هُوَ السَّمِيعُ الْبَصِيرُ ۝

57. Assuredly the creation
Of the heavens
And the earth
Is a greater (matter)
Than the creation of men:
Yet most men understand not.

٥٧ - لَخَلْقُ السَّمَوَاتِ وَالْأَرْضِ

أَكْبَرُ مِنْ خَلْقِ النَّاسِ

وَلَٰكِنَّ أَكْثَرَ النَّاسِ لَا يَعْلَمُونَ ۝

58. Not equal are the blind
And those who (clearly) see:
Nor are (equal) those
Who believe and work
Deeds of righteousness, and
Those who do evil.
Little do ye learn
By admonition!

٥٨ - وَمَا يَسْتَوِي الْأَعْمَىٰ وَالْبَصِيرُ

وَالَّذِينَ آمَنُوا وَعَمِلُوا الصَّالِحَاتِ

وَلَا الْمُسِيءُ

قَلِيلًا مَّا تَتَذَكَّرُونَ ۝

59. The Hour will certainly come:
Therein is no doubt:
Yet most men believe not.

٥٩ - إِنَّ السَّاعَةَ لَآتِيَةٌ لَّا رَيْبَ فِيهَا

وَلَٰكِنَّ أَكْثَرَ النَّاسِ لَا يُؤْمِنُونَ ۝

60. And your Lord says:
"Call on Me; I
Will answer your (Prayer):
But those who are
Too arrogant to serve Me
Will surely find themselves
In Hell—in humiliation!"

SECTION 7.

٦٠ - وَقَالَ رَبُّكُمُ ادْعُونِي

أَسْتَجِبْ لَكُمْ

إِنَّ الَّذِينَ يَسْتَكْبِرُونَ عَنْ عِبَادَتِي

سَيَدْخُلُونَ جَهَنَّمَ دَاخِرِينَ ۝

61. It is Allah Who has
Made the Night for you,
That ye may rest therein,
And the Day, as that
Which helps (you) to see.
Verily Allah is Full of
Grace and Bounty to men:
Yet most men give
No thanks.

٦١ - اللَّهُ الَّذِي جَعَلَ لَكُمُ اللَّيْلَ

لِتَسْكُنُوا فِيهِ

وَالنَّهَارَ مُبْصِرًا

إِنَّ اللَّهَ لَذُو فَضْلٍ عَلَى النَّاسِ

وَلَٰكِنَّ أَكْثَرَ النَّاسِ لَا يَشْكُرُونَ ۝

62. Such is Allah, your Lord,
The Creator of all things.
There is no god but He:
Then how ye are deluded
Away from the Truth!

63. Thus are deluded those
Who are wont to reject
The Signs of Allah.

64. It is Allah Who has
Made for you the earth
As a resting place,
And the sky as a canopy,
And has given you shape—
And made your shapes
Beautiful—and has provided
For you Sustenance.
Of things pure and good—
Such is Allah your Lord.
So Glory to Allah,
The Lord of the Worlds!

65. He is the Living (One):
There is no god but He:
Call upon Him, giving Him
Sincere devotion. Praise be
To Allah, Lord of the Worlds!

66. Say: "I have been forbidden
To invoke those whom ye
Invoke besides Allah   seeing that
The Clear Signs have come
To me from my Lord;
And I have been commanded
To bow (in Islam)
To the Lord of the Worlds."

67. It is He Who has
Created you from dust,
Then from a sperm-drop,
Then from a leech-like clot;
Then does He get you
Out (into the light)
As a child; then lets you
(Grow and) reach your age
Of full strength; then
Lets you become old—

Though of you there are
Some who die before—
And lets you reach
A Term appointed;
In order that ye
May learn wisdom.

وَمِنْكُمْ مَّنْ يُتَوَفّٰى مِنْ قَبْلُ
وَلِتَبْلُغُوْۤا اَجَلًا مُّسَمًّى
وَّلَعَلَّكُمْ تَعْقِلُوْنَ ۟

68. It is He Who gives Life
And Death; and when He
Decides upon an affair,
He says to it, "Be",
And it is.
SECTION 8.

٦٨- هُوَ الَّذِيْ يُحْيٖ وَيُمِيْتُ ۚ
فَاِذَا قَضٰۤى اَمْرًا
فَاِنَّمَا يَقُوْلُ لَهٗ كُنْ فَيَكُوْنُ ۟

69. Seest thou not those
That dispute concerning
The Signs of Allah?
How are they turned away
(From Reality)?—

٦٩- اَلَمْ تَرَ اِلَى الَّذِيْنَ يُجَادِلُوْنَ
فِيْۤ اٰيٰتِ اللّٰهِ ۚ
اَنّٰى يُصْرَفُوْنَ ۟

70. Those who reject the Book
And the (revelations) with
           which
We sent Our messengers:
But soon shall they know—

٧٠- اَلَّذِيْنَ كَذَّبُوْا بِالْكِتٰبِ وَبِمَاۤ اَرْسَلْنَا
بِهٖ رُسُلَنَا ۛ فَسَوْفَ يَعْلَمُوْنَ ۟

71. When the yokes (shall be)
Round their necks,
And the chains;
They shall be dragged along—

٧١- اِذِ الْاَغْلٰلُ فِيْۤ اَعْنَاقِهِمْ وَالسَّلٰسِلُ ۗ
يُسْحَبُوْنَ ۟

72. In the boiling fetid fluid;
Then in the Fire
Shall they be burned;

٧٢- فِى الْحَمِيْمِ ۛ ثُمَّ فِى النَّارِ يُسْجَرُوْنَ ۟

73. Then shall it be said
To them: "Where are
The (deities) to which
Ye gave part-worship—

٧٣- ثُمَّ قِيْلَ لَهُمْ
اَيْنَ مَا كُنْتُمْ تُشْرِكُوْنَ ۟

74. "In derogation of Allah?"
They will reply: "They have
Left us in the lurch:
Nay, we invoked not,
Of old, anything (that had
Real existence)." Thus
Does Allah leave
The Unbelievers to stray.

٧٤- مِنْ دُوْنِ اللّٰهِ ۗ
قَالُوْا ضَلُّوْا عَنَّا
بَلْ لَّمْ نَكُنْ نَّدْعُوْا مِنْ قَبْلُ شَيْئًا ۚ
كَذٰلِكَ يُضِلُّ اللّٰهُ الْكٰفِرِيْنَ ۟

75. "That was because
Ye were wont to rejoice
On the earth in things
Other than the Truth,
And that ye were wont
To be insolent.

76. "Enter ye the gates
Of Hell, to dwell therein:
And evil is (this) abode
Of the arrogant!"

77. So persevere in patience;
For the Promise of Allah
Is true: and whether
We show thee (in this life)
Some part of what We
Promise them—or We
Take thy soul (to Our Mercy)
(Before that)—(in any case)
It is to Us that
They shall (all) return.

78. We did aforetime send
Messengers before thee: of
　　　　　　　　them
There are some whose story
We have related to thee,
And some whose story
We have not related
To thee. It was not
(Possible) for any messenger
To bring a Sign except
By the leave of Allah:
But when the Command
Of Allah issued,
The matter was decided
In truth and justice,
And there perished,
There and then, those
Who stood on Falsehoods.
　　　　SECTION 9.

79. It is Allah who made
Cattle for you, that ye
May use some for riding
And some for food;

80. And there are (other)
　　　　　　　advantages

In them for you (besides);
That ye may through them
Attain to any need
(There may be) in your hearts;
And on them and on ships
Ye are carried.

81. And He shows you (always)
His Signs: then which
Of the Signs of Allah
Will ye deny?

82. Do they not travel through
The earth and see what
Was the End of those
Before them? They were
More numerous than these
And superior in strength
And in the traces
(They have left) in the land:
Yet all that they accomplished
Was of no profit to them.

83. For when their messengers
Came to them
With Clear Signs, they
              exulted
In such knowledge (and skill)
As they had; but
That very (Wrath) at which
They were wont to scoff
Hemmed them in.

84. But when they saw
Our Punishment, they said:
"We believe in Allah—
The One God—and we
Reject the partners we used
To join with Him."

85. But their professing the
              Faith
When they (actually) saw
Our Punishment was not going
To profit them.
(Such has been) Allah's way
Of dealing with His servants
(From the most ancient times).
And even thus did
The rejecters of Allah
Perish (utterly)!

وَلِتَبْلُغُوا عَلَيْهَا حَاجَةً
فِي صُدُورِكُمْ
وَعَلَيْهَا وَعَلَى الْفُلْكِ تُحْمَلُونَ ۝

٨١- وَيُرِيكُمْ آيَاتِهِ فَأَيَّ
آيَاتِ اللهِ تُنْكِرُونَ ۝

٨٢- أَفَلَمْ يَسِيرُوا فِي الْأَرْضِ فَيَنْظُرُوا
كَيْفَ كَانَ عَاقِبَةُ الَّذِينَ مِنْ قَبْلِهِمْ
كَانُوا أَكْثَرَ مِنْهُمْ وَأَشَدَّ قُوَّةً
وَآثَارًا فِي الْأَرْضِ
فَمَا أَغْنَى عَنْهُمْ مَا كَانُوا يَكْسِبُونَ ۝

٨٣- فَلَمَّا جَاءَتْهُمْ رُسُلُهُمْ بِالْبَيِّنَاتِ
فَرِحُوا بِمَا عِنْدَهُمْ مِنَ الْعِلْمِ
وَحَاقَ بِهِمْ
مَا كَانُوا بِهِ يَسْتَهْزِئُونَ ۝

٨٤- فَلَمَّا رَأَوْا بَأْسَنَا قَالُوا
آمَنَّا بِاللهِ وَحْدَهُ
وَكَفَرْنَا بِمَا كُنَّا بِهِ مُشْرِكِينَ ۝

٨٥- فَلَمْ يَكُ يَنْفَعُهُمْ إِيمَانُهُمْ
لَمَّا رَأَوْا بَأْسَنَا
سُنَّتَ اللهِ
الَّتِي قَدْ خَلَتْ فِي عِبَادِهِ
وَخَسِرَ هُنَالِكَ الْكَافِرُونَ ۝

INTRODUCTION TO SURA XLI. (*Ḥā - Mīm*) — 54 Verses

This is the second of the series of seven Sūras bearing the Abbreviated Letters *Ḥā-Mīm*, as explained in the Introduction to S. xl. To prevent confusion with other Suras of the *Ḥā-Mīm* series the word *Sajda* is sometimes added to the title, making it *Ḥā-Mīm as-Sajda*, the double title being necessary as there is another Sūra called Sajda (S.xxxii). To avoid the double title, it is sometimes called *Fuṣṣilat*, from the occurrence of the word in verse 3.

The meaning of *Ḥā-Mīm* has been explained in the Introduction to S. xl. where will also be found a note on the chronology and general theme of the seven *Ḥā-Mīm* Sūras.

For this particular Sūra the theme is that the basis of Faith and Revelation is God's Power and Goodness, and the fruit of both is man's righteousness and healing.

Fuṣṣilat (Expounded), or *Ḥā Mīm*

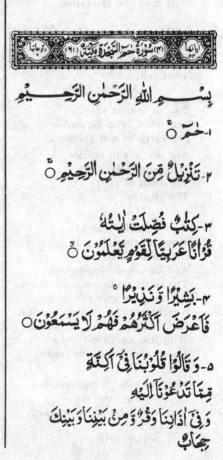

In the name of Allah, Most Gracious, Most Merciful.

1. Ḥa Mīm.

2. A revelation from (Allah),
   Most Gracious, Most
   Merciful—

3. A Book, whereof the verses
   Are explained in detail—
   A Qur'ān in Arabic,
   For people who understand—

4. Giving Good News
   And Admonition: yet most
   Of them turn away,
   And so they hear not.

5. They say: "Our hearts are
   Under veils, (concealed)
   From that to which thou
   Dost invite us, and
   In our ears is a deafness,
   And between us and thee
   Is a screen: so do

Thou (what thou wilt);
For us, we shall do
(What we will!)"

6. Say thou: "I am
But a man like you:
It is revealed to me
By inspiration, that your God
Is One God: so stand
True to Him, and ask
For His forgiveness."
And woe to those who
Join gods with Allah—

7. Those who practise not
Regular Charity, and who
Even deny the Hereafter.

8. For those who believe
And work deeds of righteousness
Is a reward that will
Never fail.

SECTION 2.

9. Say: Is it that ye
Deny Him Who created
The earth in two Days?
And do ye join equals
With Him? He is
The Lord of (all)
The Worlds.

10. He set on the (earth).
Mountains standing firm,
High above it,
And bestowed blessings on
The earth, and measured therein
All things to give them
Nourishment in due proportion,
In four Days,　　in accordance
With (the needs of)
Those who seek (sustenance).

11. Moreover, He Comprehended
In His design the sky,
And it had been (as) smoke:
He said to it
And to the earth:

"Come ye together,
Willingly or unwillingly."
They said: "We do come
(Together), in willing obedience."

12. So He completed them
As seven firmaments
In two Days   and He
Assigned to each heaven
Its duty and command.
And We adorned
The lower heaven
With lights, and (provided it)
With guard. Such
Is the Decree of (Him)
The Exalted in Might,
Full of knowledge.

13. But if they turn away,
Say thou: "I have warned
You of a stunning Punishment
(As of thunder and lightning)
Like that which (overtook)
The 'Ād and the Thamūd!"

14. Behold, the messengers came
To them, from before them
And behind them, (preaching):
"Serve none but Allah."
They said, "If our Lord
Had so pleased, He would
Certainly have sent down angels
(To preach): now we reject
Your mission (altogether)."

15. Now the 'Ād behaved
Arrogantly through the land,
Against (all) truth and reason,
And said: "Who is superior
To us in strength?" What!
Did they not see that
Allah, Who created them,
Was superior to them
In strength? But they
Continued to reject Our Signs!

16. So We sent against them
A furious Wind through days

Of disaster, that We might
Give them a taste
Of a Penalty of humiliation
In this Life; but the Penalty
Of the Hereafter will be
More humiliating still:
And they will find
No help.

17. As to the Thamūd,
We gave them guidance,
But they preferred blindness
(Of heart) to Guidance:
So the stunning Punishment
Of humiliation seized them,
Because of what they had earned.

18. But We delivered those
Who believed and practised
righteousness.

SECTION 3.

19. On the Day that
The enemies of Allah
Will be gathered together
To the Fire, they will
Be marched in ranks.

20. At length, when they reach
The (Fire), their hearing,
Their sight, and their skins
Will bear witness against them,
As to (all) their deeds.

21. They will say to their skins:
"Why bear ye witness
Against us?" They will say:
"Allah hath given us speech —
(He) Who giveth speech
To everything: He created
You for the first time,
And unto Him were ye
To return.

22. "Ye did not seek
To hide yourselves, lest
Your hearing, your sight,
And your skins should bear
Witness against you! But

صَرْصَرًا فِىٓ أَيَّامٍ نَّحِسَاتٍ

لِّنُذِيقَهُمْ عَذَابَ الْخِزْيِ فِى الْحَيَوٰةِ الدُّنْيَا

وَلَعَذَابُ الْأَخِرَةِ أَخْزَىٰ

وَهُمْ لَا يُنْصَرُونَ ○

١٦- وَأَمَّا ثَمُودُ فَهَدَيْنَٰهُمْ

فَاسْتَحَبُّوا الْعَمَىٰ عَلَى الْهُدَىٰ

فَأَخَذَتْهُمْ صَٰعِقَةُ الْعَذَابِ الْهُونِ

بِمَا كَانُوا يَكْسِبُونَ ○

١٨- وَنَجَّيْنَا الَّذِينَ

ءَامَنُوا وَكَانُوا يَتَّقُونَ ○

١٩- وَيَوْمَ يُحْشَرُ أَعْدَآءُ اللّٰهِ

إِلَى النَّارِ فَهُمْ يُوزَعُونَ ○

٢٠- حَتَّىٰ إِذَا مَا جَآءُوهَا

شَهِدَ عَلَيْهِمْ سَمْعُهُمْ وَأَبْصَٰرُهُمْ وَجُلُودُهُم

بِمَا كَانُوا يَعْمَلُونَ ○

٢١- وَقَالُوا لِجُلُودِهِمْ لِمَ شَهِدتُّمْ عَلَيْنَا

قَالُوٓا أَنطَقَنَا اللّٰهُ الَّذِىٓ

أَنطَقَ كُلَّ شَىْءٍ

وَهُوَ خَلَقَكُمْ أَوَّلَ مَرَّةٍ

وَإِلَيْهِ تُرْجَعُونَ ○

٢٢- وَمَا كُنتُمْ تَسْتَتِرُونَ أَن يَشْهَدَ عَلَيْكُمْ

سَمْعُكُمْ وَلَآ أَبْصَٰرُكُمْ وَلَا جُلُودُكُمْ

وَلَٰكِن ظَنَنتُمْ أَنَّ اللّٰهَ

Ye did think that Allah
Knew not many of the things
That ye used to do!

لَا يَعْلَمُ كَثِيرًا مِّمَّا تَعْمَلُوْنَ ٥

23. "But this thought of yours
Which ye did entertain
Concerning your Lord, hath
Brought you to destruction,
And (now) have ye become
Of those utterly lost!"

٢٣- وَ ذٰلِكُمْ ظَنُّكُمُ الَّذِىْ
ظَنَنْتُمْ بِرَبِّكُمْ أَرْدٰىكُمْ
فَأَصْبَحْتُمْ مِّنَ الْخٰسِرِيْنَ ٥

24. If, then, they have patience,
The Fire will be
A Home for them!
And if they beg
To be received into favour
Into favour will they not
(Then) be received

٢٤- فَإِنْ يَّصْبِرُوْا
فَالنَّارُ مَثْوًى لَّهُمْ ۚ
وَ اِنْ يَّسْتَعْتِبُوْا
فَمَا هُمْ مِّنَ الْمُعْتَبِيْنَ ٥

25. And We have destined
For them intimate companions
(Of like nature), who made
Alluring to them what was
Before them and behind them;
And the sentence among
The previous generations of
              Jinns
And men, who have passed away,
Is proved against them;
For they are utterly lost.

٢٥- وَقَيَّضْنَا لَهُمْ قُرَنَآءَ
فَزَيَّنُوْا لَهُمْ مَّا بَيْنَ أَيْدِيْهِمْ وَ مَا خَلْفَهُمْ
وَحَقَّ عَلَيْهِمُ الْقَوْلُ فِىْ أُمَمٍ
قَدْ خَلَتْ مِنْ قَبْلِهِمْ مِّنَ الْجِنِّ وَالْإِنْسِ ۚ
إِنَّهُمْ كَانُوْا خٰسِرِيْنَ ٥

SECTION 4.

26. The Unbelievers say;
"Listen not to this Qur-ān,
But talk at random
In the midst
Of its (reading), that ye
May gain the upper hand!"

٢٦- وَقَالَ الَّذِيْنَ كَفَرُوْا لَا تَسْمَعُوْا لِهٰذَا
الْقُرْاٰنِ وَالْغَوْا فِيْهِ
لَعَلَّكُمْ تَغْلِبُوْنَ ٥

27. But We will certainly
Give the Unbelievers a taste
Of a severe Penalty,
And We will requite them
For the worst of their deeds.

٢٧- فَلَنُذِيْقَنَّ الَّذِيْنَ كَفَرُوْا
عَذَابًا شَدِيْدًا ۙ
وَلَنَجْزِيَنَّهُمْ أَسْوَأَ الَّذِىْ كَانُوْا يَعْمَلُوْنَ ٥

28. Such is the requital
Of the enemies of Allah—
The Fire: therein will be
For them the Eternal Home:

٢٨- ذٰلِكَ جَزَآءُ أَعْدَآءِ اللّٰهِ النَّارُ ۚ
لَهُمْ فِيْهَا دَارُ الْخُلْدِ ۚ

A (fit) requital, for
That they were wont
To reject Our Signs.

جَزَآءً بِمَا كَانُوْا بِاٰيٰتِنَا يَجْحَدُوْنَ ۝

29.   And the Unbelievers will say:
"Our Lord! Show us those,
Among Jinns and men,
Who misled us: we shall
Crush them beneath our feet,
So that they become
The vilest (before all)."

٢٩- وَقَالَ الَّذِيْنَ كَفَرُوْا رَبَّنَا أَرِنَا الَّذَيْنِ
اَضَلّٰنَا مِنَ الْجِنِّ وَالْإِنْسِ
نَجْعَلْهُمَا تَحْتَ اَقْدَامِنَا
لِيَكُوْنَا مِنَ الْاَسْفَلِيْنَ ۝

30.   In the case of those
Who say, "Our Lord
Is Allah", and, further,
Stand straight and steadfast,
The angels descend on them
(From time to time):
"Fear ye not!" (they suggest),
"Nor grieve! But receive
The Glad Tidings
Of the Garden (of Bliss),
That which ye were promised!

٣٠- اِنَّ الَّذِيْنَ قَالُوْا رَبُّنَا
اللّٰهُ ثُمَّ اسْتَقَامُوْا
تَتَنَزَّلُ عَلَيْهِمُ الْمَلٰئِكَةُ
اَلَّا تَخَافُوْا وَلَا تَحْزَنُوْا
وَاَبْشِرُوْا بِالْجَنَّةِ الَّتِيْ
كُنْتُمْ تُوْعَدُوْنَ ۝

31.   "We are your protectors
In this life and
In the Hereafter:
Therein shall ye have
All that your souls
Shall desire; therein
Shall ye have all
That ye ask for!—

٣١- نَحْنُ اَوْلِيَآؤُكُمْ
فِى الْحَيٰوةِ الدُّنْيَا وَفِى الْاٰخِرَةِ ۚ
وَلَكُمْ فِيْهَا مَا تَشْتَهِيْ اَنْفُسُكُمْ
وَلَكُمْ فِيْهَا مَا تَدَّعُوْنَ ۝

32.   "A hospitable gift from One
Oft-Forgiving, Most Merciful!"
SECTION 5.

٣٢- نُزُلًا مِّنْ غَفُوْرٍ رَّحِيْمٍ ۝ ع

33.   Who is better in speech
Than one who calls (men)
To Allah, works righteousness,
And says, "I am of those
Who bow in Islam"?

٣٣- وَمَنْ اَحْسَنُ قَوْلًا مِّمَّنْ
دَعَآ اِلَى اللّٰهِ وَعَمِلَ صَالِحًا وَّقَالَ
اِنَّنِيْ مِنَ الْمُسْلِمِيْنَ ۝

34.   Nor can Goodness and Evil
Be equal. Repel (Evil)
With what is better:
Then will he between whom
And thee was hatred
Become as it were

٣٤- وَلَا تَسْتَوِى الْحَسَنَةُ وَلَا السَّيِّئَةُ ؕ
اِدْفَعْ بِالَّتِيْ هِيَ اَحْسَنُ
فَاِذَا الَّذِيْ بَيْنَكَ

Thy friend and intimate!

35. And no one will be
Granted such goodness
Except those who exercise
Patience and self-restraint—
None but persons of
The greatest good fortune.

36. And if (at any time)
An incitement to discord
Is made to thee
By the Evil One,
Seek refuge in Allah.
He is the One
Who hears and knows
All things.

37. Among His Signs are
The Night and the Day,
And the Sun and the Moon.
Adore not the sun
And the moon, but adore
Allah, Who created them,
If it is Him ye wish
To serve.

38. But if the (Unbelievers)
Are arrogant, (no matter):
For in the presence
Of thy Lord are those
Who celebrate His praises
By night and by day.
And they never flag
(Nor feel themselves
Above it).

39. And among His Signs
Is this: thou seest
The earth barren and desolate;
But when We send down
Rain to it, it is stirred
To life and yields increase.
Truly, He Who gives life
To the (dead) earth
Can surely give life
To (men) who are dead.
For He has power
Over all things.

وَبَيْنَهُ عَدَاوَةٌ كَأَنَّهُ وَلِيٌّ حَمِيمٌ ۝

٣٥- وَمَا يُلَقَّاهَآ

إِلَّا الَّذِينَ صَبَرُوا ۚ

وَمَا يُلَقَّاهَآ إِلَّا ذُو حَظٍّ عَظِيمٍ ۝

٣٦- وَإِمَّا يَنْزَغَنَّكَ

مِنَ الشَّيْطَٰنِ نَزْغٌ

فَاسْتَعِذْ بِاللَّهِ ۖ

إِنَّهُ هُوَ السَّمِيعُ الْعَلِيمُ ۝

٣٧- وَمِنْ آيَٰتِهِ الَّيْلُ وَالنَّهَارُ وَالشَّمْسُ وَ

الْقَمَرُ ۚ لَا تَسْجُدُوا لِلشَّمْسِ وَلَا لِلْقَمَرِ

وَاسْجُدُوا لِلَّهِ الَّذِي خَلَقَهُنَّ

إِنْ كُنْتُمْ إِيَّاهُ تَعْبُدُونَ ۝

٣٨- فَإِنِ اسْتَكْبَرُوا

فَالَّذِينَ عِنْدَ رَبِّكَ

يُسَبِّحُونَ لَهُ بِالَّيْلِ وَالنَّهَارِ

وَهُمْ لَا يَسْأَمُونَ ۩ ۝

٣٩- وَمِنْ آيَٰتِهِ أَنَّكَ تَرَى الْأَرْضَ خَاشِعَةً

فَإِذَآ أَنْزَلْنَا عَلَيْهَا الْمَآءَ

اهْتَزَّتْ وَرَبَتْ ۚ

إِنَّ الَّذِي أَحْيَاهَا

لَمُحْيِ الْمَوْتَىٰ ۚ

إِنَّهُ عَلَىٰ كُلِّ شَيْءٍ قَدِيرٌ ۝

40. Those who pervert
The Truth in Our Signs
Are not hidden from Us.
Which is better?—he that
Is cast into the Fire,
Or he that comes safe through,
On the Day of Judgement?
Do what ye will:
Verily He seeth (clearly)
All that ye do.

41. Those who reject the Message
When it comes to them
(Are not hidden from Us).
And indeed it is a Book
Of exalted power.

42. No falsehood can approach it
From before or behind it:
It is sent down
By One Full of Wisdom,
Worthy of all Praise.

43. Nothing is said to thee
That was not said
To the messengers before thee:
That thy Lord has
At His command (all) Forgiveness
As well as a most
Grievous Penalty.

44. Had We sent this as
A Qur'ān (in a language)
Other than Arabic, they would
Have said: "Why are not
Its verses explained in detail?
What! (a Book) not in Arabic?
And (a Messenger) an Arab?"
Say: "It is a guide
And a healing to those
Who believe; and for those
Who believe not, there is
A deafness in their ears,
And it is blindness in their (eyes):
They are (as it were)
Being called from a place
Far distant!"

SECTION 6.

45. We certainly gave Moses

The Book aforetime: but disputes
Arose herein. Had it not
Been for a Word
That went forth before
From thy Lord, (their differences)
Would have been settled
Between them: but they
Remained in suspicious
Disquieting doubt thereon.

وَلَوْلَا
كَلِمَةٌ سَبَقَتْ مِنْ رَّبِّكَ
لَقُضِيَ بَيْنَهُمْ
وَإِنَّهُمْ لَفِي شَكٍّ مِنْهُ مُرِيبٍ ۝

46. Whoever works righteousness
Benefits his own soul;
Whoever works evil, it is
Against his own soul:
Nor is thy Lord ever
Unjust (in the least)
To His servants.

٤٦ ـ مَنْ عَمِلَ صَالِحًا فَلِنَفْسِهِ
وَمَنْ أَسَاءَ فَعَلَيْهَا
وَمَا رَبُّكَ بِظَلَّامٍ لِلْعَبِيدِ ۝

47. To Him is referred
The Knowledge of the Hour
(Of Judgement: He knows all):
No date-fruit comes out
Of its sheath, nor does
A female conceive (within
Her womb) nor bring forth
(Young), but by His Knowledge,
The Day that (Allah) will
                propound
To them the (question),
"Where are the Partners
(Ye attributed) to Me?"
They will say, "We do
Assure Thee, not one
Of us can bear witness!"

٤٧ ـ إِلَيْهِ يُرَدُّ عِلْمُ السَّاعَةِ
وَمَا تَخْرُجُ مِنْ ثَمَرَاتٍ مِنْ أَكْمَامِهَا
وَمَا تَحْمِلُ مِنْ أُنْثَى
وَلَا تَضَعُ إِلَّا بِعِلْمِهِ
وَيَوْمَ يُنَادِيهِمْ أَيْنَ شُرَكَائِي
قَالُوا آذَنَّاكَ
مَا مِنَّا مِنْ شَهِيدٍ ۝

48. The (deities) they used to invoke
Aforetime will leave them
In the lurch, and they
Will perceive that they
Have no way of escape.

٤٨ ـ وَضَلَّ عَنْهُمْ مَا كَانُوا يَدْعُونَ
مِنْ قَبْلُ
وَظَنُّوا مَا لَهُمْ مِنْ مَحِيصٍ ۝

49. Man does not weary
Of asking for good (things),
But if ill touches him,
He gives up all hope
(And) is lost in despair.

٤٩ ـ لَا يَسْأَمُ الْإِنْسَانُ مِنْ دُعَاءِ الْخَيْرِ
وَإِنْ مَسَّهُ الشَّرُّ
فَيَئُوسٌ قَنُوطٌ ۝

50. When We give him a taste
Of some mercy from Ourselves

٥٠ ـ وَلَئِنْ أَذَقْنَاهُ رَحْمَةً مِنَّا

After some adversity has
Touched him, he is sure
To say, "This is due
To my (merit): I think not
That the Hour (of Judgement)
Will (ever) be established;
But if I am brought back
To my Lord, I have
(Much) good (stored) in His sight!"
But We will show
The Unbelievers the truth
Of all that they did,
And We shall give them
The taste of a severe
Penalty.

مِنْ بَعْدِ ضَرَّآءَ مَسَّتْهُ

لَيَقُوْلَنَّ هٰذَا لِيْ

وَمَآ أَظُنُّ السَّاعَةَ قَآئِمَةً

وَلَئِنْ رُّجِعْتُ إِلٰى رَبِّيْ

إِنَّ لِيْ عِنْدَهُ لَلْحُسْنٰى

فَلَنُنَبِّئَنَّ الَّذِيْنَ كَفَرُوْا بِمَا عَمِلُوْا

وَلَنُذِيْقَنَّهُمْ مِنْ عَذَابٍ غَلِيْظٍ ٥

51. **W**hen We bestow favours
On man, he turns away,
And gets himself remote
On his side (instead of⁴⁵²⁴
Coming to Us); and when
Evil seizes him, (he comes)
Full of prolonged prayer!

٥١۔ وَإِذَآ أَنْعَمْنَا عَلَى الْإِنْسَانِ

أَعْرَضَ وَنَأَى بِجَانِبِهٖ وَإِذَا

مَسَّهُ الشَّرُّ فَذُوْ دُعَآءٍ عَرِيْضٍ ٥

52. **S**ay: "See ye if
The (Revelation) is (really)
From Allah, and yet do ye
Reject it? Who is more
Astray than one who
Is in a schism
Far (from any purpose)?"

٥٢۔ قُلْ أَرَءَيْتُمْ إِنْ كَانَ مِنْ عِنْدِ اللّٰهِ

ثُمَّ كَفَرْتُمْ بِهٖ

مَنْ أَضَلُّ مِمَّنْ

هُوَ فِيْ شِقَاقٍ بَعِيْدٍ ٥

53. Soon will We show them
Our Signs in the (furthest)
Regions (of the earth), and
In their own souls, until
It becomes manifest to them
That this is the Truth.
Is it not enough that
Thy Lord doth witness
All things?

٥٣۔ سَنُرِيْهِمْ أٰيٰتِنَا فِي

الْاٰفَاقِ وَفِيْ أَنْفُسِهِمْ حَتّٰى

يَتَبَيَّنَ لَهُمْ أَنَّهُ الْحَقُّ

أَوَلَمْ يَكْفِ بِرَبِّكَ

أَنَّهُ عَلٰى كُلِّ شَيْءٍ شَهِيْدٌ ٥

54. Ah indeed! are they
In doubt concerning

٥٤۔ أَلَآ إِنَّهُمْ فِيْ مِرْيَةٍ مِنْ لِقَآءِ رَبِّهِمْ

The Meeting with their Lord?
Ah indeed! it is He
That doth encompass
All things!

اَلَاۤ اِنَّهٗ
بِكُلِّ شَيۡءٍ مُّحِيۡطٌ ۞

INTRODUCTION TO SŪRA XLII. (*Shūrā*) — 53 Verses

This is the third Sūra of the *Ḥā-Mīm* series of seven Sūras, for which see the Introduction to S. xl.

The theme is how evil and blasphemy can be cured by the Mercy and Guidance of God, which come through His Revelation, Men are asked to settle their differences in patience by mutual Consultation (xliii. 38), which explains the title of the Sūra.

Al Shūrā (Consultation)

In the name of Allah, Most Gracious,
Most Merciful.

بِسْمِ اللهِ الرَّحْمٰنِ الرَّحِيْمِ

1. Ḥā Mīm;

حٰمٓ ۚ

2. 'Ain Sīn Qāf.

عٓسٓقٓ ۚ

3. Thus doth (He) send
Inspiration to thee
As (He did) to those before
                    thee—
Allah, Exalted in Power,
Full of Wisdom.

كَذٰلِكَ يُوْحِيۡۤ اِلَيۡكَ وَاِلَى الَّذِيۡنَ مِنۡ قَبۡلِكَ ۙ اللهُ الۡعَزِيۡزُ الۡحَكِيۡمُ ۚ

4. To Him belongs all
That is in the heavens
And on earth: and He
Is Most High, Most Great.

لَهٗ مَا فِى السَّمٰوٰتِ وَمَا فِى الۡاَرۡضِ ؕ وَهُوَ الۡعَلِىُّ الۡعَظِيۡمُ ۚ

5. The heavens are almost
Rent asunder from above them
(By His Glory):
And the angels celebrate
The Praises of their Lord,
And pray for forgiveness
For All beings on earth:
Behold! Verily Allah is He,
The Oft-Forgiving,
Most Merciful.

تَكَادُ السَّمٰوٰتُ يَتَفَطَّرۡنَ مِنۡ فَوۡقِهِنَّ وَالۡمَلٰٓئِكَةُ يُسَبِّحُوۡنَ بِحَمۡدِ رَبِّهِمۡ وَيَسۡتَغۡفِرُوۡنَ لِمَنۡ فِى الۡاَرۡضِ ؕ اَلَاۤ اِنَّ اللهَ هُوَ الۡغَفُوۡرُ الرَّحِيۡمُ ۚ

6. And those who take
As protectors others besides
                    Him—
Allah doth watch over them;
And thou art not
The disposer of their affairs.

وَالَّذِيۡنَ اتَّخَذُوۡا مِنۡ دُوۡنِهٖۤ اَوۡلِيَآءَ اللهُ حَفِيۡظٌ عَلَيۡهِمۡ ۖ وَمَاۤ اَنۡتَ عَلَيۡهِمۡ بِوَكِيۡلٍ ۚ

7. Thus have We sent
By inspiration to thee
An Arabic Qur'ān:
That thou mayest warn
The Mother of Cities
And all around her—
And warn (them) of
The Day of Assembly,
Of which there is no doubt:
(When) some will be
In the Garden, and some
In the Blazing Fire.

٧- وَكَذٰلِكَ أَوْحَيْنَاۤ إِلَيْكَ قُرْآنًا عَرَبِيًّا
لِتُنْذِرَ أُمَّ الْقُرٰى
وَمَنْ حَوْلَهَا
وَتُنْذِرَ يَوْمَ الْجَمْعِ لَا رَيْبَ فِيهِ
فَرِيقٌ فِى الْجَنَّةِ
وَفَرِيقٌ فِى السَّعِيرِ ۝

8. If Allah had so willed,
He could have made them
A single people: but He
Admits whom He will
To His Mercy:
And the wrongdoers
Will have no protector
Nor helper.

٨- وَلَوْ شَاۤءَ اللّٰهُ لَجَعَلَهُمْ
أُمَّةً وَّاحِدَةً
وَّلٰكِنْ يُّدْخِلُ مَنْ يَّشَاۤءُ فِى رَحْمَتِهِ
وَالظّٰلِمُونَ مَا لَهُمْ مِّنْ وَّلِيٍّ وَّلَا نَصِيرٍ ۝

9. What! Have they taken
(For worship) protectors
Besides Him? But it is
Allah—He is the Protector,
And it is He Who
Gives life to the dead:
It is He Who has power
Over all things.

٩- أَمِ اتَّخَذُوا مِنْ دُونِهِ أَوْلِيَاۤءَ
فَاللّٰهُ هُوَ الْوَلِىُّ
وَهُوَ يُحْيِ الْمَوْتٰى
وَهُوَ عَلٰى كُلِّ شَىْءٍ قَدِيرٌ ۝

SECTION 2.

10. Whatever it be wherein
Ye differ, the decision
Thereof is with Allah:
Such is Allah my Lord:
In Him I trust,
And to Him I turn.

١٠- وَمَا اخْتَلَفْتُمْ فِيهِ مِنْ شَىْءٍ فَحُكْمُهُ
إِلَى اللّٰهِ ذٰلِكُمُ اللّٰهُ رَبِّى عَلَيْهِ تَوَكَّلْتُ
وَإِلَيْهِ أُنِيبُ ۝

11. (He is) the Creator
Of the heavens and
The earth: He has made
For you pairs
From among yourselves,
And pairs among cattle:
By this means does He
Multiply you: there is nothing
Whatever like unto Him,
And He is the One
That hears and sees (all things).

١١- فَاطِرُ السَّمٰوٰتِ وَالْأَرْضِ
جَعَلَ لَكُمْ مِّنْ أَنْفُسِكُمْ أَزْوَاجًا
وَّمِنَ الْأَنْعَامِ أَزْوَاجًا
يَذْرَؤُكُمْ فِيهِ
لَيْسَ كَمِثْلِهِ شَىْءٌ
وَهُوَ السَّمِيعُ الْبَصِيرُ ۝

12. To Him belongs the keys
Of the heavens and the earth:
He enlarges and restricts
The Sustenance to whom
He will: for He knows
Full well all things.

١٢- لَهُ مَقَالِيدُ السَّمٰوٰتِ وَ الْأَرْضِ ۚ
يَبْسُطُ الرِّزْقَ لِمَنْ يَّشَآءُ وَ يَقْدِرُ ۚ
إِنَّهُ بِكُلِّ شَيْءٍ عَلِيْمٌ ۞

13. The same religion has He
Established for you as that
Which He enjoined on
                    Noah—
That which We have sent
By inspiration to thee—
And that which We enjoined
On Abraham, Moses, and
                    Jesus:
Namely, that ye should remain
Steadfast in Religion, and make
No divisions therein:
To those who worship
Other things than Allah,
Hard is the (way)
To which thou callest them.
Allah chooses to Himself
Those whom He pleases,
And guides to Himself
Those who turn (to Him).

١٣- شَرَعَ لَكُمْ مِّنَ الدِّيْنِ
مَا وَصّٰى بِهٖ نُوْحًا
وَّ الَّذِيْ أَوْحَيْنَآ إِلَيْكَ
وَمَا وَصَّيْنَا بِهٖ إِبْرٰهِيْمَ وَمُوْسٰى وَعِيْسٰى
أَنْ أَقِيْمُوا الدِّيْنَ وَلَا تَتَفَرَّقُوْا فِيْهِ ۚ
كَبُرَ عَلَى الْمُشْرِكِيْنَ
مَا تَدْعُوْهُمْ إِلَيْهِ ۚ
اللّٰهُ يَجْتَبِيْ إِلَيْهِ مَنْ يَّشَآءُ
وَيَهْدِيْ إِلَيْهِ مَنْ يُّنِيْبُ ۞

14. And they became divided
Only after knowledge
Reached them—through selfish
Envy as between themselves.
Had it not been
For a Word that
Went forth before
From thy Lord,
(Tending) to a Term appointed,
The matter would have
Been settled between them:
But truly those who have
Inherited the Book after them
Are in suspicious (disquieting)
Doubt concerning it.

١٤- وَمَا تَفَرَّقُوْا إِلَّا مِنْ بَعْدِ مَا جَآءَهُمُ
الْعِلْمُ بَغْيًا بَيْنَهُمْ ۚ
وَلَوْ لَا كَلِمَةٌ
سَبَقَتْ مِنْ رَّبِّكَ
إِلٰى أَجَلٍ مُّسَمًّى لَّقُضِيَ بَيْنَهُمْ ۚ
وَإِنَّ الَّذِيْنَ أُوْرِثُوا الْكِتٰبَ مِنْ بَعْدِهِمْ
لَفِيْ شَكٍّ مِّنْهُ مُرِيْبٍ ۞

15. Now then, for that (reason),
Call (them to the Faith),
And stand steadfast

١٥- فَلِذٰلِكَ فَادْعُ ۚ وَاسْتَقِمْ كَمَآ أُمِرْتَ ۚ
وَلَا تَتَّبِعْ أَهْوَآءَهُمْ ۚ

As thou art commanded,
Nor follow thou their vain
Desires; but say: "I believe
In the Book which
Allah has sent down;
And I am commanded
To judge justly between you.
Allah is our Lord
And your Lord: For us
(Is the reponsibility for)
Our deeds, and for you
For your deeds. There is
No contention between us
And you. Allah will
Bring us together,
And to Him is
(Our) final goal."

16. But those who dispute
Concerning Allah after He
Had been accepted—
Futile is their dispute
In the sight of
Their Lord: on them
Is Wrath, and for them
Will be a Penalty
Terrible.

17. It is Allah Who has
Sent down the Book in truth,
And the Balance
(By which to weigh conduct).
And what will make thee
Realise that perhaps the Hour
Is close at hand?

18. Only those wish to
Hasten it who believe not
In it: those who believe
Hold it in awe,
And know that it is
The Truth. Behold, verily
Those that dispute concerning
The Hour are far astray.

19. Gracious is Allah
To His servants:

He gives Sustenance
To whom He pleases:
And He has Power
And can carry out
His Will.

SECTION 3.

20. To any that desires
The tilth of the Hereafter,
We give increase
In his tilth; and to any
That desires the tilth
Of this world, We grant
Somewhat thereof, but he
Has no share or lot
In the Hereafter.

يَرْزُقُ مَنْ يَشَآءُ ۚ
وَهُوَ الْقَوِيُّ الْعَزِيزُ ۞

٢٠- مَنْ كَانَ يُرِيدُ حَرْثَ الْأَخِرَةِ نَزِدْ لَهُ
فِي حَرْثِهٖ ۚ
وَمَنْ كَانَ يُرِيدُ حَرْثَ الدُّنْيَا نُؤْتِهٖ مِنْهَا
وَمَا لَهٗ فِي الْأَخِرَةِ مِنْ نَصِيبٍ ۞

21. What! Have they partners
(In godhead), who have
Established for them some
Religion without the permission
Of Allah? Had it not
Been for the Decree
Of Judgement, the matter
Would have been decided
Between them (at once).
But verily the wrongdoers
Will have a grievous Penalty.

٢١- أَمْ لَهُمْ شُرَكَٰٓؤُا۟ شَرَعُوا۟ لَهُمْ مِّنَ الدِّينِ
مَا لَمْ يَأْذَنْ بِهِ اللّٰهُ ۚ
وَلَوْلَا كَلِمَةُ الْفَصْلِ
لَقُضِيَ بَيْنَهُمْ ۗ
وَإِنَّ الظّٰلِمِينَ
لَهُمْ عَذَابٌ أَلِيمٌ ۞

22. Thou wilt see the wrongdoers
In fear on account of what
They have earned, and (the burden
Of) that must (necessarily)
Fall on them. But those
Who believe and work
Righteous deeds will be
In the luxuriant meads
Of the Gardens: they shall
Have, before their Lord,
All that they wish for.
That will indeed be
The magnificent Bounty
(Of Allah).

٢٢- تَرَى الظّٰلِمِينَ مُشْفِقِينَ مِمَّا
كَسَبُوا۟
وَهُوَ وَاقِعٌ بِهِمْ ۗ
وَالَّذِينَ أَمَنُوا۟ وَعَمِلُوا۟ الصّٰلِحٰتِ
فِي رَوْضَاتِ الْجَنّٰتِ ۚ
لَهُمْ مَّا يَشَآءُونَ عِنْدَ رَبِّهِمْ ۚ
ذٰلِكَ هُوَ الْفَضْلُ الْكَبِيرُ ۞

23. That is (the Bounty) whereof
Allah gives Glad Tidings
To His Servants who

٢٣- ذٰلِكَ الَّذِي يُبَشِّرُ اللّٰهُ عِبَادَهُ

Believe and do righteous deeds.
Say: "No reward do I
Ask of you for this
Except the love
Of those near of kin."
And if anyone earns
Any good, We shall give
Him an increase of good
In respect thereof: for Allah
Is Oft-Forgiving, Most Ready
To appreciate (service).

الَّذِينَ اٰمَنُوا وَعَمِلُوا الصّٰلِحٰتِ
قُلْ لَّا اَسْئَلُكُمْ عَلَيْهِ اَجْرًا
اِلَّا الْمَوَدَّةَ فِى الْقُرْبٰى
وَمَنْ يَّقْتَرِفْ حَسَنَةً
نَّزِدْ لَهُ فِيْهَا حُسْنًا
اِنَّ اللّٰهَ غَفُوْرٌ شَكُوْرٌ ۝

24. What! Do they say,
"He has forged a falsehood
Against Allah?" But if Allah
Willed, He could seal up
Thy heart. And Allah
Blots out Vanity, and proves
The Truth by His Words.
For He knows well
The secrets of all hearts.

٢٤- اَمْ يَقُوْلُوْنَ افْتَرٰى عَلَى اللّٰهِ كَذِبًا
فَاِنْ يَّشَاِ اللّٰهُ يَخْتِمْ
عَلٰى قَلْبِكَ
وَيَمْحُ اللّٰهُ الْبَاطِلَ وَيُحِقُّ الْحَقَّ بِكَلِمٰتِهٖ
اِنَّهٗ عَلِيْمٌ بِذَاتِ الصُّدُوْرِ ۝

25. He is the One that accepts
Repentance from His Servants
And forgives sins:
And He knows all
That ye do.

٢٥- وَهُوَ الَّذِيْ يَقْبَلُ التَّوْبَةَ عَنْ عِبَادِهٖ
وَيَعْفُوْا عَنِ السَّيِّاٰتِ
وَيَعْلَمُ مَا تَفْعَلُوْنَ ۝

26. And He listens to
Those who believe and
Do deeds of righteousness,
And gives them increase
Of His Bounty: but
For the Unbelievers there is
A terrible Penalty.

٢٦- وَيَسْتَجِيْبُ الَّذِيْنَ اٰمَنُوْا
وَعَمِلُوا الصّٰلِحٰتِ وَيَزِيْدُهُمْ مِّنْ
فَضْلِهٖ
وَالْكٰفِرُوْنَ لَهُمْ عَذَابٌ شَدِيْدٌ ۝

27. If Allah were to enlarge
The provision for His Servants,
They would indeed transgress
Beyond all bounds
Through the earth;
But He sends (it) down
In due measure
As He pleases.
For He is with His Servants
Well-Acquainted, Watchful.

٢٧- وَلَوْ بَسَطَ اللّٰهُ الرِّزْقَ لِعِبَادِهٖ
لَبَغَوْا فِى الْاَرْضِ
وَلٰكِنْ يُّنَزِّلُ بِقَدَرٍ
مَّا يَشَاءُ
اِنَّهٗ بِعِبَادِهٖ خَبِيْرٌ بَصِيْرٌ ۝

28. He is the One that sends down
Rain (even) after (men) have

٢٨- وَهُوَ الَّذِيْ يُنَزِّلُ الْغَيْثَ مِنْ بَعْدِ

Given up all hope,
And scatters His Mercy
(Far and wide). And He
Is the Protector, Worthy
Of all Praise.

مَا قَنَطُوا
وَ يَنْشُرُ رَحْمَتَهُ ۚ
وَ هُوَ الْوَلِيُّ الْحَمِيدُ ۞

29. And among His Signs
Is the creation of
The heavens and the earth,
And the living creatures
That He has scattered
Through them: and He
Has Power to gather them
Together when He wills.

٢٩- وَ مِنْ اٰيٰتِهٖ خَلْقُ السَّمٰوٰتِ وَ الْاَرْضِ
وَ مَا بَثَّ فِيْهِمَا مِنْ دَآبَّةٍ ۚ
وَ هُوَ
عَلٰى جَمْعِهِمْ اِذَا يَشَآءُ قَدِيْرٌ ۞

SECTION 4.

30. Whatever misfortune
Happens to you, is because
Of the things your hands
Have wrought, and for many
(Of them) He grants forgiveness.

٣٠- وَ مَا اَصَابَكُمْ مِّنْ مُّصِيْبَةٍ فَبِمَا
كَسَبَتْ اَيْدِيْكُمْ
وَ يَعْفُوا عَنْ كَثِيْرٍ ۗ

31. Nor can ye frustrate (aught),
(Fleeing) through the earth;
Nor have ye, besides Allah,
Anyone to protect
Or to help.

٣١- وَ مَا اَنْتُمْ بِمُعْجِزِيْنَ فِى الْاَرْضِ ۚ
وَ مَا لَكُمْ مِّنْ دُوْنِ اللّٰهِ
مِنْ وَّلِيٍّ وَّ لَا نَصِيْرٍ ۞

32. And among His Signs
Are the ships, smooth-running
Through the ocean, (tall)
As mountains.

٣٢- وَ مِنْ اٰيٰتِهِ الْجَوَارِ
فِى الْبَحْرِ كَالْاَعْلَامِ ۚ

33. If it be His Will,
He can still the Wind:
Then would they become
Motionless on the back
Of the (ocean). Verily
In this are Signs
For everyone who patiently
Perseveres and is grateful.

٣٣- اِنْ يَّشَاْ يُسْكِنِ الرِّيْحَ
فَيَظْلَلْنَ رَوَاكِدَ عَلٰى ظَهْرِهٖ ۗ
اِنَّ فِيْ ذٰلِكَ لَاٰيٰتٍ
لِّكُلِّ صَبَّارٍ شَكُوْرٍ ۞

34. Or He can cause them
To perish because of
The (evil) which (of men)
Have earned; but much
Doth He forgive.

٣٤- اَوْ يُوْبِقْهُنَّ بِمَا كَسَبُوْا
وَ يَعْفُ عَنْ كَثِيْرٍ ۞

35. But let those know, who

٣٥- وَ يَعْلَمَ الَّذِيْنَ

Dispute about Our Signs,
That there is for them
No way of escape.

يُجَادِلُوْنَ فِيْ اٰيٰتِنَا
مَا لَهُمْ مِنْ مَّحِيْصٍ ۝

36. Whatever ye are given (here)
Is (but) a convenience
Of this Life: but that
Which is with Allah
Is better and more lasting:
(It is) for those who believe
And put their trust
In their Lord;

٣٦- فَمَآ اُوْتِيْتُمْ مِّنْ شَيْءٍ فَمَتَاعُ الْحَيٰوةِ
الدُّنْيَا ۚ وَمَا عِنْدَ اللّٰهِ خَيْرٌ وَّاَبْقٰى
لِلَّذِيْنَ اٰمَنُوْا
وَعَلٰى رَبِّهِمْ يَتَوَكَّلُوْنَ ۝

37. Those who aviod the greater
Crimes and shameful deeds,
And, when they are angry
Even then forgive;

٣٧- وَالَّذِيْنَ يَجْتَنِبُوْنَ كَبٰئِرَ الْاِثْمِ وَ
الْفَوَاحِشَ وَاِذَا مَا غَضِبُوْا هُمْ يَغْفِرُوْنَ ۝

38. Those who harken
To their Lord, and establish
Regular prayer; who (conduct)
Their affairs by mutual
                    Consultation;
Who spend out of what
We bestow on them
For Sustenance;

٣٨- وَالَّذِيْنَ اسْتَجَابُوْا لِرَبِّهِمْ وَاَقَامُوا
الصَّلٰوةَ ۚ
وَاَمْرُهُمْ شُوْرٰى بَيْنَهُمْ ۚ
وَمِمَّا رَزَقْنٰهُمْ يُنْفِقُوْنَ ۝

39. And those who, when
An oppressive wrong is inflicted
On them, (are not cowed
But) help and defend
                    themselves.

٣٩- وَالَّذِيْنَ اِذَآ اَصَابَهُمُ الْبَغْيُ
هُمْ يَنْتَصِرُوْنَ ۝

40. The recompense for an injury
Is an injury equal thereto
(In degree): but if a person
Forgives and makes reconciliation,
His reward is due
From Allah: for (Allah)
Loveth not those who
Do wrong.

٤٠- وَجَزٰٓؤُا سَيِّئَةٍ سَيِّئَةٌ مِّثْلُهَا ۚ
فَمَنْ عَفَا وَاَصْلَحَ
فَاَجْرُهٗ عَلَى اللّٰهِ ۚ
اِنَّهٗ لَا يُحِبُّ الظّٰلِمِيْنَ ۝

41. But indeed if any do help
And defend themselves
After a wrong (done)
To them, against such
There is no cause
Of blame.

٤١- وَلَمَنِ انْتَصَرَ بَعْدَ ظُلْمِهٖ
فَاُولٰٓئِكَ مَا عَلَيْهِمْ
مِّنْ سَبِيْلٍ ۚ

42. The blame is only
Against those who oppress
Men with wrongdoing
And insolently transgress
Beyond bounds through the land,
Defying right and justice:
For such there will be
A Penalty grievous.

٤٢- اِنَّمَا السَّبِيلُ عَلَى الَّذِيْنَ يَظْلِمُوْنَ النَّاسَ وَيَبْغُوْنَ فِى الْاَرْضِ بِغَيْرِ الْحَقِّ ؕ اُولٰٓئِكَ لَهُمْ عَذَابٌ اَلِيْمٌ ۞

43. But indeed if any
Show patience and forgive,
That would truly be
An exercise of courageous will
And resolution in the conduct
Of affairs.

٤٣- وَلَمَنْ صَبَرَ وَغَفَرَ اِنَّ ذٰلِكَ لَمِنْ عَزْمِ الْاُمُوْرِ ۞

SECTION 5.

44. For any whom Allah
Leaves astray, there is
No protector thereafter.
And thou wilt see
The wrongdoers, when
In sight of the Penalty,
Say: "Is there any way
(To effect) a return?"

٤٤- وَمَنْ يُّضْلِلِ اللّٰهُ فَمَا لَهٗ مِنْ وَّلِيٍّ مِّنْ بَعْدِهٖ ؕ وَتَرَى الظّٰلِمِيْنَ لَمَّا رَاَوُا الْعَذَابَ يَقُوْلُوْنَ هَلْ اِلٰى مَرَدٍّ مِّنْ سَبِيْلٍ ۞

45. And thou wilt see them
Brought forward to the (Penalty),
In a humble frame of mind
Because of (their) disgrace,
(And) looking with a stealthy
Glance. And the Believers
Will say: "Those are indeed
In loss who have given
To perdition their own selves
And those belonging to them
On the Day of Judgement.
Behold! Truly the wrongdoers
Are in a lasting Penalty!"

٤٥- وَتَرٰىهُمْ يُعْرَضُوْنَ عَلَيْهَا خٰشِعِيْنَ مِنَ الذُّلِّ يَنْظُرُوْنَ مِنْ طَرْفٍ خَفِيٍّ ؕ وَقَالَ الَّذِيْنَ اٰمَنُوْۤا اِنَّ الْخٰسِرِيْنَ الَّذِيْنَ خَسِرُوْۤا اَنْفُسَهُمْ وَاَهْلِيْهِمْ يَوْمَ الْقِيٰمَةِ ؕ اَلَاۤ اِنَّ الظّٰلِمِيْنَ فِيْ عَذَابٍ مُّقِيْمٍ ۞

46. And no protectors have they
To help them,
Other than Allah.
And for any whom Allah
Leaves to stray, there is
No way (to the Goal).

٤٦- وَمَا كَانَ لَهُمْ مِّنْ اَوْلِيَآءَ يَنْصُرُوْنَهُمْ مِّنْ دُوْنِ اللّٰهِ ؕ وَمَنْ يُّضْلِلِ اللّٰهُ فَمَا لَهٗ مِنْ سَبِيْلٍ ۞

47. Hearken ye to your Lord,
Before there come a Day

٤٧- اِسْتَجِيْبُوْا لِرَبِّكُمْ مِّنْ قَبْلِ

Which there will be
No putting back, because
Of (the ordainment of) Allah!
That Day there will be
For you no place of refuge
Nor will there be for you
Any room for denial
(Of your sins)!

اَنْ يَّأْتِىَ يَوْمٌ لَّا مَرَدَّ لَهٗ
مِنَ اللّٰهِ ؕ
مَا لَكُمْ مِّنْ مَّلْجَاٍ يَّوْمَئِذٍ
وَّمَا لَكُمْ مِّنْ نَّكِيْرٍ ۝

48. If then they turn away,
We have not sent thee
As a guard over them.
Thy duty is but to convey
(The Message). And truly,
When We give man
A taste of a Mercy
From ourselves, he doth
Exult thereat, but
When some ill happens
To him, on account
Of the deeds which
His hands have sent forth,
Truly then is man ungrateful!

۴۸۔ فَاِنْ اَعْرَضُوْا فَمَا اَرْسَلْنٰكَ عَلَيْهِمْ
حَفِيْظًا ؕ اِنْ عَلَيْكَ اِلَّا الْبَلٰغُ ؕ
وَاِنَّا اِذَآ اَذَقْنَا الْاِنْسَانَ مِنَّا رَحْمَةً
فَرِحَ بِهَا ۚ
وَاِنْ تُصِبْهُمْ سَيِّئَةٌ ۢ
بِمَا قَدَّمَتْ اَيْدِيْهِمْ
فَاِنَّ الْاِنْسَانَ كَفُوْرٌ ۝

49. To Allah belongs the dominion
Of the heavens and the earth.
He creates what He wills
(And plans). He bestows
(Children) male or female
According to His Will (and Plan),

۴۹۔ لِلّٰهِ مُلْكُ السَّمٰوٰتِ وَالْاَرْضِ ؕ
يَخْلُقُ مَا يَشَآءُ ؕ يَهَبُ لِمَنْ يَّشَآءُ اِنَاثًا
وَّيَهَبُ لِمَنْ يَّشَآءُ الذُّكُوْرَ ۝

50. Or He bestows both males
And females, and He leaves
Barren whom He will:
For He is full
Of knowledge and power.

۵۰۔ اَوْ يُزَوِّجُهُمْ ذُكْرَانًا وَّاِنَاثًا ۚ
وَيَجْعَلُ مَنْ يَّشَآءُ عَقِيْمًا ؕ
اِنَّهٗ عَلِيْمٌ قَدِيْرٌ ۝

51. It is not fitting
For a man that Allah
Should speak to him
Except by inspiration,
Or from behind a veil,
Or by the sending
Of a Messenger
To reveal, with Allah's permission,
What Allah wills: for He
Is Most High, Most Wise.

۵۱۔ وَمَا كَانَ لِبَشَرٍ
اَنْ يُّكَلِّمَهُ اللّٰهُ اِلَّا وَحْيًا
اَوْ مِنْ وَّرَآئِ حِجَابٍ اَوْ يُرْسِلَ رَسُوْلًا
فَيُوْحِىَ بِاِذْنِهٖ مَا يَشَآءُ ؕ
اِنَّهٗ عَلِيٌّ حَكِيْمٌ ۝

52. And thus have We,
By Our command, sent
Inspiration to thee:
Thou knewest not (before)
What was Revelation, and
What was Faith; but We
Have made the (Qur'ān)
A Light, wherewith We
Guide such of Our servants
As We will; and verily
Thou dost guide (men)
To the Straight Way—

٥٢ - وَكَذٰلِكَ اَوْحَيْنَاۤ اِلَيْكَ
رُوْحًا مِّنْ اَمْرِنَا ؕ مَا كُنْتَ تَدْرِىْ
مَا الْكِتٰبُ وَلَا الْاِيْمَانُ
وَلٰكِنْ جَعَلْنٰهُ نُوْرًا
نَّهْدِىْ بِهٖ مَنْ نَّشَآءُ مِنْ عِبَادِنَا ؕ
وَاِنَّكَ لَتَهْدِىْۤ اِلٰى صِرَاطٍ مُّسْتَقِيْمٍ ۙ

53. The Way of Allah,
To Whom belongs
Whatever is in the heavens
And whatever is on earth.
Behold (how) all affairs
Tend towards Allah!

٥٣ - صِرَاطِ اللّٰهِ الَّذِىْ
لَهٗ مَا فِى السَّمٰوٰتِ وَمَا فِى الْاَرْضِ ؕ
اَلَاۤ اِلَى اللّٰهِ تَصِيْرُ الْاُمُوْرُ ۟

INTRODUCTION TO SŪRA XLIII. (*Zukhruf*) — 89 Verses

This is the fourth Sūra of the *Ḥā-Mīm* series of seven Sūras. For their chronology and general theme see the Introduction to *S. xl.*

This Sūra deals with the contrast between the real glory of Truth and Revelation and the false glitter of what people like to believe and worship. It cites the examples of Abraham, Moses and Jesus, as exposing the False and holding up the Truth. The key-word *Zukhruf* (Gold Adornments) occurs in verse 38, but the idea occurs all through the Sūra.

Al Zukhruf (The Gold Adornments)

In the name of Allah, Most Gracious,
Most Merciful.

بِسْمِ اللهِ الرَّحْمٰنِ الرَّحِيمِ

1. Ḥā Mīm.

١- حٰمٓ ۚ

2. By the Book that
Makes things clear—

٢- وَالْكِتٰبِ الْمُبِيْنِ ۙ

3. We have made it
A Qur'ān in Arabic,
That ye may be able
To understand (and learn
wisdom).

٣- اِنَّا جَعَلْنٰهُ قُرْءٰنًا عَرَبِيًّا لَّعَلَّكُمْ تَعْقِلُوْنَ ۚ

4. And verily, it is
In the Mother of the Book,
In Our Presence, high
(In dignity), full of wisdom.

٤- وَاِنَّهٗ فِيْٓ اُمِّ الْكِتٰبِ لَدَيْنَا لَعَلِيٌّ حَكِيْمٌ ۚ

5. Shall We then
Take away the Message
From you and repel (you),
For that ye are a people
Transgressing beyond bounds?

٥- اَفَنَضْرِبُ عَنْكُمُ الذِّكْرَ صَفْحًا اَنْ كُنْتُمْ قَوْمًا مُّسْرِفِيْنَ ۚ

6. But how many were
The prophets We sent
Amongst the peoples of old?

٦- وَكَمْ اَرْسَلْنَا مِنْ نَّبِيٍّ فِى الْاَوَّلِيْنَ ۚ

7. And never came there
A prophet to them
But they mocked him.

٧- وَمَا يَأْتِيْهِمْ مِّنْ نَّبِيٍّ اِلَّا كَانُوْا بِهٖ يَسْتَهْزِءُوْنَ ۚ

8. So We destroyed (them)—

٨- فَاَهْلَكْنَآ اَشَدَّ مِنْهُمْ بَطْشًا

Stronger in power than these—
And (thus) has passed on
The Parable of the peoples
Of old.

وَمَضٰى مَثَلُ الْاَوَّلِيْنَ ۟

9. If thou wert
To question them, 'Who created
The heavens and the earth?'
They would be sure to reply,
'They were created by (Him),
The Exalted in Power,
Full of Knowledge'—

٩- وَلَئِنْ سَاَلْتَهُمْ مَّنْ خَلَقَ السَّمٰوٰتِ وَالْاَرْضَ لَيَقُوْلُنَّ خَلَقَهُنَّ الْعَزِيْزُ الْعَلِيْمُ ۟

10. (Yea, the same that)
Has made for you
The earth (like a carpet)
Spread out, and has made
For you roads (and channels)
Therein, in order that ye
May find guidance (on the way);

١٠- الَّذِيْ جَعَلَ لَكُمُ الْاَرْضَ مَهْدًا وَّجَعَلَ لَكُمْ فِيْهَا سُبُلًا لَّعَلَّكُمْ تَهْتَدُوْنَ ۟

11. That sends down
(From time to time)
Rain from the sky
In due measure—
And We raise to life
Therewith a land that is
Dead; even so will ye
Be raised (from the dead)—

١١- وَالَّذِيْ نَزَّلَ مِنَ السَّمَاءِ مَآءً بِقَدَرٍ ۚ فَاَنْشَرْنَا بِهٖ بَلْدَةً مَّيْتًا ۚ كَذٰلِكَ تُخْرَجُوْنَ ۟

12. That has created pairs
In all things, and has made
For you ships and cattle
On which ye ride,

١٢- وَالَّذِيْ خَلَقَ الْاَزْوَاجَ كُلَّهَا وَجَعَلَ لَكُمْ مِّنَ الْفُلْكِ وَالْاَنْعَامِ مَا تَرْكَبُوْنَ ۟

13. In order that ye may
Sit firm and square
On their backs, and when
So seated, ye may
Celebrate the (kind) favour
Of your Lord, and say,
"Glory to Him Who
Has subjected these
To our (use), for we
Could never have accomplished
This (by ourselves)".

١٣- لِتَسْتَوٗا عَلٰى ظُهُوْرِهٖ ثُمَّ تَذْكُرُوْا نِعْمَةَ رَبِّكُمْ اِذَا اسْتَوَيْتُمْ عَلَيْهِ وَتَقُوْلُوْا سُبْحٰنَ الَّذِيْ سَخَّرَ لَنَا هٰذَا وَمَا كُنَّا لَهٗ مُقْرِنِيْنَ ۟

14. "And to our Lord, surely,
Must we turn back!"

١٤- وَاِنَّآ اِلٰى رَبِّنَا لَمُنْقَلِبُوْنَ ۟

15. Yet they attribute
To some of His servants
A share with Him
(In His godhead)!
Truly is man a blasphemous
Ingrate avowed!

SECTION 2.

16. What! Has He taken
Daughters out of what He
Himself creates, and granted
To you sons for choice?

17. When news is brought
To one of them of (the birth
Of) what he sets up
As a likeness to (Allah)
Most Gracious, his face
Darkens, and he is filled
With inward grief!

18. Is then one brought up
Among trinkets, and unable
To give a clear account
In a dispute (to be
Associated with Allah)?

19. And they make into females
Angels who themselves serve
Allah. Did they witness
Their creation? Their evidence
Will be recorded, and they
Will be called to account!

20. ("Ah!") they say, "If
It had been the Will
Of (Allah) Most Gracious,
We should not have
Worshipped such (deities)!"
Of that they have
No knowledge! they
Do nothing but lie!

21. What! have We given them
A Book before this,
To which they are
Holding fast?

22. Nay! they say: "We found

١٥- وَجَعَلُوْا لَهُ مِنْ عِبَادِهٖ جُزْءًا ۚ
اِنَّ الْاِنْسَانَ
لَكَفُوْرٌ مُّبِيْنٌ ۞

١٦- اَمِ اتَّخَذَ مِمَّا يَخْلُقُ بَنٰتٍ
وَّاَصْفٰكُمْ بِالْبَنِيْنَ ۞

١٧- وَاِذَا بُشِّرَ اَحَدُهُمْ
بِمَا ضَرَبَ لِلرَّحْمٰنِ مَثَلًا
ظَلَّ وَجْهُهٗ مُسْوَدًّا
وَّهُوَ كَظِيْمٌ ۞

١٨- اَوَمَنْ يُّنَشَّؤُا فِي الْحِلْيَةِ
وَهُوَ فِي الْخِصَامِ
غَيْرُ مُبِيْنٍ ۞

١٩- وَجَعَلُوا الْمَلٰٓئِكَةَ الَّذِيْنَ هُمْ عِبٰدُ الرَّحْمٰنِ
اِنَاثًا ۚ اَشَهِدُوْا خَلْقَهُمْ ۗ
سَتُكْتَبُ شَهَادَتُهُمْ وَيُسْئَلُوْنَ ۞

٢٠- وَقَالُوْا لَوْ شَاءَ الرَّحْمٰنُ
مَا عَبَدْنٰهُمْ ؕ
مَا لَهُمْ بِذٰلِكَ مِنْ عِلْمٍ ۗ
اِنْ هُمْ اِلَّا يَخْرُصُوْنَ ۞

٢١- اَمْ اٰتَيْنٰهُمْ كِتٰبًا مِّنْ قَبْلِهٖ
فَهُمْ بِهٖ مُسْتَمْسِكُوْنَ ۞

٢٢- بَلْ قَالُوْٓا اِنَّا وَجَدْنَآ

Our fathers following
A certain religion,
And we do guide ourselves
By their footsteps."

ابَآءَنَا عَلَى اُمَّةٍ
وَّ اِنَّا عَلَى اٰثٰرِهِمْ مُّهْتَدُوْنَ ۟

23. Just in the same way,
Whenever We sent a Warner
Before thee to any people,
The wealthy ones among
            them
Said: "We found our fathers
Following a certain religion,
And we will certainly
Follow in their footsteps."

٢٣- وَكَذٰلِكَ مَآ اَرْسَلْنَا مِنْ قَبْلِكَ فِىْ
قَرْيَةٍ مِّنْ نَّذِيْرٍ اِلَّا قَالَ مُتْرَفُوْهَآ ۖ
اِنَّا وَجَدْنَآ اٰبَآءَنَا عَلٰٓى اُمَّةٍ
وَّ اِنَّا عَلٰٓى اٰثٰرِهِمْ مُّقْتَدُوْنَ ۟

24. He said: "What!
Even if I brought you
Better guidance than that
Which ye found
Your fathers following?"
They said: "For us,
We deny that ye (prophets)
Are sent (on a mission
At all)."

٢٤- قٰلَ اَوَلَوْ جِئْتُكُمْ بِاَهْدٰى
مِمَّا وَجَدْتُّمْ عَلَيْهِ اٰبَآءَكُمْ ۭ
قَالُوْٓا اِنَّا
بِمَآ اُرْسِلْتُمْ بِهٖ
كٰفِرُوْنَ ۟

25. So We extracted retribution
From them: now see
What was the end
Of those who rejected (Truth)!

٢٥- فَانْتَقَمْنَا مِنْهُمْ فَانْظُرْ
كَيْفَ كَانَ عَاقِبَةُ الْمُكَذِّبِيْنَ ۧ

SECTION 3.

26. Behold! Abraham said
To his father and his people:
"I do indeed clear myself
Of what ye worship:"

٢٦- وَاِذْ قَالَ اِبْرٰهِيْمُ لِاَبِيْهِ وَقَوْمِهٖٓ
اِنَّنِىْ بَرَآءٌ مِّمَّا تَعْبُدُوْنَ ۟

27. "(I worship) only Him
Who made me, and He
Will certainly guide me."

٢٧- اِلَّا الَّذِىْ فَطَرَنِىْ
فَاِنَّهٗ سَيَهْدِيْنِ ۟

28. And he left it
As a Word
To endure among those
Who came after him,
That they may turn back
(To Allah).

٢٨- وَجَعَلَهَا كَلِمَةً
بَاقِيَةً فِىْ عَقِبِهٖ
لَعَلَّهُمْ يَرْجِعُوْنَ ۟

29. Yea, I have given
The good things of this life

٢٩- بَلْ مَتَّعْتُ هٰٓؤُلَآءِ

To these (men) and
Their fathers, until the Truth
Has come to them,
And a Messenger
Making things clear.

وَاٰبَآءَهُمْ حَتّٰى جَآءَهُمُ الْحَقُّ
وَرَسُوْلٌ مُّبِيْنٌ ۟

30. But when the Truth came
To them, they said:
"This is sorcery, and we
Do reject it."

٣٠- وَلَمَّا جَآءَهُمُ الْحَقُّ قَالُوْا
هٰذَا سِحْرٌ وَّ اِنَّا بِهٖ كٰفِرُوْنَ ۟

31. Also, they say: "Why
Is not this Qur'ān sent
Down to some leading man
In either of the two
(Chief) cities?"

٣١- وَقَالُوْا لَوْلَا نُزِّلَ هٰذَا الْقُرْاٰنُ
عَلٰى رَجُلٍ مِّنَ الْقَرْيَتَيْنِ
عَظِيْمٍ ۟

32. Is it they who would portion out
The Mercy of thy Lord?
It is We Who portion out
Between them their livelihood
In the life of this world:
And We raise some of them
Above others in ranks,
So that some may command
Work from others.
But the Mercy of thy Lord
Is better than the (wealth)
Which they amass.

٣٢- اَهُمْ يَقْسِمُوْنَ رَحْمَتَ رَبِّكَ ؕ
نَحْنُ قَسَمْنَا بَيْنَهُمْ مَّعِيْشَتَهُمْ
فِى الْحَيٰوةِ الدُّنْيَا
وَرَفَعْنَا بَعْضَهُمْ فَوْقَ بَعْضٍ دَرَجٰتٍ
لِّيَتَّخِذَ بَعْضُهُمْ بَعْضًا سُخْرِيًّا ؕ
وَرَحْمَتُ رَبِّكَ خَيْرٌ مِّمَّا يَجْمَعُوْنَ ۟

33. And were it not that
(All) men might become
Of one (evil) way of life,
We would provide,
For everyone that blasphemes
Against (Allah) Most Gracious,
Silver roofs for their houses,
And (silver) stairways
On which to go up,

٣٣- وَلَوْلَا اَنْ يَّكُوْنَ النَّاسُ
اُمَّةً وَّاحِدَةً
لَّجَعَلْنَا لِمَنْ يَّكْفُرُ بِالرَّحْمٰنِ
لِبُيُوْتِهِمْ سُقُفًا مِّنْ فِضَّةٍ
وَّمَعَارِجَ عَلَيْهَا يَظْهَرُوْنَ ۟

34. And (silver) doors
To their houses, and thrones
(Of silver) on which
They could recline,

٣٤- وَلِبُيُوْتِهِمْ اَبْوَابًا وَّسُرُرًا
عَلَيْهَا يَتَّكِئُوْنَ ۟

35. And also adornments
Of gold. But all this
Were nothing but conveniences
Of the present life:

٣٥- وَزُخْرُفًا ؕ وَاِنْ كُلُّ ذٰلِكَ
لَمَّا مَتَاعُ الْحَيٰوةِ الدُّنْيَا ؕ

The Hereafter, in the sight
Of thy Lord, is
For the Righteous.

SECTION 4.

وَالْأَخِرَةُ عِنْدَ رَبِّكَ لِلْمُتَّقِيْنَ ۞

36. **I**f anyone withdraws himself
From remembrance
Of (Allah) Most Gracious,
We appoint for him
An evil one, to be
An intimate companion to him.

٣٦- وَمَنْ يَعْشُ عَنْ ذِكْرِ
الرَّحْمٰنِ نُقَيِّضْ لَهُ
شَيْطٰنًا فَهُوَ لَهُ قَرِيْنٌ ۞

37. Such (evil ones) really
Hinder them from the Path,
But they think that they
Are being guided aright!

٣٧- وَإِنَّهُمْ لَيَصُدُّوْنَهُمْ عَنِ السَّبِيْلِ
وَيَحْسَبُوْنَ أَنَّهُمْ مُّهْتَدُوْنَ ۞

38. At length, when (such a one)
Comes to Us, he says
(To his evil companion):
"Would that between me
And thee were the distance
Of East and West!"   Ah!
Evil is the companion (indeed)!

٣٨- حَتّٰى إِذَا جَاءَنَا قَالَ
يٰلَيْتَ بَيْنِيْ وَبَيْنَكَ بُعْدَ الْمَشْرِقَيْنِ
فَبِئْسَ الْقَرِيْنُ ۞

39. When ye have done wrong,
It will avail you nothing,
That day, that ye shall be
Partners in punishment!

٣٩- وَلَنْ يَّنْفَعَكُمُ الْيَوْمَ إِذْ ظَّلَمْتُمْ
أَنَّكُمْ فِى الْعَذَابِ مُشْتَرِكُوْنَ ۞

40. **C**anst thou then make
The deaf to hear, or give
Direction to the blind
Or to such as (wander)
In manifest error?

٤٠- أَفَأَنْتَ تُسْمِعُ الصُّمَّ
أَوْ تَهْدِى الْعُمْىَ
وَمَنْ كَانَ فِىْ ضَلٰلٍ مُّبِيْنٍ ۞

41. Even if We take thee
Away, We shall be sure
To exact retribution from them,

٤١- فَإِمَّا نَذْهَبَنَّ بِكَ
فَإِنَّا مِنْهُمْ مُّنْتَقِمُوْنَ ۞

42. Or We shall show thee
That (accomplished) which We
Have promised them:
For verily We shall
Prevail over them.

٤٢- أَوْ نُرِيَنَّكَ الَّذِىْ وَعَدْنٰهُمْ
فَإِنَّا عَلَيْهِمْ مُّقْتَدِرُوْنَ ۞

43. So hold thou fast
To the Revelation sent down

٤٣- فَاسْتَمْسِكْ بِالَّذِىْ أُوْحِىَ إِلَيْكَ

To thee: verily thou
Art on a Straight Way.

اِنَّكَ عَلٰى صِرَاطٍ مُّسْتَقِيمٍ ۟

44. The (Qur'an) is indeed
The Message,   for thee
And for thy people;
And soon shall ye
(All) be brought to account.

وَاِنَّهٗ لَذِكْرٌ لَّكَ وَلِقَوْمِكَ ۚ
وَسَوْفَ تُسْئَلُوْنَ ۟

45. And question thou our
                            messengers
Whom We sent before thee;
Did We appoint any deities
Other than (Allah) Most Gracious,
To be worshipped?

وَسْئَلْ مَنْ اَرْسَلْنَا مِنْ قَبْلِكَ مِنْ
رُّسُلِنَآ اَجَعَلْنَا مِنْ دُوْنِ الرَّحْمٰنِ اٰلِهَةً
يُّعْبَدُوْنَ ۟

SECTION 5.

46. We did send Moses
Aforetime, with Our Signs,
To Pharaoh and his Chiefs:
He said, "I am a messenger
Of the Lord of the Worlds."

وَلَقَدْ اَرْسَلْنَا مُوْسٰى بِاٰيٰتِنَآ
اِلٰى فِرْعَوْنَ وَمَلَائِهٖ
فَقَالَ اِنِّيْ رَسُوْلُ رَبِّ الْعٰلَمِيْنَ ۟

47. But when he came to them
With Our Signs, behold,
They ridiculed them.

فَلَمَّا جَآءَهُمْ
بِاٰيٰتِنَآ اِذَا هُمْ مِّنْهَا يَضْحَكُوْنَ ۟

48. We showed them Sign
After Sign, each greater
Than its fellow, and We
Seized them with Punishment,
In order that they
Might turn (to Us).

وَمَا نُرِيْهِمْ مِّنْ اٰيَةٍ
اِلَّا هِيَ اَكْبَرُ مِنْ اُخْتِهَا ۖ
وَاَخَذْنٰهُمْ بِالْعَذَابِ لَعَلَّهُمْ يَرْجِعُوْنَ ۟

49. And they said, "O thou
Sorcerer! Invoke thy Lord
For us according to
His covenant with thee;
For we shall truly
Accept guidance."

وَقَالُوْا يٰٓاَيُّهَ السّٰحِرُ ادْعُ لَنَا رَبَّكَ
بِمَا عَهِدَ عِنْدَكَ ۚ
اِنَّنَا لَمُهْتَدُوْنَ ۟

50. But when We removed
The Penalty from them,
Behold, they broke their word.

فَلَمَّا كَشَفْنَا عَنْهُمُ الْعَذَابَ
اِذَا هُمْ يَنْكُثُوْنَ ۟

51. And Pharaoh proclaimed
Among his people, saying:
"O my people! Does not
The dominion of Egypt

وَنَادٰى فِرْعَوْنُ فِيْ قَوْمِهٖ قَالَ
يٰقَوْمِ اَلَيْسَ لِيْ مُلْكُ مِصْرَ

Belong to me, (witness)
These streams flowing
Underneath my (palace)? What!
See ye not then?

وَهٰذِهِ الْاَنْهٰرُ تَجْرِىْ مِنْ تَحْتِىْ ۚ
اَفَلَا تُبْصِرُوْنَ ۝

52. "Am I not better
Than this (Moses), who
Is a contemptible wretch
And can scarcely
Express himself clearly?

٥٢- اَمْ اَنَا خَيْرٌ مِّنْ هٰذَا الَّذِىْ
هُوَ مَهِيْنٌ ۙ
وَّلَا يَكَادُ يُبِيْنُ ۝

53. "Then why are not
Gold bracelets bestowed
On him, or (why)
Come (not) with him
Angels accompanying him
In procession?"

٥٣- فَلَوْلَا اُلْقِىَ عَلَيْهِ اَسْوِرَةٌ مِّنْ ذَهَبٍ
اَوْ جَآءَ مَعَهُ الْمَلٰٓئِكَةُ
مُقْتَرِنِيْنَ ۝

54. Thus did he make
Fools of his people,
And they obeyed him:
Truly were they a people
Rebellious (against Allah).

٥٤- فَاسْتَخَفَّ قَوْمَهٗ
فَاَطَاعُوْهُ ۚ
اِنَّهُمْ كَانُوْا قَوْمًا فٰسِقِيْنَ ۝

55. When at length they
Provoked Us, We exacted
Retribution from them, and
We drowned them all.

٥٥- فَلَمَّا اٰسَفُوْنَا انْتَقَمْنَا مِنْهُمْ
فَاَغْرَقْنٰهُمْ اَجْمَعِيْنَ ۙ

56. And We made them
(A people) of the Past
And an Example
To later ages.

SECTION 6.

٥٦- فَجَعَلْنٰهُمْ سَلَفًا
وَّمَثَلًا لِّلْاٰخِرِيْنَ ۝ ع

57. When (Jesus) the son
Of Mary is held up
As an example, behold
Thy people raise a clamour
Thereat (in ridicule)!

٥٧- وَلَمَّا ضُرِبَ ابْنُ مَرْيَمَ مَثَلًا
اِذَا قَوْمُكَ مِنْهُ يَصِدُّوْنَ ۝

58. And they say, "Are
Our gods best, or he?"
This they set forth
To thee, only by way
Of disputation: yea, they
Are a contentious people.

٥٨- وَقَالُوْٓا ءَاٰلِهَتُنَا خَيْرٌ اَمْ هُوَ ۚ
مَا ضَرَبُوْهُ لَكَ
اِلَّا جَدَلًا ۚ بَلْ هُمْ قَوْمٌ خَصِمُوْنَ ۝

59. He was no more than

٥٩- اِنْ هُوَ اِلَّا عَبْدٌ

A servant: We granted
Our favour to him,
And We made him
An example to the Children
Of Israel.

اَنْعَمْنَا عَلَيْهِ
وَجَعَلْنَاهُ مَثَلًا لِّبَنِيِّ اِسْرَآءِيْلَ ۞

60. And if it were Our Will,
We could make angels
From amongst you, succeeding
Each other on the earth.

٦٠۔ وَلَوْ نَشَآءُ لَجَعَلْنَا مِنْكُمْ مَّلٰئِكَةً
فِي الْاَرْضِ يَخْلُفُوْنَ ۞

61. And (Jesus) shall be
A Sign (for the coming
Of) the Hour (of Judgement):
Therefore have no doubt
About the (Hour), but
Follow ye Me: this
Is a Straight Way.

٦١۔ وَاِنَّهٗ لَعِلْمٌ لِّلسَّاعَةِ
فَلَا تَمْتَرُنَّ بِهَا وَاتَّبِعُوْنِ ۚ
هٰذَا صِرَاطٌ مُّسْتَقِيْمٌ ۞

62. Let not the Evil One
Hinder you: for he is
To you an enemy avowed.

٦٢۔ وَلَا يَصُدَّنَّكُمُ الشَّيْطٰنُ ۚ
اِنَّهٗ لَكُمْ عَدُوٌّ مُّبِيْنٌ ۞

63. When Jesus came
With Clear Signs, he said:
"Now have I come
To you with Wisdom,
And in order to make
Clear to you some
Of the (points) on which
Ye dispute: therefore fear Allah
And obey me.

٦٣۔ وَلَمَّا جَآءَ عِيْسٰى بِالْبَيِّنٰتِ قَالَ
قَدْ جِئْتُكُمْ بِالْحِكْمَةِ
وَلِاُبَيِّنَ لَكُمْ بَعْضَ الَّذِيْ تَخْتَلِفُوْنَ
فِيْهِ ۚ
فَاتَّقُوا اللّٰهَ وَاَطِيْعُوْنِ ۞

64. "For Allah, He is my Lord
And your Lord: so worship
Ye Him: this is
A Straight Way."

٦٤۔ اِنَّ اللّٰهَ هُوَ رَبِّيْ وَرَبُّكُمْ فَاعْبُدُوْهُ ۚ
هٰذَا صِرَاطٌ مُّسْتَقِيْمٌ ۞

65. But sects from among
Themselves fell into disagreement:
Then woe to the wrongdoers,
From the Penalty
Of a Grievous Day!

٦٥۔ فَاخْتَلَفَ الْاَحْزَابُ مِنْ بَيْنِهِمْ ۚ
فَوَيْلٌ لِّلَّذِيْنَ ظَلَمُوْا
مِنْ عَذَابِ يَوْمٍ اَلِيْمٍ ۞

66. Do they only wait
For the Hour—that it
Should come on them
All of a sudden,
While they perceive not?

٦٦۔ هَلْ يَنْظُرُوْنَ اِلَّا السَّاعَةَ
اَنْ تَأْتِيَهُمْ بَغْتَةً
وَّهُمْ لَا يَشْعُرُوْنَ ۞

67. Friends on that Day
Will be foes, one
To another—except
The Righteous.

SECTION 7.

68. My devotees!
No fear shall be
On you that Day,
Nor shall ye grieve—

69. (Being) those who have believed
In Our Signs and bowed
(Their wills to Ours) in Islam.

70. Enter ye the Garden,
Ye and your wives,
In (beauty and) rejoicing.

71. To them will be passed
Round, dishes and goblets
Of gold: there will be
There all that the souls
Could desire, all that
The eyes could delight in:
And ye shall abide
Therein (for aye).

72. Such will be the Garden
Of which ye are made
Heirs for your (good) deeds
(In life).

73. Ye shall have therein
Abundance of fruit,   from
                 which
Ye shall have satisfaction.

74. The sinners will be
In the Punishment of Hell,
To dwell therein (for aye):

75. Nowise will the (punishment)
Be lightened for them,
And in despair will they
Be there overwhelmed.

76. Nowise shall We
Be unjust to them:

But it is they who
Have been unjust themselves.

وَلٰكِنْ كَانُوْا هُمُ الظَّالِمِيْنَ ○

77. They will cry: "O Mālik!
Would that thy Lord
Put an end to us!"
He will say, "Nay, but
Ye shall abide!"

٧٧- وَنَادَوْا يٰمٰلِكُ
لِيَقْضِ عَلَيْنَا رَبُّكَ ۚ
قَالَ اِنَّكُمْ مَّاكِثُوْنَ ○

78. Verily We have brought
The Truth to you:
But most of you
Have a hatred for Truth.

٧٨- لَقَدْ جِئْنٰكُمْ بِالْحَقِّ
وَلٰكِنَّ اَكْثَرَكُمْ لِلْحَقِّ كَارِهُوْنَ ○

79. What! Have they settled
Some Plan (among themselves)?
But it is We Who
Settle things.

٧٩- اَمْ اَبْرَمُوْٓا اَمْرًا
فَاِنَّا مُبْرِمُوْنَ ۚ

80. Or do they think
That We hear not
Their secrets and their
Private counsels? Indeed
(We do), and Our Messengers
Are by them, to record.

٨٠- اَمْ يَحْسَبُوْنَ اَنَّا لَا نَسْمَعُ
سِرَّهُمْ وَ نَجْوٰىهُمْ ۚ
بَلٰى وَ رُسُلُنَا لَدَيْهِمْ يَكْتُبُوْنَ ○

81. Say: "If (Allah) Most Gracious
Had a son, I would
Be the first to worship."

٨١- قُلْ اِنْ كَانَ لِلرَّحْمٰنِ وَلَدٌ ۖ
فَاَنَا اَوَّلُ الْعٰبِدِيْنَ ○

82. Glory to the Lord
Of the heavens and the earth,
The Lord of the Throne
(Of Authority)! (He is
Free) from the things
They attribute (to Him)!

٨٢- سُبْحٰنَ رَبِّ السَّمٰوٰتِ وَالْاَرْضِ
رَبِّ الْعَرْشِ
عَمَّا يَصِفُوْنَ ○

83. So leave them to babble
And play (with vanities)
Until they meet that Day
Of theirs, which they
Have been promised.

٨٣- فَذَرْهُمْ يَخُوْضُوْا وَيَلْعَبُوْا
حَتّٰى يُلٰقُوْا يَوْمَهُمُ الَّذِيْ
يُوْعَدُوْنَ ○

84. It is He Who is God
In heaven and God on earth;
And He is Full
Of Wisdom and Knowledge.

٨٤- وَهُوَ الَّذِيْ فِى السَّمَآءِ اِلٰهٌ وَّ فِى الْاَرْضِ
اِلٰهٌ ۚ وَهُوَ الْحَكِيْمُ الْعَلِيْمُ ○

85. And blessed is He
To Whom belongs the dominion
Of the heavens and the earth,
And all between them:
With Him is the knowledge
Of the Hour (of Judgement):
And to Him shall ye
Be brought back.

٨٥- وَتَبَارَكَ الَّذِى لَهُ مُلْكُ
السَّمٰوٰتِ وَالْأَرْضِ وَمَا بَيْنَهُمَا ۚ
وَعِنْدَهٗ عِلْمُ السَّاعَةِ ۚ
وَإِلَيْهِ تُرْجَعُوْنَ ۝

86. And those whom they invoke
Besides Allah have no power
Of intercession—only he
Who bears witness to the Truth,
And they know (him).

٨٦- وَلَا يَمْلِكُ الَّذِينَ يَدْعُوْنَ مِنْ دُوْنِهِ
الشَّفَاعَةَ
إِلَّا مَنْ شَهِدَ بِالْحَقِّ وَهُمْ يَعْلَمُوْنَ ۝

87. If thou ask them, Who
Created them, they will
Certainly say, Allah: how
Then are they deluded
Away (from the Truth)?

٨٧- وَلَئِنْ سَأَلْتَهُمْ مَّنْ خَلَقَهُمْ
لَيَقُوْلُنَّ اللّٰهُ
فَأَنّٰى يُؤْفَكُوْنَ ۝

88. (Allah has knowledge)
Of the (Prophet's) cry,
"O my Lord! Truly
These are a people
Who will not believe!"

٨٨- وَقِيْلِهٖ يٰرَبِّ
إِنَّ هٰؤُلَاءِ قَوْمٌ لَّا يُؤْمِنُوْنَ ۝

89. But turn away from them,
And say "Peace!"⁴⁶⁸⁷
But soon shall they know!

٨٩- فَاصْفَحْ عَنْهُمْ وَقُلْ سَلٰمٌ ۚ
فَسَوْفَ يَعْلَمُوْنَ ۝

INTRODUCTION TO SŪRA XLIV. (*Al Dukhān*) — 59 Verses

For the chronology and the general theme of the Sūras of the *Ḥā-Mīm* series, of which this is the fifth, see the Introduction to S. xl.

The theme of this particular Sūra is how worldly pride and power are humbled in the dust if they resist spiritual forces, and how Evil and Good find their true setting in the Hereafter.

The title-word *Dukhān* occurs in verse 10. It means smoke or mist, and may refer to a drought or famine, as explained in the notes to that verse.

Al Dukhān (The Smoke)

In the name of Allah, Most Gracious,
Most Merciful.

1. Ḥā Mīm.

2. By the Book that
   Makes things clear—

3. We sent it down
   During a blessed night:
   For We (ever) wish
   To warn (against Evil).

4. In that (night) is made
   Distinct every affair
   Of wisdom,

5. By command, from Our
   Presence. For We (ever)
   Send (revelations),

6. As a Mercy
   From thy Lord:
   For He hears and knows
   (All things);

7. The Lord of the heavens
   And the earth and all
   Between them, if ye (but)
   Have an assured faith.

8. There is no god but He:

It is He Who gives life
And gives death—
The Lord and Cherisher
To you and your earliest
Ancestors.

يُحىِ وَيُمِيتُ
رَبُّكُمْ وَرَبُّ اٰبَآئِكُمُ الْأَوَّلِينَ ۝

9. Yet they play about
In doubt.

٩- بَلْ هُمْ فِى شَكٍّ يَلْعَبُونَ ۝

10. Then watch thou
For the Day
That the sky will
Bring forth a kind
Of smoke (or mist)
Plainly visible,

١٠- فَارْتَقِبْ
يَوْمَ تَأْتِى السَّمَآءُ بِدُخَانٍ
مُّبِينٍ ۝

11. Enveloping the people:
This will be a Penalty
Grievous.

١١- يَغْشَى النَّاسَ
هٰذَا عَذَابٌ أَلِيمٌ ۝

12. (They will say:)
"Our Lord! Remove
The Penalty from us,
For we do really believe!"

١٢- رَبَّنَا اكْشِفْ
عَنَّا الْعَذَابَ إِنَّا مُؤْمِنُونَ ۝

13. How shall the Message
Be (effectual) for them,
Seeing that a Messenger
Explaining things clearly
Has (already) come to them—

١٣- أَنّٰى لَهُمُ الذِّكْرَى
وَقَدْ جَآءَهُمْ رَسُولٌ مُّبِينٌ ۝

14. Yet they turn away
From him and say: "Tutored
(By others), a man possessed!"

١٤- ثُمَّ تَوَلَّوْا عَنْهُ
وَقَالُوا مُعَلَّمٌ مَّجْنُونٌ ۝

15. We shall indeed remove
The Penalty for a while,
(But) truly ye will revert
(To your ways).

١٥- إِنَّا كَاشِفُوا الْعَذَابِ قَلِيلًا
إِنَّكُمْ عَآئِدُونَ ۝

16. One day We shall seize
You with a mighty onslaught:
We will indeed (then)
Exact Retribution!

١٦- يَوْمَ نَبْطِشُ الْبَطْشَةَ الْكُبْرَى
إِنَّا مُنْتَقِمُونَ ۝

17. We did, before them,
Try the people of Pharoah:
There came to them

١٧- وَلَقَدْ فَتَنَّا قَبْلَهُمْ قَوْمَ فِرْعَوْنَ

A messenger most honourable,

وَجَآءَهُمْ رَسُوْلٌ كَرِيْمٌ ۙ

18. Saying: "Restore to me
The servants of Allah:
I am to you a messenger
Worthy of all trust;

١٨- اَنْ اَدُّوْٓا اِلَيَّ عِبَادَ اللّٰهِ ؕ
اِنِّيْ لَكُمْ رَسُوْلٌ اَمِيْنٌ ۙ

19. "And be not arrogant
As against Allah:
For I come to you
With authority manifest.

١٩- وَّاَنْ لَّا تَعْلُوْا عَلَى اللّٰهِ ۚ
اِنِّيْٓ اٰتِيْكُمْ بِسُلْطٰنٍ مُّبِيْنٍ ۚ

20. "For me, I have sought
Safety with my Lord
And your Lord, against
Your injuring me.

٢٠- وَاِنِّيْ عُذْتُ بِرَبِّيْ
وَرَبِّكُمْ اَنْ تَرْجُمُوْنِ ۙ

21. "If ye believe me not,
At least keep yourselves
Away from me"

٢١- وَاِنْ لَّمْ تُؤْمِنُوْا لِيْ
فَاعْتَزِلُوْنِ ۟

22. (But they were aggressive:)
Then he cried
To his Lord:
"These are indeed
A people given to sin."

٢٢- فَدَعَا رَبَّهٗٓ
اَنَّ هٰٓؤُلَآءِ قَوْمٌ مُّجْرِمُوْنَ ۟

23. (The reply came:)
"March forth with my servants
By night: for ye are
Sure to be pursued.

٢٣- فَاَسْرِ بِعِبَادِيْ لَيْلًا
اِنَّكُمْ مُّتَّبَعُوْنَ ۙ

24. "And leave the sea
As a furrow (divided):
For they are a host
(Destined) to be drowned."

٢٤- وَاتْرُكِ الْبَحْرَ رَهْوًا ؕ
اِنَّهُمْ جُنْدٌ مُّغْرَقُوْنَ ۟

25. How many were the gardens
And springs they left behind,

٢٥- كَمْ تَرَكُوْا مِنْ جَنّٰتٍ وَّعُيُوْنٍ ۙ

26. And cornfields
And noble buildings,

٢٦- وَّزُرُوْعٍ وَّمَقَامٍ كَرِيْمٍ ۙ

27. And wealth (and conveniences
Of life), wherein they
Had taken such delight!

٢٧- وَّنَعْمَةٍ كَانُوْا فِيْهَا فٰكِهِيْنَ ۙ

28. Thus (was their end)!
And We make other people
Inherit (those things)!

٢٨- كَذَٰلِكَ ۖ
وَاَوْرَثْنٰهَا قَوْمًا اٰخَرِيْنَ ۟

29. And neither heaven
Nor earth shed a tear
Over them: nor were
They given a respite (again).

٢٩- فَمَا بَكَتْ عَلَيْهِمُ السَّمَآءُ وَالْاَرْضُ
وَمَا كَانُوْا مُنْظَرِيْنَ ۟

SECTION 2.

30. We did deliver aforetime
The Children of Israel
From humiliating Punishment,

٣٠- وَلَقَدْ نَجَّيْنَا بَنِيْ اِسْرَآءِيْلَ
مِنَ الْعَذَابِ الْمُهِيْنِ ۟

31. Inflicted by Pharaoh, for he
Was arrogant (even) among
Inordinate transgressors.

٣١- مِنْ فِرْعَوْنَ ۚ
اِنَّهٗ كَانَ عَالِيًا مِّنَ الْمُسْرِفِيْنَ ۟

32. And We chose them aforetime
Above the nations, knowingly,

٣٢- وَلَقَدِ اخْتَرْنٰهُمْ عَلٰى عِلْمٍ عَلَى الْعٰلَمِيْنَ ۟

33. And granted them Signs
In which there was
A manifest trial.

٣٣- وَاٰتَيْنٰهُمْ مِّنَ الْاٰيٰتِ
مَا فِيْهِ بَلٰٓؤُا مُّبِيْنٌ ۟

34. As to these (Quraysh),
They say forsooth:

٣٤- اِنَّ هٰٓؤُلَآءِ لَيَقُوْلُوْنَ ۟

35. "There is nothing beyond
Our first death,
And we shall not
Be raised again.

٣٥- اِنْ هِيَ اِلَّا مَوْتَتُنَا الْاُوْلٰى
وَمَا نَحْنُ بِمُنْشَرِيْنَ ۟

36. "Then bring (back)
Our forefathers, if what
Ye say is true!"

٣٦- فَأْتُوْا
بِاٰبَآئِنَآ اِنْ كُنْتُمْ صٰدِقِيْنَ ۟

37. What! are they better
Than the people of Tubba'
And those who were
Before them? We destroyed
Them because they were
Guilty of sin.

٣٧- اَهُمْ خَيْرٌ اَمْ قَوْمُ تُبَّعٍ ۙ
وَّالَّذِيْنَ مِنْ قَبْلِهِمْ ۚ اَهْلَكْنٰهُمْ ۖ
اِنَّهُمْ كَانُوْا مُجْرِمِيْنَ ۟

38. We created not
The heavens, the earth,
And all between them,
Merely in (idle) sport;

٣٨- وَمَا خَلَقْنَا السَّمٰوٰتِ وَالْاَرْضَ
وَمَا بَيْنَهُمَا لٰعِبِيْنَ ۟

39. We created them not
Except for just ends:
But most of them
Do not understand.

٣٩- مَا خَلَقْنَاهُمَآ إِلَّا بِالْحَقِّ
وَلٰكِنَّ أَكْثَرَهُمْ لَا يَعْلَمُوْنَ ۟

40. Verily the Day of
Sorting Out is the time
Appointed for all of them—

٤٠- إِنَّ يَوْمَ الْفَصْلِ
مِيْقَاتُهُمْ أَجْمَعِيْنَ ۟

41. The Day when no protector
Can avail his client
In aught, and no help
Can they receive,

٤١- يَوْمَ لَا يُغْنِيْ مَوْلًى عَنْ مَوْلًى شَيْئًا
وَّلَا هُمْ يُنْصَرُوْنَ ۟

42. Except such as receive
Allah's Mercy: for He is
Exalted in Might, Most Merciful.
SECTION 3.

٤٢- إِلَّا مَنْ رَّحِمَ اللّٰهُ ۚ
إِنَّهُ هُوَ الْعَزِيْزُ الرَّحِيْمُ ۟ ؏

43. Verily the tree
Of Zaqqūm

٤٣- إِنَّ شَجَرَتَ الزَّقُّوْمِ ۙ

44. Will be the food
Of the Sinful—

٤٤- طَعَامُ الْأَثِيْمِ ۙ

45. Like molten brass;
It will boil
In their insides,

٤٥- كَالْمُهْلِ ۚ
يَغْلِيْ فِي الْبُطُوْنِ ۟ ۙ

46. Like the boiling
Of scalding water.

٤٦- كَغَلْيِ الْحَمِيْمِ ۟

47. (A voice will cry:)
"Seize ye him
And drag him
Into the midst
Of the Blazing Fire!"

٤٧- خُذُوْهُ
فَاعْتِلُوْهُ إِلٰى سَوَآءِ الْجَحِيْمِ ۟ ۙ

48. "Then pour over his head
The Penalty of Boiling Water.

٤٨- ثُمَّ صُبُّوْا فَوْقَ رَأْسِهِ مِنْ عَذَابِ الْحَمِيْمِ ۟

49. "Taste thou (this)!
Truly wast thou
Mighty, full of honour!

٤٩- ذُقْ ۚ
إِنَّكَ أَنْتَ الْعَزِيْزُ الْكَرِيْمُ ۟

50. "Truly this is what
Ye used to doubt!"

٥٠- إِنَّ هٰذَا مَا كُنْتُمْ بِهٖ تَمْتَرُوْنَ ۟

51. As to the Righteous

٥١- إِنَّ الْمُتَّقِيْنَ ۙ

(They will be) in
A position of Security.

فِىۡ مَقَامٍ اَمِيۡنٍ ۙ

52. Among Gardens and Springs;

۵۲- فِىۡ جَنّٰتٍ وَّعُيُوۡنٍ ۙ

53. Dressed in fine silk
And in rich brocade,
They will face each other;

۵۳- يَلۡبَسُوۡنَ مِنۡ سُنۡدُسٍ وَّ اِسۡتَبۡرَقٍ
مُّتَقٰبِلِيۡنَ ۚ

54. Moreover, We shall
Join them to Companions
With beautiful, big,
And lustrous eyes.

۵۴- كَذٰلِكَ ۚ وَ زَوَّجۡنٰهُمۡ
بِحُوۡرٍ عِيۡنٍ ۚ

55. There can they call
For every kind of fruit
In peace and security;

۵۵- يَدۡعُوۡنَ فِيۡهَا بِكُلِّ فَاكِهَةٍ
اٰمِنِيۡنَ ۚ

56. Nor will they there
Taste Death, except the first
Death; and He will preserve
Them from the Penalty
Of the Blazing Fire—

۵۶- لَا يَذُوۡقُوۡنَ فِيۡهَا الۡمَوۡتَ اِلَّا الۡمَوۡتَةَ
الۡاُوۡلٰى ۚ
وَوَقٰهُمۡ عَذَابَ الۡجَحِيۡمِ ۙ

57. As a Bounty from thy Lord!
That will be
The supreme achievement!

۵۷- فَضۡلًا مِّنۡ رَّبِّكَ ۚ
ذٰلِكَ هُوَ الۡفَوۡزُ الۡعَظِيۡمُ ۞

58. Verily, We have made
This (Qur'an) easy,
In thy tongue,
In order that they
May give heed.

۵۸- فَاِنَّمَا يَسَّرۡنٰهُ بِلِسَانِكَ
لَعَلَّهُمۡ يَتَذَكَّرُوۡنَ ۞

59. So wait thou and watch;
For they (too) are waiting.

۵۹- فَارۡتَقِبۡ اِنَّهُمۡ مُّرۡتَقِبُوۡنَ ۞

INTRODUCTION TO SŪRA XLV. (*Jāthīya*) — 37 Verses

This is the sixth Sūra of the *Hā-Mīm* series: for their general theme and chronology, see the Introduction to S. xl.

Al Jāthiyah (The Kneeling Down)

In the name of Allah, Most Gracious,
Most Merciful.

بِسْمِ اللهِ الرَّحْمٰنِ الرَّحِيمِ

1. Ḥā Mīm.

١- حٰمٓ ۚ

2. The revelation
Of the Book
Is from Allah
The Exalted in Power,
Full of Wisdom.

٢- تَنْزِيلُ الْكِتٰبِ مِنَ اللهِ
الْعَزِيزِ الْحَكِيمِ ۟

3. Verily in the heavens
And the earth, are Signs
For those who believe.

٣- إِنَّ فِى السَّمٰوٰتِ وَالْأَرْضِ لَاٰيٰتٍ
لِّلْمُؤْمِنِينَ ۟

4. And in the creation
Of yourselves and the fact
That animals are scattered
(Through the earth), are Signs
For those of assured Faith.

٤- وَفِى خَلْقِكُمْ وَمَا يَبُثُّ مِنْ دَآبَّةٍ
اٰيٰتٌ لِّقَوْمٍ يُوقِنُونَ ۟

5. And in the alternation
Of Night and Day,
And the fact that Allah
Sends down Sustenance from
The sky, and revives therewith
The earth after its death,
And in the change
Of the winds—are Signs
For those that are wise.

٥- وَاخْتِلٰفِ الَّيْلِ وَالنَّهَارِ
وَمَآ أَنْزَلَ اللهُ مِنَ السَّمَآءِ مِنْ رِّزْقٍ
فَأَحْيَا بِهِ الْأَرْضَ بَعْدَ مَوْتِهَا
وَتَصْرِيفِ الرِّيٰحِ اٰيٰتٌ
لِّقَوْمٍ يَعْقِلُونَ ۟

6. Such are Signs
Of Allah, which We rehearse to
thee
In truth: then in what
Exposition will they believe
After (rejecting) Allah
And His Signs?

٦- تِلْكَ اٰيٰتُ اللهِ نَتْلُوهَا عَلَيْكَ بِالْحَقِّ ۖ
فَبِأَيِّ حَدِيثٍ بَعْدَ اللهِ
وَاٰيٰتِهِ يُؤْمِنُونَ ۟

7. Woe to each sinful
Dealer in Falsehoods:

٧- وَيْلٌ لِّكُلِّ أَفَّاكٍ أَثِيْمِ ۙ

8. He hears the Signs
Of Allah rehearsed to him,
Yet is obstinate and lofty,
As if he had not
Heard them: then announce
To him a Penalty Grievous!

٨- يَّسْمَعُ أَيْتِ اللهِ تُتْلَى عَلَيْهِ
ثُمَّ يُصِرُّ مُسْتَكْبِرًا كَأَنْ لَّمْ يَسْمَعْهَا ۚ
فَبَشِّرْهُ بِعَذَابٍ أَلِيْمٍ ۝

9. And when he learns
Sonmething of Our Signs,
He takes them in jest:
For such there will be
A humiliating Penalty.

٩- وَإِذَا عَلِمَ مِنْ أَيٰتِنَا شَيْئًا
اتَّخَذَهَا هُزُوًا ۚ
أُولٰٓئِكَ لَهُمْ عَذَابٌ مُّهِيْنٌ ۝

10. In front of them is
Hell: and of no profit
To them is anything
They may have earned,
Nor any protectors they
May have taken to themselves
Besides Allah: for them
Is a tremendous Penalty.

١٠- مِنْ وَّرَآئِهِمْ جَهَنَّمُ ۚ
وَلَا يُغْنِيْ عَنْهُمْ مَّا كَسَبُوْا شَيْئًا
وَّلَا مَا اتَّخَذُوْا مِنْ دُوْنِ اللهِ أَوْلِيَآءَ ۚ
وَلَهُمْ عَذَابٌ عَظِيْمٌ ۝

11. This is (true) Guidance:
And for those who reject
The Signs of their Lord,
Is a grievous Penalty
Of abomination.

١١- هٰذَا هُدًى ۚ
وَالَّذِيْنَ كَفَرُوْا بِأٰيٰتِ رَبِّهِمْ
لَهُمْ عَذَابٌ مِّنْ رِّجْزٍ أَلِيْمٌ ۝ ع

SECTION 2.

12. It is Allah Who has
Subjected the sea to you,
That ship may sail
Through it by His command,
That ye may seek
Of His Bounty, and that
Ye may be gateful.

١٢- اَللهُ الَّذِيْ سَخَّرَ لَكُمُ الْبَحْرَ
لِتَجْرِيَ الْفُلْكُ فِيْهِ بِأَمْرِهٖ
وَلِتَبْتَغُوْا مِنْ فَضْلِهٖ
وَلَعَلَّكُمْ تَشْكُرُوْنَ ۝

13. And He has subjected
To you, as from Him,
All that is in the heavens
And on earth: behold,
In that are Signs indeed
For those who reflect.

١٣- وَسَخَّرَ لَكُمْ
مَّا فِي السَّمٰوٰتِ وَمَا فِي الْأَرْضِ جَمِيْعًا مِّنْهُ ۚ
إِنَّ فِيْ ذٰلِكَ لَأٰيٰتٍ لِّقَوْمٍ يَّتَفَكَّرُوْنَ ۝

14. Tell those who believe,

١٤- قُلْ لِّلَّذِيْنَ أٰمَنُوْا

To forgive those who
Do not look forward
To the Days of Allah:
It is for Him to recompense
(For good or ill) each People
According to what
They have earned.

يَغْفِرُوا لِلَّذِيْنَ
لَا يَرْجُوْنَ اَيَّامَ اللّٰهِ لِيَجْزِىَ
قَوْمًا بِمَا كَانُوْا يَكْسِبُوْنَ ۝

15. If anyone does
A righteous deed,
It enures to the benefit
Of his own soul;
If he does evil,
It works against
(His own soul).
In the end will ye
(All) be brought back
To your Lord.

١٥- مَنْ عَمِلَ صَالِحًا
فَلِنَفْسِهٖ
وَمَنْ اَسَآءَ
فَعَلَيْهَا
ثُمَّ اِلٰى رَبِّكُمْ تُرْجَعُوْنَ ۝

16. We did aforetime
Grant to the Children
Of Israel the Book,
The Power of Command,
And Prophethood; We gave
Them, for Sustenance, things
Good and pure; and We
Favoured them above the nations.

١٦- وَلَقَدْ اٰتَيْنَا بَنِىْ اِسْرَآءِيْلَ الْكِتٰبَ
وَالْحُكْمَ وَالنُّبُوَّةَ
وَرَزَقْنٰهُمْ مِّنَ الطَّيِّبٰتِ
وَفَضَّلْنٰهُمْ عَلَى الْعٰلَمِيْنَ ۝

17. And We granted them
Clear Signs in affairs
(Of Religion): it was only
After knowledge had been
Granted to them that they
Fell into schisms, through
Insolent envy among themselves
Verily thy Lord will judge
Between then on the Day
Of Judgement as to those
Matters in which they
Set up differences.

١٧- وَاٰتَيْنٰهُمْ بَيِّنٰتٍ مِّنَ الْاَمْرِ
فَمَا اخْتَلَفُوْا اِلَّا مِنْ بَعْدِ
مَا جَآءَهُمُ الْعِلْمُ بَغْيًا بَيْنَهُمْ
اِنَّ رَبَّكَ يَقْضِىْ بَيْنَهُمْ يَوْمَ
الْقِيٰمَةِ فِيْمَا كَانُوْا فِيْهِ يَخْتَلِفُوْنَ ۝

18. Then We put thee
On the (right) Way
Of Religion: so follow
Thou that (Way),
And follow not the desires
Of those who know not.

١٨- ثُمَّ جَعَلْنٰكَ عَلٰى شَرِيْعَةٍ مِّنَ الْاَمْرِ
فَاتَّبِعْهَا
وَلَا تَتَّبِعْ اَهْوَآءَ الَّذِيْنَ لَا يَعْلَمُوْنَ ۝

19. They will be of no

١٩- اِنَّهُمْ لَنْ يُّغْنُوْا

Use to thee in the sight
Of Allah: it is only
Wrongdoers (that stand as)
Protectors, one to another:
But Allah is the Protector
Of the Righteous.

عَنْكَ مِنَ اللّٰهِ شَيْئًا ۚ
وَإِنَّ الظّٰلِمِيْنَ بَعْضُهُمْ أَوْلِيَآءُ بَعْضٍ ۚ
وَاللّٰهُ وَلِيُّ الْمُتَّقِيْنَ ۝

20. These are clear evidences
To men, and a Guidance
And Mercy to those
Of assured Faith.

٢٠- هٰذَا بَصَآئِرُ لِلنَّاسِ وَهُدًى
وَّرَحْمَةٌ لِّقَوْمٍ يُّوْقِنُوْنَ ۝

21. What! do those who
Seek after evil ways
Think that We shall
Hold them equal with
Those who believe and
Do righteous deeds—that
Equal will be their
Life and their death?
Ill is the judgement
That they make.

٢١- أَمْ حَسِبَ الَّذِيْنَ اجْتَرَحُوا السَّيِّاٰتِ
أَنْ نَّجْعَلَهُمْ
كَالَّذِيْنَ اٰمَنُوْا وَعَمِلُوا الصّٰلِحٰتِ ۙ سَوَآءً
مَّحْيَاهُمْ وَمَمَاتُهُمْ ۗ
سَآءَ مَا يَحْكُمُوْنَ ۝

SECTION 3.

22. Allah created the heavens
And the earth for
Just ends, and in order
That each soul may find
The recompense of what
It has earned, and none
Of them be wronged.

٢٢- وَخَلَقَ اللّٰهُ السَّمٰوٰتِ وَالْأَرْضَ بِالْحَقِّ
وَلِتُجْزٰى كُلُّ نَفْسٍ
بِمَا كَسَبَتْ وَهُمْ لَا يُظْلَمُوْنَ ۝

23. Then seest thou such
A one as takes
As his god his own
Vain desire? Allah has,
Knowing (him as such),
Left him astray, and sealed
His hearing and his heart
(And understanding), and put
A cover on his sight.
Who, then, will guide him
After Allah (has withdrawn
Guidance)? Will ye not
Then receive admonition?

٢٣- أَفَرَءَيْتَ مَنِ اتَّخَذَ إِلٰهَهُ هَوٰهُ
وَأَضَلَّهُ اللّٰهُ
عَلٰى عِلْمٍ وَّخَتَمَ عَلٰى سَمْعِهٖ وَقَلْبِهٖ
وَجَعَلَ عَلٰى بَصَرِهٖ غِشٰوَةً ۗ
فَمَنْ يَّهْدِيْهِ مِنْ بَعْدِ اللّٰهِ ۗ
أَفَلَا تَذَكَّرُوْنَ ۝

24. And they say: "What is
There but our life

٢٤- وَقَالُوْا مَا هِيَ إِلَّا حَيَاتُنَا الدُّنْيَا

In this world?
We shall die and we live,
And nothing but Time
Can destroy us." But
Of that they have no
Knowledge: they merely
          conjecture:

25. And when Our Clear
Signs are rehearsed to them,
Their argument is nothing
But this: they say, "Bring
(Back) our forefathers, if
What ye say is true!"

26. Say: "It is Allah Who
Gives you life, then
Gives you death; then
He will gather you together
For the Day of Judgement
About which there is
No doubt": but most
Men do not understand.
         SECTION 4.

27. To Allah belongs
The dominion of the heavens
And the earth, and
The Day that the Hour
Of Judgement is established—
That Day will the dealers
In Falsehood perish!

28. And thou wilt see
Every sect bowing the knee:
Every sect will be called
To its Record: "This Day
Shall ye be recompensed
For all that ye did!

29. "This Our Record speaks
About you with truth:
For We were wont
To put on record
All that ye did."

30. Then, as to those who
Believed and did righteous
Deeds, their Lord will

Admit them to His Mercy:
That will be the Achievement
For all to see.

ذٰلِكَ هُوَ الْفَوْزُ الْمُبِينُ ۝

31. But as to those who
Rejected Allah, (to them
Will be said): "Were not
Our Signs rehearsed to you?
But ye were arrogant,
And were a people
Given to sin!

٣١- وَأَمَّا الَّذِينَ كَفَرُوا ۗ
أَفَلَمْ تَكُنْ اٰيٰتِي تُتْلٰى عَلَيْكُمْ
فَاسْتَكْبَرْتُمْ
وَكُنْتُمْ قَوْمًا مُّجْرِمِينَ ۝

32. "And when it was said
That the promise of Allah
Was true, and that the Hour—
There was no doubt
About its (coming), ye
Used to say, 'We
Know not what is
The Hour: we only think
It is an idea, and we
Have no firm assurance.'"

٣٢- وَإِذَا قِيلَ إِنَّ وَعْدَ اللهِ حَقٌّ
وَّالسَّاعَةُ لَا رَيْبَ فِيهَا
قُلْتُمْ مَا نَدْرِي مَا السَّاعَةُ ۙ
إِنْ نَّظُنُّ إِلَّا ظَنًّا
وَّمَا نَحْنُ بِمُسْتَيْقِنِينَ ۝

33. Then will appear to them
The evil (fruits) of what
They did, and they will be
Completely encircled by that
Which they used to mock at!

٣٣- وَبَدَا لَهُمْ سَيِّئَاتُ مَا
عَمِلُوا وَحَاقَ بِهِمْ
مَّا كَانُوا بِهِ يَسْتَهْزِءُونَ ۝

34. It will also be said:
"This Day We will forget
You as ye forgot
The meeting of this Day
Of yours! And your
Abode is the Fire, and
No helpers have ye!

٣٤- وَقِيلَ الْيَوْمَ نَنْسٰكُمْ
كَمَا نَسِيتُمْ لِقَاءَ يَوْمِكُمْ هٰذَا
وَمَأْوٰكُمُ النَّارُ وَمَا لَكُمْ مِّنْ نّٰصِرِينَ ۝

35. "This, because ye used
To take the Signs of Allah
In jest, and the life
Of the world deceived you:"
(From) that Day, therefore,
They shall not be taken out
Thence, nor shall they be
Received into Grace.

٣٥- ذٰلِكُمْ بِأَنَّكُمُ اتَّخَذْتُمْ اٰيٰتِ اللهِ
هُزُوًا وَّغَرَّتْكُمُ الْحَيٰوةُ الدُّنْيَا ۚ
فَالْيَوْمَ لَا يُخْرَجُونَ مِنْهَا
وَلَا هُمْ يُسْتَعْتَبُونَ ۝

36. Then Praise be to Allah,
Lord of the heavens

٣٦- فَلِلّٰهِ الْحَمْدُ رَبِّ السَّمٰوٰتِ

And Lord of the earth—
Lord and Cherisher
Of all the worlds!

وَرَبِّ الْأَرْضِ
رَبِّ الْعَالَمِينَ ٥

37. To Him be Glory
Throughout the heavens
And the earth: and He
Is Exalted in Power,
Full of Wisdom!

٣٧- وَلَهُ الْكِبْرِيَاءُ فِي السَّمَوَاتِ وَالْأَرْضِ
وَهُوَ الْعَزِيزُ الْحَكِيمُ ٥

INTRODUCTION TO SŪRA XLVI. (*Aḥqāf*) — 35 Verses

This is the seventh and last Sūra of the *Ḥā-Mīm* series. For the general theme and chronological place of these Sūras see the Introduction to S. xl.

The *Aḥqāf* (mentioned in verse 21) are the long and winding crooked tracts of sand-hills, characteristic of the country of the 'Ād people, adjoining Haḍhramaut and Yaman: see vii. 65, n. 1040. These people had, at that time, probably a fertile irrigated country, but their sins brought on the calamity mentioned in xlvi.24-25. The lesson of this Sūra is that if the Truth is challenged, the challenge will be duly answered, and Truth vindicated.

Al Aḥqāf [4773-A] (Winding Sand-tracts)

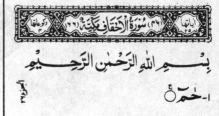

In the name of Allah, Most Gracious, Most Merciful.

1. Ḥā Mīm.

2. The revelation
Of the Book
Is from Allah
The Exalted in Power,
Full of Wisdom.

3. We created not
The heavens and the earth
And all between them
But for just ends, and
For a term appointed:
But those who reject Faith
Turn away from that
Whereof they are warned.

4. Say: "Do ye see
What it is ye invoke
Besides Allah? Show me
What it is they
Have created on earth,
Or have they a share
In the heavens?
Bring me a Book
(Revealed) before this,
Or any remnant of knowledge
(Ye may have), if ye
Are telling the truth!

5. And who is more astray
Than one who invokes,
Besides Allah, such as will
Not answer him to the Day
Of Judgement, and who
(In fact) are unconscious
Of their call (to them)?

٥- وَمَنْ أَضَلُّ
مِمَّنْ يَدْعُوا مِنْ دُونِ اللهِ
مَنْ لَا يَسْتَجِيبُ لَهُ إِلَى يَوْمِ الْقِيَامَةِ
وَهُمْ عَنْ دُعَائِهِمْ غَافِلُونَ ۝

6. And when mankind
Are gathered together
(At the Resurrection),
They will be hostile
To them and reject
Their worship (altogether)!

٦- وَإِذَا حُشِرَ النَّاسُ
كَانُوا لَهُمْ أَعْدَاءً
وَكَانُوا بِعِبَادَتِهِمْ كَافِرِينَ ۝

7. When Our Clear Signs
Are rehearsed to them,
The Unbelievers say,
Of the Truth
When it comes to them:
"This is evident sorcery!"

٧- وَإِذَا تُتْلَى عَلَيْهِمْ آيَاتُنَا بَيِّنَاتٍ
قَالَ الَّذِينَ كَفَرُوا لِلْحَقِّ
لَمَّا جَاءَهُمْ هَذَا سِحْرٌ مُبِينٌ ۝

8. Or do they say,
"He has forged it"?
Say: "Had I forged it,
Then can ye obtain
No single (blessing) for me
From Allah. He knows best
Of that whereof ye talk
(So glibly)! Enough is He
For a witness between me
And you! And He is
Oft-Forgiving, Most Merciful."

٨- أَمْ يَقُولُونَ افْتَرَاهُ
قُلْ إِنِ افْتَرَيْتُهُ فَلَا تَمْلِكُونَ لِي مِنَ
اللهِ شَيْئًا
هُوَ أَعْلَمُ بِمَا تُفِيضُونَ فِيهِ كَفَى بِهِ
شَهِيدًا بَيْنِي وَبَيْنَكُمْ وَهُوَ الْغَفُورُ
الرَّحِيمُ ۝

9. Say: "I am no bringer
Of new-fangled doctrine
Among the messengers, nor
Do I know what will
Be done with me or
With you. I follow
But that which is revealed
To me by inspiration:
I am but a Warner
Open and clear."

٩- قُلْ مَا كُنْتُ بِدْعًا
مِنَ الرُّسُلِ
وَمَا أَدْرِي مَا يُفْعَلُ بِي وَلَا بِكُمْ
إِنْ أَتَّبِعُ إِلَّا مَا يُوحَى إِلَيَّ
وَمَا أَنَا إِلَّا نَذِيرٌ مُبِينٌ ۝

10. Say: "See ye?
If (this teaching) be
From Allah, and ye reject it,

١٠- قُلْ أَرَأَيْتُمْ إِنْ كَانَ مِنْ عِنْدِ اللهِ

And a witness from among
The Children of Israel testifies
To its similarity
(With earlier scripture),
And has believed
While ye are arrogant,
(How unjust ye are!)
Truly, Allah guides not
A people unjust."

SECTION 2.

11. The Unbelievers say
Of those who believe:
"If (this Message) were
A good thing, (such men)
Would not have gone
To it first, before us!"
And seeing that they
Guide not themselves thereby,
They will say, "This is
An (old), old falsehood!"

12. And before this, was
The Book of Moses
As a guide and a mercy:
And this Book confirms (it)
In the Arabic tongue;
To admonish the unjust,
And as Glad Tidings
To those who do right.

13. Verily those who say,
"Our Lord is Allah,"
And remain firm
(On that Path)—
On them shall be no fear,
Nor shall they grieve.

14. Such shall be Companions
Of the Garden, dwelling
Therein (for aye): a recompense
For their (good) deeds.

15. We have enjoined on man
Kindness to his parents:
In pain did his mother

وَكَفَرْتُمْ بِهِ

وَشَهِدَ شَاهِدٌ مِّنْ
بَنِيٓ إِسْرَآءِيلَ عَلَىٰ مِثْلِهِ
فَـَٔامَنَ وَٱسْتَكْبَرْتُمْ ۖ
إِنَّ ٱللَّهَ لَا يَهْدِى ٱلْقَوْمَ ٱلظَّٰلِمِينَ ۞

١١- وَقَالَ ٱلَّذِينَ كَفَرُوا۟ لِلَّذِينَ ءَامَنُوا۟
لَوْ كَانَ
خَيْرًا مَّا سَبَقُونَآ إِلَيْهِ ۚ
وَإِذْ لَمْ يَهْتَدُوا۟ بِهِ
فَسَيَقُولُونَ هَٰذَآ إِفْكٌ قَدِيمٌ ○

١٢- وَمِن قَبْلِهِ كِتَٰبُ مُوسَىٰٓ إِمَامًا وَرَحْمَةً ۚ
وَهَٰذَا كِتَٰبٌ مُّصَدِّقٌ لِّسَانًا عَرَبِيًّا
لِّيُنذِرَ ٱلَّذِينَ ظَلَمُوا۟ ۖ
وَبُشْرَىٰ لِلْمُحْسِنِينَ ○

١٣- إِنَّ ٱلَّذِينَ قَالُوا۟ رَبُّنَا ٱللَّهُ
ثُمَّ ٱسْتَقَٰمُوا۟
فَلَا خَوْفٌ عَلَيْهِمْ وَلَا هُمْ يَحْزَنُونَ ○

١٤- أُو۟لَٰٓئِكَ أَصْحَٰبُ ٱلْجَنَّةِ خَٰلِدِينَ فِيهَا
جَزَآءًۢ بِمَا كَانُوا۟ يَعْمَلُونَ ○

١٥- وَوَصَّيْنَا ٱلْإِنسَٰنَ بِوَٰلِدَيْهِ إِحْسَٰنًا ۖ
حَمَلَتْهُ أُمُّهُۥ كُرْهًا

Bear him, and in pain
Did she give him birth.
The carrying of the (child)
To his weaning is
(A period of) thirty months.
At length, when he reaches
The age of full strength
And attains forty years,
He says, "O my Lord!
Grant me that I may be
Grateful for Thy favour
Which Thou hast bestowed
Upon me, and upon both
My parents, and that I
May work righteousness
Such as Thou mayest approve;
And be gracious to me
In my issue. Truly
Have I turned to Thee
And truly do I bow
(To Thee) in Islam."

وَوَضَعَتْهُ كُرْهًا ۚ

وَحَمْلُهُ وَفِصَالُهُ ثَلَاثُونَ شَهْرًا ۚ

حَتَّى إِذَا بَلَغَ أَشُدَّهُ

وَبَلَغَ أَرْبَعِينَ سَنَةً ۙ

قَالَ رَبِّ أَوْزِعْنِي

أَنْ أَشْكُرَ نِعْمَتَكَ الَّتِي

أَنْعَمْتَ عَلَيَّ وَعَلَى وَالِدَيَّ

وَأَنْ أَعْمَلَ صَالِحًا تَرْضَاهُ

وَأَصْلِحْ لِي فِي ذُرِّيَّتِي ۚ

إِنِّي تُبْتُ إِلَيْكَ

وَإِنِّي مِنَ الْمُسْلِمِينَ ۝

16. Such are they from whom
We shall accept the best
Of their deeds and pass by
Their ill deeds: (they shall
Be) among the Companions
Of the Garden: a promise
Of truth, which was
Made to them
(In this life).

١٦- أُولَٰئِكَ الَّذِينَ نَتَقَبَّلُ عَنْهُمْ أَحْسَنَ

مَا عَمِلُوا وَنَتَجَاوَزُ عَنْ سَيِّئَاتِهِمْ

فِي أَصْحَابِ الْجَنَّةِ ۚ

وَعْدَ الصِّدْقِ الَّذِي

كَانُوا يُوعَدُونَ ۝

17. But (there is one)
Who says to his parents,
"Fie on you! Do ye
Hold out the promise
To me that I
Shall be raised up,
Even though generations
Have passed before me
(Without rising again)?"
And they two seek
Allah's aid, (and rebuke
The son): "Woe to thee!

١٧- وَالَّذِي قَالَ لِوَالِدَيْهِ

أُفٍّ لَكُمَا أَتَعِدَانِنِي أَنْ أُخْرَجَ

وَقَدْ خَلَتِ

الْقُرُونُ مِنْ قَبْلِي

وَهُمَا يَسْتَغِيثَانِ اللَّهَ

وَيْلَكَ آمِنْ ۖ

إِنَّ وَعْدَ اللَّهِ حَقٌّ ۖ

Have Faith! For the promise
Of Allah is true."
But he says, "This is
Nothing but tales
Of the ancients!"

18. Such are they against whom
Is proved the Sentence
Among the previous generations
Of Jinns and men, that have
Passed away; for they will
Be (utterly) lost.

19. And to all
Are (assigned) degrees
According to the deeds
Which they (have done),
And in order that (Allah)
May recompense their deeds,
And no injustice be done
To them.

20. And on the Day that
The Unbelievers will be
Placed before the Fire,
(It will be said to them):
"Ye received your good
          things
In the life of the world,
And ye took your pleasure
Out of them: but today
Shall ye be recompensed
With a Penalty of humiliation:
For that ye were arrogant
On earth without just cause,
And that ye (ever) transgressed."

SECTION 3.

21. Mention (Hūd)
One of 'Ād's (own) brethren:
Behold, he warned his people
About the winding Sand-tracts:
But there have been Warners
Before him and after him:
"Worship ye none other
Than Allah: truly I fear
For you the Penalty
Of a Mighty Day."

فَيَقُولُ مَا هٰذَآ
إِلَّآ أَسَاطِيرُ الْأَوَّلِينَ ٠

١٨- أُولٰٓئِكَ الَّذِينَ حَقَّ عَلَيْهِمُ الْقَوْلُ
فِىٓ أُمَمٍ قَدْ خَلَتْ مِنْ قَبْلِهِمْ مِنَ الْجِنِّ
وَالْإِنْسِ إِنَّهُمْ كَانُوا خٰسِرِينَ ٠

١٩- وَ لِكُلٍّ دَرَجٰتٌ
مِّمَّا عَمِلُوا ۚ
وَلِيُوَفِّيَهُمْ أَعْمَالَهُمْ
وَهُمْ لَا يُظْلَمُونَ ٠

٢٠- وَيَوْمَ يُعْرَضُ الَّذِينَ كَفَرُوا عَلَى النَّارِ
أَذْهَبْتُمْ طَيِّبٰتِكُمْ فِى حَيَاتِكُمُ الدُّنْيَا
وَاسْتَمْتَعْتُمْ بِهَا ۚ
فَالْيَوْمَ تُجْزَوْنَ عَذَابَ الْهُونِ
بِمَا كُنْتُمْ تَسْتَكْبِرُونَ فِى الْأَرْضِ بِغَيْرِ
الْحَقِّ
وَبِمَا كُنْتُمْ تَفْسُقُونَ ٠ ع

٢١- وَاذْكُرْ أَخَا عَادٍ
إِذْ أَنْذَرَ قَوْمَهُ بِالْأَحْقَافِ
وَقَدْ خَلَتِ النُّذُرُ مِنْ بَيْنِ يَدَيْهِ وَمِنْ
خَلْفِهِ أَلَّا تَعْبُدُوا إِلَّا اللّٰهَ ۚ
إِنِّىٓ أَخَافُ عَلَيْكُمْ عَذَابَ يَوْمٍ عَظِيمٍ ٠

22. They said: "Hast thou come
In order to turn us aside
From our gods? Then bring
Upon us the (calamity)
With which thou dost
Threaten us, if thou
Art telling the truth!"

٢٢ - قَالُوا أَجِئْتَنَا لِتَأْفِكَنَا عَنْ آلِهَتِنَا ۚ
فَأْتِنَا بِمَا تَعِدُنَا
إِنْ كُنْتَ مِنَ الصَّادِقِينَ ۝

23. He said: "The Knowledge
(Of when it will come)
Is only with Allah: I
Proclaim to you the mission
On which I have been sent:
But I see that ye
Are a people in ignorance!"...

٢٣ - قَالَ إِنَّمَا الْعِلْمُ عِنْدَ اللّٰهِ ۖ
وَأُبَلِّغُكُمْ مَا أُرْسِلْتُ بِهِ
وَلٰكِنِّي أَرَاكُمْ قَوْمًا تَجْهَلُونَ ۝

24. Then, when they saw
The (Penalty in the shape of)
A cloud traversing the sky,
Coming to meet their valleys,
They said, "This cloud
Will give us rain!"
"Nay, it is the (calamity)
Ye were asking to be
Hastened!—a wind
Wherein is a Grievous Penalty!

٢٤ - فَلَمَّا رَأَوْهُ
عَارِضًا مُسْتَقْبِلَ أَوْدِيَتِهِمْ
قَالُوا هٰذَا عَارِضٌ مُمْطِرُنَا ۚ
بَلْ هُوَ مَا اسْتَعْجَلْتُمْ بِهِ ۖ
رِيحٌ فِيهَا عَذَابٌ أَلِيمٌ ۝

25. "Everything will it destroy
By the command of its Lord!"
Then by the morning
they
Nothing was to be seen
But (the ruins of) their houses!
Thus do We recompense
Those given to sin!

٢٥ - تُدَمِّرُ كُلَّ شَيْءٍ بِأَمْرِ رَبِّهَا
فَأَصْبَحُوا لَا يُرَىٰ إِلَّا مَسَاكِنُهُمْ ۚ
كَذٰلِكَ نَجْزِي الْقَوْمَ الْمُجْرِمِينَ ۝

26. And We had firmly established
Them in a (prosperity and)
power
Which We have not given
To you (ye Quraysh!)
And We had endowed them
With (faculties of)
Hearing, seeing, heart and
intellect:
But of no profit to them
Were their (faculties of)
Hearing, sight, and heart
And intellect, when they

٢٦ - وَلَقَدْ مَكَّنَّاهُمْ
فِيمَا إِنْ مَكَّنَّاكُمْ فِيهِ
وَجَعَلْنَا لَهُمْ سَمْعًا وَأَبْصَارًا وَأَفْئِدَةً ۖ
فَمَا أَغْنَىٰ عَنْهُمْ
سَمْعُهُمْ وَلَا أَبْصَارُهُمْ وَلَا أَفْئِدَتُهُمْ
مِنْ شَيْءٍ إِذْ كَانُوا يَجْحَدُونَ بِآيَاتِ اللّٰهِ

Went on rejecting the Signs
Of Allah: and they were
(Completely) encircled
By that which they
Used to mock at!

SECTION 4.

27. We destroyed aforetime
Populations round about you;
And We have shown
The Signs in various ways,
That they may turn (to Us).

28. Why then was no help
Forthcoming to them from those
Whom they worshipped as gods,
Besides Allah, as a means
Of access (to Allah)? Nay,
They left them in the lurch:
But that was their
Falsehood and their invention.

29. Behold, We turned
Towards thee a company
Of Jinns (quietly) listening
To the Qur'ān: when they
Stood in the presence
Thereof, they said, "Listen
In silence!" When the (reading)
Was finished, they returned
To their people, to warn
(Them of their sins).

30. They said, "O our people!
We have heard a Book
Revealed after Moses,
Confirming what came
Before it: it guides (men)
To the Truth and
To a Straight Path.

31. "O our people, hearken
To the one who invites
(You) to Allah, and believe
In him: He will forgive
You your faults,
And deliver you from
A Penalty Grievous.

وَحَاقَ بِهِمْ
مَّا كَانُوْا بِهٖ يَسْتَهْزِءُوْنَ ۚ ۞

٢٧- وَلَقَدْ أَهْلَكْنَا مَا حَوْلَكُمْ مِّنَ الْقُرٰى
وَصَرَّفْنَا الْاٰيٰتِ لَعَلَّهُمْ يَرْجِعُوْنَ ۟

٢٨- فَلَوْلَا نَصَرَهُمُ الَّذِيْنَ اتَّخَذُوْا مِنْ
دُوْنِ اللّٰهِ قُرْبَانًا اٰلِهَةً ۗ
بَلْ ضَلُّوْا عَنْهُمْ ۚ
وَذٰلِكَ إِفْكُهُمْ وَمَا كَانُوْا يَفْتَرُوْنَ ۟

٢٩- وَإِذْ صَرَفْنَا إِلَيْكَ نَفَرًا
مِّنَ الْجِنِّ يَسْتَمِعُوْنَ الْقُرْاٰنَ ۚ
فَلَمَّا حَضَرُوْهُ قَالُوْا أَنْصِتُوْا ۚ
فَلَمَّا قُضِيَ
وَلَّوْا إِلٰى قَوْمِهِمْ مُّنْذِرِيْنَ ۟

٣٠- قَالُوْا يٰقَوْمَنَا إِنَّا سَمِعْنَا كِتٰبًا
أُنْزِلَ مِنْ بَعْدِ مُوْسٰى
مُصَدِّقًا لِّمَا بَيْنَ يَدَيْهِ
يَهْدِيْ إِلَى الْحَقِّ وَإِلٰى طَرِيْقٍ مُّسْتَقِيْمٍ ۟

٣١- يٰقَوْمَنَا أَجِيْبُوْا دَاعِيَ اللّٰهِ
وَاٰمِنُوْا بِهٖ
يَغْفِرْ لَكُمْ مِّنْ ذُنُوْبِكُمْ
وَيُجِرْكُمْ مِّنْ عَذَابٍ أَلِيْمٍ ۟

32. "If any does not hearken
To the one who invites
(Us) to Allah, he cannot
Frustrate (Allah's Plan) on earth,
And no protectors can he have
Besides Allah: such men
(Wander) in manifest error."

٣٢- وَمَن لَّا يُجِبْ دَاعِيَ اللَّهِ
فَلَيْسَ بِمُعْجِزٍ فِي الأَرْضِ
وَلَيْسَ لَهُ مِن دُونِهِ أَوْلِيَاءُ
أُولَٰئِكَ فِي ضَلَٰلٍ مُّبِينٍ ۝

33. See they not that
Allah, Who created the heavens
And the earth, and never
Wearied with their creation,
Is able to give life
To the dead? Yea, verily
He has power over all things.

٣٣- أَوَلَمْ يَرَوْا أَنَّ اللَّهَ الَّذِي
خَلَقَ السَّمَٰوَٰتِ وَالأَرْضَ
وَلَمْ يَعْيَ بِخَلْقِهِنَّ بِقَٰدِرٍ عَلَىٰ أَن يُحْيِيَ
المَوْتَىٰ بَلَىٰ إِنَّهُ عَلَىٰ كُلِّ شَيْءٍ قَدِيرٌ ۝

34. And on the Day that
The Unbelievers will be
Placed before the Fire,
(They will be asked,)
"Is this not the Truth?"
They will say, "Yea,
By our Lord!"
(One will say:)
"Then taste ye
The Penalty, for that ye
Were wont to deny (Truth)!"

٣٤- وَيَوْمَ يُعْرَضُ الَّذِينَ كَفَرُوا عَلَى النَّارِ
أَلَيْسَ هَٰذَا بِالْحَقِّ
قَالُوا بَلَىٰ وَرَبِّنَا
قَالَ فَذُوقُوا الْعَذَابَ
بِمَا كُنتُمْ تَكْفُرُونَ ۝

35. Therefore patiently persevere,
As did (all) messengers
Of inflexible purpose;
And be in no haste
About the (Unbelievers). On
the Day
That they see the
(Punishment)
Promised them, (it will be)
As if they had not
Tarried more than an hour
In a single day. (Thine
But) to proclaim the
Message:
But shall any be destroyed
Except those who transgress?

٣٥- فَاصْبِرْ كَمَا صَبَرَ
أُولُو الْعَزْمِ مِنَ الرُّسُلِ
وَلَا تَسْتَعْجِل لَّهُمْ
كَأَنَّهُمْ يَوْمَ يَرَوْنَ
مَا يُوعَدُونَ
لَمْ يَلْبَثُوا إِلَّا سَاعَةً مِّن نَّهَارٍ
بَلَٰغٌ
فَهَلْ يُهْلَكُ إِلَّا
الْقَوْمُ الْفَاسِقُونَ ۝

INTRODUCTION TO SŪRA XLVII. (*Muḥammad*) — 38 Verses

We have examined and followed the current arrangement of the Sūras according to subject-matter and independently of chronology, ad we have found that a logical thread runs through them. We have now finished more than five-sixths of the Qur-ān. The remaining sixth consists of short Sūras, but these are again grouped according to subject-matter.

We begin the first of such groups with a group of three Sūras (xlvii. to xlix.), which deal with the organisation of the Muslim Ummat or community both for external defence and in internal relations. The present Sūra deals with the necessity of defence against external foes by courage and strenuous fighting, and dates from about the first year of the Hijra, when the Muslims were under threat of extinction by invasion from Mecca.

Muḥammad

*In the name of Allah, Most Gracious,
Most Merciful.*

بِسْمِ اللّٰهِ الرَّحْمٰنِ الرَّحِيْمِ

1. Those who reject Allah
And hinder (men) from
The Path of Allah—
Their deeds will Allah
Render astray
(From their mark).

١- اَلَّذِيْنَ كَفَرُوْا
وَصَدُّوْا عَنْ سَبِيْلِ اللّٰهِ
اَضَلَّ اَعْمَالَهُمْ ۝

2. But those who believe
And work deeds of
Righteousness, and believe
In the (Revelation) sent down
To Muhammad—for it is
The Truth from their Lord—
He will remove from them
Their ills and improve
Their condition.

٢- وَالَّذِيْنَ اٰمَنُوْا وَعَمِلُوا الصّٰلِحٰتِ
وَاٰمَنُوْا بِمَا نُزِّلَ عَلٰى مُحَمَّدٍ
وَهُوَ الْحَقُّ مِنْ رَّبِّهِمْ
كَفَّرَ عَنْهُمْ سَيِّاٰتِهِمْ
وَاَصْلَحَ بَالَهُمْ ۝

3. This because those who
Reject Allah follow vanities,
While those who believe follow
The Truth from their Lord:
Thus does Allah set forth
For men their lessons
By similitudes.

٣- ذٰلِكَ بِاَنَّ الَّذِيْنَ كَفَرُوا اتَّبَعُوا الْبَاطِلَ
وَاَنَّ الَّذِيْنَ اٰمَنُوا اتَّبَعُوا الْحَقَّ مِنْ رَّبِّهِمْ
كَذٰلِكَ يَضْرِبُ اللّٰهُ لِلنَّاسِ اَمْثَالَهُمْ ۝

4. Therefore, when ye meet[4820]

٤- فَاِذَا لَقِيْتُمُ الَّذِيْنَ كَفَرُوْا

The Unbelievers (in fight),
Smite at their necks;
At length, when ye have
Thoroughly subdued them,
Bind a bond
Firmly (on them): thereafter
(Is the time for) either
Generosity or ransom:
Until the war lays down
Its burdens. Thus (are ye
Commanded): but if it
Had been Allah's Will,
He could certainly have exacted
Retribution from them (Himself);
But (He lets you fight)
In order to test you,
Some with others.
But those who are slain
In the way of Allah—
He will never let
Their deeds be lost.

5. Soon will He guide them
And improve their condition,

6. And admit them to
The Garden which He
Has announced for them.

7. O ye who believe!
If ye will aid
(The cause of) Allah,
He will aid you,
And plant your feet firmly.

8. But those who reject (Allah—
For them is destruction,
And (Allah) will render
Their deeds astray
(From their mark).

9. That is because they
Hate the Revelation of Allah;
So He has made
Their deeds fruitless.

10. Do they not travel
Through the earth, and see
What was the End

فَضَرْبَ الرِّقَابِ ۚ حَتَّىٰ

إِذَآ أَثْخَنتُمُوهُمْ

فَشُدُّوا الْوَثَاقَ ۚ

فَإِمَّا مَنًّا بَعْدُ

وَإِمَّا فِدَآءً

حَتَّىٰ تَضَعَ الْحَرْبُ أَوْزَارَهَا ۚ ذَٰلِكَ ۚ

وَلَوْ يَشَآءُ اللَّهُ لَانتَصَرَ مِنْهُمْ

وَلَٰكِن لِّيَبْلُوَا۟ بَعْضَكُم بِبَعْضٍ ۗ

وَالَّذِينَ قُتِلُوا۟ فِى سَبِيلِ اللَّهِ

فَلَن يُضِلَّ أَعْمَالَهُمْ ۝

٥- سَيَهْدِيهِمْ وَيُصْلِحُ بَالَهُمْ ۝

٦- وَيُدْخِلُهُمُ الْجَنَّةَ

عَرَّفَهَا لَهُمْ ۝

٧- يَٰٓأَيُّهَا الَّذِينَ آمَنُوٓا۟

إِن تَنصُرُوا۟ اللَّهَ

يَنصُرْكُمْ وَيُثَبِّتْ أَقْدَامَكُمْ ۝

٨- وَالَّذِينَ كَفَرُوا۟ فَتَعْسًا لَّهُمْ

وَأَضَلَّ أَعْمَالَهُمْ ۝

٩- ذَٰلِكَ بِأَنَّهُمْ كَرِهُوا۟ مَآ أَنزَلَ اللَّهُ

فَأَحْبَطَ أَعْمَالَهُمْ ۝

١٠- أَفَلَمْ يَسِيرُوا۟ فِى الْأَرْضِ فَيَنظُرُوا۟

Of those before them
(Who did evil)?
Allah brought utter destruction
On them, and similar
(Fates await) those who
Reject Allah.

كَيْفَ كَانَ عَاقِبَةُ الَّذِيْنَ مِنْ قَبْلِهِمْ
دَمَّرَ اللّٰهُ عَلَيْهِمْ
وَلِلْكَافِرِيْنَ أَمْثَالُهَا ۞

11. That is because Allah
Is the Protector of those
Who believe, but
Those who reject Allah
Have no protector.

١١- ذٰلِكَ بِأَنَّ اللّٰهَ مَوْلَى الَّذِيْنَ اٰمَنُوْا
وَأَنَّ الْكَافِرِيْنَ لَا مَوْلٰى لَهُمْ ۞

SECTION 2.

12. Verily Allah will admit
Those who believe and do
Righteous deeds, to Gardens
Beneath which rivers flow;
While those who reject Allah
Will enjoy (this world)
And eat as cattle eat;
And the Fire will
Be their abode.

١٢- إِنَّ اللّٰهَ يُدْخِلُ الَّذِيْنَ اٰمَنُوْا وَعَمِلُوا
الصّٰلِحٰتِ جَنّٰتٍ تَجْرِيْ مِنْ تَحْتِهَا الْأَنْهَارُ
وَالَّذِيْنَ كَفَرُوْا
يَتَمَتَّعُوْنَ وَيَأْكُلُوْنَ كَمَا تَأْكُلُ الْأَنْعَامُ
وَالنَّارُ مَثْوًى لَهُمْ ۞

13. And how many cities,
With more power than
Thy city which has
Driven thee out,
Have We destroyed
(For their sins)?
And there was none
To aid them.

١٣- وَكَأَيِّنْ مِّنْ قَرْيَةٍ هِيَ أَشَدُّ قُوَّةً
مِّنْ قَرْيَتِكَ الَّتِيْ أَخْرَجَتْكَ
أَهْلَكْنٰهُمْ
فَلَا نَاصِرَ لَهُمْ ۞

14. Is then one who is
On a clear   (Path)
From his Lord,
No better than one
To whom the evil
Of his conduct seems pleasing,
And such as follow
Their own lusts?

١٤- أَفَمَنْ كَانَ عَلٰى بَيِّنَةٍ
مِّنْ رَّبِّهٖ
كَمَنْ زُيِّنَ لَهُ سُوْءُ عَمَلِهٖ
وَاتَّبَعُوْا أَهْوَاءَهُمْ ۞

15. (Here is) a Parable
Of the Garden which
The righteous are promised:
In it are rivers
Of water incorruptible;
Rivers of milk
Of which the taste

١٥- مَثَلُ الْجَنَّةِ الَّتِيْ وُعِدَ الْمُتَّقُوْنَ
فِيْهَا أَنْهَارٌ مِّنْ مَّاءٍ غَيْرِ اٰسِنٍ
وَأَنْهَارٌ مِّنْ لَّبَنٍ
لَّمْ يَتَغَيَّرْ طَعْمُهُ وَأَنْهَارٌ

Never changes; rivers
Of wine, a joy
To those who drink;
And rivers of honey
Pure and clear. In it
There are for them
All kinds of fruits;
And Grace from their Lord.
(Can those in such Bliss)
Be compared to such as
Shall dwell forever
In the Fire, and be given,
To drink, boiling water,
So that it cuts up
Their bowels (to pieces)?

مِنْ خَمْرٍ لَّذَّةٍ لِّلشَّارِبِينَ ۚ
وَأَنْهَارٌ مِّنْ عَسَلٍ مُّصَفًّى ۖ
وَلَهُمْ فِيهَا مِنْ كُلِّ الثَّمَرَاتِ
وَمَغْفِرَةٌ مِّنْ رَّبِّهِمْ ۖ
كَمَنْ هُوَ
خَالِدٌ فِي النَّارِ وَسُقُوا مَآءً حَمِيمًا
فَقَطَّعَ أَمْعَآءَهُمْ ۞

16. And among them are men
Who listen to thee,
But in the end, when they
Go out from thee,
They say to those who
Have received Knowledge,
"What is it he said
Just then?" Such are
Men whose hearts Allah
Has sealed, and who
Follow their own lusts.

١٦- وَمِنْهُمْ مَّنْ يَسْتَمِعُ إِلَيْكَ ۖ
حَتَّى إِذَا خَرَجُوا مِنْ عِنْدِكَ
قَالُوا لِلَّذِينَ أُوتُوا الْعِلْمَ
مَاذَا قَالَ آنِفًا ۚ
أُولَٰئِكَ الَّذِينَ طَبَعَ اللَّهُ عَلَىٰ قُلُوبِهِمْ
وَاتَّبَعُوا أَهْوَآءَهُمْ ۞

17. But to those who receive
Guidance, He increases
The (light of) Guidance,
And bestows on them
Their Piety and Restraint
(From evil).

١٧- وَالَّذِينَ اهْتَدَوْا
زَادَهُمْ هُدًى
وَآتَاهُمْ تَقْوَاهُمْ ۞

18. Do they then only wait
For the Hour—that it
Should come on them
Of a sudden? But already
Have come some tokens
Thereof, and when it
(Actually) is on them,
How can they benefit
Then by their admonition?

١٨- فَهَلْ يَنْظُرُونَ إِلَّا السَّاعَةَ
أَنْ تَأْتِيَهُمْ بَغْتَةً ۖ
فَقَدْ جَآءَ أَشْرَاطُهَا ۚ
فَأَنَّى لَهُمْ إِذَا جَآءَتْهُمْ ذِكْرَاهُمْ ۞

19. Know, therefore, that
There is no god
But Allah, and ask

١٩- فَاعْلَمْ أَنَّهُ لَا إِلَٰهَ إِلَّا اللَّهُ

Forgiveness for thy fault,
And for the men
And women who believe:
For Allah knows how ye
Move about and how
Ye dwell in your homes.

SECTION 3.

20. ⑳hose who believe say,
"Why is not a Sūrah
Sent down (for us)?"
But when a Sūrah
Of basic or categorical
Meaning is revealed,
And fighting is mentioned
Therein, thou wilt see those
In whose hearts is a disease
Looking at thee with a look
Of one in swoon at
The approach of death.
But more fitting for them—

21. Were it to obey
And say what is just,
And when a matter
Is resolved on, it were
Best for them if they
Were true to Allah.

22. Then, is it
To be expected of you,
If ye were put in authority,
That ye will do mischief,
In the land, and break
Your ties of kith and kin?

23. Ⓢuch are the men
Whom Allah has cursed
For He has made them
Deaf and blinded their sight.

24. Do they not then
Earnestly seek to understand
The Qur'ān, or are
Their hearts locked up
By them?

25. Those who turn back

وَاسْتَغْفِرْ لِذَنْۢبِكَ
وَلِلْمُؤْمِنِيْنَ وَالْمُؤْمِنٰتِ ؕ
وَاللّٰهُ يَعْلَمُ مُتَقَلَّبَكُمْ وَمَثْوٰىكُمْ ۞

٢٠- وَيَقُوْلُ الَّذِيْنَ اٰمَنُوْا لَوْلَا نُزِّلَتْ سُوْرَةٌ ۚ
فَاِذَاۤ اُنْزِلَتْ سُوْرَةٌ مُّحْكَمَةٌ
وَّذُكِرَ فِيْهَا الْقِتَالُ ۙ
رَاَيْتَ الَّذِيْنَ فِيْ قُلُوْبِهِمْ مَّرَضٌ
يَنْظُرُوْنَ اِلَيْكَ نَظَرَ
الْمَغْشِيِّ عَلَيْهِ مِنَ الْمَوْتِ ؕ
فَاَوْلٰى لَهُمْ ۚ

٢١- طَاعَةٌ وَّقَوْلٌ مَّعْرُوْفٌ ۟
فَاِذَا عَزَمَ الْاَمْرُ ۟
فَلَوْ صَدَقُوا اللّٰهَ لَكَانَ خَيْرًا لَّهُمْ ۚ

٢٢- فَهَلْ عَسَيْتُمْ اِنْ تَوَلَّيْتُمْ
اَنْ تُفْسِدُوْا فِى الْاَرْضِ
وَتُقَطِّعُوْۤا اَرْحَامَكُمْ ۝

٢٣- اُولٰٓئِكَ الَّذِيْنَ لَعَنَهُمُ اللّٰهُ
فَاَصَمَّهُمْ وَاَعْمٰٓى اَبْصَارَهُمْ ۝

٢٤- اَفَلَا يَتَدَبَّرُوْنَ الْقُرْاٰنَ
اَمْ عَلٰى قُلُوْبٍ اَقْفَالُهَا ۝

٢٥- اِنَّ الَّذِيْنَ ارْتَدُّوْا عَلٰٓى اَدْبَارِهِمْ

As apostates after Guidance
Was clearly shown to them—
The Evil One has instigated
Them and buoyed them up
With false hopes.

مِنْۢ بَعْدِ مَا تَبَيَّنَ لَهُمُ الْهُدَى ۙ
الشَّيْطٰنُ سَوَّلَ لَهُمْ ۚ وَاَمْلٰى لَهُمْ ۝

26. This, because they said
To those who hate what
Allah has revealed, "We
Will obey you in part
Of (this) matter"; but Allah
Knows their (inner) secrets.

٢٦- ذٰلِكَ بِاَنَّهُمْ قَالُوا لِلَّذِيْنَ كَرِهُوْا مَا
نَزَّلَ اللّٰهُ سَنُطِيْعُكُمْ فِيْ بَعْضِ الْاَمْرِ ۚ
وَاللّٰهُ يَعْلَمُ اِسْرَارَهُمْ ۝

27. But how (will it be)
When the angels take
Their souls at death,
And smite their faces
And their backs?

٢٧- فَكَيْفَ اِذَا تَوَفَّتْهُمُ الْمَلٰٓئِكَةُ
يَضْرِبُوْنَ وُجُوْهَهُمْ وَاَدْبَارَهُمْ ۝

28. This because they followed
That which called forth
The Wrath of Allah, and
They hated Allah's good pleasure;
So He made their deeds
Of no effect.

SECTION 4.

٢٨- ذٰلِكَ بِاَنَّهُمُ اتَّبَعُوْا مَا اَسْخَطَ اللّٰهَ
وَكَرِهُوْا رِضْوَانَهُ
فَاَحْبَطَ اَعْمَالَهُمْ ۝

29. Or do those in whose
Hearts is a disease, think
That Allah will not bring
To light all their rancour?

٢٩- اَمْ حَسِبَ الَّذِيْنَ فِيْ قُلُوْبِهِمْ مَّرَضٌ
اَنْ لَّنْ يُّخْرِجَ اللّٰهُ اَضْغَانَهُمْ ۝

30. Had We so willed,
We could have shown them
Up to thee, and thou
Shouldst have known them
By their marks: but surely
Thou wilt know them
By the tone of their speech!
And Allah knows
All that ye do.

٣٠- وَلَوْ نَشَآءُ لَاَرَيْنٰكَهُمْ
فَلَعَرَفْتَهُمْ بِسِيْمٰهُمْ ۚ
وَلَتَعْرِفَنَّهُمْ فِيْ لَحْنِ الْقَوْلِ ۚ
وَاللّٰهُ يَعْلَمُ اَعْمَالَكُمْ ۝

31. And We shall try you
Until We test those
Among you who strive
Their utmost and persevere
In patience; and We shall
Try your reported (mettle).

٣١- وَلَنَبْلُوَنَّكُمْ حَتّٰى نَعْلَمَ
الْمُجٰهِدِيْنَ مِنْكُمْ وَالصّٰبِرِيْنَ ۙ
وَنَبْلُوَا اَخْبَارَكُمْ ۝

32. Those who reject Allah,
Hinder (men) from
The Path of Allah, and resist
The Messenger, after Guidance
Has been clearly shown to
              them,
Will not injure Allah
In the least, but He
Will make their deeds
Of no effect.

٣٢- اِنَّ الَّذِیْنَ کَفَرُوْا وَصَدُّوْا عَنْ سَبِیْلِ
اللّٰهِ وَشَآقُّوا الرَّسُوْلَ مِنْ بَعْدِ مَا تَبَیَّنَ لَهُمُ
الْهُدٰی لَنْ یَّضُرُّوا اللّٰهَ شَیْئًا ۖ
وَسَیُحْبِطُ اَعْمَالَهُمْ ۟

33. O ye who believe!
Obey Allah, and obey
The Messenger, and make
Not vain your deeds!

٣٣- یٰۤاَیُّهَا الَّذِیْنَ اٰمَنُوْۤا اَطِیْعُوا اللّٰهَ وَاَطِیْعُوا
الرَّسُوْلَ وَلَا تُبْطِلُوْۤا اَعْمَالَکُمْ ۟

34. Those who reject Allah,
And hinder (men) from the Path
Of Allah, then die rejecting
             Allah—
Allah will not forgive them.

٣٤- اِنَّ الَّذِیْنَ کَفَرُوْا وَصَدُّوْا عَنْ سَبِیْلِ اللّٰهِ
ثُمَّ مَاتُوْا وَهُمْ کُفَّارٌ فَلَنْ یَّغْفِرَ اللّٰهُ لَهُمْ ۟

35. Be not weary and
Fainthearted, crying for peace,
When ye should be
Uppermost: for Allah is
With you, and will never
Put you in loss
For your (good) deeds.

٣٥- فَلَا تَهِنُوْا وَتَدْعُوْۤا اِلَی السَّلْمِ ۖ وَاَنْتُمُ
الْاَعْلَوْنَ ۖ
وَاللّٰهُ مَعَکُمْ وَلَنْ یَّتِرَکُمْ اَعْمَالَکُمْ ۟

36. The life of this world
Is but play and amusement:
And if ye believe
And guard against evil,
He will grant you
Your recompense, and will not
Ask you (to give up)
your possessions.

٣٦- اِنَّمَا الْحَیٰوةُ الدُّنْیَا لَعِبٌ وَّلَهْوٌ ؕ
وَاِنْ تُؤْمِنُوْا وَتَتَّقُوْا
یُؤْتِکُمْ اُجُوْرَکُمْ وَلَا
یَسْئَلْکُمْ اَمْوَالَکُمْ ۟

37. If He were to ask you
For all of them, and
Press you, ye would
Covetously withhold, and He
             would
Bring out all your ill-feeling.

٣٧- اِنْ یَّسْئَلْکُمُوْهَا
فَیُحْفِکُمْ تَبْخَلُوْا
وَیُخْرِجْ اَضْغَانَکُمْ ۟

38. Behold, ye are those

٣٨- هٰۤاَنْتُمْ هٰۤؤُلَآءِ

Invited to spend
(Of your substance)
In the Way of Allah:
But among you are some
That are niggardly. But any
Who are niggardly are so
At the expense of
Their own souls.
But Allah is free
Of all wants,
And it is ye that are needy.
If ye turn back
(From the Path), He will
Substitute in your stead
Another people; then they
Would not be like you!

تُدْعَوْنَ لِتُنْفِقُوْا فِىْ سَبِيْلِ اللّٰهِ ۚ
فَمِنْكُمْ مَّنْ يَّبْخَلُ ۚ
وَمَنْ يَّبْخَلْ فَإِنَّمَا يَبْخَلُ عَنْ نَّفْسِهٖ ۚ
وَاللّٰهُ الْغَنِىُّ
وَأَنْتُمُ الْفُقَرَآءُ ۚ
وَإِنْ تَتَوَلَّوْا يَسْتَبْدِلْ قَوْمًا غَيْرَكُمْ
ثُمَّ لَا يَكُوْنُوْٓا أَمْثَالَكُمْ ۞

INTRODUCTION TO SŪRA XLVIII. (*Fataḥ*) — 29 Verses

1.   This is the second of the group of three Medina Sūras described in the Introduction to S. xlvii. Its date is fixed by the mention of the Treaty of *Hudaibīya*, *Ẓul-qa'd* A.H. 6 = Feb. 628 (see. n. 1261 to ix. 13).

2.   Ḥudaibīya is a plain, a short day's march to the north of Mecca, a little to the west of the Medina - Mecca road, as used in the Prophet's time. Six years had passed since the Prophet had left his beloved City, and it had been in the hands of the Pagan autocracy. But Islam had grown during these six years. Its Qibla was towards the Ka'ba. The Pagans had tried to attack Islam at various times and had been foiled. By Arab custom every Arab was entitled to visit the Sacred enclosure unarmed, and fighting of any kind was prohibited during the Sacred Months (see n. 209 to ii. 194), which included the month of *Ẓul-qa'd*. In *Ẓul-qa'd* A.H. 6, therefore, the Prophet desired to perform the 'Umra or lesser pilgrimage (n. 212 to ii. 196), unarmed, but accompanied with his followers. A large following joined him, to the number of fourteen to fifteen hundred.

3.   This was not to the liking of the Pagan autocracy at Mecca, which took alarm, and in breach of all Arab tradition and usage, prepared to prevent the peaceful party from performing the rites of pilgrimage. They marched out to fight the unarmed party. The Prophet turned a little to the west of the road, and encamped at *Ḥudaibīya*, where negotiations took place. On the one hand the Prophet was unwilling to give the Quraish any pretended excuse for violence in the Sacred Territory; on the other, the Quraish had learnt, by six years' bitter experience, that their power was crumbling on all sides, and Islam was growing with its moral and spiritual forces, which were also reflected in its powers of organisation and resistance. The enthusiasm with which the Covenant of Fealty was entered into under a tree in *Ḥudaibīya* (xlviii. 18) by that great multitude united in devotion to their great leader, was evidence of the great power which he commanded even in a worldly sense if the Quraish had chosen to try conclusions with him.

4.   A peaceful Treaty was therefore concluded, known as the Treaty of *Hudaibīya*. It stipulated: (1) that there was to be peace between the parties for ten years; (2) that any tribe or person was free to join either party or make an alliance with it; (3) that if a Quraish person from Mecca, under guardianship, should join the Prophet without the guardian's permission, he (or she) should be sent back to the guardian, but in the contrary case, they should not be sent back and (4) that the Prophet and his party were not to enter Mecca that year, but that they could enter unarmed the following year.

5.   Item (3), not being reciprocal, was objected to in the Muslim camp, but it really was of little importance. Muslims under guardianship, sent back to Mecca, were not likely to renounce the blessings of Islam; on the other hand Muslims going to Mecca would be centres of influence for Islam, and it was more important that they should be allowed to remain there than that they should be sent back to Medina. It was impossible to think that there would be apostates or renegades to Paganism! "Look on this picture, and on that!"

6.　　The Muslims faithfully observed the terms of the Treaty. The following year (A.H. 7) they performed the lesser Pilgrimage in great state for three days. It is true that the Meccans later on broke the Peace in the attack which one of their allied tribes (the Banū Bakr) made on the Muslim Banū Khuza'a (who were in alliance with the Prophet), but this led to the conquest of Mecca and the sweeping away of the autocracy. Meanwhile Hudaibiya was a great victory, moral and social, as well as political, and its lessons are expounded in this Sūra, as the lessons of Badr were expounded in viii. 42-48, and of Uhud in iii. 121-129, 149-180.

Al Fatḥ (The Victory)

In the name of Allah, Most Gracious,
Most Merciful.

1.　Verily We have granted
　　Thee a manifest Victory:

2.　That Allah may forgive thee
　　Thy faults of the past
　　And those to follow;
　　Fulfil His favour to thee;
　　And guide thee
　　On the Straight Way;

3.　And that Allah may help
　　Thee with powerful help.

4.　It is He Who sent
　　Down Tranquillity
　　Into the hearts of
　　The Believers, that they may
　　Add Faith to their Faith—
　　For to Allah belong
　　The Forces of the heavens
　　And the earth; and Allah is
　　Full of Knowledge and Wisdom—

5.　That He may admit
　　The men and women
　　Who believe, to Gardens
　　Beneath which rivers flow,
　　To dwell therein for aye,
　　And remove their ills
　　From them—and that is,
　　In the sight of Allah,

The highest achievement
(For man)—

وَكَانَ ذٰلِكَ عِنْدَ اللّٰهِ فَوْزًا عَظِيْمًا ۟

6. And that He may punish
The Hypocrites, men and
Women, and the Polytheists,
Men and women, who imagine
An evil opinion of Allah.
On them is a round
Of Evil: the Wrath of Allah
Is on them: He has cursed
Them and got Hell ready
For them: and evil
Is it for a destination.

٦- وَّيُعَذِّبَ الْمُنٰفِقِيْنَ وَالْمُنٰفِقٰتِ
وَالْمُشْرِكِيْنَ وَالْمُشْرِكٰتِ
الظَّآنِّيْنَ بِاللّٰهِ ظَنَّ السَّوْءِ
عَلَيْهِمْ دَآئِرَةُ السَّوْءِ ۚ وَغَضِبَ اللّٰهُ عَلَيْهِمْ
وَلَعَنَهُمْ وَاَعَدَّ لَهُمْ جَهَنَّمَ ۚ
وَسَآءَتْ مَصِيْرًا ۟

7. For to Allah belong
The Forces of the heavens
And the earth; and Allah is
Exalted in Power,
Full of Wisdom.

٧- وَلِلّٰهِ جُنُوْدُ السَّمٰوٰتِ وَالْاَرْضِ ۚ
وَكَانَ اللّٰهُ عَزِيْزًا حَكِيْمًا ۟

8. We have truly sent thee
As a witness, as a
Bringer of Glad Tidings,
And as a Warner:

٨- اِنَّآ اَرْسَلْنٰكَ شَاهِدًا
وَّمُبَشِّرًا وَّنَذِيْرًا ۟

9. In order that ye
(O men) may believe
In Allah and His Messenger,
That ye may assist
And honour Him,
And celebrate His praises
Morning and evening.

٩- لِّتُؤْمِنُوْا بِاللّٰهِ وَرَسُوْلِهٖ
وَتُعَزِّرُوْهُ وَتُوَقِّرُوْهُ ۚ
وَتُسَبِّحُوْهُ بُكْرَةً وَّاَصِيْلًا ۟

10. Verily those who plight
Their fealty to thee
Do no less than plight
Their fealty to Allah:
The Hand of Allah is
Over their hands:
Then anyone who violates
His oath, does so
To the harm of his own
Soul, and anyone who
Fulfils what he has
Covenanted with Allah—
Allah will soon grant him
A great Reward.

١٠- اِنَّ الَّذِيْنَ يُبَايِعُوْنَكَ
اِنَّمَا يُبَايِعُوْنَ اللّٰهَ ۚ
يَدُ اللّٰهِ فَوْقَ اَيْدِيْهِمْ ۚ
فَمَنْ نَّكَثَ
فَاِنَّمَا يَنْكُثُ عَلٰى نَفْسِهٖ ۚ
وَمَنْ اَوْفٰى بِمَا عٰهَدَ عَلَيْهُ اللّٰهَ
فَسَيُؤْتِيْهِ اَجْرًا عَظِيْمًا ۟

ع

SECTION 2.

11. The desert Arabs who
Lagged behind will
Say to thee:
"We were engaged in
(Looking after) our flocks
And herds, and our families:
Do thou then ask
Forgiveness for us,"
They say with their tongues
What is not in their hearts.
Say: "Who then has
Any power at all
(To intervene) on your behalf
With Allah, if His Will
Is to give you some loss
Or to give you some profit?
But Allah is well acquainted
With all that ye do.

١١- سَيَقُوْلُ لَكَ الْمُخَلَّفُوْنَ مِنَ الْاَعْرَابِ
شَغَلَتْنَا اَمْوَالُنَا وَاَهْلُوْنَا
فَاسْتَغْفِرْ لَنَا ۚ
يَقُوْلُوْنَ بِاَلْسِنَتِهِمْ
مَّا لَيْسَ فِيْ قُلُوْبِهِمْ ۚ
قُلْ فَمَنْ يَّمْلِكُ لَكُمْ مِّنَ اللهِ شَيْئًا
اِنْ اَرَادَ بِكُمْ ضَرًّا
اَوْ اَرَادَ بِكُمْ نَفْعًا ۚ
بَلْ كَانَ اللهُ بِمَا تَعْمَلُوْنَ خَبِيْرًا ۞

12. "Nay, ye thought that
The Messenger and the Believers
Would never return to
Their families; this seemed
Pleasing in your hearts,

and
Ye conceived an evil thought,
For ye are a people
Lost (in wickedness)."

١٢- بَلْ ظَنَنْتُمْ اَنْ لَّنْ يَّنْقَلِبَ الرَّسُوْلُ
وَالْمُؤْمِنُوْنَ اِلٰۤى اَهْلِيْهِمْ اَبَدًا
وَّزُيِّنَ ذٰلِكَ فِيْ قُلُوْبِكُمْ وَظَنَنْتُمْ ظَنَّ
السَّوْءِ ۚ وَكُنْتُمْ قَوْمًا بُوْرًا ۞

13. And if any believe not
In Allah and His Messenger,
We have prepared,
For those who reject Allah,
A Blazing Fire!

١٣- وَمَنْ لَّمْ يُؤْمِنْ بِاللهِ وَرَسُوْلِهٖ
فَاِنَّا اَعْتَدْنَا لِلْكٰفِرِيْنَ سَعِيْرًا ۞

14. To Allah belongs the dominion
Of the heavens and the earth:
He forgives whom He
wills,
And He punishes whom He
Wills: but Allah is
Oft-Forgiving, Most Merciful.

١٤- وَلِلّٰهِ مُلْكُ السَّمٰوٰتِ وَالْاَرْضِ ۚ
يَغْفِرُ لِمَنْ يَّشَآءُ وَيُعَذِّبُ مَنْ يَّشَآءُ ۚ
وَكَانَ اللهُ غَفُوْرًا رَّحِيْمًا ۞

15. Those who lagged behind
(Will say), when ye (are
Free to) march and take

١٥- سَيَقُوْلُ الْمُخَلَّفُوْنَ اِذَا انْطَلَقْتُمْ اِلٰى

Booty (in war): "Permit us
To follow you." They wish
To change Allah's decree:
Say: "Not thus
Will ye follow us:
Allah has already declared
(This) beforehand": then they
Will say, "But ye are
Jealous of us." Nay,
But little do they understand
(Such things).

مَغَانِمَ لِتَأْخُذُوْهَا ذَرُوْنَا نَتَّبِعُكُمْ ۚ
يُرِيْدُوْنَ اَنْ يُّبَدِّلُوْا كَلَامَ اللّٰهِ ۚ
قُلْ لَّنْ تَتَّبِعُوْنَا كَذٰلِكُمْ
قَالَ اللّٰهُ مِنْ قَبْلُ ۚ
فَسَيَقُوْلُوْنَ بَلْ تَحْسُدُوْنَنَا ۚ
بَلْ كَانُوْا لَا يَفْقَهُوْنَ اِلَّا قَلِيْلًا ۟

16. Say to the desert Arabs
Who lagged behind: "Ye
Shall be summoned (to fight)
Against a people given to
Vehement war: then shall ye
Fight, or they shall submit.
Then if ye show obedience,
Allah will grant you
A goodly reward, but if
Ye turn back as ye
Did before, He will punish
You with a grievous Penalty."

١٦- قُلْ لِّلْمُخَلَّفِيْنَ مِنَ الْاَعْرَابِ
سَتُدْعَوْنَ اِلٰى قَوْمٍ اُولِيْ بَأْسٍ شَدِيْدٍ
تُقَاتِلُوْنَهُمْ اَوْ يُسْلِمُوْنَ ۚ
فَاِنْ تُطِيْعُوْا يُؤْتِكُمُ اللّٰهُ اَجْرًا حَسَنًا ۚ
وَاِنْ تَتَوَلَّوْا كَمَا تَوَلَّيْتُمْ
مِّنْ قَبْلُ يُعَذِّبْكُمْ عَذَابًا اَلِيْمًا ۟

17. No blame is there
On the blind, nor is
There blame on the lame,
Nor on one ill (if he
Joins not the war):
But he that obeys Allah
And His Messenger—(Allah)
Will admit him to Gardens
Beneath which rivers flow;
And he who turns back,
(Allah) will punish him
With a grievous Penalty.

١٧- لَيْسَ عَلَى الْاَعْمٰى حَرَجٌ
وَّلَا عَلَى الْاَعْرَجِ حَرَجٌ
وَّلَا عَلَى الْمَرِيْضِ حَرَجٌ ۚ
وَمَنْ يُّطِعِ اللّٰهَ وَرَسُوْلَهٗ
يُدْخِلْهُ جَنّٰتٍ تَجْرِيْ مِنْ تَحْتِهَا الْاَنْهٰرُ ۚ
وَمَنْ يَّتَوَلَّ يُعَذِّبْهُ عَذَابًا اَلِيْمًا ۟

SECTION 3.

18. Allah's Good Pleasure
Was on the Believers
When they swore Fealty
To thee under the Tree:
He knew   what was
In their hearts, and He
Sent down Tranquillity
To them; and He rewarded
Them with a speedy Victory;

١٨- لَقَدْ رَضِيَ اللّٰهُ عَنِ الْمُؤْمِنِيْنَ
اِذْ يُبَايِعُوْنَكَ تَحْتَ الشَّجَرَةِ
فَعَلِمَ مَا فِيْ قُلُوْبِهِمْ
فَاَنْزَلَ السَّكِيْنَةَ عَلَيْهِمْ
وَاَثَابَهُمْ فَتْحًا قَرِيْبًا ۟

19. And many gains will they
Acquire (besides): and Allah
Is Exalted in Power,
Full of Wisdom.

١٩- وَمَغَانِمَ كَثِيرَةً يَأْخُذُونَهَا ۗ
وَكَانَ اللّٰهُ عَزِيزًا حَكِيمًا ۝

20. Allah has promised you
Many gains that ye shall
Acquire, and He has given
You these beforehand; and
He has restrained the hands
Of men from you; that it
May be a Sign for
The Believers, and that
He may guide you
To a Straight Path;

٢٠- وَعَدَكُمُ اللّٰهُ مَغَانِمَ كَثِيرَةً تَأْخُذُونَهَا
فَعَجَّلَ لَكُمْ
هٰذِهٖ وَكَفَّ أَيْدِىَ النَّاسِ عَنْكُمْ ۚ
وَلِتَكُونَ اٰيَةً لِّلْمُؤْمِنِينَ
وَيَهْدِيَكُمْ صِرَاطًا مُّسْتَقِيمًا ۝

21. And other gains (there are),
Which are not within
Your power, but which
Allah has compassed: and Allah
Has power over all things.

٢١- وَأُخْرٰى لَمْ تَقْدِرُوا عَلَيْهَا
قَدْ أَحَاطَ اللّٰهُ بِهَا ۚ
وَكَانَ اللّٰهُ عَلٰى كُلِّ شَيْءٍ قَدِيرًا ۝

22. If the Unbelievers
Should fight you, they would
Certainly turn their backs;
Then would they find
Neither protector nor helper.

٢٢- وَلَوْ قَاتَلَكُمُ الَّذِينَ كَفَرُوا
لَوَلَّوُا الْأَدْبَارَ
ثُمَّ لَا يَجِدُونَ وَلِيًّا وَلَا نَصِيرًا ۝

23. (Such has been) the practice
(Approved) of Allah already
In the past: no change
Wilt thou find in
The practice (approved) of Allah.

٢٣- سُنَّةَ اللّٰهِ الَّتِى
قَدْ خَلَتْ مِنْ قَبْلُ ۖ
وَلَنْ تَجِدَ لِسُنَّةِ اللّٰهِ تَبْدِيلًا ۝

24. And it is He Who
Has restrained their hands
From you and your hands
From them in the midst
Of Makkah, after that He
Gave you the victory
Over them. And Allah sees
Well all that ye do.

٢٤- وَهُوَ الَّذِى كَفَّ أَيْدِيَهُمْ
عَنْكُمْ وَأَيْدِيَكُمْ عَنْهُمْ بِبَطْنِ مَكَّةَ
مِنْ بَعْدِ أَنْ أَظْفَرَكُمْ عَلَيْهِمْ ۚ
وَكَانَ اللّٰهُ بِمَا تَعْمَلُونَ بَصِيرًا ۝

25. They are the ones who
Denied revelation and hindered
you
From the Sacred Mosque
And the sacrificial
animals,

٢٥- هُمُ الَّذِينَ كَفَرُوا
وَصَدُّوكُمْ عَنِ الْمَسْجِدِ الْحَرَامِ
وَالْهَدْىَ مَعْكُوفًا

Detained from reaching their
Place of sacrifice. Had there
Not been believing men
And believing women whom
Ye did not know that
Ye were trampling down
And on whose account
A crime would have accrued
To you without (your)
              knowledge,
(Allah would have allowed you
To force your way, but
He held back your hands)
That He may admit
To His Mercy whom He
              will.
If they had been
Apart, We should
Certainly have punished
The Unbelievers among them
With a grievous punishment.

26. While the Unbelievers
Got up in their hearts
Heat and cant—the heat
And cant of Ignorance—
Allah sent down His
              Tranquillity
To his Messenger and to
The Believers, and made them
Stick close to the command
Of self-restraint; and well
Were they entitled to it
And worthy of it.
And Allah has full knowledge
Of all things.

SECTION 4.

27. Truly did Allah fulfil
The vision for His Messenger:
Ye shall enter the Sacred
Mosque, if Allah wills,
With minds secure, heads shaved,
Hair cut short, and without fear.
For He knew what ye
Knew not, and He granted,
Besides this, a speedy victory.

28. It is He Who has sent

أَن يَبْلُغَ مَحِلَّهُ ۚ
وَلَوْلَا رِجَالٌ مُّؤْمِنُونَ وَنِسَاءٌ مُّؤْمِنَاتٌ
لَّمْ تَعْلَمُوهُمْ أَن تَطَئُوهُمْ
فَتُصِيبَكُم مِّنْهُم مَّعَرَّةٌ
بِغَيْرِ عِلْمٍ ۚ
لِيُدْخِلَ اللَّهُ فِي رَحْمَتِهِ
مَن يَشَاءُ ۚ
لَوْ تَزَيَّلُوا
لَعَذَّبْنَا الَّذِينَ كَفَرُوا مِنْهُمْ
عَذَابًا أَلِيمًا ۝

٢٦- إِذْ جَعَلَ الَّذِينَ كَفَرُوا فِي قُلُوبِهِمُ
الْحَمِيَّةَ حَمِيَّةَ الْجَاهِلِيَّةِ
فَأَنزَلَ اللَّهُ سَكِينَتَهُ
عَلَى رَسُولِهِ وَعَلَى الْمُؤْمِنِينَ
وَأَلْزَمَهُمْ كَلِمَةَ التَّقْوَى
وَكَانُوا أَحَقَّ بِهَا وَأَهْلَهَا ۚ
وَكَانَ اللَّهُ بِكُلِّ شَيْءٍ عَلِيمًا ۝

٢٧- لَقَدْ صَدَقَ اللَّهُ رَسُولَهُ الرُّؤْيَا بِالْحَقِّ ۖ
لَتَدْخُلُنَّ الْمَسْجِدَ الْحَرَامَ إِن شَاءَ اللَّهُ
آمِنِينَ مُحَلِّقِينَ رُؤُوسَكُمْ وَمُقَصِّرِينَ لَا
تَخَافُونَ ۖ فَعَلِمَ مَا لَمْ تَعْلَمُوا
فَجَعَلَ مِن دُونِ ذَلِكَ فَتْحًا قَرِيبًا ۝

٢٨- هُوَ الَّذِي أَرْسَلَ رَسُولَهُ بِالْهُدَى

His Messenger with Guidance
And the Religion of Truth,
To proclaim it over
All religion: and enough
Is Allah for a Witness.

29. Muhammad is the Messenger
Of Allah; and those who are
With him are strong
Against Unbelievers, (but)
Compassionate amongst each
other.

Thou wilt see them bow
And prostrate themselves
(In prayer), seeking Grace
From Allah and (His) Good
Pleasure.

On their faces are their
Marks,-(being) the traces
Of their prostration.
This is their similitude
In the Tawrah;
And their similitude
In the Gospel is
Like a seed which sends
Forth its blade, then
Makes it strong; it then
Becomes thick, and it stands
On its own stem, (filling)
The sowers with wonder
And delight. As a result,
It fills the Unbelievers
With rage at them.
Allah has promised those
Among them who believe
And do righteous deeds
Forgiveness,
And a great Reward.

وَدِيْنِ الْحَقِّ لِيُظْهِرَهُ عَلَى
الدِّيْنِ كُلِّهِ ۚ وَكَفٰى بِاللّٰهِ شَهِيْدًا ۟

٢٩ - مُحَمَّدٌ رَّسُوْلُ اللّٰهِ ؕ
وَالَّذِيْنَ مَعَهُ أَشِدَّآءُ عَلَى الْكُفَّارِ
رُحَمَآءُ بَيْنَهُمْ
تَرٰهُمْ رُكَّعًا سُجَّدًا
يَّبْتَغُوْنَ فَضْلًا مِّنَ اللّٰهِ وَرِضْوَانًا ۫
سِيْمَاهُمْ فِيْ وُجُوْهِهِمْ مِّنْ أَثَرِ السُّجُوْدِ ؕ
ذٰلِكَ مَثَلُهُمْ فِى التَّوْرٰىةِ ۛۖ
وَمَثَلُهُمْ فِى الْإِنْجِيْلِ ۛۚ
كَزَرْعٍ
أَخْرَجَ شَطْـٔهٗ فَأٰزَرَهٗ
فَاسْتَغْلَظَ فَاسْتَوٰى
عَلٰى سُوْقِهٖ
يُعْجِبُ الزُّرَّاعَ
لِيَغِيْظَ بِهِمُ الْكُفَّارَ ؕ
وَعَدَ اللّٰهُ الَّذِيْنَ أٰمَنُوْا
وَعَمِلُوا الصّٰلِحٰتِ
مِنْهُمْ مَّغْفِرَةً
وَّ أَجْرًا عَظِيْمًا ۟ ۧ

INTRODUCTION TO SŪRA XLIX. (*Ḥujurāt*) — 18 Verses

This is the third of the group of three Medina Sūras, which began with S. xlvii. See the Introduction to that Sūra.

Its subject-matter is the manners to be observed by the members of the rapidly growing Muslim community, among themselves and towards its Leader. The key-word "*Ḥujurāt*" (Inner Apartments) occurs in verse 4.

Its date is referred to the Year of Deputations, A.H. 9, when a large number of deputations of all kinds visited Medina to offer their allegiance to Islam.

Al Ḥujurāt (The Chambers)

In the name of Allah, Most Gracious, Most Merciful.

بِسْمِ اللهِ الرَّحْمٰنِ الرَّحِيْمِ

1. O ye who believe!
Put not yourselves forward
Before Allah and His Messenger;
But fear Allah: for Allah
Is He Who hears
And knows all things.

١- يَاۤيُّهَا الَّذِيْنَ اٰمَنُوْا لَا تُقَدِّمُوْا بَيْنَ يَدَيِ اللهِ وَرَسُوْلِهٖ وَاتَّقُوا اللهَ ۚ اِنَّ اللهَ سَمِيْعٌ عَلِيْمٌ ۝

2. O ye who believe!
Raise not your voices
Above the voice of the Prophet,
Nor speak aloud to him
In talk, as ye may
Speak aloud to one another,
Lest your deeds become
Vain and ye perceive not.

٢- يَاۤيُّهَا الَّذِيْنَ اٰمَنُوْا لَا تَرْفَعُوْۤا اَصْوَاتَكُمْ فَوْقَ صَوْتِ النَّبِيِّ وَلَا تَجْهَرُوْا لَهٗ بِالْقَوْلِ كَجَهْرِ بَعْضِكُمْ لِبَعْضٍ اَنْ تَحْبَطَ اَعْمَالُكُمْ وَاَنْتُمْ لَا تَشْعُرُوْنَ ۝

3. Those that lower their voice
In the presence of
Allah's Messenger—their hearts
Has Allah tested for piety:
For them is Forgiveness
And a great Reward.

٣- اِنَّ الَّذِيْنَ يَغُضُّوْنَ اَصْوَاتَهُمْ عِنْدَ رَسُوْلِ اللهِ اُولٰٓئِكَ الَّذِيْنَ امْتَحَنَ اللهُ قُلُوْبَهُمْ لِلتَّقْوٰى ۚ لَهُمْ مَغْفِرَةٌ وَّاَجْرٌ عَظِيْمٌ ۝

4. Those who shout out
To thee from without
The Inner Apartments
Most of them lack understanding.

٤- اِنَّ الَّذِيْنَ يُنَادُوْنَكَ مِنْ وَّرَآءِ الْحُجُرَاتِ اَكْثَرُهُمْ لَا يَعْقِلُوْنَ ۝

5. If only they had patience
   Until thou couldst
   Come out to them,
   It would be best
   For them: but Allah is
   Oft-Forgiving, Most Merciful.

٥- وَلَوْ اَنَّهُمْ صَبَرُوْا حَتّٰى تَخْرُجَ اِلَيْهِمْ
لَكَانَ خَيْرًا لَّهُمْ ۖ
وَاللهُ غَفُوْرٌ رَّحِيْمٌ ٥

6. O ye who believe!
   If a wicked person comes
   To you with any news,
   Ascertain the truth, lest
   Ye harm people unwittingly,
   And afterwards become
   Full of repentance for
   What ye have done.

٦- يٰاَيُّهَا الَّذِيْنَ اٰمَنُوْٓا
اِنْ جَآءَكُمْ فَاسِقٌۢ بِنَبَاٍ
فَتَبَيَّنُوْٓا اَنْ تُصِيْبُوْا قَوْمًا بِجَهَالَةٍ
فَتُصْبِحُوْا عَلٰى مَا فَعَلْتُمْ نٰدِمِيْنَ ٥

7. And know that among you
   Is Allah's Messenger: were he,
   In many matters, to follow
   Your (wishes), ye would
   Certainly fall into misfortune:
   But Allah has endeared
   The Faith to you, and
   Has made it beautiful
   In your hearts, and He
   Has made hateful to you
   Unbelief, wickedness, and
   Rebellion: such indeed are
   Those who walk in righteousness —

٧- وَاعْلَمُوْٓا اَنَّ فِيْكُمْ رَسُوْلَ اللهِ ۖ
لَوْ يُطِيْعُكُمْ فِيْ كَثِيْرٍ مِّنَ الْاَمْرِ لَعَنِتُّمْ
وَلٰكِنَّ اللهَ حَبَّبَ اِلَيْكُمُ الْاِيْمَانَ
وَزَيَّنَهٗ فِيْ قُلُوْبِكُمْ
وَكَرَّهَ اِلَيْكُمُ الْكُفْرَ وَالْفُسُوْقَ وَالْعِصْيَانَ ۚ
اُولٰٓئِكَ هُمُ الرّٰشِدُوْنَ ۙ

8. A grace and favour
   From Allah; and Allah
   Is full of Knowledge
   And Wisdom,

٨- فَضْلًا مِّنَ اللهِ وَنِعْمَةً ۚ
وَاللهُ عَلِيْمٌ حَكِيْمٌ ٥

9. If two parties among
   The Believers fall into
   A quarrel, make ye peace
   Between them: but if
   One of them transgresses
   Beyond bounds against the other,
   Then fight ye (all) against
   The one that transgresses
   Until it complies with
   The command of Allah;
   But if it complies, then
   Make peace between them
   With justice, and be fair:

٩- وَاِنْ طَآئِفَتٰنِ مِنَ الْمُؤْمِنِيْنَ اقْتَتَلُوْا
فَاَصْلِحُوْا بَيْنَهُمَا ۚ
فَاِنْۢ بَغَتْ اِحْدٰىهُمَا عَلَى الْاُخْرٰى
فَقَاتِلُوا الَّتِيْ تَبْغِيْ
حَتّٰى تَفِيْٓءَ اِلٰٓى اَمْرِ اللهِ ۚ
فَاِنْ فَآءَتْ
فَاَصْلِحُوْا بَيْنَهُمَا بِالْعَدْلِ وَاَقْسِطُوْا ۖ

For Allah loves those
Who are fair (and just).

إِنَّ اللهَ يُحِبُّ الْمُقْسِطِينَ ۞

10. The Believers are but
A single Brotherhood:
So make peace and
Reconciliation between your
Two (contending) brothers;
And fear Allah, that ye
May receive Mercy.

١٠- إِنَّمَا الْمُؤْمِنُونَ إِخْوَةٌ
فَأَصْلِحُوا بَيْنَ أَخَوَيْكُمْ
وَاتَّقُوا اللهَ لَعَلَّكُمْ تُرْحَمُونَ ۞

SECTION 2.

11. ⓞ ye who believe!
Let not some men
Among you laugh at others:
It may be that
The (latter) are better
Than the (former):
Nor let some women
Laugh at others:
It may be that
The (latter) are better
Than the (former):
Nor defame nor be
Sarcastic to each other,
Nor call each other
By (offensive) nicknames:
Ill-seeming is a name
Connoting wickedness,
(To be used of one)
After he has believed:
And those who
Do not desist are
(Indeed) doing wrong.

١١- يَا أَيُّهَا الَّذِينَ آمَنُوا
لَا يَسْخَرْ قَوْمٌ مِنْ قَوْمٍ
عَسَى أَنْ يَكُونُوا خَيْرًا مِنْهُمْ
وَلَا نِسَاءٌ مِنْ نِسَاءٍ
عَسَى أَنْ يَكُنَّ خَيْرًا مِنْهُنَّ
وَلَا تَلْمِزُوا أَنْفُسَكُمْ
وَلَا تَنَابَزُوا بِالْأَلْقَابِ
بِئْسَ الِاسْمُ الْفُسُوقُ
بَعْدَ الْإِيمَانِ
وَمَنْ لَمْ يَتُبْ
فَأُولَٰئِكَ هُمُ الظَّالِمُونَ ۞

12. ⓞ ye who believe!
Avoid suspicion as much
(As possible): for suspicion
In some cases is a sin:
And spy not on each other,
Nor speak ill of each other
Behind their backs. Would any
Of you like to eat
The flesh of his dead
Brother? Nay, ye would
Abhor it . . . But fear Allah:
For Allah is Oft-Returning,
Most Merciful.

١٢- يَا أَيُّهَا الَّذِينَ آمَنُوا
اجْتَنِبُوا كَثِيرًا مِنَ الظَّنِّ
إِنَّ بَعْضَ الظَّنِّ إِثْمٌ وَلَا تَجَسَّسُوا
وَلَا يَغْتَبْ بَعْضُكُمْ بَعْضًا
أَيُحِبُّ أَحَدُكُمْ أَنْ يَأْكُلَ لَحْمَ أَخِيهِ مَيْتًا
فَكَرِهْتُمُوهُ وَاتَّقُوا اللهَ
إِنَّ اللهَ تَوَّابٌ رَحِيمٌ ۞

13. ⓞ mankind! We created
You from a single (pair)
Of a male and a female,
And made you into
Nations and tribes, that
Ye may know each other
(Not that ye may despise
(Each other). Verily
The most honoured of you
In the sight of Allah
Is (he who is) the most
Righteous of you.
And Allah has full knowledge
And is well-acquainted
(With all things).

١٣ - يٰۤاَيُّهَا النَّاسُ اِنَّا خَلَقْنٰكُمْ
مِّنْ ذَكَرٍ وَّ اُنْثٰى وَجَعَلْنٰكُمْ
شُعُوْبًا وَّقَبَآئِلَ لِتَعَارَفُوْا
اِنَّ اَكْرَمَكُمْ
عِنْدَ اللّٰهِ اَتْقٰكُمْ
اِنَّ اللّٰهَ عَلِيْمٌ خَبِيْرٌ ۝

14. ⓣhe desert Arabs say,
"We believe." Say, "Ye
Have no faith; but ye
(Only) say, 'We have submitted
Our wills to Allah,'
For not yet has Faith
Entered your hearts.
But if ye obey Allah
And His Messenger, He
Will not belittle aught
Of your deeds: for Allah
Is Oft-Forgiving, Most Merciful."

١٤ - قَالَتِ الْاَعْرَابُ اٰمَنَّا
قُلْ لَّمْ تُؤْمِنُوْا وَلٰكِنْ قُوْلُوْۤا اَسْلَمْنَا
وَلَمَّا يَدْخُلِ الْاِيْمَانُ فِىْ قُلُوْبِكُمْ
وَاِنْ تُطِيْعُوا اللّٰهَ وَ رَسُوْلَهٗ
لَا يَلِتْكُمْ مِّنْ اَعْمَالِكُمْ شَيْئًا
اِنَّ اللّٰهَ غَفُوْرٌ رَّحِيْمٌ ۝

15. Only those are Believers
Who have believed in Allah
And His Messenger, and have
Never since doubted, but
Have striven with their
Belongings and their persons
In the Cause of Allah:
Such are the sincere ones.

١٥ - اِنَّمَا الْمُؤْمِنُوْنَ الَّذِيْنَ اٰمَنُوْا بِاللّٰهِ وَ
رَسُوْلِهٖ ثُمَّ لَمْ يَرْتَابُوْا
وَجَاهَدُوْا بِاَمْوَالِهِمْ وَ اَنْفُسِهِمْ فِىْ
سَبِيْلِ اللّٰهِ اُولٰٓئِكَ هُمُ الصّٰدِقُوْنَ ۝

16. Say: "What! Will ye
Instruct Allah about your
Religion? But Allah knows
All that is in the heavens
And on earth: He has
Full knowledge of all things.

١٦ - قُلْ اَتُعَلِّمُوْنَ اللّٰهَ بِدِيْنِكُمْ
وَاللّٰهُ يَعْلَمُ مَا فِى السَّمٰوٰتِ
وَمَا فِى الْاَرْضِ وَاللّٰهُ بِكُلِّ شَىْءٍ عَلِيْمٌ ۝

17. They impress on thee

١٧ - يَمُنُّوْنَ عَلَيْكَ اَنْ اَسْلَمُوْا

قُل لَّا تَمُنُّوا عَلَىَّ إِسْلَامَكُمۡ
بَلِ اللَّهُ يَمُنُّ عَلَيۡكُمۡ
أَنۡ هَدَىٰكُمۡ لِلۡإِيمَانِ
إِن كُنتُمۡ صَٰدِقِينَ ۝

As a favour that they
Have embraced Islam.
Say, "Count not your Islam
As a favour upon me:
Nay, Allah has conferred
A favour upon you
That He has guided you
To the Faith, if ye
Be true and sincere.

18. "Verily Allah Knows
The secrets of the heavens
And the earth: and Allah
Sees well all
That ye do."

١٨ ـ إِنَّ اللَّهَ يَعۡلَمُ غَيۡبَ السَّمَٰوَٰتِ وَ
الۡأَرۡضِ ۚ وَاللَّهُ بَصِيرٌۢ بِمَا تَعۡمَلُونَ ۝

INTRODUCTION TO SŪRA L. (*Qāf*) — 45 Verses

We now come to a group of seven Meccan Sūras (*l,-lvi.*), dealing with God's revelation through nature, through history, and through the mouths of the Prophets, and pointing to the Hereafter. We saw that the last group of three (*xlvii,-xlix*) dealt with the external and internal relations of the Ummat when formed. In the present group our attention is more particularly directed to aspects eschatological,— the Future before us when this life is done.

This particular Sūra belongs to the early Meccan period. After an appeal to nature and to the fate of wicked peoples in history, it removes as it were the veil (verse 22) from the Future after death.

Qaf 4939

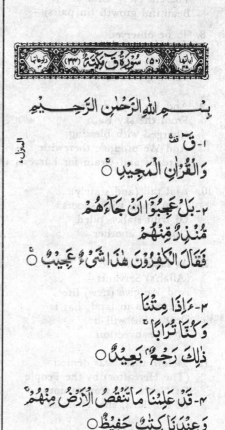

In the name of Allah, Most Gracious, Most Merciful.

1. Qaf:
   By the Glorious   Qur'ān
   (Thou art Allah's Messenger).

2. But they wonder that
   There has come to them
   A Warner from among
   Themselves.
   So the Unbelievers say:
   "This is a wonderful thing!

3. "What! When we die
   And become dust, (shall we
   Live again?) That is
   A (sort of) Return
   Far (from our understanding)."

4. We already know
   How much of them
   The earth takes away:
   With Us is a Record
   Guarding (the full account).

5. But they deny the truth
   When it comes to them:
   So they are in
   A confused state.

6. Do they not look
At the sky above them?—
How We have made it
And adorned it,
And there are no
Flaws in it?

٦- أَفَلَمْ يَنْظُرُوا إِلَى السَّمَاءِ فَوْقَهُمْ كَيْفَ بَنَيْنَاهَا وَزَيَّنَّاهَا وَمَا لَهَا مِنْ فُرُوجٍ ۝

7. And the earth—
We have spread it out,
And set thereon mountains
Standing firm, and produced
Therein every kind of
Beautiful growth (in pairs)—

٧- وَالْأَرْضَ مَدَدْنَاهَا وَأَلْقَيْنَا فِيهَا رَوَاسِيَ وَأَنْبَتْنَا فِيهَا مِنْ كُلِّ زَوْجٍ بَهِيجٍ ۝

8. To be observed
And commemorated
By every devotee
Turning (to Allah).

٨- تَبْصِرَةً وَذِكْرَى لِكُلِّ عَبْدٍ مُنِيبٍ ۝

9. And We send down
From the sky Rain
Charged with blessing,
And We produce therewith
Gardens and Grain for harvests;

٩- وَنَزَّلْنَا مِنَ السَّمَاءِ مَاءً مُبَارَكًا فَأَنْبَتْنَا بِهِ جَنَّاتٍ وَحَبَّ الْحَصِيدِ ۝

10. And tall (and stately)
Palm trees, with shoots
Of fruit stalks, piled
One over another—

١٠- وَالنَّخْلَ بَاسِقَاتٍ لَهَا طَلْعٌ نَضِيدٌ ۝

11. As sustenance for
(Allah's) Servants—
And We give (new) life
Therewith to land that is
Dead: thus will be
The Resurrection.

١١- رِزْقًا لِلْعِبَادِ وَأَحْيَيْنَا بِهِ بَلْدَةً مَيْتًا كَذَلِكَ الْخُرُوجُ ۝

12. Before them was denied
(The Hereafter) by the People
Of Noah, the Companions
Of the Rass, the Thamūd,

١٢- كَذَّبَتْ قَبْلَهُمْ قَوْمُ نُوحٍ وَأَصْحَابُ الرَّسِّ وَثَمُودُ ۝

13. The 'Ād, Pharaoh,
The Brethren of Lūṭ,

١٣- وَعَادٌ وَفِرْعَوْنُ وَإِخْوَانُ لُوطٍ ۝

14. The Companions of the Wood,
And the People of Tubba';
Each one (of them) rejected
The messengers, and My warning

١٤- وَأَصْحَابُ الْأَيْكَةِ وَقَوْمُ تُبَّعٍ كُلٌّ كَذَّبَ الرُّسُلَ

Was duly fulfilled (in them).

15. Were We then weary
With the first Creation,
That they should be
In confused doubt
About a new Creation?

SECTION 2.

16. It was We Who
Created man, and We know
What dark suggestions his soul
Makes to him: for We
Are nearer to him
Than (his) jugular vein.

17. Behold, two (guardian angels)
Appointed to learn (his doings)
Learn (and note them),
One sitting on the right
And one on the left.

18. Not a word does he
Utter but there is
A sentinel by him,
Ready (to note it).

19. And the stupor of death
Will bring truth (before
His eyes): "This was
The thing which thou
Wast trying to escape!"

20. And the Trumpet
Shall be blown:
That will be the Day
Whereof Warning (had been
given).

21. And there will come forth
Every soul: with each
Will be an (angel) to drive,
And an (angel) to
Bear witness.

22. (It will be said:)
"Thou wast heedless
Of this; now have We
Removed thy veil,

فَحَقَّ وَعِيْدِ ۟

١٥- اَفَعَيِيْنَا بِالْخَلْقِ الْاَوَّلِ ؕ
بَلْ هُمْ فِيْ لَبْسٍ
مِّنْ خَلْقٍ جَدِيْدٍۚ ۟

١٦- وَلَقَدْ خَلَقْنَا الْاِنْسَانَ
وَنَعْلَمُ مَا تُوَسْوِسُ بِهٖ نَفْسُهٗ ۚ وَنَحْنُ
اَقْرَبُ اِلَيْهِ مِنْ حَبْلِ الْوَرِيْدِ ۟

١٧- اِذْ يَتَلَقَّى الْمُتَلَقِّيٰنِ
عَنِ الْيَمِيْنِ وَعَنِ الشِّمَالِ قَعِيْدٌ ۟

١٨- مَا يَلْفِظُ مِنْ قَوْلٍ
اِلَّا لَدَيْهِ رَقِيْبٌ عَتِيْدٌ ۟

١٩- وَجَآءَتْ سَكْرَةُ الْمَوْتِ بِالْحَقِّ ؕ
ذٰلِكَ مَا كُنْتَ مِنْهُ تَحِيْدُ ۟

٢٠- وَنُفِخَ فِى الصُّوْرِ ؕ
ذٰلِكَ يَوْمُ الْوَعِيْدِ ۟

٢١- وَجَآءَتْ كُلُّ نَفْسٍ
مَّعَهَا سَآئِقٌ وَّشَهِيْدٌ ۟

٢٢- لَقَدْ كُنْتَ فِيْ غَفْلَةٍ مِّنْ هٰذَا
فَكَشَفْنَا عَنْكَ غِطَآءَكَ

And sharp is thy sight
This Day!"

تَبْصَرُكَ الْيَوْمَ حَدِيدٌ ○

23. And his Companion   will say:
"Here is (his record) ready
With me!"

٢٣- وَقَالَ قَرِيْنُهٗ
هٰذَا مَا لَدَيَّ عَتِيدٌ ۭ

24. (The sentence will be:)
"Throw, throw   into Hell
Every contumacious Rejecter,
(Of Allah)!—

٢٤- اَلْقِيَا فِيْ جَهَنَّمَ
كُلَّ كَفَّارٍ عَنِيْدٍ ۙ

25. "Who forbade what was good,
Transgressed all bounds,
Cast doubts and suspicions;

٢٥- مَّنَّاعٍ لِّلْخَيْرِ
مُعْتَدٍ مُّرِيْبٍ ۙ

26. "Who set up another god
Beside Allah: throw him
Into a severe Penalty."

٢٦- الَّذِيْ جَعَلَ مَعَ اللّٰهِ اِلٰهًا اٰخَرَ
فَاَلْقِيٰهُ فِى الْعَذَابِ الشَّدِيْدِ ○

27. His Companion   will say:
"Our   Lord! I did not
Make him transgress,
But he was (himself)
Far astray."

٢٧- قَالَ قَرِيْنُهٗ
رَبَّنَا مَا اَطْغَيْتُهٗ
وَلٰكِنْ كَانَ فِيْ ضَلٰلٍ بَعِيْدٍ ○

28.   He will say: 'Dispute not
With each other
In My Presence:
I had already in advance
Sent you   Warning.

٢٨- قَالَ لَا تَخْتَصِمُوْا لَدَيَّ
وَقَدْ قَدَّمْتُ اِلَيْكُمْ بِالْوَعِيْدِ ○

29.   "The Word changes not
Before Me, and I do not
The least injustice
To My Servants."

SECTION 3.

٢٩- مَا يُبَدَّلُ الْقَوْلُ لَدَيَّ
وَمَا اَنَا بِظَلَّامٍ لِّلْعَبِيْدِ ۖ

30. One Day We will
Ask Hell, "Art thou
Filled to the full?"
It will say, "Are there
Any more (to come)?"

٣٠- يَوْمَ نَقُوْلُ لِجَهَنَّمَ هَلِ
امْتَلَاْتِ
وَتَقُوْلُ هَلْ مِنْ مَّزِيْدٍ ○

31. And the Garden
Will be brought nigh

٣١- وَاُزْلِفَتِ الْجَنَّةُ

To the Righteous—no more
A thing distant.

32. (A voice will say:)
"This is what was
Promised for you—
For everyone who turned
(To Allah) in sincere repentance,
Who kept (His Law),

لِلْمُتَّقِيْنَ غَيْرَ بَعِيْدٍ ۝

٣٢-هٰذَا مَا تُوْعَدُوْنَ
لِكُلِّ اَوَّابٍ
حَفِيْظٍ ۚ

33. "Who feared (Allah)
Most Gracious unseen,
And brought a heart
Turned in devotion (to Him):

٣٣-مَنْ خَشِيَ الرَّحْمٰنَ بِالْغَيْبِ
وَجَاءَ بِقَلْبٍ مُّنِيْبٍ ۙ

34. "Enter ye therein
In Peace and Security:
This is a Day
Of Eternal Life!"

٣٤-اُدْخُلُوْهَا بِسَلٰمٍ ؕ
ذٰلِكَ يَوْمُ الْخُلُوْدِ ۝

35. There will be for them
Therein all that they wish—
And more besides
In Our Presence.

٣٥-لَهُمْ مَّا يَشَاءُوْنَ فِيْهَا
وَلَدَيْنَا مَزِيْدٌ ۝

36. But how many
Generations before them
Did We destroy (for their
Sins)—stronger in power
Than they? Then did they
Wander through the land:
Was there any place
Of escape (for them)?

٣٦-وَكَمْ اَهْلَكْنَا قَبْلَهُمْ مِّنْ قَرْنٍ
هُمْ اَشَدُّ مِنْهُمْ بَطْشًا
فَنَقَّبُوْا فِى الْبِلَادِ ؕ
هَلْ مِنْ مَّحِيْصٍ ۝

37. Verily in this
Is a Message
For any that has
A heart and understanding
Or who gives ear and
Earnestly witnesses (the truth).

٣٧-اِنَّ فِيْ ذٰلِكَ لَذِكْرٰى
لِمَنْ كَانَ لَهٗ قَلْبٌ
اَوْ اَلْقَى السَّمْعَ وَهُوَ شَهِيْدٌ ۝

38. We created the heavens
And the earth and all
Between them in Six Days,
Nor did any sense
Of weariness touch Us.

٣٨-وَلَقَدْ خَلَقْنَا السَّمٰوٰتِ وَالْاَرْضَ
وَمَا بَيْنَهُمَا فِيْ سِتَّةِ اَيَّامٍ ۖ
وَّمَا مَسَّنَا مِنْ لُّغُوْبٍ ۝

39. Bear, then, with patience,

٣٩-فَاصْبِرْ عَلٰى مَا يَقُوْلُوْنَ

All that they say,
And celebrate the praises
Of thy Lord, before
The rising of the sun
And before (its) setting,

وَسَبِّحْ بِحَمْدِ رَبِّكَ
قَبْلَ طُلُوعِ الشَّمْسِ
وَقَبْلَ الْغُرُوبِ ۟

40. And during part
Of the night, (also,)
Celebrate His praises
And (so likewise)
After the postures
Of adoration.

٤٠- وَمِنَ الَّيْلِ
فَسَبِّحْهُ وَ
اَدْبَارَ السُّجُودِ ○

41. And listen for the Day
When the Caller will call
Out from a place
Quite near—

٤١- وَاسْتَمِعْ يَوْمَ يُنَادِ الْمُنَادِ
مِنْ مَّكَانٍ قَرِيبٍ ۟

42. The Day when they will
Hear a (mighty) Blast
In (very) truth: that
Will be the Day
Of Resurrection.

٤٢- يَوْمَ يَسْمَعُونَ الصَّيْحَةَ بِالْحَقِّ ۚ
ذٰلِكَ يَوْمُ الْخُرُوجِ ○

43. Verily it is We Who
Give Life and Death;
And to Us is
The Final Goal—

٤٣- اِنَّا نَحْنُ نُحْيِ وَنُمِيتُ
وَاِلَيْنَا الْمَصِيرُ ۟

44. The Day when
The Earth will be
Rent asunder, from (men)
Hurrying out: that will be
A gathering together—
Quite easy for Us.

٤٤- يَوْمَ تَشَقَّقُ الْاَرْضُ عَنْهُمْ سِرَاعًا ۚ
ذٰلِكَ حَشْرٌ
عَلَيْنَا يَسِيرٌ ○

45. We know best what they
Say; and thou art not
One to overawe them
By force. So admonish
With the Qur'an such
As fear My Warning!

٤٥- نَحْنُ اَعْلَمُ بِمَا يَقُولُونَ
وَمَا اَنْتَ عَلَيْهِمْ بِجَبَّارٍ ۟
فَذَكِّرْ بِالْقُرْآنِ مَنْ يَخَافُ وَعِيدِ ۟

INTRODUCTION TO SŪRA LI. (*Ẕāriyāt*) — 60 Verses

This is an early Meccan Sūra, with highly mystic meaning. It is the second of the seven Sūras forming a group dealing with Revelation and the Hereafter. See Introduction to S.*l*. This Sūra deals with the varying ways in which Truth prevails irresistibly even against all human probabilities.

Al Dhāriyāt (The Winds That Scatter)

In the name of Allah, Most Gracious,
Most Merciful.

بِسْمِ اللهِ الرَّحْمٰنِ الرَّحِيْمِ

1. By the (Winds)
   That scatter broadcast;

١- وَالذّٰرِيٰتِ ذَرْوًا ۟

2. And those that
   Lift and bear away
   Heavy weights;

٢- فَالْحٰمِلٰتِ وِقْرًا ۟

3. And those that
   Flow with ease
   And gentleness;

٣- فَالْجٰرِيٰتِ يُسْرًا ۟

4. And those that
   Distribute and apportion
   By Command—

٤- فَالْمُقَسِّمٰتِ اَمْرًا ۟

5. Verily that which ye
   Are promised is true;

٥- اِنَّمَا تُوْعَدُوْنَ لَصَادِقٌ ۟

6. And verily Judgement
   And Justice must
   Indeed come to pass.

٦- وَّاِنَّ الدِّيْنَ لَوَاقِعٌ ۟

7. By the Sky
   With (its) numerous Paths,

٧- وَالسَّمَآءِ ذَاتِ الْحُبُكِ ۟

8. Truly ye are in
   A doctrine discordant,

٨- اِنَّكُمْ لَفِيْ قَوْلٍ مُّخْتَلِفٍ ۟

9. Through which are deluded (away
   From the Truth) such
   As would be deluded.

٩- يُّؤْفَكُ عَنْهُ مَنْ اُفِكَ ۟

10. Woe to the falsehood-mongers—

١٠- قُتِلَ الْخَرّٰصُوْنَ ۟

11. Those who (flounder) heedless
In a flood of confusion:

١١- الَّذِيْنَ هُمْ فِيْ غَمْرَةٍ سَاهُوْنَ ۞

12. They ask, "When will be
The Day of Judgement
And Justice?"

١٢- يَسْـَٔلُوْنَ اَيَّانَ يَوْمُ الدِّيْنِ ۞

13. (It will be) a Day
When they will be tried
(And tested) over the Fire!

١٣- يَوْمَ هُمْ عَلَى النَّارِ يُفْتَنُوْنَ ۞

14. "Taste ye your trial!
This is what ye used
To ask to be hastened!"

١٤- ذُوْقُوْا فِتْنَتَكُمْ ۗ
هٰذَا الَّذِيْ كُنْتُمْ بِهٖ تَسْتَعْجِلُوْنَ ۞

15. As to the Righteous,
They will be in the midst
Of Gardens and Springs,

١٥- اِنَّ الْمُتَّقِيْنَ
فِيْ جَنّٰتٍ وَّعُيُوْنٍ ۞

16. Taking joy in the things
Which their Lord gives them,
Because, before then, they
Lived a good life.

١٦- اٰخِذِيْنَ مَآ اٰتٰىهُمْ رَبُّهُمْ ۗ
اِنَّهُمْ كَانُوْا قَبْلَ ذٰلِكَ مُحْسِنِيْنَ ۞

17. They were in the habit
Of sleeping but little
By night,

١٧- كَانُوْا قَلِيْلًا مِّنَ الَّيْلِ مَا
يَهْجَعُوْنَ ۞

18. And in the hours
Of early dawn,
They (were found) praying
For Forgiveness;

١٨- وَبِالْاَسْحَارِ
هُمْ يَسْتَغْفِرُوْنَ ۞

19. And in their wealth
And possessions (was remembered)
The right of the (needy),
Him who asked, and him
Who (for some reason) was
Prevented (from asking).

١٩- وَفِيْ اَمْوَالِهِمْ
حَقٌّ لِّلسَّائِلِ
وَالْمَحْرُوْمِ ۞

20. On the earth
Are Signs for those
Of assured Faith,

٢٠- وَفِى الْاَرْضِ اٰيٰتٌ لِّلْمُوْقِنِيْنَ ۞

21. As also in your own
Selves: will ye not
Then see?

٢١- وَفِيْ اَنْفُسِكُمْ ۗ
اَفَلَا تُبْصِرُوْنَ ۞

22. And in heaven is
Your Sustenance, as (also)
That which ye are promised.

٢٢- وَفِى السَّمَآءِ رِزْقُكُمْ
وَمَا تُوْعَدُوْنَ ۝

23. Then, by the Lord
Of heaven and earth,
This is the very Truth,
As much as the fact
That ye can speak
Intelligently to each other.

SECTION 2.

٢٣- فَوَرَبِّ السَّمَآءِ وَالْاَرْضِ
اِنَّهٗ لَحَقٌّ مِّثْلَ
مَآ اَنَّكُمْ تَنْطِقُوْنَ ۝

24. **H**as the story
Reached thee, of the honoured
Guests of Abraham?

٢٤- هَلْ اَتٰىكَ حَدِيْثُ
ضَيْفِ اِبْرٰهِيْمَ الْمُكْرَمِيْنَ ۝

25. Behold, they entered
His presence, and said:
"Peace!" He said, "Peace!"
(And thought, "These seem)
Unusual people."

٢٥- اِذْ دَخَلُوْا عَلَيْهِ فَقَالُوْا سَلٰمًا ؕ
قَالَ سَلٰمٌ ۚ
قَوْمٌ مُّنْكَرُوْنَ ۝

26. Then he turned quickly
To his household, brought
Out a fatted calf,

٢٦- فَرَاغَ اِلٰۤى اَهْلِهٖ
فَجَآءَ بِعِجْلٍ سَمِيْنٍ ۝

27. And placed it before them...
He said, "Will ye not
Eat?"

٢٧- فَقَرَّبَهٗۤ اِلَيْهِمْ
قَالَ اَلَا تَاْكُلُوْنَ ۝

28. (When they did not eat).
He conceived a fear of them.
They said, "Fear not,"
And they gave him
Glad tidings of a son
Endowed with knowledge.

٢٨- فَاَوْجَسَ مِنْهُمْ خِيْفَةً ؕ
قَالُوْا لَا تَخَفْ ؕ
وَبَشَّرُوْهُ بِغُلٰمٍ عَلِيْمٍ ۝

29. But his wife came forward
(Laughing) aloud: she smote
Her forehead and said:
"A barren old woman!"

٢٩- فَاَقْبَلَتِ امْرَاَتُهٗ فِيْ صَرَّةٍ
فَصَكَّتْ وَجْهَهَا وَقَالَتْ عَجُوْزٌ عَقِيْمٌ ۝

30. They said, "Even so
Has thy Lord spoken:
And He is full
Of Wisdom and Knowledge."

٣٠- قَالُوْا كَذٰلِكِ قَالَ رَبُّكِ ؕ
اِنَّهٗ هُوَ الْحَكِيْمُ الْعَلِيْمُ ۝

31. (Abraham) said: "And what,
O ye Messengers,
Is your errand (now)?"

٣١ - قَالَ فَمَا خَطْبُكُمْ
أَيُّهَا الْمُرْسَلُونَ ۞

32. They said, "We have
Been sent to a people
(Deep) in sin—

٣٢ - قَالُوا إِنَّا أُرْسِلْنَا إِلَى قَوْمٍ
مُّجْرِمِينَ ۞

33. "To bring on, on them,
(A shower of) stones
Of clay (brimstone),

٣٣ - لِنُرْسِلَ عَلَيْهِمْ
حِجَارَةً مِّنْ طِينٍ ۞

34. "Marked as from thy Lord
For those who trespass
Beyond bounds."

٣٤ - مُّسَوَّمَةً عِنْدَ رَبِّكَ
لِلْمُسْرِفِينَ ۞

35. Then we evacuated
Those of the Believers
Who were there,

٣٥ - فَأَخْرَجْنَا
مَنْ كَانَ فِيهَا مِنَ الْمُؤْمِنِينَ ۞

36. But We found not there
Any just (Muslim) persons
Except in one house:

٣٦ - فَمَا وَجَدْنَا فِيهَا
غَيْرَ بَيْتٍ مِّنَ الْمُسْلِمِينَ ۞

37. And We left there
A Sign for such as
Fear the Grievous Penalty.

٣٧ - وَتَرَكْنَا فِيهَا آيَةً
لِّلَّذِينَ يَخَافُونَ الْعَذَابَ الْأَلِيمَ ۞

38. And in Moses
(Was another Sign):
Behold, We sent him
To Pharaoh, with authority
Manifest.

٣٨ - وَفِي مُوسَى
إِذْ أَرْسَلْنَاهُ إِلَى فِرْعَوْنَ بِسُلْطَانٍ مُّبِينٍ ۞

39. But (Pharaoh) turned back
With his Chiefs, and said,
"A sorcerer, or
One possessed!"

٣٩ - فَتَوَلَّى بِرُكْنِهِ وَقَالَ
سَاحِرٌ أَوْ مَجْنُونٌ ۞

40. So We took him
And his forces, and
Threw them into the sea:
And his was the blame.

٤٠ - فَأَخَذْنَاهُ وَجُنُودَهُ
فَنَبَذْنَاهُمْ فِي الْيَمِّ وَهُوَ مُلِيمٌ ۞

41. And in the 'Ād (people)

٤١ - وَفِي عَادٍ

(Was another Sign):
Behold, We sent against them
The devastating Wind:

اِذْ اَرْسَلْنَا عَلَيْهِمُ الرِّيْحَ الْعَقِيْمَ ۟

42. It left nothing whatever
That it came up against,
But reduced it to ruin
And rottenness.

۴۲- مَا تَذَرُ مِنْ شَىْءٍ اَتَتْ عَلَيْهِ
اِلَّا جَعَلَتْهُ كَالرَّمِيْمِ ۟

43. And in the Thamūd
(Was another Sign):
Behold, they were told,
"Enjoy (your brief day)
For a little while!"

۴۳- وَفِىْ ثَمُوْدَ
اِذْ قِيْلَ لَهُمْ
تَمَتَّعُوْا حَتّٰى حِيْنٍ ۟

44. But they insolently defied
The Command of their Lord:
So the stunning noise
(Of an earthquake) seized
Them, even while they
Were looking on.

۴۴- فَعَتَوْا عَنْ اَمْرِ رَبِّهِمْ
فَاَخَذَتْهُمُ الصّٰعِقَةُ
وَهُمْ يَنْظُرُوْنَ ۟

45. Then they could not
Even stand (on their feet),
Nor could they help themselves.

۴۵- فَمَا اسْتَطَاعُوْا مِنْ قِيَامٍ
وَّ مَا كَانُوْا مُنْتَصِرِيْنَ ۟

46. So were the People
Of Noah before them:
For they wickedly transgressed.

۴۶- وَقَوْمَ نُوْحٍ مِّنْ قَبْلُ ۚ
اِنَّهُمْ كَانُوْا قَوْمًا فٰسِقِيْنَ ۟ ۙ؏

SECTION 8.

47. With the power and skill
Did We construct
The Firmament:
For it is We Who create
The vastness of Space.

۴۷- وَالسَّمَآءَ بَنَيْنٰهَا بِاَيْدٍ
وَّ اِنَّا لَمُوْسِعُوْنَ ۟

48. And We have spread out
The (spacious) earth:
How excellently
We do spread out!

۴۸- وَالْاَرْضَ فَرَشْنٰهَا
فَنِعْمَ الْمٰهِدُوْنَ ۟

49. And of everything
We have created pairs:
That ye may receive
Instruction.

۴۹- وَمِنْ كُلِّ شَىْءٍ خَلَقْنَا زَوْجَيْنِ
لَعَلَّكُمْ تَذَكَّرُوْنَ ۟

50. Hasten ye then (at once)

۵۰- فَفِرُّوْا اِلَى اللّٰهِ ۚ

To Allah: I am from Him
A Warner to you,
Clear and open!

اِنِّىۡ لَكُمۡ مِّنۡهُ نَذِيۡرٌ مُّبِيۡنٌ ۞

51. And make not another
An object of worship
With Allah:
I am from Him
A Warner to you,
Clear and open!

۵۱- وَلَا تَجۡعَلُوۡا مَعَ اللّٰهِ اِلٰهًا اٰخَرَ ؕ
اِنِّىۡ لَكُمۡ مِّنۡهُ
نَذِيۡرٌ مُّبِيۡنٌ ۞

52. Similarly, no messenger came
To the Peoples before them,
But they said (of him)
In like manner,
"A sorcerer, or
One possessed"!

۵۲- كَذٰلِكَ مَاۤ اَتَى الَّذِيۡنَ مِنۡ قَبۡلِهِمۡ مِّنۡ
رَّسُوۡلٍ اِلَّا قَالُوۡا
سَاحِرٌ اَوۡ مَجۡنُوۡنٌ ۞

53. Is this the legacy
They have transmitted,
One to another?
Nay, they are themselves
A people transgressing
Beyond bounds!

۵۳- اَتَوَاصَوۡا
بِهٖ ۚ
بَلۡ هُمۡ قَوۡمٌ طَاغُوۡنَ ۞

54. So turn away
From them: not thine
Is the blame.

۵۴- فَتَوَلَّ عَنۡهُمۡ
فَمَاۤ اَنۡتَ بِمَلُوۡمٍ ۞

55. But teach (thy Message):
For teaching benefits
The Believers.

۵۵- وَّ ذَكِّرۡ
فَاِنَّ الذِّكۡرٰى تَنۡفَعُ الۡمُؤۡمِنِيۡنَ ۞

56. I have only created
Jinns and men, that
They may serve Me.

۵۶- وَ مَا خَلَقۡتُ الۡجِنَّ وَالۡاِنۡسَ
اِلَّا لِيَعۡبُدُوۡنِ ۞

57. No Sustenance do I require
Of them, nor do I
Require that they should
Feed Me.

۵۷- مَاۤ اُرِيۡدُ مِنۡهُمۡ مِّنۡ رِّزۡقٍ
وَّ مَاۤ اُرِيۡدُ اَنۡ يُّطۡعِمُوۡنِ ۞

58. For Allah is He Who
Gives (all) Sustenance—
Lord of Power—
Steadfast (forever).

۵۸- اِنَّ اللّٰهَ هُوَ الرَّزَّاقُ
ذُو الۡقُوَّةِ الۡمَتِيۡنُ ۞

59. For the wrongdoers,

۵۹- فَاِنَّ لِلَّذِيۡنَ

Their portion is like
Unto the portion of their
Fellows (of earlier generations):
Then let them not ask Me
To hasten (that portion)!

ظَلَمُوْا ذَنُوْبًا
مِثْلَ ذَنُوْبِ اَصْحٰبِهِمْ
فَلَا يَسْتَعْجِلُوْنِ ○

60. Woe, then, to the Unbelievers,
On account of that Day
Of theirs which they
Have been promised!

٦٠ـ فَوَيْلٌ لِّلَّذِيْنَ كَفَرُوْا مِنْ يَّوْمِهِمُ
الَّذِيْ يُوْعَدُوْنَ ○

INTRODUCTION TO SURA LII. (*Ṭūr*) — 49 Verses

This is the third of the group of seven Meccan Sūras described in the Introduction to *S.l.*

It is, like its predecessor, an early Meccan Sūra. The points here emphasised are: that Revelation is in accord with all God's Signs, including previous Revelations, and that the Hereafter is inevitable, and we must prepare for it.

Al Ṭūr (The Mount)

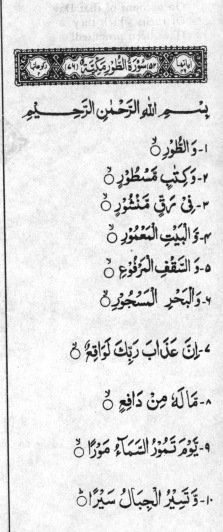

In the name of Allah, Most Gracious, Most Merciful.

1. By the Mount (of Revelation);

2. By a Decree Inscribed

3. In a Scroll unfolded;

4. By the much-frequented Fane;

5. By the Canopy Raised High;

6. And by the Ocean
Filled with Swell—

7. Verily, the Doom of thy Lord
Will indeed come to pass—

8. There is none
Can avert it—

9. On the Day when
The firmament will be
In dreadful commotion.

10. And the mountains will fly
Hither and thither.

11. Then woe that Day
To those that treat
(Truth) as Falsehood—

12. That play (and paddle)
In shallow trifles.

١٢- اَلَّذِيْنَ هُمْ فِيْ خَوْضٍ يَّلْعَبُوْنَ ۞

13. That Day shall they be
Thrust down to the Fire
Of Hell, irresistibly.

١٣- يَوْمَ يُدَعُّوْنَ اِلٰى نَارِ جَهَنَّمَ دَعًّا ۞

14. "This", it will be said,
"Is the Fire—which ye
Were wont to deny!

١٤- هٰذِهِ النَّارُ الَّتِيْ
كُنْتُمْ بِهَا تُكَذِّبُوْنَ ۞

15. "Is this then a fake,
Or is it ye that
Do not see?

١٥- اَفَسِحْرٌ هٰذَآ
اَمْ اَنْتُمْ لَا تُبْصِرُوْنَ ۞

16. "Burn ye therein:
The same is it to you
Whether ye bear it
With patience, or not:
Ye but receive the recompense
Of your (own) deeds."

١٦- اِصْلَوْهَا
فَاصْبِرُوْٓا اَوْ لَا تَصْبِرُوْا ۚ سَوَآءٌ عَلَيْكُمْ ۚ
اِنَّمَا تُجْزَوْنَ مَا كُنْتُمْ تَعْمَلُوْنَ ۞

17. As to the Righteous,
They will be in Gardens,
And in Happiness—

١٧- اِنَّ الْمُتَّقِيْنَ
فِيْ جَنّٰتٍ وَّنَعِيْمٍ ۙ

18. Enjoying the (Bliss) which
Their Lord hath bestowed
On them, and their Lord
Shall deliver them from
The Penalty of the Fire.

١٨- فٰكِهِيْنَ بِمَآ اٰتٰىهُمْ رَبُّهُمْ ۚ
وَوَقٰىهُمْ رَبُّهُمْ عَذَابَ الْجَحِيْمِ ۞

19. (To them will be said:)
"Eat and drink ye,
With profit and health,
Because of your (good) deeds."

١٩- كُلُوْا وَاشْرَبُوْا هَنِيْٓئًا
بِمَا كُنْتُمْ تَعْمَلُوْنَ ۙ

20. They will recline (with ease)
On Thrones (of dignity)
Arranged in ranks;
And We shall join them
To Companions, with beautiful
Big and lustrous eyes.

٢٠- مُتَّكِئِيْنَ عَلٰى سُرُرٍ
مَّصْفُوْفَةٍ ۚ
وَزَوَّجْنٰهُمْ بِحُوْرٍ عِيْنٍ ۞

21. And those who believe
And whose families   follow

٢١- وَالَّذِيْنَ اٰمَنُوْا وَاتَّبَعَتْهُمْ ذُرِّيَّتُهُمْ

Them in Faith—to them
Shall We join their families:
Nor shall We deprive them
(Of the fruit) of aught
Of their works:
(Yet) is each individual
In pledge for his deeds.

بِإِيْمَانٍ
أَلْحَقْنَا بِهِمْ ذُرِّيَّتَهُمْ
وَمَاۤ أَلَتْنَهُمْ مِّنْ عَمَلِهِمْ مِّنْ شَىْءٍ ۚ
كُلُّ امْرِئٍ بِمَا كَسَبَ رَهِيْنٌ ۞

22. And We shall bestow
On them, of fruit and meat,
Anything they shall desire.

٢٢- وَأَمْدَدْنَاهُمْ بِفَاكِهَةٍ وَّلَحْمٍ
مِّمَّا يَشْتَهُوْنَ ۞

23. They shall there exchange,
One with another,
A (loving) cup
Free of frivolity,
Free of all taint
Of ill.

٢٣- يَتَنَازَعُوْنَ فِيْهَا كَأْسًا
لَّا لَغْوٌ فِيْهَا
وَلَا تَأْثِيْمٌ ۞

24. Round about them will serve,
(Devoted) to them,
Youths (handsome) as Pearls
Well-guarded.

٢٤- وَيَطُوْفُ عَلَيْهِمْ غِلْمَانٌ لَّهُمْ
كَأَنَّهُمْ لُؤْلُؤٌ مَّكْنُوْنٌ ۞

25. They will advance
To each other, engaging
In mutual enquiry.

٢٥- وَأَقْبَلَ بَعْضُهُمْ عَلَى بَعْضٍ
يَتَسَاءَلُوْنَ ۞

26. They will say: "Aforetime,
We were not without fear
For the sake of our people.

٢٦- قَالُوْۤا إِنَّا كُنَّا قَبْلُ
فِيْۤ أَهْلِنَا مُشْفِقِيْنَ ۞

27. "But Allah has been good
To us, and has delivered us
From the Penalty
Of the Scorching Wind.

٢٧- فَمَنَّ اللّٰهُ عَلَيْنَا
وَوَقَانَا عَذَابَ السَّمُوْمِ ۞

28. "Truly, we did call
Unto Him from of old:
Truly it is He,
The Beneficent, the Merciful!"
SECTION 2.

٢٨- إِنَّا كُنَّا مِنْ قَبْلُ نَدْعُوْهُ ۖ
إِنَّهُ هُوَ الْبَرُّ الرَّحِيْمُ ۞

29. Therefore proclaim thou
The praises (of thy Lord):
For by the Grace
Of thy Lord, thou art
No (vulgar) soothsayer, nor

٢٩- فَذَكِّرْ
فَمَاۤ أَنْتَ بِنِعْمَتِ رَبِّكَ بِكَاهِنٍ

Art thou one possessed.

وَّلَا مَجْنُوْنٍ ۚ

30. Or do they say—
"A Poet! we await
For him some calamity
(Hatched) by Time!"

۳۰- اَمْ يَقُوْلُوْنَ شَاعِرٌ
نَّتَرَبَّصُ بِهِ رَيْبَ الْمَنُوْنِ ۝

31. Say thou: "Await ye!—
I too will wait⁵⁰⁶⁵
Along with you!"

۳۱- قُلْ تَرَبَّصُوْا
فَاِنِّيْ مَعَكُمْ مِّنَ الْمُتَرَبِّصِيْنَ ۚ

32. Is it that their faculties
Of understanding urge them
To this, or are they
But a people transgressing
Beyond bounds?

۳۲- اَمْ تَأْمُرُهُمْ اَحْلَامُهُمْ بِهٰذَاۤ
اَمْ هُمْ قَوْمٌ طَاغُوْنَ ۚ

33. Or do they say,
"He fabricated the (Message)"?
Nay, they have no faith!

۳۳- اَمْ يَقُوْلُوْنَ تَقَوَّلَهٗ ۚ
بَلْ لَّا يُؤْمِنُوْنَ ۚ

34. Let them then produce
A recital like unto it—
If (it be) they speak
The Truth!

۳۴- فَلْيَأْتُوْا بِحَدِيْثٍ مِّثْلِهٖۤ
اِنْ كَانُوْا صٰدِقِيْنَ ۚ

35. Were they created of nothing,
Or were they themselves
The creators?

۳۵- اَمْ خُلِقُوْا مِنْ غَيْرِ شَيْءٍ
اَمْ هُمُ الْخٰلِقُوْنَ ۚ

36. Or did they create
The heavens and the earth?
Nay, they have
No firm belief.

۳۶- اَمْ خَلَقُوا السَّمٰوٰتِ وَالْاَرْضَ ۚ
بَلْ لَّا يُوْقِنُوْنَ ۚ

37. Or are the Treasures
Of thy Lord with them,
Or are they managers
(Of affairs)?

۳۷- اَمْ عِنْدَهُمْ خَزَآئِنُ رَبِّكَ
اَمْ هُمُ الْمُصَيْطِرُوْنَ ۚ

38. Or have they a ladder,
By which they can (climb
Up to heaven and) listen
(To its secrets)? Then let
(Such a) listener of theirs
Produce a manifest proof.

۳۸- اَمْ لَهُمْ سُلَّمٌ
يَّسْتَمِعُوْنَ فِيْهِ ۚ
فَلْيَأْتِ مُسْتَمِعُهُمْ بِسُلْطٰنٍ مُّبِيْنٍ ۚ

39. Or has He only daughters
And ye have sons?

۳۹- اَمْ لَهُ الْبَنٰتُ وَلَكُمُ الْبَنُوْنَ ۚ

40. Or is it that thou
Dost ask for a reward,
So that they are burdened
With a load of debt?—

٤٠۔ اَمْ تَسْـَٔلُهُمْ اَجْرًا
فَهُمْ مِّنْ مَّغْرَمٍ مُّثْقَلُوْنَ ۚ

41. Or that the Unseen
Is in their hands,
And they write it down?

٤١۔ اَمْ عِنْدَهُمُ الْغَيْبُ
فَهُمْ يَكْتُبُوْنَ ۚ

42. Or do they intend
A plot (against thee)?
But those who defy Allah
Are themselves involved
In a Plot!

٤٢۔ اَمْ يُرِيْدُوْنَ كَيْدًا ۚ
فَالَّذِيْنَ كَفَرُوْا
هُمُ الْمَكِيْدُوْنَ ۚ

43. Or have they a god
Other than Allah?
Exalted is Allah
Far above the things
They associate with Him!

٤٣۔ اَمْ لَهُمْ اِلٰهٌ غَيْرُ اللّٰهِ ۚ
سُبْحٰنَ اللّٰهِ عَمَّا يُشْرِكُوْنَ ۝

44. Were they to see
A piece of the sky
Falling (on them), they
Would (only) say: "Clouds
Gathered in heaps!"

٤٤۔ وَاِنْ يَّرَوْا كِسْفًا مِّنَ السَّمَآءِ سَاقِطًا
يَّقُوْلُوْا سَحَابٌ مَّرْكُوْمٌ ۝

45. So leave them alone
Until they encounter
That Day of theirs,
Wherein they shall (perforce)
Swoon (with terror)—

٤٥۔ فَذَرْهُمْ حَتّٰى يُلٰقُوْا يَوْمَهُمُ الَّذِىْ
فِيْهِ يُصْعَقُوْنَ ۚ

46. The Day when their plotting
Will avail them nothing
And no help shall be
Given them.

٤٦۔ يَوْمَ لَا يُغْنِىْ عَنْهُمْ كَيْدُهُمْ شَيْئًا
وَّلَا هُمْ يُنْصَرُوْنَ ۚ

47. And verily, for those
Who do wrong, there is
Another punishment besides
this:
But most of them
Understand not.

٤٧۔ وَاِنَّ لِلَّذِيْنَ ظَلَمُوْا
عَذَابًا دُوْنَ ذٰلِكَ
وَلٰكِنَّ اَكْثَرَهُمْ لَا يَعْلَمُوْنَ ۝

48. Now await in patience

٤٨۔ وَاصْبِرْ لِحُكْمِ رَبِّكَ

The command of thy Lord:
For verily thou art
In Our eyes:
And celebrate the praises
Of thy Lord the while
Thou standest forth,

فَإِنَّكَ بِأَعْيُنِنَا
وَسَبِّحْ بِحَمْدِ رَبِّكَ حِينَ تَقُومُ ۝

49. And for part of the night
Also praise thou Him—
And at the retreat
Of the stars!

٤٩ـ وَمِنَ الَّيْلِ فَسَبِّحْهُ
وَإِدْبَارَ النُّجُومِ ۝

INTRODUCTION TO SŪRA LIII. *(Najm)* — 62 Verses

This is an early Meccan Sūra, and is the fourth of the series of seven which were described in the Introduction to *S.l.*

The particular theme of this Sūra is that Revelation is not an illusion : the illusion is in the minds of those who doubt and have false ideas of God: God is the source and goal of all things.

In some Sūras the consecutive arrangement is shown or suggested by a cue-word. Here the cue-word is "star". corresponding to "stars" in the last verse of the last Sūra. So in xlvi. l, the words: "Exalted in Power. Full of Wisdom": are carried forward from the last verse of S.xlv., and indeed the same words occur in the first verse of S.xlv. So, again the words: "Most Merciful, Oft-Forgiving": in xxxiv. 2, refer back to the words: "Oft-Forgiving, Most Merciful": in the last line of S.xxxiii. In S. liv. 1, the nearness of Judgement recalls the same idea at the end of the previous Sūra (liii. 57). Other examples will also be found.

Al Najm (The Star)

In the name of Allah, Most Gracious,
Most Merciful.

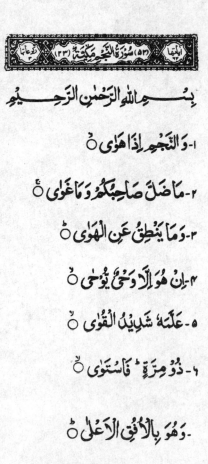

1. By the Star
When it goes down—

2. Your Companion is neither
Astray nor being misled,

3. Nor does he say (aught)
Of (his own) Desire.

4. It is no less than
Inspiration sent down to him:

5. He was taught by one
Mighty in Power,

6. Endued with Wisdom:
For he appeared
(In stately form)

7. While he was in
The highest part
Of the horizon:

8. Then he approached
   And came closer,

٨- ثُمَّ دَنَا فَتَدَلَّى ۙ

9. And was at a distance
   Of but two bow-lengths
   Or (even) nearer;

٩- فَكَانَ قَابَ قَوْسَيْنِ أَوْ أَدْنَى ۙ

10. So did (Allah) convey
    The inspiration to His Servant—
    (Conveyed) what He (meant)
    To convey.

١٠- فَأَوْحَى إِلَى عَبْدِهِ مَا أَوْحَى ۚ

11. The (Prophet's) (mind and) heart
    In no way falsified
    That which he saw.

١١- مَا كَذَبَ الْفُؤَادُ مَا رَأَى ۝

12. Will ye then dispute
    With him concerning
    What he saw?

١٢- أَفَتُمَارُونَهُ عَلَى مَا يَرَى ۝

13. For indeed he saw him
    At a second descent,

١٣- وَلَقَدْ رَآهُ نَزْلَةً أُخْرَى ۙ

14. Near the Lote-tree
    Beyond which none may pass:

١٤- عِنْدَ سِدْرَةِ الْمُنْتَهَى ۝

15. Near it is the Garden
    Of Abode.

١٥- عِنْدَهَا جَنَّةُ الْمَأْوَى ۚ

16. Behold, the Lote-tree
    Was shrouded
    (In mystery unspeakable!)

١٦- إِذْ يَغْشَى السِّدْرَةَ مَا يَغْشَى ۙ

17. (His) sight never swerved,
    Nor did it go wrong!

١٧- مَا زَاغَ الْبَصَرُ وَمَا طَغَى ۝

18. For truly did he see,
    Of the signs of his Lord,
    The Greatest!

١٨- لَقَدْ رَأَى مِنْ آيَاتِ رَبِّهِ الْكُبْرَى ۝

19. Have ye seen
    Lāt, and 'Uzzā,

١٩- أَفَرَأَيْتُمُ اللَّاتَ وَالْعُزَّى ۙ

20. And another,
    The Third (goddess), Manāt?

٢٠- وَمَنَاةَ الثَّالِثَةَ الْأُخْرَى ۝

21. What! For you
    The male sex,
    And for Him, the female?

٢١- اَلَكُمُ الذَّكَرُ وَلَهُ الْاُنْثٰى ٥

22. Behold, such would be
    Indeed a division
    Most unfair!

٢٢- تِلْكَ اِذًا قِسْمَةٌ ضِيْزٰى ٥

23. These are nothing but names
    Which ye have devised—
    Ye and your fathers—
    For which Allah has sent
    Down no authority (whatever).
    They follow nothing but
    Conjecture and what
    Their own souls desire!—
    Even though there has already
    Come to them Guidance
    From their Lord!

٢٣- اِنْ هِىَ اِلَّا اَسْمَاءٌ
سَمَّيْتُمُوْهَا اَنْتُمْ وَ اٰبَآؤُكُمْ
مَّا اَنْزَلَ اللهُ بِهَا مِنْ سُلْطٰنٍ
اِنْ يَّتَّبِعُوْنَ اِلَّا الظَّنَّ وَمَا تَهْوَى الْاَنْفُسُ
وَلَقَدْ جَآءَهُمْ
مِّنْ رَّبِّهِمُ الْهُدٰى ٥

24. Nay, shall man have (just)
    Anything he hankers after?

٢٤- اَمْ لِلْاِنْسَانِ مَا تَمَنّٰى ٥

25. But it is to Allah
    That the End and
    The Beginning (of all things)
    Belong.

٢٥- فَلِلّٰهِ
الْاٰخِرَةُ وَ الْاُوْلٰى ٥

SECTION 2.

26. How many so ever be
    The angels in the heavens,
    Their intercession will avail
                         nothing
    Except after Allah has given
    Leave for whom He pleases
    And that he is acceptable
    To Him.

٢٦- وَكَمْ مِّنْ مَّلَكٍ فِى السَّمٰوٰتِ
لَا تُغْنِىْ شَفَاعَتُهُمْ شَيْئًا
اِلَّا مِنْ بَعْدِ اَنْ يَّاْذَنَ اللهُ
لِمَنْ يَّشَآءُ وَ يَرْضٰى ٥

27. Those who believe not
    In the Hereafter, name
    The angels with female names.

٢٧- اِنَّ الَّذِيْنَ لَا يُؤْمِنُوْنَ بِالْاٰخِرَةِ
لَيُسَمُّوْنَ الْمَلٰئِكَةَ تَسْمِيَةَ الْاُنْثٰى ٥

28. But they have no knowledge
    Therein. They follow nothing
    But conjecture; and conjecture
    Avails nothing against Truth.

٢٨- وَمَا لَهُمْ بِهٖ مِنْ عِلْمٍ اِنْ يَّتَّبِعُوْنَ اِلَّا
الظَّنَّ وَ اِنَّ الظَّنَّ لَا يُغْنِىْ مِنَ الْحَقِّ شَيْئًا ٥

29. Therefore shun those who
    Turn away from Our Message

٢٩- فَاَعْرِضْ عَنْ مَّنْ تَوَلّٰى عَنْ ذِكْرِنَا

And desire nothing but
The life of this world.

وَلَمْ يُرِدْ اِلَّا الْحَيٰوةَ الدُّنْيَا ۗ

30. That is as far as
Knowledge will reach them.
Verily thy Lord knoweth best
Those who stray from
His Path, and He knoweth
Best those who receive guidance.

٣٠- ذٰلِكَ مَبْلَغُهُمْ مِّنَ الْعِلْمِ ؕ
اِنَّ رَبَّكَ هُوَ اَعْلَمُ بِمَنْ ضَلَّ عَنْ
سَبِيْلِهٖ ۙ وَهُوَ اَعْلَمُ بِمَنِ اهْتَدٰى ۞

31. Yea, to Allah belongs all
That is in the heavens
And on earth: so that
He rewards those who do
Evil, according to their deeds,
And He rewards those who
Do good, with what is best.

٣١- وَلِلّٰهِ مَا فِى السَّمٰوٰتِ وَمَا فِى الْاَرْضِ ۙ
لِيَجْزِىَ الَّذِيْنَ اَسَآءُوْا بِمَا عَمِلُوْا
وَيَجْزِىَ الَّذِيْنَ اَحْسَنُوْا بِالْحُسْنٰى ۚ

32. Those who aviod
Great sins and shameful deeds,
Only (falling into) small faults—
Verily thy Lord is ample
In forgiveness. He knows
You well when He brings
You out of the earth,
And when ye are hidden
In your mothers' wombs.
Therefore justify not yourselves:
He knows best who it is
That guards against evil.

٣٢- اَلَّذِيْنَ يَجْتَنِبُوْنَ كَبٰٓئِرَ الْاِثْمِ وَالْفَوَاحِشَ
اِلَّا اللَّمَمَ ؕ اِنَّ رَبَّكَ وَاسِعُ الْمَغْفِرَةِ ؕ
هُوَ اَعْلَمُ بِكُمْ اِذْ اَنْشَاَكُمْ مِّنَ الْاَرْضِ
وَاِذْ اَنْتُمْ اَجِنَّةٌ فِىْ بُطُوْنِ اُمَّهٰتِكُمْ ۚ
فَلَا تُزَكُّوْٓا اَنْفُسَكُمْ ؕ
هُوَ اَعْلَمُ بِمَنِ اتَّقٰى ۞

SECTION 3.

33. Seest thou one
Who turns back,

٣٣- اَفَرَءَيْتَ الَّذِىْ تَوَلّٰى ۙ

34. Gives a little,
Then hardens (his heart)?

٣٤- وَاَعْطٰى قَلِيْلًا وَّاَكْدٰى ۞

35. What! Has he knowledge
Of the Unseen
So that he can see?

٣٥- اَعِنْدَهٗ عِلْمُ الْغَيْبِ فَهُوَ يَرٰى ۞

36. Nay, is he not acquainted
With what is in the books
Of Moses—

٣٦- اَمْ لَمْ يُنَبَّأْ بِمَا فِىْ صُحُفِ مُوْسٰى ۞

37. And of Abraham
Who fulfilled his
engagements—

٣٧- وَاِبْرٰهِيْمَ الَّذِىْ وَفّٰى ۞

38. Namely, that no bearer
    Of burdens can bear
    The burden of another;

٣٨- اَلَّا تَزِرُ وَازِرَةٌ وِّزْرَ اُخْرٰى ۙ

39. That man can have nothing
    But what he strives for;

٣٩- وَاَنْ لَّيْسَ لِلْاِنْسَانِ اِلَّا مَا سَعٰى ۙ

40. That (the fruit of) his striving
    Will soon come in sight;

٤٠- وَاَنَّ سَعْيَهٗ سَوْفَ يُرٰى ۙ

41. Then will he be rewarded
    With a reward complete;

٤١- ثُمَّ يُجْزٰىهُ الْجَزَآءَ الْاَوْفٰى ۙ

42. That to thy Lord
    Is the final Goal;

٤٢- وَاَنَّ اِلٰى رَبِّكَ الْمُنْتَهٰى ۙ

43. That it is He Who
    Granteth Laughter and Tears;

٤٣- وَاَنَّهٗ هُوَ اَضْحَكَ وَاَبْكٰى ۙ

44. That it is He Who
    Granteth Death and Life;

٤٤- وَاَنَّهٗ هُوَ اَمَاتَ وَاَحْيَا ۙ

45. That He did create
    In pairs—male and female,

٤٥- وَاَنَّهٗ خَلَقَ الزَّوْجَيْنِ الذَّكَرَ وَالْاُنْثٰى ۙ

46. From a seed when lodged
    (In its place);

٤٦- مِنْ نُّطْفَةٍ اِذَا تُمْنٰى ۙ

47. That He hath promised
    A Second Creation
    (Raising of the Dead);

٤٧- وَاَنَّ عَلَيْهِ النَّشْاَةَ الْاُخْرٰى ۙ

48. That it is He Who
    Giveth wealth and satisfaction;

٤٨- وَاَنَّهٗ هُوَ اَغْنٰى وَاَقْنٰى ۙ

49. That He is the Lord
    Of Sirius (the Mighty Star);

٤٩- وَاَنَّهٗ هُوَ رَبُّ الشِّعْرٰى ۙ

50. And that it is He
    Who destroyed the (powerful)
    Ancient 'Ād (people),

٥٠- وَاَنَّهٗ اَهْلَكَ عَادَنِ الْاُوْلٰى ۙ

51. And the Thamūd,
    Nor gave them a lease
    Of perpetual life.

٥١- وَثَمُوْدَا فَمَا اَبْقٰى ۙ

52. And before them,
The people of Noah,
For that they were (all)
Most unjust
And most insolent transgressors,

٥٢ - وَقَوْمَ نُوْحٍ مِّنْ قَبْلُ اِنَّهُمْ كَانُوْا هُمْ اَظْلَمَ وَاَطْغٰى ۚ

53. And He destroyed
The Overthrown Cities
(Of Sodom and Gomorrah),

٥٣ - وَالْمُؤْتَفِكَةَ اَهْوٰى ۙ

54. So that (ruins unknown)
Have covered them up.

٥٤ - فَغَشّٰهَا مَا غَشّٰى ۚ

55. Then which of the gifts
Of thy Lord, (O man,)
Wilt thou dispute about?

٥٥ - فَبِاَيِّ اٰلَآءِ رَبِّكَ تَتَمَارٰى

56. This is a Warner,
Of the (series of) Warners
Of old!

٥٦ - هٰذَا نَذِيْرٌ مِّنَ النُّذُرِ الْاُوْلٰى

57. The (Judgement) ever
                   approaching
Draws nigh:

٥٧ - اَزِفَتِ الْاٰزِفَةُ ۚ

58. No (soul) but Allah
Can lay it bare.

٥٨ - لَيْسَ لَهَا مِنْ دُوْنِ اللّٰهِ كَاشِفَةٌ ۚ

59. Do ye then wonder
At this recital?

٥٩ - اَفَمِنْ هٰذَا الْحَدِيْثِ تَعْجَبُوْنَ ۙ

60. And will ye laugh
And not weep,—

٦٠ - وَتَضْحَكُوْنَ وَلَا تَبْكُوْنَ ۙ

61. Wasting your time
In vanities?

٦١ - وَاَنْتُمْ سٰمِدُوْنَ

62. But fall ye down in prostration
To Allah and adore (Him)!

٦٢ - فَاسْجُدُوْا لِلّٰهِ وَاعْبُدُوْا ۩

INTRODUCTION TO SŪRA LIV. (*Qamar*) — 55 Verses

This is an early Meccan Sūra, the fifth in the series dealing with Judgment, and the truth of Revelation, as explained in the Introduction to *S.l.*

The theme of the Sūra is explained by the refrain: "Is there any that will receive admonition?" which occurs six times, at the end of each reference to a past story of sin and rejection of warnings and in the appeal to the simplicity of Qur-ān (verses 15, 17, 22, 32, 40 and 51). There is an invitation to listen to the Message and turn to Truth and Righteousness.

Al Qamar (The Moon)

In the name of Allah, Most Gracious,
Most Merciful.

1. The Hour (of Judgement)
   Is nigh, and the moon
   Is cleft asunder.

2. But if they see
   A Sign, they turn away,
   And say, "This is
   (But) transient magic."

3. They reject (the warning)
   And follow their (own) lusts
   But every matter has
   Its appointed time.

4. There have already come
   To them Recitals wherein
   There is (enough) to check (them),

5. Mature wisdom—but
   (The preaching of) Warners
   Profits them not.

6. Therefore, (O Prophet)
   Turn away from them.
   The Day that the Caller
   Will call (them)
   To a terrible affair,

7. They will come forth—
   Their eyes humbled—

From (their) graves, (torpid)
Like locusts scattered abroad,

مِنَ الْأَجْدَاثِ كَأَنَّهُمْ جَرَادٌ مُّنْتَشِرٌ ۝

8. Hastening, with eyes transfixed,
Towards the Caller!—
"Hard is this Day!"
The Unbelievers will say.

٨- مُّهْطِعِيْنَ إِلَى الدَّاعِ ۖ
يَقُوْلُ الْكٰفِرُوْنَ هٰذَا يَوْمٌ عَسِرٌ ۝

9. Before them the People
Of Noah rejected (their
messenger):
They rejected Our servant,
And said, "Here is
One possessed!", and he
Was driven out.

٩- كَذَّبَتْ قَبْلَهُمْ قَوْمُ نُوْحٍ
فَكَذَّبُوْا عَبْدَنَا وَقَالُوْا مَجْنُوْنٌ وَّازْدُجِرَ ۝

10. Then he called on his Lord:
"I am one overcome:
Do Thou then help (me)!"

١٠- فَدَعَا رَبَّهٗۤ
أَنِّيْ مَغْلُوْبٌ فَانْتَصِرْ ۝

11. So We opened the gates
Of heaven, with water
Pouring forth.

١١- فَفَتَحْنَاۤ أَبْوَابَ السَّمَاءِ بِمَاءٍ
مُّنْهَمِرٍ ۗ

12. And We caused the earth
To gush forth with springs.
So the waters met (and rose)
To the extent decreed.

١٢- وَّفَجَّرْنَا الْأَرْضَ عُيُوْنًا
فَالْتَقَى الْمَاءُ عَلٰۤى أَمْرٍ قَدْ قُدِرَ ۝

13. But We bore him
On an (Ark) made of
Broad planks and caulked
With palm-fibre:

١٣- وَحَمَلْنٰهُ عَلٰى
ذَاتِ أَلْوَاحٍ وَّدُسُرٍ ۝

14. She floats under Our eyes
(And care): a recompense
To one who had been
Rejected (with scorn)!

١٤- تَجْرِيْ بِأَعْيُنِنَا ۚ
جَزَاءً لِّمَنْ كَانَ كُفِرَ ۝

15. And We have left
This as a Sign
(For all time): then
Is there any that will
Receive admonition?

١٥- وَلَقَدْ تَّرَكْنٰهَاۤ اٰيَةً
فَهَلْ مِنْ مُّدَّكِرٍ ۝

16. But how (terrible) was
My Penalty and My Warning?

١٦- فَكَيْفَ كَانَ عَذَابِيْ وَنُذُرِ ۝

17. And We have indeed
Made the Qur'ān easy
To understand and remember:
Then is there any that
Will receive admonition?

18. The 'Ād (people) (too)
Rejected (Truth): then
How terrible was
My Penalty and My Warning?

19. For We sent against them
A furious wind, on a Day
Of violent Disaster,

20. Plucking out men as if
They were roots of palm-trees
Torn up (from the ground).

21. Yea, how (terrible) was
My Penalty and My Warning!

22. But We have indeed
Made the Qur'ān easy
To understand and remember:
Then is there any that
Will receive admonition?

SECTION 2.

23. The Thamūd (also)
Rejected (their) Warners.

24. For they said: "What!
A man! A solitary one
From among ourselves!
Shall we follow such a one?
Truly should we then be
Straying in mind, and mad!

25. "Is it that the Message
Is sent to *him*,
Of all people amongst us?
Nay, he is a liar
An insolent one!"

26. Ah! they will know
On the morrow, which is
The liar, the insolent one!

27. For We will send
The she-camel
By way of trial for them.
So watch them, (O Ṣāliḥ),
And possess thyself in patience!

٢٧- اِنَّا مُرْسِلُوا النَّاقَةِ فِتْنَةً لَّهُمْ
فَارْتَقِبْهُمْ وَاصْطَبِرْ ۞

28. And tell them that
The water is to be
Divided between them:
Each one's right to drink
Being brought forward
(By suitable turns).

٢٨- وَنَبِّئْهُمْ اَنَّ الْمَآءَ
قِسْمَةٌ بَيْنَهُمْ ۚ
كُلُّ شِرْبٍ مُّحْتَضَرٌ ۞

29. But they called
To their companion,
And he took a sword
In hand, and hamstrung (her)

٢٩- فَنَادَوْا صَاحِبَهُمْ
فَتَعَاطَى فَعَقَرَ ۞

30. Ah! how (terrible) was
My Penalty and My Warning!

٣٠- فَكَيْفَ كَانَ عَذَابِي وَنُذُرِ ۞

31. For We sent against them
A single Mighty Blast,
And they became
Like the dry stubble used
By one who pens cattle.

٣١- اِنَّا اَرْسَلْنَا عَلَيْهِمْ صَيْحَةً وَّاحِدَةً
فَكَانُوا كَهَشِيمِ الْمُحْتَظِرِ ۞

32. And We have indeed
Made the Qur'ān easy
To understand and remember:
Then is there any that
Will receive admonition?

٣٢- وَلَقَدْ يَسَّرْنَا الْقُرْاٰنَ لِلذِّكْرِ
فَهَلْ مِنْ مُّدَّكِرٍ ۞

33. The People of Lūṭ
Rejected (his) Warning.

٣٣- كَذَّبَتْ قَوْمُ لُوطٍ بِالنُّذُرِ ۞

34. We sent against them
A violent tornado
With showers of stones,
(Which destroyed them), except
Lūṭ's household: them We
Delivered by early Dawn—

٣٤- اِنَّا اَرْسَلْنَا عَلَيْهِمْ حَاصِبًا
اِلَّا اٰلَ لُوطٍ ۗ
نَجَّيْنٰهُمْ بِسَحَرٍ ۞

35. As a Grace from Us:
Thus do We reward
Those who give thanks.

٣٥- نِعْمَةً مِّنْ عِنْدِنَا ۚ
كَذٰلِكَ نَجْزِي مَنْ شَكَرَ ۞

36. And (Lūt) did warn them
Of Our Punishment, but
They disputed about the
Warning.

٣٦- وَلَقَدْ اَنْذَرَهُمْ بَطْشَتَنَا
فَتَمَارَوْا بِالنُّذُرِ ۞

37. And they even sought
To snatch away his guests
From him, but We blinded
Their eyes. (They heard:)
"Now taste ye My Wrath
And My Warning."

٣٧- وَلَقَدْ رَاوَدُوْهُ عَنْ ضَيْفِهٖ
فَطَمَسْنَا اَعْيُنَهُمْ
فَذُوْقُوْا عَذَابِيْ وَنُذُرِ ۞

38. Early on the morrow
An abiding Punishment
Seized them:

٣٨- وَلَقَدْ صَبَّحَهُمْ
بُكْرَةً عَذَابٌ مُّسْتَقِرٌّ ۞

39. "So taste ye My Wrath
And My Warning."

٣٩- فَذُوْقُوْا عَذَابِيْ وَنُذُرِ ۞

40. And We have indeed
Made the Qur'ān easy
To understand and remember:
Then is there any that
Will receive admonition?

٤٠- وَلَقَدْ يَسَّرْنَا الْقُرْاٰنَ لِلذِّكْرِ
فَهَلْ مِنْ مُّدَّكِرٍ ۞   ع

SECTION 3.

41. To the People
Of Pharaoh, too, aforetime,
Came Warners (from Allah).

٤١- وَلَقَدْ جَآءَ اٰلَ فِرْعَوْنَ النُّذُرُ ۞

42. The (people) rejected all
Our Signs; but We
Seized them with such Penalty
(As comes) from One
Exalted in Power,
Able to carry out His Will.

٤٢- كَذَّبُوْا بِاٰيٰتِنَا كُلِّهَا
فَاَخَذْنٰهُمْ اَخْذَ
عَزِيْزٍ مُّقْتَدِرٍ ۞

43. Are your Unbelievers,
(O Quraysh), better than they?
Or have ye an immunity
In the Sacred Books?

٤٣- اَكُفَّارُكُمْ خَيْرٌ مِّنْ اُولٰٓئِكُمْ
اَمْ لَكُمْ بَرَآءَةٌ فِى الزُّبُرِ ۞

44. Or do they say:
"We acting together
Can defend ourselves"?

٤٤- اَمْ يَقُوْلُوْنَ نَحْنُ جَمِيْعٌ مُّنْتَصِرٌ ۞

45. Soon will their multitude
Be put to flight,

٤٥- سَيُهْزَمُ الْجَمْعُ

And they will show
Their backs.

وَيُوَلُّوْنَ الدُّبُرَ ۞

46. Nay, the Hour (of Judgement)
Is the time promised them
(For their full recompense):
And that Hour will be
Most grievous and most bitter.

٤٦- بَلِ السَّاعَةُ مَوْعِدُهُمْ
وَالسَّاعَةُ اَدْهٰى وَاَمَرُّ ۞

47. Truly those in sin
Are the ones
Straying in mind, and mad.

٤٧- اِنَّ الْمُجْرِمِيْنَ فِىْ ضَلٰلٍ وَّسُعُرٍ ۙ

48. The Day they will be
Dragged through the Fire
On their faces,   (they
Will hear:) "Taste ye
The touch of Hell!"

٤٨- يَوْمَ يُسْحَبُوْنَ فِى النَّارِ عَلٰى وُجُوْهِهِمْ ؕ
ذُوْقُوْا مَسَّ سَقَرَ ۞

49. Verily, all things
Have We created
In proportion and measure.

٤٩- اِنَّا كُلَّ شَىْءٍ خَلَقْنٰهُ بِقَدَرٍ ۞

50. And Our Command
Is but a single (Act)—
Like the twinkling
Of an eye.

٥٠- وَمَآ اَمْرُنَآ اِلَّا وَاحِدَةٌ
كَلَمْحٍ بِالْبَصَرِ ۞

51. And (oft) in the past,
Have We destroyed gangs
Like unto you; then
Is there any that
Will receive admonition?

٥١- وَلَقَدْ اَهْلَكْنَآ اَشْيَاعَكُمْ
فَهَلْ مِنْ مُّدَّكِرٍ ۞

52. All that they do
Is noted in (their)
Books (of Deeds):

٥٢- وَكُلُّ شَىْءٍ فَعَلُوْهُ فِى الزُّبُرِ ۞

53. Every matter, small and great,
Is a record.

٥٣- وَكُلُّ صَغِيْرٍ وَّكَبِيْرٍ مُّسْتَطَرٌ ۞

54. As to the Righteous,
They will be in the midst
Of Gardens and Rivers,

٥٤- اِنَّ الْمُتَّقِيْنَ فِىْ جَنّٰتٍ وَّنَهَرٍ ۙ

55. In an Assembly to Truth,
In the Presence of
A Sovereign Omnipotent.

٥٥- فِىْ مَقْعَدِ صِدْقٍ
عِنْدَ مَلِيْكٍ مُّقْتَدِرٍ ۞

INTRODUCTION TO SŪRA LV. (*Raḥmān*) — 78 Verses

The majority of Commentators consider this an early Meccan Sūra, though some consider at least a part of it as dating from Medina. The greater part of it is undoubtedly early Meccan.

It is highly poetical and mystical, and the refrain "Then which of the favours of your Lord will ye deny?" is interspersed 31 times among its 78 verses.

It is the sixth of the series of seven dealing with Revelation, the favours of God, and the Hereafter: see Introduction to S.l.

Here is the special theme is indicated by the refrain. The rhyme in most cases is in the dual grammatical form, and the Argument implies that though things are created in pairs, there is an underlying Unity, through the Creator, in the favours which He bestows, and in the goal to which they are marching.

Al Raḥmān (The Most Gracious)

In the name of Allah, Most Gracious,
Most Merciful.

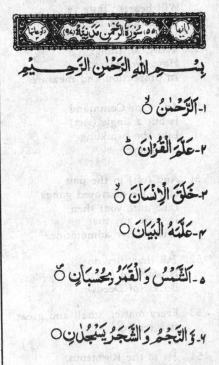

1. (Allah) Most Gracious!

2. It is He Who has
   Taught the Qur'ān.

3. He has created man:

4. He has taught him speech
   (And Intelligence).

5. The sun and the moon
   Follow courses (exactly)
                 computed;

6. And the herbs   and the trees—
   Both (alike) bow in adoration.

7. And the Firmament has He
   Raised high, and He has set up
   The Balance (of Justice),

8. In order that ye may
   Not transgress (due) balance.

9. So establish weight with justice
And fall not short
In the balance.

٩- وَأَقِيمُوا الْوَزْنَ بِالْقِسْطِ
وَلَا تُخْسِرُوا الْمِيزَانَ ۟

10. It is He Who has
Spread out the earth
For (His) creatures:

١٠- وَالْأَرْضَ وَضَعَهَا لِلْأَنَامِ ۟

11. Therein is fruit
And date palms, producing
Spathes (enclosing dates):

١١- فِيهَا فَاكِهَةٌ ۖ
وَالنَّخْلُ ذَاتُ الْأَكْمَامِ ۖ

12. Also corn, with (its)
Leaves and stalk for fodder,
And sweet-smelling plants.

١٢- وَالْحَبُّ ذُو الْعَصْفِ
وَالرَّيْحَانُ ۖ

13. Then which of the favours
Of your Lord will ye deny?

١٣- فَبِأَيِّ آلَاءِ رَبِّكُمَا تُكَذِّبَانِ ۟

14. He created man
From sounding clay
Like unto pottery,

١٤- خَلَقَ الْإِنْسَانَ
مِنْ صَلْصَالٍ كَالْفَخَّارِ ۖ

15. And He created Jinns
From fire free of smoke:

١٥- وَخَلَقَ الْجَانَّ مِنْ مَارِجٍ مِنْ نَارٍ ۖ

16. Then which of the favours
Of your Lord will ye deny?

١٦- فَبِأَيِّ آلَاءِ رَبِّكُمَا تُكَذِّبَانِ ۟

17. (He is) Lord
Of the two Easts
And Lord
Of the two Wests:

١٧- رَبُّ الْمَشْرِقَيْنِ
وَرَبُّ الْمَغْرِبَيْنِ ۖ

18. Then which of the favours
Of your Lord will ye deny?

١٨- فَبِأَيِّ آلَاءِ رَبِّكُمَا تُكَذِّبَانِ ۟

19. He has let free
The two bodies
Of flowing water,
Meeting together:

١٩- مَرَجَ الْبَحْرَيْنِ
يَلْتَقِيَانِ ۖ

20. Between them is a Barrier
Which they do not transgress:

٢٠- بَيْنَهُمَا بَرْزَخٌ لَا يَبْغِيَانِ ۖ

الجزء السابع والعشرون سُوْرَةُ الرَّحْمٰن

21. Then which of the favours
Of your Lord will ye deny?

٢١- فَبِأَيِّ اٰلَاءِ رَبِّكُمَا تُكَذِّبٰنِ ۝

22. Out of them come
Pearls and Coral:

٢٢- يَخْرُجُ مِنْهُمَا اللُّؤْلُؤُ وَالْمَرْجَانُ ۚ

23. Then which of the favours
Of your Lord will ye deny?

٢٣- فَبِأَيِّ اٰلَاءِ رَبِّكُمَا تُكَذِّبٰنِ ۝

24. And His are the Ships
Sailing smoothly through the seas,
Lofty as mountains:

٢٤- وَلَهُ الْجَوَارِ الْمُنْشَاٰتُ فِي الْبَحْرِ
كَالْأَعْلَامِ ۚ

25. Then which of the favours
Of your Lord will ye deny?

٢٥- فَبِأَيِّ اٰلَاءِ رَبِّكُمَا تُكَذِّبٰنِ ۝

SECTION 2.

26. All that is on earth
Will perish:

٢٦- كُلُّ مَنْ عَلَيْهَا فَانٍ ۝

27. But will abide (forever)
The Face of thy Lord—
Full of Majesty,
Bounty and Honour.

٢٧- وَيَبْقٰى وَجْهُ رَبِّكَ
ذُو الْجَلَالِ وَالْإِكْرَامِ ۚ

28. Then which of the favours
Of your Lord will ye deny?

٢٨- فَبِأَيِّ اٰلَاءِ رَبِّكُمَا تُكَذِّبٰنِ ۝

29. Of Him seeks (its need)
Every creature in the heavens
And on earth:
Every day in (new) Splendour
Doth He (shine)!

٢٩- يَسْأَلُهُ مَنْ فِي السَّمٰوٰتِ وَالْأَرْضِ
كُلَّ يَوْمٍ هُوَ فِي شَأْنٍ ۝

30. Then which of the favours
Of your Lord will ye deny?

٣٠- فَبِأَيِّ اٰلَاءِ رَبِّكُمَا تُكَذِّبٰنِ ۝

31. Soon shall We
Settle your affairs,
O both ye worlds!

٣١- سَنَفْرُغُ لَكُمْ أَيُّهَ الثَّقَلَانِ ۚ

32. Then which of the favours
Of your Lord will ye deny?

٣٢- فَبِأَيِّ اٰلَاءِ رَبِّكُمَا تُكَذِّبٰنِ ۝

33. O ye assembly of Jinns
And men! If it be
Ye can pass beyond
The zones of the heavens

٣٣- يٰمَعْشَرَ الْجِنِّ وَالْإِنْسِ إِنِ اسْتَطَعْتُمْ
أَنْ تَنْفُذُوْا مِنْ أَقْطَارِ السَّمٰوٰتِ وَالْأَرْضِ

And the earth, pass ye!
Not without authority
Shall ye be able to pass!

فَانْفُذُوْا ۚ

لَا تَنْفُذُوْنَ اِلَّا بِسُلْطٰنٍ ۚ

34. Then which of the favours
Of your Lord will ye deny?

٣٤- فَبِاَىِّ اٰلَاءِ رَبِّكُمَا تُكَذِّبٰنِ ۚ

35. On you will be sent
(O ye evil ones twain!)
A flame of fire (to burn)
And a smoke (to choke):
No defence will ye have:

٣٥- يُرْسَلُ عَلَيْكُمَا شُوَاظٌ مِّنْ نَّارٍ ۙ
وَّ نُحَاسٌ فَلَا تَنْتَصِرٰنِ ۚ

36. Then which of the favours
Of your Lord will ye deny?

٣٦- فَبِاَىِّ اٰلَاءِ رَبِّكُمَا تُكَذِّبٰنِ ۚ

37. When the sky is rent
Asunder, and it becomes red
Like ointment:

٣٧- فَاِذَا انْشَقَّتِ السَّمَآءُ
فَكَانَتْ وَرْدَةً كَالدِّهَانِ ۚ

38. Then which of the favours
Of your Lord will ye deny?

٣٨- فَبِاَىِّ اٰلَاءِ رَبِّكُمَا تُكَذِّبٰنِ ۚ

39. On that Day
No question will be asked
Of man or Jinn
As to his sin,

٣٩- فَيَوْمَئِذٍ لَّا يُسْئَلُ عَنْ ذَنْبِهٖۤ
اِنْسٌ وَّ لَاجَآنٌّ ۚ

40. Then which of the favours
Of your Lord will ye deny?

٤٠- فَبِاَىِّ اٰلَاءِ رَبِّكُمَا تُكَذِّبٰنِ ۚ

41. (For) the sinners will be
Known by their Marks:
And they will be seized
By their forelocks and
Their feet.

٤١- يُعْرَفُ الْمُجْرِمُوْنَ بِسِيْمٰهُمْ
فَيُؤْخَذُ بِالنَّوَاصِىْ وَالْاَقْدَامِ ۚ

42. Then which of the favours
Of your Lord will ye deny?

٤٢- فَبِاَىِّ اٰلَاءِ رَبِّكُمَا تُكَذِّبٰنِ ۚ

43. This is the Hell which
The Sinners deny:

٤٣- هٰذِهٖ جَهَنَّمُ الَّتِىْ يُكَذِّبُ بِهَا الْمُجْرِمُوْنَ ۘ

44. In its midst
And in the midst
Of boiling hot water
Will they wander round!

٤٤- يَطُوْفُوْنَ بَيْنَهَا
وَبَيْنَ حَمِيْمٍ اٰنٍ ۚ

45. Then which of the favours
    Of your Lord will ye deny?
    SECTION 3.

46. But for such as fear
    The time when they will
    Stand before (the Judgement
                        Seat
    Of) their Lord,
    There will be two Gardens—

٤٥ - فَبِأَيِّ آلَاءِ رَبِّكُمَا تُكَذِّبٰنِ ۞

٤٦ - وَلِمَنْ خَافَ مَقَامَ رَبِّهٖ جَنَّتٰنِ ۚ

47. Then which of the favours
    Of your Lord will ye deny?

٤٧ - فَبِأَيِّ آلَاءِ رَبِّكُمَا تُكَذِّبٰنِ ۙ

48. Containing all kinds
    (Of trees and delights)—

٤٨ - ذَوَاتَآ اَفْنَانٍ ۚ

49. Then which of the favours
    Of your Lord will ye deny?

٤٩ - فَبِأَيِّ آلَاءِ رَبِّكُمَا تُكَذِّبٰنِ ۙ

50. In them (each) will be
    Two Springs flowing (free);

٥٠ - فِيْهِمَا عَيْنٰنِ تَجْرِيٰنِ ۚ

51. Then which of the favours
    Of your Lord will ye deny?

٥١ - فَبِأَيِّ آلَاءِ رَبِّكُمَا تُكَذِّبٰنِ ۙ

52. In them will be Fruits
    Of every kind, two and two.

٥٢ - فِيْهِمَا مِنْ كُلِّ فَاكِهَةٍ زَوْجٰنِ ۚ

53. Then which of the favours
    Of your Lord will ye deny?

٥٣ - فَبِأَيِّ آلَاءِ رَبِّكُمَا تُكَذِّبٰنِ ۙ

54. They will recline on Carpets,
    Whose inner linings will be
    Of rich brocade: the Fruit
    Of the Gardens will be
    Near (and easy of reach).

٥٤ - مُتَّكِئِيْنَ عَلٰى فُرُشٍ بَطَائِنُهَا مِنْ اِسْتَبْرَقٍ ۚ وَجَنَا الْجَنَّتَيْنِ دَانٍ ۚ

55. Then which of the favours
    Of your Lord will ye deny?

٥٥ - فَبِأَيِّ آلَاءِ رَبِّكُمَا تُكَذِّبٰنِ ۙ

56. In them will be (Maidens),
    Chaste, restraining their
                        glances,
    Whom no man or Jinn
    Before them has touched—

٥٦ - فِيْهِنَّ قٰصِرٰتُ الطَّرْفِ ۙ لَمْ يَطْمِثْهُنَّ اِنْسٌ قَبْلَهُمْ وَلَا جَآنٌّ ۚ

57. Then which of the favours

٥٧ - فَبِأَيِّ آلَاءِ رَبِّكُمَا

Of your Lord will ye deny?

تُكَذِّبٰنِ ۟

58. Like unto rubies and coral.

۵۸- كَاَنَّهُنَّ الْيَاقُوْتُ وَالْمَرْجَانُ ۟

59. Then which of the favours
Of your Lord will ye deny?

۵۹- فَبِاَيِّ اٰلَاءِ رَبِّكُمَا تُكَذِّبٰنِ ۝

60. Is there any Reward
For Good—other than Good?

۶۰- هَلْ جَزَآءُ الْاِحْسَانِ اِلَّا الْاِحْسَانُ ۟

61. Then which of the favours
Of your Lord will ye deny?

۶۱- فَبِاَيِّ اٰلَاءِ رَبِّكُمَا تُكَذِّبٰنِ ۝

62. And besides these two,
There are two other Gardens—

۶۲- وَ مِنْ دُوْنِهِمَا جَنَّتٰنِ ۟

63. Then which of the favours
Of your Lord will ye deny?

۶۳- فَبِاَيِّ اٰلَاءِ رَبِّكُمَا تُكَذِّبٰنِ ۟

64. Dark green in colour
(From plentiful watering).

۶۴- مُدْهَآمَّتٰنِ ۟

65. Then which of the favours
Of your Lord will ye deny?

۶۵- فَبِاَيِّ اٰلَاءِ رَبِّكُمَا تُكَذِّبٰنِ ۟

66. In them (each) will be
Two Springs pouring forth
                water
In continuous abundance:

۶۶- فِيْهِمَا عَيْنٰنِ نَضَّاخَتٰنِ ۟

67. Then which of the favours
Of your Lord will ye deny?

۶۷- فَبِاَيِّ اٰلَاءِ رَبِّكُمَا تُكَذِّبٰنِ ۝

68. In them will be Fruits,
And dates and pomegranates:

۶۸- فِيْهِمَا فَاكِهَةٌ وَّ نَخْلٌ وَّ رُمَّانٌ ۟

69. Then which of the favours
Of your Lord will ye deny?

۶۹- فَبِاَيِّ اٰلَاءِ رَبِّكُمَا تُكَذِّبٰنِ ۟

70. In them will be
Fair (Companions), good,
                beautiful—

۷۰- فِيْهِنَّ خَيْرٰتٌ حِسَانٌ ۟

71. Then which of the favours
Of your Lord will ye deny?

۷۱- فَبِاَيِّ اٰلَاءِ رَبِّكُمَا تُكَذِّبٰنِ ۟

72. Companions restrained (as to

۷۲- حُوْرٌ مَّقْصُوْرٰتٌ

Their glances), in (goodly)
pavilions—

في الْخِيَامِ ۞

73. Then which of the favours
Of your Lord will ye deny?

٧٣. فَبِأَيِّ آلَاءِ رَبِّكُمَا تُكَذِّبَانِ ۞

74. Whom no man or Jinn
Before them has touched—

٧٤. لَمْ يَطْمِثْهُنَّ إِنْسٌ قَبْلَهُمْ وَلَا جَانٌّ ۞

75. Then which of the favours
Of your Lord will ye deny?

٧٥. فَبِأَيِّ آلَاءِ رَبِّكُمَا تُكَذِّبَانِ ۞

76. Reclining on green Cushions
And rich Carpets of beauty.

٧٦. مُتَّكِئِينَ عَلَى رَفْرَفٍ خُضْرٍ وَعَبْقَرِيٍّ حِسَانٍ

77. Then which of the favours
Of your Lord will ye deny?

٧٧. فَبِأَيِّ آلَاءِ رَبِّكُمَا تُكَذِّبَانِ ۞

78. Blessed be the name
Of thy Lord;
Full of Majesty,
Bounty and Honour.

٧٨. تَبَارَكَ اسْمُ رَبِّكَ
ذِى الْجَلَالِ وَالْإِكْرَامِ ۞

INTRODUCTION TO SŪRA LVI. (*Wāqi'ah*) — 96 Verses

This is the seventh and last Sūra of the series devoted to Revelation and the Hereafter, as explained in the Introduction to *S.l,*

It belongs to the early Meccan period, with the possible exception of one or two verses.

The theme is the certainty of the Day of Judgment and its adjustment of true Values (lvi. 1-56): God's Power, Goodness and Glory (lvi. 57-74); and the truth of Revelation (lvi. 75-96).

Al Wāqi'ah (The Inevitable)

In the name of Allah, Most Gracious, Most Merciful.

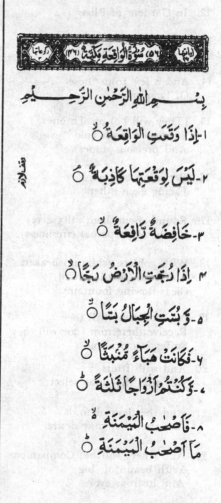

1. When the Event Inevitable
   Cometh to pass,

2. Then will no (soul)
   Entertain falsehood
   Concerning its coming.

3. (Many) will it bring low;
   (Many) will it exalt;

4. When the earth shall be
   Shaken to its depths,

5. And the mountains shall
   Be crumbled to atoms,

6. Becoming dust scattered abroad,

7. And ye shall be sorted out
   Into three classes.

8. Then (there will be)
   The Companions of
   The Right Hand—
   What will be
   The Companions of
   The Right Hand?

9. And the Companions of
   The Left Hand—

What will be
The Companions of
The Left Hand?

مَا أَصْحَبُ الْمَشْئَمَةِ ۞

10. And those Foremost
(In Faith) will be
Foremost (in the Hereafter).

١٠- وَالسّٰبِقُوْنَ السّٰبِقُوْنَ ۞

11. These will be
Those Nearest to Allah:

١١- أُولٰٓئِكَ الْمُقَرَّبُوْنَ ۞

12. In Gardens of Bliss:

١٢- فِيْ جَنّٰتِ النَّعِيْمِ ۞

13. A number of people
From those of old,

١٣- ثُلَّةٌ مِّنَ الْأَوَّلِيْنَ ۞

14. And a few from those
Of later times.

١٤- وَقَلِيْلٌ مِّنَ الْأٰخِرِيْنَ ۞

15. (They will be) on Thrones
Encrusted (with gold
And precious stones),

١٥- عَلٰى سُرُرٍ مَّوْضُوْنَةٍ ۞

16. Reclining on them,
Facing each other.

١٦- مُتَّكِئِيْنَ عَلَيْهَا مُتَقٰبِلِيْنَ ۞

17. Round about them will (serve)
Youths of perpetual (freshness),

١٧- يَطُوْفُ عَلَيْهِمْ وِلْدَانٌ مُّخَلَّدُوْنَ ۞

18. With goblets, (shining) beakers,
And cups (filled) out of
Clear-flowing fountains:

١٨- بِأَكْوَابٍ وَّأَبَارِيْقَ ۞
وَكَأْسٍ مِّنْ مَّعِيْنٍ ۞

19. No after-ache will they
Receive therefrom, nor will they
Suffer intoxication:

١٩- لَّا يُصَدَّعُوْنَ عَنْهَا
وَلَا يُنْزِفُوْنَ ۞

20. And with fruits,
Any that they may select;

٢٠- وَفَاكِهَةٍ مِّمَّا يَتَخَيَّرُوْنَ ۞

21. And the flesh of fowls,
Any that they may desire.

٢١- وَلَحْمِ طَيْرٍ مِّمَّا يَشْتَهُوْنَ ۞

22. And (there will be) Companions
With beautiful, big,
And lustrous eyes—

٢٢- وَحُوْرٌ عِيْنٌ ۞

23. Like unto Pearls
Well-guarded.

٢٣- كَأَمْثَالِ اللُّؤْلُؤِ الْمَكْنُوْنِ ۞

24. A Reward for the Deeds
Of their past (Life).

٢٤ـ جَزَآءً بِمَا كَانُوْا يَعْمَلُوْنَ ۝

25. No frivolity will they
Hear therein, nor any
Taint of ill—

٢٥ـ لَا يَسْمَعُوْنَ فِيْهَا لَغْوًا
وَّلَا تَأْثِيْمًا ۝

26. Only the saying,
"Peace! Peace".

٢٦ـ اِلَّا قِيْلًا سَلٰمًا سَلٰمًا ۝

27. The Companions of
The Right Hand—
What will be
The Companions of
The Right Hand!

٢٧ـ وَ أَصْحٰبُ الْيَمِيْنِ ۙ مَآ
أَصْحٰبُ الْيَمِيْنِ ۝

28. (They will be) among
Lote trees without thorns,

٢٨ـ فِيْ سِدْرٍ مَّخْضُوْدٍ ۝

29. Among Talh trees
With flowers (or fruits)
Piled one above another—

٢٩ـ وَّطَلْحٍ مَّنْضُوْدٍ ۝

30. In shade long-extended,

٣٠ـ وَّ ظِلٍّ مَّمْدُوْدٍ ۝

31. By water flowing constantly,

٣١ـ وَّ مَآءٍ مَّسْكُوْبٍ ۝

32. And fruit in abundance,

٣٢ـ وَّ فَاكِهَةٍ كَثِيْرَةٍ ۝

33. Whose season is not limited,
Nor (supply) forbidden,

٣٣ـ لَّا مَقْطُوْعَةٍ وَّلَا مَمْنُوْعَةٍ ۝

34. And on Thrones (of Dignity),
Raised high.

٣٤ـ وَّ فُرُشٍ مَّرْفُوْعَةٍ ۝

35. We have created
(their Companions)
Of special creation,

٣٥ـ اِنَّآ أَنْشَأْنٰهُنَّ اِنْشَآءً ۝

36. And made them
Virgin-pure (and undefiled)—

٣٦ـ فَجَعَلْنٰهُنَّ أَبْكَارًا ۝

37. Beloved (by nature),
Equal in age—

٣٧ـ عُرُبًا أَتْرَابًا ۝

38. For the Companions
Of the Right Hand.

٣٨ـ لِّأَصْحٰبِ الْيَمِيْنِ ۝

SECTION 2.

39. A (goodly) number
From those of old,

٣٩- ثُلَّةٌ مِّنَ الْأَوَّلِيْنَ ۞

40. And a (goodly) number
From those of later times.

٤٠- وَثُلَّةٌ مِّنَ الْأَخِرِيْنَ ۞

41. The Companions of
The Left Hand—
What will be
The Companions of
The Left Hand?

٤١- وَأَصْحٰبُ الشِّمَالِ ۙ
مَا أَصْحٰبُ الشِّمَالِ ۞

42. (They will be) in the midst
Of a fierce Blast of Fire
And in Boiling Water,

٤٢- فِيْ سَمُوْمٍ وَّحَمِيْمٍ ۞

43. And in the shades
Of Black Smoke:

٤٣- وَّظِلٍّ مِّنْ يَّحْمُوْمٍ ۞

44. Nothing (will there be)
To refresh, nor to please:

٤٤- لَّا بَارِدٍ وَّلَا كَرِيْمٍ ۞

45. For that they were wont
To be indulged, before that,
In wealth (and luxury),

٤٥- إِنَّهُمْ كَانُوْا قَبْلَ ذٰلِكَ مُتْرَفِيْنَ ۞

46. And persisted obstinately
In wickedness supreme!

٤٦- وَكَانُوْا يُصِرُّوْنَ عَلَى الْحِنْثِ الْعَظِيْمِ ۞

47. And they used to say,
"What! when we die
And become dust and bones,
Shall we then indeed
Be raised up again?—

٤٧- وَكَانُوْا يَقُوْلُوْنَ ۞
أَئِذَا مِتْنَا وَكُنَّا تُرَابًا وَّعِظَامًا
ءَإِنَّا لَمَبْعُوْثُوْنَ ۞

48. "(We) and our fathers of old?"

٤٨- أَوَ آبَاؤُنَا الْأَوَّلُوْنَ ۞

49. Say: "Yea, those of old
And those of later times,

٤٩- قُلْ إِنَّ الْأَوَّلِيْنَ وَالْأَخِرِيْنَ ۞

50. "All will certainly be
Gathered together for the meeting
Appointed for a Day
Well-known.

٥٠- لَمَجْمُوْعُوْنَ إِلٰى مِيْقَاتِ
يَوْمٍ مَّعْلُوْمٍ ۞

51. "Then will ye truly—
O ye that go wrong,.
And treat (Truth) as Falsehood!—

٥١- ثُمَّ اِنَّكُمْ اَيُّهَا الضَّآلُّوْنَ الْمُكَذِّبُوْنَ ۙ

52. "Ye will surely taste
Of the Tree of Zaqqūm.

٥٢- لَاٰكِلُوْنَ مِنْ شَجَرٍ مِّنْ زَقُّوْمٍ ۙ

53. "Then will ye fill
Your insides therewith,

٥٣- فَمَالِئُوْنَ مِنْهَا الْبُطُوْنَ ۚ

54. "And drink Boiling Water
On top of it:

٥٤- فَشَارِبُوْنَ عَلَيْهِ مِنَ الْحَمِيْمِ ۚ

55. "Indeed ye shall drink
Like diseased camels
Raging with thirst!"

٥٥- فَشَارِبُوْنَ شُرْبَ الْهِيْمِ ؕ

56. Such will be their entertainment
On the Day of Requital!

٥٦- هٰذَا نُزُلُهُمْ يَوْمَ الدِّيْنِ ؕ

57. It is We Who have
Created you: why will ye
Not witness the Truth?

٥٧- نَحْنُ خَلَقْنٰكُمْ فَلَوْلَا تُصَدِّقُوْنَ ۞

58. Do ye then see?—
The (human Seed) that
Ye throw out,—

٥٨- اَفَرَءَيْتُمْ مَّا تُمْنُوْنَ ؕ

59. Is it ye who create it,
Or are We the Creators?

٥٩- ءَاَنْتُمْ تَخْلُقُوْنَهٗ اَمْ نَحْنُ الْخٰلِقُوْنَ

60. We have decreed Death
To be your common lot,
And We are not
To be frustrated

٦٠- نَحْنُ قَدَّرْنَا بَيْنَكُمُ الْمَوْتَ وَمَا نَحْنُ بِمَسْبُوْقِيْنَ ۙ

61. From changing your Forms
And creating you (again)
In (Forms) that ye know not.

٦١- عَلٰى اَنْ نُّبَدِّلَ اَمْثَالَكُمْ وَنُنْشِئَكُمْ فِيْ مَا لَا تَعْلَمُوْنَ

62. And ye certainly know already
The first form of creation:
Why then do ye not
Celebrate His praises?

٦٢- وَلَقَدْ عَلِمْتُمُ النَّشْاَةَ الْاُوْلٰى فَلَوْلَا تَذَكَّرُوْنَ

63. See ye the seed that
Ye sow in the ground?

٦٣- اَفَرَءَيْتُمْ مَّا تَحْرُثُوْنَ ؕ

64. Is it ye that cause it
    To grow, or are We
    The Cause?

٦٤- ءَاَنْتُمْ تَزْرَعُوْنَهُ
اَمْ نَحْنُ الزَّارِعُوْنَ ٠

65. Were it Our Will,
    We could crumble it
    To dry powder, and ye would
    Be left in wonderment,

٦٥- لَوْ نَشَاءُ لَجَعَلْنَهُ حُطَامًا
فَظَلْتُمْ تَفَكَّهُوْنَ ٠

66. (Saying), "We are indeed
    Left with debts (for nothing):

٦٦- اِنَّا لَمُغْرَمُوْنَ ۞

67. "Indeed are we shut out
    (Of the fruits of our labour)".

٦٧- بَلْ نَحْنُ مَحْرُوْمُوْنَ ٠

68. See ye the water
    Which ye drink?

٦٨- اَفَرَءَيْتُمُ الْمَآءَ الَّذِيْ تَشْرَبُوْنَ ۞

69. Do ye bring it Down
    (In rain) from the Cloud
    Or do We?

٦٩- ءَاَنْتُمْ اَنْزَلْتُمُوْهُ مِنَ الْمُزْنِ
اَمْ نَحْنُ الْمُنْزِلُوْنَ ٠

70. Were it Our Will,
    We could make it
    Salt (and unpalatable):
    Then why do ye not
    Give thanks?

٧٠- لَوْ نَشَاءُ جَعَلْنَهُ
اُجَاجًا
فَلَوْلَا تَشْكُرُوْنَ ٠

71. See ye the Fire
    Which ye kindle?

٧١- اَفَرَءَيْتُمُ النَّارَ الَّتِيْ تُوْرُوْنَ ۞

72. Is it ye who grow
    The tree which feeds
    The fire, or do We
    Grow it?

٧٢- ءَاَنْتُمْ اَنْشَأْتُمْ شَجَرَتَهَا
اَمْ نَحْنُ الْمُنْشِئُوْنَ ٠

73. We have made it
    A memorial (of Our
                    handiwork),
    And an article of comfort
    And convenience for
    The denizens of deserts.

٧٣- نَحْنُ جَعَلْنَهَا تَذْكِرَةً
وَّ مَتَاعًا لِّلْمُقْوِيْنَ ۞

74. Then celebrate with praises
    The name of thy Lord,
    The Supreme!

٧٤- فَسَبِّحْ بِاسْمِ رَبِّكَ
الْعَظِيْمِ ۩

SECTION 3.

75. Furthermore I call
To witness the setting
Of the Stars—

٧٥ـ فَلَا أُقْسِمُ بِمَوٰقِعِ النُّجُوْمِ ۞

76. And that is indeed
A mighty adjuration
If ye but knew—

٧٦ـ وَإِنَّهٗ لَقَسَمٌ لَّوْ تَعْلَمُوْنَ عَظِيْمٌ ۞

77. That this is indeed
A Qur'ān most honourable,

٧٧ـ إِنَّهٗ لَقُرْاٰنٌ كَرِيْمٌ ۞

78. In a Book well-guarded,

٧٨ـ فِيْ كِتٰبٍ مَّكْنُوْنٍ ۞

79. Which none shall touch
But those who are clean:

٧٩ـ لَّا يَمَسُّهٗ إِلَّا الْمُطَهَّرُوْنَ ۞

80. A Revelation from the Lord
Of the Worlds.

٨٠ـ تَنْزِيْلٌ مِّنْ رَّبِّ الْعٰلَمِيْنَ ۞

81. Is it such a Message
That ye would hold
In light esteem?

٨١ـ أَفَبِهٰذَا الْحَدِيْثِ أَنْتُمْ مُّدْهِنُوْنَ ۞

82. And have ye made it
Your livelihood that ye
Should declare it false?

٨٢ـ وَتَجْعَلُوْنَ رِزْقَكُمْ
أَنَّكُمْ تُكَذِّبُوْنَ ۞

83. Then why do ye not
(Intervene) when (the soul
Of the dying man)
Reaches the throat—

٨٣ـ فَلَوْلَا إِذَا
بَلَغَتِ الْحُلْقُوْمَ ۞

84. And ye the while
(Sit) looking on—

٨٤ـ وَأَنْتُمْ حِيْنَئِذٍ تَنْظُرُوْنَ ۞

85. But We are nearer
To him than ye,
And yet see not—

٨٥ـ وَنَحْنُ أَقْرَبُ إِلَيْهِ مِنْكُمْ
وَلٰكِنْ لَّا تُبْصِرُوْنَ ۞

86. Then why do ye not—
If you are exempt
From (future) account—

٨٦ـ فَلَوْلَا إِنْ كُنْتُمْ غَيْرَ مَدِيْنِيْنَ ۞

87. Call back the soul,
If ye are true
(In your claim of Independence)?

٨٧ـ تَرْجِعُوْنَهَا إِنْ كُنْتُمْ صٰدِقِيْنَ ۞

88. Thus, then, if he
Be of those Nearest to Allah,

٨٨- فَأَمَّآ إِنْ كَانَ مِنَ الْمُقَرَّبِيْنَ ۞

89. (There is for him) Rest
And Satisfaction, and
A Garden of Delights.

٨٩- فَرَوْحٌ وَّرَيْحَانٌ ۚ
وَّجَنَّتُ نَعِيْمٍ ۞

90. And if he be
Of the Companions of
The Right Hand,

٩٠- وَأَمَّآ إِنْ كَانَ مِنْ أَصْحَبِ الْيَمِيْنِ ۞

91. (For him is the salutation),
"Peace be unto thee,"
From the Companions
Of the Right Hand.

٩١- فَسَلَمٌ لَّكَ
مِنْ أَصْحَبِ الْيَمِيْنِ ۞

92. And if he be
Of those who treat
(Truth) as Falsehood,
Who go wrong,

٩٢- وَأَمَّآ إِنْ كَانَ
مِنَ الْمُكَذِّبِيْنَ الضَّآلِّيْنَ ۞

93. For him is Entertainment
With Boiling Water,

٩٣- فَنُزُلٌ مِّنْ حَمِيْمٍ ۞

94. And burning in Hell-Fire.

٩٤- وَّتَصْلِيَةُ جَحِيْمٍ ۞

95. Verily, this is
The very Truth
And Certainty.

٩٥- إِنَّ هٰذَا لَهُوَ حَقُّ الْيَقِيْنِ ۞

96. So celebrate with praises
The name of thy Lord,
The Supreme.

٩٦- فَسَبِّحْ بِاسْمِ رَبِّكَ الْعَظِيْمِ ۞

INTRODUCTION TO SŪRA LVII. (*Ḥadīd*) — 29 Verses

We have now studied the contents of nearly nine-tenths of the Qur-ān. We have found that the arrangement of the Sūras in the present Text is not haphazard, but that they follow a distinct logical order more helpful for study than the chronological order. The comprehensive scheme of building up the new *Ummat* or Brotherhood and its spiritual implications is now complete. The remaining tenth of the Qur-ān may be roughly considered in two parts. The first contains ten Sūras (S.lvii. to S. lxvi.), all revealed in Medina, and each dealing with some special point which needs emphasis in the social life of the Ummat. The second (S.lxvii. to cxiv.) contains short Meccan lyrics, each dealing with some aspect of spiritual life, expressed in language of great mystic beauty.

The present Medina Sūra is chiefly concerned with spiritual humility and the avoidance of arrogance, and a warning that retirement from the world may not be the best way of seeking the good pleasure of God. Its probable date is after the Conquest of Mecca, A.H. 8.

Al Ḥadīd (Iron)

In the name of Allah, Most Gracious,
Most Merciful.

1. Whatever is in
The heavens and on earth—
Let it declare
The Praises and Glory of Allah:
For He is the Exalted
In Might, the Wise.

2. To Him belongs the dominion
Of the heavens and the earth:
It is He Who gives
Life and Death; and He
Has Power over all things.

3. He is the First
And the Last,
The Evident
And the Hidden:
And He has full knowledge
Of all things.

4. He it is Who created
The heavens and the earth
In six Days,   and is moreover

بِسۡمِ اللهِ الرَّحۡمٰنِ الرَّحِيۡمِ

١- سَبَّحَ لِلّٰهِ
مَا فِى السَّمٰوٰتِ وَالۡاَرۡضِ
وَهُوَ الۡعَزِيۡزُ الۡحَكِيۡمُ ۞

٢- لَهُ مُلۡكُ السَّمٰوٰتِ وَالۡاَرۡضِ
يُحۡىٖ وَيُمِيۡتُ
وَهُوَ عَلٰى كُلِّ شَىۡءٍ قَدِيۡرٌ ۞

٣- هُوَ الۡاَوَّلُ وَالۡاٰخِرُ
وَالظَّاهِرُ وَالۡبَاطِنُ
وَهُوَ بِكُلِّ شَىۡءٍ عَلِيۡمٌ ۞

٤- هُوَ الَّذِىۡ خَلَقَ السَّمٰوٰتِ وَالۡاَرۡضَ فِىۡ
سِتَّةِ اَيَّامٍ ثُمَّ اسۡتَوٰى عَلَى الۡعَرۡشِ يَعۡلَمُ

Firmly established on the
              Throne
(Of authority),   He knows
What enters within the earth
And what comes forth out
Of it, what comes down
From heaven and what mounts
Up to it. And He is
With you wheresoever ye
May be. And Allah sees
Well all that ye do.

مَا يَلِجُ فِى الْأَرْضِ وَمَا يَخْرُجُ مِنْهَا
وَمَا يَنْزِلُ مِنَ السَّمَآءِ وَمَا يَعْرُجُ فِيْهَا ۖ
وَهُوَ مَعَكُمْ اَيْنَ مَا كُنْتُمْ ۚ
وَاللّٰهُ بِمَا تَعْمَلُوْنَ بَصِيْرٌ ۞

5. To Him belongs the dominion
Of the heavens and the earth:
And all affairs are
Referred back to Allah.

٥ ـ لَهٗ مُلْكُ السَّمٰوٰتِ وَالْأَرْضِ ۚ
وَاِلَى اللّٰهِ تُرْجَعُ الْأُمُوْرُ ۞

6. He merges Night into Day,
And He merges Day into Night;
And He has full knowledge
Of the secrets of (all) hearts.

٦ ـ يُوْلِجُ الَّيْلَ فِى النَّهَارِ وَيُوْلِجُ النَّهَارَ
فِى الَّيْلِ ۚ وَهُوَ عَلِيْمٌۢ بِذَاتِ الصُّدُوْرِ ۞

7. Believe in Allah
And His Messenger,
And spend (in charity)
Out of the (substance)
Whereof He has made you
Heirs. For, those of you
Who believe and spend
(In charity)—for them
Is a great Reward.

٧ ـ اٰمِنُوْا بِاللّٰهِ وَرَسُوْلِهٖ
وَاَنْفِقُوْا مِمَّا جَعَلَكُمْ مُّسْتَخْلَفِيْنَ فِيْهِ ۖ
فَالَّذِيْنَ اٰمَنُوْا مِنْكُمْ وَاَنْفَقُوْا
لَهُمْ اَجْرٌ كَبِيْرٌ ۞

8. What cause have ye
Why ye should not believe
In Allah?—And the Messenger
Invites you to believe
In your Lord, and has
Indeed taken your Covenant,
If ye are men of faith.

٨ ـ وَمَا لَكُمْ لَا تُؤْمِنُوْنَ بِاللّٰهِ ۙ
وَالرَّسُوْلُ يَدْعُوْكُمْ لِتُؤْمِنُوْا
بِرَبِّكُمْ
وَقَدْ اَخَذَ مِيْثَاقَكُمْ اِنْ كُنْتُمْ مُّؤْمِنِيْنَ

9. He is the One Who
Sends to His Servant
Manifest Signs, that He
May lead you from
The depths of Darkness
Into the Light. And verily,

٩ ـ هُوَ الَّذِىْ يُنَزِّلُ عَلٰى عَبْدِهٖ اٰيٰتٍۭ بَيِّنٰتٍ
لِّيُخْرِجَكُمْ مِّنَ الظُّلُمٰتِ اِلَى النُّوْرِ ۚ
وَاِنَّ اللّٰهَ بِكُمْ

Allah is to you
Most Kind and Merciful.

لَرَءُوْفٌ رَّحِيْمٌ ۞

10. And what cause have ye
Why ye should not spend
In the cause of Allah?—
For to Allah belongs
The heritage of the heavens
And the earth.
Not equal among you
Are those who spent (freely)
And fought, before the
　　　　　　　　Victory,
(With those who did so later).
Those are higher in rank
Than those who spent (freely)
And fought afterwards.
But to all has Allah promised
A goodly (reward). And Allah
Is well-acquainted
With all that ye do.

١٠- وَمَا لَكُمْ
اَلَّا تُنْفِقُوْا فِيْ سَبِيْلِ اللهِ
وَلِلّٰهِ مِيْرَاثُ السَّمٰوٰتِ وَالْاَرْضِ ۚ
لَا يَسْتَوِىْ مِنْكُمْ
مَّنْ اَنْفَقَ مِنْ قَبْلِ الْفَتْحِ وَقٰتَلَ ۚ
اُولٰٓئِكَ اَعْظَمُ دَرَجَةً
مِّنَ الَّذِيْنَ اَنْفَقُوْا مِنْ بَعْدُ وَقٰتَلُوْا ۚ
وَكُلًّا وَّعَدَ اللهُ الْحُسْنٰى ۚ
وَاللهُ بِمَا تَعْمَلُوْنَ خَبِيْرٌ ۞

SECTION 2.

11. Who is he that will
Loan to Allah a beautiful
Loan? For (Allah) will
Increase it manifold
To his credit,
And he will have (besides)
A liberal reward.

١١- مَنْ ذَا الَّذِىْ
يُقْرِضُ اللهَ قَرْضًا حَسَنًا
فَيُضٰعِفَهٗ لَهٗ
وَلَهٗ اَجْرٌ كَرِيْمٌ ۞

12. One Day shalt thou see
The believing men and
The believing women—
How their Light runs
Forward before them
And by their right hands:
(Their greeting will be):
"Good News for you this Day!
Gardens beneath which flow
　　　　　　　　rivers!
To dwell therein for aye!
This is indeed
The highest Achievement!"

١٢- يَوْمَ تَرَى الْمُؤْمِنِيْنَ وَالْمُؤْمِنٰتِ
يَسْعٰى نُوْرُهُمْ بَيْنَ اَيْدِيْهِمْ
وَبِاَيْمَانِهِمْ بُشْرٰىكُمُ الْيَوْمَ
جَنّٰتٌ تَجْرِىْ مِنْ تَحْتِهَا الْاَنْهٰرُ
خٰلِدِيْنَ فِيْهَا ۚ
ذٰلِكَ هُوَ الْفَوْزُ الْعَظِيْمُ ۞

13. One Day will the Hypocrites—
Men and women—say
To the Believers: "Wait

١٣- يَوْمَ يَقُوْلُ الْمُنٰفِقُوْنَ وَالْمُنٰفِقٰتُ لِلَّذِيْنَ

For us! Let us borrow
(A light) from your Light!"
It will be said: "Turn
Ye back to your rear!
Then seek a light (where
Ye can)!" So a wall⁵²⁹¹
Will be put up betwixt them,
With a gate therein.
Within it will be Mercy
Throughout, and without it,
All alongside, will be
(Wrath and) Punishment!

14. (Those without) will call out,
"Were we not with you?"
(The others) will reply, "True!
But ye led yourselves
Into temptation; ye looked forward
(To our ruin); ye doubted
(Allah's Promise); and (your false)
Desires deceived you; until
There issued the Command
Of Allah. And the Deceiver
Deceived you in respect of
Allah.

15. "This Day shall no ransom
Be accepted of you, nor
Of those who rejected Allah
Your abode is the Fire:
That is the proper place
To claim you: and an evil
Refuge it is!"

16. Has not the time arrived
For the Believers that
Their hearts in all humility
Should engage in the
remembrance
Of Allah and of the Truth
Which has been revealed (to
them),
And that they should not
Become like those to whom
Was given Revelation
aforetime,
But long ages passed over them
And their hearts grew hard?

For many among them
Are rebellious transgressors.

وَكَثِيرٌ مِّنْهُمْ فَاسِقُونَ ۝

17. Know ye (all) that
Allah giveth life
To the earth after its death!
Already have We shown
The Signs plainly to you,
That ye may learn wisdom.

١٧- اِعْلَمُوٓا اَنَّ اللهَ يُحْيِ الْاَرْضَ بَعْدَ مَوْتِهَا قَدْ بَيَّنَّا لَكُمُ الْاٰيٰتِ لَعَلَّكُمْ تَعْقِلُونَ ۝

18. For those who give
In Charity, men and women,
And loan to Allah
A Beautiful Loan,
It shall be increased manifold
(To their credit),
And they shall have (besides)
A liberal reward.

١٨- اِنَّ الْمُصَّدِّقِينَ وَالْمُصَّدِّقٰتِ وَاَقْرَضُوا اللهَ قَرْضًا حَسَنًا يُّضٰعَفُ لَهُمْ وَلَهُمْ اَجْرٌ كَرِيمٌ ۝

19. And those who believe
In Allah and His messengers—
They are the Sincere
(Lovers of Truth), and
The Witnesses (who testify),
In the eyes of their Lord:
They shall have their Reward
And their Light.
But those who reject Allah
And deny Our Signs—
They are the Companions
Of Hell-Fire.

١٩- وَالَّذِينَ اٰمَنُوا بِاللهِ وَرُسُلِهٖٓ اُولٰٓئِكَ هُمُ الصِّدِّيقُونَ وَ الشُّهَدَآءُ عِنْدَ رَبِّهِمْ لَهُمْ اَجْرُهُمْ وَنُورُهُمْ وَالَّذِينَ كَفَرُوا وَكَذَّبُوا بِاٰيٰتِنَا اُولٰٓئِكَ اَصْحٰبُ الْجَحِيمِ ۝

SECTION 3.

20. Know ye (all), that
The life of this world
Is but play and amusement,
Pomp and mutual boasting
And multiplying, (in rivalry)
Among yourselves, riches
And children.
Here is a similitude;
How rain and the growth
Which it brings forth, delight
(The hearts of) the tillers;
Soon it withers; thou
Wilt see it grow yellow;
Then it becomes dry
And crumbles away.

٢٠- اِعْلَمُوٓا اَنَّمَا الْحَيٰوةُ الدُّنْيَا لَعِبٌ وَّلَهْوٌ وَّزِينَةٌ وَّتَفَاخُرٌۢ بَيْنَكُمْ وَتَكَاثُرٌ فِي الْاَمْوَالِ وَالْاَوْلَادِ كَمَثَلِ غَيْثٍ اَعْجَبَ الْكُفَّارَ نَبَاتُهٗ ثُمَّ يَهِيجُ فَتَرٰىهُ مُصْفَرًّا ثُمَّ يَكُونُ حُطَامًا

But in the Hereafter
Is a Penalty severe
(For the devotees of wrong).
And Forgiveness from Allah
And (His) Good Pleasure
(For the devotees of Allah).
And what is the life
Of this world, but
Goods and chattels
Of deception?

وَفِى الْآخِرَةِ عَذَابٌ شَدِيدٌ

وَمَغْفِرَةٌ مِّنَ اللّٰهِ وَرِضْوَانٌ

وَمَا الْحَيَوةُ الدُّنْيَا

إِلَّا مَتَاعُ الْغُرُورِ ۝

21. Be ye foremost (in seeking)
Forgiveness from your Lord,
And a Garden (of Bliss),
The width whereof is
As the width of
Heaven and earth,
Prepared for those who believe
In Allah and His messengers:
That is the Grace of Allah,
Which He bestows on whom
He pleases: and Allah is
The Lord of Grace abounding.

٢١- سَابِقُوا إِلَى مَغْفِرَةٍ مِّن رَّبِّكُمْ
وَجَنَّةٍ
عَرْضُهَا كَعَرْضِ السَّمَاءِ وَالْأَرْضِ
أُعِدَّتْ لِلَّذِينَ آمَنُوا بِاللّٰهِ وَرُسُلِهِ
ذٰلِكَ فَضْلُ اللّٰهِ يُؤْتِيهِ مَن يَشَاءُ
وَاللّٰهُ ذُو الْفَضْلِ الْعَظِيمِ ۝

22. No misfortune can happen
On earth or in your souls
But is recorded in
A decree before We bring
It into existence:
That is truly easy for Allah:

٢٢- مَا أَصَابَ مِن مُّصِيبَةٍ فِى الْأَرْضِ وَ
لَا فِى أَنفُسِكُمْ إِلَّا فِى كِتَابٍ مِّن قَبْلِ أَن
نَّبْرَأَهَا إِنَّ ذٰلِكَ عَلَى اللّٰهِ يَسِيرٌ ۝

23. In order that ye may
Not despair over matters
That pass you by,
Nor exult over favours
Bestowed upon you.
For Allah loveth not
Any vainglorious boaster—

٢٣- لِكَيْلَا تَأْسَوْا عَلَى مَا فَاتَكُمْ
وَلَا تَفْرَحُوا بِمَا آتَاكُمْ
وَاللّٰهُ لَا يُحِبُّ
كُلَّ مُخْتَالٍ فَخُورٍ ۝

24. Such persons as are
Covetous and commend
Covetousness to men,
And if any turn back
(From Allah's Way), verily
Allah is free of all needs,
Worthy of all praise.

٢٤- الَّذِينَ يَبْخَلُونَ
وَيَأْمُرُونَ النَّاسَ بِالْبُخْلِ وَمَن يَتَوَلَّ
فَإِنَّ اللّٰهَ هُوَ الْغَنِيُّ الْحَمِيدُ ۝

25. We sent aforetime

٢٥- لَقَدْ أَرْسَلْنَا

Our messengers with Clear Signs
And sent down with them
The Book and the Balance
(Of Right and Wrong), that men
May stand forth in justice;
And We sent down　　Iron,
In which is (material for)
Mighty war, as well as
Many benefits for mankind,
That Allah may test who
It is that will help,
Unseen,　　Him and His
　　　　　　messengers:
For Allah is Full of Strength,
Exalted in Might
(And able to enforce His Will).

SECTION 4.

26. And We sent Noah
And Abraham, and established
In their line Prophethood
And Revelation: and some of
　　　　　　them
Were on right guidance,
But many of them
Became rebellious transgressors.

27. Then, in their wake,
We followed them up
With (others of) Our mesengers:
We sent after them
Jesus the son of Mary,
And bestowed on him
The Gospel; and We ordained
In the hearts of those
Who followed him
Compassion and Mercy,
But the Monasticism
Which they invented
For themselves, We did not
Prescribe for them:
(We commanded) only
The seeking for the Good
Pleasure of Allah; but that
They did not foster
As they should have done.
Yet We bestowed, on those
Among them who believed,
Their (due) reward, but

Many of them are
Rebellious transgressors.

وَكَثِيرٌ مِّنْهُمْ فٰسِقُونَ ۟

28 O ye that believe!
Fear, Allah, and believe
In His Messenger, and He will
Bestow on you a double
Portion of His Mercy:
He will provide for you
A Light by which ye
Shall walk (straight
In your path), and He
Will forgive you (your past);
For Allah is Oft-Forgiving,
Most Merciful:

٢٨ ـ يٰٓاَيُّهَا الَّذِينَ اٰمَنُوا اتَّقُوا اللّٰهَ وَاٰمِنُوا
بِرَسُولِهٖ يُؤْتِكُمْ
كِفْلَيْنِ مِنْ رَّحْمَتِهٖ
وَيَجْعَلْ لَّكُمْ نُورًا
تَمْشُونَ بِهٖ وَيَغْفِرْ لَكُمْ ؕ
وَاللّٰهُ غَفُورٌ رَّحِيمٌ ۙ

29. That the People of
The Book may know
That they have no power
Whatever over the Grace
Of Allah, that (His) Grace
Is (entirely) in His Hand,
To bestow it on
Whomsoever He wills.
For Allah is the Lord
Of Grace abounding.

٢٩ ـ لِئَلَّا يَعْلَمَ اَهْلُ الْكِتٰبِ
اَلَّا يَقْدِرُونَ عَلٰى شَيْءٍ مِّنْ فَضْلِ اللّٰهِ
وَاَنَّ الْفَضْلَ بِيَدِ اللّٰهِ
يُؤْتِيهِ مَنْ يَّشَاءُ ؕ
وَاللّٰهُ ذُو الْفَضْلِ الْعَظِيمِ ۟

INTRODUCTION TO SŪRA LVIII. (*Mujādala*) — 22 Verses

This is the second of the ten Medina Sūras referred to in the Introduction to the last Sūra. Its subject-matter is the acceptance of a woman's Plea on behalf of herself and her children (see n. 5330 to lviii. 1 below), and a condemnation of all secret counsels and intrigues in the Muslim Brotherhood.

The date is somewhat close to that of S.xxxiii., say between A.H.5 and A.H.7.

Al Mujādilah (The Woman Who Pleads)

In the name of Allah, Most Gracious, Most Merciful.

1. Allah has indeed
Heard (and accepted) the
        statement
Of the woman who pleads
With thee concerning her husband
And carries her complaint
(In prayer) to Allah:
And Allah (always) hears
The arguments between both
Sides among you: for Allah
Hears and sees (all things).

2. If any men among you
Divorce their wives by Zihar
(Calling them mothers),
They cannot be their mothers:
None can be their mothers
Except those who gave them
Birth. And in fact
They use words (both)
        iniquitous
And false: but truly
Allah is One that blots out
(Sins), and forgives
(Again and again).

3. But those who divorce
Their wives by Zihar,
Then wish to go back
On the words they uttered—
(It is ordained that

Such a one)
Should free a slave
Before they touch each other:
This are ye admonished
To perform: and Allah is
Well-acquainted with (all)
That ye do.

مِنْ قَبْلِ أَنْ يَتَمَاسَّا ۚ
ذٰلِكُمْ تُوعَظُونَ بِهٖ ۚ
وَاللّٰهُ بِمَا تَعْمَلُونَ خَبِيرٌ ٥

4. And if any has not
(The wherewithal),
He should fast for
Two months consecutively
Before they touch each other.
But if any is unable
To do so, he should feed
Sixty indigent ones.
This, that ye may show
Your faith in Allah
And His Messenger,
Those are limits (set
By) Allah. For those who
Reject (Him), there is
A grievous Penalty.

٤ۣ فَمَنْ لَّمْ يَجِدْ فَصِيَامُ شَهْرَيْنِ مُتَتَابِعَيْنِ
مِنْ قَبْلِ أَنْ يَتَمَاسَّا ۚ
فَمَنْ لَّمْ يَسْتَطِعْ
فَإِطْعَامُ سِتِّينَ مِسْكِينًا ۚ
ذٰلِكَ لِتُؤْمِنُوا بِاللّٰهِ
وَرَسُولِهٖ ۚ
وَتِلْكَ حُدُودُ اللّٰهِ ۚ
وَلِلْكٰفِرِينَ عَذَابٌ أَلِيمٌ ٥

5. Those who resist Allah
And His Messenger will be
Humbled to dust, as were
Those before them: for We
Have already sent down
Clear Signs. And the
                    Unbelievers
(Will have) a humiliating
                        Penalty,

٥ۣ إِنَّ الَّذِينَ يُحَادُّونَ اللّٰهَ وَرَسُولَهٗ
كُبِتُوا كَمَا كُبِتَ الَّذِينَ مِنْ قَبْلِهِمْ
وَقَدْ أَنْزَلْنَا آيَاتٍ بَيِّنٰتٍ ۚ
وَلِلْكٰفِرِينَ عَذَابٌ مُّهِينٌ ۚ

6. On the Day that
Allah will raise them
All up (again) and show
Them the truth (and
                  meaning)
Of their conduct. Allah has
Reckoned its (value), though
They may have forgotten it,
For Allah is Witness
To all things.
            SECTION 2.

٦ۣ يَوْمَ يَبْعَثُهُمُ اللّٰهُ جَمِيعًا
فَيُنَبِّئُهُمْ بِمَا عَمِلُوا ۚ
أَحْصَاهُ اللّٰهُ وَنَسُوهُ ۚ
وَاللّٰهُ عَلٰى كُلِّ شَيْءٍ شَهِيدٌ ۚ

7. Seest thou not that
Allah doth know (all) that is
In the heavens and

٧ۣ أَلَمْ تَرَ أَنَّ اللّٰهَ يَعْلَمُ

On earth? There is not
A secret consultation
Between three, but He
Makes the fourth among
　　　　　　　them—
Nor between five but
He makes the sixth—
Nor between fewer nor more,
But He is with them,
Wheresoever they be:
In the end will He
Tell them the truth
Of their conduct, on the Day
Of Judgement. For Allah
Has full knowledge
Of all things.

8. Turnest thou not thy sight
Towards those who were
Forbidden secret counsels
Yet revert to that which
They were forbidden (to do)?
And they hold secret counsels
Among themselves for iniquity
And hostility, and disobedience
To the Messenger. And when
They come to thee,
They salute thee,
Not as Allah salutes thee,
(But in crooked ways):
And they say to themselves,
"Why does not Allah
Punish us for our words?"
Enough for them is Hell:
In it will they burn,
And evil is that destination!

9. O ye who believe!
When ye hold secret counsel,
Do it not for iniquity
And hostility, and disobedience
To the Messenger; but do it
For righteousness and self-
　　　　　　　restraint;
And fear Allah, to Whom
Ye shall be brought back.

10. Secret counsels are only
(Inspired) by the Evil One,

In order that he may
Cause grief to the ·Believers;
But he cannot harm them
In the least, except as
Allah permits; and on Allah
Let the Believers
Put their trust.

لِيَحْزُنَ الَّذِيْنَ اٰمَنُوْا
وَلَيْسَ بِضَآرِّهِمْ شَيْئًا اِلَّا بِاِذْنِ اللّٰهِ
وَعَلَى اللّٰهِ فَلْيَتَوَكَّلِ الْمُؤْمِنُوْنَ ۝

11. ۞ ye who believe!
When ye are told
To make room
In the assemblies,
(Spread out and) make room:
(Ample) room will Allah provide
For you. And when
Ye are told to rise up,
Rise up: Allah will
Raise up, to (suitable) ranks
(And degrees), those of you
Who believe and who have
Been granted Knowledge.
And Allah is well-acquainted
With all ye do.

١١- يٰٓاَيُّهَا الَّذِيْنَ اٰمَنُوْٓا اِذَا قِيْلَ لَكُمْ
تَفَسَّحُوْا فِى الْمَجٰلِسِ
فَافْسَحُوْا يَفْسَحِ اللّٰهُ لَكُمْ
وَاِذَا قِيْلَ انْشُزُوْا فَانْشُزُوْا
يَرْفَعِ اللّٰهُ
الَّذِيْنَ اٰمَنُوْا مِنْكُمْ ۙ وَالَّذِيْنَ
اُوْتُوا الْعِلْمَ دَرَجٰتٍ ؕ
وَاللّٰهُ بِمَا تَعْمَلُوْنَ خَبِيْرٌ ۝

12. ۞ ye who believe!
When ye consult
The Messenger in private,
Spend something in charity
Before your private consultation.
That will be best for you,
And most conducive
To purity (of· conduct).
But if ye find not
(The wherewithal), Allah is
Oft-Forgiving, Most Merciful.

١٢- يٰٓاَيُّهَا الَّذِيْنَ اٰمَنُوْٓا اِذَا نَاجَيْتُمُ الرَّسُوْلَ
فَقَدِّمُوْا
بَيْنَ يَدَيْ نَجْوٰىكُمْ صَدَقَةً ؕ
ذٰلِكَ خَيْرٌ لَّكُمْ وَاَطْهَرُ ؕ
فَاِنْ لَّمْ تَجِدُوْا
فَاِنَّ اللّٰهَ غَفُوْرٌ رَّحِيْمٌ ۝

13. Is it that ye are
Afraid of spending sums
In charity before your
Private consultation (with him)?
If, then, ye do not so,
And Allah forgives you,
Then (at least) establish
Regular prayer; practise
Regular charity; and obey
Allah and His Messenger.
And Allah is well-acquainted
With all that ye do.

١٣- ءَاَشْفَقْتُمْ اَنْ تُقَدِّمُوْا
بَيْنَ يَدَيْ نَجْوٰىكُمْ صَدَقٰتٍ ؕ
فَاِذْ لَمْ تَفْعَلُوْا وَتَابَ اللّٰهُ عَلَيْكُمْ
فَاَقِيْمُوا الصَّلٰوةَ وَاٰتُوا الزَّكٰوةَ
وَاَطِيْعُوا اللّٰهَ وَرَسُوْلَهٗ ؕ
وَاللّٰهُ خَبِيْرٌ ۢ بِمَا تَعْمَلُوْنَ ۝

SECTION 3.

14. Turnest thou not
Thy attention to those
Who turn (in friendship)
To such as have the Wrath
Of Allah upon them?
They are neither of you
Nor of them, and they
Swear to falsehood knowingly.

١٤- اَلَمْ تَرَ اِلَى الَّذِيْنَ
تَوَلَّوْا قَوْمًا غَضِبَ اللهُ عَلَيْهِمْ
مَا هُمْ مِنْكُمْ وَلَا مِنْهُمْ
وَيَحْلِفُوْنَ عَلَى الْكَذِبِ وَهُمْ يَعْلَمُوْنَ ۝

15. Allah has prepared for them
A severe Penalty: evil
Indeed are their deeds.

١٥- اَعَدَّ اللهُ لَهُمْ عَذَابًا شَدِيْدًا
اِنَّهُمْ سَاءَ مَا كَانُوْا يَعْمَلُوْنَ ۝

16. They have made their oaths
A screen (for their misdeeds):
Thus they obstruct (men)
From the Path of Allah:
Therefore shall they have
A humiliating Penalty.

١٦- اِتَّخَذُوْا اَيْمَانَهُمْ جُنَّةً
فَصَدُّوْا عَنْ سَبِيْلِ اللهِ
فَلَهُمْ عَذَابٌ مُهِيْنٌ ۝

17. Of no profit whatever
To them, against Allah,
Will be their riches
Nor their sons:
They will be Companions
Of the Fire, to dwell
Therein (for aye)!

١٧- لَنْ تُغْنِيَ عَنْهُمْ
اَمْوَالُهُمْ وَلَا اَوْلَادُهُمْ مِنَ اللهِ شَيْئًا
اُولٰئِكَ اَصْحَابُ النَّارِ
هُمْ فِيْهَا خَالِدُوْنَ ۝

18. One Day will Allah
Raise them all up
(For Judgement): then
Will they swear to Him
As they swear to you:
And they think that they
Have something (to stand upon).
No, indeed! they are
But liars!

١٨- يَوْمَ يَبْعَثُهُمُ اللهُ جَمِيْعًا
فَيَحْلِفُوْنَ لَهُ كَمَا يَحْلِفُوْنَ لَكُمْ
وَيَحْسَبُوْنَ اَنَّهُمْ عَلَى شَيْءٍ
اَلَا اِنَّهُمْ هُمُ الْكَذِبُوْنَ ۝

19. The Evil One has
Got the better of them:
So he has made them
Lose the remembrance
Of Allah. They are the Party
Of the Evil One. Truly,
It is the Party
Of the Evil One
That will Perish!

١٩- اِسْتَحْوَذَ عَلَيْهِمُ الشَّيْطٰنُ
فَاَنْسٰهُمْ ذِكْرَ اللهِ
اُولٰئِكَ حِزْبُ الشَّيْطٰنِ اَلَا اِنَّ حِزْبَ
الشَّيْطٰنِ هُمُ الْخٰسِرُوْنَ ۝

20. Those who resist
Allah and His Messenger
Will be among those
Most humiliated.

٢٠- اِنَّ الَّذِيْنَ يُحَآدُّوْنَ اللهَ وَرَسُوْلَهٗ
اُولٰٓئِكَ فِى الْاَذَلِّيْنَ ۟

21. Allah has decreed:
"It is I and My messengers
Who must prevail":
For Allah is One
Full of strength,
Able to enforce His Will.

٢١- كَتَبَ اللهُ
لَاَغْلِبَنَّ اَنَا وَرُسُلِيْ ؕ
اِنَّ اللهَ قَوِيٌّ عَزِيْزٌ ۟

22. Thou wilt not find
Any people who believe
In Allah and the Last Day,
Loving those who resist
Allah and His Messenger,
Even though they were
Their fathers or their sons,
Or their brothers, or
Their kindred. For such
He has written Faith
In their hearts, and strengthened
Them with a spirit
From Himself. And He
Will admit them to Gardens
Beneath which Rivers flow,
To dwell therein (forever).
Allah will be well pleased
With them, and they with Him.
They are the Party
Of Allah. Truly it is
The Party of Allah that
Will achieve Felicity.

٢٢- لَا تَجِدُ قَوْمًا يُّؤْمِنُوْنَ بِاللهِ وَالْيَوْمِ الْاٰخِرِ
يُوَآدُّوْنَ مَنْ حَآدَّ اللهَ وَرَسُوْلَهٗ
وَلَوْ كَانُوْۤا اٰبَآءَهُمْ اَوْ اَبْنَآءَهُمْ
اَوْ اِخْوَانَهُمْ اَوْ عَشِيْرَتَهُمْ ؕ
اُولٰٓئِكَ كَتَبَ فِيْ قُلُوْبِهِمُ الْاِيْمَانَ
وَاَيَّدَهُمْ بِرُوْحٍ مِّنْهُ ؕ
وَيُدْخِلُهُمْ جَنّٰتٍ
تَجْرِيْ مِنْ تَحْتِهَا الْاَنْهٰرُ خٰلِدِيْنَ فِيْهَا ؕ
رَضِيَ اللهُ
عَنْهُمْ وَرَضُوْا عَنْهُ ؕ
اُولٰٓئِكَ حِزْبُ اللهِ ؕ
اَلَاۤ اِنَّ حِزْبَ اللهِ هُمُ الْمُفْلِحُوْنَ ۟ ۼ

INTRODUCTION TO SŪRA LIX. (*Ḥashr*) — 24 Verses

This is the third of the series of ten short Medina Sūras, dealing each with a special point in the life of the Ummat: see Introduction to S. lvii. The special theme here is how treachery to the Ummat on the part of its enemies recoils on the enemies themselves, while it strengthens the bond between the different sections of the Ummat itself, and this is illustrated by the story of the expulsion of the Jewish tribe of the Banu Nadhīr in Rabi' I, A.H. 4.

This fixes the date of the Sūra.

Al Ḥashr (The Mustering)

In the name of Allah, Most Gracious,
Most Merciful.

1. **W**hatever is
In the heavens and
On earth, let it declare
The Praises and Glory
Of Allah: for He is
The Exalted in Might,
The Wise.

2. **I**t is He Who got out
The Unbelievers among
The People of the Book
From their homes
At the first gathering
(Of the forces).
Little did ye think
That they would get out:
And they thought
That their fortresses
Would defend them from Allah!
But the (Wrath of) Allah
Came to them from quarters
From which they little
Expected (it), and cast
Terror into their hearts,
So that they destroyed
Their dwellings by their own
Hands and the hands
Of the Believers.
Take warning, then,
O ye with eyes (to see)!

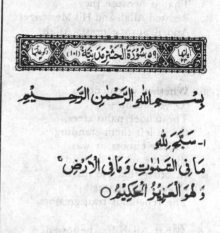

3. And had it not been
That Allah had decreed
Banishment for them,
He would certainly have
Punished them in this world:
And in the Hereafter
They shall (certainly) have
The Punishment of the Fire.

٣- وَلَوْلَا أَنْ كَتَبَ اللهُ عَلَيْهِمُ الْجَلَاءَ
لَعَذَّبَهُمْ فِي الدُّنْيَا ۖ
وَلَهُمْ فِي الْآخِرَةِ
عَذَابُ النَّارِ ۟

4. That is because they
Resisted Allah and His Messenger:
And if anyone resists Allah,
Verily Allah is severe
In Punishment.

٤- ذَٰلِكَ بِأَنَّهُمْ شَاقُّوا اللهَ وَرَسُولَهُ ۖ
وَمَنْ يُشَاقِّ اللهَ
فَإِنَّ اللهَ شَدِيدُ الْعِقَابِ ۟

5. Whether ye cut down
(O ye Muslims!)
The tender palm trees,
Or ye left them standing
On their roots, it was
By leave of Allah, and
In order that He might
Cover with shame
The rebellious transgressors.

٥- مَا قَطَعْتُمْ مِنْ لِينَةٍ
أَوْ تَرَكْتُمُوهَا قَائِمَةً عَلَى أُصُولِهَا
فَبِإِذْنِ اللهِ
وَلِيُخْزِيَ الْفَاسِقِينَ ۟

6. What Allah has bestowed
On His Messenger (and taken
Away) from them—for this
Ye made no expedition
With either cavalry or camelry:
But Allah gives power
To His messengers over
Any He pleases: and Allah
Has power over all things.

٦- وَمَا أَفَاءَ اللهُ عَلَىٰ رَسُولِهِ مِنْهُمْ
فَمَا أَوْجَفْتُمْ عَلَيْهِ مِنْ خَيْلٍ وَلَا رِكَابٍ
وَلَٰكِنَّ اللهَ يُسَلِّطُ رُسُلَهُ عَلَىٰ مَنْ يَشَاءُ ۚ
وَاللهُ عَلَىٰ كُلِّ شَيْءٍ قَدِيرٌ ۟

7. What Allah has bestowed
On His Messenger (and taken
Away) from the people
Of the townships—belongs
To Allah—to His Messenger
And to kindred and orphans,
The needy and the wayfarer;
In order that it may not
(Merely) make a circuit
Between the wealthy among you.
So take what the Messenger
Assigns to you, and deny
Yourselves that which he

٧- مَا أَفَاءَ اللهُ عَلَىٰ رَسُولِهِ
مِنْ أَهْلِ الْقُرَىٰ
فَلِلَّهِ وَلِلرَّسُولِ وَلِذِي الْقُرْبَىٰ وَالْيَتَامَىٰ
وَالْمَسَاكِينِ وَابْنِ السَّبِيلِ ۙ
كَيْ لَا يَكُونَ دُولَةً بَيْنَ الْأَغْنِيَاءِ مِنْكُمْ ۚ
وَمَا آتَاكُمُ الرَّسُولُ فَخُذُوهُ ۖ
وَمَا نَهَاكُمْ عَنْهُ فَانْتَهُوا ۚ

Withholds from you.
And fear Allah; for Allah
Is strict in Punishment.

وَاتَّقُوا اللَّهَ ۚ إِنَّ اللَّهَ شَدِيدُ الْعِقَابِ ۝

8. (Some part is due)
To the indigent Muhājirs,
Those who were expelled
From their homes and their
         property,
While seeking Grace from Allah
And (His) Good Pleasure,
And aiding Allah and His
         Messenger:
Such are indeed
The sincere ones—

٨ـ لِلْفُقَرَآءِ الْمُهَاجِرِينَ
الَّذِينَ أُخْرِجُوا مِن دِيَارِهِمْ وَأَمْوَالِهِمْ
يَبْتَغُونَ فَضْلًا مِّنَ اللَّهِ وَرِضْوَانًا
وَّيَنصُرُونَ اللَّهَ وَرَسُولَهُ ۚ
أُولَٰئِكَ هُمُ الصَّادِقُونَ ۝

9. But those who
Before them, had homes
(In Madīnah)
And had adopted the Faith—
Show their affection to such
As came to them for refuge,
And entertain no desire
In their hearts for things
Given to the (latter),
But give them preference
Over themselves, even though
Poverty was their (own lot).
And those saved from
The covetousness of their own
Souls—they are the ones
That achieve prosperity.

٩ـ وَالَّذِينَ تَبَوَّءُو الدَّارَ
وَالْإِيمَانَ مِن قَبْلِهِمْ
يُحِبُّونَ مَنْ هَاجَرَ إِلَيْهِمْ
وَلَا يَجِدُونَ فِى صُدُورِهِمْ حَاجَةً مِّمَّا
أُوتُوا وَيُؤْثِرُونَ عَلَىٰ أَنفُسِهِمْ
وَلَوْ كَانَ بِهِمْ خَصَاصَةٌ ۚ
وَمَن يُوقَ شُحَّ نَفْسِهِ
فَأُولَٰئِكَ هُمُ الْمُفْلِحُونَ ۝

10. And those who came
After them say: "Our Lord!
Forgive us, and our brethren
Who came before us
Into the Faith,
And leave not,
In our hearts,
Rancour (or sense of injury)
Against those who have believed.
Our Lord! Thou art
Indeed Full of Kindness,
Most Merciful."
        SECTION 2.

١٠ـ وَالَّذِينَ جَآءُو مِنۢ بَعْدِهِمْ يَقُولُونَ رَبَّنَا
اغْفِرْ لَنَا وَلِإِخْوَانِنَا الَّذِينَ سَبَقُونَا
بِالْإِيمَانِ
وَلَا تَجْعَلْ فِى قُلُوبِنَا غِلًّا
لِّلَّذِينَ آمَنُوا
رَبَّنَا إِنَّكَ رَءُوفٌ رَّحِيمٌ ۝

11. Hast thou not observed
The Hypocrites say

١١ـ أَلَمْ تَرَ إِلَى الَّذِينَ نَافَقُوا يَقُولُونَ

To their misbelieving brethren
Among the People of the
          Book?—
"If ye are expelled,
We too will go out
With you, and we will
Never hearken to any one
In your affair; and if
Ye are attacked (in fight)
We will help you".
But Allah is witness
That they are indeed liars.

لِإِخْوَانِهِمُ الَّذِينَ كَفَرُوا مِنْ أَهْلِ الْكِتَبِ
لَئِنْ أُخْرِجْتُمْ لَنَخْرُجَنَّ مَعَكُمْ
وَلَا نُطِيعُ فِيكُمْ أَحَدًا أَبَدًا
وَإِنْ قُوتِلْتُمْ
لَنَنْصُرَنَّكُمْ
وَاللهُ يَشْهَدُ إِنَّهُمْ لَكَذِبُونَ ۝

12. If they are expelled,
Never will they go out
With them; and if they
Are attacked (in fight),
They will never help them;
And if they do help them,
They will turn their backs;
So they will receive no help.

١٢- لَئِنْ أُخْرِجُوا لَا يَخْرُجُونَ مَعَهُمْ
وَلَئِنْ قُوتِلُوا لَا يَنْصُرُونَهُمْ
وَلَئِنْ نَصَرُوهُمْ لَيُوَلُّنَّ الْأَدْبَارَ
ثُمَّ لَا يُنْصَرُونَ ۝

13. Of a truth ye are
Stronger (than they)
Because of the terror
In their hearts,
(Sent) by Allah.
This is because they are
Men devoid of understanding.

١٣- لَأَنْتُمْ أَشَدُّ
رَهْبَةً فِي صُدُورِهِمْ مِنَ اللهِ
ذَلِكَ بِأَنَّهُمْ قَوْمٌ لَا يَفْقَهُونَ ۝

14. They will not fight you
(Even) together, except
In fortified townships,
Or from behind walls.
Strong is their fighting (spirit)
Amongst themselves:
Thou wouldst think
They were united,
But their hearts are divided:
That is because they
Are a people devoid
Of wisdom.

١٤- لَا يُقَاتِلُونَكُمْ جَمِيعًا
إِلَّا فِي قُرًى مُحَصَّنَةٍ أَوْ مِنْ وَرَاءِ جُدُرٍ
بَأْسُهُمْ بَيْنَهُمْ شَدِيدٌ
تَحْسَبُهُمْ جَمِيعًا وَقُلُوبُهُمْ شَتَّى
ذَلِكَ بِأَنَّهُمْ
قَوْمٌ لَا يَعْقِلُونَ ۝

15. Like those who lately
Preceded them, they have
Tasted the evil result
Of their conduct; and
(In the Hereafter there is)

١٥- كَمَثَلِ الَّذِينَ مِنْ قَبْلِهِمْ قَرِيبًا
ذَاقُوا وَبَالَ أَمْرِهِمْ
وَلَهُمْ

For them a grievous Penalty—

16. (Their allies deceived them),
Like the Evil One,
When he says to man,
"Deny Allah": but when
(Man) denies Allah,
(The Evil One) says,
"I am free of thee:
I do fear Allah,
The Lord of the Worlds!"

عَذَابٌ أَلِيمٌ ۝

١٦- كَمَثَلِ الشَّيْطَنِ
إِذْ قَالَ لِلْإِنْسَانِ
اكْفُرْ فَلَمَّا كَفَرَ
قَالَ إِنِّي بَرِيءٌ مِّنكَ
إِنِّي أَخَافُ اللَّهَ رَبَّ الْعَلَمِينَ ۝

17. The end of both will be
That they will go
Into the Fire, dwelling
Therein forever.
Such is the reward
Of the wrongdoers.

١٧- فَكَانَ عَاقِبَتَهُمَآ أَنَّهُمَا فِي النَّارِ
خَالِدَيْنِ فِيهَا ۚ
وَذَلِكَ جَزَؤُا الظَّلِمِينَ ۝

SECTION 3.

18. O ye who believe!
Fear Allah,
And let every soul look
To what (provision) he has
Sent forth for the morrow.
Yea, fear Allah:
For Allah is well-acquainted
With (all) that ye do.

١٨- يَٰٓأَيُّهَا الَّذِينَ ءَامَنُوا اتَّقُوا اللَّهَ
وَلْتَنظُرْ نَفْسٌ مَّا قَدَّمَتْ لِغَدٍ ۖ
وَاتَّقُوا اللَّهَ ۚ
إِنَّ اللَّهَ خَبِيرٌ بِمَا تَعْمَلُونَ ۝

19. And be ye not like
Those who forgot Allah;
And He made them forget
Their own souls! Such
Are the rebellious transgressors!

١٩- وَلَا تَكُونُوا كَالَّذِينَ نَسُوا اللَّهَ
فَأَنسَىٰهُمْ أَنفُسَهُمْ ۚ
أُوْلَٰٓئِكَ هُمُ الْفَٰسِقُونَ ۝

20. Not equal are
The Companions of the Fire
And the Companions
Of the Garden:
It is the Companions
Of the Garden,
That will achieve Felicity.

٢٠- لَا يَسْتَوِي أَصْحَٰبُ النَّارِ
وَأَصْحَٰبُ الْجَنَّةِ ۚ
أَصْحَٰبُ الْجَنَّةِ هُمُ الْفَآئِزُونَ ۝

21. Had We sent down
This Qur'ān on a mountain,
Verily, thou wouldst have seen
It humble itself and cleave
Asunder for fear of Allah.
Such are the similitudes

٢١- لَوْ أَنزَلْنَا هَٰذَا الْقُرْءَانَ عَلَىٰ جَبَلٍ
لَّرَأَيْتَهُ خَاشِعًا مُّتَصَدِّعًا
مِّنْ خَشْيَةِ اللَّهِ ۚ وَتِلْكَ الْأَمْثَٰلُ نَضْرِبُهَا

Which We propound to men,
That they may reflect.

22. Allah is He, than Whom
There is no other god—
Who knows (all things)
Both secret and open;
He, Most Gracious,
Most Merciful.

23. Allah is He, than Whom
There is no other god—
The Sovereign, the Holy One,
The Source of Peace
　　　　(and Perfection),
The Guardian of Faith,
The Preserver of Safety,
The Exalted in Might,
The Irresistible, the Supreme:
Glory to Allah!
(High is He)
Above the partners
They attribute to Him.

24. He is Allah, the Creator,
The Evolver,
The Bestower of Forms
(Or Colours).
To Him belong
The Most Beautiful Names:
Whatever is in
The heavens and on earth,
Doth declare
His Praises and Glory;
And He is the Exalted
In Might, the Wise.

لِلنَّاسِ لَعَلَّهُمْ يَتَفَكَّرُونَ ۝

٢٢- هُوَ اللّٰهُ الَّذِى لَا إِلٰهَ إِلَّا هُوَ ۚ
عٰلِمُ الْغَيْبِ وَالشَّهَادَةِ ۚ
هُوَ الرَّحْمٰنُ الرَّحِيمُ ۝

٢٣- هُوَ اللّٰهُ الَّذِى لَا إِلٰهَ إِلَّا هُوَ ۚ
الْمَلِكُ الْقُدُّوسُ السَّلٰمُ
الْمُؤْمِنُ الْمُهَيْمِنُ
الْعَزِيزُ الْجَبَّارُ الْمُتَكَبِّرُ ۚ
سُبْحٰنَ اللّٰهِ
عَمَّا يُشْرِكُونَ ۝

٢٤- هُوَ اللّٰهُ الْخَالِقُ
الْبَارِئُ الْمُصَوِّرُ
لَهُ الْأَسْمَاءُ الْحُسْنٰى ۚ
يُسَبِّحُ لَهُ
مَا فِى السَّمٰوٰتِ وَالْأَرْضِ ۚ
وَهُوَ الْعَزِيزُ الْحَكِيمُ ۝

INTRODUCTION TO SŪRA LX. (*Mumtaḥina*) — 13 Verses

This is the fourth of the ten Medina Sūras, each dealing with a special point in the life of the Ummat.

Here the point is: What social relations are possible with the Unbelievers? A distinction is made between those who persecute you for your Faith and want to destroy you and your Faith, and those who have shown no such rancour. For the latter there is hope of mercy and forgiveness. The question of women and cross-marriages is equitably dealt with.

The date is after the Pagans had broken the treaty of Ḥudaibīya, for which see Introduction to S. xlviii.—say about A.H. 8, not long before the conquest of Mecca.

Al Mumtaḥinah (That Which Examines)

In the name of Allah, Most Gracious, Most Merciful.

1. O ye who believe!
   Take not My enemies
   And yours as friends
   (Or protectors)—offering them
   (Your) love, even though
   They have rejected the Truth
   That has come to you,
   And have (on the contrary)
   Driven out the Messenger
   And yourselves (from your
                              homes),
   (Simply) because ye believe
   In Allah your Lord!
   If ye have come out
   To strive in My Way
   And to seek My Good Pleasure,
   (Take them not as friends),
   Holding secret converse
   Of love (and friendship)
   With them: for I know
   Full well all that ye
   Conceal and all that ye
   Reveal. And any of you
   That does this has strayed
   From the Straight Path.

2. If they were to get
   The better of you,
   They would behave to you
   As enemies, and stretch forth
   Their hands and their tongues
   Against you for evil;
   And they desire that ye
   Should reject the Truth.

٢- اِنْ يَّثْقَفُوْكُمْ
يَكُوْنُوْا لَكُمْ اَعْدَآءً
وَّيَبْسُطُوْا اِلَيْكُمْ اَيْدِيَهُمْ وَاَلْسِنَتَهُمْ بِالسُّوْءِ
وَوَدُّوْا لَوْ تَكْفُرُوْنَ ۞

3. Of no profit to you
   Will be your relatives
   And your children
   On the Day of Judgement:
   He will judge between you:
   For Allah sees well
   All that ye do.

٣- لَنْ تَنْفَعَكُمْ اَرْحَامُكُمْ
وَلَاۤ اَوْلَادُكُمْ يَوْمَ الْقِيٰمَةِ ۚ
يَفْصِلُ بَيْنَكُمْ ۚ
وَاللّٰهُ بِمَا تَعْمَلُوْنَ بَصِيْرٌ ۞

4. There is for you
   An excellent example (to follow)
   In Abraham and those with
                           him,
   When they said
   To their people:
   "We are clear of you
   And of whatever ye worship
   Besides Allah: we have rejected
   You, and there has arisen,
   Between us and you, enmity
   And hatred forever—unless
   Ye believe in Allah
   And Him alone":
   But not when Abraham
   Said to his father:
   "I will pray for forgiveness
   For thee, though I have
   No power (to get) aught
   On thy behalf from Allah."
   (They prayed): "Our Lord!
   In Thee do we trust,
   And to Thee do we turn
   In repentance: to Thee
   Is (our) final Goal.

٤- قَدْ كَانَتْ لَكُمْ اُسْوَةٌ حَسَنَةٌ
فِيْۤ اِبْرٰهِيْمَ وَالَّذِيْنَ مَعَهٗ ۚ
اِذْ قَالُوْا لِقَوْمِهِمْ
اِنَّا بُرَءٰٓؤُا مِنْكُمْ وَمِمَّا تَعْبُدُوْنَ مِنْ دُوْنِ
اللّٰهِ كَفَرْنَا بِكُمْ وَبَدَا
بَيْنَنَا وَبَيْنَكُمُ الْعَدَاوَةُ وَالْبَغْضَآءُ اَبَدًا
حَتّٰى تُؤْمِنُوْا بِاللّٰهِ وَحْدَهٗۤ
اِلَّا قَوْلَ اِبْرٰهِيْمَ لِاَبِيْهِ لَاَسْتَغْفِرَنَّ
لَكَ وَمَاۤ اَمْلِكُ لَكَ
مِنَ اللّٰهِ مِنْ شَيْءٍ ۗ رَبَّنَا عَلَيْكَ تَوَكَّلْنَا
وَاِلَيْكَ اَنَبْنَا
وَاِلَيْكَ الْمَصِيْرُ ۞

5. "Our Lord! Make us not
   A (test and) trial
   For the Unbelievers,
   But forgive us, our Lord!
   For Thou are the Exalted
   In Might, the Wise."

٥- رَبَّنَا لَا تَجْعَلْنَا فِتْنَةً لِّلَّذِيْنَ كَفَرُوْا
وَاغْفِرْ لَنَا رَبَّنَا ۚ
اِنَّكَ اَنْتَ الْعَزِيْزُ الْحَكِيْمُ ۞

6. There was indeed in them
An excellent example for you
To follow—for those
Whose hope is in Allah
And in the Last Day.
But if any turn away,
Truly Allah is Free of all
Wants, Worthy of all Praise.

SECTION 2.

7. It may be that Allah
Will grant love (and friendship)
Between you and those whom
Ye (now) hold as enemies.
For Allah has power
(Over all things); And Allah is
Oft-Forgiving, Most Merciful.

8. Allah forbids you not,
With regard to those who
Fight you not for (your) Faith
Nor drive you out
Of your homes,
From dealing kindly and
                              justly
With them: For Allah loveth
Those who are just.

9. Allah only forbids you,
With regard to those who
Fight you for (your) Faith,
And drive you out,
Of your homes, and support
(Others) in driving you out,
From turning to them
(For friendship and protection).
It is such as turn to them
(In these circumstances),
That do wrong.

10. O ye who believe!
When there come to you
Believing women refugees,
Examine (and test) them:
Allah knows best as to
Their Faith: if ye ascertain
That they are Believers,
Then send them not back
To the Unbelievers.

٦- لَقَدْ كَانَ لَكُمْ فِيهِمْ أُسْوَةٌ حَسَنَةٌ لِّمَنْ كَانَ يَرْجُوا اللّٰهَ وَالْيَوْمَ الْآخِرَ وَمَنْ يَتَوَلَّ فَإِنَّ اللّٰهَ هُوَ الْغَنِيُّ الْحَمِيدُ ۝

٧- عَسَى اللّٰهُ أَنْ يَجْعَلَ بَيْنَكُمْ وَبَيْنَ الَّذِينَ عَادَيْتُمْ مِّنْهُمْ مَّوَدَّةً وَاللّٰهُ قَدِيرٌ وَاللّٰهُ غَفُورٌ رَّحِيمٌ ۝

٨- لَا يَنْهَاكُمُ اللّٰهُ عَنِ الَّذِينَ لَمْ يُقَاتِلُوكُمْ فِي الدِّينِ وَلَمْ يُخْرِجُوكُمْ مِّنْ دِيَارِكُمْ أَنْ تَبَرُّوهُمْ وَتُقْسِطُوا إِلَيْهِمْ إِنَّ اللّٰهَ يُحِبُّ الْمُقْسِطِينَ ۝

٩- إِنَّمَا يَنْهَاكُمُ اللّٰهُ عَنِ الَّذِينَ قَاتَلُوكُمْ فِي الدِّينِ وَأَخْرَجُوكُمْ مِّنْ دِيَارِكُمْ وَظَاهَرُوا عَلَى إِخْرَاجِكُمْ أَنْ تَوَلَّوْهُمْ وَمَنْ يَتَوَلَّهُمْ فَأُولَٰئِكَ هُمُ الظَّالِمُونَ ۝

١٠- يَا أَيُّهَا الَّذِينَ آمَنُوا إِذَا جَاءَكُمُ الْمُؤْمِنَاتُ مُهَاجِرَاتٍ فَامْتَحِنُوهُنَّ اللّٰهُ أَعْلَمُ بِإِيمَانِهِنَّ فَإِنْ عَلِمْتُمُوهُنَّ مُؤْمِنَاتٍ فَلَا تَرْجِعُوهُنَّ إِلَى الْكُفَّارِ لَا هُنَّ حِلٌّ لَهُمْ

They are not lawful (wives)
For the Unbelievers, nor are
The (Unbelievers) lawful
                    (husbands)
For them. But pay
The Unbelievers what they

وَلَا هُمْ يَحِلُّوْنَ لَهُنَّ

وَاٰتُوْهُمْ

مَّاۤ اَنْفَقُوْا ۗ

Have spent (on their dower).
And there will be no blame
On you if ye marry them
On payment of their dower
To them. But hold not
To the guardianship of
Unbelieving women: ask
For what ye have spent
On their dowers, and let
The (Unbelievers) ask for
What they have spent
(On the dowers of women
Who come over to you).
Such is the command
Of Allah: He judges
(With justice) between you.
And Allah is Full of
Knowledge and Wisdom.

وَلَا جُنَاحَ عَلَيْكُمْ اَنْ تَنْكِحُوْهُنَّ

اِذَاۤ اٰتَيْتُمُوْهُنَّ اُجُوْرَهُنَّ ۗ

وَلَا تُمْسِكُوْا بِعِصَمِ الْكَوَافِرِ

وَسْـَٔلُوْا مَاۤ اَنْفَقْتُمْ

وَلْيَسْـَٔلُوْا مَاۤ اَنْفَقُوْا ۗ

ذٰلِكُمْ حُكْمُ اللّٰهِ ۗ

يَحْكُمُ بَيْنَكُمْ ۗ

وَاللّٰهُ عَلِيْمٌ حَكِيْمٌ ۝

11. And if any
Of your wives deserts you
To the Unbelievers,
And ye have an accession
(By the coming over of
A woman from the other side),
Then pay to those
Whose wives have deserted
The equivalent of what they
Had spent (on their dower).
And fear Allah,
In Whom ye believe.

١١- وَاِنْ فَاتَكُمْ شَيْءٌ مِّنْ اَزْوَاجِكُمْ

اِلَى الْكُفَّارِ

فَعَاقَبْتُمْ

فَاٰتُوا الَّذِيْنَ ذَهَبَتْ اَزْوَاجُهُمْ

مِّثْلَ مَاۤ اَنْفَقُوْا ۗ

وَاتَّقُوا اللّٰهَ الَّذِيْۤ اَنْتُمْ بِهٖ مُؤْمِنُوْنَ ۝

12. Prophet!
When believing women come
To thee to take the oath
Of fealty to thee, that they
Will not associate in worship
Any other thing whatever
With Allah, that they

١٢- يٰۤاَيُّهَا النَّبِيُّ اِذَا جَاءَكَ الْمُؤْمِنٰتُ

يُبَايِعْنَكَ عَلٰۤى

اَنْ لَّا يُشْرِكْنَ بِاللّٰهِ شَيْئًا

وَّلَا يَسْرِقْنَ وَلَا يَزْنِيْنَ

Will not steal, that they
Will not commit adultery
(Or fornication), that they
Will not kill their children,
That they will not utter
Slander, intentionally forging
Falsehood,   and that they
Will not disobey thee
In any just matter—
Then do thou receive
Their fealty, and pray to Allah
For the forgiveness (of
Their sins): for Allah is
Oft-Forgiving, Most Merciful.

وَلَا يَقْتُلْنَ أَوْلَادَهُنَّ
وَلَا يَأْتِينَ بِبُهْتَانٍ
يَفْتَرِينَهُ بَيْنَ أَيْدِيهِنَّ وَأَرْجُلِهِنَّ
وَلَا يَعْصِينَكَ فِي مَعْرُوفٍ فَبَايِعْهُنَّ
وَاسْتَغْفِرْ لَهُنَّ اللّٰهَ
إِنَّ اللّٰهَ غَفُورٌ رَحِيمٌ ۝

13. O ye who believe!
Turn not (for friendship)
To people on whom
Is the Wrath of Allah.
Of the Hereafter they are
Already in despair, just as
The Unbelievers are
In despair about those
(Buried) in graves.

١٣- يَٰأَيُّهَا الَّذِينَ آمَنُوا
لَا تَتَوَلَّوْا قَوْمًا غَضِبَ اللّٰهُ عَلَيْهِمْ
قَدْ يَئِسُوا مِنَ الْآخِرَةِ كَمَا
يَئِسَ الْكُفَّارُ مِنْ أَصْحَابِ الْقُبُورِ ۝

INTRODUCTION TO SURA LXI. (*Ṣaff*) — 14 Verses

This is the fifth Sūra of the series of short Medina Sūras beginning with S.lvii. Its subject-matter is the need for discipline, practical work, and self-sacrifice in the cause of the Ummat. Its date is uncertain, but it was probably shortly after the battle of Uḥud, which was fought in Shawwāl, A.H.3.

Al Ṣaff (The Battle Array)

In the name of Allah, Most Gracious,
Most Merciful.

1. Whatever is
   In the heavens and
   On earth, let it declare
   The Praises and Glory
   Of Allah: for He is
   The Exalted in Might,
   The Wise.

2. O ye who believe!
   Why say ye that
   Which ye do not?

3. Grievously odious is it
   In the sight of Allah
   That ye say that
   Which ye do not.

4. Truly Allah loves those
   Who fight in His Cause
   In battle array, as if
   They were a solid
   Cemented structure.

5. And remember, Moses said
   To his people: "O my people!
   Why do ye vex and insult
   Me, though ye know

   That I am the messenger
   Of Allah (sent) to you?"
   Then when they went wrong,
   Allah let their hearts go wrong.
   For Allah guides not those
   Who are rebellious transgressors.

6. And remember, Jesus,
The son of Mary, said:
"O Children of Israel!
I am the messenger of Allah
(Sent) to you,   confirming
The Law (which came)
Before me, and giving
Glad Tidings of a Messenger
To come after me,
Whose name shall be Ahmad."
But when he came to them
With Clear Signs,
They said, "This is
Evident sorcery!"

٦- وَإِذْ قَالَ عِيْسَى ابْنُ مَرْيَمَ
يٰبَنِىٓ اِسْرَآءِيْلَ اِنِّى رَسُوْلُ اللهِ اِلَيْكُمْ
مُّصَدِّقًا لِّمَا بَيْنَ يَدَيَّ مِنَ التَّوْرٰةِ
وَمُبَشِّرًا بِرَسُوْلٍ يَّأْتِىْ مِنْ بَعْدِى
اسْمُهٗٓ اَحْمَدُ
فَلَمَّا جَآءَهُمْ بِالْبَيِّنٰتِ
قَالُوْا هٰذَا سِحْرٌ مُّبِيْنٌ ۝

7. Who doth greater wrong
Than one who invents
Falsehood against Allah,
Even as he is being invited
To Islam? And Allah
Guides not those
Who do wrong.

٧- وَمَنْ اَظْلَمُ مِمَّنِ افْتَرٰى
عَلَى اللهِ الْكَذِبَ وَهُوَ يُدْعٰىٓ اِلَى الْاِسْلَامِ
وَاللهُ لَا يَهْدِى الْقَوْمَ الظّٰلِمِيْنَ ۝

8. Their intention is
To extinguish Allah's Light
(By blowing) with their mouths:
But Allah will complete
(The revelation of) His Light,
Even though the Unbelievers
May detest (it)

٨- يُرِيْدُوْنَ لِيُطْفِئُوْا نُوْرَ اللهِ بِاَفْوَاهِهِمْ
وَاللهُ مُتِمُّ نُوْرِهٖ
وَلَوْ كَرِهَ الْكٰفِرُوْنَ ۝

9. It is He Who has sent
His Messenger with Guidance
And the Religion of Truth,
That he may proclaim it
Over all religion,
Even though the Pagans
May detest (it).
SECTION 2.

٩- هُوَ الَّذِىٓ اَرْسَلَ رَسُوْلَهٗ بِالْهُدٰى
وَدِيْنِ الْحَقِّ
لِيُظْهِرَهٗ عَلَى الدِّيْنِ كُلِّهٖ
وَلَوْ كَرِهَ الْمُشْرِكُوْنَ ۩

10. O ye who believe!
Shall I lead you
To a bargain   that will
Save you from
A grievous Penalty?—

١٠- يٰٓاَيُّهَا الَّذِيْنَ اٰمَنُوْا
هَلْ اَدُلُّكُمْ عَلٰى تِجَارَةٍ
تُنْجِيْكُمْ مِّنْ عَذَابٍ اَلِيْمٍ ۝

11. That ye believe in Allah
And His Messenger, and that

١١- تُؤْمِنُوْنَ بِاللهِ وَرَسُوْلِهٖ وَتُجَاهِدُوْنَ

Ye strive (your utmost)
In the Cause of Allah,
With your property
And your persons:
That will be best for you,
If ye but knew!

12. He will forgive you
Your sins, and admit you
To Gardens beneath which
Rivers flow, and to beautiful
Mansions in Gardens
Of Eternity: that is indeed
The supreme Achievement.

13. And another (favour
Will He bestow), which ye
Do love—help from Allah
And a speedy victory.
So give the Glad Tidings
To the Believers.

14. O ye who believe!
Be ye helpers of Allah:
As said Jesus, the son of Mary,
To the Disciples, "Who will be
My helpers to (the work
Of) Allah?" Said the Disciples,
"We are Allah's helpers!"
Then a portion of the Children
Of Israel believed, and
A portion disbeleived:
But We gave power
To those who believed
Against their enemies,
And they became
The ones that prevailed.

في سَبِيلِ اللهِ بِأَمْوَالِكُمْ وَأَنْفُسِكُمْ
ذٰلِكُمْ خَيْرٌ لَّكُمْ إِن
كُنْتُمْ تَعْلَمُونَ ۞

١٢- يَغْفِرْ لَكُمْ ذُنُوبَكُمْ
وَيُدْخِلْكُمْ جَنَّاتٍ تَجْرِي مِنْ تَحْتِهَا الْأَنْهَارُ
وَمَسَاكِنَ طَيِّبَةً فِي جَنَّاتِ عَدْنٍ
ذٰلِكَ الْفَوْزُ الْعَظِيمُ ۞

١٣- وَأُخْرَى تُحِبُّونَهَا
نَصْرٌ مِّنَ اللهِ وَفَتْحٌ قَرِيبٌ
وَبَشِّرِ الْمُؤْمِنِينَ ۞

١٤- يَا أَيُّهَا الَّذِينَ آمَنُوا كُونُوا أَنْصَارَ اللهِ
كَمَا قَالَ عِيسَى ابْنُ مَرْيَمَ لِلْحَوَارِيِّينَ
مَنْ أَنْصَارِي إِلَى اللهِ قَالَ الْحَوَارِيُّونَ
نَحْنُ أَنْصَارُ اللهِ
فَآمَنَتْ طَائِفَةٌ مِّنْ بَنِي إِسْرَائِيلَ
وَكَفَرَتْ طَائِفَةٌ
فَأَيَّدْنَا الَّذِينَ آمَنُوا عَلَى عَدُوِّهِمْ
فَأَصْبَحُوا ظَاهِرِينَ ۞

INTRODUCTION TO SŪRA LXII. (*Jumu'ah*) — 11 Verses

This is the sixth Sūra in the Medina series of short Sūras which began with S.lvii.

The special theme here is the need for mutual contact in the Community for worship and understanding: for the spirit of the Message is for all, ignorant and learned, in order that they may be purified and may learn wisdom.

The date has no special significance; it may be placed in the early Medina period, say between A.H. 2 and 5.

Al Jumu'ah (Friday)

In the name of Allah, Most Gracious,
Most Merciful.

بِسْمِ اللهِ الرَّحْمٰنِ الرَّحِيْمِ

1. Whatever is
   In the heavens and
   On earth, doth declare
   The Praises and Glory
   Of Allah—the Sovereign,
   The Holy One, the Exalted
   In Might, the Wise.

١- يُسَبِّحُ لِلّٰهِ
مَا فِى السَّمٰوٰتِ وَمَا فِى الْأَرْضِ
الْمَلِكِ الْقُدُّوْسِ
الْعَزِيْزِ الْحَكِيْمِ ۞

2. It is He Who has sent
   Amongst the Unlettered
   A messenger from among
   Themselves, to rehearse
   To them His Signs,
   To sanctify them, and
   To instruct them in Scripture
   And Wisdom—although[5454]
   They had been, before,
   In manifest error—

٢- هُوَ الَّذِىْ بَعَثَ فِى الْأُمِّيِّنَ رَسُوْلًا مِّنْهُمْ
يَتْلُوْا عَلَيْهِمْ اٰيٰتِهٖ
وَيُزَكِّيْهِمْ وَيُعَلِّمُهُمُ الْكِتٰبَ
وَالْحِكْمَةَ ۙ وَإِنْ
كَانُوْا مِنْ قَبْلُ لَفِىْ ضَلٰلٍ مُّبِيْنٍ ۞

3. As well as (to confer
   All these benefits upon)
   Others of them,　who
   Have not already joined them:
   And He is Exalted
   In Might, Wise.

٣- وَّاٰخَرِيْنَ مِنْهُمْ
لَمَّا يَلْحَقُوْا بِهِمْ ۚ
وَهُوَ الْعَزِيْزُ الْحَكِيْمُ ۞

4. Such is the Bounty of Allah,
   Which He bestows
   On whom He will:

٤- ذٰلِكَ فَضْلُ اللهِ يُؤْتِيْهِ مَنْ يَّشَاءُ ۚ

And Allah is the Lord
Of the highest bounty.

وَاللّٰهُ ذُو الفَضلِ العَظِيمِ ۞

5. The similitude of those
Who were charged
With the (obligations
Of the) Mosaic Law,
But who subsequently failed
In those (obligations), is
That of a donkey
Which carries huge tomes
(But understands them not).
Evil is the similitude
Of people who falsify
The Signs of Allah:
And Allah guides not
People who do wrong.

٥ ـ مَثَلُ الَّذِينَ
حُمِّلُوا التَّورٰىةَ
ثُمَّ لَم يَحمِلُوهَا كَمَثَلِ الحِمَارِ
يَحمِلُ أَسفَارًا ۗ
بِئسَ مَثَلُ القَومِ الَّذِينَ
كَذَّبُوا بِآيٰتِ اللّٰهِ ۚ
وَاللّٰهُ لَا يَهدِى القَومَ الظّٰلِمِينَ ۝

6. Say: "O ye that
Stand on Judaism!
If ye think that ye
Are friends to Allah,
To the exclusion of
(Other) men, then express
Your desire for Death,
If ye are truthful!"

٦ ـ قُل يٰأَيُّهَا الَّذِينَ هَادُوا
إِن زَعَمتُم أَنَّكُم أَولِيَاءُ لِلّٰهِ مِن دُونِ
النَّاسِ
فَتَمَنَّوُا المَوتَ إِن كُنتُم صٰدِقِينَ ۝

7. But never will they
Express their desire
(For Death), because of
The (deeds) their hands
Have sent on before them!
And Allah knows well
Those that do wrong!

٧ ـ وَلَا يَتَمَنَّونَهُ أَبَدًا
بِمَا قَدَّمَت أَيدِيهِم ۚ
وَاللّٰهُ عَلِيمٌ بِالظّٰلِمِينَ ۝

8. Say: "The Death from which
Ye flee will truly
Overtake you: then will
Ye be sent back
To the Knower of things
Secret and open: and He
Will tell you (the truth
Of) the things that ye did!"

SECTION 2.

٨ ـ قُل إِنَّ المَوتَ الَّذِى تَفِرُّونَ مِنهُ
فَإِنَّهُ مُلٰقِيكُم ۖ
ثُمَّ تُرَدُّونَ إِلَىٰ عٰلِمِ الغَيبِ وَالشَّهَادَةِ
فَيُنَبِّئُكُم بِمَا كُنتُم تَعمَلُونَ ۝

9. O ye who believe!
When the call is proclaimed

٩ ـ يٰأَيُّهَا الَّذِينَ آمَنُوا إِذَا نُودِىَ

To prayer on Friday
(The Day of Assembly),
Hasten earnestly to the
              Remembrance
Of Allah, and leave off
Business (and traffic):
That is best for you
If ye but knew!

للصَّلٰوةِ مِن يَّوْمِ الْجُمُعَةِ
فَاسْعَوْا إِلٰى ذِكْرِ اللّٰهِ وَذَرُوا
الْبَيْعَ ۚ ذٰلِكُمْ خَيْرٌ لَّكُمْ إِنْ
كُنْتُمْ تَعْلَمُونَ ۝

10. And when the Prayer
Is finished, then may ye
Disperse through the land,
And seek of the Bounty
Of Allah: and celebrate
The Praises of Allah
Often (and without stint):
That ye may prosper.

١٠- فَإِذَا قُضِيَتِ الصَّلٰوةُ فَانْتَشِرُوا فِى الْأَرْضِ
وَابْتَغُوا مِنْ فَضْلِ اللّٰهِ
وَاذْكُرُوا اللّٰهَ كَثِيرًا
لَّعَلَّكُمْ تُفْلِحُونَ ۝

11. But when they see
Some bargain or some
Amusement, they disperse
Headlong to it, and leave
Thee standing. Say:
"The (blessing) from the Presence
Of Allah is better than
Any amusement or bargain!
And Allah is the Best
To provide (for all needs)."

١١- وَإِذَا رَأَوْا تِجَارَةً أَوْ لَهْوًا
انْفَضُّوا إِلَيْهَا وَتَرَكُوكَ قَائِمًا ۚ
قُلْ مَا عِنْدَ اللّٰهِ خَيْرٌ
مِّنَ اللَّهْوِ وَمِنَ التِّجَارَةِ ۚ
وَاللّٰهُ خَيْرُ الرَّازِقِينَ ۝

INTRODUCTION TO SŪRA LXIII. (*Munāfiqūn*) — 11 Verses

This is the seventh of the ten short Medina Sūras dealing with a special feature in the social life of the Brotherhood.

The special feature here dealt with is the wiles and mischief of the Hypocrite element in any community, and the need of guarding it against the temptation it throws in the way of the Believers.

The battle of Uḥud (Shawwāl A.H. 3) unmasked the Hypocrites in Medina: see iii. 167, n. 746. This Sūra may be referred to sometime after that event, say about 4 A.H. or possibly 5 A.H. if the words reported in verse 8 were uttered in the expedition against the Banū Muṣṭaliq, A.H. 5. (See. n. 5475 below).

Al Munāfiqūn (The Hypocrites)

In the name of Allah, Most Gracious,
Most Merciful.

1. When the Hypocrites
   Come to thee, they say,
   "We bear witness that thou
   Art indeed the Messenger
   Of Allah." Yea, Allah
   Knoweth that thou art
   Indeed His Messenger,
   And Allah beareth witness
   That the Hypocrites are
   Indeed liars.

2. They have made their oaths
   A screen (for their misdeeds):
   Thus they obstruct (men)
   From the Path of Allah:
   Truly evil are their deeds.

3. That is because they believed,
   Then they rejected Faith:
   So a seal was set
   On their hearts: therefore
   They understand not.

4. When thou lookest
   At them, their exteriors
   Please thee; and when
   They speak, thou listenest

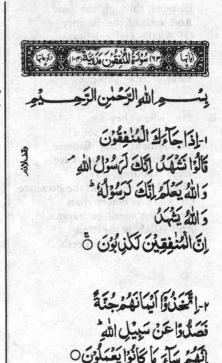

To their words. They are
As (worthless as hollow)
Pieces of timber propped up,
(Unable to stand on their own).
They think that every
Cry is against them. [5471]
They are the enemies;
So beware of them.
The curse of Allah be
On them! How are they
Deluded (away from the Truth)!

كَأَنَّهُمْ خُشُبٌ مُّسَنَّدَةٌ ۖ
يَحْسَبُونَ كُلَّ صَيْحَةٍ عَلَيْهِمْ ۚ
هُمُ الْعَدُوُّ فَاحْذَرْهُمْ ۚ
قَاتَلَهُمُ اللّٰهُ ۖ
أَنّٰى يُؤْفَكُونَ ۞

5. And when it is said
To them, "Come, the Messenger
Of Allah will pray for your
Forgiveness", they turn aside
Their heads, and thou wouldst
See them turning away
Their faces in arrogance.

٥- وَإِذَا قِيلَ لَهُمْ تَعَالَوْا
يَسْتَغْفِرْ لَكُمْ رَسُولُ اللّٰهِ
لَوَّوْا رُءُوسَهُمْ وَرَأَيْتَهُمْ يَصُدُّونَ
وَهُمْ مُّسْتَكْبِرُونَ ۞

6. It is equal to them
Whether thou pray for
Their forgiveness or not.
Allah will not forgive them.
Truly Allah guides not
Rebellious transgressors.

٦- سَوَآءٌ عَلَيْهِمْ أَسْتَغْفَرْتَ لَهُمْ أَمْ لَمْ
تَسْتَغْفِرْ لَهُمْ لَنْ يَغْفِرَ اللّٰهُ لَهُمْ ۚ
إِنَّ اللّٰهَ لَا يَهْدِى الْقَوْمَ الْفٰسِقِينَ ۞

7. They are the ones who say,
"Spend nothing on those
Who are with Allah's
                    Messenger,
To the end that they
May disperse (and quit
                    Madīnah)."
But to Allah belong
The treasures of the heavens
And the earth; but
The Hypocrites understand not.

٧- هُمُ الَّذِينَ يَقُولُونَ
لَا تُنْفِقُوا عَلٰى مَنْ عِنْدَ رَسُولِ اللّٰهِ حَتّٰى
يَنْفَضُّوا ۗ
وَلِلّٰهِ خَزَآئِنُ السَّمٰوٰتِ وَالْأَرْضِ
وَلٰكِنَّ الْمُنٰفِقِينَ لَا يَفْقَهُونَ ۞

8. They say, "If we
Return to Madīnah, surely
The more honourable (element)
Will expel therefrom the meaner".
But honour belongs to Allah
And His Messenger, and
To the Believers; but
The Hypocrites know not.

٨- يَقُولُونَ لَئِنْ رَّجَعْنَآ إِلَى الْمَدِينَةِ
لَيُخْرِجَنَّ الْأَعَزُّ مِنْهَا الْأَذَلَّ ۚ
وَلِلّٰهِ الْعِزَّةُ وَلِرَسُولِهِ وَلِلْمُؤْمِنِينَ
وَلٰكِنَّ الْمُنٰفِقِينَ لَا يَعْلَمُونَ ۞

SECTION 2.

9. O ye who believe!
Let not your riches
Or your children divert you
From the remembrance of Allah.
If any act thus,
The loss is their own.

٩- يٰٓاَيُّهَا الَّذِيْنَ اٰمَنُوْا لَا تُلْهِكُمْ
اَمْوَالُكُمْ وَلَاۤ اَوْلَادُكُمْ عَنْ ذِكْرِ اللّٰهِ وَمَنْ
يَّفْعَلْ ذٰلِكَ فَاُولٰٓئِكَ هُمُ الْخٰسِرُوْنَ ۞

10. And spend something (in charity)
Out of the substance
Which We have bestowed
On you, before Death
Should come to any of you
And he should say,
"O my Lord! Why didst
Thou not give me
Respite for a little while?
I should then have given
(Largely) in charity, and I
Should have been one
Of the doers of good".

١٠- وَاَنْفِقُوْا مِنْ مَّا رَزَقْنٰكُمْ
مِّنْ قَبْلِ اَنْ يَّاْتِيَ اَحَدَكُمُ الْمَوْتُ
فَيَقُوْلَ رَبِّ لَوْلَاۤ اَخَّرْتَنِيْۤ
اِلٰٓى اَجَلٍ قَرِيْبٍ
فَاَصَّدَّقَ
وَاَكُنْ مِّنَ الصّٰلِحِيْنَ ۞

11. But to no soul
Will Allah grant respite
When the time appointed
(For it) has come; and Allah
Is well-acquainted
With (all) that ye do.

١١- وَلَنْ يُّؤَخِّرَ اللّٰهُ نَفْسًا
اِذَا جَاۤءَ اَجَلُهَا ۚ
وَاللّٰهُ خَبِيْرٌۢ بِمَا تَعْمَلُوْنَ ۞

INTRODUCTION TO SŪRA LXIV. (*Taghābun*) — 18 Verses

This is the eighth of the short Medina Sūras, each dealing with a special aspect of the life of the Community.

The special aspect spoken of here is the mutual gain and loss of Good and Evil, contrasted in this life and in the Hereafter.

It is an early Medina Sūra, of the year 1 of the Hijra or possibly even of the Meccan period just before the Hijrat. (See n. 5494 below).

Al Taghābun (The Mutual Loss and Gain)

In the name of Allah, Most Gracious, Most Merciful.

بِسْمِ اللهِ الرَّحْمٰنِ الرَّحِيمِ

1. Whatever is
In the heavens and
On earth, doth declare
The Praises and Glory
Of Allah: to Him belongs
Dominion, and to Him belongs
Praise: and He has power
Over all things.

١- يُسَبِّحُ لِلّٰهِ
مَا فِي السَّمٰوٰتِ وَمَا فِي الْأَرْضِ
لَهُ الْمُلْكُ وَلَهُ الْحَمْدُ
وَهُوَ عَلٰى كُلِّ شَيْءٍ قَدِيْرٌ ۞

2. It is He Who has
Created you; and of you
Are some that are
Unbelievers, and some
That are Believers:
And Allah sees well
All that ye do.

٢- هُوَ الَّذِيْ خَلَقَكُمْ
فَمِنْكُمْ كَافِرٌ وَّمِنْكُمْ مُّؤْمِنٌ ۚ
وَاللهُ بِمَا تَعْمَلُوْنَ بَصِيْرٌ ۞

3. He has created the heavens
And the earth
In just proportions,
And has given you shape,
And made your shapes
Beautiful: and to Him
Is the final Goal.

٣- خَلَقَ السَّمٰوٰتِ وَالْأَرْضَ بِالْحَقِّ
وَصَوَّرَكُمْ فَأَحْسَنَ صُوَرَكُمْ ۚ
وَإِلَيْهِ الْمَصِيْرُ ۞

4. He knows what is
In the heavens
And on earth;
And He knows what
Ye conceal and what

٤- يَعْلَمُ مَا فِي السَّمٰوٰتِ وَالْأَرْضِ
وَيَعْلَمُ مَا تُسِرُّوْنَ وَمَا تُعْلِنُوْنَ ۚ

Ye reveal: yea, Allah
Knows well the (secrets)
Of (all) hearts.

وَاللّٰهُ عَلِيمٌ
بِذَاتِ الصُّدُوْرِ ۟

5. Has not the story
Reached you, of those
Who rejected Faith aforetime?
So they tasted the evil
Result of their conduct;
And they had
A grievous Penalty.

٥۔ اَلَمْ يَأْتِكُمْ نَبَؤُا الَّذِيْنَ كَفَرُوْا مِنْ قَبْلُ
فَذَاقُوْا وَبَالَ اَمْرِهِمْ
وَلَهُمْ عَذَابٌ اَلِيْمٌ ۟

6. That was because there
Came to them messengers
With Clear Signs,
But they said:
"Shall (mere) human beings
Direct us?" So they rejected
(The Message) and turned away.
But Allah can do without (them):
And Allah is
Free of all needs,
Worthy of all praise.

٦۔ ذٰلِكَ بِاَنَّهٗ كَانَتْ تَأْتِيْهِمْ رُسُلُهُمْ
بِالْبَيِّنٰتِ
فَقَالُوْۤا اَبَشَرٌ يَّهْدُوْنَنَا ۪
فَكَفَرُوْا وَتَوَلَّوْا
وَّاسْتَغْنَى اللّٰهُ ۭ
وَاللّٰهُ غَنِيٌّ حَمِيْدٌ ۟

7. The Unbelievers think
That they will not be
Raised up (for Judgement).
Say: "Yea, by my Lord,
Ye shall surely be
Raised up: then shall ye
Be told (the truth) of
All that ye did.
And that is easy for Allah."

٧۔ زَعَمَ الَّذِيْنَ كَفَرُوْۤا اَنْ لَّنْ يُّبْعَثُوْا ۭ
قُلْ بَلٰى وَرَبِّيْ
لَتُبْعَثُنَّ ثُمَّ لَتُنَبَّؤُنَّ بِمَا عَمِلْتُمْ ۭ
وَذٰلِكَ عَلَى اللّٰهِ يَسِيْرٌ ۟

8. Believe, therefore, in Allah
And His Messenger, and
In the Light which We
Have sent down. And Allah
Is well-acquainted
With all that ye do.

٨۔ فَاٰمِنُوْا بِاللّٰهِ وَرَسُوْلِهٖ
وَالنُّوْرِ الَّذِيْۤ اَنْزَلْنَا ۭ
وَاللّٰهُ بِمَا تَعْمَلُوْنَ خَبِيْرٌ ۟

9. The Day that He assembles
You (all) for a Day
Of Assembly—that will be
A day of mutual loss
And gain (among you).
And those who believe
In Allah and work righeousness—

٩۔ يَوْمَ يَجْمَعُكُمْ لِيَوْمِ الْجَمْعِ
ذٰلِكَ يَوْمُ التَّغَابُنِ ۭ
وَمَنْ يُّؤْمِنْ بِاللّٰهِ وَيَعْمَلْ صَالِحًا
يُّكَفِّرْ عَنْهُ سَيِّاٰتِهٖ

He will remove from them
Their ill, and He will admit
Them to gardens beneath
which
Rivers flow, to dwell therein
Forever: that will be
The Supreme Achievement.

وَيُدْخِلْهُ جَنّٰتٍ تَجْرِىْ مِنْ تَحْتِهَا
الْاَنْهٰرُ خٰلِدِيْنَ فِيْهَاۤ اَبَدًاؕ
ذٰلِكَ الْفَوْزُ الْعَظِيْمُ ۟

10. But those who reject Faith
And treat Our Signs
As falsehoods, they will be
Companions of the Fire,
To dwell therein for aye:
And evil is that Goal.

١٠- وَالَّذِيْنَ كَفَرُوْا وَكَذَّبُوْا بِاٰيٰتِنَاۤ
اُولٰٓئِكَ اَصْحٰبُ النَّارِ خٰلِدِيْنَ فِيْهَاؕ
وَبِئْسَ الْمَصِيْرُ ۟

· SECTION 2.

11. No kind of calamity
Can occur, except
By the leave of Allah:
And if anyone believes
In Allah, (Allah) guides his
Heart (aright): for Allah
Knows all things.

١١- مَاۤ اَصَابَ مِنْ مُّصِيْبَةٍ اِلَّا بِاِذْنِ اللّٰهِؕ
وَمَنْ يُّؤْمِنْ بِاللّٰهِ يَهْدِ قَلْبَهٗؕ
وَاللّٰهُ بِكُلِّ شَىْءٍ عَلِيْمٌ ۟

12. So obey Allah, and obey
His Messenger: but if
Ye turn back, the duty
Of Our Messenger is but
To proclaim (the Message)
Clearly and openly.

١٢- وَاَطِيْعُوا اللّٰهَ وَاَطِيْعُوا الرَّسُوْلَۚ
فَاِنْ تَوَلَّيْتُمْ
فَاِنَّمَا عَلٰى رَسُوْلِنَا الْبَلٰغُ الْمُبِيْنُ ۟

13. Allah! There is no god
But He: and on Allah,
Therefore, let the Believers
Put their trust.

١٣- اَللّٰهُ لَاۤ اِلٰهَ اِلَّا هُوَؕ
وَعَلَى اللّٰهِ فَلْيَتَوَكَّلِ الْمُؤْمِنُوْنَ ۟

14. O ye who believe!
Truly, among your wives
And your children are (some
That are) enemies to
Yourselves: so beware
Of them! But if ye
Forgive and overlook,
And cover up (their faults),
Verily Allah is
Oft-Forgiving, Most Merciful.

١٤- يٰۤاَيُّهَا الَّذِيْنَ اٰمَنُوۤا اِنَّ مِنْ اَزْوَاجِكُمْ
وَاَوْلَادِكُمْ عَدُوًّا لَّكُمْ
فَاحْذَرُوْهُمْۚ
وَاِنْ تَعْفُوْا وَتَصْفَحُوْا وَتَغْفِرُوْا
فَاِنَّ اللّٰهَ غَفُوْرٌ رَّحِيْمٌ ۟

15. Your riches and your children
May be but a trial:
But in the Presence of Allah
Is the highest Reward.

١٥ـ اِنَّمَاۤ اَمْوَالُكُمْ وَاَوْلَادُكُمْ فِتْنَةٌ ۚ
وَاللّٰهُ عِنْدَهٗۤ اَجْرٌ عَظِيْمٌ ۟

16. So fear Allah
As much as ye can;
Listen and obey;
And spend in charity
For the benefit of
Your own souls.
And those saved from
The covetousness of their own
Souls—they are the ones
That achieve prosperity.

١٦ـ فَاتَّقُوا اللّٰهَ مَا اسْتَطَعْتُمْ
وَاسْمَعُوْا وَاَطِيْعُوْا
وَاَنْفِقُوْا خَيْرًا لِّاَنْفُسِكُمْ ۗ
وَمَنْ يُّوْقَ شُحَّ
نَفْسِهٖ فَاُولٰٓئِكَ هُمُ الْمُفْلِحُوْنَ ۟

17. If ye loan to Allah
A beautiful loan, He
Will double it to
Your (credit), and He
Will grant you Forgiveness:
For Allah is most Ready
To appreciate (service),
Most Forbearing—

١٧ـ اِنْ تُقْرِضُوا اللّٰهَ قَرْضًا حَسَنًا
يُّضٰعِفْهُ لَكُمْ
وَيَغْفِرْ لَكُمْ ۗ
وَاللّٰهُ شَكُوْرٌ حَلِيْمٌ ۟

18. Knower of what is hidden
And what is open,
Exalted in Might,
Full of Wisdom.

١٨ـ عٰلِمُ الْغَيْبِ وَالشَّهَادَةِ
الْعَزِيْزُ الْحَكِيْمُ ۟

INTRODUCTION TO SŪRA LXV. (*Ṭalāq*) — 12 Verses

This is the ninth of the ten short Medina Sūras dealing with the social life of the Community. The aspect dealt with here is Divorce and the necessity of precautions to guard against its abuse. The relations of the sexes are an important factor in the social life of the Community, and this and the following Sūra deal with certain aspects of it. "Of all things permitted by law," said the Prophet, "divorce is the most hateful in the sight of God" (Abū Da'ūd. *Sunan*, xiii. 3.) While the sanctity of marriage is the essential basis of family life, the incompatibility of individuals and the weaknesses of human nature require certain outlets and safeguards if that sanctity is not to be made into a fetish at the expense of human life. That is why the question of Divorce is in the Sūra linked with the question of insolent impiety and its punishment.

The date is somewhere about A.H. 6; but the chronology has no significance.

Al Ṭalāq (Divorce)

In the name of Allah, Most Gracious,
Most Merciful.

1. ⬤ Prophet!   When ye
Do divorce women,
Divorce them at their
Prescribed periods,
And count (accurately)
Their prescribed periods:
And fear Allah your Lord:
And turn them not out
Of their houses, nor shall
They (themselves) leave,
Except in case they are
Guilty of some open lewdness,
Those are limits
Set by Allah: and any
Who transgresses the limits
Of Allah, does verily
Wrong his (own) soul:
Thou knowest not if
Perchance Allah will
Bring about thereafter
Some new situation.

2. Thus when they fulfil

Their term appointed,
Either take them back
On equitable terms
Or part with them
On equitable terms;
And take for witness
Two persons from among you,
Endued with justice,
And establish the evidence
(As) before Allah. Such
Is the admonition given
To him who believes
In Allah and the Last Day.
And for those who fear
Allah, He (ever) prepares
A way out,

فَاَمْسِكُوْهُنَّ بِمَعْرُوْفٍ
اَوْ فَارِقُوْهُنَّ بِمَعْرُوْفٍ
وَّاَشْهِدُوْا ذَوَيْ عَدْلٍ مِّنْكُمْ وَاَقِيْمُوا
الشَّهَادَةَ لِلّٰهِ
ذٰلِكُمْ يُوْعَظُ بِهٖ
مَنْ كَانَ يُؤْمِنُ بِاللّٰهِ وَالْيَوْمِ الْاٰخِرِ
وَمَنْ يَّتَّقِ اللّٰهَ
يَجْعَلْ لَّهٗ مَخْرَجًا ۟

3. And He provides for him
From (sources) he never
Could imagine. And if
Anyone puts his trust
In Allah, sufficient is (Allah)
For him. For Allah will
Surely accomplish His purpose:
Verily, for all things
Has Allah appointed
A due proportion.

٣- وَّيَرْزُقْهُ مِنْ حَيْثُ لَا يَحْتَسِبُ ۖ
وَمَنْ يَّتَوَكَّلْ عَلَى اللّٰهِ فَهُوَ حَسْبُهٗ ۖ
اِنَّ اللّٰهَ بَالِغُ اَمْرِهٖ ۖ
قَدْ جَعَلَ اللّٰهُ لِكُلِّ شَيْءٍ قَدْرًا ۟

4. Such of your women
As have passed the age
Of monthly courses, for them
The prescribed period, if ye
Have any doubts, is
Three months, and for those
Who have no courses
(It is the same):
For those who carry
(Life within their wombs),
Their period is until
They deliver their burdens:
And for those who
Fear Allah, He will
Make their path easy.

٤- وَالّٰٓـِٔيْ يَئِسْنَ مِنَ الْمَحِيْضِ مِنْ نِّسَآئِكُمْ
اِنِ ارْتَبْتُمْ
فَعِدَّتُهُنَّ ثَلٰثَةُ اَشْهُرٍ ۙ
وَّالّٰٓـِٔيْ لَمْ يَحِضْنَ ۚ
وَاُولَاتُ الْاَحْمَالِ
اَجَلُهُنَّ اَنْ يَّضَعْنَ حَمْلَهُنَّ ۚ
وَمَنْ يَّتَّقِ اللّٰهَ
يَجْعَلْ لَّهٗ مِنْ اَمْرِهٖ يُسْرًا ۟

5. That is the Command
Of Allah, which He
Has sent down to you:
And if anyone fears Allah,

٥- ذٰلِكَ اَمْرُ اللّٰهِ اَنْزَلَهٗ اِلَيْكُمْ ۚ
وَمَنْ يَّتَّقِ اللّٰهَ يُكَفِّرْ عَنْهُ سَيِّاٰتِهٖ

He will remove his ills
From him, and will enlarge
His reward.

وَيُعْظِمْ لَهُ أَجْرًا ٥

6. Let the women live
(In 'iddah) in the same
Style as ye live,
According to your means:
Annoy them not, so as
To restrict them.
And if they carry (life
In their wombs), then
Spend (your substance) on them
Until they deliver
Their burden: and if
They suckle your (offspring),
Give them their recompense:
And take mutual counsel
Together, according to
What is just and reasonable.
And if ye find yourselves
In difficulties, let another
Woman suckle (the child)
On the (father's) behalf.

٦- أَسْكِنُوهُنَّ مِنْ حَيْثُ
سَكَنْتُمْ مِنْ وُجْدِكُمْ
وَلَا تُضَآرُّوهُنَّ لِتُضَيِّقُوا عَلَيْهِنَّ ؕ
وَإِنْ كُنَّ أُولَاتِ حَمْلٍ
فَأَنْفِقُوا عَلَيْهِنَّ حَتَّى يَضَعْنَ حَمْلَهُنَّ ۚ
فَإِنْ أَرْضَعْنَ لَكُمْ فَأَتُوهُنَّ أُجُوْرَهُنَّ ۚ
وَأْتَمِرُوا بَيْنَكُمْ بِمَعْرُوْفٍ ۚ
وَإِنْ تَعَاسَرْتُمْ
فَسَتُرْضِعُ لَهُ أُخْرَى ۖ

7. Let the man of means
Spend according to
His means: and the man
Whose resources are restricted,
Let him spend according
To what Allah has given him.
Allah puts no burden
On any person beyond
What He has given him.
After a difficulty, Allah
Will soon grant relief.

٧- لِيُنْفِقْ ذُوْ سَعَةٍ مِنْ سَعَتِهٖ ؕ
وَمَنْ قُدِرَ عَلَيْهِ رِزْقُهٗ
فَلْيُنْفِقْ مِمَّا آتَاهُ اللّٰهُ ؕ
لَا يُكَلِّفُ اللّٰهُ نَفْسًا إِلَّا مَا آتَاهَا ؕ
سَيَجْعَلُ اللّٰهُ بَعْدَ عُسْرٍ يُّسْرًا ۖ

SECTION 2.

8. How many populations
That insolently opposed
The command of their Lord
And of His messengers,
Did We not then
Call to account—
To severe account?—
And We imposed on them
An exemplary Punishment.

٨- وَكَأَيِّنْ مِّنْ قَرْيَةٍ عَتَتْ
عَنْ أَمْرِ رَبِّهَا
وَرُسُلِهٖ
فَحَاسَبْنَاهَا حِسَابًا شَدِيْدًا ۙ
وَّعَذَّبْنَاهَا عَذَابًا نُّكْرًا ٥

9. Then did they taste
The evil result of
Their conduct, and the End
Of their conduct
Was Perdition.

٩- فَذَاقَتْ وَبَالَ أَمْرِهَا
وَكَانَ عَاقِبَةُ أَمْرِهَا خُسْرًا ۝

10. Allah has prepared for them
A severe Punishment
(In the Hereafter).
Therefore fear Allah,
O ye men of understanding—
Who have believed!—
For Allah hath indeed
Sent down to you
A Message—

١٠- أَعَدَّ اللهُ لَهُمْ عَذَابًا شَدِيدًا ۙ
فَاتَّقُوا اللهَ يَا أُولِي الْأَلْبَابِ ۛ
الَّذِيْنَ آمَنُوا ۛ
قَدْ أَنْزَلَ اللهُ إِلَيْكُمْ ذِكْرًا ۝

11. A Messenger, who rehearses
To you the Signs of Allah
Containing clear explanations,
That he may lead forth
Those who believe
And do righteous deeds
From the depths of Darkness
Into Light. And those who
Believe in Allah and work
Righteousness, He will admit
To Gardens beneath which rivers
Flow, to dwell therein
Forever: Allah has indeed
Granted for them
A most excellent provision.

١١- رَسُوْلًا يَتْلُوا عَلَيْكُمْ آيَاتِ اللهِ
مُبَيِّنَاتٍ
لِيُخْرِجَ الَّذِيْنَ آمَنُوا وَعَمِلُوا الصَّالِحَاتِ
مِنَ الظُّلُمَاتِ إِلَى النُّوْرِ ۚ
وَمَنْ يُؤْمِنْ بِاللهِ وَيَعْمَلْ صَالِحًا
يُدْخِلْهُ جَنَّاتٍ تَجْرِيْ مِنْ تَحْتِهَا الْأَنْهَارُ
خَالِدِيْنَ فِيْهَا أَبَدًا ۗ
قَدْ أَحْسَنَ اللهُ لَهُ رِزْقًا ۝

12. Allah is He Who
Created seven Firmaments
And of the earth
A similar number.
Through the midst
Of them (all) descends
His Command: that ye may
Know that Allah has power
Over all things, and that
Allah comprehends all things
In (His) Knowledge.

١٢- اللهُ الَّذِيْ خَلَقَ سَبْعَ سَمَاوَاتٍ
وَمِنَ الْأَرْضِ مِثْلَهُنَّ ۗ
يَتَنَزَّلُ الْأَمْرُ بَيْنَهُنَّ
لِتَعْلَمُوا أَنَّ اللهَ عَلَى كُلِّ شَيْءٍ قَدِيْرٌ ۙ
وَأَنَّ اللهَ قَدْ أَحَاطَ بِكُلِّ شَيْءٍ عِلْمًا ۝

INTRODUCTION TO SŪRA LXVI. (*Taḥrīm*) — 12 Verses

This is the tenth and last of the series of short Medina Sūras which began with S.lvii: see Introduction to that Sūra. The point dealt with here is: how far harmony between the sexes may injure the higher interests of society.

The date may be taken to be somewhere about A.H.7.

Al Taḥrīm (Prohibition)

In the name of Allah, Most Gracious, Most Merciful.

بِسْمِ اللهِ الرَّحْمٰنِ الرَّحِيمِ

1. ⓞ Prophet! Why
   Holdest thou to be forbidden
   That which Allah has
   Made lawful to thee?
   Thou seekest to please
   Thy consorts. But Allah
   Is Oft-Forgiving, Most Merciful.

يَا أَيُّهَا النَّبِيُّ لِمَ تُحَرِّمُ
مَا أَحَلَّ اللهُ لَكَ
تَبْتَغِي مَرْضَاتَ أَزْوَاجِكَ
وَاللهُ غَفُورٌ رَّحِيمٌ ٠

2. Allah has already ordained
   For you, (O men),
   The dissolution of your oaths
   (In some cases): and Allah
   Is your Protector, and He
   Is Full of Knowledge
   And Wisdom.

قَدْ فَرَضَ اللهُ لَكُمْ
تَحِلَّةَ أَيْمَانِكُمْ
وَاللهُ مَوْلَاكُمْ
وَهُوَ الْعَلِيمُ الْحَكِيمُ ٠

3. When the Prophet disclosed
   A matter of confidence
   To one of his consorts,
   And she then divulged it
   (To another), and Allah made it
   Known to him, he confirmed
   Part thereof and repudiated
   A part. Then when he
   Told her thereof, she said,
   "Who told thee this?"
   He said, "He told me
   Who knows and is well-acquainted
   (With all things)"

وَإِذْ أَسَرَّ النَّبِيُّ
إِلَى بَعْضِ أَزْوَاجِهِ حَدِيثًا
فَلَمَّا نَبَّأَتْ بِهِ وَأَظْهَرَهُ اللهُ عَلَيْهِ
عَرَّفَ بَعْضَهُ وَأَعْرَضَ عَنْ بَعْضٍ
فَلَمَّا نَبَّأَهَا بِهِ
قَالَتْ مَنْ أَنْبَأَكَ هٰذَا
قَالَ نَبَّأَنِيَ الْعَلِيمُ الْخَبِيرُ ٠

4. If ye two turn in repentance

إِنْ تَتُوبَا إِلَى اللهِ

To Him, your hearts
Are indeed so inclined;
But if ye back up
Each other against him,
Truly Allah is his Protector,
And Gabriel, and (every)
Righteous one among those
Who believe—and
     furthermore,
The angels—will back (him) up.

5. It may be, if he
Divorced you (all),
That Allah will give him
In exchange Consorts
Better than you—
Who submit (their wills),
Who believe, who are devout,
Who turn to Allah in repentance,
Who worship (in humility),
Who travel (for Faith) and
     fast—
Previously married or virgins.

6. O ye who believe!
Save yourselves and your
Families from a Fire
Whose fuel is Men
And Stones, over which
Are (appointed) angels
Stern (and) severe,
Who flinch not (from
Executing) the Commands
They receive from Allah,
But do (precisely) what
They are commanded.

7. (They will say),
"O ye Unbelievers!
Make no excuses
This Day! Ye are being
But requited for
All that ye did!"
   SECTION 2.

8. O ye who believe!
Turn to Allah

With sincere repentance:
In the hope that
Your Lord will remove
From you your ills
And admit you to Gardens
Beneath which Rivers flow—
The Day that Allah
Will not permit
To be humiliated
The Prophet and those
Who believe with him.
Their Light will run
Forward before them
And by their right hands,
While they say, "Our Lord!
Perfect our Light for us,
And grant us Forgiveness:
For Thou has power
Over all things."

تُوبُوا إِلَى اللهِ تَوْبَةً نَّصُوحًا ۖ
عَسَى رَبُّكُمْ
أَنْ يُّكَفِّرَ عَنْكُمْ سَيِّئَاتِكُمْ
وَيُدْخِلَكُمْ جَنَّاتٍ تَجْرِي مِنْ تَحْتِهَا الْأَنْهَارُ
يَوْمَ لَا يُخْزِي اللهُ النَّبِيَّ
وَالَّذِينَ آمَنُوا مَعَهُ ۖ
نُورُهُمْ يَسْعَى بَيْنَ أَيْدِيهِمْ وَبِأَيْمَانِهِمْ
يَقُولُونَ رَبَّنَا أَتْمِمْ لَنَا نُورَنَا وَاغْفِرْ لَنَا ۖ
إِنَّكَ عَلَى كُلِّ شَيْءٍ قَدِيرٌ ○

9. **O** Prophet! Strive hard
Against the Unbelievers
And the Hypocrites,
And be firm against them.
Their abode is Hell—
An evil refuge (indeed).

٩- يَا أَيُّهَا النَّبِيُّ جَاهِدِ الْكُفَّارَ
وَالْمُنَافِقِينَ وَاغْلُظْ عَلَيْهِمْ ۚ
وَمَأْوَاهُمْ جَهَنَّمُ ۖ وَبِئْسَ الْمَصِيرُ ○

10. **A**llah sets forth,
For an example
To the Unbelievers,
The wife of Noah
And the wife of Lut:
They were (respectively)
Under two of our righteous
Servants, but they were
False to their (husbands),
And they profited nothing
Before Allah on their account,
But were told: "Enter ye
The Fire along with
(Others) that enter!"

١٠- ضَرَبَ اللهُ مَثَلًا لِّلَّذِينَ كَفَرُوا
امْرَأَتَ نُوحٍ وَامْرَأَتَ لُوطٍ ۖ
كَانَتَا تَحْتَ عَبْدَيْنِ
مِنْ عِبَادِنَا صَالِحَيْنِ
فَخَانَتَاهُمَا
فَلَمْ يُغْنِيَا عَنْهُمَا مِنَ اللهِ شَيْئًا
وَقِيلَ ادْخُلَا النَّارَ مَعَ الدَّاخِلِينَ ○

11. And Allah sets forth,
As an example
To those who believe,
The wife of Pharaoh:
Behold she said:
"O my Lord! build

١١- وَضَرَبَ اللهُ مَثَلًا
لِّلَّذِينَ آمَنُوا امْرَأَتَ فِرْعَوْنَ ۘ
إِذْ قَالَتْ رَبِّ ابْنِ لِي عِنْدَكَ

For me, in nearness
To Thee, a mansion
In the Garden,
And save me from Pharaoh
And his doings,
And save me from
Those that do wrong";

بَيْتًا فِى الْجَنَّةِ

وَنَجِّنِى مِنْ فِرْعَوْنَ وَعَمَلِهِ

وَنَجِّنِى مِنَ الْقَوْمِ الظّٰلِمِيْنَ ۟

12: And Mary the daughter
Of 'Imrān, who guarded
Her chastity; and We
Breathed into (her body)
Of Our spirit; and she
Testified to the truth
Of the words of her Lord
And of his Revelations,
And was one of the
Devout (Servants).

١٢ ۔ وَمَرْيَمَ ابْنَتَ عِمْرٰنَ

الَّتِىۤ اَحْصَنَتْ فَرْجَهَا

فَنَفَخْنَا فِيْهِ مِنْ رُّوْحِنَا

وَصَدَّقَتْ بِكَلِمٰتِ رَبِّهَا

وَكُتُبِهٖ وَكَانَتْ مِنَ الْقٰنِتِيْنَ ۟ ۖ

INTRODUCTION AND SUMMARY: SŪRA LXVII. (*Mulk*) — 30 Verses

We have now done fourteen-fifteenths of the Qur-ān, and have followed by step the development of its argument establishing the Ummat or Brotherhood of Islam.

There is a logical break here. The remaining fifteenth consists of short spiritual Lyrics, mostly of the Meccan period, dealing mainly with the inner life of man, and in its individual aspects. They may be compared to Hymns or Psalms in other religious literature. But these short Quranic Sūras have a grandeur, a beauty, a mystic meaning, and a force of earnestness under persecution, all their own. With their sources in the sublimest regions of the Empyrean, their light penetrates into the darkest recesses of Life, into the concrete facts which are often mistaken for the whole of Reality, though they are but an insignificant portion and on the surface and fleeting. There is much symbolism in language and thought, in describing the spiritual in terms of the things we see and understand.

It is the contrast between the shadows of Reality here and the eternal Reality, between the surface world and the profound inner World, that is urged on our attention here.

This Sūra of 30 verses belongs to the Middle Meccan period, just before S.lxix. and S.lxx. God is mentioned here by the name *Rahmān* (Most Gracious), as He is mentioned by the names of *Rabb* (Lord and Cherisher) and *Rahman* (Most Gracious) in S.xix.

Al Mulk (The Dominion)

In the name of Allah, Most Gracious, Most Merciful.

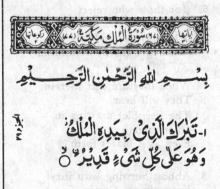

1. Blessed[5554] be He
In Whose hands
Is Dominion;
And He over all things
Hath Power —

2. He Who created Death
And Life, that He
May try which of you
Is best in deed;[5557]
And He is the Exalted
In Might, Oft-Forgiving —

3. He Who created
The seven heavens

29/30

One above another:
No want of proportion
Wilt thou see
In the Creation
Of (Allah) Most Gracious.
So turn thy vision again:
Seest thou any flaw?

طِبَاقًا ۗ
مَّا تَرَىٰ فِى خَلْقِ الرَّحْمَٰنِ مِن تَفَٰوُتٍ
فَارْجِعِ الْبَصَرَ
هَلْ تَرَىٰ مِن فُطُورٍ ۝

4. Again turn thy vision
A second time: (thy) vision
Will come back to thee
Dull and discomfited,
In a state worn out.

٤ - ثُمَّ ارْجِعِ الْبَصَرَ كَرَّتَيْنِ
يَنقَلِبْ إِلَيْكَ الْبَصَرُ خَاسِئًا
وَّهُوَ حَسِيرٌ ۝

5. And We have,
(From of old),
Adorned the lowest heaven
With Lamps, and We
Have made such (Lamps)
(As) missiles to drive
Away the Evil Ones,
And have prepared for them
The Penalty
Of the Blazing Fire.

٥ - وَلَقَدْ زَيَّنَّا السَّمَاءَ الدُّنْيَا
بِمَصَٰبِيحَ
وَجَعَلْنَٰهَا رُجُومًا لِّلشَّيَٰطِينِ
وَأَعْتَدْنَا لَهُمْ
عَذَابَ السَّعِيرِ ۝

6. For those who reject
Their Lord (and Cherisher)
Is the Penalty of Hell:
And evil is (such) destination.

٦ - وَلِلَّذِينَ كَفَرُوا بِرَبِّهِمْ
عَذَابُ جَهَنَّمَ ۖ وَبِئْسَ الْمَصِيرُ ۝

7. When they are cast therein,
They will hear
The (terrible) drawing in
Of its breath
Even as it blazes forth,

٧ - إِذَا أُلْقُوا فِيهَا سَمِعُوا
لَهَا شَهِيقًا وَّهِىَ تَفُورُ ۝

8. Almost bursting with fury:
Every time a Group
Is cast therein, its Keepers
Will ask, "Did no Warner
Come to you?"

٨ - تَكَادُ تَمَيَّزُ مِنَ الْغَيْظِ ۖ
كُلَّمَا أُلْقِىَ فِيهَا فَوْجٌ سَأَلَهُمْ خَزَنَتُهَا
أَلَمْ يَأْتِكُمْ نَذِيرٌ ۝

9. They will say: "Yes indeed;
A Warner did come to us,
But we rejected him
And said, 'Allah never
Sent down any (Message):

٩ - قَالُوا بَلَىٰ قَدْ جَاءَنَا نَذِيرٌ
فَكَذَّبْنَا وَقُلْنَا مَا نَزَّلَ اللَّهُ مِن شَىْءٍ ۚ

Ye are in nothing but
An egregious delusion!'"

اِنْ اَنْتُمْ اِلَّا فِیْ ضَلٰلٍ كَبِیْرٍ

10. They will further say:
"Had we but listened
Or used our intelligence,
We should not (now)
Be among the Companions
Of the Blazing Fire!"

١٠ ـ وَقَالُوْا لَوْ كُنَّا نَسْمَعُ
اَوْ نَعْقِلُ مَا كُنَّا فِیْۤ
اَصْحٰبِ السَّعِیْرِ ۟

11. They will then confess
Their sins: but far
Will be (Forgiveness)
From the Companions
Of the Blazing Fire!

١١ ـ فَاعْتَرَفُوْا بِذَنْۢبِهِمْ ۚ
فَسُحْقًا لِّاَصْحٰبِ السَّعِیْرِ ۟

12. As for those who
Fear their Lord unseen,
For them is Forgiveness
And a great Reward.

١٢ ـ اِنَّ الَّذِیْنَ یَخْشَوْنَ رَبَّهُمْ بِالْغَیْبِ
لَهُمْ مَّغْفِرَةٌ وَّاَجْرٌ كَبِیْرٌ ۟

13. And whether ye hide
Your word or publish it,
He certainly has (full) knowledge,
Of the secrets of (all) hearts.

١٣ ـ وَاَسِرُّوْا قَوْلَكُمْ اَوِ اجْهَرُوْا بِهٖ ؕ
اِنَّهٗ عَلِیْمٌۢ بِذَاتِ الصُّدُوْرِ ۟

14. Should He not know—
He that created?
And He is the One
That understands the finest
Mysteries (and) is
Well-acquainted (with them).

١٤ ـ اَلَا یَعْلَمُ
مَنْ خَلَقَ ؕ
وَهُوَ اللَّطِیْفُ الْخَبِیْرُ ۠ ؏

SECTION 2.

15. It is He Who has
Made the earth manageable
For you, so traverse
Ye through its tracts
And enjoy of the Sustenance
Which He furnishes: but
Unto Him is the Resurrection.

١٥ ـ هُوَ الَّذِیْ جَعَلَ لَكُمُ الْاَرْضَ ذَلُوْلًا
فَامْشُوْا فِیْ مَنَاكِبِهَا
وَكُلُوْا مِنْ رِّزْقِهٖ ؕ
وَاِلَیْهِ النُّشُوْرُ ۟

16. Do ye feel secure that
He Who is in Heaven
Will not cause you
To be swallowed up
By the earth when it
Shakes (as in an earthquake)?

١٦ ـ ءَاَمِنْتُمْ مَّنْ فِی السَّمَآءِ
اَنْ یَّخْسِفَ بِكُمُ الْاَرْضَ
فَاِذَا هِیَ تَمُوْرُ ۟

17. Or do ye feel secure
That He Who is in Heaven
Will not send against you
A violent tornado
(With showers of stones),
So that ye shall
Know how (terrible)
Was My warning?

١٧ـ اَمۡ اَمِنۡتُمۡ مَّنۡ فِى السَّمَآءِ اَنۡ يُّرۡسِلَ عَلَيۡكُمۡ حَاصِبًا ۖ فَسَتَعۡلَمُوۡنَ كَيۡفَ نَذِيۡرِ ۝

18. But indeed men before them
Rejected (My warning):
Then how (terrible) was
My rejection (of them)?

١٨ـ وَلَقَدۡ كَذَّبَ الَّذِيۡنَ مِنۡ قَبۡلِهِمۡ فَكَيۡفَ كَانَ نَكِيۡرِ ۝

19. Do they not observe
The birds above them,
Spreading their wings
And folding them in?
None can uphold them
Except (Allah) Most Gracious:
Truly it is He
That watches over all things.

١٩ـ اَوَلَمۡ يَرَوۡا اِلَى الطَّيۡرِ فَوۡقَهُمۡ صٰفّٰتٍ وَّيَقۡبِضۡنَ ۘ مَا يُمۡسِكُهُنَّ اِلَّا الرَّحۡمٰنُ ۚ اِنَّهٗ بِكُلِّ شَىۡءٍۭ بَصِيۡرٌ ۝

20. Nay, who is there
That can help you,
(Even as) an army,
Besides (Allah) Most Merciful?
In nothing but delusion
Are the Unbelievers.

٢٠ـ اَمَّنۡ هٰذَا الَّذِىۡ هُوَ جُنۡدٌ لَّكُمۡ يَنۡصُرُكُمۡ مِّنۡ دُوۡنِ الرَّحۡمٰنِ ۚ اِنِ الۡكٰفِرُوۡنَ اِلَّا فِىۡ غُرُوۡرٍ ۝

21. Or who is there
That can provide you
With Sustenance if He
Were to withhold His provision?
Nay, they obstinately persist
In insolent impiety
And flight (from the Truth).

٢١ـ اَمَّنۡ هٰذَا الَّذِىۡ يَرۡزُقُكُمۡ اِنۡ اَمۡسَكَ رِزۡقَهٗ ۚ بَلۡ لَّجُّوۡا فِىۡ عُتُوٍّ وَّنُفُوۡرٍ ۝

22. Is then one who
Walks headlong, with his face
Grovelling, better guided —
Or one who walks
Evenly on a Straight Way?

٢٢ـ اَفَمَنۡ يَّمۡشِىۡ مُكِبًّا عَلٰى وَجۡهِهٖ اَهۡدٰى اَمَّنۡ يَّمۡشِىۡ سَوِيًّا عَلٰى صِرَاطٍ مُّسۡتَقِيۡمٍ ۝

23. Say: "It is He Who
Has created you (and made
You grow), and made
For you the faculties

٢٣ـ قُلۡ هُوَ الَّذِىۡ اَنۡشَاَكُمۡ وَجَعَلَ لَكُمُ

Of hearing, seeing,
Feeling and understanding:
Little thanks it is ye give.

السَّمْعَ وَالْأَبْصَارَ وَالْأَفْئِدَةَ ۖ
قَلِيلًا مَّا تَشْكُرُونَ ۝

24. Say: "It is He Who
Has multiplied you
Through the earth,
And to Him shall ye
Be gathered together."

٢٤۔ قُلْ هُوَ الَّذِى ذَرَأَكُمْ
فِى الْأَرْضِ وَإِلَيْهِ تُحْشَرُونَ ۝

25. They ask: When will
This promise be (fulfilled)?
If ye are telling
The truth.

٢٥۔ وَيَقُولُونَ مَتَى هَذَا الْوَعْدُ
إِنْ كُنْتُمْ صَادِقِينَ ۝

26. Say: "As to the knowledge
Of the time, it is
With Allah alone:
I am (sent) only
To warn plainly in public."

٢٦۔ قُلْ إِنَّمَا الْعِلْمُ عِنْدَ اللَّهِ ۖ
وَإِنَّمَا أَنَا نَذِيرٌ مُّبِينٌ ۝

27. At length, when they
See it close at hand,
Grieved will be the faces
Of the Unbelievers,
And it will be said
(To them): "This is
(The promise fulfilled),
Which ye were calling for!"

٢٧۔ فَلَمَّا رَأَوْهُ زُلْفَةً
سِيئَتْ وُجُوهُ الَّذِينَ كَفَرُوا
وَقِيلَ هَذَا الَّذِى
كُنْتُمْ بِهِ تَدَّعُونَ ۝

28. Say: "See ye?—
If Allah were
To destroy me,
And those with me,
Or if He bestows
His mercy on us—
Yet who can deliver
The Unbelievers from
A grievous Penalty?"

٢٨۔ قُلْ أَرَأَيْتُمْ
إِنْ أَهْلَكَنِيَ اللَّهُ وَمَنْ مَّعِيَ
أَوْ رَحِمَنَا ۖ فَمَنْ يُّجِيرُ
الْكَافِرِينَ مِنْ عَذَابٍ أَلِيمٍ ۝

29. Say: "He is (Allah)
Most Gracious: we have
Believed in Him,
And on Him have we
Put our trust:
So, soon will ye know
Which (of us) it is
That is in manifest error."

٢٩۔ قُلْ هُوَ الرَّحْمَنُ آمَنَّا بِهِ
وَعَلَيْهِ تَوَكَّلْنَا ۖ
فَسَتَعْلَمُونَ
مَنْ هُوَ فِى ضَلَالٍ مُّبِينٍ ۝

30. Say: "See ye?—
If your stream be
Some morning lost
(In the underground earth),
Who then can supply you
With clear-flowing water?"

٣٠ـ قُلْ أَرَأَيْتُمْ
إِنْ أَصْبَحَ مَاؤُكُمْ غَوْرًا
فَمَنْ يَأْتِيكُمْ بِمَاءٍ مَعِينٍ ۞

INTRODUCTION TO SŪRA LXVIII. (*Qalam*) — 52 Verses

This is a very early Meccan revelation. The general Muslim opinion is that a great part of it was second in order of revelation, the first being S. xcvi. (*Iqraa*), verses 1-5: *Itqān*, Chapter 7.

The last Sūra having defined the true Reality in contrast with the false standards set up by men, this illustrates the theme by an actual historical example. Our Holy Prophet was the sanest and wisest of men: those who could not understand him called him mad or possessed. So, in every age, it is the habit of the world to call Truth Falsehood and Wisdom Madness, and, on the other hand, to exalt Selfishness as Planning, and Arrogance as Power. The contrast is shown up between the two kinds of men and their real inner worth.

Al Qalam (The Pen), or *Nūn*

In the name of Allah, Most Gracious,
Most Merciful.

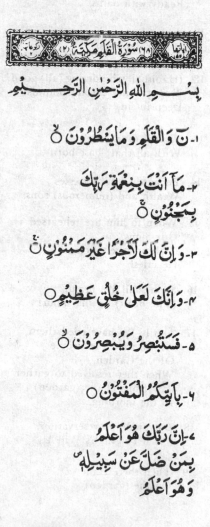

1. **Nūn.** [5592-A] By the Pen
   And by the (Record)
   Which (men) write—

2. Thou art not,
   By the grace of thy Lord,
   Mad or possessed.

3. Nay, verily for thee
   Is a Reward unfailing!

4. And thou (standest)
   On an exalted standard
   Of character.

5. Soon wilt thou see,
   And they will see,

6. Which of you is
   Afflicted with madness.

7. Verily it is thy Lord
   That knoweth best,
   Which (among men)
   Hath strayed from His Path:
   And He knoweth best
   Those who receive

(True) Guidance.

بِالْمُهْتَدِينَ ٠

8. So hearken not
To those who
Deny (the Truth).

٨ـ فَلَا تُطِعِ الْمُكَذِّبِينَ ٠

9. Their desire is that
Thou shouldst be pliant:
So would they be pliant.

٩ـ وَدُّوا لَوْ تُدْهِنُ فَيُدْهِنُونَ ٠

10. Heed not the type
Of despicable man—
Ready with oaths,

١٠ـ وَلَا تُطِعْ كُلَّ حَلَّافٍ مَهِينٍ ٠

11. A slanderer, going about
With calumnies,

١١ـ هَمَّازٍ مَشَّاءٍ بِنَمِيمٍ ٠

12. (Habitually) hindering (all) good,
Transgressing beyond bounds,
Deep in sin,

١٢ـ مَنَّاعٍ لِلْخَيْرِ مُعْتَدٍ أَثِيمٍ ٠

13. Violent (and cruel)—
With all that, base-born—

١٣ـ عُتُلٍّ بَعْدَ ذَلِكَ زَنِيمٍ ٠

14. Because   he possesses
Wealth and (numerous) sons.

١٤ـ أَنْ كَانَ ذَا مَالٍ وَبَنِينَ ٠

15. When to him are rehearsed
Our Signs,
"Tales of the Ancients",
He cries!

١٥ـ إِذَا تُتْلَى عَلَيْهِ آيَاتُنَا قَالَ أَسَاطِيرُ الْأَوَّلِينَ ٠

16. Soon shall We brand
(The beast) on the snout!

١٦ـ سَنَسِمُهُ عَلَى الْخُرْطُومِ ٠

17. Verily We have tried them
As We tried the People
Of the Garden,
When they resolved to gather
The fruits of the (garden)
In the morning,

١٧ـ إِنَّا بَلَوْنَاهُمْ كَمَا بَلَوْنَا أَصْحَابَ الْجَنَّةِ إِذْ أَقْسَمُوا لَيَصْرِمُنَّهَا مُصْبِحِينَ ٠

18. But made no reservation,
("If it be Allah's Will").

١٨ـ وَلَا يَسْتَثْنُونَ ٠

19. Then there came
On the (garden)

١٩ـ فَطَافَ عَلَيْهَا

A visitation from thy Lord,
(Which swept away) all around,
While they were asleep.

طَآئِفٌ مِّنْ رَّبِّكَ وَهُمْ نَآئِمُوْنَ ۝

20. So the (garden) became,
By the morning, like
A dark and desolate spot,
(Whose fruit had been gathered).

٢٠- فَأَصْبَحَتْ كَالصَّرِيْمِ ۝

21. As the morning broke,
They called out,
One to another—

٢١- فَتَنَادَوْا مُصْبِحِيْنَ ۝

22. "Go ye to your tilth
(Betimes) in the morning,
If ye would gather
The fruits."

٢٢- أَنِ اغْدُوْا عَلَى حَرْثِكُمْ
إِنْ كُنْتُمْ صَارِمِيْنَ ۝

23. So they departed, conversing
In secret low tones, (saying)—

٢٣- فَانْطَلَقُوْا وَهُمْ يَتَخَافَتُوْنَ ۝

24 "Let not a single indigent
Person break in upon you
Into the (garden) this day."

٢٤ أَنْ لَّا يَدْخُلَنَّهَا الْيَوْمَ عَلَيْكُمْ
مِّسْكِيْنٌ ۝

25. And they opened the morning,
Strong in an (unjust) resolve.

٢٥- وَّغَدَوْا عَلَى حَرْدٍ قَادِرِيْنَ ۝

26. But when they saw
The (garden), they said:
"We have surely lost our way:

٢٦- فَلَمَّا رَأَوْهَا
قَالُوْا إِنَّا لَضَآلُّوْنَ ۝

27. "Indeed we are shut out
(Of the fruits of our labour)!"

٢٧- بَلْ نَحْنُ مَحْرُوْمُوْنَ ۝

28. Said one of them,
More just (than the rest):
"Did I not say to you,
'Why not glorify (Allah)?'"

٢٨- قَالَ أَوْسَطُهُمْ
أَلَمْ أَقُلْ لَّكُمْ لَوْلَا تُسَبِّحُوْنَ ۝

29. They said: "Glory
To our Lord! Verily we
Have been doing wrong!"

٢٩- قَالُوْا سُبْحَانَ رَبِّنَا إِنَّا كُنَّا ظَالِمِيْنَ ۝

30. Then they turned, one
Against another, in reproach.

٣٠- فَأَقْبَلَ بَعْضُهُمْ عَلَى بَعْضٍ يَتَلَاوَمُوْنَ ۝

31. They said: "Alas for us!
We have indeed transgressed!

٣١- قَالُوا يَاوَيْلَنَا إِنَّا كُنَّا طَاغِينَ ۟

32. "It may be that our Lord
Will give us in exchange
A better (garden) than this:
For we do turn to Him
(In repentance)!"

٣٢- عَسَى رَبُّنَا أَنْ يُبْدِلَنَا خَيْرًا مِّنْهَا إِنَّا إِلَى رَبِّنَا رَاغِبُونَ ۟

33. Such is the Punishment
(In this life); but greater
Is the Punishment
In the Hereafter—
If only they knew!

٣٣- كَذَلِكَ الْعَذَابُ ۖ وَلَعَذَابُ الْآخِرَةِ أَكْبَرُ ۚ لَوْ كَانُوا يَعْلَمُونَ ۟

SECTION 2.

34. Verily, for the Righteous,
Are Gardens of Delight,
In the Presence
Of their Lord.

٣٤- إِنَّ لِلْمُتَّقِينَ عِنْدَ رَبِّهِمْ جَنَّاتِ النَّعِيمِ ۟

35. Shall We then treat
The People of Faith
Like the People of Sin?

٣٥- أَفَنَجْعَلُ الْمُسْلِمِينَ كَالْمُجْرِمِينَ ۟

36. What is the matter
With you? How judge ye?

٣٦- مَا لَكُمْ ۖ كَيْفَ تَحْكُمُونَ ۟

37. Or have ye a Book
Through which ye learn—

٣٧- أَمْ لَكُمْ كِتَابٌ فِيهِ تَدْرُسُونَ ۟

38. That ye shall have,
Through it whatever
Ye choose?

٣٨- إِنَّ لَكُمْ فِيهِ لَمَا تَخَيَّرُونَ ۟

39. Or have ye Covenants
With Us on oath,
Reaching to the Day
Of Judgement, (providing)
That ye shall have
Whatever ye shall demand?

٣٩- أَمْ لَكُمْ أَيْمَانٌ عَلَيْنَا بَالِغَةٌ إِلَى يَوْمِ الْقِيَامَةِ ۙ إِنَّ لَكُمْ لَمَا تَحْكُمُونَ ۟

40. Ask thou of them,
Which of them will stand
Surety for that!

٤٠- سَلْهُمْ أَيُّهُمْ بِذَلِكَ زَعِيمٌ ۟

41. Or have they some

٤١- أَمْ لَهُمْ شُرَكَاءُ ۚ

"Partners" (in Godhead)?
Then let them produce
Their "partners"
If they are truthful!

فَلْيَأْتُوا بِشُرَكَآئِهِمْ اِنْ
كَانُوا صٰدِقِيْنَ ۟

42. The Day that the Shin
Shall be laid bare,
And they shall be summoned
To bow in adoration,
But they shall not be able—

۴۲- يَوْمَ يُكْشَفُ عَنْ سَاقٍ
وَّيُدْعَوْنَ اِلَى السُّجُوْدِ
فَلَا يَسْتَطِيعُوْنَ ۟

43. Their eyes will be
Cast down—ignominy will
Cover them; seeing that
They had been summoned
Aforetime to bow in adoration,
While they were whole,
(And had refused).

۴۳- خَاشِعَةً اَبْصَارُهُمْ تَرْهَقُهُمْ ذِلَّةٌ ؕ
وَقَدْ كَانُوا يُدْعَوْنَ اِلَى السُّجُوْدِ
وَهُمْ سٰلِمُوْنَ ۟

44. Then leave Me   alone
With such as reject
This Message: by degrees
Shall We punish them
From directions they perceive
                    not.

۴۴- فَذَرْنِيْ وَمَنْ يُّكَذِّبُ بِهٰذَا الْحَدِيْثِ ؕ
سَنَسْتَدْرِجُهُمْ
مِّنْ حَيْثُ لَا يَعْلَمُوْنَ ۟

45. A (long) respite will I
Grant them: truly
Powerful is My Plan.

۴۵- وَاُمْلِيْ لَهُمْ ؕ
اِنَّ كَيْدِيْ مَتِيْنٌ ۟

46. Or is it that thou dost
Ask them for a reward,
So that they are burdened
With a load of debt?—

۴۶- اَمْ تَسْـَٔلُهُمْ اَجْرًا
فَهُمْ مِّنْ مَّغْرَمٍ مُّثْقَلُوْنَ ۟

47. Or that the Unseen
Is in their hands, so that
They can write it down?

۴۷- اَمْ عِنْدَهُمُ الْغَيْبُ فَهُمْ يَكْتُبُوْنَ ۟

48. So wait with patience
For the Command
Of thy Lord, and be not
Like the Companion
Of the Fish—when he
Cried out in agony.

۴۸- فَاصْبِرْ لِحُكْمِ رَبِّكَ
وَلَا تَكُنْ كَصَاحِبِ الْحُوْتِ ۘ
اِذْ نَادٰى وَهُوَ مَكْظُوْمٌ ؕ

49. Had not Grace
From His Lord

۴۹- لَوْلَا اَنْ تَدَارَكَهُ

Reached him, he
Would indeed have been
Cast off on the naked
Shore, in disgrace.

نِعْمَةٌ مِّنْ رَّبِّهِ
لَنُبِذَ بِالْعَرَآءِ وَهُوَ مَذْمُومٌ ۝

50. Thus did his Lord
Choose him and make him
Of the company
Of the Righteous.

٥٠- فَاجْتَبٰهُ رَبُّهُ
فَجَعَلَهُ مِنَ الصّٰلِحِينَ ۝

51. And the Unbelievers
Would almost trip thee up
With their eyes when they
Hear the Message; and they
Say: "Surely he is possessed!"

٥١- وَإِنْ يَّكَادُ الَّذِينَ كَفَرُوا لَيُزْلِقُوْنَكَ
بِأَبْصَارِهِمْ لَمَّا سَمِعُوا الذِّكْرَ
وَيَقُولُونَ إِنَّهُ لَمَجْنُونٌ ۝

52. But it is nothing less
Than a Message
To all the worlds.

٥٢- وَمَا هُوَ إِلَّا ذِكْرٌ لِّلْعٰلَمِينَ ۝

INTRODUCTION TO SURA LXIX. (*Ḥāqqa*) — 52 Verses

This Sūra belongs to the early middle period of Meccan Revelation. The eschatological argument is pressed home: 'the absolute Truth cannot fail; it must prevail: therefore be not lured by false appearances in this life: it is Revelation that points to the sure and certain Reality.

Al Ḥāqqah (The Sure Reality) *

In the Name of Allah, Most Gracious
Most Merciful.

1. The Sure Reality!

2. What is the Sure Reality?

3. And what will make
   Thee realise what
   The Sure Reality is?

4. The Thamūd
   And the 'Ad people
   (Branded) as false
   The Stunning Calamity!

5. But the Thamūd—
   They were destroyed
   By a terrible Storm
   Of thunder and lightning!

6. And the 'Ad—
   They were destroyed
   By a furious Wind,
   Exceedingly violent;

7. He made it rage
   Against them seven nights
   And eight days in succession:
   So that thou couldst see
   The (whole) people lying
   Prostrate in its (path),
   As if they had been
   Roots of hollow palm trees
   Tumbled down!

8. Then seest thou any

Of them left surviving? مِنْ بَاقِيَةٍ ۝

9. And Pharaoh,
And those before him,
And the Cities Overthrown,
Committed habitual Sin,

٩- وَجَآءَ فِرْعَوْنُ وَمَنْ قَبْلَهُ وَالْمُؤْتَفِكَاتُ بِالْخَاطِئَةِ ۝

10. And disobeyed (each)
The messenger of their Lord;
So He punished them
With an abundant Penalty.

١٠- فَعَصَوْا رَسُوْلَ رَبِّهِمْ فَأَخَذَهُمْ أَخْذَةً رَّابِيَةً ۝

11. We, when the water
(Of Noah's Flood) overflowed
Beyond its limits,
Carried you (mankind),
In the floating (Ark),

١١- إِنَّا لَمَّا طَغَا الْمَآءُ حَمَلْنَاكُمْ فِي الْجَارِيَةِ ۝

12. That We might
Make it a Message
Unto you, and that ears
(That should hear the tale
And) retain its memory
Should bear its (lessons)
In remembrance.

١٢- لِنَجْعَلَهَا لَكُمْ تَذْكِرَةً وَّتَعِيَهَا أُذُنٌ وَّاعِيَةٌ ۝

13. Then, when one
Blast is sounded
On the Trumpet,

١٣- فَإِذَا نُفِخَ فِي الصُّوْرِ نَفْخَةٌ وَّاحِدَةٌ ۝

14. And the earth is moved,
And its mountains,
And they are crushed to powder
At one stroke—

١٤- وَحُمِلَتِ الْأَرْضُ وَالْجِبَالُ فَدُكَّتَا دَكَّةً وَّاحِدَةً ۝

15. On that Day
Shall the (Great) Event
Come to pass,

١٥- فَيَوْمَئِذٍ وَّقَعَتِ الْوَاقِعَةُ ۝

16. And the sky will be
Rent asunder, for it will
That Day be flimsy,

١٦- وَانْشَقَّتِ السَّمَآءُ فَهِيَ يَوْمَئِذٍ وَّاهِيَةٌ ۝

17. And the angels will be
On its sides,
And eight will, that Day,
Bear the Throne

١٧- وَالْمَلَكُ عَلَى أَرْجَائِهَا وَيَحْمِلُ عَرْشَ رَبِّكَ فَوْقَهُمْ يَوْمَئِذٍ

Of thy Lord above them.

18. That Day shall ye be
Brought to Judgement:
Not an act of yours
That ye hide will be hidden.

19. Then he that will be
Given his Record
In his right hand
Will say: "Ah here!
Read ye my Record!

20. "I did really understand
That my Account would
(One Day) reach me!"

21. And he will be
In a life of Bliss,

22. In a Garden on high,

23. The Fruits whereof
(Will hang in bunches)
Low and near.

24. "Eat ye and drink ye,
With full satisfaction;
Because of the (good)
That ye sent before you,
In the days that are gone!"

25. And he that will
Be given his Record
In his left hand,
Will say: "Ah! would
That my record had not
Been given to me!

26. "And that I had never
Realised how
My account (stood)!

27. "Ah! would that (Death)
Had made an end of me!

28. "Of no profit to me
Has been my wealth!

١٨‏ ثَمَنِيَةٌ ۗ

يَوْمَئِذٍ تُعْرَضُونَ
لَا تَخْفَى مِنكُمْ خَافِيَةٌ ٥

١٩‏ فَأَمَّا مَنْ أُوتِىَ كِتَٰبَهُۥ بِيَمِينِهِۦ
فَيَقُولُ هَآؤُمُ ٱقْرَءُوا۟ كِتَٰبِيَهْ ۚ

٢٠‏ إِنِّى ظَنَنتُ أَنِّى مُلَٰقٍ حِسَابِيَهْ ۚ

٢١‏ فَهُوَ فِى عِيشَةٍ رَّاضِيَةٍ ۚ

٢٢‏ فِى جَنَّةٍ عَالِيَةٍ ۚ

٢٣‏ قُطُوفُهَا دَانِيَةٌ ٥

٢٤‏ كُلُوا۟ وَٱشْرَبُوا۟ هَنِيٓـًٔۢا
بِمَآ أَسْلَفْتُمْ فِى ٱلْأَيَّامِ ٱلْخَالِيَةِ٥

٢٥‏ وَأَمَّا مَنْ أُوتِىَ كِتَٰبَهُۥ بِشِمَالِهِۦ
فَيَقُولُ يَٰلَيْتَنِى
لَمْ أُوتَ كِتَٰبِيَهْ ۚ

٢٦‏ وَلَمْ أَدْرِ مَا حِسَابِيَهْ ۚ

٢٧‏ يَٰلَيْتَهَا كَانَتِ ٱلْقَاضِيَةَ ۚ

٢٨‏ مَآ أَغْنَىٰ عَنِّى مَالِيَهْ ۚ

29. "My power has
Perished from me!". ...

٢٩- هَلَكَ عَنِّى سُلْطَانِيَهْ ۚ

30. (The stern command will say):
"Seize ye him,
And bind ye him,

٣٠- خُذُوهُ فَغُلُّوهُ ۚ

31. "And burn ye him
In the Blazing Fire.

٣١- ثُمَّ الْجَحِيمَ صَلُّوهُ ۚ

32. "Further, make him march
In a chain, whereof
The length is seventy cubits!

٣٢- ثُمَّ فِى سِلْسِلَةٍ
ذَرْعُهَا سَبْعُونَ ذِرَاعًا فَاسْلُكُوهُ ۚ

33. "This was he that
Would not believe
In Allah Most High,

٣٣- إِنَّهُ كَانَ لَا يُؤْمِنُ
بِاللّٰهِ الْعَظِيمِ ۙ

34. "And would not encourage
The feeding of the indigent!

٣٤- وَلَا يَحُضُّ عَلَى طَعَامِ الْمِسْكِينِ ۚ

35. "So no friend hath he
Here this Day.

٣٥- فَلَيْسَ لَهُ الْيَوْمَ هٰهُنَا حَمِيمٌ ۙ

36. "Nor hath he any food
Except the corruption
From the washing of wounds,

٣٦- وَلَا طَعَامٌ
إِلَّا مِنْ غِسْلِينٍ ۙ

37. "Which none do eat
But those in sin."

SECTION 2.

٣٧- لَا يَأْكُلُهُ إِلَّا الْخَاطِئُونَ ۚ ۧ

38. So I do
Call to witness
What ye see

٣٨- فَلَا أُقْسِمُ بِمَا تُبْصِرُونَ ۙ

39. And what ye see not,

٣٩- وَمَا لَا تُبْصِرُونَ ۙ

40. That this is
Verily the word
Of an honoured messenger;

٤٠- إِنَّهُ لَقَوْلُ رَسُولٍ كَرِيمٍ ۙ

41. It is not the word
Of a poet:
Little it is
Ye believe!

٤١- وَمَا هُوَ بِقَوْلِ شَاعِرٍ ۚ
قَلِيلًا مَّا تُؤْمِنُونَ ۙ

42. Nor is it the word
Of a soothsayer:

٤٢- وَلَا بِقَوْلِ كَاهِنٍ ۚ

Little admonition it is
Ye receive.

قَلِيْلًا مَّا تَذَكَّرُوْنَ ۞

43. (This is) a Message
Sent down from the Lord
Of the Worlds.

۴۳- تَنْزِيْلٌ مِّنْ رَّبِّ الْعٰلَمِيْنَ ۞

44. And if the messenger
Were to invent
Any sayings in Our name,

۴۴- وَلَوْ تَقَوَّلَ عَلَيْنَا بَعْضَ الْأَقَاوِيْلِ ۞

45. We should certainly seize him
By his right hand,

۴۵- لَأَخَذْنَا مِنْهُ بِالْيَمِيْنِ ۞

46. And We should certainly
Then cut off the artery
Of his heart:

۴۶- ثُمَّ لَقَطَعْنَا مِنْهُ الْوَتِيْنَ ۞

47. Nor could any of you
Withhold him
(From Our wrath).

۴۷- فَمَا مِنْكُمْ مِّنْ أَحَدٍ عَنْهُ حٰجِزِيْنَ ۞

48. But verily this
Is a Message for
The God-fearing.

۴۸- وَإِنَّهُ لَتَذْكِرَةٌ لِّلْمُتَّقِيْنَ ۞

49. And We certainly know
That there are amongst you
Those that reject (it).

۴۹- وَإِنَّا لَنَعْلَمُ أَنَّ مِنْكُمْ مُّكَذِّبِيْنَ ۞

50. But truly (Revelation)
Is a cause of sorrow
For the Unbelievers.

۵۰- وَإِنَّهُ لَحَسْرَةٌ عَلَى الْكٰفِرِيْنَ ۞

51. But verily it is Truth
Of assured certainty.

۵۱- وَإِنَّهُ لَحَقُّ الْيَقِيْنِ ۞

52. So glorify the name
Of thy Lord Most High.

۵۲- فَسَبِّحْ بِاسْمِ رَبِّكَ الْعَظِيْمِ ۞

INTRODUCTION AND SUMMARY: LXX. (*Ma'arij*) — 44 Verses

This is another eschatological Sūra closely connected in subject-matter with the last one. Patience and the mystery of Time will show the ways that climb to Heaven. Sin and Goodness must each eventually come to its own.

Chronologically it belongs to the late early or early middle Meccan period, possibly soon after S.lxix.

Al Ma'arij (The Ways of Ascent)

In the name of Allah, Most Gracious,
Most Merciful.

بِسْمِ اللهِ الرَّحْمٰنِ الرَّحِيْمِ

1. A questioner asked
About a Penalty
To befall—

١-سَاَلَ سَآئِلٌ بِعَذَابٍ وَّاقِعٍ ۙ

2. The Unbelievers,
The which there is none
To ward off—

٢-لِّلْكٰفِرِيْنَ لَيْسَ لَهٗ دَافِعٌ ۙ

3. (A Penalty) from Allah,
Lord of the Ways
Of Ascent.

٣-مِّنَ اللهِ ذِى الْمَعَارِجِ ؕ

4. The angels and
The Spirit   ascend
Unto Him in a Day
The measure whereof
Is (as) fifty thousand years:

٤-تَعْرُجُ الْمَلٰٓئِكَةُ وَالرُّوْحُ اِلَيْهِ فِىْ يَوْمٍ كَانَ مِقْدَارُهٗ خَمْسِيْنَ اَلْفَ سَنَةٍ ۚ

5. Therefore do thou hold
Patience—a Patience
Of beautiful (contentment).

٥-فَاصْبِرْ صَبْرًا جَمِيْلًا ۟

6. They see the (Day) indeed
As a far-off (event):

٦-اِنَّهُمْ يَرَوْنَهٗ بَعِيْدًا ۙ

7. But We see it
(Quite) near.

٧-وَّنَرٰىهُ قَرِيْبًا ۟

8. The Day that
The sky will be like
Molten brass,

٨-يَوْمَ تَكُوْنُ السَّمَآءُ كَالْمُهْلِ ۙ

9. And the mountians will be
Like wool,

٩- وَتَكُوْنُ الْجِبَالُ كَالْعِهْنِ ۝

10. And no friend will ask
After a friend,

١٠- وَلَا يَسْئَلُ حَمِيْمٌ حَمِيْمًا ۚ۞

11. Though they will be put
In sight of each other—
The sinner's desire will be:
Would that he could
Redeem himself from
The Penalty of that Day
By (sacrificing) his children,

١١- يُبَصَّرُوْنَهُمْ ۚ
يَوَدُّ الْمُجْرِمُ لَوْ
يَفْتَدِيْ مِنْ عَذَابِ يَوْمِئِذٍ بِبَنِيْهِ ۝

12. His wife and his brother,

١٢- وَصَاحِبَتِهٖ وَاَخِيْهِ ۝

13. His kindred who sheltered him.

١٣- وَفَصِيْلَتِهِ الَّتِيْ تُؤْوِيْهِ ۝

14. And all, all that is
On earth—so it could
Deliver him:

١٤- وَمَنْ فِى الْاَرْضِ جَمِيْعًا ۙ
ثُمَّ يُنْجِيْهِ ۝

15. By no means!
For it would be
The Fire of Hell!—

١٥- كَلَّا ۚ اِنَّهَا لَظٰى ۝

16. Plucking out (his being)
Right to the skull!—

١٦- نَزَّاعَةً لِّلشَّوٰى ۚ۞

17. Inviting (all) such
As turn their backs
And turn away their faces
(From the Right),

١٧- تَدْعُوْا مَنْ اَدْبَرَ
وَتَوَلّٰى ۝

18. And collect (wealth)
And hide it (from use)!

١٨- وَجَمَعَ فَاَوْعٰى ۝

19. Truly man was created
Very impatient—

١٩- اِنَّ الْاِنْسَانَ خُلِقَ هَلُوْعًا ۝

20. Fretful when evil
Touches him;

٢٠- اِذَا مَسَّهُ الشَّرُّ جَزُوْعًا ۝

21. And niggardly when
Good reaches him—

٢١- وَاِذَا مَسَّهُ الْخَيْرُ مَنُوْعًا ۝

22. Not so those devoted
    To Prayer—

٢٢- اِلَّا الْمُصَلِّيْنَ ۙ

23. Those who remain steadfast
    To their prayer;

٢٣- الَّذِيْنَ هُمْ عَلٰى صَلَاتِهِمْ دَآئِمُوْنَ ۙ

24. And those in whose wealth
    Is a recognised right

٢٤- وَالَّذِيْنَ فِيْٓ اَمْوَالِهِمْ حَقٌّ مَّعْلُوْمٌ ۙ

25. For the (needy) who asks
    And him who is prevented
    (For some reason from asking);

٢٥- لِلسَّآئِلِ وَالْمَحْرُوْمِ ۙ

26. And those who hold
    To the truth of the Day
    Of Judgement;

٢٦- وَالَّذِيْنَ يُصَدِّقُوْنَ بِيَوْمِ الدِّيْنِ ۙ

27. And those who fear
    The displeasure of their Lord—

٢٧- وَالَّذِيْنَ هُمْ مِّنْ عَذَابِ رَبِّهِمْ مُّشْفِقُوْنَ ۚ

28. For their Lord's displeasure
    Is the opposite of Peace
    And Tranquility—

٢٨- اِنَّ عَذَابَ رَبِّهِمْ غَيْرُ مَأْمُوْنٍ ۚ

29. And those who guard
    Their chastity,

٢٩- وَالَّذِيْنَ هُمْ لِفُرُوْجِهِمْ حٰفِظُوْنَ ۙ

30. Except with their wives
    And the (captives) whom
    Their right hands possess—
    For (then) they are not
    To be blamed,

٣٠- اِلَّا عَلٰٓى اَزْوَاجِهِمْ اَوْ مَا مَلَكَتْ
اَيْمَانُهُمْ
فَاِنَّهُمْ غَيْرُ مَلُوْمِيْنَ ۚ

31. But those who trespass
    Beyond this are transgressors—

٣١- فَمَنِ ابْتَغٰى وَرَآءَ ذٰلِكَ فَاُولٰٓئِكَ هُمُ الْعَادُوْنَ ۚ

32. And those who respect
    Their trusts and covenants;

٣٢- وَالَّذِيْنَ هُمْ لِاَمٰنٰتِهِمْ وَعَهْدِهِمْ رٰعُوْنَ ۙ

33. And those who stand firm
    In their testimonies;

٣٣- وَالَّذِيْنَ هُمْ بِشَهٰدٰتِهِمْ قَآئِمُوْنَ ۙ

34. And those who guard
    (The sacredness) of their
                    worship—

٣٤- وَالَّذِيْنَ هُمْ عَلٰى صَلَاتِهِمْ يُحَافِظُوْنَ ۚ

35. Such will be
The honoured ones
In the Gardens (of Bliss).

SECTION 2.

٣٥- أُولٰۤئِكَ فِيْ جَنّٰتٍ مُّكْرَمُوْنَ ۝ ع

36. Now what is
The matter with the Unbelievers
That they rush madly
Before thee—

٣٦- فَمَالِ الَّذِيْنَ كَفَرُوْا قِبَلَكَ مُهْطِعِيْنَ ۝

37. From the right
And from the left,
In crowds?

٣٧- عَنِ الْيَمِيْنِ وَعَنِ الشِّمَالِ عِزِيْنَ ۝

38. Does every man of them
Long to enter
The Garden of Bliss?

٣٨- أَيَطْمَعُ كُلُّ امْرِئٍ مِّنْهُمْ أَنْ يُّدْخَلَ جَنَّةَ نَعِيْمٍ ۝

39. By no means!
For We have created them
Out of the (base matter)
They know!

٣٩- كَلَّا ۗ إِنَّا خَلَقْنٰهُمْ مِّمَّا يَعْلَمُوْنَ ۝

40. Now I do
Call to witness
The Lord of all points
In the East and the West
That We can certainly—

٤٠- فَلَآ أُقْسِمُ بِرَبِّ الْمَشٰرِقِ وَالْمَغٰرِبِ إِنَّا لَقٰدِرُوْنَ ۝

41. Substitute for them
Better (men) than they;
And We are not
To be defeated
(In Our Plan).

٤١- عَلٰۤى أَنْ نُّبَدِّلَ خَيْرًا مِّنْهُمْ ۙ وَمَا نَحْنُ بِمَسْبُوْقِيْنَ ۝

42. So leave them
To plunge in vain talk
And play about,
Until they encounter
That Day of theirs which
They have been promised!—

٤٢- فَذَرْهُمْ يَخُوْضُوْا وَيَلْعَبُوْا حَتّٰى يُلٰقُوْا يَوْمَهُمُ الَّذِيْ يُوْعَدُوْنَ ۝

43. The Day whereon
They will issue
From their sepulchres
In sudden haste
As if they were

٤٣- يَوْمَ يَخْرُجُوْنَ مِنَ الْأَجْدَاثِ سِرَاعًا

Rushing to a goalpost
(Fixed for them)—

كَأَنَّهُمْ إِلَىٰ نُصُبٍ يُوفِضُونَ ۝

44. Their eyes lowered
In dejection—
Ignominy covering them
(All over)!
Such is the Day
The which they
Are promised!

٤٤ خَاشِعَةً أَبْصَارُهُمْ
تَرْهَقُهُمْ ذِلَّةٌ ۚ ذَٰلِكَ الْيَوْمُ الَّذِى
كَانُوا يُوعَدُونَ ۝

INTRODUCTION AND SUMMARY: LXXI. (*Nūḥ*) — 28 Verses

This is another early Meccan Sūra, of which the date has no significance. The theme is that while Good must uphold the standard of Truth and Righteousness, a stage is reached when it must definitely part company with Evil, lest Evil should spread its corruption abroad. This theme is embodied in the prayer of Noah just before the Flood. The story of Noah's agony is almost a Parable for the Holy Prophet's persecution in the Meccan period.

Nūḥ (Noah)

In the name of Allah, Most Gracious, Most Merciful.

بِسْمِ اللهِ الرَّحْمٰنِ الرَّحِيْمِ

1. We sent Noah
To his People
(With the Command):
"Do thou warn thy People
Before there comes to them
A grievous Penalty."

١- اِنَّآ اَرْسَلْنَا نُوْحًا اِلٰى قَوْمِهٖٓ
اَنْ اَنْذِرْ قَوْمَكَ مِنْ قَبْلِ
اَنْ يَّأْتِيَهُمْ عَذَابٌ اَلِيْمٌ ۞

2. He said: "O my People!
I am to you
A Warner, clear and open:

٢- قَالَ يٰقَوْمِ
اِنِّيْ لَكُمْ نَذِيْرٌ مُّبِيْنٌ ۞

3. "That ye should worship
Allah, fear Him,
and obey me:

٣- اَنِ اعْبُدُوا اللهَ
وَاتَّقُوْهُ وَاَطِيْعُوْنِ ۞

4. "So He may forgive you
Your sins and give you
Respite for a stated Term:
For when the Term given
By Allah is accomplished,
It cannot be put forward:
If ye only knew."

٤- يَغْفِرْ لَكُمْ مِّنْ ذُنُوْبِكُمْ
وَيُؤَخِّرْكُمْ اِلٰٓى اَجَلٍ مُّسَمًّى
اِنَّ اَجَلَ اللهِ اِذَا جَاءَ لَا يُؤَخَّرُ
لَوْ كُنْتُمْ تَعْلَمُوْنَ ۞

5. He said: "O my Lord!
I have called to my People
Night and day:

٥- قَالَ رَبِّ
اِنِّيْ دَعَوْتُ قَوْمِيْ لَيْلًا وَّنَهَارًا ۞

6. "But my call only

٦- فَلَمْ يَزِدْهُمْ

Increases (their) flight
(From the Right)."

دُعَآئِى إِلَّا فِرَارًا ۝

7. "And every time I have
Called to them, that Thou
Mightest forgive them,
They have (only) thrust
Their fingers into their ears,
Covered themselves up with
Their garments, grown obstinate,
And given themselves up
To arrogance.

٧- وَإِنِّى كُلَّمَا دَعَوْتُهُمْ لِتَغْفِرَ لَهُمْ
جَعَلُوا أَصَابِعَهُمْ فِى آذَانِهِمْ
وَاسْتَغْشَوْا ثِيَابَهُمْ وَأَصَرُّوا
وَاسْتَكْبَرُوا اسْتِكْبَارًا ۝

8. "So I have called to them
Aloud;"

٨- ثُمَّ إِنِّى دَعَوْتُهُمْ جِهَارًا ۝

9. "Further I have spoken
To them in public
And secretly in private,"

٩- ثُمَّ إِنِّى أَعْلَنْتُ لَهُمْ
وَأَسْرَرْتُ لَهُمْ إِسْرَارًا ۝

10. "Saying, 'Ask forgiveness
From your Lord;
For He is Oft-Forgiving;'"

١٠- فَقُلْتُ اسْتَغْفِرُوا رَبَّكُمْ
إِنَّهُ كَانَ غَفَّارًا ۝

11. "'He will send rain
To you in abundance;

١١- يُرْسِلِ السَّمَآءَ عَلَيْكُمْ مِّدْرَارًا ۝

12. "'Give you increase
In wealth and sons;
And bestow on you
Gardens and bestow on you
Rivers (of flowing water).

١٢- وَيُمْدِدْكُمْ بِأَمْوَالٍ وَبَنِينَ وَيَجْعَلْ لَّكُمْ
جَنَّاتٍ وَيَجْعَلْ لَّكُمْ أَنْهَارًا ۝

13. "'What is the matter
With you, that ye
Place not your hope
For kindness and long-suffering
In Allah—

١٣- مَا لَكُمْ
لَا تَرْجُونَ لِلَّهِ وَقَارًا ۝

14. "'Seeing that it is He
That has created you
In diverse stages?

١٤- وَقَدْ خَلَقَكُمْ أَطْوَارًا ۝

15. "'See ye not
How Allah has created
The seven heavens
One above another,

١٥- أَلَمْ تَرَوْا كَيْفَ خَلَقَ اللَّهُ
سَبْعَ سَمَوَاتٍ طِبَاقًا ۝

16. "'And made the moon
A light in their midst,
and made the sun
As a (Glorious) Lamp?

١٦- وَجَعَلَ الْقَمَرَ فِيهِنَّ نُوْرًا
وَجَعَلَ الشَّمْسَ سِرَاجًا ۟

17. "'And Allah has produced
You from the earth,
Growing (gradually),

١٧- وَاللّٰهُ اَنْبَتَكُمْ
مِنَ الْاَرْضِ نَبَاتًا ۟

18. "'And in the End
He will return you
Into the (earth),
And raise you forth
(Again at the Resurrection)?

١٨- ثُمَّ يُعِيْدُكُمْ فِيْهَا
وَيُخْرِجُكُمْ اِخْرَاجًا ۟

19. "'And Allah has made
The earth for you
As a carpet (spread out),

١٩- وَاللّٰهُ جَعَلَ لَكُمُ الْاَرْضَ بِسَاطًا ۟

20. "'That ye may go about
Therein, in spacious roads.'"

٢٠- لِتَسْلُكُوْا مِنْهَا سُبُلًا فِجَاجًا ۟ ع

SECTION 2.

21. Noah said: "O my Lord!
They have disobeyed me,
But they follow (men)
Whose wealth and children
Give them no Increase
But only Loss.

٢١- قَالَ نُوْحٌ رَّبِّ اِنَّهُمْ عَصَوْنِيْ
وَاتَّبَعُوْا مَنْ لَّمْ يَزِدْهُ مَالُهٗ وَوَلَدُهٗ
اِلَّا خَسَارًا ۟

22. "And they have devised
A tremendous Plot.

٢٢- وَمَكَرُوْا مَكْرًا كُبَّارًا ۟

23. "And they have said
(To each other),
'Abandon not your gods:
Abandon neither Wadd
Nor Suwā', neither
Yaghūth nor Ya'ūq,
Nor Nasr—

٢٣- وَقَالُوْا لَا تَذَرُنَّ اٰلِهَتَكُمْ
وَلَا تَذَرُنَّ وَدًّا وَّلَا سُوَاعًا ۟
وَّلَا يَغُوْثَ وَيَعُوْقَ وَنَسْرًا ۟

24. "They have already
Misled many, and
Grant Thou no increase
To the wrongdoers but in
Staying (from their mark)."

٢٤- وَقَدْ اَضَلُّوْا كَثِيْرًا ۟
وَلَا تَزِدِ الظّٰلِمِيْنَ اِلَّا ضَلٰلًا ۟

25. Because of their sins
They were drowned
(In the flood),
And were made to enter
The Fire (of Punishment);
And they found—
In lieu of Allah—
None to help them.

٢٥- مِمَّا خَطِيئَاتِهِمْ أُغْرِقُوا
فَأُدْخِلُوا نَارًا ۚ
فَلَمْ يَجِدُوا لَهُمْ
مِّن دُونِ اللَّهِ أَنصَارًا ۞

26. And Noah said:
"O my Lord! Leave not
Of the Unbelievers,
A single one on earth!

٢٦- وَقَالَ نُوحٌ رَّبِّ لَا تَذَرْ
عَلَى الْأَرْضِ مِنَ الْكَافِرِينَ دَيَّارًا ۞

27. "For, if Thou dost leave
(Any of) them, they will
But mislead Thy devotees,
And they will breed none
But wicked ungrateful ones.

٢٧- إِنَّكَ إِن تَذَرْهُمْ
يُضِلُّوا عِبَادَكَ
وَلَا يَلِدُوا إِلَّا فَاجِرًا كَفَّارًا ۞

28. "O my Lord! Forgive me,
My parents, all who
Enter my house in Faith,
And (all) believing men
And believing women:
And to the wrongdoers
Grant Thou no increase
But in Perdition!"

٢٨- رَبِّ اغْفِرْ لِي وَلِوَالِدَيَّ
وَلِمَن دَخَلَ بَيْتِيَ مُؤْمِنًا
وَلِلْمُؤْمِنِينَ وَالْمُؤْمِنَاتِ ۖ
وَلَا تَزِدِ الظَّالِمِينَ إِلَّا تَبَارًا ۞

INTRODUCTION AND SUMMARY: SŪRA LXXII. (*Jinn*) — 28 Verses

This is a late Meccan Sūra, of which we can be tolerably certain of the date. It was two years before Hijrat, when the Prophet, despised and rejected in his native city of Mecca, went to evangelise the lordly men of *Ṭā-if*. They maltreated him and nearly killed him; what caused him even greater pain was the maltreatment of the humble and lowly men who went with him. Ṭabarī has handed down that memorable Prayer of faith and humility which he offered in the midst of his suffering. On his return journey to Mecca, a glorious vision was revealed to him,— hidden spiritual forces working for him,—people not known to him accepting his mission while his own people were still rejecting him. Within two months some strangers from Medina had privately met him and laid the foundations of that Hijrat which was to change the fate of Arabia and the course of world history.

Al Jinn (The Spirits)

In the name of Allah, Most Gracious, Most Merciful.

بِسْمِ اللهِ الرَّحْمٰنِ الرَّحِيْمِ

1. Say: It has been
Revealed   to me that
A company of Jinns
Listened (to the Qur'ān).
They said, 'We have
Really heard a wonderful
Recital!

قُلْ اُوْحِيَ اِلَيَّ
اَنَّهُ اسْتَمَعَ نَفَرٌ مِّنَ الْجِنِّ
فَقَالُوْا اِنَّا سَمِعْنَا قُرْاٰنًا عَجَبًا ۙ

2. 'It gives guidance
To the Right,
And we have believed therein:
We shall not join (in worship)
Any (gods) with our Lord.

يَّهْدِيْ اِلَى الرُّشْدِ
فَاٰمَنَّا بِهٖ ۗ
وَلَنْ نُّشْرِكَ بِرَبِّنَا اَحَدًا ۙ

3. 'And exalted is the Majesty
Of our Lord: He has
Taken neither a wife
Nor a son.

وَّاَنَّهٗ تَعٰلٰى جَدُّ رَبِّنَا
مَا اتَّخَذَ صَاحِبَةً وَّلَا وَلَدًا ۙ

4. 'There were some foolish ones
Among us, who used
To utter extravagant lies
Against Allah;

وَّاَنَّهٗ كَانَ يَقُوْلُ سَفِيْهُنَا
عَلَى اللهِ شَطَطًا ۙ

5. 'But we do think
That no man or spirit
Should say aught that is

وَّاَنَّا ظَنَنَّا اَنْ لَّنْ تَقُوْلَ الْاِنْسُ وَالْجِنُّ

Untrue against Allah.

عَلَى اللهِ كَذِبًا ۟

6. 'True, there were persons
Among mankind who took shelter
With persons among the Jinns,
But they increased them
In folly.

٦- وَّ اَنَّهُ كَانَ رِجَالٌ مِّنَ الْاِنْسِ
يَعُوْذُوْنَ بِرِجَالٍ مِّنَ الْجِنِّ
فَزَادُوْهُمْ رَهَقًا ۟

7. 'And they (came to) think
As ye thought, that Allah
Would not raise up
Any one (to Judgement).

٧- وَّ اَنَّهُمْ ظَنُّوْا كَمَا ظَنَنْتُمْ
اَنْ لَّنْ يَّبْعَثَ اللهُ اَحَدًا ۟

8. 'And we pried into
the secrets of heaven;
But we found it filled
With stern guards
And flaming fires.

٨- وَّ اَنَّا لَمَسْنَا السَّمَآءَ
فَوَجَدْنٰهَا مُلِئَتْ حَرَسًا
شَدِيْدًا وَّ شُهُبًا ۟

9. 'We used, indeed, to sit there
In (hidden) stations, to (steal)
A hearing; but any
Who listens now
Will find a flaming fire
Watching him in ambush.

٩- وَّ اَنَّا كُنَّا نَقْعُدُ مِنْهَا مَقَاعِدَ لِلسَّمْعِ
فَمَنْ يَّسْتَمِعِ الْاٰنَ يَجِدْ لَهُ
شِهَابًا رَّصَدًا ۟

10. 'And we understand not
Whether ill is intended
To those on earth,
Or whether their Lord
(Really) intends to guide
Them to right conduct.

١٠- وَّ اَنَّا لَا نَدْرِيْ اَشَرٌّ
اُرِيْدَ بِمَنْ فِى الْاَرْضِ
اَمْ اَرَادَ بِهِمْ رَبُّهُمْ رَشَدًا ۟

11. 'There are among us
Some that are righteous,
And some the contrary:
We follow divergent paths.

١١- وَّ اَنَّا مِنَّا الصّٰلِحُوْنَ وَ مِنَّا دُوْنَ ذٰلِكَ
كُنَّا طَرَآئِقَ قِدَدًا ۟

12. 'But we think that we
Can by no means frustrate
Allah throughout the earth,
Nor can we frustrate Him
By flight.

١٢- وَّ اَنَّا ظَنَنَّا اَنْ لَّنْ نُّعْجِزَ اللهَ فِى الْاَرْضِ
وَ لَنْ نُّعْجِزَهٗ هَرَبًا ۟

13. 'And as for us,
Since we have listened

١٣- وَّ اَنَّا لَمَّا سَمِعْنَا الْهُدٰى

To the Guidance, we have
Accepted it: and any
Who believes in his Lord
Has no fear, either
Of a short (account)
Or of any injustice.

14. 'Amongst us are some
That submit their wills
(To Allah), and some
That swerve from justice.
Now those who submit
Their wills—they have
Sought out (the path)
Of right conduct:

15. 'But those who swerve—
They are (but) fuel
For Hell-fire'—

16. (And Allah's Message is):
"If they (the Pagans)
Had (only) remained
On the (right) Way,
We should certainly have
Bestowed on them Rain
In abundance.

17. "That We might try them
By that (means).
But if any turns away
From the remembrance
Of his Lord, He will
Cause him to undergo
A severe Penalty.

18. "And the places of worship
Are for Allah (alone).
So invoke not anyone
Along with Allah;

19. "Yet when the Devotee
Of Allah stands forth
To invoke Him, they   just
Make round him a dense crowd."

أمثالها ۚ

فَمَن يُؤْمِن بِرَبِّهِ

فَلَا يَخَافُ بَخْسًا وَلَا رَهَقًا ۟

١٤ - وَأَنَّا مِنَّا الْمُسْلِمُونَ

وَمِنَّا الْقَاسِطُونَ ۖ

فَمَنْ أَسْلَمَ فَأُولَٰئِكَ

تَحَرَّوْا رَشَدًا ۟

١٥ - وَأَمَّا الْقَاسِطُونَ فَكَانُوا لِجَهَنَّمَ

حَطَبًا ۟

١٦ - وَأَن لَّوِ اسْتَقَامُوا

عَلَى الطَّرِيقَةِ

لَأَسْقَيْنَاهُم مَّاءً غَدَقًا ۟

١٧ - لِّنَفْتِنَهُمْ فِيهِ ۚ

وَمَن يُعْرِضْ عَن ذِكْرِ رَبِّهِ

يَسْلُكْهُ عَذَابًا صَعَدًا ۟

١٨ - وَأَنَّ الْمَسَاجِدَ لِلَّهِ

فَلَا تَدْعُوا مَعَ اللَّهِ أَحَدًا ۟

١٩ - وَأَنَّهُ لَمَّا قَامَ عَبْدُ اللَّهِ يَدْعُوهُ كَادُوا

يَكُونُونَ عَلَيْهِ لِبَدًا ۟ ع

SECTION 2.

20. Say: "I do
No more than invoke
My Lord, and I join not
With Him any (false god)."

٢٠- قُلْ إِنَّمَا أَدْعُوا
رَبِّيْ وَلَا أُشْرِكُ بِهِ أَحَدًا ۟

21. Say: "It is not
In my power to cause
You harm, or to bring
You to right conduct."

٢١- قُلْ إِنِّيْ لَا أَمْلِكُ
لَكُمْ ضَرًّا وَّلَا رَشَدًا ۟

22. Say: "No one can
Deliver me from Allah
(If I were to disobey Him),
Nor should I find refuge
Except in Him.

٢٢- قُلْ إِنِّيْ لَنْ يُّجِيْرَنِيْ مِنَ اللهِ أَحَدٌ ۙ
وَّلَنْ أَجِدَ مِنْ دُوْنِهِ مُلْتَحَدًا ۙ

23. "Unless I proclaim what
I receive from Allah
And His Messages:
For any that disobey Allah
And His Messenger—for them
Is Hell: they shall dwell
Therein forever."

٢٣- إِلَّا بَلٰغًا مِّنَ اللهِ وَرِسٰلٰتِهٖ ۗ
وَمَنْ يَّعْصِ اللهَ وَرَسُوْلَهٗ
فَإِنَّ لَهٗ نَارَ جَهَنَّمَ
خٰلِدِيْنَ فِيْهَا أَبَدًا ۟

24. At length, when they
See (with their own eyes)
That which they are
                        promised—
Then will they know
Who it is that is
Weakest in (his) helper
And least important
In point of numbers.

٢٤- حَتّٰى إِذَا رَأَوْا مَا يُوْعَدُوْنَ
فَسَيَعْلَمُوْنَ مَنْ أَضْعَفُ نَاصِرًا
وَّأَقَلُّ عَدَدًا ۟

25. Say: "I know not whether
The (Punishment) which ye
Are promised is near,
Or whether my Lord
Will appoint for it
A distant term.

٢٥- قُلْ إِنْ أَدْرِيْٓ
أَقَرِيْبٌ مَّا تُوْعَدُوْنَ
أَمْ يَجْعَلُ لَهٗ رَبِّيْٓ أَمَدًا ۟

26. "He (alone) knows the Unseen,
Nor does He make anyone
Acquainted with His
                        Mysteries—

٢٦- عٰلِمُ الْغَيْبِ
فَلَا يُظْهِرُ عَلٰى غَيْبِهٖٓ أَحَدًا ۙ

27. "Except a messenger

٢٧- إِلَّا مَنِ ارْتَضٰى مِنْ رَّسُوْلٍ

Whom He has chosen:
And then he makes
A band of watchers
March before him
And behind him,

28. "That he may know
That they have (truly)
Brought and delivered
The Messages of their Lord:
And He surrounds
(All the mysteries) that are
With them, and takes account
Of every single thing."

فَإِنَّهُ يَسْلُكُ
مِنْ بَيْنِ يَدَيْهِ وَمِنْ خَلْفِهِ رَصَدًا ۝

٢٨۔ لِيَعْلَمَ
أَنْ قَدْ أَبْلَغُوا رِسَالَاتِ رَبِّهِمْ
وَأَحَاطَ بِمَا لَدَيْهِمْ
وَأَحْصَى كُلَّ شَيْءٍ عَدَدًا ۝

INTRODUCTION AND SUMMARY: SŪRA LXXIII. (*Muzzammil*) — 20 Verses

This is one of the earliest Sūras to have been revealed. The first was S.xcvi. 1-5 (*Iqraa*), in the fortieth year of the Prophet's life, say about 12 years before the Hijra. Then there was an interruption (*Fatra*)' of which the duration cannot be exactly ascertained, as there was no external history connected with it. The usual estimate puts it at about six months, but it may have been a year or two years. The years were then counted by the luni-solar calender: see Appendix XI., p. 1077. The second Sūra in chronological order was probably a great portion of S.lxviii. (*Qalam*), which came after the *Fatra* was over. About the same time came this Sūra (say third) and S. lxxiv., which follows (say fourth), and the remainder of xcvi. We may roughly put the date of this Sūra at about 11 to 10 years before the' Hijra.

The subject-matter is the significance of Prayer and Humility in spiritual life and the terrible fate of those who reject Faith and Revelation.

Al Muzzammil (The Enfolded One)

In the name of Allah, Most Gracious, Most Merciful.

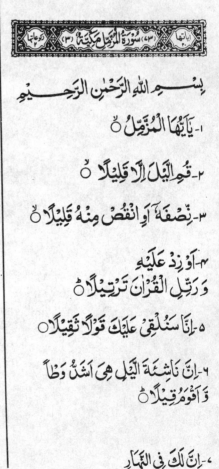

1. ⑩ thou folded
   In garments!

2. Stand (to prayer) by night,
   But not all night—

3. Half of it—
   Or a little less,

4. Or a little more;
   And recite the Qur'ān
   In slow, measured rhythmic tones

5. Soon shall We send down
   To thee a weighty Message.

6. Truly the rising by night
   Is most potent for governing
   (The soul), and most suitable
   For (framing) the Word
   (Of Prayer and Praise).

7. True, there is for thee
   By day prolonged occupation

With ordinary duties:

سَبْحًا طَوِيْلًا ۟

8. But keep in remembrance
The name of thy Lord
And devote thyself
To Him wholeheartedly.

٨- وَاذْكُرِ اسْمَ رَبِّكَ
وَتَبَتَّلْ اِلَيْهِ تَبْتِيْلًا ۟

9. (He is) Lord of the East
And the West: there is
No god but He:
Take Him therefore
For (thy) Disposer of Affairs.

٩- رَبُّ الْمَشْرِقِ وَالْمَغْرِبِ
لَآ اِلٰهَ اِلَّا هُوَ
فَاتَّخِذْهُ وَكِيْلًا ۟

10. And have patience with what
They say, and leave them
With noble (dignity).

١٠- وَاصْبِرْ عَلٰى مَا يَقُوْلُوْنَ
وَاهْجُرْهُمْ هَجْرًا جَمِيْلًا ۟

11. And leave Me
(Alone to deal with)
Those in possession of
The good things of life,
Who (yet) deny the Truth;
And bear with them
For a little while.

١١- وَذَرْنِيْ
وَالْمُكَذِّبِيْنَ اُولِي النَّعْمَةِ
وَمَهِّلْهُمْ قَلِيْلًا ۟

12. With Us are Fetters
(To bind them), and a Fire
(To burn them),

١٢- اِنَّ لَدَيْنَآ اَنْكَالًا وَّجَحِيْمًا ۟

19. And a Food that chokes,
And a Penalty Grievous,

١٣- وَّطَعَامًا ذَا غُصَّةٍ وَّعَذَابًا اَلِيْمًا ۟

14. One Day the earth
And the mountains
Will be in violent commotion,
And the mountains will be
As a heap of sand
Poured out and flowing down.

١٤- يَوْمَ تَرْجُفُ الْاَرْضُ وَالْجِبَالُ
وَكَانَتِ الْجِبَالُ
كَثِيْبًا مَّهِيْلًا ۟

15. We have sent to you,
(O men!) a messenger,
To be a witness concerning you,
Even as We sent
A messenger to Pharaoh.

١٥- اِنَّآ اَرْسَلْنَآ اِلَيْكُمْ رَسُوْلًا ۙ ة
شَاهِدًا عَلَيْكُمْ
كَمَآ اَرْسَلْنَآ اِلٰى فِرْعَوْنَ رَسُوْلًا ۟

16. But Pharaoh disobeyed
The messenger; so We
Seized him with
A heavy Punishment.

١٦- فَعَصٰى فِرْعَوْنُ الرَّسُوْلَ
فَاَخَذْنٰهُ اَخْذًا وَّبِيْلًا ۟

17: Then how shall ye,
If ye deny (Allah)
Guard yourselves against
A Day that will make
Children hoary-headed?—

١٧- فَكَيْفَ تَتَّقُوْنَ اِنْ كَفَرْتُمْ
يَوْمًا يَّجْعَلُ الْوِلْدَانَ شِيْبًا ۨ

18. Whereon the sky will be
Cleft asunder?
His Promise needs must
Be accomplished.

١٨- السَّمَاءُ مُنْفَطِرٌ بِهٖ
كَانَ وَعْدُهُ مَفْعُوْلًا ۟

19. Verily this is an Admonition;
Therefore, whoso will, let him
Take a (straight) path
To his Lord!

١٩- اِنَّ هٰذِهٖ تَذْكِرَةٌ
فَمَنْ شَاءَ اتَّخَذَ اِلٰى رَبِّهٖ سَبِيْلًا ۟ ۙ

SECTION 2.

20. Thy Lord doth know
That thou standest forth
(To prayer) nigh two-thirds
Of the night, or half
The night, or a third
Of the night, and so doth
A party of those with thee.
But Allah doth appoint Night
And Day in due measure.
He knoweth that ye are
Unable to keep count therof.
So He hath turned to you
(In mercy): read ye,
Therefore, of the Qur'ān
As much as may be
Easy for you. He knoweth
That there may be (some)
Among you in ill-health;
Others travelling through the land,
Seeking of Allah's bounty;
Yet others fighting
In Allah's Cause. Read ye,
Therefore, as much of the Qur'ān
As may be easy (for you);
And establish regular Prayer
And give regular Charity;

٢٠- اِنَّ رَبَّكَ يَعْلَمُ اَنَّكَ تَقُوْمُ اَدْنٰى
مِنْ ثُلُثَيِ الَّيْلِ وَنِصْفَهٗ
وَثُلُثَهٗ وَطَائِفَةٌ مِّنَ الَّذِيْنَ مَعَكَ
وَاللّٰهُ يُقَدِّرُ الَّيْلَ وَالنَّهَارَ
عَلِمَ اَنْ لَّنْ تُحْصُوْهُ
فَتَابَ عَلَيْكُمْ
فَاقْرَءُوْا مَا تَيَسَّرَ مِنَ الْقُرْاٰنِ
عَلِمَ اَنْ سَيَكُوْنُ مِنْكُمْ مَّرْضٰى
وَاٰخَرُوْنَ يَضْرِبُوْنَ فِى الْاَرْضِ
يَبْتَغُوْنَ مِنْ فَضْلِ اللّٰهِ
وَاٰخَرُوْنَ يُقَاتِلُوْنَ فِىْ سَبِيْلِ اللّٰهِ
فَاقْرَءُوْا مَا تَيَسَّرَ مِنْهُ
وَاَقِيْمُوا الصَّلٰوةَ وَاٰتُوا الزَّكٰوةَ

And loan to Allah
A Beautiful Loan.
And whatever good
Ye send forth
For your souls,
Ye shall find it
In Allah's Presence —
Yea, better and
Greater, in Reward,
And seek ye the Grace
Of Allah: for Allah is
Oft-Forgiving, Most Merciful.

وَأَقْرِضُوا اللّٰهَ قَرْضًا حَسَنًا ۚ

وَمَا تُقَدِّمُوا لِأَنْفُسِكُمْ مِّنْ خَيْرٍ

تَجِدُوْهُ عِنْدَ اللّٰهِ

هُوَ خَيْرًا وَّأَعْظَمَ أَجْرًا ۚ

وَاسْتَغْفِرُوا اللّٰهَ ۚ

إِنَّ اللّٰهَ غَفُوْرٌ رَّحِيْمٌ ۞

INTRODUCTION AND SUMMARY: SURA LXXIV. (*Muddaththir*) — 56 Verses

This Sūra dates from about the same time as the last one. Its subject-matter is also similar: Prayer and Praise, and the need of patience in a period of great spiritual stress: the unjust who cause sorrow and suffering now will themselves experience agony in the Hereafter.

Al Muddaththir (The One Wrapped Up)

In the name of Allah, Most Gracious, Most Merciful.

بِسْمِ اللهِ الرَّحْمٰنِ الرَّحِيْمِ

1. O thou wrapped up
   (In a mantle)!

١- يَا أَيُّهَا الْمُدَّثِّرُ ۙ

2. Arise and deliver thy warning!

٢- قُمْ فَأَنْذِرْ ۙ

3. And thy Lord
   Do thou magnify!

٣- وَرَبَّكَ فَكَبِّرْ ۙ

4. And thy garments
   Keep free from stain!

٤- وَثِيَابَكَ فَطَهِّرْ ۙ

5. And all abomination shun!

٥- وَالرُّجْزَ فَاهْجُرْ ۙ

6. Nor expect, in giving,
   Any increase (for thyself)!

٦- وَلَا تَمْنُنْ تَسْتَكْثِرُ ۙ

7. But, for thy Lord's (Cause)
   Be patient and constant!

٧- وَلِرَبِّكَ فَاصْبِرْ ۙ

8. Finally, when the Trumpet
   Is sounded,

٨- فَإِذَا نُقِرَ فِى النَّاقُوْرِ ۙ

9. That will be—that Day—
   A Day of Distress—

٩- فَذٰلِكَ يَوْمَئِذٍ يَّوْمٌ عَسِيْرٌ ۙ

10. Far from easy
    For those without Faith.

١٠- عَلَى الْكٰفِرِيْنَ غَيْرُ يَسِيْرٍ ۟

11. Leave Me alone, (to deal)
    With the (creature) whom
    I created (bare and) alone!—

١١- ذَرْنِيْ وَمَنْ خَلَقْتُ وَحِيْدًا ۙ

12. To whom I granted
Resources in abundance,

١٢- وَّجَعَلْتُ لَهُ مَالًا مَّمْدُوْدًا ۙ

13. And sons to be
By his side!—

١٣- وَّبَنِيْنَ شُهُوْدًا ۙ

14. To whom I made
(Life) smooth and comfortable!

١٤- وَّمَهَّدْتُّ لَهُ تَمْهِيْدًا ۙ

15. Yet is he greedy—
That I should add
(Yet more)—

١٥- ثُمَّ يَطْمَعُ اَنْ اَزِيْدَ ۙ

16. By no means!
For to Our Signs
He has been refractory!

١٦- كَلَّا ۚ
اِنَّهُ كَانَ لِاٰيٰتِنَا عَنِيْدًا ۙ

17. Soon will I visit him
With a mount of calamities!

١٧- سَاُرْهِقُهُ صَعُوْدًا ۙ

18. For he thought
And he plotted—

١٨- اِنَّهُ فَكَّرَ وَقَدَّرَ ۙ

19. And woe to him!
How he plotted!—

١٩- فَقُتِلَ كَيْفَ قَدَّرَ ۙ

20. Yea, woe to him;
How he plotted!—

٢٠- ثُمَّ قُتِلَ كَيْفَ قَدَّرَ ۙ

21. Then he looked round;

٢١- ثُمَّ نَظَرَ ۙ

22. Then he frowned
And he scowled;

٢٢- ثُمَّ عَبَسَ وَبَسَرَ ۙ

23. Then he turned back
And was haughty;

٢٣- ثُمَّ اَدْبَرَ وَاسْتَكْبَرَ ۙ

24. Then said he:
"This is nothing but magic,
Derived from of old;"

٢٤- فَقَالَ
اِنْ هٰذَآ اِلَّا سِحْرٌ يُّؤْثَرُ ۙ

25. "This is nothing but
The word of a mortal!"

٢٥- اِنْ هٰذَآ اِلَّا قَوْلُ الْبَشَرِ ۙ

26. Soon will I
Cast him into Hell-Fire!

٢٦- سَاُصْلِيْهِ سَقَرَ ۙ

27. And what will explain
To thee what Hell-Fire is?

٢٧- وَمَآ أَدْرٰىكَ مَا سَقَرُ ۚ

28. Naught doth it permit
To endure, and naught
Doth it leave alone!—

٢٨- لَا تُبْقِىْ وَلَا تَذَرُ ۚ

29. Darkening and changing
The colour of man!

٢٩- لَوَّاحَةٌ لِّلْبَشَرِ ۚ

30. Over it are Nineteen.

٣٠- عَلَيْهَا تِسْعَةَ عَشَرَ ۚ

31. And We have set none
But angels as guardians
Of the Fire; and We
Have fixed their number
Only as a trial
For Unblievers—in order
That the People of the Book
May arrive at certainty,
And the Believers may increase
In Faith—and that no doubts
May be left for the People
Of the Book and the Believers,
And that those in whose hearts
Is a disease and the Unbelievers
May say, "What symbol
Doth Allah intend by this?"
Thus doth Allah leave to stray
Whom He pleaseth, and guide
Whom He pleaseth; and none
Can know the forces
Of thy Lord, except He.
And this is no other than
A warning to mankind.

٣١- وَمَا جَعَلْنَآ أَصْحٰبَ النَّارِ الَّا مَلٰٓئِكَةً ۖ وَّمَا جَعَلْنَا عِدَّتَهُمْ الَّا فِتْنَةً لِّلَّذِيْنَ كَفَرُوْا ۙ لِيَسْتَيْقِنَ الَّذِيْنَ أُوْتُوا الْكِتٰبَ وَيَزْدَادَ الَّذِيْنَ اٰمَنُوْا اِيْمَانًا ۙ وَّلَا يَرْتَابَ الَّذِيْنَ أُوْتُوا الْكِتٰبَ وَالْمُؤْمِنُوْنَ ۙ وَلِيَقُوْلَ الَّذِيْنَ فِىْ قُلُوْبِهِمْ مَّرَضٌ وَّالْكٰفِرُوْنَ مَاذَآ أَرَادَ اللهُ بِهٰذَا مَثَلًا ۚ كَذٰلِكَ يُضِلُّ اللهُ مَنْ يَّشَآءُ وَيَهْدِىْ مَنْ يَّشَآءُ ۚ وَمَا يَعْلَمُ جُنُوْدَ رَبِّكَ الَّا هُوَ ۚ وَمَا هِىَ الَّا ذِكْرٰى لِلْبَشَرِ ۚ ع

SECTION 2.

32. Nay, verily:
By the Moon,

٣٢- كَلَّا وَالْقَمَرِ ۚ

33. And by the Night
As it retreateth,

٣٣- وَالَّيْلِ اِذْ أَدْبَرَ ۚ

34. And by the Dawn
As it shineth forth—

٣٤- وَالصُّبْحِ اِذَآ أَسْفَرَ ۚ

35. This is but one
Of the mighty (Portents),

٣٥- اِنَّهَا لَاِحْدَى الْكُبَرِ ۚ

36. A warning to mankind—

٣٦- نَذِيرًا لِّلْبَشَرِ ۝

37. To any of you that
Chooses to press forward,
Or to follow behind

٣٧- لِمَنْ شَآءَ مِنكُمْ أَن يَتَقَدَّمَ أَوْ يَتَأَخَّرَ ۝

38. Every soul will be (held)
In pledge for its deeds.

٣٨- كُلُّ نَفْسٍ بِمَا كَسَبَتْ رَهِينَةٌ ۝

39. Except the Companions
Of the Right Hand,

٣٩- إِلَّا أَصْحَبَ الْيَمِينِ ۛ

40. (They will be) in Gardens
(Of Delight); they will
Question each other,

٤٠- فِى جَنَّتٍ ۛ يَتَسَآءَلُونَ ۝

41. And (ask) of the Sinners:

٤١- عَنِ الْمُجْرِمِينَ ۝

42. "What led you
Into Hell-Fire?"

٤٢- مَا سَلَكَكُمْ فِى سَقَرَ ۝

43. They will say;
"We were not of those
Who prayed;"

٤٣- قَالُوا لَمْ نَكُ مِنَ الْمُصَلِّينَ ۝

44. "Nor were we of those
Who fed the indigent;"

٤٤- وَلَمْ نَكُ نُطْعِمُ الْمِسْكِينَ ۝

45. "But we used to talk
Vanities with vain talkers;"

٤٥- وَكُنَّا نَخُوضُ مَعَ الْخَآئِضِينَ ۝

46. "And we used to deny
The Day of Judgement,"

٤٦- وَكُنَّا نُكَذِّبُ بِيَوْمِ الدِّينِ ۝

47. "Until there came to us
(The Hour) that is certain."

٤٧- حَتَّى أَتَانَا الْيَقِينُ ۝

48. Then will no intercession
Of (any) intercessors
Profit them.

٤٨- فَمَا تَنفَعُهُمْ شَفَاعَةُ الشَّفِعِينَ ۝

49. Then what is
The matter with them

٤٩- فَمَا لَهُمْ عَنِ

That they turn away
From admonition?—

التَّذْكِرَةِ مُعْرِضِيْنَ ۟

50. As if they were
Affrighted asses,

٥٠- كَأَنَّهُمْ حُمُرٌ مُّسْتَنْفِرَةٌ ۟

51. Fleeing from a lion!

٥١- فَرَّتْ مِنْ قَسْوَرَةٍ ۖ

52. Forsooth, each one of them
Wants to be given
Scrolls (of revelation) spread out!

٥٢- بَلْ يُرِيْدُ كُلُّ امْرِئٍ مِّنْهُمْ
اَنْ يُّؤْتَى صُحُفًا مُّنَشَّرَةً ۟

53. By no means! But
They fear not the Hereafter.

٥٣- كَلَّا ۖ بَلْ لَّا يَخَافُوْنَ الْاٰخِرَةَ ۟

54. Nay, this surely
Is an admonition:

٥٤- كَلَّا اِنَّهُ تَذْكِرَةٌ ۚ

55. Let any who will,
Keep it in remembrance!

٥٥- فَمَنْ شَآءَ ذَكَرَهُ ۟

56. But none will keep it
In rememberance except
As Allah wills: He
Is the Lord of Righteousness,
And the Lord of Forgiveness.

٥٦- وَمَا يَذْكُرُوْنَ اِلَّا اَنْ يَّشَآءَ اللّٰهُ ۖ
هُوَ اَهْلُ التَّقْوٰى
وَاَهْلُ الْمَغْفِرَةِ ۟

INTRODUCTION AND SUMMARY: SURA LXXV. (*Qiyāmat*) — 40 Verses

This Sūra belongs to the early Meccan period, but comes chronologically a good deal later than the last two Sūras.

Its subject-matter is the Resurrection, viewed from the point of view of Man, especially unregenerate Man as he is now, and as he will be then,—his inner and psychological history.

Al Qiyāmah (The Resurrection)

*In the name of Allah, Most Gracious,
Most Merciful.*

بِسْمِ اللهِ الرَّحْمٰنِ الرَّحِيْمِ

1. I do call to witness
   The Resurrection Day;

١- لَا أُقْسِمُ بِيَوْمِ الْقِيٰمَةِ ۞

2. And I do call to witness
   The self-reproaching spirit;
   (Eschew Evil).

٢- وَلَا أُقْسِمُ بِالنَّفْسِ اللَّوَّامَةِ ۞

3. Does man think that We
   Cannot assemble his bones?

٣- أَيَحْسَبُ الْإِنْسَانُ أَنْ لَنْ نَجْمَعَ عِظَامَهُ ۞

4. Nay, We are able to put
   Together in perfect order
   The very tips of his fingers.

٤- بَلٰى قٰدِرِيْنَ عَلٰى أَنْ نُّسَوِّيَ بَنَانَهُ ۞

5. But man wishes to do
   Wrong (even) in the time
   In front of him.

٥- بَلْ يُرِيْدُ الْإِنْسَانُ لِيَفْجُرَ أَمَامَهُ ۞

6. He questions: "When
   Is the Day of Resurrection?"

٦- يَسْئَلُ أَيَّانَ يَوْمُ الْقِيٰمَةِ ۞

7. At length, when
   The Sight is dazed,

٧- فَإِذَا بَرِقَ الْبَصَرُ ۞

8. And the moon is
   Buried in darkness.

٨- وَخَسَفَ الْقَمَرُ ۞

9. And the sun and moon
   Are joined together—

٩- وَجُمِعَ الشَّمْسُ وَالْقَمَرُ ۞

10. That Day will Man say;
    "Where is the refuge?"

١٠- يَقُوْلُ الْإِنْسَانُ يَوْمَئِذٍ أَيْنَ الْمَفَرُّ ۞

11. By no means!
No place of safety!

١١- كَلَّا لَا وَزَرَ

12. Before thy Lord (alone),
That Day will be
The place of rest.

١٢- إِلَى رَبِّكَ يَوْمَئِذٍ الْمُسْتَقَرُّ

13. That Day will Man
Be told (all) that he
Put forward, and all
That he put back.

١٣- يُنَبَّؤُا الْإِنْسَانُ يَوْمَئِذٍ بِمَا قَدَّمَ وَأَخَّرَ

14. Nay, man will be
Evidence against himself,

١٤- بَلِ الْإِنْسَانُ عَلَى نَفْسِهِ بَصِيرَةٌ

15. Even though he were
To put up his excuses.

١٥- وَلَوْ أَلْقَى مَعَاذِيرَهُ

16. Move not thy tongue
Concerning the (Qur'ān)
To make haste therewith.

١٦- لَا تُحَرِّكْ بِهِ لِسَانَكَ لِتَعْجَلَ بِهِ

17. It is for Us to collect it
And to promulgate it:

١٧- إِنَّ عَلَيْنَا جَمْعَهُ وَقُرْآنَهُ

18. But when We have
Promulgated it, follow thou
Its recital (as promulgated):

١٨- فَإِذَا قَرَأْنَاهُ فَاتَّبِعْ قُرْآنَهُ

19. Nay more, it is
For us to explain it
(And make it clear):

١٩- ثُمَّ إِنَّ عَلَيْنَا بَيَانَهُ

20. Nay, (ye men!)
But ye love
The fleeting life,

٢٠- كَلَّا بَلْ تُحِبُّونَ الْعَاجِلَةَ

21. And leave alone
The Hereafter.

٢١- وَتَذَرُونَ الْآخِرَةَ

22. Some faces, that Day,
Will beam (in brightness
And beauty)—

٢٢- وُجُوهٌ يَوْمَئِذٍ نَاضِرَةٌ

23. Looking towards their Lord;

٢٣- إِلَى رَبِّهَا نَاظِرَةٌ

24. And some faces, that Day,

٢٤- وَوُجُوهٌ يَوْمَئِذٍ

Will be sad and dismal,

بَاسِرَةٌ ۙ

25. In the thought that some
Backbreaking calamity was about
To be inflicted on them;

۲۵- تَظُنُّ اَنْ يُّفْعَلَ بِهَا فَاقِرَةٌ ؕ

26. Yea, when (the soul)
Reaches to the collarbone
(In its exit),

۲۶- كَلَّاۤ اِذَا بَلَغَتِ التَّرَاقِيَ ۙ

27. And there will be a cry,
"Who is a magician
(To restore him)?"

۲۷- وَقِيْلَ مَنْ ٚ رَاقٍ ۙ

28. And he will conclude
That it was (the Time)
Of Parting;

۲۸- وَّظَنَّ اَنَّهُ الْفِرَاقُ ۙ

29. And one leg will be
Joined with another:

۲۹- وَالْتَفَّتِ السَّاقُ بِالسَّاقِ ۙ

30. That Day the Drive
Will be (all) to thy Lord!

SECTION 2.

۳۰- اِلٰى رَبِّكَ يَوْمَئِذِ ٱلْمَسَاقُ ؕ ۚ

31. So he gave nothing
In charity, nor
Did he pray!—

۳۱- فَلَا صَدَّقَ وَلَا صَلّٰى ۙ

32. But on the contrary,
He rejected Truth
And turned away!

۳۲- وَلٰكِنْ كَذَّبَ وَتَوَلّٰى ۙ

33. Then did he stalk
To his family
In full conceit!

۳۳- ثُمَّ ذَهَبَ اِلٰۤى اَهْلِهٖ يَتَمَطّٰى ؕ

34. Woe to thee,
(O man!), yea, woe!

۳۴- اَوْلٰى لَكَ فَاَوْلٰى ۙ

35. Again, woe to thee,
(O man!), yea, woe!

۳۵- ثُمَّ اَوْلٰى لَكَ فَاَوْلٰى ؕ

36. Does Man think
That he will be left
Uncontrolled, (without
purpose)?

۳۶- اَيَحْسَبُ الْاِنْسَانُ
اَنْ يُّتْرَكَ سُدًى ؕ

37. Was he not a drop

۳۷- اَلَمْ يَكُ نُطْفَةً

Of sperm emitted
(In lowly form)?

مِنْ مَّنِيٍّ يُّمْنٰى ۙ

38. Then did he become
A clinging clot;
Then did (Allah) make
And fashion (him)
In due proportion.

٣٨- ثُمَّ كَانَ عَلَقَةً
فَخَلَقَ فَسَوّٰى ۙ

39. And of him He made
Two sexes, male
And female.

٣٩- فَجَعَلَ مِنْهُ الزَّوْجَيْنِ
الذَّكَرَ وَالْاُنْثٰى ؕ

40. Has not He, (the same),
The power to give life
To the dead?

٤٠- اَلَيْسَ ذٰلِكَ بِقٰدِرٍ
عَلٰى اَنْ يُّحْيِۦَ الْمَوْتٰى ۩

INTRODUCTION AND SUMMARY: SURA LXXVI. (*Dahr*) — 31 Verses

The revelation of this Sūra was probably in the early Meccan period, with the possible exception of some verses, but its date has no significance.

Its theme is the contrast between the two classes of men, those who choose good and those who choose evil, with special reference to the former.

The title of the Sūra recalls a Pagan Arab idea, which personified Time as existing spontaneously from eternity to eternity and responsible for the misery or the happiness of mankind. In xlv. 24 we read: "They say... 'nothing but Time can destroy us'". This attitude is not course wrong. Time is a created thing: it has its mysteries, but it is no more eternal than matter. It is also relative to our conceptions and not absolute, as Einstein has proved. It is only God Who is Self-Subsisting, Eternal from the beginning and Eternal to the end, the absolute Existence and Reality. We must not transfer His attributes to any figments of our imagination.

This deification of Time (*Dahr*) as against a living personal God has given rise to the term *dahriya*, as applied to an atheist or a materialist.

The whole of the Sūra is full of the highest symbolism, as is generally the case with Meccan Sūras, and this should always be remembered in their interpretation.

Al Insān (Man), or *Al Dahr* (The Time)

In the name of Allah, Most Gracious,
Most Merciful.

1. Has there not been
   Over Man a long period
   Of Time,　when he was
   Nothing—(not even) mentioned?

2. Verily We created
   Man from a drop
   Of mingled sperm,
   In order to try him:
   So We gave him (the gifts),
   Of Hearing and Sight.

3. We showed him the Way:
   Whether he be grateful
   Or ungrateful (rests
   On his will).

4. For the Rejecters
   We have prepared

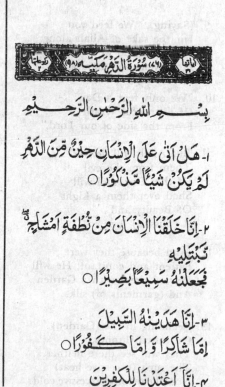

Chains, Yokes, and
A Blazing Fire.

سَلَاسِلَا وَاَغْلَالًا وَسَعِيْرًا ۝

5. As to the Righteous.
They shall drink
Of a Cup (of Wine)
Mixed with *Kāfūr*—

٥-اِنَّ الْاَبْرَارَ يَشْرَبُوْنَ

مِنْ كَاْسٍ كَانَ مِزَاجُهَا كَافُوْرًا ۝

6. A Fountain where
The Devotees of Allah
Do drink, making it
Flow in unstinted abundance.

٦-عَيْنًا يَّشْرَبُ بِهَا عِبَادُ اللهِ

يُفَجِّرُوْنَهَا تَفْجِيْرًا ۝

7. They   perform (their) vows,
And they fear a Day
Whose evil flies far and wide.

٧-يُوْفُوْنَ بِالنَّذْرِ

وَيَخَافُوْنَ يَوْمًا كَانَ شَرُّهُ مُسْتَطِيْرًا ۝

8. And they feed, for the love
Of Allah, the indigent,
The orphan, and the captive—

٨-وَيُطْعِمُوْنَ الطَّعَامَ عَلَى حُبِّهِ مِسْكِيْنًا

وَّيَتِيْمًا وَّاَسِيْرًا ۝

9. (Saying), "We feed you
For the sake of Allah alone:
No reward do we desire
From you, nor thanks."

٩-اِنَّمَا نُطْعِمُكُمْ لِوَجْهِ اللهِ

لَا نُرِيْدُ مِنْكُمْ جَزَآءً وَّلَا شُكُوْرًا ۝

10. "We only fear a Day
Of distressful Wrath
From the side of our Lord."

١٠-اِنَّا نَخَافُ مِنْ رَّبِّنَا

يَوْمًا عَبُوْسًا قَمْطَرِيْرًا ۝

11. But Allah will deliver
Them from the evil
Of that Day, and will
Shed over them a Light
Of Beauty and
A (blissful) Joy.

١١-فَوَقٰهُمُ اللهُ شَرَّ ذٰلِكَ الْيَوْمِ

وَلَقّٰهُمْ نَضْرَةً

وَّسُرُوْرًا ۝

12. And because they were
Patient and constant, He will
Reward them with a Garden
And (garments of) silk.

١٢-وَجَزٰهُمْ بِمَا صَبَرُوْا

جَنَّةً وَّحَرِيْرًا ۝

13. Reclining in the (Garden)
On raised thrones,
They will see there neither
The sun's (excessive heat)
Nor (the moon's) excessive cold.

١٣-مُّتَّكِئِيْنَ فِيْهَا عَلَى الْاَرَآئِكِ

لَا يَرَوْنَ فِيْهَا شَمْسًا

وَّلَا زَمْهَرِيْرًا ۝

14. And the shades of the (Garden)
Will come low over them,
And the bunches (of fruit),
There, will hang low
In humility.

١٤- وَدَانِيَةً عَلَيْهِمْ ظِلَالُهَا وَذُلِّلَتْ قُطُوفُهَا تَذْلِيلًا ۝

15. And amongst them will be
Passed round vessels of silver
And goblets of crystal—

١٥- وَيُطَافُ عَلَيْهِمْ بِآنِيَةٍ مِنْ فِضَّةٍ وَأَكْوَابٍ كَانَتْ قَوَارِيرَا۠ ۝

16. Crystal-clear, made of silver:
They will determine
The measure thereof
(According to their wishes).

١٦- قَوَارِيرَا۠ مِنْ فِضَّةٍ قَدَّرُوهَا تَقْدِيرًا ۝

17. And they will be given
To drink there of a Cup
(Of Wine) mixed
With *Zanjabīl*—

١٧- وَيُسْقَوْنَ فِيهَا كَأْسًا كَانَ مِزَاجُهَا زَنْجَبِيلًا ۝

18. A fountain there,
Called *Salsabīl*.

١٨- عَيْنًا فِيهَا تُسَمَّى سَلْسَبِيلًا ۝

19. And round about them
Will (serve) youths
Of perpetual (freshness):
If thou seest them,
Thou wouldst think them
Scattered Pearls.

١٩- وَيَطُوفُ عَلَيْهِمْ وِلْدَانٌ مُخَلَّدُونَ إِذَا رَأَيْتَهُمْ حَسِبْتَهُمْ لُؤْلُؤًا مَنْثُورًا ۝

20. And when thou lookest,
It is there thou wilt see
A Bliss and
A Realm Magnificent.

٢٠- وَإِذَا رَأَيْتَ ثَمَّ رَأَيْتَ نَعِيمًا وَمُلْكًا كَبِيرًا ۝

21. Upon them will be
Green Garments of fine silk
And heavy brocade,
And they will be adorned
With Bracelets of silver;
And their Lord will
Give to them to drink
Of a Wine
Pure and Holy.

٢١- عَلِيَهُمْ ثِيَابُ سُنْدُسٍ خُضْرٌ وَإِسْتَبْرَقٌ وَحُلُّوا أَسَاوِرَ مِنْ فِضَّةٍ وَسَقَاهُمْ رَبُّهُمْ شَرَابًا طَهُورًا ۝

22. "Verily this is a Reward

٢٢- إِنَّ هَذَا كَانَ لَكُمْ جَزَاءً

For you, and your Endeavour
Is accepted and recognised."

SECTION 2.

23. It is We Who
Have sent down the Qur'ān
To thee by stages.

24. Therefore be patient
With constancy to the Command
Of thy Lord, and hearken not
To the sinner or the ingrate
Among them.

25. And celebrate the name
Of thy Lord morning
And evening,

26. And part of the night,
Prostrate thyself to Him;
And glorify Him
A long night through.

27. As to these, they love
The fleeting life,
And put away behind them
A Day (that will be) hard.

28. It is We Who created
Them, and We have made
Their joints strong;
But, when We will,
We can substitute
The like of them
By a complete change.

29. This is an admonition;
Whosoever will, let him
Take a (straight) Path
To his Lord.

30. But ye will not,
Except as Allah wills:
For Allah is full of
Knowledge and Wisdom.

31. He will admit
To His Mercy Whom He will;

وَكَانَ سَعْيُكُمْ مَّشْكُوْرًا ۞

٢٣- اِنَّا نَحْنُ نَزَّلْنَا عَلَيْكَ الْقُرْاٰنَ
تَنْزِيْلًا ۞

٢٤- فَاصْبِرْ لِحُكْمِ رَبِّكَ
وَلَا تُطِعْ مِنْهُمْ
اٰثِمًا اَوْ كَفُوْرًا ۞

٢٥- وَاذْكُرِ اسْمَ رَبِّكَ بُكْرَةً وَّاَصِيْلًا ۞

٢٦- وَمِنَ الَّيْلِ فَاسْجُدْ لَهٗ
وَسَبِّحْهُ لَيْلًا طَوِيْلًا ۞

٢٧- اِنَّ هٰؤُلَاءِ يُحِبُّوْنَ الْعَاجِلَةَ
وَيَذَرُوْنَ وَرَآءَهُمْ يَوْمًا ثَقِيْلًا ۞

٢٨- نَحْنُ خَلَقْنٰهُمْ
وَشَدَدْنَا اَسْرَهُمْ
وَاِذَا شِئْنَا
بَدَّلْنَا اَمْثَالَهُمْ تَبْدِيْلًا ۞

٢٩- اِنَّ هٰذِهٖ تَذْكِرَةٌ
فَمَنْ شَاءَ اتَّخَذَ اِلٰى رَبِّهٖ سَبِيْلًا ۞

٣٠- وَمَا تَشَاءُوْنَ اِلَّا اَنْ يَّشَاءَ اللّٰهُ
اِنَّ اللّٰهَ كَانَ عَلِيْمًا حَكِيْمًا ۞

٣١- يُّدْخِلُ مَنْ

But the wrongdoers—
For them has He prepared
A grievous Penalty.

يَشَآءُ فِى رَحْمَتِهِ ۚ
وَالظّٰلِمِينَ أَعَدَّ لَهُمْ عَذَابًا أَلِيمًا ۝

INTRODUCTION AND SUMMARY: SŪRA LXXVII. (*Mursalāt*) — 50 Verses

This Sūra belongs to the early Meccan period, somewhere near to S.lxxv. (*Qiyāmat*). The theme is somewhat similar. It denounces the horrors of the Hereafter, for those who rejected Truth. The refrain. "Ah woe, that Day, to the Rejecters of Truth!" which occurs ten times in its fifty verses, or, on an average, once in every five verses, indicates the *leit-motif*.

Al Mursalāt (Those Sent Forth)

In the name of Allah, Most Gracious,
Most Merciful.

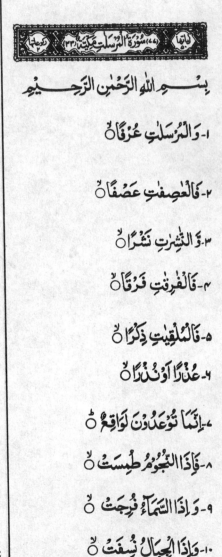

1. By the (Winds) Sent Forth
   One after another
   (To man's profit);

2. Which then blow violently
   In tempestuous Gusts,

3. And scatter (things)
   Far and wide;

4. Then separate them,
   One from another,

5. Then spread abroad
   A Message,

6. Whether of Justification
   Or of Warning—

7. Assuredly, what ye are
   Promised must come to pass.

8. Then when the stars
   Become dim;

9. When the heaven
   Is cleft asunder;

10. When the mountains are
    Scattered (to the winds) as dust;

11. And when the messengers
    Are (all) appointed a time
    (To collect)—

١١- وَ اِذَا الرُّسُلُ اُقِّتَتْ ۚ

12. For what Day are these
    (Portents) deferred?

١٢- لِاَىِّ يَوْمٍ اُجِّلَتْ ۚ

13. For the Day of Sorting out.

١٣- لِيَوْمِ الْفَصْلِ ۚ

14. And what will explain
    To thee what is
    The Day of Sorting out?

١٤- وَ مَآ اَدْرٰىكَ مَا يَوْمُ الْفَصْلِ ۚ

15. Ah woe, that Day,
    To the Rejecters of Truth!

١٥- وَيْلٌ يَّوْمَئِذٍ لِّلْمُكَذِّبِيْنَ ۟

16. Did We not destroy
    The men of old
    (For their evil)?

١٦- اَلَمْ نُهْلِكِ الْاَوَّلِيْنَ ۚ

17. So shall We make
    Later (generations)
    Follow them.

١٦- ثُمَّ نُتْبِعُهُمُ الْاٰخِرِيْنَ ۟

18. Thus do We deal
    With men of sin.

١٨- كَذٰلِكَ نَفْعَلُ بِالْمُجْرِمِيْنَ ۟

19. Ah woe, that Day,
    To the Rejecters of Truth!

١٩- وَيْلٌ يَّوْمَئِذٍ لِّلْمُكَذِّبِيْنَ ۟

20. Have We not created
    You from a fluid
    (Held) despicable?—

٢٠- اَلَمْ نَخْلُقْكُّمْ
مِّنْ مَّآءٍ مَّهِيْنٍ ۙ

21. The which We placed
    In a place of rest,
    Firmly fixed,

٢١- فَجَعَلْنٰهُ فِيْ قَرَارٍ مَّكِيْنٍ ۙ

22. For a period (of gestation),
    Determined (according to
    need)?

٢٢- اِلٰى قَدَرٍ مَّعْلُوْمٍ ۙ

23. For We do determine
    (According to need); for We
    Are the Best to determine (things).

٢٣- فَقَدَرْنَا ۖ فَنِعْمَ الْقٰدِرُوْنَ ۟

24. Ah woe, that Day!

٢٤- وَيْلٌ يَّوْمَئِذٍ

To the Rejecters of Truth!

للْمُكَذِّبِينَ ٥

25. Have We not made
The earth (as a place)
To draw together

٢٥-أَلَمْ نَجْعَلِ الْأَرْضَ كِفَاتًا ۟

26. The living and the dead,

٢٦-أَحْيَآءً وَّأَمْوَاتًا ۟

27. And made therein
Mountains standing firm,
Lofty (in stature);
And provided for you
Water sweet (and wholesome)?

٢٧-وَّجَعَلْنَا فِيهَا رَوَاسِيَ شٰمِخٰتٍ
وَّأَسْقَيْنٰكُمْ مَّآءً فُرَاتًا ۟

28. Ah woe, that Day,
To the Rejecters of Truth!

٢٨-وَيْلٌ يَّوْمَئِذٍ لِّلْمُكَذِّبِينَ ٥

29. (It will be said:)
"Depart ye to that
Which ye used to reject
As false!"

٢٩-إِنْطَلِقُوَا إِلٰى
مَا كُنْتُمْ بِهٖ تُكَذِّبُونَ ۟

30. "Depart ye to a Shadow
(Of smoke ascending)
In three columns,

٣٠-إِنْطَلِقُوَا إِلٰى ظِلٍّ ذِى ثَلٰثِ شُعَبٍ ۟

31. "(Which yields) no shade
Of coolness, and is
Of no use against
The fierce Blaze.

٣١-لَّا ظَلِيلٍ
وَّلَا يُغْنِى مِنَ اللَّهَبِ ۟

32. "Indeed it throws about
Sparks (huge) as Forts,

٣٢-إِنَّهَا تَرْمِى بِشَرَرٍ كَالْقَصْرِ ۟

33. "As if there were
(A string of) yellow camels
(Marching swiftly)."

٣٣-كَأَنَّهٗ جِمٰلَتٌ صُفْرٌ ۟

34. Ah woe, that Day,
To the Rejecters of Truth!

٣٤-وَيْلٌ يَّوْمَئِذٍ لِّلْمُكَذِّبِينَ ٥

35. That will be a Day
When they shall not
Be able to speak,

٣٥-هٰذَا يَوْمُ لَا يَنْطِقُونَ ۟

36. Nor will it be
Open to them

٣٦-وَلَا يُؤْذَنُ لَهُمْ

To put forth pleas.

فَيَعْتَذِرُوْنَ ۝

37. Ah woe, that Day,
To the Rejecters of Truth!

۳۷- وَيْلٌ يَّوْمَئِذٍ لِّلْمُكَذِّبِيْنَ ۝

38. That will be a Day
Of Sorting out! We shall
Gather you together
And those before (you)!

۳۸- هٰذَا يَوْمُ الْفَصْلِ ۚ
جَمَعْنٰكُمْ وَالْاَوَّلِيْنَ ۝

39. Now, if ye have
A trick (or plot),
Use it against Me!

۳۹- فَاِنْ كَانَ لَكُمْ كَيْدٌ فَكِيْدُوْنِ ۝

40. Ah woe, that Day,
To the Rejecters of Truth!
SECTION 2.

۴۰- وَيْلٌ يَّوْمَئِذٍ لِّلْمُكَذِّبِيْنَ ۝ ۵

41. As to the Righteous,
They shall be amidst
(Cool) shades and springs
(Of water).

۴۱- اِنَّ الْمُتَّقِيْنَ
فِيْ ظِلٰلٍ وَّعُيُوْنٍ ۝

42. And (they shall have)
Fruits—all they desire.

۴۲- وَّفَوَاكِهَ مِمَّا يَشْتَهُوْنَ ۝

43. Eat ye and drink ye
To your heart's content:
For that ye worked
(Righteousness).

۴۳- كُلُوْا وَاشْرَبُوْا هَنِيْٓئًا
بِمَا كُنْتُمْ تَعْمَلُوْنَ ۝

44. Thus do We certainly
Reward the Doers of Good.

۴۴- اِنَّا كَذٰلِكَ نَجْزِى الْمُحْسِنِيْنَ ۝

45. Ah woe, that Day,
To the Rejecters of Truth!

۴۵- وَيْلٌ يَّوْمَئِذٍ لِّلْمُكَذِّبِيْنَ ۝

46. (O ye Unjust!)
Eat ye and enjoy yourselves
(But) a little while,
For that ye are Sinners.

۴۶- كُلُوْا وَتَمَتَّعُوْا قَلِيْلًا
اِنَّكُمْ مُّجْرِمُوْنَ ۝

47. Ah woe, that Day,
To the Rejecters of Truth!

۴۷- وَيْلٌ يَّوْمَئِذٍ لِّلْمُكَذِّبِيْنَ ۝

48. And when it is said

۴۸- وَاِذَا قِيْلَ لَهُمُ

To them, "Prostrate yourselves!"
They do not so.

اركَعُوْا لَا يَرْكَعُوْنَ ٥

49. Ah woe, that Day,
To the Rejecters of Truth!

٤٩- وَيْلٌ يَّوْمَىِٕذٍ لِّلْمُكَذِّبِيْنَ ٥

50. Then what Message,
After that,
Will they believe in?

٥٠- فَبِاَيِّ حَدِيْثٍ بَعْدَهٗ
يُؤْمِنُوْنَ ۩

INTRODUCTION AND SUMMARY: SŪRA LXXVIII. (*Nabaa*) — 40 Verses

This beautiful Meccan Sūra is not quite so early as the last (S.lxxvii.) nor quite so late as S.lxxvi, but nearer in time to the latter.

Its sets forth God's loving care in the fine nature-passage, and deduces from it the Promise of the Future, when Evil will be destroyed and Good will come to its own; and invites all who have the will to seek refuge with their Lord.

Al Naba' (The Great News)

In the name of Allah, Most Gracious, Most Merciful.

1. Concerning what
   Are they disputing?

2. Concerning the Great News,

3. About which they
   Cannot agree.

4. Verily, they shall soon
   (Come to) know!

5. Verily, verily they shall
   Soon (come to) know!

6. Have We not made
   The earth as a wide
   Expanse,

7. And the mountains as pegs?

8. And (have We not) created
   you in pairs,

9. And made your sleep
   For rest,

10. And made the night
    As a covering,

11. And made the day
    As a means of subsistence?

12. And (have We not)

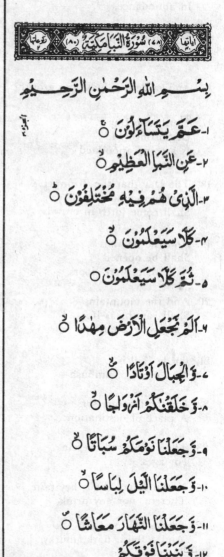

بِسْمِ اللهِ الرَّحْمٰنِ الرَّحِيْمِ

١- عَمَّ يَتَسَآءَلُوْنَ ۚ

٢- عَنِ النَّبَاِ الْعَظِيْمِ ۙ

٣- الَّذِيْ هُمْ فِيْهِ مُخْتَلِفُوْنَ ۗ

٤- كَلَّا سَيَعْلَمُوْنَ ۙ

٥- ثُمَّ كَلَّا سَيَعْلَمُوْنَ ۝

٦- اَلَمْ نَجْعَلِ الْاَرْضَ مِهٰدًا ۙ

٧- وَّالْجِبَالَ اَوْتَادًا ۙ

٨- وَّخَلَقْنٰكُمْ اَزْوَاجًا ۙ

٩- وَّجَعَلْنَا نَوْمَكُمْ سُبَاتًا ۙ

١٠- وَّجَعَلْنَا الَّيْلَ لِبَاسًا ۙ

١١- وَّجَعَلْنَا النَّهَارَ مَعَاشًا ۙ

١٢- وَّبَنَيْنَا فَوْقَكُمْ

Built over you
The seven firmaments,

سَبْعًا شِدَادًا ۞

13. And placed (therein)
A Light of Splendour?

١٣- وَجَعَلْنَا سِرَاجًا وَهَّاجًا ۞

14. And do We not send down
From the clouds water
In abundance,

١٤- وَّ أَنْزَلْنَا مِنَ الْمُعْصِرَاتِ مَاءً
ثَجَّاجًا ۞

15. That We may produce
Therewith corn and vegetables,

١٥- لِنُخْرِجَ بِهِ حَبًّا وَّنَبَاتًا ۞

16. And gardens of luxurious growth?

١٦- وَّجَنَّاتٍ أَلْفَافًا ۞

17. Verily the Day
Of Sorting Out
Is a thing appointed—

١٧- إِنَّ يَوْمَ الْفَصْلِ كَانَ مِيْقَاتًا ۞

18. The Day that the Trumpet
Shall be sounded, and ye
Shall come forth in crowds;

١٨- يَوْمَ يُنْفَخُ فِي الصُّوْرِ
فَتَأْتُوْنَ أَفْوَاجًا ۞

19. And the heavens
Shall be opened
As if there were doors,

١٩- وَّفُتِحَتِ السَّمَاءُ فَكَانَتْ أَبْوَابًا ۞

20. And the mountains
Shall vanish, as if
They were a mirage.

٢٠- وَّسُيِّرَتِ الْجِبَالُ فَكَانَتْ سَرَابًا ۞

21. Truly Hell is
As a place of ambush—

٢١- إِنَّ جَهَنَّمَ كَانَتْ مِرْصَادًا ۞

22. For the transgressors
A place of destination:

٢٢- لِّلطَّاغِيْنَ مَآبًا ۞

23. They will dwell therein
For ages.

٢٣- لّٰبِثِيْنَ فِيْهَا أَحْقَابًا ۞

24. Nothing cool shall they taste
Therein, nor any drink,

٢٤- لَا يَذُوْقُوْنَ فِيْهَا بَرْدًا وَّلَا شَرَابًا ۞

25. Save a boiling fluid
And a fluid, dark, murky,
Intensely cold—

٢٥- إِلَّا حَمِيْمًا وَّغَسَّاقًا ۞

26. A fitting recompense
(For them).

٢٦- جَزَآءً وِفَاقًا ۟

27. For that they used not
To fear any account
(For their deeds),

٢٧- إِنَّهُمْ كَانُوْا لَا يَرْجُوْنَ حِسَابًا ۟

28. But they (impudently) treated
Our Signs as false.

٢٨- وَكَذَّبُوْا بِاٰيٰتِنَا كِذَّابًا ۟

29. And all things have We
Preserved on record.

٢٩- وَكُلَّ شَيْءٍ أَحْصَيْنٰهُ كِتٰبًا ۟

30. "So taste ye (the fruits
Of your deeds);
For no increase
Shall We grant you,
Except in Punishment."

SECTION 2.

٣٠- فَذُوْقُوْا
فَلَنْ نَّزِيْدَكُمْ إِلَّا عَذَابًا ۟ ۚع

31. Verily for the Righteous
There will be
A fulfilment of
(The Heart's) desires;

٣١- إِنَّ لِلْمُتَّقِيْنَ
مَفَازًا ۟

32. Gardens enclosed, and
Grapevines;

٣٢- حَدَآئِقَ وَأَعْنَابًا ۟

33. Companions of Equal Age;

٣٣- وَّكَوَاعِبَ أَتْرَابًا ۟

34. And a Cup full
(To the Brim).

٣٤- وَّكَأْسًا دِهَاقًا ۟

35. No Vanity shall they hear
Therein, not Untruth—

٣٥- لَا يَسْمَعُوْنَ فِيْهَا لَغْوًا وَّلَا كِذَّابًا ۟

36. Recompense from thy Lord,
A Gift, (amply) sufficient —

٣٦- جَزَآءً مِّنْ رَّبِّكَ عَطَآءً حِسَابًا ۟

37. (From) the Lord
Of the heavens
And the earth,
And all between—
(Allah) Most Gracious:
None shall have power
To argue with Him.

٣٧- رَّبِّ السَّمٰوٰتِ وَالْأَرْضِ
وَمَا بَيْنَهُمَا الرَّحْمٰنِ
لَا يَمْلِكُوْنَ
مِنْهُ خِطَابًا ۟

38. The Day that
    The Spirit and the angels
    Will stand forth in ranks,
    None shall speak
    Except any who is
    Permitted by (Allah) Most
                    Gracious,
    And he will say
    What is right.

٣٨- يَوْمَ يَقُومُ الرُّوحُ وَالْمَلَائِكَةُ صَفًّا ۖ
لَا يَتَكَلَّمُونَ
إِلَّا مَنْ أَذِنَ لَهُ الرَّحْمَٰنُ
وَقَالَ صَوَابًا ۝

39. That Day will be
    The sure Reality:
    Therefore, whoso will, let him
    Take a (straight) Return
    To his Lord!

٣٩- ذَٰلِكَ الْيَوْمُ الْحَقُّ ۖ
فَمَن شَاءَ اتَّخَذَ إِلَىٰ رَبِّهِ مَآبًا ۝

40. Verily, We have warned you
    Of a Penalty near—
    The Day when man will
    See (the Deeds) which
    His hands have sent forth,
    And the Unbeliever will say,
    "Woe unto me! Would that
    I were (mere) dust!"

٤٠- إِنَّا أَنذَرْنَاكُمْ عَذَابًا قَرِيبًا ۚ
يَوْمَ يَنظُرُ الْمَرْءُ مَا قَدَّمَتْ يَدَاهُ
وَيَقُولُ الْكَافِرُ
يَا لَيْتَنِي كُنتُ تُرَابًا ۝

INTRODUCTION AND SUMMARY: SŪRA LXXIX. (*Nāzi'āt*) — 46 Verses

    This is also an early Meccan Sūra, of about the same date as the last, and deals with the mystic theme of Judgment from the point of view of Pride and its Fall. The parable of Pharaoh occupies a central place in the argument: for he said, "I am your Lord Most High." and perished with his followers.

Al Nāzi'āt (Those Who Tear Out)

In the name of Allah, Most Gracious, Most Merciful.

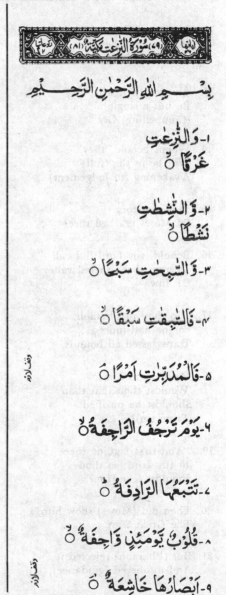

1. By the (angels)
Who tear out
(The souls of the wicked)
With violence;

2. By those who gently
Draw out (the souls
Of the blessed);

3. And by those who glide
Along (on errands of mercy),

4. Then press forward
As in a race,

5. Then arrange to do
(The Commands of their
Lord)—

6. One Day everything that
Can be in commotion will
Be in violent commotion,

7. Followed by oft-repeated
(Commotions):

8. Hearts that Day
Will be in agitation;

9. Cast down will be
(Their owners') eyes.

10. They say (now): "What!
Shall we indeed be
Returned to (our) former state?"—

١٠۔ يَقُوْلُوْنَ ءَاِنَّا
لَمَرْدُوْدُوْنَ فِي الْحَافِرَةِ ؕ

11. "What!—when we shall
Have become rotten bones?"

١١۔ءَاِذَا كُنَّا عِظَامًا نَّخِرَةً ؕ

12. They say: "It would,
In that case, be
A return with loss!"

١٢۔ قَالُوْا تِلْكَ اِذًا كَرَّةٌ خَاسِرَةٌ ۘ

13. But verily, it will
Be but a single
(Compelling) Cry,

١٣۔ فَاِنَّمَا هِيَ زَجْرَةٌ وَّاحِدَةٌ ۙ

14. When, behold, they
Will be in the (full)
Awakening (to Judgement)..

١٤۔ فَاِذَا هُمْ بِالسَّاهِرَةِ ؕ

15. Has the story
Of Moses reached thee?

١٥۔ هَلْ اَتٰىكَ حَدِيْثُ مُوْسٰى ۘ

16. Behold, thy Lord did call
To him in the sacred valley
Of Tuwā—

١٦۔اِذْ نَادٰىهُ
رَبُّهٗ بِالْوَادِ الْمُقَدَّسِ طُوًى ۚ

17. "Go thou to Pharaoh,
For he had indeed
Transgressed all bounds.

١٧۔اِذْهَبْ اِلٰى فِرْعَوْنَ
اِنَّهٗ طَغٰى ۖ

18. "And say to him,
'Wouldst thou that thou
Shouldst be purified
(From sin)?—

١٨۔ فَقُلْ هَلْ لَّكَ اِلٰى
اَنْ تَزَكّٰى ۙ

19. "'And that I guide thee
To thy Lord, so thou
Shouldst fear Him?'"

١٩۔ وَاَهْدِيَكَ اِلٰى رَبِّكَ
فَتَخْشٰى ۚ

20. Then did (Moses) show him
The Great Sign.

٢٠۔ فَاَرٰىهُ الْاٰيَةَ الْكُبْرٰى ۖ

21. But (Pharaoh) rejected it
And disobeyed (guidance);

٢١۔ فَكَذَّبَ وَعَصٰى ۖ

22. Further, he turned his back,
Striving hard (against Allah).

٢٢- ثُمَّ اَدْبَرَ يَسْعٰى ۚ

23. Then he collected (his men)
And made a proclamation,

٢٣- فَحَشَرَ فَنَادٰى ۚ

24. Saying, "I am your Lord,
Most High".

٢٤- فَقَالَ اَنَا رَبُّكُمُ الْاَعْلٰى ۗ

25. But Allah did punish him
(And made an) example
Of him—in the Hereafter,
As in this life.

٢٥- فَاَخَذَهُ اللّٰهُ نَكَالَ الْاٰخِرَةِ وَالْاُوْلٰى ۗ

26. Verily in this is
An instructive warning
For whosoever feareth (Allah):

SECTION 2.

٢٦- اِنَّ فِيْ ذٰلِكَ لَعِبْرَةً لِّمَنْ يَّخْشٰى ۚ

27. What! Are ye the more
Difficult to create
Of the heaven (above)?
(Allah) hath constructed it:

٢٧- ءَاَنْتُمْ اَشَدُّ خَلْقًا اَمِ السَّمَآءُ ۚ بَنٰهَا ۗ

28. On high hath He raised
Its canopy, and He hath
Given it order and perfection.

٢٨- رَفَعَ سَمْكَهَا فَسَوّٰىهَا ۗ

29. Its night doth He
Endow with darkness,
And its splendour doth He
Bring out (with light).

٢٩- وَاَغْطَشَ لَيْلَهَا وَاَخْرَجَ ضُحٰىهَا ۗ

30. And the earth, moreoever,
Hath He extended
(To a wide expanse);

٣٠- وَالْاَرْضَ بَعْدَ ذٰلِكَ دَحٰىهَا ۗ

31. He draweth out
Therefrom its moisture
And its pasture;

٣١- اَخْرَجَ مِنْهَا مَآءَهَا وَمَرْعٰهَا ۗ

32. And the mountians
Hath He firmly fixed—

٣٢- وَالْجِبَالَ اَرْسٰهَا ۗ

33. For use and convenience
To you and your cattle.

٣٣- مَتَاعًا لَّكُمْ وَلِاَنْعَامِكُمْ ۗ

34. Therefore, when there comes
The great, overwhelming
(Event)—

٣٤- فَاِذَا جَآءَتِ الطَّآمَّةُ الْكُبْرٰى ۖ

35. The Day when Man
Shall remember (all)
That he strove for,

٣٥- يَوْمَ يَتَذَكَّرُ الْاِنْسَانُ مَا سَعٰى ۙ

36. And Hell-Fire shall be
Placed in full view
For (all) to see—

٣٦- وَبُرِّزَتِ الْجَحِيْمُ
لِمَنْ يَّرٰى ۗ

37. Then, for such as had
Transgressed all bounds,

٣٧- فَاَمَّا مَنْ طَغٰى ۙ

38. And had preferred
The life of this world,

٣٨- وَاٰثَرَ الْحَيٰوةَ الدُّنْيَا ۙ

39. The Abode will be Hell-Fire;

٣٩- فَاِنَّ الْجَحِيْمَ هِيَ الْمَاْوٰى ۗ

40. And for such as had
Entertained the fear
Of standing before
Their Lord's (tribunal)
And had restrained
(Their) souls from lower Desires,

٤٠- وَاَمَّا مَنْ خَافَ مَقَامَ رَبِّهٖ
وَنَهَى النَّفْسَ
عَنِ الْهَوٰى ۙ

41. Their Abode will be
The Garden.

٤١- فَاِنَّ الْجَنَّةَ هِيَ الْمَاْوٰى ۗ

42. They ask thee
About the Hour—'When
Will be its appointed time?'

٤٢- يَسْـَٔلُوْنَكَ عَنِ السَّاعَةِ
اَيَّانَ مُرْسٰىهَا ۗ

43. Wherein art thou (concerned)
With the declaration thereof?

٤٣- فِيْمَ اَنْتَ مِنْ ذِكْرٰىهَا ۗ

44. With thy Lord is
The Limit   fixed therefor.

٤٤- اِلٰى رَبِّكَ مُنْتَهٰىهَا ۗ

45. Thou art but a Warner
For such as fear it.

٤٥- اِنَّمَآ اَنْتَ مُنْذِرُ مَنْ يَّخْشٰىهَا ۗ

46. The Day they see it,
(It will be) as if they
Had tarried but a single
Evening, or (at most 'till)
The following morn!

٤٦- كَاَنَّهُمْ يَوْمَ يَرَوْنَهَا
لَمْ يَلْبَثُوا اِلَّا
عَشِيَّةً اَوْ ضُحٰهَا ۝

INTRODUCTION AND SUMMARY: SŪRA LXXX. ('Abasa) — 42 Verses

This is an early Meccan Sūra, and is connected with an incident which reflects the highest honour on the Prophet's sincerity in the Revelations that were vouchsafed to him even if they seemed to reprove him for some natural and human zeal that led him to a false step in his mission according to his own high standard.

He was once deeply and earnestly engaged in trying to explain the Holy Qur-ān to Pagan Quraish leaders, when he was interrupted by a blind man, 'Abdullah ibn Ummi-i-Maktūm, one who was also poor, so that no one took any notice of him. He wanted to learn the Qur-ān. The Holy Prophet naturally disliked the interruption and showed impatience. Perhaps the poor man's feelings were hurt. But he whose gentle heart ever sympathized with the poor and the afflicted, got new Light from above, and without the least hesitation published this revelation, which forms part of the sacred scripture of Islam, as described in verses 13-16. And the Prophet always afterwards held the man in high honour.

The incident was only a passing incident, but after explaining the eternal principles of revelation, the Sūra recapitulates the Mercies of God to man and the consequences of a good or a wicked life here, as seen in the spiritual world to come, in the Hereafter.

'Abasa (He Frowned)

In the name of Allah, Most Gracious, Most Merciful.

1. (The Prophet) frowned
   And turned away,

2. Because there came to him
   The blind man (interrupting).

3. But what could tell thee
   But that perchance he might
   Grow (in spiritual understanding)?

4. Or that he might receive
   Admonition, and the teaching
   Might profit him?

5. As to one who regards
   Himself as self-sufficient,

6. To him dost thou attend;

7. Though it is no blame

On thee if he grow not
(In spiritual understanding).

اَلَّا يَزَّكَّى ۚ

8. But as to him who came
To thee striving earnestly,

٨- وَاَمَّا مَنْ جَاءَكَ يَسْعَى ۙ

9. And with fear
(In his heart),

٩- وَهُوَ يَخْشَى ۙ

10. Of him wast thou unmindful.

١٠- فَاَنْتَ عَنْهُ تَلَهَّى ۗ

11. By no means
(Should it be so)!
For it is indeed
A Message of instruction:

١١- كَلَّا
اِنَّهَا تَذْكِرَةٌ ۚ

12. Therefore let whoso will,
Keep it in remembrance.

١٢- فَمَنْ شَاءَ ذَكَرَهُ ۘ

13. (It is) in Books
Held (greatly) in honour,

١٣- فِىْ صُحُفٍ مُّكَرَّمَةٍ ۙ

14. Exalted (in dignity),
Kept pure and holy,

١٤- مَرْفُوْعَةٍ مُّطَهَّرَةٍ ۙ

15. (Written) by the hands
Of scribes—

١٥- بِاَيْدِىْ سَفَرَةٍ ۙ

16. Honourable and
Pious and Just.

١٦- كِرَامٍ بَرَرَةٍ ۗ

17. Woe to man!
What hath made him
Reject Allah?

١٧- قُتِلَ الْاِنْسَانُ مَا اَكْفَرَهُ ۗ

18. From what stuff
Hath He created him?

١٨- مِنْ اَىِّ شَىْءٍ خَلَقَهُ ۗ

19. From a sperm drop:
He hath created him, and then
Mouldeth him in due proportions;

١٩- مِنْ نُّطْفَةٍ ۗ خَلَقَهُ فَقَدَّرَهُ ۙ

20. Then doth He make
His path smooth for him;

٢٠- ثُمَّ السَّبِيْلَ يَسَّرَهُ ۙ

21. Then He causeth him to die,
And putteth him in his Grave;

٢١- ثُمَّ اَمَاتَهُ فَاَقْبَرَهُ ۙ

22. Then, when it is
His Will, He will
Raise him up (again).

٢٢ - ثُمَّ إِذَا شَاءَ أَنْشَرَهُ ۞

23. By no means hath he
Fulfilled what Allah
Hath commanded him.

٢٣ - كَلَّا لَمَّا يَقْضِ
مَا أَمَرَهُ ۞

24. Then let man look
At his Food,
(And how We provide it):

٢٤ - فَلْيَنْظُرِ الْإِنْسَانُ إِلَى طَعَامِهِ ۞

25. For that We pour forth
Water in abundance,

٢٥ - أَنَّا صَبَبْنَا الْمَاءَ صَبًّا ۞

26. And We split the earth
In fragments,

٢٦ - ثُمَّ شَقَقْنَا الْأَرْضَ شَقًّا ۞

27. And produce therein   Corn,

٢٧ - فَأَنْبَتْنَا فِيهَا حَبًّا ۞

28. And Grapes and nutritious Plants,

٢٨ - وَعِنَبًا وَقَضْبًا ۞

29. And Olives and Dates,

٢٩ - وَزَيْتُونًا وَنَخْلًا ۞

30. And enclosed Gardens,
Dense with lofty trees,

٣٠ - وَحَدَائِقَ غُلْبًا ۞

31. And Fruits and Fodder—

٣١ - وَفَاكِهَةً وَأَبًّا ۞

32. For use and convenience
To you and your cattle.

٣٢ - مَتَاعًا لَكُمْ وَلِأَنْعَامِكُمْ ۞

33. At length, when there
Comes the Deafening Noise—

٣٣ - فَإِذَا جَاءَتِ الصَّاخَّةُ ۞

34. That Day shall a man
Flee from his own brother,

٣٤ - يَوْمَ يَفِرُّ الْمَرْءُ مِنْ أَخِيهِ ۞

35. And from his mother
And his father,

٣٥ - وَأُمِّهِ وَأَبِيهِ ۞

36. And from his wife
And his children.

٣٦ - وَصَاحِبَتِهِ وَبَنِيهِ ۞

37. Each one of them,
That Day, will have
Enough concern (of his own)
To make him indifferent
To the others.

٣٤ـ لِكُلِّ امْرِئٍ مِّنْهُمْ يَوْمَئِذٍ شَأْنٌ يُغْنِيهِ ۚ

38. Some Faces that Day
Will be beaming,

٣٨ـ وُجُوهٌ يَوْمَئِذٍ مُّسْفِرَةٌ ۙ

39. Laughing, rejoicing.

٣٩ـ ضَاحِكَةٌ مُّسْتَبْشِرَةٌ ۚ

40. And other faces that Day
Will be dust stained;

٤٠ـ وَوُجُوهٌ يَوْمَئِذٍ عَلَيْهَا غَبَرَةٌ ۙ

41. Blackness will cover them:

٤١ـ تَرْهَقُهَا قَتَرَةٌ ۚ

42. Such will be
The Rejecters of Allah,
The Doers of Iniquity.

٤٢ـ أُولَٰئِكَ هُمُ الْكَفَرَةُ الْفَجَرَةُ ۚ ۝

INTRODUCTION AND SUMMARY: SŪRA LXXXI. (*Takwīr*) — 29 Verses

This is quite an early Meccan Sūra, perhaps the sixth or seventh in chronological order. It opens with a series of highly mystical metaphors suggesting the break-up of the world as we know it (verses 1-13) and the enforcement of complete personal responsibility for each soul (verse 14). Then there is a mystical passage showing how the Quranic Revelation was true, and revealed through the angel Gabriel, and not merely a rhapsody from one possessed. Revelation is given for man's spiritual guidance (verses 15-29).

Comparable with this Sūra are the Sūras lxxxii, and lxxxiv, which may be read with this.

Al Takwīr (The Folding Up)

In the name of Allah, Most Gracious,
Most Merciful.

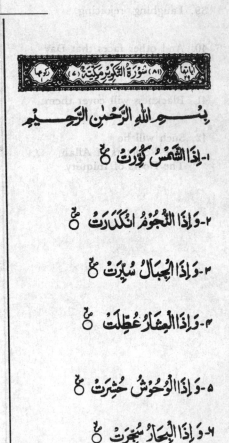

1. **W**hen the sun
   (With its spacious light)
   Is folded up;

2. When the stars
   Fall, losing their lustre;

3. When the mountains vanish
   (Like a mirage);

4. When the she-camels,
   Ten months with young,
   Are left untended;

5. When the wild beasts
   Are herded together
   (In human habitations);

6. When the oceans
   Boil over with a swell;

7. When the souls
   Are sorted out,
   (Being joined, like with like);

8. When the female (infant),
   Buried alive, is questioned—

9. For what crime
She was killed;

٩ـ بِاَیِّ ذَنۢبٍ قُتِلَتۡ ۝

10. When the Scrolls
Are laid open;

١٠ـ وَ اِذَا الصُّحُفُ نُشِرَتۡ ۝

11. When the World on High
Is unveiled;

١١ـ وَ اِذَا السَّمَآءُ كُشِطَتۡ ۝

12. When the Blazing Fire
Is kindled to fierce heat;

١٢ـ وَ اِذَا الۡجَحِیۡمُ سُعِّرَتۡ ۝

13. And when the Garden
Is brought near—

١٣ـ وَ اِذَا الۡجَنَّةُ اُزۡلِفَتۡ ۝

14. (Then) shall each soul know
What it has put forward.

١٤ـ عَلِمَتۡ نَفۡسٌ مَّاۤ اَحۡضَرَتۡ ۝

15. So verily I call
To witness the Planets—
That recede,

١٥ـ فَلَاۤ اُقۡسِمُ بِالۡخُنَّسِ ۝

16. Go straight, or hide;

١٦ـ الۡجَوَارِ الۡكُنَّسِ ۝

17. And the Night
As it dissipates;

١٧ـ وَ الَّیۡلِ اِذَا عَسۡعَسَ ۝

18. And the Dawn
As it breathes away
The darkness—

١٨ـ وَ الصُّبۡحِ اِذَا تَنَفَّسَ ۝

19. Verily this is the word
Of a most honourable
                 Messenger,

١٩ـ اِنَّهٗ لَقَوۡلُ رَسُوۡلٍ كَرِیۡمٍ ۝

20. Endued with Power,
With rank before
The Lord of the Throne,

٢٠ـ ذِیۡ قُوَّةٍ عِنۡدَ ذِی الۡعَرۡشِ مَكِیۡنٍ ۝

21. With authority there,
(And) faithful to his trust.

٢١ـ مُّطَاعٍ ثَمَّ اَمِیۡنٍ ۝

22. And (O people)!
Your Companion is not
One possessed;

٢٢ـ وَ مَا صَاحِبُكُمۡ بِمَجۡنُوۡنٍ ۝

23. And without doubt he saw him

٢٣ـ وَ لَقَدۡ رَاٰهُ بِالۡاُفُقِ

In the clear horizon.

الْمُبِينِ ٥

24. Neither doth he withhold
Grudgingly a knowledge
Of the Unseen.

٢٤- وَمَا هُوَ عَلَى الْغَيْبِ بِضَنِينٍ ٥

25. Nor is it the word
Of an evil spirit accursed.

٢٥- وَمَا هُوَ بِقَوْلِ شَيْطَنٍ رَّجِيمٍ ٥

26. Then whither go ye?

٢٦- فَأَيْنَ تَذْهَبُونَ ٥

27. Verily this is no less
Than a Message
To (all) the Worlds:

٢٧- إِنْ هُوَ إِلَّا ذِكْرٌ لِّلْعَلَمِينَ ٥

28. (With profit) to whoever
Among you wills
To go straight:

٢٨- لِمَنْ شَآءَ مِنْكُمْ أَنْ يَسْتَقِيمَ ٥

29. But ye shall not will
Except as Allah wills—
The Cherisher of the Worlds.

٢٩- وَمَا تَشَآءُونَ إِلَّا أَنْ يَشَآءَ اللهُ رَبُّ الْعَلَمِينَ ٥

INTRODUCTION AND SUMMARY: SŪRA LXXXII. (*Infiṭār*) — 19 Verses

In subject-matter this Sūra is cognate to the last, though the best authorities consider it a good deal later in chronology in the early Meccan Period.

Its argument is subject to the threefold interpretation mentioned in n.5982 to lxxxi.13.viz, as referring (1) to the final Day of Judgment, (2) to the Lesser Judgment, on an individual's death, and (3) to the awakening of the Inner Light in the soul at any time, that being considered as Death to the Falsities of this life and a Rebirth to the true spiritual Reality.

Al Infiṭār (The Cleaving Asunder)

In the Name of Allah, Most Gracious,
Most Merciful

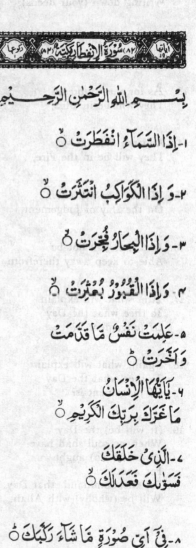

1. When the Sky
   Is cleft asunder;

2. When the Stars
   Are scattered;

3. When the Oceans
   Are suffered to burst forth;

4. And when the Graves
   Are turned upside down—

5. (Then) shall each soul know
   What it hath sent forward
   And (what it hath) kept back.

6. O man! what has
   Seduced thee from
   Thy Lord Most Beneficent?—

7. Him Who created thee,
   Fashioned thee in due
   proportion,
   And gave thee a just bias;

8. In whatever Form He wills,
   Does He put thee together.

9. Nay! but ye do
Reject Right and Judgement!

٩- كَلَّا بَلْ تُكَذِّبُونَ بِالدِّينِ ۞

10. But verily over you
(Are appointed angels)
To protect you—

١٠- وَإِنَّ عَلَيْكُمْ لَحَافِظِينَ ۞

11. Kind and honourable—
Writing down (your deeds):

١١- كِرَامًا كَاتِبِينَ ۞

12. They know (and understand)
All that ye do.

١٢- يَعْلَمُونَ مَا تَفْعَلُونَ ۞

13. As for the Righteous,
They will be in Bliss;

١٣- إِنَّ الْأَبْرَارَ لَفِي نَعِيمٍ ۞

14. And the Wicked—
They will be in the Fire,

١٤- وَإِنَّ الْفُجَّارَ لَفِي جَحِيمٍ ۞

15. Which they will, enter
On the Day of Judgement,

١٥- يَصْلَوْنَهَا يَوْمَ الدِّينِ ۞

16. And they will not be
Able to keep away therefrom.

١٦- وَمَا هُمْ عَنْهَا بِغَائِبِينَ ۞

17. And what will explain
To thee what the Day
Of Judgement is?

١٧- وَمَا أَدْرَاكَ مَا يَوْمُ الدِّينِ ۞

18. Again, what will explain
To thee what the Day
Of Judgement is?

١٨- ثُمَّ مَا أَدْرَاكَ مَا يَوْمُ الدِّينِ ۞

19. (It will be) the Day
When no soul shall have
Power (to do) aught
For another:
For the Command, that Day,
Will be (wholly) with Allah.

١٩- يَوْمَ لَا تَمْلِكُ نَفْسٌ
لِنَفْسٍ شَيْئًا ۚ
وَالْأَمْرُ يَوْمَئِذٍ لِلَّهِ ۞

INTRODUCTION AND SUMMARY: SŪRA LXXXIII. (*Taṭfīf*) — 36 Verses

This Sūra is close in time to the last one and the next one.

It condemns all fraud—in daily dealings, as well as and especially in matters of Religion and the higher spiritual Life.

Al Muṭaffifīn (The Dealers in Fraud)

In the name of Allah, Most Gracious,
Most Merciful.

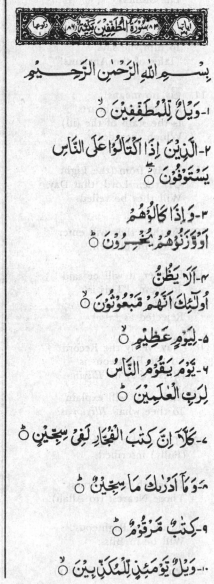

بِسْمِ اللهِ الرَّحْمٰنِ الرَّحِيمِ

1. Woe to those
That deal in fraud—

١- وَيْلٌ لِّلْمُطَفِّفِينَ ۙ

2. Those who, when they
Have to receive by measure
From men, exact full measure,

٢- الَّذِينَ إِذَا اكْتَالُوا عَلَى النَّاسِ
يَسْتَوْفُونَ ۫

3. But when they have
To give by measure
Or weight to men,
Give less than due.

٣- وَإِذَا كَالُوهُمْ
أَوْ وَّزَنُوهُمْ يُخْسِرُونَ ۫

4. Do they not think
That they will be called
To account?—

٤- أَلَا يَظُنُّ
أُولٰئِكَ أَنَّهُمْ مَّبْعُوثُونَ ۙ

5. On a Mighty Day,

٥- لِيَوْمٍ عَظِيمٍ ۙ

6. A Day when (all) mankind
Will stand before
The Lord of the Worlds?

٦- يَوْمَ يَقُومُ النَّاسُ
لِرَبِّ الْعٰلَمِينَ ۫

7. Nay! Surely the Record
Of the Wicked is
(Preserved) in *Sijjīn.*

٧- كَلَّا إِنَّ كِتٰبَ الْفُجَّارِ لَفِي سِجِّينٍ ۫

8. And what will explain
To thee what *Sijjīn* is?

٨- وَمَا أَدْرٰكَ مَا سِجِّينٌ ۙ

9. (There is) a Register
(Fully) inscribed.

٩- كِتٰبٌ مَّرْقُومٌ ۙ

10. Woe, that Day, to those
That deny—

١٠- وَيْلٌ يَوْمَئِذٍ لِّلْمُكَذِّبِينَ ۙ

11. Those that deny
The Day of Judgement.

١١- اَلَّذِيْنَ يُكَذِّبُوْنَ بِيَوْمِ الدِّيْنِ ۟

12. And none can deny it
But the Transgressor
Beyond bounds,
The Sinner!

١٢- وَمَا يُكَذِّبُ بِهٖۤ اِلَّا
كُلُّ مُعْتَدٍ اَثِيْمٍ ۟

13. When Our Signs are rehearsed
To him, he says,
"Tales of the Ancients!"

١٣- اِذَا تُتْلٰى عَلَيْهِ اٰيٰتُنَا
قَالَ اَسَاطِيْرُ الْاَوَّلِيْنَ ۟

14. By no means!
But on their hearts
Is the stain of the (ill)
Which they do!

١٤- كَلَّا بَلْ ۜ
رَانَ عَلٰى قُلُوْبِهِمْ مَّا كَانُوْا يَكْسِبُوْنَ ۟

15. Verily, from (the Light
Of) their Lord, that Day,
Will they be veiled.

١٥- كَلَّا اِنَّهُمْ عَنْ رَّبِّهِمْ
يَوْمَئِذٍ لَّمَحْجُوْبُوْنَ ۟

16. Further, they will enter
The Fire of Hell.

١٦- ثُمَّ اِنَّهُمْ لَصَالُوا الْجَحِيْمِ ۟

17. Further, it will be said
To them: "This is
The (reality) which ye
Rejected as false!

١٧- ثُمَّ يُقَالُ هٰذَا الَّذِيْ
كُنْتُمْ بِهٖ تُكَذِّبُوْنَ ۟

18. Nay, verily the Record
Of the Righteous is
(Preserved) in 'Illiyīn.

١٨- كَلَّا اِنَّ كِتٰبَ الْاَبْرَارِ
لَفِيْ عِلِّيِّيْنَ ۟

19. And what will explain
To thee what 'Illiyūn is?

١٩- وَمَاۤ اَدْرٰىكَ مَا عِلِّيُّوْنَ ۟

20. (There is) a Register
(Fully) inscribed,

٢٠- كِتٰبٌ مَّرْقُوْمٌ ۟

21. To which bear witness
Those Nearest (to Allah).

٢١- يَشْهَدُهُ الْمُقَرَّبُوْنَ ۟

22. Truly the Righteous
Will be in Bliss:

٢٢- اِنَّ الْاَبْرَارَ لَفِيْ نَعِيْمٍ ۟

23. On Thrones (of Dignity)

٢٣- عَلَى الْاَرَآئِكِ

Will they command a sight
(Of all things):

ينظرون ۞

24. Thou wilt recognise
In their Faces
The beaming brightness of Bliss.

٢٤- تَعْرِفُ فِي وُجُوهِهِمْ
نَضْرَةَ النَّعِيمِ ۞

25. Their thirst will be slaked
With Pure Wine sealed:

٢٥- يُسْقَوْنَ مِنْ رَحِيقٍ مَخْتُومٍ ۞

26. The seal thereof will be
Musk: and for this
Let those aspire,
Who have aspirations:

٢٦- خِتَمُهُ مِسْكٌ ۚ
وَفِي ذَلِكَ فَلْيَتَنَافَسِ الْمُتَنَافِسُونَ ۞

27. With it will be (given)
A mixture of *Tasnīm:*

٢٧- وَمِزَاجُهُ مِنْ تَسْنِيمٍ ۞

28. A spring, from (the waters)
Whereof drink
Those Nearest to Allah.

٢٨- عَيْنًا يَشْرَبُ بِهَا الْمُقَرَّبُونَ ۞

29. Those in sin used
To laugh at those
Who believed,

٢٩- إِنَّ الَّذِينَ أَجْرَمُوا
كَانُوا مِنَ الَّذِينَ آمَنُوا يَضْحَكُونَ ۞

30. And whenever they passed
By them, used to wink
At each other (in mockery);

٣٠- وَإِذَا مَرُّوا بِهِمْ يَتَغَامَزُونَ ۞

31. And when they returned
To their own people,
They would return jesting;

٣١- وَإِذَا انْقَلَبُوا إِلَى أَهْلِهِمُ
انْقَلَبُوا فَكِهِينَ ۞

32. And whenever they saw them,
They would say, "Behold!
These are the people
Truly astray!"

٣٢- وَإِذَا رَأَوْهُمْ قَالُوا
إِنَّ هَؤُلَاءِ لَضَالُّونَ ۞

33. But they had not been
Sent as Keepers over them!

٣٣- وَمَا أُرْسِلُوا عَلَيْهِمْ حَافِظِينَ ۞

34. But on this Day
The Believers will laugh
At the Unbelievers:

٣٤- فَالْيَوْمَ الَّذِيْنَ اٰمَنُوْا مِنَ الْكُفَّارِ
يَضْحَكُوْنَ ۞

35. On Thrones (of Dignity)
They will command (a sight)
(Of all things).

٣٥- عَلَى الْاَرَآئِكِ يَنْظُرُوْنَ ۞

36. Will not the Unbelievers
Have been paid back
For what they did?

٣٦- هَلْ ثُوِّبَ الْكُفَّارُ
مَا كَانُوْا يَفْعَلُوْنَ ۞

INTRODUCTION AND SUMMARY: SŪRA LXXXIV. (*Inshiqāq*) — 25 Verses

Chronologically this Sūra is closely connected with the last one. In subject-matter it resembles more S.lxxxii. and lxxxi, with which it may be compared.

By a number of mystic metaphors it is shown that the present phenomenal order will not last, and God's full Judgement will certainly be established: men should therefore strive for that World of Eternity and True Values.

Al Inshiqāq (The Rending Asunder)

In the name of Allah, Most Gracious, Most Merciful.

بِسْمِ اللهِ الرَّحْمٰنِ الرَّحِيْمِ

1. When the Sky is
Rent asunder,

١- اِذَا السَّمَآءُ انْشَقَّتْ ۙ

2. And hearkens to
(The Command of) its Lord—
And it must needs
(Do so)—

٢- وَاَذِنَتْ لِرَبِّهَا
وَحُقَّتْ ۙ

3. And when the Earth
Is flattened out,

٣- وَاِذَا الْاَرْضُ مُدَّتْ ۙ

4. And casts forth
What is within it
And becomes (clean) empty,

٤- وَاَلْقَتْ مَافِيْهَا
وَتَخَلَّتْ ۙ

5. And hearkens to
(The Command of) its Lord—
And it must needs
(Do so)—(then will come
Home the full Reality).

٥- وَاَذِنَتْ لِرَبِّهَا
وَحُقَّتْ ۙ

6. O thou man!
Verily thou art ever
Toiling on towards thy Lord—
Painfully toiling—but thou
Shalt meet Him.

٦- يَآيُّهَا الْاِنْسَانُ اِنَّكَ
كَادِحٌ اِلٰى رَبِّكَ كَدْحًا فَمُلٰقِيْهِ ۚ

7. Then he who is given
His Record in his
Right hand,[6037]

٧- فَاَمَّا مَنْ اُوْتِيَ كِتٰبَهٗ بِيَمِيْنِهٖ ۙ

8. Soon will his account
Be taken by an easy reckoning,

٨- فَسَوْفَ يُحَاسَبُ حِسَابًا يَسِيرًا ۞

9. And he will turn
To his people,[6038] rejoicing!

٩- وَيَنْقَلِبُ إِلَى أَهْلِهِ مَسْرُورًا ۞

10. But he who is given
His Record behind his back—

١٠- وَأَمَّا مَنْ أُوتِيَ كِتَابَهُ وَرَاءَ ظَهْرِهِ ۞

11. Soon will he cry
For Perdition,

١١- فَسَوْفَ يَدْعُوا ثُبُورًا ۞

12. And he will enter
A Blazing Fire.

١٢- وَيَصْلَى سَعِيرًا ۞

13. Truly, did he go about
Among his people, rejoicing!

١٣- إِنَّهُ كَانَ فِي أَهْلِهِ مَسْرُورًا ۞

14. Truly, did he think
That he would not
Have to return (to Us)!

١٤- إِنَّهُ ظَنَّ أَنْ لَنْ يَحُورَ ۞

15. Nay, nay! for his Lord
Was (ever) watchful of him!

١٥- بَلَى ۚ إِنَّ رَبَّهُ كَانَ بِهِ بَصِيرًا ۞

16. So I do call
To witness the ruddy glow
Of Sunset;

١٦- فَلَا أُقْسِمُ بِالشَّفَقِ ۞

17. The Night and its Homing;

١٧- وَالَّيْلِ وَمَا وَسَقَ ۞

18. And the Moon
In her Fulness:

١٨- وَالْقَمَرِ إِذَا اتَّسَقَ ۞

19. Ye shall surely travel
From stage to stage.

١٩- لَتَرْكَبُنَّ طَبَقًا عَنْ طَبَقٍ ۞

20. What then is the matter
With them, that they
Believe not?—

٢٠- فَمَا لَهُمْ لَا يُؤْمِنُونَ ۞

21. And when the Qur'ān
Is read to them, they
Fall not prostrate,

٢١- وَإِذَا قُرِئَ عَلَيْهِمُ الْقُرْآنُ لَا يَسْجُدُونَ ۩ ۞

22. But on the contrary
The Unbelievers reject (it).

٢٢- بَلِ الَّذِيْنَ كَفَرُوْا يُكَذِّبُوْنَ ۚ ۖ

23. But Allah has full Knowledge
Of what they secrete
(In their breasts).

٢٣- وَاللهُ أَعْلَمُ بِمَا يُوْعُوْنَ ۚ ۖ

24. So announce to them
A Penalty Grievous,

٢٤- فَبَشِّرْهُمْ بِعَذَابٍ أَلِيْمٍ ۙ ۖ

25. Except to those who believe
And work righteous deeds:
For them is a Reward
That will never fail.

٢٥- إِلَّا الَّذِيْنَ اٰمَنُوْا وَعَمِلُوا الصّٰلِحٰتِ
لَهُمْ أَجْرٌ غَيْرُ مَمْنُوْنٍ ۚ ۖ

INTRODUCTION AND SUMMARY: SŪRA LXXXV. (*Burūj*) — 22 Verses

This is one of the earlier Meccan Sūras, chronologically cognate with S. xci.
The subject-matter is the persecution of God's votaries. God watches over His own,
and will deal with the enemies of Truth as He dealt with them in the past.

Al Burūj (The Constellations)

In the name of Allah, Most Gracious,
Most Merciful.

بِسْمِ اللهِ الرَّحْمٰنِ الرَّحِيْمِ ۞

1. By the Sky, (displaying)
   The Zodiacal Signs;

١-وَالسَّمَاءِ ذَاتِ الْبُرُوجِ ۞

2. By the promised Day
   (Of Judgement);

٢-وَالْيَوْمِ الْمَوْعُوْدِ ۞

3. By one that witnesses,
   And the subject of the
                  witness—

٣-وَشَاهِدٍ وَّمَشْهُوْدٍ ۞

4. Woe to the makers
   Of the pit (of fire),

٤-قُتِلَ أَصْحَابُ الْأُخْدُوْدِ ۞

5. Fire supplied (abundantly)
   With Fuel:

٥-النَّارِ ذَاتِ الْوَقُوْدِ ۞

6. Behold! They sat
   Over against the (fire),

٦-إِذْ هُمْ عَلَيْهَا قُعُوْدٌ ۞

7. And they witnessed
   (All) that they were doing
   Against the Believers.

٧-وَّهُمْ عَلٰى مَا يَفْعَلُوْنَ بِالْمُؤْمِنِيْنَ شُهُوْدٌ ۞

8. And they ill-treated them
   For no other reason than
   That they believed in Allah,
   Exalted in Power,
   Worthy of all Praise!—

٨-وَمَا نَقَمُوْا مِنْهُمْ إِلَّا أَنْ يُّؤْمِنُوْا بِاللهِ الْعَزِيْزِ الْحَمِيْدِ ۞

9. Him to Whom belongs
   The dominion of the heavens
   And the earth!
   And Allah is Witness
   To all things.

٩-الَّذِيْ لَهُ مُلْكُ السَّمٰوٰتِ وَالْأَرْضِ وَاللهُ عَلٰى كُلِّ شَيْءٍ شَهِيْدٌ ۞

10. Those who persecute (or draw
into temptation)
The Believers, men and women,
And do not turn
In repentance, will have
The Penalty of Hell:
They will have the Penalty
Of the Burning Fire.

١٠- اِنَّ الَّذِيْنَ فَتَنُوا الْمُؤْمِنِيْنَ وَالْمُؤْمِنٰتِ
ثُمَّ لَمْ يَتُوْبُوا فَلَهُمْ عَذَابُ جَهَنَّمَ
وَلَهُمْ عَذَابُ الْحَرِيْقِ ۞

11. For those who believe
And do righteous deeds,
Will be Gardens,
Beneath which Rivers flow:
That is the great Salvation,
(The fulfilment of all desires),

١١- اِنَّ الَّذِيْنَ اٰمَنُوْا وَعَمِلُوا الصّٰلِحٰتِ
لَهُمْ جَنّٰتٌ تَجْرِيْ مِنْ تَحْتِهَا الْاَنْهٰرُ
ذٰلِكَ الْفَوْزُ الْكَبِيْرُ ۞

12. Truly strong is the Grip
(And Power) of thy Lord.

١٢- اِنَّ بَطْشَ رَبِّكَ لَشَدِيْدٌ ۞

13. It is He Who Creates
From the very beginning,
And He can restore (life).

١٣- اِنَّهٗ هُوَ يُبْدِئُ وَيُعِيْدُ ۞

14. And He is the Oft-Forgiving,
Full of loving-kindness,

١٤- وَهُوَ الْغَفُوْرُ الْوَدُوْدُ ۞

15. Lord of the Throne of Glory,

١٥- ذُو الْعَرْشِ الْمَجِيْدُ ۞

16. Doer (without let)
Of all that He intends.

١٦- فَعَّالٌ لِّمَا يُرِيْدُ ۞

17. Has the story
Reached thee,
Of the Forces—

١٧- هَلْ اَتٰكَ حَدِيْثُ الْجُنُوْدِ ۞

18. Of Pharaoh
And the Thamūd?

١٨- فِرْعَوْنَ وَثَمُوْدَ ۞

19. And yet the Unbelievers
(Persist) in rejecting
(The Truth)!

١٩- بَلِ الَّذِيْنَ كَفَرُوْا فِيْ تَكْذِيْبٍ ۞

20. But Allah doth
Encompass them
From behind!

٢٠- وَاللّٰهُ مِنْ وَّرَآئِهِمْ مُّحِيْطٌ ۞

21. Nay, this is
A Glorious Qur'ān

٢١ـ بَلْ هُوَ قُرْآنٌ مَجِيدٌ ۖ ۝

22. (Inscribed) in
A Tablet Preserved!

٢٢ـ فِى لَوْحٍ مَحْفُوظٍ ۖ ۝　ع

INTRODUCTION AND SUMMARY: SŪRA LXXXVI. (*Ṭāriq*) — 17 Verses

This Sūra also belongs to the early Meccan period, perhaps not far removed from the last Sūra.

Its subject-matter is the protection afforded to every soul in the darkest period of its spiritual history. The physical nature of man may be insignificant, but the soul given to him by God must win a glorious Future in the end.

Al Ṭāriq (The Night Star)

In the name of Allah, Most Gracious, Most Merciful.

1. By the Sky
   And the Night-Visitant
   (Therein)—

2. And what will explain to thee
   What the Night-Visitant is?—

3. (It is) the Star
   Of piercing brightness—

4. There is no soul but has
   A protector over it.

5. Now let man but think
   From what he is created!

6. He is created from
   A drop emitted—

7. Proceeding from between
   The backbone and the ribs:

8. Surely (Allah) is able
   To bring him back
   (To life)!

9. The Day that
   (All) things secret
   Will be tested,

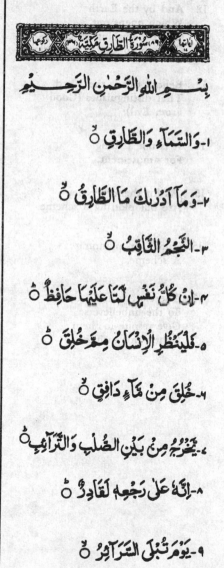

بِسْمِ اللهِ الرَّحْمٰنِ الرَّحِيْمِ

١- وَالسَّمَآءِ وَالطَّارِقِ ۙ

٢- وَمَآ اَدْرٰىكَ مَا الطَّارِقُ ۙ

٣- النَّجْمُ الثَّاقِبُ ۙ

٤- اِنْ كُلُّ نَفْسٍ لَّمَّا عَلَيْهَا حَافِظٌ ؕ

٥- فَلْيَنْظُرِ الْاِنْسَانُ مِمَّ خُلِقَ ؕ

٦- خُلِقَ مِنْ مَّآءٍ دَافِقٍ ۙ

٧- يَّخْرُجُ مِنْ بَيْنِ الصُّلْبِ وَالتَّرَآئِبِ ؕ

٨- اِنَّهٗ عَلٰى رَجْعِهٖ لَقَادِرٌ ؕ

٩- يَوْمَ تُبْلَى السَّرَآئِرُ ۙ

10. (Man) will have
    No power,
    And no helper

١٠- فَمَا لَهُ مِنْ قُوَّةٍ وَّلَا نَاصِرٍ ۗ

11. By the Firmament
    Which returns (in its round),

١١- وَالسَّمَاءِ ذَاتِ الرَّجْعِ ۗ

12. And by the Earth
    Which opens out
    (For the gushing of springs
    Or the sprouting of vegetation)—

١٢- وَالْأَرْضِ ذَاتِ الصَّدْعِ ۗ

13. Behold this is the Word
    That distinguishes (Good
    From Evil):

١٣- إِنَّهُ لَقَوْلٌ فَصْلٌ ۗ

14. It is not a thing
    For amusement.

١٤- وَّمَا هُوَ بِالْهَزْلِ ۗ

15. As for them,[6077] they
    Are but plotting a scheme,

١٥- إِنَّهُمْ يَكِيدُوْنَ كَيْدًا ۗ

16. And I am planning
    A scheme.

١٦- وَّأَكِيدُ كَيْدًا ۖ

17. Therefore grant a delay
    To the unbelievers:
    Give respite to them
    Gently (for awhile).

١٧- فَمَهِّلِ الْكَافِرِيْنَ أَمْهِلْهُمْ رُوَيْدًا ۖ ؏

INTRODUCTION AND SUMMARY: SŪRA LXXXVII. (*A'la*) — 19 Verses

This is one of the earliest of the Meccan Sūras, being usually placed eighth in chronological order, and immediately after S.lxxxi.

The argument is that God has made man capable of progress by ordered steps, and by His Revelation will lead him still higher to purification and perfection.

Al A'la (The Most High)

In the name of Allah, Most Gracious, Most Merciful.

بِسۡمِ اللهِ الرَّحۡمٰنِ الرَّحِيۡمِ

1. Glorify the name
Of thy Guardian-Lord
Most High,

١- سَبِّحِ اسۡمَ رَبِّكَ الۡاَعۡلَى ۙ

2. Who hath created,
And further, given
Order and proportion;

٢- الَّذِىۡ خَلَقَ فَسَوّٰى ۙ

3. Who hath ordained laws.
And granted guidance;

٣- وَالَّذِىۡ قَدَّرَ فَهَدٰى ۙ

4. And Who bringth out
The (green and luscious) pasture,

٤- وَالَّذِىۡۤ اَخۡرَجَ الۡمَرۡعٰى ۙ

5. And then doth make it
(But) swarthy stubble.

٥- فَجَعَلَهٗ غُثَآءً اَحۡوٰى ۙ

6. By degrees shall We
Teach thee to declare
(The Message), so thou
Shalt not forget,

٦- سَنُقۡرِئُكَ فَلَا تَنۡسٰى ۙ

7. Except as Allah wills:
For He knoweth
What is manifest
And what is hidden.

٧- اِلَّا مَا شَآءَ اللهُ ؕ اِنَّهٗ يَعۡلَمُ الۡجَهۡرَ وَمَا يَخۡفٰى ؕ

8. And We will make it

٨- وَنُيَسِّرُكَ

Easy for thee (to follow)
The simple (Path).

لِلْيُسْرٰى ۗ

9. Therefore give admonition
In case the admonition
Profits (the hearer).

٩- فَذَكِّرْ اِنْ نَّفَعَتِ الذِّكْرٰى ۗ

10. The admonition will be received
By those who fear (Allah):

١٠- سَيَذَّكَّرُ مَنْ يَّخْشٰى ۙ

11. But it will be avoided
By those most unfortunate ones,

١١- وَيَتَجَنَّبُهَا الْاَشْقَى ۙ

12. Who will enter
The Great Fire,

١٢- الَّذِيْ يَصْلَى النَّارَ الْكُبْرٰى ۙ

13. In which they will then
Neither die nor live.

١٣- ثُمَّ لَا يَمُوْتُ فِيْهَا وَلَا يَحْيٰى ۗ

14. But those will prosper
Who purify themselves,

١٤- قَدْ اَفْلَحَ مَنْ تَزَكّٰى ۙ

15. And glorify the name
Of their Guardian-Lord,
And (lift their hearts)
In Prayer.

١٥- وَذَكَرَ اسْمَ رَبِّهٖ فَصَلّٰى ۗ

16. Nay (behold), ye prefer
The life of this world;

١٦- بَلْ تُؤْثِرُوْنَ الْحَيٰوةَ الدُّنْيَا ۖ

17. But the Hereafter
Is better and more enduring.

١٧- وَالْاٰخِرَةُ خَيْرٌ وَّاَبْقٰى ۗ

18. And this is
In the Books
Of the earliest (Revelations)—

١٨- اِنَّ هٰذَا لَفِى الصُّحُفِ الْاُوْلٰى ۙ

19. The Books of
Abraham and Moses.

١٩- صُحُفِ اِبْرٰهِيْمَ وَمُوْسٰى ۗ

INTRODUCTION AND SUMMARY: SŪRA LXXXVIII. (*Gāshiya*) — 26 Verses

This is a late Sūra of the early Meccan period, perhaps close in date to S.lii. Its subject-matter is the contrast between the destinies of the Good and the Evil in the Hereafter,—on the Day when the true balance will be restored: the Signs of God even in this life should remind us of the Day of Account, for God is good and just, and His creation is for a just Purpose.

Al Ghashiyah (The Overwhelming Event)

In the name of Allah, Most Gracious,
Most Merciful.

بِسْمِ اللهِ الرَّحْمٰنِ الرَّحِيْمِ

1. Has the story
Reached thee, of
The Overwhelming (Event)?

١- هَلْ أَتٰىكَ حَدِيْثُ الْغَاشِيَةِ ۝

2. Some faces, that Day,
Will be humiliated,

٢- وُجُوْهٌ يَّوْمَئِذٍ خَاشِعَةٌ ۝

3. Labouring (hard), weary—

٣- عَامِلَةٌ نَّاصِبَةٌ ۝

4. The while they enter
The Blazing Fire—

٤- تَصْلٰى نَارًا حَامِيَةً ۝

5. The while they are given
To drink, of a boiling hot spring,

٥- تُسْقٰى مِنْ عَيْنٍ اٰنِيَةٍ ۝

6. No food will there be
For them but a bitter *Dari'*

٦- لَيْسَ لَهُمْ طَعَامٌ إِلَّا مِنْ ضَرِيْعٍ ۝

7. Which will neither nourish
Nor satisfy hunger.

٧- لَا يُسْمِنُ وَلَا يُغْنِيْ مِنْ جُوْعٍ ۝

8. (Other) faces that Day
Will be joyful,

٨- وُجُوْهٌ يَّوْمَئِذٍ نَّاعِمَةٌ ۝

9. Pleased with their Striving—

٩- لِسَعْيِهَا رَاضِيَةٌ ۝

10. In a Garden on high,

١٠- فِيْ جَنَّةٍ عَالِيَةٍ ۝

11. Where they shall hear
No (word) of vanity:

١١- لَا تَسْمَعُ فِيْهَا لَاغِيَةً ۝

12. Therein will be
A bubbling spring:

١٢- فِيْهَا عَيْنٌ جَارِيَةٌ ۝

13. Therein will be Thrones
(Of dignity), raised on high,

١٣- فِيْهَا سُرُرٌ مَّرْفُوْعَةٌ ۝

14. Goblets placed (ready),

١٤- وَّاَكْوَابٌ مَّوْضُوْعَةٌ ۝

15. And Cushions set in rows,

١٥- وَّنَمَارِقُ مَصْفُوْفَةٌ ۝

16. And rich carpets
(All) spread out.

١٦- وَّزَرَابِيُّ مَبْثُوْثَةٌ ۝

17. Do they not look
At the Camels,
How they are made?—

١٧- اَفَلَا يَنْظُرُوْنَ
اِلَى الْاِبِلِ كَيْفَ خُلِقَتْ ۝

18. And at the Sky,
How it is raised high?—

١٨- وَاِلَى السَّمَآءِ كَيْفَ رُفِعَتْ ۝

19. And at the Mountains,
How they are fixed firm?—

١٩- وَاِلَى الْجِبَالِ كَيْفَ نُصِبَتْ ۝

20. And at the Earth,
How it is spread out?

٢٠- وَاِلَى الْاَرْضِ كَيْفَ سُطِحَتْ ۝

21. Therefore do thou give
Admonition, for thou art
One to admonish.

٢١- فَذَكِّرْ ۫
اِنَّمَاۤ اَنْتَ مُذَكِّرٌ ۝

22. Thou art not one
To manage (men's) affairs.

٢٢- لَسْتَ عَلَيْهِمْ بِمُصَيْطِرٍ ۝

23. But if any turns away
And rejects Allah—

٢٣- اِلَّا مَنْ تَوَلَّى وَكَفَرَ ۝

24. Allah will punish him
With a mighty Punishment.

٢٤- فَيُعَذِّبُهُ اللهُ الْعَذَابَ الْاَكْبَرَ ۝

25. For to Us will be
Their Return;

٢٥- اِنَّ اِلَيْنَاۤ اِيَابَهُمْ ۝

26. Then it will be for Us
To call them to account.

٢٦- ثُمَّ اِنَّ عَلَيْنَا حِسَابَهُمْ ۝

INTRODUCTION AND SUMMARY: SŪRA LXXXIX. (*Fajr*) — 30 Verses

This is one of the earliest of the Sūras to be revealed,— probably within the first ten in chronological order.

Its mystic meaning is suggested by contrasts,—contrasts in nature and in man's long history. Thus does it enforce the lesson of Faith in the Hereafter to "those who understand". Man's history and legendary lore show that greatness does not last and the proudest are brought low. For enforcing moral and spiritual truths, the strictest history is no better than legend. Indeed all artistic history is legend, for it is written from a special point of view.

Man is easily cowed by contrasts in his own fortunes, and yet he does not learn from them the lesson of forbearance and kindness to others, and the final elevation of goodness in the hereafter. When all the things on which his mind and heart are set on this earth shall be crushed to nothingness, he will see the real glory and power, love and beauty, of God, for these are the light of the Garden of Paradise.

Al Fajr (The Dawn)

In the name of Allah, Most Gracious,
Most Merciful.

1. By the Break of Day;

2. By the Nights twice five;

3. By the Even
And Odd (contrasted);

4. And by the Night
When it passeth away —

5. Is there (not) in these
An adjuration (or evidence)
For those who understand?

6. Seest thou not
How thy Lord dealt
With the 'Ād (people) —

7. Of the (city of) Iram,
With lofty pillars,

8. The like of which

Were not produced
In (all) the land?

9. And with the Thamūd
(People), who cut out
(Huge) rocks in the valley?—

٩- وَثَمُوْدَ الَّذِيْنَ
جَابُوا الصَّخْرَ بِالْوَادِ ۞

10. And with Pharaoh,
Lord of Stakes?

١٠- وَفِرْعَوْنَ ذِى الْأَوْتَادِ ۞

11. (All) these transgressed
Beyond bounds in the lands.

١١- الَّذِيْنَ طَغَوْا فِى الْبِلَادِ ۞

12. And heaped therein
Mischief (on mischief).

١٢- فَأَكْثَرُوا فِيْهَا الْفَسَادَ ۞

13. Therefore did thy Lord
Pour on them a scourge
Of diverse chastisements:

١٣- فَصَبَّ عَلَيْهِمْ رَبُّكَ
سَوْطَ عَذَابٍ ۞

14. For thy Lord is
(As a Guardian)
On a watchtower.

١٤- إِنَّ رَبَّكَ لَبِالْمِرْصَادِ ۞

15. Now, as for man,
When his Lord trieth him,
Giving him honour and gifts,
Then saith he, (puffed up),
"My Lord hath honoured me"

١٥- فَأَمَّا الْإِنْسَانُ إِذَا مَا ابْتَلَاهُ رَبُّهُ
فَأَكْرَمَهُ وَنَعَّمَهُ ەۨ
فَيَقُوْلُ رَبِّيْ أَكْرَمَنِ ۞

16. But when he trieth him,
Restricting his subsistence
For him, then saith he
(In despair), "My Lord
Hath humiliated me!"

١٦- وَأَمَّا إِذَا مَا ابْتَلَاهُ
فَقَدَرَ عَلَيْهِ رِزْقَهُ ەۨ
فَيَقُوْلُ رَبِّيْ أَهَانَنِ ۞

17. Nay, nay! But ye
Honour not the orphans!

١٧- كَلَّا بَلْ لَا تُكْرِمُوْنَ الْيَتِيْمَ ۞

18. Nor do ye encourage
One another
To feed the poor!—

١٨- وَلَا تَحَاضُّوْنَ عَلَى طَعَامِ الْمِسْكِيْنِ ۞

19. And ye devour Inheritance—
All with greed,

١٩- وَتَأْكُلُوْنَ التُّرَاثَ أَكْلًا لَّمًّا ۞

20. And ye love wealth
With inordinate love!

٢٠ـ وَتُحِبُّونَ الْمَالَ حُبًّا جَمًّا ۚ

21. Nay! When the earth
Is pounded to powder,

٢١ـ كَلَّا إِذَا دُكَّتِ الْأَرْضُ دَكًّا دَكًّا ۚ

22. And thy Lord cometh,
And His angels,
Rank upon rank,

٢٢ـ وَجَآءَ رَبُّكَ
وَالْمَلَكُ صَفًّا صَفًّا ۚ

23. And Hell, that Day,
Is brought (face to face)—
On that Day will man
Remember, but how will
That remembrance profit him?

٢٣ـ وَجِائَءَ يَوْمَئِذٍ بِجَهَنَّمَ ۚ
يَوْمَئِذٍ يَتَذَكَّرُ الْإِنْسَانُ
وَأَنَّى لَهُ الذِّكْرَى ۚ

24. He will say: "Ah!
Would that I had
Sent forth (Good Deeds)
For (this) my (Future) Life!"

٢٤ـ يَقُولُ يَٰلَيْتَنِي
قَدَّمْتُ لِحَيَاتِي ۚ

25. For, that Day,
His Chastisement will be
Such as none (else)
Can inflict,

٢٥ـ فَيَوْمَئِذٍ لَّا يُعَذِّبُ
عَذَابَهُ أَحَدٌ ۚ

26. And His bonds
Will be such as
None (other) can bind.

٢٦ـ وَلَا يُوثِقُ وَثَاقَهُ أَحَدٌ ۚ

27. (To the righteous soul
Will be said:)
"O (thou) soul,
In (complete) rest
And satisfaction!

٢٧ـ يَٰأَيَّتُهَا النَّفْسُ
الْمُطْمَئِنَّةُ ۚ

28. "Come back thou
To thy Lord—
Well pleased (thyself),
And well-pleasing
Unto Him!

٢٨ـ ارْجِعِي إِلَى رَبِّكِ
رَاضِيَةً مَّرْضِيَّةً ۚ

29. "Enter thou, then,
Among my Devotees!

٢٩ـ فَادْخُلِي فِي عِبَادِي ۚ

30. "Yea, enter thou
My Heaven!"

٣٠ـ وَادْخُلِي جَنَّتِي ۚ

INTRODUCTION AND SUMMARY: SŪRA XC. (*Balad*) — 20 Verses

This is an early Meccan revelation, and refers to the mystic relation (by divine sanction) of the Holy Prophet with the city of Mecca. He was born in that City, which had already been sacred for ages before. He was nurtured in that City and had (to use a modern phrase) the freedom of that City, belonging, as he did, to the noble family which held the government of its sacred precincts in its hands. But he was an orphan, and orphans in his day had a poor time. But his mind was turned to things divine. He protested against the prevailing idolatry and sin, and his parent City persecuted him and cast him out. He made another City, Yathrib, his own: it became the *Madīnat-un-Nabī*, the City of the Prophet, and it has ever since been called Medina. We can speak of Medina as the Prophet's child. But the Prophet ever cherished in his heart the love of his parent City of Mecca, and in the fulness of time was received in triumph there. He purified it from all idols and abominations, re-established the worship of the One True God, overthrew the purse-proud selfish autocracy, restored the sway of the righteous (people of the Right Hand), the liberty of the slave, and the rights of the poor and downtrodden. What a wonderful career centring round a City! It becomes a symbol of the world's spiritual history.

Al Balad (The City)

In the name of Allah, Most Gracious, Most Merciful.

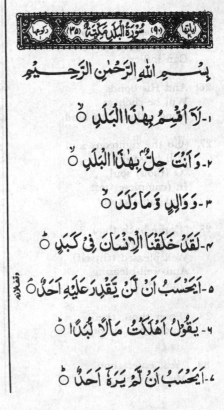

1. ❡ I do call to witness
This City—

2. And thou art a freeman
Of this City—

3. And (the mystic ties
Of) Parent and Child)—

4. Verily We have created
Man into toil and struggle.

5. ❡Thinketh he, that none
Hath power over him?

6. He may say (boastfully):
Wealth have I squandered
In abundance!"

7. Thinketh he that none
Beholdeth him?

8. Have We not made
For him a pair of eyes?—

٨ـ اَلَمْ نَجْعَلْ لَّهٗ عَيْنَيْنِ ۙ

9. And a tongue,
And a pair of lips?—

٩ـ وَلِسَانًا وَّشَفَتَيْنِ ۙ

10. And shown him
The two highways?

١٠ـ وَهَدَيْنٰهُ النَّجْدَيْنِ ۚ

11. But he hath made no haste
On the path that is steep.

١١ـ فَلَا اقْتَحَمَ الْعَقَبَةَ ۖ

12. And what will explain
To thee the path that is steep?—

١٢ـ وَمَآ اَدْرٰىكَ مَا الْعَقَبَةُ ۗ

13. (It is:) freeing the bondman;

١٣ـ فَكُّ رَقَبَةٍ ۙ

14. Or the giving of food
In a day of privation

١٤ـ اَوْ اِطْعٰمٌ فِيْ يَوْمٍ ذِيْ مَسْغَبَةٍ ۙ

15. To the orphan
With claims of relationship,

١٥ـ يَتِيْمًا ذَا مَقْرَبَةٍ ۙ

16. Or to the indigent
(Down) in the dust.

١٦ـ اَوْ مِسْكِيْنًا ذَا مَتْرَبَةٍ ۗ

17. Then will he be
Of those who believe,
And enjoin patience, (constancy,
And self-restraint), and enjoin
Deeds of kindness and
                              compassion.

١٧ـ ثُمَّ كَانَ مِنَ الَّذِيْنَ اٰمَنُوْا
وَتَوَاصَوْا بِالصَّبْرِ
وَتَوَاصَوْا بِالْمَرْحَمَةِ ۗ

18. Such are the Companions
Of the Right Hand.

١٨ـ اُولٰٓئِكَ اَصْحٰبُ الْمَيْمَنَةِ ۗ

19. But those who reject
Our Signs, they are
The (unhappy) Companions
Of the Left Hand.

١٩ـ وَالَّذِيْنَ كَفَرُوْا بِاٰيٰتِنَا
هُمْ اَصْحٰبُ الْمَشْئَمَةِ ۗ

20. On them will be Fire
Vaulted over (all round).

٢٠ـ عَلَيْهِمْ نَارٌ مُّؤْصَدَةٌ ۗ

INTRODUCTION AND SUMMARY: SŪRA XCI. (*Shams*) — 15 Verses

This is one of the early Meccan revelations. Beginning with a fine nature passage, and leading up to man's need of realising his spiritual responsibility, it ends with a warning of the terrible consequences for those who fear not the Hereafter.

Al Shams (The Sun)

In the name of Allah, Most Gracious, Most Merciful.

بِسْمِ اللهِ الرَّحْمٰنِ الرَّحِيْمِ

1. By the Sun
And its (glorious) splendour;

١- وَالشَّمْسِ وَضُحٰهَا ۪

2. By the Moon
As it follows (the Sun);

٢- وَالْقَمَرِ إِذَا تَلٰهَا ۪

3. By the Day as it
Shows up (the Sun's) glory;

٣- وَالنَّهَارِ إِذَا جَلّٰهَا ۪

4. By the Night as it
Conceals it;

٤- وَالَّيْلِ إِذَا يَغْشٰهَا ۪

5. By the Firmament
And its (wonderful) structure;

٥- وَالسَّمَاءِ وَمَا بَنٰهَا ۪

6. By the Earth
And its (wide) expanse;

٦- وَالْأَرْضِ وَمَا طَحٰهَا ۪

7. By the Soul,
And the proportion and order
Given to it;

٧- وَنَفْسٍ وَّمَا سَوّٰهَا ۪

8. And its enlightenment
As to its wrong
And its right—

٨- فَأَلْهَمَهَا فُجُوْرَهَا
وَتَقْوٰهَا ۪

9. Truly he succeeds
That purifies it,

٩- قَدْ أَفْلَحَ مَنْ زَكّٰهَا ۪

10. And he fails
That corrupts it!

١٠- وَقَدْ خَابَ مَنْ دَسّٰهَا ۪

11. The Thamūd (people)
Rejected (their prophet)
Through their inordinate
Wrongdoing.

١١-كَذَّبَتْ ثَمُوْدُ بِطَغْوٰىهَآ ۗ

12. Behold, the most wicked
Man among them was
Deputed (for impiety).

١٢-اِذِ انْۢبَعَثَ اَشْقٰىهَا ۗ

13. But the Messenger of Allah
Said to them: "It is
A She-camel of Allah!
And (bar her not
From) having her drink!"

١٣-فَقَالَ لَهُمْ رَسُوْلُ اللّٰهِ نَاقَةَ اللّٰهِ وَسُقْيٰهَا ۗ

14. Then they rejected him
(As a false prophet),
And they hamstrung her.
So their Lord, on account
Of their crime, obliterated
Their traces and made them
Equal (in destruction,
High and low)!

١٤-فَكَذَّبُوْهُ فَعَقَرُوْهَا ۗ فَدَمْدَمَ عَلَيْهِمْ رَبُّهُمْ بِذَنْۢبِهِمْ فَسَوّٰىهَا ۗ

15. And for Him
Is no fear
Of its consequences.

١٥-وَلَا يَخَافُ عُقْبٰهَا ۗ

INTRODUCTION AND SUMMARY: SURA XCII. (*Lail*) — 21 Verses

This was one of the first Sūras to be revealed—within the first ten; and may be placed in date close to S.lxxxix, and S.xciii. Note that in all these three Sūras the mystery and the contrast as between Night and Day are appealed to for the consolation of man in his spiritual yearning. Here we are told to strive our utmost towards God, and He will give us every help and satisfaction.

Al Layl (The Night)

In the name of Allah, Most Gracious,
Most Merciful.

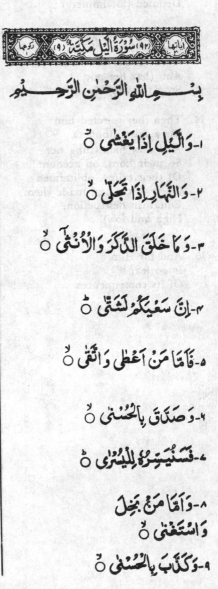

1. By the Night as it
   Conceals (the light);

2. By the Day as it
   Appears in glory;

3. By (the mystery of)
   The creation of male
   And female—

4. Verily, (the ends) ye
   Strive for are diverse.

5. So he who gives
   (In charity) and fears (Allah)

6. And (in all sincerity)
   Testifies to the Best—

7. We will indeed
   Make smooth for him
   The path to Bliss.

8. But he who is
   A greedy miser
   And thinks himself
   Self-sufficient,

9. And gives the lie
   To the Best—

10. We will indeed
Make smooth for him
The Path to Misery;

١٠- فَسَنُيَسِّرُهُ لِلْعُسْرَى ۞

11. Nor will his wealth
Profit him when he
Falls headlong (into the Pit).

١١- وَمَا يُغْنِي عَنْهُ مَالُهُ
إِذَا تَرَدَّى ۞

12. Verily We take
Upon Ourselves to guide,

١٢- إِنَّ عَلَيْنَا لَلْهُدَى ۞

13. And verily unto Us
(Belong) the End
And the Beginning.

١٣- وَإِنَّ لَنَا لَلْآخِرَةَ وَالْأُولَى ۞

14. Therefore do I warn you
Of a Fire blazing fiercely;

١٤- فَأَنْذَرْتُكُمْ نَارًا تَلَظَّى ۞

15. None shall reach it
But those most unfortunate ones

١٥- لَا يَصْلَاهَا إِلَّا الْأَشْقَى ۞

16. Who give the lie to Truth
And turn their backs.

١٦- الَّذِي كَذَّبَ وَتَوَلَّى ۞

17. But those most devoted
To Allah shall be
Removed far from it—

١٧- وَسَيُجَنَّبُهَا الْأَتْقَى ۞

18. Those who spend their wealth
For increase in self-purification,

١٨- الَّذِي يُؤْتِي مَالَهُ يَتَزَكَّى ۞

19. And have in their minds
No favour from anyone
For which a reward
Is expected in return,

١٩- وَمَا لِأَحَدٍ عِنْدَهُ
مِنْ نِعْمَةٍ تُجْزَى ۞

20. But only the desire
To seek for the Countenance
Of their Lord Most High;

٢٠- إِلَّا ابْتِغَاءَ وَجْهِ رَبِّهِ الْأَعْلَى ۞

21. And soon will they
Attain (complete) satisfaction.

٢١- وَلَسَوْفَ يَرْضَى ۞

INTRODUCTION AND SUMMARY: SŪRA XCIII. (*Dhuḥā*) — 11 Verses

This Sūra is close in date to Sūras lxxxix, and xcii, and the imagery drawn from the contrast of Night and Day is common to all three. In this Sūra the vicissitudes of human life are referred to, and a message of hope and consolation is given to man's soul from God's past mercies, and he is bidden to pursue the path of goodness and proclaim the bounties of God. This is the general meaning. In particular, the Sūra seems to have been revealed in a dark period in the outer life of the Holy Prophet, when a man of less resolute will might have been discouraged. But the Prophet is told to hold the present of less account than the glorious Hereafter which awaited him like the glorious morning after a night of stillness and gloom. The Hereafter was, not only in the Future Life, but in his later life on this earth, full of victory and satisfaction.

Al Ḍuḥā (The Glorious Morning Light)

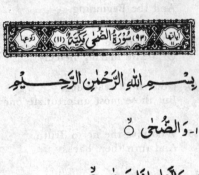

In the name of Allah, Most Gracious, Most Merciful.

1. By the Glorious
   Morning Light,

2. And by the Night
   When it is still—

3. Thy Guardian-Lord
   Hath not forsaken thee,
   Nor is He displeased.

4. And verily the hereafter
   Will be better for thee
   Than the present.

5. And soon will thy
   Guardian-Lord give thee
   (That wherewith) thou
   Shalt be well-pleased.

6. Did He not find thee
   An orphan and give thee
   Shelter (and care)?

7. And He found thee

Wandering, and He gave
Thee guidance.

8. And He found thee
In need, and made
Thee independent.

9. Therefore treat not
The orphan with harshness,

10. Nor repulse the petitioner
(Unheard);

11. But the Bounty
Of thy Lord—
Rehearse and proclaim!

ضَآلًّا فَهَدٰى ۞

٨- وَوَجَدَكَ عَآئِلًا فَاَغْنٰى ۞

٩- فَاَمَّا الْيَتِيْمَ فَلَا تَقْهَرْ ۞

١٠- وَاَمَّا السَّآئِلَ فَلَا تَنْهَرْ ۞

١١- وَاَمَّا بِنِعْمَةِ رَبِّكَ فَحَدِّثْ ۞ ۚۙ

INTRODUCTION AND SUMMARY: SŪRA XCIV. (*Inshirāḥ*) — 8 Verses

This short Sūra gives a message of hope and encouragement in a time of darkness and difficulty. It was revealed to The Holy Prophet soon after the last Sura (*Dhuḥā*), whose argument it supplements.

Al Sharḥ or *Al Inshirāḥ* (The
Expansion of the Breast)

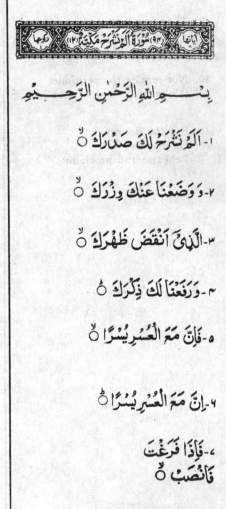

*In the name of Allah, Most Gracious,
Most Merciful.*

1. Have We not
   Expanded thee thy breast?

2. And removed from thee
   Thy burden

3. The which did gall
   Thy back?—

4. And raised high the esteem
   (In which) thou (art held)?

5. So, verily,
   With every difficulty,
   There is relief:

6. Verily, with every difficulty
   There is relief.

7. Therefore, when thou art
   Free (form thine immediate task),
   Still labour hard,

8. And to thy Lord
   Turn (all) thy attention.

INTRODUCTION AND SUMMARY: SŪRA XCV. (*Tīn*) — 8 Verses

This is also a very early Sūra. It appeals to the most sacred symbols to show that God created man in the best of moulds, but that man is capable of the utmost degradation unless he has Faith and leads a good life. In subject-matter this Sūra closely resembles S.ciii.

Al Tīn (The Fig)

In the name of Allah, Most Gracious, Most Merciful.

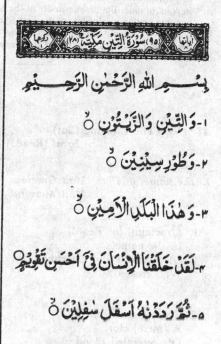

1. By the Fig
   And the Olive,

2. And the Mount
   Of Sinai,

3. And this City
   Of security—

4. We have indeed created man
   In the best of moulds,

5. Then do We abase him
   (To be) the lowest
   Of the low

6. Except such as believe
   And do righteous deeds:
   For they shall have
   A reward unfailing.

7. Then what can,
   After this, contradict thee,
   As to the Judgement
   (To come)?

8. Is not Allah
   The wisest of Judges?

INTRODUCTION AND SUMMARY: SŪRA XCVI.(*Iqraa,or 'Alaq*) — 19 Verses

Verses 1-5 of this Sūra were the first direct Revelation to the Holy Prophet. The circumstances, material and physical, in which they came, are described in C.28-30, which should be referred to.

After that there was an interval or break (*Fatra*), extending over some months or perhaps over a year. S.lxviii. is usually considered to have been the next revelation in point of time. But the remainder of the Sūra (xcvi. 6-19) came soon after the *Fatra*, and that portion is joined on to the first five verses containing the command to preach, because it explains that chief obstacle to the delivery of the message to man, *viz.*, man's own obstinacy, vanity, and insolence.

Al 'Alaq (The Clinging Clot) or
　　　　Iqra' (Read!)

In the name of Allah, Most Gracious,
　　　　　　Most Merciful.

بِسْمِ اللهِ الرَّحْمٰنِ الرَّحِيْمِ

1. Proclaim! (or Read!)
   In the name
   Of thy Lord and Cherisher,
   Who created—

١- اقْرَأْ بِاسْمِ رَبِّكَ الَّذِيْ خَلَقَ ۚ

2. Created man, out of
   A (mere) clot
   Of congealed blood:

٢- خَلَقَ الْإِنْسَانَ مِنْ عَلَقٍ ۚ

3. Proclaim! And thy Lord
   Is Most Bountiful—

٣- اقْرَأْ وَرَبُّكَ الْأَكْرَمُ ۙ

4. He Who taught
   (The use of) the Pen—

٤- الَّذِيْ عَلَّمَ بِالْقَلَمِ ۙ

5. Taught man that
   Which he knew not.

٥- عَلَّمَ الْإِنْسَانَ مَا لَمْ يَعْلَمْ ۚ

6. Nay, but man doth
   Transgress all bounds,

٦- كَلَّا إِنَّ الْإِنْسَانَ لَيَطْغٰى ۙ

7. In that he looketh
   Upon himself as self-sufficient.

٧- أَنْ رَّآهُ اسْتَغْنٰى ۚ

8. Verily, to thy Lord
   Is the return (of all).

٨- اِنَّ اِلٰى رَبِّكَ الرُّجْعٰى ۗ

9. Seest thou one
   Who forbids—

٩- اَرَءَيْتَ الَّذِىْ يَنْهٰى ۙ

10. A votary when he
    (Turns) to pray?

١٠- عَبْدًا اِذَا صَلّٰى ۗ

11. Seest thou if
    He is on (the road
    Of) Guidance?—

١١- اَرَءَيْتَ اِنْ كَانَ عَلَى الْهُدٰٓى ۙ

12. Or enjoins Righteousness?

١٢- اَوْ اَمَرَ بِالتَّقْوٰى ۗ

13. Seest thou if he
    Denies (Truth) and turns away?

١٣- اَرَءَيْتَ اِنْ كَذَّبَ وَتَوَلّٰى ۗ

14. Knoweth he not
    That Allah doth see?

١٤- اَلَمْ يَعْلَمْ بِاَنَّ اللّٰهَ يَرٰى ۗ

15. Let him beware! If he
    Desist not, We will
    Drag him by the forelock—

١٥- كَلَّا لَئِنْ لَّمْ يَنْتَهِ ۙ لَنَسْفَعًا بِالنَّاصِيَةِ ۙ

16. A lying, sinful forelock!

١٦- نَاصِيَةٍ كَاذِبَةٍ خَاطِئَةٍ ۗ

17. Then, let him call
    (For help) to his council
    (Of comrades):

١٧- فَلْيَدْعُ نَادِيَهٗ ۙ

18. We will call
    On the angels of punishment
    (To deal with him)!

١٨- سَنَدْعُ الزَّبَانِيَةَ ۙ

19. Nay, heed him not:
    But bow down in adoration,
    And bring thyself
    The closer (to Allah)!

١٩- كَلَّا لَا تُطِعْهُ وَاسْجُدْ وَاقْتَرِبْ ۩

INTRODUCTION AND SUMMARY: SŪRA XCVII. (*Qadr*) 5 — Verses

The chronology of this Sūra has no significance. It is probably Meccan, though some hold that it was revealed in Medina.

The subject-matter is the mystic Night of Power (or Honour), in which Revelation comes down to a benighted world,—it may be to the wonderful Cosmos of an individual—and transforms the conflict of wrong-doing into Peace and Harmony—through the agency of the angelic host, representing the spiritual powers of the Mercy of God.

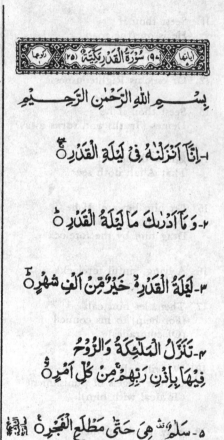

Al Qadr (The Night of Power or Honour)

In the name of Allah, Most Gracious, Most Merciful.

1. We have indeed revealed
This (Message)
In the Night of Power:

2. And what will explain
To thee what the Night
Of Power is?

3. The Night of Power
Is better than
A thousand Months.

4. Therein come down
The angels and the Spirit
By Allah's permission,
On every errand:

5. Peace!...This
Until the rise of Morn!

INTRODUCTION AND SUMMARY: SŪRA XCVIII. (*Baiyina*) — 8 Verses

This Sūra was probably an early Medina Sūra, or possibly a late Meccan Sūra.

In subject-matter it carries forward the argument of the last Sūra. The mystic night of revelation is indeed blessed: but those who reject Truth are impervious to God's Message, however clear may be the evidence in support of it.

Al Bayyinah (The Clear Evidence)

*In the name of Allah, Most Gracious,
Most Merciful.*

بِسْمِ اللهِ الرَّحْمٰنِ الرَّحِيْمِ

1. Those who reject (Truth),
Among the People of the Book
And among the Polytheists,
Were not going to depart
(From their ways) until
There should come to them
Clear Evidence —

١-لَمْ يَكُنِ الَّذِيْنَ كَفَرُوْا مِنْ اَهْلِ الْكِتٰبِ وَالْمُشْرِكِيْنَ مُنْفَكِّيْنَ حَتّٰى تَأْتِيَهُمُ الْبَيِّنَةُ ۙ

2. A messenger from Allah,
Rehearsing scriptures
Kept pure and Holy:

٢-رَسُوْلٌ مِّنَ اللهِ يَتْلُوْا صُحُفًا مُّطَهَّرَةً ۙ

3. Wherein are laws (or decrees)
Right and straight.

٣-فِيْهَا كُتُبٌ قَيِّمَةٌ ۙ

4. Nor did the People
Of the Book
Make schisms,
Until after there came
To them Clear Evidence.

٤-وَمَا تَفَرَّقَ الَّذِيْنَ اُوْتُوا الْكِتٰبَ اِلَّا مِنْ بَعْدِ مَا جَاءَتْهُمُ الْبَيِّنَةُ ۙ

5. And they have been commanded
No more than this:
To worship Allah,
Offering Him sincere devotion,
Being True (in faith);
To establish regular Prayer;
And to practise regular Charity;
And that is the Religion
Right and Straight.

٥-وَمَا أُمِرُوْا اِلَّا لِيَعْبُدُوا اللهَ مُخْلِصِيْنَ لَهُ الدِّيْنَ ۙ حُنَفَاءَ وَيُقِيْمُوا الصَّلٰوةَ وَيُؤْتُوا الزَّكٰوةَ وَذٰلِكَ دِيْنُ الْقَيِّمَةِ ۙ

6. Those who reject (Truth),
Among the People of the Book
And among the Polytheists,
Will be in Hellfire,
To dwell therein (for aye).
They are the worst
Of creatures.

٧- اِنَّ الَّذِيْنَ كَفَرُوْا
مِنْ اَهْلِ الْكِتٰبِ وَالْمُشْرِكِيْنَ
فِيْ نَارِجَهَنَّمَ خٰلِدِيْنَ فِيْهَا ؕ
اُولٰٓئِكَ هُمْ شَرُّ الْبَرِيَّةِ ؕ

7. Those who have faith
And do righteous deeds—
They are the best
Of creatures.

٧- اِنَّ الَّذِيْنَ اٰمَنُوْا وَعَمِلُوا الصّٰلِحٰتِ
اُولٰٓئِكَ هُمْ خَيْرُ الْبَرِيَّةِ ؕ

8. Their reward is with Allah:
Gardens of Eternity,
Beneath which rivers flow;
They will dwell therein
Forever; Allah well pleased
With them, and they with Him:
All this for such as
Fear their Lord and Cherisher.

٨- جَزَآؤُهُمْ عِنْدَ رَبِّهِمْ جَنّٰتُ عَدْنٍ
تَجْرِيْ مِنْ تَحْتِهَا الْاَنْهٰرُ خٰلِدِيْنَ فِيْهَا
اَبَدًا ؕ رَضِيَ اللّٰهُ عَنْهُمْ وَرَضُوْا عَنْهُ ؕ
ذٰلِكَ لِمَنْ خَشِيَ رَبَّهٗ ؕ ۶

INTRODUCTION AND SUMMARY: SŪRA XCIX. (Zilzāl) — 8 Verses

    This Sūra is close in date to the last: it is generally referred to the early Medina period, though it may possibly be of the late Meccan period.

    It refers to the tremendous convulsion and uprooting which will take place when the present order of the world is dissolved and the new spiritual world of Justice and Truth takes its place. The symbol used is that of an earthquake which will shake our present material and phenomenal world to its very foundations. The mystic words in which the earthquake is described are remarkable for both power and graphic aptness. With that shaking all hidden mysteries will be brought to light.

Al Zalzalah (The Earthquake)

In the name of Allah, Most Gracious, Most Merciful.

1. When the Earth is
Shaken to its (utmost)
               convulsion,

2. And the Earth throws up
Its burdens (from within),

3. And man cries (distressed);
'What is the matter with it?'—

4. On that Day will it
Declare its tidings:

5. For that thy Lord will
Have given it inspiration.

6. On that Day will men
Proceed in companies sorted
               out,
To be shown the Deeds
That they (had done).

7. Then shall anyone who
Has done an atom's weight
Of good, see it!

8. And anyone who
Has done an atom's weight
Of evil, shall see it.

INTRODUCTION AND SUMMARY: SŪRA C. (*ʿĀdiyāt*) — 11 Verses

This is one of the earlier Meccan Sūras. In the depth of its mystery and the rhythm and sublimity of its language and symbolism, it may be compared with S.lxxix. Its subject-matter is the irresistible nature of spiritual power and knowledge, contrasted with unregenerate man's ingratitude, pettiness, helplessness, and ignorance.

Al ʿĀdiyāt (Those That Run)

In the name of Allah, Most Gracious,
Most Merciful.

بِسْمِ اللهِ الرَّحْمٰنِ الرَّحِيمِ

1. By the (Steeds)
   That run, with panting (breath),

١- وَالْعٰدِيٰتِ ضَبْحًا ۚ

2. And strike sparks of fire,

٢- فَالْمُوْرِيٰتِ قَدْحًا ۙ

3. And push home the charge
   In the morning,

٣- فَالْمُغِيْرٰتِ صُبْحًا ۙ

4. And raise the dust
   In clouds the while,

٤- فَأَثَرْنَ بِهٖ نَقْعًا ۙ

5. And penetrate forthwith
   Into the midst (of the foe)
   En masse—

٥- فَوَسَطْنَ بِهٖ جَمْعًا ۙ

6. Truly Man is,
   To his Lord,
   Ungrateful;

٦- إِنَّ الْإِنْسَانَ لِرَبِّهٖ لَكَنُوْدٌ ۚ

7. And to that (fact)
   He bears witness
   (By his deeds);

٧- وَإِنَّهٗ عَلٰى ذٰلِكَ لَشَهِيْدٌ ۚ

8. And violent is he
   In his love of wealth.

٨- وَإِنَّهٗ لِحُبِّ الْخَيْرِ لَشَدِيْدٌ ۚ

9. Does he not know—
   When that which is

٩- أَفَلَا يَعْلَمُ

In the graves is
Scattered abroad

اِذَا بُعْثِرَ مَا فِى الْقُبُوْرِ ۙ

10. And that which is
(Locked up) in (human) breasts
Is made manifest—

۱۰- وَ حُصِّلَ مَا فِى الصُّدُوْرِ ۙ

11. That their Lord had been
Well-acquainted with them,
(Even to) that Day?

۱۱- اِنَّ رَبَّهُمْ بِهِمْ يَوْمَئِذٍ لَّخَبِيْرٌ ۙ

INTRODUCTION AND SUMMARY: SŪRA CI. (*Al-Qāri'a*) — 11 Verses

This Meccan Sūra describes the Judgment Day as the Day of Clamour, when men will be distracted and the landmarks of this world will be lost, but every deed will be weighed in a just balance, and find its real value and setting.

Al Qāri'ah (The Great Calamity)

In the name of Allah, Most Gracious, Most Merciful.

بِسْمِ اللهِ الرَّحْمٰنِ الرَّحِيْمِ

1. The (Day) of
Noise and Clamour:

١- اَلْقَارِعَةُ ۟

2. What is the (Day)
Of Noise and Clamour?

٢- مَا الْقَارِعَةُ ۟

3. And what will explain
To thee what the (Day)
Of Noise and Clamour is?

٣- وَمَآ اَدْرٰىكَ مَا الْقَارِعَةُ ۟

4. (It is) a Day whereon
Men will be like moths
Scattered about,

٤- يَوْمَ يَكُوْنُ النَّاسُ كَالْفَرَاشِ الْمَبْثُوْثِ ۟

5. And the mountains
Will be like carded wool.

٥- وَتَكُوْنُ الْجِبَالُ كَالْعِهْنِ الْمَنْفُوْشِ ۟

6. Then, he whose
Balance (of good deeds)
Will be (found) heavy,

٦- فَاَمَّا مَنْ ثَقُلَتْ مَوَازِيْنُهُ ۟

7. Will be in a Life
Of good pleasure and
satisfaction.

٧- فَهُوَ فِيْ عِيْشَةٍ رَّاضِيَةٍ ۟

8. But he whose
Balance (of good deeds)
Will be (found) light—

٨- وَاَمَّا مَنْ خَفَّتْ مَوَازِيْنُهُ ۟

9. Will have his home
In a (bottomless) Pit.

٩- فَاُمُّهُ هَاوِيَةٌ ۟

10. And what will explain
To Thee what this is?

١٠۔ وَمَآ اَدْرٰىكَ مَاهِيَهْ ۠

11. (It is) a Fire
Blazing fiercely!

١١۔ نَارٌ حَامِيَةٌ ۠

INTRODUCTION AND SUMMARY: SŪRA CII. (*Takāthur*) — 8 Verses

This probably early Meccan Sūra gives a warning against acquisitiveness, i.e, the passion for piling up quantities or numbers, whether in the good things of this world, or in man-power or in other forms of megalomania, which leave no time or opportunity for pursuing the higher things of life.

Al Takāthur (The Piling Up)

In the name of Allah, Most Gracious,
Most Merciful.

بِسْمِ اللهِ الرَّحْمٰنِ الرَّحِيْمِ

1. The mutual rivalry
For piling up (the good things
Of this world) diverts you
(From the more serious things),

١- اَلْهٰكُمُ التَّكَاثُرُ ۞

2. Until ye visit the graves.

٢- حَتّٰى زُرْتُمُ الْمَقَابِرَ ۞

3. But nay, ye soon shall
Know (the reality).

٣- كَلَّا سَوْفَ تَعْلَمُوْنَ ۞

4. Again, ye soon shall know!

٤- ثُمَّ كَلَّا سَوْفَ تَعْلَمُوْنَ ۞

5. Nay, were ye to know
With certainty of mind,
(Ye would beware!)

٥- كَلَّا لَوْ تَعْلَمُوْنَ عِلْمَ الْيَقِيْنِ ۞

6. Ye shall certainly see
Hellfire!

٦- لَتَرَوُنَّ الْجَحِيْمَ ۞

7. Again, ye shall see it
With certainty of sight!

٧- ثُمَّ لَتَرَوُنَّهَا عَيْنَ الْيَقِيْنِ ۞

8. Then, shall ye be
Questioned that Day
About the joy
(Ye indulged in!)

٨- ثُمَّ لَتُسْئَلُنَّ يَوْمَئِذٍ عَنِ النَّعِيْمِ ۞

ع

INTRODUCTION AND SUMMARY: SŪRA CIII. ('Aṣr) — 3 Verses

This early Meccan Sūra refers to the testimony of Time through the Ages. All history shows that Evil came to an evil end. But time is always in favour of those who have Faith, live clean and pure lives, and know how to wait, in patience and constancy. *Cf.* the theme of S. xcv.

Al 'Aṣr (Time Through the Ages)

In the name of Allah, Most Gracious, Most Merciful.

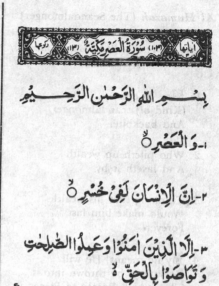

بِسْمِ اللهِ الرَّحْمٰنِ الرَّحِيمِ

1. By (the Token of)
   Time (through the Ages),

١- وَالْعَصْرِ ۟

2. Verily Man
   Is in loss,

٢- اِنَّ الْاِنْسَانَ لَفِىْ خُسْرٍ ۟

3. Except such as have Faith,
   And do righteous deeds,
   And (join together)⁶²⁶⁵
   In the mutual teaching
   Of Truth, and of
   Patience and Constancy.

٣- اِلَّا الَّذِيْنَ اٰمَنُوْا وَعَمِلُوا الصّٰلِحٰتِ
وَتَوَاصَوْا بِالْحَقِّ ۙ۬
وَتَوَاصَوْا بِالصَّبْرِ ۟

INTRODUCTION AND SUMMARY: SŪRA CIV. (*Humaza*) — 9 Verses

This Meccan Sūra condemns all sorts of scandal, backbiting and selfish hoarding of wealth, as destroying the hearts and affections of men.

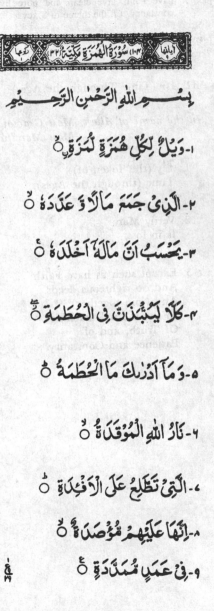

Al Humazah (The Scandalmonger)

In the name of Allah, Most Gracious, Most Merciful.

1. Woe to every
(Kind of) scandalmonger
And backbiter,

2. Who pileth up wealth
And layeth it by,

3. Thinking that his wealth
Would make him last
Forever!

4. By no means! He will
Be sure to be thrown into
That which Breaks to Pieces.

5. And what will explain
To thee That which Breaks
To Pieces?

6. (It is) the Fire
Of (the Wrath of) Allah
Kindled (to a blaze),

7. The which doth mount
(Right) to the Hearts:

8. It shall be made
Into a vault over them,

9. In columns outstretched.

INTRODUCTION AND SUMMARY: SURA CV. (*Fīl*) — 5 Verses

　　　　This early Meccan Sūra refers to an event that happened in the year of the birth of our Holy Prophet, say about 570 A.D. Yaman was then under the rule of the Abyssinians (Christian), who had driven out the Jewish Ḥimyar rulers. Abraha Ashram was the Abyssinian governor of viceroy. Intoxicated with power and fired by religious fanaticism, he led a big expedition against Mecca, intending to destroy the Kaʿba. He had an elephant or elephants in his train. But his sacrilegious intentions were defeated by a miracle. No defence was offered by the custodians of the Kaʿba as the army was too strong for them, but it was believed that a shower of stones, thrown by flocks of birds, destroyed the invading army almost to a man. The stones produced sores and pustules on the skin, which spread like a pestilence.

Al Fīl (The Elephant)

In the name of Allah, Most Gracious,
Most Merciful.

1. **S**eest[6270] thou not
   How thy Lord dealt
   With the Companions
   Of the Elephant?

2. Did He not make
   Their treacherous plan
   Go astray?

3. And He sent against them
   Flights of Birds,

4. Striking them with stones
   Of baked clay.

5. Then did He make them
   Like an empty field
   Of stalks and straw,
   (Of which the corn)
   Has been eaten up.

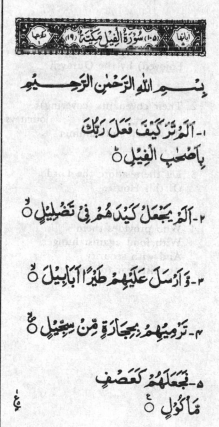

INTRODUCTION AND SUMMARY: SŪRA CVI. (*Quraish*) — 4 Verses

This Meccan Sūra may well be considered as a pendant to the last. If the Quraish were fond of Mecca and proud of it, if they profited, by its central position and its guaranteed security, from their caravans of trade and commerce, let them be grateful, adore the One True God, and accept His Message.

Quraysh (The Tribe of Quraysh)

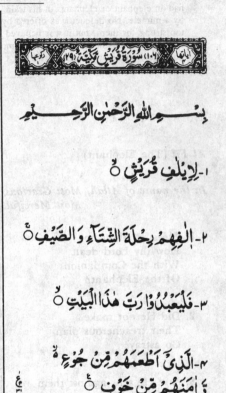

In the name of Allah, Most Gracious, Most Merciful.

1. For the covenants
   (Of security and safeguard
   Enjoyed) by the Quraysh,

2. Their covenants (covering)
   journeys
   By winter and summer—

3. Let them adore the Lord
   Of this House,

4. Who provides them
   With food against hunger,
   And with security
   Against fear (of danger).

INTRODUCTION AND SUMMARY: SŪRA CVII. (*Mā'ūn*) — 7 Verses

This Sūra—at least the first half of it—belongs to the early Meccan period. The subject-matter is the meaning of true worship, which requires Faith, the practical and helpful love of those in need, and sincerity rather than show in devotion and charity.

Al Mā'ūn (The Neighbourly Assistance)

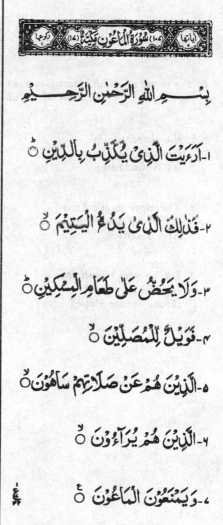

*In the name of Allah, Most Gracious,
Most Merciful.*

بِسْمِ اللهِ الرَّحْمٰنِ الرَّحِيْمِ

1. Seest thou one
   Who denies the Judgement
   (To come)?

١- أَرَءَيْتَ الَّذِيْ يُكَذِّبُ بِالدِّيْنِ ۚ

2. Then such is the (man)
   Who repulses the orphan
   (With harshness),

٢- فَذٰلِكَ الَّذِيْ يَدُعُّ الْيَتِيْمَ ۚ

3. And encourages not
   The feeding of the indigent.

٣- وَلَا يَحُضُّ عَلٰى طَعَامِ الْمِسْكِيْنِ ۚ

4. So woe to the worshippers

٤- فَوَيْلٌ لِّلْمُصَلِّيْنَ ۚ

5. Who are neglectful
   Of their Prayers,

٥- الَّذِيْنَ هُمْ عَنْ صَلَاتِهِمْ سَاهُوْنَ ۚ

6. Those who (want but)
   To be seen (of men),

٦- الَّذِيْنَ هُمْ يُرَآءُوْنَ ۚ

7. But refuse (to supply)
   (Even) neighbourly needs.

٧- وَيَمْنَعُوْنَ الْمَاعُوْنَ ۚ

INTRODUCTION AND SUMMARY: SŪRA CVIII. (*Kawthar*) — 3 Verses

This very brief early Meccan Sūra sums up in the single mystic word *Kawthar* (Abundance) the doctrine of spiritual Riches through devotion and sacrifice. The converse also follows; indulgence in hatred means the cutting off of all hope of this life and the Hereafter.

Al Kawthar (The Abundance)

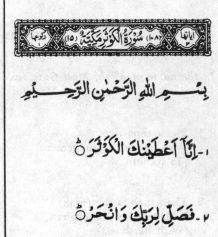

In the name of Allah, Most Gracious, Most Merciful.

بِسْمِ اللهِ الرَّحْمٰنِ الرَّحِيْمِ

1. To thee have We
   Granted the Fount
   (of Abundance).

١ ـ اِنَّاۤ اَعْطَيْنٰكَ الْكَوْثَرَ ۗ

2. Therefore to thy Lord
   Turn in Prayer
   And Sacrifice.

٢ ـ فَصَلِّ لِرَبِّكَ وَانْحَرْ ۗ

3. For he who hateth thee—
   He will be cut off
   (From Future Hope).

٣ ـ اِنَّ شَانِئَكَ هُوَ الْاَبْتَرُ ۗ

INTRODUCTION AND SUMMARY: SURA CIX. (*Kāfirūn*) — 6 Verses

This is another early Meccan Sūra. It defines the right attitude to those who reject Faith: in matters' of Truth we can make no compromise, but there is no need to persecute or abuse anyone for his faith or belief.

Al Kāfirūn (Those Who Reject Faith)

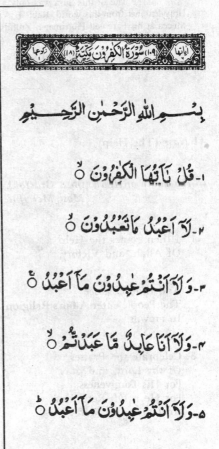

*In the name of Allah, Most Gracious,
Most Merciful.*

1. Say: O ye
   That reject Faith!

2. I worship not that
   Which ye worship,

3. Nor will ye worship
   That which I worship.

4. And I will not worship
   That which ye have been
   Wont to worship,

5. Nor will ye worship
   That which I worship.

6. To you be your Way,
   And to me mine.

INTRODUCTION AND SUMMARY: SŪRA CX. (Naṣr) — 3 Verses

This beautiful Sūra was the last of the Sūras to be revealed *as a whole*, though the portion of the verse v.4. "This day have I perfected your religion for you," etc., contains probably the last *words* of the Qur-ān to be revealed.

The date of this Sūra was only a few months before the passing away of the Holy Prophet from this world, Rabi' I, A.H. 11. The place was either the precincts of Mecca at his Farewell Pilgrimage, Zulhijja, A.H. 10, or Medina after his return from the Farewell Pilgrimage.

Victory is the crown of service, not an occasion for exultation. All victory comes from the help of God.

Al Naṣr (The Help)

In the name of Allah, Most Gracious,
Most Merciful.

بِسْمِ اللهِ الرَّحْمٰنِ الرَّحِيْمِ

1. When comes the Help
   Of Allah, and Victory,

١- اِذَا جَآءَ نَصْرُ اللهِ وَالْفَتْحُ ۙ

2. And thou dost see
   The People enter Allah's Religion
   In crowds,

٢- وَرَاَيْتَ النَّاسَ يَدْخُلُوْنَ فِيْ دِيْنِ اللهِ اَفْوَاجًا ۙ

3. Celebrate the Praises
   Of thy Lord, and pray
   For His Forgiveness:
   For He is Oft-Returning
   (In Grace and Mercy).

٣- فَسَبِّحْ بِحَمْدِ رَبِّكَ وَاسْتَغْفِرْهُ ۭ اِنَّهٗ كَانَ تَوَّابًا ۙ

INTRODUCTION AND SUMMARY: SŪRA CXI. (*Lahab*) — 5 Verses

This very early Meccan Sūra, though it referred in the first instance to a particular incident in a cruel and relentless persecution, carries the general lesson that cruely ultimately ruins itself. The man who rages against holy things is burnt up in his own rage. His hands, which are the instruments of his action, perish, and he perishes himself. No boasted wealth or position will save him. The women, who are made for nobler emotions, may, if they go wrong, feed unholy rage with fiercer fuel to their own loss. For they may twist the torturing rope round their own neck. It is a common experience that people perish by the very means by which they seek to destroy others.

Al Masad (The Plaited Rope) or
Al Lahab (The Flame)

In the name of Allah, Most Gracious,
Most Merciful.

بِسْمِ اللهِ الرَّحْمٰنِ الرَّحِيْمِ

1. Perish the hands
   Of the Father of Flame!
   Perish he!

١- تَبَّتْ يَدَا أَبِي لَهَبٍ وَّتَبَّ ۖ

2. No profit to him
   From all his wealth,
   And all his gains!

٢- مَا أَغْنَىٰ عَنْهُ مَالُهُ
وَمَا كَسَبَ ۖ

3. Burnt soon will he be
   In a Fire
   Of blazing Flame!

٣- سَيَصْلَىٰ نَارًا ذَاتَ لَهَبٍ ۖ

4. His wife shall carry
   The (crackling) wood —
   As fuel! —

٤- وَّامْرَأَتُهُ حَمَّالَةَ الْحَطَبِ ۖ

5. A twisted rope
   Of palm leaf fibre
   Round her (own) neck!

٥- فِيْ جِيْدِهَا حَبْلٌ مِّنْ مَّسَدٍ ۖ

INTRODUCTION AND SUMMARY: SŪRA XCII. (*Ikhlas*) — 4 Verses

This early Meccan Sūra sums up in a few terse verse words the Unity of the Godhead—often professed, but frequently mixed up in the popular mind with debasing superstitions.

Al Ikhlās (The Purity of Faith)

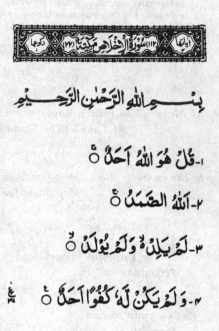

In the name of Allah, Most Gracious,
Most Merciful.

بِسْمِ اللهِ الرَّحْمٰنِ الرَّحِيْمِ

1. Say: He is Allah,
   The One and Only;

١- قُلْ هُوَ اللهُ أَحَدٌ ۚ

2. Allah, the Eternal, Absolute;

٢- اَللهُ الصَّمَدُ ۚ

3. He begetteth not,
   Nor is He begotten;

٣- لَمْ يَلِدْ ۙ وَلَمْ يُوْلَدْ ۙ

4. And there is none
   Like unto Him.

٤- وَلَمْ يَكُنْ لَّهٗ كُفُوًا أَحَدٌ ۚ

INTRODUCTION AND SUMMARY: SŪRA CXIII. (*Falaq*) — 5 Verses

This early Meccan Sūra provides the antidote to superstition and fear by teaching us to seek refuge in God from every kind of ill arising from outer nature and from dark and evil plottings and envy on the part of others.

Al Falaq (The Daybreak)

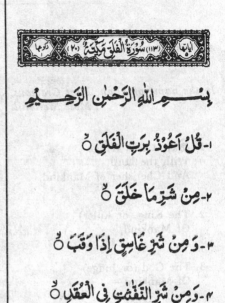

In the name of Allah, Most Gracious, Most Merciful.

بِسْمِ اللهِ الرَّحْمٰنِ الرَّحِيْمِ

1. Say: I seek refuge
   With the Lord of the Dawn,

١- قُلْ أَعُوْذُ بِرَبِّ الْفَلَقِ ۙ

2. From the mischief
   Of created things;

٢- مِنْ شَرِّ مَا خَلَقَ ۙ

3. From the mischief
   Of Darkness as it overspreads;

٣- وَمِنْ شَرِّ غَاسِقٍ إِذَا وَقَبَ ۙ

4. From the mischief
   Of those who practise
   Secret Arts;

٤- وَمِنْ شَرِّ النَّفّٰثٰتِ فِى الْعُقَدِ ۙ

5. And from the mischief
   Of the envious one
   As he practises envy.

٥- وَمِنْ شَرِّ حَاسِدٍ إِذَا حَسَدَ ۙ

INTRODUCTION AND SUMMARY: SŪRA CXIV. (*Nās*) — 6 Verses

This early Maccan Sūra is a pendant to the last Sūra, and concludes the Holy Qur-ān, with an appeal to us to trust in God, rather than man, as our sure shield and protection. It warns us specially against the secret whispers of evil within our own hearts.

Al Nās (Mankind)

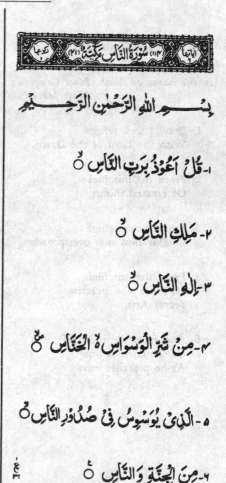

In the name of Allah, Most Gracious, Most Merciful.

1. Say: I seek refuge
   With the Lord
   And Cherisher of Mankind,

2. The King (or Ruler)
   Of Mankind,

3. The God (or Judge)
   Of Mankind—

4. From the mischief
   Of the Whisperer
   (Of Evil), who withdraws
   (After his whisper)—

5. (The same) who whispers
   Into the hearts of Mankind—

6. Among Jinns
   And among Men.